European Theories
of the Drama

TO
MY WIFE
A COLLABORATOR WHO INSPIRED
AND MADE POSSIBLE
THIS WORK

B. H. C.

European Theories of the Drama

WITH A SUPPLEMENT ON THE
AMERICAN DRAMA

AN ANTHOLOGY OF DRAMATIC THEORY
AND CRITICISM FROM ARISTOTLE TO THE
PRESENT DAY, IN A SERIES OF SELECTED
TEXTS, WITH COMMENTARIES, BIOGRA-
PHIES, AND BIBLIOGRAPHIES

by
Barrett H. Clark

newly revised
by Henry Popkin

CROWN PUBLISHERS, INC., NEW YORK

PRINTED IN THE UNITED STATES OF AMERICA

INTRODUCTION TO THE 1947 EDITION

European Theories of the Drama in its present form is a new book: the addition of a substantial body of new material from the United States not included in the earlier editions justifies that statement. It is also an old book, including the entire text as it appeared in the latest revised edition of 1929.

In its earliest form *European Theories of the Drama* was publishd in 1918; it was revised to a greater or less extent three times during the following few years. In the Introduction to the 1929 edition I wrote that the "early years of the 20th Century are still too close to us, and any attempt to select the most important theories promulgated since 1900 would prove unwise because we cannot yet determine exactly how important any new theory is going to be." I added that even though I had included certain theories written since 1900, the authors of them were "products of the 19th Century."

I had hoped that by 1947 it would be possible to bring the entire book up to date by printing a representative, if not a fairly complete collection of dramatic theories from among the many pronouncements that have reflected or influenced the work of playwrights in Europe since 1900, particularly in Russia, France, England, Italy, Spain and Germany. It is possible that if war had not intervened I might have been able to carry out such a plan; I even attempted it, but after two years I gave up. I consulted scholars and other specialists in this country; I corresponded with playwrights and critics, directors and managers abroad, but I found that even a preliminary investigation of texts covering many important dramatic movements in certain countries could not be undertaken. It would, of course, be possible to bring this section or that up to date, but I felt that such a course would be unsatisfactory and offer only a distorted picture without balance or truth, and I therefore decided to leave the European part of the book as it was.

However, it seemed to me that the phenomenal growth of a native drama in the United States since 1900, and particularly since 1920, should somehow be allowed to reflect itself in a book, or shall we say, be added to a book which in 1918 could be accurately described only as *European Theories of the Drama*. And so this new volume, still designated by the same title, carries a supplement. The work could more accurately be described as *European and American* (or shall we say *United States?*) *Theories of the Drama,* but I am allowing the old title to stand, because in its original form with its first title the book seems to have fixed itself firmly in the minds of those who have already used it.

It will be noticed that I have not followed the somewhat elaborate scheme of bibliographical and editorial classification adopted in the older part of the volume. To do this would give an air of finality to my selections which I have not intended. The amount of dramatic theorizing which has found its way into print in the United States is staggering. Aside from the periodical writing of critics in the newspapers and magazines, and counting only prefaces, books, and essays in books, I have read over twenty-five hundred items in order to choose the twelve pieces that go into my Supplement, and I print these with the reservation that they are still more or less tentative exhibits chosen from among many others, some of which are of equal importance.

In my original Introduction to *European Theories of the Drama* I wrote that it was "an attempt to set before the reader the development of the theory of dramatic technique in Europe from Aristotle to the present time. It has been my purpose to select such texts and parts of texts as have been influential in shaping the form of plays." I now add that the aims and implications of the book are somewhat wider, and that the texts included in it are likewise a reflection of the ideas and ideals on playwriting which their authors often attempt to set before the drama's practitioners.

I had imagined, when the book first appeared, that it would prove useful only, or chiefly, to students curious about the hows and whys of playwriting. I did not think it could be of much practical use to playwrights. But I have been surprised to learn from several writers who were "required" to read the book in college that it somehow furnished hints that helped them, and in one case a well-known and successful playwright told me that the book had actually made him decide to become a playwright. The late Thomas Wolfe told me ruefully that he too had been made to use the book as a college text, and if he had not turned to novel writing he might have tried more seriously to become the playwright I think he could have been. I have similar evidence from several other playwrights, but I will name no names, and I leave the drawing of conclusions to others. If *European Theories of the Drama* proves useful in any way to any playwright, I shall be happy. That is more than I ever hoped for.

Before listing my formal acknowledgments of help and encouragement, I should like to thank the many college and university instructors and special non-academic lecturers who have used the book as a text; nct so much for using it as for telling me how they have used it and how it has proved helpful to them and their students; I cannot mention here the names of all who have urged me to revise the book or (during the difficult war years) simply to keep it in print. But I must mention in particular John Mason Brown and Arthur Edwin Krows. Playwrights who have made similar requests are nearly as numerous.

Many who helped me nearly thirty years ago are now dead; my gratitude to them is deep and abiding. Among them are the late Sir Arthur Pinero, Henry Arthur Jones, J. E. Spingarn, Brander Matthews, George Pierce Baker, Montrose J. Moses, and Clayton Hamilton. Aside from the standard histories of literature and cyclopedias, the books to which I am most indebted are George Saintsbury's *History of Criticism* and J. E. Spingarn's *A History of Literary Criticism in the Renaissance.*

Special thanks are due to several persons in advising me on points affecting the selection and preparation of the texts in the Supplement. The following have given help and advice, both by letter and in person: Arthur Edwin Krows, Ludwig Lewisohn, George Jean Nathan, Joseph Wood Krutch, Eugene O'Neill, John Howard Lawson, Maxwell Anderson, John Mason Brown, and John Gassner. This book was originally dedicated to my wife, Cecile S. Clark. It is now re-dedicated to her, twenty-nine years later. And with reason. I am under the greatest obligation to her for doing a vast amount of stale, if not unprofitable reading; for transcribing texts, collating MS, and for the immense labor of preparing a large part of the index.

The text.—In almost every case I have been able to get the best published translation of standard and classic works originally written in a foreign language, but when this was out of the question, I have had to use the next best, and I have not scrupled to modify these after referring to the original and, in a few exceptional cases, to make use—with proper permission—of a phrase or note from the unobtainable standard translation. For convenience' sake I have modernized the spelling throughout, and to a certain extent standardized such matters as punctuation, paragraphing and capitalization.

BARRETT H. CLARK   1947.

PREFACE TO THE REVISED EDITION

For nearly half a century, while wars and revolutions have changed the great world and also altered the small world of the theatre, Barrett H. Clark's *European Theories of the Drama* has continued to be indispensable to students of drama. Mr. Clark's erudition and taste have stood the test of time so well that this book was still in demand even when the greater part of it, the European section, had gone without any substantial emendation for several decades. In revising this durable volume, I find that I have been able to leave Mr. Clark's work virtually unchanged, except for new bibliography, a few omissions to help make room for new material, and an occasional substitution, as in the selections from Samuel Johnson, Shaw, and O'Neill. But Mr. Clark, at every point, knew what he was doing, and, having carefully examined his book, I can only express admiration for his industry and his good sense.

This revision has been undertaken to bring *European Theories of the Drama* up to date. Those contributors who have been added fall into several categories: dramatists who had unmistakably established their importance in 1918 but were omitted, evidently because Mr. Clark could not justify sections on their nations—Ibsen, Strindberg, and Chekhov; representatives of important movements in modern thought, movements that have both influenced and interpreted the drama, reflecting the thought of Marx, Nietzsche, Freud, Jung, existentialism, and the Cambridge school of anthropology (I note parenthetically that, while Freud and Nietzsche themselves wrote on the drama, the masters did not always furnish us with usable passages, and so I have sometimes reprinted the disciples, e. g., Plekhanov for Marx and Northrop Frye for Jung); representatives of the new and continuing schools of drama—realism, the problem play, poetic drama, "folk" drama, epic theatre, the theatre of cruelty, and the theatre of the absurd; and the individual creators of the new drama—Pirandello, Lorca, Yeats, Synge, Eliot, O'Casey, Brecht, Sartre, Ionesco, Duerrenmatt, Miller, and Williams. If, at the end, I have leaned toward drama criticism by American academics (Fergusson, Frye, Bentley), I have done so in order to continue Mr. Clark's special interest in American critics and to balance his attention to critics who wrote for a larger audience.

Like any other editor, I have misgivings about omissions. The inevitable and correct explanation for any serious omission is lack of space. I worry especially about the absence of comment on the new British theatre; I think this new movement is here to stay, but I feel that the character of its contribution is not yet established.

I owe more thanks than I can express to friends both here and in Europe. In particular, I must express my gratitude for what I have learned about the drama from John Gassner and Eric Bentley and what I have learned about literature in general from Harry Levin. I wish also to compliment the consummate efficiency of my editor, Miss Lucile Wilder.

HENRY POPKIN   1964.

CONTENTS

CONTENTS

EUROPEAN THEORIES OF THE DRAMA

GREEK DRAMATIC CRITICISM

With the exception of the more or less fragmentary *Poetics* of Aristotle there is very little in Greek literature touching upon the subject of dramatic theory. What we possess are (1) quotations from Greek writers like Theophrastus (in the *Ars Grammatica* of Diomedes), and from Greek dramatists (in *The Deipnosophists* of Athenæus); (2) passages from Aristophanes; and (3) works or fragments of a more general character, of such writers as Plato and Dionysius of Halicarnassus; and (4) the Scholia, or commentaries on the dramatists.

Of dramatic criticism proper there is nothing either in Plato or Aristophanes; Plato's *Republic, Phædrus, Ion, Laws,* and other dialogues contain a good deal on the subject of poetry, and much on dramatic poetry, but, as might be expected, the philosopher is concerned rather with the moral and philosophic than the purely literary and dramatic aspects. Aristophanes' *Frogs* in particular is full of dramatic criticism of an indirect kind, but it is neither so objective nor so organized as to entitle it to serious consideration as a distinct theory of the drama. It is only by inference that the student may form any definite idea of Aristophanes' esthetic ideals. In M. Egger's indispensable *Histoire de la Critique chez les Grecs* there is quoted a passage attributed to Antiphanes on tragedy and comedy. Another short passage, attributed to Simylus, practically completes the list.

It was not likely that any considerable body of dramatic theory should be formulated before the close of the great dramatic epoch ushered in by Æschylus, so that the absence of any such work as the *Poetics* during that period is not surprising. Aristotle had before him the masterpieces of his country and was able to set forth a complete body of doctrine. While it has been pointed out that he was at a decided disadvantage in not knowing the literature of at least one other nation besides his own, it is doubly fortunate that so well-balanced a philosopher should have happened at the right time to sum up the dramatic theory of the age which immediately preceded him.

Of the rhetoricians and grammarians who followed Aristotle, of the great mass of Scholia on the tragedians and Aristophanes, there is very little to be said. Most of the commentators were concerned almost altogether with questions of philology, grammar, and the more formal aspects of the drama. Much later, Plutarch—in his *Comparison of Aristophanes and Menander* and elsewhere—turns to the drama, but his remarks are applicable mainly to the moral and stylistic side. Athenæus (in the third century A. D.) did no more than collect passages from earlier writers, some few of which are concerned with the drama.

ARISTOTLE

Aristotle was born at Stagira in the year 384 B. C. The most trustworthy biographical account of his life is by Dionysius of Halicarnassus, in his *Epistle on Demosthenes and Aristotle*: "Aristotle was the son of Nichomachus, who traced back his descent and his art to Machaon. son of Esculapius; his mother being Phæstis, a descendant of one of those who carried tne colony from Chalcis to Stagira. He was born in the 99th Olympiad in the archonship at Athens of Diotrephes (384–383), three years before Demosthenes. In the archonship of Polyzelus (367–366), after the death of his father, in his eighteenth year, he came to Athens, and having joined Plato, spent twenty years with him. On the death of Plato (May 347), in the archonship of Theophilus (348–347) he departed to Hermias, tyrant of Atarneus and, after three years' stay, during the archonship of Eubulus (345–344) he moved to Mitylene, whence he went to Philip of Macedon in the archonship of Pythodotus (343–342), and spent eight years with him as tutor of Alexander. After the death of Philip (336), in the archonship of Euænetus (335–334), he returned to Athens and kept a school in the Lyceum for twelve years. In the thirteenth, after the death of Alexander (June 323), in the archonship of Cephisodorus (323–322) having departed to Chalcis, he died of disease (322), after a life of three-and-sixty years."

The Poetics (or, *The Poetic*, according to the translation of the present version) of Aristotle is the earliest critical treatise extant dealing with dramatic practice and theory. Besides being a summing-up of the first great age of dramatic activity, it has exercised incalculable influence over the dramatists of all European and many other nations. There are few if any important contributions to dramatic theory and criticism which fail to take account of the work, but owing to its obviously incomplete form, the many corrupt portions of the text, its compact and elliptical style, it has been constantly misinterpreted, misquoted, and misunderstood. The famous Unities, the terms "Imitation" and "Purgation," have in particular proved troublesome to the Italian critics of the Renaissance and to their followers in France. Of late years, however, a number of valuable annotated editions, with copious notes and explanatory matter, have gone far to clear up the misunderstanding. Among the recent English editions, the most significant is S. H. Butcher's *Aristotle's Theory of Poetry and Fine Art*, containing the original text, a translation, and a commentary.

While Aristotle based his treatise upon the Greek poets with whose work he was acquainted, his general premises and his conclusions are in the main applicable to drama in general. Although there was an abridged version of the *Poetics* extant in the late Middle Ages, it cannot properly be maintained to have made its appearance until 1498, when Giorgio Valla published at Venice a Latin translation of it. This was followed by the Greek text, in the Aldine *Rhetores Græci* (1508). From that time forward, the text was translated into the vernacular, commented upon, and criticized; its influence was soon to become of the greatest importance, not only in Italy, but in France, Germany, and England.

THE POETIC [1]

[360–322 B. C.]

CHAP. I

Let us speak concerning poetry itself, and its [different] species; what power each possesses, and how fables must be composed, in order that poetry may be such as is fitting: further still, [let us show] of how many and what kind of parts it consists; and in like manner [let us treat] concerning such other things as pertain to this method, beginning, conformably to nature, first from such things as are first.

The epic, therefore, and tragic poetry, and moreover comedy, and dithyrambic

1 The present translation, by Theodore Buckley, is reprinted from the Bohn edition (London and New York, late ed., 1914). The foot-notes, unless otherwise designated and signed "Ed." are from that edition. Those parts of the text enclosed in brackets (by the editor of the Bohn edition) are considered either by him or by some other editor either as of doubtful authenticity or else are merely aids to render the sense clearer. Sections XX, XXI, and XXII are omitted. They deal with diction, language, grammar, and the like. Section XX is, according to Butcher "probably interpolated"; also a passage in section XXI. Section XXII is for the most part authentic, but is concerned with minor points of language. Section XXV is also omitted, as it deals mainly with objections, or "Problems."— Ed.

poetry, and the greatest part of the art pertaining to the flute and the lyre,[2] are all entirely imitations. They differ, however, in three things; for [they differ] either by imitating through means different in kind, or by imitating different objects, or in a different, and not after the same manner. For as certain persons assimilating, imitate many things by colors and figures, some indeed through art, but others through custom, [and others through voice]; thus also in the aforementioned arts, all of them indeed produce imitation in rhythm, words, and harmony; and in these, either distinctly, or mingled together, as, for instance, the arts of the flute and the lyre alone employ harmony and rhythm; and this will also be the case with any other arts which possess a power of this kind, such as the art of playing on reed-pipes. But the arts pertaining to dancing imitate by rhythm, without harmony; for dancers, through figured rhythms, imitate manners, and passions, and actions. But the epic alone imitates by mere words[3] or meters, and by these either mingling them with each other, or employing one certain kind of meters, which method has been adopted up to the present time. For otherwise we should have no common name by which we could denominate the Mimes of Sophron and Xenarchus, and the dialogues of Socrates; or those who imitate by trimeters, or elegies, or certain other things of this kind; except that men joining with meter the verb *to make*,[4] call some of these *makers of elegies*, but others epic *makers*, not as poets according to imitation, but denominating them in common according to measure. For they are accustomed thus to denominate them, if they write anything medical

or musical in verse. There is, however, nothing common to Homer and Empedocles except the measure; on which account, it is right indeed to call the former a poet; but the latter a physiologist rather than a poet. In like manner, though some one mingling all the measures, should produce imitation, as Chæremon has done in his *Centaur*, a mixed rhapsody of all the meters, yet he must not be called a poet. Let it then be thus laid down concerning these particulars. But there are some kinds of poetry which employ all the before-mentioned means, I mean, rhythm, melody and measure, such as dithyrambic poetry and the Nomes,[5] and also tragedy and comedy. But these differ, because some of them use all these at once, but others partially. I speak, therefore, of these differences of the arts in respect to the means by which they produce imitation.

CHAP. II

ON IMITATION AND ITS USUAL OBJECTS

But since imitators imitate those who do something, and it is necessary that these should either be worthy or depraved persons (for manners nearly always depend on these alone, since all men differ in their manners by vice and virtue); it is necessary either [to imitate] those who are better than we are, or those who are worse, or such as are like ourselves,[6] in the same manner as painters do. For Polygnotus, indeed, painted men more beautiful than they are, but Pauson less so, and Dionysius painted them as they are.[7] But it is evident that each of the before-mentioned imitations will have these differences; and imitation is different, by imitating different things after this manner. For there may be differences of this kind in dancing, in

---

2 Cithern playing was one of the favorite accomplishments of the Athenian youth.

3 There is much difficulty about this definition of ἐποποιία, as λόγοις ψιλοῖς is supposed by some to mean *prose* (see Robortello, p. 14), by others, *verse without music*. The sense is, therefore, " by *prose* or by *meter*, but unaccompanied by song."

4 It may be necessary to observe, that the Greek word (ποιητης — *poiétes*) whence *poeta*, and *poet*, is, literally, *maker*; and maker, it is well known, was once the current term for *poet* in our language; and to write verses, was, to *make*. Sir Philip Sidney, speaking of the Greek word, says, " wherein, I know not whether by luck or wisdom, we Englishmen have *met* with the Greeks, in calling him *maker*." *Defense of Poesy.*— Twining.

5 In dithyrambic or *Bacchic* hymns, and in the *Nomes*, which were also a species of hymns to Apollo and other deities, *all* the means of imitation were employed *together*, and *throughout* in tragedy and comedy, *separately*; some of them in one part of the drama, and some in another. In the *choral* part, however, at least, if nowhere else, *all*, melody, rhythm, and words, must probably have been used *at once*, as in the hymns.— Twining.

6 Or, " those who are commonly found."

7 Polygnotus and Dionysius lived about Ol. 80; Pauson about Ol. 90.

playing on the flute, on the lyre, and also
in orations and mere measure. Thus
Homer imitates better men [8] [than exist],
but Cleophon men as they are; and Heg-
emon the Thasian, who first made parodies,. and Nicochares, who wrote the
Deliad, imitate worse characters. In
like manner in dithyrambics and the
Nomi, [as Timotheus and Philoxenus
have imitated the Persians and the Cyclops,] one may imitate. By this very
same difference, also, tragedy differs
from comedy. For the one seeks to imitate worse, but the other better men than
are.

CHAP. III

THE THIRD DIFFERENCE OF POETRY ACCORD-
ING TO THE MANNER OF IMITATING

There is also a third difference of
these, consisting in the manner in which
one may imitate each of them. For by
the same instruments the same things
may be imitated, the poet sometimes
himself narrating, and sometimes assuming another person [as Homer does [9]];
or speaking as the same person without
any change; or as all imitate [who do so]
by deed and action. But imitation consists in these three differences, as we said
in the beginning; viz. in the means, the
objects, or the manner. Hence, Sophocles will in one respect be the same imitator as Homer, for both of them imitate
elevated characters; and in another the
same as Aristophanes, for both of them
imitate persons engaged in acting;
[[10] whence also it is said that certain
persons call their works *dramas,* because
they imitate those who are engaged in
doing something. On this account the
Dorians lay claim to the invention of
tragedy and comedy; of comedy indeed
the Megarians, as well those who are na-

tives of Greece, as being invented by
them at the time when their government
was a democracy, as those of Sicily. For
thence was the poet Epicharmus, who
was much prior to Chonides and Magnes.
But some of those Dorians who inhabit
Peloponnesus lay claim to tragedy, making names an evidence. For they allege
that they call their villages *komai,* but
the Athenians *demoi;* as if comedians
were not so denominated from *komazein,*
[i. e. *to revel*] but from their wandering
through villages, being ignominiously expelled from the cities. The verb *poiein*
also, or *to make,* is by the Dorians denominated *dran,* but by the Athenians
prattein.] And thus much concerning
the differences of imitation, as to their
number and quality.

CHAP. IV

THE CAUSES AND PROGRESS OF POETRY

Two causes, however, and these physical, appear to have produced poetry in
general. For to imitate is congenial to
men from childhood. And in this they
differ from other animals, that they are
most imitative, and acquire the first dis-
ciplines through imitation; and that all
men delight in imitations. But an evidence of this is that which happens in
the works [of artists]. For we are delighted on surveying very accurate images, the realities of which are painful
to the view; such as the forms of the
most contemptible animals, and dead
bodies. The cause, however, of this is
that learning is not only most delightful
to philosophers, but in like manner to
other persons, though they partake of it
but in a small degree. For on this account, men are delighted on surveying
images, because it happens that by surveying they learn and infer what each
particular is; as, that *this* is an image
of *that man;* since, unless one happen
to have seen [the reality], it is not the
imitation that pleases, but [it is through]
either the workmanship, or the color, or
some other cause of the like kind. But
imitation, harmony, and rhythm being
natural to us, (for it is evident that
measures or meters are parts of
rhythms [11]), the earliest among mankind,

---

8 Superior, that is, in courage, strength, wisdom, prudence, etc.— in *any* laudable, useful,
or admirable quality, whether such as we denominate *moral,* or not. If superiority of
moral character only were meant, the assertion
would be false.— It is necessary to remember
here, the *wide* sense in which the ancients used
the terms *virtue, vice — good, bad,* etc.—
Twining.

9 But this assertion is not correct, and Ritter
shows that the words are spurious.

10 The learned note of Ritter seems to condemn the whole of this passage as spurious.

11 " RHYTHM differs from METER, inasmuch
as RHYTHM is *proportion, applied to any mo-*

making a gradual progress in these things from the beginning, produced poetry from extemporaneous efforts. But poetry was divided according to appropriate manners. For men of a more venerable character imitated beautiful actions, and the actions of such men; but the more ignoble imitated the actions of depraved characters, first composing vituperative verses, in the same manner as the others composed hymns and encomiums. Of the authors, therefore, before Homer, we cannot mention any poem of this kind; though it is probable that there were many such writers. But if we begin from Homer, there are such for instance as his *Margites,* and some others, in which, as being suited, the measure is Iambic. Hence, also, the Iambic verse is now called, because in this meter they used to *Iambize* (i. e. defame) each other. Of ancient poets, likewise, some composed heroic poems, and others Iambic. But as Homer was the greatest of poets on serious subjects, (and this not only because he alone imitated well, but also because he made dramatic imitations), thus too he first demonstrated the figures of comedy, not dramatically exhibiting invective, but ridicule. For the *Margites* bears the same analogy to comedy, as the *Iliad* and *Odyssey* to tragedy. But when tragedy and comedy had appeared, those poets who were naturally impelled to each kind of poetry, some, instead of writing Iambics, became comic poets, but others, instead of [writing] epic poems, became the authors of tragedies, because these forms [of poetry] are greater and more esteemed than those. To consider, therefore, whether tragedy is now perfect in its species or not, regarded as well with reference to itself as to the theaters, is the business of another treatise. Both tragedy and comedy, therefore, at first originated from extemporaneous efforts.

tion whatever; METER *is proportion. applied to* *the motion of* WORDS SPOKEN. Thus, in the drumming of a march, or the dancing of a hornpipe, there is *rhythm,* or the dancing of a hornpipe, there is *rhythm,* no *meter;* in Dryden's celebrated *Ode* there is METER as well as RHYTHM, because the poet with the *rhythm* has associated certain *words.* And hence it follows, that, though ALL METER is RHYTHM, yet ALL RHYTHM IS NOT METER." Harris's *Philol. Inquiries.* p. 67,— where it is also observed, very truly, that " no English word expresses *rhythmus* better than the word *time.*" P. 69, note.— Twining.

And tragedy, indeed, originated from those who led the dithyramb, but comedy from those who sung the Phallic verses, which even now in many cities remain in use; and it gradually increased as obvious improvements became known. And tragedy, having experienced many changes, rested when it had arrived at its proper nature. Æschylus, also, first increased the number of players from one to two, abridged the functions of the chorus, and made one of the players act the chief part. But Sophocles introduced three players into the scene, and added scenic painting. Further still, the magnitude [of tragedy increased] from small fables and ridiculous diction, in consequence of having been changed from satyric [12] composition, it was late before it acquired dignity. The meter also of tragedy, from tetrameter, became Iambic (for at first they used tetrameter in tragedy, because poetry was then satyrical, and more adapted to the dance, but dialogue being adopted, nature herself discovered a suitable meter; for the Iambic measure is most of all adapted to conversation. And as an evidence of this, we most frequently speak in Iambics in familiar discourse with each other; but we seldom speak in hexameters, and then only when we depart from that harmony which is adapted to conversation). Again, tragedy is said to have been further adorned, with a multitude of episodes, and other particulars. Let, therefore, thus much said suffice concerning these things; for it would perhaps be a great toil to discuss every particular.

CHAP. V

ON COMEDY AND ITS ORIGIN — DIFFERENCE OF EPIC AND TRAGEDY

But comedy is, as we have said, an imitation indeed of bad characters, yet it does not imitate them according to every vice, [but the ridiculous only]; since the

12 *Satyric,* from the share which those fantastic beings called *Satyrs,* the companions and *play-fellows* of *Bacchus,* had in the earliest Tragedy, of which they formed the chorus. *Joking* and *dancing* were essential attributes of these rustic semi-deities. Hence the " *ludicrous language* " and the " *dancing genius* " of the old Tragedy, to which the TROCHAIC or *running* meter here spoken of was peculiarly adapted.— Twining.

ridiculous is a portion of turpitude. For *the ridiculous is a certain error, and turpitude unattended with pain, and not destructive.* Thus, for instance, a ridiculous face is something deformed and distorted without pain. The transitions, therefore, of tragedy, and the causes through which they are produced, are not unknown; but [those of] comedy have escaped our knowledge, because it was not at first an object of attention. For it was late before the magistrate gave a chorus to comedians [13]; but prior to that period, the choruses were voluntary. Comedy, however, at length having obtained a certain form, those who are said to have been poets therein are commemorated. But it is unknown who it was that introduced masks or prologues, or a multitude of players, and such like particulars. But Epicharmus and Phormis [were the first] to compose fables; which, therefore, originated from Sicily. But among the Athenians, Crates, rejecting the Iambic form, first began generally to compose speeches and fables. The epic, therefore, is an attendant on tragedy, [with the exception of the long meter,] since through this it is an imitation of worthy characters and actions. But it differs from tragedy in that it has a simple meter, and is a narration. It also [differs from it] in length. For tragedy is especially limited by one period of the sun, or admits but a small variation from this period; but the epic is not defined within a certain time, and in this it differs; though at first they observed the same conduct with tragedy, no less than epic poetry. With respect to the parts, however, [of the epic and tragedy,] some are the same in both, but others are peculiar to tragedy. Hence he who knows what is a good or bad tragedy, knows the same in respect to epic poetry. For those things which the epic possesses are to be found in tragedy; but everything which tragedy contains is not in the epic.

CHAP. VI

ON THE FORM AND END OF TRAGEDY, AND
ON ITS SIX PARTS, ESPECIALLY
THE PLOT

13 This was almost equivalent to the modern "licensing" of plays, but was probably conducted with more taste and less absurdity.

Concerning, therefore, imitative poetry in hexameters, and comedy, we shall speak hereafter. Let us now, however, speak concerning tragedy, assuming the definition of its essence as arising from what has been already said.[14] *Tragedy, therefore, is an imitation of a worthy or illustrious and perfect action, possessing magnitude, in pleasing language, using separately the several species of imitation in its parts, by men acting, and not through narration, through pity and fear effecting a purification from such like passions.* But by *pleasing language,* I mean language possessing rhythm, harmony, and melody. And it *uses separately the several species [of imitation],* because some parts of the tragedy are alone perfected through meters, and others again through melody. But since they produce imitation by acting, in the first place the ornament of the spectacle [15] will be a certain part of the tragedy, and in the next place the *melopœia* [16] and the diction. For by these they produce imitation. But I call diction, indeed, the composition of the meters; and *melopœia* that, the whole power of which is apparent. Since, however, [tragedy] is an imitation of action, and action is effected by certain agents, who must needs be persons of a certain description both as to their manners and their sentiments, (for from these we say that actions derive their quality), hence there are naturally two causes of actions, sen-

14 This much discussed definition of tragedy is thus rendered by Butcher: " Tragedy, then, is an imitation of an action that is serious, complete, and of a certain magnitude; in language embellished with each kind of artistic ornament, the several kinds being found in separate parts of the play; in the form of action, not of narrative; through pity and fear effecting the proper purgation of these emotions."— Ed.

15 " *Decoration* — literally, the decoration of the *spectacle,* or *sight.* In other places it is called the *spectacle,* or *sight* only — ὄψις· It comprehends *scenery, dresses* — the whole visible apparatus of the theater I do not know any single English word that answers fully to the Greek word."— Twining.

16 *Melopœia* — literally, the *making,* or the *composition, of the Music;* as we use *Epopœia,* or according to the French termination, which we have naturalized, *Epopee,* to signify epic *poetry,* or *epic-making,* in general.— I might have rendered it, at once, the MUSIC: but that it would have appeared ridiculous to observe, of a word so familiar to us, even that " *its meaning is obvious.*"— Twining.

timents and moral habit, and through these actions all men obtain or fail of the object of their wishes. But a fable, indeed, is an imitation of action; for I mean by a *fable* here, the composition of incidents. By *manners,* I mean those things according to which we say that agents are persons of a certain charac ter; and by *sentiment,* that through which those who speak demonstrate any thing, or explain their meaning. It is necessary, therefore, that the parts of every tragedy should be six, from which the tragedy derives its quality. But these are, fable and manners, diction and sentiment, spectacle and *melopœia.* Of these parts, however, two pertain to the means by which they imitate; one, to the manner; and three, to the objects. And besides these, there are no other. [Not a few [tragic poets], therefore, as I may say, use all these parts.] For every tragedy has scenic apparatus, manners, and a fable, and melody, and, in a similar manner, sentiment. But the greatest of these is the combination of the incidents. For tragedy is an imitation not of men, but of actions, [of life, and of felicity. For infelicity consists in action, and the end is a certain action, and not a quality]. Men, however, are persons of a certain character, according to their manners; but according to their actions, they are happy, or the contrary. The end of tragedy, therefore, does not consist in imitating manners, but it embraces manners on account of actions; so that the action and the fable are the end of tragedy. But the end is the greatest of all things. Moreover, without action, tragedy cannot exist; but it may exist without manners. For most modern tragedies are without manners; and in short, many poets are such as among painters Zeuxis is when compared with Polygnotus. For Polygnotus, indeed, painted the manners of the good; but the pictures of Zeuxis are without manners. Further still, if any one place in a continued series moral speeches, sayings, and sentiments well framed, he will not produce that which is the work of tragedy; but that will be much more a tragedy which uses these things as subordinate, and which contains a fable and combination of incidents. Add to that the greatest parts by which allures the soul, are the *revolutions* and

discoveries. Again, it is likewise an evidence of this, that those who attempt to write tragedies acquire the power of expressing a thing in tragic diction and manners accurately, before they can compose a fable, as was the case with nearly all the first poets. The fable, therefore, is the principal part, and as it were the soul of tragedy; but the manners are next in rank. [Just as in painting, if any one were to spread the most beautiful pigments on promiscuously, he would not please the view so much as by outlining an image with white color only. Tragedy also is an imitation of action, and on this account, especially, [an imitation] of agents. But the sentiments rank third. And by them [I mean] *the power of explaining what is inherent in the subject, and adapted to it,* which is the peculiar province of politics [17] and rhetoric. For the ancient poets represent those whom they introduce as speaking politically; but those of the present day, rhetorically. But the manners are whatever shows what the deliberate choice is. Hence those speeches are without manners, in which there is altogether nothing that the speaker may choose or avoid. But *sentiment is that* **through which they show that a certain** *thing is, or is not, or by which they universally enunciate something.* And the fourth part of tragedy is diction. But I say, as was before observed, that *diction is interpretation by the means of words, and which also has the same power in verse and prose.* But of the remaining five, the *melopœia* is the greatest of the embellishments. But the scenic decoration is alluring indeed; yet it is most inartificial, and is in the smallest degree akin to poetry. For the power of tragedy remains, even when unaccompanied with scenic apparatus and players. And further still, the art of the mechanic possesses more power in constructing the scenic apparatus than that of the poet.]

17 The reader here must not think of our modern *politics.*— The *political,* or *civil art,* or *science,* was, in Aristotle's view, of wide extent and high importance. It comprehended *ethics* and *eloquence,* or the art of public speaking; everything, in short, that concerned the well-being of a *state.*— Twining.

CHAP. VII

ON THE REQUISITES AND LENGTH OF TRAGIC ACTION

These things being defined, let us in the next place show what the combination of the incidents ought to be, since this is the first and greatest part of tragedy. But it is granted to us that tragedy is the imitation of a perfect and whole action, and of one which possesses a certain magnitude; for there may be a whole which has no magnitude. But a whole is that which has a beginning, middle, and end. And the beginning is that which necessarily is not itself posterior to another thing; but another thing is naturally expected to follow it. On the contrary, the end is that which is itself naturally adapted to be posterior to another thing, either from necessity, or for the most part; but after this there is nothing else. But the middle is that which is itself after another thing, and after which there is something else. Hence, it is necessary that those who compose fables properly, should neither begin them casually, nor end them casually, but should employ the above-mentioned forms [of beginning, middle, and end]. Further still, since that which is beautiful, whether it be an animal, or any thing else which is composed from certain parts, ought not only to have these parts arranged, but a magnitude also which is not casual. For the beautiful consists in magnitude and order. Hence, neither can any very small animal be beautiful; for the survey of it is confused, since it is effected in a time nearly insensible. Nor yet a very large animal; for it is not surveyed at once, but its subsistence as one and a whole escapes the view of the spectators; such as if, for instance, it should be an animal of ten thousand stadia in length. Hence, as in bodies and in animals it is necessary there should be magnitude; but such as can easily be seen; thus also in fables, there should be length, but this such as can easily be remembered.[18] The defini-

18 The unity here spoken of, it must be remembered, is not *absolute* and *simple*, but *relative* and *compound*, unity: a unity consisting of different *parts*, the relation of which to each other and to the whole, is easily perceived at one view. On this depends the perception of beauty in *form*.— In objects too extended, you may be said to have *parts*, but no *whole*: in very minute objects the *whole*, but no *parts*.—**Twining.**

tion, however, of the length with reference to contests 19 and the senses, does not fall under the consideration of art. For if it were requisite to perform a hundred tragedies, [as is said to have been the case more than once], the performance ought to be regulated by a clepsydra. But the definition [of the length of the fable] according to the nature of the thing, is this, that the fable is always more beautiful the greater it is, if at the same time it is perspicuous. Simply defining the thing, however, we may say, [that a fable has an appropriate magnitude], when the time of its duration is such as to render it probable that there can be a transition from prosperous to adverse, or from adverse to prosperous fortune, according to the necessary or probable order of things as they take place. This is a sufficient definition of magnitude.

CHAP. VIII

ON UNITY OF THE FABLE

The fable, however, is one, not as some suppose, if one person is the subject of it; for many things which are infinite in kind happen [to one man], from a certain number of which no one event arises. Thus, also, there are many actions of one man, from which no one action is produced. Hence all those poets appear to have erred who have written the *Heracleid*, and *Theseid*, and such like poems. For they suppose that because Hercules was one person, it was fit that the fable should be one. Homer, however, as he excelled in other things, appears likewise to have seen this clearly, whether from art, or from nature. For in composing the *Odyssey*, he has not related every thing which happened to Ulysses; such as the being wounded in Parnassus,[20] and pretending to be insane 21 at

19 i. e. to its representation at the dramatic contests.

20 *This* incident is, however, related, and at considerable length, in the xixth book of the *Odyssey* (v. 563 of Pope's translation), but digressively, and incidentally; it made no essential part of his *general plan*.— Twining.

21 A ridiculous story.—" To avoid going to the Trojan war, Ulysses pretended to be mad; and, to prove his insanity, went to plow with an *ox* and a *horse;* but Palamedes, in order to detect him, laid his infant son, Telemachus, in the way of the plow; upon which Ulysses immediately stopped, and thereby proved himself to be in his right senses."— Twining.

the muster of the Greeks; one of which taking place, it was not necessary or probable that the other should happen; but he composed the *Odyssey,* as also his *Iliad,* upon one action. It is requisite, therefore, that as in other imitative arts one imitation is the imitation of one thing, thus, also, [in tragedy], the fable, since it is an imitation of action, should be the imitation of one action, and of the whole of this, and that the parts of the transactions should be so arranged, that any one of them being transposed, or taken away, the whole would become different and changed. For that which when present or not present produces no sensible [difference], is not a part of the fable.

CHAP. IX

ON THE DIFFERENCE BETWEEN HISTORY AND
POETRY, AND HOW HISTORICAL MATTER
SHOULD BE USED IN POETRY

But it is evident from what has been said, that it is not the province of a poet to relate things which have happened, but such as might have happened, and such things as are possible according to probability, or which would necessarily have happened. For an historian and a poet do not differ from each other because the one writes in verse and the other in prose; for the history of Herodotus might be written in verse, and yet it would be no less a history with meter than without meter. But they differ in this, that the one speaks of things which have happened, and the other of such as might have happened. Hence, poetry is more philosophic, and more deserving of attention, than history. For poetry speaks more of universals, but history of particulars. But *universal* consists indeed in relating or performing certain things which happen to a man of a certain description, either probably or necessarily, [to which the aim of poetry is directed in giving names [22]]; but *particular* consists in narrating what, [for example], Alcibiades did, or what he suffered. In comedy, therefore, this is now become evident. For [comic poets] having composed a fable through things of a

probable nature, they thus give whatever names they please [23] to their characters, and do not, like Iambic poets, write poems about particular persons. But in tragedy they cling to real names. The cause, however, of this is that the possible is credible. Things, therefore, which have not yet been done, we do not yet believe to be possible; but it is evident that things which have been done are possible; for they would not have been done if they were impossible. Not, indeed, but that in some tragedies there are one or two of known names, and the rest are feigned; but in others there is no known name; as, for instance, in *The Flower* of Agatho. For in this tragedy, the things and the names are alike feigned, and yet it delights no less. Hence, one must not seek to adhere entirely to traditional fables, which are the subjects of tragedy. For it is ridiculous to make this the object of search, because even known subjects are known but to a few, though at the same time they delight all men. From these things, therefore, it is evident that a poet ought rather to be the author of fables than of meters, inasmuch as he is a poet from imitation, and he imitates actions. Hence, though it should happen that he relates things which have happened, he is no less a poet. For nothing hinders but that some actions which have happened are such as might both probably [24] and

22 Ritter well observes that the perspicuity of this otherwise clear passage is destroyed by this absurd interpolation.

23 Thus nearly all the names in the comedies of Terence and Plautus, thus Dromo and Sosia are applied to slaves, Pamphilus to a lover, Glycerium or Philumena to a lady, Pyrgopolinices or Thraso to soldiers.

24 It may appear to the reader to be a strange observation, that "*some true* events MAY be *probable.*" But he will recollect what sort of *events,* and what sort of *probability,* Aristotle here speaks of: i.e. of *extraordinary events,* such as Poetry requires, and of that more *strict* and *perfect probability,* that closer connection and *visible* dependence of circumstances, which are always required from the *poet,* though in *such* events, not often to be found in *fact,* and real life, and therefore not expected from the *historian.*

This general, and, if I may call it so, *possible* sort of *probability,* may be termed, *the probability of romance;* and these lines of Agatho furnish a good apologetical motto for the novel writer. It might be prefixed, perhaps, without impropriety, even to the best productions of the kind — to a CLARISSA or a CECILIA. Nothing is so commonly complained of in such works, as their *improbability;* and often, no doubt, the complaint is well-founded: often, however, the criticism means nothing more than that the events are *uncommon,* and possibly have happened, and by [the narration of] such he is a poet.

But of simple plots and actions, the episodic are the worst. But I call the plot episodic, in which it is neither probable nor necessary that the episodes follow each other. Such plots, however, are composed by bad poets indeed, through their own want of ability; but by good poets, on account of the players. For, introducing [dramatic] contests, and extending the plot beyond its capabilities, they are frequently compelled to distort the connexion of the parts. But, since tragedy is not only an imitation of a perfect action, but also of actions which are terrible and piteous, and actions principally become such, [and in a greater degree, when they happen contrary to opinion], on account of each other. . . . For thus they will possess more of the marvelous, than if they happened from chance and fortune; since, also, of things which are from fortune, those appear to be most admirable, which seem to happen as it were by design. Thus the statue of Mityus at Argos killed him who was the cause of the death of Mityus by falling as he was surveying it. For such events as these seem not to take place casually. Hence it is necessary that fables of this kind should be more beautiful.

CHAP. X

FABLES, EITHER SIMPLE OR COMPOUND

Of fables, however, some are simple, and others complex; for so also are the actions of which fables are the imitations. But I call the action *simple,* from which taking place, as it has been defined, with continuity and unity, there is a transition without either revolution or *discovery;* but complex, from which there is a transition, together with discovery, or revolution, or both. It is necessary, however, that these should be effected from the composition itself of the fable, so that from what has formerly happened it may come to pass that the same things take place either necessarily or probably. For it makes a great difference whether

proves nothing more than the want of fancy, and an extended view of human life in the reader. If the events were *not* uncommon, where would the book find readers? — Twining.

these things are effected on account of these, or after these.

CHAP. XI

Now, revolution is a mutation, as has been stated, of actions into a contrary condition; and this, as we say, according to the probable, or the necessary. Thus in the *Œdipus* the messenger who comes with an intention of delighting Œdipus and liberating him from his fear respecting his mother, when he makes himself known, produces a contrary effect. Thus, too, in the *Lynceus,* he indeed is introduced as one who is to die, and Danaus follows with an intention of killing him; but it happens from the course of incidents, that Lynceus is saved, and Danaus is slain. And discovery is, as the name signifies, a change from ignorance to knowledge, or into the friendship or hatred of those who are destined to prosperous or adverse fortune. The discovery, however, is most beautiful, when at the same time there are, as in the *Œdipus,* revolutions. There are, therefore, other discoveries also. For sometimes it happens, as has been before observed, that there are discoveries of things inanimate and casual; or if some one has performed, or has not performed, a thing, there is a recognition of it; but the discovery which especially pertains to the fable and the action is that before mentioned. For a discovery and revolution of this kind will excite either pity or fear; and tragedy is supposed to be an imitation of such actions [as excite fear and pity]. Again, it will happen that infelicity and felicity will be in such like discoveries. But since discovery is a discovery of certain persons, some [discoveries] are of one person only with reference to another, when it is evident who the other person is, but sometimes it is necessary to discover both persons. Thus Iphigenia was recognized by Orestes through the sending of an epistle; but another discovery was requisite to his being known by Iphigenia. [Two parts of the fable, therefore, viz. revolution and discovery, are conversant with these things; but the third part is pathos. And of these, revolution and discovery have been already discussed. Pathos, however, is an action destructive, or lamentable; such as death when it is obvious, grievous pains, wounds, and such like particulars.]

CHAP. XII

ON THE PARTS OF TRAGEDY

[But we have before spoken of the parts of tragedy which are requisite to constitute its quality. The parts of tragedy, however, according to quantity, and into which it is separately divided, are as follows: prologue,[25] episode,[26] exode,[27] and chorus, of the parts of which one is the *parados*,[28] but the other is the *stasimon*.[29] These [five] parts, therefore, are common to all [tragedies]; but the peculiar parts are [the songs] from the scene and the *kommoi*. And the prologue, indeed, is the whole part of the tragedy, prior to the entrance of the chorus. The episode is the whole part of the tragedy between two complete odes of the chorus. The exode is the whole part of the tragedy, after which there is no further melody of the chorus. And of the chorus, the parados, indeed, is the first speech of the whole chorus; but the stasimon is the melody of the chorus, without anapæst and trochee: and the commos [30] is the common lamentation of the chorus and from the scene. But we have before shown what the parts of tragedy are which must necessarily be used; but the parts of it according to quantity, and into which it is separately divided, are these.[31]]

25 *Prologue* — This may be compared to our *first act.* — Twining.
26 *Episode* — i. e. *a part introduced, inserted,* etc., as all the *dialogue* was, originally, between the choral odes.— Twining.
27 *Exode* — i. e. *the going out,* or *exit;* the concluding *act,* as we should term it. The Greek tragedies never *finished* with a choral ode.— Twining.
28 *Parode* — i. e. *entry* of the chorus upon the stage: and hence the term was applied to *what they first sung,* upon their entry.— Twining.
29 *Stasimon* — i. e., *stable;* because, as it is explained, these odes were sung by the choral troop when fixed on the stage, and at rest: whereas the *parode* is said to have been sung *as they came on.* Hence, the *trochaic* and *anapæstic* measures, being lively and full of motion, were adapted to the *parode,* but not to the *stasimon.*— Twining.
30 From a verb signifying to *beat* or *strike;* alluding to the gestures of violent grief.
31 Ritter, who has illustrated this whole chapter with great learning and taste, allows its utility, but doubts that it is the work of Aristotle.

CHAP. XIII

THE ESSENTIALS FOR A TRAGIC PLOT

In the next place we must show, as consequent to what has been said, what those who compose fables ought to aim at, and beware of, and whence the purpose of tragedy is effected. Since, therefore, it is necessary that the composition of the most beautiful tragedy should not be simple, but complex, and that it should be imitative of fearful and piteous actions — (for this is the peculiarity of such imitation) — in the first place it is evident that it is not proper that worthy men should be represented as changed from prosperity to adversity, (for this is neither a subject of terror nor commiseration, but is impious,) nor should depraved characters [be represented as changed] from adversity to prosperity; for this is the most foreign from tragedy of all things, since it possesses nothing which is proper; for it neither appeals to moral sense, nor is piteous, nor fearful. Nor, again, must a very depraved man be represented as having fallen from prosperity into adversity. For such a composition will indeed possess moral tendency, but not pity or fear. For the one is conversant with a character which does not deserve to be unfortunate; but the other, with a character similar [to one's own]. [And pity, indeed, is excited for one who does not deserve to be unfortunate; but fear, for one who resembles oneself]; so that the event will neither appear to be commiserable, nor terrible. There remains therefore the character between these. But a character of this kind is one who neither excels in virtue and justice, nor is changed through vice and depravity, into misfortune, from a state of great renown and prosperity, but has experienced this change through some [human] error; such as Œdipus and Thyestes, and other illustrious men of this kind. Hence it is necessary that a plot which is well constructed, should be rather single [32] than twofold, (though some say it should be

32 What is here meant by a *single* fable, will appear presently from the account of its opposite — the *double* fable. It must not be confounded with the *simple* fable, though in the original both are expressed by the same word. The *simple* fable is only a fable *without revolution, or discovery.*—Twining.

the latter,) and that the change should not be into prosperity from adversity, but on the contrary into adversity from prosperity, not through depravity, but through some great error, either of such a character [as we have mentioned], or better rather than worse. But the proof of this is what has taken place. For of old the poets adopted any casual fables; but now the most beautiful tragedies are composed about a few families; as for instance, about Alcmæon, Œdipus, Orestes, Meleager, Thyestes, and Telephus, and such other persons as happen either to have suffered or done things of a dreadful nature. The tragedy, therefore, which is most beautiful according to art, is of this construction. Hence they erroneously blame Euripides, who accuse him of having done this in his tragedies, and for making many of them terminate in misfortune. For this method, as we have said, is right; of which this is the greatest evidence, that in the scenes, and contests of the players, simple fables which terminate unhappily appear to be most tragical, if they are properly acted. And Euripides, though he does not manage other things well, yet appears to be the most tragic of poets.[33] The fable, however, ranks in the second place, though by some it is said to be the first composition, which has a twofold construction, such as the *Odyssey*, and which terminates in a contrary fortune, both to the better and worse characters. It appears, however, to rank in the first place, through the imbecility of the spectators.[34] For the poets, in composing their plots, accommodate themselves to the wish of the spectators. This pleasure, however, is not [properly] derived from tragedy, but is rather suited to comedy. For there, though the greatest enemies be introduced, as Orestes and Ægisthus,

yet in the end they depart friends, and no one falls by the hand of the other.

CHAP. XIV

OF TERROR AND PITY

Terror and pity, therefore, may be produced from the sight. But they may also arise from the combination of the incidents, which is preferable, and the province of a better poet. For it is necessary that the fable should be so composed that he who hears the things which are transacted, may be seized with horror, and feel pity, from the events, without the assistance of the sight; and in this manner any one who hears the fable of Œdipus is affected. But to effect this through spectacle is more inartificial, and requires great expense. But they who produce not the terrible, but the monstrous alone, through scenic representation, have nothing in common with tragedy. For it is not proper to expect every kind of pleasure from tragedy, but that which is appropriate. Since, however, it is necessary that the poet should procure pleasure from pity and fear through imitation, it is evident that this must be effected by the circumstances. Let us, then, ascertain what kind of events appear to be dreadful or lamentable. But it is necessary that actions of this kind should either be those of friends towards each other, or of enemies, or of neither. If, therefore, an enemy kills an enemy, he does not show any thing which is an object of pity, neither while he does the deed, nor when he is about to do it, except what arises from the deed itself. And this will be the case when one of those who are neither friends nor enemies do the same. But when these things happen in friendships, as when a brother kills a brother, or a son his father, or a mother her son, or a son his mother, or intends to do it, or does any thing else of the like kind — such subjects are to be sought for. One must not, therefore, [completely] alter the received fables. I mean, for instance, such as the fable of Clytemnestra being slain by Orestes, and of Eriphyle by Alcmæon. But it is necessary that the poet should invent the plot, and use in a becoming manner those fables which are handed down. What, however, we

---

33 But below, xv. 5. Euripides is justly charged with the improper introduction of comic characters and language. The praise applies only to the catastrophe.

34 That weakness which cannot bear strong emotions, even from fictitious distress. To some minds, everything that is not *cheerful* is *shocking*.— But, might not the preference here attributed to *weakness*, be attributed to better causes — the gratification of philanthropy, the love of justice, order, etc.? — the same causes which, just before, induced Aristotle himself to condemn as *shocking* and *disgusting*, those fables which involve the virtuous in calamity.— Twining.

mean by [using fables] in a becoming manner, let us explain more clearly. Now, the action may take place in such a way as the ancients have represented it, viz. knowingly with intent; as Euripides represents Medea killing her children. Men may also do an action, who are ignorant of, and afterwards discover their connexion [with, the injured party,] as in the *Œdipus* of Sophocles. This, therefore, is extraneous to the drama,[35] but is in the tragedy itself; as in the *Alcmæon* of Astydamas, or Telegonus in the *Ulysses Wounded*.[36] Further still, besides these there is a third mode, when some one is about to perpetrate, through ignorance, an atrocious deed, but makes the discovery before he does it. And besides these there is no other mode. For it is necessary to act, or not; and that knowing, or not knowing. But of these, to intend to perpetrate the deed knowingly, and not to perpetrate it, is the worst; for it is wicked and not tragical; because it is void of pathos. [Hence, no poet introduces a character of this kind except rarely; as in the *Antigone*, in which Hæmon [endeavors to kill his father] Creon, [but does not effect his purpose.][37] For the action here ranks in the second place. But it is better to perpetrate the deed ignorantly, and having perpetrated to discover; for then it is not attended with wickedness, and the discovery excites horror. The last mode, however, is the best; I mean, as in the *Cresphontes,* in which Merope is about to kill her son, but does not, in consequence of discovering that he was her son. Thus, too, in the *Iphigenia in Tauris,* in which the sister is going to kill the brother, [but recognizes him]; and in the *Helle,* the son is about to betray his mother, but is prevented by recognizing

her. Hence, as has been formerly observed, tragedies are not conversant with many families; for poets were enabled to discover incident of this kind in fables, not from art, but from fortune.[38] They were compelled, therefore, to direct their attention to those families in which calamities of this kind happened.

And thus we have spoken sufficiently concerning the combination of the incidents, and have shown what kind of fables ought to be employed.

CHAP. XV

With respect to manners, however, there are four things to which one ought to direct attention: one, indeed, and the first, that they be good. But the tragedy will indeed possess manners, if, as was said, the words or the action render any deliberate intention apparent; containing good manners, if the deliberate intention is good. But manners are to be found in each genus; for both a woman and a slave may be good; though perhaps of these, the one is less good, and the other is wholly bad.[39] In the second place, the manners must be adapted to the persons. For there are manners which are characterized by fortitude, but it is not suited to a woman to be either brave or terrible. In the third place, the manners must be similar. For this, as was before observed, differs from making the manners to be good and adapted. In the fourth place, they must be uniform; for if he is anomalous who exhibits the imitation, and expresses such like manners, at the same time it is necessary that he should be uniformly unequal. The example, however, of depraved manners is indeed not necessary; such, for instance, as that of Menelaus in the *Orestes,* but an example of unbecoming and unappropriate manners is, the lamentation of Ulysses in

35 The murder of Laius by Œdipus, his son, is supposed to have happened a considerable time before the beginning of the action.— Twining.

36 Of these two dramas nothing more is known than the little that Aristotle here tells us. In the first, the poet adhered so far to history, as to make Alcmæon *kill* his mother Eriphyle, but with the improvement (according to Aristotle's idea), of making him do it *ignorantly.* The story of Telegonus is, that he was a son of Ulysses by Circe; was sent by her in quest of his father, whom he wounded, without knowing him, in a skirmish relative to some sheep, that he attempted to carry off from the island of Ithaca.— Twining.

37 Ritter condemns this passage.

38 i. e. to history or tradition.

39 This is observed, to show the consistence of this *first* precept with the next. The manners must be drawn *as* good as may be, consistently with the observance of *propriety,* with respect to the *general* character of different sexes, ages, conditions, etc. It might have been objected —" You say the character must be *good.* But suppose the poet has to represent, for instance, a slave? — the character of slaves in general is *notoriously bad.*"— The answer is — *anything* may be good *in its kind.*— Twining.

the tragedy of *Scylla*,[40] and the speech of Menalippe; and the example of anomalous manners in the *Iphigenia in Aulis*. For Iphigenia supplicating does not at all resemble the Iphigenia in the latter part of the tragedy. It is requisite, however, in the manners as well as in the combination of the incidents, always to investigate, either the necessary or the probable; so that such a person should say or do such things, either necessarily or probably; and that it be necessary or probable that this thing should be done after that. It is evident, therefore, that the solutions of fables ought to happen from the fable itself, and not as in the *Medea*,[41] from the machinery, and in the tragedy called the *Iliad*, from the particulars respecting the sailing away [from Troy]. But we must employ machinery in things which are external to the drama, which either happened before, and which it is not possible for men to know, or which happened afterwards, and require to be previously foretold and announced. For we ascribe to the gods the power of seeing all things, but we do not admit the introduction of anything absurd in the incidents,[42] but if it is introduced it must be external to the tragedy; as in the *Œdipus* of Sophocles. Since, however, tragedy is an imitation of better things, it is necessary that we should imitate good painters. For these, in giving an appropriate form to the image, depict the similitude, but increase the beauty.[43] Thus, also, it is requisite that the poet, in imitating the wrathful and the indolent, and those who are similarly affected in their manners, should form an example of equity, as asperity; such as Agatho and Homer have represented Achilles. These things, indeed, it is nec-

40 Of the *Scylla* nothing is known.— Some fragments remain of *Menalippe the Wise* (for this was the title), a tragedy of Euripides, the subject of which is a curiosity.

41 Of Euripides. Medea is carried off, at the end of the tragedy, in a chariot drawn by flying dragons.— Twining.

42 By *incidents of the fable*, Aristotle here plainly means all those actions or events which are *essential parts* of the *subject* or *story*, whether previous to the action, and necessary to be known, or included in it, and actually represented *in* the drama.

43 This seems intended to explain his *third* precept, of *resemblance* in the manners; to reconcile it with his *first*, and to show what *sort* of likeness the nature of tragic imitation requires.— Twining.

essary to observe; and besides these, such perceptions of the senses as are attendant upon poetry, besides the necessary ones.[44] For in these, errors are frequently committed. But concerning these things enough has been said in the treatises already published.

CHAP. XVI

[45 What discovery, however, is, has been before stated. But with respect to the species of recognition, the first indeed is the most inartificial, and that which most poets use through being at a loss, and is effected through signs. But of these, some are natural, such as the "lance with which the earth-born [46] race are marked," or the stars [on the bodies of the sons] in the *Thyestes* of Carcinus. Others are adventitious, and of these some are in the body, as scars; but others are external, such as necklaces; and such as [the discovery] through a small boat, in the *Tyro*.[47] These signs also may be used in a better or worse manner. Thus Ulysses, through his scar, is in one way known by his nurse, and in another by the swineherds. For the discoveries which are for the sake of credibility, are more inartificial, and all of them are of this kind; but those which are from revolution, as in the "Washing of Ulysses," [48] are better. And those recogni-

44 i. e. to the *sight*, and the *hearing*; in other words, to actual *representation*.

45 The reader, who recollects the conclusion of Sect. 14, where the author took a formal leave of the "*fable* and *its requisites*," and proceeded to the *second* essential part of tragedy, the *manners*, will hardly be of Dacier's opinion, who contends that this section is rightly placed. His reasons are perfectly unsatisfactory.— Twining.

46 The descendants of the original Thebans, who, according to the fabulous history, sprung from the earth when Cadmus sowed the dragon's teeth, etc.— This *noble race* are said to have been distinguished by the natural mark of a lance upon their bodies.

47 Sophocles wrote two tragedies of this name, neither of them preserved.— The story of Tyro leads us to suppose, that Aristotle means the little boat, trough, or, as some render it, *cradle*, in which Tyro had exposed her children, on, or near, the river: the particular manner of the discovery it would be in vain to guess.

48 The ancients distinguished the different parts of Homer's poems by different titles accommodated to the different subjects, or episodes; and, in referring to him, they made use of these, not of the division into *books*. Thus, the part of the xixth book of the *Odyssey* above

tions rank in the second place, which are invented by the poet, on which account they are inartificial. Thus Orestes in the *Iphigenia* discovers that he is Orestes.[49] For she indeed recognizes her brother through a letter, but Orestes himself speaks what the poet designs, but not what the fable requires; on which account it is near to the above-mentioned error; since he might have introduced some [of the real things as signs]. Thus, too, in the *Tereus* of Sophocles, the "voice of the shuttle [produced a recognition]." But the third mode of discovery is through memory, from the sensible perception of something by sight, as in the *Cyprii* of Dicæogenes; for on seeing the picture a certain person weeps. And in the *Tale of Alcinous;* for Ulysses, on hearing the lyrist, and recollecting the story, weeps; whence also [all these] were recognized. The fourth mode of discovery is derived from syllogism,[50] as in the *Choephoræ* — a person like me is arrived — there is no person like me but Orestes.— Orestes, therefore, is arrived. Thus too in the *Iphigenia* [51] of Polyides the sophist. For it was probable that Orestes would syllogistically conclude that because his sister had been immolated, it would likewise happen to him to be sacrificed. Thus also in the *Tydeus*[52] of Theodectes, a certain person comes to discover his son, and himself perishes.[53] Another example also is in the *Phinidæ*. For the women, on seeing the place, inferred what their fate would be, viz. that they must needs perish in this place; for they were exposed in it from their infancy. There is also a certain compound

referred to was called *The Washing*. The *Tale of Alcinous* was another title, which will presently be mentioned.— Twining.
[49] I follow Ritter, who supplies "to Iphigenia." The older editors interpolated the passage.
[50] *Occasioned* by reasoning; — i. e. by reasoning (or rather, *inference*, or *conclusion*), *in the person discovered.*
[51] The subject appears to have been the same as that of the *Iphigenia in Tauris* of Euripides. We are to suppose, that *Orestes* was discovered to his sister by his natural exclamation, at the moment when he was led to the altar of Diana to be sacrificed.— Twining.
[52] Of this and the preceding tragedy, we know nothing but what we learn here: i. e. that in the one, *a father*, and in the other, the *daughters* of *Phineus*, were discovered, and, probably, saved, by those exclamations.— Twining.
[53] Nothing of this play is known.

[discovery], which is produced from the false inference of the spectator, as in the *Ulysses the False Messenger*. For he says he should know the bow, which he had not seen; but the [audience], as if he must be known through this, on this account infer falsely. The best recognition, however, of all, is that which arises from the things themselves, astonishment being excited through the probable circumstances; as in the *Œdipus* of Sophocles and the *Iphigenia;* (for it is probable that she would be willing to send letters); since such things alone are without fictitious signs and necklaces.[54] But the recognitions which rank in the second place, are those which are derived from syllogism.]

CHAP. XVII

It is necessary, however, that the poet should form the plots, and elaborate his diction, in such a manner that he may as much as possible place the thing before his own eyes.[55] For thus the poet perceiving most acutely, as if present with the transactions themselves, will discover what is becoming, and whatever is repugnant will be least concealed from his view. An evidence of this is the fault with which Carcinus is reproached. For Amphiaraus had left the temple, which was concealed from the spectator, who did not perceive it, and the piece was driven from the stage in consequence of the indignation of the spectators. For the poet as much as possible should co-operate with the gestures [of the actor]; since those are naturally most adapted to persuade who are themselves under the influence of passion. Hence, also, he agitates others who is himself agitated, and he excites others to anger who is himself most truly enraged. Hence, poetry is the province either of one who is naturally clever, or of one who is insane. For these characters, the one is easily fashioned, but the other is prone to ecstasy. It is likewise necessary that the poet should in a general way lay down the fables composed by others, and those which he composes himself, and afterwards introduce episodes and

[54] All this passage is hopelessly corrupt.
[55] i. e. place himself in the position of a spectator.

lengthen out [the play]. But I say that he should give a general sketch after this manner. Thus, for instance, in the *Iphigenia*, a certain virgin on the point of being sacrificed, and vanishing from the view of those who were to sacrifice her, and being brought to another country in which it was a law to sacrifice strangers to a certain goddess, she is appointed the priestess of these rites. Some time after, it happened that the brother of the priestess came to this place; [but on what account? Because some god had ordered him, for a certain reason which does not pertain to the general view of the tragedy,] to come thither, [but why he did so is foreign to the fable]. The brother, therefore, coming, and being made captive, discovered [his sister], when he is going to be sacrificed; whether, as Euripides says, [by an epistle,] or, as Polyides feigns, speaking according to probability, because he said, it was not only requisite that the sister, but that he also should be sacrificed: — and hence safety arises. After these things, the poet having given names to the persons, should insert the episodes; and he must be careful that the episodes be appropriate; as that of the insanity through which Orestes was taken captive, and his being saved through expiation. In dramas, therefore, the episodes are short, but by these the epopee is lengthened. For the fable of the *Odyssey* is short, viz. a certain man wandering for many years, and persecuted by Neptune, and left alone. And besides this, his domestic affairs being so circumstanced, that his wealth is consumed by suitors, and stratagems are plotted against his son. But driven by a tempest, he returns, and making himself known to certain persons, he attacks the suitors, and is himself saved, but destroys his enemies. This, therefore, is the peculiarity of the fable, but the rest is episode.

CHAP. XVIII

[In every tragedy, however, there is a complication and development.56 And

external circumstances indeed, and some of those that are internal, frequently form the complication; but the rest the development. I call, however, the complication, the whole of that which extends from the beginning to the last part, from which there is a transition to good fortune; but I call the development that part which extends from the beginning of the transition to the end. Thus in the *Lynceus* of Theodectes, the past transactions, and the capture of the son, are the complication; but the part which extends from the charge of murder to the end, is the development. But of tragedy there are four species; for so many parts of it have also been enumerated. And one species is the complicated, of which the whole is revolution and discovery; another, the pathetic, such as the tragedies of *Ajax* and *Ixion*; another, the moral,57 such as the *Phthiotides* and the *Peleus*; but the fourth is another such as the *Phorcides* 58 and the *Prometheus*, and tragedies which represent what passes in Hades. It is especially necessary, therefore, that the poet should endeavor to have all these species; or at least that he should have the greatest and most of them, especially since men of the present age calumniate the poets. For as there have been good poets in each part of tragedy, they now expect one poet to excel in all the parts. But it is right to call tragedy different and the same, though not perhaps with any reference to the fable; but this [may be the case with those] of which there is the same plot and solution. But many poets complicate well, and develop badly.59 But

57 i. e. in which the delineation of *manners* or *character* is predominant. Our language, I think, wants a word to express *this* sense of the Greek ἠθικὸν, and the Latin, *moratum*. *Mannered* has, I believe, sometimes been used in this sense; but so seldom, as to sound awkwardly. We know nothing of the subjects here given as examples.— Twining.

58 Æschylus wrote a tragedy so named. It is difficult to imagine what he could make of these three curious personages, who were *born old women*. lived underground, and had but one eye among them, which they used by turns; carrying it, I suppose, in a case, like a pair of spectacles. Such is the tale! — Twining.

59 No fault so common. It was with the Greek tragedians, probably, as with Shakspeare.—"In many of his plays the latter part is evidently neglected. When he found himself near the end of his work, and in view of his reward, he shortened the labor, to snatch the profit. He therefore remits his efforts where he should most vigorously exert

56 Literally, the *tying* and *untying*. With the French, *Nœud* and *Dénouement* are convenient and established terms. I hope I shall be pardoned for avoiding our awkward expressions of the *intrigue* and *unraveling* of a plot, etc. I could find no terms less exceptionable than those I have used.— Twining.

both these should always be applauded.60 But it is necessary to recollect, as has been often observed, that we must not make tragedy an epic system. Now, I call that tragedy an epic system, which consists of many fables; as if some one should compose a tragedy from the whole fable of the *Iliad*. For in the *Iliad,* on account of its length, the parts receive an appropriate magnitude. But in dramas, the effect produced would be very contrary to expectation. The truth of this is indicated by such as have represented [in one tragedy] the whole destruction of Troy, and not some part of it, as the *Niobe* or *Medea* of Euripides, and who have not acted like Æschylus; for these have either been condemned, or contend without success; since Agatho also failed in this alone. But in revolutions, and in simple actions, those poets admirably effect their aim. For this is tragical, and has a moral tendency. This, however, takes place when a wise but a depraved man, such as Sisyphus, is deceived; and a brave but unjust man is vanquished. But this is probable, as Agatho says. For it is probable that many things may take place contrary to probability. It is necessary likewise to conceive the chorus to be one of the players and a part of the whole, and that it coöperates with the players, not as in Euripides,61 but as in Sophocles. But with other tragedians, the choral songs do not more belong to that fable, than to any other tragedy; on which account the chorus sing detached pieces, inserted at pleasure,62 of which Agatho was the

them, and his catastrophe is improbably produced, or imperfectly represented." Johnson's Pref. to Shakspeare.— Twining.

60 This passage is contradictory and unintelligible. Ritter condemns the whole as spurious.

61 This expression does not, I think, necessarily imply any stronger censure of Euripides, than that the choral odes of his tragedies were, in general, more loosely connected with the subject than those of Sophocles; which, on examination, would, I believe, be found true. For that *this* is the fault here meant, not the improper " *choice of the persons who compose the chorus,*" as the ingenious translator of Euripides understands, is, I think, plain from what immediately follows; the connection being this: —" Sophocles is, in this respect, *most* perfect; Euripides *less* so; as to the *others,* *their* choral songs are *totally foreign* to the subject of their tragedies."

62 It is curious to trace the gradual extinction of the chorus. At first, it was *all;* then, relieved by the intermixture of dialogue, but

inventor. What difference, however, does it make, to sing inserted pieces, or to adapt the diction of one drama to another, or the whole episode?

CHAP. XIX

Of the other parts of tragedy enough has now been said. But it remains that we should speak concerning the diction and the sentiments. The particulars, therefore, respecting the sentiments, are unfolded in the treatise on *Rhetoric,* to which it more properly belongs. But those things pertain to the sentiments, which it is requisite to procure by a reasoning process. And the parts of these are, to demonstrate, to refute, and to excite the passions; such as pity, or fear, or anger, and such like; and besides these, to amplify and extenuate. It is evident, however, that in things, also, it is requisite to derive what is useful from the same forms, when it is necessary to procure objects of pity, or things that are dreadful, or great, or probable. Except that there is this difference, that things in tragedy ought to be rendered apparent without teaching, but in an oration they are to be shown by the speaker, and in consequence of the speech. For what employment would there be for the orator, if the things should appear [of themselves] pleasing, and not through the speech? But of things pertaining to diction, there is one species of theory respecting the forms of speech, which it is the province of the actor to know, and of him who is a master artist in this profession. Thus, for instance, [it is requisite he should know,] what a mandate is, what a prayer, narration, threats, interrogation and answer are, and whatever else there may be of this kind. For from the knowledge or ignorance of these, the poetic art incurs no blame of any moment. For who would think that Homer errs in what he is reproved for

still *principal;* then, *subordinate* to the dialogue; then, digressive, and *ill connected* with the piece; then, borrowed from *other pieces* at pleasure — and *so on,* to the fiddles and the act-tunes. The performers in the *orchestra* of a modern theater are little, I believe, aware, that they occupy the *place,* and may consider themselves as the lineal descendants, of the ancient *chorus. Orchestra* was the name of that part of the ancient theater which was appropriated to the chorus.

by Protagoras? viz. that while he fancies he prays, he commands, when he says, " The wrath, O goddess, sing." For, says he, to order a thing to be done, or not to be done, is a mandate. Hence, this must be omitted as a theorem pertaining to another art, and not to poetry.

*　　　*　　　*　　　*　　　*

CHAP. XXIII

ON THE EPIC POEM

Concerning the poetry, however, which is narrative and imitative in meter, it is evident that it ought to have dramatic fables, in the same manner as tragedy, and should be conversant with one whole and perfect action, which has a beginning, middle, and end, in order that, like one whole animal, it may produce its appropriate pleasure; [63] and that it may not be like the custom of histories, in which it is not necessary to treat of one action, but of one time, viz. of such things as have happened in that time, respecting one or more persons, the relation of each of which things to the other is just as it may happen. For as the sea-fight at Salamis, and the battle with the Carthaginians in Sicily, though they happened at the same time, tend nothing to the same end; thus also in successive times, one thing may sometimes be connected with another, from which no one end is produced. But nearly all poets do this. Hence, as we have before observed, in this respect also Homer will appear to be divine, when compared with other poets, because he did not attempt to sing of the whole of the Trojan war, though it had a beginning and an end. For if he had, it would have been very great, and not sufficiently conspicuous; or if it had been of a moderate size, it would have been intricate through the variety of incidents.[64] But now, having selected one part of the war, he has made use of many episodes; such as the catalogue of

the ships, and other episodes, with which he has adorned his poem. Other poets, however, have composed a fable about one man, and one time, and one action, consisting of many parts; as the authors of the *Cyprias,* and the *Lesser Iliad.* [With respect to the *Iliad* and *Odyssey,* therefore, one or two tragedies only could be made from each. But many might be made from the *Cypriacs;* and from the *Lesser Iliad* more than eight; such as the *Judgment of the Arms, Philoctetes, Neoptolemus, Eurypylus, The Begging* [*of Ulysses*], the *Lacænæ,* the *Destruction of Troy,* the *Return of the Greeks, Sinon,* and the *Troades.*

CHAP. XXIV

ON THE SPECIES, PARTS, ETC. OF EPIC POETRY

Again, it is requisite that the epic should have the same species as tragedy. [For it is necessary that it should be either simple, or complex, or ethical, or pathetic.] The parts also are the same, except the music and the scenery. For it requires revolutions, discoveries, and disasters; and besides these, the sentiments and the diction should be well formed; all which were first used by Homer, and are used by him fitly. For of his two poems, the *Iliad* indeed contains the simple and pathetic; but the *Odyssey,* the complex; for through the whole of it there is discovery [65] and moral. And besides these things, he excelled all poets in diction and sentiment. The epic, however, differs from tragedy in the length of the composition, and in the meter. But the proper boundary of its length has been before described; for it should be such that the beginning and the end may be seen at one view. [And this will be effected if the compositions are shorter than those of the ancient poets, and brought to the same length with the multitude of tragedies that are recited at one hearing.[66]]

63 i. e. opposed (as appears from what follows) to that which *history* gives. *Unity* of *interest* is essential to the pleasure we expect from the epic poem; and this cannot exist, at least in the degree required, without *unity* of *action.*— Twining.

64 Because " *the length of the whole would* " then " *not admit of a proper magnitude in the parts* "; and thus an *epic poem* constructed upon an *historical plan,* would be exactly in the same case with a *tragedy* " constructed on an *epic plan.*"— Twining.

65 See Pope's translation, xvi. 206, etc., where Ulysses discovers himself to Telemachus — xxi. 212, to the shepherds — xxiii. 211, to Penelope — xxiv. 375, to his father — ix. 17, to Alcinous — iv. 150, etc., Telemachus is discovered to Menelaus by his tears — v. 189, to Helen, by his resemblance to his father — xix. 545, Ulysses is discovered to the old nurse, by the scar.— Twining.

66 This is quite contrary to Aristotle's own opinion.

But it is the peculiarity of the epic to possess abundantly the power of extending its magnitude; for tragedy is not capable of imitating many actions that are performed at the same time, but that part only which is represented in the scene, and acted by the players. But in the epic, in consequence of its being a narration, many events may be introduced which have happened at the same time, which are properly connected with the subject, and from which the bulk of the poem is increased. Hence, this contributes to its magnificence, transports the hearer to different places, and adorns the poem with dissimilar episodes. For similitude of events rapidly produces satiety, and causes tragedies to fail. But heroic meter is established by experience as adapted to the epic. For if any one should attempt narrative imitation in any other meter, or in many meters mingled together, the unfitness of it would be apparent. For heroic meter is of all others the most stable and ample. [Hence it especially receives foreign words and metaphors. For narrative imitation excels all others.] But Iambics and tetrameters have more motion; the one being adapted to dancing, but the other to acting. It would, however, be still more absurd, to mingle them together, as Chæremon did. Hence, no one has composed a long poem in any other measure than the heroic; but, as we have said, Nature herself teaches us to distinguish the measure best suited. Homer, indeed, deserves to be praised for many other things, and also because he is the only poet who was not ignorant what he ought to do himself. For it is requisite that the poet should speak in his own person as little as possible; for so far as he does so he is not an imitator. Other poets, therefore, take an active part through the whole poem, and they only imitate a few things, and seldom. But Homer, after a short preface, immediately introduces a man or a woman, or something else that has manners; for

there is nothing in his poem unattended with manners. It is necessary, therefore, in tragedies to produce the wonderful; but that which is contrary to reason (whence the wonderful is best produced) is best suited to the epopee, from the agent not being seen. In the next place, the particulars respecting the pursuit of Hector would appear ridiculous in the scene; the Greeks indeed standing still, and not pursuing, and Achilles making signs to them, by the motion of his head, not to engage.[67] But in the epic this is concealed. Now, the wonderful pleases; of which this is an indication, that all men, when they wish to gratify their hearers, add something to what they relate. Homer also in the highest degree taught others how to feign in a proper manner. But this is a paralogism. For men fancy that when the consequent followers or results from the antecedent, the consequent may be converted, and that the antecedent will follow from the consequent. This, however, is false. [But why, if the antecedent be false, so long as this other be otherwise, should the consequent necessarily follow? For through knowing the consequent to be true, our soul paralogizes, and concludes that the antecedent also is true. And there is an example of this in *The Washing*.] Again, one should prefer things which are impossible but probable, to such as are possible but improbable. Fables also should not be composed from irrational parts, [but as much as possible, indeed, they should have nothing irrational in them: if, however, this is impossible, care should be taken that the irrational circumstance does not pertain to the fable, as in the case of Œdipus not knowing how Laius died. For it must not be brought into the drama, like the narration of the Pythian games in the *Electra*, or him who, in the tragedy of the Mysians, comes from Tegea to Mysia without speaking.] It is ridiculous, therefore, to say, that otherwise the fable would be destroyed; for such fables should not at first be composed. But if they are composed, and it appears more reasonable that they should be, the absurdity also must be admitted; since the irrational circumstances in the *Odyssey*, such as Ulysses being left [on the shore of Ithaca by the Phœacians], would evidently have been intolerable, if they had been fabri-

67 Pope's *Iliad*, xxii. 267.— Perhaps the idea of stopping a whole army by a nod, or shake of the head (a circumstance distinctly mentioned by Homer, but sunk in Mr. Pope's version), was the absurdity here *principally* meant. If this whole Homeric scene were represented on our stage, in the best manner possible, there can be no doubt that the effect would justify Aristotle's observation. It would certainly set the audience in a roar.— Twining.

cated by a bad poet. But now the poet conceals the absurdity, and renders it pleasing by the addition of other beauties. The diction, likewise, should be labored in the sluggish parts of the poem, and which exhibit neither manners nor sentiment. For a very splendid diction conceals the manners and the reasoning.

CHAP. XXVI

One may, however, question whether epic or tragic imitation is the more excellent. For if that imitation is the better which is less troublesome to the spectator, and such an imitation pertains to better spectators, that which imitates every thing is evidently attended with molestation. For, as if the spectators will not perceive what is acted without the addition of much movement, they make great gesticulations; just as bad players on the flute turn themselves round, when it is requisite to imitate the action of the discus, or when they sing of Scylla, draw to themselves the coryphæus, or leader of the band. Such, then, is tragedy, as the modern actors are in the estimation of their predecessors. Hence, Myniscus called Callipides an ape, in consequence of carrying his imitation to a great excess. And there was also a similar opinion respecting Pindar [the player]. But as these latter actors are to the former, so is the whole art of tragedy to the epopee. They say, therefore, that the epopee is calculated for hearers of the better sort, on which account it does not require scenery; but that tragedy is calculated for the vulgar. Hence, tragic imitation, which is troublesome to the spectator, will evidently be inferior to epic imitation.

In the first place, however, this accusation does not pertain to the poet, but the actor; since it is possible in reciting epic poetry to overdo action, as Sosistratus did, and singing likewise, as Mnastheus of Opus did. In the next place, neither is all motion to be despised, since neither is every kind of dancing, but only that which is bad; and hence Callipedes was blamed, as others now are for imitating light women. Further still, tragedy, in the same manner as the epopee, may ful-fil its purpose without gesture; for by reading, it is manifest what kind of thing it is. If, therefore, it is in other respects better, it is not necessary that it should be accompanied [by motion and gesture]. In the next place, tragedy has every thing which the epic possesses. For it may use meter, and it has also music and scenery, as no small parts, through which the pleasure it produces is most apparent. To which may be added, that it possesses perspicuity, both when it is read, and when it is acted. The end, too, of its imitation is confined in less extended limits. For being crowded into a narrower compass, it becomes more pleasing than if it were diffused through a long period of time. Thus, for instance, if one were to put the Œdipus of Sophocles into as many verses as the Iliad, [it would be less pleasing]. Again, the imitation of the epic has less unity [than tragic imitation]; of which this is an indication, that from any kind of [epic] imitation, many tragedies may be produced. Hence, if he who writes an epic poem should choose a fable perfectly one, the poem would necessarily either appear short, as if curtailed, or if it should be accompanied with length of meter, it would seem to be languid. But if he should compose one fable from many fables, I mean, if the poem should consist of many actions, it would not possess unity. Thus, the Iliad and Odyssey contain many such parts, which of themselves possess magnitude, though these poems are composed, as much as possible, in the most excellent manner, and are most eminently the imitation of one action. If, therefore, tragedy excels in all these particulars, and besides this, in the work of art, (for neither tragic nor epic imitation ought to produce a casual pleasure, but that which has been stated), it is evident that it will be more excellent than the epopee, in consequence of attaining its end in a greater degree. And thus much concerning tragedy, and the epic, as to themselves, their species, and their parts, their number, and their difference, what the causes are of their being good or bad, and also concerning the objections which may be made to them, and the solutions of the objections.

LATIN DRAMATIC CRITICISM

Latin literature yields little more material in dramatic criticism and theory than Greek. As is pointed out in another place, there is but one complete treatise extant — the *Ars Poetica* of Horace — and that is far from satisfactory as a unified and clear statement of the aims or achievements of the Latin drama. From the beginnings of Latin literary criticism with Cicero, to the time of Horace, there is practically nothing relating to the subject. Cicero himself, in his *Letters, Orations,* and various treatises, evolves interesting ideas on the drama, but nowhere sums up any sort of complete theory of body of doctrine. If the works of Varro and Lucilius had been preserved, it is doubtful whether Horace would have occupied his present position of solitary grandeur and importance, but in the absence of anything but fragments from these authors and from the numerous other critics of his time and anterior to him, we must assign to him a place of the first magnitude. Mention ought perhaps be made of a few paragraphs on the rise of comedy in Livy's history, *Ab urbe condita Libri* (vii, ii, iv, and following), written about the time of Christ. Not until Quintilian is there anything approaching a systematic study of dramatists, while Quintilian himself—in the *Institutiones Oratoriae,* Books VI and X — adopts an historical rather than theoretical method, and passes brief judgments on Greek and Latin authors. The *Noctes Atticae* of Aulus Gellius is the last of the Latin writings with any pretension to originality concerned with our subject.

A careful study of Henry Nettleship's second series of *Lectures and Essays* — chapter on *Latin Criticism*—, and of Saintsbury's *History of Criticism* — first volume — will enlighten the student as to the details of the subject, but he will find little other than fragments and titles of lost works if he goes to original sources.

HORACE

Quintus Horatius Flaccus, known in English as Horace, was born at Venusia, near the border of Apulia, in 65 B. C. His father, a former slave who had freed himself before the birth of his son, sent him to school in Rome. As a young man Horace went to Athens and studied philosophy at the famous schools. When the Civil War broke out he enlisted in the army of Brutus, served at Philippi, and came back to Rome not long after. Deprived of his property as a result of the proscriptions, he began life anew at the age of twenty-four as clerk in a public office. Not long after, he attracted the attention of Mæcenas, and soon became acquainted with Varius and Vergil, henceforth devoting himself to literary pursuits. His first work, the first book of *Satires,* was published 35 B. C. About a year later, Mæcenas presented him with the celebrated Sabine Farm, and Horace was at liberty to the end of his life to do as he liked. Before he died he was famous: the Emperor Augustus commissioned him to write the fourth book of *Odes.* He died eight years before the birth of Christ.

The *Epistle to the Pisos,* or *Art of Poetry,* has been assigned by various authorities to the period between 24 and 7 B. C. Professor Nettleship (in his *Lectures and Essays*) believes it to have been written between 24 and 20 B. C. Its interest and value are considerably enhanced in view of the fact that it is, in

Professor Saintsbury's words, "the only complete example of literary criticism that we have from any Roman." It is significant that the greater part of its subject-matter is concerned with the drama. While it has been clearly substantiated that Horace drew upon a non-extant treatise by Neoptolemus of Parium, an Alexandrian critic of uncertain date, the fact that Horace made use of and molded the ideas of his predecessor is important. The *Art of Poetry* is on the whole a somewhat arbitrary manual; the greatest importance is there attached to the purely formal side of writing; the dramatist must adhere closely to the five

acts, the chorus, and so on; proportion, good sense, decorum, cannot be neglected. Of the practical value of the work before the Renaissance, it is impossible to know; of its influence since that time, it can only be said that it was as widespread as that of Aristotle. Horace's doctrine of "pleasure and profit" was to be repeated innumerable times, and is still a criterion of criticism. Mr. Spingarn's statement that "critical activity in nearly all the countries of western Europe seems to have been ushered in by the translation of Horace's *Ars Poetica* into the vernacular tongues" is but another proof of the popularity of the work.

THE ART OF POETRY [1]
[EPISTOLA AD PISONES]
(24–20 B. C.?)

If a painter should wish to unite a horse's neck to a human head, and spread a variety of plumage over limbs [of different animals] taken from every part [of nature], so that what is a beautiful woman in the upper part terminates unsightly in an ugly fish below — could you, my friends, refrain from laughter, were you admitted to such a sight? Believe, ye Pisos, the book will be perfectly like such a picture, the ideas of which, like a sick man's dreams, are all vain and fictitious: so that neither head nor foot can correspond to any one form. "Poets and painters [you will say] have ever had equal authority for attempting any thing." We are conscious of this, and this privilege we demand and allow in turn: but not to such a degree that the tame should associate with the savage; nor that serpents should be coupled with birds, lambs with tigers.

In pompous introductions, and such as promise a great deal, it generally happens that one or two verses of purple patch-work, that may make a great show, are tagged on; as when the grove and the altar of Diana and the meandering

of a current hastening through pleasant fields, or the river Rhine, or the rainbow, is described. But here there was no room for these [fine things]: perhaps, too, you know how to draw a cypress: but what is that to the purpose, if he who is painted for the given price, is [to be represented as] swimming hopeless out of a shipwreck? A large vase at first was designed: why, as the wheel revolves, turns out a little pitcher? In a word, be your subject what it will, let it be merely simple and uniform.

The great majority of us poets — father, and youths worthy such a father — are misled by the appearance of right. I labor to be concise, I become obscure: nerves and spirit fail him that aims at the easy: one, that pretends to be sublime, proves bombastical: he who is too cautious and fearful of the storm, crawls along the ground: he who wants to vary his subject in a marvelous manner, paints the dolphin in the woods, the boar in the sea. The avoiding of an error leads to a fault, if it lack skill.

A statuary about the Æmilian school shall of himself, with singular skill, both express the nails, and imitate in brass the flexible hair; unhappy yet in the main, because he knows not how to finish a complete piece. I would no more choose to be such a one as this, had I a mind to compose any thing, than to

1 Translated, complete, by C. Smart, from *The Works of Horace literally translated into English Prose* (New York, n. d.). Unsigned footnotes are by the translator. The brackets enclose words or phrases by the translator intended to complete the sense of the original. —Ed.

live with a distorted nose, [though] remarkable for black eyes and jetty hair.

Ye who write, make choice of a subject suitable to your abilities; and revolve in your thoughts a considerable time what your strength declines, and what it is able to support. Neither elegance of style nor a perspicuous disposition, shall desert the man by whom the subject matter is chosen judiciously.

This, or I am mistaken, will constitute the merit and beauty of arrangement, that the poet just now say what ought just now to be said, put off most of his thoughts, and waive them for the present.

In the choice of his words, too, the author of the projected poem must be delicate and cautious, he must embrace one and reject another: you will express yourself eminently well, if a dexterous combination should give an air of novelty to a well-known word. If it happen to be necessary to explain some abstruse subjects by new-invented terms, it will follow that you must frame words never heard of by the old-fashioned Cethegi: and the license will be granted, if modestly used: and new and lately-formed words will have authority, if they descend from a Greek source, with a slight deviation. But why should the Romans grant to Plautus and Cæcilius a privilege denied to Vergil and Varius? Why should I be envied, if I have it in my power to acquire a few words, when the language of Cato and Ennius has enriched our native tongue, and produced new names of things? It has been, and ever will be, allowable to coin a word marked with the stamp in present request. As leaves in the woods are changed with the fleeting years; the earliest fall off first: in this manner words perish with old age, and those lately invented flourish and thrive, like men in the time of youth. We and our works are doomed to death: whether Neptune, admitted into the continent, defends our fleet from the north winds, a kingly work; or the lake, for a long time unfertile and fit for oars, now maintains its neighboring cities and feels the heavy plow; or the river, taught to run in a more convenient channel, has changed its course which was so destructive to the fruits. Mortal works must perish: much less can the honor and elegance of language be long-lived. Many words shall revive, which now have fallen off; and many words are now in esteem shall fall off, if it be the will of custom, in whose power is the decision and right and standard of language.

Homer has instructed us in what measure the achievements of kings, and chiefs, and direful war might be written.

Plaintive strains originally were appropriated to the unequal numbers [of the elegiac]: afterwards [love and] successful desires were included. Yet what author first published humble elegies, the critics dispute, and the controversy still waits the determination of the judge.

Rage armed Archilochus with the iambic of his own invention. The sock and the majestic buskin assumed this measure as adapted for dialogue, and to silence the noise of the populace, and calculated for action.

To celebrate gods, and the sons of gods, and the victorious wrestler, and the steed foremost in the race, and the inclination of youths, and the free joys of wine, the muse has allotted to the lyre.

If I am incapable and unskillful to observe the distinction described, and the complexions of works [of genius], why am I accosted by the name of " Poet "? Why, out of false modesty, do I prefer being ignorant to being learned?

A comic subject will not be handled in tragic verse: in like manner the banquet of Thyestes will not bear to be held in familiar verses, and such as almost suit the sock. Let each peculiar species [of writing] fill with decorum its proper place. Nevertheless sometimes even comedy exalts her voice, and passionate Chremes rails in a tumid strain: and a tragic writer generally expresses grief in a prosaic style. Telephus and Peleus, when they are both in poverty and exile, throw aside their rants and gigantic expressions if they have a mind to move the heart of the spectator with their complaint.

It is not enough, that poems be beautiful; let them be tender and affecting, and bear away the soul of the auditor whithersoever they please. As the human countenance smiles on those that smile, so does it sympathize with those that weep. If you would have me weep you must first express the passion of grief yourself; then, Telephus or Peleus, your misfortunes hurt me: if you pronounce the parts assigned you ill, I shall either fall asleep or laugh.

Pathetic accents suit a melancholy countenance; words full of menace, an angry one; wanton expressions, a sportive look; and serious matter, an austere one. For nature forms us first within to every modification of circumstances; she delights or impels us to anger, or depresses us to the earth and afflicts us with heavy sorrow: then expresses those emotions of the mind by the tongue, its interpreter. If the words be discordant to the station of the speaker, the Roman knights and plebeians will raise an immoderate laugh. It will make a wide difference, whether it be Davus that speaks, or a hero; a man well-stricken in years, or a hot young fellow in his bloom; and a matron of distinction, or an officious nurse; a roaming merchant, or the cultivator of a verdant little farm; a Colchian, or an Assyrian; one educated at Thebes, or one at Argos.

You that write, either follow tradition, or invent such fables as are congruous to themselves. If as a poet you have to represent the renowned Achilles; let him be indefatigable, wrathful, inexorable, courageous, let him deny that laws were made for him, let him arrogate everything to force of arms. Let Medea be fierce and untractable, Ino an object of pity, Ixion perfidious, Io wandering, Orestes in distress.

If you offer to the stage anything unattempted, and venture to form a new character, let it be preserved to the last such as it set out at the beginning, and be consistent with itself. It is difficult to write with propriety on subjects to which all writers have a common claim; and you with more prudence will reduce the *Iliad* into acts, than if you first introduce arguments unknown and never treated of before. A public story will become your own property, if you do not dwell upon the whole circle of events, which is paltry and open to every one; nor must you be so faithful a translator, as to take the pains of rendering [the original] word for word; nor by imitating throw yourself into straits, whence either shame or the rules of your work may forbid you to retreat.

Nor must you make such an exordium,

as the Cyclic writer of old: "I will sing the fate of Priam, and the noble war." What will this boaster produce worthy of all this gaping? The mountains are in labor, a ridiculous mouse will be brought forth. How much more to the purpose he, who attempts nothing improperly? "Sing for me, my muse, the man who, after the time of the destruction of Troy, surveyed the manners and cities of many men." He meditates not [to produce] smoke from a flash, but out of smoke to elicit fire, that he may thence bring forth his instances of the marvelous with beauty, [such as] Antiphates, Scylla, the Cyclops, and Charybdis. Nor does he date Diomed's return from Meleager's death, nor trace the rise of the Trojan war from [Leda's] eggs: he always hastens on to the event: and hurries away his reader into the midst of interesting circumstances, no otherwise than as if they were [already] known; and what he despairs of, as to receiving a polish from his touch, he omits; and in such a manner forms his fictions, so intermingles the false with the true, that the middle is not inconsistent with the beginning, nor the end with the middle.

Do you attend to what I, and the public in my opinion, expect from you [as a dramatic writer]. If you are desirous of an applauding spectator, who will wait for [the falling of] the curtain, and till the chorus calls out "your plaudits"; the manners of every age must be marked by you, and a proper decorum assigned to men's varying dispositions and years. The boy, who is just able to pronounce his words, and prints the ground with a firm tread, delights to play with his fellows, and contracts and lays aside anger without reason, and is subject to change every hour. The beardless youth, his guardian being at length discharged, joys in horses, and dogs, and the verdure of the sunny Campus Martius; pliable as wax to the bent of vice, rough to advisers, a slow provider of useful things, prodigal of his money, high-spirited, and amorous, and hasty in deserting the objects of his passion. [After this,] our inclinations being changed, the age and spirit of manhood seeks after wealth, and [high] connections, is subservient to points of honor; and is cautious of committing any action which he would subsequently be industrious to correct. Many inconveniences encompass a man in years; either because he seeks [eagerly] for gain, and abstains from what he has gotten and is afraid to make use of it: or because he transacts every thing in a timorous and dispassionate manner, dilatory, slow in hope, remiss, and greedy of futurity. Peevish, querulous, a panegyrist of former times when he was a boy, and chastiser and censurer of his juniors. Our advancing years bring many advantages along with them. Many our declining ones take away. That the parts [therefore] belonging to age may not be given to a youth, and those of a man to a boy, we must dwell upon those qualities which are joined and adapted to each person's age.

An action is either represented on the stage, or, being done elsewhere, is there related. The things which enter by the ear affect the mind more languidly, than such as are submitted to the faithful eyes, and what a spectator presents to himself. You must not, however, bring upon the stage things fit only to be acted behind the scenes: and you must take away from view many actions, which elegant description may soon after deliver in presence [of the spectators]. Let not Medea murder her sons before the people; nor the execrable Atreus openly dress human entrails; nor let Progne be metamorphosed into a bird, Cadmus into a serpent. Whatever you show to me in this manner, not able to give credit to, I detest.

Let a play which would be inquired after, and though seen, represented anew, be neither shorter nor longer than the fifth act. Neither let a god interfere, unless a difficulty worthy a god's unraveling should happen; nor let a fourth person be officious to speak.[2]

Let the chorus[3] sustain the part and

---

2 The poet does not forbid a fourth person to speak, but would have him say very little, as the Scholiast understands the precept. Indeed, a conversation of three people is most agreeable, because it is less confused and less divides the attention of an audience.— Rodell.

3 The chorus was not introduced between the acts, merely to relieve the audience, but had a part in the play, and concurred with the other actors to carry on the plot, and support the probability of it. The Choriphæus, or first person of the chorus, entered in the acts, and spoke for all those of whom the chorus was composed; "officiumque virile defendat."

---

manly character of an actor: nor let them sing anything between the acts which is not conducive to, and fitly coherent with, the main design. Let them both patronize the good,[4] and give them friendly advice, and regulate the passionate, and love to appease those who swell [with rage]: let them praise the repast of a short meal, the salutary effects of justice, laws, and peace with her open gates: let them conceal what is told to them in confidence, and supplicate and implore the gods that prosperity may return to the wretched, and abandon the haughty. The flute (not as now, begirt with brass and emulous of the trumpet, but), slender and of simple form, with few stops, was of service to accompany and assist the chorus, and with its tone was sufficient to fill the rows that were not as yet too crowded, where an audience, easily numbered, as being small and sober, chaste and modest, met together. But when the victorious Romans began to extend their territories, and an ampler wall encompassed the city, and their genius was indulged on festivals by drinking wine in the day-time without censure; a greater freedom arose both to the numbers [of poetry], and the measure [of music]. For what taste could an unlettered clown and one just dismissed from labors have, when in company with the polite; the base, with the man of honor? Thus the musician added new movements and a luxuriance to the ancient art, and strutting backward and forward, drew a length of train over the stage: thus likewise new notes were added to the severity of the lyre, and precipitate eloquence produced an unusual language [in the theater]: and the sentiments [of the chorus, then] expert in teaching useful things and prescient of futurity, differ hardly from the oracular Delphi.

The poet who first tried his skill in tragic verse for the paltry [prize of a] goat, soon after exposed to view wild satyrs naked, and attempted raillery with severity, still preserving the gravity [of

---

The chorus filled up the intervals of the acts with their songs, which were composed of reflections upon what was past, or their apprehensions of what might happen.— Francis.

4 The chorus, says the poet, is to take the side of the good and virtuous; i. e. is always to sustain a moral character.

tragedy]: because the spectator on festivals, when heated with wine and disorderly, was to be amused with captivating shows and agreeable novelty. But it will be expedient so to recommend the bantering, so the rallying satyrs, so to turn earnest into jest; that none who shall be exhibited as a god, none who is introduced as a hero lately conspicuous in regal purple and gold, may deviate into the low style of obscure, mechanical shops; or, [on the contrary] while he avoids the ground, affect cloudy mist and empty jargon. Tragedy, disdaining to prate forth trivial verses, like a matron commanded to dance on festival days, will assume an air of modesty, even in the midst of wanton satyrs. As a writer of satire, ye Pisos, I shall never be fond of unornamented and reigning terms: nor shall I labor to differ so widely from the complexion of tragedy, as to make no distinction, whether Davus be the speaker. And the bold Pythias, who gained a talent by gulling Simo; or Silenus, the guardian and attendant of his pupil-god [Bacchus]. I would so execute a fiction taken from a well-known story, that anybody might entertain hopes of doing the same thing; but, on trial, should sweat and labor in vain. Such power has a just arrangement and connection of the parts: such grace may be added to subjects merely common. In my judgment, the Fauns, that are brought out of the woods, should not be too gamesome with their tender strains, as if they were educated in the city, and almost at the bar; nor, on the other hand, should blunder out their obscene and scandalous speeches. For [at such stuff] all are offended, who have a horse, a father, or an estate: nor will they receive with approbation, nor give the laurel crown, as the purchasers of parched peas and nuts are delighted with.

A long syllable put after a short one is termed an iambus, a lively measure, whence also it commanded the name of trimeters to be added to iambics, though it yielded six beats of time, being similar to itself from first to last. Not long ago, that it might come somewhat slower and with more majesty to the ear, it obligingly and contentedly admitted into its paternal heritage the steadfast spondees; agreeing, however, by social league,

that it was not to depart from the second [5] and fourth place. But this [kind of measure] rarely makes its appearance in the notable [6] trimeters of Accius, and brands the verse of Ennius brought upon the stage with a clumsy weight of spondees, with the imputation of being too precipitate and careless, or disgracefully accuses him of ignorance in his art.

It is not every judge that discerns inharmonious verses, and an undeserved indulgence is [in this case] granted to the Roman poets. But shall I on this account run riot and write licentiously? Or should not I rather suppose, that all the world are to see my faults; secure, and cautious [never to err] but with hope of being pardoned? Though, perhaps, I have merited no praise, I have escaped censure.

Ye [who are desirous to excel], turn over the Grecian models by night, turn them by day. But our ancestors commended both the numbers of Plautus, and his strokes of pleasantry; too tamely, I will not say foolishly, admiring each of them; if you and I but know how to distinguish a coarse joke from a smart repartee, and understand the proper cadence, by [using] our fingers and ears.

Thespis [7] is said to have invented a new kind of tragedy, and to have carried his pieces about in carts, which [certain strollers] who had their faces besmeared with lees of wine, sang and acted. After him Æschylus, the inventor of the vizard mask and decent robe, laid the stage over with boards of a tolerable size, and taught to speak in lofty tone, and strut in the buskin. To these succeeded the old comedy, not

---

5 The iambic yields only the odd places to the spondee, the first, third, and fifth, but preserves the second, fourth, and sixth for itself. This mixture renders the verse more noble, and it may be still *trimeter*, the second foot being iambic. The comic poets, better to disguise their verse, and make it appear more like common conversation, inverted the tragic order, and put spondees in the even places.—Dacier.

6 Ironically spoken.

7 *Thespis.* A native of Icarius, a village in Attica, to whom the invention of the drama has been ascribed. Before his time there were no performers except the chorus. He led the way to the formation of a dramatic plot and language, by directing a pause in the performance of the chorus, during which he came forward and recited with gesticulation a very theological story — Wheeler.

without considerable praise: but its personal freedom degenerated into excess and violence, worthy to be regarded by law; a law was made accordingly, and the chorus, the right of abusing being taken away, disgracefully became silent.

Our poets have left no species of the art unattempted; nor have those of them merited the least honor, who dared to forsake the footsteps of the Greeks, and celebrate domestic facts; whether they have instructed us in tragedy, or in comedy. Nor would Italy be raised higher by valor and feats of arms, than by its language, did not the fatigue and tediousness of using the file disgust every one of our poets. Do you, the descendants of Pompilius, reject that poem, which many days and many a blot have not ten times subdued to the most perfect accuracy. Because Democritus believes that genius is more successful than wretched art, and excludes from Helicon all poets who are in their senses, a great number do not care to part with their nails or beard, frequent places of solitude, shun the baths. For he will acquire, [he thinks,] the esteem and title of a poet, if he neither submits his head, which is not to be cured by even three Anticyras, to Licinius the barber. What an unlucky fellow am I, who am purged for the bile in spring-time! Else nobody would compose better poems; but the purchase is not worth the expense. Therefore I will serve instead of a whetstone, which though not able of itself to cut, can make steel sharp: so I, who can write no poetry myself, will teach the duty and business [of an author]; whence he may be stocked with rich materials; what nourishes and forms the poet; what gives grace, what not; what is the tendency of excellence, what that of error.

To have good sense, is the first principle and fountain of writing well. The Socratic papers will direct you in the choice of your subjects; and words will spontaneously accompany the subject, when it is well conceived. He who has learned what he owes to his country, and what to his friends; with what affection a parent, a brother, and a stranger, are to be loved; what is the duty of a senator, what of a judge; what the duties of a general sent out to war; he, [I say,] certainly knows how to give suitable attributes to every character. I should direct the learned imitator to have a regard to the mode of nature and manners, and thence draw his expressions to the life.[8] Sometimes a play, that is showy with common-places, and where the manners are well marked, though of no elegance, without force or art, gives the people much higher delight and more effectually commands their attention, than verse void of matter, and tuneful trifles.

To the Greeks, covetous of nothing but praise, the muse gave genius; to the Greeks the power of expressing themselves in round periods. The Roman youth learn by long computation to subdivide a pound into an hundred parts. Let the son of Albinus tell me, if from five ounces one be subtracted, what remains? He would have said the third of a pound.— Bravely done! you will be able to take care of your own affairs. An ounce is added: what will that be? Half a pound. When this sordid rust and hankering after wealth has once tainted their minds, can we expect that such verses should be made as are worthy of being anointed with the oil of cedar, and kept in the well-polished cypress?[9]

Poets wish either to profit or to delight; or to deliver at once both the pleasures and the necessaries of life. Whatever precepts you give, be concise, that docile minds may soon comprehend what is said, and faithfully retain it. All superfluous instructions flow from the too full memory. Let whatever is imagined for the sake of entertainment, have as much likeness to truth as possible; let not your play demand belief for whatever [absurdities] it is inclinable [to exhibit]: nor take out of a witch's belly a living child, that she had dined upon. The tribes of the seniors rail against everything that is void of edification: the exalted knights disregard poems which are austere. He who joins the instructive with the agreeable, car-

8 Truth, in poetry, means such an expression, as conforms to the general nature of things; falsehood, that which, however suitable to the particular instance in view, doth yet not correspond to such general nature.— Tr.
9 To preserve their books, the ancients rubbed them with oil of cedar, and kept them in cases of cypress, because these kinds of wood were not liable to corruption.

ries off every vote,[10] by delighting and at the same time admonishing the reader. This book gains money for the Sosii; this crosses the sea, and continues to its renowned author a lasting duration.

Yet there are faults, which we should be ready to pardon: for neither does the string [always] form the sound which the hand and conception [of the performer] intends, but very often returns a sharp note when he demands a flat; nor will the bow always hit whatever mark it threatens. But when there is a great majority of beauties in a poem, I will not be offended with a few blemishes, which either inattention has dropped, or human nature has not sufficiently provided against. What therefore [is to be determined in this matter]? As a transcriber, if he still commits the same fault though he has been reproved, is without excuse; and the harper who always blunders on the same string, is sure to be laughed at; so he who is excessively deficient becomes another Chœrilus; whom, when I find him tolerable in two or three places, I wonder at with laughter; and at the same time am I grieved whenever honest Homer grows drowsy? But it is allowable, that sleep should steal upon [the progress of] a long work.

As is painting, so is poetry: some pieces will strike you more if you stand near, and some if you are at a greater distance: one loves the dark; another, which is not afraid of the critic's subtile judgment, chooses to be seen in the light; the one has pleased once; the other will give pleasure if ten times repeated.

O you elder of the youths, though you are framed to a right judgment by your father's instructions, and are wise in yourself, yet take this truth along with you, [and] remember it; that in certain things a medium and tolerable degree of eminence may be admitted: a counselor and pleader at the bar of the middle rate is far removed from the merit of eloquent Messala, nor has so much knowledge of the law as Cassellius Aulus, but yet he is in request; [but] a mediocrity in poets neither gods, nor men, nor [even] the booksellers' shops have endured. As at an agreeable entertainment discordant music, and muddy perfume, and poppies mixed with Sardinian [11] honey give offense, because the supper might have passed without them; so poetry, created and invented for the delight of our souls, if it comes short ever so little of the summit, sinks to the bottom.

He who does not understand the game, abstains from the weapons of the Campus Martius: and the unskillful in the tennis ball, the quoit, and the troques, keeps himself quiet; lest the crowded ring should raise a laugh at his expense: notwithstanding this, he who knows nothing of verses presumes to compose. Why not! He is free-born, of a good family; above all, he is registered at an equestrian sum of monies, and clear from every vice. You, [I am persuaded,] will neither say nor do anything in opposition to Minerva: such is your judgment, such your disposition. But if ever you shall write anything, let it be submitted to the ears of Metius [Tarpa], who is a judge, and your father's, and mine; and let it be suppressed till the ninth year, your papers being laid up within your own custody. You will have it in your power to blot out what you have not made public: a word once sent abroad can never return.

Orpheus, the priest and interpreter of the gods, deterred the savage race of men from slaughters and inhuman diet; hence said to tame tigers and furious lions. Amphion, too, the builder of the Theban wall, was said to give the stones motion with the sound of his lyre, and to lead them whithersoever he would, by engaging persuasion. This was deemed wisdom of yore, to distinguish the public from private weal; things sacred from things profane; to prohibit a promiscuous commerce between the sexes; to give laws to married people; to plan out cities; to engrave laws on [tables of] wood. This honor accrued to divine poets, and their songs. After these, excellent Homer and Tyrtæus animated the manly mind to martial achievements with their verses. Oracles were delivered in poetry, and the economy of life pointed out, and the favor of sovereign

---

10 *Omne tulit punctum.* Alluding to the manner of voting at the comitia by putting a point over the name of a candidate.— Tr.

11 Sardinia was full of bitter herbs, from whence the honey was bitter. White poppy seed, roasted, was mingled with honey by the ancients.

princes was solicited by Pierian strains, games were instituted, and a [cheerful] period put to the tedious labors of the day; [this I remind you of,] lest haply you should be ashamed of the lyric muse, and Apollo the god of song.

It has been made a question, whether good poetry be derived from nature or from art. For my part, I can neither conceive what study can do without a rich natural vein, nor what rude genius can avail of itself: so much does the one require the assistance of the other, and so amicably do they conspire [to produce the same effect]. He who is industrious to reach the wished-for goal, has done and suffered much when a boy; he has sweated, and shivered with cold; he has abstained from love and wine; he who sings the Pythian strains, was first a learner, and in awe of a master. But [in poetry] it is now enough for a man to say to himself: "I make admirable verses: a murrain seize the hindmost: it is scandalous for me to be outstripped, and fairly to acknowledge that I am ignorant of that which I never learned."

As a crier who collects the crowd together to buy his goods, so a poet rich in land, rich in money put out at interest, invites flatterers to come [and praise his works] for a reward. But if he be one who is well able to set out an elegant table, and give security for a poor man, and relieve him when entangled in gloomy lawsuits; I shall wonder if with his wealth he can distinguish a true friend from a false one. You, whether you have made, or intend to make, a present to any one, do not bring him full of joy directly to your finished verses: for then he will cry out: "Charming, excellent, judicious"; he will turn pale; at some parts he will even distill the dew from his friendly eyes; he will jump about; he will beat the ground [with ecstasy]. As those who mourn friends at funerals for pay, do and say more than those that are afflicted from their hearts; so the sham admirer is more moved than he that praises with sincerity. Certain kings are said to ply with frequent bumpers, and by wine make trial of a man whom they are sedulous to know, whether he be worthy of their friendship or not. Thus, if you compose verses, let not the fox's concealed intentions impose upon you.

If you had recited anything to Quintilius, he would say, "Alter, I pray, this and this": if you replied, you could do it no better, having made the experiment twice or thrice in vain; he would order you to blot out, and once more apply to the anvil your ill-formed verses: if you choose rather to defend than correct a fault, he spent not a word more nor fruitless labor, but you alone might be fond of yourself and your own works, without a rival. A good and sensible man will censure spiritless verses, he will condemn the rugged, on the incorrect he will draw across a black stroke with his pen; he will lop off ambitious [and redundant] ornaments; he will make him throw light on the parts that are not perspicuous; he will arraign what is expressed ambiguously; he will mark what should be altered; [in short,] he will be an Aristarchus:[12] he will not say, "Why should I give my friend offense about mere trifles?" These trifles will lead into mischiefs of serious consequence, when once made an object of ridicule, and used in a sinister manner.

Like one whom an odious plague or jaundice, fanatic phrensy or lunacy, distresses; those who are wise avoid a mad poet, and are afraid to touch him: the boys jostle him, and the incautious pursue him. If, like a fowler intent upon his game, he should fall into a well or a ditch while he belches out his fustian verses and roams about, though he should cry out for a long time, "Come to my assistance, O my country-men"; not one would give himself the trouble of taking him up. Were any one to take pains to give him aid, and let down a rope; "How do you know, but he threw himself in hither on purpose?" I shall say: and will relate the death of the Sicilian poet. Empedocles, while he was ambitious of being esteemed an immortal god, in cold blood leaped into burning Etna. Let poets have the privilege and license to die [as they please]. He who saves a man against his will, does the same with him who kills him [against his

12 Aristarchus was a critic, who wrote above four score volumes of comments on the Greek poets. His criticisms on Homer were so much esteemed that no line was thought genuine until he had acknowledged it. He was surnamed the prophet or diviner, for his sagacity.— Francis.

will]. Neither is it the first time that he has behaved in this manner; nor, were he to be forced from his purposes, would he now become a man, and lay aside his desire of such a famous death. Neither does it appear sufficiently, why he makes verses: whether he has defiled his father's ashes, or sacrilegiously removed the sad enclosure of the vindictive thunder: it is evident that he is mad, and like a bear that has burst through the gates closing his den, this unmerciful rehearser chases the learned and unlearned. And whomsoever he seizes, he fastens on and assassinates with recitation: a leech that will not quit the skin, till satiated with blood.

DRAMATIC CRITICISM OF THE MIDDLE AGES

The absence of any body of dramatic work, and the unsettled conditions of Europe between the disintegration of the Roman Empire and the earliest dawn of the Renaissance, easily account for the dearth of dramatic criticism during the Middle Ages. Such doctrine as exists is in the form of more or less cut-and-dried commentary, most of it based on other work of a similar nature. Or else we have the altogether moral—chiefly non-literary—treatises of Tertullian (*De Spectaculis*) and of St. Cyprian on the same subject, dating respectively from the second and third centuries. The greater part of these treatises and fragments are little more than repetitions of the ideas of Aristotle and Horace or of other early Greek and Latin writers. The chief interest of the fragmentary tractates of Donatus, Evanthìus, and Diomedes, is due to their preserving stray sentences from Cicero and Theophrastus. Donatus quotes Cicero's famous saying on comedy—that it is "imitatio vitae, speculum consuetudinis, imago veritatis" —Diomedes, Theophrastus' definitions of comedy and tragedy. Donatus (together with Evanthius—the commentaries *De Comœdia et Tragœdia* are often printed together) acquired no small degree of fame for his *Commentary* on Terence, which appeared for many years in nearly every edition of the Latin dramatist. Diomedes, another fourth century grammarian, devotes sections of the Third Book of his *Ars Grammatica* to a sum-

mary treatment of dramatic principles. This is based upon the non-extant *De Poetis* of Suetonius. The early Church Fathers — St. Ambrose, Lactantius, Chrysostom, Prudentius and even Augustine—had written on the drama, but their attitude, needless to say, was almost exclusively a moral one. The Seventh century scholar, Isidore of Seville, in his encyclopedic *Origines* — or *Etymologiae* — gives two small sections to drama, but these yield nothing new. They merely help bridge the gap from Horace to the Renaissance. The Moorish philosopher Averroës made an abridged version of Aristotle's *Poetics* in the Twelfth century, and added his commentary. Mr. Spingarn mentions Johannes Januensis de Balbis, who in the year 1286, distinguishes tragedy and comedy in his *Catholicon*. Horace who, as has been pointed out, was the chief inspiration of these sporadic treatises, is at least referred to by John of Salisbury (Twelfth century), in his *Policraticus*. The *Magnae Derivationes* of Uguccione da Pisa has been pointed out as a source of Dante's definitions of comedy and tragedy. Dante himself, in the fourteenth century, on the threshold of the Renaissance, still adheres to the Horatian theory. The brevity, the tone of final authority, the dependence on classical precedent in Dante's *Epistle* may well serve to illustrate the state of mind of mediæval scholars so far as they were concerned with dramatic theory.

ÆLIUS DONATUS

The only facts known about Donatus are that he flourished in the middle of the fourth century, A. D., and that he was the teacher of St. Jerome. His best known works are the various grammatical and rhetorical treatises recently gathered together under the title of *Ars Grammatica;* the *Enarrationes* and

scholia on the plays of Terence, and the fragment *De Comœdia et Tragœdia.* The *Grammar* was used for centuries and the word *Donat* became a common noun designating an elementary grammar. The *Commentaries* and fragment on *Comedy and Tragedy* were included in all the early printed editions of Terence. The influence exerted by these works extended throughout the Middle Ages into the seventeenth century, until the *Poetics* of Aristotle was known and accepted throughout the greater part of civilized Europe. Giraldi Cintio in Italy, and Lope de Vega in Spain, owe not a little to the *Commentaries* and the *De Comœdia et Tragœdia*.

The fragment here printed contains little that is new and original; the references and quotations from Horace are sufficient indication of the source of most of his ideas. His importance lies rather in the fact that he is the last of the Latins to formulate any theory, even a derived one, of the drama. He belongs to the Middle Ages in spirit; his scholastic mind and temper were evidently what appealed to his followers. He is the connecting link between Horace and Dante: Donatus is the last of the Romans: Dante, though his meager reference to drama is of the spirit of the Middle Ages is chronologically the immediate precursor of the early Renaissance critics.

ON COMEDY AND TRAGEDY [1]
[*De Comœdia et Tragœdia*]
(4th Century A. D.)

Comedy is a story treating of various habits and customs of public and private affairs, from which one may learn what is of use in life, on the one hand, and what must be avoided, on the other. The Greeks defined it as follows: κωμωδία ἐστὶν ἰδιωτικῶν καὶ πολιτικῶν πραγμάτων ἀκίνδυνος περιοχή. Cicero says that comedy is " a copy of life, a mirror of custom, a reflection of truth." Comedies, moreover, are so named from early custom; since in country towns compositions of this sort were originally played among the Greeks; as in Italy the people used to be held at crossroads by games where a measure of speech was introduced while the acts were being changed. Or ἀπὸ των κωμῶν; this is, from the acts of the lives of men who inhabit country towns because of the mediocrity of the happy; not in kingly halls, like tragic characters. Comedy, indeed, comprises action and speech, since it is verse based upon a representation of life and an imitation of customs. It is uncertain which of the Greeks first invented comedy; of the Latins there is no doubt. Livius Andronicus first invented comedy and the national drama; he said, " Comedy is the mirror of everyday life," nor was this without reason. For as we gaze into a mirror we easily perceive the features of the truth in the reflection; and so, in reading a comedy do we easily observe the reflection of life and of custom. The plan of its origin moreover comes all the way from foreign states and customs, for the Athenians, preserving the culture of Attica, when they wished to observe people living evil lives, used to come from every quarter with joy and alacrity to the country towns and there used to make known the life of individuals using their names; hence the name is made, as it is called in a comedy. These compositions, moreover, were first acted in pleasant meadows. Nor were rewards lacking whereby the talents of learned men might be incited to the art of writing; prizes were offered to the actors as well, that they might practice the pleasing modulations of speech for the pleasure of praise. Also a goat was given to them, because this animal was considered a charm against mistakes; hence the name of tragedy. Some, however, preferred that tragedy should be spoken of and called from the lees, or dregs of oil, which is a watery fluid. When these plays were first acted by artists for the glory of Father Liber, the actual authors of the comedies and tragedies began to worship and adore the divinity of this god as to a paternal deity. A probable explanation of this exists; for these unfinished verses were so produced that it was best for his glory and wondrous deeds to be thereby honored and proclaimed; then, little by little the renown of this art spread. Thespis, however, first brought these writings to the notice of every one. Afterwards, Æschylus, following the ex-

1 Translated, complete, for the present collection by Mildred Rogers. It has not before appeared in English.— Ed.

ample, made some public. Of these Horace speaks thus in his *De Arte Poetica:*

Ignotum tragicae genus invenisse Camaenae dicitur, et plaustris vexisse Poemata Thespis, quae canerent, agerentque peruncti faecibus ora post hunc personae, pallaeque repertor honestae Æschylus, et modicis instravit pulpita tignis: Et docuit magnumque loqui, nitique cothurno. Successit vetus hic Comoedia non sine multa laude: sed in vitium libertas excidit, et vim Dignam lege regi: lex est accepta: chorusque turpiter obticuit sublato jure nocendi. Nil. intentatum nostri liquere Poetae: nec minimum meruere decus, vestigia Graeca ausi deserere, et celebrare domestica facta, vel qui praetextas, vel qui docuere togatas.

[see p. 28]

Story [fabula] is the generic term, and its two chief divisions are comedy and tragedy. If the plot be Latin it is called *Praetexta;* comedy has, moreover, many subdivisions. For it may be in Greek dress; in Roman, it may be a comedy of the booths — Atellanian — or farcical — *Rhintonica* — or the *bare-foot* — *Planipedia.* This term of *Bare-foot* is applied because of the low order of the plot or the poorness of the players, who wear no sock or buskin on the stage or platform, but go bare-footed; or it may be because these comedies are not concerned with the affairs of people in towers or attics but of the inhabitants of low humble places. Cincius and Faliscus are said to have been the first actors who played comedy; Minutius and Prothonius the first who played tragedy.

All comedies are subdivided into four classes: the title-rôle, the scene of action, the situation, and the outcome. Here follow certain examples: of the title rôle, are the *Phormio,* the *Hecyra,* the *Curculio,* the *Epidicus.* Of the scene are the *Andria,* the *Leucadia,* and the *Brundisina.* Of the situation are the *Eunuchus,* the *Asinaria,* and the *Captivi.* Of the outcome are the *Commorientes,* the *Adelphi,* and the *Heautontimorumenos.* There are three kinds of comedy: the *Palliata,* in which the actors wear Greek costumes; by some this is called the *Tabernaria.* Secondly, the *To-*

gata, in which the actors wish to wear togas. Thirdly, the *Atellana;* this sort of comedy is full of witticisms and jokes; this is a time-honored form. Every comedy is divided into four parts: the prologue, the *Protasis,* the *Epitasis,* and the *Catastrophe.* The prologue is the first speech, called πρόλογος by the Greeks; that is, an address preceding the actual structure of the story. There are four kinds of prologues: Συσατικὸs, a laudatory passage wherein the author or the story is praised; Αναπορικὸs, one in which an opponent is cursed or the audience thanked; Ὑποθετικὸs, one telling the plot of the play; and one, Μικτὸs, a composite which contains all of the above elements. There were some who wished this to be between a prologue and a preface, inasmuch as a prologue is to a certain extent the introduction of the story wherein something more is told than in the plot, to the audience; either from the poet or from needs of the drama itself or the actor. The preface is where an account of the plot is given. The first part, or *Protasis,* is the beginning of the action of the drama, wherein part of the play is developed, and part withheld in order to create suspense. The second part, or *Epitasis* marked the ascent and further development of difficulties or, as I have said, the knot of the entire coil. The last part, or *Catastrophe,* is the solution, pleasing to the audience, and made clear to every one by an explanation of what has passed.

In a great many stories the titles themselves stand before the authors' names; in some, the authors precede the titles. Antiquity explains this variety of usage, for when certain narratives were first given out their titles were mentioned before their authors, so that no unpopularity could harm them because of the author. When, however, after the publication of many works the author had gained some renown, their names stood first, so that through the attraction of their names their works were successful.

It is obvious that acts were written for various games. For there are four kinds of games which the Curule Ædiles provided for the public. There are the *Megalenses* games, sacred to the great gods; these are called μεγαλεσίος by the Greeks. There are the funeral games instituted to keep back the populace while the funeral rites decreed for a Patrician were being carried out. There are the plebeian games given for the benefit of the plebs. There are the Apollonian games sacred to Apollo. On the stage there were always two altars; one to the right for Liber, one to the left for the god in whose honor the festival was held. Hence Terence's Andrian says, *Ex ara hac sume verbenas.* [Take some foliage from the altar.]

They always bring on Ulysses in Greek costume either because he finally pretended madness when he wanted to be ruler so that he should not be forced ignorantly to go to war, or because of his unusual wisdom under the cover of which he was of such great help to his comrades. For his nature was always that of a deceitful person. Some say that the inhabitants of Ithaca, like the Locrians, always wore *pallas.* The actors impersonating Achilles and Neoptolemus wear diadems, though never royal scepters. The reason of this convention is held to be that they never entered the rites of conspiracy with the other Greek youths to carry on the war with Troy, nor were they ever under the command of Agamemnon.

The old men in comedies wear white costumes, because they are held to be the oldest sort. Young men wear a variety of colors. The slaves in comedy wear thick shawls, either as a mark of their former poverty, or in order that they may run the faster. Parasites wear twisted *pallas.* Those who are happy wear white robes; the unhappy wear soiled robes; the rich wear royal purple, paupers wear reddish-purple; the soldier carries a purple *chlamys;* a girl wears a foreign robe; a procurer, a robe of many colors; yellow, to designate greed, is given to the courtesan. These garments are called *syrmata* — attired in trains because they are dragged. This custom originated from the luxuriant extravagances of the stage. The same garments worn by mourning characters denote neglect through carelessness.

Woven curtains are spread on the stage as ornament; they are painted in many colors, and were used in Rome after the custom of the Attalian kingdom; in place of these, Liparian hangings were used at a later period. There is also a curtain used for farces; this is hung before the audience while the sets of the production are being changed.

The actors speak the dialogue. The songs are arranged in measures, not by the author, but by some one skilled in music of this sort. For all the songs are not sung throughout in the same measures, but in different ones, in order to mark which group of three are singing the reciprocal measures of the song. The people who used to make this sort of measures placed their name at the front, above the title and the author and the cast.

Songs of this sort were arranged for flutes so that when these had been heard, many of the people could learn what play was going to be acted before the title was announced to the audience. They were, moreover, played on "equal" or, "unequal" flutes, and right- or left-handed. The right-handed, or Lydian, ones proclaimed the production of a comedy of serious and solemn character; the left-handed, or Serranian, ones announced humor in the comedy in the lightness of its catastrophe. In cases, though, where a "right" and "left" ceremony was required, it meant that the play combined seriousness and gayety combined.

DANTE ALIGHIERI

Dante Alighieri was born at Florence in May, 1265. His family was of noble extraction, though they had been for some time in reduced circumstances. Little is known of the poet's early years except what is told in the *Vita Nuova:* his love for Beatrice, whom he first saw when he was nine years old. His second meeting, nine years later, resulted in the writing of his first known work, a sonnet.

This sonnet, copies of which he sent to various poets, brought him friends, chief among whom was Guido Cavalcanti. Beatrice died in 1290, and the young Dante devoted himself heart and soul to the study of philosophy and literature. At the same time, however, he engaged in business and political enterprises. In 1289 he fought with the Florentine Guelfs in the Battle of Campaldino. In the *Divina Commedia* he relates that he was engaged in other battles. Not later than 1298 Dante married. Of his married life little is known, except that when he settled at Ravenna in later years his wife was not with him. They had four children, all of whom were born in Florence before 1304. In 1295, or the year after, he enrolled in the Guild of Physicians and Apothecaries, and began an active political career, which was to end in disaster. In the year 1300 he went as ambassador to San Gimignano on a special mission. Soon after, in the same year, he was elected one of the six Priors, who stood highest in the government of Florence. It was not long before one of the numerous political feuds — between the Blacks and the Whites — broke out. The leaders of both factions were banished, and Dante was sent on a mission to Rome. In his absence from home, in 1301, Charles of Valois entered Florence and sowed seeds of discord. The next year Dante learned that he had been fined on a false charge of corrupt dealings. He disregarded the fine and was condemned to exile on pain of death. He never saw Florence again. For nearly twenty years he lived in poverty, wandering from city to city. Very little is known of these last years. He went first to Siena, where he joined other conspirators in an attempt to return, but in 1304 he left the conspirators, and went to Verona and later Padua. He was in Paris, and perhaps in England during the following years, but was again in Italy in 1310 and 1311. The letters he wrote to the Florentines at that time, full of imprecations and threats, resulted in his exclusion from the number of exiles who were finally allowed to return in 1311. After further wanderings, he went to Verona again, where he was the guest of Can Grande della Scala, to whom he wrote his famous *Epistle*. In 1317 or 1318 he went to Ravenna, where he lived with his children and finished the *Divina Commedia,* on which he had been working many years. Toward the end of his life he visited Mantua and Piacenza. In 1321 he was sent as ambassador to Venice to settle a dispute, but the Venetians, refusing to allow the ambassadors to return by sea, forced them to pursue a difficult and unhealthy route; Dante was taken ill in consequence, and in September, 1321, died at Ravenna.

The *Epistle to Can Grande* was written not later than 1318, and was first printed, in very corrupt form, by G. Baruffaldi (Venice, 1700). It contains a full explanation of the scope and purpose of the *Divina Commedia.* Dante's remarks on comedy, which are here re-printed, are incidental. They are interesting rather as a link in the dramatic tradition extending from Donatus to the early Renaissance critics, than as an intrinsically valuable document. Dante reiterates the usual philological statement as to the etymology of the word " Comedy " and quotes Horace in support of his use of the word in connection with his poem.

EPISTLE TO CAN GRANDE [1]

[Epistola XI]

(Written about 1318)

Section 10.— The title of the book is: " Here beginneth the Comedy of Dante Alighieri, a Florentine by birth, but not

[1] Extract from *A Translation of Dante's Eleven Letters,* by C. S. Latham (Boston, 1892).

by character." And for the comprehension of this it must be understood that the word " Comedy " is derived from κώμη, village, and ᾠδή, which meaneth song; hence comedy is, as it were, a *village song.* Comedy is in truth a certain kind of poetical narrative that differeth

from all others. It differeth from tragedy in its subject-matter,— in this way,
that Tragedy in its beginning is admirable and quiet, in its ending or catastrophe foul and horrible; and because of
this the word " Tragedy " is derived from
τράγος, which, meaneth *goat*, and ὠδή.
Tragedy is, then, as it were, a *goatish
song;* that is, foul like a goat, as doth
appear in the tragedies of Seneca. Comedy, indeed, beginneth with some adverse
circumstances, but its theme hath a
happy termination, as doth appear in
the comedies of Terence. And hence certain writers were accustomed to say in
their salutations in place of a greeting,
" a tragic beginning and a comic ending." Likewise they differ in their style
of language, for Tragedy is lofty and

sublime, Comedy mild and humble,— as
Horace says in his *Poetica,* where he con-
cedeth that sometimes comedians speak
like tragedians and conversely:

*Interdum tamen et vocem comoedia tollit,
Iratusque Chremes tumido delitigat ore;
Et tragicus plerumque dolet sermone pe-
    destri.*

From which it is evident why the present
work is called a comedy. For if we consider the theme, in its beginning it is horrible and foul, because it is Hell; in its
ending, fortunate, desirable, and joyful,
because it is Paradise; and if we consider the style of language, the style is
careless and humble, because it is the
vulgar tongue in which even housewives
hold converse. . . .

ITALIAN DRAMATIC CRITICISM OF THE RENAISSANCE

The Italian Renaissance, bringing with
it as it did a re-birth of interest in the
art and literature of antiquity, is the
starting point of modern literary criticism. After the discovery of the ancient
texts, commentators, translators, editors
were not wanting, and it was not long
before they began to expound theories
of their own. It has already been shown
(p. 28) how the *Ars Poetica* of Horace
had been the basis of what was written
on the subject of the drama between
the Augustan period and the early Renaissance. Donatus and Diomedes both
quote largely from it, and most of their
ideas were based upon it. Aristotle, on
the other hand, was practically unknown;
his influence in classical antiquity was,
according to Spingarn, " so far as it is
possible to judge, very slight." The
manuscript of the *Poetics* was preserved
in the East. The first Oriental version
was translated from the Syriac into Arabic (about 935 A. D.) by Abu-Baschar.
In the twelfth century Averroës made an
abridged version; this in turn was translated into Latin in the thirteenth century
by a German of the name of Hermann,
and by Mantinus of Tortosa in Spain in
the fourteenth. One of the extremely
rare references to Aristotle is found in

Roger Bacon; Petrarch just mentions
him.

Giorgio Valla published his Latin translation of the *Poetics* at Venice in 1498.
This was followed by the Aldine edition
of the original Greek text in 1508. In
1536 Allessandro de' Pazzi published the
Greek original together with a revised
Latin text, and in 1548 Robortello published the first commentary (with a Latin
translation). Bernardo Segni, in 1549,
was the first to publish an Italian translation.

Among the earliest treatises on the art
of poetry was that of Vida, whose *De
Arte Poetica* appeared in 1527; contrary to practically every other work of
similar title, this influential poem contains no reference to the drama. Two
years later, however, Trissino published
the first four books of his *Poetica,* but
not until 1563, when two books were
added, did he consider the drama.
Dolce's translation of Horace in 1535
was followed the next year by the vernacular *Poetica* of Daniello, whose few
references to tragedy and comedy, based
upon Horace and Aristotle, are the first
of their kind to appear in the Italian
language. The same year saw Pazzi's
edition and Trincaveli's Greek text.

From this time on, the influence of Aristotle as an arbiter in the art of poetry was to spread. Robortello's *In Librum Aristotelis de Arte Poetica Explicationes* (1548) is the first complete commentary on the *Poetics*. Segni's translation was published the next year. In 1550 appeared Maggi's *Explicationes* (written with Lombardi), similar to the commentary of Robortello. Both are diffuse, detailed, and pedantic, and rarely depart from what the authors understood, or misunderstood, in Aristotle. Muzio [Mutio] published an *Arte Poetica* in 1551. Varchi in his *Lezzioni* (1553) upheld the Aristotelian ideals of tragedy. The *Discorso sulle Comedie e sulle Tragedie* of the famous novelist Giraldi Cintio, which was written in 1543, but not published until 1554, carried on the Aristotelian tradition begun by Daniello. This was to continue in one form or another throughout the Renaissance and be taken up later in France. Minturno's two treatises, *De Poeta* (1559) and *Arte Poetica* (1564), the first in Latin, the second in Italian, were the fullest discussions of the theory of poetry and drama yet written. The influence of Aristotle and Horace is everywhere evident, but, as will be seen from the extracts here printed, the Italian critic has expounded and amplified after his own manner. The *Commentarii* of Vettori [Victorius], printed in 1560, was another Latin treatise explaining the *Poetics*. The following year Julius Cæsar Scaliger, one of the most influential theorists since antiquity, published his Latin work, *Poetices Libri Septem*. As Scaliger had lived in France for some years (his book was published at Lyons) and was acquainted with many contemporary writers, his influence was widespread, though not so much so during the sixteenth as the seventeenth century. The *Poetics* of Scaliger, which was an "attempt to reconcile Aristotle's *Poetics*, not only with the precepts of Horace and the definitions of the Latin grammarians, but with the whole practice of Latin tragedy, comedy, and epic poetry," is a long, erudite and dogmatic treatise in which the canons of Aristotle are narrowed and confined to rules of the strictest sort. In 1563 the last two parts of Trissino's *Poetica* appeared. Castelvetro was the next to enter the field of criticism. His *Poetica* (a commentary on

and translation of Aristotle's *Poetics*) was published in 1570. This work was of prime importance, for one reason because it contained the first formulation of the unity of place, supposed to have been derived from Aristotle. The immediate effect of this, as will be seen later, was to start the endless discussion in France of the famous "three Unities." Jean de la Taille, in 1572, was the first to insist on them in that country. Castelvetro was likewise the first to consider a play as limited and directly affected by stage representation. The Italian critics from the time of Castelvetro to the end of the century, carried on discussions of varying degrees of importance, though none of them exerted an influence equal to that of Scaliger, Castelvetro or Minturno. Piccolomini's edition of the *Poetics* was published in 1575, Viperano's *De Arte Poetica* in 1579. Patrizzi's *Della Poetica* (1586), Tasso's *Discorsi dell' Arte Poetica* (1587), Denores' *Poetica* (1588), Buonamici's *Discorsi Poetici* (1597), Ingegneri's *Poesia Rappresentativa* (1598), and Summo's *Discorsi Poetici* (1600), testify to the prodigious activity of the period.

Such are the outstanding works which treat in greater or less degree the theory of the drama. If we add the prefaces and prologues to the plays of Cecchi, Giraldi Cintio, Gelli, Aretino, and Il Lasca (the *Gelosia, Strega,* and *L'Arzigoglio* in particular) and the references in the works of Speroni,[1] Luisino,[2] Partenio,[3] Fracastoro,[4] Capriano,[5] Michele,[6] Beni,[7] and Zinano[8] are included, the list of writers on the subject of the drama is nearly exhausted.

---

[1] A letter, written in 1565, on the interpretation of the word *katharsis*. (Sperone Speroni, vol. V, *Opere*, Venezia, 1740.) Also *Giudizio sopra la tragedia de Canace*, etc. (1550).

[2] F. Luisino, *In Librum Q. Horatii Flacci de Arte Poetica Commentarius* (1554).

[3] B. Partenio, *Della Imitatione Poetica* (1560).

[4] G. Fracastoro, *Naugerius, sive de Poetica Dialogus* (1555).

[5] G. P. Capriano, *Della Vera Poetica* (1555).

[6] Agostino Michele, *Discorso in cui si dimostra come si possono scrivere le Commedie e le Tragedie in Prosa* (1592).

[7] Paolo Beni, *Disputatio in qua ostenditur præstare Comœdiam atque Tragœdiam metrorum vinculis solvere* (1600).

[8] Zinano, *Discorso della Tragedia* (Reggio, 1590).

The Renaissance critics had discovered Aristotle; the study of the *Poetics,* and that of the *Ars Poetica* of Horace, was the basis of their commentaries. Much of the great mass of this material is textual comment, more or less intelligent and illuminating; much is repetition, classification, philological analysis; but out of it all there emerges the true spirit of enlightened criticism. The beginning of the sixteenth century was a period of darkness; the end found Italy the fountain-head of Europe. France, Spain; and England, followed in her wake, adopting with modifications what she had been the first to discover and discuss.

BERNARDINO DANIELLO

Nothing is known of the life of Bernardino Daniello except that he was a native of Lucca and that he died at Padua in 1565. He was a scholar, he made translations from and commentaries on classical works, and wrote on Dante. His *Poetica* was his most famous work.

Daniello's *Poetica* (1536) is without doubt the first work of its sort since antiquity, and the few passages relating to the drama are of great historical importance. Daniello's ideas are of course derived from the ancients, but they are clearly stated, and must have exercised a profound influence over his contemporaries and successors. Saintsbury says: " The first author of one [a theory of poetry] is generally taken to be Daniello . . . it has such good claims to be among the very earliest vernacular disputations of a general character on poetry in Italy." There is a mixture of Aristotle and Horace in the work. According to Spingarn, " In the *Poetica* of Daniello (1536) occurs the first allusion in modern literary criticism to the Aristotelian notion of ideal imitation." The idea that it is the function of the poet to teach and to delight is decidedly Horatian. as are indeed the critic's rules for tragedy and comedy.

POETICS [1]
[*La Poetica*]
(1536)

. . . And the materials and subjects may be many and varied, for to some, as to the writers of comedy, they may be of more common stuff: every-day occurrences, not to say lowly and commonplace, while the tragic poets treat of deaths of high kings and the ruin of great empires. . . .   [p. 34.]

. . . Similarly, one must be careful that the plot of tragedies be clearly put together, and as tragedy is an imitation of the most terrible and pitiful things, it does not seem to me permissible to introduce into it just and virtuous men changed into unjust and wicked ones

---

[1] Translated selections by Lander MacClintock.—Ed.

through the adversity of fortune — a thing rather shocking than pitiful or fearful. On the contrary, one must show the wicked and the evil changed by fortune into good and just men. Nor does one deny the right to the tragic poet to lower himself when he wishes, to humble speech, in order to weep and lament. For it does not seem right for a man who is banished from his country, however great and noble his lineage, to use pompous and proud words to other people. Nor is the writer of comedy to be prevented from using some of the grandiloquence of the tragic poet, on occasion. As for instance, an angry father to his son in order to have more power and influence over him. And since some things are done on the stage and some only referred to, it behoves us to see what can be acted, and what cannot. The things which cannot be done are the cruel deeds, the impossible, and the unseemly. As if Medea, in full view of the gaping multitude should kill her own children and then tear the murdered ones limb from limb. And as if Progne with her husband and sister and sons should, in full view of the spectators, grow wings and become birds; and in comedies there should be lascivious kisses, embraces, and the like. Comedy should not exceed the limit of five acts, nor comprise less; four characters must not speak at once, but only two or three at most, while the others stand to one side quietly listening. Nor must any deity be brought in, except in cases where man is unable by his own efforts to unravel some tangle without divine aid and intercession. Let the chorus in tragedy (since they are no longer employed in comedy, but in their stead, and between the acts music and songs and *Moresche* and jesters, in order that the stage may not remain empty)— let the chorus in tragedy, I say, take the part of the just and the good, wrongfully oppressed, and favor these. Let them advise friends, favor those who hate sin, laud sobriety, justice, law, and peace, and pray the gods that, disdaining fortune, lofty palaces and proud towers with their summits menacing heaven, they descend to console the miserable and the afflicted.   [p. 38.]

ANTONIO SEBASTIANO (MINTURNO)

Antonio Sebastiano, better known under the name of Minturno, was born at Trajetto. Very little is known of his life, which was spent in the church. He was Bishop of Ugento, and assisted at the Council of Trent. In 1565 he was transferred to Crotone in Calabria, where he died in 1574. Besides his *Poetica* and *De Poeta,* he wrote a number of religious works and some *Rime.* In his day, he was considered a man of great learning.

To the contributions to the Renaissance theory of poetry Minturno has added the Horatian element of "delight," as well as instruction. Minturno's interpretation of Aristotle is on the whole intelligent and illuminating. The first of Minturno's two treatises was the *De Poeta,* written in Latin and published in 1559. It is a long and thoroughgoing Art of Poetry, based upon Latin literature; the *Arte Poetica,* in Italian, published in 1563, takes its examples to a certain extent from Italian literature, though of necessity most of the plays discussed are Greek and Latin. While both works are similar in character, there is, on the whole, very little repetition in the *Poetica,* which is a much clearer and more interesting treatment of the subject than the *De Poeta.* Minturno's treatises soon became known abroad, and his influence was felt in Spain, France, and England, at a comparatively early date.

THE ART OF POETRY [1]

[*Arte Poetica*]

(1563)

. . . .

Ang. What is dramatic poetry?
Min. Imitations of things — to be presented in the theater — complete and per-

[1] Extracts here translated — by Ida Treat O'Neil — for the first time in English. The treatise is in dialogue form.— Ed.

fect in form and circumscribed as to length. Its form is not that of narration; it introduces several persons who act and converse. Their speech is suave and pleasing, and they may dance or sing, since dramatic poetry employs the three mediums of expression, using them individually or conjointly. Nor should there be lacking a proper stage equipment for the pleasure and profit of the onlooker.

Ang. How many kinds of subjects are treated in the theater?

Min. Three in all. One class records serious and grave happenings and concerns those of high rank — the great and the illustrious. This is the field of the tragic poet. A second recognizes the middle strata of society — common folk of the city or the country: the farmer, the common soldier, the petty merchant, and similar persons. These afford matter for comedy. The third division has to do with humble persons, mean and ludicrous, with all those in fact who seem most fitted to provoke merriment, thus supplying subject matter for satirical poetry.

Ang. So, then, dramatic poetry is divided into three parts?

Min. It has in truth three divisions. The first of these is called tragedy, the second comedy, and the third by the ancients was termed satyric drama.

Ang. A little later I will question you in detail concerning the nature of each of these forms. But now I should like to have you elucidate further the general definition of dramatic poetry.

Min. You will understand it clearly if you remember that during our conversation of yesterday I said that the dramatic poet differs in technique from the lyric or the epic poet. The lyric poet simply narrates, without laying aside his own personality; the epic poet sometimes retains his personality and sometimes abandons it, speaking at times for himself, and as often introducing other persons who speak. But the dramatic poet, of whom we are now speaking, from first to last speaks through the lips of others. This may be observed not only in the tragedies of Sophocles and of Euripides but also in some of our own — notably the work of Dolce and of Alemanni, two of the brightest ornaments of our literature — as well as in the comedies of Terence and Plautus.

·   ·   ·   ·   ·   ·

Min. The common purpose of all poets is, as Horace teaches, that of providing pleasure and profit. But the manner in which each poet may delight and instruct will be demonstrated when we discuss the different forms of poetry. And although

stage apparatus is a necessary complement of dramatic poetry, however, since dramatic poetry has three divisions, we can better understand what each division demands in the way of apparatus when discussing each of the three forms separately. So that, reserving the discussion of these two topics to a fitting place and time, there now remains for me to answer your question concerning the length of the dramatic form.

Ang. That, indeed, remains for discussion.

Min. How long a time should be given to the actual performance of the dramatic poem is not for the poet to determine. For even if there were a hundred tragedies or a hundred comedies to be presented, each would demand a certain definite period of time. Just as when there are many speakers and lawyers concerned in a single case, each must be given an opportunity for expression. But in so far as the nature of the subject is concerned, the action should be prolonged until there ensues some change of fortune — from good to ill, or from grievous to gay. One who carefully studies the works of the greatest among the ancients will discover that the action of the dramatic poem transpires in a day, or is never prolonged beyond two, just as it is said that the action of the longest epic poem should transpire in a year.

Ang. How much time shall we give to the performance of these poems, since their action takes place in less than two days?

Min. Not less than three hours nor more than four; lest neither too great brevity rob the work of its beauty and leave the desire of the hearers unsatisfied, nor excessive length deprive the poem of its proportion, spoil its charm, and render it boresome to the beholders. And indeed the wise poet should so measure the time with the matter to be presented that those who hear the work should rather deplore its brevity than regret having remained too long to listen.

Ang. I now understand perfectly the definition of dramatic poetry. Now will you tell me how many divisions there are to the dramatic poem, that I may better understand its composition?

Min. I shall answer you as I answered Signor Vespasiano yesterday when he questioned me concerning the parts of the epic poem, that the divisions are not of the same nature, since some concern the quality and some the quantity — that is, the body — of the work. And since the quality of the poem is due partly to the very essence of the work and partly to chance, there are six essential parts of such a poem: the plot, the manners or customs, the sentiments expressed, the words, the singing, and the apparatus of the stage. I shall not attempt to define four of these divisions, for they are characteristic of every form of poetry, and I have already spoken sufficiently concerning them during the discussion of epic poetry yesterday. I shall refer to them when it is necessary during the explanation of the individual poems. If you have no objection I shall postpone until that time the discussion of the singing and of the stage apparatus

Ang. And why not?

Min. It is a most reasonable arrangement, for dramatic poetry is either tragedy, or comedy, or satyric drama; that is to say, the genus is found in each of its species, nor can it be separated from them, as you may easily understand. Just as the animal is to be found in man, in the horse, in the lion, and in every other sort of animal, so it cannot exist independently, separated from them, except in the mind, or according to Plato, where mortal eye may not see.

Ang. I shall not ask you how the accidental quality of the poem may be divided, for I remember well that yesterday you informed Signor Vespasiano that such divisions are the episodes. These, like the plot, are imitations of the deeds and the sayings of others; they are garnished with the same ornaments as the plot, adorned with like colors, and tending toward the same end. And since the action of the poem must transpire in one or two days, and must arrive speedily at its conclusion in order to satisfy the impatience of the onlookers who cannot remain indefinitely in the theater, these episodes should be neither so frequent nor so long as in epic poetry, which may include the happenings of a year as well as many other incidents brought from without to render the poem longer and more varied. The episodes in a dramatic poem should be few and brief. But I should

like to inquire how many and of what nature are the parts into which the body of the poem may be divided?

Min. We may say that there are four of them, since that was the opinion of Aristotle, and we shall name them as he did: Prologues, Discourses, Choruses, and Exits. I will reserve the explanation of each of these until I come to treat the different forms of dramatic poetry, since each of them has its prologues, its discourses, its choruses, and its exits.

. . . . .

Min. Tragedy is concerned with the imitation of serious and weighty happenings, embodied in a complete and perfect form, circumscribed as to length. The language of tragedy is suave. The divisions of the poem are so organized that each has its place. It does not simply narrate, but introduces persons who act and speak, arousing feelings of pity and terror, and tending to purge the mind of the beholder of similar passions, to his delight and profit.

Ang. Will you elucidate all the parts of the definition?

Min. In yesterday's discussion I spoke at length of the meaning of " imitation," which may be regarded as the basis of all poetry, as well as of painting and sculpture. In the same discourse I explained in full how the form, in every sort of poetry, must be unified, complete, and perfect, and of a given length. Today I have said enough concerning the length. But since every complete action has a beginning, a middle, and an end, as I demonstrated yesterday, we should consider not only how long the action should be prolonged and where it should finish, but also where it should begin. And truly, he who would make a good beginning in narrating an incident, should begin where it is fitting, neither commencing his narration with the most recent details, nor going back to those most remote and faraway.

. . . . .

Min. You are doubtless aware already that what distinguishes tragedy from comedy and satyric drama is the imitation of grave and weighty happenings, together with the ennobling influence upon manners. Thus, since these grave and weighty happenings furnish the matter for tragedy, the ennobling or purification of manners is the end toward which all effort is directed.

Ang. I should like you to speak at greater length concerning the matter and the purpose, particularly the purpose.

Min. Then, you will understand the purpose of tragic poetry when you have learned the mission of the tragic poet. His mission is no other than that of employing verses so instructive, so pleasing, and so moving, that they tend to purge of passion the mind of the hearer. All dramatic poets whose plays are presented in the theater declare that their mission is to instruct, but the tragic poet creates before our eyes an image of life, showing us the behavior of those who, remarkable among men for their rank, their position, and for the favors of fortune, have fallen into extreme misery through human error. From this we learn not to place too great trust in worldly prosperity, that nothing here below is so durable and stable that it may not fall and perish, no happiness but may change to misery, nothing so high but that it may become base and infamous. And seeing others endure such changes of fortune, we learn to guard against unexpected evil, and if misfortune does come, we may learn to endure it patiently. The tragic poet aside from the suavity of his verse and the elegance of his speech, affords much pleasure to the onlooker by the use of singing and dancing. In fact, he presents nothing that does not please us, nor does he move us without charm; but with the force of his words and the weight of his thoughts, he can stir up passions in the mind, producing wonder, fear, and pity. What is more tragic than to move others? What is so moving as the terrible unexpected, such as the cruel death of Hippolytus, the wild and piteous madness of Hercules, the unhappy exile of Œdipus? And all this terror and pity frees us most pleasantly from similar passions, for nothing else so curbs the indomitable frenzy of our minds. No one is so completely the victim of unbridled appetites, that, being moved by fear and pity at the unhappiness of others, he is not impelled to throw off the habits that have been the cause of such unhappiness. And the memory

of the grave misfortunes of others not only renders us more ready and willing to support our own; it makes us more wary in avoiding like ills. The physician who with a powerful drug extinguishes the poisonous spark of the malady that afflicts the body, is no more powerful than the tragic poet who purges the mind of its troubles through the emotions aroused by his charming verses.

. . . . . .

Min. Before I define comedy, I shall speak briefly of its three general divisions and how and when they came into being. During the feasts of Bacchus, or of the pastoral Apollo, the young men warmed with food and wine used to jest among themselves, speaking often of the defects of the great men of those days when the Republic was in the hands of the people, who listened eagerly to slander of the nobles and of the prominent citizens. It was this that gave the idea of comedy to the poets, already given to attacking the evil customs of the age. So it was that these poets, possessing a certain erudition and charm of style, following the custom of the young men at the feasts of their gods, began to write little plays and present them publicly.

. . . .

Ang. But before you define comedy, tell me what is the mission of the comic poet?

Min. What else but that of teaching and pleasing? According to Plato, the gods took pity on the tedious life of mortals, wearied with never-ending tasks and labors, and that they might not lack recreations and that they might take heart again, the gods established festivals, banquets, and games, favored by Bacchus, Apollo, and the Muses. Then mankind, celebrating these holidays with poetry and with music, discovered comedy. And comedy not only delighted the hearer with imitations of pleasant things and with the charm of words, but since in those days poetry afforded a certain way in which to educate children to a proper manner of living — it even bettered their lives, affording as it did an image of their customs and everyday existence. It pleased them greatly to see the happenings of their own lives enacted by other persons. I shall not speak of the suavity of the language which is always one of the delights of comedy. The comic poet moves his hearers, though he does not stir them as deeply as the tragic poet. The comic poet awakes in the souls of those who listen pleasant and humane feelings.

.   .   .   .   .

Ang. Will you define comedy for us?
Min. Though Cicero may define comedy as an imitation of life, a mirror of manners, an image of truth, nevertheless according to the opinion of Aristotle, we might say that it is no other than an imitation of pleasing and amusing happenings, whether public or private. It must be presented in a complete and perfect form, and is circumscribed as to length. It does not consist of simple narration, but introduces persons of humble or mediocre fortune, who act and converse just as do the others. Its language is suave and pleasing, and it lacks neither singing nor dancing. . . . Its construction is even, and each part has its proper place.

Ang. Explain to me the divisions of the definition.

Min. I shall not speak of its presentation — in verses, with dancing and singing, sometimes with all three forms and sometimes with only part — nor concerning the subject matter or the form (that it should be unified and perfect and of a given length). I have already said enough concerning these things. Nor will I lose time in explaining that the incidents adapted to comedy are amusing and ludicrous, and that the persons are of humble station and equal rank; for this is the very nature of comedy, and is what distinguishes it from tragedy.

.   .   .   .   .   .

JULIUS CÆSAR SCALIGER

Julius Cæsar Scaliger, as he called himself, was born probably at Padua in 1484. He was the son of Benedetto Bordoni, a miniature painter. His own version of his noble parentage and life's adventures has been discredited and it has been established that he studied at the University of Padua, was graduated with a degree of M.D., and left home to seek his fortune. He went to Verona, where he made many acquaintances. In 1525 the Bishop of Agen induced him to come to Agen, where he continued his practice. In France, where he spent the last part of his life, he fell in love with a young woman, and in 1528 became a naturalized Frenchman and married her. He pursued literary and scientific studies, which occupied him to the end of his life. Among his first literary efforts are his tracts attacking Erasmus; but the great scholar refused to reply. He then attacked Cardan, who died shortly after. During his long residence at Agen he gradually became known not only in France, but throughout Europe. One of the few facts in his life of which any record exists is a charge of heresy in 1538, but Scaliger was acquitted. He died at Agen in 1558, one of the most celebrated men of his time.

Besides the *Poetices,* Scaliger's literary works include a number of rather crude poems, several letters, dissertations and commentaries on Hippocrates, Aristotle. and Theophrastus, various fragments of treatises on botany, and a tractate on comic meters, *De comicis dimensionibus.* Few similar works have enjoyed such universal renown as the *Poetices Libri Septem,* first published at Lyons in 1561. The work, written in Latin, is long, rambling, sketchy, violent in tone, dogmatic, scholastic, and pedantic, but with all its imperfections it was the first work to attempt a standardization of literary form and content. Aristotle was not only Scaliger's guiding light; he was so twisted and misinterpreted as to become the most rigorous of taskmasters.

POETICS [1]

[Poetices Libri Septem]

(1561)

Tragedy, like comedy, is patterned after real life, but it differs from comedy in the rank of the characters, in the nature of the action, and in the outcome. These differences demand, in turn, differences in style. Comedy employs characters from rustic, or low city life, such as Chremes, Davus, and Thais. The beginning of a comedy presents a confused state of affairs, and this confusion is happily cleared up at the end. The language is that of everyday life. Tragedy, on the other hand, employs kings and princes, whose affairs are those of the city, the fortress, and the camp. A tragedy opens more tranquilly than a comedy, but the outcome is horrifying. The language is grave, polished, removed from the colloquial. All things wear a troubled look; there is a pervading sense of doom, there are exiles and deaths. Tradition has it that the Macedonian king Archelaus, the intimate friend and patron of Euripides, asked the poet to make him the hero of a tragedy, but that Euripides replied: "Indeed, I cannot do it; your life presents no adequate misfortune."

.   .   .   .   .

The definition of tragedy given by Aristotle is as follows: "Tragedy is an imitation of an action that is illustrious, complete, and of a certain magnitude, in embellished language, the different kinds of embellishments being variously employed in the different parts, and not in the form of narration, but through pity and fear effecting the purgation of suchlike passions." I do not wish to attack this definition other than by adding my own: A tragedy is the imitation of the adversity of a distinguished man; it employs the form of action, presents a disastrous dénouement, and is expressed in impressive metrical language. Though Aristotle adds harmony and song, they are not, as the philosophers say, of the essence of tragedy; its one and only essential is acting. Then the phrase "of

1 Re-printed from *Select Translations from Scaliger's Poetics*, by F. M. Padelford (Yale University Press, New Haven, 1905).— Ed.

a certain magnitude" is put in to differentiate the tragedy from the epic, which is sometimes prolix. It is not always so, however, as the work of Musæus illustrates. Further, the mention of purgation is too restrictive, for not every subject produces this effect. "A certain magnitude," to return to the phrase, means not too long and not too short, for a few verses would not satisfy the expectant public, who are prepared to atone for the disgusting prosiness of many a day by the enjoyment of a few hours. Prolixity, however, is just as bad, when you must say with Plautus: "My legs ache with sitting, and my eyes with looking." (I, 6.)

.   .   .   .   .

Although tragedy resembles this epic poetry, it differs in rarely introducing persons of the lower classes, such as messengers, merchants, sailors, and the like. Comedies, on the other hand, never admit kings, save in such a rare instance as the *Amphitryon* of Plautus. I would limit this generalization, of course, to those plays which employ Greek characters and the Greek dress, for the Romans have admitted at will the dignified toga and *trabea*. . . . Tragedy and comedy are alike in mode of representation, but differ in subject-matter and treatment. The matters of tragedy are great and terrible, as commands of kings, slaughters, despair, suicides, exiles, bereavements, parricides, incests, conflagrations, battles, the putting out of eyes, weeping, wailing, bewailing, eulogies, and dirges. In comedy we have jests, revelling, weddings with drunken carousals, tricks played by slaves, drunkenness, old men deceived and cheated of their money. . . .

Now, a tragedy, provided it is a genuine tragedy, is altogether serious, but there have been some satyrical plays which differed little from comedies. Save in the gravity of some of the characters. We have an illustration in the *Cyclops* of Euripides, where all is wine and jesting, and where the outcome is so happy that all the companions of Ulysses are released, and the Cyclops alone suffers in the loss of his eye. The conclusion of this play was not unlike that of a mime, for the stage was wholly deserted on the exit of Ulysses, the giant with the rock alone remaining.

There are, on the other hand, many comedies which end unhappily for some of the characters. . . . Hence it is by no means true, as has hitherto been taught, that an unhappy issue is essential to tragedy. It is enough that the play contain horrible events.

When authors take their plots from history, they must be careful not to depart too widely from the records. In the early writers such care was by no means taken. Thus Æschylus followed Greek history in binding Prometheus to the rock, but he invented the fiction of his undoing by the thunderbolt, for tragic effect. There should be no dire event at the end, but only at the beginning, where he is bound to Caucasus. However, some have it that the eagle was driven away by Hercules; others that he killed it with his arrows; and still others that Prometheus was set free by Jupiter himself, because he warned the god not to cohabit with Thetis, lest she should bear him a son more illustrious than the father. Euripides invented stories about Helen which were utterly contrary to well-known history. The same author has been censured for bringing wicked and impure women into his plays. What is viler, the critic says, than Phædra, Jocasta, Canace, and Pasiphae, by whose infamy society is corrupted? But we reply that these women were not creatures of his imagination, but were taken from life. Forsooth, if we are to hear of no wickedness, history must be done away with. So those comedies should be prized which make us condemn the vices which they bring to our ears, especially when the life of impure women ends in an unhappy death.

. . . . .

The events themselves should be made to have such sequence and arrangement as to approach as near as possible to truth, for the play is not acted solely to strike the spectator with admiration or consternation — a fault of which, according to the critics, Æschylus was often guilty — but should also teach, move, and please. We are pleased either with jests, as in comedy, or with things serious, if rightly ordered. Disregard of truth is hateful to almost every man. Therefore neither those battles or sieges at Thebes which are fought through in two hours please me, nor do I take it to be the part of a discreet poet to pass from Delphi to Athens, or from Athens to Thebes, in a moment of time. Thus Æschylus has Agamemnon killed and buried so suddenly that the actor has scarcely time to breathe. Nor is the casting of Lichas into the sea by Hercules to be approved, for it cannot be represented without doing violence to truth.

The content of a play should be as concise as possible, yet also as varied and manifold as possible; for example, Hecuba in Thrace, Achilles forbidding her return, Polydorus already killed, the murder of Polyxena, and the blinding of Polymnestor. Since dead persons cannot be introduced, their apparitions, or ghosts, or specters, are substituted. Thus, as noted above, Æschylus introduces the apparitions of Polydorus and Darius, and in Ovid, Ceÿx appears to Alcyone. If a tragedy is to be composed from this last story, it should not begin with the departure of Ceÿx, for as the whole time for stage-representation is only six or eight hours, it is not true to life to have a storm arise, and the ship founder, in a part of the sea from which no land is visible. Let the first act be a passionate lamentation, the chorus to follow with execrations of sea-life; the second act, a priest with votive offerings conversing with Alcyone and her nurse, altars, fire, pious sentiments, the chorus following with approbation of the vows; the third act, a messenger announcing the rising of a storm, together with rumors as to the ship, the chorus to follow with mention of shipwrecks, and much apostrophizing of Neptune; the fourth act tumultuous, the report found true, the shipwrecks described by sailors and merchants, the chorus bewailing the event as though all were lost; the fifth act, Alcyone peering anxiously over the sea and sighting far off a corpse, followed by the resolution, when she was about to take her own life. This sample outline can be expanded by the introduction of other characters. (III, 97.)

LODOVICO CASTELVETRO

Lodovico Castelvetro was born at Modena in 1505 of an old and noble family.
His education was thorough and varied.
He attended the universities of Bologna,
Ferrara, Padua, and Siena. He studied
law and took a degree at Siena in that
profession out of deference to his father's wishes. After making a trip to
Rome, he returned to Siena, where he
applied himself to the studies for which
he felt himself best suited. His relin-
quishment of the law displeased his parents, and he returned, in bad health, to
Modena. There he engaged in literary
pursuits, in spite of his poor health. He
was a conspicuous figure in Modena in
what practically amounted to an academy. In 1553 he began the bitter literary quarrel with Caro which resulted
eventually in his exile. It began with a
criticism of a poem of Caro's, and soon
both parties resorted to intrigue and
even violence. Caro is said to have
started the inquiry which led to the arrest of several members of the "academy" on the suspicion of heresy. While
Castelvetro himself was not arrested, he
decided to go to Rome and defend himself, but seeing that he was not likely to
make out a good case he escaped and
went to Chiavenna on the Swiss-Italian
frontier. In 1561 he was excommunicated. He then appealed to the Council of Trent and was advised to return
to Rome. He determined, however, to
leave the country, and went to Lyons,
but the war of the Catholics and Prot-
estants, then in progress, soon forced
him to leave. He went to Geneva, and
thence to Chiavenna, where he lectured.
Not long after, Castelvetro's brother,
who was in the good graces of Maximilian II, urged Lodovico to come to
Vienna. In that city he published his
Poetica, dedicating it to Maximilian. On
the outbreak of the plague he returned to
Chiavenna, where he died in 1571.

Castelvetro's translation of Aristotle's
Poetics and his lengthy commentary are,
like the work of Scaliger, a landmark in
modern dramatic criticism. Like Scaliger's treatise, Castelvetro's is crude, pedantic, and inaccurate, but to the scholars of the time it was infinitely suggestive. Castelvetro not only interpreted
Aristotle too freely, he frequently mis-
translated him in order to establish a
point. Castelvetro's formulation of the
three Unities was the beginning of innumerable disputes throughout Europe.

POETICS [1]

[Poetica d'Aristotele vulgarizzata e esposta]

(1570)

Tragedy cannot effect its proper function with a reading, without staging and
acting.

In poetry there are possible two modes
of representing action, viz., either by
words and things, or by words alone;
one of these modes is more similar to the
thing represented, the other less; words
and things together are the more similar mode, words alone the less; for in
the former, words are represented by
words and things by things, whilst in

1 Re-printed from *Castelvetro's Theory of
Poetry,* by H. B. Charlton (Manchester, 1913).
— Ed.

the latter both words and things are
represented by words alone.

. . . . .

The time of the representation and
that of the action represented must be
exactly coincident . . . and the scene of
the action must be constant, being not
merely restricted to one city or house,
but indeed to that one place alone which
could be visible to one person.

. . . . .

Tragedy ought to have for subject an
action which happened in a very limited
extent of place and in a very limited
extent of time, that is, in that place
and in that time, in which and for which

the actors representing the action remain occupied in acting; and in no other place and in no other time. . . .

. . . . . .

The time of action ought not to exceed the limit of twelve hours.

. . . . . .

There is no possibility of making the spectators believe that many days and nights have passed, when they themselves obviously know that only a few hours have actually elapsed; they refuse to be so deceived.

. . . . . .

It is more marvelous when a great mutation of a hero's fortune is made, in a very limited time and a very limited place, than when it is made in a longer time and in varied and larger places.

. . . . . .

It was Aristotle's opinion that the plot of tragedy and comedy ought to comprise one action only, or two whose interdependence makes them one, and ought rather to concern one person than a race of people. But he ought to have justified this, not by the fact that a plot is incapable of comprising more actions, but by the fact that the extreme temporal limit of twelve hours and the restriction of the place for the performance, do not permit a multitude of actions nor the action of a whole race, nor indeed do they permit the whole of one complete action, if it is of any length: and this is the principal reason and the necessary one for the unity of action, that is, for the limitation of the plot to but one action of one person, or two actions, which by their interdependence can be counted one.

. . . . . .

No drama can be praiseworthy which has not two actions, that is, two plots, though one is principal and the other accessory.

. . . . . .

There is no doubt that there is more pleasure in listening to a plot containing many and diverse actions than in listening to that which contains but one.

. . . . . .

Singleness of plot is not in the least introduced on account of its necessity, but on account of the poet's eagerness for glory, and to demonstrate the excellence and the singularity of his genius

. . . for the judgment and the industry of the poet is demonstrated when with a plot comprising but a single action of a single person, that is, with a plot apparently without any promise of success in it, he nevertheless furnishes the spectators with as much delight as other poets can scarcely do with plots comprising many persons. . . . The plot of drama should necessarily comprise one action of one person, or two, interdependent on each other. . . .

. . . . . .

Tragedy is an imitation of an action, magnificent, complete, which has magnitude, and comprises each of those species, which represent with speech made delightful separately in its parts, and not by narration, and, moreover, induces through pity and fear, the purgation of such passions.

. . . . . .

Tragedy can have either a happy or a sorrowful ending, as can comedy; but the joy or the sorrow of the tragic ending is different from the joy or the sorrow of the comic ending. The joyful dénouement of tragedy is formed by the cessation to the hero or to one dear to him, of impending death or sorrowful life or threatened loss of kingship; and the sorrowful dénouement is formed by the occurrence of these things. The happy dénouement of comedy is formed by the removal of insult from the hero or from one dear to him, or by the cessation of a longstanding shame, or by the recovery of an esteemed person or possession which was lost, or by the fulfillment of his love; and the sorrowful dénouement of comedy is formed by the occurrence of the opposite of these things.

. . . . . .

Tragedy without a sad ending cannot excite and does not excite, as experience shows, either fear or pity.

. . . . . .

The solution of the plot ought to be brought about by the plot itself, i.e., the striking of the danger and the ceasing of the difficulty should themselves be constituents of the plot, following the nature of the danger and of the difference by verisimilitude.

. . . . . .

. . . Tragedy is not imitation of men,

but of actions.

* * * * *

The plot is the constitution of the things, i.e., the invention of the things or the subject: which invention or subject comprises the invention of the visible things and the invention of the invisible things.

* * * * *

In most actions, men do not hide their character, but exhibit them.

* * * * *

Poets who make tragedies without character and thought, do not really imitate human action; for in the operation of human action, character and thought are always revealed, though sometimes more, sometimes less.

* * * * *

I fail to see how there could be a good tragedy without character.

* * * * *

If the plot is the end of tragedy and of all poetry, if it is not a thing accessory to character, but on the contrary, character is necessary to the plot, then many authors of great fame, ancient and modern, including Julius Cæsar Scaliger, have gravely erred in their opinion that it was the intention of good poets like Homer and Vergil to depict and demonstrate to the world, let us say, an indignant captain as excellently as possible, a valiant soldier, a wise man, and their moral natures; with much more of the same twaddle: for if this were true, then character would not be, as Aristotle says, secondary to action, but action would be secondary to character. Moreover, such a subject could not be really poetic: it is much rather philosophic.

* * * * *

Character comes in because persons come in in action; but persons are not introduced in action because a display of character is required.

* * * * *

Though character is not a part of the action, yet it accompanies it inseparably, being revealed together with the action: hence character ought not to be considered as part separate from the action, for without it the action would not be performed.

* * * * *

In questions constituting the species of poetry, no account at all should be taken of goodness or badness, extreme or moderate: these things should be considered only in so far as the aim is to arouse pity and fear in the minds of the audience.

* * * * *

If poetry has been fashioned primarily for delight, and not for utility, why in one species of poetry, i.e., tragedy, is utility chiefly sought? Why is not delight sought primarily in this species, without regard to utility?

* * * * *

According to Aristotle, there are four kinds of pleasure. The first is the pleasure arising from the sad state of a person, good or moderately good, who falls from happiness to misery: this pleasure we have called oblique, and shown that it is caused obliquely. The second is the pleasure arising from the happy fate of a person, good or moderately good, and from the sad state of the wicked; this pleasure we have called direct, and shown that it arises directly. The third is the pleasure of the happy fate common to persons of all kinds, friends and enemies: this pleasure can be called direct popular pleasure. The fourth is the pleasure caused by a fearful and monstrous spectacle; this can be called artificial spectacular pleasure. Now, Aristotle accepts in tragedy the first and second kinds of pleasure, and commends them, the first, however, more than the second; but he will not have them in comedy: the third and the fourth, as far as tragedy is concerned, he dismisses with blame.

* * * * *

[In the same work Castelvetro states in tabular form the various functions and parts of comedy.]

* * * * *

The function of comedy is the being moved by pleasing things appealing to the sentiments or the imagination. Comedy has to do with human turpitude, either of mind or of body; but if of the mind, arising from folly, not from vice; if of the body, a turpitude neither painful nor harmful.

* * * * *

The greatest source of the comic is deception, either through folly, drunkenness, a dream, or delirium; or through ignorance of the arts, the sciences, and one's own powers; or through the novelty of the good being turned in a wrong direction or of the engineer hoist with his own petard; or through deceits fashioned by man or by fortune.

. . . . .

Its plot comprises only actions possible to happen, those which have actually

happened having no place in it at all.[2]

. . . . .

[From the *Opere Varie Critiche*, p. 81][3]

The private action of a private citizen is the subject of comedy, as the actions of kings are the subject of tragedy.

FRENCH DRAMATIC CRITICISM OF THE RENAISSANCE

While many of the ideas incorporated into the dramatic treatises of the later Renaissance in France were derived from Minturno, Scaliger, Castelvetro, and other Italian theorists, the beginnings in France hark back to the Middle Ages and antiquity. The commentaries and fragments of Donatus and Diomedes were first published toward the end of the fifteenth century. Horace was also known to the grammarians and scholars, while the architectural treatises of Vitruvius and Alberti, containing chapters on the theater, were freely drawn upon. As in Italy, Aristotle's *Poetics* was seldom referred to; not until the middle of the sixteenth century does he become a force to be reckoned with. Among the earliest French writings on the drama was the introductory matter — *Praenotamenta* — to Jodocus Badius' edition of Terence (1504). This is practically a summing-up of the doctrines of the Middle Ages. Badius' edition of Seneca (1514), in which he was aided by others, contains commentaries, and the usual excerpts from Donatus and Diomedes. These preliminary and running commentaries constituted a veritable "practical dramaturgy." Meantime, foreign influences were at work: Polydorus Vergil's *De rerum inventori-*

bus (1513), with its section on comedy, was known, and later (1544) translated into French; Erasmus' *Adages, Colloquies,* and *Letters,* however meager in their references to Aristotle, helped to disseminate the ideas of preceding ages. Lazare de Baïf, one of the first translators of Greek plays, composed a *Diffinition de la tragédie* which he prefixed to his version of the *Electra* (1537). His conception in this note, as in the *Dedication* to his *Hecuba* (1544), was purely classical. In Buchanan's *Dedication* to his Latin translation of the *Alcestis* (printed 1554), there is a new note: the poet urges the tragic writer to turn aside from the conventional themes of murder, parricide, etc. Meanwhile, the numerous editions of Terence (1529, 1542, and 1552) were reprinted with the commentaries of Donatus, Diomedes, and quotations from Horace. In Jean Bouchet's *Epistre responsive au Roy de la Basoche de Bordeaux* (written in 1526, and published in 1545) the usual classification of drama into the two categories of Comedy. and Tragedy is modified to include the *Satyre.*

The very earliest Rhetorics and Arts of Poetry are of little importance as regards dramatic theory. The first of these is Eustache Deschamps' *Art de*

---

2 By way of comparison with the theoretical treatises above-printed, a few lines are here included from the *Prologue* to Gianmaria Cecchi's play, *La Romanesca* (1574): "The *Farsa* is a new third species between tragedy and comedy. It enjoys the liberties of both and shuns their limitations; for it receives into its ample boundaries great lords and princes, which comedy does not, and, like a hospital or inn, welcomes the vilest and most plebeian of the people, to whom Dame Tragedy has never stooped. It is not restricted to certain motives; for it accepts all subjects — grave

and gay, profane and sacred, urbane and crude, sad and pleasant. It does not care for time or place. The scene may be laid in a church, or a public square, or where you will; and if one day is not long enough, two or three may be employed. What, indeed, does it matter to the *Farsa?* In a word, this modern mistress of the stage is the most amusing, most convenient, the sweetest, prettiest country lass that can be found upon our earth." (From J. A. Symonds' *Renaissance in Italy,* vol. 2. New York, n. d.).— Ed.

3 From Charlton's translation, cited above. —Ed.

dictier (finished in 1392). Together with the numerous treatises on versification, they may be ignored. Pierre Fabri's manual, *Le Grand et vray art de pleine Rhetorique,* was published in 1521; this was followed in 1539 by Gracian du Pont's *L'Art poétique,* which contains little that is not found in Fabri's work. Both Arts belong in spirit to the late Middle Ages. The *Art poétique* of Thomas Sebillet, published in 1548, is interesting chiefly because of the parallel made between the old French "moralité" and the tragedies of antiquity. The work likewise contains probably the first trace of the influence of Aristotle's *Poetics* in France. Sebillet, whose work appeared only a year before Du Bellay's *Deffense,* foreshadows, in spirit at least, some of the reforms advocated by the spokesman of the *Pléiade.* Joachim Du Bellay's *Deffense et illustration de la langue françoise* (1549) heralded the opening of a new era and announced the close of the old. Of vast importance in the realm of French literature, it contains nothing but a single brief reference to drama — in which he urges dramatists to write plays after the manner of the ancients. This manifesto was answered in 1550 by the *Quintil Horatian sur la Deffense et illustration de la langue françoise,* the author of which was recently proved to be Barthélemy Aneau, instead of Charles Fontaine, to whom it had been ascribed as late as 1898. Among the early distinct references to Aristotle's theory is the three-line sentence [1] from a speech in Jodelle's *Cléopâtre,* the first French tragedy (1552); it states the famous Unity of Time, derived and developed from a passage in the *Poetics.* Another *Art Poétique,* that of Jacques Peletier du Mans (1555), though based to a great extent so far as drama is concerned, upon Horace, Donatus, and Diomedes, incorporates many of the theories of the *Pléiade.* It was up to that date the fullest exposition of dramatic theory in France. One of the few independent-minded dramatists of the period was Jacques Grévin who, in his prefatory *Bref Discours pour l'intelligence de ce*

théâtre, printed with his tragedy, *La Mort de César* (1562), maintained that he was justified in using the soldiers in his play as a chorus, that he should not be blamed for refusing to follow the example of the ancients, because "different nations demand different ways of doing things." While he mentions Aristotle, he is hopelessly ignorant of the meaning and significance of the *Poetics.* Pierre Ronsard, the chief of the *Pléiade,* makes a few references to drama in his three short treatises on poetry: *Abrégé de l'Art poétique françois* (1565), and the first and second *Préfaces* to the *Franciade* (1572 and 1587, respectively). But by all odds the most significant treatise of the period was Jean de la Taille's *Art de la Tragédie,* prefixed to his play *Saül le furieux* (1572). By this time Aristotle was an authority, and his Italian commentators well known in France. As has already been pointed out, Taille was influenced by Castelvetro, from whom he received and stated the theory of the three unities, which were for the first time in France distinctly formulated in his short preface. Two important works, the *Arts poétiques* of Pierre de Laudun d'Aigaliers (1598), and of Vauquelin de la Fresnaye (published 1605), are among the last works of their kind of the French Renaissance. Laudun was "probably the first European critic to argue formally against"[2] the twenty-four rule supposed to have been laid down by Aristotle. Vauquelin practically translates the whole of Horace's *Ars Poetica* in his treatise, while the rest of his work is based on Aristotle and his Italian commentators.

It is impossible to mention every writer of this period who in a preface, an Art of Poetry, or letter, refers to the drama. There are, however, a number of dramatists and a few others whose casual references are of value and interest. To the two books on architecture already mentioned as containing sections on the theater may be added Serlio's work on perspective, which was translated into French in 1545 by Jehan Martin. The prefaces, dedications, etc., of many printed plays of Alexandre Hardy and Robert Garnier may be consulted; like-

---

[1] *Avant que ce soleil, qui vient ores de naitre,*
Ayant tracé son jour chez sa tante se plonge,
Cléopâtre mourra!

[2] J. E. Spingarn, *A History of Literary Criticism in the Renaissance* (1908).

wise the prefaces to the following plays: *Les Abuzez* (1543), by Charles Étienne; *Abraham sacrifiant* (1550) by Théodore de Bèze; *Les Corrivaux* (1562) by Jean de la Taille; *Aman*, by André de Rivaudeau; *Les Jaloux, Les Esprits,* and *Dedication* to *Monsieur d'Ambroise* (all of 1579) by Pierre de Larivey, also the same author's *Prologue* to *La Constance*, printed in 1611; *Régulus* (1582) by Jean de Beaubreuil; *Les Néapolitaines* (1584) by François d'Amboise; and *Esther* (1585) by P. Mathieu.

THOMAS SEBILLET

Thomas Sebillet — or Sibilet, as it is often spelled — was born in 1512, probably at Paris. The little that is known of his life has been gleaned from his writings. He studied for the law and was an "avocat" in the Parlement de Paris, but he soon turned to literary pursuits. He went to Italy in 1549. He was the friend of some of the most prominent literary men of his day, among them Du Bellay, Pasquier, and L'Estoile. He was imprisoned for political reasons. A speech of his, made in Parlement in 1589, gives evidence of his more or less reactionary attitude toward the political movements of his day. He died at Paris the same year.

Sebillet's *Art Poétique* is a distinct departure from the Rhetorics and Poetics which preceded it. Sebillet, as the friend of Du Bellay, must have been influenced by many of the ideas which were about to be promulgated by the members of the *Pléiade.* It is highly significant that his book, which precedes Du Bellay's *Deffense* by one year, advocates some of the reforms suggested in that epoch-making manifesto. Spingarn says that Sebillet's passage about the French Morality "exhibits perhaps the earliest trace of the influence of Italian ideas on French criticism." He also remarks that it exhibits in all probability the "first trace of Aristotelianism in French critical literature." Sebillet's work may, therefore, stand as a sort of dramatic manifesto of the *Pléiade,* for as has been said, Du Bellay scarcely touches upon the drama.

ART OF POETRY [1]

[Art poétique]

(1548)

(Book 2. Chapter VIII)

Dialogue and its Kinds. The Eclogue, the Morality, and the Farce

A common and successful sort of poem is that written in the "prosomilitical" or conversational style, which, by prosopopœia employs personalities speaking in their own persons. This sort of poem is called by the Greeks a Dialogue.

Dialogue.— The Dialogue includes a number of sub-divisions, which we shall consider in due order. But you must notice that each of these kinds has a common and particular name by which it is known: as, for instance, *Eclogue, Morality,* and *Farce.* But, exclusive of these particular terms, the poem in which characters are introduced, speaking to each other, goes under the generic term of Dialogue. What, I ask, is Marot's *Le Jugement de Minos?* And what are many other such poems which you will find in reading the French poets? Indeed, you will find the Dialogue utilized even in epigrams, as in the second book of Marot's *Epigrammes,* the one beginning:

MAROT

Muse, dy moy, pourquoy à ma maitresse
Tu n'as sceu dire Adieu à son depart?

---

1 Here translated, with omissions, for the first time into English, by the editor.— Ed.

SA MUSE

Pource que lors je mouru de déstresse,
Et que d'un mort un mot jamais ne part.

MAROT

Muse, dy moy, comment donques Dieu-
gard
Tu luy peus dire ainsi de mort ravie?

SA MUSE

Va pauvre sot, son céleste regard
La revoyant m'a redonné la vie.

And Saint-Gelays' *Epitaphe de feu
Monsieur Budé,* which is as follows:

A. Qui est ce corps que si grand peuple
suyt?
B. Las c'est Budé au cercœil estendu.
A. Que ne font donc lés cloches plus
grand bruit.
B. Son bruit sans cloche est asséz en-
tendu.
A. Que n'a lon plus en torches de-
spendu,
    Selon la mode acoustumée et saint?
B. A fin qu'il soit par l'obscur entendu
    Que dés François la lumiére est
esteinte.

The Eclogue.— The Eclogue is Greek
by invention, Latin by usurpation, and
French by imitation. For Theocritus the
Greek poet is the one whom Vergil used
as a model in his *Eclogues,* and these
works of Vergil were the models of
Marot and other French poets. All
three sorts [that is, Greek, Latin, and
French] must be your example. Notice
now that this poem, which they called
Eclogue, is more often than not in dialogue form, in which shepherds and the
like are introduced, in pastoral settings,
conversing of deaths of princes, the calamities of the times, the overthrow of
republics, the happy outcomes and events
of fortune, poetic praises, or the like, in
the form of very obvious allegory, so
obvious that the names of the characters,
the people themselves and the rightful
application of the pastoral dialogue will
stand revealed like painting under a glass
— as in the *Tityre* of M. de Vergile and
in the *Eclogue* he wrote on the death of
Madame Loyse [de Savoye] mother of
the late King François, first of his name
and of glorious memory; and in that
which he wrote at the request of the late
King, the characters in which went under

the names of Pan and Robin. . . .
The Morality.— *Greek or Latin Tragedy.*— The French Morality in some way
represents Greek and Latin tragedy,
principally in that it treats of grave and
important subjects. If the French had
managed to make the ending of the Morality invariably sad and dolorous, the
Morality would now be a tragedy.
The Temper of the French.— But in
this, as in everything else, we have followed our temperament, which is to take
from what is foreign not everything we
see, but only what we judge will be to
'our advantage. For in the Morality, as
the Greeks and Latins did in their tragedies, we show illustrious deeds, magnificent and virtuous, true, or at least true
to life; and otherwise as regards what is
useful for information on our customs
and life, not binding ourselves to any
sadness or pleasure of the issue. . . .
The Second Kind of Morality.— There
is another sort of Morality, besides the
one I have already spoken about, in
which we follow the allegory, or moral
sense (hence the name Morality), which
treats either a moral proposition, in
which some charaĉter, neither man nor
woman, represents some attributed abstraction, or else some other allegory intended for our instruction, or guidance
in our manners.
The Virtue of the Morality.— In spite
of everything, I believe that the first virtue of the Morality, and of every other
sort of Dialogue, is the expression of the
moral sense of the piece, or allegory. . . .
In spite of the fact that, as Horace says
in his *Ars Poetica* the poet mingles the
delightful with the profitable and earns
the applause and approbation of every
one, we to-day do not write pure Moralities nor pure and simple farces, desiring rather to mix the two, and derive
pleasure and profit, by employing consecutive and alternate rhyme, short and
long lines, and making of our plays· a
hotch-potch.
Farce. Latin Comedy.— Our farce
has little of the Latin Comedy in it.
And, to tell the truth, the acts and
scenes of Latin comedy would result only
in a tiresome polixity. For the true
subject of the French Farce or *Sottie* is
a trifling, broad piece, inciting pleasure
and laughter.
The subjects of Greek and Latin com-

edy were far different, for in them there was more morality than laughter, and often as much of truth as of fable. Our Moralities stand midway between comedy and tragedy and our Farces are in reality what the Latins called *Mimes,* or *Priapees,* the purpose and end of which was unrestrained laughter, for every licence was permitted, as is nowadays the case with our own farces.

JEAN DE LA TAILLE

Jean de la Taille was born at Bondaroy about 1540. His noble birth and good education enabled him to make a name for himself, which he did, both as soldier and man of letters. He studied at first under Muret, then entered the law department of the University of Orléans. But his interest in literature led him to abandon his profession. It is sure that he was influenced by Ronsard and Du Bellay. Regarding his military exploits, we know that he was in camp near Blois in 1563, in the battle of Dreux, at Arnay-le-Duc with the Prince of Navarre, and at Loudun in 1568. After Arnay-le-Duc he entered the service of the Prince. He took cold after the battle of Coutras, and died.

Taille was not merely a theorist, like Sebillet, but a practising dramatist as well. Although he disagreed with Sebillet and maintained that the old French farce and morality were *amères épiceries,* and that the true drama had scarcely begun in France, he was none the less an innovator. Perhaps his chief importance consists in his having formulated the third Unity, that of *place.* It is probable that this was derived from Castelvetro's *Poetica,* which had just appeared (1570). In common with other theorists, he upheld the dignity of tragedy, and forbade the dramatist's introducing violence and bloodshed on the stage. His references to Aristotle mark the final acceptance in France of the *Poetics.*

THE ART OF TRAGEDY [1]

[*Art de la tragédie* (in) *Saül le furieux*]

(1572)

Madame, the pitiable disasters falling to the lot of France during your Civil Wars, and the death of King Henry, and the King his son, and the King of Navarre your uncle, and the deaths of so many other princes, lords, knights and gentlemen, are all so great and sorrowful that one needs no other material with which to make tragedies. Although such things are the proper material for tragedy, they would only remind us of past and present sorrows, and I shall willingly leave them ,aside, preferring rather to describe the unhappiness of others than our own. . . . I now wish to dedicate to you a tragedy about the most miserable prince who ever wore crown, the first

whom God chose to rule over His people. This is the first play I have ever written. I wish here, in making this dedication, to reveal to all one of the most marvelous secrets of the whole Bible, one of the greatest mysteries of that great Lord of the World, and one of His most terrible providences. In order that you may enjoy the pleasure I desire for you without further delay, it has occurred to me to give you a sort of overture, and some foretaste of the tragedy, by clarifying the principal points, merely in touching upon them.

Tragedy is by no means a vulgar kind of poetry; it is rather the most elegant, beautiful, and excellent of all. Its true province is the depiction of the pitiful ruin of lords, the inconstancy of fortune, banishments, wars, pests, famines,

[1] Translated for the first time, with slight abridgments, by the editor.— Ed.

captivity, and the execrable cruelties of tyrants; in short, tears and extreme misery. It does not treat of those things which happen every day and for clear reasons — such as a natural death, or the death of a man by the hand of his enemy, or an execution according to law, — the result of one's just deserts. Such occurrences do not easily move us, would scarcely bring a tear to the eye. This is because the true and only end of tragedy is to move and arouse keenly the passions of each of us; and to this end the subject must be pitiful and poignant in itself, and able at once to arouse in us some passion. Such a subject is the story of him who was made to eat his own sons, the father, though unwittingly, being the sepulchre of his children; or of him who could find no executioner to end his days and his sorrows, and was forced to perform the terrible deed with his own hand. Nor must the story treat of very bad lords, who deserve punishment for their horrible crimes; nor, for the same reason, must it treat of the wholly good, men of pure and upright lives, like Socrates — even though he was unjustly poisoned. This is why subjects of the sort will always be cold, and unworthy the name of tragedy. This is why the story of Abraham, in which God merely tries Abraham and pretends to make him sacrifice Isaac, is not a fit subject, because there is no misfortune at the end. Likewise with the story of Goliath, the enemy of Israel and of our religion; when Goliath is killed by his enemy David, we are so far from feeling compassion that we are rather delighted and relieved. The story, or play, must always be presented as occurring on the same day, in the same time, and in the same place. One must also be careful to do nothing on the stage but what can easily and decently be performed; no murders or other forms of death, pretended or otherwise, for the audience will invariably detect the trick. It was not art when some one, with too little reverence, performed the crucifixion of our great Savior on the stage. As to those who declare that a tragedy must always be joyous at the first and sad at the end,

and a comedy (which is like a tragedy as regards the art and general form, but not the subject) be just the reverse, let me tell them that this is not always the case, among the great diversity of subjects and manner of treating them in both kinds. The principal point in tragedy is to know how to dispose and construct it well, so that the story may change, rise and fall, turning the minds of the spectators hither and thither, allowing them to see joy suddenly turned to sorrow, and sorrow to joy, as happens in actual life. The story must be well combined, interlaced, broken up, and begun again, and most especially, conducted at the end to the resolution and point which the author originally designed. Nor must there be anything in it useless, superfluous, or out of place. If the subject be taken from the divine writings, avoid long discourses on theology, for these are what detract from the plot; they belong rather to a sermon. And for the same reason, do not introduce that sort of character which is called *Faincte* [*Invented*] which never existed, like Death, Truth, Avarice, the World, and suchlike, for it would be necessary to have people " invented " in the same way to take pleasure in them. So much for the subject. As for the art necessary to treat it and write it down, it must be divided into five acts, at end of each of which the stage is free of actors, and the sense perfectly clear. There must be a chorus, that is, a company of men or women who, at the end of the act, hold discourse upon what has been said during it, and, above all, to keep silent and yet express without words what is happening off-stage. The tragedy must not start with the very beginning of the story or subject, but toward the middle, or the end (and this is one of the principal secrets of the art I am speaking of), after the manner of the best ancient poets and their great heroical works, in order that the audience may not listen coldly, but with the attention, born of the knowledge of the beginning, and being in sight of the end afterward. But it would take me too long to outline in detail that which the great Aristotle in his *Poetics,* and Horace after him (though not so adroitly) has written at greater length than I, who am attempting only to make clear this matter to you; my discourse is not intended for the ears of the very serious and learned. I shall treat only of the tragedies, comedies, farces, and moralities (wherein there is often neither sense nor reason, but only ridiculous discourses and nonsense), and other sorts of plays which are not constructed with true art, as were the plays of Sophocles, Euripides, and Seneca, and are consequently ignorant, ill-made, and insignificant things, good merely as pastimes for the lower classes, the common people, and frivolous-minded. I wish that all such trivial nonsense which spoils the purity of our language, could be banished from France, and that we had adopted and naturalized true tragedy and comedy, which have scarcely become known to us, and which would indeed in French form possess what grace they now have in Latin and Greek. I would to heaven that our kings and great ones knew what pleasure there is in hearing recited and seeing acted a real tragedy or comedy on a stage such as I could devise, and which was formerly held in such high esteem as a pleasure for the Greeks and Romans. And I venture to assert that such plays, simply acted by intelligent actors who, with the propriety of their acting and recitation, in a language not smacking of Latin, by a direct and fearless pronunciation not reminiscent of the student nor the pedant, and with none of the nonsense of farce, would serve as the most pleasant pastime to the great — when they come for rest to the city, after exercising, hunting and hawking. Besides, I do not care (in thus writing) about the bitter malice and brutal contempt of those who, because they are fighters, look down upon men of letters, as if knowledge and virtue, which reside only in the spirit, enfeebled the body, the heart, and the arms; and nobility were dishonored by another sort of nobility, to wit, knowledge.

．　　．　　．　　．

Now, as France has not yet a true tragedy, unless it be a translation, I publish this one, under your protecting favor, Madame, as you are one of the few of our time who protect the arts and sciences, and in order to make your name known to posterity, your kindness, your knowledge and courtesy, and that future generations may know that you sometimes took notice of those who had something to say besides the usual vulgarities and barbarities of the ignorant.[2] . . .

[2] It may be well to record the words of at least one critic, probably the first in Europe, who vigorously protested against the Unity of Time. In the *Art poétique* (1598) of Pierre de Laudun d'Aigaliers, the author says: " In the first place, this law, if it is observed by any of the ancients, need not force us to restrict our tragedies in any way, since we are not bound by their manner of writing or by the measure of feet and syllables with which they compose their verses. In the second place, if we were forced to observe this rigorous law, we should fall into one of the greatest of absurdities, by being obliged to introduce impossible and incredible things in order to enhance the beauty of our tragedies, or else they would lack all grace; for besides being deprived of matter, we could not embellish our poems with long discourses and various interesting events. In the third place, the action of the *Troades*, an excellent tragedy by Seneca, could not have occurred in one day, nor could even some of the plays of Euripides or Sophocles. In the fourth place, according to the definition already given [on the authority of Aristotle], tragedy is the recital of the lives of heroes, the fortune and grandeur of kings, princes, and others; and all this could not be accomplished in one day. Besides, a tragedy must contain five acts, of which the first is joyous, and the succeeding ones exhibit a gradual change as I have already indicated above; and this change a single day would not suffice to bring about. In the fifth and last place, the tragedies in which this rule is observed are not any better than the tragedies in which it is not observed; and the tragic poets, Greek and Latin, or even French, do not and need not and cannot observe it, since very often in a tragedy the whole life of a prince, king, emperor, noble, or other person is represented; — besides a thousand other reasons which I could advance if time permitted, but which must be left for a second edition." Translated by J. E. Spingarn, in his *History of Literary Criticism in the Renaissance*.

Ronsard's brief plea on behalf of the Unity of Time (in the *Première Préface* to *La Franciade*, 1572) runs as follows: " Tragedy and comedy are circumscribed and limited to a short space of time, that is, to one whole day. The most excellent masters of this craft commence their works from one midnight to another, and not from sunrise to sunset, in order to have greater compass and length of time." (Translated by Spingarn, in the book cited above.) — Ed.

SPANISH DRAMATIC CRITICISM OF THE GOLDEN AGE

Spanish literature as a whole has been rather freer from outside influence than that of other nations. The drama of the great age — the late sixteenth and early seventeenth centuries — was decidedly unclassic. The masterpieces of Lope de Vega and Calderon are, compared with the masterpieces of Corneille and Racine, shapeless and crude; they resemble rather the plays of the Elizabethans. The earliest Spanish criticism touching upon the theory of the drama are: the *Arte de Trobar* (written 1423, and later known as the *Arte cisoria*) of Enrique, Marquis (?) de Villena; the *Preface* to *The Proverbs* (1437) the *Letter* to the Constable of Portugal, of the Marquis de Santillana; and the *Arte* of Juan del Encina. The first of these was finished in 1434, the next two about the same time, while the last was published in 1496. Agore de Molina wrote a treatise on poetics which he prefixed to his *Conde Lucanor* (1575). But Spanish criticism proper did not begin until toward the close of the sixteenth century. Juan Diaz (or Alfonso) Rengifo's *Arte Poética Española* (1592), was a standard treatise on rhetoric, and was derived for the most part from Italian Renaissance critics.[1] Alfonso Lopez [*El Pinciano*] published in 1596 his *Filosofia Antigua Poética*, in effect a protest against the prevailing "irregular" drama; Juan de la Cueva finished the writing of his *Egemplar poético* about 1606 (published in 1774); Carvallo published his *Cisne de Apolo* in 1602; Luis Carrillo his *Libro de Erudicion Poética* in 1611; while Cascales' *Tablas poéticas* did not appear until 1616. All these works are unmistakably Italian in origin, and such elements of classicism as are found in them are derived through Minturno, Scaliger, Robortello, and their contemporaries

Juan de Mariana's *Tratado contra los Juegos Públicos* (1609) may be mentioned among the attacks on the drama of the day. (An earlier attack, *De Rege*, appeared ten years before.) In 1609 Lope de Vega published his famous manifesto, the *Arte nuevo de hazer comedias en este tiempo*, which was a protest against the rules, especially the Unities. Cervantes' attack on Lope's practice appeared in the 48th chapter of *Don Quixote*, part I, which was published in 1605. Lope had already won his case, however, and a number of "defenders" of the form in which he had succeeded, published their justifications of his dramatic methods. The most interesting of these defenses is found in the *Cigarrales de Toledo* of the dramatist Tirso de Molina, which was published in 1624. Before this defense appeared, however, Lope had been defended by Francisco de la Barreda (in his *Invectiva y Apologia*, 1622), Julius Columbarius (in his *Expostulatio Spongiae*—1618), Alfonso Sanchez; and by Carlos Boil and "Ricardo de Turia" (Pedro Juan de Rejanle y Toledo). Boil's *Romance a un licenciado que deseaba hacer comedias*, and Turia's *Apologético de las comedias españolas* both appeared in the *Norte de la Poesía española* (1616). In the Dedication to his play *Pompeyo* (1618) Cristóbal de Mesa protests against the licence of Lope's dramas. There is another in Cristóbal Suarez de Figueroa's *El Pasagero* (1618). Among the later manifestos may be mentioned Diego de Colmenares' *Censura de Lope de Vega Carpio, o discurso de la nueva poesía, con una respuesta* (1630), Gonzales de Salas' *Nueva Idea de la Tragedia Antigua*, etc. (1633), and Juan Perez de Montalban's *Prologue* to the first volume of his *Comedias* (1638), his *Para Todos* (1632), José Pellicer de Salas y Tovar's *Idea de la Comedia de Castilla* (1639). Calderon, the dominating figure of the mid-seventeenth century, is said to have

---

[1] A curious and valuable document of the time, though not dealing with dramatic technique, is *El viage entrenido* (1603–04) of Agustin de Rojas Villandrando.— Ed.

written on the drama, but his *Defensa de la comedia* has not yet been published. The various *Prefaces* contain very little dramatic theory. One of the most important critics of the period was the celebrated Balthazar Gracián, whose *Agudeza y certe de ingenio* was published in 1648. In 1650 appeared Diego Vich's *Breve discurso de las Comedias y de su representacion.* With the decline of the drama came a corresponding decline of dramatic criticism and theory. Not until the advent of Luzan was there any outstanding Art of Poetry, criticism, or preface.

THE EIGHTEENTH CENTURY

The eighteenth century in Spain marks the decline of the Golden Age of Spanish drama, and the ascendancy of foreign, chiefly French, influence. The outstanding figure is Luzan, whose *Poética* was published in 1737. It was the author's purpose to make Spanish poetry conform to " rules prevailing among the cultured nations." He drew largely upon Boileau, Aristotle and the contemporary Italian critics: Muratori, Gravina, etc. His ideas were opposed in the *Diario de los Literatos de España,* founded in 1737 by Francisco Manuel de Huerta y Vega and Juan Martinez Salafranca, and Leopoldo Geronimo Puig. He was likewise defended, in the same paper, by José Gerardo de Hervás y Cobo de la Torre, who in 1742 wrote a *Sátira contra los malos escritores de su tiempo.* Feyjoo's magazine, in imitation of the *Spectator,* the *Teatro Critico universal,* first appeared in 1726, and continued until 1739. His *Cartas eruditas y curiosas* (1740–60) went far to disseminate European ideas of literature into Spain. Martin Sarmiento is the author of a posthumous *Memorias para la historia de la poesia, y poetas espanoles* (1745). In 1749 Blas de Nasarre wrote a preface (*Dissertacion o prólogo*) to two of Cervantes' plays, and attempted to discredit the old plays of Spain. José Carrillo then attacked Nasarre the following year in his *Sinrazon impugnada,* and Zabaleta in his *Discurso crítico* (1750) defended Lope and his school. In the same year, Tomas de Iriarte published a translation of Horace's *Ars Poetica.* Mon-

tiano y Luyando furthered the work of gallicizing Spanish literature in his defense of the French rules as used in his plays; his *Discurso sobre las Tragedias* appeared in 1750; one of comedies being published the same year, and a third in 1753. Among the more pedantic writings was the *Retórica* (1757) of Gregorio Mayans y Siscar, chiefly derived from the Latins. Luis Joseph Velazquez published his *Orígines de la Poesía Castellana* three years before. Nicolás Fernandez de Moratin, a dramatist of unequal power, wrote a number of tractates and prefaces, some of which defended his own plays, while others attacked the old *autos,* which were at the time prohibited. In 1762 he pleaded for the French rules in the preface of his unsuccessful play, *La Petimetra.* The same year he published three discourses, chief among which was the *Desengaño al Teatro Español.* In 1770 he published the preface to his play *Hormesinda,* which was written, however, by Bernascone. It was attacked by Juan Pelaez in the *Reparos sobre la Tragedia intitulada Hormesinda.* The quarrel continued, and in 1773 Sebastian y Latre issued a defense of the Unities in his *Ensayo sobre el Teatro Español.* The publication, in 1785–86, of Vicente Garcia de la Huerta's selection of old plays in his *Teatro Español,* and the prefaces, especially the *Escena Española defendida* (1786), called down upon him the wrath of a number of writers, who blamed him for omitting such dramatists as Lope de Vega, Tirso, and Alarcón. The tracts and pamphlets of the time were numerous, though few of them are of any value. Among Huerta's antagonists may be mentioned Forner, Samaniego, Iriarte and Jovellanos. The popular dramatist, Ramon de la Cruz, especially in his preface to the *Teatro* (1786–91), did much to free the drama from formal restrictions. He was also the first to introduce Shakespeare to his country. His version of *Hamlet* is dated 1772. Leandro Fernandez de Moratin, one of the best dramatists of the late eighteenth century, was an ardent admirer of Shakespeare (he made a version of *Hamlet* in 1798), and of Molière. His early plays were written according to the French " rules," but in his prefaces and pamphlets he soon declared his independence. His plays *Derrota de los Pedantes* (1789), and *Comedia Nueva* (1792) are attacks on dramatists and outworn rules. In the *Prólogo* of the first part of the second volume of his Works, he further discusses his theories. The Duke of Almodóvar went still further in destroying the old Spanish tradition; his *Década Epistolar sobre el Estado de las Letras en Francia* appeared in 1781.

NINETEENTH AND TWENTIETH CENTURIES

The modern epoch in Spain produced many dramatists: from the very beginnings to the present time Spain's dramatic output has been uninterrupted. The nineteenth century, however, contributed little beyond the plays themselves, and a mass of historical erudition. The Romantic impetus from France was felt early in Spain, with the dramatist Martinez de la Rosa, who was followed by the Duke de Révas, and Antonio Garcia Gutierrez (author of *El Trovador*), Hartzenbusch, Zorilla, and Tamayo y Baus, all representatives, save only Tamayo, of the first half of the century.

In the early 1900's—with José Échegaray, Benito Pérez-Galdós, and Jacinto Benavente—Spain held its own with other modern nations. Chief among the critics and historians was Marcelino Menéndez y Peláyo, whose *Historia de las ideas estéticas en España* belongs to the eighties.

The Spanish theatre of the mid-twentieth century has won attention with the plays of the philosopher Miguel de Unamuno, Ramón del Valle-Inclán, Antonio Buero Vallejo, Alfonso Sastre, and especially Federico García Lorca, who now seems to be the only permanently interesting dramatist Spain has produced in this century, his fame far eclipsing Benavente's.

MIGUEL DE CERVANTES SAAVEDRA

Miguel de Cervantes Saavedra was born at Alcalá de Henares in 1547. In all probability Miguel was with his father and the rest of the family in their various residences, in Valladolid, Madrid, Seville, and again, in 1556, Madrid. It was in this city that he first met Lope de Rueda, one of the early Spanish dramatists. In 1569 Cervantes' first work — six small poems — appeared in a large collection edited by Cervantes' supposed schoolmaster, Juan Lopez de Hoyos. Toward the end of the same year, Cervantes was in Rome with Cardinal Acquaviva. It is probable that in 1570 he enlisted in the regular army, that the following year he was on board the *Marquesa* during the Battle of Lepanto, and that he was wounded. He returned to Messina and recuperated, and was, in 1572, transferred to another regiment. He spent the greater part of the ensuing three years in Palermo and Naples. In 1575 he was granted leave to return to Spain, but the ship in which he and his brother embarked was captured by pirates, the passengers carried into slavery and placed under guard at Algiers. During the next two years he made two or three unsuccessful attempts to escape, and in 1577 was bought by the Viceroy. Several attempts on the part of Cervantes and his family to free him, proved fruitless, until in 1580 a ransom was raised and he went to Constantinople; thence he returned to Spain. During the next few years he wrote a number of plays. In 1584 he married and the following year published his novel, *Galatea*. In 1587 Cervantes went to Seville to assist in the provisioning of the Armada, for he found it impossible to make a living by writing. He was employed in the commissary department until 1590, when he applied to the king for a position in the American colonies, but was refused. Two years later he was imprisoned for an unknown reason, but was soon released. He was continually getting into financial difficulties with the government, and was finally dismissed. Between the publication of the *Galatea* and *Don Quixote*, in 1605, Cervantes had written only a few occasional poems. *Don Quixote* was immediately successful, though the author received little compensation. During the next few years he wrote very little. In 1612 he became reconciled with Lope de Vega, whom he had criticized in *Don Quixote*. The next year he published his *Novelas exemplares*, in 1614 the *Viaje del Parnaso*. In 1615 he published a volume of plays and *entremeses*, with an interesting preface. Meanwhile a second part of the *Don Quixote* had made its appearance in 1614, in which the author, who called himself Alonso Fernandez de Avellaneda, tried to cover the subjects which Cervantes had announced in the first part. In all probability this imposture set Cervantes to work, for in 1615 the true second part appeared. While he was engaged in publishing his *Persiles y Sigismunda* he died, in 1616.

Cervantes' importance as a critic of the drama lies in his having set himself against the national type of play. There may have been some personal animus in his attack, as Lope de Vega had referred slightingly to him a short time before the publication of *Don Quixote,* and Lope was the chief representative of the popular drama. It is rather odd, too, that many of Cervantes' own plays were written more or less in the manner of Lope. The famous passage on the drama (Chapter 48 of the first part) contains, as has been pointed out, a curious parallel to Sidney's strictures on English drama, particularly where he speaks of the absurdity of the violation of the Unity of Time.

DON QUIXOTE [1]

[*Don Quixote*]

(1605)

". . . . I was discouraged, too, whenever I reflected on the present state of the drama, and the absurdity and incoherence of most of our modern comedies, whether fictitious or historical; for the actor and author both say that they must please the people, and not produce compositions which can only be appreciated by half a score of men of sense; and that they would rather gain subsistence by the many than reputation by the few. What other fate, then, could I expect but that, after racking my brains to produce a reasonable work, I should get nothing but my labor for my pains? I have occasionally endeavored to persuade theatrical managers that they would not only gain more credit, but eventually find it much more advantageous to produce better dramas; but they will not listen to reason. Conversing one day with a fellow of this kind, I said, ' Do you not remember that, a few years since, three tragedies were produced which were universally admired; that delighted both the ignorant and the wise, the vulgar as well as the cultivated; and that by those three pieces the players gained

more than by thirty of the best which have since been represented?' 'I suppose you mean the *Isabella, Phyllis,* and *Alexandra,*' he replied. ' The same,' said I ; ' And pray recollect, that although they were written in strict conformity to the rules of art, they were successful: the whole blame, therefore, is not to be ascribed to the taste of the vulgar. There is nothing absurd, for instance, in the play of *Ingratitude Revenged,* nor in the *Numantia,* nor in the *Merchant Lover,* much less in the *Favorable Enemy,* or in some others composed by ingenious poets, to their own renown and the profit of those who acted them.' To these I added other arguments, which I thought in some degree perplexed him, but were not so convincing as to make him reform his erroneous practice."

" Signor Canon," said the priest, " you have touched upon a subject which has revived in me an old grudge I have borne against our modern plays, scarcely less than I feel towards books of chivalry; for though the drama, according to Cicero, ought to be the mirror of human life, an exemplar of manners and an image of truth, those which are now produced are mirrors of inconsistency, patterns of folly, and images of licentiousness. What, for instance, can be more

[1] Re-printed extracts from the anonymous translation of *Don Quixote* (New York, n. d.). — Ed.

absurd than the introduction in the first scene of the first act of a child in swaddling clothes, that in the second makes his appearance as a bearded man? Or to represent an old man valiant, a young man cowardly, a footman rhetorician, a page a privy councillor, a king a water carrier, and a princess a scullion? Nor are they more observant of place than of time. I have seen a comedy, the first act of which was laid in Europe, the second in Asia, and the third in Africa; and had there been four acts, the fourth would doubtless have been in America. If truth of imitation be an important requisite in dramatic writing, how can anyone with a decent share of understanding bear to see an action which passed in the reign of King Pepin or Charlemagne ascribed to the Emperor Heraclius, who is introduced carrying the cross into Jerusalem, or receiving the holy sepulchre, like Godfrey of Boulogne, though numberless years had elapsed between these actions? and, when the piece is founded on fiction, to see historical events mingled with facts relating to different persons and times? — and, all this without any appearance of probability, but, on the contrary, full of the grossest absurdity? And yet there are people who think all this perfection, and call everything else mere pedantry. The sacred dramas, too — how they are made to abound with faults and incomprehensible events, frequently confounding the miracles of one saint with those of another; indeed, they are often introduced in plays on profane subjects, merely to please the people. Thus is our natural taste degraded in the opinion of cultivated nations, who, judging by the extravagance and absurdity of our productions, conceive us to be in a state of ignorance and barbarism. It is not a sufficient excuse to say that the object in permitting theatrical exhibitions being chiefly to provide innocent recreation for the people, it is unnecessary to limit and restrain the dramatic author within strict rules of composition; for I affirm that the same object is, beyond all compar-

ison, more effectually attained by legitimate work. The spectator of a good drama is amused, admonished, and improved by what is diverting, affecting and moral in the representation; he is cautioned against deceit, corrected by example, incensed against vice, stimulated to the love of virtue. Such are the effects produced by dramatic excellence; but they are not to be expected on our present stage, although we have many authors perfectly aware of the prevailing defects, but who justify themselves by saying that, in order to make their works saleable, they must write what the theater will purchase. We have a proof of this even in the happiest genius of our country, who has written an infinite number of dramatic works with such vivacity and elegance of style, such loftiness of sentiment, and richness of elocution, that his fame has spread over the world; nevertheless, in conforming occasionally to the bad taste of the present day, his productions are not all equally excellent. Besides the errors of taste, some authors have indulged in public and private scandal, insomuch that the actors have been obliged to abscond. These and every other inconvenience would be obviated if some intelligent and judicious person of the court were appointed to examine all plays before they are acted, and without whose approbation none should be performed. Thus guarded, the comedian might act without personal risk, and the author would write with more circumspection; and by such a regulation, works of merit might be more frequent, to the benefit and honor of the country. And, in truth, were the same or some other person appointed to examine all future books of chivalry, we might hope to see some more perfect productions of this kind to enrich our language, and which, superseding the old romances, would afford rational amusement, not only to the idle alone, but to the active; for the bow cannot remain always bent, and relaxion both of body and mind, is indispensable to all."

(I, 48).

FELIX LOPE DE VEGA CARPIO

Lope Felix de Vega Carpio — better known simply as Lope de Vega — was born at Madrid in 1562. According to all accounts, he was very precocious; he himself claims to have written a four-act play at the age of twelve. Very little is known of his youth except that he became a page in the service of the Bishop of Carthagena, and that he went to the University at Alcalá de Henares. When he left the University — probably in 1581 — he worked under Gerónimo Velazquez, a theater manager in Madrid. In 1583 he became a member of the Expedition to the Azores. On his return, he had begun to acquire a reputation as a poet and dramatist. In 1588 he was banished temporarily for writing libels. He went to Valencia, but shortly after returned to Madrid, and carried off and married the daughter of a former regidor of the city. They went to Lisbon, whence Lope embarked in the Armada, on the San Juan. During the stormy voyage and in the midst of the combat Lope was writing with the utmost assiduity. When he returned to Spain he settled at Valencia, where he continued to write. In 1590 he left and went to Alba de Tórmes, where he became secretary to the Duke of Alba. After the death of his wife, probably in 1595, Lope left Alba de Tórmes and went to Madrid, where he married again in 1598,

the same year in which he published his novel, the *Arcadia*. He continued to publish poems, novels and epics. About the year 1609 Lope seems to have turned his thoughts toward religion, and in that year he describes himself as a *Familiar* of the Inquisition. The following year he entered a monastery and in 1614 was admitted to the order, after the death of his son and wife. But, as ever, he found time to make love, write poems and plays, and participate in state functions. Toward the end of his life, he seems to have been overcome by remorse, after the death of one of his favorite mistresses and the drowning of another son. He died in 1635. Throughout his long career he wrote plays, the number of which ranges somewhere between twelve and twenty-five hundred.

Lope is primarily important as a dramatist, though in his prefaces, dedications, and verses, and above all in his *Arte nuevo de hacer comedias en este tiempo* (probably 1609), he showed clear vision and common sense as a critic of his own work. His *Arte nuevo* is a document of the utmost importance, because it voices the sentiments of the greater part of the dramatists and public of the time. It is an explanation and justification of the free and unclassic romantic drama of the Golden Age of Spain.

THE NEW ART OF WRITING PLAYS IN THIS AGE[1]
[*Arte nuevo de hacer comedias en este tiempo*]
(1609)

1. You command me, noble spirits, flower of Spain,— who in this congress and renowned academy will in short space of time surpass not only the assemblies of Italy which Cicero, envious of Greece, made famous with his own name, hard by the Lake of Avernus, but also Athens, where in the Lyceum of Plato was seen high conclave of philosophers,— to write you an art of the play

[1] Translated by William T. Brewster in the *Papers on Play-Making I*, with an introduction by Brander Matthews (Dramatic Museum of Columbia University, New York. 1914).

which is to-day acceptable to the taste of the crowd.

2. Easy seems this subject, and easy it would be for any one of you who had written very few comedies, and who knows more about the writing of them and of all these things; for what condemns me in this task is that I have written them without art.

3. Not because I was ignorant of the precepts; thank God, even while I was a tyro in grammar, I went through the books which treated the subject, before I had seen the sun run its course ten

times from the Ram to the Fishes;

4. But because, in fine, I found that comedies were not at that time, in Spain, as their first devisers in the world thought that they should be written; but rather as many rude fellows managed them, who confirmed the crowd in its crudeness; and so they were introduced in such wise that he who now writes them artistically dies without fame and guerdon; for custom can do more among those who lack light of art than reason and force.

5. True it is that I have sometimes written in accordance with the art which few know; but, no sooner do I see coming from some other source the monstrosities full of painted scenes where the crowd congregates and the women who canonize this sad business, than I return to that same barbarous habit; and when I have to write a comedy I lock in the precepts with six keys, I banish Terence and Plautus from my study, that they may not cry out at me; for truth, even in dumb books, is wont to call aloud; and I write in accordance with that art which they devised who aspired to the applause of the crowd; for, since the crowd pays for the comedies, it is fitting to talk foolishly to it to satisfy its taste.

6. Yet the comedy has its end established like every kind of poem or poetic art, and that has always been to imitate the actions of men and to paint the customs of their age. Furthermore, all poetic imitation whatsoever is composed of three things, which are discourse, agreeable verse, harmony, that is to say music, which so far was common also to tragedy; comedy being different from tragedy in that it treats of lowly and plebeian actions, and tragedy of royal and great ones. Look whether there be in our comedies few failings.

7. *Auto* was the name given to them, for they imitate the actions and the doings of the crowd. Lope de Rueda was an example in Spain of these principles, and to-day are to be seen in print prose comedies of his so lowly that he introduces into them the doings of mechanics and the love of the daughter of a smith; whence there has remained the custom of calling the old comedies *entremeses,* where the art persists in all its force, there being one action and

that between plebeian people; for an *entremes* with a king has never been seen. And thus it is shown how the art, for very lowness of style, came to be held in great disrepute, and the king in the comedy to be introduced for the ignorant.

8. Aristotle depicts in his *Poetics,*—although obscurely,— the beginning of comedy; the strife between Athens and Megara as to which of them was the first inventor; they of Megara say that it was Epicarmus, while Athens would have it that Maynetes was the man. Ælius Donatus says it had its origin in ancient sacrifices. He names Thespis as the author of tragedy,— following Horace, who affirms the same,— as of comedies, Aristophanes. Homer composed the *Odyssey* in imitation of comedy, but the *Iliad* was a famous example of tragedy, in imitation of what I called my *Jerusalem* an epic, and added the term *tragic;* and in the same manner all people commonly term the *Inferno,* the *Purgatorio,* and the *Paradiso* of the celebrated poet, Dante Alighieri, a comedy, and this Manetti recognizes in his prologue.

9. Now, everybody knows that comedy, as if under suspicion, was silenced for a certain time, and that hence also satire was born, which being more cruel, more quickly came to an end, and gave place to the New Comedy. The choruses were the first things; then the fixed number of the characters was introduced; but Menander, whom Terence followed, held the choruses in despite, as offensive. Terence was more circumspect as to the principles; since he never elevated the style of comedy to the greatness of tragedy, which many have condemned as vicious in Plautus; for in this respect Terence was more wary.

10. Tragedy has as its argument history, and comedy fiction; for this reason it was called flat-footed, of humble argument, since the actor performed without buskin or stage. There were comedies with the *pallium*, mimes, comedies with the toga, *fabulae atellanae,* and comedies of the tavern, which were also, as now, of various sorts.

11. With Attic elegance the men of Athens chided vice and evil custom in their comedies, and they gave their prizes both to the writers of verse and to the devisers of action. For this Tully called

comedies "the mirror of custom and a living image of the truth,"— a very high tribute, in that comedy ran even with history. Look whether it be worthy of this crown and glory!

12. But now I perceive that you are saying that this is merely translating books and wearying with painting this mixed-up affair. Believe me, there has been a reason why you should be reminded of some of these things; for you see that you ask me to describe the art of writing plays in Spain, where whatever is written is in defiance of art; and to tell how they are now written contrary to the ancient rule and to what is founded on reason, is to ask me to draw on my experience, not on art, for art speaks truth which the ignorant crowd gainsays.

13. If, then, you desire art, I beseech you, men of genius, to read the very learned Robortello of Udine and you will see in what he says concerning Aristotle and especially in what he writes about comedy, as much as is scattered among many books; for everything of to-day is in a state of confusion.

14. If you wish to have my opinion of the comedies which now have the upper hand and to know why it is necessary that the crowd with its laws should maintain the vile chimera of this comic monster, I will tell you what I hold, and do you pardon me, since I must obey whoever has power to command me,— that, gilding the error of the crowd, I desire to tell you of what sort I would have them; for there is no recourse but to follow art, observing a mean between the two extremes.

15. Let the subject be chosen and do not be amused,— may you excuse these precepts!— if it happens to deal with kings; though, for that matter, I understand that Philip the Prudent, King of Spain and our lord, was offended at seeing a king in them; either because the matter was hostile to art or because the royal authority ought not to be represented among the lowly and the vulgar.

16. This is merely turning back to the Old Comedy, where we see that Plautus introduced gods, as in his *Amphitryon* he represents Jupiter. God knows that I have difficulty in giving this my approbation, since Plutarch, speaking of Menander, does not highly esteem Old Comedy. But since we are so far away from art and in Spain do it a thousand wrongs, let the learned this once close their lips.

17. Tragedy mixed with comedy and Terence with Seneca, though it be like another minotaur of Pasiphae, will render one part grave, the other ridiculous; for this variety causes much delight. Nature gives us good example, for through such variety it is beautiful.

18. Bear in mind that this subject should contain one action only, seeing to it that the story in no manner be episodic; I mean the introduction of other things which are beside the main purpose; nor that any member be omitted which might ruin the whole of the context. There is no use in advising that it should take place in the period of one sun, though this is the view of Aristotle; but we lose our respect for him when we mingle tragic style with the humbleness of mean comedy. Let it take place in as little time as possible, except when the poet is writing history in which some years have to pass; these he can relegate to the space between the acts, wherein, if necessary, he can have a character go on some journey; a thing that greatly offends whoever perceives it. But let not him who is offended go to see them.

19. Oh! how lost in admiration are many at this very time at seeing that years are passed in an affair to which an artificial day sets a limit; though for this they would not allow the mathematical day! But, considering that the wrath of a seated Spaniard is immoderate, when in two hours there is not presented to him everything from Genesis to the Last Judgment, I deem it most fitting if it be for us here to please him, for us to adjust everything so that it succeeds.

20. The subject once chosen, write in prose, and divide the matter into three acts of time, seeing to it, if possible, that in each one the space of the day be not broken. Captain Virués, a worthy wit, divided comedy into three acts, which before had gone on all fours, as on baby's feet, for comedies were then infants. I wrote them myself, when eleven or twelve years of age, of four acts and of four sheets of paper, for a sheet contained each act; and then it was the fashion that for the three intermissions

were made three little *entremeses,* but
to-day scarce one, and then a dance, for
the dancing is so important in comedy
that Aristotle approves of it, and Athenæus, Plato and Xenophon treat of it,
though this last disapproves of indecor-
ous dancing; and for this reason he is
vexed at Callipides, wherein he pretends to ape the ancient chorus. The
matter divided into two parts, see to the
connection from the beginning until the
action runs down; but do not permit the
untying of the plot until reaching the
last scene; for the crowd, knowing what
the end is, will turn its face to the door
and its shoulder to what it has awaited
three hours face to face; for in what appears, nothing more is to be known.

21. Very seldom should the stage remain without some one speaking, because the crowd becomes restless in these
intervals and the story spins itself out
at great length; for, besides its being a
great defect, the avoidance of it increases
grace and artifice.

22. Begin then, and, with simple language, do not spend sententious thoughts
and witty sayings on family trifles, which
is all that the familiar talk of two or
three people is representing. But when
the character who is introduced persuades, counsels or dissuades, then there
should be gravity and wit; for then
doubtless is truth observed, since a man
speaks in a different style from what is
common when he gives counsel, or persuades, or argues against anything.
Aristides, the rhetorician, gave us warrant for this; for he wishes the language
of comedy to be pure, clear, and flexible,
and he adds also that it should be taken
from the usage of the people, this being
different from that of polite society; for
in the latter case the diction will be elegant, sonorous, and adorned. Do not
drag in quotations, nor let your language
offend because of exquisite words; for,
if one is to imitate those who speak, it
should not be by the language of Pan-
chaia, of the Metaurus, of hippogriffs,
demi-gods and centaurs.

23. If the king should speak, imitate as
much as possible the gravity of a king;
if the sage speak, observe a sententious
modesty; describe lovers with those passions which greatly move whomever lis-
tens to them; manage soliloquies in such
a manner that the recitant is quite trans-

formed, and in changing himself, changes
the listener. Let him ask questions and
reply to himself, and if he shall make
plaints, let him observe the respect due
to women. Let not ladies disregard
their character, and if they change costumes, let it be in such wise that it may
be excused; for male disguise usually is
very pleasing. Let him be on his guard
against impossible things, for it is of the
chiefest importance that only the likeness of truth should be represented. The
lackey should not discourse of lofty affairs, not express the conceits which we
have seen in certain foreign plays; and
in no wise let the character contradict
himself in what he has said; I mean to
say, forget,— as in Sophocles one blames
Œdipus for not remembering that he has
killed Laius with his own hand. Let the
scenes end with epigram, with wit, and
with elegant verse, in such wise that, at
his exit, he who spouts leave not the audience disgusted. In the first act set for
the case. In the second weave together
the events, in such wise that until the
middle of the third act one may hardly
guess the outcome. Always trick ex-
pectancy; and hence it may come to pass
that something quite far from what is
promised may be left to the understanding. Tactfully suit your verse to the
subjects being treated. *Décimas* are
good for complainings; the sonnet is good
for those who are waiting in expectation; recitals of events ask for *romances,*
though they shine brilliantly in *octavas.*
Tercets are for grave affairs and *redon-
dillas* for affairs of love. Let rhetorical
figure be brought in, as repetition or
anadiplosis, and in the beginning of these
same verses the various forms of ana-
phora; and also irony, questions, apos-
trophes, and exclamations.

24. To deceive the audience with the
truth is a thing that has seemed well, as
Miguel Sánchez, worthy of this memorial
for the invention, was wont to do in all
his comedies. Equivoke and the uncertainty arising from ambiguity have always held a large place among the crowd,
for it thinks that it alone understands
what the other one is saying. Better still
are the subjects in which honor has a
part, since they deeply stir everybody;
along wth them go virtuous deeds, for
virtue is everywhere loved; hence we see,
if an actor chance to represent a traitor,

he is so hateful to every one that what he wishes to buy is not sold him, and the crowd flees when it meets him; but if he is loyal, they lend to him and invite him, and even the chief men honor him, love him, seek him out, entertain him, and acclaim him.

25. Let each act have but four sheets, for twelve are well suited to the time and the patience of him who is listening. In satirical parts, be not clear or open, since it is known that for this very reason comedies were forbidden by law in Greece and Italy; wound without hate, for if, perchance, slander be done, expect not applause, nor aspire to fame.

26. These things you may regard as aphorisms which you get not from the ancient art, which the present occasion allows no further space for treating; since whatever has to do with the three kinds of stage properties which Vitruvius speaks of, concerns the impresario; just as Valerius Maximus, Petrus Crinitus, Horace in his *Epistles,* and others describe these properties, with their drops, trees, cabins, houses, and simulated marbles.

27. Of costume Julius Pollux would tell us if it were necessary, for in Spain it is the case that the comedy of to-day is replete with barbarous things: a Turk wearing the neck-gear of a Christian, and a Roman in tight breeches.

28. But of all, nobody can I call more barbarous than myself, since in defiance of art I dare to lay down precepts, and

I allow myself to be borne along in the vulgar current, wherefore Italy and France call me ignorant. But what can I do if I have written four hundred and eighty-three comedies, along with one which I have finished this week? For all of these, except six, gravely sin against art. Yet, in fine, I defend what I have written, and I know that, though they might have been better in another manner, they would not have had the vogue which they have had; for sometimes that which is contrary to what is just, for that very reason, pleases the taste.

How Comedy reflects this life of man,
　How true her portraiture of young and
　　old;
How subtle wit, polished in narrow span,
　And purest speech, and more too you
　　behold;
What grave consideration mixed with
　smiles,
　What seriousness, along with pleasant
　　jest;
Deceit of slaves; how woman oft beguiles
　How full of slyness is her treacherous
　　breast;
How silly, awkward swains to sadness
　run,
　How rare success, though all seems
　　well begun.

Let one hear with attention, and dispute not of the art; for in comedy everything will be found of such a sort that in listening to it everything becomes evident.

TIRSO DE MOLINA

Gabriel Tellez, known as Tirso de Molina, was born at Madrid probably in 1570. He was graduated from the University of Alcalá, and in 1613 he took orders. Very little is known of his life, though it is likely that he traveled a great deal and was a soldier. Toward the end of his life he became prior of the Monastery at Soria. He was a prolific playwright, whose chief claim lies in his having created the character of Don Juan. He died at Soria in 1648.

Tirso was one of the defenders of the free romantic *comedia,* and his few references to the drama are in defense of Lope de Vega, the greatest of the writers of that sort of play. In his *Cigarrales de Toledo* (1624), he includes a play, *El Vergonzoso en Palacio,* and after it, introduces a fictitious discussion in dialogue-form. One person attacks Tirso for violating the Unities. Another, Tirso himself, speaking through him, assails the critic and defends the free form. Tirso's criticism is rather a reflection of the spirit of the time than a true defense of a form which very few writers adhered to or wished for.

THE ORCHARDS OF TOLEDO [1]

[*Cigarrales de Toledo*]

(1624)

". . . Among the many blemishes (pardon my presumption!) what tries my patience is to see how ruthlessly the poet disregards in this play the limits and laws with which the first inventors of drama [*comedia*] so carefully defined its cardinal principle, namely, that a play must concern itself with an action whose beginning, middle, and end occupy at the most twenty-four hours, and one and the same place. He has cunningly given us a spectacle of the conquest of love covering a period of at least a month and a half. And yet, even in that time, it seems to us impossible (with the preservation of any decency) that so illustrious and discreet a lady should bring herself so blindly to pursue a shepherd, make him her secretary, declare her purpose through riddles, and finally risk her reputation to the bold ruthlessness of a man of such humble origin." The ill-natured disputant was continuing when Don Alejo, interrupting him, answered: "Your point is not well taken, since the play under discussion has observed the laws which are now recognized; and it seems to me that the position merited by our modern Spanish plays, which are comparable to those of antiquity, marks a distinct step in advance, however they fail to take into account the cardinal principle of the Masters. What if these Masters did maintain that a play must represent an action which could logically take place within twenty-four hours? What greater inconvenience can there be than that within that short time a discreet gallant should fall in love with a prudent lady, court her, make love to her, woo her — all within a single day, if you please, and after claiming her for the morrow, must needs marry her that very night? What opportunity is there to arouse jealousy, engender despair, bring hope to the lover, and depict all the other uncertainties and accidents without which love is a matter of no importance? Or how can a lover boast that he is constant and loyal, if there be not

allowed several days to elapse,— months, even years,— in which he may prove his constancy? These inconveniences are greater in the judgment of any one of moderate intelligence, than that which would ensue were the audience allowed to witness everything without leaving their seats, in order to follow the happenings of many days. Just as he who reads a story in a few pages covering the events of a protracted period and occuring in many places, so the spectator at a play — which is an image and representation of the story's action — can see it interpret and shadow forth the ortunes of the lovers, depicting to the life what happens to them. Now, since these things cannot happen in the space of a single day, the dramatist must assume that everything happens as he shows it, in order that the action may be perfect. Not in vain is poetry called a living picture, imitating the passive picture which, in the small space of a yard and a half of plane surface shows perspective and distance in manner to bestow upon the beholder an illusion of reality. It is not just that the license granted to the pencil be withheld from the pen. And if you argue by way of reply that we of the same craft owe it to the initiators to guard their principles intact, I answer that although veneration is due the masters for having set out in difficulty — which hampers all things in their beginning — yet it is undeniable that, adding perfection to *their* invention (a thing necessary, but at the same time easy), it is Genius which, when the fundamental laws fail to help, knows how to change the accidental, improving it by experience. There is this difference between Nature and Art: that what the former began, cannot be changed; thus the pear-tree will bear pears to eternity, and the oak the uncouth acorn, and notwithstanding the difference of soil and the varying influences of the atmosphere and climate to which they are subject, she produces them over and over again. Amid other changes, species is constant. Does it matter how much the Drama may modify the laws of its ancestors, ingeniously mix-

1 Especially translated sections for this collection by Winifred Ayres Hope.— Ed.

ing tragedy with comedy and producing a pleasant type of play of the two — and partaking of the character of each — introducing serious characters from the one, and waggish and absurd characters from the other? I claim that if the pre-eminence in Greece of Æschylus and Euripides (as among the Latins of Seneca and Terence) suffices to establish the laws of these Masters who are now so vigorously upheld, the excellence of our Spanish Lope de Vega makes his improvements in both styles of play so conspicuous that the authority he brings to this improvement is sufficient to reform the old laws. And since the Drama is so

highly esteemed for subtlety and perfection, that fact makes it a school in itself, and gives us, who are proud to be followers, the right to be proud of such a Master, and gladly to defend his doctrine against whosoever shall violently impugn it. As to the fact that in many passages of his writings he says that he does not observe the ancient art, in order that he may make his own acceptable to the people, that is only the result of his innate modesty; it is said so that malicious ignorance may not attribute to arrogance what is as a matter of fact well-bred perfection. As for us, it is right that we should look to him as the reformer of the New Drama; and such we esteem him.

FEDERICO GARCÍA LORCA

Born near Granada in 1898, Lorca studied law at the University of Granada. From 1919, he lived in Madrid, writing poetry and editing a little magazine; later he traveled occasionally in the United States (1929–30) and Latin America. His first volume of verse in 1921 was followed by *Gypsy Ballads* in 1928. His first play to win favor was *Mariana Pineda* (1927), but Lorca seriously devoted himself to the drama after his comedy *The Shoemaker's Prodigious Wife* was produced in 1930. In the following year, he founded a theatre, La

Barraca (the Hut). Both his plays and his verse usually embodied experimental forms and folk themes. Subsequent plays included *Blood Wedding,* (1933), a love tragedy arising out of a peasant feud; *The Love of Don Perlimplín* (written some years before its première in 1933), which Francis Fergusson has called "a romantic farce"; *Yerma* (1934), a tragedy of sterility; and a posthumous tragedy, *The House of Bernarda Alba.* Lorca was executed by rebel soldiers in 1936, during the Spanish Civil War.

THE AUTHORITY OF THE THEATRE[1]
(1934)

My Dear Friends: Some time ago I made a solemn promise to refuse every kind of tribute, banquet, or celebration which might be made in my honor, first, because I know that each of them drives another nail into our literary coffin, and second, because I have found that there is nothing more depressing than a formal speech made in our honor, and nothing sadder

[1] "The Prophecy of Lorca," translated by Albert E. Sloman, *Theatre Arts,* October, 1950. Reprinted by permission of *Theatre Arts.* This address was delivered after the opening of *Yerma.*

than organized applause, however sincere.

Besides, between ourselves, I hold that banquets and scrolls bring bad luck upon the one who receives them, bad luck springing from the relief of his friends who think: "Now we have done our duty by him."

A banquet is a gathering of professional people who eat with us, and where we find thrown together every kind of person who likes us least.

Rather than do honor to poets and dramatists, I should prepare challenges and attacks, in which we should be told roundly and passionately: "Are you afraid of doing this?" "Are you incapable of expressing a person's anguish at the sea?" "Daren't you show the despair of soldiers who hate war?"

Necessity and struggle, grounded on a critical love, temper the artist's soul, which easy flattery makes effeminate and destroys. The theatres are full of deceiving sirens, garlanded with hothouse roses, and the public is content, and applauds dummy hearts and superficial dialogue; but the dramatic poet who wishes to save himself from oblivion must not forget the open fields with their wild roses, fields moistened by the dawn where peasants toil, and the pigeon, wounded by a mysterious hunter, which is dying amongst the rushes with no one to hear its grief.

Shunning sirens, flattery, and congratulations, I have accepted nothing in my honor, on the occasion of the first night of *Yerma;* but it has been the greatest pleasure of my short life as a writer to learn that the theatre world of Madrid was asking the great Margarita Xirgu, an actress with an impeccable artistic career, luminary of the Spanish theatre, and admirable interpreter of the part of Yerma, together with the company which so brilliantly supports her, for a special production.

For the interest and attention in a notable theatrical endeavor which this implies, I wish, now that we are all together, to give to you my deepest and sincerest thanks. I am not speaking tonight as an author, nor as a poet, nor as a simple student of the rich panorama of man's life, but as an ardent lover of the theatre of social action. The theatre is one of the most useful and expressive instruments for a country's edification, the barometer which registers its greatness or its decline. A theatre which in every branch, from tragedy to vaudeville, is sensitive and well oriented, can in a few years change the sensibility of a people, and a broken-down theatre, where wings have given way to cloven hoofs, can coarsen and benumb a whole nation.

The theatre is a school of weeping and of laughter, a rostrum where men are free to expose old and equivocal standards of conduct, and explain with living examples the eternal norms of the heart and feelings of man.

A nation which does not help and does not encourage its theatre is, if not dead, dying; just as the theatre which does not feel the social pulse, the historical pulse, the drama of its people, and catch the genuine color of its landscape and of its spirit, with laughter or with tears, has no right to call itself a theatre, but an amusement hall, or a place for doing that dreadful thing known as "killing time." I am referring to no one, and I want to offend no one; I am not speaking of actual fact, but of a problem that has yet to be solved.

Every day, my friends, I hear about the crisis in the theatre, and I feel always that the defect is not one before our eyes, but deep down in its very nature; it is not a defect of the flower we have before us, of a play, that is, but deeply rooted; in short, a defect of organization. Whilst actors and authors are in the hands of managements that are completely commercial, free, without either literary or state control of any kind, managements devoid of all judgment and offering no kind of safeguard, actors, authors, and the whole theatre will sink lower every day, beyond all hope of salvation.

The delightful light theatre of revue, vaudeville, and farce, forms of which I am a keen spectator, could maintain and even save itself; but plays in verse, the historical play, and the so-called Spanish *zarzuela,* will suffer more and more setbacks, because they are forms which make great demands and which admit of real innovations, and there is neither the authority nor the spirit of sacrifice to impose them on a public which has to be overruled from above, and often contradicted and attacked. The theatre must impose itself on the public, not the public on the theatre. To do this, authors and actors must, whatever the cost, again assume great authority, because the theatre-going public is like a school child; it reveres the stern, severe teacher who demands justice and sees justice done; and puts pins on the chairs of the timid and flattering ones who neither teach themselves nor allow anyone else to teach.

The public can be taught—I say public, of course, not people—it can be taught; for, some years ago, I saw Debussy and Ravel howled down, and I have been present since at loud ovations given by a public of ordinary people to the very works which were earlier rejected. These authors were imposed by the high judgment of authority, superior to that of the ordinary public, just as were Wedekind in Germany and Pirandello in Italy, and so many others.

This has to be done for the good of the theatre and for the glory and status of its interpreters. Dignity must be maintained, in the conviction that such dignity will be amply repaid. To do otherwise is to tremble behind the flies, and kill the fantasies, imagination, and charm of the theatre, which is always, always an art, and will always be a lofty art, even though there may have been a time when everything which pleased was labeled art, so that the tone was lowered, poetry destroyed, and the stage itself a refuge for thieves.

Art above all else. A most noble art, and you, my actor friends, artists above all else. Artists from head to foot, since through love and vocation you have risen to the make-believe and pitiful world of the boards. Artists by occupation and by preoccupation. From the smallest theatre to the most eminent, the word "Art" should be written in auditoriums and dressing rooms, for if not we shall have to write the word "Commerce" or some other that I dare not say. And distinction, discipline, and sacrifice and love.

I don't want to lecture you, because I should be the one receiving a lecture. My words are dictated by enthusiasm and conviction. I labor under no delusion. As a good Andalusian I can think coolly, because I come of an ancient stock. I know that truth does not lie with him who says, "Today, today, today," eating his bread close to the hearth, but with him who watches calmly at a distance the first light of dawn in the country.

I know that those people who say, "Now, now, now," with their eyes fixed on the small jaws of the box office are not right, but those who say, "Tomorrow, tomorrow, tomorrow," and feel the approach of the new life which is hovering over the world.

ELIZABETHAN DRAMATIC CRITICISM

English literary criticism is derived partly from the ancients, and partly from the Italian scholars. Recent research has revealed many Italian sources drawn upon by Sidney and Jonson. The earliest formal treatise touching upon literature in England is Leonard Coxe's *Arte or Crafte of Rhetoryke*, written about 1524; this was derived in part from Melanchthon. Thomas Wilson's *Arte of Rhetorike* followed in 1553. More important still is Roger Ascham's *Scholemaster* (1570) which contains the first reference in English to Aristotle's *Poetics*. George Whetstone's *Dedication* to *Promos and Cassandra* (1578) is a curious criticism of the drama of other nations and an attempt to reconcile Platonism and the drama. The English stage was at several times the subject of controversies between the dramatists and their adherents, and the Puritanical element. The first of these controversies called forth a number of interesting attacks and defenses, among them three or four of some value as criticism of the drama. In 1577 John Northbrooke published his *Treatise wherein Dicing, Dauncing, vaine Playes or Enterluds, with other idle Pastimes, &c., commonly used on the Sabaoth Day, and reproued by the Authoritie of the Word of God and auntient Writers.* Then followed Stephen Gosson's *The Schoole of Abuse* (1579), another attack. Thomas Lodge replied in his *Defence of Poetry, Music, and Stage Plays* (1579). Later in the same year Gosson published his *A Short Apologie of the Schoole of Abuse*, etc. Henry Denham's *A Second and Third Blast of Retreat from Plays and Theatres* appeared in 1580. Gosson's *Playes confuted in five Actions*, etc., was published about 1582. About this time Sir Philip Sidney wrote his *Defence of Poesy*, or *Apologie for Poetry* (published 1595), a reply to the Puritan attacks on the stage. Three further attacks may be mentioned: Philip Stubbes' *The Anatomie of Abuses* (1583), George Whetstone's *A Touchstone for the Time* (1584), and William Rankins' *A Mirrour of Monsters* (1587). William Webbe's *A Discourse of English Poetrie* (1586) is a more ambitious formal treatise on writing, while Puttenham's *Arte of English Poesie* (1589) furthered the work of classification and introducing foreign — chiefly Italian — meters and forms. Sir John Harington's *Apologie of Poetry* (1591) was, like Sidney's similar work, a defense against the Puritan attacks. When Sidney's *Defence* was published in 1595, it was already fairly well known, as it had circulated in manuscript for some years. It is rigidly classical in its sections on the drama, and follows the Italian Renaissance scholars in requiring greater verisimilitude, and an adherence to the Unities. It is curious to note the absence of any such declaration of independence as Lope de Vega's *New Art* among the Elizabethan dramatists, most of whom were opposed in practice to all formulas. The greatest critical treatises of the period were classic in tendency, and the two most important — Sidney's and Jonson's — are directed against current practices in playwriting. Bacon's remarks on the drama — in the *Essays*, the *Advancement of Learning*, and the *De Augmentis* — could be condensed into one or two pages. The dramatists themselves had comparatively little to say of their art; a dozen Dedications and a few Prologues of Jonson,[1] Chapman,[2] Fletcher,[3] Marston,[4] Middleton,[5] Heywood,[6] Webster,[7] and Field,[8] are practically all that have direct bearing upon the subject. Ben Jonson's *Discoveries*

1 Prologue to *Every Man in His Humour* (printed 1616). *To the Readers* in *Sejanus* (printed 1605); Dedication to *Volpone* (printed 1607); *Prologue to Epicœne* (printed 1609?).

2 Dedication to *The Revenge of Bussy d'Ambois* (printed 1613).

3 *Preface* to *The Faithful Shepherdess* (printed 1609).

4 *To the General Reader,* in *Sophronisba* (printed 1606).

5 Preface to *The Roaring Girl* (printed 1611).

6 Dedication to *The Iron Age* (printed 1632).

7 *To the Reader,* in *The White Devil* (printed 1612).

8 *To the Reader* in *A Woman is a Weathercock* (1612).

closes the period. This work (published in 1641) is of prime importance, though unfortunately it is, as has been said, not a representative apology or explanation of the current practice, but an attack upon it.

NOTE. If only to prove the scantiness of dramatic theory among the dramatists of the Elizabethan period, I have below re-printed a few brief extracts from the most important prefaces to plays:

John Webster, *To the Reader* (in *The White Devil,* 1612): ". . . If it be objected this is no true dramatic poem, I shall easily confess it; *non potes in nugas dicere plura meas, ipse ego quam dixi.* Willingly, and not ignorantly, in this kind have I faulted; for should a man present to such an auditory the most sententious tragedy that ever was written, observing all the critical laws, as height of style and gravity of person, enrich it with the sententious chorus, and, as it were, liven death in the passionate and weighty Nuntius; yet, after all this divine rapture, *O dura messorum ilia,* the breath that comes from the uncapable multitude is able to poison it; and, ere it be acted, let the author resolve to fix to every scene this of Horace, *Haec porcis hodie comedenda relinques. . . .*"

John Fletcher, *To the Reader* (in *The Faithful Shepherdess,* 1609): "If you be not reasonably assured of your knowledge in this kind of poem, lay down the book, or read this, which I would wish had been the prologue. It is a pastoral tragicomedy, which the people seeing when it was played, having ever had a singular gift in defining, concluded to be a play of country hired shepherds in gray cloaks, with curtailed dogs in strings, sometimes laughing together, and sometimes killing one another; and, missing Whitsun-ales, cream, wassail, and morris-dances, began to be angry. In their error I would not have you fall, lest you incur their censure. Understand, therefore, a pastoral to be a representation of shepherds and shepherdesses with their actions and passions, which must be such as may agree with their natures, at least not exceeding former fictions and vulgar traditions; they are not to be adorned with any art, but such improper ones as nature is said to bestow, as singing and poetry; or such as experience may teach them as the virtues of herbs and fountains, the ordinary course of the sun, moon, and stars, and such like. But you are ever to remember shepherds to be such as all the ancient poets, and modern, of understanding, have received them; that is, the owners of flocks, and not hirelings. A tragicomedy is not so called in respect of mirth and killing, but in respect it wants death, which is enough to make it no tragedy, yet it brings some near it, which is enough to make it no comedy, which must be a representation of familiar people, with such kind of trouble as no life be questioned; so that a god is as lawful in this as in a tragedy, and mean people as in a comedy. Thus much I hope will serve to justify my poem, and make you understand it; to teach you more for nothing, I do not know that I am in conscience bound."

Thomas Middleton, *To the Comic Play-*

readers, Venery and Laughter (in *The Roaring Girl,* 1611): "The fashion of play-making I can properly compare to nothing so naturally as the alteration of apparel; for in the time of the great crop-doublet, your huge bombastic plays, quilted with mighty words to lean purpose, was only then in fashion: and as the doublet fell, neater inventions began to set up. Now, in the time of spruceness, our plays follow the niceness of our garments, single plots, quaint conceits, lecherous jests, dressed up in hanging sleeves; and those are fit for the times and termers. Such a kind of light-color stuff, mingled with divers colors, you shall find this published comedy; good to keep you in an afternoon from dice at home in your chambers; and for venery, you shall find enough for sixpence, but well couched an you mark it. . . ."

SIR PHILIP SIDNEY

Philip Sidney was born at Penshurst in 1554. He came of a noble and well-known family, his father being Deputy of Ireland. He attended school at Shrewsbury and later went to Oxford, which he left in 1571 without taking his degree, and went to stay with his father at Ludlow. The next year he went to Paris with a commission to negotiate for the marriage of the Queen with the Duke d'Alençon. He remained there in the King's service and was a witness of the Massacre of St. Bartholomew, and escaped with his life only by taking refuge in the English Embassy. From Paris the young Philip escaped to Germany, visiting Strassburg, Heidelberg, and Frankfurt. Together with his friend Languet, he traveled for the next three years, through Austria, Hungary, and Italy; he returned through Bohemia and Germany, and was again at Ludlow in 1575. His uncle Leicester readily took the young man under his protection, and Sidney became a courtier. In 1577 he was sent to confer with Rudolf II and the Elector Palatine in Germany on political business, and returned home by way

of the Netherlands, where he met William of Orange. His diplomatic missions were highly successful, and before long he found himself in the Queen's confidence. He was later involved in trouble incident to attacks made upon his father's administration in Ireland. In 1579 the Queen was again considering an alliance with the former Duke d'Alençon, now the Duke d'Anjou. His opposition to the match brought him into disfavor, and in 1580 he retired from Court, and began work on his *Arcadia.* Soon, however, the disgraced Leicester induced his nephew to return to Court. In 1583 he was knighted, and the same year his marriage to a daughter of Walsingham caused him to relinquish certain claims he had in America. But two years after, he was planning an expedition to the New World, and would have gone had not Drake informed the Queen that he was about to sail — contrary to her wishes. Two months later Sidney went to the Low Countries, and the following year engaged in war. He died from a wound received at Zutphen.

Sidney's only work concerned with the

drama was the *Apologie for Poetry* — or *Defence of Poesie*. This was begun in all probability in 1581, as a reply to Gosson's *The Schoole of Abuse* (1579), a Puritan attack on plays and poetry. Sidney's *Defence* is more than a reply, it is a glorification of art and its influence on the mind and conduct of human beings. He touches, incidentally, as it were, on the various forms of literature, and his remarks on the drama reveal an extensive knowledge of the classics and the Italian commentators on Aristotle.

Aristotle first became an influence in English literature through the *Apologie*, and the first mention of the Unities is likewise found in this work. It must be borne in mind that the *Apologie* was written before the great period of activity in the field of Elizabethan drama, and that the plays upon which Sidney might base his judgments or make strictures, were the indigenous interludes, moralities, farces, and classical tragedies written prior to 1580.

AN APOLOGIE FOR POETRY [1]

(or *A Defence of Poesie*)

(1595)

. . . .

No, perchance it is the Comic, whom naughty play-makers and stage-keepers have justly made odious. To the argument of abuse, I will answer after. Only thus much now is to be said, that the comedy is an imitation of the common errors of our life, which he representeth in the most ridiculous and scornful sort that may be; so as it is impossible that any beholder can be content to be such a one.

Now, as in Geometry the oblique must be known as well as the right, and in Arithmetic the odd as well as the even, so in the actions of our life, who seeth not the filthiness of evil wanteth a great foil to perceive the beauty of virtue. This doth the comedy handle so in our private and domestical matters, as with hearing it we get as it were an experience, what is to be looked for of a niggardly Demea, of a crafty Davus, of a flattering Gnato, of a vainglorious Thraso, and not only to know what effects are to be expected, but to know who be such, by the signifying badge given them by the comedian. And little reason hath any man to say that men learn by seeing it so set out, sith, as I said before, there is no man living but, by the force truth hath in nature, no sooner seeth these men play their parts, but wisheth them in Pistrinum; although

perchance the sack of his own faults lie so behind his back that he seeth not himself dance the same measure; whereto yet nothing can more open his eyes than to find his own actions contemptibly set forth. So that the right use of comedy (I think) by nobody be blamed, and much less of the high and excellent tragedy, that openeth the greatest wounds, and showeth forth the ulcers that are covered with tissue; that maketh kings fear to be tyrants, and tyrants manifest their tyrannical humors; that with stirring the effects of admiration and commiseration, teacheth the uncertainty of this world, and upon how weak foundations guilden roofs are builded; that maketh us know

Qui sceptra saevus duro imperio regit,
Timet timentes, metus in auctorem
redit.

But how much it can move, Plutarch yieldeth a notable testimony of the abominable tyrant Alexander Pheræns, from whose eyes a tragedy well made and represented, drew abundance of tears, who, without all pity, had murdered infinite numbers, and some of his own blood. So as he, that was not ashamed to make matters for tragedies, yet could not resist the sweet violence oi a tragedy. And if it wrought no further good in him, it was that he, in despite of himself, withdrew himself from hearkening to that which might mollify his hardened heart.

. . . .

1 Re-printed, with omissions, from Smith's *Elizabethan Critical Essays* (Oxford, 1904).— Ed.

Our Tragedies, and Comedies (not without cause cried out against), observing rules neither of honest civility nor of skillful poetry, excepting *Gorboduc* (again, I say, of those that I have seen), which notwithstanding, as it is full of stately speeches and well sounding phrases, climbing to the height of Seneca's style, and as full of notable morality, which it doth most delightfully teach, and so obtain the very end of poesy; yet in truth it is very defectious in the circumstances: which grieveth me, because it might not remain as an exact model of all tragedies. For it is faulty both in place and time, the two necessary companions of all corporal actions. For where the stage should always represent but one place, and the uttermost time presupposed in it should be, both by Aristotle's precept and common reason, but one day: there is both many days, and many places, inartificially imagined. But if it be so in *Gorboduc,* how much more in all the rest? Where you shall have Asia of the one side, and Afric of the other, and so many other underkingdoms, that the player, when he cometh in, must ever begin with telling where he is, or else the tale will not be conceived. Now ye shall have three ladies walk to gather flowers, and then we must believe the stage to be a garden. By and by we hear news of shipwreck in the same place, and then we are to blame, if we accept it not for a rock. Upon the back of that, comes out a hideous monster, with fire and smoke, and then the miserable beholders are bound to take it for a cave. While in the meantime, two armies fly in, represented with four swords and bucklers, and then what hard heart will not receive it for a pitched field?

Now, of time they are much more liberal. For ordinary it is that two young princes fall in love: after many traverses, she is got with child, delivered of a fair boy; he is lost, groweth a man, falls in love, and is ready to get another child, and all this in two hours' space: which how absurd it is in sense, even sense may imagine, and art hath taught, and all ancient examples justified: and at this day, the ordinary players in Italy will not err in. Yet will some bring in an example of *Eunuchus* in Terence, that containeth matter of two days, yet far short of

twenty years. True it is, and so was it to be played in two days, and so fitted to the time it set forth. And though Plautus hath in one place done amiss, let us hit with him, and not miss with him.

But they will say, how then shall we set forth a story, which containeth both many places, and many times? And do they not know that a tragedy is tied to the laws of poesy, and not of history? not bound to follow the story, but having liberty either to feign a quite new matter, or to frame the history to the most tragical conveniency? Again, many things may be told which cannot be shewed, if they know the difference betwixt reporting and representing. As for example, I may speak (though I am here) of Peru, and in speech digress from that to the description of Calcutta: but in action, I cannot represent it without Pacolet's horse: and so was the manner the ancients took, by some *Nuncius* to recount things done in former time, or other place.

Lastly, if they will represent an history, they must not (as Horace saith) begin *Ab ovo:* but they must come to the principal point of that one action, which they will represent. By example this will be best expressed. I have a story of young Polydorus delivered for safety's sake, with great riches, by his father Priam to Polymnestor, king of Thrace, in the Trojan War time. He, after some years, hearing the overthrow of Priam, for to make the treasure his own, murdereth the child: the body of the child is taken up by Hecuba; she the same day findeth a sleight to be revenged most cruelly of the tyrant. Where now would one of our tragedy-writers begin but with the delivery of the child? Then should he sail over into Thrace, and so spend I know not how many years, and travel numbers of places. But where doth Euripides? Even with the finding of the body, leaving the rest to be told by the spirit of Polydorus. This need no further to be enlarged, the dullest wit may conceive it.

But besides these gross absurdities, how all their plays be neither right tragedies, nor right comedies: mingling kings and clowns, not because the matter so carrieth it: but thrust in clowns by head and shoulders, to play a part in majestical matters, with neither decency nor discretion. So as neither the admiration and commiseration, nor the right sportfulness, is by their mongrel Tragi-comedy obtained. I know Apuleius did somewhat so, but that is a thing recounted with space of time, not represented in one moment: and I know, the ancients have one or two examples of Tragi-comedies, as Plautus hath *Amphitryo*. But if we mark them well, we shall find that they never, or very daintily, match hornpipes and funerals. So falleth it out, that, having indeed no right comedy, in that comical part of our tragedy we have nothing but scurrility, unworthy of any chaste ears: or some extreme shew of doltishness indeed fit to lift up a loud laughter and nothing else: where the whole tract of a comedy should be full of delight, as the tragedy should be still maintained in a well-raised admiration.

But our comedians think there is no delight without laughter: which is very wrong, for though laughter may come with delight, yet cometh it not of delight, as though delight should be the cause of laughter. But well may one thing breed both together. Nay, rather in themselves they have as it were a kind of contrariety: for delight we scarcely do, but in things that have a conveniency to ourselves or to the general nature: laughter almost ever cometh of things most disproportioned to ourselves and nature. Delight hath a joy in it, either permanent or present. Laughter hath only a scornful tickling. For example, we are ravished with delight to see a fair woman, and yet are far from being moved to laughter. We laugh at deformed creatures, wherein certainly we cannot delight. We delight in good chances, we laugh at mischances; we delight to hear the happiness of our friends or country, at which he were worthy to be laughed at that would laugh; we shall contrarily laugh sometimes to find a matter quite mistaken and go down the hill against the bias, in the mouth of some such men, as for the respect of them, one shall be heartily sorry, yet he cannot choose but laugh; and so is rather pained, than delighted with laughter. Yet I deny not, but that they may go well together; for as in Alexander's picture well set out, we delight without laughter, and in twenty mad antics we laugh without delight: so in Hercules, painted with his great beard and furious countenance, in woman's attire, spinning at Omphale's commandment, it breedeth both delight and laughter.

But I speak to this purpose, that all the end of the comical part be not upon such scornful matters as stirreth laughter only: but, mixt with it, that delightful teaching which is the end of poesy. And the great fault even in that point of laughter, and forbidden plainly by Aristotle, is, that they stir laughter in sinful things, which are rather execrable than ridiculous; or in miserable, which are rather to be pitied than scorned. For what is it to make folks gape at a wretched beggar, or a beggarly clown; or, against law of hospitality, to jest at strangers because they speak not English so well as we do? What do we learn? Sith it is certain

Nil habet infelix paupertas durius in se,
Quam quod ridiculos homines facit.

But rather a busy loving courtier, a heartless threatening Thraso; a self-wise-seeming schoolmaster; an awry-transformed traveler: these if we saw walk in stage names, which we play naturally, therein were delightful laughter, and teaching delightfulness: as in the other, the tragedies of Buchanan do justly bring forth a divine admiration. But I have lavished out too many words of this play matter. I do it because, as they are excelling parts of poesy, so is there none so much used in England, and none can be more pitifully abused. Which like an unmannerly daughter, shewing a bad education, causeth her mother Poesy's honesty to be called into question.

*   *   *   *   *   *

BEN JONSON

Ben Jonson was born at Westminster in 1573. His first education was received at a school near his home, and continued at the Westminister School, where he received a thorough training. It has sometimes been said that he went to Cambridge, but this has never been proved. It is likely that he applied himself to a trade, probably bricklaying — his stepfather's trade. Either a few years before or after 1592 he was a soldier in the Low Countries. He was married no later than that year. About five years after, he had become an actor, and in 1597 was engaged to revise plays. The next year he produced *Every Man in his Humour*, in which Shakespeare acted. *The Case is Altered* also belongs to the same year. At this time he was in prison as the result of a duel in which he had killed his adversary. He was released by benefit of clergy — having turned Catholic meanwhile — and again set to work for the stage. In *Cynthia's Revels* (1600) he gave offense to two of his fellow-dramatists, Dekker and Marston, and forestalled their attack by writing *The Poetaster* (1601). Dekker replied with his *Histriomastrix* (1602). Jonson next turned his attention to tragedy, and produced *Sejanus* in 1603. He then turned his hand to masques for the court of King James, recently called to the throne, and was associated for years with Inigo Jones. By 1604 he had become reconciled with Dekker and Marston and collaborated with them in the writing of the comedy *Eastward Ho* (1604). Together with his collaborators, Jonson was again sent to prison for some offense caused by the play, and the next year he and Chapman were imprisoned for the same reason, but were soon after freed. The next few years saw the production of Jonson's best works: *Volpone,*

or the Fox (1605), *Epicœne* (1609), *The Alchemist* (1610), *Bartholomew Fair* (1614), and a number of his finest masques. In 1616 Jonson determined to write no more for the stage, except to compose occasional masques. In 1618 he went to Scotland, remaining there a year and a half and making the acquaintance of Drummond of Hawthornden, who has preserved the famous *Conversations* with Jonson. His return to England was marked by several visits to his noble friends and patrons, for he had become a well-known figure. After the accession of Charles I, Jonson turned once more to the stage, and produced his later comedies. He died in 1637.

Jonson's attitude toward poetry and drama was largely influenced by Sidney's *Defence.* In the Introduction to his *Seventeenth Century Essays,* Mr. Spingarn quotes parallel passages from the two poets. Jonson's critical utterances, in his *Prologues, Prefaces,* his *Conversations* with Drummond, and, throughout the *Discoveries,* were to a great extent the result of definite literary influences. He was a classic, no doubt, and sought support in the doctrines of Aristotle, Horace, and their modern imitators. The influence exerted on him by Heinsius has been pointed out. Jonson had himself translated Horace's *Ars Poetica.* Mr. Spingarn regards Jonson as "perhaps the first Englishman with the critical temper." Jonson's criticism is to be found in many places, but its crystallization is in the *Discoveries,* published in 1641. But it was left to Dryden to develop a well-defined system of criticism.

TIMBER; OR DISCOVERIES MADE UPON MEN AND MATTER [1]
(1641)

. . . .

The parts of a comedy and tragedy.— The parts of a comedy are the same with a tragedy, and the end is partly the same, for they both delight and teach; the comics are called διδάσκαλοι of the Greeks no less than the tragics.

Aristotle. — *Plato.* — *Homer.* — Nor is

the moving of laughter always the end of comedy; that is rather a fowling for the people's delight, or their fooling. For, as Aristotle says rightly, the moving of laughter is a fault in comedy, a kind of turpitude that depraves some part of a man's nature without a disease. As a wry face without pain moves laughter, or a deformed vizard, or a rude clown dressed in a lady's habit and using her actions; we dislike and scorn such

1 Re-printed, with omissions, from Schelling's edition of the *Discoveries* (Boston, 1892).— Ed.

representations which made the ancient philosophers ever think laughter unfitting in a wise man. And this induced Plato to esteem of Homer as a sacrilegious person, because he presented the gods sometimes laughing. As also it is divinely said of Aristotle, that to seem ridiculous is a part of dishonesty, and foolish.

The wit of the old comedy.— So that what either in the words or sense of an author, or in the language or actions of men, is awry or depraved does strangely stir mean affections, and provoke for the most part to laughter. And therefore it was clear that all insolent and obscene speeches, jests upon the best men, injuries to particular persons, perverse and sinister sayings (and the rather unexpected) in the old comedy did move laughter, especially where it did imitate any dishonesty, and scurrility came forth in the place of wit, which, who understands the nature and genius of laughter cannot but perfectly know.

Aristophanes. — *Plautus.* — Of which Aristophanes affords an ample harvest, having not only outgone Plautus or any other in that kind, but expressed all the moods and figures of what is ridiculous oddly. In short, as vinegar is not accounted good until the wine be corrupted, so jests that are true and natural seldom raise laughter with the beast, the multitude. They love nothing that is right and proper. The farther it runs from reason or possibility with them the better it is.

Socrates. — *Theatrical wit.* — What could have made them laugh, like to see Socrates presented, that example of all good life, honesty, and virtue, to have him hoisted up with a pulley, and there play the philosopher in a basket; measure how many foot a flea could skip geometrically, by a just scale, and edify the people from the engine. This was theatrical wit, right stage jesting, and relishing a playhouse, invented for scorn and laughter; whereas, if it had savored of equity, truth, perspicuity, and candor, to have tasten a wise or a learned palate,— spit it out presently! this is bitter and profitable: this instructs and would inform us: what need we know anything, that are nobly born, more than a horse-race, or a hunting-match, our day to break with citizens, and such innate mysteries?

The cart.— This is truly leaping from the stage to the tumbril again, reducing all wit to the original dung-cart.

Of the magnitude and compass of any fable, epic or dramatic.

What the measure of a fable is.— The fable or plot of a poem defined.— The epic fable, differing from the dramatic.— To the resolving of this question we must first agree in the definition of the fable. The fable is called the imitation of one entire and perfect action, whose parts are so joined and knit together, as nothing in the structure can be changed, or taken away, without impairing or troubling the whole, of which there is a proportionable magnitude in the members. As for example: if a man would build a house, he would first appoint a place to build it in, which he would define within certain bounds; so in the constitution of a poem, the action is aimed at by the poet, which answers place in a building, and that action hath his largeness, compass, and proportion. But as a court or king's palace requires other dimensions than a private house, so the epic asks a magnitude from other poems, since what is place in the one is action in the other; the difference is in space. So that by this definition we conclude the fable to be the imitation of one perfect and entire action, as one perfect and entire place is required to a building. By perfect, we understand that to which nothing is wanting, as place to the building that is raised, and action to the fable that is formed. It is perfect, perhaps not for a court or king's palace, which requires a greater ground, but for the structure he would raise; so that space of the action may not prove large enough for the epic fable, yet be perfect for the dramatic, and whole.

What we understand by whole.— Whole we call that, and perfect, which hath a beginning, a midst, and an end. So the place of any building may be whole and entire for that work, though too little for a palace. As to a tragedy or a comedy, the action may be convenient and perfect that would not fit an epic poem in magnitude. So a lion is a perfect creature in himself, though it be less than that of a buffalo or a rhinocerote. They differ but in specie: either in the kind is absolute; both have

their parts, and either the whole. Therefore, as in every body so in every action,
which is the subject of a just work, there
is required a certain proportionable
greatness, neither too vast nor too minute. For that which happens to the
eyes when we behold a body, the same
happens to the memory when we contemplate an action. I look upon a monstrous giant, as Tityus, whose body covered nine acres of land, and mine eye
sticks upon every part; the whole that
consists of those parts will never be
taken in at one entire view. So in a
fable, if the action be too great, we can
never comprehend the whole together in
our imagination. Again, if it be too little, there ariseth no pleasure out of the
object; it affords the view no stay; it is
beheld, and vanisheth at once. As if we
should look upon an ant or pismire, the
parts fly the sight, and the whole considered is almost nothing. The same
happens in action, which is the object of
memory, as the body is of sight. Too
vast oppresseth the eyes, and exceeds the
memory; too little scarce admits either.

What is the utmost bounds of a fable.—
Now, in every action it behooves the poet
to know which is his utmost bound, how
far with fitness and a necessary proportion he may produce and determine it;
that is, till either good fortune change
into the worse, or the worse into the
better. For as a body without proportion cannot be goodly, no more can the
action, either in comedy or tragedy, without his fit bounds: and every bound, for
the nature of the subject, is esteemed the
best that is largest, till it can increase
no more; so it behooves the action in
tragedy or comedy to be let grow till
the necessity ask a conclusion; wherein
two things are to be considered: first,
that it exceed not the compass of one
day; next, that there be place left for
digression and art. For the episodes and
digressions in a fable are the same that
household stuff and furniture are in a
house. And so far from the measure and
extent of a fable dramatic.

What by one and entire.— Now that it
should be one and entire. One is considerable two ways; either as it is only
separate, and by itself, or as being composed of many parts, it begins to be one
as those parts grow or are wrought together. That it should be one the first

away alone, and by itself, no man that
hath tasted letters ever would say, especially having required before a just magnitude and equal proportion of the parts
in themselves. Neither of which can possibly be, if the action be single and separate, not composed of parts, which laid
together in themselves, with an equal
and fitting proportion, tend to the same
end; which thing out of antiquity itself
hath deceived many, and more this day
it doth deceive.

*Hercules. — Theseus. — Achilles. —
Ulysses.— Homer and Vergil.— Æneas.—
Venus.*— So many there be of old that
have thought the action of one man to
be one, as of Hercules, Theseus, Achilles,
Ulysses, and other heroes; which is both
foolish and false, since by one and the
same person many things may be sever-
ally done which cannot fitly be referred
or joined to the same end: which not
only the excellent tragic poets, but the
best masters of the epic, Homer and
Vergil, saw. For though the argument
of an epic poem be far more diffused
and poured out than that of tragedy,
yet Vergil, writing of Æneas, hath pre-
termitted many things. He neither tells
how he was born, how brought up, how
he fought with Achilles, how he was
snatched out of the battle by Venus;
but that one thing, how he came into
Italy, he prosecutes in twelve books.
The rest of his journey, his error by sea,
the sack of Troy, are put not as the
argument of the work, but episodes of
the argument. So Homer laid by many
things of Ulysses, and handled no more
than he saw tended to one and the same
end.

*Theseus. — Hercules. — Juvenal. —
Codrus.— Sophocles.— Ajax.— Ulysses.—*
Contrary to which, and foolishly, those
poets did, whom the philosopher taxeth,
of whom one gathered all the actions of
Theseus, another put all the labors of
Hercules in one work. So did he whom
Juvenal mentions in the beginning,
" hoarse Codrus," that recited a volume
compiled, which he called his *Theseide*,
not yet finished, to the great trouble
both of his hearers and himself; amongst
which there were many parts had no
coherence nor kindred one with another,
so far they were from being one action,
one fable. For as a house, consisting of
divers materials, becomes one structure

and one dwelling, so an action, composed of divers parts, may become one fable, epic or dramatic. For example, in a tragedy, look upon Sophocles his *Ajax:* Ajax, deprived of Achilles' armor, which he hoped from the suffrage of the Greeks, disdains; and, growing impatient of the injury, rageth, and runs mad. In that humor he doth many senseless things, and at last falls upon the Grecian flock and kills a great ram for Ulysses: returning to his senses, he grows ashamed of the scorn, and kills himself; and is by the chiefs of the Greeks forbidden burial. These things agree and hang together, not as they were done, but as seeming to be done, which made the action whole, entire, and absolute.

The conclusion concerning the whole, and the parts.— Which are episodes.— Ajax and Hector.— Homer.— For the whole, as it consisteth of parts, so without all the parts it is not the whole; and

to make it absolute is required not only the parts, but such parts as are true. For a part of the whole was true; which, if you take away, you either change the whole or it is not the whole. For if it be such a part, as, being present or absent, nothing concerns the whole, it cannot be called a part of the whole; and such are the episodes, of which hereafter. For the present here is one example: the single combat of Ajax and Hector, as it is at large described in Homer, nothing belongs to this Ajax of Sophocles.

You admire no poems but such as run like a brewer's cart upon the stones, hobbling:

Et, quae per salebras, altaque saxa cadunt,
Accius et quidquid Pacuviusque vomunt
Attonitusque legis terrai, frugiferai.

.   .   .   .

TO THE READERS [2]

(Dedication of *Sejanus: His Fall*)

(1605)

. . . First, if it be objected that what I publish is no true poem in the strict laws of time, I confess it: as also in the want of a proper chorus; whose habit and moods are such and so different, as not any, whom I have seen since the ancients, no, not they who have most presently affected laws, have yet come in the way of. Nor is it needful, or almost possible in these our times, and to such auditors as commonly things are presented, to observe the old state and splendor of dramatic poems, with preservation of any

2 Re-printed, with omissions, from the Gifford-Cunningham edition of Jonson's *Works.*— Ed.

popular delight. But of this I shall take more seasonable cause to speak, in my observations upon Horace his *Art of Poetry,* which, with the text translated, I intend shortly to publish. In the meantime, if in truth of argument, dignity of persons, gravity and height of elocution, fullness and frequency of sentence, I have discharged the other offices of a tragedy writer, let not the absence of these forms be imputed to me, wherein I shall give you occasion hereafter, and without my boast, to think I could better prescribe, than omit the due use for want of convenient knowledge. . . .

DEDICATION TO VOLPONE, OR THE FOX [3]

[*To the Most Noble and Most Equal Sisters,*
The Two Famous Universities,
For Their Love and Acceptance Shown to His Poem in the Presentation,

3 Re-printed, with omissions, from the Gifford-Cunningham edition of the *Works.*— Ed.

Ben Jonson,
The Grateful Acknowledger,
Dedicates both it and Himself]
(1607)

. . . I have labored for their instruction and amendment, to reduce not only the ancient forms, but manners of the scene, the easiness, the propriety, the innocence, and last, the doctrine, which is the principal end of poesy, to inform men in the best reason of living. And though my catastrophe may, in the strict rigor of comic law, meet with censure, as turning back to my promise; I desire the learned and charitable critic to have so much faith in me, to think it was done of industry: for, with what ease I could have varied it nearer his scale (but that I fear to boast my own faculty) I could here insert. But my special aim being to put the snaffle in their mouths that cry out, We never punish vice in our interludes, ·&c., I took the more liberty; though not without some lines of example, drawn even in the ancients themselves, the goings out of whose comedies are not always joyful, but oft-times the bawds, the servants, the rivals, yea, and the masters are mulcted; and fitly, it being the office of a comic poet to imitate justice, and instruct to life, as well as purity of language, or stir up gentle affections: to which I shall take the occasion elsewhere to speak. . . .

FRENCH DRAMATIC CRITICISM OF THE SEVENTEENTH CENTURY

While no very distinct line of demarcation can be drawn between the end of the sixteenth and beginning of the seventeenth centuries in French literary criticism, it is at least convenient to consider the sixteenth as marking the end of a stage in the development from the traditions of the Middle Ages and an important connecting link with the century in which the classic ideal received its final impetus in the *Art Poétique* of Boileau (1674). The main current was in favor of classicism, i. e., an adherence to the precepts, however misunderstood, of Aristotle and Horace; but from time to time there arose a voice in protest; Grévin and Laudun d'Aigaliers, among others, objected to the rigid Rules, and declared in favor of greater liberty. The same sort of protest was heard occasionally in the following century, from Ogier, in his *Préface* to Schélandre's *Tyr et Sidon* (1628), from Hardy, rather by his practice, however, than in his prefaces; from Durval in his preface to *Agarite* (1636), from Molière later in the century; and from numerous others. But in spite of these more or less sporadic manifestos, the main current was rigidly classic. The earlier prefaces, like that of Pierre Troterel to his play *Les Corrivaux* (1612), of Maréschal to, *La Généreuse Allemande* (1621), Isnard's preface to Pichou's *La Filis de Scire* (1631), Gombauld's to *Amaranthe* (1631), Jean de Mairet's veritable Poetic prefixed to his *Silvanire* (1631), the occasional prefaces to Du Ryer's, Claveret's, and Desmarets de Saint-Sorlin's plays — all helped to pave the way for Jean Chapelain's many and oft-repeated pleas for the Unities, and the famous *Cid* Controversy. This controversy, which will be treated at greater length in connection with Chapelain, called forth a large number of pamphlets, for and against the young Corneille, whose " irregular " *Cid,* produced in 1636, was one of the most successful plays of the century. Georges de Scudéry's *Observations sur le Cid* (published in 1637, when nearly all the controversial tracts appeared) was followed in quick succession by Faret's (?) *Deffense du Cid,* further attacks and defenses by Corneille himself, Mairet, Scudéry again, Sorel, the anonymous *Discours à Cliton,* and finally by the *Sentimens de l'Académie françoise sur la tragi-comédie du Cid* (1638), written principally and edited by Chapelain. Corneille's *Préfaces, Avertissements,* and the like, begun in 1632 in *Clitandre* — were appearing meanwhile, but his most important critical and theoretical contributions, the *Discours* and *Examens,* were not printed until the edition of 1660. Other indications of the general trend of ideas on the drama may be found in works of less importance from the viewpoint of actual influence on contemporaries; in the *Lettres* of Chapelain and of Jean-Louis Guez de Balzac, many of which are concerned with the question of the Rules and the *Cid* Controversy, while a single letter of Racan (to Ménage, 1654) registers another protest against the strict regulations of classicism. Following immediately upon the *Cid* controversy came Sarasin's *Discours sur la Tragédie* (1639), a formal treatise founded upon Aristotelian principles, and, the next year, La Mesnardière's *Art Poétique,* a pedantic and voluminous ultra-classic work. Another pedantic work, but of vaster importance and fame, appeared in 1657, the *Pratique du théâtre,* of François Hédelin, Abbé d'Aubignac. This was the first work attempting to treat of the actual writing of plays, though the author more often than not strays from his professed purpose and theorizes at great length. Corneille, who had long struggled to reconcile his practice with his theory, and his theory with his practice, replied to d'Aubignac and his other critics in his famous *Discours* and *Examens* (1660). Molière, on the other hand, whose first critical words appeared in 1659, nowhere attempts to "justify" himself in like manner, but roundly declares that to please is the great and only rule. Racine, whose *Préface* to *La Thébaïde* was first printed in 1664, is in his own way a follower of Aristotle. Rapin's *Réflexions sur la Poétique* (1674), translated into English by Rymer almost immediately after its publication in French, is a rather heavy and scholastic piece of work. But the same year (1674) saw the publication of the celebrated *Art Poétique* of Boileau, which contains in concise form all the more or less consistent attempts to formulate a definite classic standard. Boileau stands for order, "good sense," and reason. Among the earliest French "essays" are the handful of short writings of Saint-Evremond, composed between 1666 and 1677, on Racine and Corneille, on ancient, French, English, and Italian drama. Toward the end of the century there appeared a number of larger treatises, dealing with aspects of the drama, none of which, however, was of great importance. Baillet's *Jugement des savants* (1687), and Bayle's celebrated *Dictionnaire historique et critique* (1697), and the welter of pamphlets and books occasioned by the *Ancients and Moderns Quarrel,* are not primarily concerned with the drama, though they may be consulted on particular points.

FRANÇOIS OGIER

François Ogier (who signs himself in one place as a "native of Paris") was born early in the seventeenth century. Nothing is known of him except through his various writings. He entered the church at an early age and became "prédicateur du roi." He manifested an early liking for letters, and began his literary career with an attack on Garasse's *Doctrine curieuse* (1623). The argument was continued, and resulted in Ogier's *Jugement et Censure* of the *Doctrine.* After a good deal of controversy the opponents were reconciled. J.-L. G. de Balzac took part in the quarrel and sided with Ogier, who later defended Balzac in the *Apologie,* in 1627. In 1628 he published the *Préface* to Jean de Schélandre's play, *Tyr et Sidon,* orig-inally published in 1608. In 1648 Ogier went to Munster and was present at the signing of the Treaty of Westphalia. The next year he returned to Paris, preached for some time, and finally retired, devoting his efforts entirely to writing and the publishing of his works. He died at Paris in 1670.

With the exception of the *Préface* to Schélandre's play, Ogier's works consist of poems, sermons, and various criticisms of literature. Ogier was not a man of the theater, though his interest in the drama is manifest in the *Préface.* He was, indeed, little more than an amateur, but perhaps as such he was better able to realize the futility of subjecting poets and dramatists to rules. It was he, rather than Chapelain and Boileau, who applied the standard of reason and commonsense to works of art. But, as has been pointed out,

the current of the time was against him, and it did not turn until the early years of the nineteenth century.

PREFACE TO TYRE AND SIDON [1]

[*Préface au Lecteur* (to) *Tyr et Sidon*]

(1628)

. . . Those who favor the ancient poets will find something to criticize in our author's invention, and those who follow the moderns will find some little fault with his style. These former, who are the erudite, for whose criticism we have the highest regard, say that our tragi-comedy is not composed according to the rules that the ancients have prescribed for the stage, on which they were willing to perform nothing but events which can take place in the course of one day. And yet, in the first as well as in the second part of our play, there are found things which cannot be included in a single day, but which require an interval of several days to be put into execution.

But then, too, the ancients, in order to avoid this inconvenience of connecting in a few hours events far removed in time, have fallen into two errors as important as those that they wished to avoid: the one, in the fact that, fore-seeing very well that a variety of events is necessary to render the performance pleasing, they cause a number of incidents and encounters to take place in one and the same day, which probably cannot have happened in such a short space of time. That offends the judicious spectator who desires a real or imaginary interval between those events, in order that in his mind he may not discover anything too unnatural in them, and that it may not seem that the characters are assigned to appear at a given moment, like *Dei ex Machinâ*, which were also used very often out of season. This fault is noticeable in nearly all the plays of the ancients, and especially in those in which there occurs some recognition of a child formerly abandoned; for directly, in order to strengthen some

conjecture founded on age, features, or on some ring or other clew, the person who was employed to lose it, the shepherd who has reared it, the old woman who has nursed it, etc., all meet and suddenly appear on the stage, as if by magic, although it is probable that all these people can be assembled only after the expenditure of much time and pains. All the tragedies and comedies of the ancients are full of examples of this kind.

Sophocles himself, the most regular of all, in his *Œdipus Rex*, which is offered to us by the experts as the model of a perfect tragedy, has fallen into this error: for, at the very moment when Creon has returned from the Delphian oracle, when great difficulty is being experienced in attempting to discover the author of Laïus' death, at the moment when they have sent for a former servant who may have some information concerning it, and who is to arrive forthwith, suddenly the poet brings upon the scene the old man who had formerly carried off the child Œdipus, and who had received him from the hands of this old servant whom they are expecting. So that the entire affair is revealed in a moment, for fear that the action of the tragedy may exceed in length the time of one day. Who does not see at this point that the unexpected arrival of the old man from Corinth has been prepared beforehand and is too farfetched, and that it is not at all likely that a man who was not called in for this purpose, should arrive and converse with Œdipus just in the short interval of time which elapses since Laïus' old servant has been sent for? Is not this to bring these two characters together in spite of themselves, and to discover at one moment the secret of the death of this unfortunate prince?

Because of this consideration for putting off nothing to an imaginary mor-

[1] Translated, with minor omissions, for the first time in English, by August Odebrecht.—Ed.

row, it happens, too, that the poets cause certain actions to follow one other immediately, although of necessity they require an appreciable interval between them in order to be appropriately carried out. As when Æschylus brings in Agamemnon with funeral ceremony, accompanied by a long train of mourners and by libations, at the very moment when he has just been killed. Whereas this murder must have thrown the entire royal house and the whole city into disorder, when the body is to be concealed or abandoned by the murderers, and when the whole stage should be filled with violent outbursts of compassion and of vengeance, they march in great solemnity and in good order in the funeral procession of this unhappy prince, whose blood is still warm and who, so to speak, is only half dead.

The second disadvantage that the ancient poets have incurred because they wish to confine the events of a tragedy within one day, is their being compelled continually to introduce messengers in order to relate the events which have occurred on the preceding days, and the purpose of the events which are taking place on the stage at the moment. So that, in nearly all the acts, these gentlemen entertain the audience with a lengthy enumeration of tiresome intrigues which make the spectator lose patience, however well disposed he may be to listen. Indeed it is a tedious thing, that one and the same person should occupy the stage all the time, and it is more suitable for a good inn than becoming to an excellent tragedy to see messengers continually arriving there. Here it is necessary to avoid as much as possible those tiresome speakers who relate the adventures of others, and to put the persons themselves into action, leaving these long narrations to the historians or to those who have taken charge of composing the plots and the subjects of the plays that are being performed. What difference is there, pray, between *The Persians* of Æschylus and a simple narrative of what occurred between Xerxes and the Greeks? Is there anything so dull or so uninteresting? And the disgust of the reader, whence comes it if not from the fact that a messenger plays in it the part of all the characters, and that the poet has re-

fused to violate that law that we are wrongfully accused of having violated? But I am in no mood to criticize further the works of a poet who had the courage to fight valiantly for the liberty of his country, during those famous days of Marathon, of Salamis and of Platæa. Let us leave him to hold forth in such a way as may please him concerning the flight of the Persians, since he had such a good share in their defeat, and let us pass on.

Poetry, and especially that which is written for the theater, is composed only for pleasure and amusement, and this pleasure can arise only from the variety of the events which are represented on the stage, which events, not being able to occur easily in the course of one day, the poets have been constrained to abandon gradually the practice of their predecessors who confined themselves within too narrow limits; and this change is not so recent that we have no examples of it from antiquity. Whoever will carefully consider the *Antigone* of Sophocles will find that a night intervenes between the first and the second burial of Polynices; otherwise, how could Antigone have deceived the guards of the body of this unfortunate prince the first time, and avoid being seen by so many people, except in the darkness of the night? For on the second occasion she comes to the body aided by a heavy rain which causes all the guards to retire, while she, in the midst of the storm, buries her brother and pays her last respects to him. Whence it happens that the tragedy of *Antigone* represents the events of two days at least; since the pretended crime of that princess presupposes Creon's law which is proclaimed publicly and in broad daylight, on the stage and in the presence of the elders of Thebes. Here then is the order of this tragedy: the law or the interdiction of Creon, made and proclaimed during the day; the first burial of Polynices, that I maintain took place at night; the second during a great storm in broad daylight; that is the second day.

But we have a much more famous example of a comedy by Menander (for our critics demand that we observe the same rule in comedies as in tragedies in relation to the difficulty that we are considering) entitled 'Εαυτοντιμορυμένος, translated by Terence, in which, without any doubt, the poet includes the events of two days, and introduces the actors who bear witness to the fact in very plain terms. In act one, scene two, Chremes warns his son not to stray too far from the house, in view of the fact that it is already very late. In act two, scene four, Clitipho and his band enter the house to sup with the old man, and the night is spent there in pleasant occupations. The next day Chremes rises early to inform Menedemus of the return of his son, and he goes out of the house rubbing his eyes and uttering these words: *Luces cit hoc iam,* etc., *the day is beginning to dawn,* etc. For if there is any one bold enough to say that Menander and Terence have erred in this passage, and that they have forgotten themselves in respect to the proprieties that must be preserved in the theater, let him beware lest he offend as well the leading men among the Romans, Scipio and Lælius, whom Cornelius Nepos considers to be the real authors of this comedy, rather than Terence.

It can be seen, then, by this, that the ancients and the most excellent masters of the profession have not always observed that rule which our critics desire to make us so religiously preserve at the present time. For if, however, they have nearly always observed it, it is not because they believed themselves absolutely compelled to do so in order to satisfy the spectator's imagination, to which they had done just as much violence in the two ways that I have pointed out, but it was their custom to dare to deviate only very slightly from the path that had been marked out for them by their predecessors. Which appears in the fact that the least innovations in the theater are cited by the ancients as very important and very remarkable changes in the state. Sophocles invented the buskin and added three actors to the choruses that before his time consisted only of twelve. This change is of very little importance and concerns only the stature of the actor and the size of the choruses, which are always unpleasant of whatever size or quality they appear.

Now, in my opinion, there are two reasons why the ancient writers of tragedy have not dared to deviate, un-less it be very little and by degrees, from their first models. The first is that their tragedies formed a part of the worship of the gods and of the ceremonies of religion, in which, innovations being always offensive and changes hard to appreciate, unless they take place of their own accord and, as it were, imperceptibly, it happened that the poets dared undertake nothing that was not in keeping with the usual custom. And perhaps that is also the reason why, although they represent atrocious deeds, accompanied and followed by murders and other kinds of cruelty, on the other hand, they never shed blood in the presence of the audience, and all those bloody executions are understood to take place behind the scenes, and that, for fear that the solemnity of the occasion may be desecrated by the sight of some homicide; for, if one consider well, the Ajax of Sophocles does not kill himself on the stage, but in a neighboring thicket, from which his voice and his last sighs can be easily heard.

The second reason why ancient tragedies are nearly all alike and are, nearly all of them, full of choruses and of messengers, arises from the fact that the poets, wishing to carry off the prize destined to the one who composed the best work, forced themselves to write according to the desire and taste of the people and of the judges, who, without doubt, would have refused to admit among the number of contestants any one who had not followed the rules of composition observed before his time on such occasions. The subject matter itself, on which the poets were to work that year, was prescribed and suggested. From which it can be seen that nearly all ancient tragedies have the same subject, and that the same plots are treated by Æschylus, Sophocles, and Euripides, tragic authors of whom alone a few complete works have come down to us. From this it has also happened that these subjects and plots have been taken from a small number of Greek tales or stories well known to the people, who would not have been contented to being entertained by other exhibitions than those based upon events that had occurred at Thebes and at Troy. Add to this that the Athenians who had received the tragedies of Æschylus with extraordinary applause, desired as a special favor that they might still be performed in public after the death of their author. A fact which gave them such a reputation that the tragic poets who followed concluded that they must not deviate from a model that was held in such high repute, and that it was necessary to conform to public opinion since it was that of the master.

Since then, the Latins, who had submitted themselves to the inventions of the Greeks, as holding the arts and the sciences from them, did not dare to disturb the limits that had been prescribed, for them, and especially in regard to the subject of which we are speaking. For the Romans, who had imitated the Greeks in other kinds of poetry, and who had even competed with them for the prize in epic and lyric poetry, confined themselves, or very nearly so, to mere translation of their tragedies, and they have treated no subject which had not been exhibited several times on the stages of Greece.

I will not mention Accius, Nævius, Pacuvius, and a few others, of whose works we possess many fragments classed by the grammarians under the title of Greek tales; the only Latin tragedies which were composed in a better age, and that remain to us, are nearly all Greek, as well in subject matter as in form, except the *Thebaïd*, in the fact that it does not introduce any choruses, and the *Octavia*, because its subject is a roman story; but the latter is the work of an amateur, if we are to believe Justus Lipsius, and scarcely deserves to be taken into consideration.

After the Latins, the drama, as well as the other forms of more polite literature having been abandoned, barbarism succeeded this long interregnum of the humanities, that resumed their authority only within the memory of our fathers. In this restoration, however, several errors were committed, but it is not my purpose to speak of that in this place, and I cannot undertake it without making a volume out of a preface, and saying many good things that are not to the point. Only, I should wish that Francis Bacon, the public critic of human knowledge, had made some mention of it in his books, for it seems that his subject obliged him to do so.

I confine myself here to poetry alone, and say that the too intense eagerness of wishing to imitate the ancients has caused our best poets to fail to attain either the reputation or the excellence of the ancients. They did not consider that the taste of nations is different, as well in matters pertaining to the mind as in those of the body, and that, just as the Moors, and without going so far, the Spaniards, imagine and prefer a type of beauty quite different from that which we prize in France, and just as they desire their sweethearts to have a different figure, and features other than those that we desire to see in ours, to such a degree that there are some men who will form an idea of their beauty from the same features that we should consider homely, just so, it must not be doubted that the minds of nations have preferences quite different from one another, and altogether dissimilar feelings for the beauty of intellectual things, such as poetry; but philosophy, nevertheless, has no part in this matter: for it expects, to be sure, that the minds of all men, under whatever sky they may be born, shall agree in one and the same opinion concerning the things necessary for the sovereign good, and it strives as far as possible to unite them in the search after truth, because there can be but one truth; but as for matters that are merely amusing and unimportant, such as this of which we are speaking, it allows our opinions to take whatever direction they please, and does not extend its jurisdiction over this matter.

This truth granted, it opens a gentle and pleasing way to settle the quarrels that arise daily between those who attack and those who defend the works of the ancient poets; for, as I cannot refrain from censuring two or three scribblers who call Pindar stupid and extravagant, Homer a dreamer, etc., etc., and those who have imitated them in these latter days, so too, I think it remarkable that they should be proposed to us as perfect models, from which we are not permitted to deviate ever so little. To this we must reply, that the Greeks worked for Greece, and were successful in the judgment of the cultured people of their day, and that we shall imitate them much better if we grant something to the genius of our own country and to the preferences of our own language, than if we compel ourselves to follow step by step their plan and their style as a few of our writers have done. Here it is that the judgment must be brought into play as in everything else, choosing from the ancients that which can adapt itself to our own times and to the temperament of our nation, without, however, finding fault with the works that, during so many centuries, have met with public approval. They were considered in their day from a point of view different from that of the present time, and people perceived a certain charm in them which is concealed from us and to discover which it would be necessary to have breathed the air of Attica at birth and to have been reared in the midst of those excellent men of ancient Greece.

Surely, just as our stomachs refuse some meats and fruits which are considered delicacies in foreign countries, in the same manner our minds fail to enjoy a certain passage or a certain composition by a Greek or by a Latin which, in former times, has been held in high admiration. The Athenians must certainly have found other beauties in the verses of Pindar than those which our minds of the present day discover in them, since they rewarded a single word with which this poet favored their city, more generously than would the princes of to-day recompense an *Iliad* composed in their honor.

We must not then be so infatuated with the theories that the ancients have held, nor with the art which they have set up, allowing ourselves to be led like the blind; but we must examine and consider these theories themselves by the circumstances of time, place, and the persons for whom they were composed, adding to them and taking away in order to adapt them to our use, a method that Aristotle would have sanctioned: for this philosopher, who demands that supreme reason be obeyed on all occasions, and who concedes nothing to popular opinion, does not refrain from admitting at this point that poets should grant something to the convenience of the actors, in order to facilitate their acting, and should make many allowances for the stupidity and the mood of the spectators. Surely he would have conceded

much more to the preference and to the judgment of a whole nation, and if he had laid down rules for a play which was to have been performed before a people as impatient and fond of change and novelty as we are, he would have been very careful not to weary us with those narrations of the messengers, so frequent and so tiresome, nor would he have made a chorus recite almost a hundred and fifty lines at a stretch, as does Euripides in his *Iphigenia in Aulis*.

Hence, the ancients themselves, recognizing the faults of their drama, and that the little variety observed in their plays depressed the spectators, were compelled to introduce satyrs as a form of interlude, which, by virtue of an unrestrained license to slander and abuse persons of the highest rank, held the attention of the people, who delight ordinarily to hear ill spoken of others.

This plan of ordering and arranging, which they used, is our reason for not hesitating to justify the invention of tragi-comedies, introduced by the Italians, in view of the fact that it is much more reasonable, in the course of the same conversation, to mingle grave matters with the least serious, and to bring them together in a single plot for a play or for a story, than to mingle extraneously satyrs with tragedies that have no connection with one another, and that confuse and disturb the sight and the understanding of the audience; for, to say that it is improper to show in a single play the same persons speaking now of serious, important, and tragic matters, and immediately after of commonplace, vain, and humorous things, is to be unacquainted with the nature of human life, whose days and hours are very often interrupted by laughter and by tears, by joy and by sorrow, according as they are filled with happiness or troubled by misfortune. Some one of the gods endeavored formerly to mingle joy with sorrow in order to make of them a single compound; he was unable to accomplish this, but then he joined them behind one another. That is why they ordinarily follow so closely after one another, and nature herself has shown us that there is scarcely any difference between them, since artists note that the movements of muscles and nerves that give an expression of laughter to the countenance, are the same that serve to make us weep and to assume the expression of sorrow by which we manifest extreme grief. And then, after all, those who demand no variation or change in the inventions of the ancients, are arguing here merely about the word and not about the thing itself: for, what is the *Cyclops* of Euripides but a tragi-comedy full of jests and wine, of satyrs and Silenus, on the one hand; of blood and rage and baffled Polyphemus on the other?

The question, then, is an old one, although it goes by a new name; it merely remains to treat it as is fitting, to make each character speak in a manner that is becoming to the subject, and to know how to step down appropriately from the cothurnus of tragedy (for it is permissible in this discussion to make use of these terms) to the slipper of comedy, as our author has done.

Everybody knows how different should be the style that is used in such different matters: the one lofty, elevated, superb; the other, mediocre and less serious. That is why Pliny the Younger rather humorously nicknamed two of his country homes *Tragedy* and *Comedy*, because one was situated on a mountain, and the other below on the sea-shore. . . .

JEAN CHAPELAIN

Jean Chapelain, the son of a notary and an ambitious mother, was born at Paris in 1595. From the first, Jean was destined by his parents for a literary career. He studied early under the famous Nicolas Bourbon. As a young man, his knowledge and his ability as a conversationalist afforded him a place in many of the literary salons of the day. His *Préface* to the *Adone* of Marini increased his already growing reputation. He was the friend and counsellor of the Précieux, and a welcome guest at the Hôtel de Rambouillet. Among his friends and admirers were Balzac, Malherbe, Corneille, Richelieu, while the Duc de Longueville pensioned him in order that he might devote all his time to writing. The work upon which he most prided himself was the famous *La Pucelle*, upon which he worked for twenty-five years. The first twelve cantos were published in 1656, and proved a disastrous failure. The criticisms and attacks on the poem did much to destroy Chapelain's reputation as the greatest poet of his time, though he was still considered an important critic. He died at Paris in 1674.

Ever since Boileau's venomous attacks, Chapelain has presented a rather ridiculous figure in French literature. But that he was a man of great importance — and even paved the way for much of Boileau's own work — is un-

questioned. His work in connection with the foundation of the *Académie française*, his formulation of various critical dogmas and the rôle he played in the *Cid* Controversy, entitle him to a position of the utmost importance in seventeenth century French criticism.

The Cid Controversy [1]

The enormous success of Corneille's *Le Cid*, first produced in 1636, occasioned considerable jealousy among the so-called "arbiters of taste." Georges de Scudéry, a rival of the author's, published early in 1637 his *Observations sur le Cid*, in which he set out to prove that the subject of the play was worthless, that it violated the chief rules of the drama, that the handling of the subject was not good, that it contained many bad lines, and that its chief beauties were stolen. Corneille answered this onslaught in his *Lettre apologétique*, which was rather a counter-attack in Scudéry's manner, than a dignified response. Several others took up the quarrel, some championing Corneille and some his opponent. Of less importance were the *Deffense du Cid*, considered by some to have been written by Faret; *Le Souhait du Cid*, possibly from the hand of Sir-

[1] For a history of the Quarrel and re-print of the principal pamphlets, see Armand Gasté, *La Querelle du Cid* (Paris. 1898).

mond; then Scudéry's own *La Preuve des passages alléguez dans les Observations sur le Cid,* and Sorel's (?) *Le Jugement du Cid.* Of considerable interest is the anonymous *Discours à Cliton* — which has been attributed in turn to the Comte de Belin, Claveret, and Mairet — containing the *Traicté de la disposition du Poème Dramatique, et de la prétendue Règle de vingt-quatre heures.* Mairet's *Epistre familière au Sieur Corneille sur la Tragi-comédie du Cid* was answered by Corneille, or a friend of his, in the *Advertissement au Besançonnois Mairet.* Then came the famous *Les Sentimens de l'Académie française sur la Tragi-comédie du Cid,* published at the end of the year 1637. Among the many comments on this document the most interesting are letters of Balzac to Scudéry (1638), Scudéry's reply, and Scudéry's *Lettre de Monsieur de Scudéri à Messieurs de l'Académie française;* and, finally, Chapelain's twenty-six *Lettres* (re-printed in the Thamizey de Larroque edition, cited below) written in 1637, all touching upon the Quarrel.

After Corneille's first reply to Scudéry, the latter suggested referring the matter to the recently-founded Academy, and Corneille at least made no protest. The Academy accepted the task, and Chapelain wrote out a first draft of what was afterwards to become the *Sentimens.* The committee appointed to collaborate with Chapelain seems to have done nothing, and Chapelain presented his draft to Richelieu, to whose advantage it was to bring discredit upon Corneille's play. The Cardinal was pleased with the work in general, but suggested changes and asked Chapelain to make it more "worthy of the Academy." For some time the Academy deliberated and finally passed the MS, which was sent to press; but Richelieu, finding it too "flowery," stopped the printing, revised certain sections, and at last allowed the whole to be published in December, 1637.

That the *Sentimens* is essentially the work of Chapelain seems sure; he was a man of integrity, and he himself declares that the "whole idea" and "all the reasoning" are his. Possibly some allowance must be made for Chapelain's "absolute deference" and "blind obedience" to the Cardinal's wishes; Richelieu undoubtedly saw in Corneille a dangerous rival, and not only requested but commanded that the Academy bring an adverse criticism against *Le Cid.* Still, Chapelain's conscience forced him to acknowledge the many beauties of the "irregular" play.

In this work, as well as in the *Lettres,* prefaces, dissertations, and other miscellaneous work, he went far to establish that set of absolute rules which guided — and cramped — French drama and literature for many years. In the words of Lanson, Chapelain "practically founded dogmatic criticism." He was the disciple of Good-Sense and Reason, the cornerstones of Neo-classicism.

OPINIONS OF THE FRENCH ACADEMY ON THE TRAGI COMEDY "THE CID"[2]

(*Les Sentimens de l'Académie françoise sur la Tragi-comédie du Cid*)

(1637)

. . . Nature and Truth have put a certain value to things, which cannot be altered by that which chance or opinion set up; to attempt to judge them by what they seem, and not what they are, is to condemn oneself at the outset. It is true enough that the great Masters are not themselves in very close agreement on this point. Some, too much inclined, it seems, toward pleasure, hold that delight is the true purpose of dramatic poetry; others, more sparing of men's time and holding it too dear to be given over to amusements which yield only pleasure and no profit, maintain that its real end is to instruct. Though each expresses himself in such different terms, it will on closer examination be seen that both are in agreement; and if we judge them with what favor we should,

[2] Here translated for the first time, by the editor.— Ed.

we shall see that those who claim pleasure as the sole end are too reasonable to exclude anything that is not conformable to reason. We must believe — if we would do them justice — that by pleasure they mean the pleasure which is not the enemy but the instrument of virtue, and which purges men, insensibly and without disgust, of their vicious practices, and which is useful because it is good, and which can never leave regret in the mind for having surprised it, nor in the soul for having corrupted it. And so they only seem to disagree with the others, for it is true that if the pleasure they demand be not profit itself, it is at least the source whence of necessity it flows; and that wherever there is pleasure there is profit, and that both are produced from the same sources.

Hence, they are at one, and we agree with them both, and we can all of us together say that a play is good when it produces a feeling of reasonable content. But, as in music and painting, we should not consider every concert and every picture good if it please the people but fail in the observance of the rules of their respective arts, and if the experts, who are the sole judges, did not by their approval confirm that of the multitude. Hence we must not say with the crowd that a poem is good merely because it pleases, unless the learned and the expert are also pleased. Indeed, it is impossible that there can be pleasure contrary to reason, unless it be to a depraved taste — as, for instance, a liking for the bitter and the acid. We are not here concerned with satisfying the libertine and the vicious man, who only laughs at adulteries and incests, and who does not object to violations of the laws of nature, provided he is amused. Nor have we to do with pleasing those who are ignorant and untutored, who would be no more moved at seeing the sufferings of Penelope than of Clytemnestra. Evil examples are contagious, even in the theater; the representations even of feigned acts produce only too many real crimes; and there is great danger in diverting the people with pleasures which may some day result in public catastrophes. We must be careful to guard their eyes and ears against things of which they should not know, and keep them from learning of cruelty or perfidy,

unless at the same time examples are accompanied with the just retribution, so that they may take home with them after the performance at least some fear mixed with their pleasure. But, for that matter, it is impossible to please any one with disorder and confusion, and if it happens that irregular plays sometimes please, it is only by reason of what is regular in them, because of certain unquestioned and extraordinary beauties which transport the soul so far that for a long time after, it is incapable of detecting the deformities which accompany them, and which serve, imperceptibly, to bring out the faults, while the understanding is yet dazzled by the brilliancy of the good. And on the other hand, if certain regularly-constructed plays give little pleasure, it must not be thought that this is the fault of the rules, but of the ·author, whose sterile wit was unable to exercize his art upon sufficently rich material. . . .

. . . Now, the natural, rather than the true is, according to Aristotle, the province of epic and dramatic poetry, which, having for its purpose the pleasure and profit of the auditor or the spectator, the epic or dramatic poet can the more surely encompass by making use of the natural, or verisimilar, rather than what is simply true, or matter of fact, because it convinces men the more easily as it finds no resistance in them, which it would if the poet adhered to mere facts, and which might well be so strange and incredible that they would think them false and refuse to be persuaded of them. But since several things are required to make a story natural — that is, observation of time, of place, of the condition, age, manners and customs, and passions,— the principal point of all is that each personage must behave according to his character as set forth early in the poem. For instance, an evil man must not do good deeds. And the reason why this exact observation is required is that there is no other way of producing the Marvelous, which delights the mind with astonishment and pleasure, and is the perfect means adopted by poetry to arrive at the end of profit. It is indeed a great undertaking to try to create the rare effect of the Marvelous from so common a thing as the natural. And so, we believe with the Masters that herein lies the greatest merit for him who knows well how to do it; and as the difficulty is great, there are few who can succeed. And that is why so many, despairing of success, resort to that false Marvelous which re- sults in the unnatural, what is not true to life, and which may be called the Monstrous, and try to pass off on the crowd as the true Marvelous that which deserves only the name of Miraculous.

SUMMARY OF A POETIC OF THE DRAMA[3]
(*Sommaire d'une Poétique dramatique*)
(Posthumous)

The object of representative as well as of narrative poetry is the imitation of human action; their necessary condition is truth to life [*le vraysemblable*]; in its perfection it strives for the marvelous.

From the judicious union of the verisimilar and the marvelous springs the excellence of works of this sort. Both these elements belong to invention.

In Tragedy, which is the noblest form of drama, the poet imitates the actions of the great; in Comedy, those of people in middle or low condition. The ending of Comedy is happy.

Tragi-comedy was known to the Ancients only as tragedy with a happy ending. Witness the *Iphigenia in Tauris*. The modern French have made the form very popular, and as a result of the characters and the action have put it into a class nearer to tragedy than to comedy.

The Pastoral was invented and introduced by the Italians less than a hundred years after the Eclogue; it is a sort of Tragi-comedy, imitating the actions of shepherds, but in a more elevated manner and with higher sentiments than can be employed in the Eclogue.

In plays, poets depict, besides action, the various manners, customs, and passions of human beings.

They take particular care to make each personage speak according to his condition, age, and sex; and by propriety they mean not only that which is decent, but what is fitting and appropriate to the characters — be they good or evil — as they are at first set forth in the play.

In their tragedies and comedies a good plot never had more than one principal action, to which the others are related. This is what is termed Unity of Action.

They have allowed to the development of the action of a play the space of a single natural day. This is what is termed the Twenty-four-hour rule.

They have set the physical limit of their action to a single place. This is what is termed the Unity of Place.

All this is a necessary corollary to the verisimilar, without which the mind is neither moved nor persuaded.

The action of the play consists in exposition of the story, its complication [*embrouillement*] and its development.

The most worthy and agreeable effect that can be produced by a play, is that as a result of the artful conduct of the story the spectator is left suspended and puzzled to know the outcome, and cannot decide what the end of the adventure will be.

The Latins divided plays into five acts, while the Greeks divided them only into scenes.

Each act has several scenes. It will seem too short if it have only four, and too long if more than seven.

In the first act the principal points of the story are made clear; in the second, complications arise; in the third, the trouble deepens; in the fourth, matters look desperate; in the fifth, the knot is loosed — in a natural way, however, but in an unforeseen manner — and from this results the Marvelous.

There are some who insist that no more than three characters should appear on the stage at the same time in the same scene, in order to avoid confusion. I approve of this, except when it applies to the last scenes of the last act, where everything ought to point toward the end and where confusion only renders the unraveling more noble and more beautiful.

Others insist that each scene be intimately bound to the other. This, it is

3 Translated complete, for the first time, by the editor.— Ed.

true, produces a more agreeable effect; but the practice of the Ancients proves how unnecessary it is.

What seems most necessary to me is that no character should enter or leave without apparent reason.

FRANÇOIS HÉDELIN, ABBÉ D'AUBIGNAC

François Hédelin, better known as the Abbé d'Aubignac, was born at Paris in 1604. His father was an "avocat" in the Parlement and his mother a daughter of the famous Ambroise Paré. In 1610 the family moved to Nemours. At an early age François took part in the conversations of the Précieux and literary people with whom his father, a man of some literary taste and accomplishments, was acquainted. His own education, which was partly a study of modern and ancient languages, was, according to him, of his own making; his precocity was the wonder and delight of his parents and their friends. In his twenty-third year he was made an "avocat au Parlement"; the same year, 1627, he published his first work, a study, *Des Satyres, brutes, monstres et démons.* For a time he practiced law at Nemours, with some success, but before long went to Paris and entered the Church. Just after his ordination as a priest, he was appointed private tutor to the Duc de Fronsac, a nephew of Cardinal Richelieu, and son of the Marshal de Brézé. This was a turning-point in his life, for in the house of the Duke he became acquainted with the great men of his time, chief among them the Cardinal himself, who did much toward the shaping of his career. He was given the Abbey of Aubignac in recognition of his services, but in the meantime he had spent his patrimony on the education of the Duke. He experienced considerable difficulty in securing the pension to which he was entitled. His political opinions seemed sufficient reason to Condé for a refusal. As a result, d'Aubignac says (in 1663) that for seventeen years he had not been to court. He preached, wrote plays, pamphlets, a novel, dissertations of various kinds, and his celebrated *Pratique du*

théâtre. He founded an *Académie des belles lettres,* probably in 1654. His last years were filled with disappointments. He died in 1676.

D'Aubignac touched the life of his time at many diverse points. A recognized arbiter of taste, a scholar, an author, a Précieux, a man of the world and an abbé, he was for many years regarded as one of the foremost men of his age. Even after his death his opinions were respected by such men as Corneille and Racine. His principal title to fame rests on the famous *Pratique du théâtre* (1657), which was studied by many practicing dramatists. Racine's copy of the book is still in existence and his annotations are re-printed in M. Arnaud's life of d'Aubignac. (See below.) The curious mixture of pedantry and absurdity which goes hand in hand with much that is wise and sane, has done great harm to the author's reputation, while possibly Condé's mot, "I am obliged to Monsieur d'Aubignac for having so exactly followed Aristotle's rules, but I will never forgive the rules of Aristotle for having put Monsieur d'Aubignac upon writing so bad a tragedy," has served to call attention to the great disparity between the author's theory and his practice. The *Pratique* was intended, and to a certain extent is, a practical manual, the first of its kind. Its importance lies in the author's having insisted that a play is intended to be performed, and not merely read. This is by no means a new idea; Aristotle himself had laid down the principle, though he had not developed it, while Castelvetro was the first in modern times to insist on the close relation between the dramatist and the performance of a play in a theater before an audience.

THE WHOLE ART OF THE STAGE [1]

[La Pratique du théâtre]

(1657)

OF THE RULES OF THE ANCIENTS
CHAPTER IV

. . . Therefore, here are five objections which have been ordinarily made to me against the rules of the Ancients:

First, that we are not to make laws to ourselves from custom and example, but from reason; which ought to prevail over any authority.

Secondly, that the Ancients themselves have often violated their own rules.

Thirdly, that divers poems of the Ancients had been translated and acted upon our stage with very ill success.

Fourthly, that divers of our modern plays, though quite contrary to these rules, have been acted with great applause.

And last of all, that if these rigorous maxims should be followed, we should very often lose the greatest beauty of all true stories, their incidents having most commonly happened at different times and in different places.

As to the first objection, I answer that the rules of the stage are not founded upon authority, but upon reason; they are not so much settled by example as by the natural judgment of mankind, and if we call them the rules and the art of the Ancients 'tis only because they have practiced them with great regularity and much to their glory; having first made many observations upon the nature of moral actions and upon the probability of human accidents in this life and thereby drawing the pictures after the truth of the original and observing all due circumstances, they reduce to an art this kind of poem whose progress was very slow, though it were much in use among them and much admired all the world over. But, however, I am very sparing of citing their poems and when I do it it is only to show with what agreeable artifice they kept to these rules, and not to buoy up my opinion by their authority.

As for the second objection, it seems not considerable; for reason, being alike

1 Re-printed from the anonymous translation, *The Whole Art of the Stage* (London, 1684).

all the world over, does equally require everybody's submission to it, and if our modern authors cannot without offense be dispensed from the rules of the stage, no more could the Ancients; and where they have failed I do not pretend to excuse them. My observations upon Plautus show very well that I do propose the Ancients for models only in such things as they appear to have followed reason; and their example will always be an ill pretext for faults, for there is no excuse against reason. In things which are founded only in custom, as in grammar, or in the art of making a verse with long or short syllables, the learned may often use a license against the received practice and be imitated in it by others, because custom may often have countenanced a thing not well of itself. But in all that depends upon commonsense and reason, such as are the rules of the stage, there to take a license is a crime; because it offends not custom but natural light, which ought never to suffer an eclipse.

I must not omit, for the glory of the Ancients, that if they have sometimes violated the art of dramatic poems, they have done it for some more powerful and inducing reason than all the interest of the play could amount to. As for example, Euripides in *The Suppliants* has preferred the glory of his country to that of his art, of which I have spoken elsewhere.

The third objection has no force but in the ignorance of those that allege it. For if some poems of the Ancients, and even those which were most in esteem with them, have not succeeded upon our stage, the subject and not the want of art, has been the cause of it; and sometimes likewise the changes made by the translators, which destroyed all the graces of the original; they have added improbable scenes between princes and have showed out of time that which the Ancients had carefully concealed with art; and very often changed a fine relation into an impertinent, ridiculous spectacle. But that which is more worthy our consideration is that there were certain stories, fitted for the stage of Athens with great ornaments, which would be an abomination upon ours. For example, the story of Thyestes, so that we may say that either the moderns have corrupted the Ancients, by changing their whole economy, or the imperfection of the matter stifled the excellency of the art.

To destroy the fourth objection, we need only to remember that those plays of ours which took with the people and with the Court, were not liked in all their parts, but only in those things which were reasonable and in which they were conformable to the rules. When there were any passionate scenes they were praised; and when there was any great appearance or noble spectacle, it was esteemed; and if some notable event was well managed, there was great satisfaction shown; but if in the rest of the play or even in these beauties of it, any irregularities were discovered or any fault against probability and decency, either in the persons, time, or place, or as to the state of the things represented, they were condemned as faults. And all the favor that was shown the poet was that out of the desire of preserving what was fine, the spectators were somewhat more indulgent to what was amiss.

There, that success so much bragged on is so far from contradicting the rules of the stage that, quite contrary, it established their authority. For these rules being nothing but an art, to cause the finest incidents to please with decency and probability, it sufficiently appears how necessary they are since by common consent all that comes up to them is approved of and all that varies from them is in some measure condemned. Examples would extremely illustrate this truth if I were not afraid to anger some of our poets by instructing the others at their cost.

The fifth objection is absolutely ridiculous. For the rules of the stage do not at all reject the most notable incidents of any story, but they furnish us with inventions, how so to adjust the circumstances of the action, time, and place as not to go against all probable appearance, and yet not to represent them always as they are in story, but such as they ought to be, to have nothing but what's agreeable in them. 'Tis that, then, that we are to seek, and of which in the following Discourse I shall communicate my thoughts.

OF THE SUBJECT OF DRAMATIC POEMS
(Book 2, Chapter 1)

Supposing here what the poet ought to know of that part of a drama which the Ancients called the Fable, we, the Story or Romance, and I in this place the Subject — I will only say that for subjects merely invented and of which one may as well make a tragedy as a comedy, if they do not take, 'tis perfectly the poet's fault, and a fault without excuse or pretext, which he can never clear himself of; for, being master as well of the matter as of the form, the miscarriage of the play can be attributed to nothing but to his want of conduct in the thing and to the errors of his own imagination. But, as for subjects drawn from story or from the fables of the Ancients, he is more excusable if he misses of success in the representation of them, for he may be many ways constrained; as if a great man command him to preserve certain circumstances, not so fit for the stage, or that he does it himself out of some consideration more important to him than the glory of being a good poet would be. But if he be free of his choice, he may be sure that he shall be blamed if his play does not take, it being certain that art out of an ill story may make an excellent drama; as for example, if there be no plot, the poet must make one; if it be too intricate, he must make it looser and easier, if too open and weak, he must strengthen it by invention, and so for the rest. On the other side, there is no story so rich in itself but an ill poet may so spoil the beauty of it that it will be hardly known to be the same story.

Besides, one is not to think that all fine stories are fit to appear with success upon the stage, for very often the beautifullest part of them depends upon some circumstance which the theater cannot suffer; and it was for this that I advised one who had a mind to undertake the loves of Antiochus and Stratonica to let it alone; for the most considerable incident in it being the cunning of the physician in discovering the prince's passion by causing all the ladies in the court to pass one by one before the prince's bed that so by the emotion of his pulse he might judge which of them it was that caused his disease. I thought it would be very odd to make a play where the hero of it should always be abed, and that it would be hard to change the circumstance so as to preserve the beauty of it, and that besides, the time and place of the scene would be difficult to bring together; for if Antiochus be supposed sick abed in the morning, 'twould be improbable to lay much action upon him all the rest of that day; and to place the scene in a sick man's chamber or at his door would be as unlikely.

'Twas for the same reason that the *Théodore* of Corneille had not all the approbation it deserved; 'tis in itself a most ingenious play, the plot being well carried and full of variety, where all the hints of the true story are made use of to advantage, the changes and turns very judicious and the passions and verse worthy the name of so great a man. But because the whole business turns upon the prostitution of Theodora to the public stews, it would never please; not but that the poet, in that too, has taken care to expose things with great modesty and nicety, but still one is forced to have the idea of that ugly adventure so often in one's imagination, particularly in the narrations of the fourth act, that the spectators cannot but have some disgust at it.

There are a hundred stories like these, and harder yet to manage for the stage; and likewise, on the contrary, there are lucky ones which seem to have happened on purpose, as that of Sophonisba, who is a widow, and married again, loses her kingdom and recovers it, all in one day.

The way, therefore, of choosing a subject is to consider whether it be founded upon one of these three things; either upon noble passions, as *Mariamne* and the *Cid;* or upon an intricate and pleasing plot, as *Cleomedon or The Disguis'd Prince;* or upon some extraordinary spectacle and show, as *Cyminda or The Two Victims;* and if the story will bear more circumstances of this nature or that the poet's imagination can fitly supply the play with them, it will be still the better, provided he observe a just moderation, for though a poem ought not to be without a plot nor without passions or noble spectacles, yet to load a subject with any of them, is a thing to be avoided. Vio-

lent passions too often repeated do, as it were, numb the soul and its sympathy: the multitude of incidents and intrigues distract the mind and confound the memory, and much show takes up more time than can be allowed it, and is hard to bring on well. 'Tis for this reason that some of our poets who had contrived in every act a memorable incident and a moving passion did not find that the success answered their expectation.

I am asked what is the measure of employing those things? I shall answer, 'tis every one's natural judgment; and it may happen that a drama may be so luckily contrived that the preparation of the incidents and the variety of the passions shall correct the defect of the abundance of them, and that the art of the machines shall be so well understood that they may easily be made use of in every act, as I formerly propounded to Cardinal Richelieu, but hitherto they are little in use in our ordinary theaters.

'Tis besides most commonly asked here how far the poet may venture in the alterations of a true story, in order to the fitting of it for the stage. Upon which we find different opinions among both the ancient and modern critics; but my opinion is that he may do it not only in the circumstances but in the principal action itself, provided he make a very good play of it; for as the dramatic poet does not much mind the time, because he is no chronologist, no more does he nor the epic poet much mind the true story, because they are no historians. They take out of the story so much as serves their turn and change the rest, not expecting that anybody should be so ridiculous as to come to the theater to be instructed in the truth of history.

The stage, therefore, does not present things as they have been, but as they ought to be, for the poet must in the subject he takes reform everything that is not accommodated to the rules of his art; as a painter does when he works upon an imperfect model.

'Twas for this reason that the death of Camilla by the hands of her brother Horatius was never liked of upon the stage, though it be a true adventure; and I for my part gave my opinion that to save in some measure the truth of the story and yet not to offend against the decency of the stage, it would have been better that that unfortunate maid, seeing her brother come towards her with his sword drawn, had run upon it of herself, for by that means she would still have died by the hand of Horatius, and yet he might have deserved some compassion, as unfortunate but innocent, and so the story and the stage would have agreed.

In a word, the historian ought to recite matter of fact, and if he judges of it he does more than he ought to do; the epic poet is to magnify all events by great fictions where truth is, as it were, sunk and lost; and the dramatic poet ought to show all things in a state of decency, probability, and pleasingness. 'Tis true that if story is capable of all the ornaments of dramatic poetry, the poet ought to preserve all the true events; but if not, he is well grounded to make any part of it yield to the rules of his art and to the design he has to please.

Many against this do allege the authority of Horace, who says that " he ought in story to follow the common received opinion, or at least to invent things that may be as conformable to it as possible." But I answer that Horace in that place does not treat of the subject of the play, but of the customs and morals that ought to be given the actors [characters], who ought not to be represented different from what they were believed; as it would be to make Cæsar a coward, or Messalina chaste. And this Vossius has well observed in his *Poetic Art,* and I wonder that people should be abused by citations applied quite contrary to the sense of the author; and yet I am not of opinion that a known story yet fresh in the minds of the people can suffer to be considerably changed without great caution; but in such a case I should advise the poet rather to abandon such a subject than to make an ill play of it out of a humor of following truth; or at least to manage it so as not to check directly the received opinion among the vulgar. If we examine well the sense of Aristotle, I believe he will be found to be of this opinion; and as for the Ancient poets, they have always taken that liberty, the same story having hardly ever been treated the same way by different poets. As for example, the adventures of Polydorus are very different in Euripides and Vergil. Sophocles kills Hemon and Antigone, but Euripides, who has made the same story

in two plays, marries them together in one, contrary to what he himself had done before in the other called *The Phœnician Ladies.* The same Sophocles in *Œdipus* makes Jocasta strangle herself, and Euripides makes her live till the combat of her sons Eteocles and Polynices, and then kill herself upon their dead bodies. *Orestes* and *Electra* are very different in many circumstances, though both works of the same poet. In a word, the four [three] tragic poets of the Greeks whose works we have, are all different in the disposition of the same stories, and I believe that they were the cause of that grand disorder and confusion there is in story and chronology in those old times, because that they having changed both the times and events for their own ends, have influenced some historians who thought to pick out of them the truth of story, and so made all things uncertain. Anybody that will read the *Electra* of Euripides, that of Sophocles, and the *Choephorœ* of Æschylus, will easily see that they made no difficulty of contradicting one another and themselves.

As for the different kinds of subjects, letting alone those ordinary divisions of Aristotle and his commentators, I here propose three sorts of subjects.

The first consists of incidents, intrigues, and new events, when almost from act to act there is some sudden change upon the stage which alters all the face of affairs, when almost all the actors have different designs; and the means they take to make them succeed come to cross one another and produce new and unforeseen accidents, all which gives a marvelous satisfaction to the spectators, it being a continual diversion, accompanied with an agreeable expectation of what the event will be.

The second sort of subjects are of those raised out of passions; when out of a small fund the poet does ingeniously draw great sentiments and noble passions to entertain the auditory; and when out of incidents that seem natural to his subject, he takes occasion to transport his actors into extraordinary and violent sentiments, by which the spectators are ravished and their soul continually moved with some new impression.

The last sort of subjects are the mixed or compound of incidents and passions, when by unexpected events, but noble ones, the actors break out into different passions; and that infinitely delights the auditory, to see at the same time surprising accidents and noble and moving sentiments, to which they cannot but yield with pleasure.

Now, 'tis certain that in all these three sorts of subjects the poet may succeed, provided the disposition of his play be ingenious; but yet I have observed some difference, according to which they take more or less.

Subjects full of plot and intrigue are extreme agreeable at first, but being once known, they do not the second time please us so well, because they want the graces of novelty, which made them charm us at first, all our delight consisting in being surprised, which we cannot be twice.

The subjects full of passions last longer and affect us more, because the soul which received the impression of them does not keep them so long nor so strongly as our memory does the events of things; nay, it often happens that they please us more at second seeing, because that the first time we are employed about the event and disposition of the play, and by consequent do less enter into the sentiments of the actors; but having once no need of applying our thoughts to the story, we busy them about the things that are said, and so receive more impressions of grief or fear.

But it is out of doubt that the mixed or compound are the most excellent sort, for in them the incidents grow more pleasing by the passions which do as it were uphold them, and the passions seem to be renewed and spring afresh, by the variety of the unthought-of incidents; so that they are both lasting and require a great time to make them lose their graces.

We are not to forget here (and I think it one of the best observations that I have made upon this subject) that if the subject is not conformable to the customs and manners as well as opinions of the spectators, it will never take, what pains soever the poet himself take, and whatsoever ornaments he employs to set his play off. For all dramatic poems must be different according to the people before whom they are represented; and from thence often proceeds that the success is different though the play be still the same. Thus the Athenians delighted

to see upon their theater the cruelties of kings and the misfortunes befalling them, the calamities of illustrious and noble families, and the rebellion of the whole nation for an ill action of the prince, because the state in which they lived being popular, they loved to be persuaded that monarchy was always tyrannical, hoping thereby to discourage the noble men of their own commonwealth from the attempt of seizing the sovereignty, out of fear of being exposed to the fury of a commonalty who would think it just to murder them. Whereas, quite contrary among us, the respect and love which we have for our princes cannot endure that we should entertain the public with such spectacles of horror. We are not willing to believe that kings are wicked, nor that their subjects, though with some appearance of ill-usage, ought to rebel against their power, or touch their persons, no, not in effigy. And I do not believe that upon our stage a poet could cause a tyrant to be murdered, with any applause, except he had very cautiously laid the thing. As for example, that the tyrant were an usurper and the right heir should appear and be owned by the people, who should take that occasion to revenge the injuries they had suffered from the tyrant. But usurpation alone against the will of the people, would not justify without horror the death of the sovereign by the hands of his rebellious subjects. We have seen the trial of it in a play called *Timoleon*, whom no consideration of state or common good, no love nor generosity towards his country, could hinder from being considered as the murderer of his brother and his prince; and for my part, I esteem that author who avoided to have Tarquin killed upon the stage after the violence he had offered to Lucretia. The cruelty of Alboin inspired horror into the whole French Court, though otherwise it were a tragedy full of noble incidents and lofty langauage.

We have had upon our stage the *Esther* of Mr. Du Ryer, adorned with great events, fortified with strong passions, and composed in the whole with great art; but the success was much unluckier at Paris than at Rouen; and when the players at their return to Paris told us the good fortune they had had at Rouen, everybody wondered at it without being able to guess the cause; but for my part I think that Rouen, being a town of great trade, is full of a great number of Jews, some known and some concealed, and that by that reason they making up a good part of the audience, took more delight in a piece which seemed entirely Jewish, by the conformity it had to their manners and customs.

We may say the same thing of comedies, for the Greeks and Romans, with whom the debauches of young people with courtesans was but a laughing matter, took pleasure to see their intrigues represented, and to hear the discourses of those public women, with the tricks of those ministers of their pleasures countenanced by the laws. They were also delighted to see old covetous men overreached and cheated of their money by the circumvention of their slaves in favor of their young masters. They were sensible to all these things because they were subject to them one time or another. But amongst us all this would be ill received, for as Christian modesty does not permit persons of quality to approve of those examples of vice, so neither do the rules by which we govern our families all of those flights of our servants, nor do we need to defend ourselves against them. 'Tis for the same reason that we see in the French Court tragedies take a great deal better than comedies, and that on the contrary, the people are more affected with the latter and particularly with the farces and buffooneries of the stage; for in this Kingdom the persons of good quality and education have generous thoughts and designs, to which they are carried either by the motives of virtue or ambition, so that their life has a great conformity with the characters of tragedy, but the people, meanly born and dirtily bred, have low sentiments and are thereby disposed to approve of the meanness and filthiness represented in farces, as being the image of those things which they both use to say and do; and this ought to be taken notice of, not only in the principal part of the poem, but in all its parts and particularly in passions, as we shall say more amply in a chapter about them; for, if there be any act or scene that has not that conformity of manners to the spectators, you will suddenly see the applause cease and in its place a discontent succeed, though they

themselves do not know the cause of it. For the stage and eloquence are alike in this, that when even it triumphs and overcomes, it is in abomination with the audience who thereupon are apt to conclude with themselves, *That 'tis better to embrace virtue through the hazard of persecution, than to follow vice even with hopes of impunity.*

'Tis thus principally that the stage ought to be instructive to the public by the knowledge of things represented; and I have always observed that it is not agreeable to the audience that a man who swerves from the way of virtue should be set right, and repent, by the strength of precepts and sentences: we rather desire it should be by some adventure that presses him, and forces him to take up reasonable and virtuous sentiments. We should hardly endure that Herod should recall his sentence against Mariamne upon a remonstrance of one of the seven wise men of Greece: but we are pleased to see that after the death of the Queen, his love becomes his tormentor; and, having opened his eyes, drives him into so sincere a repentance, that he is ready to sacrifice his life to the regret he has for his crime.

As for the other way of teaching morality, it depends much on the ingeniousness of the poet, when he strengthens his theatrical action with divers pithy and bold truths, which being imperceptibly worked into his play, are as it were the nerves and strength of it. For, in a word, that which I condemn in common didactics, is their style and manner of expression, not the things themselves, since those great truths which are as it were the foundation of the conduct of human actions, I am so far from banishing them off the stage, that quite contrary, I think them very necessary and ornamental, which to attain, I give these following observations.

First, these general maxims must be so fastened to the subject, and linked by many circumstances with the persons acting, that the actor may seem to think more of that concern of his he is about, than of saying fine things; that is, to speak in terms of rhetoric, he must reduce the thesis to the hypothesis, and of universal propositions make particular applications; for by this means the poet avoids the suspicion of aiming to instruct pedantically, since his actors do not leave their business which they are about. For example, I would not have an actor spend many words to prove that Virtue is always persecuted; but he may say to the party concerned:

Do you think to have better measure than virtue has always had, and can you expect to be privileged from persecution more than Socrates or Cato?

And so continue a little speaking still to the party present, and upon the subject in hand, by which means these discourses seem a little to keep off from being too general precepts, and so disgust the less.

Secondly, in all these occasions the poet must use figurative speech, either by interrogation, irony, or others that his fancy shall suggest; for these figures, by not circumstancing minutely the general propositions, make them more florid, and so by ornaments free them from the didactic character. As, for example, if there be a design of advising a young woman to obey her parents: instead of preaching downright obedience to her, I think an irony would do better. As thus:

That's a fine way indeed, for a virtuous young lady to attain the reputation of a good daughter, to be carried away by her own passions, and neglect not only the censure of the best sort of people, but break through the fences of duty and honor!

My third observation is, that when any of these great maxims are to be proposed bluntly and in plain words, it be done in as few words as may be; by that means they do not cool the stage, but add something to the variety of it; but there must be care taken that this do not happen in the midst of a violent passion; for besides that in those cases men do not naturally speak sentences, the actor cannot then appear with that moderation which those reflections require. Seneca is very guilty of this fault in all his tragedies, where most commonly in the heat of passion all his fine commonplaces are bestowed upon the audience.

We have nevertheless some examples of didactic propositions made in direct terms and at length not without some success in Corneille, which to attain as well as he, requires the same ingenuity and art. The expressions must be strong, and seem to have been said only for that particular subject to which they are applied, and that requires a particular genius and much study to accomplish.

I have observed besides, that common truths, though in a didactic style, yet do very well upon the stage in the mouth of a rogue or a cheat, when his character is known; for the spectator is delighted to see him cunningly use all the maxims and discourses of a good man to intents and purposes quite contrary, so that by that means 'tis all figurative, and moves the attention of the audience.

One may likewise successfully enough burlesque all these common truths, but that can be performed nowhere but in comedy, where by that means they forsake their natural state, and are disguised under a new appearance, which causes both variety and ornament. But tragedy in its own nature is too grave to admit of anything so low and buffoon as this would be; neither do I remember to have met with anything of that kind in any serious tragedy; I say serious tragedy, because that in satirical tragedy there was admitted a mixture of heroic actions and low buffooneries; and therefore this disguising of serious precepts might have room among the rest in them.

PIERRE CORNEILLE

Pierre Corneille was born at Rouen in 1606. He came of a middle-class family of lawyers and petty officials. He attended the Jesuit College at Rouen, where he received a sound training in the classics; he later studied law and received a degree in 1624, and practiced at least part of the time, both as lawyer and in an official capacity in the department of waters and forests and the marine. During his early years he was a student of literature, and at the age of twenty-three he wrote his first play, *Mélite*. This was successfully produced by Mondory in Paris. It was followed in quick succession by five comedies, a tragi-comedy, and a tragedy, all of which appeared and were produced between 1629 and 1636. Although he went to Paris occasionally, Corneille resided in Rouen until 1662. In 1636, or early in 1637, he produced *Le Cid,* which marked not only the beginning of the poet's success, but the veritable beginning of modern French tragedy. Aside from its incalculable influence on the drama of the time and of succeeding times, it precipitated the famous *Cid* Controversy. The success of the play and the honors heaped upon Corneille brought the poet into disfavor with Richelieu, who sought to discredit the author of the "irregular" *Cid.* But the public would be influenced by no Academic attacks, and the poet's future was assured. And yet Corneille was troubled and discouraged by the many attacks on his work, and we find him years afterward attempting to justify himself and reconcile his theory with his practice. In his next play, *Horace* (1640), he replied to his critics by writing a "regular" play, which is little below *Le Cid* in power. Then followed *Cinna* (1640), *Polyeucte* (1642 or 1643), and *La Mort de Pompée* (1643–44). After this play, there is a noticeable diminution in the poet's power, followed by discouragement and what practically amounted to poverty, together with a certain measure of neglect. His last play, *Suréna,* was produced in 1674. His later years were once more troubled with a quarrel, this time over his *Sophonisbe* (1663), in which the Abbé d'Aubignac and Donneau de Visé were his adversaries. In 1647 Corneille, after two unsuccessful attempts to secure election,

was admitted to the Academy. He died at Paris in 1684.

The theoretical works of Molière and Racine are only relatively important; those of Corneille would entitle him to fame had he written no plays. Corneille's various prefaces, his *Examens,* and three *Discours,* are indicative of the trend of classicism in the literature of the seventeenth century. Together with the similar writings of Chapelain, Boileau, and d'Aubignac, they established the pseudo-Aristotelian and Horatian precepts in France. That these commentators on and idolators of Aristotle understood the *Poetics* imperfectly, makes little difference. Jules Lemaître, in his *Corneille et la Poétique d'Aristote* says, "Corneille's critical work taken as a whole is nothing but an ingenious, and in turn triumphant and despairing commentary on Aristotle's *Poetics;* or, rather a lengthy duel with Aristotle." Lemaître very wisely goes on to say that Corneille boasts in places of having dared do what no one before him had done, and elsewhere prides himself on having observed the Rules more rigorously than any one else. But out of the great mass of Corneille's controversial writing there emerges the basic ideal of the century: to please, but please according to the Rules.

Corneille was influenced by the Italian Renaissance critics — Robortello, Minturno, Castelvetro, and Scaliger — and by the Dutch scholar, Daniel Heinsius, whose *De Tragœdiae Constitutione,* an Aristotelian treatise, appeared in 1611 at Leyden. Heinsius, together with his fellow-countryman Vossius [or Voss], who published a *De Arte Poetica* in 1609, exercised considerable influence throughout Europe.

FIRST DISCOURSE [1]

ON THE USES AND ELEMENTS OF DRAMATIC POETRY

[Premier Discours. De l'Utilité et des Parties du Poème dramatique]

(1660)

Although, according to Aristotle, the sole end of dramatic poetry is to please

1 Translated, with occasional omissions, especially for this collection by Beatrice Stewart MacClintock. Never before translated.— Ed.

the audience, and although the majority of these poems have pleased, nonetheless I maintain that many of them have failed to achieve their end. "It must not be claimed," says this philosopher, "that dramatic poetry gives us every sort of pleasure, but only that which is fitting," and continues to say that in order to find that pleasure which it fitting to the audience, the poet must follow the precepts of the art and give that pleasure according to them. It is evident that there are precepts because there is an art, but it is not evident just what the precepts are. We agree on the name but not on the thing; on the words but not on their meaning. The poet must observe unity of action, time and place. No one denies this, but it is a matter of no small difficulty to determine what unity of action is and to realize the extent and limit of the allotted unity of time and place. The poet must treat his subject according to "the probable" and "the necessary." This is what Aristotle says, and all his commentators repeat the words which appear to them so clear and intelligible that not one of them has deigned any more than Aristotle himself to tell us what the "probable" and the "necessary" are. And many of them have so neglected the latter requisite, which in all cases save one,— in connection with the discussion on comedy,— is always mentioned in company with the former, that a false maxim has been established. "The subject of a tragedy must be probable"; thus applying only half of the philosopher's precept to the matter of subject and the manner in which it is to be treated. A subject of tragedy must not be merely probable. Aristotle himself cites as an example *The Flower* of Agatho wherein the names of people and things were purely fictitious, as in comedy. The great subjects which appeal to our emotions and in which our inclinations are set in conflict with the laws of duty and humanity, ought always to extend beyond the limits of the probable.

Such plays would indeed find no audience capable of believing, unless they were aided by the authority of history, which is empirically persuasive, or by common knowledge, which supplies an audience of those whose attitudes are already formed. It is not "probable" that Medea should kill her children; that Clytemnestra should murder her husband; or Orestes stab his mother, but historical legend states these facts, and the representation of these great crimes excites no incredulity in the minds of the audience.

It is neither true nor "probable" that Andromeda, at the mercy of a sea-monster, was rescued from her perilous situation by a flying knight with wings on his feet; but this is a story which has been handed down, and which was accepted by the ancients; and, since it has been transmitted even to us, no one would think of taking offense when he sees the story represented on the stage. In giving these instances I do not mean to imply that the poet may invent at haphazard: that which truth or common belief takes for granted would be rejected were there no other basis for a play than mere versimilitude or public opinion. That is why our wise man says "Subjects come from fortune, or chance,"— which causes things to happen,—"and not from art," which imagines them. She is the mistress of happenings, and the choice she allows us to make among those happenings which she presents to us contains a mystic warning not to take advantage of her, nor to utilize for dramatic purposes any happenings which are not to her liking. And so "the ancient tragedies are concerned with the stories of very few families, because very few families were fit subjects for tragedies." Succeeding generations have, however, afforded us a sufficient number of other family tragedies to enable us to go beyond the limits of ancient times and not follow in the footsteps of the Greeks, but this does not mean that we should overstep their precepts. We should, if possible, accommodate ourselves to them and make them applicable to our practice. We have in our plays left out the chorus, and this has forced us to substitute more episodes than the Greeks used. This is an instance of going beyond the precepts. We should never go against them, even though in practice we do go beyond.

We should know what these precepts are, but unfortunately, Aristotle, and Horace after him, wrote in so obscure a fashion that they needed interpreters; but also, unfortunately, those who have endeavored to act in that capacity have, for the most part, considered the text from a philosophical and dramatic viewpoint. Since these men were better versed in scholarship and metaphysics than in a knowledge of the theater, their commentaries are likely rather to render us more learned but not one jot more enlightened as to the actual meaning. With fifty years of practical experience of the theater I shall make bold to set forth in a straightforward manner some of my ideas on the subject without attempting any definite evidence and with no intention of trying to persuade any one to reject his theories for mine.

At the opening of this *Discourse,* when I said that " the sole end of the drama is to please the audience," I did not mean to enforce this maxim arbitrarily upon those who strive to ennoble dramatic art by considering it as a means to supply moral purpose as well as pleasure. A dispute on this question would be useless because it is impossible to please according to the rules without at the same time supplying a moral purpose, [" utilité"] of some sort. It is a fact that from one end to the other of Aristotle's *Poetics* not once does he make use of the word; on the contrary, he says that the end of drama is the pleasure we experience in observing the actions of men imitated. He prefers that part of the drama which has to do with the subject rather than with the " manners " portrayed, because the former contained what was most pleasing, like the " agnitions " and the " peripeties." Also, in his definition of tragedy, he includes the elements of pleasure in the subject which is at the bottom of it. And, finally, he preferred tragedy to the epic because it included material decoration and music,— both powerful agents of pleasure — because it was the shortest and least diffuse of literary forms, and the pleasure he derived made it therefore the more perfect. But let us remember that we learned from Horace that we cannot please the greatest number unless we include in our work a moral purpose. Grave and serious people, old men and lovers of virtue, will be bored if they find nothing of profit for them. *Centuriae seniorum,* etc. Thus, if the moral purpose does not enter into it unless it is decked out in pleasant style, it is none the less needful and much wiser, as I have already said, to endeavor to find just what place it should assume, than to start a useless dispute regarding the value of plays of this kind. It appears that there are four kinds of plays in which there is some sort of moral intent.

The first sort of play is that which contains maxims and moral instructions, scattered throughout. These should be sparingly used and only on the rarest occasions inserted in general discourses, and then in small doses, especially when they are put into the mouth of an impassioned character, or into the mouth of another with whom he is speaking, for, under the circumstances, he would not have the patience to listen or peace of mind to conceive and speak them. Instinct counsels, for instance, where a man of importance who is trained and sure of himself, is being consulted by a king, and then speeches of this sort may be found more frequently and be of greater extent, but it is always well to reduce them from the general to the specific. I vastly prefer having my character say, " Love gives you great cause for uneasiness," than " Love gives those who are in its power great cause for uneasiness." Be it understood, I do not wish to do away entirely with this latter method of pronouncing moral and political maxims.

Every one of my poems would present a sorry appearance if I eliminated that which I mixed into it; but again one must not accentuate them too much without applying the general to the particular, otherwise it is an ordinary situation which never fails to tire the listener, because it slackens the action. However well this exhibition of morality succeeds, we must always suspect it of being one of the vain ornaments which Horace orders us to curtail.

The second use of dramatic poetry is in the simple description of the vices and virtues, which never misses its effect if well conceived, and if the marks of it are so clear that one cannot confuse the two nor take vice for virtue.

The one, though unhappy, is loved, and the other is hated, though triumphant. The ancients were often satisfied with this description without troubling to have good actions rewarded and bad ones punished. Clytemnestra and her lover kill Agamemnon with impunity. Medea does the same with her own children and Atreus with those of her brother, Thyestes, which are served to him to eat.

It is true that, on carefully considering these actions which they chose for the climax of their tragedies, they who were punished were criminals in crimes greater than their own. Thyestes had abused the wife of his brother, but the vengeance which he exacts has something more horrible in it than the first crime. Jason was a traitor to abandon Medea, to whom he owed all; but for her to kill his children under his eyes is too strong a punishment. Clytemnestra complained of the concubines which Agamemnon brought from Troy, but he had not attempted to take her life as she attempts to take his; and these masters of art have found the crime of his son, Orestes, who kills her to avenge his father, still greater than the first, since they gave him avenging Furies to torment him and gave none to his mother who peaceably enjoys with her Ægisthus the kingdom of the husband whom she assassinated.

Our theater rarely allows such subjects. The *Thyestes* of Seneca did not have great success. *Medea* was more popular at the same time. To understand it rightly, the perfidy of Jason and the violence of the king of Corinth, makes her appear so unjustly oppressed that the listener takes her side very easily and considers her vengeance as a just act which she commits herself against those who oppress her. It is this interest which one has in the virtuous which forces one to come to this other manner of ending the dramatic poem, by the punishment of wicked actions and the reward of good ones which is not an art precept but a custom which we have adopted, which one can abandon only at one's own risk. It has existed since the time of Aristotle, and it may be that it did not please this philosopher to excess, since he says,—" It has had a vogue only by the imbecility of the judgment of the spectators, and those who practice it are gratifying the tastes of the populace and write according to the desires of their audience. Truly it is certain that we could not see an honest man in our theater without wishing him prosperity and regretting his misfortune. That is why when he.(the honest man) remains overcome by them, we leave with sorrow and carry away a kind of indignation against the author and the actor, but when the plot fills our expectations and virtue is rewarded, we leave with complete joy, and carry with us entire satisfaction, both of the work and those who represent it. The success of virtue against misfortunes and perils excites us to embrace it, and the fatal success of crime or injustice is capable of enlarging the natural of it, through the fear of like misfortune." It is in this that the third use of the theater consists, just as the fourth consists in the purgation of the passions through the means of pity and fear. But since this use is peculiar to tragedy I shall explain myself on that subject in the second volume, where I shall treat of tragedy in particular, and proceed now to the examination of the parts which Aristotle attributes to the dramatic poem.

I say the dramatic poem in general, as in treating this material, he speaks only of tragedy, since all that he says of it is applicable to comedy also, and that the difference in these two kinds of poetry consists only in the dignity of the characters and in the actions which they imitate and not in the manner of the imitation nor in the things which serve in this imitation. The poem is composed of two kinds of parts.

The first are called parts of quantity or extension, and Aristotle names four of them,— the prologue, the episode, the exodus and the chorus. The others can be called integral parts; they meet each other in each of these first to form the whole. This philosopher finds six of them,— the subject, the manners, the sentiments, the diction, the music and the stage decoration. Of these six only the technique of the subjects depends rightly on the art of poetry. The others need subsidiary arts. The manners on moral, the sentiments on rhetoric, the diction on grammar, and the two other parts have each their art of which the poet need not be instructed because he can have it supplied by others. That is why Aristotle does not treat of them. But since it is necessary that he execute everything concerning the first four himself, the knowledge of the arts on which they depend is absolutely necessary unless he has received from nature sufficiently strong and deep judgment to supply that lack. The requirements of the subject are different for tragedy and comedy. I shall speak only on that which concerns the latter, which Aristotle defines simply an imitation of low and knavish persons. I cannot refrain from saying that this definition does not satisfy me, and since many scholars hold that his treatise on Poetry has not come to us in its entirety I want to believe that in that which time has stolen of it there was a more complete one. Dramatic Poetry, according to him, is an imitation of actions, and he stops here at the condition of the person, without saying what must be the actions. However, this definition is in agreement with the custom of his time when only people of very mediocre condition were made to speak in comedy. But it (the definition) is not entirely just for our time, in which even kings may come into comedy when their actions are not above it. When one puts on the scene a simple love intrigue between kings, and when they run no risk either of their life or of their State, I do not think that even though the characters are illustrious the action is sufficiently important to aspire to the dignity of tragedy. The dignity of tragedy needs some great State interest or passion nobler and more virile than love, such as ambition or vengeance, which leads us to expect greater misfortune than the loss of a mistress. It is fit to mix love in it because it always has much attraction and can serve as a basis to those other interests and other passions of which I speak. But it must content itself with second rank in the poem and leave the first to the other.

This maxim will at first seem new. It is, however, a practice of the ancients, with whom we see no tragedy in which there is only a love-interest to unravel. Quite the contrary: they often banished it completely from their poems, and those who wish to consider mine will acknowledge that, following their example, I have never let it take the first place, and that in Le Cid, which is without doubt the play most full of love which I have made, the duty of birth and the care of honor assume a more important place than the two lovers inspire.

I shall go further, even though there are big State interests, and a royal character stills his passion through the care he must have of his glory, as in Don Sanche, if one does not meet the risk of death, loss of States, or banishments, I do not think that it has a right to a higher name than comedy, but to answer at all to

the dignity of which it (comedy) represents the actions, I have thought to call it heroic to distinguish it from ordinary comedies. This is without example amongst the ancients, but is it also without example amongst them that put kings on the stage without one of those great hazards. We must not bind ourselves slavishly to the imitation of them so that we dare not try something of our own when this does not go contrary to the rules of art, were it only to deserve that praise Horace gave the poets of his time: *Nec minimum meruere decus,* etc., and not to come under the shameful judgment: *O imitatores, servum pe₁ cus!* "What will serve now as an example," says Tacitus, "has been once without example, and what we do without example may serve as such one day."

Comedy, then, differs from tragedy in that the latter requires an illustrious, extraordinary, serious subject, while the former stops at a common, playful subject. The latter demands great dangers for its hero; the former contents itself with the worry and displeasures of those to whom it gives the first rank amongst the actors. Both have this in common, that the action must be complete and finished, that is, in the event which finishes it the spectator must be so clearly informed of the feelings of all who have had a part in it that he leaves with his mind quiet and doubting of nothing. Cinna conspires against Augustus. His conspiracy is discovered. Augustus has him arrested. If the poem stopped there the action would be incomplete, because the listener would leave in the uncertainty of what this Emperor would have commanded of the ungrateful favorite. Ptolemy fears that Cæsar, who comes to Egypt, will favor his sister, with whom he is in love, and forces him to give her her part of the kingdom which her father left her in his will. To attract favor on his side by great sacrifice, he slays Pompey. This is not enough. We must see how Cæsar receives this great sacrifice. He arrives, becomes angry and threatens Ptolemy, and wants to force him to slay the inciters of this attack and illustrious death. The latter, surprised at the unexpected welcome, resolves to anticipate Cæsar, and conspires against him to avoid, by his loss, the misfortune with which he sees himself threatened. That is still not enough. We must know what will result from this conspiracy. Cæsar is warned and Ptolemy, dying in a combat with his ministers, leaves Cleopatra in peaceful possession of the kingdom of which she demanded half. Cæsar is out of danger. The listener has nothing more to ask, and leaves satisfied because the action is complete. For comedy, Aristotle demands as the only precept that it may have as ending, the enemies becoming friends. Which must be understood in a more general sense than what the words seem to carry and to extend it to a reconciliation, as when one sees his son returning into the good favor of a father who has been angry with him for his debauchery, which was the usual end to ancient comedies; or two lovers separated by some trick done them, or by some controlling power, are reunited by the unraveling of that trick or by the consent of those who placed the obstacle there, as nearly always happens in our comedy, which very rarely has other endings than marriages. We must be careful, however, that this agreement does not come by a simple change of will but by an event which furnishes the occasion for it. Otherwise there would be no great art to the " dénouement " of a play, if, after having upheld it during two acts, on the authority of a father who does not approve the love of his son or daughter, he should suddenly consent to it in the fifth for the sole reason that it is the fifth and that the author would not dare to make six. It needs a considerable motive which forces him to it as say, his daughter's lover saved his life in some meeting or when, on the point of being assassinated by his enemies or that by some un-hoped for incident he should be recognized as being of high rank and greater fortune than he appeared.

Since it is necessary that the action be complete, one must also not add anything further, since when the effect has been attained, the listener desires nothing more and is bored by all the rest. So it is that the expressions of joy which two lovers show on being reunited after many obstacles, must be very short. I know not what beauty the arguments between Menelaus and Teucer on the burial of Ajax, whom Sophocles has pass

away in the fourth act, could have had for the Athenians, but I do know that in our time the quarrel between Ajax and Ulysses for the weapons of Achilles after the latter's death wearied many ears, although it (the subject) came from a good hand. I have not been able to see how one can bear the fifth act of *Mélite* and of *La Veuve*. One only sees the first actors reunited and they have no place there but to be made acquainted with the authors of the treachery and the violence which has separated them. Nevertheless, they could have been informed of them already, had I wished It, and they seemed to be on the stage only to serve as witnesses to those of secondary importance, which makes all this end slackened in which they have no part. I dare not attribute the success of these two comedies to ignorance of the rules — which was very general at that time — inasmuch as those rules, well or poorly observed, must make their good or bad effect on those who, even without knowing them, abandon themselves to the current of natural feeling. But I can only acknowledge that that old habit which was observed at the time, of not seeing anything better ordered, was the cause of the lack of indignation against these defects and the newness of an agreeable kind of comedy which up to that time had not appeared on the scene, has caused the admiration, all the parts of the whole pleasing at sight even though it did not have all the just proportions.

Comedy and tragedy resemble each other again in that their subjects " must have the requisite size, that is, that it must not be so little that it escapes from sight at an atom, nor so vast that it confuses the memory of the listener and bewilders his imagination." In such manner does Aristotle explain the conditions of a poem, and he adds that " to be of the proper size it must have a beginning, a middle, and an end." These terms are so general that they seem to signify nothing, but, to understand them well, they exclude the momentary actions which have not these three parts. A poem must have, then, to be of the right size, a beginning, a middle and an end. Cinna conspires against Augustus and tells of his conspiracy to Emilia. This is the beginning. Maximus warns Augustus of it.

This is the middle. Augustus forgives him. This is the end. Therefore, in the comedies of this first volume I have nearly always had two lovers on good terms, then I had them quarrel as a result of some treachery. I reunited them by the unraveling of this treachery which had separated them. . . . Enough on the subject of comedy and the requirements necessary to it. Truth to nature is one of which I shall speak later. Besides, the developments of it must always be happy — which is not a requirement of tragedy, where we have the choice of making a change from happiness to unhappiness, and *vice versa*. This needs no remark. I come to the second part of the poem, which is *Manners*. Aristotle prescribes four conditions: that they be good, suitable, similar, and equal. These are terms which he says so little about that he leaves great occasion to doubt his meaning.

I cannot imagine how one can conceive " good " to mean " virtuous." Most poems, ancient as well as modern, would remain in a pitiful state if one cut out all in the way of bad or vicious character, or characters stained by some weakness which does not comport with virtue. Horace took great care generally to describe the " manners " of every age, and attributes to them more faults than virtues, and when he advises us to describe Medea as proud and indomitable, Ixion as treacherous, Achilles carried away by anger to the point of holding that laws are not made for him and declaring that he takes right by might, Horace allows us very few virtues. One must therefore find a goodness compatible with this kind of manners; and if I may express my conjectures on what Aristotle requires by that, I believe it is the brilliant and elevated character of a criminal or virtuous habit. Just as much as is proper and suitable to the person that one presents. Cleopatra in *Rodogune* is very wicked. There is no parasite which repels her so long as she can be kept on her throne, which she prefers to everything, so great is her attachment to power; but all her crimes are accompanied by a loftiness of soul which has something so high in it that, while one despises her actions, one admires the source from which they spring. I dare say the same of *Le Men-*

teur. Lying is doubtless a vicious habit, but the chief character in this play utters his lies with such presence of mind and quickness that this imperfection acquires grace and makes the listeners acknowledge that to lie in such a manner is a vice of which imbeciles are incapable. As a third example, those who wish to consider the way in which Horace describes the anger of Achilles will not be far from my idea. It has for foundation a passage of Aristotle's which follows closely enough the one I am trying to explain. " Poetry," says he, " is an imitation of people better than in actual life, and, as painters often make flattering portraits which are more beautiful than the original and still keep the resemblance, in such a manner the poets representing choleric or slovenly men must idealize these qualities which they give them, so that from them a beautiful example of equity and stoicism can be drawn. It is thus that Homer made Achilles good." These last words should be noticed to show that Homer gave to Achilles' transports of anger that goodness necessary to manners which I think consists in that loftiness of character, of which Robortello speaks in the following manner,—" *Unum quodque genus per se supremos quosdam habet decoris gradus, et absolutissimam recipit formam, non tamen degenerans a sua natura, et effigie pristina.*" This text of Aristotle's which I mentioned may present some difficulty in that it says that the manners of choleric or slovenly men must be depicted with such a degree of excellence that one sees in them a high example of equity and austerity. There is a likeness between austerity and anger, and that is what Horace attributes to Achilles in this verse: *Iracundus inexorabilis acer.* But there is no likeness between equity and slovenliness. I cannot see what it has to do in his character. It is that which causes me to doubt if the Greek word ῥᾳθυμά has been given the meaning of Aristotle's by the Latin interpreter which I have followed. Pacius says, *Desides;* Victorius, *Inertes;* Heinsius, *Segnes;* and the word *Fainéants* of which I have made use to put it into our language, answers these three versions well enough, but Castelvetro expresses it in his by *mansueti,* or *debonnair,* or *full of mildness;* and not only does this word mean the opposite of anger, but also it would agree better with what Aristotle calls ἐπιεικεία, of which he requires a good example from us. These three interpreters translate the Greek word by that of *equity* or *integrity*, which would agree better with the *soave* [*mild*] of the Italian, than with their *segnes, desides, inertes,* provided one understands by that only a natural kindness which slowly angers, but I would still prefer that of *good humor,* of which the other makes use to express it in his language, and I think that to keep its value in our language one could change it to *compliance,* or *equitable facility* — to approve, to excuse and to support everything that happens. It is not that I wish to be judged among such great men, but I cannot deny the Italian version of this passage seems to me to have something more correct than any of the three Latin versions. Among this diversity of interpretations everyone is free to choose, since one has the right even to put them all aside, when a new one appears. Another idea comes to me concerning what Aristotle means by this goodness that he imposes on them as a first condition. That is, that they must be• as virtuous as possible, so that we do not exhibit the vicious and criminal on the stage if the subject which we are treating does not require them. He himself expresses this thought when wishing to mark an example of mistake against this rule, he uses that of Menelaus in Euripedes' *Orestes,* whose fault is not in being unjust but in being unjust without necessity.

.   .   .   .   .

In the second place, morals must be suitable. This requirement is easier to understand than the first. The poet must consider the age, dignity, birth, occupation and country of those whom he paints; he must know what one owes to one's country, to one's parents, to one's friends, to one's king; what the office of a magistrate or an army general, so that he may verify and then show what he wants his public to love, and eliminate those whom he wants it to hate, because it is an infallible maxim that to achieve success one must get the audience on the side of the important characters. It is well to remark also that what Horace says of the morals of each age is not a

rule that one can dispose of without scruple. He makes young men prodigal and old men avaricious. The contrary often happens each day without causing surprise, but one must not act like the other even though he sometimes has passions and habits which would be more suitable to him. It is only natural for a young man to be in love; not so, an old man. This does not prevent an old man from falling in love. We have enough proof before us, but he would be considered insane if he wanted to court like a youth, and if he tried to win by his personal charm. He may hope that he will be listened to, but this hope must be founded on his wealth or his qualities, but not on his person, and his pretentions cannot be reasonable if he does not think to have to do with the soul interested sufficiently to put aside everything for the attraction of riches or the ambition of rank. The quality of "equalness" which Aristotle asks of morals refers particularly to the people which history or fable teach us to know and which we must always depict such as we find them. That is what Horace means by this verse, *Sit Medea,* etc. He who should depict Ulysses as a great warrior or Achilles as a great orator or Medea as a mild and humble woman would commit himself to public ridicule. Therefore, these two qualities between which some interpreters have great pains in finding the difference, but which Aristotle finds without pointing it out, will agree easily as long as one separates them and uses the word "seemly" to designate persons who have never existed except in the soul of the poet, reserving the other who are known through history or through fable as I have just said. There remains to speak of equality, which forces us to keep in our character the manners which we gave them in the beginning: *Servetur,* etc. Inequality can enter into it all the same, not only when we bring persons of a light and uncertain spirit, but also when in keeping the equality inside, we show inequality on the exterior, according to the occasion. Such is Chimène in the matter of her love. She still strongly loves Rodrigue in her heart, but this love acts differently in the presence of the King and differently in the presence of Rodrigue, and that is what Aristotle calls "manners," unequally equal. One difficulty presents itself which must be cleared up as to what Aristotle means when he says, "that tragedy can be made without morals and that most of those of the moderns of his time have none." The meaning of this passage is quite difficult to understand, seeing that, according to him, it is by morals that a man is a wicked man or a good man, witty or stupid, timid or bold, constant or irresolute, good or bad politically, and that it is impossible to put any on the stage who is not good or wicked and that he have not any of those other qualities. To make these two sentiments agree which seem so opposed to each other, I notice that this philosopher goes on to say that " if a poet has done some fine moral narrations and very sententious discourses, he has not by that done anything yet which concerns tragedy." This has made me consider that " manners " are not only the foundation of action, but also of reasoning. A man of condition thinks and acts as such; a wicked man acts and thinks as such, and both the one and the other depict divers moral maxims according to his habit. It is, therefore, these maxims of conduct that tragedy can do without, not the conduct itself, since it is the essence of action, and that action is the soul of tragedy, where one must speak only in and for the action of the tragedy. Therefore, to explain this passage of Aristotle's by the other, we can say that when he speaks of a tragedy without " manners " he means a tragedy in which the actors simply announce their feelings or base them only on reasonings drawn from fact as Cleopatra in the second act of *Rodogune,* and not on maxims of morality or politics, as Rodogune in the first act. I must repeat again: to create a theatrical poem in which none of the actors are either good or bad, prudent or imprudent, is entirely impossible. After " manners " come sentiments, by which the actor makes known what he wishes or does not wish, and in which he can content himself with a simple acknowledgment of what he proposes to do, without strengthening it with moral reasoning, as I have just said. This part requires rhetoric to depict the passions and troubles of the soul, to consult, deliberate, exaggerate or extenuate; but there is this difference, between the dramatic poet and the orator, that the latter can exhibit his art and make it extraordinary with full freedom, and the other must hide with care, because it is never he who speaks, and those whom he has speak are not orators. To complete this *Discourse* I need only speak of the parts, of quantity, which are,— the prologue, the episode, the exodus and the chorus. The prologue is that which is recited before the first song of the chorus. The episode is that which is recited between the songs of the chorus and the exodus, that which is recited after the last song of the chorus. That is all Aristotle tells us of it; he gives us an idea of the position of the parts and their order, in representation, rather than the part of the action which they contain. Therefore, to apply them to our use, the prologue is our first act, the episode constitutes the three following, and the exodus the last. I reduce this prologue to our first act following the intention of Aristotle and to supplement in part what he has not told us or what the years have robbed from his books. I say that it must contain the seed of all that is going to happen, as much for the principal action as for the episode, so that no actors come into the following act who are not known by this first, or at least named by someone who shall have been brought into it. This maxim is new and rather strict; I have not always kept it, but I judge that it helps a great deal to create a veritable unity of action by the binding of all those which come in the poem. The ancients often have left it particularly in the *Agnitions,* for which they nearly always use people who appeared by chance in the fifth act, and would have appeared in the tenth if the piece had had ten acts. Such is that old man of Corinth in the *Œdipus* of Sophocles and Seneca where he seems to fall from a cloud by a miracle, at a time when the actors would not know what to do next nor what pose to take if he came an hour later. I have brought him in only in the fifth, just as they did, but I have prepared his coming from the first in making Œdipus say that he expects him. In like manner in *La Veuve,* though Célidan does not appear until the third act, he is brought in by Alcidon, who is of the first. It is not the same with the Moors in *Le Cid,* for which there is no preparation whatsoever in the first act. The litigant of Poitiers in *Le Menteur* had the same fault, but I found the means of correcting it in this edition where the dénouement is prepared by Philiste and not by the litigant. I desire, then, that the first act contain the basis of all the acts and shut the door to all other extraneous matter. Though this first act often does not give all the necessary information for the entire understanding of the subject and all the actors do not appear in it it is sufficient if they are spoken of, which they must be in this act. That which I say must only be understood of the characters who act in the piece through some important personal interest or carry important news to produce a notable effect. A servant who acts only by his master's order, a father who shows himself only to consent to or prevent a marriage of his children, a wife who consoles or advises her husband; in a word, all those people without action do not have to be introduced in the first act. This first act was called the prologue in Aristotle's time and ordinarily one made it the opening of the subject, to instruct the listener in all that happened before the beginning of the action, and in all that he would have to know in order to understand what he was going to see. The method of giving this instruction has changed with the times. Euripides used it quite boldly in bringing in now a god in a machine through whom the listeners received this knowledge, now one of the principal characters who instructed them himself, as in *Iphigenia* and *Helena,* where his two heroines first tell all their history to the listener without having any actor to whom to address her speech. I do not mean to say that when an actor speaks he cannot inform the listener about many things, but he must do so through the passion which moves him, and not through a simple narration. The monologue of Emilia which opens the play of *Cinna* acquaints the public with the fact that Augustus killed her father, and that to avenge his death she forces her lover to plot against him; but it is by the unrest and fear which the danger to which he exposes

Cinna arouses in her mind that we have the knowledge of it. The poet especially must remember that when an actor is alone in the theater it is taken for granted that he is thinking to himself, and speaks but to let the listener know what he thinks. Therefore it would be an unforgivable error if another actor should by this means learn his secret. One excuses that in a passion which is so violent that it is forced to burst out, even though one has no one to listen to; I should not want to condemn it in another, but I would have difficulty in bearing it myself. Our century has also invented a sort of prologue for plays of the *Deus ex Machinâ* type, but they do not bear upon the subject and are only a clever eulogy of the prince before whom these plays are to be enacted. In *Andromède,* Melpomene borrows rays from the sun in order to light up her theater for the king for whom she has prepared a magnificent pageant. The prologue of *La Toison d'or* referring to His Majesty's wedding and the peace with Spain has something still more brilliant. These prologues must be full of invention and I believe to do them justice only imaginary gods of antiquity may play a part in them. These, however, also talk about matters relating to our time in poetic fiction, which is a great help to our theater. The episodes according to Aristotle at this point are three middle acts, but as he applies this name elsewhere to actions which have nothing to do with the principal one and which are ornaments of no value whatsoever, I shall say that, although these three acts are called episodes, it does not mean that they are only made up of episodes. Augustus' consultation in the second act of *Cinna,* the remorse of this ungrateful one, that which he tells Emilia, Maximus' effort to persuade the object of his hidden love to flee with him, are only episodes, but Maximus' advice to the emperor through Euphorbus, the prince's uncertainties and Livia's advice belong to the principal action, and in *Héraclius* those three acts have more principal action than episode. These episodes are of two kinds and can be made up of the principal actors' special acts. These acts, however, are not needed in the principal action, or else they are made up of the secondary lovers' interests. These people are commonly called episodic characters. Both of these must start in the first act and be part of the principal action, that is, be of some use, and especially the episodic characters must be so closely intermingled with the principal ones that but one intrigue embroils them all. Aristotle condemns detached episodes and says, " that poor poets write them through ignorance and good ones in favor of the actors to furnish them with work." The Infante of *Le Cid* belongs to this number and she can be condemned or exonerated by Aristotle's words according to the rank that I shall be given among our moderns. I shall not mention the exodus, which is nothing more than our fifth act. I think I have explained the principal use of it when I say that the action of the Dramatic Poem must be complete. I shall only add this word, that one must if one can, reserve all the climax and even defer it until the end. The more one defers it the more the mind will remain in expec-

tancy and the desire to know to which side it will turn, creates the impatience which causes it to be received with more pleasure. This does not happen when it begins with this act. The listeners who know too much have no more curiosity, and their attention wanes during all the rest, which tells nothing new. The opposite is seen in *Mariamne* whose death, though coming in the interval which separates the fourth act from the fifth, has not prevented the displeasure of Herod which occupies all the latter to please extraordinarily, but I would not advise every one to depend on this example. Miracles do not occur every day, and though the author has well deserved the great success on account of the great mental effort he made to depict the despair of the monarch, perhaps the excellency of the author which upheld this character contributed much to this. That is what came to me in thinking of the uses and elements of the Dramatic Poem.

.　　.　　.　　.　　.

JEAN-BAPTISTE POQUELIN MOLIÈRE

Jean-Baptiste Poquelin, known as Molière, was born in Paris in 1622. He came of a good middle-class family, his father being an upholsterer, and one of the king's *valets de chambre tapissiers*. About 1636 the boy was sent to the best "college" of the time, the Collège de Clermont, where his first instruction was received from the Jesuits. After a four years' course he went to Orléans to study law, and there he may have received a degree. His movements are little known, though it is fairly certain that for a while he worked in his father's shop in Paris, while there is evidence of his having definitely given up in 1643 what intention he may have had of pursuing his father's calling. In that year he joined ten actors and actresses and helped to found a company called *L'Illustre Théâtre*. Not long after, he took the stage name of Molière. The strolling players were not very successful in their attempts to win the public, and after three years, what was left of the original troupe decided to leave

Paris and tour the provinces. The twelve years which the young actor spent in this way were full of valuable experiences. When he returned to Paris he was the head of a company of highly trained actors, an artist himself, and a good man of business. The first of his plays, with the exception of a few purely imitative attempts, was *L'Etourdi*, which was produced at Lyon in 1653. The second play, *Le Dépit amoureux*, was produced at Béziers in 1656. Two years later, after having secured the protection of the Duc d'Anjou, Molière brought his troupe to Paris and presented Corneille's *Nicomède* before the King and Queen in the Louvre. A little interlude of Molière's, now lost, followed the tragedy; this so pleased the King that he allowed the company to remain in Paris and play on alternate nights in the Théâtre du Petit-Bourbon. From this time on, Molière was firmly established in the favor of the King and the Court, and put forth his dramatic masterpieces in quick succession. In the year 1673, during a production of *Le Malade imaginaire,* in which he was himself playing, he was stricken and taken home, where he died soon after.

Compared with his work as a practicing playwright, Molière's critical contributions are not of prime importance. In his neglect of the Rules, and in his principle that to please is the best criterion of success, he seems distinctly modern. He has no creed but this, and in the few placcs (in his plays and prefaces) where he states it, he never tries to impose his theories, or want of them, upon others. His practice came first, and the theory after.

SCHOOL FOR WIVES CRITICIZED [1]

[*La Critique de l'Ecole des femmes*]

(1663)

(Scene vi.)

. . . . . .

Dorante.— You are, then, Marquis, one of those grand gentlemen who will not allow the pit to have common sense, and who would be vexed to join in their laugh, though it were at the best thing conceivable? . . . Speaking generally, I would place considerable reliance on the applause of the pit, because, amongst those who go there, many are capable of judging the piece according to rule, whilst others judge it as they ought, allowing themselves to be guided by circumstances, having neither a blind prejudice, nor an affected complaisance, nor a ridiculous refinement. . . .

(Scene vii.)

. . . . . .

Uranie.— . . . Let us not apply to ourselves the points of general censure; let us profit by the lesson, if possible, without assuming that we are spoken against. All the ridiculous delineations which are drawn on the stage should be looked on by every one without annoyance. They are public mirrors, in which we must never pretend to see ourselves. To bruit it about that we are offended at being hit, is to state openly that we are at fault. . . .

Dorante.— . . . Indeed, I think that it is much easier to soar with grand sentiments, to brave fortune in verse, to arraign destiny and reproach the Gods, than to broach ridicule in a fit manner, and to make the faults of all mankind

seem pleasant on the stage. When you paint heroes you can do as you like. These are fancy portraits, in which we do not look for a resemblance; you have only to follow your soaring imagination, which often neglects the true in order to attain the marvelous. But when you paint men, you must paint after nature. We expect resemblance in these portraits; you have done nothing, if you do not make us recognize the people of your day. In a word, in serious pieces, it suffices to escape blame, to speak good sense, and to write well. But this is not enough in comedy. You must be merry; and it is a difficult undertaking to make gentlefolk laugh. . . .

Lysidas.— Those who are versed in Horace and Aristotle, Madame, see at once that this comedy sins against all the rules of Art.

Uranie.— I confess that I am not familiar with those gentlemen, and that I do not know the rules of Art.

Dorante.— You are a most amusing set with your rules of Art, with which you embarrass the ignorant, and deafen us perpetually. To hear you talk, one would suppose that those rules of Art were the greatest mysteries in the world; and yet they are but a few simple observations which good sense has made upon that which may impair the pleasure taken in that kind of poems; and the same good sense which in former days made these observations, makes them every day easily, without resorting to Horace and Aristotle. I should like to know whether the great rule of all rules is not to please; and whether a play which attains this has not followed a good method? Can the whole

---

1 Re-printed extracts from Henri Van Laun's *Dramatic Works of J. B. Poquelin Molière,* 6 vols. (Edinburgh, 1878).— Ed.

public be mistaken in these matters, and cannot every one judge what pleases him? . . . in short, if pieces according to rule do not please, and those do please which are not according to rule, then the rules must, if necessary, have been badly made. So let us laugh at the sophistry with which they would trammel public taste, and let us judge a comedy only by the effect which it produces upon ourselves. Let us give ourselves up honestly to whatever stirs us deeply, and never hunt for arguments to mar our pleasure.

Uranie.— For my part, when I see a play, I look only whether the points strike me; and when I am well entertained, I do not ask whether I have been wrong, or whether the rules of Aristotle would forbid me to laugh.

Dorante.— It is just as if a man were to taste a capital sauce, and wished to know whether it were good according to the recipe in a cookery-book.

Uranie.— Very true; and I wonder at the critical refinements of certain people about things in which we should think for ourselves.

Dorante.— You are right, Madame, in thinking all these mysterious critical refinements very odd. For really, if they are to subsist, we are reduced to discrediting ourselves. Our very senses must be slaves in everything; and, even in eating and drinking, we must no longer dare find anything good, without permission from the committee of taste.

Lysidas.— So, Monsieur, your only reason is that *The School for Wives* [*L'Ecole des femmes*] has pleased you; you care not whether it be according to rule, provided —

Dorante.— Gently, Monsieur Lysidas; I do not grant you that. I certainly say that the great art is to please; and that, as this comedy has pleased those for whom it was written, I think that is enough, and that we need not care about anything else. But at the same time, I maintain that it does not sin against any of the rules to which you allude. I have read them, thank Heaven! as well as other men, and I could easily prove that perhaps we have not on the stage a more regular play than this. . . .

Lysidas.— What, sir! when the protasis, the epitasis, the peripetia —

Dorante.— Nay, Monsieur Lysidas, you overwhelm us with your fine words. Pray, do not seem so learned. Humanize your discourse a little, and speak intelligibly. Do you fancy a Greek word gives more weight to your arguments? And do you not think that it would look as well to say, "the exposition of the subject," as the "protasis"; "the progress of the plot," as the "epitasis"; "the crowning incident," as the "peripetia"?

Lysidas.— These are terms of art that we are allowed to make use of. But as these words offend your ears, I shall explain myself in another way; and I ask you to give me a plain answer to three or four things which I have to say. Can a piece be endured which sins against the very description of a play? For, after all, the name of a dramatic poem comes from a Greek word which signifies to act, in order to show that the nature of the form consists in action. But, in this comedy, there are no actions. . . .

PREFACE TO TARTUFE [2]

[*Préface* (to) *Tartufe*]

(1669)

.   .   .   .   .   .

. . . I am well aware that, in reply, those gentlemen have endeavored to insinuate that the stage is not fit for the discussion of these subjects; but, by their leave, I ask them upon what they

[2] Re-printed extracts from Van Laun's translation (see "On Molière," ante).— Ed.

base this beautiful axiom. It is a theory which they only advance, and which they do not prove by any means; and it would doubtless not be difficult to show them that with the ancients, comedy derived its origin from religion, and was a part of their mysteries; that the Spaniards, our neighbors, never celebrate a feast in which a comedy is not mixed up; and that, even amongst us it owes its birth to the cares of a brotherhood to which the Hôtel de Bourgogne still belongs; that it was a place given to them to represent in it the most important mysteries of our faith; that comedies printed in Gothic characters, under the name of a doctor of the Sorbonne, may still be seen there; and, without carrying the matter so far, that, in our days, sacred pieces of M. de Corneille have been performed, which were the admiration of the whole of France. If it be the aim of comedy to correct man's vices, then I do not see for what reason there should be a priv-ileged class. Such a one is, in the State, decidedly more dangerous in its consequences than any other, and we have seen that the stage possesses a great virtue as a corrective medium. The most beautiful passages in a serious moral are most frequently less powerful than those of a satire; and nothing admonishes the majority of people better than the portrayal of their faults. To expose vices to the ridicule of all the world is a severe blow to them. Reprehensions are easily suffered, but not so ridicule. People do not mind being wicked; but they object to being made ridiculous. . . .

· · · · · ·

JEAN RACINE

Jean Racine was born at Ferté-Milon, Le Valois, in 1639, of middle-class parents, both of whom died within three years of his birth. The child was brought up by his grandparents. The grandfather dying when the boy was ten years old, he was left alone with his grandmother, whom he regarded thenceforth as his mother. His preliminary education was received at the College de Beauvais, where he spent the years between 1650 or 1651 and 1655, and then entered the famous school of Port-Royal, where he remained for three years. In all probability he was a good student, and when he left he possessed a wide acquaintance with and love for the Greek and Latin authors, especially the Greek tragedians. On leaving Port-Royal, he went to the College d'Harcourt to study philosophy and logic. Not finding these to his taste, he left the College and became a sort of secretary to the Duc de Luynes. One of his earliest works, an ode written on the occasion of the marriage of Louis XIV in 1660, was highly praised by the venerable Chapelain. Racine wished to write — he had also written two plays besides the ode — but his friends at Port-Royal feared that his interest in literature would prove an evil influence upon him, and persuaded him to go south and put himself under the care of his uncle, a canon. During the year or more which he spent at Uzes, he applied himself to the study of theology, although his notes on Pindar and Homer prove that his interest in his beloved authors was not dead. In fact, his first play, *La Thébaïde*, was written at this period. Even though he did more or less formally enter the Church, his subsequent actions show that he soon ceased active work in connection with it. *La Thébaïde* was accepted by Molière and produced at the *Palais-Royal* in 1664. He left Uzes in 1662 and returned to Paris. Here he made the acquaintance of Boileau, and produced his plays. After the production of *Phèdre* in 1677, for reasons which are somewhat obscure, he abandoned playwriting, and lived on the various pensions and salaries of which he was the recipient, married, and produced no work until he was commissioned by Madame de Maintenon to write a play for the girls of Saint-Cyr. He produced *Esther,* in 1689, and followed it in 1691, by *Athalie,* which was performed at Saint-Cyr and Versailles. He died in 1699.

Racine, like Molière, is important rather as a practicing dramatist than as a critic. His remarks on his own plays are full of interest, however, as they explain how and why he wrote as he did; they are, like Molière's prefaces, the theory after the performance. Racine was from first to last a classical writer;

his passion was for clearness and compactness, and it is little wonder that his critical theories are founded on Aristotle and Horace. His very first manifesto, the *Préface* to *La Thébaïde* (1664), contains a protest against the double plot. The *Première Préface* to *Alexandre le grand* (1666) is a defense of his "natural" treatment of character; likewise the *Première Préface* to *Andromaque* (1668). The various prefaces to *Britannicus* (1670), *Bajazet* (1672), *Mithridate* (1673), *Phèdre* (1677), and two or three others, are, taken as a whole, pleas for regularity, order, and reason.

PREFACE TO LA THÉBAÏDE [1]

[*Préface* (to) *La Thébaïde*]

(1664)

The reader will surely be a little more indulgent toward this play than toward those that follow, because I was very young when I wrote it. Certain verses I had previously written happened to fall into the hands of some people of culture, who urged me to write a tragedy, and proposed the subject of *La Thébaïde*. This subject had already been treated by Rotrou, in his *Antigone;* but he killed off the two brothers at the beginning of the third act. The remainder of the drama was in a way the beginning of another tragedy, introducing entirely new interests. It combined within itself two distinct plots, one of which was the plot of Euripides' *Phœnician Women,* the other that of Sophocles' *Antigone.* I saw that the double plot tended to spoil his [Rotrou's] play, which was, however, full of beautiful things. I constructed my play on practically the same plot as the *Phœnician Women* of Euripides. As to the *Thebaid* which is found among Seneca's works, I am inclined to agree with Heinsius and maintain not only that it was not written by Seneca, but that it is

1 Translated, for the first time into English by the editor.— Ed.

the work of some rhetorical declaimer who had no idea what a tragedy was.

The catastrophe of my play is possibly a little too sanguinary; indeed, there is scarcely a character who is not killed off at the end. But then, this is the story of the Thebaid, the most tragic of antiquity.

Love which, ordinarily, assumed so important a rôle in tragedy, I have practically. neglected; I doubt whether I should give it a more important place were I to re-write the play. It would be necessary to have one of the brothers in love, or else both; but what chance had I to give them any other interest but that famous hatred, which consumed them both? If I could not have either of the brothers in love, there remained for me only to place the love-interest in characters of secondary importance; and this is what I have done. But even then, the passion of love seems strangely out of place and ineffective. In short, I am of the opinion that lovers' tenderness and jealousies can have no legitimate place amid all the incest, parricide, and other horrors which go to make up the story of Œdipus and his fated family.

FIRST PREFACE TO ANDROMAQUE [2]

[*Première Préface* (to) *Andromaque*]

(1668)

. . . However that may be, the public has treated me so well that I am not bothered by the disappointment of two or three individuals who would have us re-cast all the heroes of antiquity and

2 Extracts, here translated for the first time into English, by the editor.— Ed.

make them paragons of perfection. I think their intention of putting only such impeccable examples of humanity on the stage admirable, but I beg them to remember that it is not for me to change the laws of the drama. Horace tells us to describe Achilles as ferocious, inexorable, violent — as he actually was. And Aristotle, far from asking us to portray perfect heroes, demands on the contrary that tragic characters — whose misfortunes bring about the tragic catastrophe — should be neither wholly good nor wholly bad. He does not want them to be extremely good, because the punishment of a good man would excite indignation rather than pity in the audience; nor that they be excessively bad, because there can exist no pity for a scoundrel. They must therefore stand midway between the two extremes, be virtuous and yet capable of folly, and fall into misfortune through some fault which allows us to pity without detesting them.

FIRST PREFACE TO BRITANNICUS [3]

[Première Préface (to) Britannicus]

(1670)

... Personally, I have always believed that since tragedy was the imitation of a complete action — wherein several persons participate — that action is not complete until the audience knows in what situation the characters are finally left. Sophocles always informs us of this: in the *Antigone* he writes as many lines to show Hæmon's fury and Creon's punishment after the death of the princess, as I have written in Agrippina's imprecations, the retreat of Junia, the punishment of Narcissa and the despair of Nero, after the death of Britannicus.

How could these difficult judges be pleased? It would be an easy task, had I wished to violate commonsense a little. I should have but to abandon the natural for the extraordinary. Instead of a simple plot, with very little material — as befits an action supposed to take place within the compass of a single day and which, proceeding by degrees toward the end, is sustained solely by the interest, sentiments, and passions of the characters — I could just as well have crowded the very same story with a number of incidents which could not actually have happened within a whole month, with any number of stage-tricks, as astonishing as they would be false to nature, with a number of declamatory passages wherein the actors would utter the exact opposite of what they ought to utter. I might, for instance, have represented some hero as drunk, wishing to make his mistress hate him, out of sheer caprice; or a mouthing Lacedæmonian, a conqueror scattering maxims upon love; a woman giving lessons in pride to a warrior — in any of these ways I might have satisfied the gentlemen. But what would that small group of intelligent people whom I must please, have said? How would I have dared appear, so to speak, before those great men of antiquity whom I have taken for my models? Because, when I make use of their thoughts, I think of them actually as spectators. When we take our inspiration from them we should always ask ourselves, "What would Homer and Vergil say, if they were to read these lines? What would Sophocles say if he saw this scene?" However all this may be, I have never tried to prevent any one's criticizing my works adversely; that would be impossible: *Quid de te alii loquantur ipsi videant*, says Cicero, *sed loquentur tamen:* "Others must be careful how they speak of you; but be sure that they will speak of you, in some way or other."

I only beg the reader's forgiveness for this little preface, which I wrote merely to explain and justify my tragedy. What more natural than to defend oneself when one believes oneself unjustly attacked? I think that Terence wrote his prologue solely to justify and defend himself against the critics who spoke in disparagement of the old poet of evil intentions, *malevoli veteris poetae*, and who came to raise their voices against him, up to the very moment his comedies were performed.

... *occœpta est agi:*
Exclamat, etc.

---

[3] Extracts, here translated, by the editor, for the first time into English.— Ed.

Hardly has the curtain risen, but there he is, crying out, etc. (Prologue to the "*Eunuchus*" of Terence.)

There is one objection which might have, but has not, been urged against me. Still, what escaped the spectators may become evident to the reader: I make Junia join the Vestals. Now, according to Aulus Gellius the Vestals received no one under six years of age, nor over ten. But here the people take Junia under their protection, and I thought that in consideration of her rank, her virtue, and her misfortune, an exception might be made regarding her age, as other exceptions had been made in the cases of so many men who deserved to be made consuls.

PREFACE TO BÉRÉNICE [4]
[*Préface* (to) *Bérénice*]
(1674)

... I have for some time cherished the desire to try whether I could write a tragedy with the extremely simple plot so much admired by the ancients, for simplicity is one of the first precepts which they have left us. "Whatever you write," says Horace, "it must be simple, and it must be one." The ancients admired the *Ajax* of Sophocles, which is concerned wholly with the story of Ajax killing himself with sorrow over the refusal to give him Achilles' arms. They admired the *Philoctetes,* the subject of which is merely the coming of Ulysses for the arrows of Hercules. The *Œdipus* itself, though full of incidents, is less crowded than the simplest tragedy of our times. And finally, we see those who favored Terence justly placing him above all other comic poets, for the elegance of his style and his careful observation of the manners of his day, but confessing none the less that Plautus had a distinct advantage over him, namely, in the simplicity of the majority of his plots. It was doubtless this marvelous simplicity that caused the ancients to praise him so highly. How much simpler must Menander have been, since Terence was obliged to take two of that poet's comedies to make one of his own!

Nor must one assume that this rule was based entirely upon caprice; no, nothing but what is true to life can appeal to us in tragedy. But what sort of truth to life is there when within the space of one day a multitude of things happen that would in actual life occupy many weeks? There are some who believe that this simplicity is a confession of the author's poverty of invention. They are not aware that on the contrary, an author's invention is most severely put to the test in making something out of nothing, and that the introduction of a host of incidents has always been the refuge of poets who felt their own want of genius, and power to interest their auditors through five acts of simple plot, sustained by the force of passion, beauty of ideas, and elegance of expression. I am far from believing that my play contains all these elements, but on the other hand, I do not think that the audience blamed me too much for having written a tragedy so honored with their tears, the thirtieth performance of which was as well attended as the first.

Not that certain people have not censured me for that very simplicity I strove so diligently to attain: they believed that a tragedy so denuded of intrigue could not be according to the rules of dramatic art. I wished to know whether the tragedy had bored them, and learned that they all admitted that it had not, but had moved them, and that they would willingly witness it again. What more could they demand? I beg them to think well enough of themselves not to believe that a play which stirs them and gives them pleasure, *can* be absolutely at variance with the rules. The principal rule is to please and to stir; all others are simply means to arrive at that end. The rules are long and complicated, and I advise those who criticize the play on the grounds

4 Extracts, here translated,. by the editor, for the first time into English.—Ed.

just mentioned not to bother about them: they have more important business to attend to. Let them leave to us the trouble of interpreting Aristotle's theory of poetry, and reserve for themselves the pleasure of weeping and being moved, and allow me to tell them what a musician said to King Philip of Macedon, when the latter maintained that a certain song was not written according to the rules: "Heaven keep you, Sire, from being so unfortunate as to know such things better than I do!"

PREFACE TO PHAEDRA [5]
[*Préface* (to) *Phèdre*]
(1677)

Here is another tragedy of which the subject is taken from Euripides. Although I have followed a slightly different road from that author's for the conduct of the action, I have not scrupled to enrich my play with all that seemed to me most striking in his. While I owe only the single idea of the character of Phaedra to him, I could say that I owe to him that which I could reasonably show on the stage. I am not surprised that this character had so great a success in the time of Euripides, and that it has also succeeded so well in our century, since it has all the qualities which Aristotle demanded in the heroes of a tragedy, and which are proper to excite pity and terror. Indeed, Phaedra is neither entirely guilty, nor entirely innocent; she is involved, by her fate and the wrath of the gods, in an unlawful passion, of which she is the first to feel horror; she makes every effort to overcome it; she prefers to let herself die rather than to confess it to anyone; and when she is forced to discover it, she speaks of it with a confusion that makes plain that her crime is rather a punishment of the gods than a movement of her will.

I have even taken care to render her a little less odious than she is in the tragedies of the ancients, where she resolves of herself to accuse Hippolytus. I thought that the calumny was too base and evil to put into the mouth of a princess who elsewhere displays such noble and virtuous sentiments. This baseness appeared to me more suitable to a nurse,

who could have more servile inclinations, and who nevertheless undertakes this false accusation only to save the life and honor of her mistress. Phaedra consents to it only because she is in such agitation that she is beside herself; and she comes a moment after in the action to justify innocence and declare the truth.

Hippolytus is accused, in Euripides and Seneca, of having actually violated his stepmother: *vim corpus tulit*. But he is here accused of only having had the intention. I wished to spare Theseus a confusion which would have rendered him less agreeable to the audience.

With regard to the character of Hippolytus, I have noticed among the ancients that Euripides is reproached for having represented him as a philosopher exempt of all imperfection: which made the death of the young prince cause much more indignation than pity. I thought I should give him some weakness which would make him a little guilty towards his father, without however taking away from him any of the greatness of soul with which he spares Phaedra's honor and lets himself be oppressed without accusing her. I call weakness the passion which he feels, against his will, for Aricia, who is the daughter and the sister of mortal enemies of his father.

This Aricia is not a character of my invention. Virgil says that Hippolytus married her, and had a son by her, after Æsculapius had brought him back to life. And I have also read in some authors that Hippolytus had wedded and brought to Italy a young Athenian of high birth, called Aricia, and who had given her name to a small Italian town.

I mention these authorities because I have very scrupulously set myself to fol-

5 From *Jean Racine: Five Plays* (New York, 1960), translated by Kenneth Muir. Copyright © 1960 by Kenneth Muir. Reprinted by permission of Hill and Wang, Inc. —Ed.

low the fable. I have even followed the story of Theseus as given in Plutarch.

It is in this historian that I have found that what gave occasion to believe that Theseus descended into the underworld to rescue Prosperpine was a journey that the prince had made in Epirus towards the source of the Acheron, at the home of a king whose wife Peirithous wishes to bear off, and who took Theseus prisoner after slaying Peirithous. So I have tried to keep the verisimilitude of the story, without losing anything of the ornaments of the fable, which is an abundant storehouse of poetical imagery; and the rumor of Theseus' death, based on this fabulous voyage, gives an opportunity to Phaedra to make a declaration of love which becomes one of the principal causes of her misfortune, and which she would never have dared to make so long as she believed that her husband was alive.

For the rest, I dare not yet assert that this play is indeed the best of my tragedies. I leave it to readers and to time to decide its true value. What I can assert is that I have not made one where virtue is put in a more favorable light than in this one; the least faults are severely punished; the very thought of a crime is regarded with as much horror as the crime itself; the weaknesses of love are shown as true weaknesses; the passions are displayed only to show all the disorder of which they are the cause; and vice is everywhere depicted in colors which make the deformity recognized and hated. That is properly the end which every man who works for the public should propose to himself; and it is that which the first tragic poets kept in sight above everything. Their theatre was a school where virtue was not less well taught than in the schools of the philosophers. So Aristotle was willing to give rules for the dramatic poem; and Socrates, the wisest of philosophers, did not disdain to set his hand to the tragedies of Euripides. It could be wished that our works were as solid and as full of useful instructions as those of these poets. That would perhaps be a means of reconciling tragedy with numerous people, celebrated for their piety and for their doctrine, who have condemned it in recent times, and who would doubtless judge it more favorably if the authors thought as much about instructing their audiences as about diverting them, and if they followed in this respect the true function of tragedy.

NICOLAS BOILEAU-DESPRÉAUX

Nicolas Boileau-Despréaux, the son of Gilles Boileau, was born at Paris in 1636. His mother died when he was two years old, and the lad seems to have been somewhat neglected. From his early youth he is said to have had but one passion, "the hatred of dull books." He was educated at the College de Beauvais, and later went to study theology at the Sorbonne. Giving this up, he studied law and was admitted to the bar in 1656, but the law disgusted him and the next year, on the death of his father who left him a comfortable income, he directed his attention exclusively to study and writing. Among his earliest works are a few indifferent poems. The first of his *Satires*, in which his true genious found expression, dates from 1660. Though it was "imitated" from Juvenal, it is distinctly of the poet's own time and spirit. This was followed by others, of which twelve ultimately appeared. In these he attacked many authors of the preceding generations —among them Chapelain, Scudéry, and Quinault—and went far toward destroying the earlier traditions. He was, on the other hand, friendly toward Racine and Molière. Another of his effective attacks contributed to the downfall of the elaborate romance of the Mlle. de Scudéry type, and was called *Dialogue des héros de roman*. Though it was written in 1664, it was not published until 1713. The *Satires* appeared in the first authorized edition in 1666, and the *Epitres* from 1669 on. These attracted considerable attention and brought him into Court favor. Louis XIV granted him a generous pension and in 1677 made him Historiographer to the King. In the 1674 edition of his *Œuvres diverses* he published for the first time his celebrated poems, *L'Art poétique* and mock-heroic poem *Le Lutrin.* In the same year he also published his translation of Longinus *On the Sublime,* the *Réflexions* on which appeared in 1693. He was admitted to the Academy in 1684. His last years were spent partly at Auteuil and partly at Paris. They were not very productive. He died in 1711.

The *Art poétique* was primarily the poet's justification of his attacks in the *Satires.* In it he tried to bring to the bar of reason the various "bad" poems which he had ridiculed. Though at first he had ridiculed, he was now to criticize. His Rules, his precepts, his generalities are but obiter dicta, conclusions rather than statements. But the work as a whole exercised incalculable influence until the so-called Romantic revolt in the early years of the nineteenth century.

THE ART OF POETRY [1]
[*Art poétique*]
(1674)

There's not a monster bred beneath the sky,
But, well-disposed by art, may please the eye;.
A curious workman, by his skill divine,
From an ill object makes a good design.
Thus, to delight us, Tragedy, in tears
For Œdipus, provokes our hopes and fears;
For parricide Orestes asks relief,
And to increase our pleasure, causes grief.
    You then that in this noble art would rise,
Come and in lofty verse dispute the prize.
Would you upon the stage acquire renown,
And for your judges summon all the town?
Would you your works forever should remain,
And after ages past be sought again?
In all you write observe with care and art
To move the passions and incline the heart.
If in a labored act, the pleasing rage
Cannot our hopes and fears by turns engage,
Nor in our mind a feeling pity raise,
In vain with learned scenes you fill your plays;
Your cold discourse can never move the mind
Or a stern critic, naturally unkind,
Who, justly tired with your pedantic flight,
Or falls asleep or censures all you write.
The secret is, attention first to gain,
To move our minds and then to entertain,
That, from the very opening of the scenes,
The first may show us what the author means.

    I'm tired to see an actor on the stage
That knows not whether he's to laugh or rage;
Who, an intrigue unraveling in vain,
Instead of pleasing keeps my mind in pain.
I'd rather much the nauseous dunce should say
Downright, "My name is Hector in the play,"
Than with a mass of miracles, ill-joined,
Confound my ears, and not instruct my mind.
The subject's never soon enough expressed.

    Your place of action must be fixed, and rest.
A Spanish poet may with good event
In one day's space whole ages represent;
There oft the hero of the wandering stage
Begins a child, and ends the play of age.
But we, that are by reason's rule confined,
Will that with art the poem be designed,
That unity of action, time, and place,

[1] Re-printed from Sir William Soames' edition of Boileau's *Art of Poetry* (London, 1683) — With omissions.— Ed.

Keep the stage full, and all our labors
grace.

Write not what cannot be with ease
conceived;
Some truths may be too strong to be be-
lieved.
A foolish wonder cannot entertain;
My mind's not moved if your discourse
be vain.
You may relate what would offend the
eye;
Seeing indeed would better satisfy,
But there are objects which a curious
art
Hides from the eyes, yet offers to the
heart.

The mind is most agreeably surprised,
When a well-woven subject, long dis-
guised,
You on a sudden artfully unfold,
And give the whole another face and
mold.

At first the Tragedy was void of art,
A song, where each man danced and
sung his part,
And of god Bacchus roaring out the
praise,
Sought a good vintage for their jolly
days;
Then wine and joy were seen in each
man's eyes,
And a fat goat was the best singer's
prize.
Thespis was first, who, all besmeared
with lee,
Began this pleasure for posterity,
And with his carted actors and a song
Amused the people as he passed along.
Next Æschylus the different persons
placed,
And with a better mask his players
graced,
Upon a theater his verse expressed,
And showed his hero with a buskin
dressed.
Then Sophocles, the genius of his age,
Increased the pomp and beauty of the
stage,
Fngaged the Chorus song in every part,
And polished rugged verse by rules of
art;
He in the Greek did those perfections
gain
Which the weak Latin never could at-
tain.

Our pious fathers, in their priest-rid
age,
As impious and profane abhorred the
stage.
A troop of silly pilgrims, as 'tis said,
Foolishly zealous, scandalously played,
Instead of heroes and of love's com-
plaints,
The angels, God, the Virgin, and the
saints.
At last right reason did his laws reveal,
And showed the folly of their ill-placed
zeal,
Silenced those nonconformists of the age,
And raised the lawful heroes of the
stage;
Only the Athenian mask was laid aside,
And Chorus by the music was supplied.

Ingenious love, inventive in new arts,
Mingled in plays, and quickly touched
our hearts;
This passion never could resistance find,
But knows the shortest passage to the
mind.
Paint, then, I'm pleased my hero be in
love,
But let him not like a tame shepherd
move;
Let not Achilles be like Thyrsis seen,
Or for a Cyrus show an Artamene;
That, struggling oft, his passions we
may find
The frailty, not the virtue of his mind.

Of romance heroes shun the low de-
sign,
Yet to great hearts some human frailties
join.
Achilles must with Homer's heart en-
gage —
For an affront I'm pleased to see him
rage;
Those little failings in your hero's heart
Show that of man and nature he has
part.
To leave known rules you cannot be al-
lowed;
Make Agamemnon covetous and proud,
Æneas in religious rites austere;
Keep to each man his proper character.
Of countries and of times the humors
know,
From different climates different cus-
toms grow;
And strive to shun their fault, who
vainly dress

An antique hero like a modern ass,
Who make old Romans like our English
move,
Show Cato sparkish, or make Brutus
love.[2]

In a romance those errors are excused;
There 'tis enough that, reading, we're
amused,
Rules too severe would there be useless
found;
But the strict scene must have a juster
bound,
Exact decorum we must always find.

If then you form some hero in your
mind,
Be sure your image with itself agree,
For what he first appears he still must
be.

Affected wits will naturally incline
To paint their figures by their own de-
sign;
Your bully poets bully heroes write;
Chapman in Bussy D'Ambois took de-
light,
And thought perfection was to huff and
fight.[3]

Wise nature by variety does please;
Clothe differing passions in a differing
dress;
Bold anger in rough haughty words ap-
pears;
Sorrow is humble and dissolves in tears.

Make not your Hecuba with fury rage,
And show a ranting grief upon the stage,
Or tell in vain how "the rough Tanaïs
bore
His sevenfold waters to the Euxine
shore."
These swollen expressions, this affected
noise,
Shows like some pedant that declaims
to boys.
In sorrow you must softer methods keep,
And, to excite our tears, yourself must
weep.

2 The original runs:

Gardez donc de donner, ainsi que dans Clélie,
L'air, ni l'esprit françois à l'antique Italie.
— Ed.

3 The original reads:

Tout à l'humeur gasconne en un auteur
Calprenède et-Juba parlent du même ton.

Those noisy words with which ill plays
abound
Come not from hearts that are in sadness drowned.

The theater for a young poet's rimes
Is a bold venture in our knowing times.
An author cannot easily purchase fame;
Critics are always apt to hiss and blame;
You may be judged by every ass in
town —
The privilege is bought for half-a-crown.
To please, you must a hundred chances
try,
Sometimes be humble, then must soar on
high,
In noble thoughts must everywhere
abound,
Be easy, pleasant, solid, and profound;
To these you must surprising touches
join,
And show us a new wonder in each line;
That all, in a just method well-designed
May leave a strong impression in the
mind.
These are the arts that tragedy main-
tain.

.   .   .   .   .   .

The great success which tragic writers
found
In Athens first the comedy renowned.
The abusive Grecian there, by pleasing
ways,
Dispersed his natural malice in his plays;
Wisdom and virtue, honor, wit, and
sense,
Were subject to buffooning insolence;
Poets were publicly approved and
sought,
That vice extolled and virtue set at
naught;
A Socrates himself, in that loose age,
Was made the pastime of a scoffing
stage.
At last the public took in hand the cause,
And cured this madness by the power of
laws,
Forbade, at any time or any place
To name the persons or describe the face.
The stage its ancient fury thus let fall,
And comedy diverted without gall,
By mild reproofs recovered minds dis-
eased,
And, sparing persons, innocently pleased.[4]

4 Original:

. . . Et plut innocemment dans les vers de
Ménandre.   — Ed.

Each one was nicely shown in this new glass,
And smiled to think he was not meant the ass.
A miser oft would laugh at first, to find
A faithful draught of his own sordid mind;
And fops were with such care and cunning writ,
They liked the piece for which themselves did sit.

You, then, that would the comic laurels wear,
To study nature be your only care.
Whoe'er knows man, and by a curious art
Discerns the hidden secrets of the heart;
He who observes, and naturally can paint
The jealous fool, the fawning sycophant,
A sober wit, an enterprising ass,
A humorous Otter, or a Hudibras,—
May safely in those noble lists engage,
And make them act and speak upon the stage.
Strive to be natural in all you write,
And paint with colors that may please the sight.
Nature in various figures does abound,
And in each mind are different humors found;
A glance, a touch, discovers to the wise,
But every man has not discerning eyes.

All-changing time does also change the mind,
And different ages different pleasures find.
Youth, hot and furious, cannot brook delay,
By flattering vice is easily led astray;
Vain in discourse, inconstant in desire,
In censure rash, in pleasures all on fire.
The manly age does steadier thoughts enjoy;
Power and ambition do his soul emply;
Against the turns of fate he sets his mind,
And by the past the future hopes to find.
Decrepit age, still adding to his stores,
For others heaps the treasure he adores,
In all his actions keeps a frozen pace,
Past time extols, the present to debase;
Incapable of pleasures youth abuse,
In others blames what age does him refuse.
Your actors must by reason be controlled;
Let young men speak like young, old men like old.

Observe the town and study well the court,
For thither various characters resort.
Thus 'twas great Jonson purchased his renown,
And in his art had borne away the crown,
If, less desirous of the people's praise,
He had not with low farce debased his plays,
Mixing dull buffoonry with wit refined,
And Harlequin with noble Terence joined.
When in *The Fox* I see the tortoise hissed,
I lose the author of *The Alchemist*.[5]

The comic wit, born with a smiling air,
Must tragic grief and pompous verse forbear;
Yet may he not, as on a market-place,
With bawdy jests amuse the populace.
With well-bred conversation you must please,
And your intrigue unravelled be with ease;
Your action still should reason's rules obey,
Nor in an empty scene may lose its way.
Your humble style must sometimes gently rise,
And your discourse sententious be and wise,
The passions must to nature be confined,
And scenes to scenes with artful weaving joined.
Your wit must not unseasonably play,
But follow business, never lead the way.
Observe how Terence does this evil shun:
A careful father chides his amorous son;
Then see that son whom no advice can move,
Forget those orders, and pursue his love!
'Tis not a well-drawn picture we discover,
'Tis a true son, a father, and a lover.

I like an author that reforms the age,
And keeps the right decorum of the stage,
That always pleases by just reason's rule;

5 In the above passage — beginning with "Thus 'twas," it is necessary to restore "Molière" for "Jonson"; "Tabarin" for "Harlequin"; "ridiculous sack in which Scapin is rolled," for "When in *The Fox* I see the tortoise hissed"; and "*Le Misanthrope*" for "*The Alchemist*."— Ed.

But for a tedious droll, a quibbling fool,
Who with low nauseous bawdry fills his
plays,
Let him begone, and on two trestles raise
Some Smithfield stage, where he may act
his pranks,

And make Jack-Puddings speak to
mountebanks.[6]

(Book III.)

[6] Original: "Amusing the *Pont-Neuf* with
his stale nonsense, and playing his pranks to
the assembled lackeys."— Ed.

SAINT-EVREMOND

Charles de Marguetel de Saint-Denis,
sieur de Saint-Evremond, was born of an
old and noble family at the Château de
Saint-Denis-le-Guast (near Coutances),
in 1610. He was destined to a career in
the magistrature and was sent to Paris
to study in 1619. His education was
continued, with special emphasis on philosophy, at Paris and at Caën. He began
his law study in 1628, but gave it up at
the end of a year and entered the army.
He participated in many campaigns.
After twenty years of service he was
made *maréchal de camp,* after losing his
lieutenancy as the result of an ill-advised
joke on his former friend Condé. During his military career he read and studied and wrote. The *Comédie des acadé-
miciens* (written 1642-43) and *Maximes*
(1647), belong to this period. In 1659
he wrote a letter to Créqui criticizing the
Treaty of the Pyrenees, and as a result
he was forced to leave France. He
went at first to Holland, then (1661) to
England, where he spent the remainder
of his life. His existence in England
was evidently a not unhappy exile, for
he was in particular favor with Charles
II and his two successors; and when in
1688, he was permitted to return to his
native country, he did not take advantage of the offer. He died at London in
1703, and was buried in Westminster
Abbey.

Saint-Evremond is important in the
history of dramatic criticism both relatively and intrinsically. His knowledge,
both of books and life, and his comparative freedom from prejudice, gave him
peculiar advantages over such contemporaries as Boileau. It seems that his
stay in England, besides affording him
the incalculable advantage of knowing
another nation and its literature, gave
him a vantage point from which he was
able to judge and discriminate wisely in
the questions which were being debated in
his own country. His impartiality in the
Ancients and Moderns Quarrel is an example of this detachment. He was one
of the few Frenchmen of his time who
was able, or cared, to adopt what is now
known as the comparative system of criticism. His championship of Corneille is
sane, invigorating, and interesting. The
score of writings in which he discussed
the drama are probably the earliest
specimens of the modern essay.

OF ANCIENT AND MODERN TRAGEDY [1]

[*De la Tragédie ancienne et moderne*]

(Written 1672)

There were never so many rules to
write a good tragedy by, and yet so few
good ones are now made that the players
are obliged to revive and act all the old
ones. I remember that the Abbé d'Aubignac wrote one according to the laws
he had so imperiously prescribed for the
stage. This piece had no success, notwithstanding which he boasted in all companies that he was the first French
writer that had exactly followed the precepts of Aristotle; whereupon the Prince
of Condé said wittily: "I am obliged

[1] Re-printed from the anonymous translation of the *Works* (London, 1714).— Ed.

to Monsieur d'Aubignac for having so exactly followed Aristotle's rules, but I will never forgive the rules of Aristotle for having put Monsieur d'Aubignac upon writing so bad a tragedy."

It must be acknowledged that Aristotle's *Art of Poetry* is an excellent piece of work; but, however, there's nothing so perfect in it as to be the standing rules of all nations and all ages. Descartes and Gassendi have found out truths that were unknown to Aristotle. Corneille has discovered beauties for the stage of which Aristotle was ignorant; and as our philosophers have observed errors in his *Physics,* our poets have spied out faults in his *Poetics,* at least with respect to us, considering what great change all things have undergone since his time. The gods and goddesses amongst the Ancients brought events that were great and extreme upon the theater, either by their hatred or their friendship, by their revenge or their protection; and among so many supernatural things, nothing appeared fabulous to the people, who believed there passed a familiar correspondence between gods and men. Their gods, generally speaking, acted by human passions; their men undertook nothing without the counsel of the gods, and executed nothing without their assistance. Thus in this mixture of the divinity and humanity, there was nothing which was not credible.

But all this profusion of miracles is downright romance to us at this time of day. The gods are wanting to us, and we are wanting to the gods; and if, in imitation of the Ancients, an author would introduce his angels and saints upon our stage, the bigots and puritans would be offended at it, and the libertines would certainly think him weak. Our preachers would by no means suffer a confusion of the pulpit and the theater, or that the people should go and learn those matters from the mouth of comedians which themselves deliver in their churches, with such authority to the whole people.

Besides this, it would give too great an advantage to the libertines, who might ridicule in a comedy those very things which they receive at church with a seeming submission, either out of respect to the place or to the character of the person that utters them.

But let us put the case that our doctors should leave freely leave all holy matters to the liberty of the stage; let us likewise take it for granted that men of the least devotion would hear them with as great an inclination to be edified as persons of the profoundest resignation; yet certain it is that the soundest doctrines, the most Christian actions, and the most useful truths, would produce a kind of tragedy that would please us the least of anything in the world.

The spirit of our religion is directly opposite to that of tragedy. The humility and patience of our saints carry too direct an opposition to those heroical virtues that are so necessary for the theater. What zeal, what force is there which Heaven does not bestow upon Nearchus and Polyeucte? And what is there wanting on the part of these new Christians to answer fully the end of these happy gifts? The passion and charms of a lovely young bride make not the least impression upon the mind of Polyeucte. The politic considerations of Felix, as they less affect us, so they make a less impression. Insensible both of prayers and menaces, Polyeucte has a greater desire to die for God than other men have to live for themselves. Nevertheless, this very subject, which would make one of the finest sermons in the world, would have made a wretched tragedy, if the conversation of Pauline and Sévère, heightened with other sentiments and other passions, had not preserved that reputation to the author which the Christian virtues of our martyrs had made him lose.

The theater loses all its agreeableness when it pretends to represent sacred things; and sacred things lose a great deal of the religious opinion that is due to them by being represented upon the theater.

To say the truth, the histories of the Old Testament are infinitely better suited to our stage. Moses, Samson, and Joshua would meet much better success than Polyeucte and Nearchus, for the wonders they would work there would be a fitter subject for the theater. But I am apt to believe that the priests would not fail to exclaim against the profanation of these sacred histories, with which they fill their conversations, their books, and their sermons; and to speak soberly upon the point, the miraculous passage through the Red Sea, the sun stopped in his career by the prayer of Joshua, and whole armies defeated by Samson with the jawbone of an ass — all these miracles, I say, would not be credited in a play, because we believe them in the Bible; but we should be rather apt to question them in the Bible, because we should believe nothing of them in the play.

If what I have delivered is founded on good and solid reasons, we ought to content ourselves with things purely natural, but at the same time, such as are extraordinary; and in our heroes to choose the principal actions which we may believe possible as human, and which may cause admiration in us, as being rare and of an elevated character. In a word, we should have nothing but what is great, yet still let it be human. In the human, we must carefully avoid mediocrity; and fable in that which is great.

I am by no means willing to compare the *Pharsalia* to the *Æneid;* I know the just difference of their value; but as for what purely regards elevation, Pompey, Cæsar, Cato, Curio, and Labienus, have done more for Lucan than Jupiter, Mercury, Juno, Venus, and all the train of the other gods and goddesses have done for Vergil.

The ideas which Lucan gives us of these great men are truly greater, and affect us more sensibly, than those which Vergil gives us of his deities. The latter has clothed his gods with human infirmities to adapt them to the capacity of men; the other has raised his heroes so as to bring them into competition with the gods themselves.

Victrix causa diis placuit, sed victa Catoni.

In Vergil, the gods are not so valuable as the heroes; in Lucan, the heroes equal the gods. To give you my opinion freely, I believe that the tragedy of the Ancients might have suffered a happy loss in the banishment of their gods, their oracles and their soothsayers.

For it proceeded from these gods, these oracles, and these diviners, that the stage was swayed by a spirit of superstition and terror, capable of infecting mankind with a thousand errors, and overwhelming them with numerous mischiefs. And if we consider the usual impressions which tragedy made at Athens in the minds of the spectators, we may safely affirm that Plato was more in the right, who prohibited the use of them, than Aristotle, who recommended them; for as their tragedies wholly consisted in excessive motions of fear and pity, was not this the direct way to make the theater a school of terror and of compassion, where people only learnt to be affrighted at all dangers, and to abandon themselves to despair upon every misfortune?

It will be a hard matter to persuade me that a soul accustomed to be terrified for what regards another, has strength enough to support misfortunes that concern itself. This perhaps was the reason why the Athenians became so susceptible of the impressions of fear, and that this spirit of terror which the theater inspired into them with so much art became at last but too natural to their armies.

At Sparta and Rome, where only examples of valor and constancy were publicly shown, the people were no less brave and resolute in battle than they were unshaken and constant in the calamities of the Republic. Ever since this art of fearing and lamenting was set up at Athens, all those disorderly passions which they had, as it were, imbibed at their public representations, got footing in their camps and attended them in their wars.

Thus a spirit of superstition occasioned the defeat of their armies, and a spirit of lamentation made them sit down contented with bewailing their great misfortunes, when they ought to have found out proper remedies for them. For how was it possible for them not to learn despair in this pitiful school of commiseration? The persons they usually represented upon it were examples of the greatest misery and subjects but of ordinary virtues.

So great was their desire to lament that they represented fewer virtues than misfortunes, lest a soul raised to the admiration of heroes should be less inclined to pity the distressed; and in order to imprint these sentiments of affliction the deeper in their spectators, they had always upon their theater a chorus of virgins or of old men, who furnished them upon every event, either with their terrors or with their tears.

Aristotle was sensible enough what

prejudice this might do the Athenians, but he thought he sufficiently prevented it by establishing a certain *Purgation,* which no one hitherto has understood, and which in my opinion he himself never fully comprehended. For can anything be so ridiculous as to form a science which will infallibly discompose our minds, only to set up another, which does not certainly pretend to cure us? Or to raise a perturbation in our souls for no other end than to endeavor afterwards to calm it, by obliging it to reflect upon the dejected condition it has been in?

Among a thousand persons that are present at the theater, perhaps there may be six philosophers that are capable of recovering their former tranquillity by the assistance of these prudent and useful meditations; but the multitude will scarce make any such judicious reflections, and we may be almost assured that what we see constantly represented on the theater, will not fail, at long run, to produce in us a habit of these unhappy motions.

Our theatrical representations are not subject to the same circumstances as those of the Ancients were, since our fear never goes so far as to raise this superstitious terror, which produced such ill effects upon valor. Our fear, generally speaking, is nothing else but an agreeable uneasiness, which consists in the suspension of our minds; 'tis a dear concern which our soul has for those objects that draw its affection to them.

We may almost say the same of pity as 'tis used on our stage. We divest it of all its weakness, and leave it all that we call charitable and human. I love to see the misfortune of some great unhappy person lamented; I am content with all my heart that he should attract our compassion; nay, sometimes, command our tears; but then I would have these tender and generous tears paid to his misfortunes and virtues together, and that this melancholy sentiment of pity be accompanied with vigorous admiration, which shall stir up in our souls a sort of an amorous desire to imitate him.

We were obliged to mingle somewhat of love in the new tragedy, the better to remove those black ideas which the ancient tragedy caused in us by superstition and terror. And in truth there is

no passion that more excites us to everything that is noble and generous than a virtuous love. A man who may cowardly suffer himself to be insulted by a contemptible enemy will yet defend what he loves, though to the apparent hazard of his life, against the attacks of the most valiant. The weakest and most fearful creatures — those creatures that are naturally inclined to fear and to run away — will fiercely encounter what they dread most, to preserve the object of their love. Love has a certain heat which supplies the defect of courage in those that want it most. But to confess the truth, our authors have made as ill an use of this noble passion as the Ancients did of their fear and pity; for if we except eight or ten plays where its impulses have been managed to great advantage, we have no tragedies in which both lovers and love are not equally injured.

We have an affected tenderness where we ought to place the noblest sentiments. We bestow a softness on what ought to be most moving; and sometimes when we mean plainly to express the graces of nature, we fall into a vicious and mean simplicity.

We imagine we make kings and emperors perfect lovers, but in tragedy we make ridiculous princes of them; and by the complaints and sighs which we bestow upon them where they ought neither to complain nor sigh, we represent them weak, both as lovers and as princes.

Our great heroes upon the theater generally make love like shepherds; and thus the innocence of a sort of rural passion supplies with them the place of glory and valor.

If an actress has the art to weep and bemoan herself after a moving lively manner, we give her our tears, at certain places which demand gravity; and because she pleases best when she seems to be affected, she shall put on grief all along, indifferently.

Sometimes we must have a plain, unartificial, sometimes a tender and sometimes a melancholy whining love, without regarding where that simplicity, tenderness, or grief is requisite; and the reason of it is plain: for as we must needs have love everywhere, we look for diversity in the manners, and seldom or never place it in the passions.

I am in good hopes we shall one day

find out the true use of this passion, which is now become too common. That which ought to sweeten cruel or calamitous accidents, that which ought to affect our very souls, to animate our courage and raise our spirits, will not certainly be always made the subject of a little affected tenderness or of a weak simplicity. Whenever this happens, we need not envy the Ancients; and without paying too great a respect to Antiquity, or being too much prejudiced against the present age, we shall not set up the tragedies of Sophocles and Euripides as the only models for the dramatic compositions of our times.

However, I don't say that these tragedies wanted anything that was necessary to recommend them to the palate of the Athenians; but should a man translate the Œdipus, the best performance of all Antiquity, into French, with the same spirit and force as we see it in the original, I dare be bold to affirm that nothing in the world would appear to us more cruel and more opposite to the true sentiments which mankind ought to have.

Our age has at least this advantage over theirs, that we are allowed the liberty to hate vice and love virtue. As the gods occasioned the greatest crimes on the theater of the Ancients, these crimes captivated the respect of the spectators, and the people durst not find fault with those things which were really abominable. When they saw Agamemnon sacrifice his own daughter, and a daughter too that was so tenderly loved by him, to appease the indignation of the gods, they only considered this barbarous sacrifice as a pious obedience, and the highest proof of a religious submission.

Now, in that superstitious age, if a man still preserved the common sentiments of humanity, he could not avoid murmuring at the cruelty of the gods; he must needs be cruel and barbarous to his own fellow-creatures; he must, like Agamemnon, offer the greatest violence both to nature and to his own affection.

Tantum relligio potuit suadere malorum, says Lucretius, upon the account of this barbarous sacrifice.

Nowadays we see men represented upon the theater without the interposition of the gods; and this conduct is infinitely more useful both to the public and to private persons, for in our tragedies we neither introduce any villain who is not detested, nor any hero who does not cause himself to be admired. With us, few crimes escape unpunished and few virtues go off unrewarded. In short, by the good examples we publicly represent on the theater, by the agreeable sentiments of love and admiration that are discreetly interwoven with a rectified fear and pity, we are in a capacity of arriving to that perfection which Horace desires:

Omne tulit punctum, qui miscuit utile dulci, which can never be effected by the rules of ancient tragedy.

I shall conclude with a new and daring thought of my own, and that is this: we ought, in tragedy, before all things whatever, to look after a greatness of soul well expressed, which excites in us a tender admiration. By this sort of admiration our minds are sensibly ravished, our courages elevated, and our souls deeply affected.

RESTORATION AND EIGHTEENTH CENTURY ENGLISH DRAMATIC CRITICISM

Between the publication of Jonson's *Discoveries* (1641) and that of Dryden's *Essay of Dramatick Poesie* (1668), there is no outstanding piece of dramatic criticism in English. However, Davenant's efforts to create the opera, his *Preface to Gondibert* and Hobbes' reply, in 1650, together with the former's *Dedication* and *To the Reader* prefixed to his *Siege of Rhodes* (printed 1663), deserve passing notice as connecting links. Sir Robert Howard's *Preface to Four New Playes* (1665), which called forth Dryden's reply, and Howard's further *Preface*—to

The Great Favourite (1668) — Richard Flecknoe's *A Short Discourse of the English Stage* (1664), and the various prefaces, dedications, and prologues, especially of Shadwell's *The Sullen Lovers* (1668) and of *The Humourists* (1671), are further indications of interest in dramatic controversies. Thomas Rymer entered the field a few years after Dryden. His *Preface* to his translation of Rapin's *Réflexions sur la poétique* (1674) attacked all stragglers from the narrow path prescribed by the rigid neo-classicists; he followed this with a severe criticism of the Elizabethans, in *The Tragedies of the Last Age Consider'd*, etc. (1678), and in 1693 he published his *Short View of Tragedy*, etc., containing the famous onslaught on *Othello*. Milton published his short dissertation on tragedy with his *Samson Agonistes* (1671) as a sort of apology. It is based almost entirely upon the Italian Renaissance critics' conception of Aristotle's remarks on tragedy. Other contemporaries of Dryden, who dominated the last years of the century are, among others of less importance: the Duke of Buckingham, whose *Essay upon Poetry* was published in 1682; Ravenscroft's preface to the play *Dame Dobson* (1684); Sedley, whose *Bellamira* (1687) had a short *Preface;* Sir Thomas Pope Blount, whose extensive treatise — *De Re Poetica* — with numerous excerpts from ancient and modern poets, appeared in 1694; and the dramatists, Blackmore — *Prefaces* to *Prince Arthur* (1695) and *King Arthur* (1697) — and Dilke — *Preface* to *The City Lady* (1697). Of Dryden's thirty odd prefaces, essays, etc., on the drama, the first, the *Epistle Dedicatory* to his play *The Rival Ladies*, was published in 1664. This was followed by the *Essay of Dramatick Poesie* (1668), and the *Defence*, the same year. Nearly every one of his plays carries a preface, dedication, or separate essay defending his dramatic practice, setting forth some theory, or attacking the practice or theory of others. His last word on the drama is found in the *Discourse on Epick Poetry*, prefixed to his translation of the *Æneid* in 1697, three years before his death. Dryden was a great critic, one of the greatest of all time. " He established (let us hope for all time)," says Saintsbury, " the English

fashion of criticizing, as Shakespeare did the English fashion of dramatizing,— the fashion of aiming at delight, at truth, at justice, at nature, at poetry, and letting the rules take care of themselves." The controversy between the Puritans and the stage assumed its most violent form in the famous Collier dispute. In 1696 Jeremy Collier, a Nonjuring clergyman, published his *Short View of the Profaneness and Immorality of the English Stage*. This pamphlet was aimed primarily against the dramatists who " profaned" the stage with immoral characters and situations, and who attacked the clergy. While his purpose was primarily a moral one, there is a good deal of literary criticism in his work. There is no doubt that he was a most important factor in changing the tone of the plays of his generation, and stultifying the comedies of the next. The *Short View* called forth many replies, some of which were anonymous. Congreve replied with his *Amendments upon Mr. Collier's False and Imperfect Citations,* etc., the same year. Collier at once riposted with his *Defence of the Short View,* etc. Farquhar is the probable author of *The Adventures of Covent Garden,* in which he answered Collier by suggesting that the " best way of answering Mr. Collier was not to have replied at all." Vanbrugh, who together with Congreve and Dryden, was specifically attacked, replied in his *Vindication of the Relapse,* etc. (1699). John Dennis, a critic of no mean ability, defended the stage in a lengthy treatise on *The Usefulness of the Stage to the Happiness of Mankind, to Government, and to Religion,* etc. (1698). When, in 1705, Collier published his *Dissuasive from the Play House,* Dennis again answered with *A Person of Quality's Answer to Mr. Collier's Letter.* Before the Collier controversy started, Dennis had written his first criticism, the *Impartial Critick* (1693), in reply to Rymer's *Short View of Tragedy.* Among his subsequent dramatic criticisms may be mentioned: *An Essay on the Operas* (1706), *An Essay on the Genius and Writings of Shakespeare* (1712), *Remarks upon Cato, A Tragedy* (1713), *A Defence of Sir Fopling Flutter, a Comedy* (1722), *Remarks on a Play, call'd The Conscious Lovers, a Comedy*

(1723), *The Stage Defended from Scrip-ture, Reason and the Common Sense of Mankind for Two Thousand Years* (1726). Drake's *Antient and Modern Stages survey'd* (1699) called forth Collier's *Second Defence of the Short View,* etc. (1700). E. Filmer's *A Defence of Plays,* etc. (1707), found Collier once more ready with an answer, *A Farther Vindication of the Short View,* etc. (1708). *Mr. Collier's Dissuasive from the Play House* (1703), completes the list of the clergyman's attacks on the stage. Among the many defenses of Collier may be mentioned the anonymous *A Representation of the Impiety and Immorality of the English Stage,* etc. (1704). Formal treatises on the art of poetry made their appearance early in the new century. Edward Bysshe's *Art of English Poetry* (probably 1700) is of great historical importance, and sums up the neo-classic tendencies of the time. This was followed in 1721 by Charles Gildon's *Complete Art of Poetry.* It was probably Gildon who "improved" and continued Gerard Langbaine's *Lives and Characters of the English Dramatic Poets,* etc., which was published in 1699 (?). Addison, great as he was in other fields, is not important as a dramatic critic. In the *Spectator,* however, he touches on drama at several points.[1] In *The Tatler, The Guardian,* and other papers, Richard Steele also occasionally wrote on the drama, and in the dedications and prefaces to his plays (*The Funeral,* 1702, *The Lying Lover,* 1704, *The Conscious Lovers,* 1723). Farquhar, the last of the great Restoration dramatists, made his contributions to dramatic criticism in the *Prologue* to *Sir Harry Wildair* (1701) and in the *Discourse upon English Comedy* (1702). The latter, which is of course much fuller, is a sort of summing-up of the theories of drama held by many dramatists. It contains a vigorous protest against Aristotle and the Rules, and a loose definition of comedy as a moral guide, with the Horatian ingredient of the "useful" and the "pleasing." The Shakespearean Prefaces of the seventeenth century contain interesting critical matter. The most important are collected by D. Nichol

[1] In Nos. 39 to 42, 44, 45, 58 to 63, 258, 290, 296, 419, 446.

Smith in his *Eighteenth Century Essays on Shakespeare,* which contains the following, among others: Nicholas Rowe's *Some Account of the Life . . . of Mr. William Shakespeare* (1707); Pope's *Preface* (1725); essays of Theobald (1733), Hanmer (1744), Warburton (1747), Johnson (1765), and Farmer's *Essay on the Learning of Shakespeare* (1767). Pope's *Essay on Criticism* (1711) may also be consulted for its sections relating to the drama. Many literary critics of the period referred to the drama in the course of their writings on general literature, rhetoric, and poetry. David Hume's *Essay on Tragedy* (1742), Joseph Warton's papers in *The Adventurer* (on *The Tempest,* Nos. 93 and 97, and on *King Lear,* Nos. 113, 116, and 122); Colley Cibber's *Apology* (1740) — deal with various aspects of the drama, while Blair, Hurd, and Kames are more especially concerned with the historical, rhetorical, and esthetic sides. Burke's *Essay on Tragedy,* and *On the Sublime and Beautiful* (1756), are concerned almost wholly with purely esthetic considerations, and Samuel Foote's *Roman and English Comedy Considered and Compared* (1747) is little more than a curious document on contemporary plays and acting. Dr. Johnson's contribution to the criticism of the drama is not great in extent, but is important as an indication of the spirit of the times. His essays in the *Rambler,* the *Idler,* and the *Adventurer,* the casual remarks in the *Lives of the Poets* (1789–91), and the *Preface* to his edition of Shakespeare (1765) are practically his only dramatic criticism. Goldsmith was not a great critic, but his knowledge of the stage and inborn shrewdness make his observations in *The State of Polite Learning* (1759), the *Preface* to *The Good-Natur'd Man* (1768), and the *Essay on the Theatre* (1772), dramatic manifestos, attractive and interesting. They indicate the reaction against the Sentimental Comedy, which was at that time in its heyday. The century closed with a few treatises on the more formal aspects of dramatic criticism, like Cooke's *Elements of Dramatic Criticism* (1775), J. Penn's *Letters on the Drama* (1796), B. Walwyn's *Essay on Comedy* (1782), and Samuel Wyte's *The Theatre, a Didactic Essay* (1790).

JOHN DRYDEN

John Dryden was born at Aldwinkle, Northamptonshire, in 1631. He came of a Puritan family, which had been for years very active in the political world. Dryden was sent to school at Westminster. He published some verses at the age of eighteen. In 1650 he entered Trinity College, Cambridge, and took a degree of B.A. four years later, but it is probable that he spent also the next three years at Cambridge. He went to London in 1657. His first important literary effort, *Heroic Stanzas* to the memory of Cromwell, was published in 1659. This was followed the next year by verses on the return of Charles. In order to add to his slender income, he turned to the stage, and after two unsuccessful attempts he produced his first play, *The Wild Gallant,* in 1663. This comedy was not well received, and Dryden confesses that his forte was not comedy. The same year he produced *The Rival Ladies,* and married Lady Elizabeth Howard. *The Indian Queen* (1664), written in collaboration with Sir Robert Howard, his wife's brother, enjoyed considerable success. Dryden followed this with *The Indian Emperor* (1665). During the Plague Dryden lived with his father-in-law in Wiltshire, where he wrote his *Essay of Dramatick Poesie* (1668). Howard's preface to his *Four New Playes* (1665) called forth a reply from Dryden: *A Defence of an Essay of Dramatique Poesie* (1668). From the re-opening of the theaters in 1666, to 1681, Dryden wrote little except his plays. The production of Buckingham's satirical play *The Rehearsal* in 1671, in which Dryden was the chief personage, called forth the preface *Of Heroic Plays* and *Defence of the Epilogue* (1672). *All for Love,* in all probability the poet's greatest play, was performed in 1678.

He continued to produce plays to the end of his career. In 1681 he turned to satire and wrote *Absalom and Achitophel,* which achieved instant and widespread popularity. This was followed by other satires. In 1687, after his conversion to the Catholic Church, he wrote *The Hind and the Panther,* a plea for Catholicism. His Catholic leanings lost for him the laureateship and other offices when the Revolution came. During his last ten years he translated many of the Latin classics: Vergil, Ovid, Lucretius, Horace, Theocritus, and others, and modernied Chaucer. He died in 1700, and was buried in Westminster Abbey.

Dryden's contribution to English literature, besides his poems and plays, was the invention of a direct and simple style for literary criticism. He improved upon the prose of the Elizabethan writers in the matter of ridding English of its involved forms, even if through that process he lost some of its gorgeous ornament and rugged strength. Jonson's method in criticism was after all not much more than the note-book method of jotting down stray thoughts and opinions and reactions. Dryden elaborated his ideas, sought the weight of authority, argued both sides of the question, and adduced proofs. Dryden performed an inestimable service to his countrymen in applying true standards of criticism to the Elizabethans and in showing them a genuine and sympathetic if occasionally misguided love for Shakespeare. Dryden also enjoyed the advantage of being able to bring his knowledge of the drama of Spain and France to bear on his criticism of English dramatists, while it has already been pointed out what debts he owes to Corneille as a critic.

AN ESSAY OF DRAMATICK POESIE [1]
(1668)

．　．　．　．　．　．．

6. Eugenius [2] was going to continue

this discourse, when Lisideius [3] told him that it was necessary, before they pro-

---

[1] Re-printed — with omissions of portions not relating to the drama — from the Everyman's Library edition of *Dramatic Essays by John Dryden* (London and New York, n. d.). — Ed.

[2] Generally thought to be Lord Buckhurst.— Ed.

[3] Generally thought to be Sir Charles Sedley. — Ed.

ceded further, to take a standing measure of their controversy; for how was it possible to be decided who writ the best plays, before we know what a play should be? But, this once agreed on by both parties, each might have recourse to it, either to prove his own advantages, or to discover the failings of his adversary.

He had no sooner said this, but all desired the favor of him to give the definition of a play; and they were the more importunate, because neither Aristotle, nor Horace, nor any other who had writ of that subject, had ever done it.

Lisideius, after some modest denials, at last confessed he had a rude notion of it; indeed, rather a description than a definition; but which served to guide him in his private thoughts, when he was to make a judgment of what others writ: that he conceived a play ought to be, *A just and lively image of human nature, representing its passions and humors, and the changes of fortune to which it is subject, for the delight and instruction of mankind.*

This definition, though Crites [4] raised a logical objection against it — that it was only *genere et fine,* and so not altogether perfect, was yet well received by the rest, Crites, being desired by the company to begin, spoke on behalf of the ancients, in this manner:

" If confidence presage a victory, Eugenius, in his own opinion, has already triumphed over the ancients: nothing seems more easy to him, than to overcome those whom it is our greatest praise to have imitated well; for we do not only build upon their foundations, but by their models. Dramatic Poesy had - time enough, reckoning from Thespis (who first invented it) to Aristophanes, to be born, to grow up, and to flourish in maturity. It has been observed of arts and sciences, that in one and the same century they have arrived to great perfection; and no wonder, since every age has a kind of universal genius, which inclines those that live in it to some particular studies: the work then, being pushed on by many hands, must of necessity go forward.

" Is it not evident, in these last hun-

4 Generally thought to be Sir Robert Howard.— Ed.

dred years, when the study of philosophy has been the business of all the virtuosi in Christendom, that almost a new nature has been revealed to us? That more errors of the school have been detected, more useful experiments in philosophy have been made, more noble secrets in optics, medicine, anatomy, astronomy, discovered, than in all those credulous and doting ages from Aristotle to us? — so true it is, that nothing spreads more fast than science, when rightly and generally cultivated.

" Add to this, the more than common emulation that was in those times of writing well; which though it be found in all ages and all persons that pretend to the same reputation, yet poesy, being then in more esteem than now it is, had greater honors decreed to the professors of it, and consequently the rivalship was more high betwen them; they had judges ordained to decide their merit, and prizes to reward it; and historians have been diligent to record of Æschylus, Euripides, Sophocles, Lycophron, and the rest of them, both who they were that vanquished in these wars of the theater, and how often they were crowned: while the Asian kings and Grecian commonwealths scarce afforded them a nobler subject than the unmanly luxuries of a debauched court, or giddy intrigues of a factious city: — *Alit æmulatio ingenia* (says Paterculus), *et nunc invidia, nunc admiratio incitatio nem accendit:* Emulation is the spur of wit; and sometimes envy, sometimes admiration, quickens our endeavors.

" But now, since the rewards of honor are taken away, that virtuous emulation is turned into direct malice; yet so slothful, that it contents itself to condemn and cry down others, without attempting to do better: it is a reputation too unprofitable to take the necessary pains for it; yet, wishing they had it, that desire is incitement enough to hinder others from it. And this, in short, Eugenius, is the reason why you have now so few good poets, and so many severe judges. Certainly, to imitate the ancients well, much labor and long study is required; which pains, I have already shown, our poets would want encouragement to take, if yet they had ability to go through the work. Those ancients have been faithful imitators and wise observers of that nature which is so

torn and ill represented in our plays;
they have handed down to us a perfect
resemblance of her; which we, like ill
copiers, neglecting to look on, have rendered monstrous, and disfigured. But,
that you may know how much you are
indebted to those your masters, and be
ashamed to have so ill requitted them,
I must remember you, that all the rules
by which we practice the drama at this
day (either such as relate to the just-
ness and symmetry of the plot, or the
episodical ornaments, such as descriptions, narrations, and other beauties,
which are not essential to the play),
were delivered to us from the observations which Aristotle made, of those
poets, who either lived before him, or
were his contemporaries: we have added
nothing of our own, except we have the
confidence to say our wit is better; of
which, none boast in this our age, but
such as understand not theirs. Of that
book which Aristotle has left us, περὶ
τῆς Ποιητικῆς, [*The Poetics*] Horace his
Art of Poetry is an excellent comment,
and, I believe, restores to us that Second Book of his concerning Comedy,
which is wanting in him.

"Out of these two have been extracted
the famous Rules, which the French call
Des Trois Unités, or, The Three Unities,
which ought to be observed in every
regular play; namely, of Time, Place,
and Action.

"The unity of time they comprehend
in twenty-four hours, the compass of a
natural day, or as near as it can be contrived; and the reason of it is obvious
to every one,— that the time of the
feigned action, or fable of the play,
should be proportioned as near as can
be to the duration of that time in which
it is represented: since, therefore, all
plays are acted on the theater in the
space of time much within the compass
of twenty-four hours, that play is to be
thought the nearest imitation of nature,
whose plot or action is confined within
that time; and, by the same rule which
concludes this general proportion of
time, it follows, that all the parts of it
are (as near as may be) to the equally
subdivided; namely, that one act take
not up the supposed time of half a day,
which is out of proportion to the rest;
since the other four are then to be
straitened within the compass of the re-

maining half: for it is unnatural that one
act, which being spoke or written is not
longer than the rest, should be supposed
longer by the audience; it is therefore
the poet's duty to take care that no act
should be imagined to exceed the time
in which it is represented on the stage;
and that the intervals and inequalities of
time be supposed to fall out between the
acts.

"This rule of time, how well it has
been observed by the ancients, most of
their plays will witness; you see them in
their tragedies (wherein to follow this
rule is certainly most difficult), from the
very beginning of their plays, falling
close into that part of the story which
they intend for the action or principal
object of it, leaving the former part to
be delivered by narration: so that they
set the audience, as it were, at the post
where the race is to be concluded; and,
saving them the tedious expectation of
seeing the poet set out and ride the beginning of the course, they suffer you
not to behold him till he is in sight of
the goal, and just upon you.

"For the second unity, which is that
of Place, the ancients meant by it, that
the scene ought to be continued through
the play, in the same place where it was
laid in the beginning: for, the stage on
which it is represented being but one
and the same place, it is unnatural to
conceive it many,— and those far distant from one another. I will not deny
but, by the variation of painted scenes,
the fancy, which in these cases will contribute to its own deceit, may sometimes
imagine it several places, with some appearance of probability; yet it still carries the greater likelihood of truth if
those places be supposed so near each
other as in the same town or city; which
may all be comprehended under the
larger denomination of one place; for a
greater distance will bear no proportion
to the shortness of time which is allotted,
in the acting, to pass from one of them
to another; for the observation of this,
next to the ancients, the French are to
be most commended. They tie themselves so strictly to the unity of place
that you never see in any of their plays
a scene changed in the middle of an act:
if the act begins in a garden, a street,
or chamber, 'tis ended in the same place;
and that you may know it to be the

same, the stage is so supplied with persons, that it is never empty all the time: he who enters second, has business with him who was on before; and before the second quits the stage, a third appears who has business with him. This Corneille calls *la liaison des scènes,* the continuity or joining of the scenes; and 'tis a good mark of a well-contrived play, when all the persons are known to each other, and every one of them has some affairs with all the rest.

"As for the third unity, which is that of Action, the ancients meant no other by it than what the logicians do by their *finis,* the end or scope of any action; that which is the first in intention, and last in execution: now the poet is to aim at one great and complete action, to the carrying on of which all things in his play, even the very obstacles, are to be subservient; and the reason of this is as evident as any of the former. For two actions, equally labored and driven on by the writer, would destroy the unity of the poem; it would be no longer one play, but two: not but that there may be many actions in a play, as Ben Jonson has observed in his *Discoveries;* but they must be all subservient to the great one, which our language happily expresses in the name of *under-plots:* such as in Terence's *Eunuch* is the difference and reconcilement of Thais and Phædria, which is not the chief business of the play, but promotes the marriage of Chærea and Chremes's sister, principally intended by the poet. There ought to be but one action, says Corneille, that is, one complete action, which leaves the mind of the audience in a full repose; but this cannot be brought to pass but by many other imperfect actions, which conduce to it, and hold the audience in a delightful suspense of what will be.

"If by these rules (to omit many other drawn from the precepts and practice of the ancients) we should judge our modern plays, 'tis probable that few of them would endure the trial: that which should be the business of a day, takes up in some of them an age; instead of one action, they are the epitomes of a man's life; and for one spot of ground, which the stage should represent, we are sometimes in more countries than the map can show us.

"But if we allow the Ancients to have

contrived well, we must acknowledge them to have written better. Questionless we are deprived of a great stock of wit in the loss of Menander among the Greek poets, and of Cæcilius, Afranius, and Varius, among the Romans; we may guess at Menander's excellency by the plays of Terence, who translated some of his; and yet wanted so much of him, that he was called by C. Cæsar the half-Menander; and may judge of Varius, by the testimonies of Horace, Martial, and Velleius Paterculus. 'Tis probable that these, could they be recovered, would decide the controversy; but so long as Aristophanes and Plautus are extant, while the tragedies of Euripides, Sophocles, and Seneca, are in our hands, I can never see one of those plays which are now written but it increases my admiration of the ancients. And yet I must acknowledge further, that to admire them as we ought, we should understand them better than we do. Doubtless many things appear flat to us, the wit of which depended on some custom or story, which never came to our knowledge; or perhaps on some criticism in their language, which being so long dead, and only remaining in their books, 'tis not possible they should make us understand perfectly. To read Macrobius, explaining the propriety and elegancy of many words in Vergil, which I had before passed over without consideration as common things, is enough to assure me that I ought to think the same of Terence; and that in the purity of his style (which Tully so much valued that he ever carried his works about him) there is yet left in him great room for admiration, if I knew but where to place it. In the meantime I must desire you to take notice that the greatest man of the last age, Ben Jonson, was willing to give place to them in all things: he was not only a professed imitator of Horace, but a learned plagiary of all others; you track him everywhere in their snow: if Horace, Lucan, Petronius Arbiter, Seneca, and Juvenal, had their own from him, there are few serious thoughts which are new in him: you will pardon me, therefore, if I presume he loved their fashion, when he wore their clothes. But since I have otherwise a great veneration for him, and you, Eugenius, prefer him above all other poets,

I will use no farther argument to you
than his example: I will produce before
you Father Ben, dressed in all the ornaments and colors of the ancients; you
will need no other guide to our party, if
you follow him; and whether you consider the bad plays of our age, or regard
the good plays of the last, both the best
and worst of the modern poets will
equally instruct you to admire the ancients."

Crites had no sooner left speaking,
but Eugenius, who had waited with some
impatience for it, thus began:

" I have observed in your spech, that
the former part of it is convincing as
to what the moderns have profited by
the rules of the ancients; but in the
latter you are careful to conceal how
much they have excelled them; we own
all the helps we have from them, and
want neither veneration nor gratitude,
while we acknowledge that, to overcome
them, we must make use of the advantages we have received from them: but
to these assistances we have joined our
own industry; for, had we sat down
with a dull imitation of them, we might
then have lost somewhat of the old perfection, but never acquired any that was
new. We draw not therefore after their
lines, but those of nature; and having
the life before us, besides the experience
of all they knew, it is no wonder if we
hit some airs and features which they
have missed. I deny not what you urge
of arts and sciences, that they have flourished in some ages more than others; but
your instance in philosophy makes for
me: for if natural causes be more known
now than in the time of Aristotle, because more studied, it follows that poesy
and other arts may, with the same pains,
arrive still nearer to perfection; and,
that granted, it will rest for you to prove
that they wrought more perfect images
of human life than we; which seeing
in your discourse you have avoided to
make good, it shall now be my task to
show you some part of their defects,
and some few excellencies of the moderns. And I think there is none among
us can imagine I do it enviously, or
with purpose to detract from them; for
what interest or fame or profit can the
living lose by the reputation of the dead?
On the other side, it is a great truth
which Velleius Paterculus affirms: *Au-*
*dita visis libentius laudamus; et præsen-
tia invidia præterita admiratione prose-
quimur; et his nos obrui, illis instrui
credimus:* that praise or censure is certainly the most sincere, which unbribed
posterity shall give us.

" Be pleased then in the first place to
take notice that the Greek poesy, which
Crites has affirmed to have arrived to
perfection in the reign of the old comedy,
was so far from it that the distinction of
it into acts was not known to them; or if
it were, it is yet so darkly delivered to
us that we cannot make it out.

" All we know of it is from the singing of their Chorus; and that too is so
uncertain, that in some of their plays we
have reason to conjecture they sung more
than five times. Aristotle indeed divides
the integral parts of a play into four.
First, the *Protasis,* or entrance, which
gives light only to the characters of the
persons, and proceeds very little into
any part of the action. Secondly, the
Epitasis, or working up of the plot;
where the play grows warmer, the design or action of it is drawing on, and
you see something promising that it will
come to pass. Thirdly, the *Cantastasis,*
called by the Romans, *Status,* the height
and full growth of the play: we may call
it properly the counter-turn, which destroys that expectation, imbroils the action in new difficulties, and leaves you
far distant from that hope in which it
found you; as you may have observed
in a violent stream resisted by a narrow
passage,— it runs round to an eddy, and
carries back the waters with more swift-
ness than it brought them on. Lastly,
the *Catastrophe,* which the Grecians
called λύσις, the French *le dénouement,*
and we the discovery, or unraveling of
the plot: there you see all things settling
again upon their first foundations; and,
the obstacles which hindered the design
or action of the play once removed, it
ends with that resemblance of truth and
nature, that the audience are satisfied
with the conduct of it. Thus this great
man delivered to us the image of a play;
and I must confess it is so lively, that
from thence much light has been derived
to the forming it more perfectly into
acts and scenes: but what poet first
limited to five the number of the acts,
I know not; only we see it so firmly
established in the time of Horace, that

he gives it for a rule in comedy,— *Neu brevior quinto, neu sit productior actu.* So that you see the Grecians cannot be said to have consummated this art; writing rather by entrances than by acts, and having rather a general indigested notion of a play, than knowing how and where to bestow the particular graces of it.'

"But since the Spaniards at this day allow but three acts, which they call *Jornadas,* to a play, and the Italians in many of theirs follow them, when I condemn the ancients, I declare it is not altogether because they have not five acts to every play, but because they have not confined themselves to one certain number: it is building an house without a model; and when they succeeded in such undertakings, they ought to have sacrificed to Fortune, not to the Muses.

"Next, for the plot, which Aristotle called τό μυθος, and often τῶν πραγμάτων σύνθεσις, and from him the Romans *Fabula;* it has already been judiciously observed by a late writer, that in their tragedies it was only some tale derived from Thebes or Troy, or at least something that happened in those two ages; which was worn so threadbare by the pens of all the epic poets, and even by tradition, itself of the talkative Greeklings (as Ben Jonson calls them), that before it came upon the stage it was already known to all the audience: and the people, so soon as ever they heard the name of Œdipus, knew as well as the poet, that he had killed his father by a mistake, and committed incest with his mother, before the play; that they were now to hear of a great plague, an oracle, and the ghost of Laïus: so that they sat with a yawning kind of expectation, till he was to come with his eyes pulled out, and speak a hundred or more verses in a tragic tone, in complaint of his misfortunes. But one *Œdipus, Hercules,* or *Medea,* had been tolerable: poor people, they escaped not so good cheap; they had still the *chapon bouillé* set before them, till their appetites were cloyed with the same dish, and, the novelty being gone, the pleasure vanished; so that one main end of Dramatic Poesy in its definition, which was to cause delight, was of consequence destroyed.

"In their comedies, the Romans generally borrowed their plots from the Greek poets; and theirs was commonly a little girl stolen or wandered from her parents, brought back unknown to the city, there [falling into the hands of] some young fellow, who, by the help of his servant, cheats his father; and when her time comes, to cry,— *Juno Lucina, fer opem,*— one or other sees a little box or cabinet which was carried away with her, and so discovers her to her friends, if some god do not prevent it, by coming down in a machine, and taking the thanks of it to himself.

"By the plot you may guess much of the characters of the persons. An old father, who would willingly, before he dies, see his son well married; his debauched son, kind in his nature to his mistress, but miserably in want of money; a servant or slave, who has so much wit to strike in with him, and help to dupe his father; a braggadocio captain, a parasite, and a lady of pleasure.

"As for the poor honest maid, on whom the story is built, and who ought to be one of the principal actors in the play, she is commonly a mute in it: she has the breeding of the old Elizabeth way, which was for maids to be seen and not to be heard; and it is enough you know she is willing to be married, when the fifth act requires it.

"These are plots built after the Italian mode of houses,— you see through them all at once: the characters are indeed the imitation of nature, but so narrow, as if they had imitated only an eye or an hand, and did not dare to venture on the lines of a face, or the proportion of a body.

"But in how strait a compass soever they have bounded their plots and characters, we will pass it by, if they have regularly pursued them, and perfectly observed those three unities of time, place, and action; the knowledge of which you say is derived to us from them. But in the first place give me leave to tell you, that the unity of place, however it might be practiced by them, was never any of their rules: we neither find it in Aristotle, Horace, or any who have written of it, till in our age the French poets first made it a precept of the stage. The unity of time, even Terence himself, who was the best and most regular of them, has neglected: his *Heautontimorumenos,* or *Self-Punisher,* takes up visibly two days, says Scaliger; the two first acts concluding the first day, the three last the day ensuing; and Euripides, in tying himself to one day, has committed an absurdity never to be forgiven him; for in one of his tragedies he has made Theseus go from Athens to Thebes, which was about forty English miles, under the walls of it to give battle, and appear victorious in the next act; and yet, from the time of his departure to the return of the Nuntius, who gives the relation of his victory, Æthra and the Chorus have but thirty-six verses; which is not for every mile a verse.

"The like error is as evident in Terence his *Eunuch,* when Laches, the old man, enters by mistake into the house of Thais; where, betwixt his exit and the entrance of Pythias, who comes to give ample relation of the disorders he has raised within, Parmeno, who was left upon the stage, has not above five lines to speak. *C'est bien employer un temps si court,* says the French poet, who furnished me with one of the observations: and almost all their tragedies will afford us examples of the like nature.

"It is true, they have kept the continuity, or, as you called it, *liaison des scènes,* somewhat better: two do not perpetually come in together, talk, and go out together; and other two succeed them, and do the same throughout the act, which the English call by the name of single scenes; but the reason is, because they have seldom above two or three scenes, properly so called, in every act; for it is to be accounted a new scene, not only every time the stage is empty; but every person who enters, though to others, makes it so; because he introduces a new business. Now the plots of their plays being narrow, and the persons few, one of their acts was written in a less compass than one of our well-wrought scenes; and yet they are often deficient even in this. To go no further than Terence; you find in the *Eunuch,* Antipho entering single in the midst of the third act, after Chremes and Pythias were gone off; in the same play you have likewise Dorias beginning the fourth act alone; and after she had made a relation of what was done at the Soldiers' entertainment (which by the way was very inartificial, because she was presumed to speak directly to the audience, and to

acquaint them with what was necessary to be known, but yet should have been so contrived by the poet as to have been told by persons of the drama to one another, and so by them to have come to the knowledge of the people), she quits the stage, and Phædria enters next, alone likewise: he also gives you an account of himself, and of his returning from the country, in monologue; to which unnatural way of narration Terence is subject in all his plays. In his *Adelphi,* or *Brothers,* Syrus and Demea enter after the scene was broken by the departure of Sostrata, Geta, and Canthara; and indeed you can scarce look unto any of his comedies, where you will not presently discover the same interruption.

"But as they have failed both in laying of their plots, and in the management, swerving from the rules of their own art by misrepresenting nature to us, in which they have ill satisfied one intention of a play, which was delight; so in the instructive part they have erred worse: instead of punishing vice and rewarding virtue, they have often shewn a prosperous wickedness, and an unhappy piety: they have set before us a bloody image of revenge in Medea, and given her dragons to convey her safe from punishment, a Priam and Astyanax murdered, and Cassandra ravished, and the lust and murder ending in the victory of him who acted them: in short, there is no indecorum in any of our modern plays, which if I would excuse, I could not shadow with some authority from the ancients. . . .

"But, to return from whence I have digressed, to the consideration of the ancients' writing, and their wit (of which by this time you will grant us in some measure to be fit judges). Though I see many excellent thoughts in Seneca, yet he of them who had a genius most proper for the stage, was Ovid; he had a way of writing so fit to stir up a pleasing admiration and concernment, which are the objects of a tragedy, and to show the various movements of a soul combating betwixt two different passions, that, had he lived in our age, or in his own could have writ with our advantages, no man but must have yielded to him; and therefore I am confident the *Medea* is none of his: for, though I esteem it for the gravity and sententiousness of it, which he himself concludes to be suitable to a tragedy,— *Omne genus scripti gravitate tragœdia vincit,*— yet it moves not my soul enough to judge that he, who in the epic way wrote things so near the drama as the story of Myrrha, ot Caunus and Biblis, and the rest, should stir up no more concernment where he most endeavored it. The masterpiece of Seneca I hold to be that scene in the *Troades* where Ulysses is seeking for Astyanax to kill him: there you see the tenderness of a mother so represented in Andromache, that it raises compassion to a high degree in the reader, and bears the nearest resemblance of anything in the tragedies of the ancients to the excellent scenes of passion in Shakspeare, or in Fletcher: for lovescenes, you will find few among them; their tragic poets dealt not with that soft passion, but with lust, cruelty, revenge, ambition, and those bloody actions they produced; which were more capable of raising horror than compassion in an audience: leaving love untouched, whose gentleness would have tempered them; which is the most frequent of all the passions, and which, being the private concernment of every person, is soothed by viewing its own image in a public entertainment.

"Among their comedies, we find a scene or two of tenderness, and that where you would least expect it, in Plautus; but to speak generally, their lovers say little, when they see each other, but *anima vita mea; Ζωὴ καὶ ψυχῇ,* as the women in Juvenal's time used to cry out in the fury of their kindness. Any sudden gust of passion (as an ecstasy of love in an unexpected meeting) cannot better be expressed than in a word and a sigh, breaking one another. Nature is dumb on such occasions; and to make her speak would be to represent her unlike herself. But there are a thousand other concernments of lovers, as jealousies, complaints, contrivances, and the like, where not to open their minds at large to each other, were to be wanting to their own love, and to the expectation of the audience; who watch the movements of their minds, as much as the changes of their fortunes. For the imaging of the first is properly the work of a poet; the latter he borrows from the historian."

Eugenius was proceeding in that part of his discourse, when Crites interrupted him. "I see," said he, "Eugenius and I are never like to have this question decided betwixt us; for he maintains the moderns have acquired a new perfection in writing; I can only grant they have altered the mode of it. Homer described his heroes men of great appetites, lovers of beef broiled upon the coals, and good fellows; contrary to the practice of the French Romances, whose heroes neither eat, nor drink, nor sleep, for love. Vergil makes Æneas a bold avower of his own virtues:

Sum pius Æneas, fama super æthera notus;

which, in the civility of our poets is the character of a fanfaron or Hector: for with us the knight takes occasion to walk out, or sleep, to avoid the vanity of telling his own story, which the trusty 'squire is ever to perform for him. So in their love-scenes, of which Eugenius spoke last, the ancients were more hearty, were more talkative: they writ love as it was then the mode to make it; and I will grant thus much to Eugenius, that perhaps one of their poets had he lived in our age, *si foret hoc nostrum fato delapsus in œvum* (as Horace says of Lucilius), he had altered many things; not that they were not natural before, but that he might accommodate himself to the age in which he lived. Yet in the meantime, we are not to conclude anything rashly against those great men, but preserve to them the dignity of masters, and give that honor to their memories, *quos Libitina sacravit,* part of which we expect may be paid to us in future times."

This moderation of Crites, as it was pleasing to all the company, so it put an end to that dispute; which Eugenius, who seemed to have the better of the argument, would urge no farther: but Lisideius, after he had acknowledged himself of Eugenius his opinion concerning the ancient, yet told him, he had forborne, till his discourse were ended, to ask him why he preferred the English plays above those of other nations? and whether we ought not to submit our stage to the exactness of our next neighbors?

"Though," said Eugenius, "I am at all times ready to defend the honor of my country against the French, and to maintain, we are as well able to vanquish them with our pens, as our ancestors have been with their swords; yet, if you please," added he, looking upon Neander,[5] " I will commit this cause to my friend's management; his opinion of our plays is the same with mine, and besides, there is no reason, that Crites and I, who have now left the stage, should reënter so suddenly upon it; which is against the laws of comedy."

" If the question had been stated," replied Lisideius, " who had writ best, the French or English, forty years ago, I should have been of your opinion, and adjudged the honor to our own nation; but since that time " (said he, turning towards Neander), " we have been so long together bad Englishmen that we had not leisure to be good poets. Beaumont, Fletcher, and Jonson (who were only capable of bringing us to that degree of perfection which we have), were just then leaving the world; as if in an age of so much horror, wit, and those milder studies of humanity, had no farther business among us. But the Muses, who ever follow peace, went to plant in another country: it was then that the great Cardinal Richelieu began to take them into his protection; and that, by his encouragement, Corneille, and some other Frenchmen, reformed their theater (which before was as much below ours, as it now surpasses it and the rest of Europe). But because Crites in his discourse for the ancients has prevented me, by observing many rules of the stage which the moderns have borrowed from them, I shall only, in short, demand of you, whether you are not convinced that of all nations the French have best observed them? In the unity of time you find them so scrupulous that it yet remains a dispute among their poets, whether the artificial day of twelve hours, more or less, be not meant by Aristotle, rather than the natural one of twenty-four; and consequently, whether all plays ought not to be reduced into that compass. This I can testify, that in all their dramas writ within these last twenty years and upwards, I have not observed any that have extended the time to thirty hours: in the unity of place they are full as scrupulous; for many of their critics limit it to that very

spot of ground where the play is supposed to begin; none of them exceed the compass of the same town or city. The unity of action in all plays is yet more conspicuous; for they do not burden them with under-plots, as the English do: which is the reason why many scenes of our tragi-comedians carry on a design that is nothing of kin to the main plot; and that we see two distinct webs in a play, like those in ill-wrought stuffs; and two actions, that is, two plays, carried on together, to the confounding of the audience; who, before they are warm in their concernments for one part, are diverted to another; and by that means espouse the interest of neither. From hence likewise it arises that the one half of our actors are not known to the other. They keep their distances, as if they were Montagues and Capulets, and seldom begin an acquaintance till the last scene of the fifth act, when they are all to meet upon the stage. There is no theater in the world has anything so absurd as the English tragi-comedy; 'tis a drama of our own invention, and the fashion of it is enough to proclaim it so; here a course of mirth, there another of sadness and passion, and a third of honor and a duel: thus, in two hours and a half, we run through all the fits of Bedlam. The French affords you so much variety on the same day, but they do it not so unseasonably, or *mal à propos,* as we: our poets present you the play and the farce together; and our stages still retain somewhat of the original civility of the Red Bull:

Atque ursum et pugiles media inter carmina poscunt.

The end of tragedies or serious plays, says Aristotle, is to beget admiration, compassion, or concernment; but are not mirth and compassion things incompatible? and is it not evident that the poet must of necessity destroy the former by intermingling of the latter? that is, he must ruin the sole end and object of his tragedy, to introduce somewhat that is forced into it, and is not of the body of it. Would you not think that physician mad, who, having prescribed a purge, should immediately order you take restringents?

" But to leave our plays, and return to

theirs. I have noted one great advantage they have had in the plotting of their tragedies; that is, they are always grounded upon some known history: according to that of Horace, *Ex noto fictum carmen sequar;* and in that they have so imitated the ancients that they have surpassed them. For the ancients, as was observed before, took for the foundation of their plays some poetical fiction, such as under that consideration could move but little concernment in the audience, because they already knew the event of it. But the French goes farther:

Atque ita mentitur, sic veris falsa remiscet
Primo ne medium, medio ne discrepet
*   imum.*

He so interweaves truth with probable fiction that he puts a pleasing fallacy upon us; mends the intrigues of fate, and dispenses with the severity of history, to reward that virtue which has been rendered to us there unfortunate. Sometimes the story has left the success so doubtful that the writer is free, by the privilege of a poet, to take that which of two or more relations will best suit with his design: as for example, in the death of Cyrus, whom Justin and some others report to have perished in the Scythian war, but Xenophon affirms to have died in his bed of extreme old age. Nay more, when the event is past dispute, even then we are willing to be deceived, and the poet, if he contrives it with appearance of truth, has all the audience of his party; at least during the time his play is acting: so naturally we are kind to virtue, when our own interest is not in question, that we take it up as the general concernment of mankind. On the other side, if you consider the historical plays of Shakspeare, they are rather so many chronicles of kings, or the business many times of thirty or forty years, cramped into a representation of two hours and a half; which is not to imitate or paint nature, but rather to draw her in miniature, to take her in little; to look upon her through the wrong end of a perspective, and receive her images not only much less, but infinitely more imperfect than the life: this, instead of making a play delightful, renders it ridiculous: —

Quodcunque ostendis mihi sic, incredulus
*   odi.*

For the spirit of man cannot be satisfied but with truth, or at least verisimility; and a poem is to contain, if not τὰ ἔτυμα, yet ἐτύμοισιν ὁμοῖα, as one of the Greek poets has expressed it.

"Another thing in which the French differ from us and from the Spaniards, is that they do not embarrass or cumber themselves with too much plot; they only represent so much of a story as will constitute one whole and great action sufficient for a play; we, who undertake more, do but multiply adventures which, not being produced from one another, as effects from causes, but rarely following, constitute many actions in the drama, and consequently make it many plays.

"But by pursuing closely one argument, which is not cloyed with many turns, the French have gained more liberty for verse, in which they write; they have leisure to dwell on a subject which deserves it; and to represent the passions (which we have acknowledged to be the poet's work), without being hurried from one thing to another, as we are in the plays of Calderon, which we have seen lately upon our theaters under the name of Spanish plots. I have taken notice but of one tragedy of ours whose plot has that uniformity and unity of design in it, which I have commended in the French; and that is *Rollo,* or rather, under the name of Rollo, the Story of Bassianus and Geta in Herodian: there indeed the plot is neither large nor intricate, but just enough to fill the minds of the audience, not to cloy them. Besides, you see it founded upon the truth of history,— only the time of the action is not reducible to the strictness of the rules; and you see in some places a little farce mingled, which is below the dignity of the other parts, and in this all our poets are extremely peccant: even Ben Jonson himself, in *Sejanus* and *Catiline,* has given us this oleo of a play, this unnatural mixture of comedy and tragedy; which to me sounds just as ridiculously as the history of David with the merry humors of Golia's. In *Sejanus* you may take notice of the scene betwixt Livia and the physician which is a pleasant satire upon the artificial helps of beauty: in *Catiline* you may see the parliament of women; the little envies of them to one another; and all that passes betwixt Curio and Fulvia: scenes admirable in their kind, but of an ill mingle with the rest.

"But I return again to the French writers, who, as I have said, do not burden themselves too much with plot, which has been reproached to them by an ingenious person of our nation as a fault; for, he says, they commonly make but one person considerable in a play; they dwell on him, and his concernments, while the rest of the persons are only subservient to set him off. If he intends this by it,— that there is one person in the play who is of greater dignity than the rest, he must tax, not only theirs, but those of the ancients and, which he would be loth to do, the best of ours; for it is impossible but that one person must be more conspicuous in it than any other, and consequently the greatest share in the action must devolve on him. We see it so in the management of all affairs; even in the most equal aristocracy, the balance cannot be so justly poised but some one will be superior to the rest, either in parts, fortune, interest, or the consideration of some glorious exploit; which will reduce the greatest part of business into his hands.

"But, if he would have us to imagine, that in exalting one character the rest of them are neglected, and that all of them have not some share or other in the action of the play, I desire him to produce any of Corneille's tragedies, wherein every person, like so many servants in a well-governed family, has not some employment, and who is not necessary to the carrying on of the plot, or at least to your understanding it.

"There are indeed some protatic persons in the ancients, whom they make use of in their plays, either to hear or give the relation: but the French avoid this with great address, making their narrations only to, or by such, who are some way interested in the main design. And now I am speaking of relations, I cannot take a fitter opportunity to add this in favor of the French, that they often use them with better judgment and more à propos than the English do. Not that I commend narrations in general,— but there are two sorts of them. One, of those things which are antecedent to the play, and are related to make the conduct of it more clear to us. But 'tis a fault to choose such subjects for the stage as will force us on that rock because we see they are seldom listened to by the audience and that is many times the ruin of the play; for, being once let pass without attention, the audience can never recover themselves to understand the plot: and indeed it is somewhat unreasonable that they should be put to so much trouble, as that, to comprehend what passes in their sight, they must have recourse to what was done, perhaps, ten or twenty years ago.

"But there is another sort of relations, that is, of things happening in the action of the play, and supposed to be done behind the scenes; and this is many times both convenient and beautiful; for by it the French avoid the tumult to which we are subject in England, by representing duels, battles, and the like; which renders our stage too like the theaters where they fight prizes. For what is more ridiculous than to represent an army with a drum and five men behind it; all which the hero of the other side is to drive in before him; or to see a duel fought, and one slain with two or three thrusts of the foils, which we know are so blunted that we might give a man an hour to kill another in good earnest with them.

"I have observed that in all our tragedies, the audience cannot forbear laughing when the actors are to die; it is the most comic part of the whole play. All *passions* may be lively represented on the stage, if to the well-writing of them the actor supplies a good commanded voice, and limbs that move easily, and without stiffness; but there are many *actions* which can never be imitated to a just height: dying especially is a thing which none but a Roman gladiator could naturally perform on the stage, when he did not imitate or represent, but do it; and therefore it is better to omit the representation of it.

"The words of a good writer, which describe it lively, will make a deeper impression of belief in us than all the actor can insinuate into us, when he seems to fall dead before us; as a poet in the description of a beautiful garden, or a meadow, will please our imagination more than the place itself can please our sight. When we see death represented, we are convinced it is but fiction; but when we hear it related, our eyes, the strongest witnesses, are wanting, which might have undeceived us; and we are all willing to favor the sleight, when the poet does not too grossly impose on us. They therefore who imagine these relations would make no concernment in the audience, are deceived, by confounding them with the other, which are of things antecedent to the play: those are made often in cold blood, as I may say, to the audience; but these are warmed with our concernments, which were before awakened in the play. What the philosophers say of motion, that, when it is once begun, it continues of itself, and will do so to eternity, without some stop put to it, is clearly true on this occasion: the soul being already moved with the characters and fortunes of those imaginary persons, continues going of its own accord; and we are no more weary to hear what becomes of them when they are not on the stage, than we are to listen to the news of an absent mistress. But it is objected, that if one part of the play may be related, then why not all? I answer, some parts of the action are more fit to be represented, some to be related. Corneille says judiciously that the poet is not obliged to expose to view all particular actions which conduce to the principal: he ought to select such of them to be seen, which will appear with the greatest beauty, either by the magnificence of the show, or the vehemence of passions which they produce, or some other charm which they have in them; and let the rest arrive to the audience by narration. 'Tis a great mistake in us to believe the French present no part of the action on the stage; every alteration or crossing of a design, every new-sprung passion, and turn of it, is a part of the action, and much the noblest, except we conceive nothing to be action till the players come to blows; as if the painting of the hero's mind were not more properly the poet's work than the strength of his body. Nor does this anything contradict the opinion of Horace, where he tells us,

Segnius irritant animos demissa per aurem,
Quam quæ sunt oculis subjecta fidelibus.

For he says immediately after,

Non tamen intus
Digna geri promes in scenam; *multaq;* tolles

Ex oculis, quæ mox narret facundia præsens.

Among which many he recounts some:

Nec pueros coram populo Medea trucidet,
Aut in avem Progne mutetur, Cadmus in anguem, etc.

That is, those actions which by reason of their cruelty will cause aversion in us, or by reason of their impossibility, unbelief, ought either wholly to be avoided by a poet, or only delivered by narration. To which we may have leave to add, such as, to avoid tumult (as was before hinted), or to reduce the plot into a more reasonable compass of time, or for defect of beauty in them, are rather to be related than presented to the eye. Examples of all these kinds are frequent, not only among all the ancients, but in the best received of our English poets. We find Ben Jonson using them in his *Magnetic Lady,* where one comes out from dinner, and relates the quarrels and disorders of it, to save the undecent appearance of them on the stage, and to abbreviate the story; and this in express imitation of Terence, who had done the same before him in his *Eunuch,* where Pythias makes the like relation of what had happened within at the Soldiers' entertainment. The relations likewise of Sejanus's death, and the prodigies before it, are remarkable; the one of which was hid from sight, to avoid the horror and tumult of the representation; the other, to shun the introducing of things impossible to be believed. In that excellent play, *A King and no King,* Fletcher goes yet farther; for the whole unraveling of the plot is done by narration in the fifth act, after the manner of the ancients; and it moves great concernment in the audience, though it be only a relation of what was done many years before the play. I could multiply other instances, but these are sufficient to prove that there is no error in choosing a subject which requires this sort of narrations; in the ill management of them, there may.

"But I find I have been too long in this discourse, since the French have many other excellencies not common to us; as that you never see any of their plays end with a conversion, or simple change of will, which is the ordinary way which our poets use to end theirs. It shows little art in the conclusion of a dramatic poem, when they who have hindered the felicity during the four acts, desist from it in the fifth, without some powerful cause to take them off their design; and though I deny not but such reasons may be found, yet it is a path that is cautiously to be trod, and the poet is to be sure he convinces the audience that the motive is strong enough. As for example, the conversion of the Usurer in *The Scornful Lady* seems to me a little forced; for, being an Usurer, which implies a lover of money to the highest degree of covetousness,— and such the poet has represented him,— the account he gives for the sudden change is, that he has been duped by the wild young fellow; which in reason might render him more wary another time, and make him punish himself with harder fare and coarser clothes, to get up again what he had lost: but that he should look on it as a judgment, and so repent, we may expect to hear in a sermon, but I should never endure it in a play.

" I pass by this; neither will I insist on the care they take that no person after his first entrance shall ever appear, but the business which brings him upon the stage shall be evident; which rule, if observed, must needs render all the events in the play more natural; for there you see the probability of every accident, in the cause that produced it; and that which appears chance in the play, will seem so reasonable to you, that you will there find it almost necessary: so that in the exit of the actor you have a clear account of his purpose and design in the next entrance (though, if the scene be well wrought, the event will commonly deceive you); for there is nothing so absurd, says Corneille, as for an actor to leave the stage only because he has no more to say.

. . . . . .

Lisideius concluded in this manner; and Neander, after a little pause, thus answered him:

" I shall grant Lisideius, without much dispute, a great part of what he has urged against us; for I acknowledge that the French contrive their plots more regularly, and observe the laws of comedy, and decorum of the stage (to speak generally), with more exactness than the English. Farther, I deny not but he has taxed us justly in some irregularities of ours, which he has mentioned; yet, after all, I am of opinion that neither our faults nor their virtues are considerable enough to place them above us.

" For the lively imitation of nature being in the definition of a play, those which best fulfill that law ought to be esteemed superior to the others. 'Tis true, those beauties of the French poesy are such as will raise perfection higher where it is, but are not sufficient to give it where it is not: they are indeed the beauties of a statue, but not of a man, because not animated with the soul of poesy, which is imitation of humor and passions: and this Lisideius himself, or any other, however biassed to their party, cannot but acknowledge, if he will either compare the humors of our comedies, or the characters of our serious plays, with theirs. He who will look upon theirs which have been written till these last ten years, or thereabouts, will find it a hard matter to pick out two or three passable humors amongst them. Corneille himself, their arch-poet, what has he produced except *The Liar,* and you know how it was cried up in France; but when it came upon the English stage, though well translated, and that part of Dorante acted to so much advantage as I am confident it never received in its own country, the most favorable to it would not put it in competition with many of Fletcher's or Ben Jonson's. In the rest of Corneille's comedies you have little humor; he tells you himself, his way is, first to show two lovers in good intelligence with each other; in the working up of the play to embroil them by some mistake, and in the latter end to clear it, and reconcile them.

" But of late years Molière, the younger Corneille, Quinault, and some others, have been imitating afar off the quick turns and graces of the English stage. They have mixed their serious plays with mirth, like our tragi-comedies, since the death of Cardinal Richelieu; which Lisideius and many others not observing, have commended that in them for a virtue which they themselves no longer practice. Most of their new plays are, like some of ours, derived from the Spanish novels. There is scarce one of them without a veil, and a trusty Diego, who drolls much after the rate of *The Adventures.* But their humors, if I may grace them with that name, are so thin-sown, that never above one of them comes up in any play. I dare take upon me to find more variety of them in some one play of Ben Jonson's than in all theirs together; as he who has seen *The Alchemist, The Silent Woman,* or *Bartholomew Fair,* cannot but acknowledge with me.

" I grant the French have performed what was possible on the ground-work of the Spanish plays; what was pleasant before, they have made regular: but there is not above one good play to be writ on all those plots; they are too much alike to please often; which we need not the experience of our own stage to justify. As for their new way of mingling mirth with serious plot, I do not, with Lisideius, condemn the thing, though I cannot approve their manner of doing it. He tells us, we cannot so speedily recollect ourselves after a scene of great passion and concernment, as to pass to another of mirth and humor, and to enjoy it with any relish: but why should he imagine the soul of man more heavy than his senses? Does not the eye pass from an unpleasant object to a pleasant in a much shorter time than is required to this? and does not the unpleasantness of the first commend the beauty of the latter? The old rule of logic might have convinced him, that contraries, when placed near, set off each other. A continued gravity keeps the spirit too much bent; we must refresh it sometimes, as we bait in a journey that we may go on with greater ease. A scene of mirth, mixed with tragedy, has the same effect upon us which our music has betwixt the acts; which we find a relief to us from the best plots and language of the stage, if the discourses have been long. I must therefore have stronger arguments, ere I am convinced that compassion and mirth in the same subject destroy each other; and in the meantime cannot but conclude, to the honor of our nation, that we have invented, increased, and perfected a more pleasant way of writing for the stage than was ever known to the ancients or moderns of any nation, which is tragi-comedy.

" And this leads me to wonder why Lisideius and many others should cry up the barrenness of the French plots above the variety and copiousness of the English. Their plots are single; they carry on one design, which is pushed forward by all the actors, every scene in the play contributing and moving towards it. Our plays, besides the main design, have under-plots or by-concernments, of less considerable persons and intrigues, which are carried on with the motion of the main plot: as they say the orb of the fixed stars, and those of the planets, though they have motions of their own, are whirled about by the motion of the *primum mobile,* in which they are contained. That similitude expresses much of the English stage; for if contrary motions may be found in nature to agree; if a planet can go east and west at the same time; — one way by virtue of his own motion, the other by the force of the first mover; — it will not be difficult to imagine how the under-plot, which is only different, not contrary to the great design, may naturally be conducted along with it.

" Eugenius has already shown us, from the confession of the French poets, that the unity of action is sufficiently preserved, if all the imperfect actions of the play are conducing to the main design; but when those petty intrigues of a play are so ill ordered, that they have no coherence with the other, I must grant that Lisideius has reason to tax that want of due connection; for coördination in a play is as dangerous and unnatural as in a state. In the meantime he must acknowledge, our variety, if well ordered, will afford a greater pleasure to the audience.

" As for his other argument, that by pursuing one single theme they gain an advantage to express and work up the passions, I wish any example he could bring from them would make it good; for I confess their verses are to me the coldest I have ever read. Neither, indeed, is it possible for them, in the way they take, so to express passion, as that the effects of it should appear in the concernment of an audience, their speeches being so many declamations, which tire us with the length; so that instead of persuading us to grieve for their imaginary heroes, we are concerned for our own trouble, as we are in tedious visits of bad company; we are in pain till they are gone. When the French stage came to be reformed by Cardinal Richelieu, those long harangues were introduced to comply with the gravity of a churchman. Look upon the *Cinna* and the *Pompey;* they are not so properly to be called plays, as long discourses of reason of state; and *Polyeucte* in matters of religion is as solemn as the long stops upon our organs. Since that time it is grown into a custom, and their actors speak by the hour-glass, like our parsons; nay, they account it the grace of their parts, and think themselves disparaged by the poet, if they may not twice or thrice in a play entertain the audience with a speech of an hundred lines. I deny not but this may suit well enough with the French; for as we, who are a more sullen people, come to be diverted at our plays, so they, who are of an airy and gay temper, come thither to make themselves more serious: and this I conceive to be one reason why comedies are more pleasing to us, and tragedies to them. But to speak generally: it cannot be denied that short speeches and replies are more apt to move the passions and beget concernment in us, than the other; for it is unnatural for any one in a gust of passion to speak long together, or for another in the same condition to suffer him, without interruption. Grief and passion are like floods raised in little brooks by a sudden rain; they are quickly up; and if the concernment be poured unexpectedly in upon us, it overflows us: but a long sober shower gives them leisure to run out as they came in, without troubling the ordinary current. As for comedy, repartee is one of its chiefest graces; the greatest pleasure of the audience is a chase of wit, kept up on both sides, and swiftly managed. And this our forefathers, if not we, have had in Fletcher's plays, to a much higher degree of perfection than the French poets can reasonably hope to reach.

" There is another part of Lisideius his discourse, in which he rather excused our neighbors than commended them; that is, for aiming only to make one person considerable in their plays. 'Tis very true what he has urged, that one character in all plays, even without the poet's care, will have advantage of all the others; and that the design of the whole drama will chiefly depend on it. But this hinders not that there may be more shining characters in the play: many persons of a second magnitude, nay, some so very near, so almost equal to the first, that greatness may be opposed to greatness, and all the persons be made considerable, not only by their quality, but their action. 'Tis evident that the more the persons are, the greater will be the variety of the plot. If then the parts are managed so regularly, that the beauty of the whole be kept entire, and that the variety become not a perplexed and confused mass of accidents, you will find it infinitely pleasing to be led in a labyrinth of design, where you see some of your way before you, yet discern not the end till you arrive at it. And that all this is practicable, I can produce for examples many of our English plays: as *The Maid's Tragedy, The Alchemist, The Silent Woman:* I was going to have named *The Fox,* but that the unity of design seems not exactly observed in it: for there appear two actions in the play; the first naturally ending with the fourth act; the second forced from it in the fifth; which yet is the less to be condemned in him, because the disguise of Volpone, though it suited not with his character as a crafty or covetous person, agreed well enough with that of a voluptuary; and by it the poet gained the end at which he aimed, the punishment of vice, and the reward of virtue, both which that disguise produced. So that to judge equally of it, it was an excellent fifth act, but not so naturally proceeding from the former.

" But to leave this, and pass to the latter part of Lisideius his discourse, which concerns relations: I must acknowledge with him, that the French have reason to hide that part of the action which would occasion too much tumult on the stage, and to choose rather to have it made known by narration to the audience. Farther, I think it very convenient, for the reasons he has given, that all incredible actions were removed; but whether custom has so insinuated itself into our countrymen, or nature has so formed them to fierceness, I know not; but they will scarcely suffer combats and other objects of horror to be taken from them. And indeed, the indecency of tumults is all which can be objected against fighting: for why may not our imagination as well suffer itself to be deluded with the probability of it, as with any other thing in the play? For my part, I can with as great ease persuade myself that the blows are given in good earnest, as I can that they who strike them are kings or princes, or those persons which they represent. For objects of incredibility,— I would be satisfied from Lisideius, whether we have any so removed from all appearance of truth, as are those of Corneille's *Andromède;* a play which has been frequented the most of any he has writ. If the Perseus, or the son of a heathen god, the Pegasus, and the Monster, were not capable to choke a strong belief, let him blame any representation of ours hereafter. Those indeed were objects of delight; yet the reason is the same as to the probability: for he makes it not a ballet or masque, but a play, which is to resemble truth. But for death, that it ought not to be represented, I have, besides the arguments alleged by Lisideius, the authority of Ben Jonson, who has forborne it in his tragedies; for both the death of Sejanus and Catiline are related: though in the latter I cannot but observe one irregularity of that great poet; he has removed the scene in the same act from Rome to Catiline's army, and from thence again to Rome; and besides, has allowed a very inconsiderable time, after Catiline's speech, for the striking of the battle, and the return of Petreius, who is to relate the event of it to the senate: which I should not animadvert on him, who was otherwise a painful observer of τὸ πρέπον, or the *decorum* of the stage, if he had not used extreme severity in his judgment on the incomparable Shakspeare for the same fault.— To conclude on this subject of relations; if we are to be blamed for showing too much of the action, the French are as faulty for discovering too little of it: a mean betwixt both should be observed by every judicious writer, so as the audience may neither be left unsatisfied by not seeing what is beautiful, or shocked by beholding what is either incredible or undecent.

" I hope I have already proved in this discourse, that though we are not altogether so punctual as the French in observing the laws of comedy, yet our errors are so few, and little, and those things wherein we excel them so considerable, that we ought of right to be preferred before them. But what will Lisideius say, if they themselves acknowledge they are too strictly bounded by those laws, for breaking which he has blamed the English? I will allege Corneille's words, as I find them in the end of his *Discourse of the Three Unities:* ' Il est facile aux spéculatifs d'estre sévères,' etc. ' Tis easy for speculative persons to judge severely; but if they would produce to public view ten or twelve pieces of this nature, they would perhaps give more latitude to the rules than I have done, when by experience they had known how much we are limited and constrained by them, and how many beauties of the stage they banished from it.' To illustrate a little what he has said: By their servile observations of the unities of time and place, and integrity of scenes, they have brought on themselves that dearth of plot, and narrowness of imagination, which may be observed in all their plays. How many beautiful accidents might naturally happen in two or three days, which cannot arrive with any probability in the compass of twenty-four hours? There is time to be allowed also for maturity of design, which, amongst great and prudent persons, such as are often represented in tragedy, cannot, with any likelihood of truth, be brought to pass at so short a warning. Farther; by tying themselves strictly to the unity of place, and unbroken scenes, they are forced many times to omit some beauties which cannot be shown where the act began; but might, if the scene were interrupted, and the stage cleared for the persons to enter in another place; and therefore the French poets are often forced upon absurdities; for if the act begins in a chamber, all the persons in the play must have some business or other to come thither, or else they are not to be shown that act; and sometimes their characters are very unfitting to appear there: as, suppose it were the king's bed-chamber; yet the meanest man in the tragedy must come and dispatch his business there, rather than in the lobby or courtyard (which is fitter for him), for fear the stage should be cleared, and the scenes broken. Many times they fall by it in a greater inconvenience; for they keep their scenes unbroken, and yet change the place; as in one of their newest plays, where the act begins in the street. There a gentleman is to meet his friend; he sees him with his man, coming out from his father's house; they talk together, and the first goes out: the second, who is a lover, has made an appointment with his mistress; she appears at the window, and then we are to imagine the scene lies under it. This gentleman is called away, and leaves his servant with his mistress; presently her father is heard from within; the young lady is afraid the serving-man should be discovered, and thrusts him into a place of safety, which is supposed to be her closet. After this, the father enters to the daughter, and now the scene is in a house; for he is seeking from one room to another for this poor Philipin, or French Diego, who is heard from within, drolling and breaking many a miserable conceit on the subject of his sad condition. In this ridiculous manner the play goes forward, the stage being never empty all the while: so that the street, the window, the houses, and the closet, are made to walk about, and the persons to stand still. Now what, I beseech you, is more easy than to write a regular French play, or more difficult than to write an irregular English one, like those of Fletcher, or of Shakspeare?

" If they content themselves, as Corneille did, with some flat design, which, like an ill riddle, is found out ere it be half proposed, such plots we can make every way regular, as easily as they; but whenever they endeavor to rise to any quick turns and counterturns of plot, as some of them have attempted, since Corneille's plays have been less in vogue, you see they write as irregularly as we, though they cover it more speciously. Hence the reason is perspicuous why no French plays, when translated, have, or ever can succeed on the English stage. For, if you consider the plots, our own are fuller of variety; if the writing, ours are more quick and fuller of spirit; and therefore 'tis a strange mistake in those who decry the way of writing plays in verse, as if the English therein imitated the French. We have borrowed nothing from them; our plots are weaved in English looms: we endeavor therein to follow the variety and greatness of characters which are derived to us from Shakespeare and Fletcher; the copious-

ness and well-knitting of the intrigues we have from Jonson; and for the verse itself we have English precedents of elder date than any of Corneille's plays. Not to name our old comedies before Shakespeare, which were all writ in verse of six feet, or Alexandrines, such as the French now use,—I can show in Shakespeare many scenes of rhyme together, and the like in Ben Jonson's tragedies: in Catiline and Sejanus sometimes thirty or forty lines,—I mean besides the Chorus, or the monologues; which, by the way, showed Ben no enemy to this way of writing, especially if you read his Sad Shepherd, which goes sometimes on rhyme, sometimes on blank verse, like an horse who eases himself on trot and amble. You find him likewise commending Fletcher's pastoral of The Faithful Shepherdess, which is for the most part rhyme, though not refined to that purity to which it hath since been brought. And these examples are enough to clear us from a servile imitation of the French.

" But to return whence I have digressed: I dare boldly affirm these two things of the English drama; — First, that we have many plays of ours as regular as any of theirs, and which, besides, have more variety of plot and characters; and secondly, that in most of the irregular plays of Shakspeare or Fletcher (for Ben Jonson's are for the most part regular), there is a more masculine fancy and greater spirit in the writing than there is in any of the French. I could produce, even in Shakspeare's and Fletcher's works, some plays which are almost exactly formed; as The Merry Wives of Windsor, and The Scornful Lady: but because (generally speaking) Shakspeare, who writ first, did not perfectly observe the laws of comedy, and Fletcher, who came nearer to perfection, yet through carelessness made many faults.

" If this comedy and some others of his were translated into French prose (which would now be no wonder to them, since Molière has lately given them plays out of verse, which have not displeased them), I believe the controversy would soon be decided betwixt the two nations, even making them the judges. But we need not call our heroes to our aid. Be it spoken to the honor of the English, our nation can never want in any age such who are able to dispute the empire of wit with any people in the universe. And though the fury of a civil war, and power for twenty years together abandoned to a barbarous race of men, enemies of all good learning, had buried the muses under the ruins of monarchy; yet, with the restoration of our happiness, we see revived poesy lifting up its head, and already shaking off the rubbish which lay so heavy on it. We have seen since his majesty's return, many dramatic poems which yield not to those of any foreign nation, and which deserve all laurels but the English. I will set aside flattery and envy: it cannot be denied but we have had some little blemish either in the plot or writing of all those plays which have been made within these seven years; (and perhaps there is no nation in the world so quick to discern them, or so difficult to pardon them, as ours:) yet if we can persuade ourselves to use the candor of that poet, who, though the most severe of critics, has left us this caution by which to moderate our censures —

> ubi plura nitent in carmine, non
>   ego paucis
> Offendar maculis; —

if, in consideration of their many and great beauties, we can wink at some slight and little imperfections, if we, I say, can be thus equal to ourselves, I ask no favor from the French. And if I do not venture upon any particular judgment of our late plays, 'tis out of the consideration which an ancient writer gives me: *vivorum, ut magna admiratio, ita censura difficilis:* betwixt the extremes of admiration and malice, 'tis hard to judge uprightly of the living. Only I think it may be permitted me to say, that as it is no lessening to us to yield to some plays, and those not many, of our own nation in the last age, so can it be no addition to pronounce of our present poets, that they have far surpassed all the ancients, and the modern writers of other countries. . . . For a play is still an imitation of nature; we know we are to be deceived, and we desire to be so; but no man ever was deceived but with a probability of truth; for who will suffer a gross lie to be fastened on him? Thus we sufficiently understand that the scenes which represent cities and countries to us are not really such, but only painted on boards and canvas; but shall that excuse the ill painture or designment of them? Nay, rather ought they not be labored with so much the more diligence and exactness, to help the imagination? since the mind of man does naturally tend to truth; and therefore the nearer anything comes to the imitation of it, the more it pleases."

\.   \.   \.   \.   \.   \.

PREFACE TO TROILUS AND CRESSIDA[2]

(1679)

THE GROUNDS OF CRITICISM IN TRAGEDY

Tragedy is thus defined by Aristotle (omitting what I thought unnecessary in his definition). It is an imitation of one entire, great, and probable action; not told, but represented; which, by moving in us fear and pity, is conducive to the purging of those two passions in our minds. More largely thus: Tragedy describes or paints an action, which action must have all the proprieties above named. First, it must be one or single; that is, it must not be a history of one man's life, suppose of Alexander the

Great, or Julius Cæsar, but one single action of theirs. This condemns all Shakspeare's historical plays, which are rather chronicles represented, than tragedies; and all double action of plays. As, to avoid a satire upon others, I will make bold with my own *Marriage a la Mode*, where there are manifestly two actions not depending on one another: but in *Œdipus* there cannot properly be said to be two actions, because the love of Adrastus and Eurydice has a necessary dependence on the principal design into which it is woven. The natural reason of this rule is plain; for two different independent actions distract the at-

2 'Re-printed, complete, from the Everyman's Edition of *Dramatic Essays by John Dryden* (London and New York, n. d.).— Ed.

tention and concernment of the audience, and consequently destroy the intention of the poet; if his business be to move terror and pity, and one of his actions be comical, the other tragical, the former will divert the people, and utterly make void his greater purpose. Therefore, as in perspective, so in Tragedy, there must be a point of sight in which all the lines terminate; otherwise the eye wanders, and the work is false. This was the practice of the Grecian stage. But Terence made an innovation in the Roman: all his plays have double actions; for it was his custom to translate two Greek comedies, and to weave them into one of his, yet so that both their actions were comical, and one was principal, the other but secondary or subservient. And this has obtained on the English stage, to give us the pleasure of variety.

As the action ought to be one, it ought, as such, to have order in it; that is, to have a natural beginning, a middle, and an end. A natural beginning, says Aristotle, is that which could not necessarily have been placed after another thing; and so of the rest. This consideration will arraign all plays after the new model of Spanish plots, where accident is heaped upon accident, and that which is first might as reasonably be last; an inconvenience not to be remedied, but by making one accident naturally produce another, otherwise it is a farce and not a play. Of this nature is *The Slighted Maid;* where there is no scene in the first act which might not by as good reason be in the fifth. And if the action ought to be one, the tragedy ought likewise to conclude with the action of it. Thus in *Mustapha,* the play should naturally have ended with the death of Zanger, and not have given us the grace-cup after dinner, of Solyman's divorce from Roxolana.

The following properties of the action are so easy that they need not my explaining. It ought to be great, and to consist of great persons, to distinguish it from Comedy, where the action is trivial, and the persons of inferior rank. The last quality of the action is, that it ought to be probable, as well as admirable and great. 'Tis not necessary that there should be historical truth in it; but always necessary that there should be a likeness of truth, something that is more than barely possible; *probable* being that which succeeds, or happens, oftener than it misses. To invent therefore a probability, and to make it wonderful, is the most difficult undertaking in the art of Poetry; for that which is not wonderful is not great; and that which is not probable will not delight a reasonable audience. This action, thus described, must be represented and not told, to distinguish Dramatic Poetry from Epic: but I hasten to the end or scope of Tragedy, which is, to rectify or purge our passions, fear, and pity.

To instruct delightfully is the general end of all poetry. Philosophy instructs, but it performs its work by precept; which is not delightful, or not so delightful as example. To purge the passions by example is therefore the particular instruction which belongs to Tragedy. Rapin, a judicious critic, has observed from Aristotle, that pride and want of commiseration are the most predominant vices in mankind; therefore, to cure us of these two, the inventors of Tragedy have chosen to work upon two other passions, which are fear and pity. We are wrought to fear by their setting before our eyes some terrible example of misfortune, which happened to persons of the highest quality; for such an action demonstrates to us that no condition is privileged from the turns of fortune; this must of necessity cause terror in us, and consequently abate our pride. But when we see that the most virtuous, as well as the greatest, are not exempt from such misfortunes, that consideration moves pity in us, and insensibly works us to be helpful to, and tender over, the distressed; which is the noblest and most god-like of moral virtues. Here it is observable that it is absolutely necessary to make a man virtuous, if we desire he should be pitied: we lament not, but detest, a wicked man; we are glad when we behold his crimes are punished, and that poetical justice is done upon him. Euripides was censured by the critics of his time for making his chief characters too wicked; for example, Phædra, though she loved her son-in-law with reluctancy, and that it was a curse upon her family for offending Venus, yet was thought too ill a pattern for the stage. Shall we therefore banish all characters of villainy? I confess I am not of that opinion; but it is necessary that the hero of the play be not a villain; that is, the characters, which should move our pity, ought to have virtuous inclinations, and degrees of moral goodness in them. As for a perfect character of virtue, it never was in Nature, and therefore there can be no imitation of it; but there are alloys of frailty to be allowed for the chief persons, yet so that the good which is in them shall outweigh the bad, and consequently leave room for punishment on the one side and pity on the other.

After all, if any one will ask me whether a tragedy cannot be made upon any other grounds than those of exciting pity and terror in us, [Le] Bossu, the best of modern critics, answers thus in general: That all excellent arts, and particularly that of poetry, have been invented and brought to perfection by men of a transcendent genius; and that, therefore, they who practice afterwards the same arts are obliged to tread in their footsteps, and to search in their writings the foundation of them; for it is not just that new rules should destroy the authority of the old. But Rapin writes more particularly thus, that no passions in a story are so proper to move our concernment as fear and pity; and that it is from our concernment we receive our pleasure is undoubted; when the soul becomes agitated with fear for one character, or hope for another, then it is that we are pleased in Tragedy, by the interest which we taken in their adventures.

After the plot, which is the foundation of the play, the next thing to which we ought to apply our judgment is the manners; for now the poet comes to work above ground. The ground-work, indeed, is that which is most necessary, as that upon which depends the firmness of the whole fabric; yet it strikes not the eye so much as the beauties or imperfections of the manners, the thoughts, and the expressions.

The first rule which [Le] Bossu prescribes to the writer of an Heroic Poem, and which holds too by the same reason in all Dramatic Poetry, is to make the moral of the work; that is, to lay down to yourself what that precept of morality shall be which you would insinuate into the people; as, namely, Homer's (which I have copied in my *Conquest of Granada*) was, that union preserves a commonwealth and discord destroys it; Sophocles, in his *Œdipus,* that no man is to be accounted happy before his death. 'Tis the moral that directs the whole action of the play to one center; and that action or fable is the example built upon the moral, which confirms the truth of it to our experience: when the fable is designed, then, and not before, the persons are to be introduced, with their manners, characters, and passions.

The manners, in a poem, are understood to be those inclinations, whether natural or acquired, which move and carry us to actions, good, bad, or indifferent, in a play; or which incline the persons to such or such actions. I have anticipated part of this discourse already in declaring that a poet ought not to make the manners perfectly good in his best persons; but neither are they to be more wicked in any of his characters than necessity requires. To produce a villain, without other reason than a natural inclination to villainy, is, in Poetry, to produce an effect without a cause; and to make him more a villain than he has just reason to be is to make an effect which is stronger than the cause.

The manners arise from many causes; and are either distinguished by complexion, as choleric and phlegmatic, or by the differences of age or sex, of climates, or quality of the persons, or their present condition. They are likewise to be gathered from the several virtues, vices, or passions, and many other commonplaces, which a poet must be supposed to have learned from Natural Philosophy, Ethics, and History; of all which whosoever is ignorant does not deserve the name of poet.

But as the manners are useful in this art, they may be all comprised under these general heads: first, they must be apparent; that is, in every character of the play some inclinations of the person must appear; and these are shown in the actions and discourse. Secondly, the manners must be suitable, or agreeing to the persons; that is, to the age, sex, dignity, and the other general heads of manners: thus, when a poet has given the dignity of a king to one of his persons, in all his actions and speeches that person must discover majesty, magnanimity, and jealousy of power, because these are suitable to the general manners of a king. The third property of manners is resemblance; and this is founded upon the particular characters of men as we have them delivered to us by relation or history; that is, when a poet has the known character of this or that man before him, he is bound to represent him such, at least not contrary to that which fame has reported him to have been. Thus, it is not a poet's choice to make Ulysses choleric or Achilles patient, because Homer has described 'em quite otherwise. Yet this is a rock on which ignorant writers daily split; and the absurdity is as monstrous as if a painter should draw a coward running from a battle, and tell us it was the picture of Alexander the Great.

The last property of manners is that they be constant and equal, that is, maintained the same through the whole design: thus, when Vergil had once given the name of *pious* to Æneas, he was bound to show him such, in all his words and actions, through the whole poem. All these properties Horace has hinted to a judicious observer: 1. *Notandi sunt tibi mores; 2. Aut famam sequere; 3. Aut sibi convenientia finge; 4. Servetur ad imum, qualis ab incepto processerit, et sibi constet.*

From the manners, the characters of persons are derived; for, indeed, the characters are no other than the inclinations as they appear in the several persons of the poem; a character being thus defined — that which distinguishes one man from another. Not to repeat the same things over again which have been said of the manners, I will only add what is necessary here. A character, or that which distinguishes one man from all others, cannot be supposed to consist of one particular virtue, or vice, or passion only; but 'tis a composition of qualities which are not contrary to one another in the same person; thus, the same man may be liberal and valiant, but not liberal and covetous; so in a comical character, or humor (which is an inclination to this or that particular folly), Falstaff is a liar, and a coward, a glutton, and a buffoon, because all these qualities may agree in the same man; yet it is still to be observed that one virtue, vice, and passion ought to be shown in every man as predominant over all the rest; as covetousness in Crassus, love of his country in Brutus; and the same in characters which are feigned.

The chief character or hero in a tragedy, as I have already shown, ought in prudence to be such a man who has so much more of virtue in him than of vice, that he may be left amiable to the audience, which otherwise cannot have any concernment for his sufferings; and it is on this one character that the pity and terror must be principally, if not wholly, founded: a rule which is extremely necessary, and which none of the critics, that I know, have fully enough discovered to us. For terror and compassion work but weakly when they are divided into many persons. If Creon had been the chief character in *Œdipus,* there had neither been terror nor compassion moved, but only detestation of the man and joy for his punishment; if Adrastus and Eurydice had been made more appearing characters, then the pity had been divided and lessened on the part of Œdipus: but making Œdipus the best and bravest person, and even Jocasta but an underpart to him, his virtues, and the punishment of his fatal crime, drew both the pity and the terror to himself.

By what has been said of the manners, it will be easy for a reasonable man to judge whether the characters be truly or falsely drawn in a tragedy; for if there be no manners appearing in the characters, no concernment for the persons can be raised; no pity or horror can be moved but by vice or virtue; therefore, without them, no person can have any business in the play. If the inclinations be obscure, it is a sign the poet is in the dark and knows not what manner of man he presents to you; and consequently you can have no idea, or very imperfect, of that man, nor can judge what resolutions he ought to take or what words or actions are proper for him. Most comedies made up of accidents or adventures are liable to fall into this error; and tragedies with many turns are subject to it; for the manners can never be evident where the surprises of fortune take up all the business of the stage; and where the poet is more in pain to tell you what happened to such a man than what he was. Tis one of the excellencies of Shakespeare that the manners of his persons are generally apparent, and you see their bent and inclinations. Fletcher comes far short of him in this, as indeed he does almost in everything: there are but glimmerings of manners in most of his comedies, which run upon adventures; and in his tragedies, Rollo, Otto the King and no King, Melantius, and many others of his best, are but pictures shown you in the twilight; you know not whether they resemble vice or virtue, and they are either good, bad, or indifferent, as the present scene requires it. But of all poets, this commendation is to be given to Ben Jonson, that the manners even of the most inconsiderable persons in his plays are everywhere apparent.

By considering the second quality of manners, which is, that they be suitable to the age, quality, country, dignity, etc., of the character, we may likewise judge whether a poet has followed nature. In this kind, Sophocles and Euripides have more excelled among the Greeks than Æschylus, and Terence more than Plautus among the Romans. Thus, Sophocles gives to Œdipus the true qualities of a king in both those plays which bear his name; but in the latter, which is the *Œdipus Colonæus,* he lets fall on purpose his tragic style; his hero speaks not in the arbitrary tone, but remembers, in the softness of his complaints, that he is an unfortunate blind old man, that he is banished from his country, and persecuted by his next relations. The present French poets are generally accused that, wheresoever they lay the scene, or in whatsoever age, the manners of their heroes are wholly French. Racine's Bajazet is bred at Constantinople, but his civilities are conveyed to him, by some secret passage, from Versailles into the Seraglio. But our Shakspeare, having ascribed to Henry the Fourth the character of a king and of a father, gives him the perfect manners of each relation, when either he transacts with his son or with his subjects. Fletcher, on the other side, gives neither to Arbaces nor to his king, in the *Maid's Tragedy,* the qualities which are suitable to a monarch; though he may be excused a little in the latter, for the king there is not uppermost in the character; 'tis the lover of Evadne, who is king only in a second consideration; and though he be unjust, and has other faults which shall be nameless, yet he is not the hero of the play. 'Tis true, we find him a lawful prince (though I never heard of any king that was in Rhodes), and therefore Mr. Rymer's criticism stands good, that he should not be shown in so vicious a character. Sophocles has been more judicious in his *Antigone;* for, though he represents in Creon a bloody prince, yet he makes him not a lawful king, but an usurper, and Antigona herself is the heroine of the tragedy: but when Philaster wounds Arethusa and the boy, and Perigot his mistress, in the *Faithful Shepherdess,* both these are contrary to the character of manhood. Nor is *Valentinian* managed much better; for though Fletcher has taken his picture truly, and shown him as he was, an effeminate, voluptuous man, yet he has forgotten that he was an emperor, and has given him none of those royal marks which ought to appear in a lawful successor of the throne. If it be inquired what Fletcher should have done on this occasion — ought he not to have represented Valentinian as he was? — [Le] Bossu shall answer this question for me by an instance of the like nature: Mauritius, the Greek emperor, was a prince far surpassing Valentinian, for he was endued with many kingly virtues; he was religious, merciful, and valiant, but withal he was noted of extreme covetousness, a vice which is contrary to the character of a hero or a prince: therefore, says the critic, that emperor was no fit person to be represented in a tragedy, unless his good qualities were only to be shown and his covetousness (which sullied them all) were slurred over by the artifice of the poet. To return once more to Shakspeare; no man ever drew so many characters, or generally distinguished 'em better from one another, excepting only Jonson. I will instance but in one to show the copiousness of his intention; it is that of Caliban, or the monster, in the *Tempest.* He seems there to have created a person which was not in nature, a boldness which, at first sight, would appear intolerable; for he makes him a species of himself, begotten by an incubus on a witch; but this, as I have elsewhere proved, is not wholly beyond the bounds of credibility, at least the vulgar still believe it. We have the separated notions of a spirit and of a witch (and spirits, according to Plato, are vested with a subtle body; according to some of his followers have different sexes); therefore, as from the distinct apprehensions of a horse and of a man imagination has formed a centaur, so from those of an incubus and a sorceress Shakspeare has produced his monster. Whether or no his generation can be defended I leave to philosophy; but of this I am certain, that the poet has most judiciously furnished him with a person, a language, and a character, which will suit him, both by father's and mother's side: he has all the discontents and malice of a witch and of a devil, besides a convenient proportion of the deadly sins; gluttony, sloth, and lust are manifest; the dejectedness of a slave is likewise given him, and the ignorance of one bred up in a desert island. His person is monstrous, and he is the product of unnatural lust; and his language is as hobgoblin as his person; in all things he is distinguished from other mortals. The characters of Fletcher are poor and narrow in comparison of Shakspeare's; I remember not one which is not borrowed from him, unless you will accept that strange mixture of a man in the *King and no King;* so that in this part Shakspeare is generally worth our imitation, and to imitate Fletcher is but to copy after him who was a copyer.

Under this general head of manners the passions are naturally included as belonging to the characters. I speak not of pity and of terror, which are to be moved in the audience by the plot; but of anger, hatred, love, ambition, jealousy, 'revenge, etc., as they are shown in this or that person of the play. To describe these naturally, and to move them artfully, is one of the greatest commendations which can be given to a poet: to write pathetically, says Longinus, cannot proceed but from a lofty genius. A poet must be born with this quality: yet, unless he help himself by an acquired knowledge of the passions, what they are in their own nature, and by what springs they are to be moved, he will be subject either to raise them where they ought not to be raised, or not to raise them by the just degrees of nature, or to amplify them beyond the natural bounds, or not to observe the

crises and turns of them in their cooling and decay; all which errors proceed from want of judgment in the poet, and from being unskilled in the principles of moral philosophy. Nothing is more frequent in a fanciful writer than to foil himself by not managing his strength; therefore, as in a wrestler, there is first required some measure of force, a well-knit body and active limbs, without which all instruction would be vain; yet, these being granted, if he want the skill which is necessary to a wrestler he shall make but small advantage of his natural robustuousness: so, in a poet, his inborn vehemence and force of spirit will only run him out of breath the sooner if it be not supported by the help of Art. The roar of passion, indeed, may please an audience, three parts of which are ignorant enough to think all is moving which is noise, and it may stretch the lungs of an ambitious actor who will die upon the spot for a thundering clap; but it will move no other passion than indignation and contempt from judicious men. Longinus, whom I have hitherto followed, continues thus: *If the passions be artfully employed, the discourse becomes vehement and lofty: if otherwise, there is nothing more ridiculous than a great passion out of season:* and to this purpose he animadverts severely upon Æschylus, who writ nothing in cold blood, but was always in a rapture and in fury with his audience: the inspiration was still upon him, he was ever tearing it upon the tripos; or (to run off as madly as he does from one similitude to another) he was always at highflood of passion, even in the dead ebb and lowest water-mark of the scene. He who would raise the passion of a judicious audience, says a learned critic, must be sure to take his hearers along with him; if they be in a calm, 'tis in vain for him to be in a huff: he must move them by degrees, and kindle with 'em; otherwise he will be in danger of setting his own heap of stubble on fire, and of burning out by himself, without warming the company that stand about him. They who would justify the madness of poetry from the authority of Aristotle have mistaken the text and consequently the interpretation: I imagine it to be false read where he says of poetry that it is Εὐφυοῦς ἢ μανικοῦ, that it had always somewhat in it either of a genius or of a madman. 'Tis more probable that the original ran thus, that poetry was Εὐφυοῦς οὐ μανικοῦ, that it belongs to a witty man, but not to a madman. Thus then the passions, as they are considered simply and in themselves, suffer violence when they are perpetually maintained at the same height; for what melody can be made on that instrument, all whose strings are screwed up at first to their utmost stretch and to the same sound? But this is not the worst: for the characters likewise bear a part in the general calamity if you consider the passions as embodied in them; for it follows of necessity that no man can be distinguished from another by his discourse when every man is ranting, swaggering, and exclaiming with the same excess: as if it were the only business of all the characters to contend with each other for the prize at Billingsgate, or that the scene of the tragedy lay in Bet'lem. Suppose the poet should intend this man to be choleric and that man to be patient, yet when they are confounded in the writing you cannot distinguish them from one another: for the man who was called patient and tame is only so before he speaks; but let his clack be set agoing, and he shall tongue it as impetuously, and as loudly, as the errantest hero in the play. By this means the characters are only distinct in name; but, in reality, all the men and women in the play are the same person. No man should pretend to write who cannot temper his fancy with his judgment: nothing is more dangerous to a raw horseman than a hot-mouthed jade without a curb.

It is necessary therefore for a poet, who would concern an audience by describing of a passion, first to prepare it and not to rush upon it all at once. Ovid has judiciously shown the difference of these two ways in the speeches of Ajax and Ulysses: Ajax, from the very beginning, breaks out into his exclamations, and is swearing by his Maker, — *Agimus, proh Jupiter, inquit.* Ulysses, on the contrary, prepares his audience with all the submissiveness he can practice, and all the calmness of a reasonable man; he found his judges in a tranquility of spirit, and therefore set out lei-

surely and softly with 'em, till he had warmed 'em by degrees; and then he began to mend his pace and to draw them along with his own impetuousness: yet so managing his breath that it might not fail him at his need, and reserving his utmost proofs of ability even to the last. The success, you see, was answerable; for the crowd only applauded the speech of Ajax —

Vulgique secutum
Ultima murmur erat:

but the judges awarded the prize, for which they contended, to Ulysses —

Mota manus procerum est; et quid facundia posset
Tum patuit, fortisque viri tulit arma disertus.

The next necessary rule is to put nothing into the discourse which may hinder your moving of the passions. Too many accidents, as I have said, encumber the poet as much as the arms of Saul did David; for the variety of passions which they produce are ever crossing and justling each other out of the way. He who treats of joy and grief together is in a fair way of causing neither of those effects. There is yet another obstacle to be removed, which is pointed wit, and sentences affected out of season; these are nothing of kin to the violence of passion: no man is at leisure to make sentences and similes when his soul is in an agony. I the rather name this fault that it may serve to mind me of my former errors; neither will I spare myself, but give an example of this kind from my *Indian Emperor*. Montezuma, pursued by his enemies and seeking sanctuary, stands parleying without the fort and describing his danger to Cydaria in a simile of six lines —

As on the sands the frighted traveler
Sees the high seas come rolling from afar, etc.

My Indian potentate was well skilled in the sea for an inland prince, and well improved since the first act, when he sent his son to discover it. The image had not been amiss from another man at another time: *sed nunc non erat hisce locus:* he destroyed the concernment which the audience might otherwise have had for him; for they could not think the danger near when he had the leisure to invent a simile.

If Shakspeare be allowed, as I think he must, to have made his characters distinct, it will easily be inferred that he understood the nature of the passions: because it has been proved already that confused passions make undistinguishable characters: yet I cannot deny that he has his failings; but they are not so much in the passions themselves as in his manner of expression: he often obscures his meaning by his words, and sometimes makes it unintelligible. I will not say of so great a poet that he distinguished not the blown puffy style from true sublimity; but I may venture to maintain that the fury of his fancy often transported him beyond the bounds of judgment, either in coining of new words and phrases, or racking words which were in use into the violence of a catachresis. It is not that I would explode the use of metaphors from passion, for Longinus thinks 'em necessary to raise it: but to use 'em at every word, to say nothing without a metaphor, a simile, an image, or description, is, I doubt, to smell a little too strongly of the buskin. I must be forced to give an example of expressing passion figuratively; but that I may do it with respect to Shakspeare, it shall not be taken from anything of his: 'tis an exclamation against fortune, quoted in his *Hamlet* but written by some other poet —

Out, out, thou strumpet, Fortune! all you gods,
In general synod, take away her power;
Break all the spokes and felleys from her wheel,
And bowl the round nave down the hill of Heav'n,
As low as to the fiends.

And immediately after, speaking of Hecuba, when Priam was killed before her eyes —

The mobbled queen
Threatening the flame, ran up and down
With bisson rheum; a clout about that head

Where late the diadem stood; and for a robe,
About her lank and all o'er-teemed loins,
A blanket in th' alarm of fear caught up.
Who this had seen, with tongue in venom steep'd
'Gainst Fortune's state would treason have pronounced;
But if the gods themselves did see her then,
When she saw Pyrrhus make malicious sport
In mincing with his sword her husband's limbs,
The instant burst of clamour that she made
(Unless things mortal move them not at all)
Would have made milch the burning eyes of heaven,
And passion in the gods.

What a pudder is here kept in raising the expression of trifling thoughts! Would not a man have thought that the poet had been bound prentice to a wheelwright for his first rant? and had followed a ragman for the clout and blanket in the second? Fortune is painted on a wheel, and therefore the writer, in a rage, will have poetical justice done upon every member of that engine: after this execution, he bowls the nave down-hill, from Heaven, to the fiends (an unreasonable long mark, a man would think); 'tis well there are no solid orbs to stop it in the way, or no element of fire to consume it: but when it came to the earth it must be monstrous heavy to break ground as low as the center. His making milch the burning eyes of heaven was a pretty tolerable flight too: and I think no man ever drew milk out of eyes before him: yet to make the wonder greater, these eyes were burning. Such a sight indeed were enough to have raised passion in the gods; but to excuse the effects of it, he tells you perhaps they did not see it. Wise men would be glad to find a little sense couched under all these pompous words; for bombast is commonly the delight of that audience which loves poetry but understands it not: and as commonly has been the practice of those writers who, not being able to infuse a natural passion into the mind, have made it their business to ply the ears, and to stun their judges by the noise. But Shakspeare does not often thus; for the passions in his scene between Brutus and Cassius are extremely natural, the thoughts are such as arise from the matter, the expression of 'em not viciously figurative. I cannot leave this subject before I do justice to that divine poet by giving you one of his passionate descriptions: 'tis of Richard the Second when he was deposed and led in triumph through the streets of London by Henry of Bullingbrook: the painting of it is so lively, and the words so moving, that I have scarce read anything comparable to it in any other language. Suppose you have seen already the fortunate usurper passing through the crowd, and followed by the shouts and acclamations of the people; and now behold King Richard entering upon the scene: consider the wretchedness of his condition and his carriage in it; and refrain from pity if you can —

As in a theater, the eyes of men,
After a well-graced actor leaves the
    stage,
Are idly bent on him that enters next,
Thinking his prattle to be tedious:
Even so, or with much more contempt,
    men's eyes
Did scowl on Richard: no man cried,
    God save him:
No joyful tongue gave him his welcome
    home,
But dust was thrown upon his sacred
    head,
Which with such gentle sorrow he shook
    off,
His face still combating with tears and
    smiles
(The badges of his grief and patience),
That had not God (for some strong pur-
    pose) steel'd
The hearts of men, they must perforce
    have melted,
And barbarism itself have pitied him.

To speak justly of this whole matter: 'tis neither height of thought that is discommended, nor pathetic vehemence, nor any nobleness of expression in its proper place; but 'tis a false measure of all these, something which is like them, and is not them; 'tis the Bristol-stone which appears like a diamond; 'tis an extrava-gant thought instead of a sublime one; 'tis roaring madness instead of vehemence; and a sound of words instead of sense. If Shakspeare were stripped of all the bombasts in his passions, and dressed in the most vulgar words, we should find the beauties of his thoughts remaining; if his embroideries were burnt down, there would still be silver at the bottom of the melting-pot: but I fear (at least let me fear it for myself) that we, who ape his sounding words, have nothing of his thought, but are all outside; there is not so much as a dwarf within our giant's clothes. Therefore, let not Shakspeare suffer for our sakes; 'tis our fault, who succeed him in an age which is more refined, if we imitate him so ill that we copy his failings only and make a virtue of that in our writings which in his was an imperfection.

For what remains, the excellency of that poet was, as I have said, in the more manly passions; Fletcher's in the softer: Shakspeare writ better betwixt man and man; Fletcher betwixt man and woman: consequently, the one described friendship better; the other love: yet Shakspeare taught Fletcher to write love: and Juliet and Desdemona are originals. 'Tis true the scholar had the softer soul; but the master had the kinder. Friendship is both a virtue and a passion essentially; love is a passion only in its nature, and is not a virtue but by accident: good nature makes friendship; but effeminacy love. Shakspeare had an universal mind, which comprehended all characters and passions; Fletcher a more confined and limited: for though he treated love in perfection, yet honor, ambition, revenge, and generally all the stronger passions, he either touched not, or not masterly. To conclude all, he was a limb of Shakspeare.

I had intended to have proceeded to the last property of manners, which is, that they must be constant, and the characters maintained the same from the beginning to the end; and from thence to have proceeded to the thoughts and expressions suitable to a tragedy: but I will first see how this will relish with the age. It is, I confess, but cursorily written; yet the judgment, which is given here, is generally founded upon experience; but because many men are shocked at the name of rules, as if they were a kind of magisterial prescription upon poets, I will conclude with the words of Rapin, in his *Reflections* on Aristotle's work of *Poetry:* "If the rules be well considered, we shall find them to be made only to reduce Nature into method, to trace her step by step, and not to suffer the least mark of her to escape us: 'tis only by these that probability in fiction is maintained, which is the soul of poetry. They are founded upon good sense, and sound reason, rather than on authority; for though Aristotle and Horace are produced, yet no man must argue that what they write is true, because they writ it; but 'tis evident, by the ridiculous mistakes and gross absurdities which have been made by those poets who have taken their fancy only for their guide, that if this fancy be not regulated, it is a mere caprice, and utterly incapable to produce a reasonable and judicious poem."

JOHN MILTON

John Milton was born at London in 1608. His father was an Oxford man, and a musician of note. John received a very careful education both at school and at home. He was graduated from St. Paul's at the age of fifteen. Even before that time he is said to have written verses, in Latin and in English. He attended Christ's College, Cambridge, where he remained for over seven years. Some of his earliest known poems date from his college days, especially the *Ode on the Morning of Christ's Nativity* (1629). The years between 1632 and 1638 Milton spent with his father at Horton. He intended to enter the church, but finding himself unable to subscribe to its tenets, he decided to devote his energies to literature. During his stay in the country he wrote *L'Allegro* and *Il Penseroso, Comus,* which was performed in 1634, and *Lycidas* (1638). From Horton he went to the Continent. Toward the end of the year he was brought home by news of the Civil War. He returned in August of the next year, and became imbroiled in various religious controversies. At the same time he was giving a great deal of thought to projects for an epic or tragedy he hoped to write. In 1643 he was married, but his wife deserted him soon after. This called forth his tract on divorce, *The Doctrine and Discipline of Divorce,* etc. (1643). Two years later he was reconciled with his wife, who returned to him. In 1649 he became a Latin Secretary under Cromwell, and wrote a number of political pamphlets. He became blind in 1652, and his wife died the next year. He married again in 1656. He continued as secretary until the Restoration. At that time he was considered a menace to the government, and was arrested, but soon after released. His second wife died in 1660, and he married for the third time in 1663. *Paradise Lost* was begun in 1658, and finished five years later, but not published until 1667. In 1671, together with *Paradise Found,* he published his drama *Samson Agonistes,* with the preface on tragedy. He died in 1674.

Milton's contribution to the theory of the drama is slight enough, for practically his only reference to the subject is in the preface — *Of that sort of Dramatic Poem which is call'd Tragedy* — to his unactable pseudo-Greek play, *Samson Agonistes.* This is a defense of the form, based not primarily on Greek, but on Italian Renaissance ideas. The play is an exemplification of the theory. Professor Thorndike in his *Tragedy,* says: "Though the play stands by itself, it may be said to represent a tendency to turn to Greek rather than to French models, a tendency boasted of by Dryden and Crowne, and fully manifest in the next century. And it takes its place at the head of the numerous, if sporadic, tragedies on Greek models that extend from the Restoration to the present day."

OF THAT SORT OF DRAMATIC POEM WHICH IS CALLED TRAGEDY 1

([Preface to] *Samson Agonistes*)

(1671)

Tragedy, as it was anciently composed, hath been ever held the gravest, moralest, and most profitable of all other poems; therefore said by Aristotle to be of power, by raising pity and fear, or terror, to purge the mind of those and such like passions, that is, to temper and reduce them to just measure with a kind of delight, stirred up by reading or seeing those passions well imitated. Nor is Nature wanting in her own effects to make good this assertion; for so in physic, things of melancholic hue and quality are used against melancholy, sour against sour, salt to remove salt humors. Hence philosophers and other gravest writers, as Cicero, Plutarch, and others, frequently cite out of tragic poets, both to adorn and illustrate their discourse. The Apostle Paul himself thought it not unworthy to insert a verse of Euripides into the text of Holy Scripture, *I Cor.* 15. 33; and Paræus, commenting on the Revelation, divides the whole Book, as a tragedy, into acts, distinguished each by a chorus of heavenly harpings and song between. Heretofore men in highest dignity have labored not a little to be thought able to compose a tragedy. Of that honor Dionysius the Elder was no less ambitious than before of his attaining to the Tyranny. Augustus Cæsar also had begun his *Ajax,* but, unable to please his own judgment with what he had begun, left it unfinished. Seneca the philosopher is by some thought the author of those tragedies (at least the best of them) that go under that name. Gregory Nazianzen, a Father of the Church, thought it not unbeseeming the sanctity of his person to write a tragedy, which he entitled *Christ Suffering.* This is mentioned to vindicate tragedy from the small esteem, or rather infamy, which in the account of many it undergoes at this day, with other common interludes; happening through the poets' error of in-

termixing comic stuff with tragic sadness and gravity, or introducing trivial and vulgar persons; which by all judicious hath been counted absurd and brought in without discretion, corruptly to gratify the people. And though ancient tragedy use no Prologue, yet using sometimes, in case of self-defense or explanation, that which Martial calls an *Epistle,* in behalf of this tragedy, coming forth after the ancient manner, much different from what among us passes for best, thus much beforehand may be Epistled: that Chorus is here introduced after the Greek manner, not ancient only, but modern, and still in use among the Italians. In the modeling therefore of this poem, with good reason, the Ancients and Italians are rather followed, as of much more authority and fame. The measure of verse used in the Chorus is of all sorts, called by the Greeks *Monostrophic,* or rather *Apolelymenon,* without regard had to *Strophe, Antistrophe,* or *Epode,* which were a kind of stanzas framed only for the music, then used with the chorus that sung, not essential to the poem, and therefore not material; or being divided into stanzas or pauses, they may be called *Allæostropha.* Division into act and scene, referring chiefly to the stage (to which this work never was intended) is here omitted.

It suffices if the whole drama be found not produced beyond the fifth act; of the style and uniformity, and that commonly called the plot, whether intricate or explicit — which is nothing indeed but such economy or disposition of the fable as may stand best with verisimilitude and decorum — they only will best judge who are not unacquainted with Æschylus, Sophocles, and Euripides, the three tragic poets unequaled yet by any, and the best rule to all who endeavor to write tragedy. The circumscription of time, wherein the whole drama begins and ends is, according to the ancient rule and best example, within the space of twenty-four hours.

1 Reprinted from the second volume of J. E. Spingarn's *Critical Essays of the Seventeenth Century* (Oxford, 1908).— Ed.

THOMAS RYMER

Thomas Rymer was born, probably at Yafforth Hall, Yorkshire, in 1641. He won distinction at school in his studies, and entered Cambridge in 1658. He did not, however, take his degree. He studied law and in 1673 was admitted to the bar. His first published work was a translation of Cicero's *Prince* (1668). In 1674 he published his translation of René Rapin's *Réflexions sur la poétique,* as the *Reflexions on Aristotle's Treatise of Poesie.* Three years later he published his tragedy of *Edgar,* which failed. It appeared in print the following year, when his *Tragedies of the Last Age Consider'd* was first published. The next few years he put forth a few occasional poems some political works and translations from the Latin. In 1692 he was appointed historiographer royal, and in 1693 published his *Short View of Tragedy,* which called forth considerable comment. The same year he began work on his *Fœdora,* a collection of historical documents relative to England's foreign alliances, which appeared between 1704 and 1713. Rymer died at London in 1713.

Rymer's criticism of Shakespeare has brought him into such disrepute that to this day he is regarded rather as a wild heretic than the sincere though often misguided critic he really was. He was a strict neo-classic, and the carelessness of the Elizabethans aroused all his ire as a follower of Rapin and the extremists from across the Channel. Rymer stood for verisimilitude, good sense, order, and balance; he could not see the greatness of a Shakespeare when that greatness was accompanied by absurdities and shortcomings. A great deal of what he says about the Elizabethans is quite true, and many of his remarks are sane, but he was utterly unable to make necessary allowances. In an age that could see little good in the Elizabethans, it was but natural that Pope should consider Rymer "one of the best critics we ever had," just as it was to be expected that Macaulay should think him "the worst critic that ever lived."

A SHORT VIEW OF TRAGEDY, ITS ORIGINAL EXCELLENCY AND CORRUPTION, WITH SOME REFLECTIONS ON SHAKESPEAR AND OTHER PRACTITIONERS FOR THE STAGE [1]

(1693)

CHAP. I

THE CONTENTS

The Chorus keeps the poet to rules. A show to the spectators. Two senses to be pleased. The eye, by the show and the action. Plays acted without words. Words often better out of the way. Instance in Shakespeare. Ben Jonson and Seneca noted. To the ear, pronunciation is all in all. The story of Demosthenes. Mistakes in judging. Two sorts of judges. At Athens a third sort. Judges upon oath. In France judges divided about the

"Cid." Cardinal Richelieu against majority. At the "Thomus Morus," weeping unawares. Horace angry with shows. The French opera inconsistent with nature and good sense. Burlesque verse. At Paris Christ's Passion in burlesque. A tragedy of Æschylus. The defeat of Xerxes. The subject and economy. How imitated for. our English stage. King John of France, Francis I prisoners. The Spanish Armada in '88. An imitation recommended to Mr. Dryden.

What reformation may not we expect, now that in France they see the necessity of a chorus to their tragedies? Boyer and Racine, both of the Royal Academy, have led the dance: they have tried the success in the last plays that were pre-

[1] Re-printed from the extracts in the second volume of J. E. Spingarn's *Critical Essays of the Seventeenth Century* (Oxford, 1908). This chapter is complete.— Ed.

sented by them.

The chorus was the root and original, and is certainly almost always the necessary part, of tragedy.

The spectators thereby are secured that their poet shall not juggle, or put upon them in the matter of *place* and *time* other than is just and reasonable for the representation.

And the poet has this benefit: the chorus is a goodly show, so that he need not ramble from his subject, out of his wits for some foreign toy or hobby-horse to humor the multitude.

Aristotle tells us of two senses that must be pleased: our sight and our ears. And it is in vair for a poet, with Bayes in *The Rehearsal,* to complain of injustice and the wrong judgment in his audience, unless these two senses be gratified.

The worst on it is that most people are wholly led by these senses, and follow them upon content, without ever troubling their noodle farther.

How many plays owe all their success to a rare show? Even in the days of Horace, enter on the stage a person in a costly strange habit. Lord, what clapping, what noise and thunder, as heaven and earth were coming together! Yet not one word

Dixit adhuc aliquid? Nil sane: quid placeat ergo
Lana Tarentino violas imitata veneno.

Was there aught said? Troth, no! What then did touch ye? Some Prince of Bantam, or a *Mamamouche.*

It matters not whether there be any plot, any characters, any sense, or a wise word from one end to the other, provided in our play we have the Senate of Rome, the Venetian Senate in their Pontificalibus, or a blackamoor ruffian, or Tom Dove, or other four-legged hero of the Bear-garden.

The eye is a quick sense, will be in with our fancy and prepossess the head strangely. Another means whereby the eye misleads our judgment is the action. We go to see a play acted; in tragedy is represented a memorable action, so the spectators are always pleased to see action, and are not often so ill-natured to pry into and examine whether it be proper, just, natural, in season or out

of season. Bayes in *The Rehearsal* well knew this secret. The two Kings are at their Coranto; nay, the moon and the earth dance the Hey; anything in nature or against nature, rather than allow the serious council or other dull business to interrupt or obstruct the action.

This thing of Action finds the blindside of humankind an hundred ways. We laugh and weep with those that laugh or weep; we gape, stretch, and are very *dotterels* by example.

Action is speaking to the eyes; and all Europe over, plays have been represented with great applause in a tongue unknown and sometimes without any language at all.

Many, peradventure, of the tragical scenes in Shakespeare, cried up for the action, might do yet better without words. Words are a sort of heavy baggage that were better out of the way at the push of action, especially in his bombast circumstance, where the words and action are seldom akin, generally are inconsistent, at cross purposes, embarrass or destroy each other; yet to those who take not the words distinctly, there may be something in the buzz and sound that, like a drone to a bagpipe, may serve to set off the action.

For an instance of the former, would not a rap at the door better express Iago's meaning than

> *— Call aloud.*
IAGO. *Do, with like timorous accent and dire yell*
As when, by night and negligence, the fire
Is spied in populous cities?

For what ship? Who is arrived? The answer is:

'Tis one Iago, Ancient to the General.
He has had most favorable and happy speed;
Tempests themselves, high seas, and howling winds,
The guttered rocks and congregated sands,
Traitors ensteeped to clog the guiltless keel.
As having sense of beauty, do omit
Their common natures, letting go safely by
The divine Desdemona.

Is this the language of the Exchange

or the Insuring office? Once in a man's life he might be content at Bedlam to hear such a rapture. In a play one should speak like a man of business; his speech must be Πολιτικὸς, which the French render *Agissante,* the Italians *Negotiosa* and *Operativa;* but by this gentleman's talk one may well guess he has nothing to do. And he has many companions that are

— Hey day!
I know not what to do nor what to say.

It was then a strange imagination in Ben Jonson to go stuff out a play with Tully's Orations, and in Seneca, to think his dry morals and a tedious strain of sentences might do feats or have any wonderful operation in the drama.

Some go to *see,* others to *hear,* a play. The poet should please both; but be sure the spectators are satisfied, whatever entertainment he give his audience.

But if neither the show nor the action cheats us, there remains still a notable vehicle to carry off nonsense, which is the pronunciation.

By the loud trumpet which our courage aids,
We learn, that sound as well as sense persuades.

Demosthenes had a good stock of sense, was a great master of words, could turn a period, and draw up his tropes in a line of battle; and fain would he have seen some effect of his Orations: nobody was moved, nobody minded him. He goes to the playhouse, bargains with an actor, and learned of him to speak roundly and gracefully. From that time, Who but Demosthenes? Never such a leading man! Whenever he spake, no division, not a vote to the contrary, the whole House were with him, *Nemine contradicente.* This change observed, a friend went to him for the secret. "Tell me," says he, "Your nostrum, tell me your receipt. What is the main ingredient that makes an orator?" Demosthenes answered: "Pronunciation." — "What then the next thing?"—"Pronunciation."—"Pray then what the third?"— Still was the answer, "Pronunciation."

Now, this was at Athens, where want of wit was never an objection against them. So that it is not in song only that a good voice diverts us from the wit and sense. From the stage, bar, or the pulpit, a good voice will prepossess our ears and, having seized the pass, is in a fair way to surprise our judgment.

Considering then what power the show, the action, and the pronunciation have over us, it is no wonder that wise men often mistake and give an hasty judgment, which upon a review is justly set aside.

Horace divides the judges into *Majores Numero,* and the few of *better sort;* and these for the most part were of different judgments. The like distinction may hold in all nations; only at Athens there was a third sort, who were judges upon oath, Judges in Commission, by the government sworn to do right, and determine the merits of a play without favor or affection.

But amongst the moderns never was a cause canvassed with so much heat between the play-judges as that in France about Corneille's *Tragedy of the Cid.* The majority were so fond of it that with them it became a proverb, *Cela est plus beau que le Cid.* On the other side, Cardinal Richelieu damned it, and said: "All the pudder about it was only between the ignorant people and the men of judgment."

Yet this Cardinal with so nice a taste had not many years before been several times to see acted the *Tragedy of Sir Thomas More,* and as often wept at the representation. Never were known so many people crowded to death as at that play. Yet was it the manufacture of Jehan de Serre, one about the form of our Flecknoe or Thomas Jordan, the same De Serre that dedicated a *Book of Meditations* to King Charles I and went home with pockets full of medals and reward.

By this instance we see a man the most sharp and of the greatest penetration was imposed upon by these cheating senses, the eyes and the ears, which greedily took in the impression from the show, the action, and from the emphasis and pronunciation, though there was no great matter of fable, no manners, no fine thoughts, no language; that is, nothing of a tragedy, nothing of a poet all the while.

Horace was very angry with these

empty shows and vanity, which the gentlemen of his time ran like mad after.

Insanos oculos, et gaudia vana.

What would he have said to the French opera, of late so much in vogue? There it is for you to bewitch your eyes and to charm your ears. There is a cup of enchantment, there is music and machine; Circe and Calypso in conspiracy against nature and good sense. 'Tis a debauch the most insinuating and the most pernicious; none would think an opera and civil reason should be the growth of one and the same climate. But shall we wonder at anything for a sacrifice to the Grand Monarch? Such worship, such idol! All flattery to him is insipid unless it be prodigious. Nothing reasonable or within compass can come near the matter. All must be monstrous, enormous, and outrageous to nature, to be like him, or give any echo on his appetite.

Were Rabelais alive again, he would look on his Gargantua as but a pigmy. *The hero's race excels the poet's thought.* The Academy Royal may pack up their modes and methods, and *pensées ingénieuses;* the Racines and the Corneilles must all now dance to the tune of Baptista. Here is the opera; here is Machine and Baptista, farewell Apollo and the Muses!

Away with your opera from the theater! Better had they become the heathen temples, for the Corybantian priests and (*Semiviros Gallos*) the old capons of Gaul, than a people that pretend from Charlemagne or descend from the undoubted loins of German and Norman conquerors.

In the French, not many years before, was observed the like vicious appetite and immoderate passion for *vers burlesque.*

They were current in Italy an hundred years ere they passed to this side the Alps. But when once they had their turn in France, so right to their humor, they overran all; nothing wise or sober might stand in their way. All were possessed with the spirit of burlesque, from Doll in the dairy to the matrons at Court and maids of honor. Nay, so far went the frenzy, that no bookseller would meddle on any terms without burlesque; insomuch that *Ann.* 1649 was at Paris printed a serious treatise with this title:

— *La Passion de Nostre Seigneur, En Vers Burlesques.*

If we cannot rise to the perfection of intrigue in Sophocles, let us sit down with the honesty and simplicity of the first beginners in tragedy. As for example:

One of the most simple now extant is *The Persians* by Æschylus.

Some ten years after that Darius had been beaten by the Greeks, Xerxes (his father Darius being dead) brought against them such forces by sea and land, the like never known in history; Xerxes went also in person, with all the *Maison de Roy, Satrapie,* and Gendarmerie: all were routed. Some forty years afterwards the poet takes hence his subject for a tragedy.

The Place is by Darius' tomb, in the Metropolis of Persia.

The Time is the night, an hour or two before daybreak.

First, on the stage are seen fifteen persons in robes proper for the Satrapa, or chief Princes in Persia. Suppose they met so early at the tomb, then sacred, and ordinarily resorted to by people troubled in mind, on the accounts of dreams or any thing not boding good. They talk of the state of affairs: of Greece and of the Expedition. After some time take upon them to be the Chorus.

The next on the stage comes Atossa, the Queen Mother of Persia; she could not lie in bed for a dream that troubled her, so in a fit of devotion comes to her husband's tomb, there luckily meets with so many wise men and counselors to ease her mind by interpreting her dream. This, with the Chorus, makes the Second Act.

After this, their disorder, lamentation, and wailing is such that Darius is disturbed in his tomb, so his ghost appears, and belike stays with them till daybreak. Then the Chorus concludes the Act.

In the fourth Act come the Messengers with sad tidings which, with the reflections and troubles thereupon, and the Chorus, fill out this Act.

In the last, Xerxes himself arrives, which gives occasion of condoling, howling and distraction enough to the end of the tragedy.

One may imagine how a Grecian audience that loved their country and gloried in the virtue of their ancestors, would be affected by this representation.

Never appeared on the stage a ghost of greater consequence. The Grand Monarch Darius, who had been so shamefully beaten by those petty provinces of the united Grecians, could not now lie quiet in his grave for them, but must be raised from the dead again, to be witness of his son's disgrace and of their triumph.

Were a tragedy after this model to be drawn for our stage, Greece and Persia are too far from us. The scene must be laid nearer home: as at the Louvre; and instead of Xerxes we might take John King of France, and the Battle of Poitiers. So if the Germans or Spaniards were to compose a play on the Battle of Pavia, and King Francis were there taken prisoner, the scene should not be laid at Vienna or at Madrid, but at the Louvre. For there the tragedy would principally operate, and there all the lines most naturally center.

But perhaps the memorable adventure of the Spaniards in '88 against England may better resemble that of Xerxes. Suppose, then, a tragedy called *The Invincible Armada*.

The place, then, for the action may be at Madrid, by some tomb or solemn place of resort; or, if we prefer a turn in it from good to bad fortune, then some drawing-room in the palace near the King's bed-chamber.

The time to begin, twelve at night.

The scene opening presents fifteen grandees of Spain, with their most solemn beards and accouterments, met there (suppose) after some ball or other public occasion. They talk of the state of affairs, the greatness of their power, the vastness of their dominions, and prospect to be infallibly, ere long, lords of all. With this prosperity and goodly thoughts transported, they at last form themselves into the Chorus, and walk such measures, with music, as may become the gravity of such a Chorus.

Then enter two or three of the Cabinet Council, who now have leave to tell the secret, that the preparations and the Invincible Armada was to conquer England. These, with part of the Chorus, may communicate all the particulars, the provisions, and the strength by sea and land, the certainty of success, the advantages of that accession, and the many tun of tar-barrels for the Heretics. These topics may afford matter enough, with the Chorus, for the Second Act.

In the Third Act, these gentlemen of the Cabinet cannot agree about sharing the preferments of England, and a mighty broil there is amongst them. One will not be content unless he is King of Man; another will be Duke of Lancaster. One, that had seen a coronation in England, will by all means be Duke of Acquitaine, or else Duke of Normandy. (And on this occasion two competitors have a juster occasion to work up and show the muscles of their passion than Shakespeare's Cassius and Brutus.) After — the Chorus.

The Fourth Act may, instead of Atossa, present some old Dames of the Court, used to dream dreams and see sprites, in their night-rails and forehead-clothes, to alarm our gentlemen with new apprehensions, which make distraction and disorders sufficient to furnish out this Act.

In the last Act the King enters, and wisely discourses against dreams and hobgoblins, to quiet their minds. And the more to satisfy them and take off their fright, he lets them to know that St. Loyola had appeared to him and assured him that all is well. This said, comes a Messenger of the ill news; his account is lame, suspected, he sent to prison. A Second Messenger, that came away long after but had a speedier passage; his account is distinct, and all their loss credited. So, in fine, one of the Chorus concludes with that of Euripides: "Thus you see the gods brings things to pass often otherwise than was by man proposed."

In this draft we see the fable, and the characters or manners of the Spaniards, and room for fine thoughts and noble expressions, as much as the poet can afford.

The First Act gives a review or ostentation of their strength in battle array.

In the Second, they are in motion for the attack and we see where the action falls.

In the Third, they quarrel about dividing the spoil.

In the Fourth, they meet with a repulse, are beaten off by a van-guard of dreams, goblins, and terrors of the night.

In the Fifth, they rally under their King in person, and make good their ground, till overpowered by fresh troops of conviction, and mighty Truth prevails.

For the First Act, a painter would draw Spain hovering and ready to strike at the Universe.

In the Second, just taking England in her pounces.

But it must not be forgotten, in the Second Act, that there be some Spanish Friar or Jesuit, as St. Xavier (for he may drop in by miracle anywhere), to ring in their ears the Northern Heresy, like Iago in Shakespeare —" Put money in thy purse, I say, put money in thy purse."— So often may he repeat the Northern Heresy. " Away with your secular advantages, I say, the Northern Heresy; there is roast meat for the Church; *Voto a Christo,* the Northern Heresy ! "

If Mr. Dryden might try his pen on this subject doubtless to an audience that heartily love their country and glory in the virtue of their ancestors, his imitation of Æschylus would have better success, and would pit, box, and gallery, far beyond anything now in possession of the stage, however wrought up by the unimitable Shakespeare.

WILLIAM CONGREVE

William Congreve was born at Bardsey in 1670. His father was sent, soon after the son's birth, to Ireland, where he was in command of a garrison at Youghal. William received his first schooling at Kilkenny, and later attended the University of Dublin, where he made the acquaintance of Swift. He then went to London and entered the Middle Temple as a law student. His first literary work was a novel, *Incognita.* In 1693 he was, however, to give evidence of his genius in *The Old Bachelor,* a brilliant comedy, which was eminently successful. The next year he produced *The Double Dealer,* which was not successful, but which Dryden, who had stood sponsor for the first play, highly praised. *Love for Love* (1695) and *The Mourning Bride* (1697) a tragedy, followed the unsuccessful play. Then came Collier's famous attack on the stage (1698), which called forth Congreve's *Amendments upon Mr. Collier's False and Imperfect Citations,* etc., the same year. Meanwhile he had written his *Letter Concerning Humour in Comedy* in 1696. In 1700 Congreve produced his masterpiece, *The Way of the World.* The play was not a success, and from the year 1700 to his death in 1729 Congreve never wrote another play; a small volume of indifferent verses, a sort of masque, and parts of a play translated from Molière, are the result of his literary efforts during the rest of his life. Congreve was doubtless somewhat discouraged over the Collier controversy; he was piqued over the coolness with which his last, and greatest, comedy was received, he was in poor health — and besides, he did not need money. Congreve's life during the eighteenth century contains little of interest. He spent his time in traveling, in cultivating his friends, in writing occasional verses, and a poor opera; he was a victim of the gout, and became blind by 1710. He was next employed in several minor capacities, which assured him at least a comfortable income, for when he died he left ten thousand pounds to the Duchess of Marlborough.

Congreve is the master of the English comedy of manners. His remarks on the drama possess not only some of the qualities which make his dramatic work effective, they are in addition a valuable comment on the comedies of Congreve's own age. Like Dryden, Congreve uses the comparative method, but maintains truthfully that real humor is indigenously English, and that " it does not seem to have found such increase on any other soil." The *Prefaces* and *Dedications* to the plays, in spite of their brevity, are full of interesting and suggestive remarks. For instance, in the *Epistle*

Dedicatory to The Double Dealer, he says: "I designed the moral first, and to that moral I invented the fable, and do not know that I have borrowed one hint of it anywhere. I made the plot as strong as I could, because it was single; and I made it single, because I would avoid confusion, and was resolved to preserve the three unities of the drama." Like many practicing theorists, Congreve's theory and his practice do not always coincide,

but his plea for the Unities is more sensible than that of any other theorist of the time. The same *Epistle* contains equally interesting remarks on the soliloquy and characterization. The *Dedication* to *The Way of the World* also contains sundry references to the art of the dramatist. The *Dedication* to *The Mourning Bride* contains a few of the cut-and-dried formulas on tragedy and the moral end of that form.

CONCERNING HUMOR IN COMEDY [1]

(1696)

Dear Sir:

You write to me that you have entertained yourself two or three days with reading several comedies of several authors; and your observation is that there is more of humor in our English writers than in any of the other comic poets, ancient or modern. You desire to know my opinion, and at the same time my thought, of that which is in general called *Humor* in comedy.

I agree with you in an impartial preference of our English writers in that particular. But if I tell you my thoughts of humor, I must at the same time confess that which I take for true humor has not been so often written by them as is generally believed; and some who have valued themselves and have been esteemed by others for that kind of writing, have seldom touched upon it. To make this appear to the world would require a long and labored discourse, and such as I neither am able nor willing to undertake. But such little remarks as may be within the compass of a letter, and such unpremeditated thoughts as may be communicated between friend and friend without incurring the censure of the world, or setting up for a dictator, you shall have from me, since you have enjoined it.

To define humor perhaps were as difficult as to define wit; for, like that, it is of infinite variety. To enumerate the several humors of men were a work as endless as to sum up their several opinions. And, in my mind, *Quot homines tot sententiae,* might have been more properly interpreted of humor; since there are many men of the same opinion in many things, who are yet quite different in humors. But though we cannot certainly tell what wit is, or what humor is, yet we may go near to show something which is not wit or not humor, and yet often mistaken for both. And since I have mentioned wit and humor together, let me make the first distinction between them, and observe to you that *wit is often mistaken for humor.*

I have observed that when a few things have been wittily and pleasantly spoken by any character in a comedy, it has been very usual for those who make their remarks on a play while it is acting, to say, *Such a thing is very humorously spoken; There is a great deal of humor in that part.* Thus the character of the person speaking, may be, surprisingly and pleasantly is mistaken for a character of humor, which indeed is a character of wit. But there is a great difference between a comedy wherein there are many things *humorously,* as they call it, which is *pleasantly,* spoken, and one where there are several characters of humor, distinguished by the particular and different humors appropriated to the several persons represented, and which naturally arise from the different constitutions, complexions, and dispositions of men. The saying of humorous things does not distinguish characters; for every person in a comedy may be allowed to speak them. From a witty man they are expected; and even a fool may be permitted to stumble on 'em by

[1] Re-printed from the third volume of J. E. Spingarn's *Critical Essays of the Seventeenth Century* (Oxford, 1909).— Ed.

chance. Though I make a difference betwixt wit and humor, yet I do think that humorous characters exclude wit: no, but the manner of wit should be adapted to the humor. As, for instance, a character of a splenetic and peevish humor should have a satirical wit. A jolly and sanguine humor should have a facetious wit. The former should speak positively; the latter, carelessly: for the former observes and shows things as they are; the latter rather overlooks nature, and speaks things as he would have them, and wit and humor have both of them less alloy of judgment than the others.

As wit, so its opposite, *folly, is sometimes mistaken for humor.*

When a poet brings a character on the stage committing a thousand absurdities, and talking impertinencies, roaring aloud, and laughing immoderately on every or rather upon no occasion, this is a character of humor.

Is anything more common than to have a pretended comedy stuffed with such grotesques, figures and farce fools? Things that either are not in nature, or, if they are, are monsters and births of mischance, and consequently, as such, should be stifled and huddled out of the way, like *Sooterkins.* That mankind may not be shocked with an appearing possibility of the degeneration of a godlike species. For my part, I am as willing to laugh as anybody, and as easily diverted with an object truly ridiculous; but at the same time, I can never care for seeing things that force me to entertain low thoughts of any nature. I don't know how it is with others, but I confess freely to you, I could never look long upon a monkey without very mortifying reflections, though I never heard anything to the contrary why that creature is not originally of a distinct species. As I don't think humor exclusive of wit, neither do I think it inconsistent with folly; but I think the follies should be only such as men's humors may incline 'em to, and not follies entirely abstracted from both humor and nature.

Sometimes *personal defects are misrepresented for humors.*

I mean, sometimes characters are barbarously exposed on the stage, ridiculing natural deformities, casual defects in the senses, and infirmities of age.

Sure the poet must be very ill-natured himself, and think his audience so, when he proposes by showing a man deformed, or deaf, or blind, to give them an agreeable entertainment, and hopes to raise their mirth by what is truly an object of compassion. But much need not be said upon this head to anybody, especially to you, who, in one of your Letters to me concerning Mr. Jonson's *Fox,* have justly expected against this immortal part of ridicule in Corbaccio's character; and there I must agree with you to blame him whom otherwise I cannot enough admire for his great mastery of true humor in comedy.

External habit of body is often mistaken for humor.

By *external habit* I do not mean the ridiculous dress or clothing of a character, though that goes a good way in some received characters. (But undoubtedly, a man's humor may incline him to dress differently from other people.) But I mean a singularity of manners, speech, and behavior, peculiar to all or most of the same country, trade, profession, or education. I cannot think that a humor which is only a habit or disposition contracted by use or custom; for by a disuse, or compliance with other customs, it may be worn off or diversified.

Affectation is generally mistaken for humor.

These are indeed so much alike that at a distance they may be mistaken one for the other. For what is humor in one may be affectation in another; and nothing is more common than for some to affect particular ways of saying and doing things, peculiar to others whom they admire and would imitate. Humor is the life, affectation the picture. He that draws a character of affectation shows humor at the second hand; he at best but publishes a translation, and his pictures are but copies.

But as these two last distinctions are the nicest, so it may be most proper to explain them by particular instances from some author of reputation. Humor I take either to be born with us, and so of a natural growth, or else to be grafted into us by some accidental change in the constitution, or revolution of the internal habit of body, by which it becomes, if I may so call it, naturalized.

Humor is from nature, habit from custom, and affectation from industry.

Humor shows us as we are.

Habit shows us as we appear under a forcible impression.

Affectation shows what we would be under a voluntary disguise.

Though here I would observe by the way that a continued affectation may in time become a habit.

The character of Morose in *The Silent Woman* I take to be a character of Humor. And I choose to instance this character to you from many others of the same author, because I know it has been condemned by many as unnatural and farce; and you have yourself hinted some dislike of it for the same reason, in a Letter to me concerning some of Jonson's plays.

Let us suppose Morose to be a man naturally splenetic and melancholy; is there anything more offensive to one of such a disposition than noise and clamor? Let any man that has a spleen (and there are enough in England) be judge. We see common examples of this humor, in little, every day. 'Tis ten to one but three parts in four of the company that you dine with are discomposed and startled at the cutting of a fork or scratching a plate with a knife. It is a proportion of the same humor that makes such or any other noise offensive to the person that hears it; for there are others who will not be disturbed at all by it. Well, but Morose, you will say, is so extravagant, he cannot hear any discourse or conversation above a whisper. Why, it is his excess of this humor that makes him become ridiculous, and qualifies his character 'for comedy. If the poet had given him but a moderate proportion of that humor, 'tis odds but half the audience would have sided with the character and have condemned the author for exposing a humor which was neither remarkable nor ridiculous. Besides, the distance of the stage requires the figure represented to be something larger than the life; and sure a picture may have figures larger in proportion, and yet be very like the original. If this exactness of quantity were to be observed in wit, as some would have it in humor, what would become of those comedies that are designed for men of wit? I believe that if a poet should

steal a dialogue of any length from the extempore discourse of the two wittiest men upon earth, he would find the scene but coldly received by the town. But to the purpose.

The character of Sir John Daw in the same play is a character of affectation. He everywhere discovers an affectation of learning, when he is not only conscious to himself, but the audience also plainly perceives that he is ignorant. Of this kind are the characters of Thraso in *The Eunuch* of Terence, and Pyrgopolinices in the *Miles Gloriosus* of Plautus. They affect to be thought valiant, when both themselves and the audience know they are not. Now, such a boasting of valor in men who were really valiant would undoubtedly be a humor; for a fiery disposition might naturally throw a man into the same extravagance, which is only affected in the characters I have mentioned.

The character of Cob in *Every Man in his Humour* and most of the under characters in *Bartholomew Fair,* discover only a singularity of manners, appropriate to the several educations and professions of the persons represented. They are not humors, but habits contracted by custom. Under this head may be ranged all country-clowns, sailors, tradesmen, jockeys, gamesters, and such-like, who make use of *cants* or peculiar dialects in their several arts and vocations. One may almost give a receipt for the composition of such a character: for the poet has nothing to do but to collect a few proper phrases and terms of art, and to make the person apply them by ridiculous metaphors in his conversation with characters of different natures. Some late characters of this kind have been very successful; but in my mind they may be painted without much art or labor, since they require little more than a good memory and superficial observation. But true humor cannot be shown without a dissection of nature, and a narrow search to discover the first seeds from whence it has its root and growth.

If I were to write to the world, I should be obliged to dwell longer upon each of these distinctions and examples, for I know that they would not be plain enough to all readers. But a bare hint is sufficient to inform you of the notions which I have on this subject: and I hope by this time you are of my opinion, that humor is neither wit, nor folly, nor personal defect, nor affectation, nor habit, and yet that each and all of these have been both written and received for humor.

I should be unwilling to venture even on a bare description of humor, much more to make a definition of it, but now my hand is in, I'll tell you what serves one instead of either. I take it to be *A singular and unavoidable manner of doing or saying anything, peculiar and natural to one man only, by which his speech and actions are distinguished from those of other men.*

Our humor has relation to us and to what proceeds from us, as the accidents have to a substance; it is a color, taste, and smell, diffused through all; though our actions are never so many and different in form, they are all splinters of the same wood, and have naturally one complexion, which, though it may be disguised by art, yet cannot be wholly changed: we may paint it with other colors, but we cannot change the grain. So the natural sound of an instrument will be distinguished, though the notes expressed by it are never so various, and the divisions never so many. Dissimulation may by degrees become more easy to our practice; but it can never absolutely transubstantiate us into what we would seem: it will always be in some proportion a violence upon nature.

A man may change his opinion but I believe he will find it a difficulty to part with his humor, and there is nothing more provoking than the being made sensible of that difference. Sometimes one shall meet with those who perhaps innocently enough, but at the same time impertinently, will ask the question, *Why are you not merry? Why are you not gay, pleasant, and cheerful?* then, instead of answering, could I ask such a one, *Why are you not handsome? Why have you not black eyes and a better complexion?* Nature abhors to be forced.

The two famous philosophers of Ephesus and Abdera have their different sects at this day. Some weep and others laugh, at one and the same thing.

I don't doubt but you have observed several men laugh when they are angry, others who are silent, some that are loud; yet I cannot suppose that it is the passion of anger which is in itself different, or more or less in one than in t'other, but that it is in the humor of the man that is predominant, and urges him to expect it in that manner. Demonstrations of pleasure are as various: one man has a humor of retiring from all company, when anything has happened to please him beyond expectation; he hugs himself alone, and thinks it an addition to the pleasure to keep it secret. Another is upon thorns till he has made proclamation of it, and must make other people sensible of his happiness before he can be so himself. So it is in grief and other passions. Demonstrations of love and the effects of that passion upon several humors are infinitely different; but here the ladies who abound in servants are the best judges. Talking of the ladies, methinks something should be observed of the humor of the fair sex, since they are sometimes so kind as to furnish out a character for comedy. But I must confess I have never made any observation of what I apprehend to be true humor in women. Perhaps passions are too powerful in that sex to let humor have its course; or may be by reason of their natural coldness, humor cannot exert itself to that extravagant degree which it often does in the male sex. For if ever anything does appear comical or ridiculous in a woman, I think it is little more than an acquired folly or an affectation. We may call them the weaker sex, but I think the true reason is because our follies are stronger and our faults are more prevailing.

One might think that the diversity of humor, which must be allowed to be diffused throughout mankind, might afford endless matter for the support of comedies. But when we come closely to consider that point, and nicely to distinguish the differences of humors, I believe we shall find the contrary. For though we allow every man something of his own, and a peculiar humor, yet every man has it not in quantity to become remarkable by it; or, if many do become remarkable by their humors, yet all those humors may not be diverting. Nor is it only requisite to distinguish what humor will be diverting, but also how much of it, what part of it to show in light, and what to cast in shades, how to set it off by preparatory scenes, and by opposing other humors to it in the same scene. Through a wrong judgment, sometimes, men's humors may be opposed when there is really no specific difference between them, only a greater proportion of the same in one than in t'other, occasioned by his having more phlegm, or choler, or whatever the constitution is from whence their humors derive their source.

There is infinitely more to be said on this subject, though perhaps I have already said too much; but I have said it to a friend, who I am sure will not expose it, if he does not approve of it. I believe the subject is entirely new, and was never touched upon before; and if I would have anyone to see this private essay, it should be some one who might be provoked by my errors in it to publish a more judicious treatise on the subject. Indeed I wish it were done, that the world, being a little acquainted with the scarcity of true humor and the difficulty of finding and showing it, might look a little more favorably on the labors of them who endeavor to search into nature for it and lay it open to the public view.

I don't say but that very entertaining and useful characters, and proper to comedy, may be drawn from affectation and those other qualities which I have endeavored to distinguish from humor; but I would not have such imposed on the world for humor, nor esteemed with equal value with it. It were perhaps the work of a long life to make one comedy true in all its parts, and to give every character in it a true and distinct humor. Therefore every poet must be beholding

to other helps to make out his number of ridiculous characters. But I think such a one deserves to be broke, who makes all false monsters; who does not show one true humor in a comedy, but entertains his audience to the end of the play with everything out of nature.

I will make but one observation to you more, and have done; and that is grounded upon an observation of your own, and which I mentioned at the beginning of my letter, viz., that there is more of humor in our English comic writers than in any others. I do not at all wonder at it, for I look upon humor to be almost of English growth; at least, it does not seem to have found such increase on any other soil. And what appears to me to be the reason of it is the greater freedom, privilege, and liberty which the common people of England enjoy. Any man that has a humor is under no restraint or fear of giving it vent; they have a proverb among them, which, may be, will show the bent and genius of the people as well as a longer discourse: "He that will have a may-pole, shall have a may-pole." This is a maxim with them, and their practice is agreeable to it. I believe something considerable too may be ascribed to their feeding so much on flesh, and the grossness of their diet in general. But I have done; let the physicians agree that. Thus you have my thoughts of humor, to my power of expressing them in so little time and compass. You will be kind to show me wherein I have erred; and as you are very capable of giving me instruction, so I think I have a very just title to demand it from you, being without reserve,

Your real friend,
and humble servant,
W. CONGREVE.

GEORGE FARQUHAR

George Farquhar was born in Londonderry, Ireland, in 1677 or 1678. Little is known of his early years beyond the fact that he went to school in his native town and entered Trinity College, Dublin, in 1694. He remained there about a year. Not long after he made the acquaintance of the actor Robert Wilks, through whom he obtained a position on the Dublin stage, where he acted many parts during 1696. He accidentally wounded an actor and left the stage, having decided to write plays. He went to London that or the following year. *Love and a Bottle,* his first comedy, was produced at Drury Lane in 1698, and enjoyed a fair degree of popularity. It is interesting to know that soon after his arrival he discovered Nance Oldfield and with Vanbrugh's help, secured her a place with Rich. Farquhar's next play brought him a certain fame. This was *The Constant Couple,* produced in 1699. The next year found him in Holland, probably for his health. *Sir Harry Wildair,* his next play, was produced in 1701. *The Inconstant* and *The Twin Rivals* belong to the year 1702. Later in the same year Farquhar published a little collection of miscellaneous prose and verse, in which he included his *Discourse upon Comedy.* He was married probably the next year. He spent the following three in recruiting for the army, though he collaborated with Motteux in an adaptation from the French, called *The Stage Coach* (1704). Two years later *The Recruit-*

ing Officer was performed at Drury Lane. Though it was successful, Farquhar was harassed with debts and was forced to sell a commission which he held. During an illness in 1707 he wrote *The Beaux' Stratagem,* at the instigation of his friend Wilks. He died a few weeks after the first performance.

Farquhar's importance as a dramatist consists in his having combined many of the elements of the comedy of his time and evolving them into a form which was later developed by Goldsmith and Sheridan. One of the dire results of Collier's attack on the stage was the conversion of Farquhar. *The Twin Rivals* (1702) and its *Preface* constitute Farquhar's reply to Collier; the play, in the author's words, sets out to prove that "an English comedy may answer the strictness of poetical justice." This was precisely the "poetical justice" which Addison attacked in the *Spectator,* the conventional reward of virtue and punishment of vice. The *Discourse* published the same year contains a defense of the drama against Collier and his followers, but in general, it is merely a light essay, anti-classic in its rejection of the Unities.

A DISCOURSE UPON COMEDY IN REFERENCE TO THE ENGLISH STAGE

In a Letter to a friend [1]

(1702)

But in the first place I must beg you, sir, to lay aside your superstitious veneration for antiquity, and the usual expressions on that score; that the present age is illiterate, or their taste is vitiated; that we live in the decay of time, and the dotage of the world is fallen to our share.—

'Tis a mistake, sir; the world was never more active or youthful, and true downright sense was never more universal than at this very day; 'tis neither confined to one nation in the world, nor to one part of a city; 'tis remarkable in

[1] Re-printed, with omissions, from *A Discourse Upon Comedy, The Recruiting Officer. and The Beaux' Stratagem,* by George Farquhar, edited by Louis A. Strauss (Boston, 1914).— Ed.

England as well as France, and good genuine reason is nourished by the cold of Sweden [Swedeland] as by the warmth of Italy; 'tis neither abdicated the court with the late reigns, nor expelled the city with the play-house bills; you may find it in the Grand Jury at Hick's-Hall, and upon the bench sometimes among the justices: then why should we be hampered so in our opinions, as if all the ruins of antiquity lay so heavily on the bones of us that we could not stir hand nor foot! No, no, sir, *ipse dixit* is removed long ago, and all the rubbish of old philosophy, that in a manner buried the judgment of mankind for many centuries, is now carried off; the vast tomes of Aristotle and his commentators are all taken to pieces, and their infallibility is lost with all persons of a free and unprejudiced reason.

Then above all men living, why should the poets be hoodwinked at this rate, and by what authority should Aristotle's rules of poetry stand so fixt and immutable? Why, by the authority of two thousand years' standing; because thro' this long revolution of time the world has still continued the same.— By the authority of their being received at Athens, a city the very same with London in every particular, their habits the same, their humors alike, their public transactions and private societies *A la mode France;* in short, so very much the same in every circumstance that Aristotle's criticisms may give rules to Drury Lane, the Areopagus give judgment upon a case in the King's Bench, and old Solon shall give laws to the House of Commons.

But to examine this matter a little farther: All arts and professions are compounded of these two parts, a speculative knowledge, and a practical use; and from an excellency in both these, any person is raised to eminence and authority in his calling. The lawyer has his years of student in the speculative part of his business; and when promoted to bar, he falls upon the practice, which is the trial of his ability. Without all dispute, the great Cook has had many a tug at the bar, before he could raise himself to the bench; and had made sufficiently evident his knowledge of the laws in his pleadings, before he was admitted to the authority of giving judgment upon the case.

The physician, to gain credit to his prescriptions, must labor for a reputation in the cure of such and such distempers; and before he sets up for a Galen or Hippocrates, must make many experiments upon his patients. Philosophy itself, which is a science the most abstract from practice, has its public acts and disputations; it is raised gradually, and its professor commences doctor by degrees; he has the labor of maintaining theses, methodizing his arguments, and clearing objections; his memory and understanding is often puzzled by oppositions counciled in fallacies and sophisms, in solving all which he must make himself remarkable, before he pretends to impose his own systems upon

the world. Now, if the case be thus in philosophy, or in any branch thereof, as in ethics, physics, which are called sciences, what must be done in poetry, that is denominated an art, and consequently implies a practice in its perfection?

Is it reasonable that any person that has never writ a distich of verses in his life should set up for a dictator in poetry; and without the least practice in his own performance must give laws and rules to that of others? Upon what foundation is poetry made so very cheap and so easy a task by these gentlemen? An excellent poet is the single production of an age, when we have crowds of philosophers, physicians, lawyers, divines every day, and all of them competently famous in their callings. In the two learned commonwealths of Rome and Athens, there was but one Vergil and one Homer, yet have we above a hundred philosophers in each, and most part of 'em, forsooth, must have a touch at poetry, drawing it into Divisions, Subdivisions, etc., when the wit of 'em all set together would not amount to one of Martial's *Epigrams.*

Of all these I shall mention only Aristotle, the first and great law-giver in this respect, and upon whom all that followed him are only commentators. Among all the vast tracts of this voluminous author we don't find any fragment of an epic poem, or the least scene of a play, to authorize his skill and excellence in that art. Let it not be alleged that for ought we know he was an excellent poet, but his more serious studies would not let him enter upon affairs of this nature; for everybody knows that Aristotle was no cynic, but lived in the splendor and air of the court; that he loved riches as much as others of that station, and being sufficiently acquainted with his pupils' affection to poetry, and his complaint that he wanted an Homer to aggrandize his actions, he would never have slipt such an opportunity of farther ingratiating himself in the king's favor, had he been conscious of any abilities in himself for such an undertaking; and having a more noble and copious theme in the exploits of Alexander than what inspired the blind bard in his hero Achilles. If his epistles to Alexander were always answered with a considerable present, what might he have expected from a work like Homer's upon so great a subject, dedicated to so mighty a prince, whose greatest fault was his vain glory, and that took such pains to be deified among men?

It may be objected that all the works of Aristotle are not recovered; and among those that are lost some essays of this kind might have perished. This supposition is too weakly founded; for altho' the works themselves might have 'scaped us, 'tis more than probable that some hint or other, either in the life of the conqueror, or philosopher, might appear to convince us of such a production. Besides, as 'tis believed he writ philosophy, because we have his books; so I dare swear he writ no poetry, because none is extant, nor any mention made thereof that ever I could hear of.

But stay — without any farther enquiry into the poetry of Aristotle, his ability that way is sufficiently apparent by that excellent piece he has left behind him upon that subject.— By your favor, sir, this is *Petitio Principii*, or, in plain English, give me the sword in my own hand, and I'll fight with you.— Have but a little patience till I make a flourish or two, and then, if you are pleased to demand it, I'll grant you that and everything else.

How easy were it for me to take one of Doctor Tillotson's sermons, and, out of the œconomy of one of these discourses, trump you up a pamphlet and call it *The Art of Preaching!* In the first place I must take a *Text*, and here I must be very learned upon the etymology of this word text; then this text must be divided into such and such *Partitions*, which partitions must have their hard names and derivations; then these must be spun into *Subdivisions*, and these backed by proofs of Scripture, *Ratiocinatio Oratoris, Ornamental Figurarum Rhetoricarum,* and *Authoritas Patrum Ecclesiæ,* with some rules and directions how these ought to be managed and applied. And closing up this difficult pedantry with the *Dimensions of Time* for such an occasion, you will pay me the compliment of an excellent preacher, and affirm that any sermon whatsoever, either by a Presbiter at Geneva, or Jesuit in Spain, that deviates from these rules de-

serves to be hissed, and the priest kicked out of his pulpit. I must doubt your complaisance in this point, sir; for you know the forms of eloquence are divers, and ought to be suited to the different humor and capacities of an audience. You are sensible, sir, that the fiery, choleric humor of one nation must be entertained and moved by other means than the heavy, flegmatic complexion of another; and I have observed in my little travels, that a sermon of three-quarters of an hour that might please the congregation at St. James's would never satisfy the meeting house in the City, where people expect more for their money; and, having more temptations of roguery, must have a larger portion of instruction.

Be pleased to hear another instance of a different kind, tho' to the same purpose. I go down to Woolwich, and there upon a piece of paper I take the dimensions of the Royal Sovereign, and from hence I frame a model of a man-of-war: I divide the ship into three principal parts, the keel, the hull, and the rigging; I subdivide these into their proper denominations, and by the help of a sailor, give you all the terms belonging to every rope and every office in the whole ship; will you from hence infer that I am an excellent shipwright, and that this model is proper for a trading junck upon the Volga, or a Venetian galley in the Adriatic sea?

But you'll object, perhaps, that this is no parallel case, because that Aristotle's *Ars Poetica* was never drawn from such slight observations, but was the pure effect of his immense reason, thro' a nice inspection into the very bottom and foundation of nature.

To this I answer, that verity is eternal, as that the truth of two and two making four was as certain in the days of Adam as it is now; and that, according to his own position, nature is the same *apud omnes Gentes*. Now, if his rules of poetry were drawn from certain and immutable principles, and fixed on the basis of nature, why should not his *Ars Poetica* be as efficacious now as it was two thousand years ago? And why should not a single plot, with perfect unity of time and place, do as well at Lincoln's-Inn-Fields as at the play-house in Athens? No, no, sir, I am apt to believe that the philosopher took no such pains in poetry as you imagine; the Greek was his mother tongue, and Homer was read with as much veneration among the school-boys as we learn our Catechism. Then where was the great business for a person so expert in mood and figures as Aristotle was to range into some order a parcel of terms of art, drawn from his observations upon the *Iliads,* and these to call the model of an epic poem? Here, sir, you may imagine that I am caught, and have all this while been spinning a thread to strangle myself. One of my main objections against Aristotle's criticisms is drawn from his non-performance in poetry; and now I affirm that his rules are extracted from the greatest poet that ever lived, which gives the utmost validity to the precept, and that is all we contend for.

. . . . . .

Neither is Aristotle to be allowed any farther knowledge in dramatic than in epic poetry. Euripides, whom he seems to compliment by rules adapted to the model of his plays, was either his contemporary or lived but a little before him; he was not insensible how much this author was the darling of the city, as appeared by the prodigious expense disbursed by the public for the ornament of his plays; and, 'tis probable, he might take this opportunity of improving his interest with the people, indulging their inclination by refining upon the beauty of what they admired. And besides all this, the severity of dramatic rage was so fresh in his memory in the hard usage that his brother soph not long before met with upon the stage, that it was convenient to humor the reigning wit, lest a second Aristophanes should take him to task with as little mercy as poor Socrates found at the hands of the first.

I have talked so long to lay a foundation for these following conclusions: Aristotle was no poet, and consequently not capable of giving instructions in the art of poetry; his *Ars Poetica* are only some observations drawn from the works of Homer and Euripides, which may be mere accidents resulting casually from the composition of the works, and not any of the essential principles on which they are compiled; that without giving himself the trouble of searching into the

nature of poetry, he has only complimented the heroes of wit and valor of his age, by joining with them in their approbation; with this difference, that their applause was plain, and his more scholastic.

But to leave these only as suppositions to be relished by every man at his pleasure, I shall without complimenting any author, either ancient or modern, inquire into the first invention of comedy; what were the true designs and honest intentions of that art; and from a knowledge of the *end,* seek out the *means,* without one quotation of Aristotle, or authority of Euripides.

In all productions either divine or human, the final cause is the first mover, because the end or intention of any rational action must first be considered before the material or efficient causes are put in execution. Now, to determine the final cause of comedy we must run back beyond the material and formal agents, and take it in its very infancy, or rather in the very first act of its generation, when its primary parent, by proposing such or such an end of his labor, laid down the first sketches or shadows of the piece. Now, as all arts and sciences have their first rise from a final cause, so 'tis certain that they have grown from very small beginnings, and that the current of time has swelled 'em to such a bulk that nobody can find the fountain by any proportion between the head and the body; this, with the corruption of time, which has debauched things from their primitive innocence to selfish designs and purposes, renders it difficult to find the origin of any offspring so very unlike its parent.

This is not only the case of comedy, as it stands at present, but the condition also of the ancient theaters; when great men made shows of this nature a rising step to their ambition, mixing many lewd and lascivious representations to gain the favor of the populace, to whose taste and entertainment the plays were chiefly adopted. We must therefore go higher than either Aristophanes or Menander to discover comedy in its primitive institution, if we would draw any moral design of its invention to warrant and authorize its continuance.

I have already mentioned the difficulty

of discovering the invention of any art in the different figure it makes by succession of improvements; but there is something in the nature of comedy, even in its present circumstances, that bears so great a resemblance to the philosophical mythology of the ancients, that old Æsop must wear the bays as the first and original author; and whatever alterations or improvements farther application may have subjoined, his *Fables* gave the first rise and occasion.

Comedy is no more at present than *a well-framed tale handsomely told as an agreeable vehicle for counsel or reproof.* This is all we can say for the credit of its institution, and is the stress of its charter for liberty and toleration. Then where should we seek for a foundation but in Æsop's symbolical way of moralizing upon tales and fables? with this difference: that his stories were shorter than ours. He had his tyrant Lyon, his statesman Fox, his beau Magpie, his coward Hare, his bravo Ass, and his buffoon Ape, with all the characters that crowd our stages every day; with this distinction, nevertheless, that Æsop made his beasts speak good Greek, and our heroes sometimes can't talk English.

But whatever difference time has produced in the form, we must in our own defense stick to the end and intention of his fables. *Utile Dulce* was his motto, and must be our business; we have no other defense against the presentment of the grand jury, and, for ought I know, it might prove a good means to mollify the rigor of that persecution, to inform the inquisitors that the great Æsop was the first inventor of these poor comedies that they are prosecuting with so much eagerness and fury; that the first laureate was as just, as prudent, as pious, as reforming, and as ugly as any of themselves; and that the beasts which are lugged upon the stage by the horns are not caught in the city, as they suppose, but brought out of Æsop's own forest. We should inform them, besides, that those very tales and fables which they apprehend as obstacles to reformation were the main instruments and machines used by the wise Æsop for its propagation; and as he would improve men by the policy of beasts, so we endeavor to reform brutes with the examples of men.

Fondlewife and his young spouse are no more than the eagle and cockle; he wanted teeth to break the shell himself, so somebody else run away with the meat. The fox in the play is the same with the fox in the fable, who stufft his guts so full that he could not get out at the same hole he came in; so both Reynards, being delinquents alike, come to be trussed up together. Here are precepts, admonitions, and salutary innuendoes for the ordering of our lives and conversations couched in these allegories and allusions. The wisdom of the ancients was wrapt up in veils and figures; the Ægyptian hierogliphics and the history of the heathen gods are nothing else. But if these pagan authorities give offense to their scrupulous consciences, let them but consult the tales and parables of our Savior in holy Writ, and they may find this way of instruction to be much more Christian than they imagine. Nathan's fable of the poor man's lamb had more influence on the conscience of David than any force of downright admonition. So that by ancient practice and modern example, by the authority of Pagans, Jews, and Christians, the world is furnished with this so sure, so pleasant, and expedient an art of schooling mankind into better manners. Now, here is the primary design of comedy illustrated from its first institution; and the same end is equally alleged for its daily practice and continuance.— Then, without all dispute, whatever means are most proper and expedient for compassing this end and intention, they must be the *just rules of comedy,* and the *true art of the stage.*

We must consider, then, in the first place, that our business lies not with a French or a Spanish audience; that our design is not to hold forth to ancient Greece, nor to moralize upon the vices and defaults of the Roman Commonwealth. No, no; an English play is intended for the use and instruction of an English audience, a people not only separated from the rest of the world by situation, but different also from other nations as well in the complexion and temperament of the natural body as in the constitution of our body politic. As we are a mixture of many nations, so we have the most unaccountable medley of humors among us of any people upon earth; these humors produce variety of follies, some of 'em unknown to former ages; these new distempers must have new remedies, which are nothing but new counsels and instructions.

Now, sir, if our *Utile,* which is the end, be different from the ancients, pray let our *Dulce,* which is the means, be so too; for you know that to different towns there are different ways; or, if you would have it more scholastically, *ad diversos fines non idem conducit medium;* or, mathematically, one and the same line cannot terminate in two centers. But waving this manner of concluding by induction, I shall gain my point a nearer way, and draw it immediately from the first principle I set down: *That we have the most unaccountable medley of humors among us of any nation upon earth;* and this is demonstrable from common experience. We shall find a Wildair in one corner, and a Morose in another; nay, the space of an hour or two shall create such vicissitudes of temper in the same person that he can hardly be taken for the same man. We shall have a fellow bestir his stumps from chocolate to coffee-house with all the joy and gaiety imaginable, tho' he want a shilling to pay for a hack; whilst another, drawn about in a coach and six, is eaten up with the spleen, and shall loll in state with as much melancholy, vexation, and discontent, as if he were making the Tour of Tyburn. Then what sort of a *Dulce,* (which I take for the pleasantry of the tale, or the plot of the play) must a man make use of to engage the attention of so many different humors and inclinations? Will a single plot satisfy everybody? Will the turns and surprises that may result naturally from the ancient limits of time be sufficient to rip open the spleen of some and physic the melancholy of others, screw up the attention of a rover and fix him to the stage in spight of his volatile temper and the temptation of a mask? To make the moral instructive, you must make the story diverting. The splenetic wit, the beau courtier, the heavy citizen, the fine lady, and her fine footman come all to be instructed, and therefore must all be diverted; and he that can do this best, and with most applause, writes the best

comedy, let him do it by what rules he pleases, so they be not offensive to religion and good manners.

But *hic labor, hoc opus:* how must this secret of pleasing so many different tastes be discovered? Not by tumbling over volumes of the ancients, but by studying the humor of the moderns. The rules of English comedy don't lie in the compass of Aristotle or his followers, but in the pit, box, and galleries. And to examine into the humor of an English audience, let us see by what means our own English poets have succeeded in this point. To determine a suit at law we don't look into the archives of Greece or Rome, but inspect the reports of our own lawyers, and the acts and statutes of our Parliaments; and by the same rule we have nothing to do with the models of Menander or Plautus, but must consult Shakespeare, Johnson, Fletcher, and others, who, by methods much different from the ancients, have supported the English stage and made themselves famous to posterity. We shall find that these gentlemen have fairly dispensed with the greatest part of critical formalities; the decorums of time and place, so much cried up of late, had no force of decorum with them; the economy of their plays was *ad libitum,* and the extent of their plots only limited by the convenience of action. I would willingly understand the regularities of *Hamlet, Macbeth, Henry the Fourth,* and of Fletcher's plays: and yet these have long been the darlings of the English audience, and are like to continue with the same applause, in defiance of all the criticisms that ever were published in Greek and Latin. ·

But are there no rules, no decorums, to be observed in comedy? Must we make the condition of the English stage a state of anarchy? No, sir — for there are extremes in irregularity as dangerous to an author as too scrupulous a deference to criticism; and as I have given you an instance of one, so I shall present you an example of the t'other.

There are a sort of gentlemen that have had the jaunty education of dancing, French, and a fiddle, who, coming to age before they arrive at years of discretion, make a shift to spend a handsome patrimony of two or three thousand pound, by soaking in the tavern all night, lolling a-bed all the morning, and sauntering away all the evening between the two play-houses with their hands in their pockets; you shall have a gentleman of this size, upon his knowledge of Covent-Garden and a knack of witticizing in his cups, set up immediately for a playwright. But besides the gentleman's wit and experience, here is another motive: there are a parcel of saucy, impudent fellows about the playhouse called door-keepers, that can't let a gentleman see a play in peace, without jogging and nudging him every minute. *Sir, will you please to pay? — Sir, the act's done, will you please to pay, sir?* I have broke their heads all round two or three times, yet the puppies will still be troublesome. Before gad, I'll be plagued with 'em no longer; I'll e'en write a play myself; by which means my character of wit shall be established, I shall enjoy the freedom of the house, and to pin up the basket, pretty Miss —— shall have the profits of my third night for her maidenhead. Thus we see what a great blessing is a coming girl to a play-house. Here is a poet sprung from the tail of an actress, like Minerva from Jupiter's head. But my spark proceeds: — My own intrigues are sufficient to found the plot, and the devil's in 't if I can make my character talk as wittily as those in the *Trip to the Jubilee*. But stay — What shall I call it, first? Let me see — *The Rival Theatres.* — Very good, by gad, because I reckon the two houses will have a contest about this very play. — Thus having found a name for his play, in the next place he makes a play to his name, and thus he begins.

ACT I. SCENE: *Covent-Garden. Enter* PORTICO, PIAZA, *and* TURNSTILE.

Here you must note that Portico, being a compound of practical rake and speculative gentleman, is ten to one the author's own character, and the leading card in the pack. Piaza is his mistress, who lives in the square, and is daughter to old Pillariso, an odd, out-o'the-way gentleman, something between the character of Alexander the Great and Solon, which must please because it is new.

Turnstile is maid and confident to Piaza, who, for a bribe of ten pieces, lets Portico in at the back-door; so the first act concludes.

In the second, enter Spigotoso, who was butler, perhaps, to the Czar of Muscovy, and Fossetana his wife. After these characters are run dry, he brings you in, at the third act, Whinewell and Charmarillis for a scene of love to please the ladies, and so he goes on without fear or wit till he comes to a marriage or two, and then he writes — *Finis.*

'Tis then whispered among his friends at Will's and Hippolito's, that Mr. Such-a-one has writ a very pretty comedy; and some of 'em, to encourage the young author, equip him presently with prologue and epilogue. Then the play is sent to Mr. Rich or Mr. Betterton in a fair, legible hand, with the recommendation of some gentleman that passes for a man of parts and a critic. In short, the gentleman's interest has the play acted, and the gentleman's interest makes a present to pretty Miss ——; she's made his whore, and the stage his cully, that for the loss of a month in rehearsing, and a hundred pound in dressing a confounded play, must give the liberty of the house to him and his friends for ever after.

Now, such a play may be written with all the exactness imaginable, in respect of unity in time and place; but if you inquire its character of any person, tho'. of the meanest understanding of the whole audience, he will tell you 'tis intolerable stuff; and upon your demanding his reasons, his answer is, *I don't like it.* His humor is the only rule that he can judge a comedy by, but you find that mere nature is offended with some irregularities; and tho' he be not so learned in the drama, to give you an inventory of the faults, yet I can tell you that one part of the plot had no dependence upon another, which made this simple man drop his attention, and concern for the event; and so, disengaging his thoughts from the business of the action, he sat there very uneasy, thought the time very tedious, because he had nothing to do. The characters were so uncoherent in themselves, and composed of such variety of absurdities, that in his knowledge of nature he could find no original for such a copy; and being therefore unacquainted with any folly they reproved, or any virtue that they recommended, their business was as flat and tiresome to him as if the actors had talked Arabic.

Now, these are the material irregularities of a play, and these are the faults which downright mother-sense can censure and be offended at, as much as the most learned critic in the pit. And altho' the one cannot give me the reasons of his approbation or dislike, yet I will take his word for the credit or disrepute of a comedy sooner perhaps than the opinion of some virtuosos; for there are some gentlemen that have fortified their spleen so impregnably with criticism, and hold out so stiffly against all attacks of pleasantry, that the most powerful efforts of wit and humor cannot make the least impression. What a misfortune is it to these gentlemen to be natives of such an ignorant, self-willed, impertinent island, where let a critic and a scholar find never so many irregularities in a play, yet five hundred saucy people will give him the lie to his face, and come to see this wicked play forty or fifty times in a year. But this *Vox Populi* is the devil, tho', in a place of more authority than Aristotle, it is called *Vox Dei.* Here is a play with a vengeance, (says a critic,) to bring the transaction of a year's time into the compass of three hours; to carry the whole audience with him from one kingdom to another by the changing of a scene: where's the probability, nay, the possibility of all this? The devil's in the poet, sure; he don't think to put contradictions upon us?

Look'ee, sir, don't be in a passion. The poet does not impose contradictions upon you, because he has told you no lie; for that only is a lie which is related with some fallacious intention that you should believe it for a truth. Now, the poet expects no more that you should believe the plot of his play than old Æsop designed the world should think his eagle and lion talked like you and I; which, I think, was every jot as improbable as what you quarrel with; and yet the fables took, and I'll be hanged if you yourself don't like 'em. But besides, sir, if you are so inveterate against improbabilities, you must never come near the playhouse at all; for there are several improbabilities, nay, impossibilities, that all the

criticisms in nature cannot correct: as, for instance, in the part of Alexander the Great, to be affected with the transactions of the play, we must suppose that we see that great conqueror, after all his triumphs, shunned by the woman he loves, and importuned by her he hates; crossed in his cups and jollity by his own subjects, and at last miserably ending his life in a raging madness. We must suppose that we see the very Alexander, the son of Philip, in all these unhappy circumstances, else we are not touched by the moral, which represents to us the uneasiness of human life in the greatest state, and the instability of fortune in respect of worldly pomp. Yet the whole audience at the same time knows that this is Mr. Betterton who is strutting upon the stage and tearing his lungs for a livelihood. And that the same person should be Mr. Betterton and Alexander the Great at the same time is somewhat like an impossibility, in my mind. Yet you must grant this impossibility in spite of your teeth, if you han't power to raise the old hero from the grave to act his own part.

Now for another impossibility: The less rigid critics allow to a comedy the space of an artificial day, or twenty-four hours; but those of the thorough reformation will confine it to the natural, or solar, day, which is but half the time. Now, admitting this for a decorum absolutely requisite,— this play begins when it is exactly six by your watch, and ends precisely at nine, which is the usual time of the representation. Now, is it feazible in *rerum natura,* that the same space or extent of time can be three hours by your watch and twelve hours upon the stage, admitting the same number of minutes or the same measure of sand to both? I'm afraid, sir, you must allow this for an impossibility, too; and you may with as much reason allow the play the extent of a whole year; and if you grant me a year, you may give me seven, and so to a thousand. For that a thousand years should come within the compass of three hours is no more an impossibility than that two minutes should be contained in one; *Nullum minu continet in se majus* is equally applicable to both.

So much for the decorum of Time: now for the regularity of Place. I might make the one a consequence of t'other, and allege that by allowing me any extent of time, you must grant me any change of place, for the one depends upon t'other; and having five or six years for the action of a play, I may travel from Constantinople to Denmark, so to France, and home to England, and rest long enough in each country besides. But you'll say: How can you carry us with you? Very easily, sir, if you be willing to go. As for example: here is a new play; the house is thronged, the prologue's spoken and the curtain drawn represents you the scene of Grand Cairo. Whereabouts are you now, sir? Were not you the very minute before in the pit in the English play-house talking to a wench, and now, *presto pass,* you are spirited away to the banks of the river Nile. Surely, sir, this is a most intolerable improbability; yet this you must allow me, or else you destroy the very constitution of representation. Then, in the second act, with a flourish of the fiddles, I change the scene to Astrachan. *O, this is intolerable!* Look'ee, sir, 'tis not a jot more intolerable than the other; for you'll find that 'tis much about the same distance between Egypt and Astrachan, as it is between Drury-Lane and Grand Cairo; and if you please to let your fancy take post, it will perform the journey in the same moment of time, without any disturbance in the world to your person. You can follow Quintus Curtius all over Asia in the train of Alexander, and trudge after Hannibal, like a cadet, through all Italy, Spain, and Afric, in the space of four or five hours; yet the devil a one of you will stir a step over the threshold for the best poet in Christendom, tho he make it his business to make heroes more amiable, and to surprise you with more wonderful accidents and events.

I am as little a friend to those rambling plays as anybody, nor have I ever espoused their party by my own practice; yet I could not forbear saying something in vindication of the great Shakespear, whom every little fellow can form an *A[o]ristus primus* will presume to condemn for indecorums and absurdities; sparks that are so spruce upon their Greek and·Latin that, like our fops in travel, they can relish nothing but

what is foreign, to let the world know they have been abroad forsooth; but it must be so, because Aristotle said it; now, I say it must be otherwise, because Shakespear said it, and I'm sure that Shakespear was the greater poet of the two. But you'll say that Aristotle was the greater critic.— That's a mistake, sir, for criticism in poetry is no more than judgment in poetry; which you will find in your lexicon. Now, if Shakespear was the better poet, he must have the most judgment in his art; for everybody knows that judgment is an essential part of poetry, and without it no writer is worth a farthing. But to stoop to the authority of either, without consulting the reason of the consequence, is an abuse to a man's understanding; and neither the precept of the philosopher nor example of the poet should go down with me, without exam[in]ing the weight of their assertions. We can expect no more decorum or regularity in any business than the nature of the thing will bear; now, if the stage cannot subsist without the strength of supposition and force of fancy in the audience, why should a poet fetter the business of his plot and starve his action for the nicety of an hour or the change of a scene; since the thought of man can fly over a thousand years with the same ease, and in the same instant of time, that your eye glances from the figure of six to seven on the dial-plate; and can glide from the Cape of Good-Hope to the Bay of St. Nicholas, which is quite across the world, with the same quickness and activity as between Covent-Garden Church and Will's Coffee-House. Then I must beg of these gentlemen to let our old English authors alone.— If they have left vice unpunished, virtue unrewarded, folly unexposed, or prudence unsuccessful, the contrary of which is the *Utile* of comedy, let them be lashed to some purpose; if any part of their plots have been independent of the rest, or any of their characters forced or unnatural, which destroys the *Dulce* of plays, let them be hissed off the stage. But if by a true decorum in these material points, they have writ successfully and answered the end of dramatic poetry in every respect, let them rest in peace, and their memories enjoy the encomiums due to their merit, without any reflection for waving those niceties, which are neither instructive to the world nor diverting to mankind, but are, like all the rest of critical learning, fit only to set people together by the ears in ridiculous controversies, that are not one jot material to the good of the public, whether they be true or false.

And thus you see, sir, I have concluded a very unnecessary piece of work; which is much too long if you don't like it. But let it happen any way, be assured that I intended to please you, which should partly excuse, sir,

Your most humble Servant.

JOSEPH ADDISON

Joseph Addison was born at Milston, Wiltshire, in 1672. He was a student at the Charter House, which he left in 1687, to enter Queen's College, Oxford. After two years he was transferred to Magdalen, where he was graduated in 1693. He distinguished himself while at college for his shyness and his scholarship. In the year of his graduation he published his *Account of the Greatest English Poets.* Through Dryden, to whom he addressed some complimentary verses, he was introduced to Tonson, who set him to work translating Juvenal, Persius, Vergil, and Herodotus. While he was still at Oxford, where he remained on a fellowship after his graduation, he was on the point of taking orders, but a royal pension was obtained for him, and he set forth on his travels on the Continent. He started in 1699, spent a year and a half in France, a year in Italy, and another in Switzerland, Austria, and Germany; and after a stay of some months in Holland, he returned to England toward the end of 1703. He was reduced in circumstances, and had little hope of preferment in politics, so that he was forced to join the writers in Grub Street. But, owing to a change in the tide of affairs, and to Addison's popularity after the publication of his poem, *The Campaign,* he was made Under-Secretary of State. Meantime he was engaged in literary work, and in 1706 he produced an unsuccessful opera, *Rosamond.* Two years later Addison was deprived of his position as Under-Secretary, but was offered a Secretaryship in Ireland under the Lord Lieutenant. In 1711 he lost the post owing to a change

of the Ministry. Steele's *Tatler* papers began to appear in 1709, and Addison's first contribution dates from the same year. In 1711 he and Steele brought out the first number of *The Spectator,* which continued until 1714. In 1713 his tragedy of *Cato* was performed and met with great success because rather of its political timeliness than for any dramatic power inherent in it. An unsuccessful play, *The Drummer,* was produced, anonymously, in 1714. During the winter of 1715–16 Addison was employed by the Whig Party to uphold its interests, and he published *The Freeholder,* a political paper; his reward was in all probability the position of Commissioner for Trade and Colonies. In 1716 he married the Countess of Warwick. In 1717 he was made a Secretary of State. Failing in health, he resigned the position a year later. The next year he engaged in further political controversy, which resulted in a break with Steele. The following year he died.

Of Addison's criticism as a whole it may be said that it represented a commonsense attitude based upon neo-classic ideals. Of his dramatic criticism proper, confined as it was almost wholly to five or six *Spectator* essays, there is not so much to be said. These essays were written before he had evolved the critical standards which add so materially to the value of his later contributions. However, the drama essays briefly sum up the rationalistic tendency of criticism in the early eighteenth century. Addison condemned English tragedy because it was not sufficiently moral, and he proceeded to write a dull tragedy in order

to show what beautiful and stately sentiments should go into tragedy. He was
rigidly classic in his denunciation of the
tragi-comedy. Not until Johnson published his 156th *Rambler* (in 1751) was
the classic spell broken.

THE SPECTATOR [1]

(1711)

No. 39.   Saturday, April 14.

*Multa fero, ut placem genus irritabile
    vatum.*
Cum scribo. . . .   HOR.

As a perfect tragedy is the noblest
production of human nature, so it is capable of giving the mind one of the most
delightful and most improving entertainments. A virtuous man, says Seneca,
struggling with misfortunes, is such a
spectacle as gods might look upon with
pleasure. And such a pleasure it is
which one meets with in the representation of a well-written tragedy. Diversions of this kind wear out of our
thoughts everything that is mean and
little. They cherish and cultivate that
humanity which is the ornament of our
nature. They soften insolence, soothe
affliction, and subdue the mind to the
dispensations of Providence.

It is no wonder, therefore, that in all
the polite nations of the world, this part
of the drama has met with public encouragement.

The modern tragedy excels that of
Greece and Rome in the intricacy and
disposition of the fable; but, what a
Christian writer would be ashamed to
own, falls infinitely short of it in the
moral part of the performance. . . .

.   .   .   .   .   .

No. 40.   Monday, April 16

The English writers of tragedy are
possessed with a notion that when they
represent a virtuous or innocent person
in distress, they ought not to leave him
till they have delivered him out of his
troubles, or made him triumph over his
enemies. This error they have been led

into by a ridiculous doctrine in modern
criticism, that they are obliged to an
equal distribution of rewards and punishments, and an impartial execution of
poetical justice. Who were the first that
established this rule I know not; but I
am sure it has no foundation in nature,
in reason, or in the practice of the ancients. We find that good and evil happen alike to all men on this side of the
grave; and as the principal design of
tragedy is to raise commiseration and
terror in the minds of the audience, we
shall defeat this great end if we always
make virtue and innocence happy and
successful. Whatever crosses and disappointments a good man suffers in the
body of the tragedy, they will make but
small impression on our minds, when we
know that in the last act he is to arrive
at the end of his wishes and desires.
When we see him engaged in the depth
of his afflictions, we are apt to comfort
ourselves, because we are sure he will
find his way out of them; and that his
grief, how great soever it may be at present, will soon terminate in gladness. For
this reason the ancient writers of tragedy
treated men in their plays as they are
dealt with in the world, by making virtue sometimes happy and sometimes miserable, as they found it in the fable
which they made choice of, or as it might
affect their audience in the most agreeable manner. Aristotle considers tragedies that were written in either of these
kinds, and observes that those which
ended unhappily, had always pleased the
people, and carried away the prize in
the public disputes of the stage, from
those that ended happily. Terror and
commiseration leave a pleasing anguish
in the mind, and fix the audience in such
a serious composure of thought, as is
much more lasting and delightful than
any little transient starts of joy and
satisfaction. Accordingly, we find that
more of our English tragedies have suc-

---

1 Re-printed, with omissions, from vol. 1 of
The Spectator (Everyman's Library, London
and New York, 1906).— Ed.

ceeded, in which the favorites of the audience sink under their calamities, than those in which they recover themselves out of them. The best plays of this kind are *The Orphan, Venice Preserved, Alexander the Great, Theodosius, All for Love, Œdipus, Oroonoko, Othello,* etc. *King Lear* is an admirable tragedy of the same kind as Shakespeare wrote it, but as it reformed according to the chimerical notion of poetical justice, in my humble opinion it has lost half its beauty. At the same time I must allow that there are very noble tragedies which have been framed upon the other plan and have ended happily; as indeed most of the good tragedies which have been written since the starting of the above-mentioned criticism, have taken this turn, as *The Mourning Bride, Tamerlane, Ulysses, Phædra and Hippolytus,* with most of Mr. Dryden's. I must also allow that many of Shakespeare's, and several of the celebrated tragedies of antiquity, are cast in the same form. I do not therefore dispute against this way of writing tragedies, but against the criticism that would establish this as the only method, and by that means would very much cramp the English tragedy, and perhaps give a wrong bent to the genius of our writers.

The tragi-comedy, which is the product of the English theater, is one of the most monstrous inventions that ever entered into a poet's thoughts. An author might as well think of weaving the adventures of Æneas and Hudibras into one poem, as of writing such a motley piece of mirth and sorrow. But the absurdity of these performances is so very visible that I shall not insist upon it.

The same objections which are made to tragi-comedy may in some measure be applied to all tragedies that have a double plot in them; which are likewise more frequent upon the English stage than upon any other. For though the grief of the audience in such performance be not changed into another passion, as in tragi-comedies, it is diverted upon another object, which weakens their concern for the principal action, and breaks the tide of sorrow by throwing it into different channels. This inconvenience, however, may in a great measure be cured, if not wholly removed, by the skillful choice of an under-plot, which may bear such a near relation to the principal design, as to contribute towards the completion of it, and be concluded by the same catastrophe.

SAMUEL JOHNSON

Samuel Johnson, the son of a bookseller and magistrate, was born at Lichfield, in 1709. At school he soon distinguished himself as a talented scholar and at the age of eighteen returned home, where he studied and read. The Johnson family was unable to send Samuel to college, but through the generosity of a friend he was sent to Oxford, where he remained only two years, when he reached the end of his meager resources. He spent the next five years near his home, endeavoring to make a living by hack work. In 1735 he married Elizabeth Porter, who brought him a small dowry. After his marriage he tried to secure pupils, but during a year and half only three came to him. One of these was David Garrick. In 1737 he went to London, and after many privations, in the following year was employed to write for the *Gentleman's Magazine,* for which he reported parliamentary proceedings. His first work of any importance was *London* (1738), a satirical poem in imitation of Juvenal. The book was published anonymously, but the author's name soon became known. As a result, Pope tried to get Johnson a position as teacher, but was unable to do so. Johnson again went to work as before. He had made the acquaintance of Savage, and at his death in 1743 he wrote his biography, which was published anonymously. From this time forward, Johnson's reputation grew, so that in 1747 he was employed by a number of booksellers to write the *Dictionary of the English Language*, which was the greatest monument of his life. It appeared in 1755. Meanwhile he sought relaxation in other work, and published *The Vanity of Human Wishes*, after Juvenal, in 1749. The same year Garrick produced his tragedy of *Irene*, part of which was written before Johnson's arrival in London. Although the play was scarcely successful, Johnson reaped considerable profit. In 1750 he began publishing articles and essays after the manner of *The Spectator*, and continued until two years later. *The Rambler* was at first coldly received, but after the essays had been collected into book-form, it was one of the most popular works of the day. Mrs. Johnson died in 1752, and her death left Johnson in a more melancholy mood than usual. The publication of the *Dictionary* did much for his fame, but little for his pocket, and twice in 1755 he was sent to jail for debt. He wrote miscellaneous essays for the *Literary Magazine* and planned his edition of Shakespeare, and in 1758 issued in book-form another collection of essays, *The Idler*. At this time he wrote *Rasselas* in a week, and sold it for a hundred pounds, to defray the expenses of his mother's funeral. In 1762 George III offered Johnson a pension of three hundred pounds, which the needy author accepted, and which enabled him henceforward to do work of a more congenial nature. But he had a duty to discharge: for nine years he had been planning the edition of Shakespeare and spending the money sent in by subscribers. In 1765 the work appeared. The *Introduction* and *Notes* were very unequal, and Johnson was severely criticized for the slovenliness and inadequacy of his work. His laziness was such that between 1765 and 1775 he produced nothing but three political tracts. But his personal influence was growing, and he reigned over the famous literary coterie of which Gold-

smith, Burke, Reynolds, Gibbon, Garrick, and others were members. Boswell was ever present; and it is due to his assiduity that we possess the celebrated *Life of Johnson*. In 1773 Boswell accompanied him on a trip to the Hebrides, which resulted in the publication of his *Journey to the Hebrides*, two years later. In 1777 he undertook to write brief biographical notices for an edition of the English poets which was about to be published. The short notices which he had originally intended to supply grew to considerable size. The first four volumes appeared in 1779, the last six, two years later. His last years were spent in pain and anxiety, and after a long period of ill-health, he died in 1784.

Johnson is the representative orthodox critic of the eighteenth century, and yet his orthodoxy, so far as his opinions on the drama are concerned, was not too exclusive or rigid. While he was continually insisting upon the necessity for a moral in works of art, and judging poetry by the sense rather than by the music, he was not intolerant to the authors who violated accepted rules. In his *Preface to Shakespeare* (1768) he mentions the poet's mingling of the tragic and the comic in a single play, saying that "this is a practice contrary to the rules of criticism will be readily allowed," but he adds what is of great significance: "but there is always an appeal open from criticism to nature." This sentence belongs with the famous one in the 156th *Rambler*, on *Tragi-comedy:* "It ought to be the first endeavor of a writer to distinguish nature from custom, or that which is established because it is right from that which is right only because it is established; that he may neither violate essential principles by a desire of novelty, nor debar himself from the attainment of beauties within his view by a needless fear of breaking rules which no literary dictator had authority to enact." Professor Saintsbury declares that "With this utterance, this single utterance, all the ruling doctrines of sixteenth, seventeenth, and eighteenth century criticism receive notice to quit."

PREFACE TO SHAKESPEARE [1]
(1765)

Nothing can please many, and please long, but just representations of general nature. Particular manners can be known to few, and therefore few only can judge how nearly they are copied. The irregular combinations of fanciful invention may delight awhile by that novelty of which the common satiety of life sends us all in quest; but the pleasures of sudden wonder are soon exhausted, and the mind can only repose on the stability of truth.

Shakespeare is, above all writers, at least above all modern writers, the poet of nature, the poet that holds up to his readers a faithful mirror of manners and of life. His characters are not modified by the customs of particular places, unpracticed by the rest of the world; by the peculiarities of studies or professions which can operate but upon small numbers; or by the accidents of transient fashions or temporary opinions: they are the genuine progeny of common humanity, such as the world will always supply, and observation will always find. His persons act and speak by the influence of those general passions and principles by which all minds are agitated and the whole system of life is continued in motion. In the writings of other poets a character is too often an individual; in those of Shakespeare it is commonly a species.

It is from this wide extension of design that so much instruction is derived. It is this which fills the plays of Shakespeare with practical axioms and domestic wisdom. It was said of Euripides that every verse was a precept; and it may be said of Shakespeare that from his works may be collected a system of civil and economical prudence. Yet his real power is not shown in the splendor of particular passages, but by the progress of his fable and the tenor of his dialogue; and he that tries to recommend him by select quotations will succeed like the pedant in Hierocles, who, when he offered his house to sale, carried a brick in his pocket as a specimen.

It will not easily be imagined how much Shakespeare excels in accommodating his sentiments to real life but by comparing him with other authors. It was observed of the ancient schools of declamation that the more diligently they were frequented, the more was the student disqualified for the world, because he found nothing there which he should ever meet in any other place. The same remark may be applied to every stage but that of Shakespeare. The theatre, when it is under any other direction, is peopled by such characters as were never seen, conversing in a language which was never heard, upon topics which will never arise in the commerce of mankind. But the dialogue of this author is often so evidently determined by the incident which produces it, and is pursued with so much ease and simplicity, that it seems scarcely to claim the merit of fiction, but to have been gleaned by diligent selection out of common conversation and common occurrences.

Upon every other stage the universal agent is love, by whose power all good and evil is distributed and every action quickened or retarded. To bring a lover, a lady, and a rival into the fable; to entangle them in contradictory obligations, perplex them with oppositions of interest, and harass them with violence of desires inconsistent with each other; to make them meet in rapture and part in agony, to fill their mouths with hyperbolical joy and outrageous sorrow, to distress them as nothing human ever was distressed, to deliver them as nothing human ever was delivered, is the business of a modern dramatist. For this, probability is violated, life is misrepresented, and language is depraved. But love is only one of many passions; and as it has no great influence upon the sum of life, it has little operation in the dramas of a poet who caught his ideas from the living world and exhibited only what he saw before him. He knew that any other passion, as it was regular or exorbitant, was a cause of happiness or calamity.

Characters thus ample and general were not easily discriminated and preserved, yet perhaps no poet ever kept his personages more distinct from each

1 Extracts from the Preface to Johnson's edition of *The Plays of William Shakespeare* (London, 1765).—Ed.

other. I will not say with Pope that every speech may be assigned to the proper speaker, because many speeches there are which have nothing characteristical; but, perhaps, though some may be equally adapted to every person, it will be difficult to find any that can be properly transferred from the present possessor to another claimant. The choice is right, when there is reason for choice.

Other dramatists can only gain attention by hyperbolical or aggravated characters, by fabulous and unexampled excellence or depravity, as the writers of barbarous romances invigorated the reader by a giant and a dwarf; and he that should form his expectations of human affairs from the play, or from the tale, would be equally deceived. Shakespeare has no heroes; his scenes are occupied only by men, who act and speak as the reader thinks that he should himself have spoken or acted on the same occasion. Even where the agency is supernatural, the dialogue is level with life. Other writers disguise the most natural passions and most frequent incidents; so that he who contemplates them in the book will not know them in the world. Shakespeare approximates the remote and familiarizes the wonderful; the event which he represents will not happen, but, if it were possible, its effects would probably be such as he has assigned; and it may be said that he has not only shown human nature as it acts in real exigences, but as it would be found in trials to which it cannot be exposed.

This, therefore, is the praise of Shakespeare, that his drama is the mirror of life; that he who has mazed his imagination in following the phantoms which other writers raise up before him, may here be cured of his delirious ecstasies by reading human sentiments in human language, by scenes from which a hermit may estimate the transactions of the world and a confessor predict the progress of the passions.

His adherence to general nature has exposed him to the censure of critics who form their judgments upon narrower principles. Dennis and Rymer think his Romans not sufficiently Roman; and Voltaire censures his kings as not completely royal. Dennis is offended that Menenius, a senator of Rome, should play the buffoon; and Voltaire perhaps thinks decency violated when the Danish usurper is represented as a drunkard. But Shakespeare always makes nature predominate over accident; and, if he preserves the essential character, is not very careful of distinctions superinduced and adventitious. His story requires Romans or kings, but he thinks only on men. He knew that Rome, like every other city, had men of all dispositions; and wanting a buffoon, he went into the senate house for that which the senate house would certainly have afforded him. He was inclined to show an usurper and a murderer not only odious, but despicable; he therefore added drunkenness to his other qualities, knowing that kings love wine like other men, and that wine exerts its natural power upon kings. These are the petty cavils of petty minds; a poet overlooks the casual distinction of country and condition, as a painter, satisfied with the figure, neglects the drapery.

The censure which he has incurred by mixing comic and tragic scenes, as it extends to all his works, deserves more consideration. Let the fact be first stated and then examined.

Shakespeare's plays are not in the rigorous and critical sense either tragedies or comedies, but compositions of a distinct kind; exhibiting the real state of sublunary nature, which partakes of good and evil, joy and sorrow, mingled with endless variety of proportion and innumerable modes of combination; and expressing the course of the world, in which the loss of one is the gain of another; in which, at the same time, the reveller is hasting to his wine, and the mourner burying his friend; in which the malignity of one is sometimes defeated by the frolic of another; and many mischiefs and many benefits are done and hindered without design.

Out of this chaos of mingled purposes and casualties the ancient poets, according to the laws which custom had prescribed, selected some the crimes of men, and some their absurdities; some the momentous vicissitudes of life, and some the lighter occurrences; some the terrors of distress, and some the gaieties of prosperity. Thus rose the two modes of imitation, known by the names of *tragedy* and *comedy*, compositions intended to promote different ends by contrary means, and considered as so little allied that I do not recollect among the Greeks or Romans a single writer who attempted both.

Shakespeare has united the powers of exciting laughter and sorrw not only in one mind but in one composition. Almost all his plays are divided between serious and ludicrous characters, and, in the successive evolutions of the design, sometimes produce seriousness and sorrow, and sometimes levity and laughter.

That this is a practice contrary to the rules of criticism will be readily allowed; but there is always an appeal open from criticism to nature. The end of writing is to instruct; the end of poetry is to instruct by pleasing. That the mingled drama may convey all the instruction of tragedy or comedy cannot be denied, because it includes both in its alternations of exhibition and approaches nearer than either to the appearance of life, by showing how great machinations and slender designs may promote or obviate one another, and the high and the low co-operate in the general system by unavoidable concatenation.

It is objected that by this change of scenes the passions are interrupted in their progression, and that the principal event, being not advanced by a due gradation of preparatory incidents, wants at last the power to move, which constitutes the perfection of dramatic poetry. This reasoning is so specious that it is received as true even by those who in daily experience feel it to be false. The interchanges of mingled scenes seldom fail to produce the intended vicissitudes of passion. Fiction cannot move so much but that the attention may be easily transferred; and though it must be allowed that pleasing melancholy be sometimes interrupted by unwelcome levity, yet let it be considered likewise that melancholy is often not pleasing, and that the disturbance of one man may be the relief of another; that different auditors have different habitudes; and that, upon the whole, all pleasure consists in variety.

The players, who in their edition divided our author's works into comedies, histories, and tragedies, seem not to have distinguished the three kinds by any very exact or definite ideas.

An action which ended happily to the principal persons, however serious or distressful through its intermediate incidents, in their opinion constituted a comedy. This idea of a comedy continued long amongst us; and plays were written which, by changing the catastrophe, were tragedies today and comedies tomorrow.

Tragedy was not in those times a poem of more general dignity or elevation than comedy; it required only a calamitous conclusion, with which the common criticism of the age was satisfied, whatever lighter pleasure it afforded in its progress.

History was a series of actions, with no other than chronological succession, independent on each other, and without any tendency to introduce or regulate the conclusion. It is not always very nicely distinguished from tragedy. There is not much nearer approach to unity of action in the tragedy of *Antony and Cleopatra* than in the history of *Richard the Second*. But a history might be continued through many plays; as it had no plan, it had no limits.

Through all these denominations of the drama, Shakespeare's mode of composition is the same: an interchange of seriousness and merriment, by which the mind is softened at one time and exhilarated at another. But whatever be his purpose, whether to gladden or depress, or to conduct the story, without vehemence or emotion, through tracts of easy and familiar dialogue, he never fails to attain his purpose; as he commands us, we laugh or mourn, or sit silent with quiet expectation, in tranquillity without indifference.

When Shakespeare's plan is understood, most of the criticisms of Rymer and Voltaire vanish away. The play of *Hamlet* is opened, without impropriety, by two sentinels; Iago bellows at Brabantio's window without injury to the scheme of the play, though in terms which a modern audience would not easily endure; the character of Polonius is seasonable and useful; and the gravediggers themselves may be heard with applause.

Shakespeare engaged in dramatic poetry with the world open before him; the rules of the ancients were yet known to few; the public judgment was unformed; he had no example of such fame as might force him upon imitation, nor critics of such authority as might restrain his extravagance; he therefore indulged his natural disposition; and his disposition, as Rymer has remarked, led him to comedy. In tragedy he often writes, with great appearance of toil and study, what is written at last with little felicity; but, in his comic scenes, he seems to produce, without labor, what no labor can improve. In tragedy he is always struggling after some occasion to be comic; but in comedy he seems to repose, or to luxuriate, as in a mode of thinking congenial to his nature. In his tragic scenes there is always something wanting, but his comedy often surpasses expectation or desire. His comedy pleases by the thoughts and the language, and his tragedy for the greater part by incident and action. His tragedy seems to be skill, his comedy to be instinct.

The force of his comic scenes has suffered little diminution, from the changes made by a century and a half, in manners or in words. As his personages act upon principles arising from genuine passion, very little modified by particular forms, their pleasures and vexations are communicable to all times and to all places; they are natural, and therefore durable. The adventitious peculiarities of personal habits are only superficial dyes, bright and pleasing for a little while, yet soon fading to a dim tinct, without any remains of former lustre; but the discriminations of true passion are the colors of nature; they pervade the whole mass and can only perish with the body that exhibits them. The accidental compositions of heterogeneous modes are dissolved by the chance which combined them; but the uniform simplicity of primitive qualities neither admits increase nor suffers decay. The sand heaped by one flood is scattered by another, but the rock always continues in its place. The stream of time, which is continually washing the dissoluble fabrics of other poets, passes without injury by the adamant of Shakespeare.

If there be, what I believe there is, in every nation a style which never becomes obsolete, a certain mode of phraseology so consonant and congenial to the analogy and principles of its respective language as to remain settled and unaltered; this style is probably to be sought in the common intercourse of life, among those who speak only to be understood, without ambition of elegance. The polite are always catching modish innovations, and the learned depart from established forms of speech in hope of finding or making better; those who wish for distinction forsake the vulgar, when the vulgar is right; but there is a conversation above grossness and below refinement, where propriety resides, and where this poet seems to have gathered his comic dialogue. He is therefore more agreeable to the ears of the present age than any other author equally remote and among his other excellencies deserves to be studied as one of the original masters of our language.

These observations are to be considered not as unexceptionably constant, but as containing general and predominant truth. Shakespeare's familiar dialogue is affirmed to be smooth and clear, yet not wholly without ruggedness or difficulty; as a country may be eminently fruitful, though it has spots unfit for cultivation; his characters are praised as natural, though their sentiments are sometimes forced and their actions improbable; as the earth upon the whole is spherical, though its surface is varied with protuberances and cavities.

Shakespeare with his excellencies has likewise faults, and faults sufficient to obscure and overwhelm any other merit. I shall show them in the proportion in which they appear to me, without envious malignity or superstitious veneration. No question can be more innocently discussed than a dead poet's pretensions to renown; and little regard is due to that bigotry which sets candor higher than truth.

His first defect is that to which may be imputed most of the evil in books or in men. He sacrifices virtue to convenience and is so much more careful to please than to instruct that he seems to write without any moral purpose. From his writings indeed a system of social duty may be selected, for he that thinks reasonably must think morally; but his precepts and axioms drop casually from him; he makes no just distribution of good or evil, nor is always careful to show in the virtuous a disapprobation of the wicked; he carries his persons indifferently through right and wrong and at the close dismisses them without further care and leaves their examples to operate by chance. This fault the barbarity of his age cannot extenuate; for it is always a writer's duty to make the world better, and justice is a virtue independent on time or place.

The plots are often so loosely formed that a very slight consideration may improve them, and so carelessly pursued that he seems not always fully to comprehend his own design. He omits opportunities of instructing or delighting which the train of his story seems to force upon him, and apparently rejects those exhibitions which would be more affecting, for the sake of those which are more easy.

It may be observed that in many of his plays the latter part is evidently neglected. When he found himself near the end of his work, and in view of his reward, he shortened the labor to snatch the profit. He therefore remits his efforts where he should most vigorously exert them, and his catastrophe is improbably produced or imperfectly represented.

He had no regard to distinction of time or place, but gives to one age or nation, without scruple, the customs, institutions, and opinions of another, at the expense not only of likelihood but of possibility. These faults Pope has endeavored, with more zeal than judgment, to transfer to his imagined interpolators. We need not wonder to find Hector quoting Aristotle, when we see the loves of Theseus and Hippolyta combined with the Gothic mythology of fairies. Shakespeare, indeed, was not the only violator of chronology, for in the same age Sidney, who wanted not the advantages of learning, has, in his *Arcadia,* confounded the pastoral with the feudal times, the days of innocence, quiet, and security, with those of turbulence, violence, and adventure.

In his comic scenes he is seldom very successful when he engages his characters in reciprocations of smartness and contests of sarcasm; their jests are commonly gross, and their pleasantry licentious; neither his gentlemen nor his ladies have much delicacy nor are sufficiently distinguished from his clowns by any appearance of refined manners. Whether he represented the real conversation of his time is not easy to determine. The reign of Elizabeth is commonly supposed to have been a time of stateliness, formality, and reserve; yet perhaps the relaxations of that severity were not very elegant. There must, however, have been always some modes of gaiety preferable to others, and a writer ought to choose the best.

In tragedy his performance seems constantly to be worse as his labor is more. The effusions of passion which exigence forces out are for the most part striking and energetic; but whenever he solicits his invention, or strains his faculties, the offspring of his throes is tumor, meanness, tediousness, and obscurity.

In narration he affects a disproportionate pomp of diction and a wearisome train of circumlocution and tells the incident imperfectly in many words which might have been more plainly delivered in few. Narration in dramatic poetry is naturally tedious, as it is unanimated and inactive and obstructs the progress of the action; it should therefore always be rapid and enlivened by frequent interruption. Shakespeare found it an incumbrance and, instead of lightening it by brevity, endeavored to recommend it by dignity and splendor.

His declamations or set speeches are commonly cold and weak, for his power was the power of nature; when he endeavored, like other tragic writers, to catch opportunities of amplification, and, instead of inquiring what the occasion demanded, to show how much his stores of knowledge could supply, he seldom escapes wtihout the pity or resentment of his reader.

It is incident to him to be now and then entangled with an unwieldy sentiment, which he cannot well express and will not reject; he struggles with it awhile, and, if it continues stubborn, comprises it in words such as occur and leaves it to be disentangled and evolved by those who have more leisure to bestow upon it.

Not that always where the language is intricate the thought is subtle, or the image always great where the line is bulky; the equality of words to things is very often neglected, and trivial sentiments and vulgar ideas disappoint the attention to which they are recommended by sonorous epithets and swelling figures.

But the admirers of this great poet have most reason to complain when he approaches nearest to his highest excellence and seems fully resolved to sink them in dejection and mollify them with tender emotions by the fall of greatness, the danger of innocence, or the crosses of love. What he does best, he soon ceases to do. He is not long soft and pathetic without some idle conceit or contemptible equivocation. He no sooner begins to move than he counteracts himself; and terror and pity, as they are rising in the mind, are checked and blasted by sudden frigidity.

A quibble is to Shakespeare what luminous vapors are to the traveler; he follows it at all adventures; it is sure to lead him out of his way and sure to engulf him in the mire. It has some malignant power over his mind, and its fascinations are irresistible. Whatever be the dignity or profundity of his disquisition, whether he be enlarging knowledge or exalting affection, whether he be amusing attention with incidents or enchaining it in suspense, let but a quibble spring up before him, and he leaves his work unfinished. A quibble is the golden apple for which he will always turn aside from his career or stoop from his elevation. A quibble, poor and barren as it is, gave him such delight that he was content to purchase it by the sacrifice of reason, propriety, and truth. A quibble was to him the fatal Cleopatra for which he lost the world and was content to lose it.

It will be thought strange that in enumerating the defects of this writer I have not yet mentioned his neglect of the unities, his violation of those laws which have been instituted and established by the joint authority of poets and critics.

For his other deviations from the art of writing, I resign him to critical justice, without making any other demand in his favor than that which must be indulged to all human excellence: that his virtues be rated with his failings. But from the censure which this irregularity may bring upon him, I shall, with due reverence to that learning which I must oppose, adventure to try how I can defend him.

His histories, being neither tragedies nor comedies, are not subject to any of their laws; nothing more is necessary to all the praise which they expect than that the changes of action be so prepared as to be understood, that the incidents be various and affecting, and the characters consistent, natural, and distinct. No other unity is intended, and therefore none is to be sought.

In his other works he has well enough preserved the unity of action. He has not, indeed, an intrigue regularly perplexed and regularly unraveled; he does not endeavor to hide his design only to discover it, for this is seldom the order of real events, and Shakespeare is the poet of nature; but his plan has commonly, what Aristotle requires, a beginning, a middle, and an end; one event is concatenated with another, and the conclusion follows by easy consequence. There are perhaps some incidents that might be spared, as in other poets there is much talk that only fills up time upon the stage; but the general system makes gradual advances, and the end of the play is the end of expectation.

To the unities of time and place he has shown no regard; and perhaps a nearer view of the principles on which they stand will diminish their value and withdraw from them the veneration which, from the time of Corneille, they have very generally received, by discovering that they have given more trouble to the poet than pleasure to the auditor.

The necessity of observing the unities of time and place arises from the supposed necessity of making the drama credible. The critics hold it impossible that an action of months or years can be possibly believed to pass in three hours; or that the spectator can suppose himself to sit in the theater while ambassadors go and return between distant kings, while armies are levied and towns besieged, while an exile wanders and returns, or till he whom they saw courting his mistress shall lament the untimely fall of his son. The mind revolts from evident falsehood, and fiction loses its force when it departs from the resemblance of reality.

From the narrow limitation of time necessarily arises the contraction of place. The spectator, who knows that he saw the first act at Alexandria, cannot suppose that he sees the next at Rome, at a distance to which not the dragons of Medea could, in so short a time, have transported him; he knows with certainty that he has not changed his place; and he knows that place cannot change itself; that what was a house cannot become a plain; that what was Thebes can never be Persepolis.

Such is the triumphant language with which a critic exults over the misery of an irregular poet and exults commonly without resistance or reply. It is time, therefore, to tell him by the authority of Shakespeare, that he assumes, as an unquestionable principle, a position which, while his breath is forming it into words, his understanding pronounces to be false. It is false, that any representation is mistaken for reality; that any dramatic fable in its materiality was ever credible, or, for a single moment, was ever credited.

The objection arising from the impossibility of passing the first hour at Alexandria and the next at Rome, supposes that when the play opens the spectator really imagines himself at Alexandria and believes that his walk to the theatre has been a voyage to Egypt, and that he lives in the days of Antony and Cleopatra. Surely he that imagines this may imagine more. He that can take the stage at one time for the palace of the Ptolemies may take it in half an hour for the promontory of Actium. Delusion, if delusion be admitted, has no certain limitation; if the spectator can be once persuaded that his old acquaintance are Alexander and Caesar, that a room illuminated with candles is the plain of Pharsalia or the bank of Granicus, he is in a state of elevation above the reach of reason or of truth, and from the heights of empyrean poetry may despise the circumscriptions of terrestrial nature. There is no reason why a mind thus wandering in ecstasy should count the clock, or why an hour should not be a century in that calenture of the brains that can make the stage a field.

The truth is that the spectators are always in their senses and know, from the first act to the last that the stage is only a stage, and that the players are only players. They come to hear a certain number of lines recited with just gesture and elegant modulation. The lines relate to some action, and an action must be in some place; but the different actions that complete a story may be in places very remote from each other; and where is the absurdity of allowing that space to represent first Athens and then Sicily which was always known to be

neither Sicily nor Athens, but a modern theatre.

By supposition, as place is introduced, time may be extended; the time required by the fable elapses for the most part between the acts; for, of so much of the action as is represented, the real and poetical duration is the same. If in the first act preparations for war against Mithridates are represented to be made in Rome, the event of the war may, without absurdity, be represented in the catastrophe as happening in Pontus; we know that there is neither war nor preparation for war; we know that we are neither in Rome nor Pontus; that neither Mithridates nor Lucullus are before us. The drama exhibits successive imitations of successive actions; and why may not the second imitation represent an action that happened years after the first, if it be so connected with it that nothing but time can be supposed to intervene? Time is, of all modes of existence, most obsequious to the imagination; a lapse of years is as easily conceived as a passage of hours. In contemplation we easily contract the time of real actions and therefore willingly permit it to be contracted when we only see their imitation.

It will be asked how the drama moves if it is not credited. It is credited with all the credit due to a drama. It is credited, whenever it moves, as a just picture of a real original; as representing to the auditor what he would himself feel if he were to do or suffer what is there feigned to be suffered or to be done. The reflection that strikes the heart is not that the evils before us are real evils, but that they are evils to which we ourselves may be exposed. If there be any fallacy, it is not that we fancy the players, but that we fancy ourselves unhappy for a moment; but we rather lament the possibility than suppose the presence of misery, as a mother weeps over her babe when she remembers that death may take it from her. The delight of tragedy proceeds from our consciousness of fiction; if we thought murders and treasons real, they would please no more.

Imitations produce pain or pleasure, not because they are mistaken for realities, but because they bring realities to mind. When the imagination is recreated by a painted landscape, the trees are not supposed capable to give us shade, or the fountains coolness; but we consider how we should be pleased with such fountains playing beside us and such woods waving over us. We are agitated in reading the history of *Henry the Fifth,* yet no man takes his book for the field of Agincourt. A dramatic exhibition is a book recited with concomitants that increase or diminish its effect. Familiar comedy is often more powerful in the theatre than on the page; imperial tragedy is always less. The humor of Petruchio may be heightened by grimace; but what voice or what gesture can hope to add dignity or force to the soliloquy of Cato?

A play read affects the mind like a play acted. It is therefore evident that the action is not supposed to be real; and it follows that between the acts a longer or shorter time may be allowed to pass, and that no more account of space or duration is to be taken by the auditor of a drama than by the reader of a narrative, before whom may pass in an hour the life of a hero or the revolutions of an empire.

Whether Shakespeare knew the unities and rejected them by design, or deviated from them by happy ignorance, it is, I think, impossible to decide and useless to inquire. We may reasonably suppose that, when he rose to notice, he did not want the counsels and admonitions of scholars and critics, and that he at last deliberately persisted in a practice, which he might have begun by chance. As nothing is essential to the fable but unity of action, and as the unities of time and place arise evidently from false assumptions, and, by circumscribing the extent of the drama, lessen its variety, I cannot think it much to be lamented that they were not known by him, or not observed; nor, if such another poet could arise, should I very vehemently reproach him that his first act passed at Venice and his next in Cyprus. Such violations of rules merely positive become the comprehensive genius of Shakespeare, and such censures are suitable to the minute and slender criticism of Voltaire:

Non usque adeo permiscuit imis
Longus summa dies, ut non, si voce
  Metelli
Serventur Leges, malint a Caesare tolli.[2]

2 Lucan, *Pharsalia,* III, 138–40: "A long

Yet when I speak thus slightly of dramatic rules, I cannot but recollect how much wit and learning may be produced against me; before such authorities I am afraid to stand, not that I think the present question one of those that are to be decided by mere authority, but because it is to be suspected that these precepts have not been so easily received but for better reasons than I have yet been able to find. The result of my inquiries, in which it would be ludicrous to boast of impartiality, is that the unities of time and place are not essential to a just drama; that, though they may sometimes conduce to pleasure, they are always to be sacrificed to the nobler beauties of variety and instruction; and that a play written with nice observation of critical rules is to be contemplated as an elaborate curiosity, as the product of superfluous and ostentatious art, by which is shown, rather what is possible, than what is necessary. . . .

The mind which has feasted on the luxurious wonders of fiction has no taste for the insipidity of truth. A play which imitated only the common occurrences of the world would, upon the admirers of *Palmerin* and *Guy of Warwick,* have made little impression; he that wrote for such an audience was under the necessity of looking round for strange events and fabulous transactions; and that incredibility by which maturer knowledge is offended was the chief recommendation of writings to unskillful curiosity.

Our author's plots are generally borrowed from novels; and it is reasonable to suppose that he chose the most popular, such as were read by many and related by more; for his audience could not have followed him through the intricacies of the drama, had they not held the thread of the story in their hands.

The stories which we now find only in remoter authors were in his time accessible and familiar. The fable of *As You Like It,* which is supposed to be copied from Chaucer's *Gamelyn,* was a little pamphlet of those times; and old Mr. Cibber remembered the tale of *Hamlet* in plain English prose, which the critics have now to seek in Saxo Grammaticus.

time does not so confuse the best and the worst that the laws of Metellus would not prefer to be destroyed by Caesar."

His English histories he took from English chronicles and English ballads; and as the ancient writers were made known to his countrymen by versions, they supplied him with new subjects; he dilated some of Plutarch's lives into plays, when they had been translated by North.

His plots, whether historical or fabulous, are always crowded with incidents, by which the attention of a rude people was more easily caught than by sentiment or argumentation; and such is the power of the marvelous, even over those who despise it, that every man finds his mind more strongly seized by the tragedies of Shakespeare than of any other writer. Others please us by particular speeches; but he always makes us anxious for the event and has perhaps excelled all but Homer in securing the first purpose of a writer, by exciting restless and unquenchable curiosity and compelling him that reads his work to read it through.

The shows and bustle with which his plays abound have the same original. As knowledge advances, pleasure passes from the eye to the ear, but returns, as it declines, from the ear to the eye. Those to whom our author's labors were exhibited had more skill in pomps or processions than in poetical language and perhaps wanted some visible and discriminated events as comments on the dialogue. He knew how he should most please; and whether his practice is more agreeable to nature, or whether his example has prejudiced the nation, we still find that on our stage something must be done as well as said, and inactive declamation is very coldly heard, however musical or elegant, passionate or sublime.

Voltaire expresses his wonder that our author's extravagances are endured by a nation which has seen the tragedy of *Cato.* Let him be answered that Addison speaks the language of poets; and Shakespeare, of men. We find in *Cato* innumerable beauties which enamor us of its author, but we see nothing that acquaints us with human sentiments or human actions; we place it with the fairest and the noblest progeny which judgment propagates by conjunction with learning; but *Othello* is the vigorous and vivacious offspring of observation impregnated by genius. *Cato* affords a splendid exhibition of artificial and fictitious manners and delivers just and noble sentiments, in diction easy, elevated, and harmonious, but its hopes and fears communicate no vibration to the heart; the composition refers us only to the writer; we pronounce the name of *Cato,* but we think on Addison.

The work of a correct and regular writer is a garden accurately formed and diligently planted, varied with shades, and scented with flowers; the composition of Shakespeare is a forest, in which oaks extend their branches, and pines tower in the air, interspersed sometimes with weeds and brambles, and sometimes giving shelter to myrtles and to roses; filling the eye with awful pomp and gratifying the mind with endless diversity. Other poets display cabinets of precious rarities, minutely finished, wrought into shape, and polished into brightness. Shakespeare opens a mine which contains gold and diamonds in unexhaustible plenty, though clouded by incrustations, debased by impurities, and mingled with a mass of meaner minerals.

OLIVER GOLDSMITH

Oliver Goldsmith was born, probably at Smith-Hill House, Elphin, Roscommon, Ireland, in 1728. Soon after his birth his family moved to Kilkenny West, where Oliver first went to school. At the age of nine he left the little school at Kilkenny, and attended several academies. In 1744 he went to Trinity College, Dublin, where he barely managed to make a living. His personal ungainliness and crude manners prevented his making many acquaintances, and his life at college was miserable. He was graduated in 1749, after the death of his father, and went to live with his mother. He cast about him in search of a profession. He was a tutor at one time, but lost his position as the result of a quarrel. He decided later to emigrate to America, but missed his ship. He then determined to study law, and once again set forth to Dublin, where he gambled away the fifty pounds which had been given him. When he was twenty-four he was again endowed and went to Edinburgh to study medicine, where for a year and a half he made some slight pretense at attending lectures, and then went to Leyden, presumably to continue his studies. From Holland he proceeded on a walking tour through Flanders, France, Switzerland, and the north of Italy, earning his board and keep with his flute. In 1756 he returned to England, without a penny in his pocket, although he had, according to his own statement, received a doctor's degree. In London he turned his hand to every sort of work: translation, the writing of superficial histories, children's books, and general articles. One of the works of this period which is still included in the *Works* is the *Enquiry into the State of Polite Learning in Europe.* Through the publication of *The Bee* and the *Life of Beau Nash,* Goldsmith achieved considerable popularity, and his fortunes began to mend. He belonged to the circle of Johnson, Burke, Reynolds, and was one of "The Club." *The Traveller* appeared in 1764, and his reputation as a poet was firmly established. *The Vicar of Wakefield,* published two years later, increased his popularity, and when he produced his first play, *The Good-natur'd Man* (1768), though the play was not a success, it was widely read in

book-form. In 1770 came *The Deserted Village,* and three years after his dramatic masterpiece, *She Stoops to Conquer,* which was highly successful. Goldsmith was meanwhile busy with a great deal of hack-work — the *Natural History,* the histories of England, Rome, and Greece — which was very remunerative. But Goldsmith's carelessness, his intemperance, and his habit of gambling, soon brought him into debt. Broken in health and mind, he died in 1774.

In one of his earliest works, the *Enquiry into the Present State of Polite Learning* (1759), Goldsmith gave utterance to the thought which was to be his guiding star in the field of the drama. He says: " Does the poet paint the absurdities of the vulgar, then he is *low;* does he exaggerate the features of folly, to render it more ridiculous, he is then very *low.* In short, they have proscribed the comic or satirical muse from every walk but high life, which, though abounding in fools as well as the humblest station, is by no means so fruitful in absurdity." It was Goldsmith's mission to render natural the comedy of his time, and strike a decisive blow at the *genteel* or *sentimental* comedy, which he later termed a " kind of *mulish* production, with all the defects of its opposite parents, and marked with sterility." Goldsmith wrote comparatively little on the drama — the passages in the *Enquiry* already referred to, an occasional paragraph in the *Essays,* the important *Essay on the Theatre,* and the brief *Preface* to *The Good-natur'd Man* — are practically all he had to say on the subject.

AN ESSAY ON THE THEATRE; OR, A COMPARISON BETWEEN LAUGHING AND SENTIMENTAL COMEDY [1]

(1772)

The theater, like all other amusements, has its fashions and its prejudices: and when satiated with its excellence mankind begin to mistake change for improvement. For some years tragedy was the reigning entertainment; but of late it has entirely given way to comedy,

and our best efforts are now exerted in these lighter kinds of composition. The pompous train, the swelling phrase, and the unnatural rant, are displaced for that natural portrait of human folly and frailty, of which all are judges, because all have sat for the picture.

But as in describing nature it is presented with a double face, either of mirth or sadness, our modern writers find themselves at a loss which chiefly to copy

[1] Re-printed from *The Good-Natur'd Man and She Stoops to Conquer,* by Oliver Goldsmith,, with an Introduction by Austin Dobson (Boston, 1911) — Ed.

from; and it is now debated, whether the exhibition of human distress is likely to afford the mind more entertainment than that of human absurdity?

Comedy is defined by Aristotle to be a picture of the frailties of the lower part of mankind, to distinguish it from tragedy, which is an exhibition of the misfortunes of the great. When comedy, therefore, ascends to produce the characters of princes or generals upon the stage, it is out of its walks, since low life and middle life are entirely its object. The principal question, therefore, is, whether, in describing low or middle life, an exhibition of its follies be not preferable to a detail of its calamities? Or, in other words, which deserves the preference,— the weeping sentimental comedy so much in fashion at present, or the laughing, and even low comedy, which seems to have been last exhibited by Vanbrugh and Cibber?

If we apply to authorities, all the great masters in the dramatic art have but one opinion. Their rule is, that as tragedy displays the calamities of the great, so comedy should excite our laughter by ridiculously exhibiting the follies of the lower part of mankind. Boileau, one of the best modern critics, asserts that comedy will not admit of tragic distress: —

Le comique, ennemi des soupirs et des pleurs,
N'admet point dans ses vers de tragiques douleurs.

Nor is this rule without the strongest foundation in nature, as the distresses of the mean by no means affect us so strongly as the calamities of the great. When tragedy exhibits to us some great man fallen from his height, and struggling with want and adversity, we feel his situation in the same manner as we suppose he himself must feel, and our pity is increased in proportion to the height from which he fell. On the contrary, we do not so strongly sympathize with one born in humbler circumstances, and encountering accidental distress: so that while we melt for Belisarius, we scarcely give halfpence to the beggar who accosts us in the street. The one has our pity, the other our contempt. Distress, therefore, is the proper object

of tragedy, since the great excite our pity by their fall; but not equally so of comedy, since the actors employed in it are originally so mean, that they sink but little by their fall.

Since the first origin of the stage, tragedy and comedy have run in distinct channels, and never till of late encroached upon the provinces of each other. Terence, who seems to have made the nearest approaches, always judiciously stops short before he comes to the downright pathetic; and yet he is even reproached by Cæsar for wanting the *vis comica*. All the other comic writers of antiquity aim only at rendering folly or vice ridiculous, but never exalt their characters into buskined pomp, or make what Voltaire humorously calls *a tradesman's tragedy*.

Yet notwithstanding this weight of authority, and the universal practice of former ages, a new species of dramatic composition has been introduced, under the name of *sentimental* comedy, in which the virtues of private life are exhibited, rather than the vices exposed; and the distresses rather than the faults of mankind make our interest in the piece. These comedies have had of late great success, perhaps from their novelty, and also from their flattering every man in his favorite foible. In these plays almost all the characters are good, and exceedingly generous; they are lavish enough of their *tin* money on the stage; and though they want humor, have abundance of sentiment and feeling. If they happen to have faults or foibles, the spectator is taught, not only to pardon, but to applaud them, in consideration of the goodness of their hearts; so that folly, instead of being ridiculed, is commended, and the comedy aims at touching our passions without the power of being truly pathetic. In this manner we are likely to lose one great source of entertainment on the stage; for while the comic poet is invading the province of the tragic muse, he leaves her lovely sister quite neglected. Of this, however, he is no way solicitous, as he measures his fame by his profits.

But it will be said, that the theater is formed to amuse mankind, and that it matters little, if this end be answered, by what means it is obtained. If mankind find delight in weeping at comedy, it would be cruel to abridge them in that or any other innocent pleasure. If those pieces are denied the name of comedies, yet call them by any other name and, if they are delightful, they are good. Their success, it will be said, is a mark of their merit, and it is only abridging our happiness to deny us an inlet to amusement.

These objections, however, are rather specious than solid. It is true that amusement is a great object of the theater, and it will be allowed that these sentimental pieces do often amuse us; but the question is, whether the true comedy would not amuse us more? The question is, whether a character supported throughout a piece, with its ridicule still attending, would not give us more delight than this species of bastard tragedy, which only is applauded because it is new?

A friend of mine, who was sitting unmoved at one of these sentimental pieces, was asked how he could be so indifferent? "Why, truly," says he, "as the hero is but a tradesman, it is indifferent to me whether he be turned out of his counting-house on Fish Street Hill, since he will still have enough left to open shop in St. Giles's."

The other objection is as ill-grounded; for though we should give these pieces another name, it will not mend their efficacy. It will continue a kind of *mulish* production, with all the defects of its opposite parents, and marked with sterility. If we are permitted to make comedy weep, we have an equal right to make tragedy laugh, and to set down in blank verse the jests and repartees of all the attendants in a funeral procession.

But there is one argument in favor of sentimental comedy, which will keep it on the stage, in spite of all that can be said against it. It is, of all others, the most easily written. Those abilities that can hammer out a novel are fully sufficient for the production of a sentimental comedy. It is only sufficient to raise the characters a little; to deck out the hero with a riband, or give the heroine a title; then to put an insipid dialogue, without character or humor, into their mouths, give them mighty good hearts, very fine clothes, furnish a new set of scenes, make a pathetic scene or two, with a sprinkling of tender melancholy conversation through the whole, and there is no doubt but all the ladies will cry and all the gentlemen applaud.

Humor at present seems to be departing from the stage, and it will soon happen that our comic players will have nothing left for it but a fine coat and a song. It depends upon the audience whether they will actually drive those poor merry creatures from the stage, or sit at a play as gloomy as at the Tabernacle. It is not easy to recover an art when once lost; and it will be but a just punishment, that when, by our being too fastidious, we have banished humor from the stage, we should ourselves be deprived of the art of laughing.

DAVID HUME

David Hume was born in Edinburgh in 1711. After training by Jesuits, he began to write his philosophical treatises, thus establishing himself as a philosopher with whom the modern world still reckons. His *Treatise of Human Nature* (1739–40) laid the groundwork of his extreme skepticism with regard to human knowledge. This doctrine is expanded in his *Enquiry Concerning Human Understanding* (1748), which, in the essay "Of Miracles," records his skepticism concerning supernatural events. In the present essay (1757), he applies his usual empirical method to tragedy, going without prejudice or preconception into the problem of human response to the representation of disaster. Modifying the sense of his extended quotation from Fontenelle, he advances artistry as the key to the warm response that tragedy evokes. This essay illustrates both Hume's empirical approach and the growing contemporary interest in the study that we now call psychology. Died 1776.

OF TRAGEDY [1]

(1757)

It seems an unaccountable pleasure, which the spectators of a well-written tragedy receive from sorrow, terror, anxiety, and other passions that are in themselves disagreeable and uneasy. The more they are touched and affected, the more are they delighted with the spectacle; and as soon as the uneasy passions cease to operate, the piece is at an end. One scene of full joy and contentment and security is the utmost that any composition of this kind can bear; and it is sure always to be the concluding one. If in the texture of the piece there be interwoven any scenes of satisfaction, they afford only faint gleams of pleasure, which are thrown in by way of variety, and in order to plunge the actors into deeper distress by means of that contrast and disappointment. The whole art of the poet is employed in rousing and supporting the compassion and indignation, the anxiety and resentment, of his audience. They are pleased in proportion as they are afflicted, and never are so happy as when they employ tears, sobs, and cries, to give vent to their sorrow, and relieve their heart, swollen with the tenderest sympathy and compassion.

The few critics who have had some tincture of philosophy have remarked this singular phenomenon, and have endeavored to account for it.

L'Abbé Dubos, in his reflections on poetry and painting, asserts that nothing is in general so disagreeable to the mind as the languid, listless state of indolence into which it falls upon the removal of all passion and occupation. To get rid of this painful situation, it seeks every amusement and pursuit: business, gaming, shows, executions; whatever will rouse the passions and take its attention from itself. No matter what the passion is: let it be disagreeable, afflicting, melancholy, disordered; it is still better than that insipid languor, which arises from perfect tranquillity and repose.

It is impossible not to admit this account as being, at least in part, satisfactory. You may observe, when there are

several tables of gaming, that all the company run to those where the deepest play is, even though they find not there the best players. The view, or, at least, imagination of high passions, arising from great loss or gain, affects the spectator by sympathy, gives him some touches of the same passions, and serves him for a momentary entertainment. It makes the time pass the easier with him, and is some relief to that oppression under which men commonly labor when left entirely to their own thoughts and meditations.

We find that common liars always magnify, in their narrations, all kinds of danger, pain, distress, sickness, deaths, murders, and cruelties, as well as joy, beauty, mirth, and magnificence. It is an absurd secret which they have for pleasing their company, fixing their attention, and attaching them to such marvelous relations by the passions and emotions which they excite.

There is, however, a difficulty in applying to the present subject, in its full extent, this solution, however ingenious and satisfactory it may appear. It is certain that the same object of distress which pleases in a tragedy, were it really set before us, would give the most unfeigned uneasiness; though it be then the most effectual cure to languor and indolence. Monsieur Fontenelle seems to have been sensible of this difficulty, and accordingly attempts another solution of the phenomenon; at least makes some addition to the theory above mentioned.

"Pleasure and pain," says he, "which are two sentiments so different in themselves, differ not so much in their cause. From the instance of tickling, it appears, that the movement of pleasure, pushed a little too far, becomes pain; and that the movement of pain, a little moderate, becomes pleasure. Hence it proceeds that there is such a thing as a sorrow, soft and agreeable; it is a pain weakened and diminished. The heart likes naturally to be moved and affected. Melancholy objects suit it, and even disastrous and sorrowful, provided they are softened by some circumstance. It is

---

1 From *Essays and Treatises on Several Subjects* (Edinburgh, 1809).—Ed.

certain that, on the theatre, the representation has almost the effect of reality; yet it has not altogether that effect. However we may be hurried away by the spectacle, whatever dominion the senses and imagination may usurp over the reason, there still lurks at the bottom a certain idea of falsehood in the whole of what we see. This idea, though weak and disguised, suffices to diminish the pain which we suffer from the misfortunes of those whom we love, and to reduce that affliction to such a pitch as converts it into a pleasure. We weep for the misfortune of a hero to whom we are attached. In the same instant we comfort ourselves by reflecting that it is nothing but a fiction; and it is precisely that mixture of sentiments which composes an agreeable sorrow and tears that delight us. But as that affliction which is caused by exterior and sensible objects is stronger than the consolation which arises from an internal reflection, they are the effects and symptoms of sorrow that ought to predominate in the composition."

This solution seems just and convincing; but perhaps it wants still some new addition, in order to make it answer fully the phenomenon which we here examine. All the passions, excited by eloquence, are agreeable in the highest degree, as well as those which are moved by painting and the theatre. The epilogues of Cicero are, on this account chiefly, the delight of every reader of taste; and it is difficult to read some of them without the deepest sympathy and sorrow. His merit as an orator, no doubt, depends much on his success in this particular. When he had raised tears in his judges and all his audience, they were then the most highly delighted, and expressed the greatest satisfaction with the pleader. The pathetic description of the butchery made by Verres of the Sicilian captains is a masterpiece of this kind; but I believe none will affirm that the being present at a melancholy scene of that nature would afford any entertainment. Neither is the sorrow here softened by fiction, for the audience were convinced of the reality of every circumstance. What is it, then, which in this case raises a pleasure from the bosom of uneasiness, so to speak, and a pleasure which still retains all the features and outward

symptoms of distress and sorrow?

I answer: This extraordinary effect proceeds from that very eloquence with which the melancholy scene is represented. The genius required to paint objects in a lively manner, the art employed in collecting all the pathetic circumstances, the judgment displayed in disposing them—the exercise, I say, of these noble talents, together with the force of expression, and beauty of oratorial numbers, diffuse the highest satisfaction on the audience, and excite the most delightful movements. By this means, the uneasiness of the melancholy passions is not only overpowered and effaced by something stronger of an opposite kind; but the whole impulse of those passions is converted into pleasure and swells the delight which the eloquence raises in us. The same force of oratory, employed on an uninteresting subject, would not please half so much, or rather would appear altogether ridiculous; and the mind, being left in absolute calmness and indifference, would relish none of those beauties of imagination or expression, which, if joined to passion, give it such exquisite entertainment. The impulse or vehemence arising from sorrow, compassion, indignation, receives a new direction from the sentiments of beauty. The latter, being the predominant motion, seize the whole mind, and convert the former into themselves, at least tincture them so strongly as totally to alter their nature. And the soul, being at the same time roused by passion and charmed by eloquence, feels on the whole a strong movement which is altogether delightful.

The same principle takes place in tragedy, with this addition, that tragedy is an imitation, and imitation is always of itself agreeable. This circumstance serves still further to smooth the motions of passion, and convert the whole feeling into one uniform and strong enjoyment. Objects of the greatest terror and distress please in painting, and please more than the most beautiful objects that appear calm and indifferent. The affection, rousing the mind, excites a large stock of spirit and vehemence, which is all transformed into pleasure by the force of the prevailing movement. It is thus the fiction of tragedy softens the passion, by an infusion of a new feeling, not merely by weakening or diminishing the sorrow. You may by degrees weaken a real sorrow, till it totally disappears; yet in none of its gradations will it ever give pleasure, except, perhaps, by accident, to a man sunk under lethargic indolence, whom it rouses from that languid state.

To confirm this theory, it will be sufficient to produce other instances, where the subordinate movement is converted into the predominant, and gives force to it, though of a different, and even sometimes though of a contrary nature.

Novelty naturally rouses the mind, and attracts our attention; and the movements which it causes are always converted into any passion belonging to the object, and join their force to it. Whether an event excite joy or sorrow, pride or shame, anger or good will, it is sure to produce a stronger affection, when new or unusual. And though novelty of itself be agreeable, it fortifies the painful, as well as agreeable, passions.

Had you any intention to move a person extremely by the narration of any event, the best method of increasing its effect would be artfully to delay informing him of it, and first to excite his curiosity and impatience before you let him into the secret. This is the artifice practiced by Iago in the famous scene of Shakespeare; and every spectator is sensible that Othello's jealousy acquires additional force from his preceding impatience, and that the subordinate passion is here readily transformed into the predominant one.

Difficulties increase passions of every kind; and by rousing our attention, and exciting our active powers, they produce an emotion which nourishes the prevailing affection.

Parents commonly love that child most whose sickly infirm frame of body has occasioned them the greatest pains, trouble, and anxiety, in rearing him. The agreeable sentiment of affection here acquires force from sentiments of uneasiness.

Nothing endears so much a friend as sorrow for his death. The pleasure of his company has not so powerful an influence.

Jealousy is a painful passion; yet without some share of it, the agreeable affection of love has difficulty to subsist in its full force and violence. Absence is also a great source of complaint among lovers, and gives them the greatest uneasiness; yet nothing is more favorable to their mutual passion than short intervals of that kind. And if long intervals often prove fatal, it is only because, through time, men are accustomed to them, and they cease to give uneasiness. Jealousy and absence in love compose the *dolce piccante* of the Italians, which they suppose so essential to all pleasure.

There is a fine observation of the elder Pliny, which illustrates the principle here insisted on. "It is very remarkable," says he, "that the last works of celebrated artists, which they left imperfect, are always the most prized, such as the *Iris* of Aristides, the *Tyndarides* of Nicomachus, the *Medea* of Timomachus, and the *Venus* of Apelles. These are valued even above their finished productions. The broken lineaments of the piece, and the half-formed idea of the painter, are carefully studied; and our very grief for that curious hand, which had been stopped by death, is an additional increase to our pleasure."

These instances (and many more might be collected) are sufficient to afford us some insight into the analogy of nature, and to show us that the pleasure which poets, orators, and musicians give us, by exciting grief, sorrow, indignation, compassion, is not so extraordinary or paradoxical as it may at first sight appear. The force of imagination, the energy of expression, the power of numbers, the charms of imitation—all these are naturally, of themselves, delightful to the mind. And when the object presented lays hold also of some affection, the pleasure still rises upon us, by the conversion of this subordinate movement into that which is predominant. The passion, though perhaps naturally and when excited by the simple appearance of a real object it may be painful, yet is so smoothed, and softened, and mollified, when raised by the finer arts, that it affords the highest entertainment.

To confirm this reasoning, we may observe that if the movements of the imagination be not predominant above those of the passion, a contrary effect follows; and the former, being now subordinate, is converted into the latter, and still further increases the pain and affliction of the sufferer.

Who could ever think of it as a good expedient for comforting an afflicted parent, to exaggerate, with all the force of elocution, the irreparable loss which he has met with by the death of a favorite child? The more power of imagination and expression you here employ, the more you increase his despair and affliction.

The shame, confusion, and terror of Verres, no doubt, rose in proportion to the noble eloquence and vehemence of Cicero; so also did his pain and uneasiness. These former passions were too strong for the pleasure arising from the beauties of elocution, and operated, though from the same principle, yet in a contrary manner, to the sympathy, compassion, and indignation of the audience.

Lord Clarendon, when he approaches towards the catastrophe of the royal party, supposes that his narration must then become infinitely disagreeable; and he hurries over the king's death without giving us one circumstance of it.2 He considers it as too horrid a scene to be contemplated with any satisfaction, or even without the utmost pain and aversion. He himself, as well as the readers of that age, were too deeply concerned in the events, and felt a pain from subjects which an historian and a reader of another age would regard as the most pathetic and most interesting, and, by consequence, the most agreeable.

An action represented in tragedy may be too bloody and atrocious. It may excite such movements of horror as will not soften into pleasure; and the greatest energy of expression, bestowed on descriptions of that nature, serves only to augment our uneasiness. Such is that action represented in the *Ambitious Stepmother*,3 where a venerable old man,

2 The execution of Charles I.—Ed.
3 Nicholas Rowe's first tragedy (1700). —Ed.

raised to the height of fury and despair, rushes against a pillar and, striking his head upon it, besmears it all over with mingled brains and gore. The English theatre abounds too much with such shocking images.

Even the common sentiments of compassion require to be softened by some agreeable affection, in order to give a thorough satisfaction to the audience. The mere suffering of plaintive virtue, under the triumphant tyranny and oppression of vice, forms a disagreeable spectacle, and is carefully avoided by all masters of the drama. In order to dismiss the audience with entire satisfaction and contentment, the virtue must either convert itself into a noble courageous despair, or the vice receive its proper punishment.

Most painters appear in this light to have been very unhappy in their subjects. As they wrought much for churches and convents, they have chiefly represented such horrible subjects as crucifixions and martyrdoms, where nothing appears but tortures, wounds, executions, and passive suffering, without any action or affection. When they turned their pencil from this ghastly mythology, they had commonly recourse to Ovid, whose fictions, though passionate and agreeable, are scarcely natural or probable enough for painting.

The same inversion of that principle, which is here insisted on, displays itself in common life, as in the effects of oratory and poetry. Raise so the subordinate passion that it becomes the predominant, it swallows up that affection which it before nourished and increased. Too much jealousy extinguishes love; too much difficulty renders us indifferent; too much sickness and infirmity disgusts a selfish and unkind parent.

What so disagreeable as the dismal, gloomy, disastrous stories, with which melancholy people entertain their companions. The uneasy passion being there raised alone, unaccompanied with any spirit, genius, or eloquence, conveys a pure uneasiness, and is attended with nothing that can soften it into pleasure or satisfaction.

ITALIAN DRAMATIC CRITICISM OF THE SEVENTEENTH CENTURY

For at least a century the great Renaissance critics overshadowed their successors in Italy, and the record of seventeenth century criticism is largely one of more or less pedantic compilation, classification, and repetition. The lack of a new interest in antiquity, such as served Daniello, Trissino, Scaliger and Castelvetro, and the scanty offerings of native dramatic products, are sufficient to account for the lack of outstanding contributions to dramatic theory. Beni's *Disputatio* (1600) was among the last works mentioned under Italian Renaissance Criticism. Close upon it, in 1601, came Giovanni Bernardo Brandi's *Trattato dell' Arte Poetica*. In 1613 appeared Chiodino da Monte Melone's rhetorical treatise, and in 1618 Pellegrino's *Discorso della Poetica*, and soon after, the similar works of Udeno Nisieli and Giovanni Colle Bellunese. A curious work of the time is P. M. Cecchini's *Frutti delle moderne commedie etavisi a chi le recita* (1628). An ambitious effort was Celso Zani's *Poetica ecclesiastica e civile . . . nella quale si pone in chiaro la Diffinizione della Poesia commune alla Trajedia e all' Epopeja* (1643). The list is practically complete with the minor works on poetics by Flavio Querengo and Benedetto Menzini. In 1699 A. Perrucci published his *Dell' arte rappresentativa premeditata e all' improvviso*.

ITALIAN DRAMATIC CRITICISM OF THE EIGHTEENTH CENTURY

Four critics of varying importance opened the new century with works which exerted considerable influence: Crescimbeni, Gravina, Muratori, and Quadrio, contributed historical and critical works many of which were effective in restoring Italy to a position of honor in the critical world. Giovanni Maria Crescimbeni published *La Bellezza della volgar Poesia* in 1700, but enlarged it for the edition of 1730. For the most part his work was one of compilation. Another work, a sort of historical survey, was Gianvincenzo Gravina's *Della Ragion poetica* (1704), though of course his *Della Tragedia* is of greater interest and importance as a dramatic tract. A man of greater insight and learning was Ludovico Antonio Muratori, whose *Della perfetta Poesia italiana* (1706) exerted greater influence than the works of any of his group. Scipione Maffei and F. Palesi wrote minor works on literature and the drama, while Luigi Riccoboni wrote his treatises on the theaters in Italy and elsewhere in Europe, besides a theoretical work, *Dell' arte rappresentativa* (1725). Francesco Xavier Quadrio opened the way for the comparative study and criticism of literature, and his *Della Storia della Ragione d'ogni Poesia* (1739–52) is an ambitious attempt to cover the entire field of poetry. Francesco Maria Zanotti wrote a *Poetica* in 1768, and Girolamo Tiraboschi continued, though with greater knowledge and insight, the work of Crescimbeni, in his *Storia della Letteratura italiana* (1772–82). Meantime the dramatists themselves began to explain their theories. The eighteenth century marks the dawn of a truly national Italian drama. Scipione Maffei's *Merope* was produced in 1714, and not long after Apostolo Zeno, considered the father of modern opera, came into prominence.

With the advent of Carlo Goldoni, an innovator of the greatest importance, the *Commedia dell' Arte* (*Comedy of Masks, or Improvised Comedy*), was attacked. The *Commedia dell' Arte,* in which a scenario served as the basis of a series of improvised dialogues by a number of well-recognized type characters, had been the most practiced of Italian dramatic products. Goldoni, whose aim it was to imitate Molière and introduce a sort of realistic comedy into Italy, felt it necessary to do away with the *Commedia dell' Arte,* and in his numerous prefaces, and particularly in his *Mémoires* (1787) he argued against the old form. His principal antagonist was the dramatist Carlo Gozzi, whose *fiabi,* or dramatized fairy tales, were an attempt to resuscitate the art of the old *Commedia dell' Arte.* In his *Prefaces,* or *Ragionamenti* and in his *Memorie* (1797) he maintains his theories against Goldoni's. Meanwhile Zeno's successor, Pietro Metas-tasio, carried on his work, and his operas were popular throughout the world until the nineteenth century. His chief critical contribution to the theory of the drama was a commentary on Aristotle, *Estratto dell' Arte Poetica d'Aristotile* (1782). Vittorio Alfieri, one of the greatest dramatists of Italy, touched upon dramatic matters in his autobiography (*Vita di Vittorio Alfieri scritta da esso,* 1804), and in his various *Lettere* and essays on tragedy, but his revolutionary spirit was manifest rather in his plays than in his references to the theory behind them.

Almost contemporary with Alfieri were the three great Revolutionary poets and dramatists: Manzoni, Foscolo, and Monti, each of whom contributed to the Romantic triumph in Italy. Manzoni, in particular, was an important figure; his *Preface* to the play *Carmagnola* (1820) and his *Letter on the Unities* (1823), are landmarks of dramatic theory.

ITALIAN DRAMATIC CRITICISM OF THE NINETEENTH AND TWENTIETH CENTURIES

The Italian drama of the nineteenth century — or all but the closing years — was based upon the traditions of the past. There is very little of note in the field of dramatic criticism proper, though at least two great literary critics and estheticians ought to be named: Francesco de Sanctis and Benedetto Croce. Each of these writers has contributed valuable material to esthetics and criticism, but comparatively little to dramatic theory.

The modern dramatists have likewise had little to say, though Giuseppe Giacosa has lectured widely on the subject of his own art.

Among twentieth-century Italian dramatists, the romantic Gabriele d'Annunzio and the versatile Luigi Chiarelli are important figures, but Luigi Pirandello is the one authentic giant. In very recent years, the drama critic Nicola Chiaramonte has gained a reputation in the English-speaking world.

CARLO GOLDONI

Carlo Goldoni was born at Venice in 1707. From his earliest years he appears to have been interested in the theater: his toys were puppets and his books, plays. It is said that at the age of eight he attempted to write a play. The boy's father placed him under the care of the philosopher Caldini at Ri-mini but the youth soon ran away with a company of strolling players and came to Venice. There he began to study law; he continued his studies at Pavia, though he relates in his *Memoirs* that a considerable part of his time was spent in reading Greek and Latin comedies. He had already begun writing at this time, and, as the result of a libel in which he ridiculed certain families of Pavia, he was forced to leave the city. He continued his law studies at Udine, and eventually took his degree at Modena. He was employed as law clerk at Chioggia and Feltre, after which he returned to his native city and began practicing. But his true vocation was the theater, and he made his bow with a tragedy, *Amalasunta*, produced at Milan, but this was a failure. His next play, *Belisario*, written in 1734, succeeded. He wrote other tragedies for a time, but he was not long in discovering that his bent was for comedy. He had come to realize that the Italian stage needed reforming, and adopting Molière as his model, he went to work in earnest, and in 1738 produced his first real comedy, *L'Uomo di mondo*. During his many wanderings and adventures in Italy, he was constantly at work, and when, at Leghorn, he became acquainted with the manager Medebac, he determined to pursue the profession of playwriting in order to make a living. He was employed by Medebac to write plays for his theater in Venice. He worked for other managers, and produced during his stay in that city some of his most characteristic works. In 1761 he went to Paris, where he continued to write. Among the plays which he wrote in French, the most successful was *Le Bourru bienfaisant*, produced on the occasion of the marriage of Louis XVI and Marie Antoinette in 1771. He enjoyed considerable popularity in France, and when he retired to Versailles the King gave him a pension. But when the Revolution broke out, he was deprived of it. The day after his death, however, the Convention voted to restore the pension. He died in 1793.

Goldoni was the great reformer of Italian comedy. His importance, which consisted rather in giving good examples than precepts, lay in his having regularized the drama of his country, and freed it from the conventionality of the *Commedia dell' Arte*, or improvised comedy. He rightly maintained that Italian life and manners were susceptible of artistic treatment such as had not before been given them. Although Goldoni admired Molière and often tried to emulate if not imitate him, his plays are gentler and more optimistic in tone. He relates at considerable length in his *Memoirs* the state of Italian comedy when he began writing, and his works are a lasting monument to the changes which he brought about. Goldoni's plays are themselves the justification of his theory, and need no explanation, but his theories are interesting and valuable. These he set forth in his *Memoirs*, his prefaces, and in many places throughout the play *Il Teatro comico*.

THE COMIC THEATER [1]

[*Il Teatro Comico*]

(1751)

Comedy was invented to correct foibles and ridicule disagreeable habits; when the comedy of the ancients was written in this wise, the whole world liked it, for on seeing a fac-simile of a character upon the boards, everybody saw the original either in himself or in some one else. When comedy became merely ridiculous, nobody paid further attention to it, since under the pretext of causing laughter, the most high-sounding absurdities were permitted. Now that we are again fishing comedies out of the *Mare magnum* of nature, men find themselves again searching their hearts and identifying themselves with the passion or the character which is being represented, for they know how to discern whether a passion is well depicted, whether a character is well sustained: in short, they observe. . . .

The French have triumphed in the art of comedy during a whole century; it is now time for Italy to proclaim that in her the seed of good authorship is not dried up, Italian authors having been, after the Greeks and the Romans, the

1 Re-printed from the translated passages by the author in H. C. Chatfield-Taylor's *Goldoni, A Biography* (New York, 1913).— Ed.

first to enrich and adorn the stage. The French in their comedies, it must be admitted, present fine and well-sustained characters; moreover, they delineate passions well, and their conceptions are acute, witty, and brilliant, but the public of that country is satisfied with a little. One single character is sufficient to maintain a French comedy. Around a single passion well conceived and drawn, a great number of speeches vibrate which by dint of elocution present the air of novelty. We Italians demand much more. We wish the principal character to be strong, original, and well recognized . . . that the plot shall be fertile in incidents and novelties. We demand morals mingled with quips and humor. We insist that the end be unexpected, but plainly derived from the trend of the action. We like to have an infinity of things too many to relate here, and it is only in the course of time that we can succeed in learning by practice and usage to know them and to obtain success with them.

. . . . . .

Aristotle began to write concerning comedy, but he did not finish, and we have from him but a few imperfect fragments regarding it. In his *Poetics* he prescribed the unity of place for tragedy; yet he did not mention comedy then. There are those who maintain that his statements about tragedy must be interpreted as referring to comedy also, and that if he had finished his treatise on comedy, he would have prescribed the unity of place. But my answer is, that if Aristotle were now alive, he would cancel this obnoxious precept, because a thousand absurdities, a thousand blunders and improprieties are caused by it. I distinguish two kinds of comedy: pure comedy and comedies of intrigue. Pure comedy can be written with the unity of place. Comedy of intrigue cannot be thus written without crudity and incongruity. The ancients had not, like ourselves, a way to shift scenery, and for that reason they observed the unities. We have always observed the unity of place when the action occurs in the same city, and all the more when it remains in the same house. . . . Therefore, I conclude that if comedy with the unity of places can be written without hair-splitting or unseemliness, it should be done; but if on account of the unity of place absurdities have to be introduced, it is better to change the scenes and observe the rules of probability.

MEMOIRS [2]
[*Mémoires de M. Goldoni,* etc.]
(1787)

. . . . . .

I wish that the Italian authors had continued after the appearance of this comedy [Machiavelli's *Mandragora*] to write decent and honorable comedies, and that characters taken from nature had been substituted for fantastic intrigues.

But it was left to Molière to ennoble and render useful the comic stage, in exposing the vices and the laughable side of man to ridicule, for the purpose of correction.

I was not yet acquainted with the works of that great man, for I did not understand French; but I made up my mind to learn it, and meantime I ac-

quired the habit of observing men carefully, and never lost sight of an original character. . . . (First Part, Ch. X.)

. . . "I am now," said I to myself, "perfectly at my ease, and I can give free rein to my imagination. Hitherto I have labored on old subjects, but now I must create and invent for myself. I have the advantage of very promising actors; but in order to employ them usefully I must begin with studying them. Every person has his peculiar character from nature; if the author gives him a part to represent in unison with his own, he may lay his account with success. Well, then," continued I, "this is perhaps the happy moment to set on foot the reform which I have so long meditated. Yes, I must treat subjects of character:

2 Translation by the Editor, based in part upon the John Black translation (1814) of the *Memoirs.* Selections.— Ed.

this is the source of good comedy; with this the great Molière began his career, and he carried it to a degree of perfection which the ancients merely indicated to us, and which the moderns have never seen equalled."

Was I wrong to encourage myself in this way? No, for comedy was my forte, and good comedy was my ambition. I should have been in the wrong had I been so ambitious as to set myself alongside the masters of the art, but my sole desire was to reform and correct the abuses of the stage of my country; no great scholarship was necessary to accomplish that. . . .

That any character may be productive of effect on the stage, it has always appeared to me necessary to contrast it with characters of an opposite description. . . .

This play [*Momolo Cortesan*] was eminently successful, and I was happy. I saw my compatriots turn from their old love of farce: the reformation was at hand. But I could not yet flatter myself that it was an accomplished fact, for the dialogue of the play is not written down. . . . That consistent style which is the mark of true authors, was not to be observed: I could not reform everything at once without shocking the lovers of the old style of national comedy. I then awaited a favorable moment to attack them directly with more vigor and added sureness of touch.

(First Part, Ch. XL.)

.   .   .   .   .   .

. . . And, acting upon the maxim of comedy, *ridendo castigat mores,* I imagined that the theater might be converted into a school for the prevention of abuse and the consequences resulting from it.

(First Part, Ch. XLII.)

.   .   .   .   .

The unities requisite for the perfection of theatrical works have in all times been the subject of discussion among authors and amateurs.

The censors of my plays of character had nothing to reproach me with in respect to the unity of action and of time, but they maintained that in the unity of place I had been deficient.

The action of my comedies was always confined to the same town, and the characters never departed from it. It is true that they went from one place to another; but all these places were within the same walls; and I was then and am still of the opinion that in this manner the unity of place was sufficiently observed.

In every art and every discovery, experience has always preceded precepts. In the course of time, a method had been assigned by writers to the practice of the invention, but modern authors have always possessed the right of putting an interpretation on the ancients.

For my part, not finding either in the Poetics of Aristotle or Horace a clear and absolute precept founded on reason for the rigorous unity of place, I have always adhered to it when my subject seemed susceptible of it; but I could never induce myself to sacrifice a good comedy for the sake of a prejudice which might have spoiled it. . . .

In speaking of virtue, I do not mean an heroical virtue, affecting from its distresses, and pathetic from its diction. Those works which in France are called *drames,* have certainly their merit; they are a species of theatrical representation between tragedy and comedy, and an additional subject of entertainment for feeling hearts. The misfortunes of the heroes of tragedy interest us at a distance, but those of our equals are calculated to affect us more closely.

Comedy, which is an imitation of nature, ought not to reject virtuous and pathetic sentiments, if the essential object be observed of enlivening it with those comic and prominent traits which are the very foundations of its existence.

Far be it from me to indulge the foolish presumption of setting up for a preceptor. I merely wish to impart to my readers the little I have learned, and have myself done; for in the most contemptible books we always find something deserving of attention.

(Second Part, Ch. III.)

.   .   .   .   .   .

In this city [Bologna], the mother of wisdom and the Athens of Italy, complaints had been made some years before, of my reformation, as having a tendency to suppress the Four Masks of Italian comedy.

This sort of comedy was in greater estimation at Bologna than elsewhere. There were several persons of merit in that place who took delight in composing outlines of pieces, which were very well represented there by citizens of great ability, and were the delight of their country.

The lovers of the old comedy, on seeing the rapid progress of the new, declared everywhere that it was unworthy of an Italian to give a blow to a species of comedy in which Italy had attained great distinction, and which no other nation had ever been able to imitate.

But what made the greatest impression on the discontented, was the suppression of masks, which my system seemed to threaten. It was said that these personages had been for two centuries the amusement of Italy, and that it ought not to be deprived of a species of comic diversion which it had created and so well supported.

Before venturing to give my opinion of this subject I imagine the reader will have no objection to listen for a few moments to a short account of the origin, employments, and effects, of these four masks.

Comedy, which in all ages has been the favorite entertainment of civilized nations, shared the fate of the arts and sciences, and was buried under the ruins of the empire during the decay of letters.

The germ of comedy, however, was never altogether extinguished in the fertile bosom of Italy. Those who first endeavored to bring about its revival not finding, in an ignorant age, writers of sufficient skill, had the boldness to draw out plans, to distribute them into acts and scenes and to utter extempore, the subjects, thoughts, and witticisms which they had concerted among themselves.

Those who could read (and neither the great nor the rich were of the number), finding that in the comedies of Plautus and Terence there were always duped fathers, debauched sons, enamored girls, knavish servants, and mercenary maids; and running over the different districts of Italy, they took the fathers from Venice and Bologna, the servants from Bergamo, and the lovers and waiting-maids from the dominions of Rome and Tuscany.

Written proofs are not to be expected of what took place in a time when writing was not in use: but I prove my assertion in this way: Pantaloon has always

been a Venetian, the Doctor a Bolognese, and Brighella and Harlequin, Bergamasks; and from these places, therefore, the comic personages called the Four Masks of the Italian comedy, were taken by the players.

What I say on this subject is not altogether the product of my imagination: I possess a manuscript of the Fifteenth century, in very good preservation, and bound in parchment, containing one hundred and twenty subjects, or sketches, of Italian pieces, called *commedie dell' arte*, and of which the basis of the comic humor are always Pantaloon, a Venetian merchant; the Doctor, a Bolognese lawyer; and Brighella and Harlequin, Bergamask valets, the first clever and sprightly, and the other a mere dolt. Their antiquity and their long existence indicate their origin.

With respect to their employment, Pantaloon and the Doctor, called by the Italians the two old men, represent the part of fathers, and the other parts where cloaks are worn.

The first is a merchant, because Venice in ancient times was the richest and most extensively commercial country in Italy. He has always preserved the ancient Venetian costume; the black dress and woolen bonnet are still worn in Venice; and the red under-waistcoat and breeches, cut out like drawers with red stockings and slippers, are a most exact representation of the equipment of the first inhabitants of the Adriatic marshes. The beard, which was considered an ornament in those remote ages, has been caricatured and rendered ridiculous in subsequent periods.

The second old man, called the Doctor, was taken from among the lawyers, for the sake of opposing a learned man to a merchant; and Bologna was selected, because in that city there existed a university, which, notwithstanding the ignorance of the times, still preserved the offices and emoluments of professors.

In the dress of the Doctor we observe the ancient costume of the university and bar of Bologna, which is nearly the same at this day; and the idea of the singular mask which covers his face and nose was taken from a wine stain which disfigured the countenance of a lawyer of those times. This is a tradition still existing among the lovers of the *commedia dell' arte.*

Brighella and Harlequin, called in Italy the two Zani, were taken from Bergamo; because, the former being a very sharp fellow and the other a stupid clown, these two extremes are only to be found among the lower orders of that part of the country.

Brighella represents an intriguing, deceitful and knavish valet. His dress is a species of livery: his swarthy mask is a caricature of the color of the inhabitants of those high mountains, tanned by the heat of the sun.

Some comedians in this character have taken the name of Fenocchio, Fiqueto, and Scapin; but they have always represented the same valet and the same Bergamask.

The harlequins have also assumed other names; they have been sometimes Tracagnins, Truffaldins, Gradelins, and Mezetins; but they have always been stupid Bergamasks. Their dress is an exact reproduction of that of a poor devil who has picked up pieces of stuffs of different colors to patch his dress; but his hat corresponds with his mendicity, and the hare's tail with which it is adorned is still a common article of dress of the peasantry of Bergamo.

I have thus, I trust, sufficiently demonstrated the origin and employment of the four masks of Italian comedy; it now remains for me to mention the effects resulting from them.

The mask must always be very prejudicial to the action of the performer either in joy or sorrow; whether he be in love, cross, or good-humored, the same features are always exhibited; and however he may gesticulate and vary the tone, he can never convey by the countenance, which is the interpreter of the heart, the different passions with which he is inwardly agitated.

The masks of the Greeks and Romans were a sort of speaking-trumpets, invented for the purpose of conveying the sound through the vast extent of their amphitheaters. Passion and sentiment were not, in those times, carried to the pitch of delicacy which is now necessary. The actor must, in our day, possess a soul; and the soul under a mask is like a fire under ashes.

These were the reasons which induced me to endeavor the reformation of the Italian theater, and to substitute comedies for farces.

(Second Part, Ch. XXIV.)

CARLO GOZZI

Count Carlo Gozzi was born to an impoverished family of the Venetian nobility in 1720. A dedicated literary controversialist, he began in 1757 to attack the popular writings of Carlo Goldoni and the Abbé Pietro Chiari. He charged Goldoni with vulgarity, immorality, and carelessness in his comedies. In response to a challenge from Goldoni, Gozzi himself began to write plays, beginning with *The Love of Three Oranges* (1761). His works were performed with considerable success by Sacchi's theatrical company, with which Gozzi became closely linked. He responded to Goldoni's challenge by combining plots based on traditional fairy tales with characters and comic "bits" from the *Commedia dell' Arte.* His vituperation and his success in the theater drove Goldoni from Venice, but Gozzi's plays have now come to be primarily regarded as bases for opera. *The Love for Three Oranges* was set to music by Prokofiev, *Turandot* (1762) by Puccini and Busoni, among others. He stopped writing for the stage when Sacchi left Venice in 1782; Gozzi died in 1806.

USELESS MEMOIRS [1]

[*Memorie inutili*]

(1797)

. . . To begin with Goldoni. I recognized in him an abundance of comic motives, truth, and naturalness. Yet I detected a poverty and meanness of intrigue; nature copied from the fact, not imitated; virtues and vices ill-adjusted, vice too frequently triumphant; plebian phrases of low double meaning, particularly in his Venetian plays; surcharged characters; scraps and tags of erudition, stolen Heaven knows where, and clumsily brought in to impose upon the crowd of ignoramuses. Finally, as a writer of Italian—except in the Venetian dialect, of which he showed himself a master—he seemed to me not unworthy to be placed among the dullest, basest, and least correct authors who have used our idiom.

In spite of all the praise showered upon Goldoni, paid for or gratis, by journalists, preface-writers, romancers, apologists, Voltaires, I do not think that, with the single exception of his *Beneficent Grumbler,* which he wrote at Paris, which suited the French theatre, but which had no success in its Italian translation here, he ever produced a perfect dramatic piece. At the same time I must add that he never produced one without some excellent comic trait. In my eyes he had always the appearance of a man who was born with the innate sense of how sterling comedies should be composed, but who, by defect of education, by want of discernment, by the necessity of satisfying the public and supplying new wares to the poor Italian comedians through whom he gained his livelihood, and by the hurry in which he produced so many pieces every year to keep himself afloat, was never able to fabricate a single play which does not swarm with faults.

In the course of our playful and airy polemics—polemics which had more the

1 Excerpts from *Memoirs* (1797), translated by J. A. Symonds (London, 1890).—Ed.

form of witty squibs than formal criticisms—polemics which we Granelleschi never deigned to aim directly, in due form of siege, against the outpoured torrents of Goldoni and Chiari, but which we meant to act as sinapisms on the minds of sluggish youths, besotted by that trash and froth of ignorance—I once defied the whole world to point out a single play of Goldoni's which could be styled perfect. I confined myself to one, because I did not care to be drowned in an ocean; and I felt confident that I could fulfil my part of the challenge by making even boys and children see how the public had been taken in. No one stooped to take my glove up, and to name the perfect comedy. The goad and lash of pleasantry, with which I exposed Goldoni's stupidities, only elicited the following two verses, which he wrote and printed, and which exactly illustrate the stupidity I accused him of:

Pur troppo so che buon scrittor non sono,
E che a' fonti miglior non ho bevuto.

Too well I know that I am no good writer,
And that I have not drunk at the best fountains.

. . . You cannot fabricate a drama worthy to impress the public mind for any length of time by heaping up absurdities, marvels, scurrilities, prolixities, puerilities, insipidities, and nonsense. The neglect into which the imitations of my manner speedily fell proves this. Much the same may be said about those other species—romantic or domestic, intended to move tears or laughter—those cultured and realistic kinds of drama, as people called them, though they were generally devoid of culture and of realism, and were invariably as like each other as two peas, which occupied our stage for thirty years at least. All the good and bad that has been written and printed about my fables; the fact that they still hold the stage in Italy and other countries where they are translated in spite of their comparative antiquity; the stupid criticisms which are still being vented against them by starving journalists and envious bores, who join the cry and follow these blind leaders of the blind—criticisms only based

upon the titles and arguments I chose to draw from old wives' tales and stories of the nursery—all this proves that there is real stuff in the fabulous, poetical, allegorical genre which I created. I say this without any presumptuous partiality for the children of my fancy; nor do I resent the attacks which have been made upon them, for I am humane enough to pity the hungry and the passion-blinded.

LUIGI PIRANDELLO

Pirandello was born in 1867 in the ancient town of Agrigento, Sicily. He studied in Rome and later at the University of Bonn, where he earned his doctorate in philosophy. In 1894, he agreed to a marriage arranged by his family to a girl he had not known before. They settled in Rome, where she bore him three children and where he began in 1899 to teach Italian literature at a local teachers college for women; he continued to teach here till 1923. The loss of his father's fortune brought financial worries, and his wife's physical weakness following the birth of their third child in 1899 contributed to her growing mental derangement, which made a hell of the dramatist's life till her death in 1918.

A poet in youth and later a successful novelist with such works as *The Late Mattia Pascal* in 1904, Pirandello began as a dramatist by turning some of his short stories into one-act plays. He undertook drama more seriously during World War I and in the years following. He won his lasting fame with such plays as *Right You Are! (If You Think So)*

(1916), which establishes the difficulty of knowing the truth and the need for kindness in human relations; *Six Characters in Search of an Author* (1921), a fantasy which comments on the limits of the conventional stage and the mystery of the human personality; *Henry IV* (1922), in which a seeming madman is encouraged to believe that he is a Holy Roman Emperor; *Each in His Own Way* (1924); *As You Desire Me* (1930), concerning a lady whose identity is in doubt; and *Tonight We Improvise* (1930). Pirandello received the Nobel Prize for Literature in 1934. He died in 1936.

Over and over, he investigated questions of reality, identity, intention, and sanity. He seemed to be saying, in many different ways, that a human personality cannot and must not be violated, that its true nature cannot really be known. His best-known play, *Six Characters,* turns upon the ineffective efforts of actors to interpret a difficult family tragedy. He found both comic and tragic qualities in such problems.

PREFACE TO SIX CHARACTERS IN SEARCH OF AN AUTHOR [1]

[*Sei Personaggi in cerca d'autore*]

(1925)

It seems like yesterday but is actually

1 Translated by Eric Bentley. From *Naked Masks: Five Plays* by Luigi Pirandello. Copyright, 1922, 1952, by E. P. Dutton & Co., Inc. Renewal © 1950 by Stefano, Fausto, and Lietta Pirandello. Dutton Paperback Series. Reprinted by permission of the publisher.—Ed.

many years ago that a nimble little maidservant entered the service of my art. However, she always comes fresh to the job.

She is called Fantasy.

A little puckish and malicious, if she

likes to dress in black no one will wish to deny that she is often positively bizarre and no one will wish to believe that she always does everything in the same way and in earnest. She sticks her hand in her pocket, pulls out a cap and bells, sets it on her head, red as a cock's comb, and dashes away. Here today, there tomorrow. And she amuses herself by bringing to my house—since I derive stories and novels and plays from them—the most disgruntled tribe in the world, men, women, children, involved in strange adventures which they can find no way out of; thwarted in their plans; cheated in their hopes; with whom, in short, it is often torture to deal.

Well, this little maidservant of mine, Fantasy, several years ago, had the bad inspiration or ill-omened caprice to bring a family into my house. I wouldn't know where she fished them up or how, but, according to her, I could find in them the subject for a magnificent novel.

I found before me a man about fifty years old, in a dark jacket and light trousers, with a frowning air and ill-natured, mortified eyes; a poor woman in widow's weeds leading by one hand a little girl of four and by the other a boy of rather more than ten; a cheeky and "sexy" girl, also clad in black but with an equivocal and brazen pomp, all atremble with a lively, biting contempt for the mortified old man and for a young fellow of twenty who stood on one side closed in on himself as if he despised them all. In short, the six characters who are seen coming on stage at the beginning of the play. Now one of them and now another —often beating down one another— embarked on the sad story of their adventures, each shouting his own reasons, and projecting in my face his disordered passions, more or less as they do in the play to the unhappy Manager.

What author will be able to say how and why a character was born in his fantasy? The mystery of artistic creation is the same as that of birth. A woman who loves may desire to become a mother; but the desire by itself, however intense, cannot suffice. One fine day she will find herself a mother without having any precise intimation when it began. In the same way an artist imbibes very many germs of life and can never say how and why, at a certain moment, one of these vital germs inserts itself into his fantasy, there to become a living creature on a plane of life superior to the changeable existence of every day.

I can only say that, without having made any effort to seek them out, I found before me, alive—you could touch them and even hear them breathe—the six characters now seen on the stage. And they stayed there in my presence, each with his secret torment and all bound together by the one common origin and mutual entanglement of their affairs, while I had them enter the world of art, constructing from their persons, their passions, and their adventures a novel, a drama, or at least a story.

Born alive, they wished to live.

To me it was never enough to present a man or a woman and what is special and characteristic about them simply for the pleasure of presenting them; to narrate a particular affair, lively or sad, simply for the pleasure of narrating it; to describe a landscape simply for the pleasure of describing it.

There are some writers (and not a few) who do feel this pleasure and, satisfied, ask no more. They are, to speak more precisely, historical writers.

But there are others who, beyond such pleasure, feel a more profound spiritual need on whose account they admit only figures, affairs, landscapes which have been soaked, so to speak, in a particular sense of life and acquire from it a universal value. These are, more precisely, philosophical writers.

I have the misfortune to belong to these last.

I hate symbolic art in which the presentation loses all spontaneous movement in order to become a machine, an allegory—a vain and misconceived effort because the very fact of giving an allegorical sense to a presentation clearly shows that we have to do with a fable which by itself has no truth either fantastic or direct; it was made for the demonstration of some moral truth. The spirtual need I speak of cannot be satisfied—or seldom, and that to the end of a superior irony, as for example in Ariosto —by such allegorical symbolism. This latter starts from a concept, and from a concept which creates or tries to create for itself an image. The former on the other hand seeks in the image—which

must remain alive and free throughout—
a meaning to give it value.

Now, however much I sought, I did not
succeed in uncovering this meaning in
the six characters. And I concluded
therefore that it was no use making them
live.

I thought to myself: "I have already
afflicted my readers with hundreds and
hundreds of stories. Why should I afflict
them now by narrating the sad entangle-
ments of these six unfortunates?"

And, thinking thus, I put them away
from me. Or rather I did all I could to
put them away.

But one doesn't give life to a character for nothing.

Creatures of my spirit, these six were
already living a life which was their own
and not mine any more, a life which it
was not in my power any more to deny
them.

Thus it is that while I persisted in desiring to drive them out of my spirit,
they, as if completely detached from every narrative support, characters from
a novel miraculously emerging from the
pages of the book that contained them,
went on living on their own, choosing certain moments of the day to reappear before me in the solitude of my study and
coming—now one, now the other, now
two together—to tempt me, to propose
that I present or describe this scene or
that, to explain the effects that could be
secured with them, the new interest which
a certain unusual situation could provide,
and so forth.

For a moment I let myself be won
over. And this condescension of mine,
thus letting myself go for a while, was
enough, because they drew from it a new
increment of life, a greater degree of
clarity and addition, consequently a
greater degree of persuasive power over
me. And thus as it became gradually
harder and harder for me to go back and
free myself from them, it became easier
and easier for them to come back and
tempt me. At a certain point I actually
became obsessed with them. Until, all of
a sudden, a way out of the difficulty
flashed upon me.

"Why not," I said to myself, "present
this highly strange fact of an author who
refuses to let some of his characters live
though they have been born in his fantasy, and the fact that these characters,

having by now life in their veins, do not
resign themselves to remaining excluded
from the world of art? They are detached from me; live on their own; have
acquired voice and movement; have by
themselves—in this struggle for existence
that they have had to wage with me—become dramatic characters, characters
that can move and talk on their own initiative; already see themselves as such;
have learned to defend themselves
against me; will even know how to defend themselves against others. And so
let them go where dramatic characters
do go to have life: on a stage. And let
us see what will happen."

That's what I did. And, naturally, the
result was what it had to be: a mixture
of tragic and comic, fantastic and realistic, in a humorous situation that was
quite new and infinitely complex, a
drama which is conveyed by means of
the characters, who carry it within them
and suffer it, a drama, breathing, speaking, self-propelled, which seeks at all
costs to find the means of its own presentation; and the comedy of the vain attempt at an improvised realization of the
drama on stage. First, the surprise of
the poor actors in a theatrical company
rehearsing a play by day on a bare stage
(no scenery, no flats). Surprise and incredulity at the sight of the six characters announcing themselves as such in
search of an author. Then, immediately
afterwards, through that sudden fainting
fit of the Mother veiled in black, their
instinctive interest in the drama of which
they catch a glimpse in her and in the
other members of the strange family, an
obscure, ambiguous drama, coming about
so unexpectedly on a stage that is empty
and unprepared to receive it. And gradually the growth of this interest to the
bursting forth of the contrasting passions of Father, of Step-Daughter, of
Son, of that poor Mother, passions seeking, as I said, to overwhelm each other
with a tragic, lacerating fury.

And here is the universal meaning at
first vainly sought in the six characters,
now that, going on stage of their own
accord, they succeed in finding it within
themselves in the excitement of the desperate struggle which each wages against
the other and all wage against the Manager and the actors, who do not understand them.

Without wanting to, without knowing it, in the strife of their bedevilled souls, each of them, defending himself against the accusations of the others, expresses as his own living passion and torment the passion and torment which for so many years have been the pangs of my spirit: the deceit of mutual understanding irremediably founded on the empty abstraction of the words, the multiple personality of everyone corresponding to the possibilities of being to be found in each of us, and finally the inherent tragic conflict between life (which is always moving and changing) and form (which fixes it, immutable).

Two above all among the six characters, the Father and the Step-Daughter, speak of that outrageous unalterable fixity of their form in which he and she see their essential nature expressed permanently and immutably, a nature that for one means punishment and for the other revenge; and they defend it against the factitious affectations and unaware volatility of the actors, and they try to impose it on the vulgar Manager who would like to change it and adapt it to the so-called exigencies of the theatre.

If the six characters don't all seem to exist on the same plane, it is not because some are figures of first rank and others of the second, that is, some are main characters and others minor ones—the elementary perspective necessary to all scenic or narrative art—nor is it that any are not completely created—for their purpose. They are all six at the same point of artistic realization and on the same level of reality, which is the fantastic level of the whole play. Except that the Father, the Step-Daughter, and also the Son are realized as mind; the Mother as nature; the Boy as a presence watching and performing a gesture and the Baby unaware of it all. This fact creates among them a perspective of a new sort. Unconsciously I had had the impression that some of them needed to be fully realized (artistically speaking), others less so, and others merely sketched in as elements in a narrative or presentational sequence: the most alive, the most completely created, are the Father and the Step-Daughter who naturally stand out more and lead the way, dragging themselves along beside the almost dead weight of the others—first, the Son, holding back; second, the Mother, like a victim resigned to her fate, between the two children who have hardly any substance beyond their appearance and who need to be led by the hand.

And actually! actually they had each to appear in that stage of creation which they had attained in the author's fantasy at the moment when he wished to drive them away.

If I now think about these things, about having intuited that necessity, having unconsciously found the way to resolve it by means of a new perspective, and about the way in which I actually obtained it, they seem like miracles. The fact is that the play was really conceived in one of those spontaneous illuminations of the fantasy when by a miracle all the elements of the mind answer to each other's call and work in divine accord. No human brain, working "in the cold," however stirred up it might be, could ever have succeeded in penetrating far enough, could ever have been in a position to satisfy all the exigencies of the play's form. Therefore the reasons which I will give to clarify the values of the play must not be thought of as intentions that I conceived beforehand when I prepared myself for the job and which I now undertake to defend, but only as discoveries which I have been able to make afterwards in tranquillity.

I wanted to present six characters seeking an author. Their play does not manage to get presented—precisely because the author whom they seek is missing. Instead is presented the comedy of their vain attempt with all that it contains of tragedy by virtue of the fact that the six characters have been rejected.

But can one present a character while rejecting him? Obviously, to present him one needs, on the contrary, to receive him into one's fantasy before one can express him. And I have actually accepted and realized the six characters: I have, however, accepted and realized them as rejected: in search of *another* author.

What have I rejected of them? Not themselves, obviously, but their drama, which doubtless is what interests them above all but which did not interest me—for the reasons already indicated.

And what is it, for a character—his drama?

Every creature of fantasy and art, in order to exist, must have his drama, that is, a drama in which he may be a character and for which he *is* a character. This drama is the character's *raison d'être*, his vital function, necessary for his existence.

In these six, then, I have accepted the "being" without the reason for being. I have taken the organism and entrusted to it, not its own proper function, but another more complex function into which its own function entered, if at all, only as a datum. A terrible and desperate situation especially for the two—Father and Step-Daughter—who more than the others crave life and more than the others feel themselves to be characters, that is, absolutely need a drama and therefore their own drama—the only one which they can envisage for themselves yet which meantime they see rejected: an "impossible" situation from which they feel they must escape at whatever cost; it is a matter of life and death. True, I have given them another *raison d'être,* another function: precisely that "impossible" situation, the drama of being in search of an author and rejected. But that this should be a *raison d'être,* that it should have become their real function, that it should be necessary, that it should suffice, they can hardly suppose; for they have a life of their own. If someone were to tell them, they wouldn't believe him. It is not possible to believe that the sole reason for our living should lie in a torment that seems to us unjust and inexplicable.

I cannot imagine, therefore, why the charge was brought against me that the character of the Father was not what it should have been because it stepped out of its quality and position as a character and invaded at times the author's province and took it over. I who understand those who don't quite understand me see that the charge derives from the fact that the character expresses and makes his own a torment of spirit which is recognized as mine. Which is entirely natural and of absolutely no significance. Aside from the fact that this torment of spirit in the character of the Father derives from causes, and is suffered and lived for reasons, that have nothing to do with the drama of my personal experience, a fact which alone removes all substance from the criticism, I want to make it clear

that the inherent torment of my spirit is one thing, a torment which I can legitimately—provided that it be organic—reflect in a character, and that the activity of my spirit as revealed in the realized work, the activity that succeeds in forming a drama out of the six characters in search of an author is another thing. If the Father participated in this latter activity, if he competed in forming the drama of the six characters without an author, then and only then would it by all means be justified to say that he was at times the author himself and therefore not the man he should be. But the Father suffers and does not create his existence as a character in search of an author. He suffers it as an inexplicable fatality and as a situation which he tries with all his powers to rebel against, which he tries to remedy: hence it is that he is a character in search of an author and nothing more, even if he expresses as his own the torment of my spirit. If he, so to speak, assumed some of the author's responsibilities, the fatality would be completely explained. He would, that is to say, see himself accepted, if only as a rejected character, accepted in the poet's heart of hearts, and he would no longer have any reason to suffer the despair of not finding someone to construct and affirm his life as a character. I mean that he would quite willingly accept the *raison d'être* which the author gives him and without regrets would forego his own, throwing over the Manager and the actors to whom in fact he runs as his only recourse.

There is one character, that of the Mother, who on the other hand does not care about being alive (considering being alive as an end in itself). She hasn't the least suspicion that she is *not* alive. It has never occurred to her to ask how and why and in what manner she lives. In short, she is not aware of being a character, inasmuch as she is never, even for a moment, detached from her role. She doesn't know she has a role.

This makes her perfectly organic. Indeed, her role of Mother does not of itself, in its natural essence, embrace mental activity. And she does not exist as a mind. She lives in an endless continuum of feeling, and therefore she cannot acquire awareness of her life—that is, of her existence as a character. But with all this, even she, in her own way and for her own ends, seeks an author, and at a certain stage seems happy to have been brought before the Manager. Because she hopes to take life from him, perhaps? No: because she hopes the Manager will have her present a scene with the Son in which she would put so much of her own life. But it is a scene which does not exist, which never has and never could take place. So unaware is she of being a character, that is, of the life that is possible to her, all fixed and determined, moment by moment, in every action, every phrase.

She appears on stage with the other characters but without understanding what the others make her do. Obviously, she imagines that the itch for life with which the husband and the daughter are afflicted and for which she herself is to be found on stage is no more than one of the usual incomprehensible extravagances of this man who is both tortured and torturer and—horrible, most horrible —a new equivocal rebellion on the part of that poor erring girl. The Mother is completely passive. The events of her own life and the values they assume in her eyes, her very character, are all things which are "said" by the others and which she only once contradicts, and that because the maternal instinct rises up and rebels within her to make it clear that she didn't at all wish to abandon either the son or the husband: the Son was taken from her and the husband forced her to abandon him. She is only correcting data; she explains and knows nothing.

In short, she is nature. Nature fixed in the figure of a mother.

This character gave me a satisfaction of a new sort, not to be ignored. Nearly all my critics, instead of defining her, after their habit, as "unhuman"—which seems to be the peculiar and incorrigible characteristic of all my creatures without exception—had the goodness to note "with real pleasure" that at last a *very human* figure had emerged from my fantasy. I explain this praise to myself in the following way: since my poor Mother is entirely limited to the natural attitude of a Mother with no possibility of free mental activity, being, that is, little more than a lump of flesh completely alive in all its functions—procreation, lactation,

caring for and loving its young—without any need therefore of exercising her brain, she realizes in her person the true and complete "human type." That must be how it is, since in a human organism nothing seems more superfluous than the mind.

But the critics have tried to get rid of the Mother with this praise without bothering to penetrate the nucleus of poetic values which the character in the play represents. A very human figure, certainly, because mindless, that is, unaware of being what she is or not caring to explain it to herself. But not knowing that she is a character doesn't prevent her from being one. That is her drama in my play. And the most living expression of it comes spurting out in her cry to the Manager who wants her to think all these things have happened already and therefore cannot now be a reason for renewed lamentations: "No, it's happening now, it's happening always! My torture is not a pretence, signore! I am alive and present, always, in every moment of my torture: it is renewed, alive and present, always!" This she *feels,* without being conscious of it, and feels it therefore as something inexplicable: but she feels it so terribly that she doesn't think it *can* be something to explain either to herself or to others. She feels it and that is that. She feels it as pain, and this pain is immediate; she cries it out. Thus she reflects the growing fixity of life in a form —the same thing, which in another way, tortures the Father and the Step-Daughter. In them, mind. In her, nature. The mind rebels and, as best it may, seeks an advantage; nature, if not aroused by sensory stimuli, weeps.

Conflict between life-in-movement and form is the inexorable condition not only of the mental but also of the physical order. The life which in order to exist has become fixed in our corporeal form little by little kills that form. The tears of a nature thus fixed lament the irreparable, continuous aging of our bodies. Hence the tears of the Mother are passive and perpetual. Revealed in three faces, made significant in three distinct and simultaneous dramas, this inherent conflict finds in the play its most complete expression. More: the Mother declares also the particular value of artistic form—a form which does not delimit or destroy its own life and which life does not consume—in her cry to the Manager. If the Father and Step-Daughter began their scene a hundred thousand times in succession, always, at the appointed moment, at the instant when the life of the work of art must be expressed with that cry, it would always be heard, unaltered and unalterable in its form, not as a mechanical repetition, not as a return determined by external necessities, but on the contrary, alive every time and as new, suddenly born *thus forever!* embalmed alive in its incorruptible form. Hence, always, as we open the book, we shall find Francesca alive and confessing to Dante her sweet sin, and if we turn to the passage a hundred thousand times in succession, a hundred thousand times in succession Francesca will speak her words, never repeating them mechanically, but saying them as though each time were the first time with such living and sudden passion that Dante every time will turn faint. All that lives, by the fact of living, has a form, and by the same token must die—except the work of art which lives forever in so far as it *is* form.

The birth of a creature of human fantasy, a birth which is a step across the threshold between nothing and eternity, can also happen suddenly, occasioned by some necessity. An imagined drama needs a character who does or says a certain necessary thing; accordingly this character is born and is precisely what he had to be. In this way Madame Pace is born among the six characters and seems a miracle, even a trick, realistically portrayed on the stage. It is no trick. The birth is real. The new character is alive not because she was alive already but because she is now happily born as is required by the fact of her being a character—she is obliged to be as she is. There is a break here, a sudden change in the level of reality of the scene, because a character can be born in this way only in the poet's fancy and not on the boards of a stage. Without anyone's noticing it, I have all of a sudden changed the scene: I have gathered it up again into my own fantasy without removing it from the spectator's eyes. That is, I have shown them, instead of the stage, my own fantasy in the act of creating— my own fantasy in the form of this same

stage. The sudden and uncontrollable changing of a visual phenomenon from one level of reality to another is a miracle comparable to those of the saint who sets his own statue in motion: it is neither wood nor stone at such a moment. But the miracle is not arbitrary. The stage —a stage which accepts the fantastic reality of the six characters—is no fixed, immutable datum. Nothing in this play exists as given and preconceived. Everything is in the making, is in motion, is a sudden experiment: even the place in which this unformed life, reaching after its own form, changes and changes again contrives to shift position organically. The level of reality changes. When I had the idea of bringing Madame Pace to birth right there on the stage, I felt I could do it and I did it. Had I noticed that this birth was unhinging and silently, unnoticed, in a second, giving another shape, another reality to my scene, I certainly wouldn't have brought it about. I would have been afraid of the apparent lack of logic. And I would have committed an ill-omened assault on the beauty of my work. The fervor of my mind saved me from doing so. For, despite appearances, with their specious logic, this fantastic birth is sustained by a real necessity in mysterious, organic relation with the whole life of the work.

That someone now tells me it hasn't all the value it could have because its expression is not constructed but chaotic, because it smacks of romanticism, makes me smile.

I understand why this observation was made to me: because in this work of mine the presentation of the drama in which the six characters are involved appears tumultuous and never proceeds in an orderly manner. There is no logical development, no concatenation of the events. Very true. Had I hunted it with a lamp I couldn't have found a more disordered, crazy, arbitrary, complicated, in short, romantic way of presenting "the drama in which the six characters are involved." Very true. But I have not presented that drama. I have presented another—and I won't undertake to say again what!—in which, among the many fine things that everyone, according to his tastes, can find, there is a discreet satire on romantic procedures: in the six characters thus excited to the point where they stifle themselves in the roles which each of them plays in a certain drama while I present them as characters in another play which they don't know and don't suspect the existence of, so that this inflammation of their passions—which belongs to the realm of romantic procedures—is humorously "placed," located in the void. And the drama of the six characters presented not as it would have been organized by my fantasy had it been accepted but in this way, as a rejected drama, could not exist in the work except as a "situation," with some little development, and could not come out except in indications, stormily, disorderedly, in violent foreshortenings, in a chaotic manner: continually interrupted, sidetracked, contradicted (by one of its characters), denied, and (by two others) not even seen.

There is a character indeed—he who denies the drama which makes him a character, the Son—who draws all his importance and value from being a character not of the comedy in the making—which as such hardly appears—but from the presentation that I made of it. In short, he is the only one who lives solely as "a character in search of an author"—inasmuch as the author he seeks is not a dramatic author. Even this could not be otherwise. The character's attitude is an organic product of my conception, and it is logical that in the situation it should produce greater confusion and disorder and another element of romantic contrast.

But I had precisely to *present* this organic and natural chaos. And to present a chaos is not at all to present chaotically, that is, romantically. That my presentation is the reverse of confused, that it is quite simple, clear, and orderly, is proved by the clarity which the intrigue, the characters, the fantastic and realistic, dramatic and comic levels of the work have had for every public in the world and by the way in which, for those with more searching vision, the unusual values enclosed within it come out.

Great is the confusion of tongues among men if criticisms thus made find words for their expression. No less great than this confusion is the intimate law of order which, obeyed in all points, makes this work of mine classical and typical and at its catastrophic close forbids the use of words. Though the audience eventually understands that one does not create life by artifice and that the drama of the six characters cannot be presented without an author to give them value with his spirit, the Manager remains vulgarly anxious to know how the thing turned out, and the "ending" is remembered by the Son in its sequence of actual moments, but without any sense and therefore not needing a human voice for its expression. It happens stupidly, uselessly, with the going-off of a mechanical weapon on stage. It breaks up and disperses the sterile experiment of the characters and the actors, which has apparently been made without the assistance of the poet.

The poet, unknown to them, as if looking on at a distance during the whole period of the experiment, was at the same time busy creating—with it and of it—his own play.

GERMAN DRAMATIC CRITICISM FROM THE BEGINNINGS TO LESSING

Owing to a variety of causes — the lack of political unity, among others — Germany was late in developing her literature, and what dramatic criticism exists before Lessing is more or less of the old style — Latin commentaries, statement and re-statement of the Rules, and grammatical disquisitions. Individual figures stand out, however — like Opitz, Gottsched, and Johann Elias Schlegel — but none of these contributed theories of epoch-making importance.

German dramatic criticism begins with German general criticism, somewhere toward the middle of the sixteenth century. It is doubtful just who was the beginner, though Sturm, Fabricius, and Pontanus all have just claims, while Schosser's pedantic *Disputationes de Tragœdia* antedated them all (1559). Johann Sturm was a scholar of no mean attainments, and his commentaries, letters and the work on rhetoric, exercised some influence, especially on his pupil Johann Lobart, who edited a commentary of Horace's *Ars Poetica* in 1576. Georgius Fabricius, the first part of whose *De Re Poetica* appeared in 1565 (an enlarged edition was published in 1571), was considerably influenced by Scaliger. Jacobus Pontanus [Spanmüller] wrote an *Institutiones Poeticae,* a pedantic and unoriginal treatise which appeared in 1594.[1] But the first of the truly modern and vernacular tractates was Martin Opitz' *Buch von der Deutscher Poeterei* (1624). This work, with all its shortcomings, gave rise to a good deal of more or less original work in Germany, though between its appearance and that of Gottsched's *Versuch* in 1730 there was a large amount of the usual Latin scholarship and pedantic compilation. With Andreas Gryphius, the most important dramatist of the century, the English influence, which was beginning to be felt even in the days of Opitz, became more widespread, and in his plays, lectures, and prefaces he combatted the old rules of drama. Erdmann Neumeister followed Gryphius in his disregard of convention, while Philip von Zesen (in his *De Poetica,* 1656) and Augustine Buchner, in his *Kurzer Wegweiser zur Deutsch Tichtkunst* (1663), continued the pedantic tradition. Johann Christoph Gottsched exerted considerable influence over his contemporaries and successors.

1 Some critics include two great Dutch writers — Heinsius and Voss — with the Early Germans. Daniel Heinsius published his *De Tragœdiœ Constitutione* in 1611, and Gerard Voss his *Commentariorum Rhetoricorum sive Oratoriarum Institutionum Libri Sex* in 1609, though the enlarged edition of 1643 contains much more on the drama.

He was during a great part of the first half of the eighteenth century a literary dictator, and his *Versuch einer kritischen Dichtkunst* (1730) opened the eyes of Germany to the possibility of developing her own literature. The spirit of the work was neo-classical, and Gottsched was a staunch admirer of the French critics. His quarrels with Bodmer and Breitinger, the Swiss critics, over Milton and other subjects, resulted in ignominious defeat. Johann Jakob Bodmer is the author of the famous *Diskurse der Mahler* (1721), and J. J. Breitinger of the *Kritische Dichtkunst* (1740). Gottsched's ideas were soon rejected by the public, but he had a number of followers, chiefly among the small group of writers who founded the *Bremer Beiträge* in 1745. Among these were Gellert, Klopstock, and Johann Elias Schlegel. Schlegel wrote a number of interesting essays on the drama, among the best of which is the *Gedanken zur Aufnahme des dänischen Theaters.* He was likewise a Shakespeare enthusiast, and has been called the initiator of Shakespeare study in his country. Moses Mendelssohn's *Briefe* are concerned, among other things, with Shakespeare criticism. But by all odds the greatest critic of the time, and one of the greatest of all time, was Gotthold Ephraim Lessing. While he wrote a vast amount of miscellaneous criticism and a purely esthetic work — the *Laokoon* (1776) — his chief contribution to dramatic theory is his *Hamburgische Dramaturgie* (1769). These papers were originally published as disconnected dramatic criticisms, but taken as a whole, they none the less constitute a body of dramatic theory. Lessing's principal task was to destroy the French models set up by Gottsched and others, to explain Aristotle, and to exhort his fellow dramatists to turn to England, where they would find a dramatic form more flexible and better adapted to their genius than the rigidly fixed classical dramas of France.

GOTTHOLD EPHRAIM LESSING

Gotthold Ephraim Lessing was born at Kamenz in 1729. His preliminary schooling was received at Meissen, whence he went to the University of Leipzig, where he studied theology. He was not long in discovering that his interests lay rather in literature and philosophy, and he went to Berlin, where for five years he led a precarious and hand-to-mouth existence as a literary hack. Thence he went to Wittenberg, where he took his M.A. degree. He did some miscellaneous writing alone and in collaboration with Moses Mendelssohn. He had been early attracted to the theater, and in his youth he had written a number of small plays and translated others. His first important play, *Miss Sara Sampson,* appeared in 1755. The next few years found him doing all sorts of work and in many cities, but in 1758 he returned to Berlin and edited a review, *Litteraturbriefe,* which attracted a great deal of attention. From 1760 to 1765 he was secretary to the Governor of Breslau, and in 1766 he published his famous *Laokoon.* The following year he produced *Minna von Barnhelm,* the first great German comedy. In 1767 he was called to Hamburg as critic of the new National Theater, and for two years he published the criticisms which were re-printed as the *Hamburgische Dramaturgie.* When the theater closed Lessing became librarian at Wolfenbüttel. Shortly after, he traveled in Italy and in 1772 he published *Emilia Galotti.* In 1776 he married Eva König, who died within a year of the marriage. For some time he engaged in various theological disputes, turning finally to dramatic writing. *Nathan der Weise* made its appearance in 1779. This was his last important literary work. He died in 1781.

Lessing was a dramatist of the first rank, and a critic, coming as he did at a turning-point in German literature, of supreme importance. Throughout the *Hamburgische Dramaturgie* there is a tendency to correct the fallacious notions then current, and above all a healthy note of constructive criticism. His interpretation of Aristotle and his attacks on French forms were of inestimable importance to the dramatists of his day. The *Dramaturgie* contains a mass of arguments favoring the theory that no true drama can rest upon any but Aristotelian laws. He insists especially upon unity of action. A large number of papers are devoted to attacking the French classical dramatists, and others to showing how Shakespeare was basically a follower of Aristotle. Says Lessing in his *Preface* to the *Dramaturgie:* " This *Dramaturgie* is to form a critical index of all the plays performed, and is to accompany every step made here by the art of the poet or the actor. . . . At the same time it is well that the mediocre should not pretend to be more than it is, so that the dissatisfied spectator may at least learn to judge from it. It is only needful to explain to a person of healthy mind the reasons why something has not pleased him if one desires to teach him good taste."

HAMBURG DRAMATURGY [1]

[*Hamburgische Dramaturgie*]

(1769)

No. 1.—May 1, 1767.

The theater was successfully opened on the 22nd of last month with the tragedy *Olindo and Sophronia. Olindo and Sophronia* is the work of a young poet, and is a posthumous incomplete work. Its theme is the well-known episode in Tasso. It is not easy to convert a touching little story into a touching drama. True, it

1 Re-printed, with omissions, from *Lessing's Laoköon, Dramatic Notes, and the Representation of Death by the Ancients,* translated by E. C. Beasley and Helen Zimmern (New Bohn Eds.).— Ed.

costs little trouble to invent new complications and to enlarge separate emotions into scenes. But to prevent these new complications from weakening the interest or interfering with probability; to transfer oneself from the point of view of a narrator into the real standpoint of each personage; to let passions arise before the eyes of the spectator in lieu of describing them, and to let them grow up without effort in such illusory continuity that he must sympathize, whether he will or no; this it is which is needful, and which genius does without knowing it, without tediously explaining it to itself, and which mere cleverness endeavors in vain to imitate.

Here I wish to make a double remark which, borne in mind, will save young tragic poets from committing some great faults. If heroic sentiments are to arouse admiration, the poet must not be too lavish of them, for what we see often, what we see in many persons, no longer excites astonishment. Every Christian in *Olindo and Sophronia* holds being martyred and dying as easy as drinking a glass of water. We hear these pious bravadoes so often and out of so many mouths, that they lose all their force.

The second remark concerns Christian tragedies in particular. Their heroes are generally martyrs. Now we live in an age when the voice of healthy reason resounds too loudly to allow every fanatic who rushes into death wantonly, without need, without regard for all his citizen duties, to assume to himself the title of a martyr. We know too well to-day how to distinguish the false martyr from the true, but despise the former as much as we reverence the latter, and at most they extort from us a melancholy tear for the blindness and folly of which we see humanity is capable. But this tear is none of those pleasing ones that tragedy should evoke. If therefore the poet chooses a martyr for his hero let him be careful to give to his actions the purest and most incontrovertible motives, let him place him in an unalterable necessity of taking the step that exposes him to danger, let him not suffer him to seek death carelessly or insolently challenge it. Else his pious hero becomes an object of our distaste, and even the religion that he seeks to honor may suffer thereby. I have already said that it could only be a superstition that led Olindo to steal the image from the mosque as contemptible as that which we despise in the wizard Ismenor. It does not excuse the poet that there were ages when such superstition was general and could subsist side by side with many excellent qualities, that there still are countries where it would be nothing strange for pious ignorance. For he wrote his tragedy as little for those ages as he intended that it should be performed in Bohemia or Spain. The good author, be he of whatever species he will, if he does not write

merely to show his wit and learning, has ever the best and most intelligent of his time and country before his eyes and he only condescends to write what pleases and can touch these. Even the dramatic author, if he lowers himself to the mob, lowers himself only in order that he may enlighten and improve the mass and not to confirm them in their prejudices or in their ignoble mode of thought.

No. 2

Yet another remark, also bearing on Christian tragedies might be made about the conversion of Clorinda. Convinced though we may be of the immediate operations of grace, yet they can please us little on the stage, where everything that has to do with the character of the personages must arise from natural causes. We can only tolerate miracles in the physical world; in the moral world everything must retain its natural course, because the theater is to be the school of the moral world. The motives for every resolve, for every change of opinion or even thoughts, must be carefully balanced against each other so as to be in accordance with the hypothetical character, and must never produce more than they could produce in accordance with strict probability. The poet, by beauty of details, may possess the art of deluding us to overlook misproportions of this kind, but he only deceives us once, and as soon as we are cool again we take back the applause he has lured from us.

.   .   .   .   .   .

Even Corneille's *Polyeucte* is to be condemned in view of the above remarks, and since the plays made in imitation of it are yet more faulty, the first tragedy that deserves the name of Christian has beyond doubt still to appear. I mean a play in which the Christian interests us solely as a Christian. But is such a piece even possible? Is not the character of a true Christian something quite untheatrical? Does not the gentle pensiveness, the unchangeable meekness that are his essential features, war with the whole business of tragedy that strives to purify passions by passions? Does not his expectation of rewarding happiness after this life contradict the disinterestedness with which we wish to see all great and good actions undertaken and carried out on the stage?

Until a work of genius arises that incontestably decides these objections,— for we know by experience what difficulties genius can surmount,— my advice is this, to leave all existent Christian tragedies unperformed. This advice, deduced from the necessities of art, and which deprives us of nothing more than very mediocre plays, is not the worse because it comes to the aid of weak spirits who feel I know not what shrinkage, when they hear sentiments spoken from the stage that they had only expected to hear in a holier place. The theater should give offense to no one, be he who he may, and I wish it would and could obviate all preconceived offense.

. . . . .

. . . In another still worse tragedy where one of the principal characters died quite casually, a spectator asked his neighbor, " But what did she die of? "— " Of what? Of the fifth act," was the reply. In very truth the fifth act is an ugly evil disease that carries off many a one to whom the first four acts promised a longer life.

. . . . .

. . . I know full well that the sentiments in a drama must be in accordance with the assumed character of the person who utters them. They can therefore not bear the stamp of absolute truth, it is enough if they are poetically true, if we must admit that this character under these circumstances, with these passions could not have judged otherwise. But on the other hand this poetical truth must also approach to the absolute and the poet must never think so unphilosophically as to assume that a man could desire evil for evil's sake, that a man could act on vicious principles, knowing them to be vicious and boast of them to himself and to others.

No. 9

. . . . . .

It is right and well if in every-day life we start with no undue mistrust of the character of others, if we give all credence to the testimony of honest folk. But may the dramatic poet put us off with such rules of justice? Certainly not, although he could much ease his business thereby. On the stage we want

to see who the people are, and we can only see it from their actions. The goodness with which we are to credit them, merely upon the word of another, cannot possibly interest us in them. It leaves us quite indifferent, and if we never have the smallest personal experience of their goodness it even has a bad reflex effect upon those on whose faith we solely and only accepted the opinion. Far therefore from being willing to believe Siegmund to be a most perfect and excellent young man, because Julia, her mother, Clarissa and Edward declare him to be such, we rather begin to suspect the judgment of these persons, if we never see for ourselves anything to justify their favorable opinion. It is true a private person cannot achieve many great actions in the space of four-and-twenty hours. But who demands great actions? Even in the smallest, character can be revealed, and those that throw the most light upon character, are the greatest according to poetical valuation. Moreover how came it that four-and-twenty hours was time enough to give Siegmund opportunity to compass two of the most foolish actions that could occur to a man in his position? The occasion was suitable, the author might reply, but he scarcely will reply that. They might have arisen as naturally as possible, be treated as delicately as possible; for all that the foolish actions, that we see him commit, would leave a bad impression on our minds concerning this young impetuous philosophist. That he acts badly we see; that he can act well we hear, not even by examples but in the vaguest of general terms.

No. 11

. . . For the dramatic poet is no historian, he does not relate to us what was once believed to have happened, but he really produces it again before our eyes, and produces it again not on account of mere historical truth but for a totally different and a nobler aim. Historical accuracy is not his aim, but only the means by which he hopes to attain his aim; he wishes to delude us and touch our hearts through this delusion. . . .

No. 12

. . .

I will not say that it is a fault when

the dramatic poet arranges his fable in such a manner that it serves for the exposition or confirmation of some great moral truth. But I may say that this arrangement of the fable is anything but needful; that there are very instructive and perfect plays that do not aim at such a single maxim, and that we err when we regard the moral sentences that are found at the close of many ancient tragedies, as the keynote for the existence of the entire play.

* * * * *

No. 16

. . . The only unpardonable fault of a tragic poet is this, that he leaves us cold; if he interests us he may do as he likes with the little mechanical rules.

* * * * *

No. 19

* * * * *

Now, Aristotle has long ago decided how far the tragic poet need regard historical accuracy: not farther than it resembles a well-constructed fable wherewith he can combine his intentions. He does not make use of an event because it really happened, but because it happened in such a manner as he will scarcely be able to invent more fitly for his present purpose. If he finds this fitness in a true case, then the true case is welcome; but to search through history books does not reward his labor. And how many know what has happened? If we only admit the possibility that something can happen from the fact that it has happened, what prevents us from deeming an entirely fictitious fable a really authentic occurrence, of which we have never heard before? What is the first thing that makes a history probable? Is it not its internal probability? And is it not a matter of indifference whether this probability be confirmed by no witnesses or traditions, or by such as have never come within our knowledge? It is assumed quite without reason, that it is one of the objects of the stage to keep alive the memory of great men. For that we have history and not the stage. From the stage we are not to learn what such and such an individual man has done, but what every man of a certain character would do under certain given circumstances. The object of tragedy is more philosophical than the object of history, and it is degrading her from her true dignity to employ her as a mere panegyric of famous men or to misuse her to feel national pride.

* * * * *

No. 21

Nanine belongs to pathetic comedy. It has also many laughable scenes, and only in so far as these laughable scenes alternate with the pathetic, Voltaire would admit of them in comedy. An entirely serious comedy, wherein we never laugh, not even smile, wherein we should rather always weep, is to him a monstrosity. On the other hand he finds the transition from the pathetic to the comic, and from the comic to the pathetic, very natural. Human life is nothing but a constant chain of such transitions, and comedy should be a mirror of human life.

* * * * *

No. 24

* * * * *

In short, tragedy is not history in dialogue. History is for tragedy nothing but a storehouse of names wherewith we are used to associate certain characters. If the poet finds in history circumstances that are convenient for the adornment or individualizing of his subject; well, let him use them. Only this should be counted as little a merit as the contrary is a crime.

* * * * *

No. 25

* * * * *

" In short, no single part in this tragedy is what it should be, all are perverted and yet the play has pleased. When this pleasure? Obviously out of the situation of the personages that is touching in itself. A great man who is led to the scaffold will always interest; the representation of his fate makes an impression even without the help of poetry; very nearly the same impression that reality itself would make."

So much is the tragic poet dependent on his choice of subject. Through this alone the weakest and most confused play can achieve a kind of success, and I do not know how it is that in such plays good actors always show themselves to best advantage. . . .

No. 27

. . . the tragic poet loves the unexpected, the sudden, more than any other; . . .

No. 28

.   .   .   .   .   .

There is nothing to object to in this verdict, but against another criticism that attacks the poet on the score of morality, there is the more. An absent-minded person is said to be no *motif* for a comedy. And why not? To be absent, it is said, is a malady, a misfortune and no vice. An absent man deserves ridicule as little as one who has the headache. Comedy must only concern itself with such faults as can be remedied. Whoever is absent by nature can merit this as little by means of ridicule, as though he limped.

.   .   .   .   .

Well, but now granted that absence of mind is incurable, where is it written that comedy should only laugh at moral faults, and not at incurable defects? Every absurdity, every contrast of reality and deficiency is laughable. But laughter and derision are far apart. We can laugh at a man, occasionally laugh about him, without in the least deriding him. Indisputable and well-known as this difference is, yet all the quibbles which Rousseau lately made against the use of comedy only arose from the fact that he had not sufficiently regarded it. He says, for instance, Molière makes us laugh at a misanthrope and yet the misanthrope is the honest man of the play, Molière therefore shows himself an enemy to virtue in that he makes the virtuous man contemptible. Not so; the misanthrope does not become contemptible, he remains what he was, and the laughter that springs from the situations in which the poet places him does not rob him in the least of our esteem. The same with the *distrait*, we laugh at him, but do we despise him on that account? We esteem his other good qualities as

we ought; why, without them we could not even laugh at his absence of mind. Let a bad, worthless man be endowed with this absence of mind, and then see whether we should still find it laughable? It will be disgusting, horrid, ugly, not laughable.

No. 29

Comedy is to do us good through laughter; but not through derision; not just to counteract those faults at which it laughs, nor simply and solely in those persons who possess these laughable faults. Its true general use consists in laughter itself, in the practice of our powers to discern the ridiculous, to discern it easily and quickly under all cloaks of passion and fashion; in all admixture of good and bad qualities, even in the wrinkles of solemn earnestness. Granted that Molière's *Miser* never cured a miser; nor Regnard's *Gambler*, a gambler; conceded that laughter never could improve these fools; the worse for them, but not for comedy. It is enough for comedy that, if it cannot cure an incurable disease, it can confirm the healthy in their health. *The Miser* is instructive also to the extravagant man; and to him who never plays *The Gambler* may prove of use. The follies they have not got themselves, others may have with whom they have to live. It is well to know those with whom we may come into collision; it is well to be preserved from all impressions by example. A preservative is also a valuable medicine, and all morality has none more powerful and effective, than the ridiculous.

No. 30

.   .   .   .   .   .

This triple murder should constitute only one action, that has its beginning, its center and its end in the one passion of one person. What therefore does it lack as the subject for a tragedy? Nothing for genius, everything for a bungler. Here there is no love, no entanglement, no recognition, no unexpected marvelous occurrence; everything proceeds naturally. This natural course tempts genius and repels the bungler. Genius is only busied with events that are rooted in one another, that form a chain of cause and effect. To reduce the latter to the former, to weigh the latter against the former, everywhere to exclude chance, to cause everything that occurs to occur so that it could not have happened otherwise, this is the part of genius when it works in the domains of history and converts the useless treasures of memory into nourishment for the soul. Wit, on the contrary, that does not depend on matters rooted in each other, but on the similar or dissimilar, if it ventures on a work that should be reserved to genius alone, detains itself with such events as have not further concern with one another except that they have occurred at the same time. To connect these, to interweave and confuse their threads so that we lose the one at every moment in following out the other and are thrown from one surprise into another, this is the part of wit and this only. From the incessant crossing of such threads of opposed colors results a texture, which is to art what weavers call *changeant:* a material of which we cannot say whether it be blue or red, green or yellow; it is both, it seems this from one side, that from another, a plaything of fashion, a juggling trick for children.

．　　．　　．　　．　　．　　．

No. 32

The poet finds in history a woman who murders her husband and sons. Such indeed can awaken terror and pity, and he takes hold of it to treat it as a tragedy. But history tells him no more than the bare fact and this is as horrible as it is unusual. It furnishes at most three scenes, and, devoid of all detailed circumstances, three improbable scenes. What therefore does the poet do?

As he deserves this name more or less, the improbability or the meager brevity will seem to him the greatest want in this play.

If he be in the first condition, he will consider above all else how to invent a series of causes and effects by which these improbable crimes could be accounted for most naturally. Not satisfied with resting their probability upon historical authority, he will endeavor so to construct the characters of his personages, will endeavor so to necessitate one from another the events that place his characters in action, will endeavor to define the passions of each character so accurately, will endeavor to lead these passions through such gradual steps, that we shall everywhere see nothing but the most natural and common course of events. Thus with every step we see his personages take, we must acknowledge that we should have taken it ourselves under the same circumstances and the same degree of passion, and hence nothing will repel us but the imperceptible approach to a goal from which our imagination shrinks, and where we suddenly find ourselves filled with profound pity for those whom a fatal stream has carried so far, and full of terror at the consciousness that a similar stream might also thus have borne ourselves away to do deeds which in cold blood we should have regarded as far from us. If the poet takes this line, if his genius tells him that he cannot ignobly falter in its course, then the meager brevity of his fable has vanished at once, it no longer distresses him how he shall fill his five acts with so few events, he is only afraid lest five acts should not suffice for all his material, that enlarges more and more under his treatment now that he has discovered its hidden organization and understands how to unravel it.

Meantime the poet who less deserves this name, who is nothing but an ingenious fellow, a good versifier, he, I say, will find so little obstacle in the improbability of his scheme that he actually seeks therein its claim to admiration, which he must on no account diminish if he would not deprive himself of the surest means to evoke pity and terror. For he knows so little wherein this pity and terror really consist that in order to evoke them he thinks he cannot pile up enough marvelous, unexpected, incredible and abnormal matters, and thinks he must ever have recourse to extraordinary and horrible misfortunes and crimes. Scarcely therefore has he scented in history a Cleopatra, the murderess of her husband and sons, than he sees nothing further to do, in order to form this into a tragedy, than to fill in the interstices between the two crimes and to fill it with matter as strange as the crimes themselves. All this, his invention and the historical materials, he kneads into a very long, very incomprehensible romance, and when he has kneaded it as well as flour and straw can be kneaded together, he places his paste upon the skeleton wires of acts and scenes, relates and relates, rants and rhymes, and in four to six weeks, according to rhyming is easy or difficult to him, the wonder-work is finished, is called a tragedy, is printed and performed, read and looked at, admired or hissed, retained or forgotten as good luck will have it. For *et habent sua fata libelli*.

May I presume to apply this to the great Corneille? Or must I still make this application? According to the secret fate that rules over writings as over men, his *Rodogune* has been held for more than a hundred years the greatest masterpiece of the greatest tragic poet of all France and has occasionally been admired by all Europe. Can an admiration of a hundred years be groundless? Where have mankind so long concealed their eyes, their emotions? Was it reserved from 1644 to 1767 to a Hamburg dramatic critic to see spots in the sun and to debase a planet to a meteor?

Oh no! Already in the last century a certain honest Huron was imprisoned in the Bastille at Paris; he found time hang heavy on his hands although he was in Paris, and from sheer *ennui* he studied the French poets; and this Huron could not take pleasure in *Rodogune*. After this there lived, somewhere in Italy at the beginning of this century, a pedant who had his head full of the tragedies of the Greeks and of his countrymen of the sixteenth century, and he also found much to censure in *Rodogune*. Finally, a few years ago there was a Frenchman,[2] a great admirer of Corneille's name, who because he was rich and had a good heart, took pity on the poor deserted grand-daughter of the great poet, had her educated under his eyes, taught her to make pretty verses, collected alms for her, wrote a large lucrative commentary to the works of her grandfather as her dowry, and so forth; yet even he declared *Rodogune* to be a very absurd play, and was utterly amazed how so great a man as the great Cornelle could write such wretched stuff. Under one

2 Voltaire.— Ed.

of these the above dramatic critic must have gone to school and most probably under the last named, for it is always a Frenchman who opens the eyes of a foreigner to the faults of a Frenchman. Beyond question he repeats after him; or if not after him, after the Italian, or perhaps even after Huron. From one of these he must have learnt it. For that a German should think of himself, should of himself have the audacity to doubt the excellence of a Frenchman, who could conceive such a thing? . . .

No. 33

. . . . .

But moral or no moral, it is the same thing to a dramatic poet whether a general truth can be deduced or no from his fable, . . .

No. 34

For according to the indicated conception that we make to ourselves of genius, we are justified in demanding purpose and harmony in all the characters a poet creates; that is, if he demands from us that we should regard him in the light of a genius.

Harmony; for nothing in the characters must be contradictory; they must ever remain uniform and inherently themselves; they must express themselves now with emphasis, now more slightly as events work upon them, but none of the events must be mighty enough to change black to white. . . .

To act with a purpose is what raises man above the brutes, to invent with a purpose, to imitate with a purpose, is that which distinguishes genius from the petty artists who only invent to invent, imitate to imitate. They are content with the small enjoyment that is connected with their use of these means, and they make these means to be their whole purpose and demand that we also are to be satisfied with this lesser enjoyment, which springs from the contemplation of their cunning but purposeless use of their means. It is true that genius begins to learn from such miserable imitations; they are its preliminary studies. It also employs them in larger works for amplification and to give resting-places to our warmer sympathy, but with the construction and elaboration of its chief personages it combines larger and wider intentions; the intention to instruct us what we should do or avoid; the intention to make us acquainted with the actual characteristics of good and bad, fitting and absurd. It also designs to show us the good in all their combinations and results still good and happy even in misery; the bad as revolting and unhappy even in unhappiness. When its plot admits of no such immediate imitation, no such unquestionable warning, genius still aims at working upon our powers of desire and abhorrence with objects that deserve these feelings, and ever strives to show these objects in their true light, in order that no false light may mislead us as to what we should desire, what we should abhor.

.   .   .   .   .   .

No. 35

I have once before, elsewhere, drawn the distinction that exists between the action in an Æsopian fable and a drama. What is valid for the former, is valid for every moral tale that intends to bring a general moral axiom before our contemplation. We are satisfied if this intention is fulfilled and it is the same to us whether this is so by means of a complete action that is in itself a rounded whole, or no. The poet may conclude wherever he wills as soon as he sees his goal. It does not concern him what interest we may take in the persons through whom he works out his intention; he does not want to interest but to instruct us; he has to do with our reason, not with our heart; this latter may or may not be satisfied so long as the other is illumined. Now, the drama on the contrary makes no claim upon a single definite axiom flowing out of its story. It aims at the passions which the course and events of its fable arouse and treat, or it aims at the pleasure accorded by a true and vivid delineation of characters and habits. Both require a certain integrity of action, a certain harmonious end which we do not miss in the moral tale because our attention is solely directed to the general axiom of whose especial application the story affords such an obvious instance.

.   .   .   .   .   .

No 36

.   .   .   .   .

Let us instance the *Matron of Ephesus*. This acrid fable is well known, it is unquestionably the bitterest satire that was ever made on female frivolity. It has been recounted a thousand times after Petronius, and since it pleased even in the worst copy, it was thought that the subject must be an equally happy one for the stage. Houdar de la Motte and others made the attempt, but I appeal to all good taste as to the results of these attempts. The character of the matron in the story provokes a not unpleasant sarcastic smile at the audacity of wedded love; in the drama this becomes repulsive, horrible. In the drama the soldier's persuasions do not seem nearly so subtle, importunate, triumphant, as in the story.

In the story we picture to ourselves a sensitive little woman who is really in earnest in her grief, but succumbs to temptation and to her temperament; her weakness seems the weakness of her sex, we therefore conceive no especial hatred towards her, we deem that what she does, nearly every woman would have done. Even her suggestion to save her living lover by means of her dead husband we think we can forgive her, because of its ingenuity and presence of mind; or rather its very ingenuity leads us to imagine that this suggestion may have been appended by the malicious narrator who desired to end his tale with some right poisonous sting. Now, in the drama we cannot harbor this suggestion; what we hear has happened in the story, we see really occur; what we would doubt of in the story, in the drama the evidence of our own eyes settles incontrovertibly. The mere possibility of such an action diverted us; its reality shows it in all its atrocity; the suggestion amused our fancy, the execution revolts our feelings, we turn our backs to the stage and say with the Lykas of Petronius, without being in Lykas's peculiar position: "Si justus Imperator fuisset, debuit patris familiæ corpus in monimentum referre, mulierem adfigere cruci." And she seems to us the more to deserve this punishment, the less art the poet has expended on her seduction, for we do not then condemn in her weak woman in general, but an especially volatile, worthless female in particular. In short, in order happily to bring Petronius's fable on the stage it should preserve its end and yet not preserve it; the matron should go as far and yet not as far. The explanation of this another time.

No. 38

Now, Aristotle commends nothing more to the tragic poet than a good conception of his fable, and he has endeavored to render this easy to him by various and subtle remarks. For it is the fable that principally makes a poet; ten will succeed in representing customs, reflexions, expressions, for one who is excellent and blameless in this. He declares a fable to be an imitation of an action, $\pi\rho\dot{\alpha}\xi\epsilon\omega\varsigma$, and an action by a combination of events is $\sigma\dot{\upsilon}\nu\theta\epsilon\sigma\iota\varsigma$ $\pi\rho\alpha\gamma\mu\dot{\alpha}\tau\omega\nu$. The action is the whole, the events are the parts of this whole, and as the goodness of any whole rests on the goodness and connexion of its several parts, so also tragical action is more or less perfect, according as the events of which it is composed separately and collectively coincide with the intentions of the tragedy. Aristotle classes the events that can take place in a tragic action under three main heads: change of circumstances, $\pi\epsilon\rho\iota\pi\dot{\epsilon}\tau\epsilon\iota\alpha$; recognition, $\dot{\alpha}\nu\alpha\gamma\nu\omega\rho\iota\sigma\mu\dot{\alpha}\varsigma$; and suffering, $\pi\dot{\alpha}\theta\sigma\varsigma$. What he means by the two first, the names sufficiently reveal. Under the third he comprehends all that can occur of a painful and destructive nature to the acting personages: death, wounds, martyrdom and so forth. Change of circumstances and recognition are that by which the more intricate fable, $\mu\dot{\upsilon}\theta\sigma\varsigma$ $\pi\epsilon\pi\lambda\epsilon\gamma\mu\dot{\epsilon}\nu\sigma\varsigma$, is distinguished from the simple, $\dot{\alpha}\tau\lambda\sigma\tilde{\upsilon}\varsigma$. They are therefore no essential part of the fable, they only make the action more varied and hence more interesting and beautiful, but an action can have its full unity, completion and greatness without them. But without the third we can conceive of no tragical action; every tragedy must have some form of suffering, $\pi\dot{\alpha}\theta\eta$, be its fable simple or involved, for herein lies the actual intention of tragedy, to awaken fear and pity; while not every change of outward circumstances, not every recognition, but only certain forms of these attain this end, and other forms are rather disadvantageous than profitable. While, therefore, Aristotle regards and examines separately the various parts of tragical action that he has brought under these three main divisions, explaining what are the best outward changes, the best recognition, the best treatment of suffering, he finds in regard to the former that such changes of fortune are the best and most capable of awakening and stimulating pity and fear, which change from better to worse. In regard to the latter division he finds that the best treatment of suffering in the same sense is when the persons whom suffering threatens do not know each other or only recognize each other at the moment when this suffering is to become reality and it is therefore stayed.

And this is called a contradiction? I do not understand where can be the thoughts of him who finds the least contradiction here. The philosopher speaks of various parts; why must that which he maintains of one of these parts of necessity apply to the others? Is the possible perfection of the one also the perfection of the other? Or is the perfection of a part also the perfection of the whole? If change of circumstances and that which Aristotle includes under the word suffering, are two different things, as they are indeed, why should not something quite different be said of them? Or is it impossible that a whole should have parts of opposed characteristics? Where does Aristotle say that the best tragedy is nothing but a representation of changes of fortunes from prosperity to adversity? Or where does he say that the best tragedy results from nothing but the recognition of him on whom a fearful and unnatural deed was to have been committed? He says neither one thing nor the other of tragedy generally, but each of these things of an especial part that more or less concerns the end, which may or may not have influence. Change of fortune may occur in the middle of the play, and even if it continues thus to the end of the piece, it does not therefore constitute its end. For example, the change of fortune in *Œdipus* that evinces itself already at the close of the fourth act but to which various sufferings, $\pi\dot{\alpha}\theta\eta$, are added and with which the play really concludes. In the same manner suffering can attain its accomplishment in the play and at the same moment be thwarted by recognition, so that by means of this recognition the play is far from concluded, as in the second *Iphigenia* of Euripides where Orestes is already recognized in the fourth act by his sister who was in the act of sacrificing him. And how perfectly such tragical changes of fortune can be combined with tragical treatment of suffering in one and the same fable, can be shown in *Merope* itself. It contains the latter but what hinders it from having the former also, if for instance Merope, when she recognizes her son under the dagger in her eagerness to defend him from Polyphontes, contributes to her own or to her loved son's destruction? Why should not this play close as well with the destruction of the mother as with that of the tyrant? Why should it not be open to the poet to raise to the highest point our pity for a tender mother and allow her to be unfortunate through her tenderness? Or why should it not be permissible to let the son whom a pious vengeance has torn from his mother, succumb to the pursuit of the tyrant? Would not such a *Merope* in both cases combine those two characteristics of the best tragedy, in which the critic has been found so contradictory?

I perceive very well what caused the misunderstanding. It was not easy to imagine a change of fortune from better to worse without suffering, or suffering that has been obviated by recognition otherwise than connected with change of fortune. Yet each can equally be without the other, not to mention that both need not touch the same person, and even if it touches the same person, that both may not occur at the same time, but one follows the other, and one can be caused by the other. Without considering this, people have only thought of those instances and fables in which both parts either harmonize, or in which one of necessity excludes the other. That such exist is unquestionable. But is the art critic to be censured because he composes his rules in the most general manner, without considering the cases in which his general rules come into collision and one perfection must be sacrificed to another? Does such a collision of necessity bring him into contradiction with himself? He says: This part of the fable, if it is to have its perfection, must

be of such and such a constitution, that part of another, a third again of another. But where has he said that every fable must of necessity have all these parts? Enough for him that there are fables that could have them all. If your fable is not among the number of these happy ones; if it only admits of the best changes of fortune, the best treatment of suffering, then examine with which of the two you would succeed best as a whole, and choose. That is all!

No. 41

". . . For you cannot think how severe the master is whom we must strive to please: I mean our public. They demand that in a tragedy the hero should speak everywhere and the poet nowhere, and contend that at critical junctures in assemblies, at violent scenes, at a threatening danger, no king, no minister would make poetical comparisons." Now does such a public demand anything unfair? Does it not contend the truth? Should not every public demand this? contend this? . . .

No. 42

. . . The tragedian should avoid everything that can remind the audience of their illusion, for as soon as they are reminded thereof the illusion is gone. It almost seems here as though Maffei [3] sought to strengthen this illusion by assuming the idea of a theater outside the theater. . . .

No. 46

It is one thing to circumvent the rules, another to observe them. The French do the former, the latter was only understood by the ancients.

Unity of action was the first dramatic law of the ancients; unity of time and place were mere consequences of the former which they would scarcely have observed more strictly than exigency required had not the combination with the chorus arisen. For since their actions required the presence of a large body of people and this concourse always remained the same, who could go no further from their dwellings nor remain absent

[3] The author of *Merope*.— Ed.

longer than it is customary to do from mere curiosity, they were almost obliged to make the scene of action one and the same spot and confine the time to one and the same day. They submitted *bonâ fide* to this restriction; but with a suppleness of understanding such that in seven cases out of nine they gained more than they lost thereby. For they used this restriction as a reason for simplifying the action and to cut away all that was superfluous, and thus, reduced to essentials, it became only the ideal of an action which was developed most felicitously in this form which required the least addition from circumstances of time and place.

The French, on the contrary, who found no charms in true unity of action, who had been spoilt by the wild intrigues of the Spanish school before they had learnt to know Greek simplicity, regarded the unity of time and place not as consequences of unity of action, but as circumstances absolutely needful to the representation of an action, to which they must therefore adapt their richer and more complicated actions with all the severity required in the use of a chorus which, however, they had totally abolished. When they found, however, how difficult, nay at times how impossible this was, they made a truce with the tyrannical rules against which they had not the courage to rebel. Instead of a single place, they introduced an uncertain place, under which we could imagine now this, now that spot; enough if the places combined were not too far apart and none required special scenery, so that the same scenery could fit the one about as well as the other. Instead of the unity of a day they substituted unity of duration, and a certain period during which no one spoke of sunrise or sunset, or went to bed, or at least did not go to bed more than once, however much might occur in this space, they allowed to pass as a day.

Now, no one would have objected to this, for unquestionably even thus excellent plays can be made, and the proverb says, cut the wood where it is thinnest. But I must also allow my neighbor the same privilege. I must not always show him the thickest part, and cry, " There you must cut! That is where I cut!" Thus the French critics all exclaim, espe-

cially when they speak of the dramatic works of the English. What an ado they then make of regularity, that regularity which they have made so easy to themselves! But I am weary of dwelling on this point! . . .

. . . . . .

The strictest observation of the rules cannot outweigh the smallest fault in a character. How tamely Polyphontes talks and acts in Maffei's play has not escaped Lindelle. He is right to mock at the needless maxims that Maffei places in the tyrant's mouth. . . .

. . . And finally what do we mean by the mixtures of genres? In our primers it is right we should separate them from one another as carefully as possible, but if a genius for higher purposes amalgamates several of them in one and the same work, let us forget our primer and only examine whether he has attained these higher purposes. What do I care whether a play of Euripides is neither wholly a narrative nor wholly a drama, call it a hybrid, enough that this hybrid pleases me more, edifies me more, than the most rule-correct creations of your correct Racines or whatever else they may be called. Because the mule is neither a horse nor an ass, is it therefore the less one of the most useful beasts of burden?

No. 69

. . . . . .

Nothing is more chaste and decent than simple Nature, coarseness and confusion are as far removed from her as pomposity and bombast from the sublime. The same feeling which makes the boundary there, makes it here. The most pompous poet is therefore infallibly the most vulgar. Both faults are inseparable, and no species gives more opportunities of falling into both than tragedy.

. . . . . .

No. 70

. . . There are persons who will not admit of any nature which we can imitate too faithfully, they insist that even what displeases us in nature, pleases us in a faithful imitation, by means of imitation. There are others who regard beautifying nature as a whim; a nature that intends to be more beautiful than nature is just on that account not nature. Both declare themselves to be admirers of the only nature such as she is; the one sees nothing to avoid, the other nothing to add. The former would necessarily admire the Gothic mixed plays, and the latter would find it difficult to take pleasure in the masterpieces of the ancients.

But suppose this were not the consequence? If those persons, great admirers though they are of common everyday nature, should yet declare themselves against the mixture of the farcical and interesting. If these others, monstrous as they deem everything that desires to be better and more beautiful than nature, can yet wander through the whole Greek theater without finding the least obstacle on this account, how should we explain this contradiction?

We should necessarily have to retrace our steps and retract that which we insisted on before concerning the two species, but how must we retract without involving ourselves in new difficulties? The comparison of such blood-and-thunder tragedies concerning whose worth we dispute, with human life, with the ordinary course of the world, is still so correct.

I will throw out a few thoughts, which if they are not thorough enough may suggest more thorough ones. My chief thought is this: it is true and yet not true that the comic tragedy of Gothic invention faithfully copied nature. It only imitates it faithfully in one half and entirely neglects the other, it imitates the nature of phenomena without in the least regarding the nature of our feelings and emotions.

In nature everything is connected, everything is interwoven, everything changes with everything, everything merges from one into another. But according to this endless variety it is only a play for an infinite spirit. In order that finite spirits may have their share of this enjoyment, they must have the power to set up arbitrary limits, they must have the power to eliminate and to guide their attention at will.

This power we exercise at all moments of our life; without this power there would be no life for us; from too many various feelings we should feel nothing, we should be the constant prey of present impressions, we should dream without knowing what we dream. The purpose of art is to save us this abstraction in the realms of the beautiful, and to render the fixing of our attention easy to us. All in nature that we might wish to abstract in our thoughts from an object or a combination of various objects, be it in time or in place, art really abstracts for us, and accords us this object or this combination of various objects as purely and tersely as the sensations they are to provoke allow.

If we are witnesses of an important and touching event, and another event of trifling import traverses it, we seek and evade the distractions of our attention thus threatened. We abstract from it and it must needs revolt us to find that again art which we wished away in nature.

Only if this event in its progress assumes all shades of interest and one does not merely follow upon the other, but of necessity evolves from it, if gravity provokes laughter, sadness pleasure or *vice versâ*, so directly that an abstraction of the one or the other is impossible to us, then only do we not demand it from art and art knows how to draw a profit from this impossibility.

No. 80

To what end the hard work of dramatic form? Why build a theater, disguise men and women, torture their memories, invite the whole town to assemble at one place if I intend to produce nothing more with my work and its representation, than some of those emotions that would be produced as well by any good story that every one could read by his chimney-corner at home?

The dramatic form is the only one by which pity and fear can be excited, at least in no other form can these passions be excited to such a degree. Nevertheless it is preferred to excite all others rather than these; — nevertheless it is preferred to employ it for any purpose but this, for which it is so especially adapted.

• • • • • •

FRENCH DRAMATIC CRITICISM OF THE EIGHTEENTH CENTURY

It is not surprising to find in eighteenth century French dramatic criticism and theory a good deal of the philosophical spirit which runs through the *Encyclopédie* and the works of its many contributors. The seventeenth century was on the whole religious in spirit and if not anti-, at least, un-democratic. The Ancients and Moderns quarrel, begun in 1657, became acute in 1687, on the publication of Charles Perrault's *Siècle de Louis le Grand*. La Fontaine, La Bruyère, Fontenelle, Boileau, and Fénelon, soon joined the discussion, some maintaining the superiority of the Ancients, some the Moderns, and Fénelon standing midway between the two. Fontenelle, who wrote a few unsuccessful plays, is the author of a *Vie de Corneille*, a history of the French theater, and general prefaces to his collected plays (found respectively in volume 7 of the 1751 edition of his *Œuvres* and in volume 4 of the 1790 edition). His *Remarques sur quelques comédies d'Aristophane, Sur le théâtre grec*, and the *Réflexions sur la poétique*, in the third volume of the latter, are his chief contributions to dramatic theory. Antoine Houdar de La Motte, a friend of Fontenelle, began one of the earliest literary disputes of the new century. His "up-to-date" version of the *Iliad* called forth the wrath of Madame Dacier; the quarrel became general, but La Motte was soon crushed by the straightforward reasoning of Voltaire. La Motte's theories were not confined to epic poetry; himself a dramatist (his *Inès de Castro* was produced with signal success in 1723), he evolved an interesting theory in discussing the Unities: the Unity of Interest. His *Premier Discours sur la tragédie*, the three *Discours* prefixed to the plays *Romulus, Inès*, and *Œdipe*, and the *Suite des réflexions sur la tragédie*, are all assaults upon the various literary and dramatic questions of the early eighteenth century. Among the other precursors whose work is more or less directly concerned with the drama is Pierre Bayle, whose *Dictionnaire historique et critique* appeared in 1697. Bossuet's *Maximes et réflexions sur la comédie* which, while it is concerned chiefly with the moral point of view, is partially critical, was first published in 1694. This treatise and the similar works of Conti and Nicole (*Traité de la Comédie* and *Pensées sur les spectacles*), corresponded with the puritanical outbursts by Collier and his followers in England. Cailhava's *Art de la comédie* (1722), Crébillon's *Préface* to *Electre* (1715) and other plays, the Abbé du Bos' *Réflexions critiques sur la poésie et la peinture* (1719), all contain historical, controversial, and critical matter touching upon the drama. Fénelon's *Lettre sur les occupations de l'Académie française* (1717) contains a veritable Poetic on comedy and tragedy. The figure of Voltaire dominates the century. His first play, *Œdipe*, was produced in 1718. The standard editions include seven letters on the play, containing general remarks, with comparisons of the various ways in which the story had been treated in the past. There are about forty dedications, prefaces, etc., in which Voltaire discusses his theories of the drama; the *Lettres philosophiques, Dictionnaire philosophique, Commentaires sur Corneille*, and the *Lettres*, which run to the number of ten thousand, are likewise full of references to drama. These are scattered throughout Voltaire's lifetime, and have a distinct bearing on his attempts to resuscitate tragedy to its position of former dignity and popularity. Meanwhile, other influences were at work: the spirit of philosophical inquiry, the quest for "truth," resulted in the compilation of the celebrated *Encyclopédie*, which was begun by Diderot

228 EUROPEAN THEORIES OF THE DRAMA

and his associates in the middle of the century. Somewhat earlier, Nivelle de la Chaussée's *La Fausse antipathie,* in 1733, presented a new type of play, variously called the *Comédie larmoyante,* the *Drame,* the *Comédie sérieuse,* and the *Drame sérieux.* La Chaussée's *Prologue* to his play *La Fausse antipathie* (1733), and Gresset's *Lettre sur la comédie* (1759) are interesting documents by practicing dramatists. (A typical *comédie larmoyante* was Sedaine's *Le Philosophe sans le savoir* 1765.) The theories of Diderot on this subject, and those of Beaumarchais, somewhat later, are more important than the plays themselves. It is not difficult to trace the ideas of Dumas fils and Augier to the suggestions of Diderot and his followers. Unfortunately, Diderot's theories led him far from his practice, and farther still from that Nature which he professed to follow. Among the many contributors to the *Encyclopédie* who concerned themselves with questions of dramatic theory, were Voltaire, d'Alembert, Marmontel, and Jean-Jacques Rousseau. D'Alembert and Rousseau deserve mention for their discussion of the question of the theater. D'Alembert in his article on Geneva for the *Enclyclopédie* had, at the instigation of Voltaire, criticised the law forbidding theatrical productions. In 1758 Rousseau wrote a reply known as the *Lettre à d'Alembert sur les spectacles.* This lengthy epistle belongs to the category of philosophy and morality rather than to dramatic criticism proper, but it throws a clear light upon a by no means uncommon attitude. Rousseau wrote in at least two other places on the drama: *Lettre XVII* of *La Nouvelle Héloïse,* and *De l'imitation théâtrale.* Marmontel, who contributed a number of articles on literary subjects to the *Encyclopédie,* collected them afterward in his *Eléments de Littérature* (1787). The articles on *Comique, Tragédie, Unité,* and the like, are typical eighteenth century judgments. Beaumarchais' prefaces followed close upon Diderot's discursive lucubrations: the *Essai sur le drame sérieux,* prefixed to *Eugénie* (1767), the *Lettre modérée* prefixed to *Le Barbier de Séville* (1775), and the Preface to *Le Mariage de Figaro* (1784)). Sébastien Mercier's *Du Théâtre ou nouvel essai sur l'art dramatique* (1773) and *Nouvel examen de la Tragédie française* (1778) are attempts to reduce the theory of the drama to a mechanical science. La Harpe is usually considered the last of the Neo-classicists, and his *Lycée ou Cours de littérature* (published in full in 1825) with its characteristic judgments on dramatic poetry [1] takes us almost to the nineteenth century chronologically, if not in spirit. There is little material on the drama in the Revolutionary period, although the dramatico-political utterances of Marie-Joseph Chénier are indicative of the spirit of the times. His *Discours de la liberté du théâtre* (1789) and dedication, *A la Nation Française* in *Charles IX ou l'Ecole des Rois* (1789) are very curious documents.

[1] See vols. 11, 12, and 13, which are devoted to the drama.

VOLTAIRE

François Marie Arouet — later known as Voltaire — was born at Paris in 1694. His first schooling was received under the Jesuits at the College Louis-le-Grand, where he remained until 1711. His training there seems to have been good, and he evidently benefited by his experience in the production of Latin plays. He showed considerable facility in writing satirical verses, a gift which was to involve him in trouble on many occasions. He wished to make writing his profession, but his father insisted that he study law. The youth reluctantly applied himself to his law books at Caën, returned home and entered a law office, but was soon after sent to the country for writing libelous poems. During the winter of 1714–15 he continued to study law, but spent his spare time — and more — in writing, and when he returned to Paris, he brought with him the MS. of his first play, *Œdipe*. Before its production in 1718 he was thrice practically sent into exile for writing satirical verses. In 1721 his father died, leaving him a comfortable income. The next year he became a government spy, going to Belgium and Holland. Meantime, he was at work on *La Henriade* and more plays. A few years later, as the result of a quarrel, he was sent to the Bastille and two weeks later transferred, at his own request, to England. The three years he spent there did much for his mental development. There he made the acquaintance of the most important literary men of the day — among them Pope, Congreve, and Bolingbroke — and at least made the name of Shakespeare familiar to his countrymen. He returned to France in 1729. *Brutus* was produced in 1730, and two years later, one of his best and most successful plays, *Zaïre*. In 1733 he published his *Lettres philosophiques sur les anglais,* which contained a thinly-veiled criticism of French institutions. The edition was confiscated the next year, and when the authorities came for the author, they found he had gone to Lorraine. The next few years he spent at the Château de Cirey with the Marquise du Châtelet, there devoting himself almost entirely to literary labors. He traveled a great deal during these years. In 1745 he was again at the French Court, where he was made historiographer on the recommendation of Madame de Pompadour. The following year he was admitted to the Academy. On the death of the Marquise du Châtelet in 1749, Voltaire was without a home, and spent his time in Paris and traveling about France. After many unsuccessful efforts, Frederick the Great persuaded him to come to Berlin, where he went in 1751. The Emperor's relations with the Frenchman were at first most cordial, but before long Voltaire became embroiled in quarrels, and

showed a lamentable want of tact throughout. He published libels and letters without the Emperor's permission, and was practically sent away. In 1753 Voltaire and his niece were arrested in Frankfurt by Frederick's order, but were soon after released. During his stay at the Prussian court Voltaire wrote his *Siècle de Louis XIV* and began the *Dictionnaire philosophique*. After further wanderings he established himself at Geneva, where he had a private theater, but he soon infringed the laws of that city prohibiting public performances of plays. This led to his inciting d'Alembert to write an attack on Geneva in the *Encyclopédie,* which called forth Rousseau's celebrated *Lettre à d'Alembert sur les spectacles.* In 1758 he bought the estate of Ferney, not far from Geneva, and there spent his last years, writing, interesting himself in charity, and receiving his friends. In 1778 he went to Paris to attend the first performance of his new play, *Irène.* The same year he was taken sick and died.

Compared with Diderot and Beaumarchais, the other theorists of the drama in eighteenth century France were of minor importance. Voltaire is a reactionary classicist. He advocates the adherence to rimed verse in tragedy, and to the Unities. But Voltaire's classicism is neither very deep nor very "reasoned"; in the words of M. Faguet, he is a "Classic who understands practically nothing of antiquity." His ideas on dramatic form were taken for the most part from the theory and practice of the seventeenth century. His classicism is largely a matter of exactitude in form, clarity of thought, and precision. His rigid standards naturally excluded much that was best in literature and prevented his appreciation of many "Irregulars." Hence Voltaire's occasional errors in judging Racine, and his misunderstanding of Corneille. Voltaire's practice as a dramatist was of more importance in the attempt to revive French classical tragedy than his many prefaces. But the tide was against him: the *Drame* had come, and it was to develop during the next century into one of the most striking of all dramatic forms: the middle-class drama.

PREFACE TO HEROD AND MARIAMNE [1]
[*Préface* (to) *Hérode et Mariamne*]
(1725)

I tremble in giving this edition. I have remarked so many plays applauded on the stage, which have been afterwards despised in the closet, that I am afraid lest mine should meet with the same fate. One or two interesting situations, the actor's art, and the readiness which I showed to own and correct my faults, might have gained me some approbation, when it was acted. But many more qualifications are necessary to satisfy the cool deliberate reader. A plot regularly conducted will contribute but little to that end; and though it should be affecting, yet even that will not be sufficient: all poetical performances, though ever so perfect in other points, must necessarily displease if the lines are not strong and harmonious, and if there does not run through the whole a continued elegance and inexpressible charm of verse, that genius only can inspire, that wit alone can never attain, and about which people have agreed so ill, and to so little purpose since the death of Boileau.

It is a very gross mistake to imagine that the versification is the least essential and least difficult part of a theatrical piece. M. Racine, than whom, after Vergil, no man ever knew better the art of versifying, was not of that opinion. His *Phèdre* alone employed him for two years. Pradon boasted of having finished his in three months. As the success at the acting of a play does not depend so much on the style as on the plot and the actors' performance, it happened that both *Phèdres* seemed to share the same fate; but on the reading, their difference is easily perceived and their merits were soon settled in their upper classes. It was to no purpose that Pradon published, according to the custom of all bad authors, a very insolent preface in which he abuses the critics of his piece; notwithstanding the praises it received, from himself and from his cabal, it soon fell into that contempt

which it deserves, and had it not been for the *Phèdre* of Racine it would not now be known that Pradon writ one.

Yet what is the cause of this mighty difference between the two performances? The plot is pretty much the same in both plays; Phædra expires in each; Theseus is absent during the two first acts, and supposed to have traveled to hell with Pirithous; his son Hippolytus is resolved to quit Trezena in order to shun Aricia, whom he loves; he declares his passion to her, but is struck with horror at Phædra's love for him; he dies in the same manner, and his governor gives the same account of it. Besides the personages of both plays being in the same situation, talk pretty much to the same purport; but this is what best distinguishes the great man from the bad poet. The difference between Pradon and Racine is never so conspicuous as when their thoughts are most alike. Hippolytus' declaration to Aricia is a remarkable proof of this assertion. Racine makes Hippolytus speak in this manner:

Moi qui, contre l'amour fièrement révolté,
Aux fers de ses captifs ai longtemps insulté;
Qui, des faibles mortels déplorant les naufrages,
Pensais toujours du bord contempler les orages,
Asservi maintenant sous la commune loi,
Par quel trouble me vois-je emporté loin de moi;
Un moment a vaincu mon audace imprudente,
Cette ame si superbe est enfin dépendante.
Depuis près de six mois, honteux, désespéré,
Portant partout le trait dont je suis déchiré,
Contre vous, contre moi, vainement je m'éprouve.
Présente, je vous fuis; absente, je vous trouve;
Dans le fond des forêts votre image me suit;

1 Re-printed, complete, from the anonymous *Critical Essays on Dramatic Poetry by Monsieur de Voltaire* (London, 1761).— Ed.

La lumière du jour, les ombres de la nuit,
Tout retrace à mes yeux les charmes que j'évite;
Tout vous livre à l'envi le rebelle Hippolyte.
Moi-même, pour tout fruit de mes soins superflus,
Maintenant je me cherche, et ne me trouve plus;
Mon arc, mes javelots, mon char, tout m'importune;
Je ne me souviens plus des leçons de Neptune:
Mes seuls gémissements font retentir les bois,
Et mes coursiers oisifs ont oublié ma voix.

In Pradon's play, Hippolytus expresses himself in the following manner:

Assez et trop longtemps, d'une bouche profane,
Je méprisai l'amour, et j'adorai Diane;
Solitaire, farouche, on me voyait toujours
Chasser dans nos forêts les lions et les ours.
Mais un soin plus pressant m'occupe et m'embarrasse;
Depuis que vous vois, j'abandonne la chasse.
Elle fît autrefois mes plaisirs les plus doux,
Et quand j'y vais, ce n'est que pour penser à vous.

It is impossible to compare these two speeches without admiring the one, and laughing at the other. Yet the like thought and sentiments run through each; for when the passions are to be described, nearly the same ideas occur to everybody; but it is in the expression of them that the man of genius is easily discerned from the wit, and the poet from the scribbler.

To attain to M. Racine's perfection in writing, a man must be possessed of his genius, and take as much pains as he did in finishing his works. What apprehensions must I be then under, who, born with slender parts, and continually afflicted with diseases have neither an imagination to create many beauties, nor the liberty to correct my faults by constant labor and study. I am fully con-

vinced of the many errors in the intrigue of this play, as well as in the diction. I should have corrected some, if this edition could have been retarded; but many must still have remained. There are certain limits in every art which we cannot go beyond. We are stopped by the weakness of our own talents. We spy perfection at a distance, and make but vain efforts to attain it.

I shall not enter into any particular criticisms upon the play now published; my readers will do it sufficiently without my help. But I cannot avoid mentioning a general criticism that has been made on the choice of the subject. As it is in the genius of the French to place the most serious matters in the most ridiculous light, they said the story of this play was nothing more than " a bruitish yet amorous old man whose wife obstinately refuses to comply with his desires "; and added that domestic strife can never be a proper subject for a tragedy. I beg leave to offer a few reflections on this prejudiced opinion.

All tragic pieces are founded either on the interests of a nation, or on the particular interest of princes. Of the former kind are *Iphigenia in Aulis,* in which Greece assembled, demands the blood of the child of Agamemnon; the *Horace,* where three combatants have in their hands the fate of Rome; *Œdipus,* where the safety of the Thebans depends on the discovery of the murder of Laïus. Of the latter kind are *Britannicus, Phèdre, Mithridate,* and so forth.

In these three last pieces the whole interest is confined to the family of the hero who is represented. The whole depends on passions which are equally felt by all mankind, and the intrigue is as proper for comedy as for tragedy. Change only the names, and Mithridates is but an old man in love with a young girl, who is also passionately beloved by his two sons; and he makes use of a low stratagem to find out which of the two is his happy rival. Phædra is a mother-in-law who, emboldened by her confidant, discovers her passion to her son-in-law, who happens to be engaged elsewhere. Nero is an impetuous young man who becomes enamored of a sudden, resolves immediately to get a divorce from his wife, and hides behind some hangings to listen to his mistress's conversation. These are all subjects which Molière might have handled as well as Racine. And, in fact, the intrigue of *L'Avare* is exactly the same with that of *Mithridate*. Harpagon and the King of Pontus are two amorous old men; both have their sons for rivals; both contrive in the same manner to find out the correspondence that subsists between their son and mistress; and both plays conclude with the marriage of the young fellows.

Molière and Racine have equally succeeded in handling this subject: the one amuses and diverts, the other moves us with terror and compassion. Molière exposes the ridiculous fondness of an old miser; Racine describes the foibles of a great king, and makes them even venerable. Let a wedding be drawn by Watteau and Le Brun. One will represent peasants under an arbor full of genuine and unbounded joy, at a rustic meal, where reign immoderate laughter, riot and drunkenness; the other, on the contrary, will paint the nuptials of Thetis and Peleus, the festivals of gods, and their majestic joy; and both arrive at the perfection of their art by different roads.

We may apply these different examples to *Mariamne*. The ill-humor of a wife, the fondness of an old husband, the disturbances caused by a sister-in-law, are in themselves of little importance, and well-adapted to the comic scene. But a king whom all the world have agreed to call a great man, deeply enamored of the finest woman in the universe; the vehement passion of this sovereign, so famous for his virtues and for his crimes, for his former cruelties, and for his present remorse, this continual and rapid transition from love to hatred, from hatred back to love; the ambition of his sister; the intrigues of his ministers; the grievous situation of a princess whose beauty and virtues are still celebrated in the world, who saw her father and her brother condemned to death by her own husband, and to complete her misfortune, was beloved by the murderer of her family. What a vast field! What a scope for a man of happier parts than I have! Can such a subject be deemed unworthy of tragedy? It is in these instances that it can be truly said that things change their name according to the appearance they are placed in.

LETTER TO FATHER PORÉE, JESUIT[2]

[*Lettre au Père Porée, Jésuite*]

(In *Œdipe*, 1730)

·   ·   ·   ·   ·   ·

First I wish you to know, in order that I may justify myself, that although I was young when I wrote *Œdipe,* I wrote it practically as you see it to-day: I was full-fed after having read the ancients and after receiving my lessons from you, and I knew very little about the theater of Paris; I worked, therefore, as I might have worked had I been in ancient Athens. I consulted M. Dacier, who knew the ground, and he advised me to put a chorus in every scene, after the manner of the Greeks; but this was as bad as advising me to walk about the streets of Paris in Plato's robe. And I had considerable trouble even in persuading the actors there to include the

2 Translated, with omissions, by the Editor. — Ed.

three or four choruses which I did put in; and I had more trouble in getting a tragedy accepted which contained practically no love interest. . . . No matter how many books are written on the technique of painting by those who know their subject, not one of them will afford as much instruction to the pupil as will the sight of a single head of Raphael.

The principles of all the arts, which depend upon imagination, are simple and easy; they are based upon nature and reason. Your Pradons and Boyers knew these rules as well as Racine and Corneille: the only difference — the only difference there ever will be — lying in the application of the rules. The authors of *Armide* and of *Issé,* and the worst of composers, worked according to the same musical rules. Poussin worked by the same principles as did Vignon. It would seem quite as superfluous to speak of rules in the preface to a tragedy, as it would be for a painter to prepare his public beforehand with a dissertation on painting, or a composer try to prove why his music ought to be pleasing.

But since M. de La Motte is seeking to establish laws running counter to those which have guided our great masters, it will not be amiss to defend these ancient rules, not because they are ancient, but because they are good and necessary, and because they might find, in a man of M. de La Motte's merit, a formidable adversary.

The Three Unities

M. de La Motte would first do away with the unities of action, of place, and of time.

The French were among the first of the modern nations to revive these wise rules of the drama: the other nations long remained unwilling to submit to a yoke which seemed so irksome; but as the yoke was necessary, and as reason always triumphs in the end, they all submitted. And nowadays, in England, certain dramatists have informed the audience before the play begins that the duration of the action is identical with that of its representation on the stage: they go beyond even us, who in that respect were their preceptors. All nations are beginning to consider as barbarous those ages when the rules were ignored by the greatest geniuses, such as Lope de Vega and Shakespeare; these nations even acknowledge their obligation to us for having brought the rules out of that state of barbarism. Should, therefore, a Frenchman make use of all his intelligence to lead us back to that primitive state? . . .

What is a play? The representation of an action. Why of one action only, and not of two or three? Because the human brain cannot focus its attention upon several objects at the same time; because the interest which is dispersed when there is more than one action, soon disappears; because we are shocked to observe two events in the same picture; because, finally, nature herself has given

us this precept, which ought to be like her, immutable.

For the same reason, unity of place is essential: a single action obviously cannot transpire in several places at once. If the characters which I see are at Athens in the first act, how can they be in Persia in the second? Did M. Le Brun paint Alexander at Arbela and in the Indies on the same canvas? "I should not be surprised," says M. de La Motte very cleverly, "to see an intelligent nation, but one which is less inclined toward an observance of the rules, accepting Coriolanus, condemned at Rome in the first act, received by the Volsci in the third, and besieging Rome in the fourth," and so on. To begin with, I cannot imagine an intelligent and enlightened nation *not* inclined toward an observance of the rules, which are based upon good sense, and made in order to enhance our pleasure. In the second place, is it not clear in the instance cited above, that there are three different tragedies? and even if these were written in beautiful literary style, would they ever amount to more than one of those plays à la Jodelle or Hardy, versified by a clever modern?

Unity of time naturally goes hand in hand with the other two unities. And here, I believe, is an obvious proof. I see a tragedy: that is, the representation of an action. The subject is concerned with the working-out of that action alone. There is a conspiracy against Augustus in Rome; I wish to know what will happen to Augustus and the conspirators. If the poet makes the action last fifteen days, he must account for what passes during these fifteen days, because I am in the theater to learn what happens: nothing superfluous *must* happen. Now, if he causes to pass before my eyes the events of fifteen days, there will be at least fifteen different actions, no matter how small and unimportant they may be. It is not in this case merely the bringing to a head of this conspiracy toward which the poet must quickly lead his play: he must of necessity drag out his story until it no longer interests and is no longer living. All these things are very far from the decisive moment which I am waiting for. I do not come in order to learn the whole history of the hero, I come only to see a single happening in his life. Further, the spectator is in the theater only three hours: therefore the action must not last longer than three hours. The action in *Cinna, Andromaque, Bajazet,* in *Œdipe* — whether it be in that of the great Corneille, or of M. de La Mòtte, or of my own, if I may refer to it — lasts no longer. If other plays perchance require more time, the liberty can be allowed only where the play makes up for the loss in compensating beauties. The greater the liberty, the more open it is to censure.

We often extend the limit of unity of time to twenty-four hours, and that of unity of place to the walls of a whole palace. A greater severity than this would sometimes render some beautiful subjects impracticable, while greater liberty might open the way to greater abuses. For were it once established that the action of a play could extend over a period of two days, it would not be long before one poet would take two weeks, and another two years; and if the unity of place were not limited to a comparatively confined space, we should soon see plays like the old *Julius Cæsar* of the English, where Cassius and Brutus are in Rome in the first act, and in Thessaly in the fifth.

An observance of these laws not only prevents faults, but even leads the poet to true beauty, just as the rules observed in the best sort of architecture must of necessity result in a building that is sure to please the eye. It is seen, therefore, that with unity of time, action, and place, it is difficult to write a play which shall not be simple. This is the great merit of M. Racine's plays; this was demanded by Aristotle. M. de La Motte, in defending one of his own tragedies, prefers to this noble simplicity, a large number of events, and he believes that his idea is authoritative because *Bérénice* is not well thought of, and *Le Cid* is. It is true that *Le Cid* is more touching than *Bérénice;* but *Bérénice* is open to

censure only because it is rather an elegy than a simple tragedy; and *Le Cid,* the action of which is truly tragic, surely does not owe its success to a multiplicity of events. It pleases in spite of this; it touches, in spite of the Infante, and not because of the Infante.

M. de La Motte believes that one can rise above the rules by observing a unity of interest, which he claims to have invented and which he calls a paradox, but this unity of interest seems to me to be no other than unity of action. "If many characters," he says, "are in one way and another interested in the same event, and if they all deserve that I should interest myself in their passions, then there is unity of action, and not unity of interest."

Since I took the liberty of entering into a dispute with M. de La Motte on this little question, I have re-read the great Corneille's *Discours;* it were better to consult the great master than myself. This is what he says: "I maintain, and I have already said, that unity of action consists in unity of intrigue and in unity of peril." I refer the reader to this place in Corneille's *Discours;* let him decide between M. de La Motte and me. And if that authority is not great enough, have I not a more convincing argument? It is experience. Read our best French tragedies, and you will invariably find the principal characters in one way or another interested in the same event. But, it will be observed, these diverse interests are all connected with the principal character; this is unity of action. If, on the contrary, all these diverse interests are not connected with the principal character, if they are not strings tied together at the center, then the interest is two-fold: so is what is called action on the stage. Let us, therefore, together with the great Corneille, adhere to the three unities, within which the other rules — that is to say, the other beauties — are likewise to be found.

•   •   •   •   •   •

A DISCOURSE ON TRAGEDY [3]

[Discours sur la Tragédie, à Mylord Bolingbroke]

(Prefixed to Brutus, 1731)

. . . .

All these laws — not to fill the action with bloodshed, not to allow more than three characters to speak at the same time, and so on — are laws which, it seems to me, may have exceptions among us, as they did among the Greeks. There is a difference between the rules of decorum, which are always rather arbitrary, and those fundamental rules of the theater, which are the three unities: it would result only in feebleness and sterility to extend the action of a play beyond the proper time and place. Ask any one who has crowded too many events into his play, what the reason for this fault is: if he be honest, he will tell you that he lacked the inventive genius to fill his play with a single action; and if' he uses two days and two cities in which to conduct his story, believe me, he has done so because he was unable to condense it within the space of three hours and within the walls of a single palace, a proceeding which is demanded by probability. It is otherwise with the poet who would hazard portraying a horrible spectacle on the stage: he will not insult our sense of what is probable, and his boldness, far from being considered a weakness, demands on the contrary a great genius to put into the play, by means of his words, the veritable grandeur of the story which, without a sublime literary style, would be simply disgusting or atrocious.

This is what our great Corneille dared once to attempt, in his Rodogune. He shows us a mother who, in the presence of the court and an ambassador, tries to poison her son and daughter-in-law, after having killed her other son with her own hand. She presents to the two the poisoned drink; and on their refusing and showing that they suspect her, she swallows the draught herself, and dies of the poison which she had intended for them. Such incidents should be most sparingly used, and it is not every one who dares attempt them.

These novelties must be circumspectly introduced, and handled with great mastery. The English themselves admit that Shakespeare, for instance, was the only one among them who evoked ghosts and made them speak:

Within that magic circle none durst move but he.

The more majestic and fearful a dramatic action, the more insipid does it become when it is often repeated; something like the details of battles which, while in themselves they are most terrible, become cold and tiresome, as a result of being told again and again in histories. The only play in which M. Racine has made use of this sort of spectacular scene is *Athalie*. In this play we see a child on a throne; its nurse and the priests stand about; a queen commands the soldiers to murder it; and the armed Levites come to the rescue. This is dramatic pathos; and if the style were not written to match, the whole would be puerile.

The more the dramatist wishes to appeal to the eye with striking scenes of this sort, the greater becomes the necessity to saying sublime things; otherwise he will be but a decorator, and not a tragic poet. Nearly thirty years ago the tragedy of *Montézume* was produced at Paris; the scene disclosed was something of a novelty: a palace of magnificent and barbaric splendor. Montezuma himself wore an extraordinary costume; slaves armed with arrows stood at the back of the stage. About Montezuma were eight grandees of the court, their faces bowed to the ground. Montezuma opened the play with these words which were addressed to them:

Levez-vous; votre roi vous permet aujourd'hui
Et de l'envisager et de parler à lui.

The scene charmed the audience: but this was the only beautiful thing in the tragedy.

---

[3] Translated, with omissions by the Editor. Ed.

For my part, I confess that it was not without some trepidation that I introduced to the French public the Roman Senate, in red robes, each member giving his vote. I remember that formerly when I introduced in my *Œdipe* a chorus of Thebans who said:

O mort, nous implorons ton funeste se-
cours!
O mort, viens nous sauver, viens terminer
nos jours!

the parterre, instead of being affected by the pathos which these lines should have contained, felt at first merely the ridiculous side: that is, that such words had been given to actors who were little accustomed to speak the lines — and they burst out laughing. This is what deterred me, in *Brutus,* from having the senators speak when Titus is accused in their presence, and increasing the terror of the situation, by having these fathers of Rome express their sorrow and surprise, which they would undoubtedly have done, and otherwise than by mere gesture; although they were not permitted even this.

The English dramatists have more action in their plays than we have; they speak more directly. The French aim rather at elegance, harmony, style. It is certainly more difficult to write well than to fill the play with murders, wheels, gibbets, sorcerers, and ghosts. The tragedy of *Cato,* which does such great honor to M. Addison, your successor in the ministry; this tragedy, I say, the only one your nation has produced which is well written from beginning to end — you yourself have said it — owes its great reputation to no other element than its beautiful lines, its vigorous and true thoughts, expressed in harmonious verse. It is the minor details which bolster up verse plays, and preserve them for future generations. Often the unusual way of saying ordinary things, and the art of embellishing by literary style what all men think and feel — these are what make great poets. There are neither out-of-the-way sentiments nor romantic adventures in the fourth book of Vergil; everything is natural: it is the great effort of a human mind. M. Racine stands above

others not because he has said the same things as he has, but because he has said them better than they. Corneille is not truly great except when he expresses himself as well as he thinks. Let us bear in mind the precept of Despréaux:

Et que tout ce qu'il dit, facile à retenir,
De son ouvrage en nous laisse un long
souvenir.

This precept is quite neglected in a great many of our plays, which, however, by the art of the actor, and the figure and voice of the actress, have been accepted on our stage. How many more badly-written plays are produced than *Cinna* and *Britannicus,* and yet no one ever retained two lines of such wretched compositions, while entire scenes of the other two are frequently memorized. In vain did the *Régulus* of Pradon draw tears from the audience by means of some affecting incidents; that work, and all which resembled it, are now fallen into contempt, in spite of the self-applause lavished by the authors in their prefaces.

Some judicious critics may ask why I have introduced love into a tragedy which bears the name of *Junius Brutus?* Why I have mingled that passion with the rigid virtue of a Roman senator, and the political intrigues of an ambassador?

Our nation has been reproached for having enfeebled the tragic stage by too much tenderness; and the English have merited the same accusation for nearly a century; for you have always found our fashions and faults somewhat contagious. But will you allow me to give you my opinion on this matter?

To expect love in every tragedy seems to me to argue an effeminate taste, while always to proscribe it, shows a contemptuous and unreasonable captiousness.

The stage, whether occupied by tragedy or comedy, exhibits a living picture of the human passions. In the first is represented the ambition of a prince; the object of the latter is to ridicule the vanity of the middle-class parvenu. Here we laugh at the coquetry of a citizen's wife; there we weep over the unhappy passion of Phædra. In like manner, love amuses us in romance, and transports us in the Dido of Vergil.

Love is not more essentially a fault in tragedy than it is in the *Æneid*. It is open to censure only when it is dragged in out of season, and conducted without art. . . .

That love may be deserving of a place in tragedy it must have a necessary connection with the whole piece and not be arbitrarily introduced to fill up gaps, as it does in your tragedies as well as in our own, all of which are too long. It should in reality be a tragic passion, considered as a weakness, and opposed and contrasted by remorse. It should either lead to misfortune and crime, to convince us of its perils; or else virtue should triumph over it, to show that it is not invincible. Treated in any other way, love is of the same nature as that which is the subject of pastorals or comedies.

* * * * * *

DENIS DIDEROT

Denis Diderot was born at Langres in 1713, of lower middle-class parents. At the age of eight he was sent to school in his native town under the Jesuits, with a view to entering the church. He continued his studies at the College d'Harcourt in Paris, and afterward went into a law office, where he remained for two years. His chief occupation, however, was study — mathematics, Latin and Greek, and modern languages. At this time Denis' father stopped the youth's allowance and demanded that he accept some sort of position, or return home. Denis left the law office, however, and lived in an attic, giving lessons. This life lasted for ten years, during which the father refused to help his son. But his strangely inquisitive and philosophical nature was not such as to bring him financial success, and he was forced to turn his hand to the humblest sort of hack-work: translating, writing sermons to order, and the like. He even resorted to dishonest methods to secure money from a priest who wished to help him enter a monastery. However, he was sufficiently sure of himself in 1743 to think of marriage, and accordingly in that year he married Toinette Champion. The couple lived for some time on the little Denis could make by writing, and on the savings of his wife. When Denis' parents heard of their son's marriage, Denis sent his wife home to them. They were so pleased with her, that when she returned to Paris three months later, parents and son became reconciled, and Denis was enabled to devote his efforts to his own work. The family life of the young couple was not happy; it was rendered worse, indeed, by the continual demands for money from Diderot's mistress, and it was in order to make this money that he translated various works and wrote his *Pensées philosophiques*, the *Lettre sur les aveugles*, and *Les Bijoux indiscrets*. He was meantime collecting material for the *Encyclopédie*, the "privilege" for which was granted in 1746. For many years Diderot was constantly opposed in this work, interference coming from the court, the church, and the Academy. His opponents managed to send him to prison at Vincennes in 1749. It was there that Rousseau visited him and the two became friends. Toward the end of the year, Diderot was released, and the first volume of the *Encyclopédie* was published — in 1751. Opposition continued, and after the publication of the sixth volume, the publishers were forbidden to issue any more of it. At this time, Diderot was busy with his plays. In 1757 he published *Le Fils naturel*, together with the famous *Dorval et Moi* dialogues evolving the author's ideas on the drama. *Le Père de famille* appeared the following year, accompanied by the long essay *De la Poésie dramatique*. As a result of the persecution of the editors of the *Encyclopédie*, d'Alembert left the editorial staff, and Diderot was forced to continue the work under very discouraging auspices. In 1765 further volumes of the work were distributed to subscribers. Diderot was so poor that he was on the point of selling his private library when Catherine II, informed of the author's poverty, bought the library, gave Diderot the use of it during his life, and added a generous pension. In 1772 he married off his daughter, and started traveling with his friend Falconet the next year. He visited St. Petersburg, where he was well received by the Empress. He returned to Paris in 1774. His health was undermined, but he persevered with his work, a great part of which was not published during his life-time. He died at Paris in 1784.

At his death Diderot left thirty-three volumes of MSS., which were forwarded to Russia with his library. A great part of his work was only recently published, while some of his novels and other works were translated into German from the MSS., and translated back into French before the French originals were printed. Of the three or four editions of Diderot published prior to the last half of the nineteenth century, not one contains more than a part of his characteristic work; hence the difficulty, until recent years, of arriving at a true critical evaluation of his work. In his day Diderot was best-known as editor of the *Encyclopédie;* the greater part of his work was published either anonymously or remained in manuscript. He was above all an enthusiast; no matter what subject he attacked, he was able to make it interesting. If his own plays are feeble and over-sentimental, his theories are in part sound. He demanded a return to nature, and sounded the call against what was false in the classic ideal. The age was ready for him. His influence was felt principally in Germany — through Lessing and Goethe — though Beaumarchais in France developed his ideas with greater clarity.

ON DRAMATIC POETRY [1]

[De la Poésie dramatique à monsieur Grimm]

(1758)

. . . . Vice cotis acutum
Reddere quae ferrum valet, exsors ipsa
*   secundi.*
        HORAT. *de Arte poet.,* v. 348.

I. OF THE VARIOUS KINDS OF DRAMA

If to a nation which had known only one sort of play — light and pleasing comedy — one were to propose another, serious and touching, have you any idea what it would think of it, my friend? Unless I am very much mistaken, the intelligent people, after having conceived it as a possibility, would not fail to say: " But of what use is this new form? Does not life give us enough real troubles without our inventing additional, imaginary ones? Why allow sadness to creep into the world, even of our amusements? " The remark of one who knows not the pleasure of being touched and giving way to tears.

We are the slaves of custom. Let a man with a spark of genius appear in our midst with a new work. First of all he dazzles us and causes discord among the thinking minds; gradually he gathers them together; soon after, imitations follow; they are studied; rules are formulated, art is born again, and limits fixed to it, and it is maintained that everything that does not fall within the scope of these limits is bizarre and bad: they are veritable Pillars of Hercules, beyond which none can venture but at his peril.

Nothing can prevail against the true. The evil perishes in spite of the praise of imbecility; and the good remains in spite of uncertainty and the tongue of envy. The sad part of it all is that men never obtain justice until they are gone. Only after having tormented the life out of a man does the public deign to strew a few faded flowers on his tomb. What can be done then? Either stand still, or else bow down before a law to which our betters have been forced to submit. Woe to him who produces, unless his work be the fruit of love, and unless he be content with scant praise! The number of good judges is limited. Oh, my friend, when I have published something, the sketch of a play, a philosophical idea, some bit of literature of morality —

1 Translated, for the first time, with omissions, by the Editor.—Ed.

for my mind is rested by variety — I shall come to see you. If my presence be not distasteful to you, if you appear satisfied with me, I shall patiently wait until justice — which time invariably brings — has given my work the appreciation it deserves.

If one type of art exists, it is difficult to introduce another. And suppose the new type is introduced? We have another prejudice, for before long it will be thought that the two types are closely akin to each other.

Zeno denied the existence of movement. By way of refutation, his adversary Diogenes the Cynic started to walk; and even had he been able only to limp, he would have made the same answer!

Likewise, in *Le Fils naturel*, I tried to give the idea of a drama which should stand somewhere between comedy and tragedy.

Le Père de famille, which I promised at the same time, and which continual distractions have hindered my completing, stands somewhere between the *Serious Drama* [*genre sérieux*], and comedy.

And if ever I have the time and the courage, I hope to write a play between the Serious Drama and the tragedy.

Whether these works be considered worthy or not, they will at least indicate that the gap I have observed between the two accepted types is not merely a matter of imagination.

II. OF SERIOUS COMEDY

Here is the whole field of drama: the gay comedy whose purpose it is to ridicule and chastise vice; Serious comedy, whose office it is to depict virtue and the duties of man; that sort of tragedy which is concerned with our domestic troubles; and, finally, the sort of tragedy which is concerned with public catastrophes and the misfortunes of the great.

Who now will give us powerful portrayals of the duties of man? What is demanded of the poet who takes unto himself such a task?

He must be a philosopher who has looked into his own mind and soul, he must know human nature, he must be a student of the social system, and know well its functions and importance, its advantages and its disadvantages.

"But how," it will be asked, "can all that has to do with the condition of man be compressed within the rigid limits of a play? Where is to be found the intrigue that can carry such a subject? Will the result be merely what we call an episodic comedy [*pièce à tiroir*], one disjointed scene following another? Or, at least, if there be an intrigue, can it do other than merely wind in and out of the action? There can be no unity, little action, and no interest. Each scene will of course conform to the two important points so strongly advised by Horace, but there will be no unity of effect: the whole will be without consistency and without life."

First, if the condition of man has ever furnished us a play like *Les Fâcheux* of Molière, for example, we have won at least one point; but I adhere to the belief that we can produce other such plays. The obligations and inconveniences of one's station in life are not of equal importance. I see no reason why we should not adhere to the chief problems, making them the basis of our plays, throwing details to the winds. This is precisely what I tried to do in *Le Père de famille*, where the social position of the son and that of the daughter are the two principal points. Fortune, birth, education, the duties of fathers toward their children, of the children toward their parents, marriage, celibacy — every problem arising in connection with the existence of the father of a family, is brought out in my dialogue. Let another dramatist happen along, give him the talent which I lack, and see what he will do with my play.

All the objections made against this new type prove but one thing, that it is difficult to write. It is not the sort of play that a child can write: it demands an art, a knowledge, a gravity and power of intellect, which are very rarely at the command of a dramatist.

To judge well of any work of art, you must not compare it with another work. One of our foremost critics went astray on this point. He says: "The Ancients had no opera, therefore the operatic form is bad." A more careful or a better-informed critic would have said: "The Ancients had only one form of opera, therefore our tragedy is not good." If his logical faculties had been better developed, he would in all likelihood have reasoned in neither of the above fashions. Whether or not we have models from antiquity, makes no difference. There is one rule taking precedence over the others, and that is that the right sort of poet did not exist, otherwise how could the first poem be judged? Was it good because it pleased, or did it please because it was good?

The duties of man, as well as his follies and vices, offer a rich field to the dramatist, and Serious dramas will succeed everywhere, but more especially with a people whose manners and customs are corrupt. They will go to the theater in order to escape the evil-doers by whom they are surrounded in life; there will they find people with whom they would care to live; there they will see mankind as it really is, and they will become reconciled with it. Good people do exist, though they are rare. He who believes otherwise, stands self-convicted, and proves how unfortunate he is in his wife, his relatives, his friends and acquaintances. Some one said to me one day after he had read a book which was concerned with serious and good people, and which had given him intense pleasure: "It seems that I am alone." The book deserved the praise, but the man's friends surely not the imputation.

When you write, you must always keep virtue and virtuous people in mind. When I take my pen in hand, I think of you, my friend; and when I write, your image is constantly before me. I wish to please Sophie [Sophie Voland]. If you grant me an indulgent and sympathetic smile, if she sheds a tear, if you both love me a little more, I am sufficiently rewarded.

When I saw the scenes in which The Peasant appeared in Le Faux généreux, I said to myself: This will please every one, and will continue to please forever; it will cause the shedding of tears. The success of the play has confirmed my opinion. That episode is quite in the Serious and good [honnête et sérieux] style.

It may be said: "The example of a single good episode proves nothing. If you fail to break up the monotonous discourses of virtue by the introduction of a few ridiculous or forced characters, as every other dramatist does, I fear, no matter what you say of your new form, that you will give us nothing but a few cold and colorless scenes or tiresome and

lugubrious morality — a sort of sermon in dialogue."

Let us consider the elements of a drama, and see. Do you judge a play by its subject? In the Serious and good drama the subject is of no less importance than in the gay comedy, only it is treated more truthfully. By its characters? They can be as varied and as original; and besides, the dramatist must draw them with a surer and stronger hand. By the passions? The greater the interest, the stronger will the passions be. By the style? It will be more nervous, graver, more elevated, violent, more susceptible of what we term feeling [sentiment], without which no style appeals to the heart. By the absence of ridicule? As if human folly, exhibited in human action and speech, when it is suggested by a partly understood interest or through passion, were not the true object of ridicule!

Look at the best scenes in Terence; what is the style employed in the scenes where fathers and lovers are concerned?

If in Le Père de famille I have been unable to live up to the dignity of my subject, if the action leaves one cold and the passions furnish only moralizing discourses, if the character of the Father, of his Son, of Sophie, of the Commander, of Germeuil, and of Cécile lack comic vigor, is it the fault of the style of play I tried to write, or my own?

Suppose a dramatist decides to take a judge, his social position and environment, as the subject of a play; he introduces as interesting an intrigue as is necessary; the judge is forced as a result either of his position or his function to do something unworthy his high calling, bring dishonor upon himself or others, immolate himself upon the altar of his own passions, his tastes, his fortune, his birth, his wife and his children. Who will declare after such a play that the Serious and good play is without warmth, color, and power?

There is one method I have adopted of going about work, a successful one to which I turn whenever habit or novelty obscures my judgment — both produce this effect — and it is to seize the very thought of certain objects, transport them bodily from nature to my canvas, and examine them from a point where they are neither too far from me, nor too near.

Let us apply the method. Take two comedies, one of the *Serious* type, the other of the usual gay type. Let us make two galleries of pictures, scene by scene, and see through which we more willingly wander, and in which we experience the stronger and more agreeable sensations, and to which we are the readier to return.

To the Serious, I repeat, the Serious. It touches us more intimately than that which excites our disgust and our laughter. Oh, poet, art thou a creature of sensibility and refinement? Then touch this chord, you will hear it vibrate, and stir the souls of men.

" Is human nature good, then? "

Yes, my friend, very good. Water, air, earth, fire — everything is good in nature; and the whirlwind that rises up toward the end of autumn, blowing on forests and striking the trees one against the other, breaking and blowing away the dead branches; and the tempest, lashing the waves of the sea and purifying its waters; and the volcano that pours from its opened flank a stream of molten matter, casting up vapor that cleanses the atmosphere.

It is our miserable conventions that pervert and cramp mankind, not human nature. Now, what affects us more than the recital of a generous action? Who so low that he can listen unmoved to the plea of an upright man?

The theater is the only place where the tears of the virtuous man and the rogue are mingled. There the mean man regrets the injustices he has committed, feels sorry for the evil he has done, and is indignant toward a man of his own sort. But the impression is made, and it remains in the hearts of each of us, in spite of ourselves. The evil man leaves his seat less disposed to do evil than if he had listened to a severe and pitiless orator.

The poet, the novelist, the actor, appeal to the heart by indirect means; the effect produced depends upon the extent to which the heart is open to receive impressions. The unfortunate happenings which arouse my pity are, I admit, imaginary, but they touch me none the less. Every line of *L'Homme de qualité retiré du monde,* of the *Doyen de Killerine* and of *Cleveland,* arouses in me the greatest interest in the misfortunes to which virtue is exposed, and causes me to shed tears. What art could be more harmful than that which should make me an accomplice of evil men? But on the other hand, what art more precious than that which leads me, imperceptibly, to take an interest in the lot of the good man, taking me out of the quiet and soothing position I now enjoy, and forces me into the refuge where he has gone, to take part in the trials which it has pleased the poet to throw across his path in order to try his mettle?

How mankind would be benefited were all the arts of imitation to seek a common end, and come together with laws forcing us to love virtue and despise vice! It is the philosopher's place to invite them; he it is who must turn to the poet, the painter, the musician, and cry aloud: " Men of genius, why has heaven endowed you with gifts? " If the artists give heed to him, soon the images of debauchery covering our palace walls will disappear; our voices will no longer be the organs of crime; good taste and good customs and morals will gain inestimably. Do you think that the depiction of a blind couple, who have for years each sought the other until age has come upon them, and who finally, with tears in their eyes, clasp each other on the very verge of the grave, demands as much talent, and would move me more than the spectacle of the violent and novel passions to which the same couple would be subject in their youth?

III. OF A SORT OF MORAL DRAMA

Occasionally I imagine that the theater will be a place where the most important moral problems will be discussed without interfering with the swift and violent action of the play.

How to go about it? Arrange your play as you would under ordinary circumstances, just as the abdication of the Empire is arranged in *Cinna.* Thus will the poet manage questions of suicide, honor, duels, fortune, dignity, and so on. Thus our plays would assume added gravity, in case they should lack it. If a certain scene is necessary, if it is basically required, if it is announced and if the spectator wishes it, he will give all his attention to it, and be very differently affected than by those ambiguous and paradoxical maxims with which our modern plays are littered.

I don't want clever maxims on our stage, but impressions. He who says of a play, and quotes detached sentences by way of proof, that it is mediocre, is rarely mistaken. The greatest poet is he whose work remains long in our minds.

Oh, dramatists, the true applause which you seek is not the hand-clapping which follows a brilliant verse, it is rather that profound sigh which escapes from the depths of the soul after the constraint of long silence, the sigh that brings relief. But there is another impression to make, a more violent one, which you will readily understand if you are born to your art, if you are aware of its magic, and that is to make your audience feel ill at ease. Their minds will be troubled, uncertain, distracted, and your spectators be like those who in the presence of an earthquake see the walls of their homes rock, and feel the earth yawn before them.

IV. OF A SORT OF PHILOSOPHICAL DRAMA

There is a sort of play in which moral problems can be set forth successfully. Here is an example. Let us hear what our judges have to say of it; if they declare it cold, believe me, they have no strength of soul, no idea of true eloquence, no sensibility, no character. For my part, I believe that if a man of genius makes use of it, he will allow no eye a moment in which to become dry, and that we shall owe to him the most touching of spectacles, the most instructive and interesting book imaginable. The subject is the death of Socrates.

The scene is a prison. We see the philosopher lying on a bed of straw, in shackles. He is asleep. His friends have corrupted the guards, and they come at daybreak to announce to him the news of his deliverance.

All Athens is in an uproar, but the just man slumbers.

The innocence of his life! How sweet it is to have the consolation that one has lived uprightly when he is at the point of death! *First scene.*

Socrates awakes, and sees his friends. He is surprised to see them so early. Socrates' dream.

They tell him what they have done. He discusses with them what he had best do.

His self-respect and the sacredness of the laws. *Second scene.*

The guards arrive and take off his shackles.

The fable of pain and pleasure.

The Judges enter, and with them, Socrates' accusers with a crowd. He is accused, and defends himself.

The apology. *Third scene.*

. . . The accusations must be read, and Socrates must challenge the judges, his accusers, and the people. He must question them, and they must answer. You must show exactly how it all happened: the spectacle will be all the truer, more striking, and more beautiful.

The Judges retire, and Socrates' friends remain with him. They feel that their friend will be convicted. Socrates speaks with them and consoles them. On the immortality of the soul. *Fourth scene.*

He is convicted. His death-sentence is announced to him. He sees his wife and children. The hemlock is brought. He dies. *Fifth scene.*

This is only a single act, but if it be well done, it will attain to the dimensions, or nearly so, of an ordinary play. What eloquence is required! What profound philosophy! What truth to nature! What essential truth! If the dramatist realizes the firm, tranquil, serene and elevated character of the philosopher, he will readily see how difficult it is to represent him. At every moment he will draw a smile to the lips of the spectator, and a tear to the eye. I would die happy if I could write this play as I conceive it. Once again, if critics see in it merely a string of cold philosophical discourses, how I pity the poor wretches! How I pity them!

V. OF SIMPLE AND COMPLEX DRAMAS

For my part, I consider a passion, a well developed character, culminating in the exhibition of all his strength, much more important than that combination of incidents which goes to make up the tissue of a play in which the characters and audience are equally jostled and bandied about. That sort of thing is, it seems to me, foreign to good taste and grand effects. And yet this is what we call movement. The Ancients had another idea. A simple plot, an action taken up toward its end in order that everything should be heightened in its effect, a catastrophe invariably imminent, which is only kept back by a simple and true circumstance; strong passions; tableaux; one or two characters firmly drawn; and that was all. In order to move his audience, Sophocles required no more. Those who do not care to read the Ancients, will never know how much our Racine owes to old Homer.

Have you ever noticed, as I have, that no matter how complicated a play happened to be, there is hardly anyone who thinks about this after the première? You readily recall the events, but not the discourses, and once the situations are known, the complicated play loses its effect.

If a play were meant to be produced only once and never printed, I should say to the poet: "Complicate as much as you like; you will arouse the interest and emotions of your audience; but if you desire to be read and known to posterity, be simple."

One good scene contains more ideas than is possible in a whole play of incident; and it is to ideas that we return, that we listen to and never grow tired of; these affect us in every age. The scene of Roland in the cave waiting for the perfidious Angélique; Lusignan's words to his daughter, or those of Clytemnestra to Agamemnon, are always new to me.

And even were I to allow as many complications as possible, the play would contain only the same action. It is wellnigh impossible to conduct two intrigues simultaneously, unless one interests us at the expense of the other. How many examples I might cite in modern plays! But I have no desire to offend.

Where can we find a more ingenious interlacing of scenes than those in which Terence has woven the loves of Pamphila and Charinus in the *Andria?* And yet, has not the poet sacrificed something? Do we not feel that at the beginning of the second act we are starting a new play? And does the fifth act end as interestingly as it might?

He who undertakes to develop two intrigues at once labors under the necessity of unravelling them at the same moment. If the principal intrigue ends before the other, that other cannot stand alone; or if the subsidiary plot ends first, either the characters disappear, or else they are brought in again without sufficient motive, and the play is mutilated and leaves a frigid impression.

What would have happened to Terence's *Heautontimorumenos,* or *Self-Tormentor,* unless, by an effort of genius, the poet had been able to carry on again the story of Clinia which ends in the third act, and joined it with that of Clitiphon?

Terence took the intrigue of Menander's *Perinthia* and put it into his *Andria;* of the two simple plays he made one. I adopted the opposite course in *Le Fils naturel.* Goldoni made a three-act farce, using *L'Avare* of Molière and the characters of *The True Friend* [*Il vero amico*]. I separated these subjects and made a five-act play. Whether the result be good or bad, I am sure I was right in my method.

Terence maintains that in having doubled the subject of the *Heautontimorumenos,* his play was a new one. Possibly, but whether it was a *better* play, is another question.

If I can flatter myself for any reason in *Le Père de famille,* it is for having given Germeuil and Cécile a passion which they cannot avow during the early acts, and for having so subordinated that thread of interest to the passion of Saint-Albin for Sophie, that even after the declaration, Germeuil and Cécile cannot talk of their love, although they are constantly together.

There is no middle way: you will always lose in one place what you have gained in another. If you gain interest and rapidity by a number of incidents, you will have no discourses, for your characters will have no time to speak: they will merely act instead of develop. I speak from experience.

VI. OF THE BURLESQUE DRAMA

You cannot put too much action and movement into a farce. . . . Less in gay comedy, still less in Serious comedy, and almost none at all in tragedy.

The less true to life a type is, the easier the task of making it rapid in action, and "warm." You have heat at the expense of truth and what is beautiful in human nature. The most tedious thing imaginable is a burlesque and cold play. In the Serious Drama the choice of incidents renders warmth difficult to preserve.

And yet not every one can write a good farce. It requires an original sort of gayety: the characters are like the grotesques of Callot, in which the essential features of the human being must be preserved. Not every one can so twist his point of view. If you think there are many men more capable of writing *Pourceaugnacs* than *Misanthropes*, you are mistaken.

What was Aristophanes? An original writer of farces. An author of this sort ought to prove a great boon for any government that knows how to make use of him. The various enthusiasts who trouble society from time to time ought to be left to him. If they be exposed in the public places, prisons will not be needed.

Although the movement of a play varies according to the different types, the action progresses in the same manner with all; it never stops, even during the entr'actes. It is like a mass of rock set loose from a mountain-top, whose speed increases as it descends, bounding headlong past every obstacle.

If this comparison be just, if discourses decrease in inverse proportion to the action, the characters ought to speak a great deal at first and act a great deal toward the end.

VII. OF THE PLOT AND THE DIALOGUE

Is it more difficult to make a scenario [*établir le plan*] than to write dialogue? I have often heard the question argued, and it seemed to me that each one answered rather according to his own ability than to the facts.

A man who knows the world, speaks fluently, understands men after having studied them and listened to them — and who is able to write — finds it difficult work to plan his play.

Another, who can see things generally, who has given thought to the art of poetry and who knows the theater, whose experience and taste serve as guides toward situations that interest, and who knows how to combine events, will find it no difficult task to plan his play, but the individual scenes will give him trouble. He will be less satisfied with his own invention for the particular scenes, because he is well acquainted with the masterpieces of his own country as well as of Antiquity, and he cannot help comparing his work with that of the masters whose plays he knows so well. If he set to work on a long speech, he thinks of the *Andria;* of a scene full of passion, then of the *Eunuchus;* each play will give him ten examples for one he will himself think of.

None the less, genius is required for both elements; only the genius is not of the same sort. The plot is what holds a complicated play together; the speeches and the dialogue are what make people listen to and read a simple play.

Let me observe in passing that there are more well-written than well-constructed plays. The sort of talent which can arrange a series of incidents seems rarer than that which writes a true and natural speech. How many beautiful scenes there are in Molière! But you can soon count the artfully conducted dénouements.

A good plot is the fruit of the imagination; good dialogue comes from the observing of nature.

You can formulate any number of plots on the same subject and with the same characters; but, given the characters, there is only one way in which they may speak. These will say such and such things according to the situations in which you place them, but since they are always the same people, in any situation, they must be consistent.

One might almost say that a play ought to be the work of two men of genius, one of whom should make the plot, and the other write the dialogue. But who can write dialogue for another's plot? The talent for writing dialogue is not universal: each man ventures forth and does what he can. When he constructs his plot he seeks, unconsciously, the sort of situation which he can successfully handle. Change his situations, and it will seem to him that his talent has deserted him. One man can deal with comic situations; another with moral and serious ones; a third, with eloquence and pathos. Give Corneille one of Racine's plots, and Racine one of Corneille's, and see how each will succeed!

As my own character is a sensitive and straightforward one, I confess, my friend, that I have never felt the least trepidation in attacking a scene the success of which depended upon reason and honesty. These are weapons my parents taught me to use at an early age, and I have often wielded them against others, as well as myself!

You know how well at home I am in the art of the soliloquy. If I leave some social gathering and return home, sad and chagrined, I retire to my room and ask myself, What is the matter? Just bad humor? Yes.— Are you ill? No.— I then insist, and drag forth the truth. And it seems that I have a spirit which is gay, tranquil, honest, serene; this spirit interrogates another within me, which is ashamed of some folly it has committed and which it is afraid to admit. And yet the confession comes. If it be a folly I have committed — often the case — I absolve myself. If some one has wounded me — which likewise often happens when I am with people who wish to take advantage of my good nature — I forgive. Thus my sadness disappears; I join the family, a good husband, a good father, a good master,— at least so I imagine; and no one has to suffer the ill-humor which I might have inflicted upon every one who approached me.

I advise this sort of self-communion to every one who wishes to write: it will render him at the same time a better man and a better writer.

When I wish to construct a plot, I unconsciously seek out situations which can be handled by a man of my character and ability.

" Is this the best plot? "

So it seems to me.

" But to others? "

That is a different matter.

Listen to men and women, and talk with yourself: these are the two ways of learning the art of dialogue.

The requisites for constructing a good plot are: imagination, the ability to observe the course of events and the relations between them; the courage to develop long scenes, and to work hard; to attack a subject at the vital point; to be able to see exactly where your story begins, and know how much to relegate to the past, and to recognize the most affecting scenes for representation on the stage.

Above all, you must never jot down a single detail until your plot is definitely made out.

As the plot requires a vast amount of labor and meditation, what happens to those who possess some facility in the depiction of character? They have a general view of the subject; they know fairly well what the situations are to be; and they know their characters. The moment they say to themselves, This mother is to be a coquette, this father a strict man, this lover a libertine, this young girl tender and gentle, they are seized with a mad desire to write the scenes. They write and write; they express fine and delicate thoughts, even powerful ideas; they have charming ready-made fragments, but when the time comes for constructing the plot — and that time always comes — they vainly try to incorporate their charming fragments; they are never willing to relinquish this or that delicate or powerful bit, and consequently they do precisely what they ought not to do: make the plot fit the scenes, rather than the scenes the plot. And there will result a limited and cramped plot, which will extend even to the dialogue itself, much labor and time lost, and many fragments left over. Too bad, especially if the work is in verse!

I know a young poet, not devoid of talent, who has written over three or four thousand lines of a tragedy which remains unfinished, and which will never be complete.

VIII. OF THE FIRST SKETCH

Whether you write in verse or in prose, first make out your plot; after that, you may think of the scenes.

How shall we go about making the plot? There is a splendid suggestion in Aristotle on this point. It has helped me and it may help others. Here it is:

Among the great host of authors who have written on the art of poetry, three are particularly famous: Aristotle, Horace, and Boileau. Aristotle is a philosopher who proceeds in an orderly manner, establishes general principles, and allows his readers to draw their own conclusions and apply his theories. Horace is a man of genius who affects a disregard of order and, himself a poet, speaks of his kind. Boileau is a master who tries to give both precept and example.

Somewhere in Aristotle's *Poetics* it is said that Whether you work at a known or an unknown subject, you must begin by sketching the Fable; afterward you may think of the episodes or circumstances which are to develop it. Is it to be a tragedy? Suppose a young girl is conducted to an altar to be sacrificed; all at once she disappears, and is transported to a land where it is customary to offer strangers as a sacrifice to the presiding goddess. They make her a priestess. Some years after, the brother of the princess comes to the country where she is. He is seized by the inhabitants, and as he is about to be sacrificed by his sister, he cries out: "Is it not enough that my sister has been sacrificed, but must I also be?" Whereupon he is recognized and saved.

But why was the princess condemned to die on the altar?

Why are strangers sacrificed in the barbaric land where her brother finds her?

How was he captured?

He comes to obey an oracle. But why that oracle?

He is recognized by his sister. Was there no other method of being recognized?

All these points are outside the subject. But they must be supplied in the Fable.

The subject is common property, but the poet is at liberty to handle it as his fancy directs, and he who accomplishes his task in the most simple and *necessary* way will achieve the greatest success.

Aristotle's idea is applicable to every sort of play; this is how I make use of it.

A certain father has two children, a son and a daughter. The daughter is secretly in love with a young man who lives in the same house. The son is in love with an unknown woman whom he has seen in the neighborhood. He has tried to seduce her, but was unsuccessful. He disguises himself and lives next door to her under an assumed name. There he is taken for a man of the lower classes, engaged in some sort of mechanical work. He is hard at work all day long, and sees his beloved only in the evening. But the father, who is well aware of what happens in his house, finds out that his son is never at home at night. This sort of conduct, which forbodes irregularity, worries him. He waits for the son.

This is where the play begins.

What happens next? The girl is a suitable match for his son. At the same time, he learns that his daughter loves the man he had destined for her, and he consents to their engagement. Thus he brings about two marriages, in spite of his brother-in-law, who had other views on the subject.

But why does the daughter keep her love a secret?

Why does her lover live in the same house with her? What is he doing there? Who is he?

Who is the unknown sweetheart of the son? How did she fall to such a state of poverty?

Where does she come from? Born in the country, what brought her to Paris? And what keeps her there?

Who is the brother-in-law?

Whence comes his authority in the father's house?

Why is he opposed to the marriages which the father desires?

As the stage cannot represent two places at the same time, how can the unknown young woman enter the father's house?

How does the father discover the passion of his daughter and the young man living with him?

Why must he conceal his plans?

How does it come about that the unknown woman is acceptable in his eyes?

What obstacles does the brother-in-law bring to the father's notice?

How does the double marriage come to pass in spite of these obstacles?

How many things remain to be disposed of after the poet has made his preliminary sketch! But I have given you the story in his principal outlines. Now, the next task is to divide the story into acts, select what characters are required, determine how they are to be treated, and map out the subjects of each individual scene.

I can see that this sketch will be satisfactory to me, because the father, whose character I intend to bring into evidence, will be very unhappy. He will be opposed to his son's marriage; it will seem that his daughter is avoiding the marriage he wishes; and the proud reticence of each will prevent their confessing their true feelings in the matter.

The number of characters I shall use is decided.

I am no longer uncertain as to their attributes.

The father will behave in accordance with his station in life; he will be good, vigilant, firm, yet tender. Placed in the most difficult situation in life, his whole soul will be bared.

His son must be violent. The more unreasonable the passion, the less free does it become.

His mistress is never sufficiently amiable. I have made her an innocent child, respectable and sensitive.

The brother-in-law, who is my "villain," is a hard-headed and prejudiced man, uncompromising, feeble, mean, importunate, tricky, dishonest — a trouble in the house, a thorn in the side of the father and his children, and the aversion of every one.

Who is Germeuil? He is the son of a deceased friend of the father's; the friend's affairs having been left in a bad state, he has left the young man without a penny. The father took him in after the death of the friend, and brought him up as his own son.

Cécile, who believes that her father will never allow the young man to become her husband, always keeps him at a distance, and sometimes treats him harshly; Germeuil, who is repulsed by her behavior and fearing that he might fail in respect to the father, treats the daughter with the utmost formality; but in spite of the efforts of the young people, appearances are against them, and their passion develops — in word and deed — though at first it is scarcely perceptible.

Germeuil, then, will possess a firm, tranquil, and somewhat retiring character.

And Cécile will be proud, vivacious, reserved, and sensitive.

The dissimulation practiced by the young people deceives the father. Dissuaded from his original plan by the antipathy he believes to exist between the lovers, the father will not dare propose for a husband a young man for whom she seems to have so little liking, and who seems as distant toward her as she to him.

The father will say: "Is it not enough to torment my son by taking from him the woman he loves? Must I also try to force upon my daughter a man whom she does not love?"

And the daughter will answer: "Are not my father and uncle sufficiently worried about my brother? Ought I to increase their cares by confessing something which would shock every one?"

In this way, the Germeuil-daughter thread of interest is relegated to the background, and allows place for the development of the love of the son for his mistress, and develop the uncle's bad humor and the father's sorrow.

I shall have succeeded beyond my fondest hopes if I interest these two in the son's love-affair, and forget their own for the time being. The interest in their own will not run the risk of rivalling the other interest, but will rather make their own more interesting to themselves.

I intend that the father shall be the principal character. The preliminary sketch remains the same; the episodes only would have been changed had I chosen the son, the friend, or the uncle, as my hero.

IX. OF THE INCIDENTS

If the poet be possessed of imagination, and if he adheres to his sketch, he will vitalize it and see a whole legion of incidents spring from it, finding it difficult only to make his choice from among them.

He must be rigid upon this point when the subject he treats is serious. Nowadays, we would not accept a scene where a father puts to flight a pedant with a mule-bell, or where a husband hides under a table in order to hear his wife's conversation. These incidents belong to farce.

If a young princess is led to an altar where she is to be sacrificed, we cannot but think that such a fatal situation is due to a mistake on the part of a messenger who has failed to arrive.

"Does not the fate which makes playthings of us all bring forth the greatest events from the smallest causes?"

True. But the poet ought not to imitate fate in this respect: he will make use of the incident, if it be furnished by history, but not invent it. I will judge his methods more severely than the conduct of the gods.

He must be scrupulous in the choice of his incidents and restrained in the use of them; he must make them proportionate to the importance of his story, and establish the necessary connection between them.

"The more obscure and feeble the means by which the will of the gods is exercised upon men, the greater the fear inspired in me for their lot."

I agree. But I must be made certain of what that will is — not of the poet, but the gods.

Tragedy demands dignity in the method; comedy, delicacy.

Is a jealous lover uncertain of the feelings of his beloved? In such a scene, Terence brings a Davus upon the stage to listen to the lover's discourse, and will repeat it later to his master. We French insist that the poet shall know more.

A vain and foolish old man changes his middle-class name, Arnolphe, to that of M. de La Souche; this ingenious trick is the basis of all the intrigue, and brings about the dénouement in a simple and unexpected way. The audience exclaims "Marvelous!" and they are right. But if, without the least semblance to truth, they are shown Arnolphe as the confidant of his rival and the dupe of his pupil five or six times in succession — going from Horace to Agnès and then from Agnès to Horace again — they will say, "This is no play, but a fairy-tale," and if you have not all the wit, cleverness and genius of a Molière, they will accuse you of want of invention, and say "It is a fairy-tale that will put you to sleep."

If you have few incidents, you will have few characters. Never introduce a superfluous character; and have the connecting links between your scenes invisible.

Above all, never introduce a thread that leads nowhere; if you interest me in a situation which is not developed you will scatter my attention.

An example of this, if I am not mistaken, is the Frosine incident in *L'Avare*. She attempts to dissuade the Miser from marrying Marianne, by speaking of a certain Viscountess de Basse-Bretagne, of whom she promises marvels — and the audience expects these. And yet the play ends without our seeing more of Frosine or the Viscountess, both of whom we have been waiting for.

X. OF THE PLOT IN TRAGEDY AND COMEDY

What a play it would be whose plot was open to no criticism! Is there such a play? The more complicated it is, the less true to life. I have been asked whether the plot of tragedy or of comedy be more difficult.

There are three kinds of subjects. History, which is a matter of facts; tragedy, where the poet adds to history whatever elements of interest he can; and comedy, where the poet invents everything.

Wherefore it is concluded that the comic writer is the greatest. He it is who creates. In his sphere he is what the supreme Being is in nature. He creates, snatching from the great generality of things; but with this difference, that in nature we see only a vast succession of events the causes of which are unknown to us, whereas the march of events in a play are revealed to us, or if the poet conceals a sufficient number of causes for a while, he finally initiates us into his secrets and satisfies our curiosity.

"But if comedy be an imitation of nature in all its aspects, must not the poet adhere to his model when he constructs his plot?"

Undoubtedly.

"Then what is his model?"

Before answering this, I shall ask what a plot is.

"A plot is an interesting story, constructed according to the rules of dramatic form, which is in part the invention of the tragic poet and altogether that of the comic poet."

Very well. What is the basis of dramatic art?

"Historic art."

Nothing can be more reasonable. Poetry has been compared with painting; very good, but a better comparison would be that between history and poetry. Thus we are enabled to form a more exact notion of the true, the likely, and the possible, and a clear idea of the interesting and the marvelous — which belong to all kinds of drama, and which few poets are able to define.

Every historic event is not fit material

for tragedy, nor every domestic event for comedy. The Ancients limited the subjects of their tragedies to the stories of the families of Alcmæon, Œdipus, Orestes, Meleager, Thyestes, Telephus and Hercules.

Horace is opposed to the dramatist's putting upon the stage a character who snatches a living child from the womb of Lamia. If he is shown something of that sort, he can neither believe it possible nor bear to see it represented. But exactly where shall we draw the line between such incredible incidents and those which are credible? How far can the poet venture?

There sometimes occurs in the natural order of things an extraordinary chain of incidents. It is this same order that distinguishes the marvelous from the miraculous. The rare cases are marvelous; those which are naturally impossible are miraculous. Dramatic art rejects miracles.

If nature never brought about situations of an extraordinary sort, then everything imagined by the poet outside the simple and cold uniformity about him would be unbelievable. But this is not the case. What does the poet do? He either uses the extraordinary combinations which he finds in nature, or else he invents them. But, in place of the relation of cause and effect which often escapes our notice in nature, and which, owing to our want of knowledge often seems like a fatal association of circumstances, the poet insists that throughout his work there be a visible and credible relation, and in this respect his work is less true, but more natural and true to life, than that of the historian.

" But if the mere coexistence of events is sufficient to produce the marvelous in history, why is not the poet satisfied with this? "

Sometimes he is, the tragic poet especially. But the assumption of simultaneous incidents is not always allowed to the comic poet.

" Why? "

Because the known portion which the tragic poet borrows from history makes us accept the imaginative part as if it were history. The part he invents is given a verisimiltude from the historic part. But nothing is given to the comic poet; therefore he is less able to rely upon extraordinary combinations of events. Furthermore, fate and the will of the gods, which inspire terror in the hearts of men whose destiny is in the hands of superior beings before whom they are helpless, which follows them and strikes them the moment they believe themselves secure — this is more necessary to tragedy. If there is anything sad in life, it is the spectacle of a man rendered guilty and unhappy in spite of himself.

In comedy men must play the rôle which gods play in tragedy. Fate is the basis of tragedy; human malignity that of comedy.

" And what is this veneer of romance which is decried in some of our plays? "

A play is romantic when the marvelous is caused by coincidence: if we see gods or men too malignant; if events and characters differ too greatly from what experience and history lead us to expect; and above all, if the relation of cause and effect is too complicated or extraordinary.

Whence, one may conclude that the novel from which one cannot make a good play is not for that reason bad; but on the other hand, there is no good play from which an excellent novel cannot be made. It is merely a matter of technical rules that differentiates the novel from the play.

Illusion is the end of both, but upon what does the illusion depend? On circumstances. It is these which make illusion more or less difficult.

Will you allow me to speak the language of geometry? You know what the geometrician calls an equation. Illusion stands to one side. It is an invariable quantity, equal to a sum of terms — some positive, others negative — whose number and possibility of combination can be varied in endless ways, but the total value of which is always the same. The positive terms represent ordinary circumstances and situations; the negatives, the extraordinary. One sort is compensated for by the others.

Illusion is not voluntary. The poet who says, I wish to create an illusion, is like the man who says, I have a certain experience of life to which I shall pay no attention.

When I say that an illusion is an invariable quantity, I mean to a man who judges of various productions, and not to various men. There are probably no two human beings in the world possessing the same measure of certainty, and yet the poet is forced to create an illusion for every one! The poet takes advantage of the reason and the experience of an experienced man, just as a governess takes advantage of the stupidity of a child. A good poem is a story worthy of being told to sensible men.

The novelist has the time and space which are denied the dramatist; everything else being equal, therefore, I have more admiration for a play than for a novel. There is no difficulty which cannot be avoided by the former. He will say: *"La douce vapeur du sommeil,"* etc. [a short passage from Fénelon's *Télémaque*, Book VII]. This is how the novelist extricates himself. But, no matter what the difficulty of writing this speech, the dramatist would have been forced either to change his plot completely, or else surmount the difficulty. What difference there is in the methods of painting, and producing an effect on the stage!

The Ancients possessed tragedies in which the plots were entirely the invention of the poet. History did not even furnish the names of the characters. But what difference does this make, provided the poet keeps within the limits of the marvelous? . . .

XI. OF INTEREST

In complicated plays, interest is the result rather of the plot than of the speeches; in simple plays, on the other hand, it is rather the speeches than the plot that arouse interest. But in whom is the interest to be aroused? In the characters, or in the minds of the audience?

The spectators are merely ignorant witnesses of what passes.

"Then must one keep the characters in mind and interest them?" . . .

The more I think of the drama, the more vexed I am with those who have written about it. The drama is a tissue of particular laws, from which the critics have deduced general precepts. It has been noticed that certain incidents produce great effects; and immediately it becomes a rule that all poets shall resort to the same means in order to produce like results. Now, if one had examined a little more closely, he would have seen that still greater effects might have been produced by entirely opposite means. Thus has the art of the drama become surcharged with rules; and the dramatists, in servilely subjecting themselves to them, have often gone to much pain and done less well than they might have done.

If it were only understood that, although a drama is made to be produced, it was still necessary that both author and actor forget the spectator, and that all the interest should be centered in the characters, there would be less reading of Poetics. If you do this or that, you will produce this or that effect on the spectator. They should say: If you do this or that, this is what will happen to your characters.

Those who have written on the drama are like a man who, trying to sow trouble in a family, thinks rather of what the neighbors will say, than of what ill he can bring upon the family. Never mind the neighbors, but put your characters into action and rest assured that they will suffer nothing that the others will escape.

From other models, other rules. Perhaps it may be said: let your outcome be known, and soon, and let your audience be in continual suspense anticipating the light which will be shed on all the characters — as to what they have been doing and as to what they are.

If it is necessary to arouse interest in a play toward the end, this process seems as good to me as the opposite. Ignorance and perplexity excite curiosity in the mind of the audience and keep them aroused; but it is rather the things that are known and invariably expected which trouble and move them. This means is absolutely certain to keep the catastrophe always before the audience.

If, instead of taking part with his characters and allowing the audience to take care of themselves, the poet steps down from the stage into the parterre, he will harm his plot. He will do as those painters who, instead of keeping closely to nature, lose sight of it and have recourse to pure technique, and fail to present her to me as she is and as they see her, but try to depict her relatively, by means of ordinary tricks of the trade.

Are not all points in space variously lighted? Are they not separate? Do they not go hither and thither in an arid and flat plain, as in the most varied of landscapes? If you imitate such a painter, your drama will be like his picture: he will have a few fine spots, and your play a few splendid moments, but this is not the point: the picture must be beautiful from end to end of the canvas, and your drama from start to finish.

And what will become of the actor, if you concentrate upon the audience? Do you imagine he will feel any more than what you have given him? If you think of the audience, he will think of them, too. You seek their applause; so will he. And then what will become of your illusion?

I have said that the actor performs badly what the poet wrote for the audience, and that if the parterre acted, they would say to the characters on the stage: "Whom do you blame? I am not one of you. Do I meddle in your affairs? Go home," and if the author played his part, he would have come forth from behind the scenes and answered the parterre: "I beg your pardon, Messieurs, it is my fault. 1 shall do better another time, and so will the character."

Whether you write or act, think no more of the audience than if it had never existed. Imagine a huge wall across the front of the stage, separating you from the audience, and behave exactly as if the curtain had never risen.

"But the Miser who has lost his chest asks the audience: Messieurs, is not the thief among you?"

Never mind that author. The exception taken from the work of a genius proves nothing against commonsense. Tell me whether you can speak to your audience without stopping the action, and whether the least you will have done in thus directing your attention to it, does not result in a number of lapses throughout your play, and a general loosening of its fabric?

I agree that a dramatist may introduce points in his play which the spectator may apply to himself; let him ridicule people, and predominant vices, and public events; let him instruct and please, provided he does not think about it. If the audience detects his purpose, he will fail to achieve it; he ceases to write drama, and only preaches.

.   .   .   .   .   .

BEAUMARCHAIS

Pierre-Augustin Caron was born at Paris in 1732. His father was a clock-maker, and intended that his son should follow the same profession. His early life seems to have been happily spent. He was sent to a sort of technical school at Alfort, and then brought back again at the age of thirteen to work in his father's shop. The young man, with his indomitable spirit and love of adventure, displeased the father, who sent him away, and then received him home again after extracting numerous promises for the lad's future good behavior. Pierre-Augustin from that time on diligently applied himself to his profession, and at the age of twenty he invented an appliance for watches. By 1755 he considered himself firmly established, for he was high in court favor. Soon, however, the watch-maker fell in love with one of his customers, married her and in 1757 took the name of Beaumarchais, which was that of a small estate said to be in the possession of his wife. On her death in 1757 Beaumarchais became involved in suits of various sorts, and before long found himself ruined. During the next four years fortune favored him once more, for he turned his knowledge of music to good advantage and arranged concerts for the court. The political influence which Beaumarchais was able to bring to bear upon certain personages at court resulted in his participation in many business enterprises and speculations. With his fortune, which he readily made, he purchased a court office which entitled him to rank among the nobility. A letter from his sister in Madrid interrupted his life in Paris and took him to Spain (1764) where he handled with great skill and tact the celebrated Clavijo case for breach of promise. He remained in Madrid until 1765, returned to Paris, and once again plunged into his life of adventure, intrigue, and pleasure. When in 1767 Beaumarchais produced his first play, he had acquired some skill through the writing of burlesque sketches. But the first of his plays which he deemed worthy of print was *Eugénie,* produced in 1767. The play and the *Préface* exemplified Diderot's theories on the *Drame.* This play was followed in 1770 by *Les Deux amis,* another *Drame.* The play was a failure, and Beaumarchais was ready to turn to pure comedy, but once again he became involved in difficulties. His second wife, whom he married in 1768, died in 1770. She was followed the same year by Duverney, his old business associate. Beaumarchais presented a claim upon Duverney's estate and was soon involved in his most celebrated law-suit. Further trouble ensued, Beaumarchais was imprisoned, and the celebrated Goezman trial took place, resulting in that delightful masterpiece, the *Mémoires* of Beaumarchais. The trial left him deprived of fortune and reputation. However, the king, knowing how useful Beaumarchais might be to him, took him under his protection, and made him a secret agent. He at once went to London and accomplished a delicate mission; on his return to Paris he was amply recompensed. His next mission took him to Holland, Germany, and Austria; and again, on his return to Paris, he was sent to London. He finally gained the complete confidence of Louis XVI, and in 1776 was reinstated as a noble and a citizen. Meanwhile *Le Barbier de Séville* had been written by 1772, but the production was delayed by the censors

until 1775; the play was very successful. The untiring dramatist again engaged in commercial ventures, this time sending supplies to the American government for their struggle with England, but he became so entangled in negotiations with the Americans, that not until years after his death, in 1835, did his heirs finally succeed in adjusting matters. The next play, *Le Mariage de Figaro,* after many delays, was produced in 1784, with enormous success. The Revolution was at hand, Beaumarchais was growing old, and in a pamphlet discussion with Mirabeau, he was so fiercely attacked that he retired in shame. Financial reverses set in, and further suits and fines. *Tarare,* an opera, was produced with little success, in 1787, one year after the author's third marriage. *La Mère coupable* (1792) enjoyed only a fair degree of popularity. Once again the indefatigable Beaumarchais engaged in speculations — this time selling arms to the government. Interminable proposals and counter-proposals were made, Beaumarchais was thrown into prison, freed, sent as secret agent to Holland and England, and finally, in 1796, allowed to return to Paris. In the midst of his activities, financial and political, he died, in 1799.

Beaumarchais' theory of the drama is directly derived from Diderot, but he differs from Diderot in that he is primarily a dramatist. True it is that the sort of play which Diderot had so unsuccessfully attempted to write had been feebly imitated by Beaumarchais in *Les Deux amis* and *Eugénie;* but *Le Barbier de Séville* and *Le Mariage de Figaro* are among the finest comedies in existence. Beaumarchais' greatest importance lay in his insistence upon action. It is the business of a comedy to "inspire, move, transport, and strike," the spectator. The modern note struck in Beaumarchais' prefaces was well in accord with many of Victor Hugo's ideas; and we find that revolutionary praising Beaumarchais as one of the "three great characteristic geniuses of our stage."

ESSAY ON THE SERIOUS DRAMA [1]

[*Essai sur le genre dramatique sérieux*]

(1767)

I can lay no just claim to the dignity of author: both time and talent have been denied me; but some eight years ago I amused myself by committing to paper a few ideas of the *Serious Drama,* that form which is a sort of intermediary between the heroic tragedy and the pleasing comedy. Of the several forms of the drama which I might have chosen, that was perhaps the least esteemed; and that was the very reason for my preference. I have always been so seriously occupied that I have sought nothing in the field of letters but an honorable means of recreation. *Neque sem per arcum tendit Apollo.* The subject pleased, and carried me along with it; but I was not long in learning that I was mistaken in endeavoring to convince by reason in a form where one ought rather to persuade by sentiment. I was soon seized with the desire to substitute example for precept: an infallible way of creating proselytes when one is successful, but which exposes the unfortunate mortal who is not, to the twofold chagrin of having failed to attain his object, and being the butt of ridicule for having presumed beyond his powers.

Too wrought up by my subject to be capable of this latter thought, I composed the play which I herewith publish. *Miss Fanny, Miss Jenny, Miss Polly,* and so on, charming books, my *Eugénie* would doubtless have gained much in taking you for models; but she was born before you were in existence — without which one can never serve as model at all. I refer your authors to the little Spanish novelette of the Comte de Belflor, in *Le Diable boiteux;* that was the source of my idea. The little I obtained therefrom will cause them small regret that they were unable to help me in any way.

The general outline of my plan of action — that rapid mass-work, indicating in a general way the situations, and sketching out the characters — developing very quickly under the white heat of my enthusiasm, saw no waning of my

courage; but when it came to the part where I was forced to confine the subject within a certain space, or expand it, really work at it; then my poor brain, muddled with details of execution, was cognizant of real difficulties, took fright at the whole thing, and gave up both play and dissertation. . . .

Shortly after, M. Diderot brought out his *Père de famille.* The genius of this writer, his powerful manner, the vigorous and masculine style of his play, ought to have caused me to throw down my pen; instead, the path he had opened up held forth such charms to me that I listened to the dictates of my personal inclination rather than to the voice of my own weakness and inability. I went to work on my play with renewed ardor. As soon as I had finished it, I gave the manuscript to the *Comédie Française.* . . .

Now that it has been produced, I shall proceed to inquire into all the uproarious clamor and adverse criticism which it has aroused; but I shall not linger long over those points which do not immediately concern the dramatic form which it pleased me to choose, because that is the only point which can interest the public at this time. I shall indulge in no personalities. *Jam dolor in morem venit meus* (Ovid). I shall even pass over in silence everything that has been said against the play, firmly convinced that the greatest honor that could be paid it — after the actual interest taken in it on the stage — is that it is not unworthy of critical discussion. . . .

I have seen people actually and sincerely bemoan the fact that the *Serious Drama* was gaining partisans. "An equivocal form!" they declare. "You cannot tell what it is. What sort of play is that in which there is not a single line that makes you laugh? Five mortal acts of long-drawn-out prose, with no comic relief, no moral reflections, no characters — during which we are held suspended by the thread of some romantic circumstance which has neither versimilitude nor reality! Does not the sufferance of such works rather

---

[1] Translated into English by the Editor, for the first time.— Ed.

open the gate to license, and encourage laziness? The facility of prose will tend to turn our young authors from the arduous task of writing verse, and our stage will soon fall into a state of barbarism, out of which our poets have so painfully managed to develop it. I do not mean to infer that some of these pieces have not affected me, I do not know just how; but how terrible it would be if such plays obtained a foothold! And besides, their popularity would be most unseemly in our land: every one knows what our celebrated authors have thought, and they are authorities! They have proscribed this dramatic form as belonging neither to Melpomene nor to Thalia. Must we create a new Muse to preside over this trivial cothurnus, this stilted comic form? *Tragi-comedy, Bourgeois Tragedy, Tearful Comedy* — I can find no term to designate this hybrid. And let no wretched author pride himself upon the momentary approval of the public, which is vouchsafed rather to the assiduity and talent of the actors! The public! What is this public? The moment that collective entity dissolves, and each member of it goes his own way, what remains of the general opinion, unless it becomes that of each individual, among whom the most enlightened exercise a natural influence over the others, who are brought sooner or later to think with the former? Whence it will be seen that the author must look to the few and not to the many for his "general opinion."

Enough. Now let us proceed to reply to the vast torrent of objections, which I have neither belittled nor exaggerated in my account. Let us begin by rendering our judge favorable toward us by defending his own rights. Despite the assertion of the critics to the contrary, the assembled public is none the less that sole judge of plays which are written to amuse it. Every one alike is forced to submit to it, and any effort to obstruct the efforts of genius in the creation of a new dramatic form, or in the further development of those forms which are already established, is a conspiracy against its rights, a plot to deprive it of its pleasure. I readily agree that a difficult, deep-hidden truth in a play will be sooner discovered, better understood, and more intelligently judged by a small number of enlightened individuals, than by a clamorous crowd — otherwise the truth could not be said to be "difficult"; but questions of taste and sentiment, matters pertaining to pure effects; in a word, all that regards the work as a play, since it cannot be considered apart from the powerful and instantaneous effect produced upon an audience as a whole — ought, I ask, all these things to be judged according to the same rules? When it is less a matter of discussing and analyzing than of feeling, being amused, and being touched, is it not then as questionable to say that the judgment of the public when it is under the influence of emotion, is false and mistaken, as to maintain that a certain kind of drama, which has made its emotional appeal and succeeded in pleasing, generally speaking, a whole nation, and yet is not of sufficient value and dignity for this nation? What importance are we to attach to the satires of certain writers on the *Serious Drama,* as against the weight of public taste, especially when the shafts of ridicule are directed against charming plays written in this style by the satirists themselves? The light and playful touch of sarcasm may be reasonable and consistent, but it has never decided an important question: its only reason for existence is that it merely starts discussions; it should only be permitted when it is directed against cowardly adversaries who, firmly entrenched behind a heap of authorities, refuse to struggle and reason in the open. . . . I have heard important-sounding words in connection with the sort of play I am discussing, and seen arrayed before me, opposing my plea for the serious play, Aristotle, the ancients, the *Poetics,* "the laws of the drama," the rules, above all, the rules — the eternal common meeting-ground of the critics, the scarecrow of ordinary minds. In what branch of art have rules ever produced masterpieces? Is it not rather the great examples which from the very beginnings have served as a basis of these rules, which are, inverting the natural order of things, brought forward as a positive hindrance to genius? Would mankind ever have advanced in the arts and sciences, if they had servilely followed the misleading and confining precepts laid down by their predecessors? The New World would still be utterly unknown to us had the hardy Genoese navigator not spurned the *Nec plus ultra* of the Pillars of Hercules. Was *that* rule not presumptuous and misleading? Genius that is ever on the alert for something new, that is impatient, that chafes under the restrictions of what is already known, suspects something more, something beyond the known; agitated and set in motion by this impelling force, the genius, his mind in torment, impatient, struggling to free himself, grows; and finally, breaking down the barrier of prejudice, he presses forward, out beyond the known borders. Sometimes he loses his way, but still it is he alone who carries the beacon far into the night of the possible, toward which others strive to follow him. He has made a giant stride, and the outposts of art are advanced. I must stop at this point, for I have no desire to enter into a heated argument; I wish merely to reason calmly. Let us reduce to simple terms a great question which has not hitherto been decided. If I were to submit it to a tribunal of reason, I should state it in this way: *Is it permissible to interest a theater audience and make it shed tears over a situation which, if it occurred in everyday life, would never fail to produce the same effect upon each individual in that audience?* For that, in fine, is the object of well-intentioned, *Serious Drama.*

If there exists a person so barbarous, so classic, who would dare maintain the opposite, I should like to ask him whether he does not take the word "drama" or "play" to mean a truthful picture of the actions of human beings? He ought to read the novels of Richardson; these are true dramas, since the drama is the conclusion, the most interesting moment in every novel. He should be told, if he does not know, that many scenes in *L'Enfant prodigue,* all of *Nanine, Mélanide, Célie, Le Père de famille, L'Ecossaise, Le Philosophe sans le savoir,* are living proofs of the beautiful treatment of which the *Serious* form is susceptible; that these have taught us to enjoy the touching spectacle of domestic unhappiness, which has all the greater claim upon our attention because it is something which is more likely to enter our own lives. Results of this sort can never elsewhere be hoped for — at least to so

great a degree — in the vast panorama of heroic tragedy.

Before proceeding any farther, I may say that what I am about to discuss does not apply to our celebrated writers of tragedy: they would have shone bright in any other career: genius is born of itself, it owes nothing to the themes which it treats, and is universal in its application. I am discussing fundamentals, respecting the authors at the same time. I am comparing dramatic forms, not individual dramatic talents. This is what I have to say:

The essential object of the *Serious Drama* is to furnish a more direct and appealing interest, a morality which is more applicable than can be found in heroic tragedy; and, everything else being equal, a more profound impression than light comedy.

And now I hear a thousand voices raised against me crying, "Impious!" but I ask in all fairness to be heard, before you pronounce the anathema. These ideas are too new not to demand further development.

When I see the ancient tragedies, I am seized with a feeling of personal indignation against the cruel gods who allow such terrible calamities to be heaped upon the innocent. Œdipus, Jocasta, Phædra, Ariadne, Philoctetes, Orestes, and many others, inspire more terror in me than interest. Devoted passive beings, blind instruments of the wrath and caprice of the gods, I am more horrified at, than compassionate toward them. Everything in these plays seems monstrous to me: unbridled passions, atrocious crimes, these are as far from being natural as they are unusual, in the civilization of our time. In all these tragedies we pass through nothing but ruins, oceans of blood, heaps of slain, and arrive at the catastrophe only by way of poisoning, murder, incest, and parricide. The tears shed are forced, they seldom flow, and when they do, they are burning hot: they cause the forehead to contract before tears finally flow. Unbelievably great efforts are necessary to force them, so that only the very greatest geniuses are able to accomplish the feat.

And then, the inevitable tragedies of destiny offer no moral struggle. When one can only tremble and be silent, is not thinking the very worst thing to do?

If one could evolve some sort of moral from a play of this sort, it is a terrible moral, and would indubitably encourage as many to commit crimes who might urge fate as an excuse, as it would discourage to follow in the paths of virtue, because according to this system all our efforts mean nothing at all. If it be true that no virtue can be attained without sacrifice, then it must equally stand to reason that no sacrifice can be made without hope of reward. A belief in fatalism degrades man, because it takes his personal liberty from him; and without this, there is no morality in his acts.

If we inquire into what sort of interest is aroused in us by the heroes and kings of heroic tragedy, we will soon see that the situations and pompous characters which it presents to us are no more than traps laid for our vanity; they seldom appeal to the heart. Our vanity is flattered when we are made to participate in the secrets of a magnificent court, to be present at a council which is to revolutionize the state, to enter a private room of the queen, whom in actual life we should scarcely be allowed to see.

We delight in believing ourself the confidant of an unhappy prince, because his sorrows, his tears, his weaknesses, seem to bring his position in life much nearer to our own, or else console us for being so far beneath him; and, without our being aware, each of us seeks to widen his sphere, and our pride is nourished by the pleasure we experience in judging, in the theater, these masters of the world who, anywhere else, might well walk over without noticing us. Men deceive themselves more easily than they are apt to imagine: the wisest among them is often affected by motives which, if he thought of them, would cause him to blush for shame. But if emotions enter into the interest we take in the characters of a tragedy, the reason is less because those characters are heroes and kings than that they are unfortunate men. Is it the Queen of Messina who appeals to my emotions in *Merope?* No, it is the mother of Ægisthus: nature alone claims sovereignty over our hearts.

If the drama be a faithful picture of what occurs in human society, the interest aroused in us must of necessity be closely related to our manner of observing real objects. Now, I have often noticed that a great prince, at the very height of happiness, glory, and success, excited in us nothing but the barren sentiment of admiration, which is a stranger to the heart. We perhaps never feel how dear to us he is until he falls into some disgrace. This touching enthusiasm of the people, who praise and reward good kings, never takes root in their hearts except when they realize that their king is unhappy, or when they feel they may lose him. Then their compassion for the suffering man is so true and deep that it almost seems to compensate the king for all his lost happiness. The true heart-interest, the real relationship, is always between man and man, and not between man and king. And so, far from increasing my interest in the characters of tragedy, their exalted rank rather diminishes it. The nearer the suffering man is to my station in life, the greater is his claim upon my sympathy. "Would it not be better," asks M. Rousseau, "for our authors of the sublime to descend a little from their continual elevation, and make us sympathize occasionally with suffering humanity; for fear that as a result of enlisting our sympathy for unhappy heroes, we may end by feeling sympathy for no one at all?"

What do I care, I, a peaceful subject in an eighteenth century monarchy, for the revolutions of Athens and Rome? Of what real interest to me is the death of a Pelopennesian tyrant, or the sacrifice of a young princess at Aulis? There is nothing in that for me; no morality which is applicable to my needs. For what is morality? It is the fruitful result and individual application of certain mental deductions occasioned by an actual occurrence. What is interest? It is the involuntary sensation by which we adapt that occurrence to our own ends; it puts us in the place of him who suffers, throws us into the situation for the time being. A random comparison, taken from nature, will make this idea clear to every one.

Why does the story of the earthquake which swallowed up Lima and its inhabitants, three thousand leagues away, trouble me, while the story of the political murder of Charles I, which was committed at London, merely arouse my indignation? Because the volcano which engulfed the Peruvian city might explode under Paris, and bury me beneath ruins — possibly I am threatened even at this moment; whereas I cannot conceive of a misfortune similar to the unheard-of tragedy of the King of England's happening to me. This sentiment lies in the heart of every man; it serves as basis to this absolute principle of art, that there can be neither interest nor moral appeal on the stage without some sort of connection existing between the subject of the play and ourselves. Now, it is an obvious fact that heroic tragedy appeals to us only in so far as it resembles the *Serious Drama,* and portrays men and not kings. The subjects which it treats are so foreign to our customs and manners, and the characters so different from ourselves, that the interest aroused is less vital than that in the *Serious Drama;* the moral less poignant, more abstract, so that it often remains sterile and useless to us, unless it console us for our mediocrity, in showing us that great crimes and misfortunes are the lot of those who govern the world.

After what I have said, I do not think it necessary to prove that there is more interest to be derived from the *Serious Drama* than from comedy. Every one is aware that, granting each play is of equal merit in its respective field, the *Serious Play* with an emotional appeal affects us more deeply than that which is merely amusing. It now remains for me to develop the reasons for this effect, which is as palpable as it is natural, and to inquire into the morality of the matter by comparing the two forms.

Gayety serves as a distraction for us: in one way or another it takes our souls and spreads them round about us: people never truly laugh except when they are together. But if the gay spirit of ridicule amuses us for an instant, experience teaches that the laugh which is aroused by a satiric shaft dies as it reaches its victim, without ever rebounding and affecting ourselves. Pride, zealously avoiding the personal application, hides itself amid the uproar of the assembled audience, and takes advantage of the general tumult to cast out all that might be of value to us in a sharp epigram. If matters went no further, the

evil would not be irremediable, so long as the dramatist holds up to public ridicule only such types as the pedant, the blockhead, the coquette, the pretentious man, the fool, the puppet — in a word, all those who in the life of our day are ridiculous. But is the mockery which chastises them the proper weapon with which to attack vice? Can a dramatist smite his victim with a joke? Not only would he fail to fulfill his purpose, he would achieve the exact opposite of what he set out to accomplish. We see this happen in most comic pieces: to the shame of his moral sense, the spectator often finds himself sympathizing with the rascal against the honest man, because the latter is always rendered the less attractive of the two. But if the gayety of the play has succeeded in sweeping me along for a moment, it is not long, however, before I experience a sense of humiliation at having allowed myself to be ensnared by witty lines and stage tricks; and I leave the theater displeased with the author and with myself. The essential morality of the comic play is therefore either very shallow, or else nothing at all; or finally it produced just the result which it should not produce.

Not so with a drama which appeals to our emotions, whose subject-matter is taken from our daily life. If loud laughter is the enemy of reflection, pity, on the other hand, induces silence: it invites us to meditate, and isolates us from distracting externals. He who weeps at a play is alone; and the more deeply he feels, the more genuine is his pleasure, especially in the *Serious Drama,* which moves us by true and natural means. Often, in the midst of an amusingly pleasant scene, some charming bit of emotion causes abundant and ready tears to fall, which, mingling with a graceful smile, bring sympathy and joy to the face of the spectator. Is not a touching conflict of this sort the greatest triumph of art, as well as the sweetest sensation that can be experienced by a person of sensibility?

Sympathy has this advantage over the spirit of ridicule, that it is never aroused in us without the concomitant quality of realization, which is made all the more powerful as it appeals to us directly, on the stage.

When we see an honest man who is unhappy we are touched: the spectacle opens our heart, takes possession of it, and finally forces us to examine our inmost conscience. When I see virtue persecuted, made a victim by wickedness, and yet remaining beautiful, glorious, and preferable to everything else, even when it is surrounded by misfortune — when all this is portrayed in a drama, then I am assured that that drama is not "equivocal": I am interested in virtue alone. And then, if I am not happy myself, if base envy does her best to influence me, if she attacks my person, my fortune, and my honor, then how much more interest do I take in that sort of play! And what a splendid moral can I take from it! The subject is one to interest me, naturally: since I am interested only in those who are unhappy and who suffer unjustly, I ask myself whether as a result of some carelessness of character, some fault in my conduct, some excessive ambition, or dishonorable conspiracy, I have called down upon my own head the hatred which pursues me. In any event, I shall be induced to correct my faults, and I shall leave the theater a better man than I entered, merely because I shall have been moved to tenderness and sympathy.

If the injury that has been done me cries aloud for justice, and is more the fault of others than myself, then the lesson derived from the drama will be the more consoling to me. I shall look into my own heart with pleasure, and if I conclude that I have done my full duty toward society, if I am a good parent, a just master, a kind friend, an upright man and a useful citizen, my spiritual satisfaction consoling me for injuries received from others, I shall then all the more appreciate the play which I have witnessed, because it will recall to me that in the pursuit of virtue I find the greatest happiness to which a wise man can attain: contentment with himself, and I shall return again to shed sweet tears at the spectacle of innocence and persecuted virtue. . . .

The noble and Serious drama has been criticized in turn for lacking stamina, warmth, power, and the comic element. . . . Let us see how far this criticism is justified. Every form which is too new to contain definite rules according to which it can be discussed, is judged by analogy according to the general rules governing human nature. Let us apply this method to the case in question. The *Serious* emotional drama stands midway between heroic tragedy and light comedy. If I consider that part of it which touches upon tragedy, I ask myself: do the warmth and power of a character in a play arise from his position in the state, or from the depths of his own character? A cursory glance at the models which real life furnishes to art (which is imitative), reveals that a powerful character is no more the sole possession of a prince than of any one else. Three men spring forth from the heart of Rome, and divide the world among them. The first is a pusillanimous coward; the second, valiant, presumptuous and fierce; the third, a clever rascal, who outwits the other two. But Lepidus, Antony, and Octavius, when they formed the Triumvirate, possessed characters which alone decided the different parts they were to play in their common usurpation. The softness of the first, the violence of the second, and the cleverness of the other — all these would have had their effect had it been merely a question of private succession among them. Every man is what he is because of his character; as to his station in life, that is determined by destiny; but a man's character can influence that station in life to a considerable extent. Hence, the *Serious Drama*, which shows me men who are moved by situations, is as susceptible of power, dynamic force, and elevation of thought, as heroic tragedy, which likewise shows me men who are moved, but who are above men in the ordinary walks of life. And if I consider that part of the *Serious* and noble drama which touches upon comedy, I cannot deny that the *vis comica* is indispensable to all good comedies; but then I may ask why the *Serious Drama* is criticized for a lack of warmth, which, if it exists, can be only the result of a lack of skill on the part of the dramatist? Since plays of this sort deal with people taken out of every-day life — as in light comedy — ought these characters to be treated with any less vigor, portrayed any the less forcibly, when the situation in which they find themselves involves their honor, or life itself, than when these same characters are involved in matters of less moment — say, in simple ordinary embarrassments of one kind or another, or even in comic situations? And even if all the dramas which I have referred to lack comic elements (which I am gravely inclined to doubt) . . . even then, the question revolves upon the ability or shortcomings of individual dramatists and not upon the dramatic form as such, which is in itself less bombastic and may be thought of as containing the best fiber of any. . . .

My task will have advanced considerably, if I have succeeded in convincing my readers that the *Serious Drama* exists, that it is a good form, that its interest is lively, that it contains a direct and profound appeal to the moral sense, that it can have but one style, that of

nature; that, besides enjoying the advantages common to other dramatic forms, it possesses a beauty all its own; that it blazes a new trail in the realm of the drama, where genius may soar. to heights unknown before, because the form treats all sides of life, and therefore contains every possible situation therein. And once again the dramatist will be able to succeed by utilizing the great figures of comedy, which have by now been nearly exhausted because the situations in which they have figured are out-worn. Finally, the *Serious Drama* is an endless source of amusement and morality for society in general. . . . A theory of art may evolve as the result of study and reflection, but the production of a work of art belongs only to genius, which cannot be taught.

DEDICATORY LETTER

TO THE BARBER OF SEVILLE [2]

[*Lettre Modérée sur la Chûte et la Critique du Barbier de Séville*]

(1775)

. . . I succumbed to the temptation, at two different times in the past, Monsieur, to present you with two pathetic dramas: monstrous, hybrid productions because, as is well known, there is no mean way between comedy and tragedy. The question has been decided: the master has pronounced finally upon it, and the school reëchoes with his words. And as for myself, I am so far convinced that if I wished now to portray on the stage a distressed mother, a betrayed wife, a distracted sister, or a disinherited son, I should, in order that they might decently be put before the public, begin by giving each a kingdom where they will have reigned wisely — in some distant archipelago or other far corner of the world; and be certain thereafter that the improbability of the fable, the exaggerated situations and characters, the outlandish ideas and bombast of speech, far from being a reason of reproach to me, will assure my success.

Portray ordinary men and women in difficulties and sorrow? Nonsense!

Such ought only to be scoffed at. Ridiculous citizens and unhappy kings, these are the only characters fit for treatment on the stage; such is the case, and I have no quarrel with any one.

As I say, I formerly succumbed to the temptation to write plays, monsieur, which were not in the true accepted form, and I am duly repentant.

Circumstances changed and I hazarded writing those unhappy *Mémoires,* which my enemies declared were not written in good style; I am consumed by cruel remorse.

To-day I offer for your inspection an exceedingly gay comedy, which certain arbiters of taste consider is not *de bon ton;* I am inconsolable. . . .

Next to commanding men, is not the greatest honor, monsieur, to judge them?

Of course. Now, I recognize no other judge than you, not excepting the esteemed spectators who, basing their opinions on a first impression, often find their verdict nullified before your tribunal.

The case was first plead before them in the theater, and the spectators having laughed generously, I assumed that I

2 Here translated, by the editor, for the first time — Ed.

had gained my cause with them. Nothing of the kind: a journalist who lives at Bouillon maintains that it was at me that the audience laughed. But what he said was only, as they say at the courts, the poor quibble of a lawyer, for my purpose was to amuse the audience, and whether they laughed at me or at the play, so long as they laughed wholeheartedly, my purpose has been accomplished. I call that having gained my cause with the audience. . . .

Plays, monsieur, are like children: conceived with pleasure, carried about before they are born with great fatigue, and brought forth in pain; scarcely ever do they recompense their parents, and they cost more sorrow than they give delight. Follow the career of a play; hardly does it see the light of day when, under the pretext that it is bombastic, the censors attack it; and so many a play is legally "detained." Instead of quietly enjoying a play, the parterre jeers at it and causes it to fail. Often, instead of helping, nursing it along, the actor lames it. If you once lose it from view, you will find it again, alas! anywhere, everywhere, disfigured, tattered, cut, and covered with critical remarks. Finally escaping so many ills, if it shines for a moment in public, then the greatest ill of all overtakes it: mortal oblivion kills it. So these plays die, return to the vast void, lost forever in the huge mass of books. . . .

And now, if you please, let us see whether this critic from Bouillon has maintained that much-to-be-desired character of amiability, and above all, candor.

He says: "The play is a farce."

We shall not quibble about names. The malicious word which a foreign cook uses to designate French ragouts does not change the taste; *that* is done only in passing through his hands. Let us proceed with Bouillon's farce.

He says: "The play has no form."

Is the play so simple that it escapes the sagacity of the adolescent critic?

An amorous old man intends to marry his ward to-morrow; a young lover, who is much cleverer, forestalls him, and that very day makes the girl his wife in the house and before the very eyes of the guardian. That is the basis of the play, of which might have been made, with equal success, a tragedy, a comedy, a drama, an opera, and so on. Is *L'Avare* of Molière anything else? Or *Le Grand Mithridate?* The actual form of a play, or any other sort of literature, depends less on the action than on the characters which set that action into play.

As for myself, since I intended to write nothing but an amusing play, one that could not cause fatigue, a sort of *imbroglio,* it was enough that the character about whom the action centered should be a droll fellow in place of a black villain; a carefree man who laughs alike at the success or failure of his enterprises. I wished only that the play should, far from becoming a serious drama, be merely a gay comedy. And just because the guardian is not quite so stupid as the greater part of such characters who are seen in the theater, there has resulted a great deal of movement, as well as the necessity for greater relief to those engaged in the intrigue. . . .

MODERN GERMAN DRAMATIC CRITICISM

The period before Lessing was one of groping; he it was who gave the necessary impetus to original composition in criticism and the drama. His own plays — particularly *Minna von Barnhelm* (1767), *Emilia Galotti* (1772), and *Nathan der weise* (1779) — were works of high quality. With Lessing the modern German drama was born. His criticism marked the beginning of an era which has not yet ended. During his lifetime the Romantic movement began. The inspiration was received chiefly from England, whose literature — especially Shakespeare — was read and admired. Klopstock, an epic, lyric, and dramatic poet belonged partly to the Gottsched group and partly to the new. A younger man, Wieland, exerted widespread influence in his dramatic reviews and general writings. He also translated twenty-two of Shakespeare's plays (between 1762 and 1766); the translations were not particularly good, though they undoubtedly affected the writers of his time. Next in importance to Lessing, however, was Johann Gottfried Herder, who first showed the way to original composition in his trenchant criticisms and Shakespeare study. His influence on the young Goethe was inestimable, and the *Sturm und Drang* Period dates from his meeting with the young poet at Strassburg in 1770-71. He wrote an essay on Shakespeare (1773), in which he attacked the French critical canons and demanded that Shakespeare should be judged on his own great merits. The *Sturm und Drang* was a period of violent reaction against the fetters and conventions of life and art. Shakespeare was the idol of the younger men, and Shakespeare study dates from these days. Goethe was strongly influenced by Shakespeare and an early play, *Götz von Berlichingen* (1773) was one of the results of his study of the English poet. There soon followed other romantic works, the novel of *Werther* (1774), the play *Clavigo* (1774) and the first sketch of *Faust* (1790). Then came the impetuous Schiller, whose play *Die Räuber* (1781) sounded a blast to the new Romantics. The *Prefaces* are documents of considerable interest. With this play and with its immediate successors, *Fiesco* (1783), and *Kabale und Liebe* (1784), it may be said that modern German poetic drama was born. The last play of Lessing, *Nathan der weise*, had appeared in 1779; Goethe's *Iphigenie* and Schiller's *Don Carlos* belong to the late eighties, as well as Goethe's *Torquato Tasso*. Goethe meanwhile had been contributing numerous articles on the drama, and strengthening the Shakespeare interest in his various versions of the *Wilhelm Meister* novel. Schiller had during the nineties delved into philosophy and æsthetics and delivered lectures and written essays on tragic art and the function of the drama, etc. The best of these are the *Ueber den Grund des Vergnügens an tragischen Gegenständen* (1792), and *Ueber die tragische Kunst,* of the same year. His last years were devoted to the writing

of *Wallenstein* (1800) and *Wilhelm Tell*. His death in 1805 cut short his brilliant career. For over a score of years Goethe continued to evolve his dramatic theories, but long before his death the Schlegels, August Wilhelm and Karl Wilhelm Friedrich, had begun their celebrated translations of Shakespeare, and in 1798 founded the *Athenæum*, which is usually regarded as the beginning of the truly modern Romantic movement, the influence of which was felt, through Coleridge, even in England. The brothers published in 1801 their joint work, *Charakteristiken*, containing their various literary theories, and in 1809 and 1811 August Wilhelm issued his famous lectures *Vorlesungen über dramatische Kunst und Literatur*. Among the contributors to the *Athenæum* was Novalis [Friedrich von Hardenberg], whose fragmentary remarks on Shakespeare are among the most interesting of the time. Schubarth, Uhland, and Solger belong to the period, and all made contributions to the subject. Ludwig Tieck, who collaborated in the Schlegel translation of Shakespeare, in his *Kritische Schriften* (1848-52), and his *Nachgelassene Schriften* (1855), contributed generously to dramatic criticism, especially to the subject of Shakespeare and the pre-Shakespearian drama. Among the writers on pure æsthetics, Hegel may be mentioned (though his work falls outside the scope of this collection), and Jean-Paul Richter, whose *Vorschule der Æsthetik* was published in 1813. The Austrian dramatist Franz Grillparzer wrote a number of critical reviews, essays, and the like, on the drama, the best of which are the *Zur Dramaturgie* (from 1817 on, in the *Æsthetische Studien*), the *Studien zur griechischen Literatur* (about 1860), and on other literatures; the *Studien zum spanischen Theater* (written at various times) and the *Studien zur deutschen Literatur*. It is perhaps unnecessary to mention in detail the various Shakespeare scholars, like Gervinus, and the æstheticians like Carriere. Friedrich Hebbel, the dramatist, wrote at great length on his art, and the preface to *Maria Magdalena* (1844), *Mein Wort über das Drama* (1843), and his criticisms of Kleist and Körner, went far to establish the Middle-class Drama of which he was the chief exponent. Richard Wagner carried the drama into the realm of the music-drama, and offered many ingenious and some absurd suggestions as to the Artwork of the Future. His *Oper und Drama* (1851), and later tract, *Ueber die Bestimmung der Oper* (1871) undoubtedly revolutionized the opera form; whether it effected a great change in the drama it is difficult to determine. A decidedly different theorist was the novelist and dramatist Gustav Freytag, whose *Technik des Dramas*, a handbook of practical advice, appeared in 1863. Until recently this work was a standard. Friedrich Nietzsche's *Die Geburt der Tragödie* (1877) is one of the most interesting works on the drama. The past sixty years have witnessed the publication of many hundreds of works on the drama, to the most important of which it is possible only to refer in passing: Theodor Fontane's dramatic criticisms (in the *Gesammelte Werke,* 1905–12); Ernst von Wildenbruch's *Das deutsche Drama* (1900); Otto Brahm's *Kritische Schriften über Drama und Theater* (1913); Heinrich Bulthaupt's four volumes of *Dramaturgie des Schauspiels* (1894–1908); Hugo Dinger's *Dramaturgie als Wissenschaft* (1904–05); A. Perger's *System der dramatische Technik* (1909); Paul Ernst's *Der Weg zum Form* (1906); Julius Bab's *Kritik der Bühne* (1908); *Wege zum Drama* (1906) and *Neue*

Wege zum Drama (1911); Maximilian Harden's *Literatur und Theater* (1896); Hermann Schlag's *Das Drama* (1909); Eugen Zabel's volumes *Zur modernen Dramaturgie* (1899, etc.); Arno Holz's *Die Kunst* and *Neue Folge* (1891 and 1893); Hermann Bahr's *Wiener Theater* (1899); *Dialog vom Tragischen* (1904); and Frank Wedekind's *Schauspielkunst* (1910). And still other important volumes of German dramatic criticism have appeared: Bernhard Diebold's *Anarchie im Drama* (1921); Alfred Kerr's *Die Welt im Drama* (1954); Herbert Jhering's *Von Reinhardt bis Brecht* (1958), in three volumes; and Julius Bab's *Uber den Tag Hinaus* (1960). The Viennese father of psychoanalysis, Sigmund Freud, has contributed both directly and indirectly to the criticism of literature and drama.

The two important schools of twentieth-century German drama are expressionism, which stresses abstraction, the dream state, and giving a direct voice to feeling; and epic drama, characterized by episodic form and political themes. Epic drama was founded and interpreted by the dramatist Bertolt Brecht and the director Erwin Piscator. Brecht's influence is evident in the parable drama of the Swiss dramatists Friedrich Duerrenmatt and Max Frisch.

FRIEDRICH VON SCHILLER

Johann Christoph Friedrich von Schiller was born at Marbach on the Neckar, in 1759. His father was an officer in the army, and it was while the family was in residence at Ludwigsburg and Lorch that the young Friedrich received his early education. In 1773 the Duke of Württemberg took the young man into his military school near Ludwigsburg, and taught him law. Two years after the school was transferred to Stuttgart, where Schiller was allowed to change his study to that of medicine, which was more congenial. In 1776 his first poetic efforts appeared in magazine form, and two years later he finished his first play, *Die Räuber*. In 1780 he was graduated as a surgeon, and given a position with

a regiment quartered in Stuttgart. The following year he published *Die Räuber*, which was well received. In 1782 it was produced in Mannheim. The young poet's visits to Mannheim, and what was considered an uncomplimentary reference to one of the Duke's contemporaries, incurred that nobleman's displeasure, and Schiller was placed under arrest and subsequently forbidden to leave the city. But later in the year he escaped and went to Mannheim, and thence to Bauerbach, where he finished *Kabale und Liebe* and began *Don Carlos*. The next year he was appointed "Theater poet" at Mannheim. He published meantime an address on the theater, *Die. Schaubühne als eine moralische Anstalt betrachtet*

(1784). The next year he left Mannheim and spent the summer near Leipzig, writing poetry and resting. Thence he went to Dresden with Körner, a friend who in many ways directed the education of the poet. In 1787 he went to Weimar, where he met Herder and Wieland. The next year he published the first part of his history of the Netherlands, for which, upon Goethe's recommendation, he was made a professor at Jena in 1789. In 1790 he married Charlotte von Lengefeld. Then followed sickness and financial troubles, but these latter were relieved for a time by his noble protectors. He continued his philosophic and æsthetic studies, publishing various lectures in 1792 and 1793. For some time he had edited a journal, and in 1794 he founded another, *Die Horen*, which brought him into close relations with Goethe. The two became friends and collaborators. *Die Horen* gave way to another journal in 1797, the *Musenalmanach*, in which he published many of his best lyrics. Between 1799 and 1804 he returned to the drama, and wrote the *Wallenstein* plays, *Maria Stuart, Die Jungfrau von Orleans, Wilhelm Tell*, and others of less importance. His last years were marked by ill-health and considerable popularity. In 1802 he was ennobled. He died at Weimar in 1805.

Schiller's æsthetic essays are his best-known contribution to criticism, although his occasional reviews and prefaces contain a considerable amount of pure dramatic criticism. His two important essays on the drama — *Ueber den Grund des Vergnügens an tragischen Gegenständen*, and *Ueber die tragische Kunst* — first appeared in the *Neue Thalia* in 1792. In the first of these essays the poet endeavors to prove that the sole end of tragic art is to give pleasure. The second is partly theoretical and partly practical. It is interesting to know that Schiller at this time was not acquainted with Aristotle's *Poetics*. On the whole, Schiller's theories on dramatic art are not of the epoch-making sort; Lessing was an incontestably greater critic, but Schiller's theories are significant as showing the close connection between the study of philosophy (Schiller was an ardent admirer of Kant) and the drama.

PREFACE TO THE ROBBERS [1]

[*Vorrede* (to) *Die Räuber*]

(1781)

This play is to be regarded merely as a dramatic narrative in which, for the purposes of tracing out the innermost workings of the soul, advantage has been taken of the dramatic method, without otherwise conforming to the stringent rules of theatrical composition, or seeking the dubious advantage of stage adaptation. It must be admitted as somewhat inconsistent that three very remarkable people, whose acts are dependent on perhaps a thousand contingencies, should be completely developed within three hours, considering that it would scarcely be possible, in the ordinary course of events, that three such remarkable people should, even in twenty-four hours, fully reveal their characters

to the most penetrating inquirer. A greater amount of incident is here crowded together than it was possible for me to confine within the narrow limits prescribed by Aristotle or Batteux.

It is, however, not so much the bulk of my play as its contents which banish it from the stage. Its scheme and economy require that several characters should appear who would offend the finer feelings of virtue and shock the delicacy of our manners. Every delineator of human character is placed in the same dilemma if he proposes to give a faithful picture of the world as it really is, and not an ideal fantasy, a mere creation of his own. It is the course of mortal things that the good should be shadowed by the bad, and virtue shine the brightest when contrasted with vice.

---

[1] Re-printed, complete, from *Schiller's Works*, translated by R. D. Boylan and Joseph Mellish (Boston, 1902).—Ed.

Whoever proposes to discourage vice and to vindicate religion, morality, and social order against their enemies, must unveil crime in all its deformity and place it before the eyes of men in its colossal magnitude; he must diligently expose its dark mazes, and make himself familiar with sentiments at the wickedness of which his soul revolts.

Vice is here exposed in its innermost workings. In Franz it resolves all the confused terrors of conscience into wild abstractions, destroys virtuous sentiments by dissecting them, and holds up the earnest voice of religion to mockery and scorn. He who has gone so far (a distinction by no means enviable) as to quicken his understanding at the expense of his soul — to him the holiest things are no longer holy; to him God and man are alike indifferent, and both worlds are as nothing. Of such a monster I have endeavored to sketch a striking and lifelike portrait, to hold up to abhorrence all the machinery of his scheme of vice, and to test its strength by contrasting it with truth. How far my narrative is successful in accomplishing these objects, the reader is left to judge. My conviction is that I have painted nature to the life.

Next to this man [Franz] stands another who would perhaps puzzle not a few of my readers. A mind for which the greatest crimes have only charms through the glory which attaches to them, the energy which their perpetuation requires, and the dangers which attend them. A remarkable and important personage, abundantly endowed with the power of becoming either a Brutus or a Catiline, according as that power is directed. An unhappy conjunction of circumstances determines him to choose the latter for his example, and it is only after a fearful straying that he is recalled to emulate the former. Erroneous nations of activity and power, an exuberance of strength which bursts through all the barriers of law, must of necessity conflict with the rules of social life. To these enthusiastic dreams of greatness and efficiency it needed but a sarcastic bitterness against the unpoetic spirit of the age to complete the strange Don Quixote whom, in the Robber Moor, we at once detest and love, admire and pity. It is, I hope, unnecessary to remark that I no more hold up this picture as a warning exclusively to robbers than the greatest Spanish satire was leveled exclusively at knights errant.

It is nowadays so much the fashion to be witty at the expense of religion that a man will hardly pass for a genius if he does not allow his impious satire to run a tilt at its most sacred truths. The noble simplicity of holy writ must needs be abused and turned into ridicule at the daily assembies of the so-called wits; for what is there so holy and serious that will not raise a laugh if a false sense be attached to it? Let me hope that I shall have rendered no inconsiderable service to the cause of true religion and morality in holding up these wanton misbelievers to the detestation of society, under the form of the most despicable robbers.

But still more. I have made these said immoral characters to stand out favorably in particular points and even in some measure to compensate by qualities of the head, for they are deficient in those of the heart. Herein I have done no more than literally copy nature. Every man, even the most depraved, bears in some degree the impress of the Almighty's image, and perhaps the greatest villain is not farther removed from the most upright man than the petty offender; for the moral forces keep even pace with the powers of the mind, and the greater the capacity bestowed on man, the greater and more responsible is he for his errors.

The Adramelech of Klopstock (in his Messiah) awaken in us a feeling in which admiration is blended with detestation. We follow Milton's Satan with shuddering wonder throughout the pathless realms of chaos. The Medea of the old dramatists, is, in spite of all her crimes, a great and wondrous woman, and Shakespeare's Richard III is sure to excite the admiration of the reader, much as he would hate the reality. If it is to be my task to portray men as they are, I must at the same time include their good qualities, of which even the most vicious are never totally destitute. If I would warn mankind against the tiger, I must not omit to describe his glossy, beautifully marked skin, lest, owing to this omission, the ferocious animal should not be recognized until too late. Besides this, a man who is so utterly depraved as to be without a single redeeming point is no meet subject for art, and would disgust rather than excite the interest of the reader, who would turn over with impatience the pages which concern him. A noble soul can no more endure a succession of moral discords than the musical ear the grating of knives upon glass.

And for this reason I should have been ill-advised in attempting to bring my drama on the stage A certain strength of mind is required both on the part of the poet and the reader; in the former, that he may not disguise vice, in the latter that he may not suffer brilliant qualities to beguile him into admiration of the essentially detestable. Whether the author has fulfilled his duty he leaves others to judge; that his readers will perform theirs, he by no means feels assured. The vulgar — among whom I would not be understood to mean merely the rabble — the vulgar, I say (between ourselves) extend their influence far around, and unfortunately — set the fashion. Too short-sighted to reach my full meaning, too narrow-minded to comprehend the largeness of my views, too disingenuous to admit my moral aim — they will, I fear, almost frustrate my good intentions, and pretend to discover in my work an apology for the very vice which it has been my object to condemn, and will perhaps make the poor poet, to whom anything rather than justice is usually accorded, responsible for his simplicity.

Thus we have a *Da Capo* of the old story of Democritus and Abdera, and our worthy Hippocrates would need exhaust whole plantations of hellebore, were it proposed to remedy this mischief by a healing decoction. Let as many friends of truth as you will instruct their fellow-citizens in the pulpit and on the stage, the vulgar will never cease to be vulgar, though the sun and moon may change their course, and "heaven and earth wax old as a garment."

Perhaps, in order to please tender-hearted people, I might have been less true to nature; but if a certain beetle, of whom we have all heard, could extract filth even from pearls, if we have examples that fire destroyed and water deluged, shall therefore pearls, fire and water be condemned? In consequence of the remarkable catastrophe which ends my play, I may justly claim for it a place among books of morality, for crime meets at last with the punishment it deserves; the lost one enters again within the pale of the law, and virtue is triumphant. Whoever will but be courteous enough toward me to read my work through with a desire to understand it, from him I may expect — not that he will admire the poet, but that he will esteem the honest man.

ON TRAGIC ART [2]
[*Ueber die tragische Kunst*]
(1792)

If we now form the proper deductions from the previous investigation, the following will be the conditions that form bases of the tragic art. It is necessary, in the first place, that the object of our pity should belong to our own species — I mean belong in the full sense of the term — and that the action in which it is sought to interest us be a moral action; that is, an action comprehended in the field of free will. It

2 Extract re-printed from *Essays, Æsthetical and Philosophical* by Schiller, translated anonymously (London, 1875).— Ed.

is necessary, in the second place, that suffering, its sources, its degrees, should be completely communicated by a series of events chained together. It is necessary, in the third place, that the object of the passion be rendered present to our senses, not in a mediate way and by description, but immediately and in action. In tragedy, art unites all these conditions and satisfies them.

According to these principles, tragedy might be defined as the poetic imitation of a coherent series of particular events (forming a complete action): an imitation which shows us man in a state of suffering, and which has for its end to excite our pity.

I say first that it is the *imitation* of an action; and this idea of imitation already distinguishes tragedy from the other kinds of poetry, which only narrate or describe. In tragedy, particular events are presented to our imagination or to our senses at the very time of their accomplishment; they are present, we see them immediately, without the intervention of a third person. The epos, the romance, simple narrative, even in their form, withdraw action to a distance, causing the narrator to come between the acting person and the reader. Now what is distant and past always weakens, as we know, the impression and the sympathetic affection; what is present makes them stronger. All narrative forms make of the present something past; all dramatic form makes of the past a present.

Secondly, I say that tragedy is the imitation of a succession of *events,* of an action. Tragedy has not only to represent by imitation the feelings and the affections of tragic persons, but also the events that have produced these feelings, and the occasion on which these affections are manifested. This distinguishes it from lyric poetry, and from its different forms, which no doubt offer, like tragedy, the poetic imitation of certain states of the mind, but not the poetic imitation of certain actions. An elegy, a song, an ode, can place before our eyes, by imitation, the moral state in which the poet actually is — whether he speaks in his own name, or in that of an ideal person — a state determined by particular circumstances; and up to this point these lyric forms seem certainly to be incorporated in the idea of tragedy; but they do not complete that idea, because they are confined to representing our feelings. There are still more essential differences, if the end of these lyrical forms and that of tragedy are kept in view.

I say, in the third place, that tragedy is the imitation of a complete action. A separate event, though it be ever so tragic, does not in itself constitute a tragedy. To do this, several events are required, based one on the other, like cause and effect, and suitably connected so as to form a whole; without which the

truth of the feeling represented, of the character, etc.— that is, their conformity with the nature of our mind, a conformity which alone determines our sympathy — will not be recognized. If we do not feel that we ourselves in similar circumstances should have experienced the same feelings and acted in the same way, our pity would not be awakened. It is, therefore, important that we should be able to follow in all its concatenation the action that is represented to us, that we should see it issue from the mind of the agent by a natural gradation, under the influence and with the concurrence of external circumstances. It is thus that we see spring up, grow, and come to maturity under our eyes, the curiosity of Œdipus and the jealousy of Iago. It is also the only way to fill up the great gap that exists between the joy of an innocent soul and the torments of a guilty conscience, between the proud serenity of the happy man and his terrible catastrophe; in short, between the state of calm, in which the reader is at the beginning, and the violent agitation he ought to experience at the end.

A series of several connected incidents is required to produce in our souls a succession of different movements which arrest the attention, which, appealing to all the faculties of our minds, enliven our instinct of activity when it is exhausted, and which, by delaying the satisfaction of this instinct, do not kindle it the less. Against the suffering of sensuous nature the human heart has only recourse to its moral nature as counterpoise. It is, therefore, necessary, in order to stimulate this in a more pressing manner, for the tragic poet to prolong the torments of sense, but he must also give a glimpse to the latter of the satisfaction of its wants, so as to render the victory of the moral sense so much the more difficult and glorious. This twofold end can only be attained by a succession of actions judiciously chosen and combined to this end.

In the fourth place, I say that tragedy is the poetic *imitation* of an action deserving of pity, and, therefore, tragic imitation is opposed to *historic* imitation. It would only be a historic imitation if it proposed a historic end, if its principal object were to *teach* us that a thing has taken place, and how it took place. On this hypothesis it ought to keep rigorously to historic accuracy, for it would only attain its end by representing faithfully that which really took place. But tragedy has a *poetic* end, that is to say, it represents an action to *move* us, and to *charm* our souls by the medium of this emotion. If, therefore, a matter being given, tragedy treats it conformably with this poetic end which is proper to it, it becomes, by that very thing, free in its imitation. It is a right — nay, more, it is an obligation — for tragedy to subject historic truth to the laws of poetry; and to treat its matter in conformity with requirements of this art. But as it cannot attain its end, which is emotion, except on the condition of a perfect conformity with the laws of nature, tragedy is, notwithstanding its freedom in regard to history, strictly subject to the laws of natural truth, which, in opposition to the truth of history, takes the name of poetic truth. It may thus be understood how much poetic truth may lose, in many cases, by a strict observance of historic truth, and, reciprocally, how much it may gain by even a very serious alteration of truth according to history. As the tragic poet, like poets in general, is only subject to the laws of poetic truth, the most conscientious observance of historic truth could never dispense him from his duties as poet, and could never excuse in him any infraction of poetic truth or lack of interest. It is, therefore, betraying very narrow ideas on tragic art, or rather on poetry in general, to drag the tragic poet before the tribunal of history, and to require *instruction* of the man who by his very title is only bound to move and charm you. Even supposing the poet, by a scrupulous submission to historic truth, had stripped himself of his privilege of artist, and that he had tacitly acknowledged in history a jurisdiction over his work, art retains all her rights to summon him before its bar; and pieces such as, if they could not stand the test on this side, would only be tragedies of mediocre value, notwithstanding all the minuteness of costume — of national costume — and of the manners of the time.

Fifthly, tragedy is the imitation of an action that lets us see *man suffering*. The word *man* is essential to mark the limits of tragedy. Only the suffering of a being like ourselves can move our pity. Thus, evil genii, demons — or even men like them, without morals — and again pure spirits, without our weaknesses, are unfit for tragedy. The very idea of suffering implies a man in the full sense of the term. A pure spirit cannot suffer, and a man approaching one will never awaken a high degree of sympathy. A purely sensuous being can indeed have terrible suffering; but without moral sense it is a prey to it, and a suffering with reason inactive is a disgusting spectacle. The tragedian is right to prefer mixed characters, and to place the ideal of his hero half way between utter perversity and entire perfection.

Lastly, tragedy unites all these requisites to excite pity. Many means the tragic poet takes might serve another object; but he frees himself from all requirements not relating to this end, and is thereby obliged to direct himself with a view to this supreme object.

The final aim to which all the laws tend is called the *end* of any style of poetry. The means by which it attains this are its *form*. The end and form are, therefore, closely related. The form is determined by the end, and when the form is well observed the end is generally attained. Each kind of poetry having a special end must have a distinguishing form. What it exclusively produces it does in virtue of this special nature it possesses. The end of tragedy is *emotion;* its form is the imitation of an action that leads to suffering. Many kinds may have the same object as tragedy, or emotion, though it be not their principal end. Therefore, what distinguishes tragedy is the relation of its form to its end, the way in which it attains its end by means of its subject.

If the end of tragedy is to awaken sympathy, and its form is the means of attaining it, the imitation of an action fit to move must have all that favors sympathy. Such is the form of tragedy.

The production of a kind of poetry is perfect when the form peculiar to its kind has been used in the best way. Thus, a perfect tragedy is that where the form is best used to awaken sympathy. Thus, the best tragedy is that where the pity excited results more from the treatment of the poet than the theme. Such is the ideal of a tragedy.

A good number of tragedies, though fine as poems, are bad as dramas, because they do not seek their end by the best use of tragic form. Others, because they use the form to attain an end different from tragedy. Some very popular ones only touch us on account of the subject, and we are blind enough to make this a merit in the poet. There are others in which we seem to have quite forgotten the object of the poet, and, contented with pretty plays of fancy and wit, we issue with our hearts cold from the theater. Must art, so holy and venerable, defend its cause by such champions before such judges? The indulgence of the public only emboldens mediocrity: it causes genius to blush, and discourages it.

JOHANN WOLFGANG VON GOETHE

Johann Wolfgang von Goethe was born at Frankfort-on-Main in 1749. His early education was received at home, first under his father, and then with tutors, though the influence of his mother was strongly marked. In his *Dichtung und Wahrheit* Goethe tells of his early interest in puppet-plays and theaters, and in the French company of actors which remained in his native city after the Seven Years' War. These early years were devoted to literary effort, though the youth found time for at least one love-affair before reaching the age of sixteen. In 1765 he went to Leipzig and entered the University. There a second love-affair inspired a number of juvenile lyrics. Two minor plays also belong to this period. As a result of illness he was sent home, and during his convalescence he read and studied. When, in 1770, after his recovery, he went to Strassburg to study law, he was completely changed. He took up in earnest his work of criticizing French art and standing for a truly German art. He was greatly influenced by Herder, who showed him the beauty of Shakespeare. Another love-affair went far to inspire him in his first important lyrics, which were to mark a new epoch in German poetry. *Götz von Berlichingen* was written at Strassburg (though not published until 1773). "With *Götz von Berlichingen*, Shakespeare's art first triumphed on the German stage, and the literary movement known as *Sturm und Drang* was inaugurated." Goethe received his degree in 1771 and returned to Frankfurt, where he began to practice his profession. Friendships, further love-affairs, and writing, occupied the years previous to his Weimar residence. *Die Leiden des jungen Werthers* (1774) brought Goethe widespread fame. The first studies for *Faust* also date from this time, and a number of complete plays. His trip to Weimer was made after repeated invitations by the "hereditary prince," Karl August. At Weimar Goethe was entrusted with state affairs. The years between his arrival there and his famous Italian trip are chiefly memorable for some of the poet's best lyrics, a large part of *Wilhelm Meisters theatralische Sendung,* and *Iphigenie auf Tauris.* In 1786 he went to Italy. The final version of *Iphigenie* (1787), *Torquato Tasso* (1790), *Egmont* (1788), and the *Fragment* of *Faust* (1790), were all influenced by this journey. He returned to Weimar in 1788. There he lived with Christiane Vulpius for many years, finally marrying her in 1806. During the stormy years of the French Revolution Goethe took part in the French Campaign in 1792 and the Siege of Mainz in 1793. The Revolution meant little to him but the unsettling of government and order. A few very uneven plays of his bear witness to his dissatisfaction. In 1791 he was appointed director of the Ducal theater. At the same time he was occupied with biological, physical, botanical, and chemical research, and many works appeared with the results of his inquiries. The revised and extended version of *Wilhelm Meister* was included in his *Neue Schriften* (1792–1800), and exerted great influence. In 1794 he and Schiller became friends, and Goethe collaborated with the latter in his *Horen.* Schiller stimulated Goethe and encouraged him to further literary efforts. In 1798 Goethe published his epic *Hermann und Dorothea* and many ballads. Ten years later appeared the first part of *Faust,* and the next year the novel *Die Wahlverwandtschaften,* which was very popular. *Aus meinem Leben, Dichtung und Wahrheit,* part I, was published in 1811. Additional parts appeared in 1812, 1814, and the last, after his death. His wife died in 1816. The next year he retired from his position as theater director. The second part of *Faust* appeared in 1833. He died at Weimar in 1832.

Throughout a great part of Goethe's work there is a stream of criticism which renders it difficult to re-construct a complete critical theory. The various versions of the *Wilhelm Meister* novel, even *Faust* itself, are critical in spirit. But it is in the miscellaneous prefaces, articles, letters, and the Eckermann *Gespräche — Conversations —* that his critical powers are best seen. Goethe's broad outlook, his sympathy with and his deep knowledge of man and art, gave him a most catholic view, and possibly the best statement of his creed is found in Calvin Thomas' *Goethe: . . .* "the simple creed that informs Goethe, and gives him his criteria for judging the work of others. It is that the artist as such must have no creed; that is no creed derivable from the intellect or accountable to it. Rules, conventions, theories, principles, inhibitions of any sort not born of his own immediate feeling, are no concern of his. They proceed from an inferior part of human nature, being the work of gapers and babblers."

CONVERSATIONS [1]

[*Gespräche mit Goethe in den letzten Jahren seines Lebens, 1823–1832*]

(1836–48)

[1823].

(Sup.[1])   *Fri., Apr. 3.—* . . . We talked about the theater, and the improvements which have taken place in it lately. "I have remarked it without going there," said Goethe, laughing. "Two months ago my children always came home in an ill-humor; they were never satisfied with the entertainment which had been provided. But now they have turned over a new leaf; they come with joyful countenances, *because for once and away they can have a good cry.* Yesterday, they owed this 'pleasure in weeping' to a drama by Kotzebue."

(Sup.[2])   *Wed., Apr. 13.—* . . . "still, we must at all events allow that the author [of *Die Zauberflöte*] understood, to a high degree, the art of producing great theatrical effects by means of contrasts."

Tues., Oct. 21.— . . . I then asked Goethe his opinion as to the kind of verse proper for German tragedy. "People in Germany," he replied, "will scarcely come to an agreement on that point. Every one does just as he likes, and as he finds somewhat suitable to his subject. The Iambic trimeter would be the most dignified measure, but it is too long for us Germans, who, for want of epithets, generally find five feet quite enough. The English, on account of their many monosyllables, cannot even get on so far as we do."

Sat., Oct. 25.— . . . We talked of the theater, which was one of the topics which chiefly interested me this winter. The *Erdennacht* [*Night on Earth*] of Raupach was the last piece I had seen. I gave it as my opinion that the piece was not brought before us as it existed in the mind of the poet; that the Idea

1 Extracts re-printed from *Conversations of Goethe with Eckermann and Soret,* translated by John Oxenford (latest Bohn edition, London, 1913).— Ed.
2 "Supplement" of conversations with Soret.— Ed.

was more predominant than Life; that
it was rather lyric than dramatic; and
that what was spun out through five
acts would have been far better in two
or three. Goethe added that the idea of
the whole which turned upon aristocracy
and democracy, was by no means of universal interest to humanity.

I then praised those pieces of Kotzebue's which I had seen — namely, his
Verwandschaften [*Affinities*], and his
Versöhnung [*Reconciliation*]. I praised
in them the quick eye for real life, the
dexterity at seizing its interesting side,
and the genuine and forcible representation of it. Goethe agreed with me.
" What has kept its place for twenty
years, and enjoys the favor of the people," said he, " must have something in
it. When Kotzebue contented himself
with his own sphere, and did not go beyond his powers, he usually did well.
It was the same with him as with Chodo-
wiecky, who always succeeded perfectly
with the scenes of common citizens' life,
while if he attempted to paint Greek
or Roman heroes it proved a failure."

He named several other good pieces
of Kotzebue's, especially *Die beiden
Klinsberge* [*The Two Klingsbergs*].
" None can deny," said he, " that Kotzebue has looked about a great deal in
life, and ever kept his eyes open.

" Intellect, and some poetry, cannot
be denied to our modern tragic poets,
but most of them are incapable of an
easy, living representation; they strive
after something beyond their powers;
and for that reason I might call them
forced talents."

" I doubt," said I, " whether such poets
could write a piece in prose, and am of
opinion that this would be the true touchstone of their talent." Goethe agreed
with me, adding that versification enhanced, and even called forth poetic feeling.

*   *   *   *   *   *

Fri., Nov. 14.— . . . " I have," said I,
" a peculiar feeling towards Schiller.
Some scenes of his great dramas I read
with genuine love and admiration; but
presently I meet with something which
violates the truth of nature, and I can
go no further. I feel this even in reading *Wallenstein*. I cannot but think
that Schiller's turn for philosophy in-

jured his poetry, because this led him
to consider the idea far higher than all
nature; indeed, thus to annihilate nature.
What he could conceive must happen,
whether it were in conformity with nature or not."

" It was sad," said Goethe, " to see how
so highly gifted a man tormented himself with philosophical disquisitions which
could in no way profit him. Humboldt
has shown me letters which Schiller wrote
to him in those unblest days of speculation. There we see how he plagued himself with the design of perfectly separating sentimental from *naïve* poetry.
For the former he could find no proper
soil, and this brought him into unspeak-
able preplexity. As if," continued he,
smiling, " sentimental poetry could exist at all without the *naïve* ground in
which, as it were, it has its root.

" It was not Schiller's plan," continued
Goethe, " to go to work with a certain
unconsciousness, and as it were instinctively; he was forced, on the contrary,
to reflect on all he did. Hence it was
that he never could leave off talking
about his poetical projects, and thus he
discussed with me all his late pieces,
scene after scene.

" On the other hand, it was contrary
to my nature to talk over my poetic
plans with anybody — even with Schiller.
I carried everything about with me in
silence, and usually nothing was known
to any one till the whole was completed.
When I showed Schiller my *Hermann
und Dorothea* finished, he was astonⁱ
ished, for I had said not a syllable to
him of any such plan.

" But I am curious to hear what
you will say of *Wallenstein* to-morrow.
You will see noble forms, and the piece
will make an impression on you such as
you probably do not dream of."

*   *   *   *   *   *

1824.
Tues., Mar. 30.— This evening I was
with Goethe. I was alone with him; we
talked on various subjects, and drank
a bottle of wine. We spoke of the
French drama, as contrasted with the
German.

" It will be very difficult," said Goethe,
" for the German public to come to a
kind of right judgment, as they do in
Italy and France. We have a special

obstacle in the circumstance, that on our stage a medley of all sorts of things is represented. On the same boards where we saw Hamlet yesterday, we see Staberle to-day; and if to-morrow we are delighted with *Zauberflöte,* the day after we shall be charmed with the oddities of the next lucky wight. Hence the public becomes confused in its judgment, mingling together various species, which it never learns rightly to appreciate and to understand. Furthermore, every one has his own individual demands and personal wishes, and returns to the spot where he finds them realized. On the tree where he has plucked figs to-day, he would pluck them again to-morrow, and would make a long face if sloes had grown in their stead during the night. If any one is a friend to sloes, he goes to the thorns.

"Schiller had the happy thought of building a house for tragedy alone, and of giving a piece every week for the male sex exclusively. But this notion presupposed a very large city, and could not be realized with our humble means."

We talked about the plays of Iffland and Kotzebue, which, in their way, Goethe highly commended. "From this very fault," said he, "that people do not perfectly distinguish between *kinds* in art, the pieces of these men are often unjustly censured. We may wait a long time before a couple of such popular talents come again."

I praised Iffland's *Hagestolz* [*Old Bachelor*], with which I had been highly pleased on the stage. "It is unquestionably Iffland's best piece," said Goethe; "it is the only one in which he goes from prose into the ideal."

He then told me of a piece, which he and Schiller had made as a continuation to the *Hagestolz;* that is to say, in conversation, without writing it down. Goethe told me the progress of the action, scene by scene; it was very pleasant and cheerful, and gave me great delight.

Goethe then spoke of some new plays by Platen. "In these pieces," said he, "we may see the influence of Calderon. They are very clever, and, in a certain sense, complete; but they want specific gravity, a certain weight of import. They are not of a kind to excite in the

mind of the reader a deep and abiding interest; on the contrary, the strings of the soul are touched but lightly and transiently. They are like cork, which, when it swims on the water, makes no impression, but is easily sustained by the surface.

"The German requires a certain earnestness, a certain grandeur of thought, and a certain fullness of sentiment. It is on this account that Schiller is so highly esteemed by them all. I do not in the least doubt the abilities of Platen; but those, probably from mistaken views of art, are not manifested here. He shows distinguished culture, intellect, pungent wit, and artistical completeness; but these, especially in Germany, are not enough.

"Generally, the personal character of the writer influences the public rather than his talents as an artist. Napoleon said of Corneille, '*S'il vivait, je le ferais prince*'; yet he never read him. Racine he read, but did not say this of him. Lafontaine, too, is looked upon with a high degree of esteem by the French, not on account of his poetic merits, but of the greatness of character which he manifests in his writings."

·　·　·　·　·　·

Wed., Nov. 24.—"The French," said Goethe, "do well to study and translate our writers; for, limited as they are both in form and motives, they can only look without for means. We Germans may be reproached for a certain formlessness; but in matter we are their superiors. The theatrical productions of Kotzebue and Iffland are so rich in motives that they may pluck them a long time before all is used up. But, especially, our philosophical Ideality is welcome to them; for every Ideal is serviceable to revolutionary aims.

·　·　·　·　·

1825.

We continued to converse about Byron, and Goethe admired his extraordinary talent. "That which I call invention," said he, "I never saw in any one in the world to a greater degree than in him. His manner of loosing a dramatic knot is always better than one would anticipate." . . . Goethe agreed with me [on another matter] and laughed to think that Lord Byron, who, in practical life, could never adapt himself, and never even asked about a law, finally subjected himself to the stupidest of laws — that of the *three unities.*

"He understood the purpose of this law," said he, "no better than the rest of the world. *Comprehensibility* is the purpose, and the three unities are only so far good as they conduce to this end. If the observance of them hinders the comprehension of a work, it is foolish to treat them as laws, and to try to observe them. Even the Greeks, from whom the rule was taken, did not always follow it. In the *Phaëton* of Euripides, and in other pieces, there is a change of place, and it is obvious that good representation of their subject was with them more important than blind obedience to law, which, in itself, is of no great consequence. The pieces of Shakespeare deviate, as far as possible, from the unities of time and place; but they are comprehensible — nothing more so — and on this account, the Greeks would have found no fault in them. The French poets have endeavored to follow most rigidly the laws of the three unities, but they sin against comprehensibility, inasmuch as they solve a dramatic law, not dramatically, but by narration."

"I call to mind the *Feinde* [*Enemies*] of Houwald. The author of this drama stood much in his own light, when, to preserve the unity of place, he sinned against comprehensibility in the first act, and altogether sacrificed what might have given greater effect to his piece to a whim, for which no one thanks him. I thought, too, on the other hand, of *Goetz von Berlichingen,* which deviates as far as possible from the unity of time and place; but which, as everything is visibly developed to us, and brought before our eyes, is as truly dramatic and comprehensible as any piece in the world. I thought, too, that the unities of time and place were natural, and in accordance with the intention of the Greeks, only when a subject is so limited in its range that it can develop itself before our eyes with all its details in the given time; but that with a large action, which occurs in several places, there is no reason to be confined to one place, especially as our present stage arrangements offer no obstacle to a change of scene."

Goethe continued to talk of Lord Byron. "With that disposition," said he, "which always leads him into the illimitable, the restraint which he imposed upon himself by the observance of the three unities becomes him very well. If he had but known how to endure moral restraint also! That he could not was his ruin; and it may be aptly said, that he was destroyed by his own unbridled temperament."

* * * * *

1825.

"I will not deny that it was something," returned Goethe. "The main point, however, was this, that the Grand Duke left my hands quite free, and I could do just as I liked. I did not look to magnificent scenery, and a brilliant wardrobe, but I looked to good pieces. From tragedy to farce, every species was welcome; but a piece was obliged to have something in it to find favor. It was necessary that it should be great and clever, cheerful and graceful, and, at all events, healthy and containing some pith. All that was morbid, weak, lachrymose, and sentimental, as well as all that was frightful, horrible, and offensive to decorum, was utterly excluded; I should have feared, by such expedients, to spoil both actors and audience."

* * * * *

Wed., Apr. 20.— A poet who writes for the stage must have a knowledge of the stage, that he may weigh the means at his command, and know generally what is to be done, and what is to be left alone; the opera-composer, in like manner, should have some insight into poetry, that he may know how to distinguish the bad from the good, and not apply his art to something impracticable.

"Carl Maria Von Weber," said Goethe, "should not have composed *Euryanthe.* He should have seen at once that this was a bad material, of which nothing could be made. So much insight we have a right to expect of every composer, as belonging to his art."

* * * * *

Sun., May 1.—"Even Shakespeare and Molière," returned Goethe, "had no other view. Both of them wished, above all things, to make money by their theaters. In order to attain this, their principal aim, they necessarily strove that everything should be as good as possible, and that, besides good old plays, there should be some clever novelty to please and attract. The prohibition of *Tartuffe* was a thunderbolt to Molière; but not so much for the poet as for the director Molière, who had to consider the welfare of an important troupe, and to find some means to procure bread for himself and his actors."

.   .   .   .   .

Thurs., May 12.— . . . "The great point is, that he from whom we would learn should be congenial to our nature. Now, Calderon, for instance, great as he is, and much as I admire him, has exerted no influence over me for good or for ill. But he would have been dangerous to Schiller — he would have led him astray; and hence it is fortunate that Calderon was not generally known in Germany till after Schiller's death. Calderon is infinitely great in the technical and theatrical; Schiller, on the contrary, far more sound, earnest, and great in his intention, and it would have been a pity if he had lost any of these virtues, without, after all, attaining the greatness of Calderon in other respects."

We spoke of Molière. "Molière," said Goethe, "is so great, that one is astonished anew every time one reads him. He is a man by himself — his pieces border on tragedy; they are apprehensive; and no one has the courage to imitate them. His *Miser,* where the vice destroys all the natural piety between father and son, is especially great, and in a high sense tragic. But when, in a German paraphrase, the son is changed into a relation, the whole is weakened, and loses its significance. They feared to show the vice in its true nature, as he did; but what is tragic there, or indeed anywhere, except what is intolerable?

"I read some pieces of Molière's every year, just as, from time to time, I contemplate the engravings after the great Italian masters. For we little men are not able to retain the greatness of such things within ourselves; we must therefore return to them from time to time, and renew our impressions."

.   .   .   .   .

"*Macbeth,*" said Goethe, "is Shakespeare's best acting play, the one in which he shows most understanding with respect to the stage. But would you see his mind unfettered, read *Troilus and Cressida,* where he treats the materials of the *Iliad* in his own fashion."

.   .   .   .   .

[1826].

Sun. Evening, Jan. 29.—"Molière is my strength and consolation at present," said I; "I have translated his *Avare,* and am now busy with his *Médicin malgré lui.* Molière is indeed a great, a genuine man."

"Yes," said Goethe, "a genuine man; that is the proper term. There is nothing distorted about him. He ruled the manners of his day, while, on the contrary, our Iffland and Kotzebue allowed themselves to be ruled by theirs, and were limited and confined in them. Molière chastised men by drawing them just as they were."

"I would give something," said I, "to see his plays acted in all their purity! Yet such things are much too strong and natural for the public, so far as I am acquainted with it. Is not this over-refinement to be attributed to the so-called ideal literature of certain authors?"

"No," said Goethe, "it has its source in society itself. What business have our young girls at the theater? They do not belong to it — they belong to the convent, and the theater is only for men and women, who know something of human affairs. When Molière wrote, girls were in the convent, and he was not forced to think about them. But now we cannot get rid of these young girls, and pieces which are weak, and therefore *proper,* will continue to be produced. Be wise and stay away, as I do. I was really interested in the theater only so long as I could have a practical influence upon it. It was my delight to bring the establishment to a high degree of perfection; and when there was a performance, my interest was not so much in the pieces as in observing whether the actors played as they ought. The faults I wished to point out I sent in writing to the *Regisseur,* and was sure they would be avoided on the next representation. Now I can no longer have any practical influence in the theater, I feel no calling to enter it; I should be forced to endure defects without being able to amend them; and that would not suit me. And with the reading of plays, it is no better. The young German poets are eternally sending me tragedies; but what am I to do with them? I have never read German plays except with the view of seeing whether I could act them; in every other respect they were indifferent to me. What am I to do now, in my present situation, with the pieces of these young people? I can gain nothing for myself by reading how things ought *not* to be done; and I cannot assist the young poets in the matter which is already finished. If, instead of their printed plays, they would send me the plan of a play, I could at least say, 'Do it,' or 'Leave it alone,' or 'Do it this way,' or 'Do it that'; and in this there might be some use."

.   .   .   .   .   .

Wed., July 26.— . . . I told him that one of my friends intended to arrange Lord Byron's *Two Foscari* for the stage. Goethe doubted his success.

"It is indeed a temptation," he said. "When a piece makes a deep impression on us in reading, we think it will do the same on the stage, and that we could obtain such a result with little trouble. But this is by no means the case. A piece that is not originally, by the intent and skill of the poet, written for the boards, will not succeed; but whatever is done to it, will always remain something unmanageable. What trouble have I taken with my *Götz von Berlichingen!* yet it will not go right as an acting play, but is too long; and I have been forced to divide it into two parts, of which the last is indeed theatrically effective, while the first is to be looked upon as a mere introduction. If the first part were given only once as an introduction, and then the second repeatedly, it might succeed. It is the same with *Wallenstein: Die Piccolomini* does not bear repetition, but *Wallenstein's Tod* is always seen with delight."

I asked how a piece must be constructed so as to be fit for the theater.

"It must be symbolical," replied Goethe; "that is to say, each incident must be significant in itself, and lead to another still more important. The *Tar-*

tuffe of Molière is, in this respect, a great example. Only think what an introduction is the first scene! From the very beginning everything is highly significant, and leads us to expect something still more important which is to come. The beginning of Lessing's *Minna von Barnhelm* is also admirable; but that of the *Tartuffe* comes only once into the world: it is the greatest and best thing that exists of the kind."

We then came to the pieces of Calderon.

"In Calderon," said Goethe, "you find the same perfect adaptation to the theater. His pieces are throughout fit for the boards; there is not a touch in them which is not directed towards the required effect. Calderon is a genius who had also the finest understanding."

"It is singular," said I, "that the dramas of Shakespeare are not theatrical pieces, properly so called, since he wrote them all for his theater."

"Shakespeare," replied Goethe, "wrote those pieces direct from his own nature. Then, too, his age, and the existing arrangements of the stage, made no demands upon him; people were forced to put up with whatever he gave them. But if Shakespeare had written for the court of Madrid, or for the theater of Louis XIV, he would probably have adapted himself to a severer theatrical form. This, however, is by no means to be regretted, for what Shakespeare has lost as a theatrical poet he has gained as a poet in general. Shakespeare is a great psychologist, and we learn from his pieces the secrets of human nature."

.   .   .   .   .   .

[1827].

Wed., Jan. 31.— . . . "Here again," continued Goethe, "the Greeks were so great, that they regarded fidelity to historic facts less than the treatment of them by the poet. We have, fortunately, a fine example in *Philoctetes*, which subject has been treated by all three of the great tragedians, and lastly and best by Sophocles. This poet's excellent play has, fortunately, come down to us entire, while of the *Philoctetes* of Æschylus and Euripides only fragments have been found, although sufficient to show how they have managed the subject. If time permitted, I would restore these pieces, as I did the

Phaëton of Euripides; it would be to me no unpleasant or useless task.

" In this subject the problem was very simple, namely, to bring Philoctetes, with his bow, from the island of Lemnos. But the manner of doing this was the business of the poet, and here each could show the power of his invention, and one could excel another. Ulysses must fetch him; but shall he be known by Philoctetes or not? and if not, how shall he be disguised? Shall Ulysses go alone, or shall he have companions, and who shall they be? In Æschylus there is no companion; in Euripides, it is Diomed; in Sophocles, the son of Achilles. Then, in what situation is Philoctetes to be found? Shall the island be inhabited or not? and, if inhabited, shall any sympathetic soul have taken compassion on him or not? And so with a hundred other things, which are all at the discretion of the poet, and in the selection and omission of which one may show his superiority in wisdom to another. Here is the grand point, and our present poets should do like the ancients. They should not be always asking whether a subject has been used before, and look to south and north for unheard-of adventures, which are often barbarous enough, and merely make an impression as incidents. But to make something of a simple subject by a masterly treatment requires intellect and great talent, and these we do not find."

. . . . . .

" The same law," said I, " seems to lie at the foundation of a good style, where we like to avoid a sound which we have just heard. Even on the stage a great deal might be done with this law, if it were well applied. Plays, especially tragedies, in which an uniform tone uninterrupted by change prevails, have always something wearisome about them; and if the orchestra plays melancholy, depressing music during the *entr'actes* of a melancholy piece, we are tortured by an insupportable feeling, which we would escape by all possible means."

" Perhaps," said Goethe, " the lively scenes introduced into Shakspeare's plays rest upon this ' law of required change,' but it does not seem applicable to the higher tragedy of the Greeks, where, on the contrary, a certain fundamental tone pervades the whole."

" The Greek tragedy," said I, " is not of such a length as to be rendered wearisome by one pervading tone. Then there is an interchange of chorus and dialogue; and the sublime sense is of such a kind that it cannot become fatiguing, since a certain genuine reality, which is always of a cheerful nature, constantly lies at the foundation."

" You may be right," said Goethe; " and it would be well worth the trouble to investigate how far the Greek tragedy is subject to the general ' law of required change.' You see how all things are connected with each other, and how a law respecting the theory of colors can lead to an inquiry into Greek tragedy. We must only take care not to push such a law too far, and make it the foundation for much besides. We shall go more safely if we only apply it by analogy."

. . . . .

Wed., Feb. 7.— To-day Goethe spoke severely of certain critics, who were not satisfied with Lessing, and made unjust demands upon him. " When people," said he, " compare the pieces of Lessing with those of the ancients, and call them paltry and miserable, what do they mean? Rather pity the extraordinary man for being obliged to live in a pitiful time, which afforded him no better materials than are treated in his pieces; pity him, because in his *Minna von Barnhelm,* he found nothing better to do than to meddle with the squabbles of Saxony and Prussia. His constant polemical turn, too, resulted from the badness of his time. In *Emilia Galotti,* he vented his pique against princes; in *Nathan,* against the priests."

. . . . .

(Sup.). *Wed., Mar. 21.*— . . . " You must have remarked generally," continued Goethe, " that Hinrichs, in considering Greek tragedy, sets out from the *idea;* and that he looks upon Sophocles as one who, in the invention and arrangement of his pieces, likewise set out from an idea, and regulated the sex and rank of his characters accordingly. But Sophocles, when he wrote his pieces, by no means started from an *idea;* on the contrary, he seized upon some ancient ready-made popular tradition in which a good idea existed, and then only thought of adapting it in the best and most effective manner for the theater. The Atreides will not allow Ajax to be buried; but as in Antigone the sister struggles for the brother, so in the Ajax the brother struggles for the brother. That the sister takes charge of the unburied Polyneices, and the brother takes charge of the fallen Ajax, is a contingent circumstance, and does not belong to the invention of the poet, but to the tradition, which the poet followed and was obliged to follow."

"What he says about Creon's conduct," replied I, "appears to be equally untenable. He tries to prove that, in prohibiting the burial of Polyneices, Creon acts from pure political virtue; and since Creon is not merely a man, but also a prince, he lays down the proposition, that, as a man represents the tragic power of the state, this man can be no other than he who is himself the personification of the state itself — namely, the prince; and that of all persons the man as prince must be just that person who displays the greatest political virtue."

"These are assertions which no one will believe," returned Goethe with a smile. "Besides, Creon by no means acts out of political virtue, but from hatred towards the dead. When Polyneices endeavored to reconquer his paternal inheritance, from which he had been forcibly expelled, he did not commit such a monstrous crime against the state that his death was insufficient, and that the further punishment of the innocent corpse was required.

"An action should never be placed in the category of political virtue, which is opposed to virtue in general. When Creon forbids the burial of Polyneices, and not only taints the air with the decaying corpse, but also affords an opportunity for the dogs and birds of prey to drag about pieces torn from the dead body, and thus to defile the altars — an action so offensive both to gods and men is by no means politically virtuous, but on the contrary a political crime. Besides, he has everybody in the play against him. He has the elders of the state, who form the chorus, against him; he has the people at large against him;

he has Teiresias against him; he has his own family against him; but he hears not, and obstinately persists in his impiety, until he has brought to ruin all who belong to him, and is himself at last nothing but a shadow."

"And still," said I, "when one hears him speak, one cannot help believing that he is somewhat in the right."

"That is the very thing," said Goethe, "in which Sophocles is a master; and in which consists the very life of the dramatic in general. His characters all possess this gift of eloquence, and know how to explain the motives for their action so convincingly, that the hearer is almost always on the side of the last speaker.

"One can see that, in his youth, he enjoyed an excellent rhetorical education, by which he became trained to look for all the reasons and seeming reasons of things. Still, his great talent in this respect betrayed him into faults, as he sometimes went too far.

"There is a passage in *Antigone* which I always look upon as a blemish, and I would give a great deal for an apt philologist to prove that it is interpolated and spurious.

"After the heroine has, in the course of the piece, explained the noble motives for her action, and displayed the elevated purity of her soul, she at last, when she is led to death, brings forward a motive which is quote unworthy, and almost borders upon the comic.

"She says that, if she had been a mother, she would not have done, either for her dead children or for her dead husband, what she has done for her brother. For," says she, "if my husband died I could have had another, and if my children died I could have had others by my new husband. But with my brother the case is different. I cannot have another brother; for since my mother and father are dead, there is no one to beget one.

"This is, at least, the bare sense of this passage, which in my opinion, when placed in the mouth of a heroine, going to her death, disturbs the tragic tone, and appears to me very far-fetched — to save her too much of dialectical calculation. As I said, I should like a philologist to show us that the passage is spurious."

We then conversed further upon Sophocles, remarking that in his pieces he always less considered a moral tendency than an apt treatment of the subject in hand, particularly with regard to theatrical effect.

" I do not object," said Goethe, "to a dramatic poet having a moral influence in view; but when the point is to bring his subject clearly and effectively before his audience, his moral purpose proves of little use, and he needs much more a faculty for delineation and a familiarity with the stage to know what to do and what to leave undone. If there be a moral in the subject, it will appear, and the poet has nothing to consider but the effect and artistic treatment of the subject. If a poet has as high a soul as Sophocles, his influence will always be moral, let him do what he will. Besides, he knew the stage, and understood his craft thoroughly."

" How well he knew the theater," answered I, "and how much he had in view of theatrical effect, we see in his ' Philoctetes,' and the great resemblance which this piece bears to ' Œdipus in Colonos,' both in arrangement and in course of action.

" In both pieces we see the hero in a helpless condition; both are old and suffering from bodily infirmities. Œdipus has, at his side, his daughter as a guide and a prop; Philoctetes has his bow. The resemblance is carried still further. Both have been thrust aside in their afflictions; but when the oracle declares with respect to both of them, that the victory can be obtained with their aid alone, and endeavor is made to get them back again; Ulysses comes to Philoctetes, Creon to Œdipus. Both begin their discourse with cunning and honeyed words; but when these are of no avail, they use violence, and we see Philoctetes deprived of his bow, and Œdipus of his daughter."

" Such acts of violence," said Goethe, "give an opportunity for excellent altercations, and such situations of helplessness excited the emotions of the audience, on which account the poet, whose object it was to produce an effect upon the public, liked to introduce them. In order to strengthen this effect in the Œdipus, Sophocles brings him in as a weak old man, when he still, according to all circumstances, must have been a man in the prime of life. But at this vigorous age, the poet could not have used him for his play; he would have produced no effect, and he therefore made him a weak, helpless old man."

" The resemblance to Philoctetes," continued I, "goes still further. The hero, in both pieces, does not act, but suffers. On the other hand, each of these passive heroes has two active characters against him. Œdipus has Creon and Polyneices, Philoctetes has Neoptolemus and Ulysses; two such opposing characters were necessary to discuss the subject on all sides, and to gain the necessary body and fullness for the piece."

" You might add," interposed Goethe, "that both pieces bear this further resemblance, that we see in both the extremely effective situation of a happy change, since one hero, in his disconsolate situation, has his beloved daughter restored to him, and the other, his no less beloved bow."

The happy conclusions of these two pieces are also similar; for both heroes are delivered from their sorrows: Œdipus is blissfully snatched away, and as for Philoctetes, we are forewarned by the oracle of his cure, before Troy, by Æsculapius.

" When we," continued Goethe, "for our modern purposes, who wish to learn how to conduct ourselves upon the theater, Molière is the man to whom we should apply.

" Do you know his *Malade imaginaire?* There is a scene in it which, as often as I read the piece, appears to me the symbol of a perfect knowledge of the boards. I mean the scene where the ' Malade Imaginaire ' asks his little daughter Louison, if there has not been a young man in the chamber of her eldest sister.

" Now, any other who did not understand his craft so well would have let the little Louison plainly tell the fact at once, and there would have been the end of the matter.

" But what various motives for delay are introduced by Molière into this examination for the sake of life and effect. He first makes the little Louison act as if she did not understand her father; then she denies that she knows anything;

then, threatened with the rod, she falls down as if dead; then, when her father bursts out in despair, she springs up from her feigned swoon with roguish hilarity, and at last, little by little, she confesses all.

"My explanation can only give you a very meager notion of the animation of the scene; but read the scene yourself till you become thoroughly impressed with its theatrical worth, and you will confess that there is more practical instruction contained in it than in all the theories in the world.

"I have known and loved Molière," continued Goethe, "from my youth, and have learned from him during my whole life. I never fail to read some of his plays every year, that I may keep up a constant intercourse with what is excellent. It is not merely the perfect artistic treatment which delights me; but particularly the amiable nature, the highly formed mind, of the poet. There is in him a grace and a feeling for the decorous, and a tone of good society which his innate beautiful nature could only attain by daily intercourse with the most eminent men of his age. Of Menander, I only know the few fragments; but these give me so high an idea of him, that I look upon this great Greek as the only man who could be compared to Molière."

"I am happy," returned I, "to hear you speak so highly of Molière. This sounds a little different from Herr von Schlegel! I have to-day, with great repugnance, swallowed what he says concerning Molière in his lectures on dramatic poetry. He quite looks down upon him, as a vulgar buffoon, who has only seen good society at a distance, and whose business it was to invent all sorts of pleasantries for the amusement of his lord. In these low pleasantries, Schlegel admits he was most happy, but he stole the best of them. He was obliged to force himself into the higher school of comedy, and never succeeded in it."

"To a man like Schlegel," returned Goethe, "a genuine nature like Molière's is a veritable eyesore; he feels that he has nothing in common with him, he cannot endure him. The *Misanthrope,* which I read over and over again, as one of my most favorite pieces, is repugnant to him; he is forced to praise *Tartuffe* a little, but he lets him down again as much as he can. Schlegel cannot forgive Molière for ridiculing the affectation of learned ladies; he feels, probably as one of my friends has remarked, that he himself would have been ridiculed if he had lived with Molière.

"It is not to be denied," continued Goethe, "that Schlegel knows a great deal, and one is almost terrified at his extraordinary attainments and his extensive reading. But this is not enough. All the learning in the world is still no judgment. His criticism is completely one-sided, because in all theatrical pieces he merely regards the skeleton of the plot and arrangement, and only points out small points of resemblance to great predecessors, without troubling himself in the least as to what the author brings forward of graceful life and the culture of a high soul. But of what use are all the arts of genius, if we do not find in a theatrical piece an amiable or great personality of the author. This alone influences the cultivation of the people.

"I look upon the manner in which Schlegel has treated the French drama as a sort of recipe for the formation of a bad critic, who is wanting in every organ for the veneration of excellence, and who passes over a sound nature and a great character as if they were chaff and stubble."

"Shakespeare and Calderon, on the other hand," I replied, "he treats justly, and even with decided affection."

"Both," returned Goethe, "are of such a kind that one cannot say enough in praise of them, although I should not have wondered if Schlegel had scornfully let them down also. Thus he is also just to Æschylus and Sophocles; but this does not seem to arise so much from a lively conviction of their extraordinary merit as from the tradition among philologists to place them both very high; for, in fact, Schlegel's own little person is not sufficient to comprehend and appreciate such lofty natures. If this had been the case, he would have been just to Euripides too, and would have gone to work with him in a different manner. But he knows that philologists do not estimate him very highly, and he therefore feels no little delight that he is permitted upon such high authority, to fall foul of this mighty ancient and to schoolmaster him as much as he can. I do not deny that Euripides has his faults; but he was always a very respectable competitor with Sophocles and Æschylus. If he did not possess the great earnestness and the severe artistic completeness of his two predecessors, and as a dramatic poet treated things a little more leniently and humanely, he probably knew his Athenians well enough to be aware that the chord which he struck was the right one for his contemporaries. A poet whom Socrates called his friend, whom Aristotle lauded, whom Menander admired, and for whom Sophocles and the city of Athens put on mourning on hearing of his death, must certainly have been something. If a modern man like Schlegel must pick out faults in so great an ancient, he ought only to do it upon his knees."

. . . . . .

The conversation then turned upon the *Antigone* of Sophocles, and the high moral tone prevailing in it: and, lastly, upon the question — how the moral element came into the world?

"Through God himself," returned Goethe, "like everything else. It is no product of human reflection, but a beautiful nature inherent and inborn. It is, more or less, inherent in mankind generally, but to a high degree in a few eminently gifted minds. These have, by great deeds or doctrines, manifested their divine nature; which, then, by the beauty of its appearance, won the love of men, and powerfully attracted them to reverence and emulation."

"A consciousness of the worth of the morally beautiful and good could be attained by experience and wisdom, inasmuch as the bad showed itself in its consequences as a destroyer of happiness, both in individuals and the whole body, while the noble and right seemed to produce and secure the happiness of one and all. Thus the morally beautiful could become a doctrine, and diffuse itself over whole nations as something plainly expressed."

"I have lately read somewhere," answered I, "the opinion that the Greek tragedy had made moral beauty a special object."

"Not so much morality," returned Goethe, "as pure humanity in its whole extent; especially in such positions where, by falling into contact with rude power, it could assume a tragic character. In this region, indeed, even the moral stood as a principal part of human nature.

"The morality of *Antigone*, besides, was not invented by Sophocles, but was contained in the subject, which Sophocles chose the more readily, as it united so much dramatic effect with moral beauty."

Goethe then spoke about the characters of Creon and Ismene, and on the necessity for these two persons for the development of the beautiful soul of the heroine.

"All that is noble," said he, "is in itself of a quiet nature, and appears to sleep until it is aroused and summoned forth by contrast. Such a contrast is Creon, who is brought in, partly on account of Antigone, in order that her noble nature and the right which is on her side may be brought out by him, partly on his own account, in order that his unhappy error may appear odious to us.

"But, as Sophocles meant to display the elevated soul of his heroine even before the deed, another contrast was requisite by which her character might be developed; and this is her sister Ismene. In this character, the poet has given us a beautiful standard of the commonplace, so that the greatness of *Antigone*, which is far above such a standard, is the more strikingly visible."

The conversation then turned upon dramatic authors in general, and upon the important influence which they exerted, and could exert, upon the great mass of the people.

"A great dramatic poet," said Goethe, "if he is at the same time productive, and is actuated by a strong noble purpose, which pervades all his works, may succeed in making the soul of his pieces become the soul of the people. I should think that this was something well worth the trouble. From Corneille proceeded an influence capable of forming heroes. This was something for Napoleon, who had need of an heroic people; on which account, he said of Corneille, that if he were still living he would make a prince of him. A dramatic poet who knows his vocation should therefore work incessantly at its higher development, in order that his influence on the people may be noble and beneficial.

"One should not study contemporaries and competitors, but the great men of antiquity, whose works have, for centuries, received equal homage and consideration. Indeed, a man of really superior endowments will feel the necessity of this, and it is just this need for intercourse with great predecessors, which is the sign of a higher talent. Let us study Molière, let us study Shakespeare, but above all things, the old Greeks, and always the Greeks."

"For highly endowed natures," remarked I, "the study of the authors of antiquity may be perfectly inavailable; but, in general, it appears to have little influence upon personal character. If this were the case, all philologists and theologians would be the most excellent of men. But this is by no means the case; and such connoisseurs of the ancient Greek and Latin authors are able people or pitiful creatures, according to the bad or good qualities which God has given them, or which they have inherited from their father and mother."

"There is nothing to be said against that," returned Goethe; "but it must not, therefore, be said, that the study of antiquity is entirely without effect upon the formation of character. A worthless man will always remain worthless, and a little mind will not, by daily intercourse with the great minds of antiquity, become one inch greater. But a noble man, in whose soul God has placed the capability for future greatness of character and elevation of mind, will, by a knowledge of, and familiar intercourse with, the elevated natures of ancient Greeks and Romans, every day make a visible approximation to similar greatness."

* * * * *

"Shakespeare, in writing his pieces, could hardly have thought that they would appear in print, so as to be told over, and compared one with another; he had rather the stage in view when he wrote; he regarded his plays as a lively and moving scene, that would pass rapidly before the eyes and ears upon the stage, not as one that was to be held firmly, and carped at in detail. Hence, his only point was to be effective and significant for the moment."

* * * * *

Sat., July 21.— . . . "I am in the third volume already," said he, as he laid aside the book, "and am thus getting many new thoughts. You know Aristotle says of tragedy, 'It must excite fear, if it is to be good.' This is true, not only of tragedy, but of many other sorts of poetry. You find it in my *Gott und die Bayadere.* You find it in very good comedy, even in the *Sieben Mädchen in Uniform* [*Seven Girls in Uniform*], as we do not know how the joke will turn out for the dear creatures.

"This fear may be of two sorts; it may exist in the shape of alarm [*Angst*], or in that of uneasiness [*Bangigkeit*]. The latter feeling is awakened when we see a moral evil threatening, and gradually overshadowing, the personages, as, for instance, in the *Wahlverwandtschaften;* but alarm is awakened, in reader or spectator, when the personages are threatened with physical danger, as, for instance, in the *Galley Slave,* and in *Der Freischütz;* — nay in the scene of the Wolf's-glen, not only alarm, but a sense of annihilation, is awakened in the spectators. Now, Manzoni makes use of this alarm with wonderful felicity, by resolving it into emotion, and thus leading us to admiration. The feeling of alarm is necessarily of a material character, and will be excited in every reader; but that of admiration is excited by a recognition of the writer's skill, and only the connoisseur will be blessed with this feeling. What say you to these æsthetics of mine? If I were younger, I would write something according to this theory, though perhaps not so extensive a work as this of Manzoni.

* * * * *

(1829.)

Wed., Feb. 4.— . . . "Writing for the stage," he continued, "is something peculiar, and he who does not understand it thoroughly, had better leave it alone. Every one thinks that an interesting fact will appear interesting on the boards,— nothing of the kind! Things may be very pretty to read, and very pretty to think about; but as soon as they are put upon the stage the effect is quite different, and that which has charmed us in the closet will probably fall flat on the boards. If any one reads my *Hermann und Dorothea,* he thinks it might be brought out at the theater. Töpfer has been inveigled into the experiment; but what is it, what effect does it produce, especially if it is not played in a first-rate manner, and who can say that it is in every respect a good piece? Writing for the stage is a trade that one must understand, and requires a talent that one must possess. Both are uncommon, and where they are not combined, we shall scarcely have any good result."

.　　.　　.　　.　　.　　.

(1830.)

Goethe then talked of Gozzi, and his theater at Venice, where the actors had merely subjects given them, and filled up the details impromptu. Gozzi said there were only six-and-thirty tragic situations. Schiller thought there were more, but could never succeed in finding even so many.

.　　.　　.　　.　　.　　.

(Sup.) *Wed., Mar.* 17.— This evening at Goethe's for a couple of hours. By order of the Grand Duchess I brought him back *Gemma von Art,* and told him

the good opinion I entertained of this piece.

" I am always glad," returned he, " when anything is produced which is new in invention, and bears the stamp of talent." Then, taking the volume between his hands, and looking at it somewhat askance, he added, " but I am never quite pleased when I see a dramatic author make pieces too long to be represented as they are written. This imperfection takes away half the pleasure that I should otherwise feel. Only see what a thick volume this *Gemma von Art* is."

" Schiller," returned I, " has not managed much better, and yet he is a very great dramatic author."

" He too has certainly committed this fault," returned Goethe. " His first pieces particularly, which he wrote in the fullness of youth, seem as if they would never end. He had too much on his heart, and too much to say to be able to control it. Afterwards, when he became conscious of this fault, he took infinite trouble, and endeavored to overcome it by work and study; but he never perfectly succeeded. It really requires a poetical giant, and is more difficult than is imagined, to control a subject properly, to keep it from overpowering one, and to concentrate one's attention on that alone which is absolutely necessary."

.　　.　　.　　.　　.　　.

EPIC AND DRAMATIC POETRY [3]

[*Ueber epische und dramatische Dichtung*]

(1797)

The epic poet and the dramatic poet are both subject to the general laws of poetry, and especially to the laws of unity and of progression. Furthermore, they deal with subjects that are similar, and they can avail themselves of motives of either kind. The great and essential difference between them, however, lies in the fact that, whereas the epic poet describes an action as being altogether past and completed, the dramatic poet represents it as actually occurring. The best way of deducing the laws in detail, according to which both have to act, from the nature of man, is to picture to ourselves a rhapsodist and a stage-player, both as poets, the former surrounded by a quiet and attentive circle of listeners, the latter by a crowd impatiently waiting to see and hear him. Nor would it be a difficult matter to explain what is of the greatest use to each of these respective forms of poetry; what subjects each one will preferably adopt; of what motives it will preferably avail it-

[3] Re-printed, complete, from W. B. Rönnfeldt's *Criticisms, Reflections, and Maxims of Goethe* (London, n. d.).— Ed.

self. I say *preferably;* for, as I pointed out at the commencement, neither of them can lay exclusive claim to anything.

The subjects of epic poetry and of tragedy should be altogether human, full of significance and pathos. The characters will appear to the greatest advantage if they are represented as having attained a certain stage of development, when self-activity or spontaneity makes them still appear dependent upon themselves alone, and when their influence makes itself felt, not morally, politically, or mechanically, but in a purely personal way. The legends from the heroic times of the Greeks were in this sense especially favorable to their poets.

The epic poem represents above all things circumscribed activity, tragedy, circumscribed suffering. The epic poem gives us man working outside of and beyond himself: battles, wanderings, enterprises of all kinds which demand a certain sensuous breadth. Tragedy gives us man thrown in upon himself, and the actions of genuine tragedy therefore stand in need of but little space.

Of motives I distinguish five different varieties:

1. *Progressive,* which further the action, and are for the most part employed in drama.

2. *Retrogressive,* which draw the action away from its goal; these are almost exclusively confined to epic poetry.

3. *Retardative,* which delay the course or lengthen the way; these are used in both kinds of poetry with the greatest advantage.

4. *Retrospective,* by means of which events that have happened previously to the epoch of the poem are introduced into it.

5. *Anticipatory,* which anticipate that which will happen after the epoch of the poem; the epic poet, as also the dramatic poet, uses both kinds in order to create a perfect poem.

The worlds which are to be represented to view are common to both. They are:

1. The physical; and firstly, that most nearly approaching the one to which the persons represented belong, and by which they are surrounded. Here the dramatist as a rule confines himself strictly to one single point; the epic poet has more freedom of motion and his range of lo-

cality is much greater. Secondly, there is the remoter world, in which I include the whole of nature. This one the epic poet, who, generally speaking, has recourse to the imagination, seeks to bring nearer to us by means of similes or comparisons, of which the dramatist avails himself with less frequency.

2. The moral world is equally common to both, and is most happily represented in all its physiological and pathological simplicity.

3. The world of phantasies, presentiments, apparitions, accidents, and fatalities. This lies open to both, it being of course understood that it must approximate to the world of sensuous perception. Hence there arises a special difficulty for the moderns, because, much as we may desire it, we cannot easily find a substitute for the miraculous creatures, the gods, soothsayers, and oracles of the ancients.

With regard to the treatment as a whole, we shall deem the rhapsodist who describes that which belongs altogether to the past, to be a man of wisdom surveying with a calm recollection the things which have happened. His description will tend so to compose his hearers that they find pleasure in listening to him for a long space of time. He will distribute the interest equally throughout, since he is not able to counterbalance any unduly vivid impression with the necessary rapidity. He will turn about and wander to and fro according to the impulse of his fancy; and wherever he goes, he will be closely followed, for he has to deal with the imagination alone, which fashions its own pictures and which is to a certain degree indifferent as to what pictures it summons up. The rhapsodist should not himself appear in his poem as a kind of superior being. The best method for him would be to read from behind a screen, so that his hearers might turn aside their thoughts from all personality and imagine they heard the voice of the muses in general and nothing more.

With the stage-player, on the other hand, the position is exactly reversed. He comes before us as a distinct and determined individual. He wants us to interest ourselves exclusively in him and his immediate surroundings; he wants us to share his mental and bodily sufferings, to feel his perplexities, and to forget ourselves in following him. He too will, indeed, set to work in a gradual manner; but he can venture upon far more powerful effects, because in the case of sensuous presence even an unusually strong impression may be dispelled by means of a weaker one. The contemplative listener is in reason bound to remain in a state of constant sensuous exertion; he must not pause to meditate, but must follow in a state of passionate eagerness; his fancy is entirely put to silence; no claims may be made upon it, and even that which is narrated must be so placed before the eyes of the spectator as though it were actually taking place.[4]

[4] An interesting note on *Dramatic Form,* written about 1775:
" It is well-nigh time that people ceased talking about the form of dramatic compositions, about their length and shortness, their unities, their beginning, middle, and end, and all the rest of it; and that we now began to go straightway to their contents, which hitherto, it seems, have been left to take of themselves.
" There is, however, one form which is as distinct from the other as the internal sense from the external; a form which is not tangible but requires to be felt. Our head must be able to overlook that which the head of another can grasp; our heart must be able to feel that which the heart of another can feel. The intermingling of the rules will not give rise to looseness; and, though the example should prove dangerous, yet it is at bottom better to make a confused piece than a cold one.
" Indeed, if only more persons were alive to this inner form, which comprehends within itself all forms, we should not be disgusted by so many abortive productions of the intellect; writers would not think of expanding every tragic event into a drama and of slicing up every novel into a play. I wish that some clever individual would parody this twofold nuisance by arranging, say, the Æsopian fable of the Wolf and the Lamb in the form of a tragedy in five acts.
" Every form, even that which admits of the greatest amount of feeling, has in it something that is untrue. Yet the form is invariably the glass through which we collect the holy rays of extended nature and throw them upon the heart of humanity as their focus. But as for the glass — he to whom it is not given, will not succeed in obtaining it, do what he will. Like the mysterious stone of the alchemists, it is both husk and matter, both fire and cooling draught; it is so simple, so common, it lies before every door, and yet so wonderful a thing, that just those people who possess it can as a rule make no use thereof.
" He who would work for the stage should, moreover, study the stage, the effects of scenography, of lights and rouge and other coloring matter, of glazed linen and spangles. He should leave nature in her proper place, and take careful heed not to have recourse to anything but what may be performed by children with puppets upon boards and laths, together with sheets of cardboard and linen."

AUGUST WILHELM SCHLEGEL

August Wilhelm Schlegel was born at Hannover in 1767. He received his education at the Hannover Gymnasium and the University of Göttingen. He was a tutor for some years in Amsterdam, and in 1796 he went to Jena, where he married. Two years later he was made a professor at the University. Here he began his famous translation of Shakespeare, in which he was later assisted by Ludwig Tieck and others. He also contributed articles to various periodicals, and with his brother, Karl Wilhelm Friedrich, he edited the *Athenæum.* For years the two fought consistently for the new Romantic movement in literature, and their joint book, *Charakteristiken* (1801), contains many advance-guard essays. The next year August Wilhelm went to Berlin to lecture on literature and art. The publication of his play *Ion* (1803) and the study of plays, clearly indicated his interest in dramatic literature at this time. In 1807 he published in French his *Comparaison entre la Phèdre de Racine et celle d'Euripide,* in which he attacked the French classical drama. In 1808, at Vienna, he delivered a series of lectures on the drama which were printed in 1809 and 1811, under the title *Vorlesungen über dramatische Kunst und Literatur.* After his divorce in 1804 Schlegel traveled abroad. In 1813 he became secretary to the Crown Prince of Sweden. In 1818 he was made professor of literature at Bonn. He thenceforward divided his time between Oriental studies and general literature and art. He died at Bonn in 1845.

The brothers August Wilhelm and Karl Wilhelm Friedrich von Schlegel are the recognized founders of the Romantic school in Germany. August Wilhelm was one of the earliest admirers of Shakespeare and did more to encourage the reading and acting of his plays than any other man of his day. He published seventeen of the plays (Berlin, 1798–1810). He also published an excellent edition of translations from Spanish dramatic masterpieces. His lectures on dramatic art constitute a brief history as well as a vital criticism of the drama from its beginnings. These lectures were translated into many languages.

LECTURES ON DRAMATIC ART AND LITERATURE [1]
[*Vorlesungen über dramatische Kunst und Literatur*]
(1809–11)

(LECTURE II)

Before, however, entering upon such a history as we have now described, it will be necessary to examine what is meant by *dramatic, theatrical, tragic,* and *comic.*

What is dramatic? To many the answer will seem very easy: where various persons are introduced conversing together, and the poet does not speak in his own person. This is, however, merely the first external foundation of the form; and that is dialogue. But the characters may express thoughts and sentiments without operating any change on each other, and so leave the minds of both in exactly the same state in which they were at the commencement; in such a case, however interesting the conversation may be, it cannot be said to possess a dramatic interest. I shall make this clear by alluding to a more tranquil species of dialogue, not adapted for the stage: the philosophic. When, in Plato, Socrates asks the conceited sophist Hippias, what is the meaning of the beautiful, the latter is at once ready with a superficial answer, but is afterwards compelled by the ironical objections of Socrates to give up his former definition, and to grope about him for other ideas, till, ashamed at last and irritated at the superiority of the sage who has convicted him of his ignorance, he is forced to quit the field. This dialogue is not merely philosophically instructive, but arrests the attention like a drama in miniature. And justly, therefore, has this lively movement in the thoughts, this stretch of expectation for the issue, in a word, the dramatic cast of the dialogues of Plato, been always celebrated.

From this we may conceive wherein consists the great charm of dramatic poetry. Action is the true enjoyment of life, nay, life itself. Mere passive enjoyment may lull us into a state of listless complacency, but even then, if possessed of the least internal activity, we cannot avoid being soon wearied. The great bulk of mankind merely from their situation in life, or from their incapacity for extraordinary exertion, are confined within a narrow circle of insignificant operations. Their days flow on in succession under the sleepy rule of custom, their life advances by an insensible progress, and the bursting torrent of the first passions of youth soon settles into a stagnant marsh. From the discontent which this occasions, we are compelled to have recourse to all sorts of diversions, which uniformly consist in a species of occupation that may be renounced at pleasure, and though a struggle with difficulties, yet with difficulties that are easily surmounted. But of all diversions the theater is undoubtedly the most entertaining. Here we may see others act even when we cannot act to any great purpose ourselves. The highest object of human activity is man, and in the drama we see men, measuring their powers with each other as intellectual and moral beings, either as friends or foes, influencing each other by their opinions, sentiments, and passions, and decisively

1 Re-printed from *Lectures on Dramatic Art and Literature,* translated by John Black (2nd, revised, ed., Bohn Library, London, 1914). Selections from Lectures II and III.— Ed

their reciprocal relations and circumstances. The art of the poet, accordingly, consists in separating from the fable whatever does not essentially belong to it, whatever in the daily necessities of real life and the petty occupations to which they give rise interrupts the progress of important actions, and concentrating within a narrow space a number of events calculated to attract the minds of the hearers and to fill them with attention and expectation. In this manner he gives us a renovated picture of life; a compendium of whatever is moving and progressive in human existence.

But this is not all. Even in a lively oral narration it is usual to introduce persons in conversation with each other, and to give a corresponding variety to the tone and the expression. But the gaps which these conversations leave in the story the narrator fills up in his own name with a description of the accompanying circumstances and other particulars. The dramatic poet must renounce all such expedients; but for this he is richly recompensed in the following invention. He requires each of the characters in his story to be personated by a living individual; that this individual should, in sex, age, and figure, meet as near as may be the prevalent conceptions of his fictitious original, nay, assume his entire personality; that every speech should be delivered in a suitable tone of voice, and accompanied by appropriate action and gesture; and that those external circumstances should be added which are necessary to give the hearers a clear idea of what is going forward. Moreover, these representatives of the creatures of his imagination must appear in the costume belonging to their assumed rank, and to their age and country; partly for the sake of greater resemblance, and partly because, even in dress, there is something characteristic. Lastly, he must see them placed in a locality which, in some degree, resembles that where, according to his fable, the action took place, because this also contributes to the resemblance; he places them, i.e., on a scene. All this brings us to the idea of the *theater*. It is evident that the very form of dramatic poetry, that is, the exhibition of an action by dialogue without the aid of narrative, implies the theater as its necessary complement. We allow that there are dramatic works which were not originally designed for the stage and not calculated to produce any great effect there, which, nevertheless, afford great pleasure in the perusal. I am, however, very much inclined to doubt whether they would produce the same strong impression with which they affect us, upon a person who had never seen or heard a description of a theater. In reading dramatic works we are accustomed ourselves to supply the representation.

. . . . . .

After this rapid sketch of what may be called the map of dramatic literature, we return to the examination of its fundamental ideas. Since, as we have already shown, visible representation is essential to the very form of the drama, a dramatic work may always be regarded from a double point of view — how far it is *poetical* and how far it is *theatrical*. The two are by no means inseparable. Let not, however, the expression *poetical* be misunderstood: I am not now speaking of the versification and the ornaments of language; these, when not animated by some higher excellence, are the least effective on the stage; but I speak of the poetry in the spirit and design of a piece; and this may exist in as high a degree when the drama is written in prose as in verse. What is it, then, that makes a drama poetical? The very same, assuredly, that makes other work so. It must in the first place be a connected whole, complete and satisfactory within itself. But this is merely the negative definition of a work of art, by which it is distinguished from the phenomena of nature, which run into each other, and do not possess in themselves a complete and independent existence. To be poetical it is necessary that a composition should be a mirror of ideas, that is, thoughts and feelings which in their character are necessary and eternally true, and soar above this earthly life, and also that it should exhibit them embodied before us. What the ideas are, which in this view are essential to the different departments of the drama, will hereafter be the subject of our investigation. We shall also, on the other hand, show that without them a drama becomes altogether prosaic and empirical, that is to say, patched together by the understanding out of the observations it has gathered from literal reality.

But how does a dramatic work become theatrical, or fitted to appear with advantage on the stage? In single instances it is often difficult to determine whether a work possesses such a property or not. It is indeed frequently the subject of great controversy, especially when the self-love of authors and actors comes into collision; each shifts the blame of failure on the other, and those who advocate the cause of the author appeal to an imaginary perfection of the histrionic art, and complain of the insufficiency of the existing means for its realization. But in general the answer to this question is by no means so difficult. The object proposed is to produce an impression on an assembled multitude, to rivet their attention, and to excite their interest and sympathy. In this respect the poet's occupation coincides with that of the orator. How, then, does the latter attain his end? By perspicuity, rapidity, and energy. Whatever exceeds the ordinary measure of patience or comprehension he must diligently avoid. Moreover, when a number of men are assembled together, they mutually distract each other's attention whenever their eyes and ears are not drawn to a common object without and beyond themselves. Hence the dramatic poet, as well as the orator, must from the very commencement, by strong impressions, transport his hearers out of themselves and, as it were, take bodily possession of their attention. There is a species of poetry which gently stirs a mind attuned to solitary contemplation, as soft breezes elicit melody from the Æolian harp. However excellent this poetry may be in itself, without some other accompaniments its tones would be lost on the stage. The melting *harmonica* is not calculated to regulate the march of an army, and kindle its military enthusiasm. For this we must have piercing instruments, but above all, a strongly marked rhythm, to quicken the pulsation and give a more rapid movement to the animal spirits. The grand requisite in a drama is to make this rhythm perceptible in the onward progress of the action. When this

has once been effected the poet may all the sooner halt in his rapid career and indulge the bent of his own genius. There are points, when the most elaborate and polished style, the most enthusiastic lyrics, the most profound thoughts and remote illusions, the smartest coruscations of wit, and the most dazzling flights of sportive and ethereal fancy, are all in their place, and when the willing audience, even those who cannot entirely comprehend them, follow the whole with a greedy ear, like music in unison with their feelings. Here the poet's great art lies in availing himself of the effect of contrasts, which enable him at one time to produce calm repose, profound contemplation, and even the self-abandoned indifference of exhaustion, or, at another, the most tumultuous emotions, the most violent storm of the passions. With respect to theatrical fitness, however, it must not be forgotten that much must always depend on the capacities and humors of the audience, and, consequently, on the national character in general, and the particular degree of mental culture. Of all kinds of poetry the dramatic is, in a certain sense, the most secular; for, issuing from the stillness of an inspired mind, it yet fears not to exhibit itself in the midst of the noise and tumult of social life. The dramatic poet is, more than any other, obliged to court external favor and loud applause. But of course it is only in appearance that he thus lowers himself to his hearers; while, in reality, he is elevating them to himself.

In thus producing an impression on an assembled multitude, the following circumstances deserve to be weighed, in order to ascertain the whole amount of its importance. In ordinary intercourse men exhibit only the outward man to each other. They are withheld by mistrust or indifference from allowing others to look into what passes within them; and to speak with anything like emotion or agitation of that which is nearest our heart is considered unsuitable to the tone of polished society. The orator and the dramatist find means to break through these barriers of conventional reserve. While they transport their hearers into such lively emotions that the outward signs thereof break forth involuntarily, every man perceives those around him to be affected in the same manner and degree, and those who before were strangers to one another become in a moment intimately acquainted. The tears which the dramatist or the orator compels them to shed for calumniated innocence or dying heroism make friends and brothers of them all. Almost inconceivable is the power of a visible communion of numbers to give intensity to those feelings of the heart which usually retire into privacy, or only open themselves to the confidence of friendship. The faith in the validity of such emotions becomes irrefragable from its diffusion; we feel ourselves strong among so many associates, and all hearts and minds flow together in one great and irresistible stream. On this very account, the privilege of influencing an assembled crowd is exposed to most dangerous abuses. As one may disinterestedly animate them for the noblest and best of purposes, so another may entangle them in the deceitful meshes of sophistry, and dazzle them by the glare of a false magnanimity whose vainglorious crimes may be painted as virtues and even as sacrifices. Beneath the delightful charms of oratory and poetry, the poison steals imperceptibly into ear and heart. Above all others must the comic poet (seeing that his very occupation keeps him always on the slippery brink of this precipice) take heed lest he avoid an opportunity for the lower and baser parts of human nature to display themselves without restraint. When the sense of shame which ordinarily keeps these baser propensities within the bounds of decency, is once weakened by the sight of others' participation in them, our inherent sympathy with what is vile will soon break out into the most unbridled licentiousness. . . .

. . . . . .

(LECTURE III)

. . . . .

The dramatic poet, as well as the epic, represents external events, but he represents them as real and present. In common with the lyric poet, he also claims our mental participation, but not in the same calm composedness; the feeling of joy and sorrow which the drama-

tist excites is more immediate and vehement. He calls forth all the emotions which the sight of similar deeds and fortunes of living men would elicit, and it is only by the total sum of the impression which he produces that he ultimately resolves the conflicting emotions into a harmonious tone of feeling. As he stands in such close proximity to real life, and endeavors to indue his own imaginary creations with vitality, the equanimity of the epic poet would in him be indifferent; he must decidedly take part with one or other of the leading views of human life, and constrain his audience also to participate in the same feeling.

To employ simpler and more intelligible language: the *tragic* and *comic* bear the same relation to one another as *earnest* and *sport*. Every man, from his own experience, is acquainted with both these states of mind; but to determine their essence and their source would demand deep philosophical investigation. Both, indeed, bear the stamp of our common nature, but earnestness belongs more to its moral, and mirth to its animal, part. The creatures destitute of reason are incapable either of earnest or of sport. Animals seem, indeed, at times to labor as if they were earnestly intent upon some aim and as if they made the present moment subordinate to the future; at other times they seem to sport, that is, they give themselves up without object or purpose to the pleasure of existence; but they do not possess consciousness, which alone can entitle these two conditions to the names of earnest and sport. Man alone, of all the animals with which we are acquainted, is capable of looking back towards the past and forward into futurity; and he has to purchase the enjoyment of this noble privilege at a dear rate. Earnestness, in the most extensive signification, is the direction of our mental powers to some aim. But as soon as we begin to call ourselves to account for our actions, reason compels us to fix this aim higher and higher, till we come at last to the highest end of our existence: and here that longing for the infinite which is inherent in our being is baffled by the limits of our finite existence. All that we do, all that we effect, is vain and perishable; death stands everywhere in the background, and to it every well or ill spent moment brings us nearer and closer; and, even when a man has been so singularly fortunate as to reach the utmost term of life without any grievous calamity, the inevitable doom still awaits him to leave or to be left by all that is most dear to him on earth. There is no bond of love without a separation, no enjoyment without the grief of losing it. When, however, we contemplate the relations of our existence to the extreme limit of possibilities; when we reflect on its entire dependence on a chain of causes and effects stretching beyond our ken; when we consider how weak and helpless, and doomed to struggle against the enormous powers of an unknown world, as it were ship-wrecked at our very birth; how we are subject to all kinds of errors and deceptions, any one of which may be our ruin; that in our passions we cherish an enemy in our bosoms; how every moment demands from us in the name of the most sacred duties the sacrifice of our dearest inclinations, and how at one blow we may be robbed of all that we have acquired with much toil and difficulty; that with every accession to our stores the risk of loss is proportionately increased, and we are only the more exposed to the malice of hostile force; when we think upon all this every heart which is not dead to feeling must be overpowered by an inexpressible melancholy for which there is no other counterpoise than the consciousness of a vocation transcending the limits of this earthly life. This is the tragic tone of mind; and when the thought of the possible issues out of the mind as a living reality, when this tone pervades and animates a visible representation of the most striking instances of violent revolutions in a man's fortunes, either prostrating his mental energies, or calling forth the most heroic endurance — then the result is *Tragic Poetry*. We thus see how this kind of poetry has its foundation in our nature, while to a certain extent we have also answered the question, why we are fond of such mournful representations, and even find something consoling and elevating in them. This tone of mind we have described is inseparable from strong feeling; and although poetry cannot remove these internal dissonances, she must at least endeavor to effect an ideal reconciliation of them.

As earnestness, in the highest degree, is the essence of tragic representation, so in sport of the comic. The disposition of mirth is a forgetfulness of all gloomy considerations in the pleasant feeling of present happiness. We are then inclined to view everything in a sportive light, and to allow nothing to disturb or ruffle our minds. The imperfections and the irregularities of men, are no longer an object of dislike and compassion, but serve, by their strange inconsistencies, to entertain the understanding and to amuse the fancy. The comic poet must therefore carefully abstain from whatever is calculated to excite more indignation at the conduct or sympathy with the situations of his personages, because this would inevitably bring us back again into earnestness. He must paint their irregularities as springing out of the predominance of the animal part of their nature, and the incidents which befall them as merely ludicrous distresses, which will be attended with no fatal consequences. This is uniformly what takes place in what we call Comedy, in which, however, there is still a mixture of seriousness, as I shall show in the sequel. The oldest comedies of the Greeks was, however, entirely sportive, and in that respect, formed the most complete contrast to their tragedy. Not only were the characters and situations of individuals worked up into a comic picture of real life, but the whole frame of society, the constitution, nature, and the gods, were all fantastically painted in the most ridiculous and laughable colors.

RICHARD WAGNER

Wilhelm Richard Wagner was born at Leipzig in 1813. His father died when Richard was in his infancy, and his stepfather, dramatist, actor, and painter, intended Richard to be a painter, but as he himself confesses, he had no talent. He soon developed a taste for music and played the piano before he was six. However, music was of only secondary interest, for at the age of eleven he wrote a poem which was published. He then became interested in plays, and while he was still a child he learned English in order to read Shakespeare, and even wrote a tragedy in imitation of him. It was after hearing Beethoven's *Egmont* music that Wagner determined to furnish similar music for his tragedy. At this time he decided to become a composer, and in quick succession he wrote a number of miscellaneous compositions. An orchestral overture was even performed. His schooling had been irregular, though he attended the University. He then studied composition at the Thomasschule in Leipzig. He produced his first symphony in 1833, and the next year he conducted an opera at Magdeburg. In 1836 he was looking for a position at Königsberg, and there he married. Three years later he took his unfinished *Rienzi* to Paris, but was unsuccessful in having it produced. In 1842 it was heard at Dresden, and was followed by *Der fliegende Holländer.* *Tannhäuser* was played in 1845. *Lohengrin* was completed three years after, but that year he was forced to leave Saxony for political reasons. He went to Zürich where he remained until 1859. He was constantly working at the tetralogy, *Der Ring des Nibelungen,* but wrote

Tristan und Isolde in the meantime (1865). He was pardoned in 1861 and returned to his native country. Three years after, he produced *Die Meistersinger.* In 1870 Wagner married Cosima, Liszt's daughter. Ludwig, King of Bavaria, invited him to Munich to finish the *Ring.* Six years later the whole tetralogy was performed at Bayreuth, where Wagner had worked out his plans for the celebrated opera-house. His last work was *Parsifal.* He died at Bayreuth in 1883.

Wagner wrote the librettos for all his operas, regarding the drama as inseparable from the music. Throughout his life he wrote about his theories— often obscurely, almost as obscurely as the translator of his collected works — on the new music-drama form, but these are reducible to the one theory that the art-work of the future is a combination of music and drama. Probably the best statement is found in *Ueber die Bestimmung der Oper* (1871). He once said: " A subject which is comprehended merely by the intelligence can also be expressed merely through the language of words; but the more it expands into an emotional concept, the more does it call for an expression which in its final and essential fullness can alone be obtained through the language of sounds. Hereby the essence of that which the Word-Tone-Poet has to express results quite by itself: it is the Purely Human, freed from all conventions."

THE PURPOSE OF THE OPERA [1]

[*Ueber die Bestimmung der Oper*]

(1871)

.   .   .   .   .   .

The very essence of the dramatic art, therefore, as opposed to the poetic method, appears to be at first sight entirely irrational; it is only to be grasped by a complete change in the nature of the observer. It should not be difficult for us to determine in what this change should consist, if we look at the *natural*

[1] Re-printed extract from *Art Life and Theories of Richard Wagner*, by Edward L. Burlingame (New York, 1875).— Ed.

method in the beginnings of *all* art — and this we find distinctly in *improvisation.* The poet who should show to the improvising actor a plan of the action to be represented, would stand in much the same relation in which the author of an operatic text stands to the musician; his work cannot yet have any artistic value whatever; but this will be most fully imparted to it if the poet makes the actor's improvising spirit his own, and carries out his work completely in the character of an improvisation, so that now the actor can enter with all his own peculiarity into the higher thought of the poet. Of course, a complete change in the art-product itself must take place through this means; and such a change could only be exactly described, if it were possible to have before us the actually transcribed improvisation of a great musician.

We have the testimony of excellent witnesses to the incomparable impression which Beethoven left upon his friends by improvising at the piano; and we cannot regard as exaggerated the regret expressed at the fact of not having been able to preserve these creations in writing — it cannot be called exaggerated even when we consider the master's greatest written works, if we remember the frequent occurrence, that even less gifted composers, whose compositions when written out are characterized by stiffness and constraint, can, by free improvisation, throw us into genuine amazement at a creative gift never before suspected and often most productive.

In any case, we believe we shall greatly facilitate the solution of a very difficult problem if we call the Shakespearian drama a *definitely-planned histrionic improvisation of the very highest artistic value*. For if we take this view we shall have an immediate explanation of the apparently remarkable inconsistencies in the action and language of characters who are created with the single purpose of *being*, now and at the moment when they are before us, precisely those characters they are *meant* to appear to us,— and to whom no language could possibly occur which would lie outside this *nature*, with which they are, as it were, bewitched. And it would seem absurd enough, on closer consideration, if one of these characters should suddenly seek to appear to us in the character of a poet. This element is silent, and remains a riddle to us, as Shakespeare does. Yet its work is the only true drama; and we see what importance the drama really has as a work of art, in the fact that its author will always appear to us the deepest poetic nature of all time.

To continue the considerations to which the drama so strongly urges us,

let us now look at those peculiarities of it which seem most serviceable for our purpose. Most prominent among these is the fact that, apart from all its other value, it belongs to the class of pieces which alone are effective in the *theater* — pieces that have been arranged expressly for the theater at different periods, have proceeded *from* the theater or from authors standing in direct communication with it, and have from year to year enriched the popular French stage, for example. The difference between them lies only in the *poetic* value of true dramatic products that have arisen from the same origin. This difference seems at first sight to be determined by the greatness and importance of the material selected for their action. While not only the French have succeeded in most truthfully depicting upon the stage all the events of modern life in general, but the Germans (people of much less theatrical talent) have successfully brought forward the occurrences of this life in its smaller and more domestic circle, this truly reproductive force has failed just in proportion as the events of a higher sphere of action, and the fate of historic heroes and the myths concerning them (removed to a respectful distance from matters of everyday life), were sought to be produced. For this purpose the true poet (that is, the inventor and former of myths) had to overcome the insufficient dramatic improvisation; and his genius, especially fitted for such a task, must manifest itself in raising the style of that improvisation to the height of his own poetic purpose. How Shakespeare succeeded in raising his players themselves to this height, must remain a problem; it is only certain that the capacities of our modern players would at once fail in the task thus set them. The assumption is possible, that the grotesque affectation peculiar to the English actors of the present day (to which we referred above) is a remnant of an earlier power which, since it comes from a trait lying undeniably in the nature of the nation, may have been able, in the most perfect period of national life and through the noble example of the poetic actor himself, to lead to so unprecedented a point in theatrical art that Shakespeare's conceptions could be for once fully carried out.

Or we may perhaps call to mind for the explanation of this enigma, if we do not wish to accept so extraordinary a miracle as that just supposed, the fate of the great Sebastian Bach, whose rich and difficult choral compositions would appear to lead us to the theory that the master must have had at command for their execution the most incomparable vocal forces; while on the contrary we know from undoubted documentary evidence his own complaints of the general wretched composition of his choir of schoolboys. It is certain that Shakespeare retired very early from his connection with the stage; a fact that we can easily explain by the very great fatigue the rehearsals of his pieces cost him, as well as his despair at the flight of his own genius beyond the possibilities that were open to him. The whole nature of his genius is, however, only clear to us through these very "possibilities," which certainly existed in the basis of the actor's nature, and were therefore very properly taken for granted by the author; and, considering the efforts for culture made by the genius of humanity in one great connection, we can look upon it as the task which the great dramatist in a certain sense bequeathed to his successors, to really reach those highest possibilities in the development of the capabilities of histrionic art.

To labor at this task appears to have been the truest calling of our own great German poets. Proceeding from the necessary acknowledgment of Shakespeare's inimitability, this purpose determined a direction for every form of their poetic conception, which we can well understand if we keep this hypothesis in mind. The search for the ideal form of the highest work of art — the drama — led them of necessity away from Shakespeare to the renewed and always deeper consideration of the tragedy of the ancients; we have seen in what way alone they thought to gain anything from this, and we observed that they were necessarily led from this more than doubtful path to that inexplicable new impression which the noblest creations of the opera (in other respects entirely enigmatical to them) produced upon them.

Two things were noteworthy in connection with this, namely, that the noble music of a great master could give an ideal enchantment to the work of even little-gifted dramatic performers, an enchantment which was denied to even the most admirable actors of the spoken drama; while on the other hand a true dramatic talent could so ennoble utterly worthless music that we could be struck by a performance which the same talent could not succeed in producing in a spoken play. That this phenomenon could only be explained by the power of *music,* was unavoidable. And this could be true only of music *in general;* while it remained incomprehensible how the peculiar flexibility of its forms could be attained without their subordination to the worst possible kind of dramatic poet.

We adduced the example of Shakespeare, to give us as much of a glimpse as possible into the nature, and especially the method, of the true dramatist. And mysterious as the greater part of this must be to us, we could nevertheless perceive that it was the actor's art with which the poet entirely united; and we recognized that this actor's art was the dew of life, in which the poetic purpose must be bathed, in order that it might be able, as though by a magic transformation, to appear a true mirror of life. Now, in every action, even ordinary event of life (such as not only Shakespeare but every true playwright shows us), can reveal itself to us, when reproduced as a mimic drama, in the glorified light and with the objective effect of a mirrored picture, we must accept as proved as a result of our further considerations, that this reflection in turn shows itself in the pure light of the ideal so soon as it has been dipped in the magic fountain of music; and at the same time is displayed to us as a pure form, freed from all realistic materialization.

It would no longer be needful, therefore, to take into consideration the *form of music,* but rather the forms of music *as historically developed,* if one desired to determine that highest possibility in the development of the actor's art, which seemed to the investigator and the worker a dark enigma, while on the other hand it pressed itself more and more upon him.

By "the form of music" we must undoubtedly understand *melody*. The development of this especially fills the history of our music; as the need of it determined the development of the lyric drama attempted by the Italians, into the opera. The attempt being first made to imitate in this respect the form of the Greek tragedy, this seemed at the first glance to be divided into two principal parts — the choral song, and the dramatic recitation which periodically rose into musical measure; and the actual "drama" was thus left to the recitative, the oppressive monotony of which was finally interrupted by the discovery of the "air" (an invention approved by the academy). It was only with this that music gained its independent form as *melody;* and it thus (very rightly) won such an advantage over the remaining factors of the musical drama, that this latter, no longer employed as anything but an excuse for the other, finally sank to the place of a mere scaffolding for the exhibition of the *aria*. It must be the history of melody closely limited to this *aria* form, which must therefore engage our attention, if we are not entirely content with the consideration of those of its effects merely, which it presented to our great poets when they felt themselves so deeply impressed by its power, yet so much more deeply at a loss in thinking of any poetic association with it. It was indisputably only a special form of genius that could so endue with life this narrow and empty form of melodic expression, that it could be capable of a really powerful effect. Its extension and development was therefore only to be expected from the musician; and the course of that development could be distinctly seen by a comparison of Mozart's masterpiece with Gluck's. In this comparison a rich power of purely musical invention is especially displayed as the only thing which could make pure music powerful in a dramatic sense; for in Mozart's *Don Juan* there is an abundance of dramatic elements of which the far less powerful composer Gluck had no conception. But it was reserved for German genius to elevate the musical

form, by the highest inspiration of even its least important parts to the inexhaustible variety and richness which the music of our great Beethoven now offers to a wondering world.

The musical creations of Beethoven have traits which render them as inexplicable from one point of view as those of Shakespeare are from another. While the powerful influence of both must be felt as different in kind though equal in effect, even this difference between them seems to disappear upon closer consideration, and in view of the incomprehensible peculiarity of their creations; for the only way of explaining the one appears to us in the explanation given for the other.

Let us instance in proof of this, and as the most easily intelligible point, the peculiarity of the humorous element in both, and we shall see that what often appears to us as an incomprehensible inconsistency in the humor of Shakespeare's creations, appears in precisely similar features of Beethoven's work as a natural piece of high idealism — presented as a melody which is inseparable from the mood of the listener. We cannot escape here from the assumption of a primal connection between the two, which we shall be able to properly define if we do not look upon it as existing between the musician and the poet— but as between one poetic actor or *mimic*, and another. The secret lies in the *directness* of the representation, conveyed in the one case by expression and action, and in the other by living music. That which both create and form is the true work of art, for which the poet only draws the plan — and even this unsuccessfully, unless he has taken it directly from nature.

We have seen that the Shakespearian drama is most correctly comprehended under the name of a "definite imitative improvisation"; and we were obliged to assume that the highest poetic value, though emanating at first from the dignity of the material selected, must be secured to such a work of art by the elevation of the *style* of that improvisation. We cannot be mistaken, therefore, in thinking that such an elevation, to the extent which is really needed, can only be found in that music which stands in just such a relation to it as does Beethoven's music to Shakespeare's dramas.

The very point in which the difficulty of applying music like Beethoven's to dramas like Shakespeare's is here most prominently to be seen, might, if properly adjusted, lead directly to the highest perfection of musical form, by freeing it from every fetter that may still hamper it. That which so perplexed our great poets in their consideration of the opera, and that feature in Beethoven's instrumental music which still distinctly shows the skeleton of a structure found rather in the same tendency that produced the opera *aria* and the ballet piece, than in the true nature of music — these features of conventional composition, though endowed with such wonderfully vigorous life by Beethoven's use of melody, would thus most completely disappear before an ideal method full of the truest freedom. Thus music, in this respect at least, would adapt itself closely to the thoroughly life-filled form of a Shakespearian drama which, when its noble irregularity is compared with the drama of the ancients, seems almost like a scene in nature beside an architectural work — while its thoroughly logical character nevertheless is revealed in the certainty of the effect the work of art produces. In this, too, would be shown the entire novelty of the form of such an art product which, only conceivable (as an idealized natural production) by employing in it the aid of the German language, the most cultured of modern tongues, could nevertheless deceive the judgment as long as a standard was applied to it which it had entirely outgrown — whereas the fitting new standard would be derived from the impression which the unwritten improvisation of an incomparable composer would make upon one fortunate enough to hear it. The greatest of dramatists has taught us to give definite form to such an improvisation; and in the highest conceivable work of art the noblest inspirations of both composer and dramatist should exist as the very essence of the world thus revealed to us in the mirror of the world itself.

If we adopt, for the work of art which we have in view this designation, "a dramatic-musical improvisation of perfected poetic value, embodied in a fixed form by the highest artistic thought," we shall find, if we follow the teachings of experience, a surprising light thrown upon the practical points connected with the actual execution of such a work.

In a very important sense, and interpreting the matter strictly, our great poets could only be chiefly concerned with the discovery of some method by which a heightened pathos could be added to the drama, and a technical means be found for embodying this. However certain it may be that Shakespeare derived his style from the instincts of the actor's art, he must nevertheless have been dependent for the presentation of his dramas on the accident of greater or less talent in his players, who must all have been to a certain extent Shakespeares, just as he himself was always to a certain extent the character presented; and we have no reason for the assumption that his genius could have recognized in the performance of his pieces more than the mere shadow of himself cast upon the stage.

That which so strangely attracted our great poets toward music was the fact that it was at the same time the purest form and the most sensuous realization of that form. The abstract arithmetical number, the mathematical figure, meets us here as a creation having an irresistible influence upon the emotions — that is, it appears as *melody;* and this can be as unerringly established so as to produce sensuous effect, as the poetic diction of written language, on the contrary, is abandoned to every whim in the personal character of the person reciting it. What was not practically possible for Shakespeare — to be *himself* the actor of each one of his rôles — is practicable for the musical composer, and this with great definiteness — since he speaks to us directly through each one of the musicians who execute his works. In this case the transmigration of the poet's soul into the body of the performer takes place according to the infallible laws of the most positive *technique;* and the composer who gives the correct measure for a technically right performance of his work becomes completely one with the musician who performs it, to an extent that can at most only be affirmed of the constructive artist in regard to a work which he had himself produced in color or stone — if, indeed, a transmigration of his soul into lifeless matter is a supposable case.

If we add to this wonderful power in the musician that capacity of his art which we deduced from the facts we considered in the beginning — the facts that even insignificant music (so long as it is not entirely distorted into the vulgar grotesquesness of certain kinds of opera now popular) makes otherwise unattainable performances possible to a great dramatic talent, while noble music can almost *force* from insignificant dramatic powers successes impossible in any other way — when we add the results of these facts to the musician's power, we can scarcely feel a doubt as to the reason of the complete failure which this view predicts for the poet of to-day, if he attempts to succeed in mastering the drama, in its noblest sense, by the only means at his command — the capabilities of the same language in which now even newspaper articles speak to us!

In this respect, however, our assumption that the highest perfection is reserved for the musically-arranged drama, should have a hopeful, rather than a discouraging influence upon us: for here we are primarily concerned with the purification of a great and many-sided department of art — that of the drama as a whole — the errors of which are to-day both increased and concealed by the influence of the modern opera. To gain a clean conception of this, and to accurately measure the field of their future productiveness, our dramatists might perhaps find it advisable to trace back the descent of the modern theater; but not to seek its origin in the ancient drama, which was in its form a so completely original product of the Hellenic mind, its religion, and even its form of government, that the assumption that it had been imitated by later forms would lead to the greatest errors. The origin of the modern theater, on the contrary, shows us along the path of its development such an abundance of noble productions of the greatest value, that this path may certainly be followed further without shame. The genuine theatrical " play," in its most modern sense, would

have to be the only healthful basis of all further dramatic efforts; but in order to labor successfully in this direction it is necessary first of all to form a right conception of the spirit of theatrical art, which has its basis in the art of the *actor;* and not to use it for the formulating of tendencies, but as the reflection of life-pictures such as are really seen.

The French, who have even recently contributed so much that is excellent in this respect, did not, it is true, look for the appearance of a new Molière among them every year; and for us too the birth of a Shakespeare is not to be read in every calendar.

As far as seeking to satisfy ideal demands is concerned, the limit to which such demands may properly go seems to be set, for the influence of the all-powerful dramatic work of art which we have in view, with greater certainty than has before been possible. This point may be distinctly recognized as existing where, in that art-product, song comes in contact with *spoken* words. Yet by no means an absolutely narrow sphere is indicated by this, but rather an entirely different and dissimilar one; and we may at once gain an insight into this difference if we call to mind a certain involuntary compulsion which forces even our best dramatic singers into excess; and by which they feel themselves forced to *speak* an emphatic word in the very midst of their song. Schröder-Devrient, for example, saw herself compelled to this course by a fearfully highly wrought situation in the opera of *Fidelio* where, holding her pistol before the tyrant, she suddenly positively *spoke* — and with a terrible accent of despair — the last word of the phrase —" another step — and thou art — DEAD." The indescribable effect of this acted upon every one as a harsh break from one sphere into the other; and the power of it consisted in this, that as though by a flash of lightning we gained a sudden insight into the nature of both spheres, one of them the ideal, and the other the real. It was evident that for a moment the ideal one was incapable of bearing a burden which it therefore cast upon the other; and as especially passionate and excited music is so commonly credited with a purely morbid element inherent in it, it may easily surprise us to recognize from this example how delicate and purely ideal in form its sphere really is, so that the realistic terrors of actual life cannot be contained in it — though the soul of all reality finds pure expression in music alone.

Evidently, therefore, there is a side to the world which concerns us most seriously, and the terrible teachings of which are only intelligible to us in the field of observation, in which music must be silent. This field is perhaps best estimated, if we allow ourselves to be led into it by the great actor, Shakespeare, as far as the point where we find him overcome by that despairing discouragement which we have thought it necessary to assume as the reason of his early retirement from the stage. This field may be best called, if not the basis, at least the manifestation of history; and to properly seize upon its real value for human knowledge, must always be left to the poet alone.

So important and distinct an influence as we could only attempt to indicate here by the merest outline — an influence exercised not only upon that department of the drama with which it is most closely connected with the drama in any way — such an influence could only be possible for the musically-arranged and executed dramatic work that we have referred to, if the latter, in its production before the public, can render itself outwardly intelligible in a consistent way, and thus enable an opinion of its characteristics to be formed with the necessary freedom. It is so closely related to the opera that we feel we may rightly look upon it, as far as our present consideration is concerned, as the province of that branch of art; none of the possibilities suggested to us could have been clear to us if they had not been manifested for us in the opera in general, and especially in the most admirable works of the great operatic composers. And just as certainly, it was the spirit of music which, in the constantly increasing richness of its development, could have such an influence upon the opera that these possibilities could in any way arise within it. And yet, if we desire to explain the degradation which the opera has undergone, we must seek its cause again in the peculiarities of music. As in painting and even in architecture, the merely " attractive " may displace the beautiful, so it has been not the less the less fate of music to decline from a noble to a merely pleasing art. If its sphere was that of the purest idealism — if it had so deep an influence on our emotions and freed what was realistic from everything disagreeable in its representation by the very fact that it showed itself to us as pure form alone, so that what threatened to disturb this fell or was kept away from it — even if all this was true, yet this pure form, if not placed in an entirely appropriate relation to its environment, might easily seem only suitable for a pleasant plaything and only be used for such a ·purpose. This would be the case as soon as it was used, in so unfitting a sphere as the basis of the opera could offer it, as a mere superficial method of giving pleasure to the sense of hearing or arousing the emotions.

But we are little concerned here with this view, for we began our essay with the complaint made against the effect and the influence of the opera, the unfortunate importance of which cannot be better shown than by pointing to the universal experience, that the stage of to-day has long been given up and viewed with complete indifference by the truly educated portion of the nation, who used once to look to it with every hope. If we wish, then, to secure for the work of art we have just described the only esteem which could be just and valuable for it — that of those who have turned with serious displeasure from the recent stage — this can only be possible outside of all relation with that stage. The neutral ground, however, on which it can be done, though ever so completely separated *locally* from the field of influence of our theaters, could only bear proper fruit if nourished by the real elements of our histrionic and musical arts. In these alone lies the truly productive material for genuine dramatic achievement; every attempt of every other kind must lead not to art, but to an affected artificiality.

It is our actors, singers, and musicians upon whose own instincts all hope for the attainment of artistic objects must rest, even when these objects themselves may be incomprehensible to them. For they must be the ones to whom these objects will most speedily become clear, as soon as their own artistic instincts are put upon the right path toward their recognition. That these instincts of theirs have hitherto been only guided, by the influences of our stage toward the development of the very worst qualities of dramatic ambition — this fact must inspire us with the wish to at least occasionally free these otherwise invaluable dramatic forces from such tendencies, to permit their *good* qualities to gain that practice which would quickly and decidedly make them serviceable in the realization of our proposed art-work. For it is only the peculiar will of this guild of actors, so singular in their erroneous course, from which the perfect drama we have indicated can come, just as indeed every excellent dramatic result that has ever appeared has emanated from them. The decline of theatrical art in our time has been brought about less by them than by those who have hitherto — though without any authority — been their leaders.

If we desire to point out that thing which, of all on German soil is and continues to be least worthy of the fame of our great modern triumphs, we must point to *the stage,* the whole course of which has prominently and boldly shown it to be a very betrayer of German honor.

Whoever makes any effort to sustain this course must submit to a judgment which will necessarily class him with a part of our public life that is of a most doubtful nature — and from which it will be as difficult to emerge into a sphere of pure art, as it will be to rise from the opera to the ideal drama we have supposed. It is certainly true that if, according to Schiller's remark (here apparently inexact) that " art has only declined through the fault of the artists "— it can only be *elevated again by the artists,* and not by those by whose pleasure in art that art suffers injury. To help this elevation of the art-standard by artists, and to help it from without as well, this effort should be the national atonement for the national sin: the evil influence of the modern German stage.

FRIEDRICH NIETZSCHE

Born in the German town of Röcken in 1844, Nietzsche studied at the universities of Bonn and Leipzig, then lectured on classical philology at the University of Basel. He served in the Franco-Prussian War and was invalided home. His first book, *The Birth of Tragedy from the Spirit of Music* (1872), undertook to justify the practice of Richard Wagner's operas by tracing the origin of tragedy to the fusion of Apollonian and Dionysiac qualities in art—the combination of form and inspiration respectively. In subsequent works, Nietzsche assailed

some contemporary thinkers but defended Schopenhauer and Wagner, turning against the latter when he seemed to embrace Christianity in *Parsifal.* In his late works, including *Thus Spake Zarathustra* (1883–85), *Beyond Good and Evil* (1886), and *The Genealogy of Morals* (1887), Nietzsche celebrated strength and derided the slave morality he associated with Christianity; he deplored the triumph of Christianity over healthy paganism and praised individualism, embodied in the superman. Pronounced insane in 1889, he died in 1900.

THE BIRTH OF TRAGEDY FROM THE SPIRIT OF MUSIC[1]

[Die Geburt der Tragödie]
(1870–71)

Much will have been gained for es-

1 Excerpts from the new translation by Francis Golffing, included in *The Birth of Tragedy and the Genealogy of Morals.* Copyright ©

thetics once we have succeeded in apprehending directly—rather than merely

1956 by Doubleday & Co., Inc. Used by permission of the publisher.—Ed.

ascertaining—that art owes its continuous evolution to the Apollonian-Dionysiac duality, even as the propagation of the species depends on the duality of the sexes, their constant conflicts and periodic acts of reconciliation. I have borrowed my adjectives from the Greeks, who developed their mystical doctrines of art through plausible *embodiments,* not through purely conceptual means. It is by those two art-sponsoring deities, Apollo and Dionysos, that we are made to recognize the tremendous split, as regards both origins and objectives, between the plastic, Apollonian arts and the non-visual art of music inspired by Dionysos. The two creative tendencies developed alongside one another, usually in fierce opposition, each by its taunts forcing the other to more energetic production, both perpetuating in a discordant concord that agon which the term *art* but feebly denominates: until at last, by the thaumaturgy of an Hellenic act of will, the pair accepted the yoke of marriage and, in this condition, begot Attic tragedy, which exhibits the salient features of both parents.

To reach a closer understanding of both these tendencies, let us begin by viewing them as the separate art realms of *dream* and *intoxication,* two physiological phenomena standing toward one another in much the same relationship as the Apollonian and Dionysiac. It was in a dream, according to Lucretius, that the marvelous gods and goddesses first presented themselves to the minds of men. That great sculptor, Phidias, beheld in a dream the entrancing bodies of more-than-human beings, and likewise, if anyone had asked the Greek poets about the mystery of poetic creation, they too would have referred him to dreams and instructed him much as Hans Sachs instructs us in *Die Meistersinger:*

> *My friend, it is the poet's work*
> *Dreams to interpret and to mark.*
> *Believe me that man's true conceit*
> *In a dream becomes complete:*
> *All poetry we ever read*
> *Is but true dreams interpreted.*

The fair illusion of the dream sphere, in the production of which every man proves himself an accomplished artist, is a precondition not only of all plastic art, but even, as we shall see presently, of a wide range of poetry. Here we enjoy an immediate apprehension of form, all shapes speak to us directly, nothing seems indifferent or redundant. . . . Our innermost being, the common substratum of humanity, experiences dreams with deep delight and a sense of real necessity. This deep and happy sense of the necessity of dream experiences was expressed by the Greeks in the image of Apollo. Apollo is at once the god of all plastic powers and the soothsaying god. He who is etymologically the "lucent" one, the god of light, reigns also over the fair illusion of our inner world of fantasy. The perfection of these conditions in contrast to our imperfectly understood waking reality, as well as our profound awareness of nature's healing powers during the interval of sleep and dream, furnishes a symbolic analogue to the soothsaying faculty and quite generally to the arts, which make life possible and worth living. But the image of Apollo must incorporate that thin line which the dream image may not cross, under penalty of becoming pathological, of imposing itself on us as crass reality: a discreet limitation, a freedom from all extravagant urges, the sapient tranquillity of the plastic god. His eye must be sunlike, in keeping with his origin. Even at those moments when he is angry and ill-tempered there lies upon him the consecration of fair illusion. In an eccentric way one might say of Apollo what Schopenhauer says, in the first part of *The World as Will and Idea,* of man caught in the veil of Maya: "Even as on an immense, raging sea, assailed by huge wave crests, a man sits in a little rowboat trusting his frail craft, so, amidst the furious torments of this world, the individual sits tranquilly, supported by the *principium individuationis* and relying on it." One might say that the unshakable confidence in that principle has received its most magnificent expression in Apollo, and that Apollo himself may be regarded as the marvelous divine image of the *principium individuationis,* whose looks and gestures radiate the full delight, wisdom, and beauty of "illusion."

In the same context Schopenhauer has described for us the tremendous awe which seizes man when he suddenly begins to doubt the cognitive modes of experience, in other words, when in a given

instance the law of causation seems to suspend itself. If we add to this awe the glorious transport which arises in man, even from the very depths of nature, at the shattering of the *principium individuationis,* then we are in a position to apprehend the essence of Dionysiac rapture, whose closest analogy is furnished by physical intoxication. Dionysiac stirrings arise either through the influence of those narcotic potions of which all primitive races speak in their hymns, or through the powerful approach of spring, which penetrates with joy the whole frame of nature. So stirred, the individual forgets himself completely. . . .
. . . Man now expresses himself through song and dance as the member of a higher community; he has forgotten how to walk, how to speak, and is on the brink of taking wing as he dances. Each of his gestures betokens enchantment; through him sounds a supernatural power, the same power which makes the animals speak and the earth render up milk and honey. He feels himself to be godlike and strides with the same elation and ecstasy as the gods he has seen in his dreams. . . .

At this point we need to call upon every esthetic principle so far discussed, in order to find our way through the labyrinthine origins of Greek tragedy. I believe I am saying nothing extravagant when I claim that the problem of these origins has never even been posed, much less solved, no matter how often the elusive rags of ancient tradition have been speculatively sewn together and ripped apart. That tradition tells us in no uncertain terms that tragedy arose out of the tragic chorus and was, to begin with, nothing but chorus. . . .
. . . The satyr, as the Dionysiac chorist, dwells in a reality sanctioned by myth and ritual. That tragedy should begin with him, that the Dionysiac wisdom of tragedy should speak through him, is as puzzling a phenomenon as, more generally, the origin of tragedy from the chorus. Perhaps we can gain a starting point for this inquiry by claiming that the satyr, that fictive nature sprite, stands to cultured man in the same relation as Dionysiac music does to civilization. Richard Wagner has said of the latter that it is absorbed by music as

lamplight by daylight. In the same manner, I believe, the cultured Greek felt himself absorbed into the satyr chorus, and in the next development of Greek tragedy state and society, in fact all that separated man from man, gave way before an overwhelming sense of unity which led back into the heart of nature. The metaphysical solace (with which, I wish to say at once, all true tragedy sends us away) that, despite every phenomenal change, life is at bottom indestructibly joyful and powerful, was expressed most concretely in the chorus of satyrs, nature beings who dwell behind all civilization and preserve their identity through every change of generations and historical movement.

With this chorus the profound Greek, so uniquely susceptible to the subtlest and deepest suffering, who had penetrated the destructive agencies of both nature and history, solaced himself. Though he had been in danger of craving a Buddhistic denial of the will, he was saved by art, and through art life reclaimed him.

While the transport of the Dionysiac state, with its suspension of all the ordinary barriers of existence, lasts, it carries with it a Lethean element in which everything that has been experienced by the individual is drowned. This chasm of oblivion separates the quotidian reality from the Dionysiac. But as soon as that quotidian reality enters consciousness once more it is viewed with loathing, and the consequence is an ascetic, abulic state of mind. In this sense Dionysiac man might be said to resemble Hamlet: both have looked deeply into the true nature of things, they have *understood* and are now loath to act. They realize that no action of theirs can work any change in the eternal condition of things, and they regard the imputation as ludicrous or debasing that they should set right the time which is out of joint. Understanding kills action, for in order to act we require the veil of illusion; such is Hamlet's doctrine, not to be confounded with the cheap wisdom of John-a-Dreams, who through too much reflection, as it were a surplus of possibilities, never arrives at action. What, both in the case of Hamlet and of Dionysiac man, overbalances any motive leading to action, is not reflection but understanding, the apprehension of truth and its terror. Now no comfort any longer avails, desire reaches beyond the transcendental world, beyond the gods themselves, and existence, together with its gulling reflection in the gods and an immortal Beyond, is denied. The truth once seen, man is aware everywhere of the ghastly absurdity of existence, comprehends the symbolism of Ophelia's fate and the wisdom of the wood sprite Silenus: nausea invades him.

Then, in this supreme jeopardy of the will, art, that sorceress expert in healing, approaches him; only she can turn his fits of nausea into imaginations with which it is possible to live. These are on the one hand the spirit of the *sublime,* which subjugates terror by means of art; on the other hand the *comic* spirit, which releases us, through art, from the tedium of absurdity. The satyr chorus of the dithyramb was the salvation of Greek art; the threatening paroxysms I have mentioned were contained by the intermediary of those Dionysiac attendants.

The satyr and the idlyllic shepherd of later times have both been products of a desire for naturalness and simplicity. But how firmly the Greek shaped his wood sprite, and how self-consciously and mawkishly the modern dallies with his tender, fluting shepherd! For the Greek the satyr expressed nature in a rude, uncultivated state: he did not, for that reason, confound him with the monkey. Quite the contrary, the satyr was man's true prototype, an expression of his highest and strongest aspirations. He was an enthusiastic reveler, filled with transport by the approach of the god; a compassionate companion re-enacting the sufferings of the god; a prophet of wisdom born out of nature's womb; a symbol of the sexual omnipotence of nature, which the Greek was accustomed to view with reverent wonder. The satyr was sublime and divine—so he must have looked to the traumatically wounded vision of Dionysiac man. . . . Even as tragedy, with its metaphysical solace, points to the eternity of true being surviving every phenomenal change, so does the symbolism of the satyr chorus express analogically the primordial relation between the thing in itself and appearance. The idyllic shepherd of modern man is

but a replica of the sum of cultural illusions which he mistakes for nature. The Dionysiac Greek, desiring truth and nature at their highest power, sees himself metamorphosed into the satyr.

Such are the dispositions and insights of the reveling throng of Dionysos; and the power of these dispositions and insights transforms them in their own eyes, until they behold themselves restored to the condition of genii, of satyrs. Later the tragic chorus came to be an esthetic imitation of that natural phenomenon; which then necessitated a distinction between Dionysiac spectators and votaries actually spellbound by the god. What must be kept in mind in all these investigations is that the audience of Attic tragedy discovered *itself* in the chorus of the orchestra. Audience and chorus were never fundamentally set over against each other: all was one grand chorus of dancing, singing satyrs, and of those who let themselves be represented by them. This granted, Schlegel's dictum assumes a profounder meaning. The chorus is the "ideal spectator" inasmuch as it is the only *seer*—seer of the visionary world of the proscenium. An audience of spectators, such as we know it, was unknown to the Greeks. Given the terraced structure of the Greek theater, rising in concentric arcs, each spectator could quite literally survey the entire cultural world about him and imagine himself, in the fullness of seeing, as a chorist. . . .

Dionysiac excitation is capable of communicating to a whole multitude this artistic power to feel itself surrounded by, and one with, a host of spirits. What happens in the dramatic chorus is the primary *dramatic* phenomenon: projecting oneself outside oneself and then acting as though one had really entered another body, another character. This constitutes the first step in the evolution of drama. This art is no longer that of the rhapsodist, who does not merge with his images but, like the painter, contemplates them as something outside himself; what we have here is the individual effacing himself through entering a strange being. It should be made clear that this phenomenon is not singular but epidemic: a whole crowd becomes rapt in this manner. It is for this reason that the dithyramb differs essentially from any other kind of chorus. The virgins who, carrying laurel branches and singing a processional chant, move solemnly toward the temple of Apollo, retain their identities and their civic names. The dithyrambic chorus on the other hand is a chorus of the transformed, who have forgotten their civic past and social rank, who have become timeless servants of their god and live outside all social spheres. While all the other types of Greek choric verse are simply the highest intensification of the Apollonian musician, in the dithyramb we see a community of unconscious actors all of whom see one another as enchanted.

Enchantment is the precondition of all dramatic art. In this enchantment the Dionysiac reveler sees himself as satyr, and as satyr, in turn, he sees the god. In his transformation he sees a new vision, which is the Apollonian completion of his state. And by the same token this new vision completes the dramatic act.

Thus we have come to interpret Greek tragedy as a Dionysiac chorus which again and again discharges itself in Apollonian images. Those choric portions with which the tragedy is interlaced constitute, as it were, the matrix of the *dialogue,* that is to say, of the entire stage-world of the actual drama. This substratum of tragedy irradiates, in several consecutive discharges, the vision of the drama—a vision on the one hand completely of the nature of Apollonian dream-illusion and therefore epic, but on the other hand, as the objectification of a Dionysiac condition, tending toward the shattering of the individual and his fusion with the original Oneness. Tragedy is an Apollonian embodiment of Dionysiac insights and powers, and for that reason separated by a tremendous gulf from the epic.

On this view the chorus of Greek tragedy, symbol of an entire multitude agitated by Dionysos, can be fully explained. Whereas we who are accustomed to the role of the chorus in modern theater, especially opera, find it hard to conceive how the chorus of the Greeks should have been older, more central than the dramatic action proper (although we have clear testimony to this effect); and whereas we have never been quite able to reconcile with this position of importance the fact that the chorus was composed of such lowly beings as—originally—goat-like satyrs; and whereas, further, the orchestra in front of the stage has always seemed a riddle to us—we now realize that the stage with its action was originally conceived as pure vision and that the only reality was the chorus, who created that vision out of itself and proclaimed it through the medium of dance, music, and spoken word. Since, in this vision, the chorus beholds its lord and master Dionysos, it remains forever an *attending* chorus; it sees how the god suffers and transforms himself, and it has, for that reason, no need to act. But, notwithstanding its subordination to the god, the chorus remains the highest expression of nature, and, like nature, utters in its enthusiasm oracular words of wisdom. Being compassionate as well as wise, it proclaims a truth that issues from the heart of the world. Thus we see how that fantastic and at first sight embarrassing figure arises, the wise and enthusiastic satyr who is at the same time the "simpleton" as opposed to the god. The satyr is a replica of nature in its strongest tendencies and at the same time a herald of its wisdom and art. He combines in his person the roles of musician, poet, dancer and visionary.

It is in keeping both with this insight and with general tradition that in the earliest tragedy Dionysos was not actually present but merely imagined. Original tragedy is only chorus and not drama at all. Later an attempt was made to demonstrate the god as real and to bring the visionary figure, together with the transfiguring frame, vividly before the eyes of every spectator. This marks the beginning of drama in the strict sense of the word. It then became the task of the dithyrambic chorus so to excite the mood of the listeners that when the tragic hero appeared they would behold not the awkwardly masked man but a figure born of their own rapt vision. If we imagine Admetus brooding on the memory of his recently departed wife, consuming himself in a spiritual contemplation of her form, and how a figure of similar shape and gait is led toward him in deep disguise; if we then imagine his tremor of excitement, his impetuous comparisons, his instinctive conviction—then we have an analogue for the excitement of the spectator beholding the god, with whose sufferings he has already identified himself, stride onto the stage. Instinctively he would project the shape of the god that was magically present to his mind onto that masked figure of a man, dissolving the latter's reality into a ghostly unreality. This is the Apollonian dream state, in which the daylight world is veiled and a new world—clearer, more comprehensible, more affecting than the first, and at the same time more shadowy —falls upon the eye in ever changing shapes. Thus we may recognize a drastic stylistic opposition: language, color, pace, dynamics of speech are polarized into the Dionysiac poetry of the chorus, on the one hand, and the Apollonian dream world of the scene on the other. The result is two completely separate spheres of expression. The Apollonian embodiments in which Dionysos assumes objective shape are very different from the continual interplay of shifting forces in the music of the chorus, from those powers deeply felt by the enthusiast, but which he is incapable of condensing into a clear image. The adept no longer obscurely senses the approach of the god: the god now speaks to him from the proscenium with the clarity and firmness of epic, as an epic hero, almost in the language of Homer.

Everything that rises to the surface in the Apollonian portion of Greek tragedy (in the dialogue) looks simple, transparent, beautiful. In this sense the dialogue is a mirror of the Greek mind, whose nature manifests itself in dance, since in dance the maximum power is only potentially present, betraying itself in the suppleness and opulence of movement. The language of the Sophoclean heroes surprises us by its Apollonian determinacy and lucidity. It seems to us that we can fathom their innermost being, and we are somewhat surprised that we had such a short way to go. However, once we abstract from the character of the hero as it rises to the surface and becomes visible (a character at bottom no more than a luminous shape projected onto a dark wall, that is to say, *appearance* through and through) and instead penetrate into the myth which is projected in these luminous reflections, we suddenly come up against a phenomenon which is the exact opposite of a familiar optical one. After an energetic attempt to focus on the sun, we have, by way of remedy almost, dark spots before our eyes when we turn away. Conversely, the luminous images of the Sophoclean heroes—those Apollonian masks —are the necessary productions of a deep look into the horror of nature; luminous spots, as it were, designed to cure an eye hurt by the ghastly night. Only in this way can we form an adequate notion of the seriousness of Greek "serenity"; whereas we find that serenity generally misinterpreted nowadays as a condition of undisturbed complacence.

Sophocles conceived doomed Oedipus, the greatest sufferer of the Greek stage, as a pattern of nobility, destined to error and misery despite his wisdom, yet exercising a beneficent influence upon his environment in virtue of his boundless grief. The profound poet tells us that a man who is truly noble is incapable of sin; though every law, every natural order, indeed the entire canon of ethics, perish by his actions, those very actions will create a circle of higher consequences able to found a new world on the ruins of the old. This is the poet's message, insofar as he is at the same time a religious thinker. In his capacity as poet, he presents us in the beginning with a complicated legal knot, in the slow unraveling of which the judge brings about his own destruction. The typically Greek delight in this dialectical solution is so great that it imparts an element of triumphant serenity to the work, and thus removes the sting lurking in the ghastly premises of the plot. In *Oedipus at Colonus* we meet this same serenity, but utterly transfigured. In contrast to the aged hero, stricken with excess of grief and passively undergoing his many misfortunes, we have here a transcendent serenity issuing from above and hinting that by his passive endurance the hero may yet gain a consummate energy of action. This activity (so different from his earlier conscious striving, which had resulted in pure passivity) will extend far beyond the limited experience of his own life. Thus the legal knot of the Oedipus fable, which had seemed to mortal eyes incapable of being disentangled, is slowly loosened. And we experience the most profound human joy as we witness this divine counterpart of dialectics. If this explanation has done the poet justice, it may yet be asked whether it has exhausted the implications of the myth; and now we see that the poet's entire conception was nothing more nor less than the luminous afterimage which kind nature provides our eyes after a look into the abyss. Oedipus, his father's murderer, his mother's lover, solver of the Sphinx's riddle! What is the meaning of this triple fate? An ancient popular belief, especially strong in Persia, holds that a wise *magus* must be incestuously begotten. If we examine Oedipus, the solver of riddles and liberator of his mother, in the light of this Parsee belief, we may conclude that wherever soothsaying and magical powers have broken the spell of present and future, the rigid law of individuation, the magic circle of nature, extreme unnaturalness—in this case incest—is the necessary antecedent; for how should man force nature to yield up her secrets but by successfully resisting her, that is to say, by unnatural acts? This is the recognition I find expressed in the terrible triad of Oedipean fates: the same man who solved the riddle of nature (the ambiguous Sphinx) must also, as murderer of his father and husband of his mother, break the consecrated tables of the natural order. It is as though the myth whispered to us that wisdom, and especially Dionysiac wisdom, is an unnatural crime, and that whoever, in pride of knowledge, hurls nature into the abyss of destruction, must himself experience nature's disintegration. "The edge of wisdom is turned against the wise man; wisdom is a crime committed on nature": such are the terrible words addressed to us by myth. Yet the Greek poet, like a sunbeam, touches the terrible and austere Memnon's Column of myth, which proceeds to give forth Sophoclean melodies. Now I wish to contrast to the glory of passivity the glory of action, as it irradiates the *Prometheus* of Aeschylus. Young Goethe has revealed to us, in the bold words his Prometheus addresses to Zeus, what the thinker Aeschylus meant to say, but what, as poet, he merely gave us to divine in symbol:

Here I sit, kneading men

In my image,
A race like myself,
Made to suffer, weep,
Laugh and delight,
And forget all about you—
As I have forgotten.

Man, raised to titanic proportions, conquers his own civilization and compels the gods to join forces with him, since by his autonomous wisdom he commands both their existence and the limitations of their sway. What appears most wonderful, however, in the Prometheus poem —ostensibly a hymn in praise of impiety —is its profound Aeschylean longing for *justice*. The immense suffering of the bold individual, on the one hand, and on the other the extreme jeopardy of the gods, prefiguring a "twilight of the gods" —the two together pointing to a reconciliation, a merger of their universes of suffering—all this reminds one vividly of the central tenet of Aeschylean speculation in which Moira, as eternal justice, is seen enthroned above men and gods alike. In considering the extraordinary boldness with which Aeschylus places the Olympian world on his scales of justice, we must remember that the profound Greek had an absolutely stable basis of metaphysical thought in his mystery cults and that he was free to discharge all his sceptical velleities on the Olympians. The Greek artist, especially, experienced in respect of these divinities an obscure sense of mutual dependency, a feeling which has been perfectly symbolized in the *Prometheus* of Aeschylus. The titanic artist was strong in his defiant belief that he could create men and, at the least, destroy Olympian gods; this he was able to do by virtue of his superior wisdom, which, to be sure, he must atone for by eternal suffering. The glorious power to *do*, which is possessed by great genius, and for which even eternal suffering is not too high a price to pay—the *artist's* austere pride—is of the very essence of Aeschylean poetry, while Sophocles in his *Oedipus* intones a paean to the *saint*. . . .

Once we have comprehended the substance of the Prometheus myth—the imperative necessity of *hubris* for the titanic individual—we must realize the non-Apollonian character of this pessimistic idea. It is Apollo who tranquilizes the individual by drawing boundary lines, and who, by enjoining again and again the practice of self-knowledge, reminds him of the holy, universal norms. But lest the Apollonian tendency freeze all form into Egyptian rigidity, and in attempting to prescribe its orbit to each particular wave inhibit the movement of the lake, the Dionysiac flood tide periodically destroys all the little circles in which the Apollonian will would confine Hellenism. The swiftly rising Dionysiac tide then shoulders all the small individual wave crests, even as Prometheus' brother, the Titan Atlas, shouldered the world. This titanic urge to be the Atlas of all individuals, to bear them on broad shoulders ever farther and higher, is the common bond between the Promethean and the Dionysiac forces. In this respect the Aeschylean Prometheus appears as a Dionysiac mask, while in his deep hunger for justice Aeschylus reveals his paternal descent from Apollo, god of individuation and just boundaries. We may express the Janus face, at once Dionysiac and Apollonian, of the Aeschylean Prometheus in the following formula: 'What ever exists is both just and unjust, and equally justified in both." What a world!

It is an unimpeachable tradition that in its earliest form Greek tragedy records only the sufferings of Dionysos, and that he was the only actor. But it may be claimed with equal justice that, up to Euripides, Dionysos *remains* the sole dramatic protagonist and that all the famous characters of the Greek stage, Prometheus, Oedipus, etc., are only masks of that original hero. The fact that a god hides behind all these masks accounts for the much-admired "ideal" character of those celebrated figures. Someone, I can't recall who, has claimed that all individuals, as individuals, are comic, and therefore untragic; which sems to suggest that the Greeks did not tolerate individuals at all on the tragic stage. And in fact they must have felt this way. The Platonic distinction between the idea and the eidolon is deeply rooted in the Greek temperament. If we wished to use Plato's terminology we might speak of the tragic characters of the Greek stage somewhat as follows: the one true Dionysos appears in a multiplicity of characters, in the mask of warrior hero, and enmeshed in the web of individual will. The god ascends the stage in the likeness of a striving and suffering individual. That he can *appear* at all with this clarity and precision is due to dream interpreter Apollo, who projects before the chorus its Dionysiac condition in this analogical figure. Yet in truth that hero is the suffering Dionysos of the mysteries. He of whom the wonderful myth relates that as a child he was dismembered by Titans now experiences in his own person the pains of individuation, and in this condition is worshiped as Zagreus. We have here an indication that dismemberment—the truly Dionysiac suffering—was like a separation into air, water, earth, and fire, and that individuation should be regarded as the source of all suffering, and rejected. The smile of this Dionysos has given birth to the Olympian gods, his tears have given birth to men. In his existence as dismembered god, Dionysos shows the double nature of a cruel, savage daemon and a mild, gentle ruler. Every hope of the Eleusinian initiates pointed to a rebirth of Dionysos, which we can now interpret as meaning the end of individuation; the thundering paean of the adepts addressed itself to the coming of the third Dionysos. This hope alone sheds a beam of joy on a ravaged and fragmented world—as is shown by the myth of sorrowing Demeter, who rejoiced only when she was told that she might once again bear Dionysos. In these notions we already find all the components of a profound and mystic philosophy and, by the same token, of the mystery doctrine of tragedy; a recognition that whatever exists is of a piece, and that individuation is the root of all evil; a conception of art as the sanguine hope that the spell of individuation may yet be broken, as an augury of eventual reintegration.

SIGMUND FREUD

Freud was born 1856 in Freiberg, then in the Austro-Hungarian Empire but now in Czechoslovakia. He spent most of his life in Vienna. He was at first a physician; his medical practice led him to the study of hysteria and thence to discoveries concerning the unconscious mind and repressed sexual impulses. His further discoveries and his publications established him as the father of modern psychoanalysis. He gave the world a new view of itself and a new vocabulary when he wrote of the *id* (the primitive, uncensored impulse), the *ego* and the *super-ego* (civilized elements of charac- ter that exercise restraint), the Oedipus complex (rivalry with the father and sexual love of the mother), and other psychic patterns. He found curious, unconscious patterns for investigation in the dream and in literature. Accordingly, he interpreted *Hamlet* and *Oedipus Rex* in *The Interpretation of Dreams* and recondite tendencies of the comic in *Wit and Its Relation to the Unconscious;* his writings abound in other, incidental interpretations of literature and the drama. He died in 1939 in London, a refugee from Hitler.

OEDIPUS AND HAMLET [1]

(1900)

. . . According to my already extensive experience, parents play a leading part in the infantile psychology of all persons who subsequently become psychoneurotics. Falling in love with one parent and hating the other forms part of the permanent stock of the psychic impulses which arise in early childhood, and are of such importance as the material of the subsequent neurosis. But I do not believe that psychoneurotics are to be sharply distinguished in this respect from other persons who remain normal— that is, I do not believe that they are capable of creating something absolutely new and peculiar to themselves. It is far more probable—and this is confirmed by incidental observations of normal children—that in their amorous or hostile attitude toward their parents, psychoneurotics do no more than reveal to us, by magnification, something that occurs less markedly and intensively in the minds of the majority of children. Antiquity has furnished us with legendary matter which corroborates this belief, and the profound and universal validity of the old legends is explicable only by

an equally universal validity of the above-mentioned hypothesis of infantile psychology.

I am referring to the legend of King Oedipus and the *Oedipus Rex* of Sophocles. Oedipus, the son of Laius, king of Thebes, and Jocasta, is exposed as a suckling, because an oracle had informed the father that his son, who was still unborn, would be his murderer. He is rescued, and grows up as a king's son at a foreign court, until, being uncertain of his origin, he, too, consults the oracle, and is warned to avoid his native place, for he is destined to become the murderer of his father and the husband of his mother. On the road leading away from his supposed home he meets King Laius, and in a sudden quarrel strikes him dead. He comes to Thebes, where he solves the riddle of the Sphinx, who is barring the way to the city, whereupon he is elected king by the grateful Thebans, and is rewarded with the hand of Jocasta. He reigns for many years in peace and honour, and begets two sons and two daughters upon his unknown mother, until at last a plague breaks out —which causes the Thebans to consult the oracle anew. Here Sophocles' tragedy begins. The messengers bring the reply that the plague will stop as soon as the murderer of Laius is driven from the

1 From *The Interpretation of Dreams* [*Traümdeutung*], in *The Basic Writings of Sigmund Freud*, translated and edited by A. A. Brill. Copyright 1938 by Random House, Inc. Reprinted by permission of Gioia B. Bernheim and Edmund Brill.—Ed.

country. But where is he?

> *Where shall be found,*
> *Faint, and hard to be known, the trace of*
> *the ancient guilt?*

The action of the play consists simply in the disclosure, approached step by step and artistically delayed (and comparable to the work of a psychoanalysis) that Oedipus himself is the murderer of Laius, and that he is the son of the murdered man and Jocasta. Shocked by the abominable crime which he has unwittingly committed, Oedipus blinds himself, and departs from his native city. The prophecy of the oracle has been fulfilled. The *Oedipus Rex* is a tragedy of fate; its tragic effect depends on the conflict between the all-powerful will of the gods and the vain efforts of human beings threatened with disaster; resignation to the divine will, and the perception of one's own impotence is the lesson which the deeply moved spectator is supposed to learn from the tragedy. Modern authors have therefore sought to achieve a similar tragic effect by expressing the same conflict in stories of their own invention. But the playgoers have looked on unmoved at the unavailing efforts of guiltless men to avert the fulfilment of curse or oracle; the modern tragedies of destiny have failed of their effect. If the *Oedipus Rex* is capable of moving a modern reader or playgoer no less powerfully than it moved the contemporary Greeks, the only possible explanation is that the effect of the Greek tragedy does not depend upon the conflict between fate and human will, but upon the peculiar nature of the material by which this conflict is revealed. There must be a voice within us which is prepared to acknowledge the compelling power of fate in the *Oedipus,* while we are able to condemn the situations occurring in *Die Ahnfrau* or other tragedies of fate as arbitrary inventions. And there actually is a motive in the story of King Oedipus which explains the verdict of this inner voice. His fate moves us only because it might have been our own, because the oracle laid upon us before our birth the very curse which rested upon him. It may be that we were all destined to direct our first sexual impulses toward our mothers, and our first impulses of

hatred and violence toward our fathers; our dreams convince us that we were. King Oedipus, who slew his father Laius and wedded his mother Jocasta, is nothing more or less than a wish-fulfilment— the fulfilment of the wish of our childhood. But we, more fortunate than he, in so far as we have not become psychoneurotics, have since our childhood succeeded in withdrawing our sexual impulses from our mothers, and in forgetting our jealousy of our fathers. We recoil from the person for whom this primitive wish of our childhood has been fulfilled with all the force of the repression which these wishes have undergone in our minds since childhood. As the poet brings the guilt of Oedipus to light by his investigation, he forces us to become aware of our own inner selves, in which the same impulses are still extant, even though they are suppressed. The antithesis with which the chorus departs:—

> *. . . Behold, this is Oedipus,*
> *Who unravelled the great riddle, and was*
> *first in power,*
> *Whose fortune all the townsmen praised*
> *and envied;*
> *See in what dread adversity he sank!*

—this admonition touches us and our own pride, us who since the years of our childhood have grown so wise and so powerful in our own estimation. Like Oedipus, we live in ignorance of the desires that offend morality, the desires that nature has forced upon us and after their unveiling we may well prefer to avert our gaze from the scenes of our childhood.

In the very text of Sophocles' tragedy there is an unmistakable reference to the fact that the Oedipus legend had its source in dream-material of immemorial antiquity, the content of which was the painful disturbance of the child's relations to its parents caused by the first impulses of sexuality. Jocasta comforts Oedipus—who is not yet enlightened, but is troubled by the recollection of the oracle—by an allusion to a dream which is often dreamed, though it cannot, in her opinion, mean anything:—

> *For many a man hath seen himself in*
> *dreams*

*His mother's mate, but he who gives
no heed
To suchlike matters bears the easier
life.*

The dream of having sexual intercourse with one's mother was as common then as it is to-day with many people, who tell it with indignation and astonishment. As may well be imagined, it is the key to the tragedy and the complement to the dream of the death of the father. The Oedipus fable is the reaction of phantasy to these two typical dreams, and just as such a dream, when occurring to an adult, is experienced with feelings of aversion, so the content of the fable must include terror and self-chastisement. The form which it subsequently assumed was the result of an uncomprehending secondary elaboration of the material, which sought to make it serve a theological intention. The attempt to reconcile divine omnipotence with human responsibility must, of course, fail with this material as with any other.

Another of the great poetic tragedies, Shakespeare's *Hamlet*, is rooted in the same soil as *Oedipus Rex*. But the whole difference in the psychic life of the two widely separated periods of civilization, and the progress, during the course of time, of repression in the emotional life of humanity, is manifested in the differing treatment of the same material. In *Oedipus Rex* the basic wish-phantasy of the child is brought to light and realized as it is in dreams; in *Hamlet* it remains repressed, and we learn of its existence —as we discover the relevant facts in a neurosis—only through the inhibitory effects which proceed from it. In the more modern drama, the curious fact that it is possible to remain in complete uncertainty as to the character of the hero has proved to be quite consistent with the overpowering effect of the tragedy. The play is based upon Hamlet's hesitation in accomplishing the task of revenge assigned to him; the text does not give the cause or the motive of this hesitation, nor have the manifold attempts at interpretation succeeded in doing so. According to the still prevailing conception, a conception for which Goethe was first responsible, Hamlet represents the type of man whose active energy is paralysed by excessive intellectual activity: "Sicklied

o'er with the pale cast of thought." According to another conception, the poet has endeavoured to portray a morbid, irresolute character, on the verge of neurasthenia. The plot of the drama, however, shows us that Hamlet is by no means intended to appear as a character wholly incapable of action. On two separate occasions we see him assert himself: once in a sudden outburst of rage, when he stabs the eavesdropper behind the arras, and on the other occasion when he deliberately, and even craftily, with the complete unscrupulousness of a prince of the Renaissance, sends the two courtiers to the death which was intended for himself. What is it, then, that inhibits him in accomplishing the task which his father's ghost has laid upon him? Here the explanation offers itself that it is the peculiar nature of this task. Hamlet is able to do anything but take vengeance upon the man who did away with his father and has taken his father's place with his mother—the man who shows him in realization the repressed desires of his own childhood. The loathing which should have driven him to revenge is thus replaced by self-reproach, by conscientious scruples, which tell him that he himself is no better than the murderer whom he is required to punish. I have here translated into consciousness what had to remain unconscious in the mind of the hero; if anyone wishes to call Hamlet an hysterical subject I cannot but admit that this is the deduction to be drawn from my interpretation. The sexual aversion which Hamlet expresses in conversation with Ophelia is perfectly consistent with this deduction—the same sexual aversion which during the next few years was increasingly to take possession of the poet's soul, until it found its supreme utterance in *Timon of Athens*. It can, of course, be only the poet's own psychology with which we are confronted in *Hamlet;* and in a work on Shakespeare by Georg Brandes (1896) I find the statement that the drama was composed immediately after the death of Shakespeare's father (1601)—that is to say, when he was still mourning his loss, and during a revival, as we may fairly assume, of his own childish feelings in respect of his father. It is known, too, that Shakespeare's son, who died in childhood, bore the name of Hamnet (identical with Hamlet). Just as *Hamlet* treats of the relation of the son to his parents, so *Macbeth*, which was written about the same period, is based upon the theme of childlessness. Just as all neurotic symptoms, like dreams themselves, are capable of hyper-interpretation, and even require such hyper-interpretation before they become perfectly intelligible, so every genuine poetical creation must have proceeded from more than one motive, more than one impulse in the mind of the poet, and must admit of more than one interpretation. I have here attempted to interpret only the deepest stratum of impulses in the mind of the creative poet.

BERTOLT BRECHT

Brecht was born in Augsburg, Germany, in 1898. After briefly studying at the University of Munich, he became a hospital orderly in World War I. He started writing for the stage with *Baal* (1918) followed by the prize-winning *Trommeln in der Nacht* (1922). Some of his early plays showed an inclination toward expressionism, but by the time he wrote the enormously popular play, *The Threepenny Opera* (1928, freely adapted from John Gay's *The Beggar's Opera*, with musical score by Kurt Weill), he was forging his own theatrical style, and his cynical, nihilistic view of society was somewhat tempered by Marxism. In this work he implied that crime was a characteristic kind of bourgeois enterprise. Such plays as *The Rise and Fall of the City of Mahagonny* (with another score by Weill) and *Saint Joan of the Stockyards* consolidated both his new method and his Marxism. He became an exile when Hitler rose to power in 1933. He reached the United States in 1941 and went back to Europe in 1947. During his period of exile, he continued to write, but his contact with the theatre was intermittent. Here and there, his new plays were performed—at Paris (*The Private Life of the Master Race*, 1938), Zurich (*Mother Courage*, 1941, and *The Good Woman of Setzuan*, 1943), New York (*Galileo*, 1947), and Northfield, Minnesota (*The Caucasian Chalk Circle*, 1948), among other places. Back in Germany at last, he was given a theatre in East Berlin for his company, the Berliner Ensemble, of which his wife was managing director. He had advantageous conditions for staging his own plays, and he created one of the world's great acting companies before his death in 1956.

His distinctive dramatic genre is epic drama, a play that is as free, flexible, and episodic as narrative. It is influenced by Elizabethan and Chinese stage conventions and by the practice of the short-lived German romantic Georg Buechner. Its performance, its reception, and its writing all involve the idea of *Verfremdung*, usually translated as *alienation* but sometimes as *distancing* or *estrangement* —that is to say, in theory, epic drama requires an objective attitude so that it may instruct its audience. In practice, epic drama often seems to be a superior, more exact, and selective variety of realism.

THEATRE FOR LEARNING [1]

(1957)

When anyone spoke of modern theatre a few years ago, he mentioned the Moscow, the New York or the Berlin theatre. He may also have spoken of a particular production of Jouvet's in Paris, of Cochran's in London, or the Habima performance of *The Dybbuk*, which, in fact, belonged to Russian theatre, since it was

[1] Translated by Edith Anderson. From *Mainstream* (June, 1958). © 1958 by Masses and Mainstream, Inc. Used by permission of the publisher.—Ed.

directed by Vakhtangov; but by and large, there were only three capitals as far as modern theatre was concerned.

The Russian, the American and the German theatres were very different from one another, but they were alike in being modern, i.e., in introducing technical and artistic innovations. In a certain sense they even developed stylistic similarities, probably because technique is international (not only the technique directly required for the stage, but also that which exerts an influence on it, the film, for example) and because the cities in question were great progressive cities in great industrial countries. Most recently, the Berlin theatre seemed to have taken the lead among the most advanced capitalist countries. What was common to modern theatre found there its strongest and, for the moment, most mature expression.

The last phase of the Berlin theatre, which as I said only revealed in its purest form the direction in which modern theatre was developing, was the so-called *epic theatre*. What was known as the "Zeitstueck" [play dealing with current problems—Trans.] or Piscator theatre or the didactic play all belonged to epic theatre.

EPIC THEATRE. The expression "epic theatre" seemed self-contradictory to many people, since according to the teachings of Aristotle the epic and the dramatic forms of presenting a story were considered basically different from one another. The difference between the two forms was by no means merely seen in the fact that one was performed by living people while the other made use of a book—epic works like those of Homer and the *minnesingers* of the Middle Ages were likewise theatrical performances, and dramas like Goethe's *Faust* or Byron's *Manfred* admittedly achieved their greatest effect as books. Aristotle's teachings themselves distinguished the dramatic from the epic form as a difference in construction, whose laws were dealt with under two different branches of aesthetics. This construction depended on the different way in which the works were presented to the public, either on the stage or through a book, but nevertheless, apart from that, "the dramatic" could also be found in epic works and "the epic" in dramatic

works. The bourgeois novel in the last century considerably developed "the dramatic," which meant the strong centralization of plot and an organic interdependence of the separate parts. "The dramatic" is characterized by a certain passion in the tone of the exposition and a working out of the collision of forces. The epic writer, Doblin,[2] gave an excellent description when he said that the epic, in contrast to the dramatic, could practically be cut up with a scissors into single pieces, each of which could stand alone.

I do not wish to discuss here in what way the contrasts between epic and dramatic, long regarded as irreconcilable, lost their rigidity, but simply to point out that (other causes aside) technical achievements enabled the stage to include narrative elements in dramatic presentations. The potentialities of projection, the film, the greater facility in changing sets through machinery, completed the equipment of the stage and did so at a moment when the most important human events could no longer be so simply portrayed as through personification of the moving forces or through subordinating the characters to invisible, metaphysical powers. To make the events understandable, it had become necessary to play up the "bearing" of the *environment* upon the people living in it.

Of course this environment had been shown in plays before, not, however, as an independent element but only from the viewpoint of the main figure of the drama. It rose out of the hero's reaction to it. It was seen as a storm may be "seen" if you observe on the sea a ship spreading its sails and the sails bellying. But in the epic theatre it was now to appear as an independent element.

The stage began to narrate. The narrator no longer vanished with the fourth wall. Not only did the background make its own comment on stage happenings through large screens which evoked other events occurring at the same time in other places, documenting or contradicting statements by characters through quotations projected onto a screen, lending tangible, concrete statistics to ab-

2 Alfred Doblin (1878–1957), German novelist and essayist. His best-known work was the novel *Berlin-Alexanderplatz*.

stract discussions, providing facts and figures for happenings which were plastic but unclear in their meaning; the actors no longer threw themselves completely into their roles but maintained a certain distance from the character performed by them, even distinctly inviting criticism.

Nothing permitted the audience any more to lose itself through simple empathy, uncritically (and practically without any consequences) in the experiences of the characters on the stage. The presentation exposed the subject matter and the happenings to a process of de-familiarization.[3] De-familiarization was required to make things understood. When things are "self-evident," understanding is simply dispensed with. The "natural" had to be given an element of the *conspicuous*. Only in this way could the laws of cause and effect become plain. Characters had to behave as they *did* behave, and at the same time be capable of behaving otherwise.

These were great changes.

TWO OUTLINES. The following little outlines may indicate in what respect the function of the epic is distinguished from that of the dramatic theatre.

(1)

Dramatic Form

The stage "incarnates" an event.
Involves the audience in an action, uses up its activity.
Helps it to feel.
Communicates experiences.
The audience is projected into an event.
Suggestion is used.
Sensations are preserved.
The character is a known quantity.
Man unchangeable.
His drives.
Events move in a straight line.
Natura non facit saltus.
The world as it is.

Epic Form

Relates the event.
Makes the audience an observer, but arouses its activity.
Compels it to make decisions.

3 In German, "Entfremdung," sometimes translated as "alienation," and sometimes called "Verfremdung" by Brecht. The latter is an invented word like "de-familiarization."
—Trans.

Communicates insights.
The audience is confronted with an event.
Arguments are used.
Impelled to the level of perceptions.
The character is subjected to investigation.
Man who can change and make changes.
His motives.
In "irregular" curves.
Facit saltus.
The world as it is becoming.

(2)

The audience in the dramatic theatre says:

Yes, I have felt that too.—That's how I am.—That is only natural.—That will always be so.—This person's suffering shocks me because he has no way out.—This is great art: everything in it is self-evident.—I weep with the weeping, I laugh with the laughing.

The audience in the epic theatre says:

I wouldn't have thought that.—People shouldn't do things like that.—That's extremely odd, almost unbelievable.—This has to stop.—This person's suffering shocks me, because there might be a way out for him.—This is great art: nothing in it is self-evident.—I laugh over the weeping, I weep over the laughing.

DIDACTIC THEATRE. The stage began to instruct.

Oil, inflation, war, social struggles, the family, religion, wheat, the meat-packing industry became subjects for theatrical portrayal. Choruses informed the audience about facts it did not know. In montage form, films showed events all over the world. Projections provided statistical data. As the "background" came to the fore, the actions of the characters became exposed to criticism. Wrong and right actions were exhibited. People were shown who knew what they were doing, and other people were shown who did not know. The theatre entered the province of the philosophers—at any rate, the sort of philosophers who wanted not only to explain the world but also to change it. Hence the theatre philosophized; hence it instructed. And what became of entertainment? Were the audiences put back in school, treated as illiterates? Were they to take examinations and be given marks?

It is the general opinion that a very

decided difference exists between learning and being entertained. The former may be useful, but only the latter is pleasant. Thus we have to defend the epic theatre against a suspicion that it must be an extremely unpleasant, a joyless, indeed a wearing business.

Well, we can only say that the contrast between learning and being entertained does not necessarily exist in nature, it has not always existed and it need not always exist.

Undoubtedly, the kind of learning we did in school, in training for a profession, etc., is a laborious business. But consider under what circumstances and for what purpose it is done. It is, in fact, a purchase. Knowledge is simply a commodity. It is acquired for the purpose of being re-sold. All those who have grown too old for school have to pursue knowledge on the Q.T., so to speak, because anybody who admits he still has to study depreciates himself as one who knows too little. Apart from that, the utility of learning is very much limited by factors over which the student has no control. There is unemployment, against which no knowledge protects. There is the division of labor, which makes comprehensive knowledge unnecessary and impossible. Often, those who study do it only when they see no other possibility of getting ahead. There is not much knowledge that procures power, but much knowledge is only procured through power.

Learning means something very different to people in different strata of society. There are people who cannot conceive of any improvement in conditions; conditions seem good enough to them. Whatever may happen to petroleum, they make a profit out of it. And they feel, after all, that they are getting rather old. They can scarcely expect many more years of life. So why continue to learn? They have already spoken their "Ugh!" [4] But there are also people who have not yet "had their turn," who are discontented with the way things are, who have an immense practical interest in learning, who want orientation badly, who know they are lost without learning—these are the best and most ambitious learners. Such differences also exist among nations and peoples. Thus the lust for learning is dependent on various things; in short, there *is* thrilling learning, joyous and militant learning.

If learning could not be delightful, then the theatre, by its very nature, would not be in a position to instruct.

Theatre remains theatre, even when it is didactic theatre, and if it is good theatre it will entertain.

THEATRE AND SCIENCE. "But what has science to do with art? We know very well that science can be diverting, but not everything that diverts belongs in the theatre."

I have often been told when I pointed out the inestimable services that modern science, properly utilized, could render to art, especially to the theatre, that art and science were two admirable but completely different fields of human activity. This is a dreadful platitude, of course, and the best thing to do is admit at once that it is quite right, like most platitudes. Art and science operate in very different ways—agreed. Still, I must admit—bad as this may sound—that I cannot manage as an artist without making use of certain sciences. This may make many people seriously doubt my artistic ability. They are accustomed to regarding poets as unique, almost unnatural beings who unerringly, practically like gods, perceive things that others can only perceive through the greatest efforts and hard work. Naturally, it is unpleasant to have to admit not being one of those so endowed. But it must be admitted. It must also be denied that this application to science has anything to do with some pardonable avocation indulged in the evening after work is done. Everyone knows that Goethe also went in for natural science, Schiller for history, presumably—this is the charitable assumption—as a sort of hobby. I would not simply accuse these two of having needed the science for their poetic labors, nor would I use them to excuse myself, but I must say I need the sciences. And I must even admit that I regard suspiciously all sorts of people who I know do not keep abreast of science, who, in other words, sing as the birds sing, or as

4 Reference to popular German literature about American Indians, by the author Karl May, in which, after a chieftain had given his opinion at a powwow he would conclude, "I have spoken. Ugh!"—Trans.

they imagine the birds sing. This does not mean that I would reject a nice poem about the taste of a flounder or the pleasure of a boating party just because the author had not studied gastronomy or navigation. But I think that unless every resource is employed towards understanding the great, complicated events in the world of man, they cannot be seen adequately for what they are.

Let us assume that we want to portray great passions or events which influence the fates of peoples. Such a passion today might be the drive for power. Supposing that a poet "felt" this drive and wanted to show someone striving for power—how could be absorb into his own experience the extremely complicated mechanism within which the struggle for power today takes place? If his hero is a political man, what are the workings of politics; if he is a business man, what are the workings of business? And then there are poets who are much less passionately interested in any individual's drive for power than in business affairs and politics as such! How are they to acquire the necessary knowledge? They will scarcely find out enough by going around and keeping their eyes open, although that is at least better than rolling their eyes in a fine frenzy. The establishment of a newspaper like the *Voelkische Beobachter* or a business like Standard Oil is a rather complicated matter, and these things are not simply absorbed through the pores. Psychology is an important field for the dramatist. It is supposed that while an ordinary person may not be in a position to discover, without special instruction, what makes a man commit murder, certainly a writer ought to have the "inner resources" to be able to give a picture of a murderer's mental state. The assumption is that you only need look into yourself in such a case; after all, there is such a thing as imagination. . . . For a number of reasons I can no longer abandon myself to this amiable hope of managing so comfortably. I cannot find in myself alone all the motives which, as we learn from newspapers and scientific reports, are discovered in human beings. No more than any judge passing sentence am I able to imagine adequately, unaided, the mental state of a murderer. Modern psychology, from psychoanalysis

to behaviorism, provides me with insights which help me to form a quite different judgment of the case, especially when I take into consideration the findings of sociology, and do not ignore economics or history. You may say: this is getting complicated. I must answer, it *is* complicated. Perhaps I can talk you into agreeing with me that a lot of literature is extremely primitive; yet you will ask in grave concern: Wouldn't such an evening in a theatre be a pretty alarming business? The answer to that is: No.

Whatever knowledge may be contained in a poetic work, it must be completely converted into poetry. In its transmuted form, it gives the same type of satisfaction as any poetic work. And although it does not provide that satisfaction found in science as such, a certain inclination to penetrate more deeply into the nature of things, a desire to make the world controllable, are necessary to ensure enjoyment of poetic works generated by this era of great discoveries and inventions.

IS THE EPIC THEATRE A SORT OF "MORAL INSTITUTION"? According to Friedrich Schiller the theatre should be a moral institution. When Schiller posed this demand it scarcely occurred to him that by moralizing from the stage he might drive the audience out of the theatre. In his day the audience had no objection to moralizing. Only later on did Friedrich Nietzsche abuse him as the moral trumpeter of Säckingen.[5] To Nietzsche a concern with morality seemed a dismal affair; to Schiller it seemed completely gratifying. He knew of nothing more entertaining and satisfying than to propagate ideals. The bourgeoisie was just establishing the concept of the nation. To furnish your house, show off your new hat, present your bills for payment is highly gratifying. But to speak of the decay of your house, to have to sell your old hat and pay the bills yourself is a truly dismal affair, and that was how Friedrich Nietzsche saw it a century later. It was no use talking to him about morality or, in consequence, about the

5 Nietzsche's quip referred to a banal verse tale by Viktor Scheffel, *Der Trompeter von Säckingen,* a standard favorite in Germany's "plush-sofa kultur"—a parallel of Victorianism—in the second half of the nineteenth century.—Trans.

other Friedrich. Many people also attacked the epic theatre, claiming it was too moralistic. Yet moral utterances were secondary in the epic theatre. Its intention was less to moralize than to study. And it did study, but then came the rub: the moral of the story. Naturally, we cannot claim that we began making studies just because studying was so much fun and not for any concrete reason, or that the results of our studies then took us completely by surprise. Undoubtedly there were painful discrepancies in the world around us, conditions that were hard to bear, conditions of a kind not only hard to bear for moral reasons. Hunger, cold and hardship are not only burdensome for moral reasons. And the purpose of our investigation was not merely to arouse moral misgivings about certain conditions (although such misgivings might easily be felt, if not by every member of the audience; such misgivings, for example, were seldom felt by those who profited by the conditions in question). The purpose of our investigation was to make visible the means by which those onerous conditions could be done away with. We were not speaking on behalf of morality but on behalf of the wronged. These are really two different things, for moral allusions are often used in telling the wronged that they must put up with their situation. For such moralists, people exist for morality, not morality for people.

Nevertheless it can be deduced from these remarks to what extent and in what sense the epic theatre is a moral institution.

CAN EPIC THEATRE BE PERFORMED ANY-WHERE? From the standpoint of style, the epic theatre is nothing especially new. In its character of show, of demonstration, and its emphasis on the artistic, it is related to the ancient Asian theatre. The medieval mystery play, and also the classical Spanish and Jesuit theatres, showed an instructive tendency.

Those theatre forms corresponded to certain tendencies of their time and disappeared wtih them. The modern epic theatre is also linked with definite tendencies. It can by no means be performed anywhere. Few of the great nations today are inclined to discuss their problems in the theatre. London, Paris, Tokyo and Rome maintain their theatres for quite different purposes. Only in a few places, and not for long, have circumstances been favorable to an epic, instructive theatre. In Berlin, fascism put a violent end to the development of such a theatre.[6]

Besides a certain technical standard, it presupposes a powerful social movement which has an interest in the free discussion of vital problems, the better to solve them, and can defend this interest against all opposing tendencies.

The epic theatre is the broadest and most far-reaching experiment in great modern theatre, and it has to overcome all the enormous difficulties that all vital forces in the area of politics, philosophy, science and art have to overcome.

[6] After the defeat of the Nazis in 1945, the German administrators of the then Soviet-occupied zone—now the German Democratic Republic—invited Brecht to establish his own theatre in East Berlin. This theatre is recognized today all over the world as a classical type of epic theatre.—Trans.

FRIEDRICH DUERRENMATT

The son of a pastor, Duerrenmatt was born in 1921 in the village of Konolfingen, Switzerland, near Berne. He studied at the University of Berne and turned to writing after an early beginning as a painter. Several of his novels, including *The Quarry, The Pledge* (which has been filmed), and *Traps* (which has been dramatized), have appeared in English; they share with his plays a preoccupation with suspense, violence, and the quest for justice. Following World War II, Duerrenmatt's plays, together with those of another Swiss, Max Frisch, established Zurich as the theatre center of the German-speaking world. They tend to be satirical parables, bitter and comic at the same time, owing some of their parabolic technique to such predecessors as Bertolt Brecht and Thornton Wilder. *The Visit* (1956) established Duerrenmatt's international fame. New York and London know it in the adaptation of Maurice Valency, successfully performed by Alfred Lunt and Lynn Fontanne; in its original form this tale of a vindictive woman's purchase of a belated justice is both more savage and more playful. Subsequently, in *The Physicists,* Duerrenmatt commented on international politics and atomic physics.

PROBLEMS OF THE THEATRE [1]

(1955)

. . . I love a colorful stage setting, a colorful theatre, like the stage of Teo Otto, to mention an admirable example. I have little use for a theatre that uses black curtains as was the fashion once upon a time, or for the tendency to glory in threadbare poverty which some stage designers seem to aim for. To be sure the word is important above all else in the theatre; but note: above all else. For after the word there are many other things, which also rightfully belong to the theatre, even a certain wantonness. Thus when someone asked me quite thoughtfully with respect to my play *Mississippi,* where one of the characters enters through a grandfather's clock, whether or not I thought a four-dimensional theatre possible, I could only remark that I had not thought of Einstein when I did it. It is just that in my daily life it should give me great pleasure if I could enter into a company and astonish those present by coming into the room through a grandfathers' clock or by floating in through a window. No one should deny us playwrights the opportunity to satisfy such desires now and then at least on the stage, where such whims can be fulfilled. The old argument of which came first, the chicken or the egg, can be transformed in art into the question of whether the egg or the chicken, the world as potential or as rich harvest, is to be presented. Artists might very well be divided then into those favoring the egg and those favoring the chicken. The argument is a lively one. Alfred Polgar once said to me, it was odd that while in the contemporary Anglo-Saxon drama everything came out

in the dialogue, there was always much too much happening on the stage in my plays and that he, Polgar, would sometimes like to see a simple Duerrenmatt play. Behind this truth, however, lies my refusal to say that the egg came before the chicken, and my personal prejudice of preferring the chicken to the egg. It happens to be my passion, not always a happy one perhaps, to want to put on the stage the richness, the manifold diversity of the world. As a result my theatre is open to many interpretations and appears to confuse some. Misunderstandings creep in, as when someone looks around desperately in the chicken coop of my plays, hoping to find the egg of Columbus which I stubbornly refuse to lay.

But a play is bound not only to a place, but also to a time. Just as the stage represents a place, so it also represents a time, the time *during* which the action takes place as well as the time *in* which it occurs. If Aristotle had really demanded the unity of time, place and action, he would have limited the duration of a tragedy to the time it took for the action to be carried out (a feat which the Greek tragedians nearly achieved), for which reasons, of course, everything would have to be concentrated upon that action. Time would pass "naturally," everything coming one after the other without breaks. But this does not always have to be the case. In general the actions on the stage follow one another but, to cite an example, in Nestroy's magical farce, *Death on the Wedding Day* (*Der Tod am Hochzeitstag*), there are two acts taking place simultaneously and the illusion of simultaneity is skillfully achieved by having the action of the second act form the background noise for the first, and the

1 Extracts from a lecture (Zurich, 1955), translated by Gerhard Nellhaus in the *Tulane Drama Review* (Oct., 1958). Reprinted by permission of Jonathan Cape, Ltd.—Ed.

action of the first act the background noise for the second. Other examples of how time is used as a theatrical device could be easily recalled. Time can be shortened, stretched, intensified, arrested, repeated; the dramatist can, like Joshua, call to his heaven's orbits, "Theatre-Sun, stand thou still upon Gibeon! And thou, Theatre-Moon, in the valley of Ajalon!"

It may be noted further that the unities ascribed to Aristotle were not wholly kept in Greek tragedy either. The action is interrupted by the choruses, and by this means time is spaced. When the chorus interrupts the action, it achieves as regards time—to elucidate the obvious like an amateur—the very same thing the curtain does today. The curtain cuts up and spreads out the time of an action. I have nothing against such an honorable device. The good thing about a curtain is that it so clearly defines an act, that it clears the table, so to speak. Moreover it is psychologically often extremely necessary to give the exhausted and frightened audience a rest. But a new way of binding language and time has evolved in our day.

If I cite Wilder's *Our Town* once again, I do so because I assume that this fine play is widely known. You may recall that in it different characters turn toward the audience and talk of the worries and needs of their small town. In this way Wilder is able to dispense with the curtain. The curtain has been replaced by the direct address to the audience. The epic element of description has been added to the drama. For this reason, of course, this form of theatre has been called the epic theatre.

Yet when looked at quite closely, Shakespeare's plays or Schiller's *Goetz von Berlichingen* are in a certain sense also epic theatre. Only in a different, less obvious manner. Since Shakespeare's histories often extend over a considerable period of time, this time span is divided into different actions, different episodes, each of which is treated dramatically. *Henry IV, Part I,* consists of nineteen such episodes, while by the end of the fourth act of *Goetz* there already are no less than forty-one tableaux. I stopped counting after that. If one looks at the way the over-all action has been built up, then, with respect

to time, it is quite close to the epic, like a movie that is run too slowly, so that the individual frames can be seen. The condensation of everything into a certain time has been given up in favor of an episodic form of drama.

Thus when an author in some of our modern plays turns toward the audience, he attempts to give the play a greater continuity than is otherwise possible in an episodic form. The void between the acts is to be filled; the time gap is to be bridged, not by a pause, but by words, by a description of what has gone on in the meanwhile, or by having some new character introduce himself. In other words, the expositions are handled in an epic manner, not the actions to which these expositions lead. This represents an advance of the word in the theatre, the attempt of the word to reconquer territory lost a long time ago. Let us emphasize that it is but an attempt; for all too often the direct address to the audience is used to explain the play, an undertaking that makes no sense whatever. If the audience is moved by the play, it will not need prodding by explanations; if the audience is not moved, all the prodding in the world will not be of help.

In contrast to the epic, which can describe human beings as they are, the drama unavoidably limits and therefore stylizes them. This limitation is inherent in the art form itself. The human being of the drama is, after all, a talking individual, and speech is his limitation. The action only serves to force this human being on the stage to talk in a certain way. The action is the crucible in which the human being is molten into words, must become words. This, of course, means that I, as the playwright, have to get the people in my drama into situations which force them to speak. If I merely show two people sitting together and drinking coffee while they talk about the weather, politics or the latest fashions, then I provide neither a dramatic situation nor dramatic dialogue, no matter how clever their talk. Some other ingredient must be added to their conversation, something to add pique, drama, double meaning. If the audience knows that there is some poison in one of the coffee cups, or perhaps even in both, so that the conversation is really one between two poisoners, then this little coffee-for-two idyl becomes through this artistic device a dramatic situation, out of which and on the basis of which dramatic dialogue can develop. Without the addition of some special tension or special condition, dramatic dialogue can not develop.

Just as dialogue must develop out of a situation, so it must also lead into some situation, that is to say, of course, a new situation. Dramatic dialogue effects some action, some suffering, some new situation, out of which in turn new dialogue can again develop, and so on and so forth.

However, a human being does more than just talk. The fact that a man also thinks, or at least should think, that he feels, yes, more than anything feels, and that he does not always wish to show others what he is thinking or feeling, has led to the use of another artistic device, the monologue. It is true, of course, that a person standing on a stage and carrying on a conversation with himself out loud is not exactly natural; and the same thing can be said, only more so, of an operatic aria. But the monologue (like the aria) proves that an artistic trick, which really ought not be played, can achieve an unexpected effect, to which, and rightly so, the public succumbs time and again; so much so that Hamlet's monologue, "To be or not to be," or Faust's, are among the most beloved and most famous passages in the theatre.

But not everything that sounds like a monologue is monologue. The purpose of dialogue is not only to lead a human being to a point where he must act or suffer, but at times it also leads into a major speech, to the explanation of some point of view. Many people have lost the appreciation of rhetoric since, as Hilpert maintains, some actor who was not sure of his lines discovered naturalism. That loss is rather sad. A speech can win its way across the footlights more effectively than any other artistic device. But many of our critics no longer know what to make of a speech. An author, who today dares a speech, will suffer the same fate as the peasant Dicaeopolis; he will have to lay his head upon the executioner's block. Except that instead of the Acharnians of Aristophanes, it will be the majority of critics who descend on the author—the most normal things

in the world. Nobody is more anxious to bash out someone's brains than those who haven't any. . . .

These elements and problems of place, time, and action, which are all, of course, interwoven and are but hinted at here, belong to the basic material, to the artistic devices and tools of the craft of the drama. But let me make it clear here and now, that I make war upon the notion of "the craft of the drama." The very idea that anyone who makes a sufficiently diligent and steadfast endeavor to achieve something in that art will succeed in the end or even that this craft can be learned is a notion we thought discarded long ago. . . .

Employing this—really non-existent—craft, let us try and give shape to a certain material. Usually there is a central point of reference, the hero. In theories of the drama a difference is made between a tragic hero, the hero of tragedy, and a comic hero, the hero of comedy. The qualities a tragic hero must possess are well known. He must be capable of rousing our sympathy. His guilt and his innocence, his virtues and his vices must be mixed in the most pleasant and yet exact manner, and administered in doses according to well-defined rules. If, for example, I make my tragic hero an evil man, then I must endow him with a portion of intellect equal to his malevolence. As a result of this rule, the most sympathetic stage character in German literature has turned out to be the devil. The role of the hero in the play has not changed. The only thing that has changed is the social position of the character who awakens our sympathy.

In ancient tragedy and in Shakespeare the hero belongs to the highest class in society, to the nobility. The spectators watch a suffering, acting, raving hero who occupies a social position far higher than their own. This continues still to impress audiences today.

Then when Lessing and Schiller introduced the bourgeois drama, the audience saw itself as the suffering hero on the stage. But the evolution of the hero continued. Buechner's Woyzeck is a primitive proletarian who represents far less socially than the average spectator. But it is precisely in this extreme form of human existence, in this last, most miserable form, that the audience is to see the human being also, indeed itself.

And finally we might mention Pirandello who was the first, as far as I know, to render the hero, the character on the stage, immaterial and transparent just as Wilder did the dramatic place. The audience watching this sort of presentation attends, as it were, its own dissection, its own psychoanalysis, and the stage becomes man's internal milieu, the inner space of the world.

Of course, the theatre has never dealt only with kings and generals; in comedy the hero has always been the peasant, the beggar, the ordinary citizen—but this was always in comedy. Nowhere in Shakespeare do we find a comic king; in his day a ruler could appear as a bloody monster but never as a fool. In Shakespeare the courtiers, the artisans, the working people are comic. Hence, in the evolution of the tragic hero we see a trend toward comedy. Analogously the fool becomes more and more of a tragic figure. This fact is by no means without significance. The hero of a play not only propels an action on, he not only suffers a certain fate, but he also represents a world. Therefore we have to ask ourselves how we should present our own questionable world and with what sort of heroes. We have to ask ourselves how the mirrors which catch and reflect this world should be ground and set.

Can our present-day world, to ask a concrete question, be represented by Schiller's dramatic art? Some writers claim it can be, since Schiller still holds audiences in his grip. To be sure, in art everything is possible when the art is right. But the question is if an art valid for its time could possibly be so even for our day. Art can never be repeated. If it were repeatable, it would be foolish not just to write according to the rules of Schiller.

Schiller wrote as he did because the world in which he lived could still be mirrored in the world his writing created, a world he could build as a historian. But just barely. For was not Napoleon perhaps the last hero in the old sense? The world today as it appears to us could hardly be encompassed in the form of the historical drama as Schiller wrote it, for the reason alone that we no longer have any tragic heroes, but only vast tragedies staged by world

butchers and produced by slaughtering machines. Hitler and Stalin can not be made into Wallensteins. Their power is so enormous that they themselves are no more than incidental, corporeal and easily replaceable expressions of this power; and the misfortune associated with the former and to a considerable extent also with the latter is too vast, too complex, too horrible, too mechanical and usually simply too devoid of all sense. Wallenstein's power can still be envisioned; power as we know it today can only be seen in its smallest part for, like an iceberg, the largest part is submerged in anonymity and abstraction. Schiller's drama presupposes a world that the eye can take in, that takes for granted genuine actions of state, just as Greek tragedy did. For only what the eye can take in can be made visible in art. The state today, however, can not be envisioned for it is anonymous and bureaucratic; and not only in Moscow and Washington, but also in Berne. Actions of state today have become *post hoc* satiric dramas which follow the tragedies executed in secret earlier. True representatives of our world are missing; the tragic heroes are nameless. Any small-time crook, petty government official or policeman better represents our world than a senator or president. Today art can only embrace the victims, if it can reach men at all; it can no longer come close to the mighty. Creon's secretaries close Antigone's case. The state has lost its physical reality, and just as physics can now only cope with the world in mathematical formulas, so the state can only be expressed in statistics. Power today becomes visible, material only when it explodes as in the atom bomb, in this marvelous mushroom which rises and spreads immaculate as the sun and in which mass murder and beauty have become one. The atom bomb can not be reproduced artistically since it is mass-produced. In its face all of man's art that would recreate it must fail, since it is itself a creation of man. Two mirrors which reflect one another remain empty.

But the task of art, insofar as art can have a task at all, and hence also the task of drama today, is to create something concrete, something that has form. This can be accomplished best by comedy. Tragedy, the strictest genre in art, presupposes a formed world. Comedy—insofar as it is not just satire of a particular society as in Molière—supposes an unformed world, a world being made and turned upside down, a world about to fold like ours. Tragedy overcomes distance; it can make myths originating in times immemorial seem like the present to the Athenians. But comedy creates distance; the attempt of the Athenians to gain a foothold in Sicily is translated by comedy into the birds undertaking to create their own empire before which the gods and men will have to capitulate. How comedy works can be seen in the most primitive kind of joke, in the dirty story, which, though it is of very dubious value, I bring up only because it is the best illustration of what I mean by creating distance. The subject of the dirty story is the purely sexual, which because it is purely sexual, is formless and without objective distance. To be given a form the purely sexual is transmuted, as I have already mentioned, into the dirty joke. Therefore this type of joke is a kind of original comedy, a transposition of the sexual onto the plain of the comical. In this way it is possible today in a society dominated by John Doe, to talk in an accepted way about the purely sexual. In the dirty story it becomes clear that the comical exists in forming what is formless, in creating order out of chaos.

The means by which comedy creates distance is the conceit. Tragedy is without conceit. Hence there are few tragedies whose subjects were invented. By this I do not mean to imply that the ancient tragedians lacked inventive ideas of the sort that are written today, but the marvel of their art was that they had no need of these inventions, of conceits. That makes all the difference. Aristophanes, on the other hand, lives by conceits. The stuff of his plays are not myths but inventions, which take place not in the past but the present. They drop into their world like bomb shells which, by throwing up huge craters of dirt, change the present into the comic and thus scatter the dirt for everyone to see. This, of course, does not mean that drama today can only be comical. Tragedy and comedy are but formal concepts, dramatic attitudes, figments of the esthetic imagination which can embrace one and the same thing. Only the conditions under which each is created are different, and these conditions have their basis only in small part in art.

Tragedy presupposes guilt, despair, moderation, lucidity, vision, a sense of responsibility. In the Punch-and-Judy show of our century, in this back-sliding of the white race, there are no more guilty and also, no responsible men. It is always, "We couldn't help it" and "We didn't really want that to happen." And indeed, things happen without anyone in particular being responsible for them. Everything is dragged along and everyone gets caught somewhere in the sweep of events. We are all collectively guilty, collectively bogged down in the sins of our fathers and of our forefathers. We are the offspring of children. That is our misfortune, but not our guilt: guilt can exist only as a personal achievement, as a religious deed. Comedy alone is suitable for us. Our world has led to the grotesque as well as to the atom bomb, and so it is a world like that of Hieronymus Bosch whose apocalyptic paintings are also grotesque. But the grotesque is only a way of expressing in a tangible manner, of making us perceive physically the paradoxical, the form of the unformed, the face of a world without face; and just as in our thinking today we seem to be unable to do without the concept of the paradox, so also in art, and in our world which at times seems still to exist only because the atom bomb exists: out of fear of the bomb.

But the tragic is still possible even if pure tragedy is not. We can achieve the tragic out of comedy. We can bring it forth as a frightening moment, as an abyss that opens suddenly; indeed many of Shakespeare's tragedies are already really comedies out of which the tragic arises.

After all this the conclusion might easily be drawn that comedy is the expression of despair, but this conclusion is not inevitable. To be sure, whoever realizes the senselessness, the hopelessness of this world might well despair, but this despair is not a result of this world. Rather it is an answer given by an individual to this world; another answer would be not to despair, would be an individual's decision to endure this world in which we live like Gulliver among the giants. He also achieves distance, he also steps back a pace or two who takes measure of his opponent, who prepares himself to fight his opponent or to escape him. It is still possible to show man as a courageous being.

In truth this is a principal concern of mine. The blind man, Romulus, Uebelohe, Akki, are all men of courage. The lost world order is restored within them; the universal escapes my grasp. I refuse to find the universal in a doctrine. The universal for me is chaos. The world (hence the stage which represents this world) is for me something monstrous, a riddle of misfortunes which must be accepted but before which one must not capitulate. The world is far bigger than any man, and perforce threatens him constantly. If one could but stand outside the world, it would no longer be threatening. But I have neither the right nor the ability to be an outsider to this world. To find solace in poetry can also be all too cheap; it is more honest to retain one's human point of view. Brecht's thesis, that the world is an accident, which he developed in his street

scene where he shows how this accident happened, may yield—as it in fact did—some magnificent theatre; but he did it by concealing most of the evidence! Brecht's thinking is inexorable, because inexorably there are many things he will not think about.

And lastly it is through the conceit, through comedy that the anonymous audience becomes possible as an audience, becomes a reality to be counted on, and also, one to be taken into account. The conceit easily transforms the crowd of theatre-goers into a mass which can be attacked, deceived, outsmarted into listening to things it would otherwise not so readily listen to. Comedy is a mousetrap in which the public is easily caught and in which it will get caught over and over again. Tragedy, on the other hand, predicated a true community, a kind of community whose existence in our day is but an embarrassing fiction. Nothing is more ludicrous, for instance, than to sit and watch the mystery plays of the Anthroposophists when one is not a participant.

SCANDINAVIAN DRAMATIC CRITICISM

If modern drama is the creation of Henrik Ibsen, Scandinavian drama is the creation of Ludvig Holberg (1684–1754), who, though born in Norway, is usually regarded as a Danish author. The first dramatist to write in Danish, he wrote comedies in the tradition of Molière and Plautus and was called "the Molière of the North." He was followed by two Danish dramatists who were critics as well and who therefore justified their art at length—Adam Oehlenschlaeger (1779–1850), who specialized in historical dramas influenced by Schiller and Shakespeare, and J. L. Heiberg (1791–1860), who wrote farces and romantic dramas.

The Norwegian dramatist Bjørnstjerne Bjørnson (1832–1910) turned from historical dramas to a sort of optimistic realism. He was eclipsed by Henrik Ibsen (1828–1906), who also abandoned an early attachment to romantic and historical drama, choosing to write instead

the mordant, searching realistic plays that added a serious meaning to Eugène Scribe's "well-made play" form and effectively began the history of modern drama. Although many of Ibsen's early drafts survive and provide insight into his method, his direct comments on his intentions are few and occur mainly in chance passages from his speeches and letters. At hand, however, was the first great defender of the realism of Bjørnson and Ibsen—the Danish critic Georg Brandes (1842–1927). In the tradition of H. A. Taine, Brandes offered a social interpretation of literature and demanded a literature that answered to the needs and the circumstances of the time. He interpreted the two dramatists in the widely influential *Main Currents in Nineteenth Century Literature* (6 vols., 1871–90) and in his book, *Henrik Ibsen* (1898).

The Swedish dramatist, August Strindberg (1849–1912), wrote plays in a great variety of forms, but he was himself skilled in defending his practice, whether realistic (as in his preface to *Miss Julie*) or non-realistic (as in the pamphlets he addressed to the actors of the Intimate Theatre). Modern drama in general took its tone from the rival whom Strindberg resented, Henrik Ibsen, but Strindberg, as the father of Expressionism and other avant-garde movements in the theatre, may well rank as the second most influential dramatist.

HENRIK IBSEN

Ibsen, born in Skien, Norway, in 1828, came of a wealthy family that was soon impoverished, and in this respect he resembled his own character Peer Gynt. He worked in the theatre as a stage manager and a director. His first play, *Catiline* (1850), started him on his efforts to find his own path in playwriting. The verse comedy *Love's Comedy* (1862), the historical play *The Pretenders* (1863), the episodic history of a fanatic, *Brand* (1866), and the episodic history of an audacious libertine, *Peer Gynt* (1867) all illustrate the variety of his strivings before he inaugurated his realistic period —and, indeed, founded the modern drama—with *The League of Youth* (1869). If his realistic plays followed the outward form of the well-made play that had been pioneered by Eugène Scribe, they departed from their model in offering credible, original characters and a serious view of society. If Ibsen was not a coherent critic of society, at least he touched upon timely, lively issues—the place of women in *A Doll's* *House* (1879), the taboo subjects of venereal disease, incest, and mercy killing in *Ghosts* (1881), a community's capacity to face the truth in *An Enemy of the People* (1882), and the necessity for illusion in *The Wild Duck* (1884). This last play proved something of a turning point, for thereafter Ibsen was even less directly concerned with public issues. Perhaps his attitude was reflected in *Rosmersholm* (1886), about an idealist who loses his interest in reforming his community. *Hedda Gabler* (1890), which provided many actresses with a favorite role, is a psychological study of a destructive woman. The last plays are increasingly preoccupied with symbols and sorrow: *The Master Builder* (1892), *Little Eyolf* (1894), *John Gabriel Borkman* (1896), and *When We Dead Awaken* (1899). Throughout his lifetime, Ibsen preserved a bold testiness which supported the story that, on his deathbed in 1906, his last words were: "On the other hand."

ON THE POET'S VISION [1]

(1874)

. . . My private relations I have never made the direct subject of any poetical work. In the earlier hard times these relations were of less importance to me than I have afterwards often been able

[1] From *Speeches and New Letters* (Boston, 1910), translated by Arne Kildal. During the summer of 1874 Ibsen spent a couple of months in Norway, after an absence of ten years. On the afternoon of September 10th the students marched in procession to the home of the poet and greeted him in song and word. The following passage is taken from Ibsen's speech in answer to the students.

to justify to myself. When the nest of the eider duck was robbed the first and second and third time, it was of illusions and of great hopes of life that it was robbed. When at festival gatherings I have been sensible of recollections like the bear in the hands of his tamer, it has been because I have been co-responsible in a time which buried a glorious thought amid song and feasting.

And what is it then that constitutes a poet? As for me, it was a long time before I realized that to be a poet, that is chiefly to see, but mark well, to see in such a manner that the thing seen is perceived by his audience just as the poet saw it. But thus is seen and thus is appreciated that only which has been lived through. And as regards the thing which has been lived through, that is just the secret of the literature of modern times. All that I have written, these last ten years, I have, mentally, lived through. But no poet lives through anything isolated. What he lives through all of his countrymen live through together with him. For if that were not so, what would establish the bridge of understanding between the producing and the receiving mind?

And what is it, then, that I have lived through and written on? The range has been large. Partly, I have written on that which only by glimpses and at my best moments I have felt stirring vividly within me as something great and beautiful. I have written on that which, so to speak, has stood higher than my daily self, and I have written on this in order to fasten it over against and within myself.

But I have also written on the opposite, on that which to introspective contemplation appears as the dregs and sediment of one's own nature. The work of writing has in this case been to me like a bath which I have felt to leave cleaner, healthier, and freer. Yes, gentlemen, nobody can poetically present that to which he has not to a certain degree and at least at times the model within himself. And who is the man among us who has not now and then felt and acknowledged within himself a contradiction between word and action, between will and task, between life and teaching on the whole? Or who is there among us who has not, at least in some cases, selfishly been sufficient unto himself, and half unconsciously, half in good faith, has extenuated this conduct both to others and to himself?

. . . A poet by nature belongs to the far-sighted. Never have I seen the fatherland and the actual life of the fatherland so fully, so clearly, and at a closer range than just from afar and during my absence. . . .

TO THE NORWEGIAN WOMEN'S RIGHTS LEAGUE [2]

(1898)

I am not a member of the Women's Rights League. Whatever I have written has been without any conscious thought of making propaganda. I have been more poet and less social philosopher than people generally seem inclined to believe. I thank you for the toast, but must disclaim the honor of having consciously worked for the women's rights movement. I am not even quite clear as to just what this women's rights movement really is. To me it has seemed a problem of humanity in general. And if you read my books carefully you will

2 From *Speeches and New Letters* (Boston, 1910), translated by Arne Kildal.

understand this. True enough, it is desirable to solve the problem of women's rights, along with all the others; but that has not been the whole purpose. My task has been the *description of humanity*. To be sure, whenever such a description is felt to be reasonably true, the reader will insert his own feelings and sentiments into the work of the poet. These are attributed to the poet; but incorrectly so. Every reader remolds it so beautifully and nicely, each according to his own personality. Not only those who write, but also those who read are poets; they are collaborators; they are often more poetical than the poet himself. . . .

IBSEN AND SOCIALISM [3]

(1890)

I did not, for instance, say that I have never studied the question of Socialism—the fact being that I am much interested in the question, and have endeavoured to the best of my ability to acquaint myself with its different sides. I only said that I have never had time to study the extensive literature dealing with the different socialistic systems.

Where the correspondent repeats my assertion that I do not belong to the Social-Democratic party, I wish that he had not omitted what I expressly added,

namely, that I never have belonged, and probably never shall belong, to any party whatever.

I may add here that it has become an absolute necessity to me to work quite independently and to shape my own course.

What the correspondent writes about my surprise at seeing my name put forward by socialistic agitators as that of a supporter of their dogmas is particularly liable to be misunderstood.

What I really said was that I was surprised that I, who had made it my chief life-task to depict human characters and human destinies, should, without conscious or direct intention, have arrived in several matters at the same conclusions as the social-democratic moral philosophers had arrived at by scientific processes. . . .

3 Portion of a letter to H. L. Brækstad, (born 1845), a Norwegian-English man of letters resident in London. At Ibsen's request, Mr. Brækstad inserted parts of the letter in the *Daily Chronicle* of August 28, 1890, as a reply to an article in which Ibsen had been misquoted. In *Letters of Henrik Ibsen* (New *York*, 1905), translated by J. N. Laurvik and Mary Morison.

AUGUST STRINDBERG

Johan August Strindberg was born in Stockholm in 1849. His mother was a former servant who had been his father's mistress; after his mother's death, his father married a second servant. The misery of Strindberg's early life set the keynote for further unhappiness. He studied at the University of Uppsala, taught school, returned to the university as a medical student, studied acting, and finally discovered his true métier in playwriting. One of his short plays brought a reward from the king, and soon he wrote his first full-length play, *Master Olof* (1872). From 1874 to 1882, he served as assistant librarian in the Royal Library at Stockholm.

In 1877, he married Siri von Essen. It was the first of his three unhappy marriages, all of which ended in divorce. In each case, his wife was one of those aggressive modern women whom he professed to despise. His fame grew with his woes, and not only because of the three suits for divorce. He began to draw attention with such autobiographical novels as *The Son of a Servant, The Growth of a Soul,* and *The Confession of a Fool,* but his real reputation rested

on his plays. His earlier plays were written mainly for the realistic theatre. In what may be called his middle period, he produced the intense dramas *The Father* (1887), showing a man destroyed by his wife, and *Miss Julie* (1888), about the seduction of a young noblewoman. From 1883 to 1897 he spent most of his time on the Continent and belonged to the main stream of theatre life. After a mental breakdown in the 1890's he wrote the less emphatically realistic *Crimes and Crimes* (1899), such history plays as *Erik XIV* (1899), and such frankly non-realistic plays as *To Damascus* (1898), *A Dream Play* (1902), which followed the illogical pattern of a dream, and *The Ghost Sonata* (1907), a sonata-like variation upon certain issues of guilt. In all he wrote more than fifty plays. He founded his Intimate Theatre for his own chamber plays in Stockholm in 1907. He died in 1912.

Invariably, he wrote with an intensity and vigor that must have been nurtured by his own complaints against the world. His experiments prepared the way for expressionism and the theatre of the absurd.

AUTHOR'S FOREWORD TO MISS JULIE [1]

(1888)

Theatre has long seemed to me—in common with much other art—a *Biblia Pauperum,* a Bible in pictures for those who cannot read what is written or printed; and I see the playwright as a lay preacher peddling the ideas of his time in popular form, popular enough for the middle-classes, mainstay of theatre audiences, to grasp the gist of the matter without troubling their brains too much. For this reason theatre has always been an elementary school for the young, the semi-educated and for women who still have a primitive capacity for deceiving themselves and letting themselves be deceived—who, that is to say, are susceptible to illusion and to suggestion from the author. I have therefore thought it not unlikely that in these days, when that rudimentary and immature thought-process operating through fantasy appears to be developing into reflection, research and analysis, that theatre, like religion, might be discarded as an outworn form for whose appreciation we lack the necessary conditions. This opinion is confirmed by the major crisis still prevailing in the theatres of Europe, and still more by the fact that in those countries of culture, producing the greatest thinkers of the age, namely England and Germany, drama—like other fine arts—is dead.

Some countries, it is true, have attempted to create a new drama by using the old forms with up-to-date contents, but not only has there been insufficient time for these new ideas to be popularized, so that the audience can grasp them, but also people have been so wrought up by the taking of sides that pure, disinterested appreciation has become impossible. One's deepest impressions are upset when an applauding or a hissing majority dominates as forcefully and openly as it can in the theatre. Moreover, as no new form has been devised for these new contents, the new wine has burst the old bottles.

In this play I have not tried to do any-thing new, for this cannot be done, but only to modernize the form to meet the demands which may, I think, be made on this art today. To this end I chose—or surrendered myself to—a theme which claims to be outside the controversial issues of today, since questions of social climbing or falling, of higher or lower, better or worse, of man and woman, are, have been and will be of lasting interest. When I took this theme from a true story told me some years ago, which made a deep impression, I saw it as a subject for tragedy, for as yet it is tragic to see one favoured by fortune go under, and still more to see a family heritage die out, although a time may come when we have grown so developed and enlightened that we shall view with indifference life's spectacle, now seeming so brutal, cynical and heartless. Then we shall have dispensed with those inferior, unreliable instruments of thought called feelings, which become harmful and superfluous as reasoning develops.

The fact that my heroine rouses pity is solely due to weakness; we cannot resist fear of the same fate overtaking us. The hyper-sensitive spectator may, it is true, go beyond this kind of pity, while the man with belief in the future may actually demand some suggestion for remedying the evil—in other words some kind of policy. But, to begin with, there is no such thing as absolute evil; the downfall of one family is the good fortune of another, which thereby gets a chance to rise, and, fortune being only comparative, the alternation of rising and falling is one of life's principal charms. Also, to the man of policy, who wants to remedy the painful fact that the bird of prey devours the dove, and lice the bird of prey, I should like to put the question: why should it be remedied? Life is not so mathematically idiotic as only to permit the big to eat the small; it happens just as often that the bee kills the lion or at least drives it mad.

That my tragedy depresses many people is their own fault. When we have grown strong as the pioneers of the French revolution, we shall be happy and relieved to see the national parks cleared

1 From *Six Plays of Strindberg,* translated by Elizabeth Sprigge. © 1955 by Elizabeth Sprigge. Reprinted by permission of Willis Kingsley Wing.—Ed.

of ancient rotting trees which have stood too long in the way of others equally entitled to a period of growth—as relieved as we are when an incurable invalid dies.

My tragedy *The Father* was recently criticised for being too sad—as if one wants cheerful tragedies! Everybody is clamouring for this supposed "joy of life," and theatre managers demand farces, as if the joy of life consisted in being ridiculous and portraying all human beings as suffering from St. Vitus's dance or total idiocy. I myself find the joy of life in its strong and cruel struggles, and my pleasure in learning, in adding to my knowledge. For this reason I have chosen for this play an unusual situation, but an instructive one—an exception, that is to say, but a great exception, one proving the rule, which will no doubt annoy all lovers of the commonplace. What will offend simple minds is that my plot is not simple, nor its point of view single. In real life an action—this, by the way, is a somewhat new discovery—is generally caused by a whole series of motives, more or less fundamental, but as a rule the spectator chooses just one of these—the one which his mind can most easily grasp or that does most credit to his intilligence. A suicide is committed. Business troubles, says the man of affairs. Unrequited love, say the women. Sickness, says the invalid. Despair, says the down-and-out. But it is possible that the motive lay in all or none of these directions, or that the dead man concealed his actual motive by revealing quite another, likely to reflect more to his glory.

I see Miss Julie's tragic fate to be the result of many circumstances: the mother's character, the father's mistaken upbringing of the girl, her own nature, and the influence of her fiancé on a weak degenerate mind. Also, more directly, the festive mood of Midsummer Eve, her father's absence, her monthly indisposition, her pre-occupation with animals, the excitement of dancing, the magic of dusk, the strongly aphrodisiac influence of flowers, and finally the chance that drives the couple into a room alone—to which must be added the urgency of the excited man.

My treatment of the theme, moreover, is neither exclusively physiological nor psychological. I have not put the blame wholly on the inheritance from her mother, nor on her physical condition at the time, nor on immorality. I have not even preached a moral sermon; in the absence of a priest I leave this to the cook.

I congratulate myself on this multiplicity of motives as being up-to-date, and if others have done the same thing before me, then I congratulate myself on not being alone in my "paradoxes," as all innovations are called.

In regard to the drawing of the characters, I have made my people somewhat "characterless" for the following reasons. In the course of time the word character has assumed manifold meanings. It must have originally signified the dominating trait of the soul-complex, and this was confused with temperament. Later it became the middle-class term for the automaton, one whose nature had become fixed or who had adapted himself to a particular rôle in life. In fact a person who had ceased to grow was called a character, while one continuing to develop—the skilful navigator of life's river, sailing not with sheets set fast, but veering before the wind to luff again—was called characterless, in a derogatory sense, of course, because he was so hard to catch, classify and keep track of. This middle-class conception of the immobility of the soul was transferred to the stage where the middle-class has always ruled. A character came to signify a man fixed and finished: one who invariably appeared either drunk or jocular or melancholy, and characterization required nothing more than a physical defect such as a club-foot, a wooden leg, a red nose; or the fellow might be made to repeat some such phrase as: "That's capital!" or: "Barkis is willin'!" This simple way of regarding human beings still survives in the great Molière. Harpagon is nothing but a miser, although Harpagon might have been not only a miser, but also a first-rate financier, an excellent father and a good citizen. Worse still, his "failing" is a distinct advantage to his son-in-law and his daughter, who are his heirs, and who therefore cannot criticise him, even if they have to wait a while to get to bed. I do not believe, therefore, in simple stage characters; and the summary judgments of authors—this man is stupid, that one brutal, this jealous, that stingy, and so forth—should be challenged by the Naturalists who know the richness of the soul-complex and realise that vice has a reverse side very much like virtue.

Because they are modern characters, living in a period of transition more feverishly hysterical than its predecessor at least, I have drawn my figures vacillating, disintegrated, a blend of old and new. Nor does it seem to me unlikely that, through newspapers and conversations, modern ideas may have filtered down to the level of the domestic servant.

My souls (characters) are conglomerations of past and present stages of civilization, bits from books and newspapers, scraps of humanity, rags and tatters of fine clothing, patched together as is the human soul. And I have added a little evolutionary history by making the weaker steal and repeat the words of the stronger, and by making the characters borrow ideas or "suggestions" from one another.

Miss Julie is a modern character, not that the half-woman, the man-hater, has not existed always, but because now that she has been discovered she has stepped to the front and begun to make a noise. The half-woman is a type who thrusts herself forward, selling herself nowadays for power, decorations, distinctions, diplomas, as formerly for money. The type implies degeneration; it is not a good type and it does not endure; but it can unfortunately transmit its misery, and degenerate men seem instinctively to choose their mates from among such women, and so they breed, producing offspring of indeterminate sex to whom life is torture. But fortunately they perish, either because they cannot come to terms with reality, or because their repressed instincts break out uncontrollably, or again because their hopes of catching up with men are shattered. The type is tragic, revealing a desperate fight against nature, tragic too in its Romantic inheritance now dissipated by Naturalism, which wants nothing but happiness —and for happiness strong and sound species are required.

But Miss Julie is also a relic of the old warrior nobility now giving way to the new nobility of nerve and brain. She is a victim of the discord which a mother's "crime" has produced in a family, a victim too of the day's complaisance, of circumstances, of her own defective constitution, all of which are equivalent to the Fate or Universal Law of former days. The Naturalist has abolished .guilt with God, but the consequences of the action—punishment, imprisonment or the fear of it—he cannot abolish, for the simple reason that they remain whether he is acquitted or not. An injured fellow-being is not so complacent as outsiders, who have not been injured, can afford to be. Even if the father had felt impelled to take no vengeance, the daughter would have taken vengeance on herself, as she does here, from that innate or acquired sense of honour which the upper-classes inherit—whether from Barbarism or Aryan forebears, or from the chivalry of the Middle Ages, who knows? It is a very beautiful thing, but it has become a danger nowadays to the preservation of the race. It is the nobleman's *hara-kiri*, the Japanese law of inner conscience which compels him to cut his own stomach open at the insult of another, and which survives in modified form in the duel, a privilege of the nobility. And so the valet Jean lives on, but Miss Julie cannot live without honour. This is the thrall's advantage over the nobleman, that he lacks this fatal preoccupation with honour. And in all of us Aryans there is something of the nobleman, or the Don Quixote, which makes us sympathize with the man who commits suicide because he has done something ignoble and lost his honour. And we are noblemen enough to suffer at the sight of fallen greatness littering the earth like a corpse—yes, even if the fallen rise again and make restitution by honourable deeds. Jean, the valet, is a race-builder, a man of marked characteristics. He was a labourer's son who has educated himself towards becoming a gentleman. He has learnt easily, through his well-developed senses (smell, taste, vision)— and he also has a sense of beauty. He has already bettered himself, and is thick-skinned enough to have no scruples about using other people's services. He is already foreign to his associates, despising them as part of the life he has turned his back on, yet also fearing and fleeing from them because they know his secrets, pry into his plans, watch his rise with envy, and look forward with pleasure to his fall. Hence his dual, indeterminate character, vacillating between love of the heights and hatred of those who have already achieved them. He is, he says himself, an aristocrat; he has learned the secrets of good society. He is polished, but vulgar within; he already wears his tails with taste, but there is no guarantee of his personal cleanliness.

He has some respect for his young lady, but he is frightened of Kristin, who knows his dangerous secrets, and he is sufficiently callous not to allow the night's events to wreck his plans for the future. Having both the slave's brutality and the master's lack of squeamishness, he can see blood without fainting and take disaster by the horns. Consequently he emerges from the battle unscathed, and probably ends his days as a hotel-keeper. And even if *he* does not become a Roumanian Count, his son will doubtless go to the university and perhaps become a county attorney.

The light which Jean sheds on a lower-class conception of life, life seen from below, is on the whole illuminating—when he speaks the truth, which is not often, for he says what is favourable to himself rather than what is true. When Miss Julie suggests that the lower-classes must be oppressed by the attitude of their superiors, Jean naturally agrees, as his object is to gain her sympathy; but when he perceives the advantage of separating himself from the common herd, he at once takes back his words.

It is not because Jean is now rising that he 'has the upper hand of Miss Julie, but because he is a man. Sexually he is the aristocrat because of his virility, his keener senses and his capacity for taking the initiative. His inferiority is mainly due to the social environment in which he lives, and he can probably shed it with his valet's livery.

The slave mentality expresses itself in his worship of the Count (the boots), and his religious superstition; but he worships the Count chiefly because he holds that higher position for which Jean himself is striving. And this worship remains even when he has won the daughter of the house and seen how empty is that lovely shell.

I do not believe that a love relationship in the "higher" sense could exist between two individuals of such different quality, but I have made Miss Julie imagine that she is in love, so as to lessen her sense of guilt, and I let Jean suppose that if his social position were altered he would truly love her. I think love is like the hyacinth which has to strike roots in darkness *before* it can produce a vigorous flower. In this case it shoots up quickly, blossoms and goes to seed all at the same time, which is why the plant dies so soon.

As for Kristin, she is a female slave, full of servility and sluggishness acquired in front of the kitchen fire, and stuffed full of morality and religion, which are her cloak and scape-goat. She goes to church as a quick and easy way of unloading her household thefts on to Jesus and taking on a fresh cargo of guiltlessness. For the rest she is a minor character, and I have therefore sketched her in the same manner as the Pastor and the Doctor in "The Father," where I wanted ordinary human beings, as are most country pastors and provincial doctors. If these minor characters seem abstract to some people this is due to the fact that ordinary people are to a certain extent abstract in pursuit of their work; that is to say, they are without individuality, showing, while working, only one side of themselves. And as long as the spectator does not feel a need to see them from other sides, there is nothing wrong with my abstract presentation.

In regard to the dialogue, I have departed somewhat from tradition by not making my characters catechists who ask stupid questions in order to elicit a smart reply. I have avoided the symmetrical, mathematical construction of French dialogue, and let people's minds work irregularly, as they do in real life where, during a conversation, no topic is drained to the dregs, and one mind finds in another a chance cog to engage in. So too the dialogue wanders, gathering in the opening scenes material which is later picked up, worked over, repeated, expounded and developed like the theme in a musical composition.

The plot speaks for itself, and as it really only concerns two people, I have concentrated on these, introducing only one minor character, the cook, and keeping the unhappy spirit of the father above and behind the action. I have done this because it seems to me that the psychological process is what interests people most today. Our inquisitive souls are no longer satisfied with seeing a thing happen; we must also know how it happens. We want to see the wires themselves, to watch the machinery, to examine the box with the false bottom, to take hold of the magic ring in order to find the join, and look at the cards to see how they are marked.

In this connection I have had in view the documentary novels of the brothers de Goncourt, which appeal to me more than any other modern literature.

As far as the technical side of the work is concerned I have made the experiment of abolishing the division into acts. This is because I have come to the conclusion that our capacity for illusion is disturbed by the intervals, during which the audience has time to reflect and escape from the suggestive influence of the author-hypnotist. My play will probably take an hour and a half, and as one can listen to a lecture, a sermon or a parliamentary debate for as long as that or longer, I do not think a theatrical performance will be fatiguing in the same length of time. As early as 1872, in one of my first dramatic attempts, *The Outlaw,* I tried this concentrated form, although with scant success. The play was written in five acts, and only when finished did I become aware of the restless, disjointed effect that it produced. The script was burnt and from the ashes rose a single well-knit act— fifty pages of print, playable in one hour. The form of the present play is, therefore, not new, but it appears to be my own, and changing tastes may make it timely. My hope is one day to have an audience educated enough to sit through a whole evening's entertainment in one act, but one would have to try this out to see. Meanwhile, in order to provide respite for the audience and the players, without allowing the audience to escape from the illusion, I have introduced three art forms: monologue, mime and ballet. These are all part of drama, having their origins in classic tragedy, monody having become monologue and the chorus, ballet.

Monologue is now condemned by our realists as unnatural, but if one provides

motives for it one makes it natural, and then can use it to advantage. It is, surely, natural for a public speaker to walk up and down the room practicing his speech, natural for an actor to read his part aloud, for a servant girl to talk to her cat, a mother to prattle to her child, an old maid to chatter to her parrot, and a sleeper to talk in his sleep. And in order that the actor may have a chance, for once, of working independently, free from the author's direction, it is better that the monologue should not be written, but only indicated. For since it is of small importance what is said in one's sleep or to the parrot or to the cat —none of it influences the action—a talented actor, identifying himself with the atmosphere and the situation, may improvise better than the author, who cannot calculate ahead how much may be said or how long taken without waking the audience from the illusion.

Some Italian theatres have, as we know, returned to improvisation, thereby producing actors who are creative, although within the bounds set by the author. This may well be a step forward, or even the beginning of a new art-form worthy to be called *productive.*

In places where monologue would be unnatural I have used mime, leaving here an even wider scope for the actor's imagination, and more chance for him to win independent laurels. But so as not to try the audience beyond endurance, I have introduced music—fully justified by the Midsummer Eve dance—to exercise its powers of persuasion during the dumb show. But I beg the musical director to consider carefully his choice of compositions, so that conflicting moods are not induced by selections from the current operetta or dance show, or by folk-tunes of too local a character.

The ballet I have introduced cannot be replaced by the usual kind of "crowd-scene," for such scenes are too badly played—a lot of grinning idiots seizing the opportunity to show off and thus destroying the illusion. And as peasants cannot improvise their taunts, but use ready-made phrases with a double meaning, I have not composed their lampoon, but taken a little-known song and dance which I myself noted down in the Stockholm district. The words are not quite to the point, but this too is intentional, for the cunning, i.e. weakness, of the slave prevents him from direct attack. Nor can there be clowning in a serious action, or coarse joking in a situation which nails the lid on a family coffin.

As regards the scenery, I have borrowed from impressionist painting its asymmetry and its economy; thus, I think, strengthening the illusion. For the fact that one does not see the whole room and all the furniture leaves scope for conjecture—that is to say imagination is roused and complements what is seen. I have succeeded too in getting rid of those tiresome exits through doors, since scenery doors are made of canvas, and rock at the slightest touch. They cannot even express the wrath of an irate head of the family who, after a bad dinner, goes out slamming the door behind him, "so that the whole house shakes." On the stage it rocks. I have also kept to a single set, both in order to let the characters develop in their métier and to break away from over-decoration. When one has only one set, one may expect it to be realistic; but as a matter of fact nothing is harder than to get a stage room that looks something like a room, however easily the scene painter can produce flaming volcanoes and water-falls. Presumably the walls must be of canvas; but it seems about time to dispense with painted shelves and cooking utensils. We are asked to accept so many stage conventions that we might as least be spared the pain of painted pots and pans.

I have set the back wall and the table diagonally so that the actors may play full-face and in half-profile when they are sitting opposite one another at the table. In the opera *Aïda* I saw a diagonal background, which led the eye to unfamiliar perspectives and did not look like mere reaction against boring straight lines.

Another much needed innovation is the abolition of foot-lights. This lighting from below is said to have the purpose of making the actors' faces fatter. But why, I ask, should all actors have fat faces? Does not this underlighting flatten out all the subtlety of the lower part of the face, specially the jaw, falsify the shape of the nose and throw shadows up over the eyes? Even if this were not so, one thing is certain: that the lights hurt the performers' eyes, so that the full play of their expression is lost. The footlights strike part of the retina usually protected—except in sailors who have to watch sunlight on water—and therefore one seldom sees anything other than a crude rolling of the eyes, either sideways or up towards the gallery, showing their whites. Perhaps this too causes that tiresome blinking of the eyelashes, especially by actresses. And when anyone on the stage wants to speak with his eyes, the only thing he can do is to look straight at the audience, with whom he or she then gets into direct communication, outside the framework of the set—a habit called, rightly or wrongly, "greeting one's friends."

Would not sufficiently strong sidelighting, with some kind of reflectors, add to the actor's powers of expression by allowing him to use the face's greatest asset:—the play of the eyes?

I have few illusions about getting the actors to play *to* the audience instead of *with* it, although this is what I want. That I shall see an actor's back throughout a critical scene is beyond my dreams, but I do wish crucial scenes could be played, not in front of the prompter's box, like duets expecting applause, but in the place required by the action. So, no revolutions, but just some small modifications, for to make the stage into a real room with the fourth wall missing would be too upsetting altogether.

I dare not hope that the actresses will listen to what I have to say about make-up, for they would rather be beautiful than life-like, but the actor might consider whether it is to his advantage to create an abstract character with greasepaints, and cover his face with it like a mask. Take the case of a man who draws a choleric charcoal line between his eyes and then, in this fixed state of wrath, has to smile at some repartee. What a frightful grimace the result is! And equally, how is that false forehead, smooth as a billiard ball, to wrinkle when the old man loses his temper?

In a modern psychological drama, where the subtlest reactions of a character need to be mirrored in the face rather than expressed by sound and gesture, it would be worth while experimenting with powerful side-lighting on a small stage and a cast without make-up, or at least with the minimum.

If, in addition, we could abolish the visible orchestra, with its distracting lamps and its faces turned toward the audience; if we could have the stalls raised so that the spectators' eyes were higher than the players' knees; if we could get rid of the boxes (the centre of my target), with their tittering diners and supper-parties, and have total darkness in the auditorium during the performance; and if, first and foremost, we could have a *small* stage and a *small* house, then perhaps a new dramatic art might arise, and theatre once more become a place of entertainment for educated people. While waiting for such a theatre it is as well for us to go on writing so as to stock that repertory of the future.

I have made an attempt. If it has failed, there is time enough to try again.

RUSSIAN DRAMATIC CRITICISM

The Russian drama was a thriving enterprise long before Chekhov earned for it its continuing prestige in the world theatre. Before Chekhov, the most distinctive trend is toward realistic comedy, in the works of Denis Fonvizin (1744–92), Alexander Griboyedov (1795–1829), Nikolai Gogol (1809–52), and Alexander Ostrovsky (1823–86). If the models at the beginning were such foreign dramatists as Molière and Holberg, the comic tradition rapidly became indigenously Russian. Gogol's realism perfectly harmonized with the Western-minded advocacy of realism by the leading Russian critic, Vissarion Belinsky (1811–48). Even more Western-minded was Alexander Pushkin (1799–1837), who admired especially Shakespeare and Byron and wrote the ponderous drama *Boris Godunov* in a style that he hoped was Shakespearean. If in his writing for the stage, the novelist Ivan Turgenev (1818–83) began in the comic tradition, he concluded by introducing more serious elements and thus, in *A Month in the Country,* anticipating Chekhov. In effect, Leo Tolstoy (1828–1910) provided his own dramatic criticism for his powerful, moralizing, realistic plays—in his treatise *What Is Art?,* in which he finds Shakespeare wanting by moral standards.

Anton Chekhov (1860–1904) wrote a new kind of play, casual, somber, comic, realistic, superficially shapeless but formed with the most deliberate care. It is most authentically interpreted in Chekhov's own occasional writings (mainly letters) and in the comments of the men who brought it to life on the stage, Konstantin Stanislavsky and Vladimir Nemirovich-Danchenko. Stanislavsky (1865–1938), the great innovator of modern realistic acting and directing, not only reinterpreted the drama of the past but obviously by his prestige must have encouraged the writing of drama that lent itself to his realistic approach. His fellow director Vsevolod Meyerhold (1874–1943) advocated a more stylized theatre and, accordingly, directed the fanciful but politically revolutionary plays of Vladimir Mayakovsky (1894–1930). Both Meyerhold and Stanislavsky sympathized with the revolution, but the demand for "socialist realism" doomed Meyerhold, who lost his theatre and died in circumstances that are still mysterious.

Following the revolution, Russian dramatic criticism was, naturally enough, Marxist. Marxism tended to be used as a yardstick, a guide to value-judgment. But, before the revolution, Russian Marxism produced one critic of literature and the drama who employed Marxism as a guide to understanding—Georgi Plekhanov.

ANTON CHEKHOV

Anton Pavlovich Chekhov was born in 1860 in the provincial Russian town of Taganrog. He came of a family of serfs, but his father ran a store and was able to send him to Moscow to study medicine. He became a physician and wrote short stories, little nuggets of the ironic observation of character. His first play, untitled and never performed in his lifetime, was written in 1881; it is a busy concoction of startling events. It has become known under such titles as *Platonov, Don Juan in the Russian Manner,* and *A Country Scandal.* For years, beginning in 1885 with *On the Highway,* he wrote one-act plays, effective but unassuming little entertainments. His next long play was *Ivanov* (1887), a study of Russian inertia and despair. A similar canvas in *The Wood Demon* (1889) was enlivened by the aspirations of the title character, a devotee of reforestation.

Chekhov's mature period as a dramatist began with *The Sea Gull* (1896), a play seemingly paralyzed by inaction and a total failure at its premier in St. Petersburg. Fortunately, it was revived at the new Moscow Art Theatre by Konstantin Stanislavsky, who caught its nuances, orchestrated its characters' solo speeches, and transmitted its profound reality. In gratitude, Chekhov wrote his remaining plays for the Moscow Art Theatre—*Uncle Vanya,* (1897); in which he adapted *The Wood Demon* to his new manner; *The Three Sisters* (1900); and *The Cherry Orchard* (1904). All of them show us sensitive, intelligent people cruelly trapped in ineffectual lives. The plot-lines are indistinct, the characters tend to speak in long arias rather than in conversations, and the action seems fitful at best. Yet Chekhov considered these plays comic, and, rightly played, they are. He revolutionized the stage with these seemingly casual dramas, to which critics instinctively apply metaphors based on music.

Wedded to the Moscow Art Theatre, he also married one of its leading actresses, Olga Knipper, in 1901. She created the role of Madame Ranevsky in *The Cherry Orchard* just before Chekhov's dear in 1904.

LETTERS ON THE DRAMA[1]

To M. V. Kiselev: Moscow. January 14, 1887.

I have written a play[2] on four sheets of paper. It will take from fifteen to twenty minutes to act. . . . It is much better to write small things than big ones; they are unpretentious and successful. . . . What more would you have? I wrote my play in an hour and five minutes. I began another, but have not finished it, for I have no time.

To Alex. Chekhov: Moscow. Oct., 1887.

Ask Fedorov or Byezhetsky to insert the following notice in the theatrical news:

"Comedy, *Ivanov,* by A. P. Chekhov, in four acts. Read before one of the Moscow literary circles, (or something of that kind) it produced a very strong impression; the subject is new, the characters are outstanding, noble, etc.," . . . It is not necessary to praise the play in this notice. Limit yourself to commonplaces.

I wrote the play unexpectedly, after a certain conversation with Korsh.[3] Went to bed, thought up a theme, and wrote it down. I spent less than two weeks on it. I cannot judge of the merits of the play. It is to come out in a surprisingly short time. Everybody likes it. Korsh did not find a single error or sin against the stage, which is a sad indication of how good and attentive my

---

[1] From *Letters on the Short Story, the Drama and Other Literary Topics* (New York, 1924), edited by Louis S. Friedland.—Ed.
[2] *Calchas,* later called *The Swan-Song.*

[3] Manager of a private theatre, who produced *Ivanov.*

judges are. I write a play for the first time, ergo, mistakes should be therein. The plot is complicated and not silly. I finish up each act as if it were a story: the action goes on quietly and peacefully, and at the end I give the audience a sockdologer. All my energy was spent on a few really brisk, forceful climaxes; but the bridges joining these are insignificant, loose, and not startling. Still, I am glad; no matter how bad the play is, I created a type that has literary value; I have produced a rôle which only as great a talent as Davidov will undertake to play, a rôle in which an actor can reveal himself, and display true ability. . . .

My play has fourteen characters, five of them women. I feel that my ladies, with the exception of one, are not thoroughly well developed.

Modern playwrights begin their plays with angels, scoundrels, and clowns exclusively. Well, go seek these elements in all Russia! Yes, you may find them, but not in such extreme types as the playwrights need. Unwillingly, you begin forging them out of the mind and the imagination, you perspire, and give the matter up. I wanted to be original: I did not portray a single villain, not a single angel (though I could not refrain when it came to the clown), did not accuse anyone, or exculpate. Whether all this is well done, I do not know.

To I. L. Shcheglov: Fedosia. July 18, 1888.

Send me "The Theatre Bird." You are a brave and clever chap to have written a comedy. Write at full speed, and in any manner you are moved to at the given moment. Should you be inspired to write a tragedy—write; if, on the other hand, the mood dictates a light vaudeville—write that. Your nature cannot adapt itself to the views and rules laid down by someone else. You must follow your own inner feeling; this is the best indicator for nervous and sensitive people. And the plays you write will be the better for it.

To A. S. Souvorin[4]: Moscow. Dec. 19, 1888.

[4] An editor and publisher, who became a close friend of Chekhov's.

I give you my word that I shall write no more of such intellectual and sickly plays as "Ivanov." If "Ivanov" does not succeed I shall not be surprised, and shall not lay it to intrigues and plots.

To A. S. Souvorin: Moscow. Dec. 23, 1888.

The absence of Sasha in the fourth act was very noticeable, you say. So it should be. Let the whole audience know that Sasha is not there. You insist on her appearing: the laws, forsooth, demand it. Very well, let her appear, but what will she say? Such young ladies (she is not a girl but a woman) cannot and should not speak. The former Sasha could speak and was sympathetic, but the new one will only irritate the public by appearing. She cannot really fall on Ivanov's neck and say, "I love you!" She does not love and has confessed it. To bring her on the stage at the end she would have to be completely remodeled. You say that there is not a single woman in the closing scenes, and that this makes the ending dry. I agree with you. Only two women could appear at the close and speak for Ivanov; only two women who really loved him: his mother and the Jewess. But as both of them are dead, that is out of the question. An orphan, let him remain an orphan, the devil take him.

To A. S. Souvorin: Moscow. Dec. 30, 1888.

. . . The manager thinks Ivanov a superfluous man, in the manner of Turgenev; Savina asks, "Why is Ivanov a scoundrel?" You write, "It is necessary to add something that will make it clear why two women cling to Ivanov, and why he is a scoundrel, and the doctor,— a great man." If the three of you have so understood me that my Ivanov has no good in him at all, then I suppose my wits forsook me, and I did not succeed in writing what I intended. If Ivanov appears in my play as a scoundrel or a superfluous man, and the doctor as a great man, if it is not clear why Sarra and Sasha love Ivanov, then evidently the play has not turned out as I wished, and to stage it is out of the question. This is how I understand my characters. Ivanov is a gentleman, a University man, and not remarkable in any way. He is excitable, hot-headed, easily carried away, honest and straightforward like most people of his class. He has lived on his estate and served on the Zemstvo.[5] What he has been doing and how he has behaved, what he has been interested in and enthusiastic over, can be seen from the following words of his addressed to the doctor (Act I., Scene 5): "Don't marry Jewesses or neurotic women or blue-stockings . . . don't fight with thousands single-handed, don't wage war on windmills, don't batter your head against the wall. . . . God preserve you from scientific farming, wonderful schools, enthusiastic speeches. . . ." This is what he has in his past. Sarra, who has seen his scientific farming and other crazes, says about him to the doctor: "He is a remarkable man, doctor, and I am sorry you did not meet him two or three years ago. Now he is depressed and melancholy, he doesn't talk or do anything,— but in the old days . . . how charming he was!" (Act I., Scene 7). His past is beautiful, as is generally the case with educated Russians. There is not, or there hardly is, a single Russian gentleman or University man who does not boast of his past. The present is always worse than the past. Why? Because Russian excitability has one specific characteristic: it is quickly followed by exhaustion. A man has scarcely left the classroom before he rushes to take up a burden beyond his strength; he tackles at once the schools, the peasants, scientific farming, and the *Viestnik Evropi,* he makes speeches, writes to the minister, combats evil, applauds good, falls in love, not in an ordinary, simple way, but selects either a blue-stocking, or a neurotic, or a Jewess, or even a prostitute whom he tries to save, and so on, and so on. But by the time he is thirty or thirty-five he begins to feel tired and bored. He has not got decent mustaches yet, but he already says with authority: "Don't marry, my dear fellow. . . . Trust my experience," or, "After all, what does Liberalism come to? Between ourselves, Katkov was often right. . . ." He is ready to reject the Zemstvo and scientific farming, and science and love. My Ivanov says to the doctor (Act I., Scene 5):

5 An assembly elected to administer district affairs.

"You took your degree only last year, my dear friend, you are still young and vigorous, while I am thirty-five. I have a right to advise you. . . ." That is how these prematurely exhausted people talk. Further down, sighing authoritatively, he advises: "Don't you marry in this or that way (see above), but choose something commonplace, gray, with no vivid colors or superfluous flourishes. Altogether, build your life according to the conventional pattern. The grayer and more monotonous the background, the better. . . . The life that I have led—how tiring it is! Ah, how tiring!".

Conscious of physical exhaustion and boredom, he does not understand what is the matter with him, and what has happened. Horrified, he says to the doctor (Act I., Scene 3): "Here you tell me she is going to die and I feel neither love nor pity, but a sort of emptiness and weariness. . . . If one looks at me from outside it must be horrible. I don't understand what is happening to my soul." Finding themselves in such a position, narrow and unconscientious people generally throw the whole blame on their environment, or write themselves down as Hamlets and superfluous people, and are satisfied with that. But Ivanov, a straightforward man, openly says to the doctor and to the public that he does not understand his own mind. "I don't understand! I don't understand!" That he really doesn't understand can be seen from his long monologue in Act III., where, *tête-à-tête* with the public, he opens his heart to it and even weeps.

The change that has taken place in him offends his sense of what is fitting. He looks for the causes outside himself and fails to find them; he begins to look for them inside and finds only an indefinite feeling of guilt. It is a Russian feeling. Whether there is a death or illness in his family, whether he owes money or lends it, a Russian always feels guilty. Ivanov talks all the time about being to blame in some way, and the feeling of guilt increases in him at every juncture. In Act I. he says: "Suppose I am terribly to blame, yet my thoughts are in a tangle, my soul is in bondage to a sort of sloth, and I am incapable of understanding myself. . . ." In Act II., he says to Sasha: "My conscience aches day and night, I feel that I am profoundly to blame, but in what exactly I have done wrong I cannot make out."

To exhaustion, boredom, and the feeling of guilt add one more enemy: loneliness. Were Ivanov an official, an actor, a priest, a professor, he would have grown used to his position. But he lives on his estate. He is in the country. His neighbors are either drunkards or fond of cards, or are of the same type as the doctor. None of them cares about his feelings or the change that has taken place in him. He is lonely. Long winters, long evenings, an empty garden, empty rooms, the grumbling Count, the ailing wife. . . . He has nowhere to go. This is why he is every minute tortured by the question: what is he to do with himself?

Now about his fifth enemy. Ivanov is tired and does not understand himself, but life has nothing to do with that! It makes its legitimate demands upon him, and whether he will or no, he must settle problems. His sick wife is a problem, his numerous debts are a problem, Sasha flinging herself on his neck is a problem. The way in which he settles all these problems must be evident from his monologue in Act III., and from the contents of the last two acts. Men like Ivanov do not solve difficulties, but collapse under their weight. They lose their heads, gesticulate, become nervous, complain, do silly things, and finally, giving rein to their flabby, undisciplined nerves, lose the ground under their feet and enter the class of the "broken down" and "misunderstood."

Disappointment, apathy, nervous limpness, and exhaustion are the inevitable consequences of extreme excitability, and such excitability is extremely characteristic of our young people. Take literature. Take the present time . . . Socialism is one of the forms of this excitement. But where is socialism? You see it in Tikhomirov's letter to the Tsar. The socialists are married and they criticize the Zemstvo. Where is Liberalism? Mikhailovsky himself says that all the labels have been mixed up now. And what are all the Russian enthusiasms worth? The war has wearied us, Bulgaria has wearied us till we can only be ironical about it. Zucchi has wearied us and so has the comic opera.

Exhaustion (Dr. Bertenson will con-firm this) finds expression not only in complaining or the sensation of boredom. The life of an over-tired man cannot be represented like this:

It is very unequal. Over-tired people never lose the capacity for becoming extremely excited, but cannot keep it up for long, and each excitement is followed by still greater apathy. . . . Graphically, it could be represented like this:

The fall, as you see, is not continuous but broken. Sasha declares her love and Ivanov cries out in ecstasy, "A new life!"—and next morning he believes in this new life as little as he does in spooks (the monologue in Act III.); his wife insults him, and, fearfully worked up and beside himself with anger, he flings a cruel insult at her. He is called a scoundrel. This is either fatal to his tottering brain, or stimulates him to a fresh paroxysm, and he pronounces sentence on himself.

Not to tire you out altogether I pass now to Dr. Lvov. He is the type of an honest, straightforward, hotheaded, but narrow and uncompromising man. Clever people say of such men: "He is stupid, but his heart is in the right place." Anything like breadth of outlook or unreflecting feeling is foreign to Lvov. He is the embodiment of a program, a walking tendency. He looks through a narrow frame at every person and event, he judges everything according to preconceived notions. Those who shout, "Make way for honest labor!" are an object of worship to him; those who do not shout it are scoundrels and exploiters. There is no middle. He has been brought up on Mikhailov's novels; at the theatre he has seen on the stage "new men," i.e., the exploiters and sons of our age, painted by the modern playwrights. He has stored it all up, and so much so, that when he reads *Rudin* 5a he is sure to be asking himself, "Is Rudin a scoundrel or not?" Literature and the stage have so educated him that

5a Novel by Turgenev.

he approaches every character in real life and in fiction with this question. . . . If it were given him to see your own play, he would blame you for not saying clearly: are Mmes. Kotelnikov, Sabinin, Adashev, Matvella, scoundrels, or not? That question is to him of first importance. It is not enough for him that all men are sinners. He wants saints and villains.

He was prejudiced before he came to the district. He at once classed all the rich peasants as exploiters, and Ivanov, whom he could not understand, as a scoundrel. Why, the man has a sick wife and he goes to see a rich lady-neighbor—of course he is a scoundrel! It is obvious that he is killing his wife in order to marry an heiress.

Lvov is honest and straightforward, and he blurts out the truth without sparing himself. If necessary, he will throw a bomb at a carriage, give a school inspector a blow in the face, or call a man a scoundrel. He will not stop at anything. He never feels remorse—it is his mission as "an honest worker" to fight "the powers of darkness"!

Such people are useful, and are for the most part attractive. To caricature them, even in the interests of the play, is unfair and, indeed, unnecessary. True, a caricature is more striking, and therefore easier to understand, but it is better to put your color on too faint than too strong.

Now about the women. What do they love Ivanov for? Sarra loves him because he is a fine man, because he has enthusiasm, because he is brilliant and speaks with as much heat as Lvov. (Act I., Scene 7.) She loves him while he is excited and interesting; but when he begins to grow misty in her eyes, and to lose definiteness of outline, she ceases to understand him, and at the end of Act III. speaks out plainly and sharply.

Sasha is a young woman of the newest type. She is well-educated, intelligent, honest, and so on. In the realm of the blind a one-eyed man is king, and so she favors Ivanov in spite of his being thirty-five. He is better than anyone else. She knew him when she was a child and saw his work close at hand, at the period before he was exhausted. He is a friend of her father's.

She is a female who is not won by the vivid plumage of the male, not by their courage and dexterity, but by their complaints, whinings, and failures. She is the sort of girl who loves a man when he is going downhill. The moment Ivanov loses heart the young lady is on the spot! That's just what she was waiting for. Just think of it, she now has such a holy, such a grateful task before her! She will raise up the fallen one, set him on his feet, make him happy. . . . It is not Ivanov she loves, but this mission. Argenton [6] in Daudet's book says, "Life is not a novel." Sasha does not know this. She does not know that for Ivanov love is only a fresh complication, an extra stab in the back. And what comes of it? She struggles with him for a whole year and, instead of being raised, he sinks lower and lower.

If all of this is not in the play, there can be no question of producing it. It seems that I did not write what I wished. Remove it from the boards. I do not want to preach heresy on the stage. If the audience will leave the theatre with the conviction that Ivanovs are scoundrels and that Doctors Lvov are great men, then I'll have to give up and fling my pen to the devil. You won't get anywhere with corrections and insertions. No corrections can bring down a great man from his pedestal, and no insertions can change a scoundrel into an ordinary sinful mortal. You may bring Sasha on the stage at the end, but to Ivanov and Lvov I can add nothing more. I simply don't know how. And if I should add anything, it will spoil the effect still more. Trust in my intuition; it is an author's, you know. If the public does not understand "iron in the blood," then to the devil with it, i.e., with the blood in which there is no iron.

. . . Characteristically, Ivanov often lets fall the word "Russian." Don't be cross about it. When I was writing the play I had in mind only the things that really matter—that is, only the typical Russian characteristics. Thus the extreme excitability, the feeling of guilt, the liability to become exhausted are purely Russian. Germans are never excited, and that is why Germany knows nothing of disappointed, superfluous, or over-tired people. . . . The excitability

6 In Daudet's *Jack*.

of the French is always maintained at one and the same level, and makes no sudden bounds or falls, and so a Frenchman is normally excited down to a decrepit old age. In other words, the French do not have to waste their strength in over-excitement; they spend their powers sensibly, and do not go bankrupt.

It is understood that in the play I did not use such terms as "Russian," "excitability," etc., in the full expectation that the reader and spectator would be attentive and that for them it would not be necessary to underscore these. I tried to express myself simply, was not subtle, and was far from the suspicion that the readers and spectators would fasten my characters to a phrase, would emphasize the conversations about the dowry, etc. I suppose I could not write the play. Of course, it is a pity. Ivanov and Lvov appear to my imagination to be living people. I tell you honestly, in all conscience, these men were born in my head, not by accident, not out of sea foam, or preconceived "intellectual" ideas. They are the result of observing and studying life. They stand in my brain, and I feel that I have not falsified the truth or exaggerated it a jot. If on paper they have not come out clear and living, the fault is not in them but in me, for not being able to express my thoughts. It shows it is too early for me to begin writing plays.

To A. S. Souvorin: Moscow. Jan 7, 1889.

If a skilful, energetic actor were to play Ivanov I would make many alterations and some additions. And I would have a free hand. But alas! Davidov plays the part. This means that one must write concisely, in a grayer tone, keeping in mind that all delicate shadings and "nuances" will be mingled in one gray monotone, and that they will be dull. Can Davidov be tender, and also wrathful? When he plays serious parts it is as if a mill were in his throat, a feebly-turning, monotonous mill, that acts instead of him. I pity poor Savina that she has to play the dead Sasha. I would do everything imaginable for Savina, but as long as Ivanov insists on mumbling, I shall be unable to help Sasha in spite of all my efforts. I am ashamed that Savina must play an in-

ferior rôle in the drama. Had I known in time that she would be Sasha and that Davidov would take upon him the rôle of Ivanov, I would have named my play "Sasha" and constructed the entire work about this part, and I would have made Ivanov merely incidental; but how was one to anticipate these things? There are two monologues assigned to Ivanov that are fatal to the play: one in Act III. the other at the end of Act IV. The first should be rendered lyrically, the second, read furiously. Both the one and the other are impossible for Davidov. He will read them "wisely," that is, with infinite, drowsy slowness.

I have been cherishing the bold dream of summing up all that has hitherto been written about whining, miserable people, and with my Ivanov saying the last word. It seemed to me that all Russian novelists and playwrights were drawn to depict despondent men, but that they all wrote instinctively, having no definite image or views on the subject. As far as my design goes I was on the right track, but the execution is good for nothing. I ought to have waited! I am glad I did not listen to Grigorovich two or three years ago, and write a novel! I can just imagine what a lot of good material I should have spoiled. He says: "Talent and freshness overcome everything." It is more true to say that talent and freshness can spoil a great deal. In addition to plenty of material and talent, one wants something else which is no less important. One wants to be mature—that is one thing; and for another the *feeling of personal freedom* is essential, and that feeling has only recently begun to develop in me. I used not to have it before; its place was successfully filled by my frivolity, carelessness, and lack of respect for my work.

To Alex. P. Chekhov: Moscow. April 11, 1889.

Try to be original in your play and as clever as possible; but don't be afraid to show yourself foolish; we must have freedom of thinking, and only he is an emancipated thinker who is not afraid to write foolish things. Don't round things out, don't polish,—but, be awkward and impudent. Brevity is the sister of talent. Remember, by the way, that declarations of love, the infidelity of husbands and wives, widows', orphans', and all other tears, have long since been written up. The subject ought to be new, but there need be no "fable." And the main thing is—father and mother must eat. Write. Flies purify the air, and plays,—the morals.

To Alex. P. Chekhov: Sumi. May 8, 1889.

Now about your play. You undertook to depict a man who has not a grief in the world, and then you took fright. The problem seems to me to be clear. Only he has no grief who is indifferent; and people who are indifferent and aloof are either philosophers or petty, egotistic natures. The latter should be treated negatively, the former,—positively. Of course,—those unmoved dullards who will suffer no pain even when you burn them with red-hot irons, cannot be discussed at all. Even if by a man without grief you understand one who is not indifferent to the life about him, and who bravely and patiently bears the blows of fate, and looks hopefully to the future,—there; too, the problem is comparatively simple and clear.

The large number of revisions need not trouble you, for the more of a mosaic the work is, the better. The characters stand to gain by this. The play will be worthless if all the characters resemble you. In this respect your *Money-Box* is monotonous and arouses a feeling of boredom. What are Natasha, Kolya, Tosya for? Is there no life outside of you? And who is interested in knowing my life or yours, my thoughts and your thoughts? Give people people, and not yourself.

Avoid "choice" diction. The language should be simple and forceful. The lackeys should speak simply, without elegance. Retired captains in the reserve, with huge, red noses, newspaper-reporters who drink, starving authors, consumptive women-toilers, honest young people without a flaw in their make-up, ideal maidens, good-natured nurses,— all these have been described again and again, and should be avoided as a pitfall. Still another suggestion: go to the theatre now and then and watch the stage. Compare,—that is important. The first act may last as long as a whole hour, but the rest should not be more than twenty minutes each. The crux of a play is the third act, but it must not be so strong a climax as to kill the last act.

To A. S. Souvorin: Melikhovo. June 4, 1892.

I have an interesting subject for a comedy, but I have not as yet thought of an ending. Whoever will invent new endings for plays will open a new era. The wretched endings won't come! The hero either marries or shoots himself,— there is no other way out. My future comedy is called *The Cigar-Case.* I shall not go on with it until I think of an ending as good as the beginning. And when I do get hold of the ending, I shall write the thing in two weeks.

To A. S. Souvorin: Yalta. Jan. 23, 1900.

The new play,[7] Acts 1 and 2, I liked, and I find that it is even better than *Tatyana Repiňa.* The other is closer to the theatre, this to life. The third act was not definite, because there is no action; there is not even clarity of idea. It may be that to make it more certain and clearer, a fourth act will be required. In the third act the explanation between the husband and the wife is modeled after Sumbatov's *Chains;* and I would prefer that the wife remain behind the curtain all the time, and that Varya,—as happens in life in similar circumstances, —should believe more in the father than in the mother.

I have few comments to make. A cultured nobleman entering the priesthood, —that has become stale, and no longer arouses curiosity. Those who entered the priesthood just fell into the water; some, remaining ordinary archimandrites— waxed fat and have long since forgotten every idea; others gave up all and are living in peace. Nothing definite was expected of them, and they gave nothing; and on the stage a young man preparing for the priesthood will simply be received without sympathy by the public, and in his activities and chastity they will see something of the Skoptsi.[8] And, indeed, the actor will not play the part well. You would do better to take a young, learned, mysterious Jesuit dreaming of a united church; or someone else, but

7 *The Question.*
8 A fanatic, ascetic religious sect in Russia.

someone who will appear greater than a nobleman entering the priesthood.

Varya is well done. At first sight there is an excessive hysteria in the language. She must not use witticisms; but you make all of them fall into this habit; they keep playing on words, and that tires the attention a little; it is too flashy; the language of your characters is like a white silk dress on which the sun is always shining in full force and which it hurts the eyes to look at. The words "vulgarity" and "vulgar" are hackneyed.

Natasha is very good. You make her a different person in the third act.

The families "Ratishchev" and "Muratov" are too theatrical, not simple. Give Ratishchev to a Little Russian family,— for variety.

The father is without a weakness, without a distinct appearance; he does not drink, or smoke, or gamble, or fall ill. You must stitch on to him some attribute or other, so that the actor can have something to grasp.

The father knows of Varya's sin, or does not know,—I think it makes no difference, and is of no importance. The sexual sphere, of course, plays an important part in this world, but not everything depends on it,—far from everything; and not everywhere, by far, does it have decisive significance.

When you send the fourth act I shall write more if I think of anything to say. I am glad that you have almost completed the play, and again repeat that you ought to write both plays and novels, —first because it is necessary, and second, because for you it is healthful, as it is pleasant to vary your life.

To Maxim Gorky: Moscow. Oct. 22, 1901.

Five days have passed since I read your play (*The Petty Bourgeois*). I have not written to you till now because I could not get hold of the fourth act; I have kept waiting for it, and—I still have not got it. And so I have read only three acts, but that I think is enough to judge of the play. It is, as I expected, very good, written à la Gorky, original, very interesting; and, to begin by talking of the defects, I have noticed only one, a defect incorrigible as red hair in a red-haired man—the conservatism of the form. You make new and original people sing new songs to an accompaniment that looks second-hand; you have four acts, the characters deliver edifying discourses, there is a feeling of alarm before long speeches, and so on, and so on. But all that is not important, and it is all, so to speak, drowned in the good points of the play. Perchikhin—how living! His daughter is enchanting, Tatyana and Piotr also, and their mother is a splendid old woman. The central figure of the play, Nil, is vigorously drawn and extremely interesting! In fact, the play takes hold of one from the first act. Only, God preserve you from letting anyone act Perchikhin except Artyom, while Alekseyev-Stanislavsky must certainly play Nil. Those two figures will do just what's needed; Piotr—Meierkhold. Only, Nil's part, a wonderful part, must be made two or three times as long. You ought to end the play with it, to make it the leading part. Only, do not contrast him with Piotr and Tatyana, let him be by himself and them by themselves, all wonderful, splendid people independent of one another. When Nil tries to seem superior to Piotr and Tatyana, and says of himself that he is a fine fellow,—the element so characteristic of our decent working man, the element of modesty, is lost. He boasts, he argues, but you know one can see what sort of man he is without that. Let him be merry, let him play pranks through the whole four acts, let him eat a great deal after his work— and that will be enough for him to conquer the audience with. Piotr, I repeat, is good. Most likely you don't even suspect how good he is. Tatyana, too, is a finished figure, only,—(a) she ought really to be a schoolmistress, ought to be teaching children, ought to come home from school, ought to be taken up with her pupils and exercise-books, and—(b) it ought to be mentioned in the first or second act that she has attempted to poison herself; then, after that hint, the poisoning in the third act will not seem so startling and will be more in place. Teterev talks too much: such characters ought to be shown bit by bit among others, for in any case such people are everywhere merely incidental—both in life and on the stage. Make Elena dine with all the rest in the first act, let her sit and make jokes, or else there is very little of her, and she is not clear. Her avowal to Piotr is too abrupt; on the stage it would come out in too high relief. Make her a passionate woman, if not loving, at least apt to fall in love. . . .

To Maxim Gorky: July 29, 1902.

I have read your play.[9] It is new and unmistakably fine. The second act is very good; it is the best, the strongest, and when I was reading it, especially the end, I almost danced with joy. The tone is gloomy, oppressive; the audience, unaccustomed to such subjects, will walk out of the theatre, and you may well say good-by to your reputation as an optimist, in any case. My wife will play Vasilisa, the immoral and spiteful woman; Vishnevsky walks about the house and imagines himself the Tatar— he is convinced that it is the part for him. Luka, alas! you must not give to Artyom. He will repeat himself in that part and be exhausted; but he would do the policeman wonderfully; it is his part. The part of the actor, in which you have been very successful (it is a magnificent

9 *The Lower Depths.*

part), should be given to an experienced actor, Stanislavsky perhaps. Kachalov will play the baron.

You left out of the fourth act all the most interesting characters (except the actor), and you must mind, now, that there is no ill effect from it. The act may seem boring and unnecessary, especially if, with the exit of the strongest and most interesting actors, there are left only the mediocrities. The death of the actor is awful; it is as though you gave the spectator a sudden box on the ear à propos of nothing without preparing him in any way. How the baron got into the doss-house and why he is a baron is also not quite clear.

To Vl. I. Nemirovich-Danchenko: Yalta. Nov. 2, 1903.

"Gorky" is younger than you or I; he has his life before him. As regards the Nizhni Theatre, that is merely an episode; Gorky will try it, sniff it, and give it up quickly. A propos of the popular theatres and popular literature,— all that is foolishness, sugar-candy for the people. You must not lower Gogol to the people, but raise the people to the level of Gogol.

KONSTANTIN STANISLAVSKY

This Russian actor, director, and theorist of acting was born in 1865; his real name was Alexeyev. In 1888, he helped to found a literary society for the production of plays and, with this group, arranged the first staging of Tolstoy's *The Fruits of Enlightenment.* He was influenced by the meticulous attention paid to detail by the company of the Duke of Saxe-Meiningen, and he set out to add to their technique a greater realism of acting when, together with Vladimir Nemirovich-Danchenko, he founded the Moscow Art Theatre in 1898. The Art Theatre discovered its own dramatist when it staged Chekhov's *The Sea Gull* and his subsequent plays, infusing them

with a reality which no one had anticipated. Maxim Gorky became a second dramatist peculiarly identified with this group. Following the revolution, Stanislavsky's intensely realistic practice in directing and in the theory of acting made him an international figure. The Stanislavsky method, involving full understanding of the character and his social context and requiring intense identification with him, became the most modish approach to acting. Stanislavsky, who died in 1938, recorded his life story in *My Life in Art* and his practice in *An Actor Prepares, Stanislavsky Rehearses Othello, Building a Character,* and *Creating a Role.*

THE MAGIC IFS [1]

(1930–33)

"I see a beautiful young Venetian woman, who has grown up amid luxury and is spoiled, high-spirited, full of dreams, fantasies, the way young girls are who are brought up without mothers, raised on fairy tales and romances. This scarcely opened flower, Desdemona, is bored by being shut in with household responsibilities and catering to the whims of her proud and important father. No one is allowed to come and see her and her young heart craves love. There are suitors for her hand, arrogant and dissipated young Venetians. But they do not charm this young dreamer. She is looking for the unheard of, the things you read about in fine romances. She is waiting for a fairy prince or powerful potentate, a king. He will come from some wonderful far-off country. He must be a hero, handsome, bold, unconquerable. She will give herself to him and sail away in a fine ship to some fairy-tale kingdom.

"Now you go on from there," said Tortsov turning to me. But I was so intent on listening to him that I was not prepared and could say nothing.

"I can't," I said after a pause, "I'm not primed."

"Prime yourself then," urged Tortsov.

"I haven't the wherewithal," I admitted.

"I'll give it to you," said Tortsov. "Do you see in your mind's eye the place where the action is laid, where what you are telling about all happens?"

"Yes," I replied with quickened interest. "I imagine the action taking place in a Venice that looks exactly like our Sevastopol; for some reason I see the Governor's house from Nizhny Novgorod there too. This is where Brabantio seems to live, it is on the shore of the South Bay in which little steamers scurry around, as they do to this day. Yet this does not interfere with the antique gondolas darting in all directions, with their

1 An excerpt from the discussion of *Othello* in *Creating a Role*. © 1961 by Elizabeth Reynolds Hapgood, the translator. The speakers are the fictitious teacher Tortsov and his students. Used by permission of Theatre Arts Books.—Ed.

oars splashing."

"Let us assume that is so," said Tortsov. "Who can explain the caprices of an actor's imagination! It has no use for history or geography and is not afraid of anachronisms."

"It is even more curious," I continued with my fantasy, "that in my Venice, which looks like Sevastopol, there is a bluff on the shore of the bay exactly like the one in Nizhny Novgorod, on the banks of the Volga, where there are poetic and secluded places that I used to love and of which I have tenderly unhappy memories."

After I had finished telling what I saw with my inner vision, I was immediately tempted to criticize the foolish creation of my imagination, but Tortsov waved his arms excitedly and said:

"Don't do it, for goodness sake! It is not in your power to order yourself in accordance with your own wishes to bring up these or those memories. Let them come to life of their own accord and act as powerful stimulants to your creativeness as an actor. The only proviso is that they should not essentially contradict the basic plot of the play as written by the author."

In order to further my imaginings Tortsov then gave me another clue.

"When did all this happen, which you see with your inner vision?" was his new question.

When my source dried up he stimulated me again to further work.

"How did it all happen?" he asked, and then immediately clarified his question. "I mean that I would like to know the line of this inner action, its gradual progress and development. For the time being we only know that a spoiled young woman, Desdemona, lives in a Nizhny Novgorod palace on the shore of the Volga and does not wish to marry any of the dissipated young Venetians. Tell me what she dreams of, how she lives, and what happens next."

This new stimulus was to no avail, so Tortsov carried on in my stead, thinking up all sorts of fascinating rumors deriving from the talk about the popularity of the Moor that preceded his arrival.

Tortsov would have it that the Moor's feats and all the hardships he related to Desdemona must be like fairy tales, romantically beautiful and effective so that they would excite the overheated young brain of the girl who had been waiting for the hero in her dreams.

After another pause Tortsov tried once more to set me in motion. He advised me to tell in logical order what happened: Where did they meet, how did they fall in love, get married?

I was silent because I found it far more interesting and instructive to hear Tortsov's imagination at work.

So he went on, and described how Othello had arrived in Venetian Sevastopol in a great ship. The legends concerning the general's feats drew a huge crowd to the pier. The appearance and dark skin of Othello aroused curiosity. When he rode or walked through the streets little boys ran after him in crowds, the passers-by whispered to each other and pointed their fingers at him.

The first meeting of these future lovers took place in the street and it made a great impression on the young woman. Othello fascinated her not only with his brave appearance but also and especially with his naïve ways of a savage, his modesty and his goodness, all of which shone in his eyes. This modesty and shyness joined with valor and imperviousness to fear made an unusual and beautiful combination.

Another time Desdemona saw Othello at the head of troops coming back from some military exercises. His easy seat on his horse made an even greater impression on her. That was the time she first saw Cassio riding with his general. Desdemona's imaginings kept her from sleep. One day Brabantio announced to his daughter, as mistress of the household, that he had invited the celebrated Othello to dinner. At this name the girl almost fainted away.

It is easy to imagine with what care Desdemona dressed herself and had the dinner prepared, and how she waited for this meeting with her hero.

The look in her eyes could not but go to the Moor's heart. It embarrassed him and increased his shyness, which was so becoming in this hero with his name for invincibility.

The Moor, who had not been spoiled by womanly warmth, could not at first understand the exceptional amiability of his hostess. He was accustomed to being received and tolerated in the houses of highly placed Venetians as an official personage. Yet amid the honors heaped on him he always felt himself to be in the position of a slave. No pair of wonderful eyes had ever before looked with warmth on his black and, as he believed, ugly face, until suddenly on this day. . . .

Nor did Othello sleep for many nights, and he waited with impatience for another invitation from Brabantio. It was not long in coming. Probably at the instigation of the lovelorn girl he was invited again, and yet again, so that they could listen to his stories of his exploits, of the hard life during campaigns. After dinners, over the wine, and sitting out on the terrace with a view of Sevastopol harbor with the Nizhny Novgorod bluff, the Moor would modestly but truthfully tell about his exploits, as Shakespeare himself described him doing when the Moor speaks to the Senate, and as Tortsov imaginatively painted him.

I really came to believe that such a story could not but turn the head of a high-spirited young woman in a romantic frame of mind.

"Desdemona was not one to build her life like all the others on a narrowly bourgeois pattern," continued Tortsov. "She craved the unusual, the contents of a fairy tale. One could not have imagined a better hero than Othello for a girl of her flaming nature.

"The Moor began to feel more and more at home at Brabantio's. It was his first opportunity to see a real home at close quarters. The presence of a beautiful young woman lent an added charm, and so forth." Here Tortsov broke off his story.

"Do you not find," he asked, "that this kind of re-telling of the contents of a play is more interesting than the dry recounting of the facts? If you were to make me tell you still again the contents of this tragedy and I followed the inner pattern rather than the outer form, I'd think up something more. And the more often you made me tell the story the more material would be stored up for imaginative extensions to the words of the author, for the 'magic ifs' which you will use to justify the material given you by the author.

"So now follow my example, and as often as possible relate the contents of plays and sketches which you are given to act in, approaching them each time from a different angle, from your own point of view in your own person, or from that of one of the characters, that is to say putting yourself in his stead."

"All this is fine . . . but with one proviso: You must possess a brilliant natural or highly developed imagination," I said sadly. "We have to think about what leads to the development of an imagination which is still only in an embryonic stage."

"Yes, you will have to acquire methods for prodding your imagination, which has not yet warmed up," agreed Tortsov.

"That's it, that's what we need! That is exactly what we lack," I added to what he had said.

"We have begun our analysis layer by layer, working from the top down—from the things which are more accessible to our conscious feelings down to those which are less so.

"The topmost layer consists of the *plot,* the *facts,* and *events* of the play. We have already touched on these but limited ourselves to their enumeration for the purpose of reproducing them on the stage. Now we shall continue our study of them. The word 'study' in our language means not only that we state the fact, look at it, and understand it, but also that we appraise its worth and significance.

"This new aspect of analysis is what we call *appraising the facts.*

"There are plays (poor comedies, melodramas, vaudeville, revues, farces) in which the external plot represents the principal asset of the performance. In such works the very facts of a murder, a death, a wedding, or the process of dumping flour or water on the head of one of the characters, of losing a pair of trousers, of getting into the wrong room where a peaceful guest is taken for a robber, and so forth—all such facts constitute the principal moments of the production. It would be superfluous to appraise them; they are instantly comprehended and accepted by everyone.

"But in other works the plot itself and the facts contained in it sometimes do not have much significance in themselves. In such plays it is not the facts but the attitude of the characters toward them that provides the fulcrum, the central interest, which the audience follows with thumping pulse. In such plays facts are needed only to the extent that they provide motivation and occasion for revealing the inner content. Chekhov's plays are of this kind.

"In the best plays of all, form and content are in direct relationship with each other; then the life of the spirit is indivisible from the facts and the plot. In most of Shakespeare's plays, and among them *Othello,* this complete correspondence exists, this mutual interaction between the external, factual line and the inner line.

"In such works, appraising the facts is of prime significance. As you examine the external events you come in contact with the given circumstances that give rise to the facts. As you study these circumstances you come to realize the inner reasons that relate to them. So you go deeper into the very thick of the spiritual life of a role, you reach the subtext, you come to the underlying current of the play which provokes the superficial waves of action.

"The technique of appraising the facts is very simple to start with. You begin by mentally canceling the fact to be appraised, and then you try to find out how that affects the life of the spirit in your role.

"Let us test this process in your roles," said Tortsov turning to Vanya and Grisha. "The first fact you come to in the play is your *arrival in front of Brabantio's palace.* Do I need to explain that if this fact were lacking the whole first scene would be nonexistent, and during the beginning of the tragedy you could sit quietly in your dressing room instead of moving around in excitement on the stage? It is obvious that the fact of your arrival at Brabantio's palace is an essential one and you must believe in it, and hence experience its impact.

"The second of the facts in the first scene which we have recorded is the *quarrel with Roderigo, Iago's defense of his innocence, the necessity of raising the alarm* and of starting the *pursuit of the Moor.* Remove all these facts, and what happens? The two characters would arrive on the scene in a gondola and immediately start to raise the alarm. In such a course of events we, the spectators, would be left in ignorance of the exposition of the play, that is to say of the relationship between Roderigo and Desdemona, Iago and Othello, of Iago's resentment against Othello, and the regimental intrigue which unlooses the whole tragedy.

"This would be reflected in the acting of the alarm scene. It is one thing to arrive somewhere, begin to yell, raise a racket to waken people who are sound asleep; it is quite another to do what you can to save your vanishing happiness, as in the case of Roderigo who is losing his bride, the eloping Desdemona. It is one thing to raise a row for the fun of it, and quite another when it is done in the spirit of revenge, as in the case of Iago who is venting his hatred of Othello. Every action which is carried out not merely because of some external reason but because of some inner impulse is incomparably more effective, better grounded, and therefore more moving to the actor who executes it.

"Appraising the facts is inseparable from another aspect of our analysis, namely, *the justification of the facts.* This is a necessary part of the process, because a fact without a basis dangles in midair. The fact which is not experienced, not included in the inner line of life in the play, not responsive to it, is of no use and indeed is a hindrance to proper inner development. Such an unjustified fact constitutes a blank, a break in a role. It is a spot of dead flesh in a living organism, it is a deep hole on a smooth road, it impedes free movement and the course of inner feelings. You must either fill up the hole or throw a bridge across it. That is why we need the *justification of facts.* Once a fact is justified it is automatically included in the inner line of the play, in the subtext; it promotes the free unfolding of the spiritual life of your part. Facts which are justified also promote logic and consecutiveness in feeling a part, and you already know what importance those two factors have in our work. . . .

"Now you know the facts of the first scene of the play. More than that, you have executed them more or less correctly. But you have not as yet plumbed the depths of their true validity, nor will you do this until you have *justified* them on the basis of new given circumstances, proposed by yourselves. These will compel you to visualize the course of events in the play as a human being, not just as an actor, as an initiator and author, not as a mere copyist. So let us now examine these facts and see whether you have appraised, from your own personal, human point of view, everything that happens in the first scene, putting yourselves in the place of Roderigo and Iago. As far as the external rendering of the facts is concerned, I believe what you did. They arrive, just as you did, at the landing and moor their gondola. Just as they do, you tied it up here, not just anyhow but with a purpose—*to raise the alarm.* In turn you raised the alarm with another and definite purpose in mind—to pursue and arrest the Moor, and rescue Desdemona.

GEORGI V. PLEKHANOV

Plekhanov, a Russian revolutionary and theoretician of Marxism, was born in 1857. He spent much of his life in exile, and, after 1881, he lived in Switzerland. From this vantage point, he established himself as the true founder of Russian Marxism and the teacher of Lenin, with whom he collaborated in the early years of the twentieth century in editing a revolutionary journal, *Iskra.* He combatted the cult of the peasant and other efforts to create a distinctively Russian revolutionary movement, but following the Brussels congress of the Social Democratic party, he leaned to the less militant Menshevik wing. He further alienated old comrades by urging continued Russian participation in the war in 1917. He died in 1918.

In his writing about art, Plekhanov used Marxism as a tool and not a whip. His *Art and Society* employed Marxist theory to furnish an historical context and thus to account for certain kinds of art. He applied this method more specifically in "French Drama and Painting of The Eighteenth Century" and "Ibsen, Petty Bourgeois Revolutionist."

FRENCH DRAMA OF THE EIGHTEENTH CENTURY [1]

There is no more remarkable confirmation of that principle of historical materialism which holds that man's consciousness is determined by his existence, than the history of primitive peoples. For proof of this thesis we need only refer to Bücher's well-known work, *Arbeit und Rhythmus*. "I have reached the conclusion," he writes, "that while in the first stages of their development labor, music and poetry were usually blended, labor was the predominant element, the others being only of secondary importance." According to Bücher "the origin of poetry must be sought in labor." And no one familiar with the literature of the subject will accuse him of stretching the point. The critical objections which have been made by specialists apply, not to his fundamental thesis, but only to certain minor details. In the main, Bücher is undoubtedly correct.

However, his conclusions refer only to the origin of poetry. What shall we say of poetry and art in general in their higher stages of social development? Is there a discernible causal relationship between existence and consciousness—between the means of production and economic relations in society, on the one hand, and art on the other; and at what stage of development will it be best discovered?

In the following pages we shall attempt to answer this question on the basis of the history of French art in the eighteenth century. Before proceeding, however, a preliminary statement should be made.

From a sociological viewpoint, the outstanding characteristic of French society in the eighteenth century was its *division into classes*. This condition

1 The first portion of an essay, "French Drama and Painting of the Eighteenth Century," in *Art and Society* (Critics Group Series No. 3, New York, 1936), translated by Paul S. Leitner, Alfred Goldstein, and C. H. Crout. —Ed.

could not fail to influence the development of art. Let us examine the theatre, for example.

On the medieval stage, in France as well as in the rest of western Europe, the so-called "farces" occupied an important position. These farces were written for, and performed by, the people; and they served always to express the views and aspirations of the masses, and—what is especially noteworthy—their dissatisfaction with the higher estates. But during the reign of Louis XIII, the decline of the farce sets in; it comes to be regarded as entertainment fit only for servants, unworthy of refined taste, "not approved by nice people," as one French writer expressed it in 1625.

Tragedy now replaces the farce. French tragedy, however, is quite remote from the views, aspirations and dissatisfactions of the masses. It is an aristocratic product, and expresses the views, tastes, and aspirations of the higher estates. We shall soon see how profoundly the entire character of tragedy was affected by its origin.

First, however, we wish to point out that in France at the time when tragedy arose, the aristocracy served no productive function; it was supported entirely by the economic activity of the third estate. Obviously, works of art originating in this aristocratic society and expressing its views and tastes could not fail to be influenced by this situation. For example, it is known that in some of their songs the inhabitants of New Zealand celebrate the cultivation of bananas. These songs are often accompanied by a dance which *imitates the bodily motions of the farmer tending his plants*. This illustrates clearly how man's economic activities influence his art. It is also clear that *art originating in the upper classes, who do not engage in productive work, is not directly related to economic processes*.

Does this mean that in a society divided into classes, the causal connection between man's consciousness and his existence is weakened? No, not at all; for the very division of society into classes hinges upon its economic development. And if art produced by the upper classes bears no direct relationship to the productive processes of society, that too, in the final analysis, is to be explained on economic grounds. Historical materialism holds in this case as well. However, the unmistakable causal connection between existence and consciousness—between social relationships based upon *"labor,"* on the one hand, and art, on the other, is of course not quite so apparent here; for in such a situation there are certain intermediate stages which, by drawing upon themselves the investigator's entire attention, usually constitute an obstacle to any true understanding of the situation.

Having thus cleared the ground, we can now take up our subject proper. First let us turn to tragedy.

Taine said that French tragedy appeared "at a period when a noble and well-regulated monarchy under Louis XIV established the empire of decorum and court-life, the 'pomp and circumstance' of society, and the elegant domestic phrases of aristocracy. It disappeared when the social rule of the nobility and the manners of the antechamber were swept away by the Revolution."

This is quite true. But the historical process of the origin and decay, particularly the latter, of classical French tragedy is much more complex than the famous literary critic makes it out to be.

Let us study at closer range the form and essence of this literary genre. As to form, we must first of all bear in mind the familiar unities of classic tragedy—which were later to become the subject of the controversy, immortalized in the annals of French literature, between the classicists and the romanticists. The theory of the unities had been known in France since the Renaissance; but it was not until the seventeenth century that they became the literary law and the rigid rule of "good taste." "In 1620, when he wrote *Mélite,"* says Lanson, "Corneille had never heard of them." In the early thirties of the seventeenth

century Mairet came forward as the champion of the unities; his *Sophonisbe,* the first tragedy written according to the "rules," was presented on the stage in 1634. In the controversy evoked by this play, the opponents of the unities argued very much in the manner of the romanticists. But the learned admirers of antiquity took up the cudgels in defense of the three unities and they won an unequivocal and enduring victory. To what did they owe their victory? Surely not to their erudition, which could hardly move the public; rather to the growing influence of the upper classes, who abominated the naive formlessness of the earlier drama.

"The unities," continues Lanson, "offered an idea which appealed to honest men: an imitation exactly equivalent to reality, and yet capable of creating an illusion. Essentially they represented only as much stage convention as could not be omitted in the representation of life. . . . Thus acceptance of the unities was actually a triumph of realism over imagination." It was in fact the crystallization of aristocratic taste, accompanied by the final establishment of the "noble and benign monarchy," which made the victory possible. Subsequent advances in stage technique would probably have made it possible to imitate reality without adhering to the unities; but audiences came to associate the unities with a whole series of other ideas which were near and dear to them, and the theory thus attained an almost independent value which seemed to rest upon the incontestable demands of good taste. Later on, as we shall see, other social elements upheld the three unities, and hence the theory was defended even by the enemies of the aristocracy. The struggle against the unities became all but hopeless. The romanticists in their battle to abolish them needed all their wit, perseverance, and downright revolutionary ardor.

Having mentioned the subject of stage technique, we might add that the aristocratic origin of French tragedy also had influence, among other things, upon the art of the actor. We know, for example, that even today French tragic actors have a rather stilted and artificial manner, which, to one unaccustomed to it, is extremely unpleasant. No one who has seen Sarah Bernhardt will gainsay this. French dramatic artists inherit this affectedness from the time when classic tragedy held sway on the French stage. In the seventeenth and eighteenth centuries polite society would have been highly displeased if an actor had ventured to assume on the stage that simplicity and naturalness which go to make up the bewitching qualities of an Eleonora Duse, for example. Simplicity and naturalness are opposed to every rule of aristocratic esthetics. "The French," writes Abbé du Bos, "do not depend upon dress alone for giving the actors of tragedy a suitable dignity and grandeur. We insist likewise upon their speaking in a tone of voice more elevated, graver, and more sustained than that which is used in common conversation. All the little negligences which custom authorizes in the pronunciation of familiar discourse, are forbidden in our tragedies. 'Tis true this manner of reciting is more troublesome than a pronunciation bordering upon ordinary conversation; but, besides being more majestic, it is also more advantageous for the spectators, who are better enabled thereby to understand the verse. . . . 'Tis requisite also, that the gestures of tragic actors be exacter and nobler, their step and gait more grave, and their countenance more serious than those of comic personages. In fine, we insist upon tragic actors giving an air of grandeur and dignity to whatsoever they do." But why were tragic actors obliged to give an air of grandeur and dignity? Because tragedy was the spiritual child of aristocracy; its characters were confined to kings, heroes, and exalted personages generally, whose very position, as it were, demanded that they give an air of "grandeur" and "dignity." Even a highly talented actor could expect no applause from the audiences of that day if his histrionics lacked the conventional amount of aristocratic grandeur.

This is evidenced most clearly in French estimates of Shakespeare and even, under French influence, English estimates of the great dramatist. Hume warned against overrating Shakespeare's genius, since disproportioned and misshapen things often appear more gigantic than they really are. Shakespeare was good enough for his own time, but he was ill-suited to a more refined audience. Pope deplored Shakespeare's having written for the populace and not for men of the world. Shakespeare would have written much better, he thought, had he enjoyed the patronage of the king and the support of the court. Even Voltaire, the literary precursor of a new epoch hostile to the old order, many of whose tragedies were vehicles for his philosophic ideas, bowed to the esthetic tastes of aristocratic society. He considered Shakespeare a natural genius, but a *barbarian*. The following estimate of *Hamlet* is characteristic:

"It is a gross and barbarous piece, and would never be borne by the lowest rabble in France or Italy. . . . The gravediggers make a grave for the poor girl [Ophelia]; one asking the other whether a woman who drowns herself ought to be interred in holy ground: after which they sing ballads, worthy of their profession and their manners; at the same time, throwing out the bones and skulls of the dead upon the stage. . . . In the first scene, for instance, the guards says: *"Not a mouse stirring"*! Yes, sir, a soldier might make such an answer when in the barracks; but not upon the stage, before the first persons of distinction, who express themselves nobly, and before whom every one should express himself in like manner . . . Imagine to yourself, gentlemen, Louis XIV in the gallery at Versailles, surrounded by a brilliant court; and a ragged blackguard making his way through the crowd of heroes, lofty personages, and beauties composing the court, to propose their discarding Corneille, Racine and Molière, for a merry Andrew, that cuts jokes and is a good tumbler: How do you think such a proposal would be received?"

These words provide a clue not only to the aristocratic origin of French classic drama but also to the reasons for its decline.

Mannerism easily becomes *affectation;* and affectation precludes any serious and profound dramatic treatment. Under the influence of class prejudice, not only the treatment but even the choice of subject matter was bound to suffer. Class conceptions of suitability clipped the wings of art. In this connection the artistic requirements set by Marmontel are very typical and instructive:

"A peaceful and enlightened nation in which everyone feels himself dutybound to adapt his ideas and emotions to social mores and usages, in which the rules of decorum have become a decalogue—such a nation may admit in its literature only such characters as are ennobled by their environment and only such vices as are corrected by propriety."

Aristocratic ideals came to be the criterion in judging works of art. This is reason enough for the decline of classic tragedy. It does not explain, however, the appearance of a new dramatic genre on the French stage. In the third decade of the eighteenth century we witness the appearance of a new literary genre—the so-called *comédie larmoyante*, the sentimental comedy, which for a time was rather popular. If consciousness can be explained on the basis of existence, if the so-called spiritual development of man depends upon his economic development, then eighteenth century economic life must provide an explanation, among other things, of the appearance of the sentimental comedy. Does it provide an explanation? It does; and furthermore a partial analysis is already at hand. For instance, Hettner, in his history of eighteenth century literature, proves our point; he ascribes the rise of the sentimental comedy in France to the ascendancy of the bourgeoisie. The ascendancy of the bourgeoisie, however, like that of any other class, can be explained only on the basis of the economic development of society; and Hettner, without intending it or even realizing it, employs the materialistic interpretation of history. Nor is Hettner an exception. Brunetière in *Les Epoques du Théâtre Française,* further reveals the causal dependence we are seeking:

". . . with the collapse of Law's Mississippi Bubble—to go back no further —the aristocracy, as every one knows, loses ground steadily. All that a class can do to discredit, it hastens to do. . . . But above all, it grows poorer, while the bourgeoisie, the third estate, grows richer, assumes greater importance, *acquires a new consciousness of its rights. Inequalities become more glaring, abuses more unendurable.* Hearts 'overflow with hatred,' as a poet is soon to say, and 'hunger for justice'—or equality, to

be exact . . . What possibility that with such a means of propaganda and action at their disposal as the theatre, they would not put it to good use? or that they would not regard as serious, even tragic, those inequalities that had been a source of amusement to the author of *Le Bourgeois Gentilhomme* and *Georges Dandin?* But above all, what possibility that this bourgeoisie, already triumphant, would not resign itself to seeing the center of the stage forever monopolized by emperors and kings; and that the first use to which they would put their savings would not have been to order their own portrait?"

The sentimental comedy, then, portrayed the French bourgeoisie of the eighteenth century. So much is true. Indeed, it is generally known as middle-class drama. But Brunetière's idea, although essentially correct, is too general and therefore ambiguous. We shall attempt to develop this idea in greater detail. Brunetière contends that the bourgeoisie would not have resigned itself to seeing the center of the stage forever monopolized by emperors and kings. From the above quotation this seems reasonable, but hardly convincing. Only a study of the psychology of certain literary figures of the time makes the matter a certainty. One of these is Beaumarchais, the gifted author of several sentimental comedies. What was his reaction to having emperors and kings forever monopolize the center of the stage?

Emphatically and passionately Beaumarchais reviled the aristocratic tradition. He ridiculed the custom of having kings and noblemen the heroes of tragedy, and the middle classes the butt of comedy. "Depict the middle classes crushed and miserable? None of that! One must show them only to scoff at them! The citizenry ridiculous and royalty unhappy—there's the whole theatre for you!"

This mordant irony from an important ideologist of the third estate confirms Brunetière's contention.

Beaumarchais, however, not only appeals for honesty in depicting the "crushed" bourgeoisie. He also opposes the custom of drawing upon the legends and history of antiquity for the subjects of "serious" drama. "Of what interest to me, peace-loving subject of an eighteenth century monarchy, are revolutions in Athens or Rome? What real interest can I have in the death of a Peloponnesian tyrant? Or in the sacrifice of a young princess in Aulis? There is nothing in all that I can see, not the slightest moral applicable to me."

The choosing of legendary heroes was simply a means of expressing enthusiasm for antiquity, an enthusiasm which was the ideological reflection of a great struggle. This was the struggle between feudalism and a new rising order. The love of antiquity which marked the Renaissance continued into the age of Louis XIV, which, of course, has often been compared with the age of Augustus. But when rebellion stirred the bourgeoisie, when hatred and "longing for justice" filled their hearts and minds, their enthusiasm for legendary heroes—in former years fully shared by their cultivated representatives—seemed inopportune, and the annals of ancient history scarcely instructive. "The man of the third estate" then became the hero of middle-class drama: more or less idealized by the bourgeois ideologists of the period, the accuracy of the "portrait" naturally suffered.

To proceed: the real creator of French middle-class drama is Nivelle de la Chaussée. What do we find in his numerous works? Protests against various aspects of aristocratic psychology, attacks on aristocratic prejudices, or vices if you will. His contemporaries valued mainly the morality which pervades all of his plays; even in this respect the sentimental comedy remains true to its origin.

It is commonly recognized that in endeavoring to "portray" the middle class in their dramas, the apologists of the French bourgeoisie did not show any great originality. They did not invent middle-class drama; they merely imported it from England. In England this dramatic genre had developed at the end of the seventeenth century as a reaction from the extreme moral looseness which had previously ruled the stage, reflecting the moral decay of the aristocracy. The bourgeoisie, who had risen in armed rebellion against the nobility, had demanded comedy "worthy of Christians"; and henceforth preached their own morality. French literary innovators, who as a rule borrowed freely from the English everything corresponding to the attitude and sentiments of their own rebellious bourgeoisie, introduced also this feature of the middle-class drama. (As early as 1773 Louis-Sebastien Mercier pronounced the theatre "the strongest and most effective means of providing the human mind with powerful weapons, and of enlightening the whole people at a single stroke.") This is one of the secrets of their success, and it will help us to understand something which seems incomprehensible at first glance. French middle-class drama, which by the second half of the eighteenth century has apparently become well established, disappears, succumbing to classic tragedy—something one would not expect.

We are going to see presently how this strange phenomenon is to be explained; but let us first note the following: Diderot, who, as an ardent pioneer, was unrivalled in his enthusiasm for bourgeois drama (he even tried his hand at it: *Le Fils Naturel* 1757, and *Le Père de Famille,* 1758), demanded that the drama present men not as characterizations, but as representatives of social positions. The objection was raised that social position in no way determines the man. "What," he was asked, "is a judge as such (*le juge en soi*)? What is a merchant as such (*le negociant en soi*)?" This argument, however, was based on a complete misunderstanding of Diderot's position. Diderot was not speaking of merchants or judges in the abstract, but of the merchant of his day, and particularly of the judge of that period. The judge of that period, in fact, furnished a good deal of illuminating and lively stage material, as the comedy, *Le Mariage de Figaro* so delightfully proves. Diderot's demand was simply a reflection of the revolutionary aspirations of the French bourgeoisie of that period.

Strangely enough, however, it was the revolutionary character of these aspirations that prevented middle-class drama from quite submerging classic tragedy in France. An aristocratic product, classic tragedy dominated the French stage as long as the power of the aristocracy went unchallenged—power restricted only by the feudal monarchy.

(These restrictions themselves, let it be understood, were the historical fruit of a long and bitter class struggle in France.) When the bourgeoisie rebelled and challenged the power of the aristocracy, the old literary standards began to seem inadequate and the old theatre not sufficiently "instructive." Thus there arose alongside the decaying classic tragedy the drama of the bourgeoisie. In *le drame bourgeois*, the "man of the middle class" sets up his morality in opposition to the utter depravity of the aristocracy. Preaching, however, could not solve the social contradictions that cried for solution in France. The problem was not the destruction of aristocratic vices but of the aristocracy itself. This was impossible, of course, without a severe struggle. Now a *paterfamilias*, with all his stolid respectability and middle-class morality, obviously could never serve as the prototype of the aroused and heroic fighter. The literary portrait of the middle class could not inspire valor. And the enemies of the old regime acutely felt the need for valor; they realized that the bourgeois morale of the third estate must be developed. Where could the prototypes of such heroism be found? Why, where the heroes of an earlier literary tradition had been found—in antiquity!

Thus there arose a new enthusiasm. No longer did the enemies of the aristocracy inquire, like Beaumarchais: "Of what interest to me, peace-loving subject of an eighteenth century monarchy, are revolutions in Athens or Rome?" Once again Greek and Roman history captured the interest of the public. This interest, however, was now of quite a different character. If the young bourgeois ideologists were suddenly interested in "the sacrifice of a young princess in Aulis," it was primarily with a view to "fighting superstition"; if their attention was attracted by "the death of a Peloponnesian tyrant," it was not so much the psychological as the political significance of the event which gave them pause. Moreover it was no longer the Age of Augustus but rather the republican heroes of Plutarch that fired their enthusiasm. Plutarch became the Bible of these young bourgeois, as testified by Madame Roland's memoirs, for instance. And indeed it was this enthusiasm for the republican heroes in particular which re-

vived classical interest in general. The entire body of French art of that period derived its peculiar character from the new vogue of imitating antiquity. We are going to see later what deep traces it left on the history of French painting. For the present, however, we wish merely to note that the new vogue diverted the interest of the public away from dull middle-class drama and postponed for a long time the end of classic drama.

French as well as foreign historians of literature and art have often been puzzled by the fact that the revolutionaries who fought for and in the great French revolution remained literary conservatives. Why did classicism lose its hold so long after the fall of the old regime? The truth is that these innovators were conservative only superficially. For although the form of tragedy did not change, its essence did.

For example let us take Saurin's tragedy, *Spartacus,* which appeared in 1760. The hero of this play is filled with longing for liberty. For the sake of his great ideal he even foregoes marrying the girl he loves; his conversation constantly revolves around freedom and love of mankind. One had to be anything but a literary conservative either to write or to applaud tragedies such as this. Into the old literary bottle had been poured a new and revolutionary wine.

Tragedies like those by Saurin and Lemièrre (Cf. his *Guillaume Tell*) fulfill one of Diderot's revolutionary demands: they present men not as characterizations but as representatives of social positions; and especially do they express the revolutionary social aspirations of that period. And if this new wine was poured into old bottles, it must be remembered that those bottles were an ancient legacy. The widespread enthusiasm for antiquity was a remarkable but characteristic symptom of the new social temper. Side by side with this new kind of classic tragedy there appeared the bourgeois drama, that dramatized morality, as Beaumarchais approvingly termed it. But it was too colorless, too dull, too conservative in subject matter.

Middle-class drama, despite its origin in the revolutionary temper of the French bourgeoisie, failed as an adequate medium of expression for its revolutionary aspirations. It gave a literary portrait in which certain transitory contemporary characteristics of the original were well reproduced, but when the original no longer bore these characteristics, and when these characteristics ceased to be agreeable, the public lost interest in the portrait. And that is all. Classic tragedy lived on to the time when the French bourgeoisie finally triumphed over the defenders of the old regime, and even after enthusiasm for the republican heroes of antiquity had lost every social significance.

But when the time came, middle-class drama burst into new life. After some minor changes corresponding to the new social status of the bourgeoisie, it established itself definitely and securely on the French stage. Even those who refuse to recognize the close relationship between romantic drama and middle-class drama of the eighteenth century agree that the works of the younger Dumas represent the true middle-class drama of the nineteenth century.

Social psychology is expressed in the art and esthetics of a given period. But in the psychology of a society divided into classes many things are bound to seem incomprehensible and paradoxical if we ignore—as idealist historians do, despite the better legacy of the middle-class science of history—the reciprocal relationships of classes and the meaning of the class struggle.

ALEXANDER KORNEICHUK

The plays of this Ukrainian dramatist (born 1905) are often performed in Russian translation. They completely adhere to the political demands made of them, and no one has ever accused Korneichuk of introducing any qualifying or wavering note into his treatment of political subjects. His *The Sinking of the Squadron* (1934) heroically presents the revolutionary sailors' sinking of the Black Sea squadron in 1918. He consolidated his fame with *Platon Krechet* (1935), about a heroic surgeon; *The Banker* (1936), about a philanthropic Soviet banker; *Truth* (1937), concerning a Ukrainian peasant who seeks the truth and finds Lenin; and *Bogdan Khmelnitski* (1939), celebrating a seventeenth-century Ukrainian rebel against Polish oppression. His war plays include *Guerrillas of the Ukrainian Steppes* (1942) and *The Front* (1942), the latter a play blaming old-fashioned generals for Russia's early defeats and praising Stalin's handling of the war. Korneichuk was awarded the Stalin Prize and has served as Ukrainian commissar for foreign affairs.

THE AUTHOR AND SOCIETY: THE SOVIET POINT OF VIEW [1]

(1954)

Our great Communist party entrusts to us the high mission of making our drama a true popular theatre. This noble and exacting task is based not only on the principles governing the elabora-

[1] Extracts from a report to the Second Congress of Soviet Authors in Moscow, December 1954; published in *World Theatre*, IV:4.

tion of a new art unknown to history, socialist in content and multi-nation in form, but also on the age-long experience of world culture, for those of its works that resist the test of time are those that reflect with most force and passion the life and struggle, the hopes and aspirations of the common people. That is why we still feel today the heart of dead generations beating in these great works.

How pitiable appear the unavailing efforts of all kinds of decadents and other enemies of our Soviet art, to discredit its great principles and thereby everything that is greatest and most luminous in the art of the world.

How ridiculous are the muddleheads who swear all the time by socialist realism, while at the same time seeking to impose their erroneous aesthetic criteria and raise the banner of a drama distinct from the life of the people.

These muddleheads inveigh with violence against any innovation of form or content in our theatre and give a false interpretation to the work of Constantin Stanislavski. They are content with a vulgar naturalism and brand as formalism any attempt to develop a new stage form. They refuse to understand that what we consider formalism is above all absence of content, that formalism in art is defined not by brilliant stage form but by hollowness of content, and that formalism and naturalism are equally alien and harmful to our art of the theatre . . .

Yes, our hero is the positive hero but to affirm the necessity of idealization is simply to fight against the positive hero.

The spectator does not expect from us an idealized and perfect hero, a sublime talker, but a combatant for the luminous Communist ideal who not only surmounts the forces hostile to the birth of a new world, but who also overcomes in himself the human weaknesses that are more or less inherent in everyone. . . .

For a few hours each evening, hundreds of thousands of spectators attend the theatre. Not even the most passionate lover of nightingale's trills can bear four hours of uninterrupted insipid birdchatter on the stage in place of profound and passionate speech. The true theatre has ever been a great political rostrum where human passions come into more violent collision than in other styles of literature and art. Nowhere, neither in deep valleys nor on lost heights, does the spectator's heart experience such majestic, such ineffable calm as at the theatre where, at one with author and actor, men hardened in the conflict shed burning tears or peal with laughter.

FRENCH DRAMATIC CRITICISM OF THE NINETEENTH
AND TWENTIETH CENTURIES

Madame de Staël combines the spirit of the eighteenth century—Diderot and Rousseau in particular—with the new spirit of Romanticism. The result of her association with the German writers, especially the Schlegels, was her book *De l'Allemagne* (1810), which brought over the seeds of the movement which was soon to blossom forth in the plays of Victor Hugo. It was of course not altogether due to her work that the Romanticism of 1830 came when and as it did, but her books — *De la Littérature*, etc. (1800) should be added to the first — went far to interest the writers of the time. Her chapter *De l'art dramatique* in the book on Germany was obviously an echo of the Romanticists in Germany. Her contemporary, Chateaubriand, touches upon the drama in his epoch-making *Le Génie du Christianisme* (1802) — second part. Doubtless the French Revolution, with its attempts to establish a popular theater (see the decrees of the Committee of Public Safety)[1] had its share in influencing the artistic ideals of the time, though these were not developed until the advent of Michelet, and by Ro-

[1] See Romain Rolland, *Le Théâtre du peuple* (Paris, 1903), for quotations from various Revolutionary documents.— **Ed.**

main Rolland toward 1900. Népo-mucène Lemercier did a good deal of his work in the Revolutionary period, and his *Cours de littérature générale* was published in 1817. Alexandre Duval's *Réflexions sur l'art de la comédie* (1820) might be mentioned in passing. A more or less complete treatise on the theater is J.-L. Geoffroy's *Cours de littérature dramatique* (1819-20). The earliest of the more detailed Romantic criticisms of drama are in the work of Benjamin Constant (*Réflexions sur la tragédie*, etc., 1829, and his *Quelques Réflexions* on Schiller and the German drama, 1809); Henri Beyle (Stendhal) (*Racine et Shakespeare*, 1823); and Sainte-Beuve (*Tableau historique et critique de la Poésie française et du théâtre français au XVIᵉ siècle*, 1828). This book aroused great interest in early French literature and drama. Sainte-Beuve, who is said to have disliked the theater, wrote little purely dramatic criticism, though his essays on Corneille and Racine, and some others, are acute and interesting. (See *Causeries du Lundi* (1851-62); *Portraits littéraires* (1862-64); *Port-Royal* (1840-60); *Premiers Lundis* (1875); and *Nouveaux Lundis* (1863-72).) The Romantic dramatists, with Victor Hugo at their head, exposed their theories at great length. Hugo himself in the celebrated *Préface* to *Cromwell* (1827) called the younger poets to arms, and gave them a rallying standard. Nearly all his plays were preceded by prefaces, which appeared for the most part between 1827 and 1840. His *William Shakespeare* was published in 1864. Alexandre Dumas, in his *Mémoires* (1852-54), his various prefaces (in the many volumes of his *Théâtre complet*) and *Souvenirs dramatiques* (1868) is full of interesting matter. Alfred de Vigny clearly set forth his ideas in the *Avant-Propos de l'édition de 1839 of Le More de Venise* and in the *Lettre à Lord * * * sur la soirée de 24 octobre, 1829, et sur un système dramatique*, and in the preface to his play *Chatterton*, written in 1834. Théophile Gautier, another Romantic, exposed his theories in his *Histoire du Romantisme* (1874), *Les Grotesques* (1844), and his *Histoire de l'art dramatique*, etc. (1858-59). A large number of writers, better known as poets, novelists,

and miscellaneous essayists, wrote copiously on the theater, and a casual reference to such writers as Nodier, Guizot, Villemain, Michelet, Nisard, Mérimée, George Sand, Flaubert, Taine, and Baudelaire, will here suffice. There are, besides, the numerous professional dramatic critics: Jules Janin (*Histoire de la littérature dramatique*, 1853-58); Saint-Marc Girardin (*Cours de littérature dramatique*, 1843); Paul de Saint-Victor (*Les Deux masques*, 1867); Jules Barbey d'Aurevilly (*Le Théâtre contemporain*, 1887-92); J.-J. Weiss (*Trois années de théâtre*, 1892-96, *Le Théâtre et les mœurs*, 1889, *Le Drame historique et le drame passionel*, 1894, etc.); and Francisque Sarcey (*Quarante ans de théâtre*, posthumously published, 1900-02). The æstheticians and historians, Hippolyte Taine, Crépet, Fournier, Montégut, Chasles, Magnin, and Scherer, all contributed to the theory and history of the drama. Among the dramatists who at the same time theorized on their art, the most important is Alexandre Dumas fils, who affixed prefaces to all his plays, and wrote a number of pamphlets besides. He was continually preoccupied with the moral and political "utility" of the drama. His theoretical writings cover the period between 1860 and 1890. Emile Augier wrote very little on the drama; George Sand, on the other hand, prefaced nearly all her plays. The movement toward Naturalism in the novel extended to the drama, and the earliest exponents were the brothers Goncourt, who wrote prefaces to their plays *Henriette Maréschal* (1886), *La Patrie en danger* (1873), and the *Théâtre* (1879). Henry Becque, the founder of the Naturalistic drama, wrote much concerning his literary quarrels, but his *Souvenirs d'un auteur dramatique* (1895), have little dramatic theory. The spokesman of the early Naturalistic dramatists was the novelist Emile Zola. His periodical criticisms of the sixties and seventies he collected in *Le Naturalisme au théâtre* (1881), and *Nos Auteurs dramatiques* (1881). His prefaces to his *Théâtre* (1878) and individual plays — (1873-74-78), contain clear statements of his ideals of a new drama. After the foundation of Antoine's *Théâtre libre* in 1887, Jean Jullien wrote two volumes of theory, *Le Théâtre vivant* (1892-96), exposing the "slice of life" theories then recently developed. Ferdinand Brunetière developed his Law of the Drama in the early nineties and published it in its latest form as *La Loi du théâtre*, in 1894. The critics of this century's first decades produced a vast amount of material, most of which has been collected into book-form from periodicals of the day. The most important of these are Jules Lemaître, whose ten volumes of *Impressions de théâtre* appeared between 1888 and 1898; Emile Faguet, who contributed some thirty-five or forty volumes on the theater (*Drame ancien, Drame moderne* — 1898, *Propos de théâtre* — 1903-10, are the best); Catulle Mendès, with his three volumes of *L'Art au théâtre* (1897-1900); René Doumic, with his *Théâtre nouveau* (1908), *De Scribe à Ibsen* (1893); and *Essais sur le théâtre contemporain* (1896); Adolphe Brisson, with his *Le Théâtre* (1907ff); Gustave Larroumet, with his *Etudes d'histoire et de critique dramatique* (1892), and *Nouvelles études* (1899). Among the psychological and philosophical treatises on the drama may be mentioned Gustave Le Bon's *La Psychologie des foules* (1895) and Henri Bergson's *Le Rire* (1900). Paul Bourget contributed occasional essays on the theatre, the most significant of which is the *Réflexions sur le théâtre* (1888). Late nineteenth-century France was rich in historians of the theatre; among these were Eugène Lintilhac, author of a life of Beaumarchais and of various essays on dramatic theory; Gustave Lanson, author of a history of French literature and of numerous works on dramatists; Augustin Filon, whose *De Dumas à Rostand* (1898) affords a comprehensive view of the drama of the time; Antoine Benoist, author of *Essais de critique dramatique* (1898), and *Le Théâtre d'aujourd'hui* (1911); Alphonse Séché and Jules Bertaut, authors of *L'Evolution du théâtre contemporain* (1908); Louis Veuillot, author of *Les Prédicateurs de la scène* (1904); Emile de Saint-Auban, author of *L'Idée sociale au théâtre* (1901); Hippolyte Parigot, author of *Le Théâtre d'hier* (1893) and *Génie et métier* (1894); Armand Kahn, author of *Le Théâtre social en France* (1907). More or less professional dramatic critics include: Anatole France (*La Vie littéraire*, 1888-94); Paul Flat (*Figures du théâtre contemporain*, 1911); Jean Ernest-Charles (*Les Samedis littéraires* (1903-07) and *Le Théâtre des poètes*, 1910); Gabriel Trarieux (*La Lanterne de Diogène*, n.d.); A.-E. Sorel (*Essais de psychologie dramatique*, 1911); Edmond Sée (*Le Théâtre des autres*, and *Petits dialogues sur le théâtre et l'art dramatique*, 1913); and Georges Polti (*Les Trente-six situations dramatiques*, 1895, and *L'Art d'inventer les personnages*, 1912). Both Romain Rolland and Maurice Pottecher for some years spent time and effort to found a people's theater, and each one wrote a book of theories called *Le Théâtre du peuple* (Pottecher's dating from 1899, and Rolland's from 1903). Many of the dramatists of the early 1900's wrote on the drama: chief among these are the Belgian, Maurice Maeterlinck, who in his essays (*Le Trésor des humbles*, 1896, *La Sagesse et la destinée*, 1898, and *Le double Jardin*, 1904, among others), attacked the modern drama and attempted to divert the current toward a new expression of the impalpable and sub-conscious. Henry Bataille wrote prefaces to some ten of his plays, and various articles on Shakespeare, Becque, and his own contemporaries; his dramatic essays were all printed in his *Ecrits sur le théâtre* (1917). Alfred Capus collected a number of dramatic essays into a volume, *Le Théâtre* (1912), though another, *Notre Epoque et le théâtre* (1906), has never been reprinted. Newer volumes by dramatic critics include Jacques Copeau's *Critiques d'un autre temps* (1923); Robert Kemp's *La Vie du théâtre* (1956), Gabriel Marcel's *L'Heure théâtrale*, (1960), and Jean-Jacques Gautier's *Deux Fauteuils d' orchestre* (1962).

The latest movement on the French stage has been an experimental drama that has attacked timeless issues, problems forever insoluble. Some, like Samuel Beckett, Eugène Ionesco, and Arthur Adamov (in his early work), owing what seems a common debt to the director Antonin Artaud, are grouped together under the term "theatre of the absurd." Jean Genet has some affinities with these writers. Ionesco is a voluble spokesman for them. Jean-Paul Sartre is equally serious, but his philosophical or political plays are technically more conventional.

STENDHAL

The novelist who called himself Stendhal was born Henri Beyle in Grenoble, France, in 1783. Serving in Napoleon's army, he delighted in his first visit to Italy, and after Napoleon's fall, he lived briefly in Milan. Late in life, he returned to Italy as French consul at Civitavecchia. The essays that went into his *Racine and Shakespeare* appeared in 1823 and 1825. Stendhal urged Shakespeare as a more suitable model of tragic writing than Racine and, accordingly, mounted a characteristically romantic attack upon classical practice. He attacked the unities of time and place and urged prose as the proper language and French history as the proper subject of French tragedy. He practiced his romantic theory in his novels, frank and cynical works marked by close attention to psychological detail. His two masterpieces, *The Red and the Black* (1830) and *The Charterhouse of Parma* (1839), record the conflict between worldly ambition and a churchly vocation. He died in 1842.

RACINE OR SHAKESPEARE? [1]

(1823)

. . . The entire dispute between Racine and Shakespeare comes down to whether, while observing the two unities of *time* and *place,* one can write plays that vitally interest nineteenth-century audiences—plays that make them weep and shudder or, in other words, that give them *dramatic* pleasures rather than the *epic* pleasures that make us rush to the fiftieth performance of *Le Paria* or *Régulus.*

I maintain that adherence to the two unities of *time* and *place* is a French habit; a habit with very deep roots; a habit from which we shall free ourselves only with difficulty, because Paris is the salon of Europe and sets the fashion for Europe. But I also maintain that these unities are by no means necessary for producing profound emotion and the genuine dramatic effect.

Why, I will ask the partisans of *Classicism,* do you demand that the action depicted in a tragedy cover not more than twenty-four or thirty-six hours? And that the setting represented on the stage not change—or at any rate, as Vol-

taire says, that the changes of setting not extend beyond the different rooms of a palace?

THE ACADEMICIAN: Because it is not credible that an action represented in two hours should encompass a week or a month; or that in a few moments the actors should go from Venice to Cyprus, as in Shakespeare's *Othello,* or from Scotland to the English court, as in *Macbeth.*

THE ROMANTIC: Not only is that incredible and impossible; but it is likewise impossible that the action encompass twenty-four or thirty-six hours.

THE ACADEMICIAN: Heaven forbid that we should be so absurd as to claim that the fictitious duration of the action should correspond exactly to the *material* time consumed by the performance. If this were the case, the rules would be actual fetters on genius. In the imitative arts, one must be strict but not rigorous. The spectator can easily imagine that several hours have passed during the interval of the intermissions—all the more so because he is diverted by the symphonies played by the orchestra.

THE ROMANTIC: Be careful of what you say, Monsieur. You are giving me a great advantage. You agree, then, that the spectator can *imagine* that more time is passing than that during which he is seated in the theatre. But tell me: Can he imagine a time passing that is double the real time, triple, quadruple, or a hundred times greater? Where shall we stop?

THE ACADEMICIAN: You are odd, you modern philosophers. You blame poetics because, so you say, it fetters genius. And now you want us to apply the rule of the *unity of time* with all the rigor and exactitude of mathematics, in order for it to be plausible. Is it not enough for you that it obviously contravenes all credibility for the spectator to imagine that a year, a month, or even a week has passed since he got his ticket and entered the theatre?

THE ROMANTIC: And who told you that the spectator cannot imagine that?

THE ACADEMICIAN: It is reason that tells me.

THE ROMANTIC: I beg your pardon. Reason cannot possibly teach you this. How could you know that the spectator can imagine that twenty-four hours have passed, whereas actually he has only been sitting in his box for two hours, unless experience had taught you this? How could you know that those hours that seem so long to a man who is bored, seem to fly when a person is being amused, unless experience had told you. In a word, it is *experience* alone that must settle the issue between you and me.

THE ACADEMICIAN: Yes, no doubt it is experience.

THE ROMANTIC: Well, experience has already spoken against you. In England, for two centuries now, and in Germany, during the past fifty years, they have been performing tragedies whose action covers entire months; and the spectators' imagination accommodates itself perfectly to this.

THE ACADEMICIAN: But now you are giving me the example of foreigners— and Germans at that!

THE ROMANTIC: Some other time we shall discuss this unquestionable superiority of the Frenchman in general, and the inhabitant of Paris in particular, over all the other peoples of the world. I shall be fair: this superiority is a *matter of feeling* with you. You are despots spoiled by two centuries of flattery. Fate willed that you Parisians should become responsible for making literary reputations in Europe. A woman of wit, known for her *enthusiasm* for the

beauties of nature, once exclaimed, in order to please the Parisians: "The most beautiful stream in the world is the stream of the Rue du Bac!" All the genteel writers—not only in France but throughout Europe—have flattered you in order to obtain a bit of literary fame in return. And what you call *inner feeling* and *moral evidence* is nothing more than the moral evidence of a spoiled child; in other words, the habit of being flattered.

But let us get back to the point. Can you deny that the inhabitant of London or Edinburgh, the compatriots of Fox and Sheridan, who are perhaps not utter fools, see performances of tragedies like *Macbeth,* for example, without being shocked in the slightest? Now this play, which every year is applauded an infinite number of times in England and America, begins with the assassination of the king and the flight of his sons. And it ends with the return of these same princes at the head of an army that they have assembled in England in order to dethrone the bloody Macbeth. This series of actions necessarily requires several months.

THE ACADEMICIAN: Ah! You will never persuade me that the English and the Germans, even if they are foreigners, really imagine that entire months pass while they are at the theatre.

THE ROMANTIC: Just as you will never persuade me that the French spectators believe that twenty-four hours pass while they are watching a performance of *Iphigénie en Aulide.*

THE ACADEMICIAN (*impatient*): What a difference!

THE ROMANTIC: Let us not become incensed. And please observe carefully what is going on in your head. Try to draw aside for a moment the veil that habit has thrown over acts which take place so rapidly that you have lost the ability to follow them with your eye and see them *occur*. Let us come to an agreement on the word *illusion*. When one says that the spectator imagines that the time necessary for the events represented on the stage has passed, one does not mean that the spectator's illusion extends to the point of believing that all this time has really elapsed. The fact is that the spectator, caught up and carried along by the story, is not shocked by anything. He gives no thought whatsoever to the time that has passed. Your Parisian spectator sees Agamemnon awaken Arcas at exactly seven o'clock. He witnesses the arrival of Iphigenia; and he sees her led to the altar where the Jesuitic Calchas is waiting for her. If anyone asked him, he would of course reply that these events required several hours. And yet, if during the quarrel between Achilles and Agamemnon he were to take out his watch, it would show the hour of 8:15. What spectator would be surprised by this? Nonetheless, the play that he is applauding has already lasted for several hours.

The truth of the matter is that even your Parisian spectator is accustomed to seeing time move at different rates on the stage and in the other part of the theatre. This is a fact that you cannot deny. It is clear that even in Paris, even at the Théâtre-Français in the Rue de Richelieu, the spectator's imagination lends itself easily to the poet's suppositions. The spectator, quite naturally, pays no attention to the intervals of time required by the poet; just as in sculpture he does not take it into his head to reproach Dupaty or Bosio for the fact that their figures lack movement. This is one of the infirmities of art. The spectator, when he is not a pedant, is concerned only with the acts and developments of passions that are presented to his view. Precisely the same thing happens in the head of the Parisian who applauds *Iphigénie en Aulide* and in that of the Scotsman who admires the story of his former kings, Macbeth and Duncan. The only difference is that the Parisian, being a child of good family, has acquired the habit of mocking others.

THE ACADEMICIAN: In other words, according to you the theatrical illusion is the same for both?

THE ROMANTIC: To have illusions, to be in a state of *illusion,* means to deceive oneself, according to the *Dictionary* of the Academy. An *illusion,* M. Guizot says, is the effect of a thing or an idea that deceives us by its misleading appearance. Illusion therefore means the act of a man who believes a thing that does not exist—as in dreams, for example. Theatrical illusion would be the act of a man who believes that the things that take place on the stage really exist.

Last year (August 1822) a soldier who was standing guard in the theatre in Baltimore, upon seeing Othello, in the fifth act of the tragedy of that name, about to kill Desdemona, cried out: "It will never be said that in my presence a damned nigger killed a white woman." At the same moment the soldier shot at the actor who was playing Othello and broke his arm. Not one year passes but what the newspapers report similar incidents.

Now that soldier was entertaining an *illusion:* he believed in the reality of what was happening on the stage. But an ordinary spectator at the moment when his pleasure is most intense—at the moment when he is enthusiastically. *applauding* Talma-Manlius [2] saying to his friend, "Do you recognize this writing?"—by virtue of the very fact that he applauds, does not have a *complete illusion,* because he is applauding Talma and not the Roman, Manlius. Manlius does nothing deserving of applause. His act is very simple and entirely in his own interest.

THE ACADEMICIAN: I beg your pardon, my friend, but what you have just said is a commonplace.

THE ROMANTIC: I beg your pardon, my friend, but what you have just said represents the defeat of a man made incapable of close reasoning by an ingrained habit of indulging in elegant phrases.

It is impossible for you not to agree that the illusion one seeks at the theatre is not a complete illusion. *Complete* illusion is the kind experienced by the soldier standing guard in the theatre in Baltimore. It is impossible for you not to agree that the spectators know very well that they are in a theatre and watching a work of art, not a real event.

THE ACADEMICIAN: Who would think of denying that?

THE ROMANTIC: Then you grant that there is *imperfect illusion?* You had better be on your guard.

Do you believe that from time to time —for example, two or three times in one act, and for only a second or two each time—the illusion is complete?

---

2 I.e., François-Joseph Talma, the famous tragic actor, in the leading role of *Manlius Capitolinus,* by Lafosse d' Aubigny, a playwright of the eighteenth century.—Trans.

THE ACADEMICIAN: That is by no means clear. In order to give you an answer, I should have to go back to the theatre several times and observe my actions.

THE ROMANTIC: Ah! That is a charming reply, and one full of good faith. One can easily see that you belong to the Academy and that you no longer need the votes of your colleagues to be admitted. A man who had yet to make his reputation as a learned *littérateur* would take pains to avoid being so clear and reasoning in a manner so precise. You had better be on your guard: if you continue to be of good faith, we shall agree with each other.

It seems to me that these moments of *complete illusion* are more frequent than is generally supposed, especially than is admitted in literary discussions, as a matter of fact. But these moments are of infinitely brief duration—for example, a half-second or a quarter-second. One very quickly forgets Manlius and sees only Talma. Such moments last longer with young women, and that is why they cry so copiously at a tragedy.

But let us try to discover at what moments in a tragedy the spectator can hope to find these delicious instants of *complete illusion*.

Such charming instants do not occur when there is a change of scene; nor at the precise moment when the poet requires the spectator to skip over twelve or fifteen days; nor when the poet is obliged to give a long speech to one of his characters for the sole purpose of informing the spectator of a previous fact about which he must know; nor, again, when there are three or four lines which are admirable and remarkable *as poetry*.

These delicious and very rare instants of *complete illusion* are encountered only in the warmth of a lively scene when there is a rapid exchange of lines among the actors. For example, when Hermione says to Orestes, who has just assassinated Pyrrhus by her order:

Who told you?

One will never encounter these moments of *complete illusion* at the instant when a murder is committed on the stage or when the guards come to arrest a character and take him to prison. We cannot believe any of these things to be real, and they never produce an illusion. These bits are written only to introduce the scenes in which the spectators experience those half-seconds that are so delicious. *Now I maintain that these brief moments of complete illusion are found more often in the tragedies of Shakespeare than in the tragedies of Racine.*

All the pleasure one derives from the tragic spectacle depends upon the frequency of these brief moments of illusion *and upon the state of emotion in which the spectator is left during the intervals between them.*

One of the things most opposed to the birth of these moments of illusion is admiration—however well-founded it may be—for the beautiful poetic lines of a tragedy.

It is much worse if one decides he wants to judge the *poetic lines* of a tragedy. But this is precisely the state of soul of the Parisian spectator when he first goes to see that much-lauded tragedy *Le Paria*.

Here we have the question of *romanticism* reduced to its ultimate terms. If you are of bad faith, or if you lack sensitivity, or if you have been petrified by Laharpe, you will deny me my brief moments of perfect illusion.

And I admit that there is nothing I can say in reply to you. Your feelings are not something material that I can extract from your own heart and hold up in front of your eyes to confound you.

I say to you: You should have such and such a feeling at this moment. All men who are generally well organized experience such a feeling at this moment. And you will reply: Please pardon my use of the expression, *but that is not true.*

As for me, I have nothing further to add. I have arrived at the last confines of what logic can grasp in poetry.

THE ACADEMICIAN: Your metaphysics is abominably obscure. Do you hope, with that, to make people hiss Racine?

THE ROMANTIC: First of all, only charlatans claim that they can teach algebra or extract a tooth without some pain. The question we are discussing is one of the most difficult that the human mind can undertake.

As for Racine, I am pleased that you mentioned that great man. His name has been made an insult for us; but his glory is immortal. He will always be one of the greatest geniuses to stir the astonishment and admiration of men. Is Caesar less a great general because gunpowder has been invented since his campaigns against our ancestors, the Gauls? All we claim is that if Caesar were to return to the world, his first concern would be to have cannons in his army. Would anyone say that Catinat or Luxembourg were greater generals than Caesar because they possessed a park of artillery, and because in three days they captured places that would have withstood the Roman legions for a month? It would have been a fine bit of reasoning if someone had said to Francis I at Marignan: "You must not use your artillery. Caesar had no cannons. Do you think you are more clever than Caesar?"

If persons of unquestionable talent like MM. Chénier, Lemercier, and Delavigne had dared to free themselves from rules whose absurdity has been recognized since Racine, they would have given us better plays than *Tibère, Agamemnon*, or *Les Vêpres siciliennes*. Is not *Pinto* a hundred times better than *Clovis*,

Orovèse, Cyrus, or any other very correct tragedy of M. Lemercier?

Racine did not believe that tragedies could be written any other way. If he lived in our time and dared to follow the new rules, he would do a hundred times better than *Iphigénie*. Instead of arousing only admiration, a rather cold sentiment, he would cause torrents of tears to flow. Is there any man, of even a modicum of education, who does not derive more pleasure from seeing M. Lebrun's *Marie Stuart* at the Théâtre-Français than Racine's *Bajazet?* And yet M. Lebrun's lines of poetry are very weak. The great difference in the degree of pleasure is due to the fact that M. Lebrun has dared to be quasi-romantic.

THE ACADEMICIAN: You have talked a long time. You have perhaps spoken well, but you have not convinced me.

THE ROMANTIC: I was expecting that. But then, too, this rather lengthy intermission is going to end. The curtain is going up. I merely wanted to relieve the boredom by making you a bit angry. You must agree that I have succeeded.

VICTOR HUGO

Victor-Marie Hugo was born at Besançon in 1802. His father was a general under Napoleon. His early education was received at Paris and Madrid. He returned later to Paris and studied at the *Ecole Polytéchnique*. It is said that he wrote a tragedy at the age of fourteen. Three years later he was a contributor to the *Conservateur littéraire*, but he attracted no attention until in 1822 he published his *Odes et poésies diverses.* This was followed by two novels. The *Odes et ballades* (1826) and *Orientales* (1829) brought him added fame. Meantime, his first play, the unactable *Cromwell*, was published in 1827. The famous *Préface*, in which the poet proclaimed the tenets of new Romantic drama, brought him into recognition as

the leader and champion of the new movement. In 1830 his *Hernani* was produced at the *Théâtre-Français*; it marked an epoch in the history of the French stage. For the next thirteen years he continued to produce and publish plays, prefaces, novels, and poems. In 1852 he was banished for political reasons, and spent some years on the Isle of Jersey. These he spent writing political and poetic satire, though he found time to write two of his best and most ambitious volumes of poems, *Les Contemplations* (1856), and *La Légende des siècles* (1859). A little later appeared *Les Misérables* (1862), and two years afterward, *William Shakespeare* (1864). After the political upheaval of 1870–71, he returned to France, but his imprudent political activities made it necessary for him to leave the country again, and seek refuge in Belgium. But he was sent back from that country, and lived in Paris until his death in 1885.

From the standpoint of drama, Victor Hugo is of great importance as the champion of the Romantic form, which he revived. The publication of each of his plays was accompanied with a defense of the form used. The Romantic group — of which the best-known were Alfred de Vigny, Dumas père, and Casimir Delavigne — rallied round his standard, and constituted the chief school of dramatic art in France for some years. Hugo's principal models were taken from the art of the Middle Age and Shakespeare. His method is rather inspirational than logical, and his arguments are on the whole somewhat unsound.

PREFACE TO CROMWELL [1]

[(Préface) — Cromwell]

(1827)

. . . . . .

Behold, then, a new religion, a new society; upon this twofold foundation there must inevitably spring up a new poetry. Previously — we beg pardon for setting forth a result which the reader has probably already foreseen from what has been said above — previously, following therein the course pursued by the ancient polytheism and philosophy, the purely epic muse of the ancients had studied nature in only a single aspect, casting aside without pity almost everything in art which, in the world subjected to its imitation, had not relation to a certain type of beauty. A type which was magnificent at first, but, as always happens with everything systematic, became in later times false, trivial and conventional. Christianity leads poetry to the truth. Like it, the modern muse will see things in a higher and broader light. It will realize that everything in creation is not humanely *beautiful*, that the ugly exists beside the beautiful, the unshapely beside the graceful, the grotesque on the reverse of the sublime, evil with good, darkness with light. It will ask itself if the narrow and relative sense of the artist should prevail over the infinite, absolute sense of the Creator; if it is for man to correct God; if a mutilated nature will be the more beautiful for the mutilation; if art has the right to duplicate, so to speak, man, life, creation; if things will progress better when their muscles and their vigor have been taken from them; if, in short, to be incomplete is the best way to be harmonious. Then it is that, with its eyes fixed upon events that are both laughable and redoubtable, and under the influence of that spirit of Christian melancholy and philosophical criticism which we described a moment ago, poetry will take a great step, a decisive step, a step which, like the upheaval of an earthquake, will change the whole face of the intellectual world. It will set about doing as nature does, mingling in its creations — but without confounding them — darkness and light, the grotesque and the sublime; in other words, the body and the soul, the beast and the intellect; for the starting-point of religion is always the starting-point of poetry. All things are connected.

Thus, then, we see a principle unknown to the ancients, a new type, in-

1 Re-printed from vol. 3 of the *Dramatic Works of Victor Hugo* (Boston, 1909). Translation of this *Preface* — of which the principal parts are here included — by George Burnham Ives.— Ed.

troduced in poetry; and as an additional element in anything modifies the whole of the thing, a new form of the art is developed. This type is the grotesque; its new form is comedy.

And we beg leave to dwell upon this point; for we have now indicated the significant feature, the fundamental difference which, in our opinion, separates modern from ancient art, the present form from the defunct form; or, to use less definite but more popular terms, *romantic* literature from *classical* literature.

" At last!" exclaim the people who for some time past *have seen what we were coming at*, " at last we have you — you are caught in the act. So then you put forward the ugly as a type for imitation, you make the *grotesque* an element of art. But the graces; but good taste! Don't you know that art should correct nature? that we must *ennoble* art? that we must *select?* Did the ancients ever exhibit the ugly and the grotesque? Did they ever mingle comedy and tragedy? The example of the ancients, gentlemen! And Aristotle, too; and Boileau; and La Harpe. Upon my word! "

These arguments are sound, doubtless, and, above all, of extraordinary novelty. But it is not our place to reply to them. We are constructing no system here — God protect us from systems! We are stating a fact. We are a historian, not a critic. Whether the fact is agreeable or not matters little; it is a fact. Let us resume, therefore, and try to prove that it is of the fruitful union of the grotesque and the sublime types that modern genius is born — so complex, so diverse in its forms, so inexhaustible in its creations; and therein directly opposed to the uniform simplicity of the genius of the ancients; let us show that that is the point from which we must set out to establish the real and radical difference between the two forms of literature.

Not that it is strictly true that comedy and the grotesque were entirely unknown to the ancients. In fact, such a thing would be impossible. Nothing grows without a root; the germ of the second epoch always exists in the first. In the *Iliad* Thersites and Vulcan furnish comedy, one to the mortals, the other to the gods. There is too much nature and originality in the Greek tragedy for there not to be an occasional touch of comedy in it. For example, to cite only what we happen to recall, the scene between Menelaus and the portress of the palace (*Helen,* Act I), and the scene of the Phrygian (*Orestes,* Act IV). The Tritons, the Satyrs, the Cyclops, are grotesque; Polyphemus is a terrifying, Silenus a farcical grotesque.

But one feels that this part of the art is still in its infancy. The epic, which at this period imposes its form on everything, weights heavily upon it and stifles it. The ancient grotesque is timid and forever trying to keep out of sight. It is plain that it is not on familiar ground, because it is not in its natural surroundings. It conceals itself as much as it can. The Satyrs, the Tritons, and the Sirens are hardly abnormal in form. The Fates and the Harpies are hideous in their attributes rather than in feature; the Furies are beautiful, and are called *Eumenides,* that is to say, *gentle, beneficent.* There is a veil of grandeur or of divinity over other grotesques. Polyphemus is a giant, Midas a king, Silenus a god.

Thus comedy is almost imperceptible in the great epic *ensemble* of ancient times. What is the barrow of Thespis beside the Olympian chariots? What are Aristophanes and Plautus, beside the Homeric colossi, Æschylus, Sophocles, Euripides? Homer bears them along with him, as Hercules bore the pygmies, hidden in his lion's skin?

In the idea of men of modern times, however, the grotesque plays an enormous part. It is found everywhere; on the one hand it creates the abnormal and the horrible, on the other the comic and the burlesque. It fastens upon religion a thousand original superstitions, upon poetry a thousand picturesque fancies. It is the grotesque which scatters lavishly, in air, water, earth, fire those beside the Olympian chariots? What are Aristophanes and Plautus, beside the Homeric colossi, Æschylus, Sophocles, Euripides? Homer bears them along with him, as Hercules bore the pygmies, hidden in his lion's skin?

In the idea of men of modern times, however, the grotesque plays an enormous part. It is found everywhere; on the one hand it creates the abnormal and the horrible, on the other the comic and the burlesque. It fastens upon religion a thousand original superstitions, upon poetry a thousand picturesque fancies. It is the grotesque which scatters lavishly, in air, water, earth, fire those myriads of intermediary creatures which we find all alive in the popular traditions of the Middle Ages; it is the grotesque which impels the ghastly antics of the witches' revels, which gives Satan his horns, his cloven foot and his bat's wings. It is the grotesque, still the grotesque, which now casts into the Christian hell the frightful faces which the severe genius of Dante and Milton will evoke, and again peoples it with those laughter-moving figures amid which Callot, the burlesque Michelangelo, will disport himself. If it passes from the world of imagination to the real world, it unfolds an inexhaustible supply of parodies of mankind. Creations of its fantasy are the Scaramouches, Crispins and Harlequins, grinning silhouettes of man, types altogether unknown to serious-minded antiquity, although they originated in classic Italy. It is the grotesque, lastly, which, coloring the same drama with the fancies of the North and of the South in turn, exhibits Sganarelle capering about Don Juan and Mephistopheles crawling about Faust.

And how free and open it is in its bearing! how boldly it brings into relief all the strange forms which the preceding age had timidly wrapped in swaddling-clothes! Ancient poetry, compelled to provide the lame Vulcan with companions, tried to disguise their deformity by distributing it, so to speak, upon gigantic proportions. Modern genius retains this myth of the supernatural smiths, but gives it an entirely different character and one which makes it even more striking; it changes the giants to dwarfs and makes gnomes of the Cyclops. With like originality, it substitutes for the somewhat commonplace Lernæan hydra all the local dragons of our national legends — the gargoyle of Rouen, the *gra-ouilli* of Metz, the *chair sallee* of Troyes, the *drée* of Montlhéry, the *tarasque* of Tarascon — monsters of forms so diverse, whose outlandish names are an additional attribute. All these creations draw from their own nature

that energetic and significant expression before which antiquity seems sometimes to have recoiled. Certain it is that the Greek Eumenides are much less horrible, and consequently less *true*, than the witches in *Macbeth*. Pluto is not the devil.

In our opinion a most novel book might be written upon the employment of the grotesque in the arts. One might point out the powerful effects the moderns have obtained from that fruitful type, upon which narrow-minded criticism continues to wage war even in our own day. It may be that we shall be led by our subject to call attention in passing to some features of this vast picture. We will simply say here that, as a means of contrast with the sublime, the grotesque is, in our view, the richest source that nature can offer art. Rubens so understood it, doubtless, when it pleased him to introduce the hideous features of a court dwarf amid his exhibitions of royal magnificence, coronations and splendid ceremonial. The universal beauty which the ancients solemnly laid upon everything, is not without monotony; the same impression repeated again and again may prove fatiguing at last. Sublime upon sublime scarcely presents a contrast, and we need a little rest from everything, even the beautiful. On the other hand, the grotesque seems to be a halting-place, a mean term, a starting-point whence one rises toward the beautiful with a fresher and keener perception. The salamander gives relief to the water-sprite; the gnome heightens the charm of the sylph.

And it would be true also to say that contact with the abnormal has imparted to the modern sublime a something purer, grander, more sublime, in short, than the beautiful of the ancients; and that is as it should be. When art is consistent with itself, it guides everything more surely to its goal. If the Homeric Elysium is a long, long way from the ethereal charm, the angelic pleasureableness of Milton's Paradise, it is because under Eden there is a hell far more terrible than the heathen Tartarus. Do you think that Francesca da Rimini and Beatrice would be so enchanting in a poet who should not confine us in the Tower of Hunger and compel us to share Ugolino's revolting repast. Dante would have less charm, if he had less power. Have the fleshly naiads, the muscular Tritons, the wanton Zephyrs, the diaphanous transparency of our water-sprites and sylphs? Is it not because the modern imagination does not fear to picture the ghastly forms of vampires, ogres, ghouls, snake-charmers and jinns prowling about graveyards, that it can give to its fairies that incorporeal shape, that purity of essence, of which the heathen nymphs fall so far short? The antique Venus is beautiful, admirable, no doubt; but what has imparted to Jean Goujon's faces that weird, tender, ethereal delicacy? What has given them that unfamiliar suggestion of life and grandeur, if not the proximity of the rough and powerful sculptures of the Middle Ages?

If the thread of our argument has not been broken in the reader's mind by these necessary digressions — which in truth, might be developed much further — he has realized, doubtless, how powerfully the grotesque — that germ of comedy, fostered by the modern muse — grew in extent and importance as soon as it was transplanted to a soil more propitious than paganism and the Epic. In truth, in the new poetry, while the sublime represents the soul as it is, purified by Christian morality, the grotesque plays the part of the human beast. The former type, delivered of all impure alloy, has as its attributes all the charms, all the graces, all the beauties; it must be able some day to create Juliet, Desdemona, Ophelia. The latter assumes all the absurdities, all the infirmities, all the blemishes. In this partition of mankind and of creation, to it fall the passions, vices, crimes; it is sensuous, fawning, greedy, miserly, false, incoherent, hypocritical; it is, in turn, Iago, Tartuffe, Basile, Polonius, Harpagon, Bartholo, Falstaff, Scapin, Figaro. The beautiful has but one type, the ugly has a thousand. The fact is that the beautiful, humanly speaking, is merely form considered in its simplest aspect, in its most perfect symmetry, in its most entire harmony with our nake-up. Thus the *ensemble* that it offers us is always complete, but restricted like ourselves. What we call the ugly, on the contrary, is a detail of a great whole which eludes us, and which is in harmony, not with man but with all creation. That is why it constantly presents itself to us in new but incomplete aspects.

It is interesting to study the first appearance and the progress of the grotesque in modern times. At first, it is an invasion, an irruption, an overflow, as of a torrent that has burst its banks. It rushes through the expiring Latin literature, imparts some coloring to Persius, Petronius and Juvenal, and leaves behind it the *Golden Ass* of Apuleius. Thence it diffuses itself through the imaginations of the new nations that are remodeling Europe. It abounds in the work of the fabulists, the chroniclers, the romancists. We see it make its way from the South to the North. It disports itself in the dreams of the Teutonic nations, and at the same time vivifies with its breath the admirable Spanish *romanceros*, a veritable Iliad of the age of chivalry. For example, it is the grotesque which describes thus, in the *Roman de la Rose,* an august ceremonial, the election of a king: —

" *A long-shanked knave they chose, I wis,*
Of all their men the boniest."

More especially it imposes its characteristic qualities upon that wonderful architecture which, in the Middle Ages, takes the place of all the arts. It affixes its mark on the façades of cathedrals, frames its hells and purgatories in the ogive arches of great doorways, portrays them in brilliant hues on window-glass, exhibits its monsters, its bull-dogs, its imps about capitals, along friezes, on the edges of roofs. It flaunts itself in numberless shapes on the wooden façades of houses, on the stone façades of châteaux, on the marble façades of palaces. From the arts it makes its way into the national manners, and while it stirs applause from the people for the *graciosos* of comedy, it gives to the kings court-jesters. Later, in the age of etiquette, it will show us Scarron on the very edge of Louis XIV's bed. Meanwhile, it decorates coats-of-arms, and draws upon knights' shields the symbolic hieroglyphs of feudalism. From the manners, it makes its way into the laws; numberless strange customs attest its passage through the institutions of the Middle Ages. Just as it represented Thespis, smeared with wine-lees, leaping in her tomb, it dances with the *Basoche* on the famous marble table which served at the same time as a stage for the popular farces and for the royal banquets. Finally, having made its way into the arts, the manners, and the laws, it enters even the Church. In every Catholic city we see it organizing some one of those curious ceremonies, those strange processions, wherein religion is attended by all varieties of superstition — the sublime attended by all the forms of the grotesque. To paint it in one stroke, so great is its vigor, its energy, its creative sap, at the dawn of letters, that it casts, at the outset, upon the threshold of modern poetry, three burlesque Homers: Ariosto in Italy, Cervantes in Spain, Rabelais in France.

It would be mere surplusage to dwell further upon the influence of the grotesque in the third civilization. Everything tends to show its close creative alliance with the beautiful in the so-called "romantic" period. Even among the simplest popular legends there are none which do not somewhere, with an admirable instinct, solve this mystery of modern art. Antiquity could not have produced *Beauty and the Beast.*

It is true that at the period at which we have arrived the predominance of the grotesque over the sublime in literature is clearly indicated. But it is a spasm of reaction, an eager thirst for novelty, which is but temporary; it is an initial wave which gradually recedes. The type of the beautiful will soon resume its rights and its rôle, which is not to exclude the other principle, but to prevail over it. It is time that the grotesque should be content with a corner of the picture in Murillo's royal frescoes, in the sacred pages of Veronese; content to be introduced in two marvelous *Last Judgments,* in which art will take a just pride, in the scene of fascination and horror with which Michelangelo will embellish the Vatican; in those awe-inspiring representations of the fall of man which Rubens will throw upon the arches of the Cathedral of Antwerp. The time has come when the balance between the two principles is to be established. A man, a poet-king, *Poeta soverano,* as Dante calls Homer, is about to adjust everything. The two rival genii combine their flames, and thence issues Shakespeare.

We have now reached the poetic culmination of modern times. Shakespeare is the drama; and the drama, which with the same breath molds the grotesque and the sublime, the terrible and the absurd, tragedy and comedy — the drama is the distinguishing characteristics of the third epoch of poetry, of the literature of the present day.

Thus, to sum up hurriedly the facts that we have noted thus far, poetry has three periods, each of which corresponds to an epoch of civilization: the ode, the epic, and the drama. Primitive times are lyrical, ancient times epical, modern times dramatic. The ode sings of eternity, the epic imparts solemnity to history, the drama depicts life. The characteristics of the first poetry is ingenuousness, of the second, simplicity, of the third, truth. The rhapsodists mark the transition from the lyric to the epic poets, as do the romancists that from the lyric to the dramatic poets. Historians appear in the second period, chroniclers and critics in the third. The characters of the ode are colossi — Adam, Cain, Noah; those of the epic are giants — Achilles, Atreus, Orestes; those of the drama are men — Hamlet, Macbeth, Othello. The ode lives upon the ideal, the epic upon the grandiose, the drama upon the real. Lastly, this threefold poetry flows from three great sources — the Bible, Homer, Shakespeare.

Such then — and we confine ourselves herein to noting a single result — such are the diverse aspects of thought in the different epochs of mankind and of civilization. Such are its three faces, in youth, in manhood, in old age. Whether one examines one literature by itself or all literatures *en masse,* one will always reach the same result: the lyric poets before the epic poets, the epic poets before the dramatic poets. In France, Malherbe before Chapelain, Chapelain before Corneille; in ancient Greece, Orpheus before Homer, Homer before Æschylus; in the first of all books, *Genesis* before *Kings, Kings* before *Job;* or to come back to that monumental scale of all ages of poetry, which we ran over a moment since, The Bible before the *Iliad,* the *Iliad* before Shakespeare.

In a word, civilization begins by singing of its dreams, then narrates its doings, and, lastly, sets about describing what it thinks. It is, let us say in passing, because of this last, that the drama, combining the most opposed qualities, may be at the same time full of profundity and full of relief, philosophical and picturesque.

It would be logical to add here that everything in nature and in life passes through these three phases, the lyric, the epic, and the dramatic, because everything is born, acts, and dies. If it were not absurd to confound the fantastic conceits of the imagination with the stern deductions of the reasoning faculty, a poet might say that the rising of the sun, for example, is a hymn, noon-day a brilliant epic, and sunset a gloomy drama wherein day and night, life and death, contend for mastery. But that would be poetry — folly, perhaps — and *what does it prove?*

Let us hold to the facts marshalled above; let us supplement them, too, by an important observation, namely that we have in no wise pretended to assign exclusive limits to the three epochs of poetry, but simply to set forth their predominant characteristics. The Bible, that divine lyric monument, contains in germ, as we suggested a moment ago, an epic and a drama — *Kings* and *Job*. In the Homeric poems one is conscious of a clinging reminiscence of lyric poetry and of a beginning of dramatic poetry. Ode and drama meet in the epic. There is a touch of all in each; but in each there exists a generative element to which all the other elements give place, and which imposes its own character upon the whole.

The drama is complete poetry. The ode and the epic contain it only in germ; it contains both of them in a state of high development, and epitomizes both. Surely, he who said: "The French have not the epic brain," said a true and clever thing; if he had said, "The moderns," the clever remark would have been profound. It is beyond question, however, that there is epic genius in that marvelous *Athalie,* so exalted and so simple in its sublimity that the royal century was unable to comprehend it. It is certain, too, that the series of Shakespeare's chronicle dramas presents a grand epic aspect. But it is lyric poetry above all that befits the drama; it never embarrasses it, adapts itself to all its caprices, disports itself in all forms, sometimes sublime as in Ariel, sometimes grotesque as in Caliban. Our era being above all else dramatic, is for that very reason eminently lyric. There is more than one connection between the beginning and the end; the sunset has some features of the sunrise; the old man becomes a child once more. But this second childhood is not like the first; it is as melancholy as the other is joyous. It is the same with lyric poetry. Dazzling, dreamy, at the dawn of civilization, it reappears, solemn and pensive, at its decline. The Bible opens joyously with *Genesis* and comes to a close with the threatening Apocalypse. The modern ode is still inspired, but is no longer ignorant. It meditates more than it scrutinizes; its musing is melancholy. We see, by its painful labor, that the muse has taken the drama for her mate.

To make clear by a metaphor the ideas that we have ventured to put forth, we will compare early lyric poetry to a placid lake which reflects the clouds and stars; the epic is the stream which flows from the lake, and rushes on, reflecting its banks, forests, fields and cities, until it throws itself into the ocean of the drama. Like the lake, the drama reflects the sky; like the stream, it reflects its banks; but it alone has tempests and measureless depths.

The drama, then, is the goal to which everything in modern poetry leads. *Paradise Lost* is a drama before it is an epic. As we know, it first presented itself to the poet's imagination in the first of these forms, and as a drama it always remains in the reader's memory, so prominent is the old dramatic framework still beneath Milton's epic structure! When Dante had finished his terrible *Inferno,* when he had closed its doors and nought remained save to give his work a name, the unerring instinct of his genius showed him that that multiform poem was an emanation of the drama, not of the epic; and on the front of that gigantic monument, he wrote with his pen of bronze: *Divina Commedia.*

Thus we see that the only two poets of modern times who are of Shakespeare's stature follow him in unity of design. They coincide with him in imparting a dramatic tinge to all our poetry; like him, they blend the grotesque with the sublime; and, far from standing by themselves in the great literary *ensemble* that rests upon Shakespeare, Dante and Milton are, in some sort, the two supporting abutments of the edifice of which he is the central pillar, the buttresses of the arch of which he is the keystone.

Permit us, at this point, to recur to certain ideas already suggested, which, however, it is necessary to emphasize. We have arrived, and now we must set out again.

On the day when Christianity said to man: "Thou art twofold, thou art made up of two beings, one perishable, the other immortal, one carnal, the other ethereal, one enslaved by appetites, cravings and passions, the other borne aloft on the wings of enthusiasm and reverie — in a word, the one always stooping toward the earth, its mother, the other always darting up toward heaven, its fatherland"— on that day the drama was created. Is it, in truth, anything other than that contrast of every day, that struggle of every moment, between two opposing principles which are ever face to face in life, and which dispute possession of man from the cradle to the tomb?

The poetry born of Christianity, the poetry of our time is, therefore, the drama; the real results from the wholly natural combination of two types, the sublime and the grotesque, which meet in the drama, as they meet in life and in creation. For true poetry, complete poetry, consists in the harmony of contraries. Hence, it is time to say aloud — and it is here above all that exceptions prove the rule — that everything that exists in nature exists in art.

On taking one's stand at this point of view, to pass judgment on our petty conventional rules, to disentangle all those scholastic labyrinths, to solve all those trivial problems which the critics of the last two centuries have laboriously built up about the art, one is struck by the promptitude with which the question of the modern stage is made clear and distinct. The drama has but to take a step to break all the spiders' webs with which the militia of Lilliput have attempted to fetter its sleep.

And so, let addle-pated pedants (one does not exclude the other) claim that the deformed, the ugly, the grotesque should never be imitated in art; one replies that the grotesque is comedy, and that comedy apparently makes a part of art. Tartuffe is not handsome, Pourceaugnac is not noble, but Pourceaugnac and Tartuffe are admirable flashes of art.

If, driven back from this entrenchment to their second line of customhouses, they renew their prohibition of the grotesque coupled with the sublime, of comedy melted into tragedy, we prove to them that, in the poetry of Christian nations, the first of these two types represents the human beast, the second the soul. These two stalks of art, if we prevent their branches from mingling, if we persistently separate them, will produce by way of fruit, on the one hand abstract vices and absurdities, on the other, abstract crime, heroism and virtue. The two types, thus isolated and left to themselves, will go each its own way, leaving the real between them, at the left hand of one, at the right hand of the other. Whence it follows that after all these abstractions there will remain something to represent — man; after these tragedies and comedies, something to create — the drama.

In the drama, as it may be conceived at least, if not executed, all things are connected and follow one another as in real life. The body plays its part no less than the mind; and men and events, set in motion by this twofold agent, pass across the stage, burlesque and terrible in turn, and sometimes both at once. Thus the judge will say: "Off with his head and let us go to dinner!" Thus the Roman Senate will deliberate over Domitian's turbot. Thus Socrates, drinking the hemlock and discoursing on the immortal soul and the only God, will interrupt himself to suggest that a cock be sacrificed to Æsculapius. Thus Elizabeth will swear and talk Latin. Thus Richelieu will submit to Joseph the Capuchin, and Louis XI to his barber, Maître Olivier le Diable. Thus Cromwell will say: "I have Parliament in my bag and the King in my pocket"; or, with the hand that signed the death sentence of Charles I, smear with ink the face of a regicide who smilingly returns the compliment. Thus Cæsar, in his triumphal car, will be afraid of overturning. For men of genius, however great they be, have always within them a touch of the beast which mocks at their intelligence. Therein they are akin to mankind in general, for therein they are dramatic. "It is but a step from the sublime to the ridiculous," said Napoleon, when he was convinced that he was mere man; and that outburst of a soul on fire illumines art and history at once; that cry of anguish is the résumé of the drama and of life.

It is a striking fact that all these contrasts are met with in the poets themselves, taken as men. By dint of meditating upon existence, of laying stress upon its bitter irony, of pouring floods of sarcasm and raillery upon our infirmities, the very men who make us laugh so heartily become profoundly sad. These Democrituses are Heraclituses as well. Beaumarchais was surly, Molière gloomy, Shakespeare melancholy.

The fact is, then, that the grotesque is one of the supreme beauties of the drama. It is not simply an appropriate element of it, but is oftentimes a necessity. Sometimes it appears in homogeneous masses, in entire characters, as Daudin, Prusias, Trissotin, Brid'oison, Juliet's nurse; sometimes impregnated with terror, as Richard III, Bégears, Tartuffe, Mephistopheles; sometimes, too, with a veil of grace and refinement, as Figaro, Osric, Mercutio, Don Juan. It finds its way in everywhere; for just as the most commonplace have their occasional moments of sublimity, so the most exalted frequently pay tribute to the trivial and ridiculous. Thus, often impalpable, often imperceptible, it is always present on the stage, even when it says nothing, even when it keeps out of sight. Thanks to it, there is no thought of monotony. Sometimes it injects laughter, sometimes horror, into tragedy. It will bring Romeo face to face with the apothecary, Macbeth with the witches, Hamlet with the grave-diggers. Sometimes it may, without discord, as in the scene between King Lear and his jester, mingle its shrill voice with the most sublime, the most dismal, the dreamiest music of the soul. That is what Shakespeare alone among

all has succeeded in doing, in a fashion of his own, which it would be no less fruitless than impossible to imitate — Shakespeare, the god of the stage, in whom, as in a trinity, the three characteristic geniuses of our stage, Corneille, Molière, Beaumarchais, seem united.

We see how quickly the arbitrary distinction between the species of poetry vanishes before common sense and taste. No less easily one might demolish the alleged rule of the two unities. We say *two* and not *three* unities, because unity of plot or of *ensemble,* the only true and well-founded one, was long ago removed from the sphere of discussion.

Distinguished contemporaries, foreigners and Frenchmen, have already attacked, both in theory and in practice, that fundamental law of the pseudo-Aristotelian code. Indeed, the combat was not likely to be a long one. At the first blow it cracked, so worm-eaten was that timber of the old scholastic hovel!

The strange thing is that the slaves of routine pretend to rest their rule of the two unities on probability, whereas reality is the very thing that destroys it. Indeed, what could be more improbable and absurd than this porch or peristyle or ante-chamber — vulgar places where our tragedies are obliging enough to develop themselves; whither conspirators come, no one knows whence, to declaim against the tyrant, and the tyrant to declaim against the conspirators, each in turn, as if they had said to one another in bucolic phrase: —

Alternis cantemus; amant alterna Camenæ.

Where did any one ever see a porch or peristyle of that sort? What could be more opposed — we will not say to the truth, for the scholastics hold it very cheap, but to probability? The result is that everything that is too characteristic, too intimate, too local, to happen in the ante-chamber or on the street-corner — that is to say, the whole drama — takes place in the wings. We see on the stage only the elbows of the plot, so to speak; its hands are somewhere else. Instead of scenes we have narrative; instead of tableaux, descriptions. Solemn-faced characters, placed, as in the old chorus, between the drama and ourselves, tell us what is going on in the temple, in the palace, on the public square, until we are tempted many a time to call out to them: "Indeed! then take us there! It must be very entertaining — a fine sight!" To which they would reply no doubt: "It is quite possible that it might entertain or interest you, but that isn't the question; we are the guardians of the dignity of the French Melpomene." And there you are!

"But," some one will say, "this rule that you discard is borrowed from the Greek drama." Wherein, pray, do the Greek stage and drama resemble our stage and drama? Moreover, we have already shown that the vast extent of the ancient stage enabled it to include a whole locality, so that the poet could, according to the exigencies of the plot, transport it at his pleasure from one part of the stage to another, which is practically equivalent to a change of stage-setting. Curious contradiction! the Greek theater, restricted as it was to a national and religious object, was much more free than ours, whose only object is the enjoyment, and, if you please, the instruction, of the spectator. The reason is that the one obeys only the laws that are suited to it, while the other takes upon itself conditions of existence which are absolutely foreign to its essence. One is artistic, the other artificial.

People are beginning to understand in our day that exact localization is one of the first elements of reality. The speaking or acting characters are not the only ones who engrave on the minds of the spectators a faithful representation of the facts. The place where this or that catastrophe took place becomes a terrible and inseparable witness thereof; and the absence of silent characters of this sort would make the greatest scenes of history incomplete in the drama. Would the poet dare to murder Rizzio elsewhere than in Mary Stuart's chamber? to stab Henri IV elsewhere than in Rue de la Ferronerie, all blocked with drays and carriages? to burn Jeanne d'Arc elsewhere than in the Vieux-Marché? to dispatch the Duc de Guise elsewhere than in that château of Blois where his ambition roused a popular assemblage to frenzy? to behead Charles I and Louis XVI elsewhere than in those ill-omened localities whence Whitehall or the Tuileries may be seen, as if their scaffolds were appurtenance of their palaces?

Unity of time rests on no firmer foundation than unity of place. A plot forcibly confined within twenty-four hours is as absurd as one confined within a peristyle. Every plot has its proper duration as well as its appropriate place. Think of administering the same dose of time to all events! of applying the same measure to everything! You would laugh at a cobbler who should attempt to put the same shoe on every foot. To cross unity of time and unity of place like the bars of a cage, and pedantically to introduce therein, in the name of Aristotle, all the deeds, all the nations, all the figures which Providence sets before us in such vast numbers in real life,— to proceed thus is to mutilate men and things, to cause history to make wry faces. Let us say, rather, that everything will die in the operation, and so the dogmatic mutilators reach their ordinary result: what was alive in the chronicles is dead in tragedy. That is why the cage of the unities often contains only a skeleton.

And then, if twenty-four hours can be comprised in two, it is a logical consequence that four hours may contain forty-eight. Thus Shakespeare's unity must be different from Corneille's. 'Tis pity!

But these are the wretched quibbles with which mediocrity, envy and routine has pestered genius for two centuries past! By such means the flight of our greatest poets has been cut short. Their wings have been clipped with the scissors of the unities. And what has been given us in exchange for the eagle feathers stolen from Corneille and Racine? Campistron.

We imagine that some one may say: "There is something in too frequent changes of scene which confuses and fatigues the spectator, and which produces a bewildering effect on his attention; it may be, too, that manifold transitions from place to place, from one time to another time, demand explanations which repel the attention; one should also avoid leaving, in the midst of a plot, gaps which prevent the different parts of the drama from adhering closely to one another, and which, moreover, puzzle the spectator because he does not know what there may be in those gaps." But these are precisely the difficulties which art has to meet. These are some of the obstacles peculiar to one subject or another, as to which it would be impossible to pass judgment once for all. It is for genius to overcome, not for treatises or poetry to evade them.

A final argument, taken from the very bowels of the art, would of itself suffice to show the absurdity of the rule of the two unities. It is the existence of the third unity, unity of plot — the only one that is universally admitted, because it results from a fact: neither the human eye nor the human mind can grasp more than one *ensemble* at one time. This one is as essential as the other two are useless. It is the one which fixes the viewpoint of the drama; now, by that very fact, it excludes the other two. There can no more be three unities in the drama than three horizons in a picture. But let us be careful not to confound unity with simplicity of plot. The former does not in any way exclude the secondary plots on which the principal plot may depend. It is necessary only that these parts, being skillfully subordinated to the general plan, shall tend constantly toward the central plot and group themselves about it at the various stages, or rather on the various levels of the drama. Unity of plot is the stage law of perspective.

"But," the customs-officers of thought will cry, "great geniuses have submitted to these rules which you spurn!" Unfortunately, yes. But what would those admirable men have done if they had been left to themselves? At all events they did not accept your chains without a struggle. You should have seen how Pierre Corneille, worried and harassed at his first step in the art on account of his marvelous work, *Le Cid,* struggled under Mairet, Claveret, d'Aubignac and Scudéri! How he denounced to posterity the violent attacks of those men, who, he says, made themselves "all white with Aristotle"! You should read how they said to him — and we quote from books

of the time: "Young man, you must learn before you teach; and unless one is a Scaliger or a Heinsius that is intolerable!" Thereupon Corneille rebels and asks if their purpose is to force him "much below Claveret." Here Scudéri waxes indignant at such a display of pride, and reminds the "thrice great author of *Le Cid* of the modest words in which Tasso, the greatest man of his age, began his apology for the finest of his works against the bitterest and most unjust censure perhaps that will ever be pronounced. M. Corneille," he adds, "shows in his replies that he is as far removed from that author's moderation as from his merit   The young man *so justly and gently reproved* dares to protest; thereupon Scudéri returns to the charge; he calls to his assistance the *Eminent Academy:* "Pronounce, O my Judges, a decree worthy of your eminence, which will give all Europe to know that *Le Cid* is not the masterpiece of the greatest man in France, but the least judicious performance of M. Corneille himself. You are bound to do it, both for your own private renown; and for that of our people in general, who are concerned in this matter; inasmuch as foreigners who may see this precious masterpiece — they who have possessed a Tasso or a Guarini — might think that our greatest masters were no more than apprentices."

These few instructive lines contain the everlasting tactics of envious routine against growing talent — tactics which are still followed in our own day, and which, for example, added such a curious page to the youthful essays of Lord Byron. Scudéri gives us its quintessence. In like manner the earlier works of a man of genius are always preferred to the newer ones, in order to prove that he is going down instead of up — *Mélite* and *La Galerie du Palais* placed above *Le Cid.* And the names of the dead are always thrown at the heads of the living — Corneille stoned with Tasso and Guarini (Guarini!), as, later, Racine will be stoned with Corneille, Voltaire with Racine, and as to-day, every one who shows signs of rising is stoned with Corneille, Racine and Voltaire. These tactics, as will be seen, are well-worn; but they must be effective as they are still in use. However, the poor devil of a great man still breathed. Here we cannot help but admire the way in which Scudéri, the bully of this tragic-comedy, forced to the wall, blackguards and maltreats him, how pitilessly he unmasks his classical artillery, how he shows the author of *Le Cid* "what the episodes should be, according to Aristotle, who tells us in the tenth and sixteenth chapters of his *Poetics*"; how he crushes Corneille, in the name of the same Aristotle "in the eleventh chapter of his *Art of Poetry,* wherein we find the condemnation of *Le Cid*"; in the name of Plato, "in the tenth book of his *Republic*"; in the name of Marcellinus, "as may be seen in the twenty-seventh book"; in the name of "the tragedies of *Niobe* and *Jephthah*"; in the name of the "*Ajax* of Sophocles"; in the name of "the example of Euripides"; in the name of "Heinsius, chapter six of the *Constitution of Tragedy;* and the younger Scaliger in his poems"; and finally, in the name of the Canonists and Jurisconsults, under the title "Nuptials." The first arguments were addressed to the Academy, the last one was aimed at the Cardinal. After the pin-pricks the blow with a club. A judge was needed to decide the question. Chapelain gave judgment. Corneille saw that he was doomed; the lion was muzzled, or, as was said at the time, the crow [*Corneille*] was plucked. Now comes the painful side of this grotesque performance: after he had been thus quenched at his first flash, this genius, thoroughly modern, fed upon the Middle Ages and Spain, being compelled to lie to himself and to hark back to ancient times, drew for us that Castilian Rome, which is sublime beyond question, but in which, except perhaps in *Nicomède,* which was so ridiculed by the eighteenth century for its dignified and simple coloring, we find neither the real Rome nor the true Corneille.

Racine was treated to the same persecution, but did not make the same resistance. Neither in his genius nor in his character was there any of Corneille's lofty asperity. He submitted in silence and sacrificed to the scorn of his time his enchanting elegy of *Esther,* his magnificent epic, *Athalie.* So that we can but believe that, if he had not been paralyzed as he was by the prejudices of his epoch, if he had come in contact less frequently with the classic cramp-fish, he would not have failed to introduce Locustes in his drama between Narcissus and Nero, and above all things would not have relegated to the wings the admirable scene of the banquet at which Seneca's pupil poisons Britannicus in the cup of reconciliation. But can we demand of the bird that he fly under the receiver of an air-pump? What a multitude of beautiful scenes the *people of taste* have cost us, from Scudéri to La Harpe! A noble work might be composed of all that their scorching breath has withered in its germ. However, our great poets have found a way none the less to cause their genius to blaze forth through all these obstacles. Often the attempt to confine them behind walls of dogmas and rules is vain. Like the Hebrew giant they carry their prison doors with them to the mountains.

But still the same refrain is repeated, and will be, no doubt, for a long while to come: "Follow the rules! Copy the models! It was the rules that shaped the models." One moment! In that case there are two sorts of models, those which are made according to the rules, and, prior to them, those according to which the rules were made. Now, in which of these two categories should genius seek a place for itself? Although it is always disagreeable to come in contact with pedants, is it not a thousand times better to give them lessons than to receive lessons from them? And then — copy! Is the reflection equal to the light? Is the satellite which travels unceasingly in the same circle equal to the central creative planet? With all his poetry Vergil is no more than the moon of Homer.

And whom are we to copy, I pray to know? The ancients? We have just shown that their stage has nothing in common with ours. Moreover, Voltaire, who will have none of Shakespeare, will have none of the Greeks, either. Let him tell us why: "The Greeks ventured to produce scenes no less revolting to us. Hippolytus, crushed by his fall, counts his wounds and utters doleful cries. Philoctetes falls in his paroxysms of pain; black blood flows from his wound. Œdipus, covered with the blood that still drops from the sockets of the eyes he has torn out, complains bitterly of gods and men. We hear the shrieks of Clytemnestra, murdered by her own son, and Electra, on the stage, cries: 'Strike! spare her not! she did not spare our father.' Prometheus is fastened to a rock by nails driven through his stomach and his arms. The Furies reply to Clytemnestra's bleeding shade with inarticulate roars. Art was in its infancy in the time of Æschylus, as it was in London in Shakespeare's time."

Whom shall we copy, then? The moderns? What! Copy copies! God forbid!

" But," some one else will object, " according to your conception of the art, you seem to look for none but great poets, to count always upon genius." Art certainly does not count upon mediocrity. It prescribes no rules for it, it knows nothing of it; in fact, mediocrity has no existence so far as art is concerned; art supplies wings, not crutches. Alas! d'Aubignac followed rules, Campistron copied models. What does it matter to art? It does not build its palaces for ants. It lets them make their ant-hill, without taking the trouble to find out whether they have built their burlesque imitation of its palace upon its foundation.

The critics of the scholastic school place their poets in a strange position. On the one hand they cry incessantly: " Copy the models!" On the other hand they have a habit of declaring that " the models are inimitable "! Now, if their craftsman, by dint of hard work, succeeds in forcing through this dangerous defile some colorless tracing of the masters, these ungrateful wretches, after examining the new *refaccimiento,* exclaim sometimes: " This doesn't resemble anything!" and sometimes: " This resembles everything!" And by virtue of a logic made for the occasion each of these formulæ is a criticism.

Let us then speak boldly. The time for it has come, and it would be strange if, in this age, liberty, like the light, should penetrate everywhere except to the one place where freedom is most natural — the domain of thought. Let us take the hammer to theories and poetic

systems. Let us throw down the old plastering that conceals the façade of art. There are neither rules nor models; or, rather, there are no other rules than the general laws of nature, which soar above the whole field of art, and the special rules which result from the conditions appropriate to the subject of each composition. The former are of the essence, eternal, and do not change; the latter are variable, external, and are used but once. The former are the framework that supports the house; the latter the scaffolding which is used in building it, and which is made anew for each building. In a word, the former are the flesh and bones, the latter the clothing, of the drama. But these rules are not written in the treatises on poetry. Richelet has no idea of their existence. Genius, which divines rather than learns, devises for each work the general rules from the general plan of things, the special rules from the separate *ensemble* of the subject treated; not after the manner of the chemist, who lights the fire under his furnace, heats his crucible, analyzes and destroys; but after the manner of the bee, which flies on its golden wings, lights on each flower and extracts its honey, leaving it as brilliant and fragrant as before.

The poet — let us insist on this point — should take counsel therefore only of nature, truth, and inspiration which is itself both truth and nature. "Quando he," says Lope de Vega,

Quando he de escrivir una comedia,
Encierro los preceptos con seis llaves.

To secure these precepts " six keys " are none too many, in very truth. Let the poet beware especially of copying anything whatsoever — Shakespeare no more than Molière, Schiller no more than Corneille. If genuine talent could abdicate its own nature in this matter, and thus lay aside its original personality, to transform itself into another, it would lose everything by playing this rôle of its own double. It is as if a god should turn valet. We must draw our inspiration from the original sources. It is the same sap, distributed through the soil, that produces all the trees of the forest, so different in bearing power, in fruit, in foliage. It is the same nature that fertilizes and nourishes the most diverse geniuses. The poet is a tree that may be blown about by all winds and watered by every fall of dew; and bears his works as his fruit, as the *fablier* of old bore his fables. Why attach one's self to a master, or graft one's self upon a model? It were better to be a bramble or a thistle, fed by the same earth as the cedar and the palm, than the fungus or the lichen of those noble trees. The bramble lives, the fungus vegetates. Moreover, however great the cedar and the palm may be, it is not with the sap one sucks from them that one can become great one's self. A giant's parasite will be at best a dwarf. The oak, colossus that it is, can produce and sustain nothing more than the mistletoe.

Let there be no misunderstanding: if some of our poets have succeeded in being great, even when copying, it is because, while forming themselves on the antique model, they have often listened to the voice of nature and to their own genius — it is because they have been themselves in some one respect. Their branches became entangled in those of the near-by tree, but their roots were buried deep in the soil of art. They were the ivy, not the mistletoe. Then came imitators of the second rank, who, having neither roots in the earth, nor genius in their souls, had to confine themselves to imitation. As Charles Nodier says: "After the school of Athens, the school of Alexandria." Then there was a deluge of mediocrity; then there came a swarm of those treatises on poetry, so annoying to true talent, so convenient for mediocrity. We were told that everything was done, and God was forbidden to create more Molières or Corneilles. Memory was put in place of imagination. Imagination itself was subjected to hard-and-fast rules, and aphorisms were made about it: "To imagine," says La Harpe, with his naïve assurance, "is in substance to remember, that is all."

But Nature! Nature and truth!— And here, in order to prove that, far from demolishing art, the new ideas aim only to reconstruct it more firmly and on a better foundation, let us try to point out the impassable limit which in our opinion, separates reality according to art from reality according to nature. It is careless to confuse them as some ill-informed partisans of *romanticism* do. Truth in art cannot possibly be, as several writers have claimed, *absolute* reality. Art cannot produce the thing itself. Let us imagine, for example, one of those unreflecting promoters of absolute nature, of nature viewed apart from art, at the performance of a romantic play, say *Le Cid.* "What's that?" he will ask at the first word. "The Cid speaks in verse? It isn't *natural* to speak in verse."—"How would you have him speak, pray?"—"In prose." Very good. A moment later, "How's this!" he will continue, if he is consistent; "the Cid· is speaking French!"—"Well?"— "Nature demands that he speak his own language; he can't speak anything but Spanish."

We shall fail entirely to understand, but again — very good. You imagine that this is all? By no means: before the tenth sentence in Castilian, he is certain to rise and ask if the Cid who is speaking is the real Cid, in flesh and blood. By what right does the actor, whose name is Pierre or Jacques, take the name of the Cid? That is *false.* There is no reason why he should not go on to demand that the sun should be substituted for the footlights, *real* trees and *real* houses for those deceitful wings. For, once started on that road, logic has you by the collar, and you cannot stop.

We must admit, therefore, or confess ourselves ridiculous, that the domains of art and of nature are entirely distinct. Nature and art are two things — were it not so, one or the other would not exist. Art, in addition to its idealistic side, has a terrestrial, material side. Let it do what it will, it is shut in between grammar and prosody, between Vaugelas and Richelet. For its more capricious creations, it has formulæ, methods of execution, a complete apparatus to set in motion. For genius there are delicate instruments, for mediocrity, tools.

It seems to us that some one has already said that the drama is a mirror wherein nature is reflected. But if it be an ordinary mirror, a smooth and polished surface, it will give only a dull image of objects, with no relief — faithful, but colorless; every one knows that color and light are lost in a simple reflection. The drama, therefore, must be a concentrating mirror, which, instead of weakening, concentrates and condenses the colored rays, which makes of a mere gleam a light, and of a light a flame. Then only is the drama acknowledged by art.

The stage is an optical point. Everything that exists in the world — in history, in life, in man — should be and can be reflected therein, but under the magic wand of art. Art turns the leaves of the ages, of nature, studies chronicles, strives to reproduce actual facts (especially in respect to manners and peculiarities, which are much less exposed to doubt and contradiction than are concrete facts), restores what the chroniclers have lopped off, harmonizes what they have collected, divines and supplies their omissions, fills their gaps with imaginary scenes which have the color of the time, groups what they have left scattered about, sets in motion anew the threads of Providence which work the human marionettes, clothes the whole with a form at once poetical and natural, and imparts to it that vitality of truth and brilliancy which gives birth to illusion, that prestige of reality which arouses the enthusiasm of the spectator, and of the poet first of all, for the poet is sincere. Thus the aim of art is almost divine: to bring to life again if it is writing history, to create if it is writing poetry.

It is a grand and beautiful sight to see this broad development of a drama wherein art powerfully seconds nature; of a drama wherein the plot moves on to the conclusion with a firm and unembarrassed step, without diffuseness and without undue compression; of a drama, in short, wherein the poet abundantly fulfills the multifold object of art, which is to open to the spectator a double prospect, to illuminate at the same time the interior and the exterior of mankind: the exterior by their speech and their acts, the interior, by asides and monologues; to bring together, in a word, in the same picture, the drama of life and the drama of conscience.

It will readily be imagined that, for a work of this kind, if the poet must *choose* (and he must), he should choose, not the *beautiful,* but the *characteristic.* Not that it is advisable to "make local color," as they say to-day; that is, to add as an afterthought a few discordant touches here and there to a work that is at best utterly conventional and false. The local color should not be on the surface of the drama, but in its substance, in the very heart of the work, whence it spreads of itself, naturally, evenly, and, so to speak, into every corner of the drama, as the sap ascends from the root to the tree's topmost leaf. The drama should be thoroughly impregnated with this color of the time, which should be, in some sort, in the air, so that one detects it only on entering the theater, and that on going forth one finds one's self in a different period and atmosphere. It requires some study, some labor, to attain this end; so much the better. It is well that the avenues of art should be obstructed by those brambles from which everybody recoils except those of powerful will. Besides, it is this very study, fostered by an ardent inspiration, which will ensure the drama against a vice that kills it — the *commonplace.* To be commonplace is the failing of shortsighted, short-breathed poets. In this tableau of the stage, each figure must be held down to its most prominent, most individual, most precisely defined characteristic. Even the vulgar and the trivial should have an accent of their own. Like God, the true poet is present in every part of his work at once. Genius resembles the die which stamps the king's effigy on copper and golden coins alike.

・　　・　　・　　・　　・　　・

ALEXANDRE DUMAS FILS

Alexandre Dumas, the illegitimate son of the celebrated novelist, was born at Paris in 1824. His father recognized him at an early age, and gave him his name. The youth was educated at the Institution Goubaux and the College Bourbon, and after leaving school was initiated into the riotous life his father himself was accustomed to. From these early experiences Dumas fils made ample use in his plays and prefaces, and *La Dame aux camélias* was the immediate result of his observations. It was written to extricate the young man from a mass of debts, which he was enabled to pay with the royalties. He had, however, attempted to follow his father's profession, and a number of more or less mediocre novels belong to his early period. For over thirty years he produced plays regularly and fought bravely to make the theater an instrument of public usefulness. He died at Marly-le-Roy in 1895.

Dumas fils was an incorrigible adherent of the "useful" drama — the drama which should expose vices, remedy evils, and be in general an instrument of public and private good. Somewhat late in his career he wrote an open letter to Sarcey — *A M. Sarcey,*— which has since been reprinted in the first series of the *Entr' actes*—where he clearly states his ideals as to the function of the drama.

He says: " I realize that the prime requisites of a play are laughter, tears, passion, emotion, interest, curiosity: to leave life at the cloak-room; but I maintain that if, by means of all these ingredients, and without minimizing one of them, I can exercise some influence over society; if, instead of treating effects I can treat causes; if, for example, while I satirize and describe and dramatize adultery I can find means to force people to discuss the problem, and the law-maker to revise the law, I shall have done more than my part as a poet, I shall have done my duty as a man." Dumas' many plays and more numerous prefaces and articles bear out and develop this basic idea. Together with Emile Augier, he brought the thesis-play to its highest point of development. His influence is seen in many of Ibsen's works, though the Norwegian was not so directly didactic. More especially in France has his preoccupation with moral utility borne fruit, particularly in the plays of Paul Hervieu and Eugène Brieux.

PREFACE TO A PRODIGAL FATHER [1]

[*Préface* (to) *Un Père prodigue*]

(1868)

To-day, by your leave, we shall discuss technique. We should never fail to attribute to technique the importance due it in dramatic art. Technique is so important that it sometimes happens that technique is mistaken *for* art. Of all the various forms which can be assumed by thought, the drama is that which most nearly approaches the plastic arts; dramatic art cannot be practiced before one knows all the material methods — with this difference, however, that in all the other arts these methods can be learned, but in this, one divines them, or, rather, has them within him.

One may become a painter, a sculptor, even a musician, by study — but not a dramatist. One is a dramatist at the beginning, the way one is dark or light, without wishing it. It is a freak of nature that has so constructed your vision as to enable you to see in a certain way,

1 Re-printed from *The Drama* (Feb., **1917**). Translated for the first time in English, by the editor. Complete text.— Ed.

which is not absolutely the true way, but which for the time being *appears* to be the only way whereby you can make others see what you have seen. The man who is called to write for the stage reveals this very rare faculty at his first attempt, in a farce at school or in a parlor charade. It is the science of optics and perspective which allows him to depict a human being, a character, a passion, an act of the soul, with a single scratch of the pen. The illusion is so complete that it often happens that when the spectator turns reader and wishes to revive for his personal satisfaction the emotion he has experienced together with the crowd, he not only cannot find that emotion in the *written* word and action, but he cannot find the place itself in the play where he experienced it. A word, a look, a gesture, a pause, a purely atmospheric combination of effects had held him spell-bound. That is the genius of technique — if these two words can stand side by side. A play is to other forms of literature what a ceiling fresco is to wall- or easel-paintings. Woe be unto the painter if he forgets that his fresco must be seen from a distance, with the light coming from below!

A man of no value as thinker, moralist, philosopher, writer, may be a first-rate dramatist; that is to say, as manipulator of the purely external actions of human beings; and, on the other hand, in order to be accepted in the theater as thinker, moralist, philosopher, and writer, it is indispensable that he be endowed with the same particular qualities as the man of no value (except as technician). In short, if one would be master in this art he must first be proficient in its technique.

If it be a fact that the natural endowments cannot be given to those who are without them, nothing, on the other hand, is easier than to recognize them in those who do possess them.

The first of these endowments, the most indispensable, the one that dominates and commands, is logic — which includes good sense and clearness. The truth may be absolute or relative, according to the importance of the subject and the *milieu*. But the logic must be implacable from beginning to end; it must never lose sight of this end, while developing the idea and the action. The dramatist must unflaggingly place before the spectator that part of the being or thing for or against which he aims to draw a conclusion. Then comes the science of contrasts; that is to say, the blacks, the shadows, the balancing, the totality of effect, harmony; then conciseness and tempo, which prevent the listener's being distracted or reflecting, or taking a momentary breath, to discuss in his own mind with the author; the knowledge of foreground and background, keeping the figure which ought to stand out in the high-light from falling into the shadow, and those which belong in the middle-distance from assuming a position of too great prominence; and then the mathematical precision, inexorable, fatal, which multiplies scene by scene, even by event, act by act, up to the dénouement, which must be the sum-total, the Q. E. D.; and, lastly, the exact conception of our limitations, which forbid us to make our picture larger than the frame, because the dramatist who has even the most to say must say it all between eight in the evening and midnight, out of which period he must subtract one hour for entr'-actes, and repost for the audience.

I have not mentioned imagination, because the theater — besides the author — supplies this in the actors, scenery, and accessories. It puts into flesh and bone, in spoken words, in images, before the spectator, the individuals, places, and things which he would be forced to imagine were he reading a book. Nor have I spoken of invention, because in our profession there is no such thing. We need invent nothing; we have only to observe, remember, feel, coördinate, restore, in a particular form, what every spectator ought to have recalled to him immediately after having felt or seen, without having been conscious of it. As for basis, the real; as for facts, what is possible; as for means, what is ingenious; that is all that can rightfully be asked of us.

Does the art of the drama, which requires a technique all its own, likewise demand a style of its own? Yes. No one is altogether a dramatist unless he has his manner of writing, just as he has his manner of seeing, a manner altogether personal. A play should be written as if it were never intended to be other than read. The production is nothing but a reading by many people who do not care or know how to read. A play succeeds as a result of people's going to the theater; it becomes firmly established as a result of being read. The spectator gives it a certain notoriety, the reader gives it lasting fame. The play that we have no desire to read without having seen, nor to re-read after having seen it, is dead, no matter if it enjoys a run of two thousand nights. Only, it is necessary, if the work is to survive without the aid of the interpreter, that the writer's style be such as to convey to the reader the solidity, proportions, form, and suggestions of tone, which are applauded by the spectator in a theater. The style of the greatest writers can be of no help to the dramatist except as a sort of reference: it can teach him only a few words, and there are even a number of these which he must eschew from his vocabulary, because they lack the relief, strength, character — I had almost said triviality — which are necessary to the end of setting the true human being in action on a false ground. Molière's vocabulary is very limited; he invariably uses the same expressions: he plays the gamut of the whole of the human soul on five octaves and a half.

Written style, that is, thought presented directly to the reader, can be fixed once for all. Whoever writes a story, be it merely a dialogue destined to be read and nothing more, can make use of the form of a master of his own class — Bossuet, Voltaire, Pascal, Jean-Jacques, Sand, Hugo, Lamartine, Renan, Théophile Gautier, Sainte-Beuve, Flaubert, About; and not only will he not be blamed, but rather praised for paying homage to tradition and purism. Perhaps even his original sources will not be perceived, but his influence will be felt; he will be proclaimed a writer, and will actually be one, even if his elegant and pure style fails to contain a single original idea. We see examples of this every day, books in which the style leads one to believe that there is a solid foundation of thought.

There is nothing of the sort in the drama. The moment we imitate the style of one of our masters, we are not hailed as respectful disciples; we are tiresome imitators. What we ought to imitate in those masters is their manner of observing and not of stating. Each of them has his own trade-mark, which cannot be imitated without our being accused of counterfeiting. Read Corneille, Racine, Molière, Marivaux, Beaumarchais — to speak only of the dead — and notice the difference in their styles. Notice how each one of them has poured his particular essence into the flowing river which is called language! Need this style of the drama be correct? No, so far as mere grammar is concerned. It must first of all be clear, colored, penetrating, incisive. *Je t'aimais inconstant; qu'aurais-je fait, fidèle?* is an adorable grammatical slip, which was moreover not necessitated by the meter; and yet, if he had had to express the same idea in prose, Racine, *who knew his technique,* would have written it with the same error. There are certain expressions, certain

words which in themselves possess a saliency, a sonority, a form which render them necessary, which require their use even at the risking of the author's reputation as a literary man. Academic writers understand nothing of our particular form, and consider us barbarians. It was this misunderstanding of the two different styles that caused La Bruyère to enunciate the absurd truth that, " All Molière needed was to avoid jargon, and to *write purely."*

Fénelon thought and spoke like La Bruyère when he wrote of our leader.

La Bruyère was right and wrong, that is why I said " absurd truth," in reference to the opinion of a writer whom I revere more than any one else does, the author who put our language on a firm basis, who inundated the world with truths which he would have been incapable of stating in the theater, because he would have worked everything out in detail instead of modeling it in high relief.

Suppose now that you are Fénelon — an assumption which certainly cannot wound your feelings. Your connection with the church will not allow you to go to the theater; nevertheless, you wish to keep abreast of the times, because you are a writer, a prince's tutor, and you live in the most literary age that France had yet known. You have heard a certain Molière spoken of — a fellow who has been excommunicated — an actor, a *valet de chambre* of the King, who, some say, writes immoral comedies; others — Boileau, for instance — sublime works. And you read these lines:

" Pour moi, je *vous l'avoue,* je me re-*pais* un *peu* de gloire. Les applaudissements me touchent, et je tiens *que,* dans tous les beaux-arts, c'est un supplice assez fâcheux *que* de se produire à des sots, *que* d'essuyer sur des compositions la barbarie d'un stupide. Il y a plaisir, ne m'en parlez point, a travailler pour des personnes *qui* soient capables de sentir les délicatesses d'un art, *qui* sachent faire un doux acceuil aux beautés d'un ouvrage, et, par de chatouillantes approbations, vour régaler de votre travail. Que, la récompense la plus agréable *qu'on* puisse recevoir des choses *que* l'on fait, c'est de les voir connues, de les voir caresser d'un applaudissement *qui* vous honore, il n'y a rien, à mon avis, *qui* nous paye mieux *que* cela de toutes nos fatigues; et ce sont des douceurs exquises *que* des louanges éclairées."

You are Fénelon! You stop at that point, and you throw aside *Le Bourgeois gentilhomme* and say, " A poor writer." And you think no more about it.

Now, it happens that you are not Fénelon — and the case is extremely easy; you are the first-comer and you are interested in literature; naturally you know the works of Fénelon and Molière. You are asked which one you would prefer to be; which would you choose? Molière, without a shadow of doubt. That is all I have to say.

Such errors, so shocking when they are read, not only pass unperceived in the theater beneath the intonation of the actor and the movement of the play, but even sometimes add to the life of the whole, just as small eyes, a large nose, a huge mouth and disordered hair, often add more grace, character, passion and distinction to a face, than Greek perfection of feature. That Greek type has been accepted as an ideal type of beauty because some sort of set ideal must be established in every art; but after this has been once established, each artist goes his own way according to his particular temperament, and overthrows tradition if he is sufficiently strong to do so. Thus it is that new schools are founded, and men discuss them. This is not a bad way of killing time, which has its *longueurs,* [dull periods] as we say in the theater.

" Then should we allow errors on top of errors, as in the style of M. Scribe? Is that sufficient? "

Exactly, if the style of M. Scribe expresses ideas. What do I care for the material of a dress, provided the dress itself be beautiful?

" But then, will M. Scribe perish because of his form? "

Another mistake! No one ever perishes because of his form; he lives or dies according to the matter. Translation offers a proof of my assertion. We can daily admire foreign writers in translations which are far better in style than the plays of M. Scribe, because, since the thought is strong and solid, it stands forth and takes shape above and beyond the soft and colorless form, like a mountain-peak emerging from the morning mist. Think like Æschylus and write like M. Scribe; we ask nothing more of you. Unfortunately, or rather fortunately, such a discrepancy is impossible. Expression will always, in spite of one's desires, equal thought: it will be just and firm if the thought is great; feeble and bombastic if the thought is vulgar or common. Inspiration of idea and sincerity are lacking in M. Scribe, hence the want of expression; he is not himself convinced, he cannot be eloquent. *A liqueur sans valeur, vase sans prix.* [A worthless liquid for a worthless jar.] But M. Scribe did not try to write comedies; he tried merely to write *for the theater;* he had no wish either to preach, to instruct, or to correct people; he wanted only to amuse them. He did not seek that glory which immortalizes the dead, but contented himself with success which affords popularity to the living and riches which they can enjoy. He was a prestidigitator of the first rank — a marvelous juggler. He exposed a situation to you as if it were a *muscade* [2] and led you, in tears and laughter and terror, during two, three, or five acts, through to the dénouement. It was always the same, and he never said anything. The language used in conducting these tricks was intended to throw the audience off the scent and gain time until the arrival of the promised effect, the moment when the *muscade* becomes a shell of '48, only to return to the juggler's goblet at the end. It was merely by the juggler's sleight of hand that the trick was done. The performance over, the candles were snuffed out, the *muscades* put back into the sack, goblets placed one within the other; the excitement passed, life and movement went — there remain in the mind and soul of the spectator never an idea, a thought, no enthusiasm, no hope, no remorse, no agitation, no consolation. People have seen, heard, had their curiosity aroused; laughed, wept — which is a great deal, but they have learned nothing. Perhaps they afterward referred to the play; they never discussed it. In short, M. Scribe possessed all the qualities pertaining to talent, but not one indicative of genius. Three times only did his char-

2 Ball of spice used by jugglers.— Ed.

acters assume the appearance, not of actual life, but of the epic life: and that was when Meyerbeer lent his powerful life-giving breath. Once, and once only, did he succeed in prying open the gate of the temple and stealing upon the mysteries of the Good Goddess: he bordered upon great comedy in *Camaraderie*, in which he had as much to be proud, as to be ashamed of. The day that play was performed, he proved that he might have belonged to the family of true observers, and that by concentrating his powers, thinking less of riches and more of his art, he might have been a great dramatist. But he did not will it; his will be done!

Still, the drama owes one real innovation to him, an innovation that may be taken as his own particular theory of the drama. Up to his time love and marriage with the loved woman were considered the final recompense of the comedy hero. The poet made this woman out to be as beautiful, as pure, as passionate, in short, as interesting as possible. M. Scribe thought that he ought to add to all these qualities, another quality of the first order: a good three per cent. income. There is no happiness possible in the crowning marriage unless the young lady brings the young man a fat dowry. And so well did M. Scribe's ideal coincide with that of his public, that the public recognized him at once as its representative; and during a third of a century the high-priest of this bourgeois religion celebrated mass every night on the altar of the half-crown, turning round from time to time in the midst of the ceremony, to say to his flock, with his hand on the double-columned Evangel: *Ego vobiscum!*

Collaborators, pupils, imitators, amateurs, were not lacking in this facile, agreeable, productive enterprise, which perverted public taste and led away from serious art. The Scribe had passed into the customs and manners of the times. There was no safety outside his beaten path. Unfortunately, the master abused his technique, and people ended by tiring of the everlasting colonels, widows, rich heiresses whose dowries were the object of continual pursuit; of artists supported by bankers' wives; of Legion of Honor crosses obtained in adultery; of all-powerful millionaires; of

shop-girls who led queens by the nose. People felt the need of hearing something that smacked of commonsense, which should encourage and console humanity, which is neither so selfish nor so foolish as M. Scribe would have us think. Shortly after him came a robust-minded, loyal and refined man [Emile Augier], and *Gabrielle,* with its simple and touching action, and noble and beautiful language, was the first work of revolt against the older conventional drama. The intelligent, fatherly, and eloquent husband was exalted on the same stage where for twenty years had been held up to ridicule the everlastingly foolish, blinded husband, deceived shamelessly by his amorous wife, and where had been two women, a traveling salesman, an artist, or else a diplomat dressed, warmed, and decorated by his mistress, and finally made rich by his cousin — a sop to his remorse!

"Why this prejudice against M. Scribe?" you will ask. "Why this attack?"

I am not attacking M. Scribe; I am not beating the drum in front of my own shop in order to prevent your going into my neighbor's; but, having set out to discuss this matter of technique, I am studying and explaining the man who is its living incarnation, and who has pushed the science of it so far that, as I said earlier, some have mistaken that technique for art itself. No one knew better than M. Scribe — who was without conviction, without simplicity, without any philosophic end in view — how to set into action if not a character or an idea, at least a subject, and above all a situation, and to extract from that subject and that situation, their logical theatric effect; none better than he understood how to assimilate the latest ideas and adapt them to the stage, sometimes on a scale and in a spirit absolutely opposed to the combinations of the one from whom he received the idea. He turned everything to his own advantage: the temperament, the début, the name, the beauty, the ugliness, the stoutness, the thinness, the arms, the feet, the expression, the color of the hair, the elegance, the stupidity, the cleverness, of the actor or actress; even the tastes, passions, prejudices, hypocrisies, cowardice of the public he was addressing, from which he tried to take its fortune and its liberty. He was the most extraordinary improviser we have had in the history of our drama; he was the most expert at manipulating characters that had no life. He was the shadow-Shakespeare.

Now, if among the four hundred plays he wrote, either by himself or in collaboration, you place *Il ne faut jurer de rien,* or *Un Caprice,* or *Il faut qu'une porte soit ouverte ou fermée* — that is to say, a tiny *proverbe* written by the most naïve and inexpert of dramatists [Alfred de Musset] — you will see all Scribe's plays dissolve and go up into thin air, like mercury when heated to three hundred and fifty degrees; because Scribe worked for his audience without putting into his labor anything of his soul or heart, while Musset wrote with heart and soul for the heart and soul of humanity. His sincerity gave him, though he was unaware of this, all the resources which were the sole merit of Scribe.

" And the conclusion? "

Is that the dramatist who knows *man* as Balzac did, and the *theater* as Scribe did, will be the greatest of the world's dramatists.

EMILE ZOLA

Emile Edouard Charles Antoine Zola was born at Paris in 1840. His father having died when the boy was young, he would have had little education had not he and his mother been assisted by relatives. The youth was sent to school, and showed his interest in literature by writing a short play. On leaving school, he went to work in a publisher's office. At the same time he was contributing stories and critical reviews to the newspapers. When he left the office he devoted his time to art criticism, but not succeeding very well, he turned his hand to the writing of fiction. His vast epic series of novels—*Les Rougon-Macquart*—is an imposing literary monument comparable, at least in scope, with Balzac's *Comédie humaine.* He was always a champion of Naturalism, and he tried his hand at some half-dozen Naturalistic plays, the best of which is without doubt *Thérèse Raquin,* which was produced in 1873. His *Préface* to the printed play, and the Prefaces to the volume and to the other two plays in the volume, are Zola's most trenchant contributions to the Naturalistic program. For some years he wrote dramatic criticism, and the greater part of his essays were subsequently reprinted in *Le Naturalisme au théâtre* (1881) and *Nos Auteurs dramatiques* (1881). Zola died at Paris in 1902.

Although Zola was not himself a great Naturalistic dramatist, he has contributed a body of criticism and theory fuller and more influential than that of any other Naturalist. Henry Becque would logically have been the prophet of the movement, but his non-dramatic writings, *Querelles littéraires* (1899) and *Souvenirs d'un auteur dramatique* (1895), contain little dramatic theory and are mainly of a personal and polemic character. Jean Jullien, in his two volumes of *Le Théâtre vivant* (1892–96) is, next to Zola, the greatest exponent of Naturalism in the theater, but his plays are not of great importance. Zola's dramatic theories were formed chiefly to bring literary men into the theater with plays based upon observation. He mercilessly attacked the school of the " well-made play " and pleaded for greater sincerity, a deeper appreciation of the values of life and a closer adherence to external detail.

PREFACE TO THÉRÈSE RAQUIN [1]
[*Préface* (to) *Thérèse Raquin*]
(1873)

. . . . . .

. . . It is by no means my intention to make my play a rallying standard. It has striking shortcomings, toward which no one is more severe than myself; if I were to criticize it, there would be only one thing I should not attack: the author's very obvious desire to bring the theater into closer relation with the great movement toward truth and experimental science which has since the last century been on the increase in every manifestation of the human intellect. The movement was started by the new methods of science; thence, Naturalism revolutionized criticism and history, in submitting man and his works to a system of precise analysis, taking into account all circumstances, environment, and "organic cases." Then, in turn, art and letters were carried along with the current: painting became realistic — our landscape school killed the historical school —; the novel, that social and individual study with its extremely loose frame-work, after growing and growing, took up all the activities of man, absorbing little by little the various classifications made in the rhetorics of the past. These are all undeniable facts. We have now come to the birth of the true, that is the great, the only force of the century. Everything advances in a literary epoch. Whoever wishes to retreat or turn to one side, will be lost in the general dust. This is why I am absolutely convinced that in the near future the Naturalist movement will take its place in the realm of the drama, and bring with it the power of reality, the new life of modern art.

In the theater, every innovation is a delicate matter. Literary revolutions are slow in making themselves felt. And it is only logical that this should be the last citadel of falsehood: where the true belongs. The public as a whole resents

having its habits changed, and the judgments which it passes have all the brutality of a death-sentence. But there comes a time when the public itself becomes an accomplice of the innovators; this is when, imbued with the new spirit, weary of the same stories repeated to it countless times, it feels an imperious desire for youth and originality.

I may be mistaken, but I believe that this is the situation of our public to-day. The historical drama is in its death-throes, unless something new comes to its assistance: that corpse needs new blood. It is said that the operetta and the dramatic fantasy have killed the historical drama. This is not so: the historical drama is dying a natural death, of its own extravagances, lies, and platitudes. If comedy still maintains its place amid the general disintegration of the stage it is because comedy clings closer to actual life, and is often true. I defy the last of the Romanticists to put upon the stage a heroic drama; at the sight of all the paraphernalia of armor, secret doors, poisoned wines and the rest, the audience would only shrug its shoulders. And melodrama, that bourgeois offspring of the romantic drama, is in the hearts of the people more dead than its predecessor; its false sentiment, its complications of stolen children and discovered documents, its impudent gasconnades, have finally rendered it despicable, so that any attempt to revive it proves abortive. The great works of 1830 will always remain advance-guard works, landmarks in a literary epoch, superb efforts which laid low the scaffoldings of the classics. But, now that everything is torn down, and swords and capes rendered useless, it is time to base our works on truth. To substitute the Romantic for the Classic tradition would be a refusal to take advantage of the liberty acquired by our forbears. There should no longer be any school, no more formulas, no standards of any sort; there is only life itself, an immense field where

1 Extracts translated, for the first time into English, by the editor.— Ed.

each may study and create as he likes.

I am attempting no justification of my own cause, I am merely expressing my profound conviction — upon which I particularly insist — that the experimental and scientific spirit of the century will enter the domain of the drama, and that in it lies its only possible salvation. Let the critics look about them and tell me from what direction help is to be expected, or a breath of life, to rehabilitate the drama? Of course, the past is dead. We must look to the future, and the future will have to do with the human problem studied in the frame-work of reality. We must cast aside fables of every sort, and delve into the living drama of the two-fold life of the character and its environment, bereft of every nursery tale, historical trapping, and the usual conventional stupidities. The decayed scaffoldings of the drama of yesterday will fall of their own accord. We must clear the ground. The well-known receipts for the tying and untying of an intrigue have served their time; now we much seek a simple and broad picture of men and things, such as Molière might write. Outside of a few scenic conventions, all that is now known as the " science of the theater " is merely a heap of clever tricks, a narrow tradition that serves to cramp the drama, a ready-made code of language and hackneyed situations, all known and planned out beforehand, which every original worker will scorn to use.

Naturalism is already stammering its first accents on the stage. I shall not cite any particular work, but among the plays produced during these past two years, there are many that contain the germ of the movement whose approach I have prophesied. I am not taking into account plays by new authors, I refer especially to certain plays of dramatists who have grown old in the métier, who are clever enough to realize the new transformation that is taking place in our literature. The drama will either die, or become modern and realistic.

It is under the influence of these ideas that I have dramatized *Thérèse Raquin*. As I have said, there are in that novel a subject, characters and *milieu* constituting, to my mind, excellent elements for the tentative of which I have dreamed. I tried to make of it a purely human

study, apart from every other interest, and go straight to the point; the action did not consist in any story invented for the occasion, but in the inner struggles of the characters; there was no logic of facts, but a logic of sensation and sentiment; and the dénouement was the mathematical result of the problem as proposed. I followed the novel step by step; I laid the play in the same room, dark and damp, in order not to lose relief or the sense of impending doom; I chose supernumerary fools, who were unnecessary from the point of view of strict technique, in order to place side by side with the fearful agony of my protagonists the drab life of every day; I tried continually to bring my setting into perfect accord with the occupations of my characters, in order that they might not *play,* but rather *live,* before the audience. I counted, I confess, and with good reason, on the intrinsic power of the drama to make up, in the minds of the audience, for the absence of intrigue and the usual details. The attempt was successful, and for that reason I am more hopeful for the plays I *shall* write than for *Thérèse Raquin.* I publish this play with vague regret, and with a mad desire to change whole scenes.

The critics were wild: they discussed the play with extreme violence. I have nothing to complain of, but rather thank them. I gained by hearing them praise the novel from which the play was taken, the novel which was so badly received by the press when it was first published. To-day the novel is good, and the drama is worthless. Let us hope that the play would be good were I able to extract something from it that the critics should declare bad. In criticism, you must be able to read between the lines. For instance, how could the old champions of 1830 be indulgent toward *Thérèse Raquin?* Supposing even that my merchant's wife were a queen and my murderer wore an apricot-colored cloak? And if at the last Thérèse and Laurent should take poison from a golden goblet filled to the brim with Syracusan wine? But that nasty little shop! And those lower middle-class shop-keepers that presume to participate in a drama of their own in their own house, with their oil-cloth table-cover! It is certain that the last of the Romanticists, even if they found some talent in my play, would have denied it absolutely, with the beautiful injustice of literary passion. Then there were the critics whose beliefs were in direct opposition to my own; these very sincerely tried to persuade me that I was wrong to burrow in a place which was not their own. I read these critics carefully; they said some excellent things, and I shall do my best to profit by some of their utterances which particularly appealed to me. Finally, I have to thank those sympathetic critics, of my own age, those who share my hopes, because, sad to say, one rarely finds support among one's elders: one must grow along with one's own generation, be pushed ahead by the one that follows, and attain the idea and the manner of the time. This, in short, is the attitude of the critics: they mentioned Shakespeare and Paul de Kock. Well, between these two extremes there is a sufficiently large place

into which I can step.

I must acknowledge publicly my gratitude to M. Hippolyte Hostein, who has seen fit to grant my work his artistic patronage. In him I found not a show-master, but a friend, a true collaborator, original and broad-minded. Without him, *Thérèse Raquin* would long have remained locked up in my desk. To bring it forth it was necessary for me to happen by chance upon a director who believed, as I did, in the necessity of rehabilitating the theater by going to the reality which is found in the modern world. While an operetta was making the fortune of one of his neighbors, it was really a beautiful thing to see M. Hippolyte Hostein, in the midst of the summer season, willing to lose money on my play. I am eternally grateful to him.

Paris, 25 July, 1873.

FERDINAND BRUNETIÈRE

Ferdinand Brunetière was born at Toulon in 1849. · He attended school at Lorient, and later at Marseilles. He had traveled considerably before he reached Paris in 1867, where he completed his studies at the Lycée Louis-le-Grand. He was a studious young man, and took many courses afterward — at the Louvre, in particular, and at the Ecole des Beaux-arts, where he met Taine. At the same time he was a constant attendant at the theater. Failing in 1869 to pass the examination for entrance into the Ecole Normale he found himself without funds and without a position. The war came and Brunetière enlisted. After the war he tutored in language, history, and philosophy. He met Bourget not long after, who made an opening for him on the staff of the *Revue des deux mondes,* of which Brunetière later became the editor. His first important contribution was *Le Roman naturaliste* (1875). He continued to write articles of various sorts, which were later collected in the *Essais critiques.* He later secured a position as teacher at the Ecole Normale. His theory of literary evolu-

tion was set forth in books, articles, and lectures, and applied in his important *Histoire de la littérature française classique.* In 1891 he further developed his ideas in a course of lectures at the *Odéon* on the history of the French drama. In the early nineties he taught at the Sorbonne and in 1893 was elected to membership in the Academy. Toward 1895, after he had become editor of the *Revue des deux mondes,* he practically ceased literary criticism. Among his late contributions to critical theory was his famous *Law of the Drama,* published as preface to Noël and Stoullig's *Les Annales du théâtre et de la musique.* His last years were devoted to religious and political controversy. In 1897 he came to the United States, where he lectured. He later went round the world, preaching Catholicism, to which he was converted in 1894 or before. He died in 1906.

Brunetière's writings on the drama include a large number of articles and books, but the theory for which he is perhaps best-known was not definitely formulated until his lectures, *Les*

Epoques du théâtre français, were delivered at the *Odéon* in 1891–92, and published shortly after. But the final statement is in the *Loi du théâtre,* a preface to the *Annales du théâtre et de la musique* for 1893 (published 1894). In Brander Matthews' notes to the English translation of *Brunetière's Law of the Drama,* he says: "The theory as finally stated by Brunetière is his own, although it seems to have had its origin in the doctrine of the 'tragic conflict' declared by Hegel and taken over by Schlegel and Coleridge. The idea that tragedy must present a struggle is as ancient as Aristotle. . . . But Brunetière goes beyond Hegel and Aristotle. He subordinates the idea of struggle to the idea of volition. And in so doing he broadens the doctrine to include not tragedy only but all the manifold forms of the drama. . . .

Attention was first directed to it [the law] in the opening chapter on the '*Art of the Dramatist*' in the '*Development of the Drama*' by Professor Brander Matthews, published in 1903." The Law seems to have attracted more attention in English-speaking countries, especially in America, than elsewhere. Clayton Hamilton, in *The Theory of the Theatre* (1910), and in *Studies in Stagecraft* (1914), William Archer in *Playmaking* (1912), Brander Matthews in *The Development of the Drama* (1903), Henry Arthur Jones in the Introduction to the English translation of the Law (1914), Barrett H. Clark in *The Continental Drama of To-day* (1913), and *The British and American Drama of To-day* (1914), are a few of the writers who have considered the theory.

THE LAW OF THE DRAMA [1]

[*La Loi du théâtre*]

(1894)

If some "First-Nighter" or some "Old Playgoer" who was not born when our acquaintance began, should be surprised, my dear Noël, to see me writing this preface for your *Annales du théâtre et de la musique,* certainly no one is better qualified than you to answer him, and tell him how great has been my love for the theater. That was about 1867 — more than twenty-five years ago; and we were not rich. But somehow or other we had managed to make the acquaintance of several leaders of the *claque,* and for twenty-five sous — sometimes for ten, on repertory nights — we bought the right to sit in the pit at the Comédie-Française — and to applaud as little as we chose. The Gymnase and the Vaudeville where there was no pit, cost us more. Were those, as the saying is, the "good old days"? I will not answer for you, but for my part, I am not one of those who regret their youth; and if ever I do, I shall have greatly changed. And yet we had our happy moments, particularly after the theater, along the

deserted quays, or the next day, under the trees in the Luxembourg, when we would discuss which was the better in the *Mariage de Figaro,* Got with his careful, intelligent, quiet rendering, or the broader, less studied, more spontaneous rendering of Coquelin, who since . . . but at that time he was the spoiled child of the House of Molière. Were you not translating Goethe's plays then? And for a change, you would go to see *King Lear* at the Odéon. . . . These memories are becoming a little confused to my mind. But if I remember rightly, we preferred above all the plays of Musset: the *Caprices de Marianne, Le Chandelier, On ne badine pas avec l'amour, Il ne faut jurer de rien* . . . and, to be frank, I care less, much less about him to-day, but I am not ashamed of having liked him. And how many performances, by how many actors, have we seen of *Horace* and *Britannicus, Esther* and *Athalie, Tartuffe* and the *Misanthrope,* the *Barbier de Séville,* in which no one has equaled Bressant, and the *Mariage de Figaro,* in which no one has replaced Leroux. I like to think that we thus contributed our little share to bring the classics back to their place of honor.

---

[1] Re-printed, complete, from the translation by Philip M. Hayden, from Brunetière's *The Law of The Drama* (New York, 1914).— Ed.

For they are played more often now than then. Didn't you and I wait until we were quite grown-up to see *Bajazet*, for example, or *Bérénice?* We were in despair.

If now I have almost ceased to attend the theater, if I only follow it from afar, it is my own fault, and mine alone. What would you have? The fifteen lectures which I delivered at the Odéon, nearly three years ago, on the *Époques du Théâtre français* left me sated, saturated, wearied with the subject,— gorged, if I may say so. But they were not without their usefulness for me; and, between ourselves, if some of my auditors were kind enough to like them, it was I who profited the most. Instead of applying myself, confining myself, as I had done before, and as we all do, to the examination of *Polyeucte* or of *Andromaque*, and following my personal taste or the demand of the moment, I had to try to grasp the essence and the connection of the works in the history of our stage, and to deduce from them, if I could, the theory, or, to speak more modestly, a theory of dramatic action. And so, when you invited me this year to write the Preface for your interesting *Annales* I accepted at once. The theory, uncertain and still vague in my lectures, had taken definite form. It had become broader, it seems to me, by becoming more simple. A child could understand it. And do not tell me that you are tempted to distrust it, precisely because of this simplicity! On the contrary, my dear friend, it is not art, science, nor life that are complex, it is the ideas that we form for ourselves in regard to them. Whoever grasps a principle, grasps all its applications. But the very diversity, multiplicity, perversity, and apparent contradiction of these applications, prevent him from seeing the principle. Will any argument, however ingenious, alter the fact that all poetry is either lyric, epic, or dramatic? Certainly not. And if the *Cid*, if *Phèdre*, if *Tartuffe*, if the *Légataire universel*, if the *Barbier de Séville*, if the *Camaraderie*, if the *Demi-monde*, if *Célimare le bien-aimé* are dramatic, does it not follow that all these works, so different, must nevertheless have not merely a few points of contact or vague resemblance, but an essential characteristic in common?

What is this characteristic? That is what I shall try to explain.

Observe, if you please, that I ask only one — no more — and that I leave the dramatist complete freedom in development. That is where I depart from the old school of criticism, that believed in the mysterious power of " Rules " in their inspiring virtues; and consequently we see the old-school critics struggling and striving, exercising all their ingenuity to invent additional Rules; read, for example, the *Cours de littérature analytique* by Népomucène Lemercier. But the truth is that there are no Rules in that sense; there never will be. There are only conventions, which are necessarily variable, since their only object is to fulfill the essential aim of the dramatic work, and the means of accomplishing this vary with the piece, the time, and the man. Must we, like Corneille, regularly subordinate character to situation; invent, construct, the situations first, and then, if I may so express it, put the characters inside? We may do so, certainly, since he did it, in the *Cid* and in *Horace*, in *Polyeucte* and in *Rodogune*. Or shall we, like Racine, subordinate situation to character, find the characters first, study them, master them, and then seek the situations which will best bring out their different aspects? We may do so, and that is what he did, as you know, in *Andromaque*, in *Britannicus*, in *Bajazet*, in *Phèdre*. There is an example, then, of a Rule which may be violated, and Racine's dramaturgy is none the less dramatic for being the opposite of Corneille's dramaturgy. Take another Rule. Shall we oblige the dramatic author to observe the Three Unities? I reply that he will not be hampered by them, if he can choose, like Racine, subjects which properly or necessarily adjust themselves of their own accord, so to speak, to the rule: *Bérénice*, *Iphigénie*, *Esther* . . . But if he chooses like Shakespere, subjects 'which are checked by it in their free development, or diverted merely, we will relieve him of the Rule: and *Othello*, *Macbeth*, *Hamlet*, will still be drama. This is another example of a Rule which can be turned in various ways. Or again, shall we mingle tragic and comic, tears and laughter, terror and joy, the sublime and the grotesque, Ariel and Caliban, Bottom and

Titania, Triboulet and François I, Don Guritan and Ruy Blas? Shakespere and Hugo have done it, but Euripides and Sophocles seem to have carefully avoided it; and who will deny that they were both right? We do not feel the need of a comic element to enliven or vary the severe beauty of *Œdipus at Colonus,* but we should certainly be sorry to have *King Lear* deprived of his Fool. It is unnecessary to continue. Evidently, all these alleged Rules effect or express only the most superficial characteristics of the drama. Not only are they not mysterious, they are not in the least profound. Whether we observe them or not, drama is drama with them or without them. They are only devices which may at any time give place to others. It all depends on the subject, the author, and the public. This is the point to add that there is something which does not depend on them.

To convince ourselves of that fact, let us examine more carefully two or three works whose dramatic value is universally recognized, and let us take them from species as different as the *Cid,* the *Ecole des femmes,* and *Célimare le bien-aimé.* Chimène *wants* to avenge her father; and the question is how she will succeed. Arnolphe *wants* to marry Agnès, whose stupidity will guarantee her fidelity; and the question is whether he will succeed. Célimare *wants* to get rid of the widowers of his former mistresses; and the question is what means he will employ. But Célimare is hampered in the execution of his *will* by his fear of the vengeance of his friends. Arnolphe is disturbed in the execution of his *will* by the young madcap Horace, who arouses love, and with love a *will,* in Agnès' heart. Chimène is betrayed in the execution of her *will* by the love which she feels for Rodrigue. On the other hand, Chimène's *will* is checked and broken by the insurmountable obstacle which she encounters in a *will* superior to her own. Arnolphe, who is far from being a fool, sees all the plans of his *will* tricked by the conspiracy of youth and love. And Célimare, by the power of his *will,* triumphs over the widowers of his mistresses. Nothing would be easier than to multiply examples. Take the *Tour de Nesle,* the *Demi-monde,* and the *Chapeau de paille d'Italie.* Fadinard

wants to obtain a Leghorn hat to replace that of Mme. Beauperthuis; and the whole farce consists in the remarkable character of the means which he employs. Suzanne d'Ange *wants* to marry M. de Nanjac; and the whole drama consists only in the means which she formulates. Buridan *wants* to exploit the monstrous secret which exists between him and Marguerite de Bourgogne; and the whole melodrama consists only of the succession of the means which he invents. Buridan's *will* is opposed in its work by Marguerite's pride. Suzanne's *will* is countered by that of Olivier de Jalin. And Fadinard's *will* becomes entangled in the means which he seeks to satisfy it. But chance, more powerful than Fadinard's *will,* brings success at the moment when he least expects it. Olivier's *will* wins out over Suzanne's. And by the exercise of their *will,* Marguerite and Buridan fall into the trap set by their own *will.* Is it not easy now to draw the conclusion? In drama or farce, what we ask of the theater, is the spectacle of a *will* striving towards a goal, and conscious of the means which it employs.

This essential characteristic of dramatic composition distinguishes it, in the first place, from lyric composition, which I shall not discuss, in order not to complicate the question unnecessarily, and from the composition of the novel, with which, especially in our day, it has so often been confused. "Who is not for us is against us,"— you know the phrase. The drama and the novel are not the same thing; or rather, each is exactly the opposite of the other. Read *Gil Blas* again, or go again to see the *Mariage de Figaro.* The setting and the character are the same. Beaumarchais made a trip to Spain, but Lesage's novel was none the less his principal model. I have shown elsewhere that we find in the monologue of Figaro whole sentences from *Gil Blas.* Only, whereas nothing happens to Gil Blas that he has actually willed, it is on the contrary Figaro's *will* that conducts the plot of his marriage. Let us pursue this point of comparison.

Gil Blas, like everybody else, wants to live, and if possible to live agreeably. That is not what we call having a will. But Figaro wants a certain definite thing, which is to prevent Count Almaviva from exercising on Susanne the seigneurial privilege. He finally succeeds,— and I grant, since the statement has been made, that it is not exactly through the means which he had chosen, most of which turn against him; but nevertheless he has constantly willed what he willed. He had not ceased to devise means of attaining it, and when these means have failed, he has not ceased to invent new ones. That is what may be called *will*, to set up a goal, and to direct everything toward it, to strive to bring everything into line with it. Gil Blas really has no goal. Highway robber, doctor's assistant, servant to a canon, to an actress, or to a nobleman, all the positions which he occupies one after another, come to him from fortune or chance. He has no plan, because he has no particular or definite aim. He is subject to circumstances; he does not try to dominate them. He does not *act;* he is *acted upon.* Is not the difference evident? The proper aim of the novel, as of the epic — of which it is only a secondary and derived form, what the naturalists call a sub-species or a variety — the aim of the *Odyssey,* as of *Gil Blas,* of the *Knights of the Round Table,* as of *Madame Bovary,* is to give us a picture of the influence which is exercised upon us by all that is outside of ourselves. The novel is therefore the contrary of the drama; and if I have successfully set forth this opposition, do you not see the consequences which result from it?

It is thus that one can distinguish action from motion or agitation; and that is certainly worth while. Is it action to move about? Certainly not, and there is no true action except that of a will conscious of itself, conscious, as I was saying, of the means which it employs for its fulfillment, one which adapts them to its goal, and all other forms of action are only imitations, counterfeits, or parodies. The material or the subject of a novel or of a play may therefore be the same at bottom; but they become drama or novel only by the manner in which they are treated; and the manner is not merely different, it is opposite. One will never be able, therefore, to transfer to the stage any novels except those which are already dramatic; and note well that they are dramatic only to the extent to which their heroes are truly the archi-

tects of their destiny. It follows that one could make a novel of the *Mariage de Figaro,* but one will never make a drama or a comedy of *Gil Blas.* One might make a novel of Corneille's *Rodogune,* one will never make a drama of Rousseau's *Héloïse.* The general law of the theater, thus defined, gives us, then, in the first place, a sure means of perceiving what in any subject there is of the novel or the drama. The fact is that people do not know this well enough; and the Naturalist school in France has committed no worse error than confusing the conditions of the two species.

The same law provides, further, the possibility of defining with precision the dramatic species — about as one does the biological species; and for that it is only necessary to consider the particular obstacle against which the will struggles. If these obstacles are recognized to be insurmountable, or reputed to be so, as were, for example, in the eyes of the ancient Greeks, the decrees of Fate; or, in the eyes, of the Christians, the decrees of Providence; as are, for us, the laws of nature, or the passions aroused to frenzy and becoming thus the internal fatality of Phædra and of Roxane, of Hamlet or of Othello; — it is tragedy. The incidents are generally terrifying, and the conclusion sanguinary, because in the struggle which man undertakes to make against fate, he is vanquished in advance, and must perish. Suppose now that he has a chance of victory, just one, that he still has in himself the power to conquer his passion; or suppose that, the obstacles which he is striving to overcome being the work of his fellow men, as prejudice, for example, or social conventions, a man is for that very reason capable of surmounting them,— that is the drama properly speaking, romantic drama or social drama, *Hernani* or *Antony,* the *Fils naturel* or *Madame Caverlet.* Change once more the nature of the obstacle, equalize, at least in appearance, the conditions of the struggle, bring together two opposing wills, Arnolphe and Agnès, Figaro and Almaviva, Suzanne d'Ange and Olivier de Jalin — this is comedy. *Don Sanche d'Aragon,* heroic comedy,— you know this title of one of Corneille's plays. *Bérénice,* for the same reason, is hardly a tragedy. But instead of locating the obstacle in an opposing will, conscious and mistress of its acts, in a social convention or in the fatality of destiny, let us locate it in the irony of fortune, or in the ridiculous aspect of prejudice, or again in the disproportion between the means and the end,— that is farce, that is the *Légataire universel*, the *Chapeau de paille d'Italie*.

I do not say after that, that the types are always pure. In the history of literature or of art, as in nature, a type is almost never anything but an ideal, and consequently a limit. Where is the man among us, where is the woman, who embodies the perfection of the sex and of the species? There is moreover a natural relationship, we might say a consanguinity between adjoining species. Is a mulatto or a quadroon white or black? They are related to both. Likewise there may be an alliance or mixture of farce and comedy, of drama and tragedy. *Célimare* is almost a comedy; the *Cid* is almost a melodrama. It is nevertheless useful to have carefully defined the species; and if the law should only teach authors not to treat a subject of comedy by the devices of farce, that would be something. The general law of the theater is defined by the action of a will conscious of itself; and the dramatic species are distinguished by the nature of the obstacles encountered by this will.

And the quality of will measures and determines, in its turn, the dramatic value of each work in its species. Intelligence rules in the domain of speculation, but the will governs in the field of action, and consequently in history. It is the will which gives power; and power is hardly ever lost except by a failure or relaxation of the will. But that is also the reason why men think there is nothing grander than the development of the will, whatever the object, and that is the reason for the superiority of tragedy over the other dramatic forms. One may prefer for one's own taste a farce to a tragedy; one ought even to prefer a good farce to a mediocre tragedy, that goes without saying; and we do it every day. One cannot deny that tragedy is superior to farce: *Athalie* to the *Légataire universel*, and *Ruy Blas* to the *Trois Epiciers*. Another reason sometimes given is that it implies indifference to death, but that is the same reason, if the supreme effort

of the will is to conquer the horror of death. But shall we say that comedy is superior to farce, and why? We will say that, and for the same reason, because the obstacles against which Crispin contends in the *Légataire universel* do not exist, strictly speaking; they are only an invention of Regnard; and so the will is exerting itself to no effect. The goal is only a lure, so the action is only a game. And we will say in conclusion that one drama is superior to another drama according as the quantity of will exerted is greater or less, as the share of chance is less, and that of necessity greater. Who doubts that *Bajazet* is very much superior to *Zaïre*? If you seek the true reason, you will find it here. *Zaïre* would not finish if Voltaire did not intervene at every moment in his work; but given the characters of Bajazet and Roxane, they develop as if of themselves; and does it not really seem as if Racine confined himself to observing their action?

I will not continue. But I cannot refrain from noting the remarkable confirmation that this law finds in the general history of the theater. As a matter of fact, it is always at the exact moment of its national existence when the will of a great people is exalted, so to speak, within itself, that we see its dramatic art reach also the highest point of its development, and produce its masterpieces. Greek tragedy is contemporary with the Persian wars. Æschylus fought the Mede; and while the fleets were engaꞡ d in the waters of Salamis, on that very day, the legend has it, Euripides was born. Legend is perhaps not more true, but it is often more profound than history. Consider the Spanish theater: Cervantes, Lope de Vega, Calderon, belong to the time when Spain was extending over all of Europe, as well as over the New World, the domination of her will, or rather, as great causes do not always produce their literary effects at once, they are of the time immediately following. And France in the seventeenth century? The greatest struggle that our fathers made to maintain, within as without, the unity of the French nation, or to bring it to pass, was at the end of the sixteenth century, and was under Henry IV, under Richelieu, under Mazarin. The development of the theater followed immediately. I see, indeed, that great strengthenings of the national will have not always been followed by a dramatic renaissance, in England in the eighteenth century, for example, or in Germany to-day; but what I do not see, is a dramatic renaissance whose dawn has not been announced, as it were, by some progress, or some arousing of the will. Think of the theater of Lessing, of Schiller, of Goethe and remember what Frederick the Great had done, a few years before, without knowing it perhaps, to give to the Germany of the eighteenth century a consciousness of herself and of her national genius. The converse is no less striking. If it is extremely rare that a great development of the novel is contemporary even with a great development of the theater — if in France in particular, when the Molières, the Corneilles, the Racines have appeared, we have seen the *Artamènes*, the *Faramons*, the *Astrées*, sink gently into oblivion, or again if *Gil Blas, Manon Lescaut, Marianne* are contemporary, at the beginning of the eighteenth century, with an exhaustion only too certain of the dramatic vein,— it is because in literature as in nature, the competition is always keenest between the neighboring species; and the soil is rarely rich enough for two rival varieties to prosper, develop and multiply in peace. But it is also because, being as we have seen, the contrary each of the other, drama and novel do not answer to the same conception of life. *Gil Blas* and *Figaro,* I repeat, belong to the same family; they cannot belong to the same time; and between them, if you take the trouble to examine carefully, there is all the interval that separates the relaxation of the will in the time of the Regency, from the vigorous recovery that it makes on the eve of the Revolution. What can be more singular? But if the theater has for its object to present the development of the will, what can be more natural? The Orientals have no drama, but they have novels. That is because they are fatalists, or determinists if you prefer, which amounts to the same thing, for to-day at least; and when the Greeks had a drama, they no longer had novels, I mean epics; they no longer had an *Odyssey.*

You see the reason, don't you? Are we free agents? Or are we not? Are we the masters of events? Or are we only their dupes, their playthings, their victims? I don't know; at this moment I don't care to know, and you may believe that I am not going to dabble in metaphysics here. But in any case it appears that our belief in our freedom is of no small assistance in the struggle that we undertake against the obstacles which prevent us from attaining our object. And I grant that in order to succeed in dominating nature, or even in reforming society, it is not necessary to believe one's self capable of it. There is always an acquired momentum of the human race that aids the insufficiency of individual effort. But that is not without value either; for one does not attempt the impossible. The bond between the belief in free will and the exertion of the will explains therefore pretty well the favor or the moral support given, at certain epochs to an art whose essential object is the representation of the power of the will. A question of fitness, or, as we say, of adaptation to environment. The belief in determinism is more favorable to the progress of the novel, but the belief in free will is more favorable to the progress of dramatic art. Men of action, Richelieu, Condé, Frederick, Napoleon, have always been fond of the theater.

And why may we not see here, in a sort of weakening of the will among us, one at least of the reasons for what we have generally called, for the last ten years, the dramatic crisis? Drama does not " go," they tell us. Comedy is languishing. Farce is dying out. As a matter of fact, I am sure that there is some exaggeration in the wail. Your *Annales* would suffice to prove it, if need be. But that the contemporary drama is inferior as a whole to the drama of only twenty or twenty-five years ago, it seems to me difficult not to admit. On the other hand, the philosophers, or even mere observers, complain that the power of will is weakening, relaxing, disintegrating. People no longer know how to exert their will, they say, and I am afraid that they have some right to say it. We are broken-winded, as the poet says. We are abandoning ourselves. We are letting ourselves drift with the current. Are you not tempted to see here something more than a mere coincidence? For my part, I see here the explanation of the crisis, and at the same time another proof of the truth of the Law of the theater.

Permit me to stop here. . . .

As I was saying, my dear Noël,— no, I have not yet said it — the subject is one of those which would fill a book, and I have not time to write the book, and if I did write it, you would not be able to use it. In the meantime, since you have believed that the idea of the book might deserve discussion, I have been glad to take the opportunity which you offered me to express it. I have been able only to indicate rapidly a few of its applications, but I noted others in my lectures at the Odéon; and now I see an infinite number of them. If your readers should see still more, that is about all I could desire. I say about all, for there is one thing more I should like, and that is, that they should grasp clearly the difference between the idea of Law and the idea of Rule: the Rule being always limited by its very expression, incapable of exceeding it without destroying itself, always narrow, consequently unbending, rigid, or so to speak, tyrannical; and the Law, on the contrary, inevitable by definition and so fundamentally immutable; but broad, supple, flexible in its application, very simple and very general at the same time, very rich in applications, and, without ceasing to be the Law, always ready to be enriched by whatever reflection, experience, or history contribute in confirmations to explain it, or in contradictions to be absorbed in it.

HENRI BERGSON

Henri-Louis Bergson, a leading figure in twentieth-century philosophy, was born in Paris in 1859 and lectured for many years at the Collège de France. He devoted himself especially to re-examining problems of metaphysics and asserted the importance of the *élan vital,* an animating impulse which develops in the course of human evolution. In addition, he altered and extended our understanding of the nature of time, thereby influencing the fiction of Marcel Proust. His gifts of imagination and style made him a literary figure—a fact attested by his being awarded the Nobel Prize for Literature in 1928. His best-known works in philosophy are *Creative Evolution* (1907) and *The Two Sources of Morality and Religion* (1932). His study of comedy, *Le Rire, Essai sur la signification du comique* (1900), translated as *Laughter,* interprets the phenomenon of laughter as a corrective response to rigidity, to the human being who assumes the qualities of a machine; for its examples, it draws especially upon the French tradition, notably Molière and Labiche. Bergson died in 1941.

THE COMIC ELEMENT [1]

(1900)

A man, running along the street, stumbles and falls; the passers-by burst out laughing. They would not laugh at him, I imagine, could they suppose that the whim had suddenly seized him to sit down on the ground. They laugh because his sitting down is involuntary. Consequently, it is not his sudden change of attitude that raises a laugh, but rather the involuntary element in this change,— his clumsiness, in fact. Perhaps there was a stone on the road. He should have altered his pace or avoided the obstacle. Instead of that, through lack of elasticity, through absentmindedness and a kind of physical obstinacy, *as a result,*

[1] Extracts from the essay *Laughter* [*Le Rire*], included in *Comedy* (New York, 1956), © 1956 by Wylie Sypher. Reprinted by permission of Doubleday & Co., Inc.

in fact, of rigidity or of momentum, the muscles continued to perform the same movement when the circumstances of the case called for something else. That is the reason of the man's fall, and also of the people's laughter. . . .

Now, let us go a little further. Might not certain vices have the same relation to character that the rigidity of a fixed idea has to intellect? Whether as a moral kink or a crooked twist given to the will, vice has often the appearance of a curvature of the soul. Doubtless there are vices into which the soul plunges deeply with all its pregnant potency, which it rejuvenates and drags along with it into a moving circle of reincarnations. Those are tragic vices. But the vice capable of making us comic is, on the contrary, that which is brought from without, like a ready-made frame into which we are to step. It lends us its own rigidity instead of borrowing from us our flexibility. We do not render it more complicated; on the contrary, it simplifies us. Here, as we shall see later on in the concluding section of this study, lies the essential difference between comedy and drama. A drama, even when portraying passions or vices that bear a name, so completely incorporates them in the person that their names are forgotten, their general characteristics effaced, and we no longer think of them at all, but rather of the person in whom they are assimilated; hence, the title of a drama can seldom be anything else than a proper noun. On the other hand, many comedies have a common noun as their title: *l'ovare, le Joueur,* etc. Were you asked to think of a play capable of being called *le Jaloux,* for instance, you would find that *Sganarelle* or *George Dandin* would occur to your mind, but not *Othello: le Jaloux* could only be the title of a comedy. The reason is that, however intimately vice, when comic, is associated with persons, it none the less retains its simple, independent existence, it remains the central character, present though invisible, to which the characters in flesh and blood on the stage are attached. At times it delights in dragging them down with its own weight and making them share in its tumbles. More frequently, however, it plays on them as on an instrument or pulls the strings as though they were puppets. Look closely:

you will find that the art of the comic poet consists in making us so well acquainted with the particular vice, in introducing us, the spectators, to such a degree of intimacy with it, that in the end we get hold of some of the strings of the marionette with which he is playing, and actually work them ourselves; this it is that explains part of the pleasure we feel. Here, too, it is really a kind of automatism that makes us laugh—an automatism, as we have already remarked, closely akin to mere absentmindedness. To realise this more fully, it need only be noted that a comic character is generally comic in proportion to his ignorance of himself. The comic person is unconscious. As though wearing the ring of Gyges with reverse effect, he becomes invisible to himself while remaining visible to all the world. A character in a tragedy will make no change in his conduct because he will know how it is judged by us; he may continue therein even though fully conscious of what he is and feeling keenly the horror he inspires in us. But a defect that is ridiculous, as soon as it feels itself to be so, endeavours to modify itself or at least to appear as though it did. Were Harpagon to see us laugh at his miserliness, I do not say that he would get rid of it, but he would either show it less or show in differently. Indeed, it is in this sense only that laughter "corrects men's manners." It makes us at once endeavour to appear what we ought to be, what some day we shall perhaps end in being. . . .

We will now pass from the comic element in *forms* to that in *gestures* and *movements.* Let us at once state the law which seems to govern all the phenomena of this kind. It may indeed be deduced without any difficulty from the considerations stated above.

The attitudes, gestures and movements of the human body are laughable in exact proportion as that body reminds us of a mere machine. . . .

Let us go on to society. As we are both in and of it, we cannot help treating it as a living being. Any image, then, suggestive of the notion of a society disguising itself, or of a social masquerade, so to speak, will be laughable. Now, such a notion is formed when we perceive anything inert or stereotyped, or simply ready-made, on the surface of living society. There we have rigidity over again, clashing with the inner suppleness of life. The ceremonial side of social life must, therefore, always include a latent comic element, which is only waiting for an opportunity to burst into full view. It might be said that ceremonies are to the social body what clothing is to the individual body: they owe their seriousness to the fact that they are identified, in our minds, with the serious object with which custom associates them, and when we isolate them in imagination, they forthwith lose their seriousness. For any ceremony, then, to become comic, it is enough that our attention be fixed on the ceremonial element in it, and that we neglect its matter, as philosophers say, and think only of its form. Every one knows how easily the comic spirit exercises its ingenuity on social actions of a stereotyped nature, from an ordinary prize-distribution to the solemn sitting of a court of justice. Any form or formula is a ready-made frame into which the comic element may be fitted. . . .

. . . *Any arrangement of acts and events is comic which gives us, in a single combination, the illusion of life and the distinct impression of a mechanical arrangement.*

1. *The Jack-in-the-box.*—As children we have all played with the little man who springs out of his box. You squeeze him flat, he jumps up again. Push him lower, and he shoots up still higher. Crush him down beneath the lid, and often he will send everything flying. It is hard to tell whether or not the toy itself is very ancient, but the kind of amusement it affords belongs to all time. It is a struggle between two stubborn elements, one of which, being simply mechanical, generally ends by giving in to the other, which treats it as a plaything. A cat playing with a mouse, which from time to time she releases like a spring, only to pull it up short with a stroke of her paw, indulges in the same kind of amusement.

We will now pass on to the theatre, beginning with a Punch and Judy show. No sooner does the policeman put in an appearance on the stage than, naturally enough, he receives a blow which fells him. He springs to his feet, a second blow lays him flat. A repetition of the offence is followed by a repetition of the punishment. Up and down the constable flops and hops with the uniform rhythm of the bending and release of a spring, whilst the spectators laugh louder and louder.

Now, let us think of a spring that is rather of a moral type, an idea that is first expressed, then repressed, and then expressed again; a stream of words that bursts forth, is checked, and keeps on starting afresh. Once more we have the vision of one stubborn force, counteracted by another, equally pertinacious. This vision, however, will have discarded a portion of its materiality. No longer is it Punch and Judy that we are watching, but rather a real comedy. . . .

. . . *In a comic repetition of words we generally find two terms: a repressed feeling which goes off like a spring, and an idea that delights in repressing the feeling anew.*

When Dorine is telling Orgon of his wife's illness, and the latter continually interrupts her with inquiries as to the health of Tartuffe, the question: "Et Tartuffe?" repeated every few moments, affords us the distinct sensation of a spring being released. This spring Dorine delights in pushing back, each time she resumes her account of Elmire's illness. And when Scapin informs old Géronte that his son has been taken prisoner on the famous galley, and that a ransom must be paid without delay, he is playing with the avarice of Géronte exactly as Dorine does with the infatuation of Orgon. The old man's avarice is no sooner repressed than up it springs again automatically, and it is this automatism that Molière tries to indicate by the mechanical repetition of a sentence expressing regret at the money that would have to be forthcoming: "What the deuce did he want in that galley?" The same criticism is applicable to the scene in which Valère points out to Harpagon the wrong he would be doing in marrying his daughter to a man she did not love. "No dowry wanted!" interrupts the miserly Harpagon every few moments. Behind this exclamation, which recurs automatically we faintly discern a complete repeating-machine set going by a fixed idea.

At times this mechanism is less easy

to detect, and here we encounter a fresh difficulty in the theory of the comic. Sometimes the whole interest of a scene lies in one character playing a double part, the intervening speaker acting as a mere prism, so to speak, through which the dual personality is developed. We run the risk, then, of going astray, if we look for the secret of the effect in what we see and hear,—in the external scene played by the characters,—and not in the altogether inner comedy of which this scene is no more than the outer refraction. For instance, when Alceste stubbornly repeats the words, "I don't say that!" on Oronte asking him if he thinks his poetry bad, the repetition is laughable, though evidently Oronte is not now playing with Alceste at the game we have just described. We must be careful, however, for, in reality, we have two men in Alceste: on the one hand, the "misanthropist" who has vowed henceforth to call a spade a spade, and on the other the gentleman who cannot unlearn, in a trice, the usual forms of politeness, or even, it may be, just the honest fellow who, when called upon to put his words into practice, shrinks from wounding another's self-esteem or hurting his feelings. Accordingly, the real scene is not between Alceste and Oronte, it is between Alceste and himself. The one Alceste would fain blurt out the truth, and the other stops his mouth just as he is on the point of telling everything. Each "I don't say that!" reveals a growing effort to repress something that strives and struggles to get out. And so the tone in which the phrase is uttered gets more and more violent, Alceste becoming more and more angry—not with Oronte, as he thinks—but with himself. The tension of the spring is continually being renewed and reinforced, until it at last goes off with a bang. Here, as elsewhere, we have the same identical mechanism of repetition.

For a man to make a resolution never henceforth to say what he does not think, even though he "openly defy the whole human race," is not necessarily laughable; it is a phase of life at its highest and best. For another man, through amiability, selfishness or disdain, to prefer to flatter people, is only another phase of life; there is nothing in it to make us laugh. You may even combine these two men into one, and arrange that the individual waver between offensive frankness and delusive politeness, this duel between two opposing feelings will not even then be comic, rather it will appear the essence of seriousness if these two feelings through their very distinctness complete each other, develop side by side, and make up between them a composite mental condition, adopting, in short, a *modus vivendi* which merely gives us the complex impression of life. But imagine these two feelings as *inelastic* and unvarying elements in a really living man, make him oscillate from one to the other; above all, arrange that this oscillation becomes entirely mechanical by adopting the well-known form of some habitual, simple, childish contrivance: then you will get the image we have so far found in all laughable objects, *something mechanical in something living;* in fact, something comic.

We have dwelt on this first image, the Jack-in-the-box, sufficiently to show how comic fancy gradually converts a material mechanism into a moral one. Now we will consider one or two other games, confining ourselves to their most striking aspects.

2. *The Dancing-jack.*—There are innumerable comedies in which one of the characters thinks he is speaking and acting freely, and consequently, retains all the essentials of life, whereas, viewed from a certain standpoint, he appears as a mere toy in the hands of another, who is playing with him. The transition is easily made, from the dancing-jack which a child works with a string, to Géronte and Argante manipulated by Scapin. Listen to Scapin himself: "The *machine* is all there," and again: "Providence has brought them into my net," etc. Instinctively, and because one would rather be a cheat than be cheated, in imagination at all events, the spectator sides with the knaves; and for the rest of the time, like a child who has persuaded his playmate to lend him his doll, he takes hold of the strings himself and makes the marionette come and go on the stage as he pleases. But this latter condition is not indispensable; we can remain outside the pale of what is taking place if only we retain the distinct impression of a mechanical arrangement. This is what

happens whenever one of the characters vacillates between two contrary opinions, each in turn appealing to him, as when Panurge asks Tom, Dick and Harry whether or not he ought to get married. Note that, in such a case, a comic author is always careful to *personify* the two opposing decisions. For, if there is no spectator, there must at all events be actors to hold the strings.

All that is serious in life comes from our freedom. The feelings we have matured, the passions we have brooded over, the actions we have weighed, decided upon and carried through, in short, all that comes from us and is our very own, these are the things that give life its ofttimes dramatic and generally grave aspect. What, then, is requisite to transform all this into a comedy? Merely to fancy that our seeming freedom conceals the strings of a dancing-jack, and that we are, as the poet [Sully Prudhomme] says, ". . . humble marionettes/The wires of which are pulled by Fate." So there is not a real, a serious, or even a dramatic scene that fancy cannot render comic by simply calling forth this image. Nor is there a game for which a wider field lies open.

3. *The Snow-ball.*—The farther we proceed in this investigation into the methods of comedy, the more clearly we see the part played by childhood's memories. These memories refer, perhaps, less to any special game than to the mechanical device of which that game is a particular instance. The same general device, moreover, may be met with in widely different games, just as the same operatic air is found in many different arrangements and variations. What is here of importance and is retained in the mind, what passes by imperceptible stages from the games of a child to those of a man, is the mental diagram, the skeleton outline of the combination, or, if you like, the abstract formula of which these games are particular illustrations. Take, for instance, the rolling snow-ball, which increases in size as it moves along. We might just as well think of toy soldiers standing behind one another. Push the first and it tumbles down on the second, this latter knocks down the third, and the state of things goes from bad to worse until they all lie prone on the floor. Or again,

take a house of cards that has been built up with infinite care: the first you touch seems uncertain whether to move or not, its tottering neighbour comes to a quicker decision, and the work of destruction, gathering momentum as it goes on, rushes headlong to the final collapse. These instances are all different, but they suggest the same abstract vision, that of an effect which grows by arithmetical progression, so that the cause, insignificant at the outset, culminates by a necessary evolution in a result as important as it is unexpected. Now let us open a children's picture-book; we shall find this arrangement already on the high road to becoming comic. Here, for instance, —in one of the comic chapbooks picked up by chance,—we have a caller rushing violently into a drawing-room; he knocks against a lady, who upsets her cup of tea over an old gentleman, who slips against a glass window which falls in the street on to the head of a constable, who sets the whole police force agog, etc. The same arrangement reappears in many a picture intended for grown-up persons. In the "stories without words" sketched by humorous artists we are often shown an object which moves from place to place, and persons who are closely connected with it, so that through a series of scenes a change in the position of the object mechanically brings about increasingly serious changes in the situation of the persons. Let us now turn to comedy. Many a droll scene, many a comedy even, may be referred to this simple type. Read the speech of Chicanneau in the *Plaideurs;* here we find lawsuits within lawsuits, and the mechanism works faster and faster— Racine produces in us this feeling of increasing acceleration by crowding his law terms ever closer together—until the lawsuit over a truss of hay costs the plaintiff the best part of his fortune. And again the same arrangement occurs in certain scenes of *Don Quixote;* for instance, in the inn scene, where, by an extraordinary concatenation of circumstances, the mule-driver strikes Sancho, who belabours Maritornes, upon whom the innkeeper falls, etc. Finally, let us pass to the light comedy of to-day. Need we call to mind all the forms in which this same combination appears? There is one that is employed rather frequently.

For instance a certain thing, say a letter, happens to be of supreme importance to a certain person and must be recovered at all costs. This thing, which always vanishes just when you think you have caught it, pervades the entire play, "rolling up" increasingly serious and unexpected incidents as it proceeds. All this is far more like a child's game than appears at first blush. Once more the effect produced is that of the snow-ball.

It is the characteristic of a mechanical combination to be generally *reversible*. A child is delighted when he sees the ball in a game of ninepins knocking down everything in its way and spreading havoc in all directions; he laughs louder than ever when the ball returns to its starting-point after twists and turns and waverings of every kind. In other words, the mechanism just described is laughable even when rectilinear, it is much more so on becoming circular and when every effort the player makes, by a fatal interaction of cause and effect, merely results in bringing it back to the same spot. Now, a considerable number of light comedies revolve round this idea. An Italian straw hat has been eaten up by a horse.[2] There is only one other hat like it in the whole of Paris; it *must* be secured regardless of cost. This hat, which always slips away at the moment its capture seems inevitable, keeps the principal character on the run, and through him all the others who hang, so to say, on to his coat tails, like a magnet which, by a successive series of attractions, draws along in its train the grains of iron filings that hang on to each other. And when at last, after all sorts of difficulties, the goal seems in sight, it is found that the hat so ardently sought is precisely the one that has been eaten. . . .

The truth is, the comic character may, strictly speaking, be quite in accord with stern morality. All it has to do is to bring itself into accord with society. The character of Alceste is that of a thoroughly honest man. But then he is unsociable, and, on that very account, ludicrous. A flexible vice may not be so easy to ridicule as a rigid virtue. It is *rigidity* that society eyes with suspicion. Consequently, it is the rigidity of Alceste that makes us laugh, though here rigidity

2 *The Italian Straw Hat* (Labiche).

stands for honesty. The man who withdraws into himself is liable to ridicule, because the comic is largely made up of this very withdrawal. This accounts for the comic being so frequently dependent on the manners or ideas, or, to put it bluntly, on the prejudices, of a society.

It must be acknowledged, however, to the credit of mankind, that there is no essential difference between the social ideal and the moral. We may therefore admit, as a general rule, that it is the faults of others that make us laugh, provided we add that they make us laugh by reason of their *unsociability* rather than of their immorality. What, then, are the faults capable of becoming ludicrous, and in what circumstances do we regard them as being too serious to be laughed at?

We have already given an implicit answer to this question. The comic, we said, appeals to the intelligence pure and simple; laughter is incompatible with emotion. Depict some fault, however trifling, in such a way as to arouse sympathy, fear, or pity; the mischief is done, it is impossible for us to laugh. On the other hand, take a downright vice,—even one that is, generally speaking, of an odious nature,—you may make it ludicrous if, by some suitable contrivance, you arrange so that it leaves our emotions unaffected. Not that the vice *must* then be ludicrous, but it *may*, from that time forth, become so. *It must not arouse our feelings;* that is the sole condition really necessary, though assuredly it is not sufficient. . . .

To sum up, whether a character is good or bad is of little moment; granted he is unsociable, he is capable of becoming comic. We now see that the seriousness of the case is of no importance either: whether serious or trifling, it is still capable of making us laugh, provided that care be taken not to arouse our emotions. Unsociability in the performer and insensibility in the spectator —such, in a word, are the two essential conditions. There is a third, implicit in the other two, which so far it has been the aim of our analysis to bring out. This third condition is automatism. We have pointed it out from the outset of this work, continually drawing attention to the following point: what is essentially laughable is what is done automatically. In a vice, even in a virtue, the comic is that element by which the person unwittingly betrays himself—the involuntary gesture or the unconscious remark. Absentmindedness is always comical. Indeed, the deeper the absentmindedness the higher the comedy. Systematic absentmindedness, like that of Don Quixote, is the most comical thing imaginable: it is the comic itself, drawn as nearly as possible from its very source. Take any other comic character: however unconscious he may be of what he says or does, he cannot be comical unless there be some aspect of his person of which he is unaware, one side of his nature which he overlooks; on that account alone does he make us laugh.[3] Profoundly comic sayings are those artless ones in which some vice reveals itself in all its nakedness: how could it thus expose itself were it capable of seeing itself as it is? It is not uncommon for

[3] When the humourist laughs at himself, he is really acting a double part; the self who laughs is indeed conscious, but not the self who is laughed at.

a comic character to condemn in general terms a certain line of conduct and immediately afterwards afford an example of it himself: for instance, M. Jourdain's teacher of philosophy flying into a passion after inveighing against anger; Vadius taking a poem from his pocket after heaping ridicule on readers of poetry, etc. What is the object of such contradictions except to help us to put our finger on the obliviousness of the characters to their own actions? Inattention to self, and consequently to others, is what we invariably find. And if we look at the matter closely, we see that inattention is here equivalent to what we have called unsociability. The chief cause of rigidity is the neglect to look around— and more especially within oneself: how can a man fashion his personality after that of another if he does not first study others as well as himself? Rigidity, automatism, absentmindedness and unsociability are all inextricably entwined; and all serve as ingredients to the making up of the comic in character.

MAURICE MAETERLINCK

Maurice Maeterlinck was born at Ghent of a Flemish family of ancient descent, in 1862. In accordance with the wishes of his parents he studied for the law, and practiced in his native city for some time after his graduation. In 1886 he left Belgium for Paris, where he became acquainted with a number of the younger writers — especially Villiers de l'Isle Adam — who were to exert great influence over him. It was Adam who, according to Maeterlinck, directed him toward "the spiritual, poetic, and mysterious side of things." In 1889, after his return home on the death of his father, he published his first works, a volume of verses, Serres chaudes, and La Princesse Maleine, a play which called forth the extravagant praise of Octave Mirbeau, who called the poet a Belgian Shakespeare. Until 1896 he spent most of his time in Belgium writing plays, and translating plays from the English. In that year he returned to Paris. There he devoted himself to his lifework, which

included numerous plays, essays, and poems. His best-known plays are Pelléas et Mélisande (1892), The Bluebird (1909), The Betrothal (1919), and The Burgomaster of Stilemond (1920). He died in 1949.

Maeterlinck's work is written in French and perhaps in the broadest sense of term he may be considered French, though his basic ideas are distinctly Belgian. He occupies a unique position in modern drama and literature. He attempted and for the most part succeeded in expressing moods and subconscious and half-realized feelings; to this end he invented the so-called Static drama, which he later discarded. Every step in his development as a dramatist was accompanied by a statement of his theory. On the whole it may be said that he attacks the conventional plays of the day as too obvious, and strives to express the implicit. He himself realized the futility of classification in matters of art, and he once wrote (1913) to the editor of the present volume: "You must not attach too great importance to the expression *Static;* it was an invention, a theory of my youth, worth what most literary theories are worth — that is, almost nothing. Whether a play be *static, dynamic, symbolistic,* or *realistic,* is of little consequence. What matters is that it be well written, well thought out, human and, if possible, superhuman, in the deepest significance of the term. The rest is mere rhetoric." [1]

[1] Printed, together with another letter, in *The Continental Drama of To-day,* by Barrett H. Clark, (2nd ed.. New York, 1914).— Ed.

THE TRAGICAL IN DAILY LIFE [2]
[*Le Tragique quotidien*]
(1896)

. . . In most cases, indeed, you will find that psychological action — infinitely loftier in itself than mere material action, and truly, one might think, well-nigh indispensable — that psychological action even has been suppressed, or at least vastly diminished, in a truly marvelous fashion, with the result that the interest centers solely and entirely in the individual, face to face with the universe. Here we are no longer with the barbarians, nor is the man now fretting himself in the midst of elementary passions, as though, forsooth, these were the only things worthy of note: he is at rest, and we have time to observe him. It is no longer a violent, exceptional moment of life that passes before our eyes — it is life itself. Thousands and thousands of laws there are, mightier and more venerable than those of passion; but, in common with all that is endowed with resistless force, these laws are silent, and discreet, and slow-moving; and hence it is only in the twilight that they can be seen and heard, in the meditation that comes to us at the tranquil moments of life. When Ulysses and Neoptolemus come to Philoctetes and demand of him the arms of Hercules, their action is in itself as simple and ordinary as that of a man of our day who goes into a house to visit an invalid, of a traveler who knocks at the door of an inn, or of a mother who, by the fireside, awaits the return of her child. Sophocles indicates the character of his heroes by means of the lightest and quickest of touches. But it may safely be said that the chief interest of tragedy does not lie in the struggle we witness between cunning and loyalty, between love of country, rancor and head-strong pride. There is more beyond: for it is man's loftier existence that is laid bare to us. The poet adds to ordinary life something, I know not what, which is the poet's secret: and there comes to us a sudden revelation of life in its stupendous grandeur, in its submissiveness to the unknown powers, in its endless affinities, in its awe-inspiring misery. Let but the chemist pour a few mysterious drops into a vessel that seems to contain the purest water, and at once masses of crystals will rise to the surface, thus revealing to us all that lay in abeyance there where nothing was visible before to incomplete eyes. And even thus is it in *Philoctetes;* the primitive psychology of the three leading characters would seem to be merely the sides of the vessel containing the clear water; and this itself is our ordinary life, into which the poet is about to let fall the revelation-bearing drops of his genius.

Indeed, it is not in the actions but in the words that are found the beauty and greatness of tragedies that are truly beautiful and great; and this not solely in the words that accompany and explain the action, for there must perforce be another dialogue besides the one which is superficially necessary. And indeed the only words that count in the play are those that at first seemed useless, for it is therein that the essence lies. Side by side with the necessary dialogue will you almost always find another dialogue that seems superfluous; but examine it carefully, and it will be borne home to you that this is the only one

[2] Translated sections from *The Treasure of the Humble* (translated by Alfred Sutro, New York, 1897).— Ed.

that the soul can listen to profoundly, for here alone is it the soul that is being addressed. You will see, too, that it is the quality and the scope of this unnecessary dialogue that determine the quality and the immeasurable range of the work. Certain it is that, in the ordinary drama, the indispensable dialogue by no means corresponds to reality; and it is just those words that are spoken by the side of the rigid, apparent truth, that constitute the mysterious beauty of the most beautiful tragedies, inasmuch as these are words that conform to a deeper truth, and one that lies incomparably nearer to the invisible soul by which the poem is upheld. One may even affirm that a poem draws the nearer to beauty and loftier truth in the measure that it eliminates words that merely explain the action, and substitutes for them others that reveal, not the so-called "soul-state," but I know not what intangible and unceasing striving of the soul towards its own beauty and truth. And so much the nearer, also, does it draw to the true life. To every man does it happen, in his workaday existence, that some situation of deep seriousness has to be unraveled by means of words. Reflect for an instance. At moments such as those — nay, at the most commonplace of times — is it the thing you say or the reply you receive that has the most value? Are not other forces, other words one cannot hear, brought into being, and do not these determine the event? What I say often counts for so little; but my presence, the attitude of my soul, my future and my past, that which will take birth in me and that which is dead, a secret thought, the stars that approve, my destiny, the thousands of mysteries which surround me and float about yourself — all this it is that speaks to you at that tragic moment, all this it is that brings to me your answer. There is all this beneath every one of my words, and each one of yours; it is this, above all, that we see, it is this, above all, that we hear, ourselves notwithstanding. If you have come, you, the "outraged husband," the "deceived lover," the "forsaken wife," intending to kill me, your arm will not be stayed by my most moving entreaty; but it may be that there will come towards you, at that moment, one of these unexpected forces; and my soul, knowing of their vigil near to me, may whisper a secret word whereby, haply, you shall be disarmed. These are the spheres wherein adventures come to issue, this is the dialogue whose echo should be heard. And it is this echo that one does hear — extremely attenuated and variable, it is true — in some of the great works mentioned above. But might we not try to draw nearer to the spheres where it is "in reality" that everything comes to pass?

PREFACE TO THE PLAYS [3]
[*Préface — Théâtre 1*]
(1901)

. . . . . .

. . . I do not believe that a poem should sacrifice its beauty in order to point a moral, but if, without losing any element that goes to make up its interior or exterior beauty, it leads us to truths as acceptable but more encouraging than the truth which leads us nowhere, it will possess the advantage of accomplishing a twofold, though uncertain, purpose. For centuries we have sung of the van-

ity of life and the irresistible power of emptiness and death, and summoned up sorrows that become more and more monotonous the nearer they approach to the ultimate truth. But now let us try to vary the appearance of the unknown which surrounds us and discover a new reason for living and persevering; we shall at least be able to alternate our sorrows by mixing with them our reviving or falling hopes. Granted our present conditions, it is at least as reasonable to hope that our efforts are not useless as we think they are. The su-

3 Extracts from the *Préface* to vol. 1 of the Brussels edition of Maeterlinck's *Théâtre* (1901): translated by the editor.— Ed.

preme truth of death, nothingness, and the uselessness of our existence — the point at which we arrive at the end of our inquiry — is, after all, only the limit of our human consciousness. We cannot see beyond that, because that marks the barrier of our intelligence. It only *seems* certain, but as a matter of fact, there is nothing more certain in it than our ignorance. Before we are forced to admit this truth irrevocably, we must do our best for a long time to dissipate this ignorance and do what we can to find the light. Then the great mass of our formerly conceived duties — conceived in the light of our over-hasty and mortal conclusion — will be called into question and human life begun again, with its passions that seem less futile, with its joys, its sorrows and its duties, all of which will assume an added importance, because they will help us to emerge from the obscurity and bear to look upon it without bitterness.

I do not mean to infer that we shall return to where we stood formerly, nor that love, death, destiny and the other mysterious powers of life will all occupy the place they once occupied in our actual existence, and in human works, especially — since it is with this that we are at present concerned — in dramatic works. The human mind — as I remarked in this connection in a passage which is practically unknown — the human mind has during the past three-quarters of a century undergone a transformation which we are not yet fully able to realize, but which is probably one of the most profound in the whole domain of thought. This evolution, if it has not revealed to us the end, the origin, the laws of the universe — definite certitudes — about matter, life, and the destiny of man, has at least done away with and rendered powerless a number of *uncertainties,* and these *uncertainties* were precisely those wherein the greatest thoughts flourished with the utmost freedom. They were in essence the element of beauty and the greatness of our aspirations, the hidden force that elevated our words above the words of everyday life; the poet seemed great and profound in proportion to the form, more or less triumphant, and the more or less preponderating place he was able to give to these beautiful or terrifying, peaceful

or hostile, tragic or consoling, uncertainties.

Great poetry, if we observe it closely, is made up of three principal elements: first, verbal beauty; then the contemplation and passionate portrayal of what actually exists about us and within us, that is to say, nature and our sentiments; and, finally, enveloping the whole work and creating the atmosphere proper to it, the idea which the poet forms of the unknown in which float about the beings and things which he evokes, the mystery which dominates them, judges them, and presides over their destinies. I have no doubt that this last is the most important element. Look at any beautiful poem, no matter how short it may be, or rapid. Only in the rarest instances are its beauty and grandeur limited to the known facts. Nine times out of ten it owes its beauty to an illusion to the mystery of human destiny, to some new link between the visible and the invisible, the temporal and the eternal. Now, if the possible unprecedented evolution in our ideas taking place nowadays regarding the unknown has not as yet profoundly stirred the lyric poet, and deprives him of only a part of his resources, it is not the same with the dramatic poet. Perhaps it is allowable for the lyric poet to remain a sort of theorist of the unknown; possibly he should be permitted to deal in great and vast generalities; he need not think of the practical consequences. If he is convinced that the gods of old, that justice and destiny, no longer intervene in the actions of man and direct the progress of this world, he need not give a name to the powers which he does not understand, forces which are always concerned with men and which dominate everything. It makes little difference whether it be God or the Universe which appears immense and terrible to him. What we demand of him principally is that he make us feel the immense or terrible impression which he felt. But the dramatic poet cannot limit himself to these generalities, he must bring down his own ideas of the unknown into the world of living men, into the everyday world. He must show us how, under what form and conditions, according to what laws, to what end, the superior powers act upon our destinies, the unintelligible influences, the infinite principles of which he as poet is convinced the universe is full. And since the dramatist of the present has arrived upon the scene at a time when he cannot sincerely accept the ancient truths, and when the new truths, which are to replace the old, are not yet determined, have even no name, he hesitates, feels his way and, if he wishes to remain absolutely sincere, dares not risk going beyond the immediate reality. He confines himself to the study of human feelings in their material and psychological effects. Within this sphere he can create powerful works full of observation, passion, and wisdom, but it is certain that he will never attain to the vaster and more profound beauty of the great poems wherein something of the infinite is mingled with the acts of men; and he asks himself whether or no he should cease striving for beauty of that sort.

I think he ought not. He will find a way of realizing these beauties, through difficulties with which no poet has hitherto been confronted, but not until to-morrow. Yet even to-day, when the alternative seems the most dangerous, one or two poets have succeeded in escaping from the world of obvious actuality, without returning to that of the chimeras of old — because the greatest poetry is, above all, the kingdom of the unexpected, and from the most general rules, like fragments of stars which cross the sky where no trace of brightness is looked for, spring forth the most disconcerting exceptions. For example, Tolstoy's *The Power of Darkness* is a work that floats down the most sordid river of the depths of life, like an island, grandiose in its horror, reeking with hellish odors, but enveloped at the same time by an enormous white light, pure and miraculous, springing from the simple soul of Akim. Or else, take Ibsen's *Ghosts,* where in a stuffy middle-class drawing-room, unbearable, maddening to the characters, there breaks forth one of the most terrible mysteries of human destiny. It is all very well for us to shut our eyes to the anguish of the unknown: but into these two plays enter superior powers which all of us feel weighing down upon our lives. For it is much less the action of the God of the Christians which troubles us in Tol-

stoi's poem than of the God who is in a human heart, simpler, juster, purer, greater than the others. And in Ibsen's poem it is the influence of a law of justice or injustice, formidable and only recently suspected — the law of heredity, of which very little is known, and that open to discussion, and yet plausible — the menace of which hides the greater part of what might have been a matter for doubt.

But in spite of these unexpected sallies into the realm of the uncertain, it remains a fact that mystery, the unintelligible, the superhuman, the infinite — the word, makes little difference — all this has, since we no longer admit *a priori* divine intervention in human action, become almost " unworkable," and genius itself is seldom able to cope with it. When in his other dramas Ibsen tries to combine with other mysteries the acts of his men who are a prey to an abnormal conscience, or his women who are a prey to hallucination, we must admit that if the atmosphere he creates is strange and troubling, it is healthy and breathable because it is rarely reasonable and real.

From time to time in the past a true genius, or sometimes the simple and honest man of talent, succeeded in writing a play with that profound background, that mist about the summit, that feeling of the infinite here and there which, having neither name nor form, permitted us to mingle our images of it while we spoke, and seemed necessary in order that the dramatic work might flow by, brimming to the banks, and attain its ideal. Nowadays, our drama almost always lacks the third character, enigmatic, invisible, but everywhere present, which we might well call the sublime character, and which is perhaps no other than the unconscious though powerful and undeniable concept of the poet's idea of the universe, which gives to the play a far greater reach, a certain aspiration for existence after the death of other things, and makes us return to it without ever exhausting its possibilities of beauty. Such a genius, we must also admit, is wanting in our life as well. Will he ever return? Will he arise from a new and experimental conception of justice, or from the indifference of nature, from one of those far-reaching general laws of matter or mind which we have just begun to catch sight of? In any event, let us keep a place for him. At least let us see to it that nothing else takes his place while he is getting clear of the shadows; and let us see to it that we do not set up any more phantoms. Our very waiting for him, his empty place in life, are in themselves of far greater significance than anything we could put on his throne, which our patience is now reserving for him.

For my humble part, after producing the little dramas of which I have just spoken, it seemed wise and loyal to exile death from that throne where it is by no means certain he has a right to sit. And in the last, which I had not named among the others, in *Aglavaine et Sélysette*, I wished death to give away, at least in part, to love, wisdom, and happiness. But death did not obey me, and I await, together with most of the poets of my time, the revelation of a new poet.

ANTONIN ARTAUD

Artaud, born in 1896, is important primarily as a pioneer and a theorist of the movement that became known as the theatre of the absurd and embraced the work of Samuel Beckett, Eugène Ionesco, and Arthur Adamov. A poet, director, and actor, he broke with the surrealist movement in order to write and stage surrealist plays, beginning in 1927. He aimed at a theatre of magic, myth, astonishment, and cruelty. He founded his short-lived Theatre of Cruelty in 1935, staging his own play about the Cenci with the aid of two subsequent luminaries of the French theatre, Jean-Louis Barrault and Roger Blin. His principal writings on the theatre are collected in *The Theater and Its Double* (Paris, 1938; New York, 1958). In 1937, he was judged insane and confined to an asylum at Rodez. Released in 1946, he was publicly saluted by leaders of the French stage. He died in 1948. His letters and admiring memoirs of him continued to appear, testifying to his significance in the experimental theatre.

THE THEATRE AND CRUELTY [1]

[*Le Théâtre et son Double*]
(1933)

An idea of the theatre has been lost. And as long as the theatre limits itself to showing us intimate scenes from the lives of a few puppets, transforming the public into Peeping Toms, it is no wonder the elite abandon it and the great public looks to the movies, the music hall or the circus for violent satisfactions, whose intentions do not deceive them.

At the point of deterioration which our sensibility has reached, it is certain that we need above all a theatre that wakes us up: nerves and heart.

[1] From *The Theater and Its Double*, translated by Mary Caroline Richards. Copyright © 1958 by Grove Press, Inc. Used by permission of the publisher.—Ed.

The misdeeds of the psychological theatre descended from Racine have unaccustomed us to that immediate and violent action which the theatre should possess. Movies in their turn, murdering us with second-hand reproductions which, filtered through machines, cannot *unite with* our sensibility, have maintained us for ten years in an ineffectual torpor, in which all our faculties appear to be foundering.

In the anguished, catastrophic period we live in, we feel an urgent need for a theatre which events do not exceed, whose resonance is deep within us, dominating the instability of the times.

Our long habit of seeking diversion has made us forget the idea of a serious theatre, which, overturning all our pre-conceptions, inspires us with the fiery magnetism of its images and acts upon us like a spiritual therapeutics whose touch can never be forgotten.

Everything that acts is a cruelty. It is upon this idea of extreme action, pushed beyond all limits, that theatre must be rebuilt.

Imbued with the idea that the public thinks first of all with its senses and that to address oneself first to its understanding as the ordinary psychological theatre does is absurd, the Theatre of Cruelty proposes to resort to a mass spectacle; to seek in the agitation of tremendous masses, convulsed and hurled against each other, a little of that poetry of festivals and crowds when, all too rarely nowadays, the people pour out into the streets.

The theatre must give us everything that is in crime, love, war, or madness, if it wants to recover its necessity.

Everyday love, personal ambition, struggles for status, all have value only in proportion to their relation to the terrible lyricism of the Myths to which the great mass of men have assented.

This is why we shall try to concentrate, around famous personages, atrocious crimes, superhuman devotions, a drama which, without resorting to the defunct images of the old Myths, shows that it can extract the forces which struggle within them.

In a word, we believe that there are living forces in what is called poetry and that the image of a crime presented in the requisite theatrical conditions is something infinitely more terrible for the spirit than that same crime when actually committed.

We want to make out of the theatre a believable reality which gives the heart and the senses that kind of concrete bite which all true sensation requires. In the same way that our dreams have an effect upon us and reality has an effect upon our dreams, so we believe that the images of thought can be identified with a dream which will be efficacious to the degree that it can be projected with the necessary violence. And the public will believe in the theatre's dreams on condition that it take them for true dreams and not for a servile copy of reality; on condition that they allow the public to lib-

erate within itself the magical liberties of dreams which it can only recognize when they are imprinted with terror and cruelty.

Hence this appeal to cruelty and terror, though on a vast scale, whose range probes our entire vitality, confronts us with all our possibilities.

It is in order to attack the spectator's sensibility on all sides that we advocate a revolving spectacle which, instead of making the stage and auditorium two closed worlds, without possible communication, spreads its visual and sonorous outbursts over the entire mass of the spectators.

Also, departing from the sphere of analyzable passions, we intend to make use of the actor's lyric qualities to manifest external forces, and by this means to cause the whole of nature to re-enter the theatre in its restored form.

However vast this program may be, it does not exceed the theatre itself, which appears to us, all in all, to identify itself with the forces of ancient magic.

Practically speaking, we want to resuscitate an idea of total spectacle by which the theatre would recover from the cinema, the music hall, the circus, and from life itself what has always belonged to it. The separation between the analytic theatre and the plastic world seems to us a stupidity. One does not separate the mind from the body nor the senses from the intelligence, especially in a domain where the endlessly renewed fatigue of the organs requires intense and sudden shocks to revive our understanding.

Thus, on the one hand, the mass and extent of a spectacle addressed to the entire organism; on the other, an intensive mobilization of objects, gestures, and signs, used in a new spirit. The reduced role given to the understanding leads to an energetic compression of the text; the active role given to obscure poetic emotion necessitates concrete signs. Words say little to the mind; extent and objects speak; new images speak, even new images made with words. But space thundering with images and crammed with sounds speaks too, if one knows how to intersperse from time to time a sufficient extent of space stocked with silence and immobility.

On this principle we envisage producing a spectacle where these means of direct action are used in their totality; a spectacle unafraid of going as far as necessary in the exploration of our nervous sensibility, of which the rhythms, sounds, words, resonances, and twitterings, and their united quality and surprising mixtures belong to a technique which must not be divulged.

The images in certain paintings by Grunewald or Hieronymus Bosch tell enough about what a spectacle can be in which, as in the brain of some saint, the objects of external nature will appear as temptations.

It is in this spectacle of a temptation from which life has everything to lose and the mind everything to gain that the theatre must recover its true signification.

Elsewhere we have given a program which will allow the means of pure staging, found on the spot, to be organized around historic or cosmic themes, familiar to all.

And we insist on the fact that the first spectacle of the Theatre of Cruelty will turn upon the preoccupations of the great mass of men, preoccupations much more pressing and disquieting than those of any individual whatsoever.

It is a matter of knowing whether now, in Paris, before the cataclysms which are at our door descend upon us, sufficient means of production, financial or otherwise, can be found to permit such a theatre to be brought to life—it is bound to in any case, because it is the future. Or whether a little real blood will be needed, right away, in order to manifest this cruelty.

JEAN-PAUL SARTRE

Born in Paris in 1905, Sartre is a professional philosopher and the best-known exponent of existentialism, but he is also a novelist, a dramatist, an editor, and a dedicated student of politics. He was a teacher of philosophy at the time he published his first novel, *Nausea,* in 1938 and a book of stories the following year. His careers were interrupted when he served in World War II and became a prisoner of war. His plays were first staged during the occupation of France, beginning with *The Flies* (1942), a new version of the Orestes story, and *No Exit* (1944), a parable of hell, which is found to consist of other people. He founded a periodical, *Les Temps modernes,* in 1946. More novels and plays followed, accompanied by radical political pronouncements, but Sartre won international fame primarily as the interpreter of existentialism, a philosophy which holds that man, naturally lonely and despairing, in effect creates himself, escaping from chaos only by the choices that he makes. Subsequent plays, which have tended to bear out this doctrine, have included *The Respectful Prostitute* (1946), *Dirty Hands* (1948), and *The Condemned of Altona* (1959).

FORGERS OF MYTHS [1]

(1946)

In reading the newspaper reviews of Katharine Cornell's production of Jean Anouilh's *Antigone,* I had the impression that the play had created a certain amount of discomfort in the minds of

the New York drama critics. Many expressed surprise that such an ancient myth should be staged at all. Others reproached Antigone with being neither alive nor credible, with not having what, in theatre jargon, is called "character." The misunderstanding, I believe, was due to the fact that the critics were not informed of what many young authors in France—each along differing lines and

[1] Translated by Rosamond Gilder. From *Theatre Arts Anthology.* Copyright 1946 by Theatre Arts, Inc., 1950 by Theatre Arts Books. Used by permission of Theatre Arts Books.—Ed.

without concerted aim—are attempting to do.

There has been a great deal of discussion in France about "a return to tragedy," about the "rebirth of the philosophic play." The two labels are confusing and they should both be rejected. Tragedy is, for us, an historic phenomenon which flourished between the sixteenth and eighteenth centuries; we have no desire to begin that over again. Nor are we anxious to produce philosophic plays, if by that is meant works deliberately intended to set forth on the stage the philosophy of Marx, St. Thomas, or existentialism. Nevertheless there is some truth attached to these two labels: in the first place, it is a fact that we are less concerned with making innovations than with returning to a tradition; it is likewise true that the problems we wish to deal with in the theatre are very different from those we habitually dealt with before 1940.

The theatre, as conceived of in the period between the two world wars, and as it is perhaps still thought of in the United States today, is a theatre of characters. The analysis of characters and their confrontation was the theatre's chief concern. The so-called "situations" existed only for the purpose of throwing the characters into clearer relief. The best plays in this period were psychological studies of a coward, a liar, an ambitious man or a frustrated one. Occasionally a playwright made an effort to outline the workings of a passion—usually love—or to analyze an inferiority complex.

Judged by such principles Anouilh's Antigone is not a character at all. Nor is she simply a peg on which to hang a passion calculated to develop along the approved lines of whatever psychology might be in style. She represents a naked will, a pure, free choice; in her there is no distinguishing between passion and action. The young playwrights of France do not believe that men share a ready-made "human nature" which may alter under the impact of a given situation. They do not think that individuals can be seized with a passion or a mania which can be explained purely on the grounds of heredity, environment, and situations. What is universal, to their way of thinking, is not nature but the situations in which man finds himself; that is, not the sum total of his psychological traits but the limits which enclose him on all sides.

For them man is not to be defined as a "reasoning animal," or a "social" one, but as a free being, entirely indeterminate, who must choose his own being when confronted with certain necessities, such as being already committed in a world full of both threatening and favorable factors among other men who have made their choices before him, who have decided in advance the meaning of those factors. He is faced with the necessity of having to work and die, of being hurled into a life already complete which yet is his own enterprise and in which he can never have a second chance; where he must play his cards and take risks no matter what the cost. That is why we feel the urge to put on the stage certain situations which throw light on the main aspects of the condition of man and to have the spectator participate in the free choice which man makes in these situations.

Thus, Anouilh's Antigone may have seemed abstract because she was not portrayed as a young Greek princess, formed by certain influences and some ghastly memories, but rather as a free woman without any features at all until she chooses them for herself in the moment when she asserts her freedom to die despite the triumphant tyrant. Similarly, when the burgomaster of Vauxelles in Simone de Beauvoir's *Les Bouches Inutiles* has to decide whether to save his beleaguered town by cutting off half its citizens (women, children, and old men) or to risk making them all perish in an effort to save them all, we do not care whether he is sensual or cold, whether he has an Oedipus complex, or whether he is of an irritable or jolly disposition. No doubt if he is rash or incautious, vain or pusillanimous, he will make the wrong decision. But we are not interested in arranging in advance the motivations or reasons which will inevitably force his choice. Rather, we are concerned in presenting the anguish of a man who is both free and full of good will, who in all sincerity is trying to find out the side he must take, and who knows that when he chooses the lot of others he is at the same time choosing his own pattern of behavior and is deciding once and for all whether he is to be a tyrant or a democrat.

If one of us happens to present character on the boards, it is only for the purpose of getting rid of it at once. For instance, Caligula, at the outset of Albert Camus' play of that name, has a character. One is led to believe he is gentle and well behaved, and no doubt he actually is both. But that gentleness and that modesty suddenly melt away in the face of the prince's horrifying discovery of the world's absurdity. From then on he will choose to be the man to persuade other men of that absurdity, and the play becomes only the story of how he carries out his purpose.

A man who is free within the circle of his own situations, who chooses, whether he wishes to or not, for everyone else when he chooses for himself—that is the subject matter of our plays. As a successor to the theatre of characters we want to have a theatre of situation; our aim is to explore all the situations that are most common to human experience, those which occur at least once in the majority of lives. The people in our plays will be distinct from one another— not as a coward from a miser or a miser from a brave man, but rather as actions are divergent or clashing, as right may conflict with right. In this it may well be said that we derive from the Corneillean tradition.

It is easy to understand, therefore, why we are not greatly concerned with psychology. We are not searching for the right "word" which will suddenly reveal the whole unfolding of a passion, nor yet the "act" which will seem most lifelike and inevitable to the audience. For us psychology is the most abstract of the sciences because it studies the workings of our passions without plunging them back into their true human surroundings, without their background of religious and moral values, the taboos and commandments of society, the conflicts of nations and classes, of rights, of wills, of actions. For us a man is a whole enterprise in himself. And passion is a part of that enterprise.

In this we return to the concept of tragedy as the Greeks saw it. For them, as Hegel has shown, passion was never a simple storm of sentiment but fundamentally always the assertion of a right. The fascism of Creon, the stubbornness of Antigone for Sophocles and Anouilh, the madness of Caligula for Camus, are *at one and the same time* transports of feeling which have their origin deep within us and expressions of impregnable will which are affirmations of systems of values and rights such as the rights of citizenship, the rights of the family, individual ethics, collective ethics, the right· to kill, the right to reveal to human beings their pitiable condition, and so forth. We do not reject psychology, that would be absurd; we integrate life.

For fifty years one of the most celebrated subjects for dissertation in France has been formulated as follows: "Comment on La Bruyère's saying: Racine draws man as he is; Corneille, as he should be." We believe the statement should be reversed. Racine paints psychologic man, he studies the mechanics of love, of jealousy in an abstract, pure way; that is, without ever allowing moral considerations or human will to deflect the inevitability of their evolution. His dramatis personae are only creatures of his mind, the end results of an intellectual analysis. Corneille, on the other hand, showing will at the very core of passion, gives us back man in all his complexity, in his complete reality.

The young authors I am discussing take their stand on Corneille's side. For them the theatre will be able to present man in his entirety only in proportion to the theatre's willingness to be *moral*. By that we do not mean that it should put forward examples illustrating the rules of deportment or the practical ethics taught to children, but rather that the study of the conflict of characters should be replaced by the presentation of the conflict of rights. It was not a question of the opposition of *character* between a Stalinist and a Trotskyite; it was not in their characters that an anti-Nazi of 1933 clashed with an S.S. guard; the difficulties in international politics do not derive from the characters of the men leading us; the strikes in the United States do not reveal conflicts of character between industrialists and workers. In each case it is, in the final analysis and in spite of divergent interests, the system of values, of ethics and of concepts of man which are lined up against each other.

Therefore, our new theatre definitely has drawn away from the so-called "realistic theatre" because "realism" has always offered plays made up of stories of defeat, laissez-faire, and drifting; it has always preferred to show how external forces batter a man to pieces, destroy him bit by bit, and ultimately make of him a weathervane turning with every change of wind. But we claim for ourselves the *true* realism because we know it is impossible, in everyday life, to distinguish between fact and right, the real from the ideal, psychology from ethics.

This theatre does not give its support to any one "thesis" and is not inspired by any preconceived idea. All it seeks to do is to explore the state of man in its entirety and to present to the modern man a portrait of himself, his problems, his hopes, and his struggles. We believe our theatre would betray its mission if it portrayed individual personalities, even if they were as universal types as a miser, a misanthrope, a deceived husband, because, if it is to address the masses, the theatre must speak in terms of their most general preoccupations, dispelling their anxieties in the form of myths which anyone can understand and feel deeply.

My first experience in the theatre was especially fortunate. When I was a prisoner in Germany in 1940, I wrote, staged, and acted in a Christmas play which, while pulling wool over the eyes of the German censor by means of simple symbols, was addressed to my fellow-prisoners. This drama, biblical in appearance only, was written and put on by a prisoner, was acted by prisoners in scenery painted by prisoners; it was aimed exclusively at prisoners (so much so that I have never since then permitted it to be staged or even printed), and it addressed them on the subject of their concerns as prisoners. No doubt it was neither a good play nor well acted: the work of an amateur, the critics would say, a product of special circumstances. Nevertheless, on this occasion, as I addressed my comrades across the footlights, speaking to them of their state as prisoners, when I suddenly saw them so remarkably silent and attentive, I realized what theatre ought to be—a great collective, religious phenomenon.

To be sure, I was, in this case, favored by special circumstances; it does not happen every day that your public is drawn together by one great common interest, a great loss or a great hope. As a rule, an audience is made up of the most diverse elements; a big businessman sits beside a traveling salesman or a professor, a man next to a woman, and each is subject to his own particular preoccupations. Yet this situation is a challenge to the playwright: he must create his public, he must fuse all the disparate elements in the auditorium into a single unity by awakening in the recesses of their spirits the things which all men of a given epoch and community care about.

This does not mean that our authors intend to make use of symbols in the sense that symbols are the expression either indirect or poetic of a reality one either cannot or will not grasp directly. We would feel a profound distaste today for representing happiness as an elusive bluebird, as Maeterlinck did. Our times are too austere for child's play of that sort. Yet if we reject the theatre of symbols, we still want ours to be one of myths; we want to attempt to show the public the great myths of death, exile, love. The characters in Albert Camus' *Le Malentendu* are not symbols, they are flesh and blood: *a* mother and *a* daughter, *a* son who comes back from a long journey; their tragic experiences are complete in themselves. And yet they are mythical in the sense that the misunderstanding which separates them can serve as the embodiment of all misunderstandings which separate man from himself, from the world, from other men.

The French public makes no mistake about this, as has been proved by the discussions engendered by certain plays. With *Les Bouches Inutiles,* for instance, criticism was not confined to discussing the story of the play which was based on actual events that took place frequently in the Middle Ages: it recognized in the play a condemnation of fascist procedures. The Communists, on the other hand, saw in it a condemnation of their own procedures: "The conclusion," so they said in their newspapers, "is couched in terms of petty bourgeois idealism. All useless mouths should have been sacrificed to save the city." Anouilh also stirred up a storm of discussion with *Antigone,* being charged on the one hand with being a Nazi, on the other with being an anarchist. Such violent reactions prove that our plays are reaching the public just where it is important that it should be reached.

Yet these plays are austere. To begin with, since the situation is what we care about above all, our theatre shows it at the very point where it is about to reach its climax. We do not take time out for learned research, we feel no need of registering the imperceptible evolution of a character or a plot: one does not reach death by degrees, one is suddenly confronted with it—and if one approaches politics or love by slow degrees, then acute problems, arising suddenly, call for no progression. By taking our dramatic personae and precipitating them, in the very first scene, into the highest pitch of their conflicts we turn to the well-known pattern of classic tragedy, which always seizes upon the action at the very moment it is headed for catastrophe.

Our plays are violent and brief, centered around one single event; there are few players and the story is compressed within a short space of time, sometimes only a few hours. As a result they obey a kind of "rule of the three unities," which has been only a little rejuvenated and modified. A single set, a few entrances, a few exits, intense arguments among the characters who defend their individual rights with passion—this is what sets our plays at a great distance from the brilliant fantasies of Broadway. Yet some of them find that their austerity and intensity have not lacked appreciation in Paris. Whether New York will like them is a question.

Since it is their aim to forge myths, to project for the audience an enlarged and enhanced image of its own sufferings, our playwrights turn their backs on the constant preoccupation of the realists, which is to reduce as far as possible the distance which separates the spectator from the spectacle. In 1942, in Gaston Baty's production of *The Taming of the Shrew,* there were steps going from the stage to the auditorium so that certain characters could go down among the orchestra seats. We are very far away from such concepts and methods. To us a play should not seem too *familiar.* Its greatness derives from its social and, in a certain sense, religious functions: it must remain a rite; even as it speaks to the spectators of themselves it must do it in a tone and with a constant reserve of manner which, far from breeding familiarity, will increase the distance between play and audience.

That is why one of our problems has been to search out a style of dialogue which, while utterly simple and made up of words on everyone's lips, will still preserve something of the ancient dignity of our tongue. We have all barred from our plays the digressions, the set speeches, and what we in France like to call the *"poésie de réplique";* all this chitchat debases a language. It seems to us that we shall recapture a little of the pomp of ancient tragedies if we practice the most rigorous economy of words. As for me, in *Morts Sans Sépulture,* my latest play, I did not deny myself the use of familiar turns of phrase, swearwords, even slang, whenever I felt that such speech was germane to the characters. But I did attempt to preserve, through the pace of the dialogue, an extreme conciseness of statement—ellipses, brusque interruptions, a sort of inner tension in the phrases which at once set them apart from the easy going sound of everyday talk. Camus' style in *Caligula* is different in kind but it is magnificently sober and taut. Simone de Beauvoir's language in *Les Bouches Inutiles* is so stripped that it is sometimes accused of dryness.

Dramas which are short and violent, sometimes reduced to the dimensions of a single long act (*Antigone* lasts an hour and a half, my own play, *Huis-Clos,* an hour and twenty minutes without intermission), dramas entirely centered on one event—usually a conflict of rights, bearing on some very general situation—written in a sparse, extremely tense style, with a small cast not presented for their individual characters but thrust into a conjunction where they are forced to make a choice—in brief this is the theatre, austere, moral, mythic, and ceremonial in aspect, which has given birth to new plays in Paris during the occupation and especially since the end of the war. They correspond to the needs of a people exhausted but tense, for whom liberation has not meant a return to abundance and who can live only with the utmost economy.

The very severity of these plays is in keeping with the severity of French life; their moral and metaphysical topics reflect the preoccupation of a nation which must at one and the same time reconstruct and re-create and which is searching for new principles. Are they the product of local circumstances or can their very austerity of form enable them to reach a wider public in more fortunate countries? This is a question we must ask ourselves frankly before we try to transplant them.

EUGÈNE IONESCO

Ionesco was born in 1912 in Slatina, Rumania. He was brought to Paris as a child and then taken back to Rumania, where he studied at the University of Bucharest. He returned to Paris in 1938. His first dramatic work was *The Bald Soprano,* a one-act play in which no bald soprano appears. It was inspired by the commonplace statements which occurred in his English lessons; what Ionesco did was to orchestrate these nonsense lines and create characters to speak them. Performed in 1950, it was coolly received. Ionesco appeared briefly as an actor and then, in his next plays, *The Lesson* and *Jack, or the Submission,* burlesqued, respectively, instruction and conformity. Subsequent plays, equally experimental, *The Chairs* and *Victims of Duty,* began to win him some recognition. His first full-length play, *The Killer* (1959), has death for its subject. The second full-length play, *Rhinoceros* (1959), a new attack on conformity, earned considerable international attention. Later plays include *Exit the King* and *Le Piéton de l'air.* An indefatigable controversialist, Ionesco has attacked both bourgeois and Marxist foes.

THERE IS NO AVANT-GARDE THEATRE [1]

What is meant by "avant-garde theatre"? Deliberate or not, great confusion has arisen round these words, mainly owing to prejudice. The expression itself is confusing and the idea that avant-garde theatre is "ridiculous" might even be caused merely by faulty definition. A critic in one of the foreign countries where I have been lucky enough to see my plays acted—favorable, moreover, to my work—still wondered whether this kind of theatre was not after all just a transition, a stage in the development of drama. So that is what avant-garde means: a kind of drama that opens the way to another kind of drama, which will be definitive. But nothing is

definitive, everything is just a stage in development, our very lives are essentially transitory: everything is, at one and the same time, the culmination of one thing and the announcement of something else. So one can say that the French theatre of the seventeenth century prepares the way for Romantic drama (which is not worth much anyway in France) and that Racine and Corneille are the advance guard of the theatre of Victor Hugo, who himself blazed the trail for what came after and rejected him.

And again: the mechanism governing forward and rear positions is far more complicated than the blinkered dialecticians imagine. There are some productive "avant-garde" movements which arise from opposition to the achievements of preceding generations or, on the other hand, others which are encour-

[1] A chapter, "Still About Avant-Garde Theatre," from *Notes and Counternotes,* translated by Donald Watson. Copyright © 1964 by Grove Press, Inc. Used by permission of Grove Press, Inc.—Ed.

aged or facilitated by a reappraisal of sources, of old and forgotten works. Shakespeare is always far more contemporary than Victor Hugo (cited above); Pirandello far more "avant-garde" than Roger Ferdinand; Büchner infinitely more poignant and alive than, for example, Bertolt Brecht and his imiators in Paris.

And this is where matters seem to become clearer: in reality, the avant-garde does not exist; or rather it is quite different from what it is thought to be.

As the avant-garde is, we all agree, revolutionary, it has always been and still is, like most revolutionary movements, a turning back, a reappraisal. The change is only apparent: this "apparentness" is of enormous importance, for it is this that allows (by presenting something new and yet going beyond it) reassessment and restoration of something permanent. For example: the political upheavals that appear at moments when a regime is worn out and "liberalized" —when the structure has weakened to such a point that collapse is anyway imminent, ready to take place, as one might say, unaided—prepare and allow for a strengthening and reconstitution of the social structure according to an archetypal and changeless model: there is a real change on the personal plane, obviously, on the level of superficial conditions, in idiom: that is to say things— identical in essence—assume different names, without modifying the deeper reality or the fundamental pattern of society.

What has really happened? Simply this: authority (which had been relaxed) has tightened up, "order" is re-established, tyranny clamps down again on freedom, the leaders of the state recover their taste and vocation for power with a quiet conscience, for they feel themselves to be invested with a kind of "God's Grace," with an alibi provided by a firm and reliable ideological justification for the cynicism inseparable from power. And there we have the basic hierarchical social structure, clearly reaffirmed and reconstituted, with the king (the political leaders) upheld by dogma and the church (the ideologists, the writers, the artists, the journalists, the propagandists, all back in obedience) and either supported or suffered by the ma-

jority—the people (the believers, the faithful or the passive) who are no longer capable of insurrection.

Almost the same thing happens with artistic revolutions, when there is really an attempt at revolution, or a revolutionary experiment coming from the avant-garde. This happens inevitably, of its own accord as you might say, at a moment when certain modes of expression have become exhausted and worn out, when they have deteriorated, when they have wandered too far from some forgotten model. Thus, in painting, the moderns have been able to *rediscover* in the painters we call "primitive" forms that are pure and permanent, the basic laws that govern their art. And this rediscovery, dictated by the history of art where forms and models lose their power—has been made possible thanks to an art, an *idiom* that springs from a reality lying outside history.

It is indeed in the union between the historical and the unhistorical, the topical and the untopical (that is to say the permanent) that we can seek this changeless basic material which we can also succeed in finding, instinctively, in ourselves: without it, any work of art is valueless, it keeps everything alive. So finally I maintain quite fearlessly that the true avant-garde or revolutionary art is that which, boldly setting its face against its own times, looks as if it is *untopical*. By casting off all claim to topicality, it reveals its links with this universal basic material we have already spoken of, and being universal it may be considered classical; but it should be understood that this classicism must be rediscovered by passing through and going beyond the new elements that should permeate this kind of art. Any attempt to return to some sort of "historical" classicism by turning one's back on what is new and would only encourage the development of an outdated and academic style. For example: *Endgame* by Beckett, a so-called avant-garde play, is far closer to the lamentations of *Job,* the tragedies of Sophocles or Shakespeare, than to the tawdry drama known as committed or boulevard theatre. Topical drama does not last (by definition) and it does not last for the good reason that people are not truly profoundly interested in it.

It is also worth noting that social changes are not always related to artistic revolution. Or rather: when the mystique of a revolution becomes a regime, it returns to artistic forms (and so to a mentality) that are outmoded, with the result that the new realism is bound up with the mental clichés we call bourgeois and reactionary. Conventionalism repeats itself and the bewhiskered academic portraits of the new reaction are —stylistically—no different from the academic portraits, with or without whiskers, of the bourgeois period which did not understand Cézanne. So we can say, somewhat paradoxically perhaps, *that it is the "historical" which is moribund, and the non-historical which remains alive.*

Chekhov in his drama shows us dying men in a particular dying society; the destruction, as time runs out and gnaws away, of the men of a certain period; Proust too had done this in his novels— and so had Gustave Flaubert in *L'Education sentimentale,* although he showed as a background to his characters not a declining but a rising society. So it is not the collapse or the break-up or the erosion of a social system which is the principal theme, the *truth* of these works: but man eroded by time, his destruction seen at a certain historical moment but true for *all* history; we are *all* murdered by time.

I mistrust pacifist plays, which seem to be showing us that it is war that destroys mankind and that we only die in wartime. This is more or less what one young critic seemed to be saying, obstinately dogmatic, when commenting on *Mother Courage.*

More of us die in wartime: topical truth. We die: permanent truth, not topical yet always topical, it concerns everybody, and so it also concerns people not involved in war: Beckett's *Endgame* is more true, more universal, than Schéhadé's *Histoire de Vasco* (which in no way prevents this play from having high poetic qualities).

Since at first sight "what concerns us all fundamentally" is curiously less accessible than what concerns only some people or what concerns us less—it is obvious that avant-garde plays, whose aim is (I apologize for being so insist-ent) to rediscover and make known a forgotten truth—and to reintegrate it, in an untopical way, into what is topical—it is obvious that when these works appear they cannot help being misunderstood by the majority of people. So they are not "popular." This in no way invalidates them. The plainest realities are discovered by the poet in silence and solitude. The philosopher too, in the silence of his library, discovers truths difficult to communicate: how long did it take for Karl Marx himself to be understood, and even now can *everyone* understand him? He is not "popular." How many people have succeeded in assimilating Einstein? The fact that only a few people are capable of a clear understanding of the theories of modern physicists does not make me doubt their validity; and this truth that they have discovered is neither invention nor subjective vision, but objective reality, outside time, eternal, and the scientific mind has only just touched the fringe of it. Where we are concerned with an unchanging truth, all we ever do is approach, move away and then draw closer again.

There also exists—as we are meant to be talking about the theatre—a dramatic idiom, a theatrical method of approach, a trail to blaze, if we are to reach a reality that has objective existence: and this trail to blaze (or path to find again) cannot be other than one belonging to the theatre, which will lead to a reality that can only be revealed theatrically. It is what we might agree to call laboratory research.

There is no reason why there should not be drama for *the people* (I am not quite sure who the people are, unless it is the majority, the non-specialists), boulevard theatre, a theatre of propaganda and instruction, composed in some conventional idiom: this is popularized theatre. We must not for this reason prevent the other kind of theatre from continuing its work: a drama of research, laboratory drama, the avant-garde. If it is not taken up by a large public, this in no way means that it is not of vital importance to our minds, as necessary as artistic, literary or scientific research. We do not always know *what use it is*— but as it fulfills a mental requirement, it is clearly quite indispensable. If such drama has an audience of fifty people every evening (and it can have that number) the need for it is proved. This kind of theatre is in danger. Politics, apathy, malice and jealousy are, unfortunately, a dangerous threat on every side to such writers as Beckett, Vauthier, Schéhadé, Weingarten and others, as well as to their supporters.

ENGLISH DRAMATIC CRITICISM OF THE NINETEENTH AND TWENTIETH CENTURIES

At a time when the English drama was near its lowest ebb, England could boast of at least half a dozen of her greatest critics. True it is that Coleridge and Lamb, Hazlitt, and Leigh Hunt, did not devote all their criticisms to the acted drama, but the theories they evolvea are applicable to it. Coleridge and Lamb went far to engage the interest of their contemporaries in the earlier English stage, while Hazlitt and Hunt applied themselves more particularly to the criticism of acting. Most of Coleridge's best dramatic criticism is found in the *Lectures on Shakespeare* and other poets, delivered during the first twenty years of the century. Most of Lamb's essays on the drama are of a discursive character and pertain to acting, though in the Notes to his *Specimens of English Dramatic Poets* (1808), and in occasional essays, like *On the Artificial Comedy of the Last Century*, he set forth a distinct theory of comedy. Of William Hazlitt's many hundreds of periodical criticisms, those pertaining to the drama are found for the most part in *View of the English Stage* (1818 and 1821), *Lectures on the English Comic Writers* (1819) and *Lectures on the Literature of the Age of Elizabeth* (1820). Leigh Hunt's first collection of criticisms was the *Critical Essays* (1807). He was for years a constant contributor to various papers — *The Reflector, The Indicator, The Companion*, etc. Among Robert Southey's miscellaneous essays, some of which have never been collected, *The Doctor* contains a few articles on the drama and dramatists. Sir Walter Scott wrote a long article on *Drama* in 1810. Shelley's *Defence of Poetry* (1821) contains some passages on the drama. The comparatively minor disputes of the time are reflected in James Sheridan Knowles' *Lectures on Dramatic Literature* (1820–50); John Dennant's *Appeal to the Candour and common sense of the public respecting the present controversy on the subject of plays* (1808), and *Letter to the writer of an anonymous pamphlet in defence of plays* (1808); William Hayley's *Dramatic Observations* (1811); Martin M'Dermot's *A Philosophical Inquiry into the Source of the Pleasure derived from Tragic Representations*, etc. (1824); John William Calcraft's *Defence of the Stage*, etc. (1839); and Edward Mayhew's *Stage Effect* (1840). Into the many literary quarrels of Gifford and Hazlitt, Hunt and Macaulay (see the latter's essay on *Leigh Hunt*, 1841, which contains an attack on Lamb's *Artificial Comedy*) it is not necessary to enter. The more scholarly critics, editors, commentators, historians, of the period are "Christopher North," Hartley Coleridge, Henry Hallam, all of whom at least touched upon dramatic literature, though none produced a body of doctrine on the subject. George Henry Lewes, in his occasional reviews, and in his book, *The Spanish Drama* (1845), and *On Actors and the Art of Acting* (1875), and John Forster — kept up the tradition of Hazlitt and Hunt. Mention should also be made of Percy Fitzgerald's *The Romance of the English Stage* (1874), *Principles of Comedy and Dramatic Effect* (1870), and *A New History of the Stage* (1882). Theodore Martin's *Essays on the Drama* appeared in 1874. The practicing dramatist, W. S. Gilbert, wrote *A Stage Play* (1873). Matthew Arnold included a preface to his play *Merope* in the first edition (1858). *The French Play in London* was published in *Irish Essays*. The more or less professional critics of the mid-nineteenth century often published their articles in book-form. Of outstanding interest may be mentioned: Henry Morley and his *Journal of a London Playgoer from 1851 to 1866* (1866); Morris Mowbray and his *Essays in Theatrical Criticism* (1882); Clement Scott and his *Drama of Yesterday and To-day* (1899); Dutton Cook and his *The Book of the Play* (1876), *Nights at the Play* (1883), and *On the Stage* (1883). Henry Arthur Jones and Sir Arthur Pinero began writing plays in the late seventies, and the former began lecturing on the drama in the eighties. Jones' two books, *The Renascence of the English Drama* (1895), and *Foundations of a National Drama* (1913) were instrumental in developing modern English dramatic art. Pinero wrote little, but his essay on *R. L. Stevenson: The Dramatist* (1903) is an interesting commentary on the art of the drama. Bernard Shaw's copious industry is best represented in his *Dramatic Opinions and Essays* (1906), collected from his *Saturday Review* criticisms of the nineties, and his *Prefaces*. Shaw successfully attacked artificiality and insincerity in the drama, and made way for the play of ideas. Later dramatists have stated their theories of play-writing. Among these, the following may be mentioned in passing: H. Granville-Barker, in a number of occasional magazine articles; John Masefield in his Preface to *Nan* (1911); St. John Hankin (*A Note on Happy Endings*, 1907, *Puritanism and the English Stage*, 1906, *Mr. Bernard Shaw as Critic*, 1907, *How to Run an Art Theatre for London*, 1907, and *The Collected Plays of Oscar Wilde*, 1908); and John Galsworthy in his *Some Platitudes Concerning Drama* (1909) and *The New Spirit in the Drama* (1913). Jerome K. Jerome, Israel Zangwill, and Sydney Grundy have contributed more or less interesting articles and books on their art. Arthur Symons (in his *Plays, Acting and Music,* 1909); W. L. Courtney (in his *Idea of Tragedy,* 1900, and articles on the *Idea of Comedy,* 1913–14); W. L. George (in his *Dramatic Actualities*) have all contributed to dramatic theory. The regular dramatic critics are of considerable importance, especially William Archer (*About the Theatre,* 1886, *The Theatrical World* 1894–98, *Study and Stage,* 1899, and *Playmaking,*

1912); Arthur Bingham Walkley (*Playhouse Impressions,* 1892, *Frames of Mind,* 1899, *Dramatic Criticism,* 1903, and *Drama and Life,* 1908); J. T. Grein (*Premières of the Year,* 1900, and *Dramatic Criticism,* 1899, 1901, 1904); and Max Beerbohm (*Around Theatres,* 1930). George Meredith's *Essay on Comedy and the Uses of the Comic Spirit* was first delivered as a lecture in 1877, and reprinted in book-form twenty years later. "E. F. S." (E. F. Spence) has collected a number of criticisms in his suggestive book, *Our Stage and its Critics* (1910). A later school of dramatic critics, some of whom did not publish all their work in book form, included E. A. Baughn, Ashley Dukes, P. P. Howe, Huntley Carter, C. E. Montague, James Agate, A. N. Monkhouse, Graham Sutton, Ivor Brown, Gilbert Cannan, and John Palmer, who brought certain new ideas into dramatic criticism. See especially Dukes' *Modern Dramatists* (1911), and *The World to Play With,* P. P. Howe's *Dramatic Portraits* (1914), Huntley Carter's *The New Spirit in Drama and Art* (1912); C. E. Montague's *Dramatic Values* (1911), Gilbert Cannan's *Joy of the Theatre* (1913), and John Palmer's *Comedy* (1913 or 14), and *The Future of the Theatre* (1909). The Irish Theatre movement has aroused considerable theorizing. See especially William Butler Yeats: *The Irish Dramatic Movement* (articles collected from *Samhain, The Arrow,* etc., 1901–07); *Discoveries* (1907); *Ideas of Good and Evil* (1903); *Preface* to *Plays for an Irish Theatre* (1911). George Moore: *Impressions and Opinions* (1891), and prefaces to his own play, *The Bending of the Bough* (1900), and to Martyn's *Heather Field* (1899). J. M. Synge: *Preface* to *The Tinker's Wedding* (1907) and *The Playboy of the Western World* (1907). Lord Dunsany: in *Romance and the Modern Stage* (1911). Sean O'Casey: *The Green Crow* (1956), and his multi-volume autobiography.

James Agate established himself as the most influential drama critic of the period between the two world wars, and published many volumes of collected reviews, beginning with *Buzz Buzz* (1918). In this tepid time of English drama, the Irish dramatist Sean O'Casey was one of the few who quarreled with Agate's preference for workmanlike plays that said nothing. But the nature of British drama altered sharply in 1956 with the advent of John Osborne and Brendan Behan, who heralded a new movement featuring plays of social comment. Their

prophet and interpreter was Kenneth Tynan, who collected his reviews in *Curtains* (1961). The verse plays and essays of T. S. Eliot remained apart from these shifting currents in the popular theatre.

SAMUEL TAYLOR COLERIDGE

Samuel Taylor Coleridge **was born at** Ottery St. Mary, Devon, in 1772. His father, a minister, gave Samuel an education with a view to training him to enter the church. At the age of ten he was sent to Christ's Hospital, London, where he made the acquaintance of Lamb. Here he stayed for seven years. Two years later he went to Cambridge, where he distinguished himself as a good scholar. But his studies were constantly interrupted by his preoccupation with the new ideas of the time, engendered by the French Revolution. In 1793, he left college and enlisted in the cavalry, but he was released and returned to Cambridge the next year. A little later, at Oxford, he met Southey, and the two planned an ideal republic, which came to naught. In 1794 Coleridge left Cambridge without his degree. He lectured in Bristol on political subjects, and published a few poems. The next year he married. From Bristol the Coleridges moved to Nether Stowey and enjoyed the friendship of the Wordsworths, who were their neighbors. At this time he was preaching and getting subscribers to a paper — which soon failed. Between 1796 and 1798 he wrote *The Ancient Mariner* and most of his best poems, which were published in 1798. The same year the Wedgwoods offered Coleridge an annuity, and the poet went to Germany, where he became deeply interested in philosophy and metaphysics. On his

return in 1800 he published his translations from Schiller, and soon after contributed a series of philosophical articles to the *Morning Post*. It was in 1801 that he began to take opium. In 1804 he became a secretary in Malta, and later traveled in Italy. He did comparatively little during the next few years, though he delivered lectures in London, and founded a magazine, *The Friend*. His play, *Remorse*, was produced with some success at Drury Lane. Some years after, he put himself under the care of Mr. Gillman of Highgate, who eventually cured him of his disease. Further lectures were given, and partially written down; these contain some of his best critical work. He died at Highgate in 1834.

Coleridge's critical writings are supremely important. His drama criticism is not primarily of the acted drama, but his viewpoint in general is all-embracing and inspirational. The best of his dramatic criticism is in the *Lectures on Shakespeare* and other dramatists, but it is in flashes, random notes, and in the notes of others who took down his utterances, that they are found. Matthew Arnold said of him: "That which will stand of Coleridge is this: the stimulus of his continual instinctive effort to get at and to lay bare the real truth of his matter in hand, whether that matter were literary or philosophical, or political or religious; and this in a country when at that moment such an effort was almost unknown."

GREEK DRAMA [1]

(1818)

It is truly singular that Plato,— whose

1 Re-printed extracts from the Everyman's Library Edition of the *Lectures*, etc., first delivered in **1812** and printed in the *Literary Remains*, vol. 2 (London, 1836).— Ed.

philosophy and religion were but exotic at home, and a mere opposition to the finite in all things, genuine prophet and anticipator as he was of the Protestant Christian era,— should have given in his

Dialogue of the *Banquet*, a justification of our Shakespeare. For he relates that, when all the other guests had either dispersed or fallen asleep, Socrates only, together with Aristophanes and Agathon, remained awake, and that, while he continued to drink with them out of a large goblet, he compelled them, though most reluctantly, to admit that it was the business of one and the same genius to excel in tragic and comic poetry, or that the tragic poet ought, at the same time, to contain within himself the powers of comedy. Now, as this was directly repugnant to the entire theory of the ancient critics, and contrary to all their experience, it is evident that Plato must have fixed the eye of his contemplation on the innermost essentials of the drama, abstracted from the forms of age or country. In another passage he even adds the reason, namely, that opposites illustrate each other's nature, and in their struggle draw forth the strength of the combatants, and display the conqueror as sovereign even on the territories of the rival power.

Nothing can more forcibly exemplify the separative spirit of the Greek arts than their comedy as opposed to their tragedy. But as the immediate struggle of contraries supposes an arena common to both, so both were alike ideal; that is, the comedy of Aristophanes rose to as great a distance above the ludicrous of real life, as the tragedy of Sophocles above its tragic events and passions,— and it is in this one point, of absolute ideality, that the comedy of Shakespeare and the old comedy of Athens coincide. In this also alone did the Greek tragedy and comedy unite; in everything else they were exactly opposed to each other. Tragedy is poetry in its deepest earnest; comedy is poetry in unlimited jest. Earnestness consists in the direction and convergence of all the powers of the soul to one aim, and in the voluntary restraint of its activity in consequence; the opposite, therefore, lies in the apparent abandonment of all definite aim or end, and in the removal of all bounds in the exercise of the mind,— attaining its real end, as an entire contrast, most perfectly, the greater the display is of intellectual wealth squandered in the wantonness of sport without an object, and the more abundant the life and vivacity in the creations of the arbitrary will.

The later comedy, even where it was really comic, was doubtless likewise more comic, the more free it appeared from any fixed aim. Misunderstandings of intention, fruitless struggles of absurd passion, contradictions of temper, and laughable situations there were; but still the form of the representation itself was serious; it proceeded as much according to settled laws, and used as much the same means of art, though to a different purpose, as the regular tragedy itself. But in the old comedy the very form itself is whimsical; the whole work is one great jest, comprehending a world of jests within it, among which each maintains its own place without seeming to concern itself as to the relation in which it may stand to its fellows. In short, in Sophocles, the constitution of tragedy is monarchical, but such as it existed in elder Greece, limited by laws, and therefore the more venerable,— all the parts adapting and submitting themselves to the majesty of the heroic scepter: — in Aristophanes, comedy, on the contrary, is poetry in its most democratic form, and it is a fundamental principle with it, rather to risk all the confusion of anarchy, than to destroy the independence and privileges of its individual constituents,— place, verse, characters, even single thoughts, conceits, and allusions, each turning on the pivot of its own free will.

The tragic poet idealizes his characters by giving to the spiritual part of our nature a more decided preponderance over the animal cravings and impulses, than is met with in real life: the comic poet idealizes his characters by making the animal the governing power, and the intellectual the mere instrument. But as tragedy is not a collection of virtues and perfections, but takes care only that the vices and imperfections shall spring from the passions, errors, and prejudices which arise out of the soul; — so neither is comedy a mere crowd of vices and follies, but whatever qualities it represents, even though they are in a certain sense amiable, it still displays them as having their origin in some dependence on our lower nature, accompanied with a defect in true freedom of spirit and self-subsistence, and subject to that unconnection by contradictions of the inward being, to which all folly is owing.

The ideal of earnest poetry consists in the union and harmonious melting down. and fusion of the sensual into the spiritual,— of man as an animal into man as a power of reason and self-government. And this we have represented to us most clearly in the plastic art, or statuary; where the perfection of outward form is a symbol of the perfection of an inward idea; where the body is wholly penetrated by the soul, and spiritualized even to a state of glory, and like a transparent substance, the matter, in its own nature darkness, becomes altogether a vehicle and fixture of light, a means of developing its beauties, and unfolding its wealth of various colors without disturbing its unity, or causing a division of the parts. The sportive ideal, on the contrary, consists in the perfect harmony and concord of the higher nature with the animal, as with its ruling principle and its acknowledged regent. The understanding and practical reason are represented as the willing slaves of the senses and appetites, and of the passions arising out of them. Hence we may admit the appropriateness to the old comedy, as a work of defined art, of allusions and descriptions, which morality can never justify, and, only with reference to the author himself, and only as being the effect or rather the cause of the circumstances in which he wrote, can consent even to palliate.

The old comedy rose to its perfection in Aristophanes, and in him also it died with the freedom of Greece. Then arose a species of drama, more fitly called, dramatic entertainment than comedy, but of which, nevertheless, our modern comedy (Shakespeare's altogether excepted) is the genuine descendant. Euripides had already brought tragedy lower down and by many steps nearer to the real world than his predecessors had ever done, and the passionate admiration which Menander and Philemon expressed for him, and their open avowals that he was their great master, entitle us to consider their dramas as of a middle species, between tragedy and comedy,— not the tragi-comedy, or thing of heterogeneous

parts, but a complete whole, founded on principles of its own. Throughout we find the drama of Menander distinguishing itself from tragedy, but not, as the genuine old comedy, contrasting with, and opposing it. Tragedy, indeed, carried the thoughts into the mythologic world, in order to raise the emotions, the fears, and the hopes, which convince the inmost heart that their final cause is not to be discovered in the limits of mere mortal life, and force us into a presentiment, however dim, of a state in which those struggles of inward free will with outward necessity, which form the true subject of the tragedian, shall be reconciled and solved; — the entertainment or new comedy, on the other hand, remained within the circle of experience. Instead of the tragic destiny, it introduced the power of chance; even in the few fragments of Menander and Philemon now remaining to us, we find many exclamations and reflections concerning chance and fortune, as in the tragic poets concerning destiny. In tragedy, the moral law, either as obeyed or violated, above all consequences — its own maintenance or violation constituting the most important of all consequences — forms the ground; the new comedy, and our modern comedy in general (Shakespeare excepted as before), lies in prudence or imprudence, enlightened or misled self-love. The whole moral system of the entertainment exactly like that of fable, consists in rules of prudence, with an exquisite conciseness, and at the same time an exhaustive fullness of sense. An old critic said that tragedy was the flight or elevation of life, comedy (that of Menander) its arrangement or ordonnance.

Add to these features a portrait-like truth of character,— not so far indeed as that a bona fide individual should be described or imagined, but yet so that the features which give interest and permanence to the class should be individualized. The old tragedy moved in an ideal world,— the old comedy in a fantastic world. As the entertainment, or new comedy, restrained the creative activity both of the fancy and the imagination, it indemnified the understanding in appealing to the judgment for the probability of the scenes represented. The ancients themselves acknowledged the new comedy as an exact copy of real life. The grammarian, Aristophanes, somewhat affectedly exclaimed:—" O Life and Menander! which of you two imitated the other?" In short the form of this species of drama was poetry, the stuff or matter was prose. It was prose rendered delightful by the blandishments and measured motions of the muse. Yet even this was not universal. The mimes of Sophron, so passionately admired by Plato, were written in prose, and were scenes out of real life conducted in dialogue. The exquisite *Feast of Adonis* (Συρακούσιαι ἢ Ἀδωνιάζουσαι) in Theocritus, we are told, with some others of his eclogues, were close imitations of certain mimes of Sophron — free translations of the prose into hexameters. . . .

.　　.　　.　　.　　.　　.

PROGRESS OF THE DRAMA [2]

(1818)

.　　.　　.　　.　　.　　.

And here it will be necessary to say a few words on the stage and on stage-illusion.

A theater, in the widest sense of the word, is the general term for all places of amusement through the ear or eye, in which men assembled in order to be amused by some entertainment presented to all at the same time and in common. Thus, an old Puritan divine says:— "Those who attend public worship and sermons only to amuse themselves, make a theater of the church, and turn God's house into the devil's. *Theatra ædes diabololatricæ.*" The most important and dignified species of this *genus* is, doubtless, the stage, (*res theatralis histrionica*), which, in addition to the generic definition above given, may be characterized in its idea, or according to what it does, or ought to, aim at, as a combination of several or of all the fine arts in an harmonious whole, having a distinct end of its own, to which the peculiar end of each of the component arts, taken separately, is made subordinate and subservient,— that, namely, of imitating reality — whether external things, actions, or passions — under a semblance of reality. Thus, Claude imitates a landscape at sunset, but only as a picture; while a forest-scene is not presented to the spectators as a picture, but as a forest; and though, in the full sense of the word, we are no more deceived by the one than by the other, yet are our feelings very differently affected; and the pleasure derived from the one is not composed of the same elements as that afforded by the other, even on the supposition that the *quantum* of both were equal. In the former, a picture, it is a condition of all genuine delight that we should not be deceived; in the latter, stage-scenery, (inasmuch as its principal end is not in or for itself, as is the case in a picture, but to be an assistance and means to an end out of itself) its very purpose is to produce as much illusion as its nature permits. These, and all other stage presentations, are to produce a sort of temporary half-faith, which the spectator encourages in himself and supports by a voluntary contribution on his own part, because he knows that it is at all times in his power to see the thing as it really is. I have often observed that little children are actually deceived by stage-scenery, never by pictures; though even these produce an effect on their impressible minds, which they do not on the minds of adults. The child, if strongly impressed, does not indeed positively think the picture to be the reality; but yet he does not think the contrary. As Sir George Beaumont was shewing me a very fine engraving from Rubens, representing a storm at sea without any vessel or boat introduced, my little boy, then about five years old, came dancing and singing into the room, and all at once (if I may so say) *tumbled in* upon the print. He instantly started, stood silent and motionless, with the strongest expression, first of wonder and then of grief in his eyes and countenance, and at length said,

2 Re-printed extracts from the Everyman's Library Edition of the *Lectures*. Originally delivered in 1818 and first printed in vol. 2 of the *Literary Remains* (London, 1836).—Ed.

" And where is the ship? But that is sunk, and the men are all drowned!" still keeping his eyes fixed on the print. Now what pictures are to little children, stage illusion is to men, provided they retain any part of the child's sensibility; except, that in the latter instance, the suspension of the act of comparison, which permits this sort of negative belief, is somewhat more assisted by the will, than in that of a child respecting a picture.

The true stage-illusion in this and in all other things consists — not in the mind's judging it to be a forest, but, in its remission of the judgment that it is not a forest. And this subject of stage-illusion is so important, and so many practical errors and false criticisms may arise, and indeed have arisen, either from reasoning on it as actual delusion, (the strange notion, on which the French critics built up their theory, and on which the French poets justify the construction of their tragedies), or from denying it altogether, (which seems the end of Dr. Johnson's reasoning, and which, as extremes meet, would lead to the very same consequences, by excluding whatever would not be judged probable by us in our coolest state of feeling, with all our faculties in even balance), that these few remarks will, I hope, be pardoned, if they should serve either to explain or to illustrate the point. For not only are we never absolutely deluded — or anything like it, but the attempt to cause the highest delusion possible to beings in their senses sitting in a theater, is a gross fault, incident only to low minds, which, feeling that they cannot affect the heart or head permanently, endeavor to call forth the momentary affections. There ought never to be more pain than is compatible with co-existing pleasure, and to be amply repaid by thought.

Shakespeare found the infant stage demanding an intermixture of ludicrous character as imperiously as that of Greece did the chorus, and high language accordant. And there are many advantages in this; — a greater assimilation to nature, a greater scope of power, more truths, and more feelings; — the effects of contrast. as in Lear and the Fool; and especially this, that the true language of passion becomes sufficiently elevated by your having previously heard, in the same piece, the lighter conversation of men under no strong emotion. The very nakedness of the stage, too, was advantageous,— for the drama thence became something between recitation and representation; and the absence or paucity of scenes allowed a freedom from the laws of unity of place and unity of time, the observance of which must either confine the drama to as few subjects as may be counted on the fingers, or involve gross improbabilities, far more striking than the violation would have caused. Thence, also, was precluded the danger of a false ideal,— of aiming at more than what is possible on the whole. What play of the ancients, with reference to their ideal, does not hold out more glaring absurdities than any in Shakspeare? On the Greek plan a man could more easily be a poet than a dramatist; upon our plan more easily a dramatist than a poet.

THE DRAMA GENERALLY, AND PUBLIC TASTE [3]

(1818)

. . . .

In my last address I defined poetry to be the art, or whatever better term our language may afford, of representing external nature and human thoughts, both relatively to human affections, so as to cause the production of as great immedi-

3 Re-printed extracts from the Everyman's Library Edition. Originally delivered in 1818, and first printed in vol. 2 of the *Literary Remains* (London, 1836).— Ed.

ate pleasure in each part, as is compatible with the largest possible sum of pleasure on the whole. Now this definition applies equally to painting and music as to poetry; and in truth the term poetry is alike applicable to all three. The vehicle alone constitutes the difference; and the term " poetry " is rightly applied by eminence to measured words, only because the sphere of their action is far wider, the power of giving permanence to them much more certain, and incomparably greater the facility, by which men, not defective by nature or disease, may be enabled to derive habitual pleasure and instruction from them. On my mentioning these considerations to a painter of great genius, who had been, from a most honorable enthusiasm, extolling his own art, he was so struck with their truth, that he exclaimed, " I want no other arguments; — poetry, that is, verbal poetry, must be the greatest; all that proves final causes in the world, proves this; it would be shocking to think otherwise!"— And in truth, deeply, O! far more than words can express, as I venerate the Last Judgment and the Prophets of Michel Angelo Buonarotti,— yet the very pain which I repeatedly felt as I lost myself in gazing upon them, the painful consideration that their having been painted in *fresco* was the sole cause that they had not been abandoned to all the accidents of a dangerous transportation to a distant capital, and that the same caprice, which made the Neapolitan soldiery destroy all the exquisite masterpieces on the walls of the church of the *Trinitado Monte,* after the retreat of their antagonist barbarians, might as easily have made vanish the rooms and open gallery of Raphael, and the yet more unapproachable wonders of the sublime Florentine in the Sixtine Chapel, forced upon my mind the reflection; How grateful the human race ought to be that the works of Euclid, Newton, Plato, Milton, Shakespeare, are not subjected to similar contingencies,— that they and their fellows, and the great, though inferior, peerage of undying intellect, are secured; — secured even from a second irruption of Goths and Vandals, in addition to many other safeguards, by the vast empire of English language, laws, and religion founded in America, through the overflow of the power and the virtue of my country; — and that now the great and certain works of genuine fame can only cease to act for mankind, when men themselves cease to be men, or when the planet. on which they exist, shall have altered its relations, or have ceased to be.

. . . . . .

But let us now consider what the drama should be. And first, it is not a copy, but an imitation, of nature. This is the universal principle of the fine arts. In all well laid out grounds what delight do we feel from that balance and antithesis of feelings and thoughts! How natural! we say; — but the very wonder that caused the exclamation, implies that we perceived art at the same moment. We catch the hint from nature itself. Whenever in mountains or cataracts we discover a likeness to anything artificial which yet we know is not artificial — what pleasure! And so it is in appearances known to be artificial, which appear to be natural. This applies in due degrees, regulated by steady good sense, from a clump of trees to the *Paradise Lost* or *Othello.* It would be easy to apply it to painting and even, though with greater abstraction of thought, and by more subtle yet equally just analogies — to music. But this belongs to others; suffice it that one great principle is common to all the fine arts, a principle which probably is the condition of all consciousness, without which we should feel and imagine only by discontinuous moments, and be plants or brute animals instead of men; — I mean that evervarying balance, or balancing, of images, notions, or feelings, conceived as in opposition to each other; — in short, the perception of identity and contrariety; the least degree of which constitutes likeness, the greatest absolute indifference; but the infinite gradations between these two form all the play and all the interest of our intellectual and moral being, till it leads us to a feeling and an object more awful than it seems to me compatible with even the present subject to utter aloud, though I am most desirous to suggest it. For there alone are all things at once different and the same; there alone, as the principle of all things, does distinction exist unaided by division; there are will and reason, succession of time and unmoving eternity, infinite change and ineffable rest! —

Return Alpheus! the dread voice is past
Which shrunk thy streams!

——— Thou honor'd flood,
Smooth-flowing Avon, crown'd with vocal
*   reeds,*
That strain I heard, was of a higher
*   mood! —*
But now my voice proceeds.

We may divide a dramatic poet's characteristics before we enter into the component merits of any one work, and with reference only to those things which are to be the materials of all, into language, passion, and character; always bearing in mind that these must act and react on each other,— the language inspired by the passion, and the language and the passion modified and differenced by the character. To the production of the highest excellencies in these three, there are requisite in the mind of the author; — good sense; talent; sensibility; imagination; — and to the perfection of a work we should add two faculties of lesser importance, yet necessary for the ornaments and foliage of the column and the roof — fancy and a quick sense of beauty.

. . . . .

The German tragedies have in some respects been justly ridiculed. In them the dramatist often becomes a novelist in his directions to the actors, and thus degrades tragedy into pantomime. Yet still the consciousness of the poet's mind must be diffused over that of the reader or spectator; but he himself, according to his genius, elevates us, and by being always in keeping, prevents us from perceiving any strangeness, though we feel great exultation. Many different kinds of style may be admirable, both in different men, and in different parts of the same poem.

See the different language which strong feelings may justify in Shylock, and learn from Shakespeare's conduct of that character the terrible force of every plain and calm diction, when known to proceed from a resolved and impassioned man.

It is especially with reference to the drama, and its characteristics in any given nation, or at any particular period, that the dependence of genius on the public taste becomes a matter of the deepest importance. I do not mean that taste which springs merely from caprice or fashionable imitation, and which, in fact, genius can, and by degrees will, create for itself; but that which arises out of wide-grasping and heart-enrooted causes, which is epidemic, and in the very air that all breathe. This it is which kills, or withers, or corrupts. Socrates, indeed, might walk arm and arm with

Hygeia, whilst pestilence, with a thousand furies running to and fro, and clashing against each other in a complexity and agglomeration of horrors, was shooting her darts of fire and venom all around him. Even such was Milton; yea, and such, in spite of all that has been babbled by his critics in pretended excuse for his damning, because for them too profound, excellencies,— such was Shakspeare. But alas! the exceptions prove the rule. For who will dare to force his way out of the crowd,— not of the mere vulgar,— but of the vain and banded aristocracy of intellect, and presume to join the almost supernatural beings that stand by themselves aloof?

Of this diseased epidemic influence there are two forms especially preclusive of tragic worth. The first is the necessary growth of a sense and love of the ludicrous, and a morbid sensibility of the assimilative power,— an inflammation produced by cold and weakness,— which in the boldest bursts of passion will lie in wait for a jeer at any phrase, that may have an accidental coincidence in the mere words with something base or trivial. For instance,— to express woods, not on a plain, but clothing a hill, which overlooks a valley, or dell, or river, or the sea,— the trees rising one above another, as the spectators in an ancient theater,— I know no other word in our language, (bookish and pedantic terms out of the question,) but *hanging* woods, the *sylvæ superimpendentes* of Catullus; yet let some wit call out in a slang tone,—"the gallows!" and a peal of laughter would damn the play. Hence it is that so many dull pieces have had a decent run, only because nothing unusual above, or absurd below, mediocrity furnished an occasion,— a spark for the explosive materials collected behind the orchestra. But it would take a volume of no ordinary size however laconically the sense were expressed, if it were meant to instance the effects, and unfold all the causes, of this disposition upon the moral, intellectual, and even physical character of a people, with its influences on domestic life and individual deportment. A good document upon this subject would be the history of Paris society and of French, that is, Parisian, literature from the commencement of the latter half of the reign of Louis XIV to that of Buonaparte, compared with the preceding philosophy and poetry even of Frenchmen themselves.

The second form, or more properly, perhaps, another distinct cause, of this diseased disposition is matter of exultation to the philanthropist and philosopher, and of regret to the poet, the painter, and the statuary alone, and to them only as poets, painters, and statuaries;—namely, the security, the comparative equability, and ever increasing sameness of human life. Men are now

so seldom thrown into wild circumstances, and violences of excitement, that the language of such states, the laws of association of feeling with thought, the starts and strange far-flights of the assimilative power on the slightest and least obvious likeness presented by thoughts, words, or objects,—these are all judged of by authority, not by actual experience,—by what men have been accustomed to regard as symbols of these states, and not the natural symbols, or self-manifestations of them.

NOTES ON *THE TEMPEST* [4]
(1836)

There is a sort of improbability with which we are shocked in dramatic representation, not less than in a narrative of real life. Consequently, there must be rules respecting it; and as rules are nothing but means to an end previously ascertained—(inattention to which simple truth has been the occasion of all the pedantry of the French school),—we must first determine what the immediate end or object of the drama is. And here, as I have previously remarked, I find two extremes of critical decision;—the French, which evidently presupposes that a perfect delusion is to be aimed at,—an opinion which needs no fresh confutation; and the exact opposite to it, brought forward by Dr. Johnson, who supposes the auditors throughout in the full reflective knowledge of the contrary. In evincing the impossibility of delusion, he makes no sufficient allowance for an intermediate state, which I have before distinguished by the term, illusion, and have attempted to illustrate its quality and character by reference to our mental state, when dreaming. In both cases we simply do not judge the imagery to be unreal; there is a negative reality, and no more. Whatever, therefore, tends to prevent the mind from placing itself, or being placed, gradually in that state in which the images have such negative reality for the auditor,

destroys this illusion, and is dramatically improbable.

Now the production of this effect—a sense of improbability—will depend on the degree of excitement in which the mind is supposed to be. Many things would be intolerable in the first scene of a play, that would not at all interrupt our enjoyment in the height of the interest, when the narrow cockpit may be made to hold

The vast field of France, or we may cram
Within its wooden O the very casques
That did affright the air at Agincourt.

Again, on the other hand, many obvious improbabilities will be endured, as belonging to the groundwork of the story rather than to the drama itself, in the first scenes, which would disturb or disentrance us from all illusion in the acme' of our excitement; as for instance, Lear's division of his kingdom, and the banishment of Cordelia.

But, although the other excellences of the drama besides this dramatic probability, as unity of interest, with distinctness and subordination of the characters, and appropriateness of style, are all, so far as they tend to increase the inward excitement, means towards accomplishing the chief end, that of producing and supporting this willing illusion,—yet they do not on that account cease to be ends themselves; and we must remember that, as such, they carry their own justification with them, as long as they do not

4 Re-printed, with one omission, from the Everyman's Library Edition. Originally printed in vol. 2 of the *Literary Remains* (London, 1836).— Ed.

contravene or interrupt the total illusion. It is not even always, or of necessity, an objection to them, that they prevent the illusion from rising to as great a height as it might otherwise have attained; — it is enough that they are simply compatible with as high a degree of it as is requisite for the purpose. Nay, upon particular occasions, a palpable improbability may be hazarded by a great genius for the express purpose of keeping down the interest of a merely instrumental scene, which would otherwise make too great an impression for the harmony of the entire illusion. Had the panorama been invented in the time of Pope Leo X, Raphael would still, I doubt not, have smiled in contempt at the regret, that the broom twigs and scrubby brushes at the back of some of his grand pictures were not as probable trees as those in the exhibition.

The Tempest is a specimen of the purely romantic drama, in which the interest is not historical, or dependent upon fidelity of portraiture, or the natural connection of events,— but is a birth of the imagination, and rests only on the coaptation and union of the elements granted to, or assumed by, the poet. It is a species of drama which owes no allegiance to time or space, and in which, therefore, errors of chronology and geography — no mortal sins in any species — are venial faults, and count for nothing. It addresses itself entirely to the imaginative faculty; and although the illusion may be assisted by the effect on the senses of the complicated scenery and decorations of modern times, yet this sort of assistance is dangerous. For the principal and only genuine excitement ought to come from within,— from the moved and sympathetic imagination; whereas, where so much is addressed to the mere external senses of seeing and hearing, the spiritual vision is apt to languish, and the attraction from without will withdraw the mind from the proper and only legitimate interest which is intended to spring from within.

The romance opens with a busy scene admirably appropriate to the kind of drama, and giving, as it were, the key-note to the whole harmony. It prepares and initiates the excitement required for the entire piece, and yet does not demand anything from the spectators, which their previous habits had not fitted them to understand. It is the bustle of a tempest, from which the real horrors are abstracted; — therefore it is poetical, though not in strictness natural —(the distinction to which I have so often alluded)— and is purposely restrained from concentering the interest on itself, but used merely as an induction or tuning for what is to follow.

In the second scene, Prospero's speeches, till the entrance of Ariel, contain the finest example, I remember, of retrospective narration for the purpose of exciting immediate interest, and putting the audience in possession of all the information necessary for the understanding of the plot. Observe, too, the perfect probability of the moment chosen by Prospero (the very Shakspeare himself, as it were, of the tempest) to open out the truth to his daughter, his own romantic bearing, and how completely anything that might have been disagreeable to us in the magician, is reconciled and shaded in the humanity and natural feelings of the father. In the very first speech of Miranda the simplicity and tenderness of her character are at once laid open; — it would have been lost in direct contact with the agitation of the first scene. The opinion once prevailed, but, happily, is now abandoned, that Fletcher alone wrote for women; — the truth is, that with very few, and those partial, exceptions, the female characters in the plays of Beaumont and Fletcher are, when of the light kind, not decent; when heroic, complete viragos. But in Shakspeare all the elements of womanhood are holy, and there is the sweet, yet dignified feeling of all that *continuates* society, as sense of ancestry and of sex, with a purity unassailable by sophistry, because it rests not in the analytic processes, but in that same equipoise of the faculties, during which the feelings are representative of all past experience,— not of the individual only, but of all those by whom she has been educated, and their predecessors even up to the first mother that lived. Shakspeare saw that the want of prominence, which Pope notices for sarcasm, was the blessed beauty of the woman's character, and knew that it arose not from any deficiency, but from the more exquisite harmony of all the parts of the moral being constituting one living total of head and heart. He has drawn it, indeed, in all its distinctive energies of faith, patience, constancy, fortitude,— shown in all of them as following the heart, which gives its results by a nice tact and happy intuition, without the intervention of the discursive faculty, sees all things in and by the light of the affections, and errs, if it ever err, in the exaggerations of love alone. In all the Shakspearian women there is essentially the same foundation and principle; the distinct individuality and variety are merely the result of the modification of circumstances, whether in Miranda the maiden, in Imogen the wife, or in Katherine the queen.

But to return. The appearance and characters of the super or ultra-natural servants are finely contrasted. Ariel has in everything the airy tint which gives the name; and it is worthy of remark that Miranda is never directly brought into comparison with Ariel, lest the natural and human of the one and the supernatural of the other should tend to neutralize each other; Caliban, on the other hand, is all earth, all condensed and gross in feelings and images; he has the dawnings of understanding without reason or the moral sense, and in him, as in some brute animals, this advance to the intellectual faculties, without the moral sense, is marked by the appearance of vice. For it is in the primacy of the moral being only that man is truly human; in his intellectual powers he is certainly approached by the brutes, and, man's whole system duly considered, those powers cannot be considered other than means to an end, that is, to morality.

In this scene, as it proceeds, is displayed the impression made by Ferdinand and Miranda on each other; it is

love at first sight:—

> at the first sight
> They have chang'd eyes:—

and it appears to me, that in all cases of real love, it is at one moment that it takes place. That moment may have been prepared by previous esteem, admiration, or even affection,— yet love seems to require a momentary act of volition, by which a tacit bond of devotion is imposed,— a bond not to be thereafter broken without violating what should be sacred in our nature. How finely is the true Shakspearian scene contrasted with Dryden's vulgar alteration of it in which a mere ludicrous psychological experiment, as it were, is tried — displaying nothing but indelicacy without passion. Prospero's interruption of the courtship has often seemed to me to have no sufficient motive; still his alleged reason —

> lest too light winning
> Make the prize light —

is enough for the ethereal connections of the romantic imagination, although it would not be so for the historical. The whole courting scene, indeed, in the beginning of the third act, between the lovers, is a masterpiece; and the first dawn of disobedience in the mind of Miranda to the command of her father is very finely drawn, so as to seem the working of the Scriptural command *Thou shalt leave father and mother*, &c. O! with what exquisite purity this scene is conceived and executed! Shakspeare may sometimes be gross, but I boldly say that he is always moral and modest. Alas! in this our day decency of manners is preserved at the expense of morality of heart, and delicacies for vice are allowed, whilst grossness against it is hypocritically, or at least morbidly, condemned.

·   ·   ·   ·   ·

SHAKSPEARE'S ENGLISH HISTORICAL PLAYS [5]

(1836)

The first form of poetry is the epic,

5 Re-printed extracts from the Everyman's Library Edition. Originally appeared in vol. 2 of the *Literary Remains* (London, 1836). — Ed.

the essence of which may be stated as the successive in events and characters. This must be distinguished from narration in which there must always be a narrator, from whom the objects represented receive a coloring and a manner: — whereas in the epic, as in the so called poems of Homer, the whole is completely objective, and the representation is a pure reflection. The next form into which poetry passed was the dramatic; — both forms having a common basis with a certain difference, and that difference not consisting in the dialogue alone. Both are founded on the relation of providence to the human will; and this relation is the universal element, expressed under different points of view according to the difference of religion, and the moral and intellectual cultivation of different nations. In the epic poem fate is represented as overruling the will, and making it instrumental to the accomplishment of its designs: —

$$\text{——— } \Delta\iota\grave{o}s\ \delta\grave{e}\ \tau\epsilon\lambda\epsilon\acute{\iota}\epsilon\tau o\ \beta o\upsilon\lambda\acute{\eta}.$$

In the drama, the will is exhibited as struggling with fate, a great and beautiful instance and illustration of which is the *Prometheus* of Æschylus; and the deepest effect is produced, when the fate is represented as a higher and intelligent will, and the opposition of the individual as springing from a defect.

In order that a drama may be properly historical, it is necessary that it should be the history of the people to whom it is addressed. In the composition, care must be taken that there appear no dramatic improbability, as the reality is taken for granted. It must, likewise, be poetical; — that only, I mean, must be taken which is the permanent in our nature, which is common, and therefore deeply interesting to all ages. The events themselves are immaterial, otherwise than as the clothing and manifestations of the spirit that is working within. In this mode, the unity resulting from succession is destroyed, but is supplied by a unity of a higher order, which connects the events by reference to the workers, gives a reason for them in the motives, and presents men in their causative character. It takes, therefore, that part of real history which is the least known, and infuses a principle of life and organization into the naked facts, and makes them all the framework of an animated whole.

In my happier days, while I had yet hope and onward-looking thoughts, I planned an historical drama of King Stephen, in the manner of Shakspeare. Indeed it would be desirable that some man of dramatic genius should dramatize all those omitted by Shakspeare, as far down as Henry VII. Perkin Warbeck would make a most interesting drama. A few scenes of Marlowe's *Edward II* might be preserved. After *Henry VIII*, the events are too well and distinctly known, to be, without plump inverisimilitude, crowded together in one night's exhibition. Whereas, the history of our ancient kings — the events of their reigns, I mean,— are like stars in the sky; — whatever the real interspaces may be, and however great, they seem close to each other. The stars — the events — strike us and remain in our eye, little modified by the difference of dates. An historic drama is, therefore, a collection of events borrowed from history, but connected together in respect of cause and time, poetically and by dramatic fiction. It would be a fine national custom to act such a series of dramatic histories in orderly succession, in the yearly Christmas holidays, and could not but tend to counteract that mock cosmopolitism, which under a positive term really implies nothing but a negation of, or indifference to, the particular love of our country. By its nationality must every nation retain its independence; — I mean a nationality *quoad* the nation. Better thus; — nationality in each individual, *quoad* his country, is equal to the sense of individuality *quoad* himself; but himself as subsensuous, and central. Patriotism is equal to the sense of individuality reflected from every other individual. There may come a higher virtue in both — just cosmopolitism. But this latter is not possible but by antecedence of the former.

NOTES ON *OTHELLO* [6]

(1836)

Dr. Johnson has remarked that little or nothing is wanting to render the *Othello* a regular tragedy, but to have opened the play with the arrival of Othello in Cyprus, and to have thrown the preceding act into the form of narration. Here then is the place to determine, whether such a change would or would not be an improvement; — nay, (to throw down the glove with a full challenge) whether the tragedy would or not by such an arrangement become more regular,— that is, more consonant with the rules dictated by universal reason, on the true commonsense of mankind, in its application to the particular case. For in all acts of judgment, it can never be too often recollected, and scarcely too often repeated, that rules are means to ends, and, consequently, that the end must be determined and understood before it can be known what the rules are or ought to be. Now, from a certain species of drama, proposing to itself the accomplishment of certain ends,— these partly arising from the idea of the species itself, but in part, likewise, forced upon the dramatist by accidental circumstances beyond his power to remove or control,— three rules have been abstracted; — in other words, the means most conducive to the attainment of the proposed ends have been generalized, and prescribed under the names of the three unities,— the unity of time, the unity of place, and the unity of action,— which last would, perhaps, have been as appropriately, as well as more intelligibly, entitled the unity of interest.

6 Re-printed from the Everyman's Library Edition. First published in vol. 2 of the *Literary Remains* (London, 1836).— Ed.

With this last the present question has no immediate concern: in fact, its conjunction with the former two is a mere delusion of words. It is not properly a rule, but in itself the great end not only of the drama, but of the epic poem, the lyric ode, of all poetry, down to the candle-flame cone of an epigram,— nay of poesy in general, as the proper generic term inclusive of all the fine arts as its species. But of the unities of time and place, which alone are entitled to the names of rules, the history of their origin will be their best criterion. You might take the Greek chorus to a place, but you could not bring a place to them without as palpable an equivoque as bringing Birnam wood to Macbeth at Dunsinane. It was the same, though in a less degree, with regard to the unity of time: — the positive fact, not for a moment removed from the senses, the presence, I mean, of the same identical chorus, was a continued measure of time; — and although the imagination may supersede perception, yet it must be granted to be an imperfection — however easily tolerated — to place the two in broad contradiction to each other. In truth, it is a mere accident of terms; for the Trilogy of the Greek theater was a drama in three acts, and notwithstanding this, what strange contrivances as to place there are in the Aristophanic *Frogs*. Besides, if the law of mere actual perception is once violated — as it repeatedly is even in the Greek tragedies — why is it more difficult to imagine three hours to be three years than to be a whole day and night?

* * * * * *

CHARLES LAMB

Charles Lamb was born at London in 1775. He attended school at a very early age, and at eight was sent to Christ's Hospital. There he met Coleridge, who was destined to be his lifelong friend. After seven years at Christ's Charles returned to his parents. Shortly after, he was employed at the South Sea House, and in 1792 he became a clerk in the East India House, a position he held for many years. Two years after, his first published poem appeared in a newspaper, though it was signed with the initials of Coleridge, who had corrected it. Not long afterward the letters of Lamb bear witness to those periodical attacks of madness to which his sister Mary and he were subject; Mary, indeed, killed her mother in one of her attacks, and the tragedy had a lasting effect on the pair, who lived together until the death of Charles. But in his books and in writings he soon found solace. He wrote, often in collaboration with Mary, a number of tales and poems, and in 1802 published his verse tragedy *John Woodvil*. They both wrote the celebrated *Tales from Shakespeare*, which appeared in 1807. The following year Charles issued the famous *Specimens of English Dramatic Poets*, etc. Meantime he had found time to write the farce *Mr. H.* (1806), which was a failure. Between 1809 and 1817 he contributed various essays to the *Reflector*. In 1818 he publish 1 two volumes of his *Works*. In 1820 he began contributing further essays to the *London Magazine* under the name of Elia. Many of these appeared in book-form in 1823. Two years after this

he retired from his position with a pension. His last years he was able to devote to his work, as he was comparatively well-to-do. A few months after the death of his friend Coleridge, Charles Lamb died, in 1834.

While Lamb wrote a few plays, he is not in any sense a dramatist; these plays are rather experiments from the hand of one interested in poetry and the drama, than expert products of a practicing playwright. His interest in Shakespeare and the Elizabethans was manifest in his *Specimens*, which were more influential than anything else in directing the attention of the moderns to Shakespeare's contemporaries. His love for the old drama is everywhere observable in his writings. As a critic of the drama, Lamb did not contribute much of theory, nor did he formulate any distinctly new ideas, though in the two most important essays, *On the Artificial Comedy of the Last Century*, and *On the Tragedies of Shakespeare*, he puts forward an interesting and ingenious idea.

ON THE ARTIFICIAL COMEDY OF THE LAST CENTURY [1]

[From *Essays of Elia*]

(1823)

The artificial Comedy, or Comedy of manners, is quite extinct on our stage. Congreve and Farquhar show their heads once in seven years only, to be exploded and put down instantly. The times cannot bear them. Is it for a few wild speeches, an occasional license of dialogue? I think not altogether. The business of their dramatic characters will not stand the moral test. We screw everything up to that. Idle gallantry in a fiction, a dream, the passing pageant of an evening, startles us in the same way as the alarming indications of profligacy in a son or ward in real life should startle a parent or guardian. We have no such middle emotions as dramatic interests left. We see a stage libertine playing his loose pranks of two hours' duration, and of no after consequence, with

the severe eyes which inspect real vices with their bearings upon two worlds. We are spectators to a plot or intrigue (not reducible in life to the point of strict morality), and take it all for truth. We substitute a real for a dramatic person, and judge him accordingly. We try him in our courts, from which there is no appeal to the *dramatis personæ*, his peers. We have been spoiled with — not sentimental comedy — but a tyrant far more pernicious to our pleasures which has succeeded to it, the exclusive and all-devouring drama of common life; where the moral point is everything; where, instead of the fictitious half-believed personages of the stage (the phantoms of old comedy), we recognize ourselves, our brothers, aunts, kinsfolk, allies, patrons, enemies,— the same as in life,— with an interest in what is going on so hearty and substantial, that we cannot afford our moral judgment, in its deepest and most vital results, to com-

1 Re-printed in full from the Everyman's Library Edition of *The Essays of Elia* (1906). — Ed.

promise or slumber for a moment. What is *there* transacting, by no modification is made to affect us in any other manner than the same events or characters would do in our relationships of life. We carry our fireside concerns to the theater with us. We do not go thither like our ancestors, to escape from the pressure of reality, so much as to confirm our experience of it; to make assurance double, and take a bond of fate. We must live our toilsome lives twice over, as it was the mournful privilege of Ulysses to descend twice to the shades. All that neutral ground of character, which stood between vice and virtue; or which in fact was indifferent to neither, where neither properly was called into question; that happy breathing-place from the burthen of a perpetual moral questioning — the sanctuary and quiet Alsatia of hunted casuistry — is broken up and disfranchised, as injurious to the interests of society. The privileges of the place are taken away by law. We dare not dally with images, or names, of wrong. We bark like foolish dogs at shadows. We dread infection from the scenic representation of disorder, and fear a painted pustule. In our anxiety that our morality should not take cold, we wrap it up in a great blanket surtout of precaution against the breeze and sunshine.

I confess for myself that (with no great delinquencies to answer for) I am glad for a season to take an airing beyond the diocese of the strict conscience,— not to live always in the precincts of the law-courts,— but now and then, for a dream-while or so, to imagine a world with no meddling restrictions — to get into recesses, whither the hunter cannot follow me —

> *Secret shades*
> *Of woody Ida's inmost grove,*
> *While yet there was no fear of Jove.*

I come back to my cage and my restraint the fresher and more healthy for it. I wear my shackles more contentedly for having respired the breath of an imaginary freedom. I do not know how it is with others, but I feel the better always for the perusal of one of Congreve's — nay, why should I not add, even of Wycherley's — comedies. I am the gayer at least for it; and I could never connect those sports of a witty fancy in any shape with any result to be drawn from them to imitation in real life. They are a world of themselves almost as much a fairyland. Take one of their characters, male or female (with few exceptions they are alike), and place it in a modern play, and my virtuous indignation shall rise against the profligate wretch as warmly as the Catos of the pits could desire; because in a modern play I am to judge of the right and the wrong. The standard of *police* is the measure of *political justice*. The atmosphere will blight it; it cannot live here. It has got into a moral world, where it has no business, from which it must needs fall headlong, as dizzy, and incapable of making a stand, as a Swedenborgian bad spirit that has wandered unawares into the sphere of one of his Good Men, or Angels. But in its own world do we feel the creature is so very bad? — The Fainalls and the Mirabels, the Dorimants and the Lady Touchwoods, in their own sphere, do not offend my moral sense; in fact, they do not appeal to it at all. They seem engaged in their proper element. They break through no laws or conscientious restraints. They know of none. They have got out of Christendom into the land — what shall I call it? — of cuckoldry — the Utopia of gallantry, where pleasure is duty, and the manners perfect freedom. It is altogether a speculative scene of things, which has no reference whatever to the world that is. No good person can be justly offended as a spectator, because no good person suffers on the stage. Judged morally, every character in these plays — the few exceptions only are *mistakes* — is alike essentially vain and worthless. The great art of Congreve is especially shown in this, that he has entirely excluded from his scenes — some little generosities in the part of Angelica perhaps excepted — not only anything like a faultless character, but any pretensions to goodness or good feelings whatsoever. Whether he did this designedly, or instinctively, the effect is as happy as the design (if design) was bold. I used to wonder at the strange power which his Way of the World in particular possesses of interesting you all along in the pursuits of characters, for whom you absolutely care nothing — for you neither hate nor love his personages — and I think it is owing to this very indifference for any, that you endure the whole. He has spread a privation of moral blight, I will call it, rather than by the ugly name of palpable darkness, over his creations; and his shadows flit before you without distinction or preference. Had he introduced a good character, a single gush of moral feeling, a revulsion of the judgment to actual life and actual duties, the impertinent Goshen would have only lighted to the discovery of deformities, which now are none, because we think them none.

Translated into real life, the characters of his, and his friend Wycherley's dramas, are profligates and strumpets — the business of their brief existence, the undivided pursuit of lawless gallantry. No other spring of action, or possible motive of conduct, is recognized; principles which, universally acted upon, must reduce this frame of things to a chaos. But we do them wrong in so translating them. No such effects are produced, in *their* world. When we are among them, we are amongst a chaotic people. We are not to judge them by our usages. No reverend institutions are insulted by their proceedings — for they have none among them. No peace of families is violated — for no family ties exist among them. No purity of the marriage bed is stained — for none is supposed to have a being. No deep affections are disquieted, no holy wedlock bands are snapped asunder — for affection's depth and wedded faith are not of the growth of that soil. There is neither right nor wrong — gratitude or its opposite — claim or duty — paternity or sonship. Of what consequence is it to Virtue or how is she at all concerned about it, whether Sir Simon or Dapperwit steal away Miss Martha; or who is the father of Lord Froth's or Sir Paul Pliant's children?

The whole is a passing pageant, where we should sit as unconcerned at the issues, for life or death, as at the battle of the frogs and mice. But, like Don Quixote, we take part against the puppets, and quite as impertinently. We dare not contemplate an Atlantis, a scheme, out of which our coxcombical moral sense is for a little transitory ease excluded. We have not the courage to imagine a state of things for which there

is neither reward nor punishment. We cling to the painful necessities of shame and blame. We would indict our very dreams.

Amidst the mortifying circumstances attendant upon growing old, it is something to have seen the *School for Scandal* in its glory. This comedy grew out of Congreve and Wycherley, but gathered some allays of the sentimental comedy which followed theirs. It is impossible that it should be now *acted*, though it continues, at long intervals, to be announced in the bills. Its hero, when Palmer played it at least, was Joseph Surface. When I remember the gay boldness, the graceful solemn plausibility, the measured step, the insinuating voice — to express it in a word — the downright *acted* villainy of the part, so different from the pressure of conscious actual wickedness,— the hypocritical assumption of hypocrisy,— which made Jack so deservedly a favorite in that character, I must needs conclude the present generation of playgoers more virtuous than myself, or more dense. I freely confess that he divided the palm with me with his better brother; that, in fact, I liked him quite as well. Not but there are passages,— like that, for instance, where Joseph is made to refuse a pittance to a poor relation,— incongruities which Sheridan was forced upon by the attempt to join the artificial with the comedy, either of which must destroy the other — but over these obstructions Jack's manner floated him so lightly, that a refusal from him no more shocked you, than the easy compliance of Charles gave you in reality any pleasure; you got over the paltry question as quickly as you could, to get back into the regions of pure comedy, where no cold moral reigns. The highly artificial manner of Palmer in this character counteracted every disagreeable impression which you might have received from the contrast, supposing them real, between the two brothers. You did not believe in Joseph with the same faith with which you believed in Charles. The latter was a pleasant reality, the former a no less pleasant poetical foil to it. The comedy, I have said, is incongruous; a mixture of Congreve with sentimental incompatibilities; the gayety upon the whole is buoyant; but it required the consummate art of Palmer to reconcile the discordant elements.

A player with Jack's talents, if we had one now, would not dare to do the part in the same manner. He would instinctively avoid every turn which might tend to unrealize, and so to make the character fascinating. He must take his cue from his spectators, who would expect a bad man and a good man as rigidly opposed to each other as the deathbeds of those geniuses are contrasted in the prints, which I am sorry to say have disappeared from the windows of my old friend Carrington Bowles, of St. Paul's Church-yard memory — (an exhibition as venerable as the adjacent cathedral and almost coeval) of the bad and good men at the hour of death; where the ghastly apprehensions of the former,— and truly the grim phantom with his reality of a toasting-fork is not to be despised,— so finely contrast with the meek complacent kissing of the rod,— taking it in like honey and butter, — with which the latter submits to the scythe of the gentle bleeder, Time, who wields his lancet with the apprehensive finger of a popular young ladies' surgeon. What flesh, like loving grass, would not covet to meet half-way the stroke of such a delicate mower? — John Palmer was twice an actor in this exquisite part. He was playing to you all the while that he was playing upon Sir Peter and his Lady. You had the first intimation of a sentiment before it was on his lips. His altered voice was meant to you, and you were to suppose that his fictitious co-flutterers on the stage perceived nothing at all of it. What was it to you if that half reality, the husband, was over-reached by the puppetry — or the thin thing (Lady Teazle's reputation) was persuaded it was dying of a plethory? The fortunes of Othello and Desdemona were not concerned in it. Poor Jack has passed from the stage in good time, that he did not live to this our age of seriousness. The present old Teazle *King*, too, is gone in good time. His manner would scarce have passed current in our day. We must love or hate — acquit or condemn —censure or pity — exert our detestable coxcombry or moral judgment upon everything. Joseph Surface, to go down now, must be a downright revolting villain — no compromise — his first appearance must shock and give horror — his specious plausibilities, which the pleasurable faculties of our fathers welcomed with such hearty greetings, knowing that no harm (dramatic harm, even) could come, or was meant to come, of them, must inspire a cold and killing aversion. Charles, (the real canting person of the scene — for the hypocrisy of Joseph has its ulterior legitimate ends, but his brother's professions of a good heart center in downright self-satisfaction) must be *loved*, and Joseph *hated*. To balance one disagreeable reality with another, Sir Peter Teazle must be no longer the comic idea of a fretful old bachelor bridegroom, whose teasings (while King acted it) were evidently as much played off at you, as they were meant to concern anybody on the stage,— he must be a real person, capable in law of sustaining an injury — a person towards whom duties are to be acknowledged — the genuine crim. con. antagonist of the villainous seducer Joseph. To realize him more, his sufferings under his unfortunate match must have the downright pungency of life — must (or should) make you not mirthful but uncomfortable, just as the same predicament would move you in a neighbor or old friend.

The delicious scenes which give the play its name and zest, must affect you in the same serious manner as if you heard the reputation of a dear female friend attacked in your real presence. Crabtree and Sir Benjamin — those poor snakes that live but in the sunshine of your mirth — must be ripened by this hot-bed process of realization into asps or amphisbænas; and Mrs. Candour — O! frightful! — become a hooded serpent. Oh! who that remembers Parsons and Dodd — the wasp and butterfly of the *School for Scandal* — in those two characters; and charming natural Miss Pope, the perfect gentlewoman as distinguished from the fine lady of comedy, in the latter part — would forego the true scenic delight — the escape from life — the oblivion of consequences — the holiday barring out of the pedant Reflection — those Saturnalia of two or three brief hours, well won from the world — to sit instead at one of our modern plays — to have his coward conscience (that forsooth must not be left for a moment) stimulated with perpetual appeals — dulled rather, and blunted, as a faculty without repose must be — and his moral vanity pampered with images of notional justice, notional beneficence, lives saved without the spectator's risk, and fortunes given away that cost the author nothing?

No piece was, perhaps, ever so completely cast in all its parts as this *manager's comedy*. Miss Farren had succeeded to Mrs. Abington in Lady Teazle; and Smith, the original Charles, had retired when I first saw it. The rest of the characters, with very slight exceptions, remained. I remember it was then the fashion to cry down John Kemble, who took the part of Charles after Smith; but, I thought, very unjustly. Smith, I fancy, was more airy, and took the eye with a certain gayety of person. He brought with him no somber recollections of tragedy. He had not to expiate the fault of having pleased beforehand in lofty declamation. He had no sins of Hamlet, or of Richard, to atone for. His failure in these parts was a passport to success in one of so opposite a tendency. But, as far as I could judge, the weighty sense of Kemble made up for more personal incapacity than he had to answer for. His harshest tones in this part came steeped and dulcified in good humor. He made his defects a grace. His exact declamatory manner, as he managed it, only served to convey the points of his dialogue with more precision. It seemed to head the shafts to carry them deeper. Not one of his sparkling sentences was lost. I remember minutely how he delivered each in succession, and cannot by any effort imagine how any of them could be altered for the better. No man could deliver brilliant dialogue — the dialogue of Congreve, or of Wycherley — because none understood it — half so well as John Kemble. His Valentine, in *Love for Love*, was to my recollection, faultless. He flagged sometimes in the intervals of tragic passion. He would slumber over the level parts of an heroic character. His Macbeth has been known to nod. But he always seemed to me to be particularly alive to pointed and witty dialogue. The relaxing levities of tragedy have not been touched by any since him — the playful court-bred spirit in which he condescended to the players in *Hamlet* — the sportive relief which he threw into the darker shades of Richard — disappeared with him. (Tragedy is become a uniform dead-weight. They have fashioned lead to her buskins. She never pulls them off for the ease of the moment. To invert a commonplace, from *Niobe*, she never forgets herself to liquefaction.) He had his sluggish moods, his torpors — but they were the halting-stones and resting-place of his tragedy — politic savings, and fetches of the breath — husbandry of the lungs, where nature pointed him to be an economist — rather, I think, than errors of the judgment. They were, at worst, less painful than the eternal tormenting unappeasable vigilance,— the "lidless dragon eyes," of present fashionable tragedy.[2]

[2] Macaulay's essay on Leigh Hunt's edition of the *Comic Dramatists*, contains the following paragraph relative to the above essay of Lamb:

"But it is not the fact that the world of these dramatists is a world into which no moral enters. Morality constantly enters into that world, a sound morality, and an unsound morality; the sound morality to be insulted, derided, associated with everything mean and hateful; the unsound morality to be set off to every advantage and inculcated by all methods, direct and indirect. It is not the fact that none of the inhabitants of this conventional world feel reverence for sacred institutions and family ties. Fondlewife, Pinchwife, every person in short of narrow understanding and disgusting manners, expresses that reverence strongly. The heroes and heroines, too, have a moral code of their own, an exceedingly bad one, but not, as Mr. Charles Lamb seems to think, a code existing only in the imagination of the dramatists. It is, on the contrary, a code actually received and obeyed by great numbers of people. We need not go to Utopia or Fairyland to find them. They are near at hand. Every night some of them cheat at the hells in the Quadrant, and others pace the Piazza in Covent Garden. Without flying to Nephelococcygia or to the Court of Queen Mab, we can meet with sharpers, bullies, hardhearted impudent debauchees, and women worthy of such paramours. The morality of the *Country Wife* and the *Old Bachelor* is the morality, not, as Mr. Charles Lamb maintains, of an unreal world, but of a world which is a good deal too real. It is the morality, not of a chaotic people, but of low town-rakes, and of those ladies whom the newspapers call 'dashing Cyprians.' And the question is simply this, whether a man of genius who constantly and systematically endeavors to make this sort of character attractive, by uniting it with beauty, grace, dignity, spirit, a high social position, popularity, literature, wit, taste, knowledge of the world, brilliant success in every undertaking, does or does not make an ill use of his powers. We own that we are unable to understand how this question can be answered in any way but one."

WILLIAM HAZLITT

William Hazlitt was born at Maidstone in 1778. His early education was received at home in Shropshire, whither his family had gone during his youth, and when he was fifteen he was sent to the Unitarian College at Hackney to prepare for the church. Four years' stay at Hackney, however, did not make a minister of him. At home in 1798 he heard Coleridge preach, and the poet encouraged him in his metaphysical studies. He visited Coleridge the same year, and met Wordsworth on one occasion. His interest in literature dates, he tells us, from this visit. After a short apprenticeship at painting, during 1802–03, he resumed his study of philosophy and in 1805 published the *Principles of Human Action.* He married in 1808 and went to live at Winterslow. Four years later they moved to Westminster. After his divorce, he married again in 1824. The family — Hazlitt's son by his first wife accompanied the couple — visited the Continent, after which Mrs. Hazlitt re-fused to return to her husband. He then began to write political reviews and dramatic criticisms for the *Morning Chronicle,* and later he contributed to *The Examiner, The Champion,* and many other papers. His lectures and miscellaneous writing occupied the remainder of his life. He died in 1830.

As one of the greatest critics of literature, Hazlitt has contributed a vast number of sound critical judgments. He is neither so brilliant as Lamb nor so profound as Coleridge, but his grasp of the matter in hand and his sanity are, in general, what give him the high position as a critic of the drama which he occupies. Unlike that of Lamb and Coleridge, much of his criticism is on acted plays; to that work he brought most of the readiness of mind and acute judgment that were always his. His lectures on Elizabethan literature and on the English poets are perhaps fuller and better thought out than his critiques of current plays.

ON THE COMIC WRITERS OF THE LAST CENTURY [1]

[*Lectures on the English Comic Writers*]

(1819)

The question which has been often asked, *Why there are comparatively so few good modern Comedies?* appears in a great measure to answer itself. It is because so many excellent comedies have been written, that there are none written at present. Comedy naturally wears itself out — destroys the very food on which it lives; and by constantly and successfully exposing the follies and weaknesses of mankind to ridicule, in the end leaves itself nothing worth laughing at. It holds the mirror up to nature; and men, seeing their most striking peculiarities and defects pass in gay review before them, learn either to avoid or conceal them. It is not the criticism which the public taste exercises upon the stage, but the criticism which the stage exercises upon public manners, that is fatal to comedy, by rendering the subject-matter of it tame, correct, and spiritless. We are drilled into a sort of stupid decorum, and forced to wear the same dull uniform of outward appear-

1 Re-printed, with one slight omission, from the Everyman's Library Edition of the *Lectures on the English Comic Writers and Miscellaneous Essays* (1910).— The notes are by the author.— Ed

ance; and yet it is asked, why the Comic Muse does not point, as she was wont, at the peculiarities of our gait and gesture, and exhibit the picturesque contrasts of our dress and costume, in all that graceful variety in which she delights. The genuine source of comic writing,

Where it must live, or have no life at all,

is undoubtedly to be found in the distinguishing peculiarities of men and manners. Now this distinction can subsist, so as to be strong, pointed, and general, only while the manners of different classes are formed almost immediately by their particular circumstances, and the characters of individuals by their natural temperament and situation, without being everlastingly modified and neutralized by intercourse with the world — by knowledge and education. In a certain stage of society, men may be said to vegetate like trees, and to become rooted to the soil in which they grow. They have no idea of anything beyond themselves and their immediate sphere of action; they are, as it were, circumscribed, and defined by their particular circumstances; they are what their situation makes them, and nothing more. Each is absorbed in his own profession or pursuit, and each in his turn contracts that habitual peculiarity of manners and opinions which makes him the subject of ridicule to others, and the sport of the Comic Muse. Thus the physician is nothing but a physician, the lawyer is a mere lawyer, the scholar degenerates into a pedant, the country squire is a different species of being from the fine gentleman, the citizen and the courtier inhabit a different world, and even the affectation of certain characters, in aping the follies or vices of their betters, only serves to show the immeasurable distance which custom or fortune has placed between them. Hence the earlier comic writers, taking advantage of this mixed and solid mass of ignorance, folly, pride, and prejudice, made those deep and lasting incisions into it,— have given those sharp and nice touches, that bold relief to their characters,— have opposed them in every variety of contrast and collision, of conscious self-satisfac-

tion and mutual antipathy, with a power which can only find full scope in the same rich and inexhaustible materials. But in proportion as comic genius succeeds in taking off the mask from ignorance and conceit, as it teaches us in proportion as we are brought out on the stage together, and our prejudices clash one against the other, our sharp angular points wear off; we are no longer rigid in absurdity, passionate in folly, and we prevent the ridicule directed at our habitual foibles by laughing at them ourselves.

If it be said, that there is the same fund of absurdity and prejudice in the world as ever — that there are the same unaccountable perversities lurking at the bottom of every breast,— I should answer, Be it so: but at least we keep our follies to ourselves as much as possible; we palliate, shuffle, and equivocate with them; they sneak into bye-corners, and do not, like Chaucer's Canterbury Pilgrims, march along the high road, and form a procession; they do not entrench themselves strongly behind custom and precedent; they are not embodied in professions and ranks in life; they are not organized into a system; they do not openly resort to a standard, but are a sort of straggling non-descripts, that, like Wart, " present no mark to the foeman." As to the gross and palpable absurdities of modern manners, they are too shallow and barefaced, and those who affect are too little *serious* in them, to make them worth the detection of the Comic Muse. They proceed from an idle, impudent affectation of folly in general, in the dashing *bravura* style, not from an infatuation with any of its characteristic modes. In short, the proper object of ridicule is *egotism:* and a man cannot be a very great egotist, who every day sees himself represented on the stage. We are deficient in comedy, because we are without characters in real life — as we have no historical pictures, because we have no faces proper for them.

It is, indeed, the evident tendency of all literature to generalize and *dissipate* character, by giving men the same artificial education, and the same common stock of ideas; so that we see all objects from the same point of view, and through the same reflected medium; — we learn to exist, not in ourselves, but in books; — all men become alike mere readers — spectators, not actors in the scene, and lose their proper personal identity. The templar, the wit, the man of pleasure, and the man of fashion, the courtier and the citizen, the knight and the squire, the lover and the miser — Lovelace, Lothario, Will Honeycomb, and Sir Roger de Coverley, Sparkish and Lord Foppington, Wester and Tom Jones, My Father and My Uncle Toby, Millamant and Sir Sampson Legend, Don Quixote and Sancho, Gil Blas and Guzman d'Alfarache, Count Fathom and Joseph Surface,— have met and exchanged commonplaces on the barren plains of the *haute littérature* — toil slowly on to the temple of science, " seen a long way off upon a level," and end in one dull compound of politics, criticism, and metaphysics!

We cannot expect to reconcile opposite things. If, for example, any of us were to put ourselves into the stagecoach from Salisbury to London, it is more than probable we should not meet with the same number of odd accidents, or ludicrous distresses on the road, that befel Parson Adams; but why, if we get into a common vehicle, and submit to the conveniences of modern traveling, should we complain of the want of adventures? Modern manners may be compared to a modern stage-coach; our limbs may be a little cramped with the confinement, and we may grow drowsy, but we arrive safe, without any very amusing or very sad accident, at our journey's end.

In this theory I have, at least, the authority of Sterne and the *Tatler* on my side, who attribute the greater variety and richness of comic excellence in our writers, to the greater variety and distinctness of character among ourselves; the roughness of the texture and the sharp angles not being worn out by the artificial refinements of intellect, or the frequent collision of social intercourse.— It has been argued on the other hand, indeed, that this circumstance makes against me; that the suppression of the grosser indications of absurdity ought to stimulate and give scope to the ingenuity and penetration of the comic writer who is to detect them; and that the progress of wit and humor ought to

keep pace with critical distinctions and metaphysical niceties. Some theorists, indeed, have been sanguine enough to expect a regular advance from grossness to refinement on the stage and in real life, marked on a graduated scale of human perfectibility, and have been hence led to imagine that the best of our old comedies were no better than the coarse jests of a set of country clowns — a sort of *comédies bourgeoises,* compared with the admirable productions which might but have not, been written in our times. I must protest against this theory altogether, which would go to degrade genteel comedy from a high court lady into a literary prostitute. I do not know what these persons mean by refinement in this instance. Do they find none in Millamant and her morning dreams, in Sir Roger de Coverley and his widow? Did not Etherege, Wycherley, and Congreve, approach tolerably near

> —— the ring
> *Of mimic statesmen and their merry king?*

Is there no distinction between an Angelica and a Miss Prue, a Valentine, a Tattle, and a Ben? Where, in the annals of modern literature, shall we find anything more refined, more deliberate, more abstracted in vice, than the nobleman in *Amelia?* Are not the compliments which Pope paid to his friends equal in taste and elegance to any which have been paid since? Are there no traits in Sterne? Is not Richardson minute enough? Must we part with Sophia Western and her muff, and Clarissa Harlowe's " preferable regards " for the loves of the plants and the triangles? Or shall we say that the Berinthias and Alitheas of former times were little rustics, because they did not, like our modern belles, subscribe to circulating libraries, read *Beppo,* prefer *Gertrude of Wyoming* to the *Lady of the Lake,* or the *Lady of the Lake* to *Gertrude of Wyoming,* differ in their sentiments on points of taste or systems of mineralogy, and deliver dissertations on the arts with Corinna of Italy? They had something else to do and to talk about. They were employed in reality, as we see them on the stage, in setting off their charms to the greatest advantage, in mortifying their rivals by the most pointed irony, and trifling with their lovers with infinite address. The height of comic elegance and refinement is not to be found in the general diffusion of knowledge and civilization, which tends to level and neutralize, but in the pride of individual distinction, and the contrast between the conflicting pretensions of different ranks in society.

For this reason I conceive that the alterations which have taken place in conversation and dress, in consequence of the change of manners in the same period, have been by no means favorable to comedy. The present prevailing style of conversation is not *personal*, but critical and analytical. It consists almost entirely in the discussion of general topics, in ascertaining the merits of authors and their works: and Congreve would be able to derive no better hints from the conversations of our toilettes or drawing-rooms, for the exquisite raillery or poignant repartee of his dialogues, than from a deliberation of the Royal Society. In manner, the extreme simplicity and graceful uniformity of modern dress, however favorable to the arts, has certainly stripped comedy of one of its richest ornaments and most expressive symbols. The sweeping pall and buskin, and nodding plume, were never more serviceable to tragedy, than the enormous hoops and stiff stays worn by the belles of former days, were to the intrigues of comedy. They assisted wonderfully in heightening the mysteries of the passion, and adding to the intricacy of the plot. Wycherley and Vanbrugh could not have spared the dresses of Van Dyck. These strange fancy-dresses, perverse disguises, and counterfeit shapes, gave an agreeable scope to the imagination. "That sevenfold fence" was a sort of foil to the lusciousness of the dialogue, and a barrier against the sly encroachments of *double entendre*. The greedy eye and bold hand of indiscretion were repressed, which gave a greater license to the tongue. The senses were not to be gratified in an instant. Love was entangled in the folds of the swelling handkerchief, and the desires might wander forever round the circumference of a quilted petticoat, or find a rich lodging in the flowers of a damask stomacher. There was room for years of patient contrivance, for a thousand thoughts, schemes, conjectures, hopes, fears, and wishes. There seemed no end of obstacles and delays; to overcome so many difficulties was the work of ages. A mistress was an angel, concealed behind whalebone, flounces, and brocade. What an undertaking to penetrate through the disguise! What an impulse must it give to the blood, what a keenness to the invention, what a volubility to the tongue! "Mr. Smirk, you are a brisk man," was then the most significant commendation; but nowadays — a woman can be *but undressed!* — Again, the character of the fine gentleman is at present a little obscured on the stage, nor do we immediately recognize it elsewhere, for want of the formidable *insignia* of a bagwig and sword. Without these outward credentials, the public must not only be unable to distinguish this character intuitively, but it must be "almost afraid to know itself." The present simple disguise of a gentleman is like the *incognito* of kings. The opinion of others affects our opinion of ourselves; and we can hardly expect from a modern man of fashion that air of dignity and superior gracefulness of carriage, which those must have assumed who were conscious that all eyes were upon them, and that their lofty pretensions continually exposed them either to public scorn or challenged public admiration. A lord who should take the wall of the plebeian passengers without a sword by his side, would hardly have his claim of precedence acknowledged; nor could he be supposed to have that obsolete air of self-importance about him, which should alone clear the pavement at his approach. It is curious how an ingenious actor of the present day (Mr. Farren) should play Lord Ogleby so well as he does, having never seen anything of the sort in reality. A nobleman in full costume, and in broad day, would be a phenomenon like the lord mayor's coach. The attempt at getting up genteel comedy at present is a sort of Galvanic experiment, a revival of the dead.[2]

2 I have only to add, by way of explanation on this subject, the following passage from the *Characters of Shakespear's Plays:*   "There

I have observed in a former Lecture, that the most spirited era of our comic drama was that which reflected the conversation, tone, and manners of the profligate, but witty age of Charles II. With the graver and more business-like turn which the Revolution probably gave to our minds, comedy stooped from her bolder and more fantastic flights; and the ferocious attack made by the nonjuring divine, Jeremy Collier, on the immorality and profaneness of the plays then chiefly in vogue, nearly frightened those unwarrantable liberties of wit and humor from the stage, which were no longer countenanced at court nor copied in the city. Almost the last of our writers who ventured to hold out in the prohibited track, was a female adventurer, Mrs. Centlivre, who seemed to take advantage of the privilege of her sex, and to set at defiance the cynical denunciations of the angry puritanical reformist. Her plays have a provoking spirit and volatile salt in them, which still preserves them from decay. Congreve is said to have been jealous of their success at the time, and that it was one cause which drove him in dis-

is a certain stage of society in which people become conscious of their peculiarities and absurdities, affect to disguise what they are, and set up pretensions to what they are not. This gives rise to a corresponding style of comedy, the object of which is to detect the disguises of self-love. and to make reprisals on these preposterous assumptions of vanity, by marking the contrast between the real and the affected character as severely as possible, and denying to those, who would impose on us for what they are not, even the merit which they have. This is the comedy of artificial life, of wit and satire, such as we see it in Congreve, Wycherley, Vanbrugh, etc. To this succeeds a state of society from which the same sort of affectation and pretence are banished by a greater knowledge of the world, or by their successful exposure on the stage; and which by neutralizing the materials of comic character, both natural and artificial, leaves no comedy at all — but *the sentimental*. Such is our modern comedy. There is a period in the progress of manners anterior to both these, in which the foibles and follies of individuals are of nature's planting. not the growth of art or study; in which they are therefore unconscious of them themselves. or care not who knows them, if they can but have their whim out; and in which, as there is no attempt at imposition, the spectators rather receive pleasure from humoring the inclinations of the persons they laugh at. than wish to give them pain by exposing their absurdity. This may be called the comedy of nature. and it is the comedy which we generally find in Shakespear."

gust from the stage. If so, it was without any good reason: for these plays have great and intrinsic merit in them, which entitled them to their popularity (and it is only spurious and undeserved popularity which should excite a feeling of jealousy in any well-regulated mind): and besides, their merit was of a kind entirely different from his own. *The Wonder* and *The Busy Body* are properly comedies of intrigue. Their interest depends chiefly on the intricate involution and artful *dénouement* of the plot, which has a strong tincture of mischief in it, and the wit is seasoned by the archness of the humor and sly allusion to the most delicate points. They are plays evidently written by a very clever woman, but still by a woman: for I hold, in spite of any fanciful theories to the contrary, that there is a distinction discernible in the minds of women as well as in their faces. *The Wonder* is one of the best of our acting plays. The passion of jealousy in Don Felix is managed in such a way as to give as little offense as possible to the audience, for every appearance combines to excite and confirm his worst suspicions, while we, who are in the secret, laugh at his groundless uneasiness and apprehensions. The ambiguity of the heroine's situation, which is like a continued practical *équivoque*, gives rise to a quick succession of causeless alarms, subtle excuses, and the most hair-breadth 'scapes. The scene near the end, in which Don Felix, pretending to be drunk, forces his way out of Don Manuel's house, who wants to keep him a prisoner, by producing his marriage-contract in the shape of a pocket-pistol, with the terrors and confusion into which the old gentleman is thrown by this sort of *argumentum ad hominem*, is one of the richest treats the stage affords, and calls forth incessant peals of laughter and applause. Besides the two principal characters (Violante and Don Felix) Lissardo and Flippanta come in very well to carry on the underplot; and the airs and graces of an amorous waiting-maid and conceited manservant, each copying after their master and mistress, were never hit off with more natural volubility or affected *nonchalance* than in this enviable couple. Lissardo's playing off the diamond ring before the eyes of his mortified Dulcinea, and aping his master's absent manner while repeating —" Roast me these Violantes," as well as the jealous quarrel of the two waiting-maids, which threatens to end in some very extraordinary discoveries, are among the most amusing traits in this comedy. Colonel Breton, the lover of Clara, is a spirited and enterprising soldier of fortune; and his servant Gibby's undaunted, incorrigible blundering, with a dash of nationality in it, tells in a very edifying way.— *The Busy Body* is inferior, in the interest of the story and characters, to *The Wonder;* but it is full of bustle and gayety from beginning to end. The plot never stands still; the situations succeed one another like the changes of machinery in a pantomime. The nice dove-tailing of the incidents, and cross-reading in the situations, supplies the place of any great force of wit or sentiment. The time for the entrance of each person on the stage is the moment when they are least wanted, and when their arrival makes either themselves or somebody else look as foolish as possible. The laughableness of this comedy, as well as of *The Wonder,* depends on a brilliant series of mistimed exits and entrances. Marplot is the whimsical hero of the piece, and a standing memorial of unmeaning vivacity and assiduous impertinence.

The comedies of Steele were the first that were written expressly with a view not to imitate the manners, but to reform the morals of the age. The author seems to be all the time on his good behavior, as if writing a comedy was no very creditable employment, and as if the ultimate object of his ambition was a dedication to the queen. Nothing can be better meant, or more inefficient. It is almost a misnomer to call them comedies; they are rather homilies in dialogue, in which a number of very pretty ladies and gentlemen discuss the fashionable topics of gaming, of duelling, of seduction, of scandal, etc., with a sickly sensibility, that shows as little hearty aversion to vice, as sincere attachment to virtue. By not meeting the question fairly on the ground of common experience, by slubbering over the objections, and varnishing over the answers, the whole distinction between virtue and vice (as it appears in evidence in the comic drama) is reduced to verbal professions, and a mechanical, infantine goodness. The sting is, indeed, taken out of what is bad; but what is good, at the same time, loses its manhood and nobility of nature by this enervating process. I am unwilling to believe that the only difference between right and wrong is mere cant, or *make-believe;* and I imagine, that the advantage which the moral drama possesses over mere theoretical precept or general declamation is this, that by being left free to imitate nature as it is, and not being referred to an ideal standard, it is its own voucher for the truth of the inferences it draws, for its warnings, or its examples; that it brings out the higher, as well as lower principles of action, in the most striking and convincing points of view; satisfies us that virtue is not a mere shadow; clothes it with passion, imagination, reality, and, if I may so say, translates morality from the language of theory into that of practice. But Steele, by introducing the artificial mechanism of morals on the stage, and making his characters act, not from individual motives and existing circumstances, the truth of which every one must feel, but from vague topics and general rules, the truth of which is the very thing to be proved in detail, has lost that fine 'vantage ground which the stage lends to virtue; takes away from it its best grace, the grace of sincerity; and, instead of making it a test of truth, has made it an echo of the doctrine of the schools — and "the one cries *Mum,* while t'other cries *Budget!*" The comic writer, in my judgment, then, ought to open the volume of nature and the world for his living materials, and not take them out of his ethical commonplace book; for in this way, neither will throw any additional light upon the other. In all things there is a division of labor; and I am as little for introducing the tone of the pulpit or reading-desk on the stage, as for introducing plays and interludes in church-time, according to the good old popish practice. It was a part, indeed, of Steele's plan, " by the politeness of his style and the genteelness of his expressions," [3] to bring

3 See Mandeville's *Fable of the Bees.*

about a reconciliation between things which he thought had hitherto been kept too far asunder, to wed the graces to the virtues, and blend pleasure with profit. And in this design he succeeded admirably in his *Tatler,* and some other works; but in his comedies he has failed. He has confounded, instead of harmonizing — has taken away its gravity from wisdom, and its charm from gayety. It is not that in his plays we find "some soul of goodness in things evil"; but they have no soul either of good or bad. His *Funeral* is as trite, as tedious, and full of formal grimace, as a procession of mutes and undertakers. The characters are made either affectedly good and forbearing, with "all the milk of human kindness"; or purposely bad and disgusting, for the others to exercise their squeamish charities upon them. The *Conscious Lovers* is the best; but that is far from good, with the exception of the scene between Mr. Thomas and Phillis, who are fellow-servants, and commence lovers from being set to clean the window together. We are here once more in the company of our old friend, Isaac Bickerstaff, Esq. Indiana is as listless, and as insipid, as a drooping figure on an Indian screen; and Mr. Myrtle and Mr. Bevil only just disturb the still life of the scene. I am sorry that in this censure I should have Parson Adams against me; who thought the *Conscious Lovers* the only play fit for a Christian to see, and as good as a sermon. For myself, I would rather have read, or heard him read, one of his own manuscript sermons: and if the volume which he left behind him in his saddlebags was to be had in print, for love or money, I would at any time walk ten miles on foot only to get a sight of it. Addison's *Drummer, or the Haunted House,* is a pleasant farce enough; but adds nothing to our idea of the author of the *Spectator.*
Pope's joint after-piece, called *An Hour after Marriage,* was not a successful attempt. He brought into it "an alligator stuff'd," which disconcerted the ladies, and gave just offense to the critics. Pope was too fastidious for a farce-writer; and yet the most fastidious people, when they step out of their regular routine, are apt to become the grossest. The smallest offenses against probability or decorum are, to their habitual scrupulousness, as unpardonable as the greatest. This was the rock on which Pope probably split. The affair was, however, hushed up; and he wreaked his discreet vengeance at leisure on the "odious endeavors," and more odious success of Colley Cibber in the line in which he had failed.

Gay's *What-d'ye-call-it,* is not one of his happiest things. His Polly is a complete failure, which, indeed, is the common fate of second parts. If the original Polly, in the *Beggar's Opera,* had not had more winning ways with her, she would hardly have had so many Countesses for representatives as she has had, from her first appearance up to the present moment.

Fielding was a comic writer, as well as a novelist; but his comedies are very inferior to his novels: they are particularly deficient both in plot and character. The only excellence which they have is that of the style, which is the only thing in which his novels are deficient. The only dramatic pieces of Fielding that retain possession of the stage are, the *Mock Doctor* (a tolerable translation from Molière's *Médecin malgré lui*), and his *Tom Thumb,* a very admirable piece of burlesque. The absurdities and bathos of some of our celebrated tragic writers could hardly be credited, but for the notes at the bottom of this preposterous medley of bombast, containing his authorities and the parallel passages. Dryden, Lee, and Shadwell, make no very shining figure there. Mr. Liston makes a better figure in the text. His Lord Grizzle is prodigious. What a name, and what a person! It has been said of this ingenious actor, that "he is very great in Liston"; but he is even greater in Lord Grizzle. What a wig is that he wears! How flighty, flaunting, and fantastical! Not "like those hanging locks of young Apollo," nor like the serpent-hair of the Furies of Æschylus; but as troublous, though not as tragical as the one — as imposing, though less classical than the other. "*Que terribles sont ces cheveux gris,*" might be applied to Lord Grizzle's most valiant and magnanimous curls. This sapient courtier's " fell of hair does at a dismal treatise rouse and stir as if life were in 't." His wits seem flying away with the disorder of his flowing locks, and to sit as loosely on our hero's head as the caul of his peruke. What a significant vacancy in his open eyes and mouth! what a listlessness in his limbs! what an abstraction of all thought or purpose! With what an headlong impulse of enthusiasm he throws himself across the stage when he is going to be married, crying, "Hey for Doctor's Commons," as if the genius of folly had taken whole-length possession of his person! And then his dancing is equal to the discovery of a sixth sense — which is certainly very different from *common sense!* If this extraordinary personage cuts a great figure in his life, he is no less wonderful in his death and burial. "From the sublime to the ridiculous there is but one step"; and this character would almost seem to prove, that there is but one step from the ridiculous to the sublime.— Lubin Log, however inimitable in itself, is itself an imitation of something existing elsewhere; but the Lord Grizzle of this truly original actor, is a pure invention of his own. His Caper, in the *Widow's Choice,* can alone dispute the palm with it in incoherence and volatility; for that, too, "is high fantastical," almost as full of emptiness, in as grand a gusto of insipidity, as profoundly absurd, as elaborately nonsensical! Why does not Mr. Liston play in some of Molière's farces? I heartily wish that the author of *Love, Law, and Physic,* would launch him on the London boards in Monsieur Jourdain, or Monsieur Pourceaugnac. The genius of Liston and Molière together —

———*Must bid a gay defiance to mischance.*

Mr. Liston is an actor hardly belonging to the present age. Had he lived, unfortunately for us, in the time of Colley Cibber, we should have seen what a splendid niche he would have given him in his *Apology.*

.   .   .   .   .

In his plays, his personal character perhaps predominates too much over the inventiveness of his Muse; but so far from being dull, he is everywhere light,

fluttering, and airy. His pleasure in himself made him desirous to please; but his fault was, that he was too soon satisfied with what he did, that his indolence or want of thought led him to indulge in the vein that flowed from him with most ease, and that his vanity did not allow him to distinguish between what he did best and worst. His *Careless Husband* is a very elegant piece of agreeable, thoughtless writing; and the incident of Lady Easy throwing her handkerchief over her husband, whom she finds asleep in a chair by the side of her waiting-woman, was an admirable contrivance, taken, as he informs us, from real life. His *Double Gallant,* which has been lately revived, though it cannot rank in the first, may take its place in the second or third class of comedies. It abounds in character, bustle, and stage-effect. It belongs to what may be called the composite style; and very happily mixes up the comedy of intrigue, such as we see it in Mrs. Centlivre's Spanish plots, with a tolerable share of the wit and spirit of Congreve and Vanbrugh. As there is a good deal of wit, there is a spice of wickedness in this play, which was a privilege of the good old style of comedy, not altogether abandoned in Cibber's time. The luscious vein of the dialogue is stopped short in many of the scenes of the revived play, though not before we perceive its object —

———*In hidden mazes running,*
With wanton haste and giddy cunning.

These imperfect hints of double meanings, however, pass off without any marks of reprobation; for unless they are insisted on, or made pretty broad, the audience, from being accustomed to the cautious purity of the modern drama, are not very expert in deciphering the equivocal allusion, for which they are not on the look-out. To what is this increased nicety owing? Was it that vice, from being formerly less common (though more fashionable) was less catching than at present? The first inference is by no means in our favor: for though I think that the grossness of manners prevailing in our fashionable comedies was a direct transcript of the manners of the court at the time, or in the period immediately preceding, yet the same grossness of expression and allusion existed long before, as in the plays of Shakespeare and Ben Jonson, when there was not this grossness of manners, and it has of late years been gradually refining away. There is a certain grossness or freedom of expression, which may arise as often from unsuspecting simplicity as from avowed profligacy. Whatever may be our progress either in virtue or vice since the age of Charles II certain it is, that our manners are not mended since the time of Elizabeth and Charles I. Is it, then, that vice was formerly a thing more to be wondered at than imitated; that behind the rigid barriers of religion and morality it might be exposed freely, without the danger of any serious practical consequences — whereas now that the safeguards of wholesome authority and prejudice are removed, we seem afraid to trust our eyes or ears with a single situation or expression of a loose tendency, as if the mere mention of licentiousness implied a conscious approbation of it, and the extreme delicacy of our moral sense would be debauched by the bare suggestion of the possibility of vice? But I shall not take upon me to answer this question. The characters in the *Double Gallant* are well kept up: At-All and Lady Dainty are the two most prominent characters in this comedy, and those into which Cibber has put most of his own nature and genius. They are the essence of active impertinence and fashionable frivolity. Cibber, in short, though his name has been handed down to us as a bye-word of impudent pretension and impenetrable dullness by the classical pen of his accomplished rival, who, unfortunately, did not admit of any merit beyond the narrow circle of wit and friendship in which he himself moved, was a gentleman and a scholar of the old school; a man of wit and pleasantry in conversation, a diverting mimic, an excellent actor, an admirable dramatic critic, and one of the best comic writers of his age. His works, instead of being a *caput mortuum* of literature, had a great deal of the spirit, with a little too much of the froth. His *Nonjuror* was taken from Molière's *Tartuffe,* and has

been altered to the *Hypocrite. Love's Last Shift* appears to have been his own favorite; and he received the compliments of Sir John Vanbrugh and old Mr. Southern upon it: — the latter said to him, "Young man, your play is a good one; and it will succeed, if you do not spoil it by your acting." His plays did not always take equally. It is ludicrous to hear him complaining of the ill success of one of them, *Love in a Riddle,* a pastoral comedy, "of a nice morality," and well spoken sentiments, which he wrote in opposition to the *Beggar's Opera,* at the time when its worthless and vulgar rival was carrying everything triumphantly before it. Cibber brings this, with much pathetic *naïveté,* as an instance of the lamentable want of taste in the town!

The Suspicious Husband by Hoadley, *The Jealous Wife* by Colman, and the *Clandestine Marriage* by Colman and Garrick, are excellent plays of the middle style of comedy; which are formed rather by judgment and selection, than by any original vein of genius; and have all the parts of a good comedy in degree, without having any one prominent, or to excess. The character of Ranger, in the *Suspicious Husband,* is only a variation of those of Farquhar, of the same class as his Sir Harry Wildair and others, without equal spirit. A great deal of the story of the *Jealous Wife* is borrowed from Fielding; but so faintly, that the resemblance is hardly discernible till you are apprised of it. The Jealous Wife herself is, however, a dramatic *chef-d'œuvre,* and worthy of being acted as often, and better than it is. Sir Harry Beagle is a true fox-hunting English squire. The *Clandestine Marriage* is nearly without a fault; and has some lighter theatrical graces, which I suspect Garrick threw into it. Canton is, I should think, his; though this classification of him among the ornamental parts of the play may seem whimsical. Garrick's genius does not appear to have been equal to the construction of a solid drama; but he could retouch and embellish with great gayety and knowledge of the technicalities of his art. Garrick not only produced joint-pieces and afterpieces, but often set off the plays of his friends and contemporaries with the garnish, the *sauce piquante,* of prologues and epilogues, at which he had an admirable knack.— The elder Colman's translation of Terence, I may here add, has always been considered, by good judges, as an equal proof of the author's knowledge of the Latin language, and taste in his own.

Bickerstaff's plays and comic operas are continually acted: they come under the class of mediocrity, generally speaking. Their popularity seems to be chiefly owing to the unaffected ease and want of pretension with which they are written, with a certain humorous *naïveté* in the lower characters, and an exquisite adaptation of the music to the songs. His *Love in a Village* is one of the most delghtful comic operas on the stage. It is truly pastoral; and the sense of music hovers over the very scene like the breath of morning. In his alteration of the *Tartuffe* he has spoiled the *Hypocrite,* but he has added Maw-worm.

Mrs. Cowley's comedy of the *Belles' Stratagem, Who's the Dupe,* and others, are of the second or third class: they are rather *refaccimentos* of the characters, incidents, and materials of former writers, got up with considerable liveliness and ingenuity, than original compositions, with marked qualities of their own.

Goldsmith's *Good-natur'd Man* is inferior to *She Stoops to Conquer;* and even this last play, with all its shifting vivacity, is rather a sportive and whimsical effusion of the author's fancy, a delightful and delicately managed caricature, than a genuine comedy.

Murphy's plays of *All in the Wrong* and *Know Your Own Mind,* are admirably written; with sense, spirit, and conception of character: but without any great effect of the humorous, or that truth of feeling which distinguishes the boundary between the absurdities of natural character and the gratuitous fictions of the poet's pen. The heroes of these two plays, Millamour and Sir Benjamin Constant, are too ridiculous in their caprices to be tolerated, except in farce; and yet their follies are so flimsy, so motiveless, and fine-spun, as not to be intelligible, or to have any effect in their only proper sphere. Both his principal pieces are said to have suffered by their similarity, first, to Colman's *Jealous Wife,* and next to the *School for Scandal,* though in both cases he had the undoubted priority. It is hard that the fate of plagiarism should attend upon originality: yet it is clear that the elements of the *School for Scandal* are not sparingly scattered in Murphy's comedy of *Know Your Own Mind,* which appeared before the latter play, only to be eclipsed by it. This brings me to speak of Sheridan.

Mr. Sheridan has been justly called "a dramatic star of the first magnitude": and, indeed, among the comic writers of the last century, he "shines like Hesperus among the lesser lights." He has left four several dramas behind him, all different or of different kinds, and all excellent in their way;—*The School for Scandal, The Rivals, The Duenna,* and *The Critic.* The attraction of this last piece is, however, less in the mock-tragedy rehearsed, than in the dialogue of the comic scenes, and in the character of Sir Fretful Plagiary, which is supposed to have been intended for Cumberland. If some of the characters in *The School for Scandal* were contained in Murphy's comedy of *Know Your Own Mind* (and certainly some of Dashwood's detached speeches and satirical sketches are written with quite as firm and masterly a hand as any of those given to the members of the scandalous club, Mrs. Candour or Lady Sneerwell), yet they were buried in it for want of grouping and relief, like the colors of a well-drawn picture sunk in the canvas. Sheridan brought them out, and exhibited them in all their glory. If that gem, the character of Joseph Surface, was Murphy's, the splendid and more valuable setting was Sheridan's. He took Murphy's Malvil from his lurking-place in the closet, and "dragged the struggling monster into day" upon the stage. That is, he gave interest, life, and action, or, in other words, its dramatic being, to the mere conception and written specimens of a character. This is the merit of Sheridan's comedies, that everything in them *tells;* there is no labor in vain. His Comic Muse does not go about prying into obscure corners, or collecting idle curiosities, but shows her laughing face, and points to her rich treasure — the follies of mankind. She is garlanded and crowned with roses and vine-leaves. Her eyes sparkle with delight, and her heart runs over with good-natured malice. Her step is firm and light, and her ornaments consummate! *The School for Scandal* is, if not the most original, perhaps the most finished and faultless comedy which we have. When it is acted, you hear people all around you exclaiming, "Surely it is impossible for anything to be cleverer." The scene in which Charles sells all the old family pictures but his uncle's, who is the purchaser in disguise, and that of the discovery of Lady Teazle when the screen falls, are among the happiest and most highly wrought that comedy, in its wide and brilliant range, can boast. Besides the wit and ingenuity of this play, there is a genial spirit of frankness and generosity about it, that relieves the heart as well as clears the lungs. It professes a faith in the natural goodness, as well as habitual depravity of human nature. While it strips off the mask of hypocrisy, it inspires a confidence between man and man. As often as it is acted, it must serve to clear the air of that low, creeping, pestilent fog of cant and mysticism, which threatens to confound every native impulse, or honest conviction, in the nauseous belief of a perpetual lie, and the laudable profession of systematic hypocrisy.— The character of Lady Teazle is not well made out by the author; nor has it been well represented on the stage since the time of Miss Farren.— *The Rivals* is a play of even more action and incident, but of less wit and satire than *The School for Scandal*. It is as good as a novel in the reading, and has the broadest and most palpable effect on the stage. If Joseph Surface and Charles have a smack of Tom Jones and Blifil in their moral constitution, Sir Anthony Absolute and Mrs. Malaprop remind us of honest Matthew Bramble and his sister Tabitha, in their tempers and dialect. Acres is a distant descendant of Sir Andrew Ague-cheek. It must be confessed of this author, as Falstaff says of some one, that "he had damnable iteration in him!" *The Duenna* is a perfect work of art. It has the utmost sweetness and point. The plot, the characters, the dialogue, are all complete in themselves, and they are all his own; and

the songs are the best that ever were written, except those in the *Beggar's Opera*. They have a joyous spirit of intoxication in them, and a strain of the most melting tenderness. Compare the softness of that beginning,

Had I a heart for falsehood framed,

with the spirited defiance to Fortune in the lines,

Half thy malice youth could bear,
And the rest a bumper drown.

.   .   .   .   .   .

Macklin's *Man of the World* has one powerfully written character, that of Sir Pertinax Macsycophant, but it required Cooke's acting to make it thoroughly effectual.

Mr. Holcroft, in his *Road to Ruin*, set the example of that style of comedy, in which the *slang* phrases of jockey-noblemen and the humors of the four-in-hand club are blended with the romantic sentiments of distressed damsels and philosophic waiting-maids, and in which he has been imitated by the most successful of our living writers, unless we make a separate class for the school of Cumberland, who was almost entirely devoted to the *comédie larmoyante*, and who, passing from the light, volatile spirit of his *West-Indian* to the mawkish sensibility of the *Wheel of Fortune*, linked the Muse of English comedy to the genius of German tragedy, where she has since remained, like Christabel fallen asleep in the Witch's arms, and where I shall leave her, as I have not the poet's privilege to break the spell.

There are two other writers whom I have omitted to mention, but not forgotten: they are our two immortal farce-writers, the authors of the *Mayor of Garratt* and the *Agreeable Surprise*. If Foote has been called our English Aristophanes, O'Keeffe might well be called our English Molière. The scale of the modern writer was smaller, but the spirit is the same. In light, careless laughter, and pleasant exaggerations of the humorous, we have had no one equal to him. There is no labor or contrivance in his scenes, but the drollery of his subject seems to strike irresistibly upon his fancy, and run away with his discretion as it does with ours. His Cowslip and Lingo are Touchstone and Audrey revived. He is himself a Modern Antique. His fancy has all the quaintness and extravagance of the old writers, with the ease and lightness which the moderns arrogate to themselves. All his pieces are delightful, but the *Agreeable Surprise* is the most so. There are in this some of the most felicitous blunders in situation and character that can be conceived; and in Lingo's superb replication, " A scholar! I was a master of scholars," he has hit the height of the ridiculous. Foote had more dry, sarcastic humor, and more knowledge of the world. His farces are bitter satires, more or less personal, as it happened. Mother Cole, in *The Minor,* and Mr. Smirk the Auctioneer, in *Taste,* with their coadjutors, are rich cut-and-come-again, " pleasant, though wrong." But *The Mayor of Garratt* is his *Magnum opus* in this line. Some comedies are long farces: this farce is a comedy in little. It is also one of the best acted farces that we have. The acting of Dowton and Russell, in Major Sturgeon and Jerry Sneak, cannot be too much praised: Foote himself would have been satisfied with it. The strut, the bluster, the hollow swaggering, and turkey-cock swell of the Major; and Jerry's meekness, meanness, folly, good-nature, and hen-pecked air, are assuredly done to the life. The latter character is even better than the former, which is saying a bold word. Dowton's art is only an imitation of art, of an affected or assumed character; but in Russell's Jerry you see the very soul of nature, in a fellow that is " pigeon-livered and lacks gall," laid open and anatomized. You can see that his heart is no bigger than a pin, and his head as soft as a pippin. His whole aspect is chilled and frightened, as if he had been dipped in a pond; and yet he looks as if he would like to be snug and comfortable, if he durst. He smiles as if he would be friends with you upon any terms; and the tears come in his eyes because you will not let him. The tones of his voice are prophetic as the cuckoo's under-song. His words are made of water-gruel. The scene in which he tries to make a con-

fidant of the Major is great; and his song of *Robinson Crusoe* as melancholy as the island itself. The reconciliation-scene with his wife, and his exclamation over her, " to think that I should make my Molly *veep!* " are pathetic, if the last stage of human infirmity is so. This farce appears to me to be both moral and entertaining; yet it does not take. It is considered as an unjust satire on the city, and the country at large; and there is a very frequent repetition of the word " nonsense " in the house, during the performance. Mr. Dowton was even hissed, either from the upper boxes or gallery, in his speech recounting the marching of his corps " from Brentford to Ealing, and from Ealing to Acton "; and several persons in the pit, who thought the whole *low,* were for going out. This shows well for the progress of civilization. I suppose the manners described in *The Mayor of Garratt* have, in the last forty years, become obsolete, and the characters ideal: we have no longer either hen-pecked or brutal husbands, or domineering wives; the Miss Molly Jollops no longer wed Jerry Sneaks, or admire the brave Major Sturgeons on the other side of Temple-bar; all our soldiers have become heroes, and our magistrates respectable, and the farce of life is o'er.

One more name, and I have done. It is that of Peter Pindar. The historian of Sir Joseph Banks and the Emperor of Morocco, of the Pilgrims and the Peas, of the Royal Academy, and of Mr. Whitbread's brewing-vat, the bard in whom the nation and the king delighted, is old and blind, but still merry and wise: — remembering how he has made the world laugh in his time, and not repenting of the mirth he has given; with an involuntary smile lighted up at the mad pranks of his Muse, and the lucky hits of his pen —" faint picture of those flashes of his spirit, that were wont to set the table in a roar "; like his own Expiring Taper, bright and fitful to the last; tagging a rhyme or conning his own epitaph; and waiting for the last summons, GRATEFUL and CONTENTED! [4]

I have thus gone through the history of that part of our literature, which I

[4] This ingenious and popular writer is since dead.

had proposed to myself to treat of. I have only to add, by way of explanation, that in some few parts I had anticipated myself in fugitive or periodical publications; and I thought it better to repeat what I had already stated to the best of my ability, than alter it for the worse.

These parts bear, however, a very small proportion to the whole; and I have used such diligence and care as I could, in adding to them whatever appeared necessary to complete the general view of the subject, or make it (as far as lay in my power) interesting to others.

GEORGE MEREDITH

A leading English novelist, though not a popular writer, George Meredith was born in 1828, in middle-class circumstances so ordinary that they evidently gave him subsequent cause for embarrassment. In 1849, he married the daughter of the novelist Thomas Love Peacock but was later deserted by his wife. He married again, more happily, in 1864. Pre-eminent among his mannered psychological novels are *The Ordeal of Richard Feverel* (1859), *The Egoist* (1879), and his best-received book, *Diana of the Crossways* (1885);

The Egoist in particular is an embodiment of the comic spirit. His long poem *Modern Love* (1862) is an account of an unhappy marriage. His *Essay on Comedy* (published 1897) was originally a lecture given in 1877, *The Idea of Comedy and the Uses of the Comic Spirit*. Here he characterized comedy as an expression of common sense suited to a harmonious, tolerant social world in which women participate. Its sanity curbs egoistic excess. Meredith died in 1909.

AN ESSAY ON COMEDY [1]

(1877)

The comic poet is in the narrow field, or enclosed square, of the society he depicts; and he addresses the still narrower enclosure of men's intellects, with reference to the operation of the social world upon their characters. He is not concerned with beginnings or endings or surroundings, but with what you are now weaving. To understand his work and value it, you must have a sober liking of your kind, and a sober estimate of our civilized qualities. The aim and business of the comic poet are misunderstood, his meaning is not seized nor his point of view taken, when he is accused of dishonoring our nature and being hostile to sentiment, tending to spitefulness and making an unfair use of laughter. Those who detect irony in comedy do so because they choose to see it in life. Poverty, says the satirist, "has nothing harder in

itself than that it makes men ridiculous." But poverty is never ridiculous to comic perception until it attempts to make its rags conceal its bareness in a forlorn attempt at decency, or foolishly to rival ostentation. Caleb Balderstone, in his endeavor to keep up the honor of a noble household in a state of beggary, is an exquisitely comic character. In the case of "poor relatives," on the other hand, it is the rich, whom they perplex, that are really comic; and to laugh at the former, not seeing the comedy of the latter, is to betray dulness of vision. Humorist and satirist frequently hunt together as ironists in pursuit of the grotesque, to the exclusion of the comic. That was an affecting moment in the history of the Prince Regent, when the First Gentleman of Europe burst into tears at a sarcastic remark of Beau Brummell's on the cut of his coat. Humor, satire, irony, pounce on it altogether as their common prey. The Comic Spirit eyes, but does not touch, it. Put into action, it would be farcical. It is too gross for comedy.

Incidents of a kind casting ridicule on our unfortunate nature, instead of our conventional life, provoke derisive laughter, which thwarts the comic idea. But derision is foiled by the play of the intellect. Most of doubtful causes in contest are open to comic interpretation, and any intellectual pleading of a doubtful cause contains germs of an idea of comedy.

The laughter of satire is a blow in the back or the face. The laughter of comedy is impersonal and of unrivaled politeness, nearer a smile—often no more than a smile. It laughs through the mind, for the mind directs it; and it might be called the humor of the mind.

One excellent test of the civilization of a country, as I have said, I take to be the flourishing of the comic idea and comedy; and the test of true comedy is that it shall awaken thoughtful laughter.

If you believe that our civilization is founded in common sense (and it is the first condition of sanity to believe it), you will, when contemplating men, discern a Spirit overhead; not more heavenly than the light flashed upward from glassy surfaces, but luminous and watchful; never shooting beyond them, nor lagging in the rear; so closely attached to them that it may be taken for a slavish reflex, until its features are studied. It has the sage's brows, and the sunny malice of a faun lurks at the corners of the half-closed lips drawn in an idle wariness of half-tension. That slim feasting smile, shaped like the long-bow, was once a big round satyr's laugh, that flung up the brows like a fortress lifted by gunpowder. The laugh will come again, but it will be of the order of the smile, finely-tempered, showing sunlight of the mind, mental richness rather than noisy enormity. Its common aspect is one of unsolicitous observation, as if surveying a full field and having leisure to dart on its chosen morsels, without any fluttering eagerness. Men's future upon earth does not attract it; their honesty and shapeliness in the present does; and whenever they wax out of proportion, overblown, affected, pretentious, bombastical, hypocritical, pedantic, fantastically delicate; whenever it sees them

self-deceived or hoodwinked, given to run riot in idolatries, drifting into vanities, congregating in absurdities, planning short-sightedly, plotting dementedly; whenever they are at variance with their professions, and violate the unwritten but perceptible laws binding them in consideration one to another; whenever they offend sound reason, fair justice; are false in humility, or mined with conceit, individually, or in the bulk; the Spirit overhead will look humanely malign, and cast an oblique light on them, followed by volleys of silvery laughter. That is the Comic Spirit.

Not to distinguish it is to be bull-blind to the spiritual, and to deny the existence of a mind of man where minds of men are in working conjunction.

You must, as I have said, believe that our state of society is founded in common sense, otherwise you will not be struck by the contrasts the Comic Spirit perceives, or have it to look to for your consolation. You will, in fact, be standing in that peculiar oblique beam of light, yourself illuminated to the general eye as the very object of chase and doomed quarry of the thing obscure to you. But to feel its presence, and to see it, is your assurance that many sane and solid minds are with you in what you are experiencing; and this of itself spares you the pain of satirical heat, and the bitter craving to strike heavy blows. You share the sublime of wrath, that would not have hurt the foolish, but merely demonstrate their foolishness. Molière was contented to revenge himself on the critics of the *École des Femmes* by writing the *Critique de l'École des Femmes,* one of the wisest as well as the playfullest of studies in criticism. A perception of the Comic Spirit gives high fellowship. You become a citizen of the selecter world, the highest we know of in connection with our old world, which is not supermundane. Look there for your unchallengeable upper class! You feel that you are one of this our civilized community, that you cannot escape from it, and would not if you could. Good hope sustains you; weariness does not overwhelm you; in isolation you see no charms for vanity; personal pride is greatly moderated. Nor shall your title of citizenship exclude you from worlds of imagination or of devotion. The Comic Spirit is not hostile to the sweetest songfully poetic. Chaucer bubbles with it; Shakespeare overflows; there is a mild moon's ray of it (pale with superrefinement through distance from our flesh and blood planet) in *Comus*. Pope has it, and it is the daylight side of the night half-obscuring Cowper. It is only hostile to the priestly element when that, by baleful swelling, transcends and overlaps the bounds of its office; and then, in extreme cases, it is too true to itself to speak, and veils the lamp—as, for example, the spectacle of Bossuet over the dead body of Molière, at which the dark angels may, but men do not, laugh.

We have had comic pulpits, for a sign that the laughter-moving and the worshipful may be in alliance; I know not how far comic, or how much assisted in seeming so by the unexpectedness and the relief of its appearance; at least they are popular—they are said to win the ear. Laughter is open to perversion, like other good things; the scornful and the brutal sorts are not unknown to us; but the laughter directed by the Comic Spirit is a harmless wine, conducing to sobriety in the degree that it enlivens. It enters you like fresh air into a study, as when one of the sudden contrasts of the comic idea floods the brain like reassuring daylight. You are cognizant of the true kind by feeling that you take it in, savor it, and have what flowers live on, natural air for food. That which you give out—the joyful roar—is not the better part; let that go to good-fellowship and the benefit of the lungs. Aristophanes promises his auditors that, if they will retain the ideas of the comic poet carefully, as they keep dried fruits in boxes, their garments shall smell odoriferous of wisdom throughout the year. The boast will not be thought an empty one by those who have choice friends that have stocked themselves according to his directions. Such treasuries of sparkling laughter are wells in our desert. Sensitiveness to the comic laugh is a step in civilization. To shrink from being an object of it is a step in cultivation. We know the degree of refinement in men by the matter they will laugh at, and the ring of the laugh; but we know likewise that the larger natures are distinguished by the great breadth of their power of laughter, and no one really loving Molière is refined by that love to despise or be dense to Aristophanes, though it may be that the lover of Aristophanes will not have risen to the height of Molière. Embrace them both, and you have the whole scale of laughter in your breast. Nothing in the world surpasses in stormy fun the scene in the *Frogs,* when Bacchus and Xanthias receive their thrashings from the hands of businesslike Aeacus, to discover which is the divinity of the two by his imperviousness to the mortal condition of pain, and each, under the obligation of not crying out, makes believe that his horrible bellow—the god's *"iou! iou!"* being the lustier—means only the stopping of a sneeze, or horsemen sighted, or the prelude to an invocation to some deity, and the slave contrives that the god shall get the bigger lot of blows. Passages of Rabelais, one or two in *Don Quixote,* and the supper "in the manner of the ancients" in *Peregrine Pickle,* are of a similar cataract of laughter. But it is not illuminating; it is not the laughter of the mind. Molière's laughter, in his purest comedies, is ethereal—as light to our nature, as color to our thoughts. The *Misanthrope* and the *Tartuffe* have no audible laughter, but the characters are steeped in the comic spirit. They quicken the mind through laughter, from coming out of the mind; and the mind accepts them because they are clear interpretations of certain chapters of the Book lying open before us all. Between these two stand Shakespeare and Cervantes, with the richer laugh of heart and mind in one; with much of the Aristophanic robustness, something of Molière's delicacy.

GEORGE BERNARD SHAW

George Bernard Shaw was born at Dublin in 1856. He was forced at an early age to earn his own living, as the family was in straightened circumstances. He went into a land-agent's office in his native city. But his interest in other things — chiefly music and science — made him restless, and in 1876 he went to London, where for nine years he did literary hack work. Between 1880 and 1883 he wrote four novels, which were not very successful, but during this time he met many people interested in politics and socialism, who were to exert great influence over him: Webb, Carpenter, Morris, and Archer, were guiding forces. In the early nineties he became dramatic critic of the *Saturday Review,* and carried on a campaign against the conventional plays and acting of the time. In 1892 he produced his first play, *Widowers' Houses.* This was soon followed by *The Philanderer* (1893) and *Mrs. Warren's Profession* (written a short while after, but censored and not performed until 1902). Meantime Shaw was busy lecturing, and engaged in the activities of the Fabian Society. Before long his influence began to make an effect on the English theatre, and continued to do so until his death in 1950 and afterwards. His plays are continually being revived in theatres all over the world.

Bernard Shaw's contribution to the drama has been two-fold, and that contribution is partly practical and partly theoretical. In his periodical critiques in the *Saturday Review* he was mainly concerned with destroying current notions about the well-made play, and absurd ideas about romance. Both in theory and in practice he has stood for the thesis-play: and like Tolstoy, he maintained that it is the function of the drama to teach and serve a practical and immediate purpose for the community and society. Throughout his lectures, essays, reviews, prefaces, and even in his plays he has preached his doctrines, though as Granville-Barker once commented, his own plays are often as close kin to Italian opera as to thesis-play.

THE AUTHOR'S APOLOGY FROM MRS. WARREN'S PROFESSION [1]
(1902)

. . . .
. . . Such an audience as I have described would be revolted by many of our fashionable plays. They would leave the theater convinced that the Plymouth Brother who still regards the playhouse as one of the gates of hell is perhaps the safest adviser on the subject of which he knows so little. If I do not draw the same conclusion, it is not because I am one of those who claim that art is exempt from moral obligations, and that the writing or performance of a play is not a moral act, to be treated on exactly the same footing as theft or murder if it produces equally mischievous consequences. I am convinced that fine art is

[1] Re-printed extracts from the edition with an Introduction by John Corbin (New York, 1905).— Ed.

the subtlest, the most seductive, the most effective means of propagandism in the world, excepting only the example of personal conduct; and I waive even this exception in favor of the art of the stage, because it works by exhibiting examples of personal conduct made intelligible and moving to crowds of unobservant, unreflecting people to whom real life means nothing. I have pointed out again and again that the influence of the theater in England is growing so great that whilst private conduct, religion, law, science, politics and morals are becoming more and more theatrical, the theater itself remains impervious to common sense, religion, science, politics, and morals. That is why I fight the theater, not with pamphlets and sermons and treatises, but with plays; and so effective do I find the dramatic method that I have no doubt I shall at last persuade even London to take its conscience and its brains with it when it goes to the theater, instead of leaving them at home with its prayer book as it does at present. Consequently, I am the last man in the world to deny that if the net effect of a performance of *Mrs. Warren's Profession* were an increase in the number of persons entering that profession, its performance should be dealt with accordingly.

.   .   .   .   .

. . . As to the voluptuaries, I can assure them that the playwright, whether he be myself or another, will always disappoint them. The drama can do little to delight the senses: all the apparent instances to the contrary are instances of the personal fascination of the performers. The drama of pure feeling is no longer in the hands of the playwright: it has been conquered by the musician, after whose enchantments all the verbal arts seem cold and tame. *Romeo and Juliet* with the loveliest Juliet is dry, tedious, and rhetorical in comparison with Wagner's *Tristan,* even though Isolde be fourteen stone and forty, as she often is in Germany. Indeed, it needed no Wagner to convince the public of this. The voluptuous sentimentality of Gounod's *Faust* and Bizet's *Carmen* has captured the common playgoer; and there is, flatly, no future now for any drama without music except the drama of thought. The attempt to produce a genus of opera without music — and this absurdity is what our fashionable theaters have been driving at for a long time past without knowing it — is far less hopeful than my own determination to accept problem as the normal material of the drama.

That this determination will throw me into a long conflict with our theater critics, and with the few playgoers who go to the theater as often as the critics, I well know; but I am too well equipped for the strife to be deterred from it, or to bear malice towards the losing side. In trying to produce the sensuous effects of opera, the fashionable drama has become so flaccid in its sentimentality, and the intellect of its frequenters so atrophied by disuse, that the reintroduction of problem, with its remorseless logic and iron framework of fact, inevitably produces at first an overwhelming impression of coldness and inhuman rationalism. But this will soon pass away. When the

intellectual muscle and moral nerve of the critics has been developed in the struggle with modern problem plays, the pettish luxuriousness of the clever ones, and the sulky sense of disadvantaged weakness in the sentimental ones, will clear away; and it will be seen that only in the problem play is there any real drama, because drama is no mere setting up of the camera to nature: it is the presentation in parable of the conflict between Man's will and his environment: in a word, of problem. The vapidness of such drama as the pseudo-operatic plays contain lies in the fact that in them animal passion, sentimentally diluted, is shown in conflict, not with real circumstances, but with a set of conventions and assumptions half of which do not exist off the stage, whilst the other half can either be evaded by a pretense of compliance or defied with complete impunity by any reasonably strong-minded person. Nobody can feel that such conventions are really compulsory; and consequently nobody can believe in the stage pathos that accepts them as an inexorable fate, or in the genuineness of the people who indulge in such pathos. Sitting at such plays we do not believe: we make believe. And the habit of make believe becomes at last so rooted that criticism of the theater ceases to be criticism at all, and becomes more and more a chronicle of the fashionable enterprises of the only realities left on the stage: that is, the performers in their own persons. In this phase the playwright who attempts to revive genuine drama produces the disagreeable impression of the pedant who attempts to start a serious discussion at a fashionable at-home. Later on, when he has driven the tea servies out and made the people who had come to use the theater as a drawing-room understand that it is they and not the dramatists who are the intruders, he has to face the accusation that his plays ignore human feeling, an illusion produced by that very resistance of fact and law to human feeling which creates drama. It is the *deus ex machina* who, by suspending that resistance, makes the fall of the curtain an immediate necessity, since drama ends exactly where resistance ends. Yet the introduction of this resistance produces so strong an impression of heartlessness nowadays that a distinguished critic has summed up the impression made on him by *Mrs. Warren's Profession,* by declaring that "the difference between the spirit of Tolstoy and the spirit of Mr. Shaw is the difference between the spirit of Christ and the spirit of Euclid." But the epigram would be as good if Tolstoy's name were put in place of mine and D'Annunzio's in place of Tolstoy's. At the same time I accept the enormous compliment to my reasoning powers with sincere complacency; and I promise my flatterer that when he is sufficiently accustomed to and therefore undazzled by the problem on the stage to be able to attend to the familiar factor of humanity in it as well as to the unfamiliar one of a real environment, he will both see and feel that *Mrs. Warren's Profession* is no mere theorem, but a play of instincts and temperaments in conflict with each other and with a flinty social problem that never yields an inch to mere sentiment.

I go further than this. I declare that the real secret of the cynicism and inhumanity of which shallower critics accuse me is the unexpectedness with which my characters behave like human beings, instead of conforming to the romantic logic of the stage. The axioms and postulates of that dreary mimanthropometry are so well known that it is almost impossible for its slaves to write tolerable last acts to their plays, so conventionally do their conclusions follow from their premises. Because I have thrown this logic ruthlessly overboard, I am accused of ignoring, not stage logic, but, of all things, human feeling. People with completely theatrified imaginations tell me that no

girl would treat her mother as Vivie Warren does, meaning that no stage heroine would in a popular sentimental play. They say this just as they might say that no two straight lines would inclose a space. They do not see how completely inverted their vision has become even when I throw its preposterousness in their faces, as I repeatedly do in this very play. Praed, the sentimental artist (fool that I was not to make him a playwright instead of an architect!), burlesques them by anticipating all through the piece that the feelings of the others will be logically deducible from their family relationships and from his "conventionally unconventional" social code. The sarcasm is lost on the critics: they, saturated with the same logic, only think him the sole sensible person on the stage. Thus it comes about that the more completely the dramatist is emancipated from the illusion that men and women are primarily reasonable beings, and the more powerfully he insists on the ruthless indifference of their great dramatic antagonist, the external world, to their whims and emotions, the surer he is to be denounced as blind to the very distinction on which his whole work is built. Far from ignoring idiosyncrasy, will, passion, impulse, whim, as factors in human action, I have placed them so nakedly on the stage that the elderly citizen, accustomed to see them clothed with the veil of manufactured logic about duty, and to disguise even his own impulses from himself in this way, finds the pictures as unnatural as Carlyle's suggested painting of Parliament sitting without its clothes.

. . . . . .

THE PROBLEM PLAY [2]

(1895)

I do not know who has asked the question, Should social problems be freely dealt with in the drama?—some very thoughtless person evidently. Pray what

[2] Contribution to a symposium on the question, "Should social problems be freely dealt with in the drama?" in *The Humanitarian,* VI (London), May, 1895. Used by permission of The Public Trustee and The Society of Authors, London.—Ed.

social questions and what sort of drama? Suppose I say yes, then, vaccination being a social question, and the Wagnerian music drama being the one complete form of drama in the opinion of its admirers, it will follow that I am in favor of the production of a Jennerian tetralogy at Bayreuth. If I say no, then, marriage being a social question, and also the theme of Ibsen's Doll's House, I shall be held to contemn that work as a violation of the canons of art. I therefore reply to the propounder that I am not prepared to waste my own time and that of the public in answering maladroit conundrums. What I am prepared to do is to say what I can with the object of bringing some sort of order into the intellectual confusion which has expressed itself in the conundrum.

Social questions are produced by the conflict of human institutions with human feeling. For instance, we have certain institutions regulating the lives of women. To the women whose feelings are entirely in harmony with these institutions there is no Woman Question. But during the present century, from the time of Mary Wollstonecraft onwards, women have been developing feelings, and consequently opinions, which clash with these institutions. The institutions assumed that it was natural to a woman to allow her husband to own her property and person, and to represent her in politics as a father represents his infant child. The moment that seemed no longer natural to some women, it became grievously oppressive to them. Immediately there was a Woman Question, which has produced Married Women's Property Acts, Divorce Acts, Woman's Suffrage in local elections, and the curious deadlock to which the Weldon and Jackson cases have led our courts in the matter of conjugal rights. When we have achieved reforms enough to bring our institutions as far into harmony with the feelings of women as they now are with the feelings of men, there will no longer be a Woman Question. No conflict, no question.

Now the material of the dramatist is always some conflict of human feeling with circumstances; so that, since institutions are circumstances, every social question furnishes material for drama. But every drama does not involve a social question, because human feeling may be in conflict with circumstances which are not institutions, which raise no question at all, which are part of human destiny. To illustrate, take Mr Pinero's Second Mrs. Tanqueray. The heroine's feelings are in conflict with the human institutions which condemn to ostracism both herself and the man who marries her. So far, the play deals with a social question. But in one very effective scene the conflict is between that flaw in the woman's nature which makes her dependent for affection wholly on the attraction of her beauty, and the stealthy advance of age and decay to take her beauty away from her. Here there is no social question: age, like love, death, accident, and personal character, lies outside all institutions; and this gives it a permanent and universal interest which makes the drama that deals with it independent of period and place. Abnormal greatness of character, abnormal baseness of character, love, and death: with these alone you can, if you are a sufficiently great dramatic poet, make a drama that will keep your language alive long after it has passed out of common use. Whereas a drama with a social question for the motive cannot outlive the solution of that question. It is true that we can in some cases imaginatively reconstruct an obsolete institution and sympathize with the tragedy it has produced: for instance, the very dramatic story of Abraham commanded to sacrifice his son, with the interposition of the angel to make a happy ending; or the condemnation of Antonio to lose a pound of flesh, and his rescue by Portia at the last moment, have not completely lost their effect nowadays—though it has been much modified—through the obsolescence of sacrificial rites, belief in miracles, and the conception that a debtor's person belongs to his creditors. It is enough that we still have paternal love, death, malice, moneylenders, and the tragedies of criminal law. But when a play depends entirely on a social question—when the struggle in it is between man and a purely legal institution—nothing can prolong its life beyond that of the institution. For example, Mr Grundy's Slaves of the Ring, in which the tragedy is produced solely by the conflict between the individual and the institution of indissoluble marriage, will not survive a rational law of divorce, and actually fails even now to grip an English audience because the solution has by this time become so very obvious. And that irrepressibly popular play It's Never Too Late to Mend will hardly survive our abominable criminal system. Thus we see that the drama which deals with the natural factors in human destiny, though not necessarily better than the drama which deals with the political factors, is likely to last longer.

It has been observed that the greatest dramatists shew a preference for the non-political drama, the greatest dramas of all being almost elementarily natural. But so, though for a different reason, do the minor dramatists. The minor dramatist leads the literary life, and dwells in the world of imagination instead of in the world of politics, business, law, and the platform agitations by which social questions are ventilated. He therefore remains, as a rule, astonishingly ignorant of real life. He may be clever, imaginative, sympathetic, humorous, and observant of such manners as he has any clue to; but he has hardly any wit or knowledge of the world. Compare his work with that of Sheridan, and you feel the deficiency at once. Indeed, you need not go so far as Sheridan: Mr Gilbert's Trial by Jury is unique among the works of living English playwrights, solely because it, too, is the work of a wit and a man of the world. Incidentally, it answers the inquiry as to whether social questions make good theatrical material; for though it is pointless, and, in fact, unintelligible except as a satire on a social institution (the breach-of-promise suit), it is highly entertaining, and has made the fortune of the author and his musical collaborator. The School for Scandal, the most popular of all modern comedies, is a dramatic sermon, just as Never Too Late to Mend, the most popular of modern melodramas, is a dramatic pamphlet: Charles Reade being another example of the distinction which the accomplished man of the world attains in the theatre as compared to the mere professional dramatist. In fact, it is so apparent that the best and most popular plays are dramatized sermons, pamphlets, satires, or bluebooks, that we find our popular authors, even when they have made a safe position for themselves by their success in purely imaginative drama, bidding for the laurels and the percentages of the sociologist dramatist. Mr Henry Arthur Jones takes a position as the author of The Middleman and The Crusaders, which The Silver King, enormously popular as it was, never could have gained him; and Mr Pinero, the author of The Second Mrs.

Tanqueray and The Notorious Mrs. Ebbsmith, is a much more important person, and a much richer one, than the author of Sweet Lavender. Of course, the sociology in some of these dramas is as imaginary as the names and addresses of the characters; but the imitation sociology testifies to the attractiveness of the real article.

We may take it then that the ordinary dramatist only neglects social questions because he knows nothing about them, and that he loses in popularity, standing, and money by his ignorance. With the great dramatic poet it is otherwise. Shakespear and Goethe do not belong to the order which "takes no interest in politics." Such minds devour everything with a keen appetite—fiction, science, gossip, politics, technical processes, sport, everything. Shakespear is full of little lectures of the concrete English kind, from Cassio on temperance to Hamlet on suicide. Goethe, in his German way, is always discussing metaphysical points. To master Wagner's music dramas is to learn a philosophy. It was so with all the great men until the present century. They swallowed all the discussions, all the social questions, all the topics, all the fads, all the enthusiasms, all the fashions of their day in their nonage, but their theme finally was not this social question or that social question, this reform or that reform, but humanity as a whole. To this day your great dramatic poet is never a socialist, nor an individualist, nor a positivist, nor a materialist, nor any other sort of "ist," though he comprehends all the "isms," and is generally quoted and claimed by all the sections as an adherent. Social questions are too sectional, too topical, too temporal to move a man to the mighty effort which is needed to produce great poetry. Prison reform may nerve Charles Reade to produce an effective and businesslike prose melodrama; but it could never produce Hamlet, Faust, or Peer Gynt.

It must, however, be borne in mind that the huge size of modern populations and the development of the press make every social question more momentous than it was formerly. Only a very small percentage of the population commits murder; but the population is so large that the frequency of executions is appalling. Cases which might have come under Goethe's notice in Weimar perhaps once in ten years come daily under the notice of modern newspapers, and are described by them as sensationally as possible. We are therefore witnessing a steady intensification in the hold of social questions on the larger poetic imagination. Les Misérables, with its rivulet of story running through a continent of essays on all sorts of questions, from religion to main drainage, is a literary product peculiar to the nineteenth century: it shows how matters which were trifles to Æschylus become stupendously impressive when they are multiplied by a million in a modern civilized state. Zola's novels are the product of an imagination driven crazy by a colossal police intelligence, by modern hospitals and surgery, by modern war correspondence, and even by the railway system—for in one of his books the hero is Jack the Ripper and his sweetheart a locomotive engine. What would Aristophanes have said to a city with fifteen thousand lunatics in it? Might he not possibly have devoted a comedy to the object of procuring some amelioration in their treatment? At all events, we find Ibsen, after producing, in Brand, Peer Gynt, and Emperor and Galilean, dramatic poems on the grandest scale, deliberately turning to comparatively prosaic topical plays on the most obviously transitory social questions, finding in their immense magnitude under modern conditions the stimulus which, a hundred years ago, or four thousand, he would only have received from the eternal strife of man with his own spirit. A Doll's House will be as flat as ditchwater when A Midsummer Night's Dream will still be as fresh as paint; but it will have done more work in the world; and that is enough for the highest genius, which is always intensely utilitarian.

Let us now hark back for a moment to the remark I made on Mr Grundy's Sowing the Wind [Slaves of the Ring, as above.—Ed.]: namely, that its urgency and consequently its dramatic interest are destroyed by the fact that the social question it presents is really a solved one. Its production after Les Surprises du Divorce (which Mr Grundy himself adapted for England) was an anachronism. When we succeed in adjusting our social structure in such a way as to enable us to solve social questions as fast as they become really pressing, they will no longer force their way into the theatre. Had Ibsen, for instance, had any reason to believe that the abuses to which he called attention in his prose plays would have been adequately attended to without his interference, he would no doubt have gladly left them alone. The same exigency drove William Morris in England from his tapestries, his epics, and his masterpieces of printing, to try and bring his fellow-citizens to their senses by the summary process of shouting at them in the streets and in Trafalgar Square. John Ruskin's writing began with Modern Painters; Carlyle began with literary studies of German culture and the like: both were driven to become revolutionary pamphleteers. If people are rotting and starving in all directions, and nobody else has the heart or brains to make a disturbance about it, the great writers must. In short, what is forcing our poets to follow Shelley in becoming political and social agitators, and to turn the theatre into a platform for propaganda and an arena for discussion, is that whilst social questions are being thrown up for solution almost daily by the fierce rapidity with which industrial processes change and supersede one another through the rivalry of the competitors who take no account of ulterior social consequences, and by the change in public feeling produced by popular "education," cheap literature, facilitated travelling, and so forth, the political machinery by which alone our institutions can be kept abreast of these changes is so old-fashioned, and so hindered in its action by the ignorance, the apathy, the stupidity, and the class feuds of the electorate, that social questions never get solved until the pressure becomes so desperate that even governments recognize the necessity for moving. And to bring the pressure to this point, the poets must lend a hand to the few who are willing to do public work in the stages at which nothing but abuse is to be gained by it.

Clearly, however, when the unhappy mobs which we now call nations and populations settle down into ordered commonwealths, ordinary bread-and-butter questions will be solved without troubling the poets and philosophers. The Shelleys, the Morrises, the Ruskins and Carlyles of that day will not need to spend their energies in trying to teach elementary political economy to the other members of the commonwealth; nor will the Ibsens be devising object lessons in spoiled womanhood, sickly consciences, and corrupt town councils, instead of writing great and enduring dramatic poems.

I need not elaborate the matter further. The conclusions to be drawn are:

1. Every social question, arising as it must from a conflict between human feeling and circumstances, affords material for drama.

2. The general preference of dramatists for subjects in which the conflict is between man and his apparently inevitable and eternal rather than his political and temporal circumstances, is due in the vast majority of cases to the dramatist's political ignorance (not to mention that of his audience), and in a few to the comprehensiveness of his philosophy.

3. The hugeness and complexity of modern civilizations and the development of our consciousness of them by means of the press, have the double effect of discrediting comprehensive philosophies by revealing more facts than the ablest man can generalize, and at the same time intensifying the urgency of social reforms sufficiently to set even the poetic faculty in action on their behalf.

4. The resultant tendency to drive social questions on to the stage, and into fiction and poetry, will eventually be counteracted by improvements in social organization, which will enable all prosaic social questions to be dealt with satisfactorily long before they become grave enough to absorb the energies which claim the devotion of the dramatist, the storyteller, and the poet.

WILLIAM ARCHER

William Archer was born at Perth, Scotland, in 1856. He attended Edinburgh University, and in 1883 was admitted to the bar. But before that time he had relinquished the idea of practicing, and as early as 1875 he was contributing to the *Edinburgh Evening News*. The next year he spent in Australia. He came to London in 1878, and in 1879 became dramatic critic of the *Figaro*. He occupied the same position on the *World* from 1884 to 1905. He was meantime engaged in translating the important plays of Ibsen, whom he helped to introduce to the English reading public. From 1906 to 1908 he was dramatic critic of *The Tribune*, and has since contributed to the *Star* and many other newspapers. Most of his criticisms he collected into books, the first of which, *English Dramatists of Today*, appeared in 1882. Besides his dramatic criticism, Archer has written political and social works.

Out of his long experience Archer has evolved no strikingly new theory of the drama, but in his *Playmaking* he has considered the essentials of dramatic form, and in attempting to disprove the validity of Brunetière's *Law* has laid down the dictum that crisis and not conflict is the chief requirement of the drama. Clayton Hamilton (in *Studies in Stagecraft*, 1914) justly taxes Archer in turn for limiting the field of the drama to crises, and says: " Yet I do not think it would be difficult to convince so open-minded a critic as Mr. Archer that the element of ' crisis ' is no more indispensable to a genuinely interesting drama than the element of ' conflict.' " And he adduces proofs by referring to three successful plays devoid of crisis. Archer has defined the dramatic as " Any representation of imaginary personages which is capable of interesting an average audience assembled in a theater." This is as far from Aristotle as any definition could well be.

He died in 1924.

PLAYMAKING [1]

[Chapter on] DRAMATIC AND UNDRAMATIC

(1912)

It may be well, at this point, to consider for a little what we mean when we use the term "dramatic." We shall probably not arrive at any definition that can be applied as an infallible touchstone to distinguish the dramatic from the undramatic. Perhaps, indeed, the upshot may rather be to place the student on his guard against troubling too much about the formal definitions of critical theorists.

The orthodox opinion of the present time is that which is generally associated with the name of the late Ferdinand Brunetière. "The theater in general," said that critic,[2] "is nothing but the place for the development of the human will, attacking the obstacles opposed to it by destiny, fortune, or circumstances." And again: "Drama is a representation of the will of man in conflict with the mysterious powers or natural forces which limit and belittle us; it is one of us thrown living upon the stage, there to struggle against fatality, against social law, against one of his fellow-mortals, against himself, if need be, against the interests, the prejudices, the folly, the malevolence of those who surround him."

The difficulty about this definition is that, while it describes the matter of a good many dramas, it does not lay down any true differentia — any characteristic common to all drama, and possessed by no other form of fiction. Many of the greatest plays in the world can with difficulty be brought under the formula, while the majority of romances and other stories come under it with ease. Where, for instance, is the struggle in *Agamemnon?* There is no more struggle between Clytemnestra and Agamemnon than there is between the spider and the fly who walked into his net. There is not even a struggle in Clytemnestra's mind. Agamemnon's doom is sealed from the outset, and she merely carries out a pre-arranged plot. There is contest indeed in the succeeding plays of the trilogy; but it will scarcely be argued that the *Agamemnon*,

taken alone, is not a great drama. Even the *Œdipus* of Sophocles, though it may at first sight seem a typical instance of a struggle against Destiny, does not really come under the definition. Œdipus, in fact, does not struggle at all. His struggles, in so far as that word can be applied to his misguided efforts to escape from the toils of fate, are all things of the past; in the actual course of the tragedy he simply writhes under one revelation after another of bygone error and unwitting crime. It would be a mere play upon words to recognize as a dramatic "struggle" the writhing of a worm on a hook. And does not this description apply very closely to the part played by another protagonist — Othello, to wit? There is no struggle, no conflict, between him and Iago. It is Iago alone who exerts any will; neither Othello nor Desdemona makes the smallest fight. From the moment when Iago sets his machination to work, they are like people sliding down an ice-slope to an evitable abyss. Where is the conflict in *As You Like It?* No one, surely, will pretend that any part of the interest or charm of the play arises from the struggle between the banished Duke and the Usurper, or between Orlando and Oliver. There is not even the conflict, if so it can be called, which nominally brings so many hundreds of plays under the Brunetière canon — the conflict between an eager lover and a more or less reluctant maid. Or, take again, Ibsen's *Ghosts* — in what valid sense can it be said that that tragedy shows us will struggling against obstacles? Oswald, doubtless, wishes to live, and his mother desires that he should live; but this mere will for life cannot be the differentia that makes of *Ghosts* a drama. If the reluctant descent of the "downward path to death" constituted drama, then Tolstoy's *Death of Ivan Ilytch* would be one of the greatest dramas ever written — which it certainly is not. Yet again, if we want to see will struggling against obstacles, the classic to turn to is not *Hamlet*, not *Lear*, but *Robinson Crusoe;* yet no one, except a

1 Re-printed from *Playmaking* (Boston, 1912). Sections from this chapter.— Ed.
2 *Etudes critiques*, vol. 7, pp. 153 and 207.

pantomime librettist, ever saw a drama in Defoe's narrative. In a Platonic dialogue, in *Paradise Lost,* in *John Gilpin,* there is a struggle against obstacles, there is none in *Hannele,* which, nevertheless, is a deeply moving drama. Such a struggle is characteristic of all fiction, from *Clarissa Harlowe* to *The House With the Green Shutters;* whereas, in many plays, the struggle, if there be any at all, is the merest matter of form (for instance, a quite conventional love-story), while the real interest resides in something quite different.

The plain truth seems to be that conflict is *one* of the most dramatic elements in life, and that many dramas — perhaps most — do, as a matter of fact, turn upon strife of one sort or another. But it is clearly an error to make conflict indispensable to drama, and especially to insist — as do some of Brunetière's followers — that the conflict must be between will and will. A stand-up fight between will and will — such a fight as occurs in, say, the *Hippolytus* of Euripides or Racine's *Andromaque,* or Molière's *Tartufe,* or Ibsen's *Pretenders,* or Dumas' *Francillon,* or Sudermann's *Heimat,* or Sir Arthur Pinero's *Gay Lord Quex,* or Mr. Shaw's *Candida,* or Mr. Galsworthy's *Strife* — such a stand-up fight, I say, is no doubt one of the intensest forms of drama. But it is comparatively rare, at any rate, as the formula of a whole play. In individual scenes a conflict of will is frequent enough; but it is, after all, only one among a multitude of equally telling forms of drama. No one can say that the balcony scene in *Romeo and Juliet* is undramatic, or the "Galeoto fu il libro" scene in Mr. Stephen Phillips' *Paolo and Francesca;* yet the point of these scenes is not a clash, but an ecstatic concordance, of wills. Is the death scene of Cleopatra undramatic? Or the banquet scene in *Macbeth?* Or the pastoral act in the *Winter's Tale?* Yet in none of these is there any conflict of wills. In the whole range of drama there is scarcely a passage which one would call more specifically dramatic than the Screen scene in the *School for Scandal;* yet it would be the veriest quibbling to argue that any appreciable part of its effect arises from the clash of will against will. This whole comedy, indeed, suffices

to show the emptiness of the theory. With a little strain, it is possible to bring it within the letter of the formula; but who can pretend that any considerable part of the attraction or interest of the play is due to that possibility?

The champions of the theory, moreover, place it on a metaphysical basis, finding in the will the essence of human personality, and therefore of the art which shows human personality raised to its highest power. It seems unnecessary, however, to apply to Schopenhauer for an explanation of whatever validity the theory may possess. For a sufficient account of the matter, we need go no further than the simple psychological observation that human nature loves a fight, whether it be with clubs or with swords, with tongues or with brains. One of the earliest forms of mediæval drama was the *estrif* or *flyting* — the scolding match between husband and wife, or between two rustic gossips. This motive is glorified in the quarrel between Brutus and Cassius, degraded in the patter of two "knockabout comedians." Certainly there is nothing more telling in drama than a piece of "cut-and-thrust" dialogue after the fashion of the ancient "stichomythia." When a whole theme involving conflict, or even a single scene of the nature described as a "passage-at-arms" comes naturally in the playwright's way, by all means let him seize the opportunity. But do not let him reject a theme or scene as undramatic, merely because it has no room for a clash of warring wills.

There is a variant of the *conflict* theory which underlines the word "obstacles" in the above-quoted dictum of Brunetière, and lays down the rule: "No obstacle, no drama." Though far from being universally valid, this form of the theory has a certain practical usefulness, and may well be borne in mind. Many a play would have remained unwritten if the author had asked himself, "Is there a sufficient obstacle between my two lovers?" or, in more general terms, "between my characters and the realization of their will?" There is nothing more futile than a play in which we feel that there is no real obstacle to the inevitable happy ending, and that the curtain might just as well fall in the middle of the first act as at the end of the third.

Comedies are bound (though they reach the stage only by accident) in which the obstacle between Corydon and Phyllis, between Lord Edwin and Lady Angelina, is not even a defect or peculiarity of character, but simply some trumpery misunderstanding which can be kept afoot only so long as every one concerned holds his or her commonsense in studious abeyance. "Pyramus and Thisbe without the wall" may be taken as the formula for the whole type of play. But even in plays of a much higher type, the author might often ask himself with advantage whether he could not strengthen his obstacle, and so accentuate the struggle which forms the matter of his play. Though conflict may not be essential to drama, yet, when you set forth to portray a struggle, you may as well make it as real and intense as possible. . . .

. . . . . .

What, then, is the essence of drama, if conflict be not it? What is the common quality of themes, scenes, and incidents, which we recognize as specifically dramatic? Perhaps we shall scarcely come nearer to a helpful definition than if we say that the essence of drama is crisis. A play is a more or less rapidly-developing crisis in destiny or circumstances, and a dramatic scene is a crisis within a crisis, clearly furthering the ultimate event. The drama may be called the art of crises, as fiction is the art of gradual developments. It is the slowness of its process which differentiates the typical novel from the typical play. If the novelist does not take advantage of the facilities offered by his form for portraying gradual change, whether in the way of growth or of decay, he renounces his own birthright in order to trespass on the domain of the dramatist. Most great novels embrace considerable segments of many lives; whereas the drama gives us only the culminating points — or, shall we say, the intersecting culminations? — of two or three destinies. Some novelists have excelled precisely in the art with which they have made the gradations of change in character or circumstance so delicate as to be imperceptible from page to page, and measurable, as in real life, only when we look back over a considerable period. The dramatist, on the other hand, deals in rapid and startling changes, the *peripeties*, as the Greeks called them, which may be the outcome of long, slow processes, but which actually occur in very brief spaces of time. Nor is this merely a mechanical consequence of the narrow limits of stage presentation. The crisis is as real, though not as inevitable, a part of human experience as the gradual development. Even if the material conditions of the theater permitted the presentation of a whole *Middlemarch* or *Anna Karénina* — as the conditions of the Chinese theater actually do — some dramatists, we cannot doubt, would voluntarily renounce that license of prolixity, in order to cultivate an art of concentration and crisis. The Greek drama "subjected to the faithful eyes," as Horace phrases it, the culminating points of the Greek epic; the modern drama places under the lens of theatrical presentment the culminating points of modern experience.

But, manifestly, it is not every crisis that is dramatic. A serious illness, a law-suit, a bankruptcy, even an ordinary prosaic marriage, may be a crisis in a man's life, without being necessarily, or even probably, material for drama. How, then, do we distinguish a dramatic from a non-dramatic crisis? Generally, I think, by the fact that it develops, or can be made naturally to develop, through a series of minor crises, involving more or less emotional excitement, and, if possible, the vivid manifestation of character. . . .

. . . . . .

And now, after all this discussion of the "dramatic" in theme and incident, it remains to be said that the tendency of recent theory, and of some recent practice, has been to widen the meaning of the word, until it bursts the bonds of all definition. Plays have been written, and have found some acceptance, in which the endeavor of the dramatist has been to depict life, not in moments of crisis, but in its most level and humdrum phases, and to avoid any crispness of touch in the presentation of individual incidents. "Dramatic," in the eyes of writers of this school, has become a term of reproach, synonymous with "theatrical." They take their cue from Maeterlinck's famous essay on *The Tragical in Daily Life*, in which he lays it down that: "An old man, seated in his arm-chair, waiting patiently, with his lamp beside him — submitting with bent head to the presence of his soul and his destiny — motionless as he is, does yet live in reality a deeper, more human, and more universal life than the lover who strangles his mistress, the captain who conquers in battle, or the husband who ' avenges his honor.' " They do not observe that Maeterlinck, in his own practice, constantly deals with crises, and often with violent and startling ones.

At the same time, I am far from suggesting that the reaction against the traditional " dramatic " is a wholly mistaken movement. It is a valuable corrective of conventional theatricalism; and it has, at some points, positively enlarged the domain of dramatic art. Any movement is good which helps to free art from the tyranny of a code of rules and definitions. The only really valid definition of the " dramatic " is: any representation of imaginary personages which is capable of interesting an average audience assembled in a theater. We must say, " representation of imaginary personages " in order to exclude a lecture or a prize-fight; and we must say " an average audience " (or something to that effect) in order to exclude a dialogue of Plato or of Landor, the recitation of which might interest a specially selected public. Any further attempt to limit the content of the term " dramatic " is simply the expression of an opinion that such-and-such forms of representation will not be found to interest an audience; and this opinion may always be rebutted by experiment. In all that I have said, then, as to the dramatic and non-dramatic, I must be taken as meaning: " Such and such forms and methods have been found to please and will probably please again. They are, so to speak, safer and easier than other forms and methods. But it is the part of original genius to override the dictates of experience, and nothing in these pages is designed to discourage original genius from making the attempt." We have already seen, indeed, that in a certain type of play — the broad picture of a social phenomenon or environment — it is preferable that no attempt be made to depict a marked crisis. There should be just enough story to afford a plausible excuse for raising and for lowering the curtain.

Let us not, however, seem to grant too much to the innovators and the quietists. To say that a drama should be, or tends to be, the presentation of a crisis in the life of certain characters, is by no means to insist on a mere arbitrary convention. It is to make at once an induction from the overwhelming majority of existing dramas and a deduction from the nature and inherent conditions of theatrical presentation. The fact that theatrical conditions often encourage a violent exaggeration of the characteristically dramatic elements in life does not make these elements any the less real or any the less characteristically dramatic. It is true that crispness of handling may easily degenerate into the pursuit of mere picture-poster situation; but that is no reason why the artist should not seek to achieve crispness within the bounds prescribed by nature and commonsense. There is a drama — I have myself seen it — in which the heroine, fleeing from the villain, is stopped by a yawning chasm. The pursuer is at her heels, and it seems as though she has no resource but to hurl herself into the abyss. But she is accompanied by three Indian servants, who happen, by the mercy of Providence, to be accomplished acrobats. The second climbs on the shoulders of the first, the third on the shoulders of the second; and then the whole trio falls forward across the chasm, the top one grasping some bush or creeper on the other side; so that a living bridge is formed, on which the heroine (herself, it would seem, something of an acrobat) can cross the dizzy gulf and bid defiance to the baffled villain. This is clearly a dramatic crisis within our definition; but, no less clearly, it is not a piece of rational or commendable drama. To say that such-and-such a factor is necessary, or highly desirable, in a dramatic scene, is by no means to imply that every scene which contains this factor is good drama. Let us take the case of another heroine — Nina in Sir Arthur Pinero's *His House in Order*. The second wife of Filmer Jesson, she is continually being offered up as a sacrifice on the altar dedicated to the memory of his adored first wife. Not only her husband but the relatives of the sainted Annabel make her life a burden to her. Then there comes to her knowledge — she obtains absolute proof — that Annabel was anything but the saint she was believed to be. By a single word she can overturn the altar of her martyrdom, and shatter the dearest illusion of her persecutor. Shall she speak that word, or shall she not? Here is a crisis which comes within our definition just as clearly as the other; only it happens to be entirely natural and probable, and eminently illustrative of character.

Ought we, then, to despise it because of the element it has in common with the picture-poster situation of preposterous melodrama? Surely not. Let those who have the art — the extremely delicate and difficult art — of making drama without the characteristically dramatic ingredients, do so by all means; but let them not seek to lay an embargo on the judicious use of these ingredients as they present themselves in life.

WILLIAM BUTLER YEATS

Yeats, who was born near Dublin in 1865, is the leading English-language poet of the twentieth century. He studied art in Dublin but soon essayed a literary career. His early poetry, which showed the influence of the English Pre-Raphaelite school and of Irish mythology, tended to be melodic and sensual. The poetry he published after the turn of the century tended, on the other hand, to be more austere, philosophical, and pessimistic. Most of his plays belong to the later period. His fanciful verse play *The Land of Heart's Desire* (1894) is the principal dramatic product of his early manner. The change in his writing accompanied his taking a serious interest in the theatre and his founding, with Lady Augusta Gregory, of the Irish Literary Theatre in 1899. This organization differed from the new theatres of the continent in its dedication to distinctively Irish material and, wherever possible, to poetic treatment of mythology and peasant life. By 1904 the company had moved into the Abbey Theatre, and Yeats became a devoted writer of plays essentially poetic, whether in verse or prose; among them were *Deirdre* (1906, based on a popular Irish legend), *At the Hawk's Well* (1916, the first of several plays about the Irish hero Cuchulainn), *The Player-Queen* (1922), *The Words upon the Window Pane* (1934, concerning a spiritualistic seance in which Jonathan Swift manifests his presence), and *Purgatory* (1938). Some of the plays, including *At the Hawk's Well*, reflect Yeats's interest in the highly stylized tradition of Japanese No drama and thereby serve to remind us that Yeats was consciously writing for a minority audience. He died in 1939.

EMOTION OF MULTITUDE [1]

(1903)

I have been thinking a good deal about plays lately, and I have been wondering why I dislike the clear and logical construction which seems necessary if one is to succeed on the modern stage. It came into my head the other day that this construction, which all the world has learnt

from France, has everything of high literature except the emotion of multitude. The Greek drama has got the emotion of multitude from its chorus, which called up famous sorrows, even all the gods and all heroes, to witness, as it were, some well-ordered fable, some action separated but for this from all but itself. The French play delights in the well-ordered fable, but by leaving out

1 From *Essays and Introductions*, © 1961 by Mrs. W. B. Yeats. Used by permission of The Macmillan Co. and Mrs. W. B. Yeats.—Ed.

the chorus it has created an art where poetry and imagination, always the children of far-off multitudinous things, must of necessity grow less important than the mere will. This is why, I said to myself, French dramatic poetry is so often rhetorical, for what is rhetoric but the will trying to do the work of the imagination? The Shakespearian drama gets the emotion of multitude out of the sub-plot which copies the main plot, much as a shadow upon the wall copies one's body in the firelight. We think of *King Lear* less as the history of one man and his sorrows than as the history of a whole evil time. Lear's shadow is in Gloucester, who also has ungrateful children, and the mind goes on imagining other shadows, shadow beyond shadow, till it has pictured the world. In *Hamlet,* one hardly notices, so subtly is the web woven, that the murder of Hamlet's father and the sorrow of Hamlet are shadowed in the lives of Fortinbras and Ophelia and Laertes, whose fathers, too, have been killed. It is so in all the plays, or in all but all, and very commonly the sub-plot is the main plot working itself out in more ordinary men and women, and so doubly calling up before us the image of multitude. Ibsen and Maeterlinck have, on the other hand, created a new form, for they get multitude from the wild duck in the attic, or from the crown at the bottom of the fountain, vague symbols that set the mind wandering from idea to idea, emotion to emotion. Indeed all the great masters have understood that there cannot be great art without the little limited life of the fable, which is always the better the simpler it is, and the rich, far-wandering, many-imaged life of the half-seen world beyond it. There are some who understand that the simple unmysterious things living as in a clear noon light are of the nature of the sun, and that vague, many-imaged things have in them the strength of the moon. Did not the Egyptian carve it on emerald that all living things have the sun for father and the moon for mother, and has it not been said that a man of genius takes the most after his mother?

THE REFORM OF THE THEATRE [2]

(1903)

I think the theatre must be reformed in its plays, its speaking, its acting, and its scenery. That is to say, I think there is nothing good about it at present.

First. We have to write or find plays that will make the theatre a place of intellectual excitement—a place where the mind goes to be liberated as it was liberated by the theatres of Greece and England and France at certain great moments of their history, and as it is liberated in Scandinavia to-day. If we are to do this we must learn that beauty and truth are always justified of themselves, and that their creation is a greater service to our country than writing that compromises either in the seeming service of a cause. We will, doubtless, come more easily to truth and beauty because we love some cause with all but all our heart; but we must remember when truth and beauty open their mouths to speak, that all other mouths should be as silent as Finn bade the son of Lugaidh be in the houses of the great. Truth and beauty judge and are above judgment. They justify and have no need of justification.

Such plays will require, both in writers and audiences, a stronger feeling for beautiful and appropriate language than one finds in the ordinary theatre. Sainte-Beuve has said that there is nothing immortal in literature except style, and it is precisely this sense of style, once common among us, that is hardest for us to recover. I do not mean by style words with an air of literature about them, what is ordinarily called eloquent writing. The speeches of Falstaff are as perfect in their style as the soliloquies of Hamlet. One must be able to make a king of Faery or an old countryman

2 First published in *Samhain: 1903;* included in *Explorations,* © 1962 by Mrs. W. B. Yeats. Used by permission of The Macmillan Co. and Mrs. W. B. Yeats.—Ed.

or a modern lover speak that language which is his and nobody else's, and speak it with so much of emotional subtlety that the hearer may find it hard to know whether it is the thought or the word that has moved him, or whether these could be separated at all.

If we do not know how to construct, if we cannot arrange much complicated life into a single action, our work will not hold the attention or linger in the memory, but if we are not in love with words it will lack the delicate movement of living speech that is the chief garment of life; and because of this lack the great realists seem to the lovers of beautiful art to be wise in this generation, and for the next generation, perhaps, but not for all generations that are to come.

Second. But if we are to restore words to their sovereignty we must make speech even more important than gesture upon the stage.

I have been told that I desire a monotonous chant, but that is not true, for though a monotonous chant may be a safer beginning for an actor than the broken and prosaic speech of ordinary recitation, it puts me to sleep none the less. The sing-song in which a child says a verse is a right beginning, though the child grows out of it. An actor should understand how so to discriminate cadence from cadence, and so to cherish the musical lineaments of verse or prose that he delights the ear with a continually varied music. Certain passages of lyrical feeling, or where one wishes, as in the Angel's part in *The Hour-Glass,* to make a voice sound like the voice of an Immortal, may be spoken upon pure notes which are carefully recorded and learned as if they were the notes of a song. Whatever method one adopts, one must always be certain that the work of art, as a whole, is masculine and intellectual, in its sound as in its form.

Third. We must simplify acting, especially in poetical drama, and in prose drama that is remote from real life like my *Hour-Glass.* We must get rid of everything that is restless, everything that draws the attention away from the sound of the voice, or from the few moments of intense expression, whether that expression is through the voice or through the hands; we must from time to time substitute for the movements that the eye sees the nobler movements that the heart sees, the rhythmical movements that seem to flow up into the imagination from some deeper life than that of the individual soul.

Fourth. Just as it is necessary to simplify gesture that it may accompany speech without being its rival, it is necessary to simplify both the form and colour of scenery and costume. As a rule the background should be but a single colour, so that the persons in the play, wherever they stand, may harmonise with it and preoccupy our attention. In other words, it should be thought out not as one thinks out a landscape, but as if it were the background of a portrait, and this is especially necessary on a small stage where the moment the stage is filled, the painted forms of the background are broken up and lost. Even when one has to represent trees or hills they should be treated in most cases decoratively, they should be little more than an unobtrusive pattern. There must be nothing unnecessary, nothing that will distract the attention from speech and movement. An art is always at its greatest when it is most human. Greek acting was great because it did all but everything with the voice, and modern acting may be great when it does everything with voice and movement. But an art which smothers these things with bad painting, with innumerable garish colours, with continual restless mimicries of the surface of life, is an art of fading humanity, a decaying art.

JOHN MILLINGTON SYNGE

Born in Dublin in 1871, Synge studied music before going to Paris to write. Here he was saved for his native Ireland by William Butler Yeats in 1899 and persuaded that he must write about his own land. He went off on a second trip to the isolated Aran Islands, where he studied the local dialects, characters, and folklore. He began to write plays of peasant life, employing the natural speech which he had learned. His first play, *In the Shadow of the Glen,* was performed in 1903 by the Irish National Theatre, of which Yeats and Lady Gregory were co-founders. In 1904, Synge's brief peasant tragedy, *Riders to Sea,* was staged at this company's new home, the Abbey Theatre, and Synge became the Abbey's literary adviser. Other folk plays followed, including his comedy about a mock-hero, *The Playboy of the Western World* (1907), which caused patriots to riot at the theatre. Synge died in 1909.

PREFACE TO THE PLAYBOY OF THE WESTERN WORLD [1]

(1907)

In writing *The Playboy of the Western World,* as in my other plays, I have used one or two words only that I have not heard among the country people of Ireland, or spoken in my own nursery before I could read the newspapers. A certain number of the phrases I employ I have heard also from herds and fishermen along the coast from Kerry to Mayo, or from beggar-women and ballad-singers nearer Dublin; and I am glad to acknowledge how much I owe to the folk-imagination of these fine people. Anyone who has lived in real intimacy with the Irish peasantry will know that the wildest sayings and ideas in this play are tame indeed, compared with the fancies one may hear in any little hillside cabin in Geesala, or Carraroe, or Dingle Bay. All art is a collaboration; and there is little doubt that in the happy ages of literature, striking and beautiful phrases were as ready to the story-teller's or the playwright's hand, as the rich cloaks and dresses of his time. It is probable that when the Elizabethan dramatist took his ink-horn and sat down to his work he used many phrases that he had just heard, as he sat at dinner, from his mother or his children. In Ireland, those of us who know the people have the same privilege. When I was writing *The Shadow of the Glen,* some years ago, I got more aid than any learning could have given me from a chink in the floor of the old Wicklow house where I was

staying, that let me hear what was being said by the servant girls in the kitchen. This matter, I think, is of importance, for in countries where the imagination of the people, and the language they use, is rich and living, it is possible for a writer to be rich and copious in his words, and at the same time to give the reality, which is the root of all poetry, in a comprehensive and natural form. In the modern literature of towns, however, richness is found only in sonnets, or prose poems, or in one or two elaborate books that are far away from the profound and common interests of life. One has, on one side, Mallarmé and Huysmans producing this literature; and on the other, Ibsen and Zola dealing with the reality of life in joyless and pallid words. On the stage one must have reality, and one must have joy; and that is why the intellectual modern drama has failed, and people have grown sick of the false joy of the musical comedy, that has been given them in place of the rich joy found only in what is superb and wild in reality. In a good play every speech should be as fully flavoured as a nut or apple, and such speeches cannot be written by anyone who works among people who have shut their lips on poetry. In Ireland, for a few years more, we have a popular imagination that is fiery and magnificent, and tender; so that those of us who wish to write start with a chance that is not given to writers in places where the springtime of the local life has been forgotten, and the harvest is a memory only, and the straw has been turned into bricks.

[1] Both prefaces are from *The Complete Works of John M. Synge,* © 1935 by The Modern Library, Inc. Used by permission of Random House, Inc.—Ed.

PREFACE TO THE TINKER'S WEDDING [1]

(1907)

The drama is made serious—in the French sense of the word—not by the degree in which it is taken up with problems that are serious in themselves, but by the degree in which it gives the nourishment, not very easy to define, on which our imaginations live. We should not go to the theatre as we go to a chemist's, or a dramshop, but as we go to a dinner, where the food we need is taken with pleasure and excitement. This was nearly always so in Spain and England and France when the drama was at its richest—the infancy and decay of the drama tend to be didactic—but in these days the playhouse is too often stocked with the drugs of many seedy problems, or with the absinthe or vermouth of the last musical comedy.

The drama, like the symphony, does not teach or prove anything. Analysts with their problems, and teachers with their systems, are soon as old-fashioned as the pharmacopœia of Galen,—look at Ibsen and the Germans—but the best plays of Ben Jonson and Molière can no more go out of fashion than the blackberries on the hedges.

Of the things which nourish the imagination humor is one of the most needful, and it is dangerous to limit or destroy it. Baudelaire calls laughter the greatest sign of the Satanic element in man; and where a country loses its humor, as some towns in Ireland are doing, there will be morbidity of mind, as Baudelaire's mind was morbid.

In the greater part of Ireland, however, the whole people, from the tinkers to the clergy have still a life, and view of life, that are rich and genial and humorous. I do not think that these country people, who have so much humor themselves, will mind being laughed at without malice, as the people in every country have been laughed at in their own comedies.

SEAN O'CASEY

O'Casey was born in Dublin in 1880, and worked as a common laborer before turning playwright. His first three full-length plays were performed by the Abbey Theatre, although their realistic form was contrary to the original principles of the Abbey. They are *The Shadow of a Gunman*, about a pretender to heroism during the Irish civil war (1923); *Juno and the Paycock*, about the decline and collapse of a humble family in Dublin (1924); and *The Plough and the Stars*, a view of Dublin in the Easter rebellion of 1916 (1926). A hostile audience rioted when the last play was performed. Soon after, Yeats rejected O'Casey's *The Silver Tassie*, a semi-expressionist play of English life, showing the effects of World War I. Angered, O'Casey left the Abbey and made London the center of his theatrical activity. Most of the plays that followed reflected his radical political leanings and were, in some measure, experiments in expressionism; they included, among others, *Within the Gates* (1933), *Purple Dust* (1940), *Red Roses for Me* (1942), and *Cock-a-Doodle Dandy* (1949). In London, the pugnacious O'Casey quarrelled with those drama critics—the influential James Agate in particular—who preferred the superficial realism of such dramatists as Noel Coward and Emlyn Williams, writers of entertainments. Some of his angry essays appear in *The Flying Wasp* (1937) and *The Green Crow* (1956). From 1939 to 1956, O'Casey has published several autobiographical volumes: *I Knock at the Door, Pictures in the Hallway, Drums under the Window, Inishfallen Fare Thee Well, Rose and Crown,* and *Sunset and Evening Star.* Some of these formed the basis of dramatic readings given in New York, arranged and staged by Paul Shyre.

GREEN GODDESS OF REALISM [1]

(1956)

In the theatre of today, realism is the totem pole of the dramatic critics.

Matter-of-fact plays, true true-to-life arrangement, and real, live characters are the three gods the critics adore and saturate with the incense of their commonplace praise once a day and twice on Sundays in their trimly-dressed little articles. What the dramatic critics mean by the various terms they use for Realism is the yearly ton of rubbish that falls on the English stage and is swiftly swept away into the dustbins. The critics give a cordial welcome to the trivial plays because, in my opinion, they are, oh, so easy to understand, and gorge the critics with the ease of an easy explanation. It is very dangerous for a dramatist to be superior to the critics, to be a greater dramatist than the critic is a critic. They don't like it, and so most of them do all they can to discourage any attempt in the theatre towards an imagination fancy-free, or an attempt to look on life and mold it into a form fit for the higher feeling and intelligence of the stage. They are those who compare Beaumont and Fletcher's *Philaster* with *Charley's Aunt,* and in their heart of hearts vote for the farce and shove the poetic play out of their way (a few spit the preference in our face, as Archer did). Charley's Aunt is loved by Charley's uncles. They have grown fat and lazy on triviality, so fat and so lazy that they are hardly able to move. The curse is that these critics do their best to prevent anyone else from moving either. They will have simply to be roughly shunted out of the way, and these few words are one of the first sharp prods to get them to buzz off and do their sleeping somewhere else. Realism, or what the critics childishly believe to be Realism, has had its day, and has earned a rest. It began on a sunny autumn evening in 1886, or thereabouts, as the lawyers say, at the first production of *Ours* by Robertson, when the miracle took place. "In reading the play today," says William Archer, the world-famous dramatic critic, "we recognize in Robertson —just what the stage wanted in its progress towards verisimilitude—the genius of the commonplace. The first act of *Ours* was, in intention at any rate, steeped in an atmosphere quite new to the theatre. The scene was an avenue in Shendryn Park which Robertson describes in the abhorrent prompt-book jargon of the time. But one line had, I venture to say, as yet appeared in no prompt-book in the world: '*Throughout the act the autumn leaves fall from the trees.*' How this effect was produced and whether it was successful, I cannot say. Nor can I discuss the question whether it was a desirable effect, or a mere trick of mechanical realism which the true artist would despise." Now the falling of the leaves from the trees was and could have been nothing but "a mere trick of mechanical realism," because the trees couldn't have been true-to-life trees, and, even if they were, the autumnal leaves couldn't have fallen with the regularity and rhythm required to create the desirable effect. And no true artist of the theatre would despise "a mere trick of mechanical realism" by which to get a scenic or an emotional effect out of his play and over to his audience. We remember the fine effect that the first sound of the first fall of rain had as it fell in the first act of Obey's *Noah;* and this fall of rain was a mere trick of mechanical realism as it was also the opening of the floodgates of Heaven, swelling into a flood that destroyed all life that was in the world save only those who found safe shelter in the faith of Noah; or the sudden change in the wind in *Saint Joan* that set the pennon streaming eastward, and sent Dunois and Saint Joan hurrying out to make for the flash of the guns, and drive the English out of France. You see the artist in the theatre never despises a mere trick of mechanical realism; but he knows how to keep it in its proper place. . . .

Although the bone of realism in the theatre has been picked pretty clean, the

1 Extracts from an essay in *The Green Crow,* © 1956 by Sean O'Casey. Used by permission of George Braziller, Inc.—Ed.

critics keep gnawing away at it, so that if a playwright as much as gets a character to blow his nose (preferably when "the autumn leaves are falling from the trees"), the critics delightedly nod to each other, and murmur, "An exact imitation of life, brothers." Commenting on *Call It a Day,* a play in which everything is attempted and nothing done, Mr. Agate tells us that "Miss Dodie Smith is never concerned whether 'it' is a play or not, but whether she has assembled on her stage characters so real that she might have gone into the street and compelled them into the theatre," though these characters that might have been pulled in off the street are as tender and delicate and true as the tenderest and most delicate characters wistfully wandering about in the most wistful Barrie play. J. G. B., commenting on *Love from a Stranger,* tells us that "it is written with brilliant matter-of-factness, and is a real play about real people." Here our noses are shoved up against the image of realism in the theatre. A real play about real people: here's a sentence that apparently punches home; but look well into it, and you'll find it empty of any real meaning. Week in and week out these commonplace plays are reducing the poor critics into more and more vague and vapid expressions that would give a sparkle to the mouth of a politician trying to cod his constituents—and very often succeeding. A real play about real people—what does it mean? This is something of a triumph —a real play with real people in a real theatre before a real audience. But every play is a real play whether it be good or bad, just as a real lion is a real lion and a real mouse is a real mouse, and both are animals. But the real mouse isn't a real lion, nor is the real lion a real mouse, though both are animals. I wonder do the critics get this? There is a big difference between a lion and a mouse, though both are animals, and there is a bigger difference between a good and a bad play, though both are plays just the same. What is a "real play"? Answer, according to J. G. B., *Love from a Stranger* is a real play, therefore the nearer we get to this praised play, the nearer we get to a real play. Now is *The Dream Play* by Strindberg a real play? It certainly

bears no resemblance to *Love from a Stranger,* but the imagination can handle *The Dream Play* just as well and with far fuller satisfaction. Apparently the critics think that a play to be a real play must have real people in it, though they never take breath to tell us what they mean by real people. Take people off the street or carry them out of a drawing-room, plonk them on the stage and make them speak as they speak in real, real life, and you will have the dullest thing imaginable. I suppose the critics will be shocked to hear that no real character can be put in a play unless some of the reality is taken out of him through the heightening, widening, and deepening of the character by the dramatist who creates him. Would the dramatic critics call the characters in *Hamlet* real people, or only the creations out of the mind of a poet, and isn't *Hamlet* all the better for its want of reality? Isn't it more of a play, and what has the word "play" got to do with reality? Is Caliban a real person, found in the street and compelled into the theatre? If he isn't, then, isn't the character just as powerful as if he were? What peculiar quality does this term of "real people in a real play" give to a play, seeing that many plays, some of them in step with the greatest, have in them characters far removed from this critic-quality of matter-of-factness? Isn't Caliban as real a character as Gustav Bergmann in *Close Quarters,* or the ladies and gents in *Fallen Angels,* or *Night Must Fall,* or *Call It a Day,* the author of which, as Mr. Agate tells us, assembles on her stage characters so real (again this word "real"—the spyhole through which the critics view the stage) that she might have gone into the street and compelled them into the theatre. (Though how a critic couples a play dealing with sex almost from the word "go" to the last lap, a play in which an accountant goes to the flat of an actress-client and nothing happens; in which the accountant's wife is entertained by a friend, and then entertains the friend alone in her house, and nothing happens; in which their daughter flings herself at an artist, and nothing happens; in which her brother falls for a young lassie that climbs over the garden wall to him, and nothing happens; in which the maid falls for the manservant of the family a few doors down, and nothing happens; and the bitch brought out for a walk by the manservant rubs noses with the dog 'taken out by the maid, and nothing happens—how a critic couples all this sort of thing with characters hustled in off the streets, only a critic could know, and only a critic can tell.) If all that is in this play be life, then life is a mass of sentimentally holy hokum.

As a matter-of-factness no one, least of all a playwright, can go out into the streets and lanes of the city and compel the people to come on to the stage, for the people on the stage must be of the stage and not of the streets and lanes of the city or of the highways and hedges of the country. The most realistic characters in the most realistic play cannot be true to life. Perhaps the most real character in any play we know of is the character of Falstaff done by Shakespeare. Here is realism as large as life; but it is realism larger, and a lot larger, than life. Falstaff was never pulled off the streets into the theatre by Shakespeare. God never created Falstaff—he sprang from Shakespeare's brain. God, if you like, created Shakespeare, but Shakespeare created Falstaff. Falstaff is no more real, there is no more matter-of-factness in the character of Falstaff, than there is in Caliban or Puck or Ariel. He is a bigger creation than any of these three, and that is all. A play, says Dryden, ought to be a just image of human nature, and this is true of *Hamlet*, of *John Bull's Other Island*, of *Strange Interlude*, of *Six Characters in Search of an Author*, of *Peer Gynt*, of *The Dream Play*; but it is not true of the trivial tomtit-realism in the thousand and one entertainment plays patted and praised by the dramatic critics. Why, even the sawdust characters of the Moor, Petroushka, and the Ballerina are a more just image of human nature than the characters in the matter-of-fact, exact-imitation-of-life plays that flit about on the English stage.

As it is with the play, so it is with the dressed-up stage—the critics want to be doped into the belief that the scene on the stage is as real as life itself. The stirring of the hair is more to them than the stirring of the heart. But things as real as life itself on the stage they can

never have; a room can never be a room, a tree a tree, or a death a death. These must take the nature of a child's toys and a child's play. . . .

This rage for real, real life on the stage has taken all the life out of the drama. If everything on the stage is to be a fake exact imitation (for fake realism it can only be), where is the chance for the original and imaginative artist? Less chance for him than there was for Jonah in the whale's belly. The beauty, fire, and poetry of drama have perished in the storm of fake realism. Let real birds fly through the air (not like Basil Dean's butterflies in *Midsummer Night's Dream*, fluttering over the stage and pinning themselves to trees), real animals roam through the jungle, real fish swim in the sea; but let us have the make-believe of the artist and the child in the theatre. Less of what the critics call "life," and more of symbolism; for even in the most commonplace of realistic plays the symbol can never be absent. A house on a stage can never be a house, and that which represents it must always be a symbol. A room in a realistic play must always be a symbol for a room. There can never be any important actuality on the stage, except an actuality that is unnecessary and out of place. An actor representing a cavalier may come on the stage mounted on a real horse, but the horse will always look only a little less ridiculous than the "cavalier." The horse can have nothing to do with the drama. I remember a play written round Mr. Pepys, and in this play was used "the identical snuff-box used by him when he was head of the Admiralty in the reign of Charles the Second." So much was said about the snuff-box that I expected it to be carried in on a cushion preceded by a brass band, and hawked around for all to admire before the play began. Now this snuff-box added nothing to the play, and because of this commonplace spirit in the play, the play added nothing to the drama. It seems that the closer we move to actual life, the further we move away from the drama. Drama purely imitative of life isn't drama at all. Now the critics are beginning to use the word "theatre" when they find themselves in a bit of a tangle over what they should say about a play that has a bad whiff of staleness in its theme, character, and form. For instance, Mr. Ivor Brown, writing of a recent play, said that "the play is not life, it is theatre and might be allowed to wear its flamboyant colors"; "might be allowed," mind you—he, too, isn't sure. He doesn't tell us to what theatre the play belonged. He left his readers to find that out for themselves. Was it the theatre of Shakespeare, of Shaw, of Strindberg, of Ibsen, of Goldsmith, of O'Neill, of Pirandello, or of Toller? Or the theatre of Dan Leno, Marie Lloyd, George Robey, Charlie Chaplin, Sidney Howard, or Will Hay? These are all good theatre and so they are all good life. But it is not the life that they imitate in their plays or in their actions that makes them good theatre, but the unique and original life that is in themselves. They have the life that the present dramatic critics lack, for the critics cannot, or are afraid to, be lively. They wouldn't venture to give the plays they call "theatre" their baptismal name of rubbish. . . .

T. S. ELIOT

Thomas Stearns Eliot was born in 1888 in St. Louis, Missouri, of an old New England family. Educated at Harvard, he came under the influence of Irving Babbitt, prophet of the New Humanism and leader, with Paul Elmer More, of an effort to re-establish classical principles in literature and life. Further study and travel abroad were followed by employment in a London bank. He began to publish poems, essays, and book reviews and to work as an editor. His early poems began to win him some attention during World War I, but the appearance of his long poem "The Waste Land" in 1922 made him an object of international interest and curiosity. A collection of essays, *The Sacred Wood* (1920), touched upon the question of poetic drama and re-examined such dramatists as Marlowe and Jonson; additional essays, many of them on the drama, were assembled in *Selected Essays, 1917–1932* (1932).

Since 1925, Eliot has worked as an editor for the London publisher, Faber and Faber. He became a British subject in 1927. His first play was published in 1932—*Sweeney Agonistes: Fragments of an Aristophanic Melodrama,* but his growing fame still rested on his work as poet, critic, and editor—the last because, from 1923 to 1939, he edited the distinguished London literary magazine, *Criterion. Murder in the Cathedral,* a play about the death of Thomas à Becket, first performed at the Canterbury Festival of 1935, has been widely acted. Other plays, all in verse, have included *The Family Reunion,* utilizing part of the Orestes story in a modern setting (1939); *The Cocktail Party,* a popular success (1950); *The Confidential Clerk* (1953); and *The Elder Statesman* (1958). Eliot received the Nobel Prize for Literature in 1948.

Much of Eliot's criticism is concerned to establish the impersonal, objective nature of a literary work; in connection with this effort, he used the widely borrowed term "objective correlative," first employed in his essay on *Hamlet.* In writing on the drama, Eliot has often dwelt upon the problems of poetry in the theatre.

POETRY AND DRAMA [1]

(1950)

Reviewing my critical output for the last thirty-odd years, I am surprised to find how constantly I have returned to the drama, whether by examining the

[1] The first Theodore Spencer Memorial Lecture delivered at Harvard University. From *On Poetry and Poets.* © 1951, 1957 by T. S. Eliot. Used by permission of Farrar, Straus & Co., Inc., and Faber and Faber, Ltd.—Ed.

work of the contemporaries of Shakespeare, or by reflecting on the possibilities of the future. It may even be that people are weary of hearing me on this subject. But, while I find that I have been composing variations on this theme all my life, my views have been continually modified and renewed by increasing experience; so that I am impelled to take stock of the situation afresh at every stage of my own experimentation.

As I have gradually learned more about the problems of poetic drama, and the conditions which it must fulfil if it is to justify itself, I have made a little clearer to myself, not only my own reasons for wanting to write in this form, but the more general reasons for wanting to see it restored to its place. And I think that if I say something about these problems and conditions, it should make clearer to other people whether and if so why poetic drama has anything potentially to offer the playgoer, that prose drama cannot. For I start with the assumption that if poetry is merely a decoration, an added embellishment, if it merely gives people of literary tastes the pleasure of listening to poetry at the same time that they are witnessing a play, then it is superfluous. It must justify itself dramatically, and not merely be fine poetry shaped into a dramatic form. From this it follows that no play should be written in verse for which prose is *dramatically* adequate. And from this it follows, again, that the audience, its attention held by the dramatic action, its emotions stirred by the situation between the characters, should be too intent upon the play to be wholly conscious of the medium.

Whether we use prose or verse on the stage, they are both but means to an end. The difference, from one point of view, is not so great as we might think. In those prose plays which survive, which are read and produced on the stage by later generations, the prose in which the characters speak is as remote, for the best part, from the vocabulary, syntax, and rhythm of our ordinary speech—with its fumbling for words, its constant recourse to approximation, its disorder, and its unfinished sentences—as verse is. Like verse, it has been written, and rewritten. Our two greatest prose stylists in the drama—apart from Shakespeare and the other Elizabethans who mixed prose and verse in the same play—are, I believe, Congreve and Bernard Shaw. A speech by a character of Congreve or of Shaw has—however clearly the characters may be differentiated—that unmistakable personal rhythm which is the mark of a prose style, and of which only the most accomplished conversationalists—who are for that matter usually monologuists—show any trace in their talk. We have all heard (too often!) of Molière's character who expressed surprise when told that he spoke prose. But it was M. Jourdain who was right, and not his mentor or his creator: he did not speak prose—he only talked. For I mean to draw a triple distinction: between prose, and verse, and our ordinary speech which is mostly below the level of either verse or prose. So if you look at it in this way, it will appear that prose, on the stage, is as artificial as verse: or alternatively, that verse can be as natural as prose.

But while the sensitive member of the audience will appreciate, when he hears fine prose spoken in a play, that this is something better than ordinary conversation, he does not regard it as a wholly different language from that which he himself speaks, for that would interpose a barrier between himself and the imaginary characters on the stage. Too many people, on the other hand, approach a play which they know to be in verse, with the consciousness of the difference. It is unfortunate when they are repelled by verse, but can also be deplorable when they are attracted by it—if that means that they are prepared to enjoy the play and the language of the play as two separate things. The chief effect of style and rhythm in dramatic speech, whether in prose or verse, should be unconscious.

From this it follows that a mixture of prose and verse in the same play is generally to be avoided: each transition makes the auditor aware, with a jolt of the medium. It is, we may say, justifiable when the author wishes to produce this jolt: when, that is, he wishes to transport the audience violently from one plane of reality to another. I suspect that this kind of transition was easily acceptable to an Elizabethan audience, to whose ears both prose and verse came naturally; who liked highfalutin and low comedy in the same play; and to whom it seemed perhaps proper that the more humble and rustic characters should speak in a homely language, and that those of more exalted rank should rant in verse. But even in the plays of Shakespeare some of the prose passages seem to be designed for an effect of contrast which, when achieved, is something that can never become old-fashioned. The knocking at the gate in *Macbeth* is an example that comes to everyone's mind; but it has long seemed to me that the alternation of scenes in prose with scenes in verse in *Henry IV* points an ironic contrast between the world of high politics and the world of common life. The audience probably though they were getting their accustomed chronicle play garnished with amusing scenes of low life; yet the prose scenes of both Part I and Part II provide a sardonic comment upon the bustling ambitions of the chiefs of the parties in the insurrection of the Percys.

To-day, however, because of the handicap under which verse drama suffers, I believe that in verse drama prose should be used very sparingly indeed; that we should aim at a form of verse in which everything can be said that has to be said; and that when we find some situation which is intractable in verse, it is merely because our form of verse is inelastic. And if there prove to be scenes which we cannot put in verse, we must either develop our verse, or avoid having to introduce such scenes. For we have to accustom our audiences to verse to the point at which they will cease to be conscious of it; and to introduce prose dialogue would only be to distract their attention from the play itself to the medium of its expression. But if our verse is to have so wide a range that it can say anything that has to be said, it follows that it will not be "poetry" all the time. It will only be "poetry" when the dramatic situation has reached such a point of intensity that poetry becomes the natural utterance, because then it is the only language in which the emotions can be expressed at all.

It is indeed necessary for any long poem, if it is to escape monotony, to be able to say homely things without bathos, as well as to take the highest flights without sounding exaggerated. And it is still more important in a play, especially if it is concerned with contemporary life. The reason for writing even the more pedestrian parts of a verse play in verse instead of prose is, however, not only to avoid calling the audience's attention to the fact that it is at other moments listening to poetry. It is also that the verse rhythm should have its effect upon the hearers, without their being conscious of it. A brief analysis of one scene of Shakespeare's may illustrate this point. The opening scene of *Hamlet*—as well constructed an opening scene as that of any play ever written—has the advantage of being one that everybody knows.

What we do not notice, when we witness this scene in the theatre, is the great variation of style. Nothing is superfluous, and there is no line of poetry which is not justified by its dramatic value. The first twenty-two lines are built of the simplest words in the most homely idiom. Shakespeare had worked for a long time in the theatre, and written a good many plays, before reaching the point at which he could write those twenty-two lines. There is nothing quite so simplified and sure in his previous work. He first developed conversational, colloquial verse in the monologue of the character part—Faulconbridge in *King John,* and later the Nurse in *Romeo and Juliet.* It was a much further step to carry it unobtrusively into the dialogue of brief replies. No poet has begun to master dramatic verse until he can write lines which, like these in *Hamlet,* are *transparent.* You are consciously attending, not to the poetry, but to the meaning of the poetry. If you were hearing *Hamlet* for the first time, without knowing anything about the play, I do not think that it would occur to you to ask whether the speakers were speaking in verse or prose. The verse is having a different effect upon us from prose; but at the moment, what we are aware of is the frosty night, the officers keeping watch on the battlements, and the foreboding of a tragic action. I do not say that there is no place for the situation in which part of one's pleasure will be the enjoyment of hearing beautiful poetry— providing that the author gives it, in that place, dramatic inevitability. And of course, when we have both seen a play several times and read it between performances, we begin to analyse the means by which the author has produced his effects. But in the immediate impact of this scene we are unconscious of the medium of its expression.

From the short, brusque ejaculations at the beginning, suitable to the situation and to the character of the guards—but not expressing more character than is required for their function in the play—the verse glides into a slow movement with the appearance of the courtiers Horatio and Marcellus.

Horatio says 'tis but our fantasy, . . .

and the movement changes again on the appearance of Royalty, the ghost of the King, into the solemn and sonorous

What art thou, that usurp'st this time of night, . . .

(and note, by the way, this anticipation of the plot conveyed by the use of the verb *usurp*); and majesty is suggested in a reference reminding us whose ghost this is:

So frown'd he once, when, in an angry parle,
He smote the sledded Polacks on the ice.

There is an abrupt change to staccato in Horatio's words to the Ghost on its second appearance; this rhythm changes again with the words

We do it wrong, being so majestical,
To offer it the show of violence;
For it is, as the air, invulnerable,
And our vain blows malicious mockery.

The scene reaches a resolution with the words of Marcellus:

It faded on the crowing of the cock.
Some say that ever 'gainst that season comes
Wherein our Saviour's birth is cele-brated,
The bird of dawning singeth all night long; . . .

and Horatio's answer:

So have I heard and do in part believe it.
But, look, the morn, in russet mantle clad,
Walks o'er the dew of yon high eastern hill.
Break we our watch up.

This is great poetry, and it is dramatic; but besides being poetic and dramatic, it is something more. There emerges, when we analyse it, a kind of musical design also which reinforces and is one with the dramatic movement. It has checked and accelerated the pulse of our emotion without our knowing it. Note that in these last words of Marcellus there is a deliberate brief emergence of the poetic into consciousness. When we hear the lines

But, look, the morn, in russet mantle clad,
Walks o'er the dew of yon high eastern hill,

we are lifted for a moment beyond character, but with no sense of unfitness of the words coming, and at this moment, from the lips of Horatio. The transitions in the scene obey laws of the music of dramatic poetry. Note that the two lines of Horatio which I have quoted twice are preceded by a line of the simplest speech which might be either verse or prose:

So have I heard and do in part believe it,

and that he follows them abruptly with a half line which is hardly more than a stage direction:

Break we our watch up.

It would be interesting to pursue, by a similar analysis, this problem of the double pattern in great poetic drama—the pattern which may be examined from the point of view of stagecraft or from that of the music. But I think that the examination of this one scene is enough to show us that verse is not merely a formalization, or an added decoration, but that it intensifies the drama. It should indicate also the importance of the unconscious effect of the verse upon us. And lastly, I do not think that this effect is felt only by those members of an audience who "like poetry" but also by those who go for the play alone. By the people who do not like poetry, I mean those who cannot sit down with a book of poetry and enjoy reading it: these people also, when they go to a play in verse, should be affected by the poetry. And these are the audiences whom the writer of such a play ought to keep in mind.

At this point I might say a word about those plays which we call *poetic*, though they are written in prose. The plays of John Millington Synge form rather a special case, because they are based upon the idiom of a rural people whose speech is naturally poetic, both in imagery and in rhythm. I believe that he even incorporated phrases which he had heard from these country people of Ireland. The language of Synge is not available except for plays set among that same people. We can draw more general conclusions from the plays in prose (so much admired in my youth, and now hardly even read) by Maeterlinck. These plays are in a different way restricted in their subject matter; and to say that the characterization in them is dim is an understatement. I do not deny that they have some poetic quality. But in order to be poetic in prose, a dramatist has to be so consistently poetic that his scope is very limited. Synge wrote plays about characters whose originals in life talked poetically, so he could make them talk poetry and remain real people. The poetic prose dramatist who has not this advantage, has to be too poetic. The poetic drama in prose is more limited by poetic convention or by our conventions as to what subject matter is poetic, than is the poetic drama in verse. A really dramatic verse can be employed, as Shakespeare employed it, to say the most matter-of-fact things.

Yeats is a very different case from Maeterlinck or Synge. A study of his development as a dramatist would show, I think, the great distance he went, and the triumph of his last plays. In his first period, he wrote plays in verse about subjects conventionally accepted as suitable for verse, in a metric which—though even at that early stage having the personal Yeats rhythm—is not really a form of speech quite suitable for anybody except mythical kings and queens. His middle-period *Plays for Dancers* are very beautiful, but they do not solve any problem for the dramatist in verse: they are poetic prose plays with important interludes in verse. It was only in his last play *Purgatory* that he solved his problem of speech in verse, and laid all his successors under obligation to him.

II

Now, I am going to venture to make some observations based on my own experience, which will lead me to comment on my intentions, failures, and partial successes, in my own plays. I do this in the belief that any explorer or experimenter in new territory may, by putting on record a kind of journal of his explorations, say something of use to those who follow him into the same regions and who will perhaps go farther.

The first thing of any importance that I discovered, was that a writer who has worked for years, and achieved some success, in writing other kinds of verse, has to approach the writing of a verse play in a different frame of mind from that to which he has been accustomed in his previous work. In writing other verse, I think that one is writing, so to speak, in terms of one's own voice: the way it sounds when you read it to yourself is the test. For it is yourself speaking. The question of communication, of what the reader will get from it, is not paramount: if your poem is right to you, you can only hope that the readers will eventually come to accept it. The poem can wait a little while; the approval of a few sympathetic and judicious critics is enough to begin with; and it is for future readers to meet the poet more than half way. But in the theatre, the problem of communication presents itself immediately. You are deliberately writing verse for other voices, not for your own, and you do not know whose voices they will be. You are aiming to write lines which will have an immediate effect upon an unknown and unprepared audience, to be interpreted to that audience by unknown actors rehearsed by an unknown producer. And the unknown audience cannot be expected to show any indulgence towards the poet. The poet cannot afford to write his play merely for his admirers, those who know his non-dramatic work and are prepared to receive favourably anything he puts his name to. He must write with an audience in view which knows nothing and cares nothing, about any previous success he may have had before he ventured into the theatre. Hence one finds out that many of the things one likes to do, and knows how to do, are out of place; and that every line must be judged by a new law, that of dramatic relevance.

When I wrote *Murder in the Cathedral* I had the advantage for a beginner, of an occasion which called for a subject generally admitted to be suitable for verse. Verse plays, it has been generally held, should either take their subject matter from some mythology, or else should be about some remote historical period, far enough away from the present for the characters not to need to be recognizable as human beings, and therefore for them to be licensed to talk in verse. Picturesque period costume renders verse much more acceptable. Furthermore, my play was to be produced for a rather special kind of audience—an audience of those serious people who go to "festivals" and expect to have to put up with poetry—though perhaps on this occasion some of them were not quite prepared for what they got. And finally it was a religious play, and people who go deliberately to a religious play at a religious festival expect to be patiently bored and to satisfy themselves with the feeling that they have done something meritorious. So the path was made easy.

It was only when I put my mind to thinking what sort of play I wanted to do next, that I realized that in *Murder in the Cathedral* I had not solved any general problem; but that from my point of view the play was a dead end. For one thing, the problem of language which that play had presented to me was a special problem. Fortunately, I did not have to write in the idiom of the twelfth century, because that idiom, even if I knew Norman French and Anglo-Saxon, would have been unintelligible. But the vocabulary and style could not be exactly those of modern conversation—as in some modern French plays using the plot and personages of Greek drama—because I had to take my audience back to an historical event; and they could not afford to be archaic, first because archaism would only have suggested the wrong period, and second because I wanted to bring home to the audience the contemporary relevance of the situation.

The style therefore had to be *neutral*, committed neither to the present nor to the past. As for the versification, I was only aware at this stage that the essential was to avoid any echo of Shakespeare, for I was persuaded that the primary failure of nineteenth-century poets when they wrote for the theatre (and most of the greatest English poets had tried their hand at drama) was not in their theatrical technique, but in their dramatic language; and that this was due largely to their limitation to a strict blank verse which, after extensive use for non-dramatic poetry, had lost the flexibility which blank verse must have if it is to give the effect of conversation. The rhythm of regular blank verse had become too remote from the movement of modern speech. Therefore what I kept in mind was the versification of *Everyman,* hoping that anything unusual in the sound of it would be, on the whole, advantageous. An avoidance of too much iambic, some use of alliteration, and occasional unexpected rhyme, helped to distinguish the versification from that of the nineteenth century.

The versification of the dialogue in *Murder in the Cathedral* has therefore, in my opinion, only a *negative* merit: it succeeded in avoiding what had to be avoided, but it arrived at no positive novelty: in short, in so far as it solved the problem of speech in verse for writing to-day, it solved it for this play only, and provided me with no clue to the verse I should use in another kind of play. Here, then, were two problems left unsolved: that of the idiom and that of the metric (it is really one and the same problem), for general use in any play I might want to write in future. I next became aware of my reasons for depending, in that play, so heavily upon the assistance of the chorus. There were two reasons for this, which in the circumstances justified it. The first was that the essential action of the play— both the historical facts and the matter which I invented—was somewhat limited. A man comes home, foreseeing that he will be killed, and he is killed. I did not want to increase the number of characters, I did not want to write a chronicle of twelfth-century politics, nor did I want to tamper unscrupulously with the meagre records as Tennyson did (in introducing Fair Rosamund, and in suggesting that Becket had been crossed in love in early youth). I wanted to concentrate on death and martyrdom. The introduction of a chorus of excited and sometimes hysterical women, reflecting in their emotion the significance of the action, helped wonderfully. The second reason was this: that a poet writing for the first time for the stage, is much more at home in choral verse than in dramatic dialogue. This, I felt sure, was something I could do, and perhaps the dramatic weaknesses would be somewhat covered up by the cries of the women. The use of a chorus strengthened the power, and concealed the defects of my theatrical technique. For this reason I decided that next time I would try to integrate the chorus more closely into the play.

I wanted to find out also, whether I could learn to dispense altogether with the use of prose. The two prose passages in *Murder in the Cathedral* could not have been written in verse. Certainly, with the kind of dialogue verse which I used in that play, the audience would have been uncomfortably aware that it was verse they were hearing. A sermon cast in verse is too unusual an experience for even the most regular churchgoers: nobody could have responded to it as a sermon at all. And in the speeches of the knights, who are quite aware that they are addressing an audience of people living eight hundred years after they themselves are dead, the use of platform prose is intended of course to have a special effect: to shock the audience out of their complacency. But this is a kind of trick: that is, a device tolerable only in one play and of no use for any other. I may, for aught I know, have been slightly under the influence of *St. Joan*.

I do not wish to give you the impression that I would rule out of dramatic poetry these three things: historical or mythological subject matter, the chorus, and traditional blank verse. I do not wish to lay down any law that the only suitable characters and situations are those of modern life, or that a verse play should consist of dialogue only, or that a wholly new versification is necessary. I am only tracing out the route of exploration of one writer, and that one myself. If the poetic drama is to reconquer its place, it must, in my opinion, enter into overt competition with prose drama. As I have said, people are prepared to put up with verse from the lips of personages dressed in the fashion of some distant age: therefore they should be made to hear it from peopled dressed like ourselves, living in houses and apartments like ours, and using telephones and motor cars and radio sets. Audiences are prepared to accept poetry recited by a chorus, for that is a kind of poetry recital, which it does them credit to enjoy. And audiences (those who go to a verse play because it is in verse) expect poetry to be in rhythms which have lost touch with colloquial speech. What we have to do is to bring poetry into the world in which the audience lives and to which it returns when it leaves the theatre; not to transport the audience into some imaginary world totally unlike its own, an unreal world in which poetry is tolerated. What I should hope might be achieved, by a generation of dramatists having the benefit of our experience, is that the audience should find, at the moment of awareness that it is hearing poetry, that it is saying to itself: *"I* could talk in poetry too!"* Then we should not be transported into an artificial world; on the contrary, our own sordid, dreary daily world would be suddenly illuminated and transfigured.

I was determined, therefore, in my next play to take a theme of contemporary life, with characters of our own time living in our own world. *The Family Reunion* was the result. Here my first concern was the problem of the versification, to find a rhythm close to contemporary speech, in which the stresses could be made to come wherever we should naturally put them, in uttering the particular phrase on the particular occasion. What I worked out is substantially what I have continued to employ: a line of varying length and varying number of syllables, with a caesura and three stresses. The caesura and the stresses may come at different places, almost anywhere in the line; the stresses may be close together or well separated by light syllables; the only rule being that there must be one stress on one side of the caesura and two on the other. In retrospect, I soon saw that I had given my attention to versification, at the expense of plot and character. I had, indeed, made some progress in dispensing with the chorus; but the device of using four of the minor personages, representing the Family, sometimes as individual character parts and sometimes collectively as chorus, does not seem to me very satisfactory. For one thing, the immediate transition from individual, characterized part to membership of a chorus is asking too much of the actors: it is a very difficult transition to accomplish. For another thing, it seemed to be another trick, one which, even if successful, could not have been applicable in another play. Furthermore, I had in two passages used the device of a lyrical duet further isolated from the rest of the dialogue by being written in shorter lines with only two stresses. These passages are in a sense "beyond character," the speakers have to be presented as falling into a kind of trance-like state in order to speak them. But they are so remote from the necessity of the action that they are hardly more than passages of poetry which might be spoken by anybody; they are too much like operatic arias. The member of the audience, if he enjoys this sort of thing, is putting up with a suspension of the action in order to enjoy a poetic fantasia: these passages are really less related to the action than are the choruses in *Murder in the Cathedral*.

I observed that when Shakespeare, in one of his mature plays, introduces what might seem a purely poetic line or passage, it never interrupts the action, or is out of character, but on the contrary, in some mysterious way supports both action and character. When Macbeth speaks his so often quoted words beginning

To-morrow and to-morrow and to-morrow,

or when Othello, confronted at night with his angry father-in-law and friends, utters the beautiful line

Keep up your bright swords, for the dew will rust them,

we do not feel that Shakespeare has thought of lines which are beautiful poetry and wishes to fit them in somehow, or that he has for the moment come to the end of his dramatic inspiration and has turned to poetry to fill up with. The lines are surprising, and yet they fit in with the character; or else we are compelled to adjust our conception of the character in such a way that the lines will be appropriate to it. The lines spoken by Macbeth reveal the weariness of the weak man who had been forced by his wife to realize his own half-hearted desires and her ambitions, and who, with her death, is left without the motive to continue. The line of Othello expresses irony, dignity, and fearlessness; and incidentally reminds us of the time of night in which the scene takes place. Only poetry could do this; but it is *dramatic* poetry: that is, it does not interrupt but intensifies the dramatic situation.

It was not only because of the introduction of passages which called too much attention to themselves as poetry, and could not be dramatically justified, that I found *The Family Reunion* defective: there were two weaknesses which came to strike me as more serious still. The first was, that I had employed far too much of the strictly limited time allowed to a dramatist, in presenting a situation, and not left myself enough time, or provided myself with enough material, for developing it in action. I had written what was, on the whole, a good first act; except that for a first act it was much too long. When the curtain rises again, the audience is expecting, as it has a right to expect, that something is going to happen. Instead, it finds itself treated to a further exploration of the background: in other words, to what ought to have been given much earlier if at all. The beginning of the second act presents much of the most difficult problem to producer and cast: for the audience's attention is beginning to wander. And then, after what must seem to the audience an interminable time of preparation, the conclusion comes so abruptly that we are, after all, unready for it. This was an elementary fault in mechanics.

But the deepest flaw of all, was in a failure of adjustment between the Greek story and the modern situation. I should either have stuck closer to Aeschylus or else taken a great deal more liberty with his myth. One evidence of this is the appearance of those ill-fated figures, the Furies. They must, in future, be omitted from the cast, and be understood to be visible only to certain of my characters, and not to the audience. We tried every possible manner of presenting them. We put them on the stage, and they looked like uninvited guests who had strayed in from a fancy dress ball. We concealed them behind gauze, and they suggested a still out of a Walt Disney film. We made them dimmer, and they looked like shrubbery just outside the window. I have seen other expedients tried: I have seen them signalling from across the garden, or swarming on to the stage like a football team, and they are never right. They never succeed in being either Greek goddesses or modern spooks. But their failure is merely a symptom of the failure to adjust the ancient with the modern.

A more serious evidence is that we are left in a divided frame of mind, not knowing whether to consider the play the tragedy of the mother or the salvation of the son. The two situations are not reconciled. I find a confirmation of this in the fact that my sympathies now have come to be all with the mother, who seems to me, except perhaps for the chauffeur, the only complete human being in the play; and my hero now strikes me as an insufferable prig.

Well, I had made some progress in learning how to write the first act of a play, and I had—the one thing of which I felt sure—made a good deal of progress in finding a form of versification and an idiom which would serve all my purposes, without recourse to prose, and be capable of unbroken transition between the most intense speech and the most relaxed dialogue. You will understand, after my making these criticisms of *The Family Reunion,* some of the errors that I endeavoured to avoid in designing *The Cocktail Party.* To begin with, no chorus, and no ghosts. I was still inclined to go to a Greek dramatist for my theme, but I was determined to do so merely as a point of departure, and to conceal the origins so well that nobody would identify them until I pointed them out myself. In this at least I have been successful; for no one of my acquaintance (and no dramatic critics) recognized the source of my story in the *Alcestis* of Euripides. In fact, I have had to go into detailed ex-

planation to convince them—I mean, of course, those who were familiar with the plot of that play—of the genuineness of the inspiration. But those who were at first disturbed by the eccentric behaviour of my unknown guest, and his apparently intemperate habits and tendency to burst into song, have found some consolation in having their attention called to the behaviour of Heracles in Euripides' play.

In the second place, I laid down for myself the ascetic rule to avoid poetry which could not stand the test of strict dramatic utility: with such success, indeed, that it is perhaps an open question whether there is any poetry in the play at all. And finally, I tried to keep in mind that in a play, from time to time, something should happen; that the audience should be kept in the constant expectation that something is going to happen; and that, when it does happen, it should be different, but not too different, from what the audience had been led to expect.

I have not yet got to the end of my investigation of the weaknesses of this play, but I hope and expect to find more than those of which I am yet aware. I say "hope" because while one can never repeat a success, and therefore must always try to find something different, even if less popular, to do, the desire to write something which will be free of the defects of one's last work is a very powerful and useful incentive. I am aware that the last act of my play only just escapes, if indeed it does escape, the accusation of being not a last act but an epilogue; and I am determined to do something different, if I can, in this respect. I also believe that while the self-education of a poet trying to write for the theatre seems to require a long period of disciplining his poetry, and putting it, so to speak, on a very thin diet in order to adapt it to the needs of the stage, he may find that later, when (and if) the understanding of theatrical technique has become second nature, he can dare to make more liberal use of poetry and take greater liberties with ordinary colloquial speech. I base this belief on the evolution of Shakespeare, and on some study of the language in his late plays.

In devoting so much time to an examination of my own plays, I have, I believe, been animated by a better motive than egotism. It seems to me that if we are to have a poetic drama, it is more likely to come from poets learning how to write plays, than from skilful prose dramatists learning to write poetry. That some poets can learn how to write plays, and write good ones, may be only a hope, but I believe a not unreasonable hope; but that a man who has started by writing successful prose plays should then learn how to write good poetry, seems to me extremely unlikely. And, under present-day conditions, and until the verse play is recognized by the larger public as a possible source of entertainment, the poet is likely to get his first opportunity to work for the stage only after making some sort of reputation for himself as the author of other kinds of verse. I have therefore wished to put on record, for what it may be worth to others, some account of the difficulties I have encountered, and the mistakes into which I have fallen, and the weaknesses I have had to try to overcome.

I should not like to close without attempting to set before you, though only a dim outline, the ideal towards which poetic drama should strive. It is an unattainable ideal: and that is why it interests me, for it provides an incentive towards further experiment and exploration, beyond any goal which there is prospect of attaining. It is a function of all art to give us some perception of an order in life, by imposing an order upon it. The painter works by selection, combination, and emphasis among the elements of the visible world; the musician in the world of sound. It seems to me that beyond the nameable, classifiable emotions and motives of our conscious life when directed towards action—the part of life which prose drama is wholly adequate to express—there is a fringe of indefinite extent, of feeling which we can only detect, so to speak, out of the corner of the eye and can never completely focus; of feeling of which we are only aware in a kind of temporary detachment from action. There are great prose dramatists—such as Ibsen and Chekhov —who have at times done things of which I would not otherwise have supposed prose to be capable, but who seem to me, in spite of their success, to have been hampered in expression by writing in prose. This peculiar range of sensibility can be expressed by dramatic poetry, at its moments of greatest intensity. At such moments, we touch the border of those feelings which only music can express. We can never emulate music, because to arrive at the condition of music would be the annihilation of poetry, and especially of dramatic poetry. Nevertheless, I have before my eyes a kind of mirage of the perfection of verse drama, which would be a design of human action and of words, such as to present at once the two aspects of dramatic and of musical order. It seems to me that Shakespeare achieved this at least in certain scenes—even rather early, for there is the balcony scene of *Romeo and Juliet*— and that this was what he was striving towards in his late plays. To go as far in this direction as it is possible to go, without losing that contact with the ordinary everyday world with which drama must come to terms, seems to me the proper aim of dramatic poetry. For it is ultimately the function of art, in imposing a credible order upon ordinary reality, and thereby eliciting some perception of an order *in* reality, to bring us to a condition of serenity, stillness, and reconciliation; and then leave us, as Virgil left Dante, to proceed toward a region where that guide can avail us no farther.

NOTE TO "POETRY AND DRAMA"

. . . The passage in this essay analysing the first scene of *Hamlet* was taken from a lecture delivered some years previously at Edinburgh University. From the same Edinburgh lecture I have extracted the following note on the balcony scene in *Romeo and Juliet:*

In Romeo's beginning, there is still some artificiality:

> *Two of the fairest stars in all the heaven,*
> *Having some business, do intreat her eyes*
> *To twinkle in their spheres till they return.*

For it seems unlikely that a man standing below in the garden, even on a very bright moonlight night, would see the eyes of the lady above flashing so brilliantly as to justify such a comparison.

Yet one is aware, from the beginning of this scene, that there is a musical pattern coming, as surprising in its kind as that in the early work of Beethoven. The arrangement of voices—Juliet has three single lines, followed by Romeo's three, four and five, followed by her longer speech—is very remarkable. In this pattern, one feels that it is Juliet's voice that has the leading part: to her voice is assigned the dominant phrase of the whole duet:

My bounty is as boundless as the sea,
My love as deep: the more I give to
thee
The more I have, for both are infinite.

And to Juliet is given the key-word "lightning," which occurs again in the play, and is significant of the sudden and disastrous power of her passion, when she says

'Tis like the lightning, which doth cease
to be
Ere one can say "it lightens."

In this scene, Shakespeare achieves a perfection of verse which, being perfection, neither he nor anyone else could excel—for this particular purpose. The stiffness, the artificiality, the poetic decoration, of his early verse has finally given place to a simplification to the language of natural speech, and this language of conversation again raised to great poetry, and to great poetry which is essentially dramatic: for the scene has a structure of which each line is an essential part.

AMERICAN DRAMATIC CRITICISM

As stated in the *Introduction* (see p. vii) the editorial and bibliographical apparatus of this new Supplement does not conform to that used in the earlier part of the book. What follows here is intended chiefly as a very brief summary, a bird's-eye view, of the subject to serve as general introduction to the texts that follow.

Although plays were produced in the United States before 1700, little criticism has survived from the early period. The 18th Century furnishes the first examples of native playwriting based on American themes and using dialogue of somewhat native flavor. Interesting examples of early American criticism may be found in *The American Theater as Seen by its Critics, 1752–1934*, compiled by Montrose J. Moses and John Mason Brown (1934). By far the greater part of what was written during the 19th Century was concerned with acting and anecdotes of the stage, but among the occasional lectures or articles by the playwrights Dion Boucicault, Bronson Howard and James A. Herne may be found curious and illuminating passages on the technique and philosophy of the drama. Somewhat later the playwright Augustus Thomas prefaced several of his published plays with practical treatises on technique. The regular play reviewers of the last part of the Century were largely concerned with acting and production, though William Winter (who reprinted hundreds of his reviews in several volumes) evolved more or less by implication certain dramatic theories.— During the early years of the 20th Century several "movements" were started by playwrights, poets, producers, and outsiders, intended to decentralize the theater, encourage native playwriting and develop novel forms of drama. Among the propagandists of the time who formulated their ideas in articles and books were the poet-playwright Percy MacKaye (*The Playhouse and the Play*, 1909, and *The Civic Theater*, 1912); Thomas H. Dickinson (*The Case of American Drama*, 1915; *The Insurgent Theater*, 1917; and *Playwrights of the New American Theater*, 1925); Sheldon Cheney (*The New Movement in the Theater*, 1914, and *The Art Theater*, 1925); Kenneth Macgowan (*The Theater of To-*

morrow, 1921); and Oliver M. Sayler (*Our American Theater,* 1923).

Meantime the historians and keepers of records, whose pioneer work is based largely on source materials, were keeping pace with the development of the American playwright. The basic texts in this category are Arthur Hobson Quinn's *A History of the American Drama From the Beginning to the Civil War* (1923), and *A History of the American Drama From the Civil War to the Present Day* (1936), and Montrose J. Moses' *The American Dramatist* (1925). To these should be added a few others, amplifying and modifying them so far as facts and conclusions are concerned: Richard Burton's *The New American Drama* (1913); Walter Prichard Eaton's *The Drama in English* (1930); Burns Mantle's *American Playwrights of Today* (1938); Barrett H. Clark's *A Study of the Modern Drama* (1938) and *An Hour of American Drama* (1930); Margaret G. Mayorga's *A Short History of the American Drama: Commentaries on Plays Prior to 1920* (1932); George Freedley's and John A. Reeves' *History of the Theater* (1941); Joseph Wood Krutch's *The American Drama Since 1918* (1939); John Anderson's *The American Theater* (1938) and *Box Office* (1929); Eleanor Flexner's *American Playwrights: 1918–1938* (1938); and Frank Hurlburt O'Hara's *Today in American Drama* (1939). The standard chronological record of dramatic productions is Burns Mantle's *The Best Plays of 1919–20 and the Year Book of the Drama in America* (1920), an annual published regularly from 1920 to the present time. The editor is now Henry Hewes. This series has since been supplemented, in collaboration with Garrison P. Sherwood, by *The Best Plays of 1899–1909* (1944) and *The Best Plays of 1909–1919* (1933). For references on drama and theatre in general, and especially on American drama, see Bernard Sobel's *Theatre Handbook and Digest of Plays* (1940).

Among the few regular reviewers of plays for newspapers and periodicals who have collected some of their criticisms in book form are Norman Hapgood (*The Stage in America, 1897–1900,* 1901); Arthur Ruhl (*Second Nights,* 1914); Walter Prichard Eaton (*The American Stage of Today,* 1908; *At the New Theater and Others,* 1910; *Plays and Players,* 1916); Clayton Hamilton (*Studies in Stagecraft,* 1914; *Problems of the Playwright,* 1917; *Seen on the Stage,* 1920); Alexander Woollcott (*Shouts and Murmurs,* 1922; *Enchanted Aisles,* 1924; *Going to Pieces,* 1928); Ludwig Lewisohn (*The Drama and the Stage,* 1922); Stark Young (*The Flower in Drama,* 1923; *Immortal Shadows,* 1948); Percy Hammond (*But is it Art?,* 1927; *This Atom in the Audience,* 1940); John Mason Brown (*Upstage,* 1930; *Two on the Aisle,* 1938; *Broadway in Review,* 1940; *Letters from Greenroom Ghosts,* 1934; *Seeing Things,* 1946); and George Jean Nathan (beginning with *Another Book on the Theatre,* 1915, and continuing with an average of one new book a year for many years. Collections by more recent reviewers include books by Brooks Atkinson (*Broadway Scrapbook,* 1947); Eric Bentley (*The Dramatic Event,* 1954; *What Is Theatre?,* 1956); Mary McCarthy (*Sights and Spectacles,* 1956, most of which is included in *Theatre Chronicle, 1937–1962,* 1963); Walter Kerr (*Pieces at Eight,* 1957; *The Theater in Spite of Itself,* 1963); and Harold Clurman (*Lies Like Truth,* 1958).

The books of Brander Matthews, partly composed of reprinted essays and partly larger treatises written primarily as books, extend over a fairly long period (some are mentioned in the section devoted to Matthews' work); the more formal and elaborate treatises on dramatic technique, by Matthews and others, remain to be mentioned: Brander Matthews' *Principles of Playmaking* (1919); *A Study of the Drama* (1910), and scattered essays in *The Historical Novel* (1901) and other volumes; Clayton Hamilton's *The Theory of the Theater and Other Principles of Dramatic Criticism* (newly consolidated edition including an earlier work of the same title and three other books) (1939), *So You're Writing a Play?* (1935); William T. Price's *The Technique of the Drama* (1892); *The Analysis of Play Construction and Dramatic Principle* (1908); *Why Plays Fail* (1912); and *The Philosophy of Dramatic Principle and Method* (1912); Eugene Walter's *How to Write a Play* (1925); Mark Swan's *How You*

Can Write Plays (1927); The Art of Playwriting (1928), lectures by Jesse Lynch Williams, Langdon Mitchell, Rachel Crothers, Gilbert Emery, and others; George Pierce Baker's Dramatic Technique (1919); John Howard Lawson's Theory and Technique of Playwriting (1936); Arthur Edwin Krows' Playwriting for Profit (1928); Kenneth Rowe's Write That Play (1939); Josephine Niggli's Pointers on Playwriting (1945); Alan Reynolds Thompson's The Anatomy of Drama (1946); Lajos Egri's The Art of Dramatic Writing (1946); Kenneth MacGowan's A Primer of Playwriting (1951); John Van Druten's Playwright at Work (1953); and Lawrence Langner's The Play's the Thing (1960). In books of various kinds—historical, theoretical, philosophical—are to be found more or less pertinent sections of interest so far as dramatic theory is concerned. Among the many works in this field may be mentioned Archibald Henderson's The Changing Drama (1919); Isaac Goldberg's The Drama of Transition (1922); Joseph T. Shipley's The Quest for Literature (1931); H. K. Motherwell's The Theater of Today (revised, 1927); Stark Young's The Theatre (1927); Robert Edmond Jones' The Dramatic Imagination (1941); Mordecai Gorelik's New Theatres for Old (1940); Anita Block's The Changing World in Plays and Theater (1939); Arthur Hopkins' How's Your Second Act? (revised, 1931); Lee Simonson's The Stage is Set

(1932); Paul Green's The Hawthorn Tree (1943); Harold Clurman's The Fervent Years (1945); Eric Bentley's The Playwright as Thinker (1946), In Search of Theater (1953); Francis Fergusson's The Idea of a Theater (1949), The Human Image in Dramatic Literature (1957); John Gassner's Masters of the Drama (1940), The Theatre in Our Times (1954), Theatre at the Crossroads (1960); Walter Kerr's How Not to Write a Play (1955); and Elmer Rice's The Living Theatre (1959).

It is worth while to consult the prefaces of a number of published plays, especially those written by the authors themselves; many of these are illuminating on matters affecting the writers' intentions. See especially the published plays of Paul Green, Lillian Hellman, Clifford Odets, William Saroyan, Irwin Shaw, Maxwell Anderson, John Howard Lawson, Sidney Howard, Tennessee Williams, Arthur Miller, and William Inge.

Finally, an immense amount of material on drama and occasional papers on technical practice and theory, are to be found in the files of newspapers (especially the New York Sunday Times), in trade magazines (Billboard, Variety, The Dramatic Mirror); in magazines specializing in dramatic news, like The Drama, Poet Lore, and, among magazines still functioning, Theatre Arts, Tulane Drama Review, Drama Survey, and Modern Drama.

BRANDER MATTHEWS

James Brander Matthews (the James was soon dropped) was born in New Orleans in 1852. He was educated for the most part in the North, and was graduated from Columbia College in 1871. His lifelong interest in the theater, which began before or during his undergraduate years, was stimulated by extended travel in Europe, where he did a great deal of playgoing. He wrote several plays, some for production by amateur players, and some for the professional stage. At least one of these enjoyed a commercial run.

In 1891 he lectured at Columbia University on literary subjects, and the following year he became a professor of literature. In 1899 he was appointed Professor of Dramatic Literature. This, according to a short biographical account of Matthews in Authors Today and Yesterday (1933), was a "landmark in American university development, marking the establishment of the first dramatic chair in an English-speaking university."

From 1899 to 1924, when he retired, Matthews developed, as lecturer, teacher

and writer, the principles which under-
lie his basic contentions that the drama
'was a separate art, and could be studied
not in the library, but only in the theater" (Clayton Hamilton). Matthews
died in 1929.

The importance of Brander Matthews'
teachings consisted partly in his insistence on considering playwriting as
a craft based upon more or less rigid
principles determined by the physical
shape of the actor, and the audience. His knowledge of the English, French and American theaters of his day, and his familiarity with the theoretical writings of
Brunetière and Sarcey, whose basic
principles he popularized, did much to
stimulate young critics and playwrights

in the United States to participate in
that widespread movement of the past
generation that culminated in the adult
drama that began to appear in the early
1920's. Matthews' various theoretical
writings on the drama and theater are
to be found in many volumes of his collected critical works, but particularly in
the following: *Studies of the Stage*
(1894); *The Development of the Drama*
(1903); *Molière: His Life and Works*
(1910); *A Study of the Drama* (1910);
Shakespeare as a Playwright (1913);
A Book About the Theater (1916); *The
Principles of Playmaking* (1919); *Playwrights on Playmaking* (1919); and *Rip
Van Winkle Goes to the Play* (1926).
His autobiography, *These Many Years,*
appeared in 1917.

THE ART OF THE DRAMATIST [1]
[From *The Development of the Drama*]
(1903)

III

It is, perhaps, going a little too far to
assert that the drama can be as independent of literature as painting may
be, or as sculpture; and yet this is an
overstatement only: it is not an untruth.
The painter seeks primarily for pictorial
effects, and the sculptor for plastic effects — just as the dramatist is seeking
primarily for dramatic effects. On the
other hand, there is no denying that the
masterpieces of the graphic arts have
all of them a poetic quality in addition to
their pictorial and plastic qualities. To
be recognized as masterpieces, they must
needs possess something more than
merely technical merits; but without
these technical merits they would not be
masterpieces. No fresco, no bas-relief,
is fine because of its poetic quality alone.
In like manner, we may be sure that there
is no masterpiece of the drama in which
the poetic quality, however remarkable
it may be, is not sustained by a solid
structure of dramaturgic technic. The

1 Reprinted extracts, from *The Development of the Drama*, New York, 1903, by
permission of the publishers, Charles Scrib-
ner's Sons. Copyright, 1903, by Brander
Matthews.

great dramatist must be a poet, of
course; but first of all he must be a thea-
ter-poet, to borrow the useful German
term. And it is a German critic —
Schlegel — who has drawn attention to
the difference in dramatic capacity which
subsists among nations equally distinguished for intellect, "so that theatrical
talent would seem to be a peculiar quality, essentially distinct from the poetic
gift in general." By the phrase "theatrical talent" Schlegel obviously means
the dramaturgic faculty, the skill of the
born play-maker. Voltaire says somewhere that the success of a poem lies
largely in the choice of a subject; and
it is even more certain that the success
of a play lies in the choice of the special
aspects of the subject which shall be
shown in action on the stage. If the poet
is not a playwright, or if he cannot acquire the playwright's gift of picking out
the scenes which will unfailingly move
the hearts of the spectators, then his sheer
poetic power will not save him, nor any
affluence of imagery — just as no luxuriance of decoration would avail to keep
a house standing if the foundations were
faulty.

This dramaturgic faculty, without
which the most melodious poet cannot

hope to win acceptance as a dramatist, seems to be generally instinctive. It is a birthright of the play-maker, from whom it can sometimes be acquired by poets not so gifted by nature. For example, Victor Hugo was a poet who was not a born playwright, but who managed to attain the essential principles of the craft — essential principles which poets of the power and sweep of Byron and Browning were never able to grasp. These British bards were without the dramaturgic faculty which was possessed, in some measure, by the unliterary play-makers who devised the Italian comedy-of-masks.

In the early days of any art there is always imperfect differentiation; and the polychromatic bas-reliefs of the Egyptians remind us that it was long before painting and sculpture were separated. Not only are comedy and tragedy not carefully kept apart, but the drama itself is commingled with much that is not truly dramatic, and only by slow degrees is it able to disentangle itself from these extraneous matters. Even in the days of the great Greeks a lyric element survived in their tragedies which was often quite undramatic; and even in England, under Elizabeth, the stage was sometimes made to serve as a pulpit on which a sermon was preached, or as a platform on which a lecture was delivered, while the action of the play was forced to stand still.

There is also to be noted in every period of play-making a frequent element of mere spectacle. The rhythmic movements of the Greek chorus in the orchestra and their statuesque attitudes were meant to take the eye, like the coronation processions in the English chronicle-play of "Henry VIII."

IV

. . . [These] are mere accidental accessories; and they have no vital relation to the fundamental principles of dramaturgy. By slow degrees the dramatist gets control of his material, and comes to a conscious appreciation of the necessities of his art. He may not be able to formulate the conditions which these necessities impose, but he has an intuitive perception of their requirements. These dramaturgic principles are not mere rules laid down by theoretical critics, who have rarely any acquaintance with the actual theater; they are laws, inherent in the nature of the art itself, standing eternal, as immitigable to-day as when Sophocles was alive, or Shakespere, or Molière. It is because these laws are unchanging that the observation of the modern theater helps to give us an insight into the methods of the ancient theater. And we can go a step further, and confess that the latest burlesque in a music-hall, with its topical songs and its parodies, may be of immediate assistance to us in seizing the intent and in understanding the methods of Aristophanes.

To M. Ferdinand Brunetière — who profited, perhaps, by a hint of Hegel's — we owe the clearest statement of one important law only dimly perceived by earlier critics. He declares that the drama differs from the other forms of literature in that it must always deal with some exertion of the human will. If a play is really to interest us, it must present a struggle; its chief character must desire something, striving for it with all the forces of his being. Aristotle has defined tragedy as "the imitation of an action," but by action he does not mean mere movement — the fictitious bustle often found in melodrama and in farce. Perhaps the Greek critic intended *action* to be interpreted *struggle,* a struggle in which the hero knows what he wants, and wants it with all his might, and does his best to get it. He may be thwarted by some overpowering antagonist, or may be betrayed by some internal weakness of his own soul; but the strength of the play and its interest to the spectator will lie in the balance of the contending forces. . . .

A determined will, resolute in seeking its own end, this is what we always find in the dramatic form; and this is what we do not find in the lyric or the epic. In the lyric the poet is satisfied if he is able to set forth his own sentiment. The epic poet — with whom the novelist must needs be classed nowadays — has to do mainly with adventure and with character. His narrative is not necessarily dramatic; it may, if he should so prefer, be as placid as a mill-pond. There is no obligation on the novelist to deal with what Stevenson has finely called the great passionate crises of existence "when duty and inclination come nobly to the grapple." He may do so if he chooses, and if he does, his novel is then truly dramatic; but he need not deal with this conflict unless he likes, and not a few novels of distinction are not intended to be dramatic. Gil Blas, Tom Jones, and Waverley, Mr. Pickwick and Tartarin of Tarascon, Silas Lapham and Huckleberry Finn, are none of them beings of unfaltering determination, nor do they exert a controlling influence over the conduct of the stories to which they have given their names. Each of them is more or less a creature of accident and a victim of circumstance. No one of them is master of his own fate, or even steersman of his own bark on the voyage of life. M. Brunetière has drawn our attention to the many resemblances between "Gil Blas" and the "Marriage of Figaro" in local color and in moral tone; and then he points out that the comic hero of the novel is the sport of chance—he is passive; while the comic hero of the play is active, he has made up his mind to defend his bride against his master; and this struggle is the core of the comedy. The drama of Beaumarchais might be turned into a narrative easily enough; but the story of Lesage could never be made into a play. And here we may perceive a reason why the modern novel of character-analysis can very seldom be dramatized successfully. . . .

There is yet another corollary of this law of M. Brunetière's; or at least there is a chance to use it here to elucidate a principle often insisted upon by another French critic. The late Francisque Sarcey maintained that every subject for a play, every theme, every plot, contained certain possible scenes which the playwright was bound to present on the stage. These he called the *scènes à faire,* the scenes which had to be done, which could not be shirked, but must be shown in action. He asserted that the spectator vaguely desires these scenes, and is dumbly disappointed if they take place behind closed doors and if they are only narrated. Now, if the drama deals with a struggle, then the incidents of the plot most likely to arouse and sustain the interest of the audience are those in which the contending forces are seen grappling with one another; and these

are therefore the *scenes à faire,* the scenes that have to be set upon the stage before the eyes of the spectators.

Thus it is in the presence of the public that Sophocles brings Oedipus to the full discovery of the fatal secret he has persisted in seeking. Thus Shakspere lets us behold a street-brawl of the Montagues and Capulets before making us witnesses of the love at first sight of Romeo and Juliet. Nor is Shakspere satisfied to have some minor character tell us how Iago dropped the poison of jealousy into Othello's ear: he makes us see it with our own eyes,— just as Molière makes us hear Tartuffe's casuistical pleading with Orgon's wife. One of the most obvious defects of French tragedy, especially in its decadence toward the end of the eighteenth century, is the frequent neglect or suppression of these necessary scenes and the constant use of mere messengers to narrate the episodes which the spectator would rather have beheld for himself. Victor Hugo remarked that at the performance of a tragedy of this type the audience was ever ready to say to the dramatist that what was being talked about seemed as though it might be interesting — "then why not let us see it for ourselves?"

V

M. Brunetière's law helps us to perceive the necessary subject-matter of the drama; and M. Sarcey's suggestion calls our attention to the necessary presentation of the acutest moments of the struggle before our eyes. The drama has other laws also, due to the fact that it is an art; it has its conventions by which alone it is allowed to differ from nature. In every art there is an implied contract between the artist and the public, permitting him to vary from the facts of life, and authorizing him to translate these facts and to transpose them as his special art may require. . . .

The conventions of the drama, its permitted variations from the facts of life, are some of them essential, and therefore eternal; and some of them are accidental only, and therefore temporary. It is a condition precedent to any enjoyment of a play that the fourth wall of every room shall be removed, so that we can see what is going on, also that the actors shall keep their faces turned toward us, and that they shall raise their voices so that we can hear what they have to say. It is essential, moreover, that the dramatist, having chosen his theme, shall present it to us void of all the accessories that would encumber it in real life, showing us only the vital episodes, omitting whatever may be less worthy of our attention, and ordering his plot so that everything is clear before our eyes, to enable us to understand at once every fresh development as the story unfolds itself. And as the action is thus compacted and heightened, so must the dialogue also be condensed and strengthened. It is only a brief time that we have to spend in the theater; and therefore must the speech of every character be stripped of the tautology, of the digressions, of the irrelevancies which dilute every-day conversation.

These things are essential, and we find them alike in the ancient drama and in the modern. . . .

Temporary and accidental conventions seem natural to us if we happen to be accustomed to them, but they strike us as grossly unnatural when they are unfamiliar. We do not object if a flimsy frame of canvas is lowered before our eyes to represent the castle of Elsinore, or if a stone wall suddenly becomes transparent that Faust may have a vision of Margaret. But we are inclined to smile at the black-robed attendant who hovers about the Japanese actor to provide a fan or a cushion, and who is supposed to be invisible or even non-existent. We should be taken aback if, after a murder was committed off the stage, a door suddenly flew open, revealing the criminals and the corpse posed in a living picture; and yet this is said to have been a device of the Greek theater. And we should laugh outright if we could listen to one of the medieval mysteries as they were acted in Portugal, when we heard the devil speaking Spanish, as it was always the custom of the Portuguese to represent him. . . .

GEORGE PIERCE BAKER

George Pierce Baker was born at Providence, R. I., in 1866. After his graduation from Harvard in 1887 he began his long teaching career, becoming an instructor at his Alma Mater the following year and an assistant professor in 1895. Some time toward the end of the century he began to take an active interest in the drama as a living and growing thing rather than as a subject for literary and antiquarian research. As Director of the 47 Workshop at Harvard he conducted courses in playwriting which attracted many men and women who were later on to make their marks in the professional theater as playwrights, managers, critics, directors, actors and scene designers. Among his many students only a few are here enumerated: Eugene O'Neill, George Abbott, Philip Barry, Sidney Howard, Robert Edmond Jones, John Mason Brown. Baker's work was continued at Yale when he became Professor of the History and Technique of Drama at the University Theater in 1925. Baker's writings include text-books on argumentation, prefaces to classic dramas, several volumes of student-written plays; *The Development of Shakespeare as a Dramatist* (1907), and *Dramatic Technique* (1919). In the last-named book he has attempted to summarize the results of his long years of practical teaching. (For various personal recollections of Baker and a good deal of information on his work and students, see *George Pierce Baker, A Memorial*, 1939.) He died in 1936.

THE ESSENTIALS OF DRAMA: ACTION AND EMOTION [1]

[From *Dramatic Technique*]

(1919)

What is the common aim of all dramatists? Twofold: first, as promptly as possible to win the attention of the audience; secondly, to hold that interest steady or, better, to increase it till the final curtain falls. It is the time limit to which all dramatists are subject which makes the immediate winning of attention necessary. The dramatist has no time to waste. How is he to win this attention? By what is done in the play; by characterization; by the language the people of his play speak; or by a combination of two or more of these. Today we hear much discussion whether it is what is done, *i.e.* action, or characterization, or dialogue which most interests a public. Which is the chief essential in good drama? History shows indisputably that the drama in its beginnings, no matter where we look, depended most on action. . . .

Look where we will, then, — at the beginnings of drama in Greece, in England centuries later, or among savage peoples today — the chief essential in winning and holding the attention of the spectator was imitative movement by the actors, that is, physical action. Nor, as the drama develops, does physical action cease to be central. . . . In Shakespeare's day, audiences again and again, as they watched plays of Dekker, Heywood, and many another dramatist, willingly accepted inadequate characterization and weak dialogue so long as the action was absorbing. . . . The history of the Drama shows that only rarely does even a group of people for a brief time care more for plays of characterization and dialogue than for plays of action. Throughout the ages, the great public, cultivated as

well as uncultivated, have cared for action first, then, as aids to a better understanding of the action of the story, for characterization and dialogue. Now, for more than a century, the play of mere action has been so popular that it has been recognized as a special form, namely, melodrama. This type of play, in which characterization and dialogue have usually been entirely subordinated to action, has been the most widely attended. . . . From the practice of centuries the feeling that action is really central in drama has become instinctive with most persons who write plays without preconceived theories. Watch a child making his first attempt at play-writing. In ninety-nine cases out of a hundred, the play will contain little except action. There will be slight characterization, if any, and the dialogue will be mediocre at best. The young writer has depended almost entirely upon action because instinctively, when he thinks of drama, he thinks of action.

Nor, if we paused to consider, is this dependence of drama upon action surprising. "From emotions to emotions" is the formula for any good play. To paraphrase a principle of geometry, "A play is the shortest distance from emotions to emotions." The emotions to be reached are those of the audience. The emotions conveyed are those of the people on the stage or of the dramatist as he has watched the people represented. Just herein lies the importance of action for the dramatist: it is his quickest means of arousing emotion in an audience. Which is more popular with the masses, the man of action or the thinker? The world at large believes, and rightly that, as a rule, "Actions speak louder than words." The dramatist knows that not what a man thinks he thinks, but what at a crisis he does, instinctively, sponta-

[1] Reprinted excerpts from *Dramatic Technique* (1919), by permission of the publisher, Houghton Mifflin Company. Copyright, 1919, by George Pierce Baker.

neously, best shows his character. The dramatist knows, too, that though we may think, when discussing patriotism in the abstract, that we have firm ideas about it, what reveals our real beliefs is our action at a crisis in the history of our country. . . . Is it any wonder, then, that popular vote has declared action the best revealer of feeling and, therefore, that the dramatist, in writing his plays, depends first of all upon action? If any one is disposed to cavil at action as popular merely with the masses and the less cultivated, let him ask himself, "What, primarily in other people interests me — what these people do or why they do it?" Even if he belong to the group, relatively very small in the mass of humanity, most interested by "Why did these people do this?" he must admit that till he knows clearly what the people did, he cannot take up the question which more interests him. For the majority of auditors, action is of first importance in drama: even for the group which cares far more for characterization and dialogue it is necessary as preparing the way for that characterization and dialogue on which they insist.

Consider for a moment the nature of the attention which a dramatist may arouse. Of course it may be only of the same sort which an audience gives a lecturer on a historical or scientific subject, — a readiness to hear and to try to understand what he has to present, — close but unemotional attention. Comparatively few people, however, are capable of sustained attention when their emotions are not called upon. How many lectures last over an hour? Is not the "popular lecturer" popular largely because he works into his lecture many anecdotes and dramatic illustrations in order to avoid or to lighten the strain of close, sustained attention? There is, undoubtedly, a public which can listen to ideas with the same keen enjoyment which most auditors feel when listening to something which stirs them emotionally, but as compared with the general public it is infinitesimal. Understanding this, the dramatist stirs the emotions of his hearers by the most concrete means at his command, his quickest communication from brain to

brain, — action just for itself or illustrating character. . . .

Just what, however, is this action which in drama is so essential? To most people it means physical or bodily action which rouses sympathy or dislike in an audience. The action of melodrama certainly exists largely for itself. We expect and get little but physical action for its own sake when a play is announced as was the well-known melodrama, *A Race for Life*.

As Melodramatically and Masterfully Stirring, Striking and Sensational as Phil Sheridan's Famous Ride.
Superb, Stupendous Scenes in Sunset Regions.
Wilderness Wooings Where Wild Roses Grow.
The Lights and Shades of Rugged Border Life.
Chinese Comedy to Make Confucius Chuckle.
The Realism of the Ranch and Race Track.
The Hero Horse That Won a Human Life.
An Equine Beauty Foils a Murderous Beast.
Commingled Gleams of Gladness, Grief, and Guilt.
Dope, Dynamite and Devilish Treachery Distanced.
Continuous Climaxes That Come Like Cloudbursts.

Some plays depend almost wholly upon mere bustle and rapidly shifting movement, much of it wholly unnecessary to the plot. . . .

If physical action in and of itself is so often dramatic, is all physical action dramatic? That is, does it always create emotion in an onlooker? No. It goes for naught unless it rouses his interest. Of itself, or because of the presentation given it by the dramatist, it must rouse in the onlooker an emotional response. A boy seeing "Crazy Mary" stalking the street in bedizened finery and bowing right and left, may see nothing interesting in her. More probably her actions will move him to jeer and jibe at her. Let some spectator, however, tell the boy of the tragedy in Crazy Mary's younger life which left her unbalanced, and, if he has any right feeling, the boy's attitude will begin to change. He may even give over the jeering he has begun. Reveal to him exactly what is passing in the crazed mind of the woman, and his mere interest will probably turn to sympathy. Characterization, preceding and accompanying action, creates sympathy or repulsion for the figure or figures involved. This sympathy or repulsion in turn converts mere interest into emotional response of the keenest kind. Though physical action is undoubtedly fundamental in drama, no higher form than crude melodrama or crude farce can develop till characterization appears to explain and interpret action. . . .

The first scene of Act I of *Romeo and Juliet* is full of interesting physical action — quarrels, fighting, and the halting of the fight by the angry Prince. The physical action, however, characterizes in every instance, from the servants of the two factions to Tybalt, Benvolio, the Capulets, the Montagues, and the Prince. Moreover, this interesting physical action, which is all the more interesting because it characterizes, is interesting in the third place because in every instance it helps to an understanding of the story. It shows so intense an enmity between the two houses that even the servants cannot meet in the streets without quarreling. By its characterization it prepares for the parts Benvolio and Tybalt are to play in later scenes. It motivates the edict of banishment which is essential if the tragedy of the play is to occur. . . .

Even physical action, then, may interest for itself, or because it characterizes, or because it helps on the story, or for two or more of these reasons.

If we examine other extracts from famous plays we shall, however, find ourselves wondering whether action in drama must not mean something besides mere physical action. . . .

The fact is, the greatest drama of all time . . . uses action much less for its own sake than to reveal mental states which are to rouse sympathy or repulsion in an audience. In brief, marked mental activity may be quite as dramatic

as mere physical action. Hamlet may sit quietly by his fire as he speaks the soliloquy " To be, or not to be," yet by what we already know of him and what the lines reveal we are moved to the deepest sympathy for his tortured state. . . .

Many an inexperienced dramatist fails to see the force of these words of Maeterlinck: " An old man, seated in his armchair, waiting patiently, with his lamp beside him — submitting his bent head to the presence of his soul and his destiny — motionless as he is does yet live in reality a deeper, more human, and more universal life than the lover who strangles his mistress, the captain who conquers in battle, or the husband who 'avenges his honor.' " If an audience can be made to feel and understand the strong but contained emotion of this motionless figure, he is rich dramatic material. . . .

[We] must include mental as well as physical activity in any definition of the word *dramatic*. Provided a writer can convey to his audience the excited mental state of one or more of his characters, then this mental activity is thoroughly dramatic. That is, neither physical nor mental activity is in itself dramatic; all depends on whether it naturally arouses, or can be made by the author to arouse, emotion in an audience. Just as we had to add to physical action which arouses emotional response of itself, physical action which is made to arouse response because it develops the story or illustrates character, we must now add action which is not physical, but mental.

There is even another chance for confusion. A figure sitting motionless not because he is thinking hard but because blank in mind may yet be dramatic. Utter inaction, both physical and mental, of a figure represented on the stage does not mean that it is necessarily undramatic. If the dramatist can make an audience feel the terrible tragedy of the contrast between what might have been and what is for this perfectly quiet unthinking figure, he rouses emotion in his hearers, and in so doing makes his material dramatic. Suppose, too, that the expressionless figure is an aged father or mother very dear to some one in the play who has strongly won the sympathy of the audience. The house takes fire. The flames draw nearer and nearer the unconscious figure. We are made to look at the situation through the eyes of the character — some child or relative — to whom the scene, were he present, would mean torture. Instantly the figure, because of the way in which it is represented, becomes dramatic. Here again, however, the emotion of the audience could hardly be aroused except through characterization of the figure as it was or might have been, or of the child or relative who has won our sympathy. Again, too, characterization so successful must depend a good deal on well-chosen words.

This somewhat elaborate analysis should have made three points clear. First, we may arouse emotion in an audience by mere physical action; by physical action which also develops the story, or illustrates character, or does both; by .mental rather than physical action, if clearly and accurately conveyed to the audience; and even by inaction, if characterization and dialogue by means of other figures are of high order. Secondly, as the various illustrations have been examined, it must have become steadily more clear that while action is popularly held to be central in drama, emotion is really the essential. Because it is the easiest expression of emotion to understand, physical action, which without illuminating characterization and dialogue can express only a part of the world of emotion, has been too often accepted as expressing all the emotion the stage can present. Thirdly, it should be clear that a statement one meets too frequently in books on the drama, that certain stories or characters, above all certain well-known books, are essentially undramatic material is at least dubious. The belief arises from the fact that the story, character, or idea, as usually presented, seems to demand much analysis and description, and almost to preclude illustrative action. In the past few years, however, the drama of mental states and the drama which has revealed emotional significance in seeming or real inaction, has been proving that "nothing human is foreign" to the drama. A dramatist may see in the so-called undramatic material ·emotional values. If so, he will develop

a technique which will create in his public a satisfaction equal to that which the so-called undramatic story, character, or idea could give in story form. Of course he will treat it differently in many respects because he is writing not to be read but to be heard, and to affect the emotions, not of the individual, but of a large group taken as a group. He will prove that till careful analysis has shown in a given story, character, or idea, no possibility of arousing the same or dissimilar emotions in an audience, we cannot say that this or that is dramatic or undramatic, but only: "This material will require totally different presentation if it is to be dramatic on the stage, and only a person of acumen, experience with audiences, and inventive technique can present it effectively."

The misapprehension just analyzed rests not only on the misconception that action rather than emotion is the essential in drama, but also largely on a careless use of the word *dramatic*. In popular use this word means *material for drama*, or *creative of emotional response*, or *perfectly fitted for production under the conditions of the theatre*. If we examine a little, in the light of this chapter, the nature and purpose of a play, we shall see that *dramatic* should stand only for the first two definitions, and that *theatric* must be used for the third. Avoiding the vague definition *material for drama*, use *dramatic* only as *creative of emotional response* and the confusion will disappear.

A play exists to create emotional response in an audience. The response may be to the emotions of the people in the play or the emotions of the author as he watches these people. Where would satirical comedy be if, instead of sharing the amusement, disdain, contempt or moral anger of the dramatist caused by his figures, we responded exactly to their follies or evil moods? All ethical drama gets its force by creating in an audience the feelings toward the people in the play held by the author. Dumas fils, Ibsen, Brieux prove the truth of this statement. The writer of the satirical or the ethical play, obtruding his own personality as in the case of Ben Jonson, or with fine impersonality as in the case of Congreve or

Molière, makes his feelings ours. It is an obvious corollary of this statement that the emotions aroused in an audience need not be the same as those felt by the people on the stage. They may be in the sharpest contrast. Any one experienced in drama knows that the most intensely comic effects often come from people acting very seriously. . . . In brief, the dramatic may rouse the same, allied, or even contrasting emotions in an onlooker.

Nor need the emotion roused in an audience by actor or author be exactly the same in amount. The actress who abandons herself to the emotions of the part she is playing soon exhausts her nervous vitality. It would be the same if audiences listening to the tragic were permitted to feel the scenes as keenly as the figures of the story. On the other hand, in some cases, if the comic figure on the stage felt his comicality as strongly as the audience which is speechless with laughter, he could not go on, and the scene would fail. Evidently, an audience may be made, as the dramatist wills, to feel more or less emotion than the characters of the play.

That it is duplication of emotion to the same, a less, or a greater extent or the creation of contrasting emotion which underlies all drama, from melodrama, riotous farce and even burlesque to high-comedy and tragedy, must be firmly grasped if a would-be dramatist is to steer his way clearly through the many existing and confusing definitions of *dramatic*. For instance, Brunetière said, "Drama is the representation of the will of man in contrast to the mysterious powers of natural forces which limit and belittle us; it is one of us thrown living upon the stage, there to struggle against fatality, against social law, against one of his fellow mortals, against himself, if need be, against the emotions, the interests, the prejudices, the folly, the malevolence of those around him." [1] That is, by this definition, conflict is central in drama. But we know that in recent drama particularly, the moral drifter has many a time aroused our sympathy. Surely inertness, supineness, stupidity,

and even torpor may be made to excite emotion in an audience. Conflict covers a large part of drama but not all of it.

Mr. William Archer, in his *Play-Making*, declares that "a crisis" is the central matter in drama, but one immediately wishes to know what constitutes a crisis, and we have defined without defining. When he says elsewhere that that is dramatic which "by representation of imaginary personages is capable of interesting an average audience assembled in a theatre," [2] he almost hits the truth. If we rephrase this definition: "That is dramatic which by representation of imaginary personages interests, through its emotions, an average audience assembled in a theatre," we have a definition which will better stand testing.

Is all dramatic material *theatric?* No, for *theatric* does not necessarily mean *sensational, melodramatic, artificial.* It should mean, and it will be so used in this book, *adapted for the purpose of the theatre.* Certainly all dramatic material, that is, material which arouses or may be made to arouse emotion, is not fitted for use in the theatre when first it comes to the hand of the dramatist. . . . Even material so emotional in its nature as to be genuinely dramatic may need careful reworking if it is to succeed as a play that is, if it is to become properly *theatric.* Drama, then, is presentation of an individual or group of individuals so as to move an audience to responsive emotion of the kind desired by the dramatist and the amount required. This response must be gained under the conditions which a dramatist finds or develops in a theatre; that is, dramatic material must be made theatric in the right sense of the word before it can become drama.

To summarize: accurately conveyed emotion is the great fundamental in all good drama. It is conveyed by action, characterization, and dialogue. It must be conveyed in a space of time, usually not exceeding two hours and a half, and under the existing physical conditions of the stage, or with such changes as the dramatist may bring about in them. It must be conveyed, not directly through the author, but indirectly through the actors. In order that the dramatic may

[1] *Études Critiques,* vol. VII, p. 207.

[2] *Play-Making,* p. 48. William Archer. Small, Maynard & Co., Boston.

become theatric in the right sense of the word, the dramatic must be made to meet all these conditions successfully. These conditions affect action, characterization, and dialogue. A dramatist must study the ways in which the dramatic has been and may be made theatric: that is what technique means.

GEORGE JEAN NATHAN

George Jean Nathan was born at Fort Wayne, Ind., in 1882. He was graduated from Cornell University in 1904. After a year in Europe he returned to the United States and worked for a year or two on the editorial staff of the New York *Herald.* In 1908 he began writing for *Smart Set* magazine, to which he contributed dramatic reviews and other material until 1923. Together with H. L. Mencken he was editor of the same magazine, beginning in 1914. In 1924 he and Mencken founded the *American Mercury,* but the following year he dropped his editorial work, remaining as critic and contributing editor until 1930. Nathan reviewed plays continuously during all his adult life, in various newspapers and magazines, and the best of his reviews have been reprinted in books, which appeared regularly from 1916 until his death. He tried his hand on occasion at playwriting, and also wrote essays and books on nondramatic subjects; he encouraged and championed new playwrights, native and foreign. This is especially true of his relations with O'Neill and Saroyan. A conscientious student of the history of his subject, he was familiar with the theatres and dramatic literatures of several countries, including his own. Though his style is informal, colloquial, and entertaining, he—especially in *The Critic and the Drama*—evolved a consistent theory of the drama and established critical standards of a high, if occasionally restricted and somewhat limited, order. Among his many volumes of collected criticism a few are here mentioned: *Another Book on the Theatre* (1916); *Mr. George Jean Nathan Presents* (1917); *The World in Falseface* (1923); *Materia Critica* (1924); *Art of the Night* (1928); *The Entertainment of a Nation* (1942). For a number of years, beginning in 1943, Nathan's collected reviews appeared annually in *The Theatre Book of the Year.* He died in 1958.

THE DRAMA AS AN ART[1]
[From *The Critic and the Drama*]
(1922)

I

If the best of criticism, in the familiar description of Anatole France, lies in the adventure of a soul among masterpieces, the best of drama may perhaps be described as the adventure of a masterpiece among souls. Drama is fine or impover-

[1] Reprinted in full from *The Critic and the Drama*, New York, 1922, by permission of the author and of the publisher Alfred A. Knopf. Copyright, 1922, by Alfred A. Knopf, Inc. The author made a few slight textual revisions for this book.

ished in the degree that it evokes from such souls a fitting and noble reaction.

Drama is, in essence, a democratic art in constant brave conflict with aristocracy of intelligence, soul, and emotion. When drama triumphs, a masterpiece like "Hamlet" comes to life. When the conflict ends in a draw, a drama half-way between greatness and littleness is the result — a drama, say, like "El Gran Galeoto." When the struggle ends in defeat, the result is a "Way Down East" or a "Lightnin'." This, obviously, is not to say that great drama may not be popular drama, nor popular drama great drama, for I speak of drama here not as this play or that, but as a specific art. And it is as a specific art that it finds its test and trial, not in its own intrinsically democratic soul, but in the extrinsic aristocratic soul that is taste, and connoisseurship, and final judgment. Drama that has come to be at once great and popular has ever first been given the imprimatur, not of democratic souls, but of aristocratic. Shakespeare and Molière triumphed over aristocracy of intelligence, soul and emotion before that triumph was presently carried on into the domain of inferior intelligence, soul and emotion. In our own day, the drama of Hauptmann, Shaw and the American O'Neill has come into its popular own only after it first achieved the imprimatur of what we may term the unpopular, or undemocratic, theatre. Aristocracy cleared the democratic path for Ibsen, as it cleared it, in so far as possible, for Rostand and Hugo von Hofmannsthal.

Great drama is the rainbow born when the sun of reflection and understanding smiles anew upon an intelligence and emotion which that drama has respectively shot with gleams of brilliant lightning and drenched with the rain of brilliant tears. Great drama, like great men and great women, is always just a little sad. Only idiots may be completely happy. Reflection, sympathy, wisdom, gallant gentleness, experience — the chords upon which great drama is played — these are wistful chords. The commonplace urge that drama, to be truly great, must uplift is, in the sense that the word uplift is used, childish. The mission of great drama is not to make numskulls glad that they are alive, but to make them speculate why they are permitted to be alive at all. And since this is the mission of great drama — if ts mission may, indeed, be reduced to any phrase — it combines within itself, together with this mystical and awe-struck appeal to the proletariat, a direct and agreeable appeal to such persons as are, by reason of their metaphysical perception and emotional culture, superior to and contemptuous of the proletariat. Fine drama, in truth, is usually just a trifle snobbish. It has no traffic with such souls as are readily made to feel "uplifted" by spurious philosophical nostrums and emotional sugar pills. Its business is with what the matchless Dryden hailed "souls of the highest rank and truest understanding": souls who find a greater uplift in the noble depressions of Brahms' first trio, Bartolommeo's Madonna della Misericordia, and Joseph Conrad's "Youth" than in the easy buoyancies of John Philip Sousa, Howard Chandler Christy and Rupert Hughes. The aim of great drama is not to make men happy with themselves as they are, but with themselves as they might, yet alas cannot, be. As Gautier has it, "The aim of art is not exact reproduction of nature, but creation, by means of forms and colors, of a microcosm wherein may be produced dreams, sensations, and ideas inspired by the aspect of the world." If drama is irrevocably a democratic art and uplift of the great masses of men its noblest end, Mrs. Porter's "Pollyanna" must endure as a work of dramatic art a thousand times finer than Corneille's "Polyeucte."

Drama has been strictly defined by the ritualists in a dozen different ways. "Drama," says one, "must be based on character, and the action proceed from character." "Drama," stipulates another, "is not an imitation of men, but of an action and of life: character is subsidiary to action." "Drama," promulgates still another, "is the struggle of a will against obstacles." And so on, so on. Rules, rules and more rules. Pigeon-holes upon pigeon-holes. Good drama is anything that interests an intelligently emotional group of persons assembled together in an illuminated hall. Molière, wise among dramatists, said as much, though in somewhat more, and doubtless too, sweeping words. Throughout the ages of drama there will be always Romanticists of one sort or another, brave and splendid spirits, who will have to free themselves from the definitions and limitations imposed upon them by the neo-Bossus and Boileaus, and the small portion Voltaires, La Harpes and Marmontels. Drama is struggle, a conflict of wills? Then what of "Ghosts"? Drama is action? Then what of "Nachtasyl"? Drama is character? Then what of "The Dream Play"? "A 'character' upon the stage," wrote the author of the last named, "has become a creature ready-made — a mere mechanism that drives the man — I do not believe in these theatrical 'characters.'"

Of all the higher arts, drama is organically perhaps the simplest. Its anatomy is composed of all the other arts, high and low, stripped to their elementals. It is a synthesis of those portions of these other arts that, being elemental, are most easily assimilable on the part of the multitude. It is a snatch of music, a bit of painting, a moment of dancing, a slice of sculpture, draped upon the skeleton of literature. At its highest, it ranks with literature, but never above it. One small notch below, it ranks only with itself, in its own isolated and generically peculiar field. Drama, indeed, is dancing literature: a hybrid art. It is often purple and splendid; it is often profoundly beautiful and profoundly moving. Yet, with a direct appeal to the emotions as its first and encompassing aim, it has never, even at its finest, been able to exercise the measure of direct emotional appeal that is exercised, say, by Chopin's C sharp minor Nocturne, op. 27, No. 1, or by the soft romance of the canvases of Palma Vecchio, or by Rodin's superb "Eternal Spring," or by Zola's "La Terre." It may, at its finest as at its worst, of course subjugate and triumph over inexperienced emotionalism, but the greatest drama of Shakespeare himself has never, in the truthful confession of cultivated emotionalism, influenced that emotionalism as has the greatest literature, or the greatest music, or the greatest painting or sculpture. The splendid music of "Romeo" or "Hamlet" is not so eloquent and moving as that of "Tristan" or "Lohengrin"; no situation in the whole of Hauptmann can strike in the heart so thrilling and profound a chord of pity as a single line in Allegri's obvious "Miserere." The greatest note of comedy in drama falls short of the note of comedy in the "Coffee-Cantata" of Bach; the greatest note of ironic remorse falls short of that in the scherzo in B minor of Chopin; the greatest intellectual note falls short of that in the first and last movements of the C minor symphony of Brahms. What play of Sudermann's has the direct appeal of "The Indian Lily"? What play made out of Hardy's "Tess," however adroitly contrived, retains the powerful appeal of the original piece of literature? To descend, what obvious thrill melodrama, designed frankly for dollars, has — with all its painstaking and deliberate intent — yet succeeded in provoking half the thrill and shock of the obvious second chapter of Andreas Latzko's equally obvious "Men in War"?

Art is an evocation of beautiful emotions: art is art in the degree that it succeeds in the evocation: drama succeeds in an inferior degree. Whatever emotion drama may succeed brilliantly in evoking, another art succeeds in evoking more brilliantly.

II

Although, of course, one speaks of drama here primarily in the sense of acted drama, it is perhaps not necessary so strictly to confine one's self. For when the critic confines himself in his discussion of drama to the acted drama, he regularly brings upon himself from other critics — chiefly bookish fellows whose theatrical knowledge is meagre — the very largely unwarranted embarrassment of arguments anent "crowd psychology" and the like which, while they have little or nothing to do with the case, none the less make a certain deep impression upon his readers. (Readers of criticism become automatically critics; with his first sentence, the critic challenges his critic-reader's sense of argument.) This constantly advanced contention of "crowd psychology," of which drama is supposed to be at once master and slave, has small place in a consideration of drama, from whatever sound point of view one elects to consider the latter. If "crowd psychology" operates in the case of theatre drama, it operates also in the case of concert-hall music. Yet no one so far as I know seriously maintains that, in a criticism of music, this "crowd psychology" has any place.

I have once before pointed out that, even accepting the theory of crowd psychology and its direct and indirect implications so far as drama is concerned, it is as nonsensical to assume that one thousand persons assembled together before a drama in a theatre are, by reason of their constituting a crowd, any more likely to be moved automatically than the same crowd of one thousand persons assembled together before a painting in an art gallery. Furthermore, the theory that collective intelligence and emotionalism are a more facile and ingenuous intelligence and emotionalism, while it may hold full water in the psychological laboratory, holds little in actual external demonstration, particularly in any consideration of a crowd before one of the arts. While it may be true that the Le Bon and Tarde theory applies aptly to the collective psychology of a crowd at a prize-fight or a bull-fight or a circus, one may be permitted severe doubts that it holds equally true of a crowd in a theatre or in an art gallery or in a concert hall. The tendency of such a latter group is not æsthetically downward, but upward. And not only æsthetically, but intellectually and emotionally. (I speak, of course, and with proper relevance, of a crowd assembled to hear good drama or good music, or to see good painting. The customary obscuring tactic of critics in this situation is to argue out the principles of intelligent reaction to good drama in terms of yokel reaction to bad drama. Analysis of the principles of sound theatre drama and the reaction of a group of eight hundred citizens of Marion, Ohio, to " The Two Orphans " somehow do not seem to me to be especially apposite.) The fine drama or the fine piece of music does not make its auditor part of a crowd; it removes him, and every one else in the crowd, from the crowd, and makes him an individual. The crowd ceases to exist as a crowd; it becomes a crowd of units, of separate individuals. The dramas of Mr. Owen Davis make crowds; the dramas of Shakespeare make individuals.

The argument to the contrary always somewhat grotesquely assumes that the crowd assembled at a fine play, and promptly susceptible to group psychology, is a new crowd, one that has never attended a fine play before. Such an assumption falls to pieces in two ways. First, it is beyond reason to believe that it is true in more than one instance out of a hundred; and, secondly, it would not be true even if it were true. For,

granting that a crowd of one thousand persons were seeing great drama for the first time in their lives, what reason is there for believing that the majority of persons in the crowd who had never seen great drama and didn't know exactly what to make of it would be swayed and influenced by the minority who had never seen great drama but did know what to make of it? If this were true, no great drama could ever possibly fail in the commercial theatre. Or, to test the hypothesis further, take it the other way round. What reason is there for believing that the majority in this crowd would be moved the one way or the other, either by a minority that did understand the play, or did not understand it? Or take it in another way still. What reason is there for believing that the minority in this crowd who did know what the drama was about would be persuaded emotionally by the majority who did not know what the drama was about?

Theories, and again theories. But the facts fail to support them. Take the lowest type of crowd imaginable, one in which there is not one cultured man in a thousand — the crowd, say, at a professional American baseball game — and pack it into an American equivalent of Reinhardt's Grosses Schauspielhaus. The play, let us say, is " Œdipus Rex." At the ball game, the crowd psychology of Le Bon operated to the full. But what now? Would the crowd, in the theatre and before a great drama, be the same crowd? Would it not be an entirely different crowd? Would not its group psychology promptly and violently suffer a sudden change? Whether out of curiosity, disgust, admiration, social shame or what not, would it not rapidly segregate itself, spiritually or physically, into various groups? What is the Le Bon theatrical view of the crowd psychology that somehow did not come off during the initial engagement of Barrie's " Peter Pan " in Washington, D. C.? Or of the crowd psychology that worked the other way round when Ibsen was first played in London? Or of the crowd psychology that, operating regularly, if artificially, at the New York premières, most often fails, for all its high enthusiasm, to move either the minority or the majority in its composition?

The question of sound drama and the pack psychology of a congress of ground-lings is a fatuous one: it gets nowhere. Sound drama and sound audiences are alone to be considered at one and the same time. And, as I have noted, the tendency of willing, or even semi-willing, auditors and spectators is in an upward direction, not a downward. No intelligent spectator at a performance of " Ben Hur " has ever been made to feel like throwing his hat into the air and cheering by the similar actions of the mob spectators to the left and right of him. No ignoble auditor of " The Laugh-ter of the Gods " but has been made to feel, in some part, the contagion of cul-tivated appreciation to *his* left and right. " I forget," wrote Sarcey, in a considera-tion of the subject, " what tyrant it was of ancient Greece to whom massacres were everyday affairs, but who wept copiously over the misfortunes of a heroine in a tragedy. He was the audi-ence; and for the one evening clothed himself in the sentiments of the pub-lic." A typical example of sophisti-cated reasoning. How does Sarcey know that it was not the rest of the audience — the crowd — that was influenced by this repentant and copiously lachrymose individual rather than that it was this individual who was moved by the crowd?

If fallacies perchance insinuate them-selves into these opposing contentions, it is a case of fallacy versus fallacy: my intent is not so much to prove anything as to indicate the presence of holes in the proofs of the other side. These holes seem to me to be numerous, and of con-siderable circumference. A description of two of them may suffice to suggest the rest. Take, as the first of these, the familar Castelvetro doctrine that, since a theatrical audience is not a select con-gress but a motley crowd, the dramatist, ever conscious of the group psychology, must inevitably avoid all themes and ideas unintelligible to such a gathering. It may be true that a theatrical audi-ence is not a select congress, but why confine the argument to theatrical audi-ences and seek thus to prove something of drama that may be proved as well — if one is given to such idiosyncrasies —

of music? What, as I have said before, of opera and concert hall audiences? Consider the average audience at Covent Garden, the Metropolitan, Carnegie Hall. Is it in any way culturally su-perior to the average audience•at the St. James's Theatre, or the Théâtre de l'Oeuvre, or the Plymouth—or even the Neighbourhood Playhouse down in Grand Street? What of the audiences who attended the original performances of Beethoven's " Leonore " (" Fi-delio "), Berlioz's " Benvenuto Cellini," the original performances of Wagner in France and the performances of his " Der Fliegende Holländer " in Germany, the operas of Händel in England in the years 1733–37, the work of Rossini in Italy, the concerts of Chopin during his tour of England and Scotland? . . . Again, as to the imperative necessity of the dramatist's avoidance of all themes and ideas unintelligible to a mob audi-ence, what of the success among such very audiences — to name but a few more recent profitably produced and locally readily recognizable examples — of Shaw's " Getting Married," Augustus Thomas' " The Witching Hour," Ibsen's " The Wild Duck," Dunsany's " The Laughter of the Gods," Barrie's " Mary Rose," Strindberg's " The Father," Synge's " Playboy "? . . . Surely it will be quickly allowed that however obvious the themes and ideas of these plays may be to the few, they are hardly within the ready intelligence of what the theorists picture as the imaginary mob theatre audience. Fine drama is independent of all such theories: the dramatist who sub-scribes to them should not figure in any treatise upon drama as an art.

A second illustration: the equivocation to the effect that drama, being a demo-cratic art, may not properly be evalu-ated in terms of more limited, and aris-tocratic, taste. It seems to me an idiotic assumption that drama is a more demo-cratic art than music. All great art is democratic in intention, if not in re-ward. Michelangelo, Shakespeare, Wag-ner and Zola are democratic artists, and their art democratic art. It is criticism of Michelangelo, Shakespeare, Wagner and Zola that is aristocratic. Criticism, not art, generically wears the ermine and the purple. To appraise a democratic art in terms of democracy is to attempt to effect a chemical reaction in nitrogen with nitrogen. If drama is, critically, a democratic art since it is meant not to be read by the few but to be played before the many, music must be critically no less a democratic art. Yet the theorists conveniently overlook this embarrassment. Nevertheless, if Shakespeare's dramas were designed for the heterogeneous ear, so, too, were the songs of Schumann. No great artist has ever in his heart deliberately fashioned his work for a remote and forgotten cellar, dark and stairless. He fashions it, for all his doubts, in the hope of hospitable eyes and ears, and in the hope of a sun to shine upon it. It is as ridiculous to argue that because Shakespeare's is a democratic art it must be criticized in terms of democratic reaction to it as it would be to argue that because the United States is a democracy the most acute and comprehensive criticism of that democracy must lie in a native democrat's reaction to it. " To say that the theatre is for the people," says Gordon Craig, " is necessary. But to forget to add that part and parcel of the people is the aristocracy, whether of birth or feeling, is an omission. A man of the eighteenth century, dressed in silks, in a fashionable loggia in the theatre at Versailles, looking as if he did no work (as Voltaire in his youth may have looked), presents, in essence, exactly the same picture as Walt Whitman in his rough gray suit lounging in the Bowery, also looking as if he did no work. . . . One the aristocrat, one the democrat: the two are identical."

III

" Convictions," said Nietzsche, " are prisons." Critical " theories," with negligible exception, seek to denude the arts of their splendid, gypsy gauds and to force them instead to don so many duplicated black and white striped uniforms. Of all the arts, drama has suffered most in this regard. Its critics, from the time of Aristotle, have bound and fettered it, and have then urged it impassionedly to soar. Yet, despite its shackles, it has triumphed, and each triumph has been a derision of one of its

most famous and distinguished critics. It triumphed, through Shakespeare, over Aristotle; it triumphed, through Molière, over Castelvetro; it triumphed, through Lemercier, over Diderot; it triumphed, through Lessing, over Voltaire; it triumphed, through Ibsen, over Flaubert; it has triumphed, through Hauptmann, over Sarcey and, through Schnitzler and Bernard Shaw, over Mr. Archer. The truth perhaps is that drama is an art as flexible as the imaginations of its audiences. It is no more to be bound by rules and theories than such imaginations are to be bound by rules and theories. Who so allwise that he may say by what rules or set of rules living imaginations and imaginations yet unborn are to be fanned into theatrical flame? " Imagination," Samuel Johnson's words apply to auditor as to artist, " a licentious and vagrant faculty, unsusceptible of limitations and impatient of restraint, has always endeavored to baffle the logician, to perplex the confines of distinction, and burst the inclosures of regularity." And further, " There is therefore scarcely any species of writing of which we can tell what is its essence, and what are its constituents; every new genius produces some innovation which, when invented and approved, subverts the rules which the practice of foregoing authors had established."

Does the play interest, and whom? This seems to me to be the only doctrine of dramatic criticism that is capable of supporting itself soundly. First, does the play interest? In other words, how far has the dramatist succeeded in expressing himself, and the materials before him, intelligently, eloquently, symmetrically, beautifully? So much for the criticism of the dramatist as an artist. In the second place, whom does the play interest? Does it interest inferior persons, or does it interest cultivated and artistically sensitive persons? So much for the criticism of the artist as a dramatist.

The major difficulty with critics of the drama has always been that, having once positively enunciated their critical credos, they have been constrained to devote their entire subsequent enterprise and ingenuity to defending the fallacies therein. Since a considerable number of these critics have been, and are, extraordinarily shrewd and ingenious men, these defences of error have often been contrived with such persuasive dexterity and reasonableness that they have endured beyond the sounder doctrines of less deft critics, doctrines which, being sound, have suffered the rebuffs that gaunt, grim logic, ever unprepossessing and unhypnotic, suffers always. " I hope that I am right; if I am not right, I am still right," said Brunetière. " Mr. William Archer is not only, like myself, a convinced, inflexible determinist," Henry Arthur Jones has written, " I am persuaded that he is also, unlike myself, a consistent one. I am sure he takes care that his practice agrees with his opinions — even when they are wrong." Dramatic criticism is an attempt to formulate rules of conduct for the lovable, wayward, charming, wilful vagabond that is the drama. For the drama is an art with a feather in its cap and an ironic smile upon its lips, sauntering impudently over forbidden lawns and through closed lanes into the hearts of those of us children of the world who have never grown up. Beside literature, it is the Mother Goose of the arts: a gorgeous and empurpled Mother Goose for the fireside of impressible and romantic youth that, looking upward, leans ever hushed and expectant at the knee of life. It is a fairy tale told realistically, a true story told as romance. It is the lullaby of disillusion, the chimes without the cathedral, the fears and hopes and dreams and passions of those who cannot fully fear and hope and dream and flame themselves.

"The drama must have reality," so Mr. P. P. Howe in his engaging volume of "Dramatic Portraits," "but the first essential to our understanding of an art is that we should not believe it to be actual life. The spectator who shouts his warning and advice to the heroine when the villain is approaching is, in the theatre, the only true believer in the hand of God; and he is liable to find it in a drama lower than the best." The art of the drama is one which imposes upon drama the obligation of depicting at once the inner processes of life realistically and the external aspects of life delusively. Properly and sympatheti-

cally to appreciate drama, one must look upon it synchronously with two different eyes: the one arguing against the other as to the truth of what it sees, and triumphing over this doubtful other with the full force of its sophistry. Again inevitably to quote Coleridge, "Stage presentations are to produce a sort of temporary half-faith, which the spectator encourages in himself and supports by a voluntary contribution on his own part, because he knows that it is at all times in his power to see the thing as it really is. Thus the true stage illusion as to a forest scene consists, not in the mind's judging it to be a forest, but in its remission of the judgment that it is not a forest." This obviously applies to drama as well as to dramatic investiture. One never for a moment believes absolutely that Mr. John Barrymore is Richard III; one merely agrees, for the sake of Shakespeare, who has written the play, and Mr. Hopkins, who has cast it, that Mr. John Barrymore is Richard III, so that one may receive the ocular, aural and mental sensations for which one has paid three and one-half dollars. Nor does one for a moment believe that Mr. Walter Hampden, whom that very evening one has seen dividing a brobdingnagian dish of goulash with Mr. Oliver Herford in the Players' Club and discussing the prospects of the White Sox, is actually speaking extemporaneously the rare verbal embroideries of Shakespeare; or that Miss Ethel Barrymore who is billed in front of Browne's Chop House to take a star part in the Actors' Equity Association's benefit, is really the queen of a distant kingdom.

The dramatist, in the theatre, is not a worker in actualities, but in the essence of actualities that filters through the self-deception of his spectators. There is no such thing as realism in the theatre: there is only mimicry of realism. There is no such thing as romance in the theatre: there is only mimicry of romance. There is no such thing as an automatic dramatic susceptibility in a theatre audience: there is only a volitional dramatic susceptibility. Thus, it is absurd to speak of the drama holding the mirror up to nature; all that the drama can do is to hold nature up to its own peculiar mirror which, like that in a pleasure-park, amusingly fattens up nature, or shrinks it, yet does not at any time render it unrecognizable. One does not go to the theatre to see life and nature; one goes to see the particular way in which life and nature happen to look to a cultivated, imaginative and entertaining man who happens, in turn, to be a playwright. Drama is the surprising pulling of a perfectly obvious, every-day rabbit out of a perfectly obvious, every-day silk hat. The spectator has seen thousands of rabbits and thousands of silk hats, but he has never seen a silk hat that had a rabbit concealed in it, and he is curious about it.

But if drama is essentially mimetic, so also — as Professor Gilbert Murray implies — is criticism essentially mimetic in that it is representative of the work criticized. It is conceivable that one may criticize Mr. Ziegfeld's "Follies" in terms of the "Philoctetes" of Theodectes — I myself have been guilty of even more exceptional feats; it is not only conceivable, but of common occurrence, for certain of our academic American critics to criticize the plays of Mr. Shaw in terms of Scribe and Sardou, and with a perfectly straight face; but criticism in general is a chameleon that takes on something of the colour of the pattern upon which it imposes itself. There is drama in Horace's "Epistola ad Pisones," a criticism of drama. There is the spirit of comedy in Hazlitt's essay "On the Comic Writers of the Last Century." Dryden's "Essay on Dramatic Poesy" is poetry. There is something of the music of Chopin in Huneker's critical essays on Chopin, and some of Mary Garden's spectacular histrionism in his essay on her acting. Walkley, criticizing "L'Enfant Prodigue," uses the pen of Pierrot. Criticism, more than drama with her mirror toward nature, holds the mirror up to the nature of the work it criticizes. Its end 's the revivification of the passion of art which has been spent in its behalf, but under the terms laid down by Plato. Its aim is to reconstruct a great work of art on a diminutive scale, that eyes which are not capable of gazing on high may have it within the reach of their vision. Its aim is to play again all the full richness

of the artist's emotional organ tones, in so far as is possible, on the cold cerebral xylophone that is criticism's deficient instrument. In the accomplishment of these aims, it is bound by no laws that art is not bound by. There is but one rule: there are no rules. Art laughs at locksmiths.

It has been a favorite diversion of critics since Aristotle's day to argue that drama is drama, whether one reads it from a printed page or sees it enacted in a theatre. Great drama, they announce, is great drama whether it ever be acted or not; "it speaks with the same voice in solitude as in crowds"; and "all the more then" — again I quote Mr. Spingarn — "will the drama itself 'even apart from representation and actors,' as old Aristotle puts it, speak with its highest power to the imagination fitted to understand and receive it." Upon this point of view much of the academic criticism of drama has been based. But may we not well reply that, for all the fact that Shakespeare would still be the greatest dramatist who ever lived had he never been played in the theatre, so, too, would Bach still be the greatest composer who ever lived had his compositions never been played at all? If drama is not meant for actors, may we not also argue that music is not meant for instruments? Are not such expedients less sound criticism than clever evasion of sound criticism: a frolicsome and agreeable straddling of the æsthetic see-saw? There is the printed drama — criticize it. There is the same drama acted — criticize it. Why quibble? Sometimes, as in the case of "Gioconda" and Duse, they are one. Well and good. Sometimes, as in the case of "Chantecler" and Maude Adams, they are not one. Well and good. But where, in either case, the confusion that the critics lay such stress upon? These critics deal not with theories, but with mere words. They take two dozen empty words and adroitly seek therewith to fashion a fecund theory. The result is — words. "Words which," said Ruskin, "if they are not watched, will do deadly work sometimes. There are masked words droning and skulking about us just now ... (there never were so many, owing to the teaching of catechisms and phrases at school instead of human meanings) . . . there never were creatures of prey so mischievous, never diplomatists so cunning, never poisoners so deadly, as these masked words: they are the unjust stewards of men's ideas. . . ."

As they are of men's lack of ideas.

LUDWIG LEWISOHN

Ludwig Lewisohn was born in Berlin of German-Jewish parents in 1882, and came to the United States eight years later. The rest of his boyhood was spent in South Carolina. Graduated from the College of Charleston with a Master's degree in 1901, he continued his university work at Columbia and received a Master's degree there two years later. For some years thereafter he lived in New York, writing magazine articles and working at a novel. His first novel was published in 1908. For a year he taught German at the University of Wisconsin, and from 1911 to 1919 he was on the faculty of Ohio State University. Returning to New York in 1919, he became dramatic critic for *The Nation*, where he remained until 1924. There followed several years' residence abroad, during which he wrote several novels and devoted himself to a study of the Jewish problem. He later returned to the United States.

His book *The Modern Drama*, an extended and unorthodox treatment of the subject, appeared in 1915. In 1922 he reissued several of his dramatic criticisms in the volume *The Drama and the Stage. The Creative Life*, in which only one section is concerned with the drama, was published in 1924. Lewisohn has devoted only a relatively small part of his work to dramatic and theatrical subjects. His critical activities cover a wide field, and his familiarity with European literature and philosophy enabled him to apply standards to the America drama of which few "regular" dramatic critics were aware. He died in 1955.

SPEAKING OF THE THEATER [1]

THE PROFESSOR: I've been reading Granville Barker's "The Exemplary Theater" with a good deal of satisfaction.

THE DRAMATIC CRITIC: I've read it, too. But I don't think it's important.

THE PROFESSOR: If you'll let me be frank I think I can account for your dislike of it. Barker pleads for the theater as fundamentally an educational force and a form of social service.

[1] Reprinted in full from *The Creative Life*. New York, 1924, by permission of the author. Published by Boni & Liveright, Publishers. Copyright, 1924, by Boni & Liveright, Inc.

THE DRAMATIC CRITIC: Exactly.

THE PROFESSOR: I don't at all blame you for disliking terms besmirched by every Philistine and cheap reformer. But one can carry that dislike so far as to discredit the true and fine and necessary things which those words denote.

THE DRAMATIC CRITIC: I don't discredit those things. But I'm sure the theater is not an educational force and if I'm to call it a form of social service it must be according to an interpretation of my own which will please neither Barker nor yourself.

THE PROFESSOR: Then you are content to have the theater considered an amusement?

THE DRAMATIC CRITIC: As you like.

THE PROFESSOR: You are holding an idea in reserve. You are not, after all, so largely preoccupied with something that is only an amusement.

THE DRAMATIC CRITIC: I dislike these fixed terms. They have a way of betraying you to all sorts of people and committing you to all kinds of causes.

THE PROFESSOR: Very well. But there must be some form, if not formula, by which you can communicate your sense of the value which the theater represents.

THE DRAMATIC CRITIC: It is not so simple. When I was young I was interested in art. Then the theater, except at its rare best, didn't interest me at all. Now I'm interested in life and in art primarily as it interprets and shapes life, and so the theater seems to me very important.

THE PROFESSOR: Why, on account of that shift in your interests, precisely the theater?

THE DRAMATIC CRITIC: There are two reasons. The form of the drama is no accidental one. Its struggle, crisis, resolution are of the essence of the life-process itself. It is thus that life proceeds; it is thus that single lives proceed. Therefore the mirror which the drama holds up to nature gives back an image that is closer to the inevitable laws of being than the image of the other arts.

THE PROFESSOR: But that does not apply to the popular theater.

THE DRAMATIC CRITIC: It applies in a negative sense. The popular playwright must, by an implication that is inescapable in his medium, deal with essentials. He deals with them absurdly. It is easy to shatter his structures. But always the dealing is with essentials. Even assent to the moral order of a silly play is a more tonic exercise for the crowd than mere story interest in cheap fiction. Your very shop-girl, moreover, who does not know what criticism is may look into the reviews of a piece that has moved or amused her and be plunged, upon some terms however crude, into a discussion concerning the world and the will and the true character of human action.

THE PROFESSOR: In brief, the theater's function, in your opinion, is to enlighten people.

THE DRAMATIC CRITIC: That is a terrible word. Yes, I think the theater does throw light. But I am not concerned, like your professional enlighteners, with the light. I am concerned with the thing lit. So far as I can see the worst thing in the world is the avoidable moral suffering. It can be mitigated by understanding man and human life as they really are. All art can serve that purpose; the theater can serve it more directly, swiftly, intensely.

THE PROFESSOR: I am amused to find you so much of a moralist after all.

THE DRAMATIC CRITIC: We are all concerned with conduct. It only depends how or with what intention. I don't want to lay down laws. I want people helped to discover those laws of their own being in the light of which they can live without cruelty or tyranny or rancor.

THE PROFESSOR: I think that I follow you. But did you not have a second reason?

THE DRAMATIC CRITIC: I have already stated it. The drama not only deals with the life-process upon its own terms, but does so with unexampled intensity. The theater is the instrument by which that intensity is achieved. No artistic experience, that is, no vicarious and interpretative experience of life, can cleave so deep as a theatric one. In those two hours of overwhelmingly profound absorption in something beyond the *ego,* cruelty may melt into compassion, tyranny into tolerance, blindness into vision.

THE PROFESSOR: Does it happen often?

THE DRAMATIC CRITIC: Does anything desirable or of good report happen often? It does happen; it can happen. Yes, I have heard quite simple people discuss plays and admit naïvely that they gained a clearer idea of life from them and were able to act more tolerantly and less muddily and angrily as a result.

THE PROFESSOR: But isn't that both education and social service?

THE DRAMATIC CRITIC: It has, at all events, nothing to do with either information or uplift. For what it comes to ultimately is this: the drama communicates a sense of the necessarily tragic character of human life, of its necessary and inevitable defeat upon any but spiritual terms, of the fact that its single spiritual victory consists in compassion, in understanding, in abstention from force, from moral fraud, from judgment and the execution of judgment.

THE PROFESSOR: In short, you like the theater because, in the long run, you think it will make your views of life prevail?

THE DRAMATIC CRITIC: I do. And I am yet to see a really grown-up person who likes anything very deeply for any other reason."

JOSEPH WOOD KRUTCH

Joseph Wood Krutch was born in Knoxville, Tenn., in 1893, where he received his early education, graduating from the University of Tennessee in 1915. He then entered Columbia University, where in 1916 he received his Master's degree. After serving in the United States Army in 1919–20, he spent a year in Europe, and in 1923 he received his Doctor's degree at Columbia. In 1924 he joined the editorial board of *The Nation,* and became dramatic critic for the same periodical. He began teaching shortly after his return from Europe, and from 1925 he was a member of the faculty at Columbia, where he became Brander Matthews Professor of Dramatic Literature. In 1953 he retired from both Columbia and *The Nation.*

His first published book on drama was a scholarly volume, *Comedy and Conscience after the Restoration* (1924). His *Edgar Allan Poe: A Study in Genius* (1926), has become a standard work, and his *Five Masters: A Study in the Mutations of the Novel* (1930) is another distinguished critical work. *The Modern Temper* (1929), though not dealing primarily with drama, yields however the chapter *The Tragic Fallacy,* which is reprinted in the present work. Among his other writings on the theatre are a critical and expository volume called *The American Drama Since 1918* (1939), which he calls "an informal history," and *"Modernism" in Modern Drama* (1953), in which he attacks most modern drama but defends O'Neill.

THE TRAGIC FALLACY [1]

[From *The Modern Temper, A Study and a Confession*]

(1929)

Through the legacy of their art the great ages have transmitted to us a dim image of their glorious vitality. When we turn the pages of a Sophoclean or a Shakespearean tragedy we participate

[1] Reprinted in full from *The Modern Temper* (1929), by permission of the author, and the publisher, Harcourt, Brace & Co. Copyright, 1929, by Harcourt, Brace & Co.

faintly in the experience which created it and we sometimes presumptuously say that we "understand" the spirit of these works. But the truth is that we see them, even at best and in the moments when our souls expand most nearly to their dimensions, through a glass darkly.

It is so much easier to appreciate than to create that an age too feeble to reach the heights achieved by the members of a preceding one can still see those heights towering above its impotence, and so it is that, when we perceive a Sophocles or a Shakespeare soaring in an air which we can never hope to breathe, we say that we can "appreciate" them. But what we mean is that we are just able to wonder, and we can never hope to participate in the glorious vision of human life ·out of which they were created — not even to the extent of those humbler persons for whom they were written; for while to us the triumphant voices come from far away and tell of a heroic world which no longer exists, to them they spoke of immediate realities and revealed the inner meaning of events amidst which they still lived.

When the life has entirely gone out of a work of art come down to us from the past, when we read it without any emotional comprehension whatsoever and can no longer even imagine why the people for whom it was intended found t absorbing and satisfying, then, of course, it has ceased to be a work of art at all and has dwindled into one of those deceptive "documents" from which we get a false sense of comprehending through the intellect things which cannot be comprehended at all except by means of a kinship of feeling. And though all works from a past age have begun in this way to fade there are some, like the great Greek or Elizabethan tragedies, which are still halfway between the work of art and the document. They no longer can have for us the immediacy which they had for those to whom they originally belonged, but they have not yet eluded us entirely. We no longer live in the world which they represent, but we can half imagine it and we can measure the distance which we have moved away. We write no tragedies today, but we can still talk about the tragic spirit of which we would, perhaps, have no conception were it not for the works in question.

An age which could really "appreciate" Shakespeare or Sophocles would have something comparable to put beside them — something like them, not necessarily in form, or spirit, but at least in magnitude — some vision of life which would be, however different, equally am-

ple and passionate. But when we move to put a modern masterpiece beside them, when we seek to compare them with, let us say, a *Ghosts* or a *Weavers,* we shrink as from the impulse to commit some folly and we feel as though we were about to superimpose Bowling Green upon the Great Prairies in order to ascertain which is the larger. The question, we see, is not primarily one of art but of the two worlds which two minds inhabited. No increased powers of expression, no greater gift for words, could have transformed Ibsen into Shakespeare. The materials out of which the latter created his works — his conception of human dignity, his sense of the importance of human passions, his vision of the amplitude of human life — simply did not and could not exist for Ibsen, as they did not and could not exist for his contemporaries. God and Man and Nature had all somehow dwindled in the course of the intervening centuries, not because the realistic creed of modern art led us to seek out mean people, but because this meanness of human life was somehow thrust upon us by the operation of that same process which led to the development of realistic theories of art by which our vision could be justified.

Hence, though we still apply, sometimes, the adjective "tragic" to one or another of those modern works of literature which describe human misery and which end more sadly even than they begin, the term is a misnomer since it is obvious that the works in question have nothing in common with the classical examples of the genre and produce in the reader a sense of depression which is the exact opposite of that elation generated when the spirit of a Shakespeare rises joyously superior to the outward calamities which he recounts and celebrates the greatness of the human spirit whose travail he describes. Tragedies, in that only sense of the word which has any distinctive meaning, are no longer written in either the dramatic or any other form and the fact is not to be accounted for in any merely literary terms. It is not the result of any fashion in literature or of any deliberation to write about human nature or character under different aspects, any more than it is of either any greater sensitiveness of feeling which would make us shrink from the contemplation of the suffering of Medea or Othello or of any greater optimism which would make us more likely to see life in more cheerful terms. It is, on the contrary, the result of one of those enfeeblements of the human spirit not unlike that described in the previous chapter of this essay, and a further illustration of that gradual weakening of man's confidence in his ability to impose upon the phenomenon of life an interpretation acceptable to his desires which is the subject of the whole of the present discussion.

To explain that fact and to make clear how the creation of classical tragedy did consist in the successful effort to impose such a satisfactory interpretation will require, perhaps, the special section which follows, although the truth of the fact that it does impose such an interpretation must be evident to any one who has ever risen from the reading of *Oedipus* or *Lear* with that feeling of exultation which comes when we have been able, by rare good fortune, to enter into its spirit as completely as it is possible for us of a remoter and emotionally enfeebled age to enter it. Meanwhile one anticipatory remark may be ventured. If the plays and the novels of today deal with littler people and less mighty emotions it is not because we have become interested in commonplace souls and their unglamorous adventures but because we have come, willy-nilly, to see the soul of man as commonplace and its emotions as mean.

II

Tragedy, said Aristotle, is the "imitation of noble actions," and though it is some twenty-five hundred years since the dictum was uttered there is only one respect in which we are inclined to modify it. To us "imitation" seems a rather naïve word to apply to that process by which observation is turned into art, and we seek one which would define or at least imply the nature of that interposition of the personality of the artist between the object and the beholder which constitutes his function and by means of which he transmits a modified version,

rather than a mere imitation, of the thing which he has contemplated.

In the search for this word the estheticians of romanticism invented the term "expression" to describe the artistic purpose to which apparent imitation was subservient. Psychologists, on the other hand, feeling that the artistic process was primarily one by which reality is modified in such a way as to render it more acceptable to the desires of the artist, employed various terms in the effort to describe that distortion which the wish may produce in vision. And though many of the newer critics reject both romanticism and psychology, even they insist upon the fundamental fact that in art we are concerned, not with mere imitation, but with the imposition of some form upon the material which it would not have if it were merely copied as a camera copies.

Tragedy is not, then, as Aristotle said, the *imitation* of noble actions, for, indeed, no one knows what a *noble* action is or whether or not such a thing as nobility exists in nature apart from the mind of man. Certainly the action of Achilles in dragging the dead body of Hector around the walls of Troy and under the eyes of Andromache, who had begged to be allowed to give it decent burial, is not to us a noble action, though it was such to Homer, who made it the subject of an able passage in a noble poem. Certainly, too, the same action might conceivably be made the subject of a tragedy and the subject of a farce, depending upon the way in which it was treated; so that to say that tragedy is the *imitation* of a *noble* action is to be guilty of assuming, first, that art and photography are the same, and, second, that there may be something inherently noble in an act as distinguished from the motives which prompted it or from the point of view from which it is regarded.

And yet, nevertheless, the idea of nobility is inseparable from the idea of tragedy, which cannot exist without it. If tragedy is not the imitation or even the modified representation of noble actions it is certainly a representation of actions *considered* as noble, and herein lies its essential nature, since no man can conceive it unless he is capable of believing in the greatness and importance of man. Its action is usually, if not always, calamitous, because it is only in calamity that the human spirit has the opportunity to reveal itself triumphant over the outward universe which fails to conquer it; but this calamity in tragedy is only a means to an end and the essential thing which distinguishes real tragedy from those distressing modern works sometimes called by its name is the fact that it is in the former alone that the artist has found himself capable of considering and of making us consider that his people and his actions have that amplitude and importance which make them noble. Tragedy arises then when, as in Periclean Greece or Elizabethan England, a people fully aware of the calamities of life is nevertheless serenely confident of the greatness of man, whose mighty passions and supreme fortitude are revealed when one of these calamities overtakes him.

To those who mistakenly think of it as something gloomy or depressing, who are incapable of recognizing the elation which its celebration of human greatness inspires, and who, therefore, confuse it with things merely miserable or pathetic, it must be a paradox that the happiest, most vigorous, and most confident ages which the world has ever known — the Periclean and the Elizabethan — should be exactly those which created and which most relished the mightiest tragedies; but the paradox is, of course, resolved by the fact that tragedy is essentially an expression, not of despair, but of the triumph over despair and of confidence in the value of human life. If Shakespeare himself ever had that " dark period " which his critics and biographers have imagined for him, it was at least no darkness like that bleak and arid despair which sometimes settles over modern spirits. In the midst of it he created both the elemental grandeur of Othello and the pensive majesty of Hamlet and, holding them up to his contemporaries, he said in the words of his own Miranda, "Oh, rare new world that hath *such* creatures in it."

All works of art which deserve their name have a happy end. This is indeed the thing which constitutes them art and through which they perform their function. Whatever the character of the events, fortunate or unfortunate, which they recount, they so mold or arrange or interpret them that we accept gladly the conclusion which they reach and would not have it otherwise. They may conduct us into the realm of pure fancy where wish and fact are identical and the world is remade exactly after the fashion of the heart's desire or they may yield some greater or less allegiance to fact; but they must always reconcile us in one way or another to the representation which they make and the distinctions between the genres are simply the distinctions between the means by which this reconciliation is effected.

Comedy laughs the minor mishaps of its characters away; drama solves all the difficulties which it allows to arise; and melodrama, separating good from evil by simple lines, distributes its rewards and punishments in accordance with the principles of a naïve justice which satisfies the simple souls of its audience, which are neither philosophical enough to question its primitive ethics nor critical enough to object to the way in which its neat events violate the laws of probability. Tragedy, the greatest and the most difficult of the arts, can adopt none of these methods; and yet it must reach its own happy end in its own way. Though its conclusion must be, by its premise, outwardly calamitous, though it must speak to those who know that the good man is cut off and that the fairest things are the first to perish, yet it must leave them, as *Othello* does, content that this is so. We must be and we are glad that Juliet dies and glad that Lear is turned out into the storm.

Milton set out, he said, to justify the ways of God to man, and his phrase, if it be interpreted broadly enough, may be taken as describing the function of all art, which must, in some way or other, make the life which it seems to represent satisfactory to those who see its reflection in the magic mirror, and it must gratify or at least reconcile the desires of the beholder, not necessarily, as the naïver exponents of Freudian psychology maintain, by gratifying individual and often eccentric wishes, but at least by satisfying the universally human desire to find in the world some justice, some meaning, or, at the very least, some recognizable order. Hence it is that every real tragedy, however tremendous it may be, is an affirmation of faith in life, a declaration that even if God is not in his Heaven, then at least Man is in his world.

We accept gladly the outward defeats which it describes for the sake of the inward victories which it reveals. Juliet died, but not before she had shown how great and resplendent a thing love could be; Othello plunged the dagger into his own breast, but not before he had revealed that greatness of soul which makes his death seem unimportant. Had he died in the instant when he struck the blow, had he perished still believing that the world was as completely black as he saw it before the innocence of Desdemona was revealed to him, then, for him at least, the world would have been merely damnable, but Shakespeare kept him alive long enough to allow him to learn his error and hence to die, not in despair, but in the full acceptance of the tragic reconciliation to life. Perhaps it would be pleasanter if men could believe what the child is taught — that the good are happy and that things turn out as they should — but it is far more important to be able to believe, as Shakespeare did, that however much things in the outward world may go awry, man has, nevertheless, splendors of his own and that, in a word, Love and Honor and Glory are not words but realities.

Thus for the great ages tragedy is not an expression of despair but the means by which they saved themselves from it. It is a profession of faith, and a sort of religion; a way of looking at life by virtue of which it is robbed of its pain. The sturdy soul of the tragic author seizes upon suffering and uses it only as a means by which joy may be wrung out of existence, but it is not to be forgotten that he is enabled to do so only because of his belief in the greatness of human nature and because, though he has lost the child's faith in life, he has not lost his far more important faith in human nature. A tragic writer does not have to believe in God, but he must believe in man.

And if, then, the Tragic Spirit is in reality the product of a religious faith in which, sometimes at least, faith in the greatness of God is replaced by faith in the greatness of man, it serves, of course, to perform the function of religion, to make life tolerable for those who participate in its beneficent illusion. It purges the souls of those who might otherwise despair and it makes endurable the realization that the events of the outward world do not correspond with the desires of the heart, and thus, in its own particular way, it does what all religions do, for it gives a rationality, a meaning, and a justification to the universe. But if it has the strength it has also the weakness of all faiths, since it may — nay, it must — be ultimately lost as reality, encroaching further and further into the realm of imagination, leaves less and less room in which that imagination can build its refuge.

III

It is, indeed, only at a certain stage in the development of the realistic intelligence of a people that the tragic faith can exist. A naïver people may have, as the ancient men of the north had, a body of legends which are essentially tragic, or it may have only (and need only) its happy and childlike mythology which arrives inevitably at its happy end, where the only ones who suffer "deserve" to do so and in which, therefore, life is represented as directly and easily acceptable. A too sophisticated society on the other hand — one which, like ours, has outgrown not merely the simple optimism of the child but also that vigorous, one might almost say adolescent, faith in the nobility of man which marks a Sophocles or a Shakespeare, has neither fairy tales to assure it that all is always right in the end nor tragedies to make it believe that it rises superior in soul to the outward calamities which befall it.

Distrusting its thought, despising its passions, realizing its impotent unimportance in the universe, it can tell itself no stories except those which make it still more acutely aware of its trivial miseries. When its heroes (sad misnomer for the pitiful creatures who people contemporary fiction) are struck down it is not, like Oedipus, by the gods that they are struck but only, like Oswald Alving, by syphilis, for they know that the gods, even if they existed, would not trouble with them, and they cannot attribute to themselves in art an importance in which they do not believe. Their so-called tragedies do not and cannot end with one of those splendid calamities which in Shakespeare seem to reverberate through the universe, because they cannot believe that the universe trembles when their love is, like Romeo's, cut off or when the place where they (small as they are) have gathered up their trivial treasure is, like Othello's sanctuary, defiled. Instead, mean misery piles on mean misery, petty misfortune follows petty misfortune, and despair becomes intolerable because it is no longer even significant or important.

Ibsen once made one of his characters say that he did not read much because he found reading "irrelevant," and the adjective was brilliantly chosen because it held implications even beyond those of which Ibsen was consciously aware. What is it that made the classics irrelevant to him and to us? Is it not just exactly those to him impossible premises which make tragedy what it is, those assumptions that the soul of man is great, that the universe (together with whatever gods may be) concerns itself with him and that he is, in a word, noble? Ibsen turned to village politics for exactly the same reason that his contemporaries and his successors have, each in his own way, sought out some aspect of the common man and his common life — because, that is to say, here was at least something small enough for him to be able to believe.

Bearing this fact in mind, let us compare a modern "tragedy" with one of the great works of a happy age, not in order to judge of their relative technical merits but in order to determine to what extent the former deserves its name by achieving a tragic solution capable of purging the soul or of reconciling the emotions to the life which it pictures. And in order to make the comparison as fruitful as possible let us choose *Hamlet* on the one hand and on the other a play like *Ghosts* which was not only written by perhaps the most powerful as well as the most typical of modern writers but which is, in addition, the one of his works which seems most nearly to escape

that triviality which cannot be entirely escaped by any one who feels, as all contemporary minds do, that man is relatively trivial.

In *Hamlet* a prince ("in understanding, how like a god!") has thrust upon him from the unseen world a duty to redress a wrong which concerns not merely him, his mother, and his uncle, but the moral order of the universe. Erasing all trivial fond records from his mind, abandoning at once both his studies and his romance because it has been his good fortune to be called upon to take part in an action of cosmic importance, he plunges (at first) not into action but into thought, weighing the claims which are made upon him and contemplating the grandiose complexities of the universe. And when the time comes at last for him to die he dies, not as a failure, but as a success. Not only has the universe regained the balance which had been upset by what *seemed* the monstrous crime of the guilty pair ("there is nothing either good nor ill but thinking makes it so"), but in the process by which that readjustment is made a mighty mind has been given the opportunity, first to contemplate the magnificent scheme of which it is a part, and then to demonstrate the greatness of its spirit by playing a rôle in the grand style which it called for. We do not need to despair in *such* a world if it has *such* creatures in it.

Turn now to *Ghosts* — look upon this picture and upon that. A young man has inherited syphilis from his father. Struck by a to him mysterious malady he returns to his northern village, learns the hopeless truth about himself, and persuades his mother to poison him. The incidents prove, perhaps, that pastors should not endeavor to keep a husband and wife together unless they know what they are doing. But what a world is this in which a great writer can deduce nothing more than that from his greatest work and how are we to be purged or reconciled when we see it acted? Not only is the failure utter, but it is trivial and meaningless as well.

Yet the journey from Elsinore to Skien is precisely the journey which the human spirit has made, exchanging in the process princes for invalids and gods for disease. We say, as Ibsen would say, that the problems of Oswald Alving are more " relevant " to our life than the problems of Hamlet, that the play in which he appears is more " real " than the other more glamorous one, but it is exactly because we find it so that we are condemned. We can believe in Oswald but we cannot believe in Hamlet, and a light has gone out in the universe. Shakespeare justifies the ways of God to man, but in Ibsen there is no such happy end and with him tragedy, so called, has become merely an expression of our despair at finding that such justification is no longer possible.

Modern critics have sometimes been puzzled to account for the fact that the concern of ancient tragedy is almost exclusively with kings and courts. They have been tempted to accuse even Aristotle of a certain naïveté in assuming (as he seems to assume) that the " nobility " of which he speaks as necessary to a tragedy implies a nobility of rank as well as of soul, and they have sometimes regretted that Shakespeare did not devote himself more than he did to the serious consideration of those common woes of the common man which subsequent writers have exploited with increasing pertinacity. Yet the tendency to lay the scene of a tragedy at the court of a king is not the result of any arbitrary convention but of the fact that the tragic writers believed easily in greatness just as we believe easily in meanness. To Shakespeare, robes and crowns and jewels are the garments most appropriate to man because they are the fitting outward manifestation of his inward majesty, but to us they seem absurd because the man who bears them has, in our estimation, so pitifully shrunk. We do not write about kings because we do not believe that any man is worthy to be one and we do not write about courts because hovels seem to us to be dwellings more appropriate to the creatures who inhabit them. Any modern attempt to dress characters in robes ends only by making us aware of a comic incongruity and any modern attempt to furnish them with a language resplendent like Shakespeare's ends only in bombast.

True tragedy capable of performing its function and of purging the soul by reconciling man to his woes can exist only by virtue of a certain pathetic fallacy far more inclusive than that to which the name is commonly given. The romantics, feeble descendants of the tragic writers to whom they are linked by their effort to see life and nature in grandiose terms, loved to imagine that the sea or the sky had a way of according itself with their moods, of storming when they stormed and smiling when they smiled. But the tragic spirit sustains itself by an assumption much more far-reaching and no more justified. Man as it sees him lives in a world which he may not dominate but which is always aware of him. Occupying the exact center of a universe which would have no meaning except for him and being so little below the angels that, if he believes in God, he has no hesitation in imagining Him formed as he is formed and crowned with a crown like that which he or one of his fellows wears, he assumes that each of his acts reverberates through the universe. His passions are important to him because he believes them important throughout all time and all space; the very fact that he can sin (no modern can) means that this universe is watching his acts; and though he may perish, a God leans out from infinity to strike him down. And it is exactly because an Ibsen cannot think of man in any such terms as these that his persons have so shrunk and that his " tragedy " has lost that power which real tragedy always has of making that infinitely ambitious creature called man content to accept his misery if only he can be made to feel great enough and important enough. An Oswald is not a Hamlet chiefly because he has lost that tie with the natural and supernatural world which the latter had. No ghost will leave the other world to warn or encourage him, there is no virtue and no vice which he can possibly have which can be really important, and when he dies neither his death nor the manner of it will be, outside the circle of two or three people as unnecessary as himself, any more important than that of a rat behind the arras.

Perhaps we may dub the illusion upon which the tragic spirit is nourished the Tragic, as opposed to the Pathetic, Fallacy, but fallacy though it is, upon its existence depends not merely the writing of tragedy but the existence of that religious feeling of which tragedy is an expression and by means of which a people aware of the dissonances of life manages nevertheless to hear them as harmony. Without it neither man nor his passions can seem great enough or important enough to justify the sufferings which they entail, and literature, expressing the mood of a people, begins to despair where once it had exulted. Like the belief in love and like most of the other mighty illusions by means of which human life has been given a value, the Tragic Fallacy depends ultimately upon the assumption which man so readily makes that something outside his own being, some "spirit not himself" — be it God, Nature, or that still vaguer thing called a Moral Order — joins him in the emphasis which he places upon this or that and confirms him in his feeling that his passions and his opinions are important. When his instinctive faith in that correspondence between the outer and the inner world fades, his grasp upon the faith that sustained him fades also, and Love or Tragedy or what not ceases to be the reality which it was because he is never strong enough in his own insignificant self to stand alone in a universe which snubs him with its indifference.

In both the modern and the ancient worlds tragedy was dead long before writers were aware of the fact. Seneca wrote his frigid melodramas under the impression that he was following in the footsteps of Sophocles, and Dryden probably thought that his *All for Love* was an improvement upon Shakespeare, but in time we awoke to the fact that no amount of rhetorical bombast could conceal the fact that grandeur was not to be counterfeited when the belief in its possibility was dead, and turning from the hero to the common man, we inaugurated the era of realism. For us no choice remains except that between mere rhetoric and the frank consideration of our fellow men. who may be the highest of the anthropoids but who are certainly too far below the angels to imagine either that these angels can concern themselves with them or that they can catch any glimpse of even the soles of angelic feet. We can

no longer tell tales of the fall of noble men because we do not believe that noble men exist. The best that we can achieve is pathos and the most that we can do is to feel sorry for ourselves. Man has put off his royal robes and it is only in sceptered pomp that tragedy can come sweeping by.

IV

Nietzsche was the last of the great philosophers to attempt a tragic justification of life. His central and famous dogma — "Life is good *because* it is painful" — sums up in a few words the desperate and almost meaningless paradox to which he was driven in his effort to reduce to rational terms the far more imaginative conception which is everywhere present but everywhere unanalyzed in a Sophocles or a Shakespeare and by means of which they rise triumphant over the manifold miseries of life. But the very fact that Nietzsche could not even attempt to state in any except intellectual terms an attitude which is primarily unintellectual and to which, indeed, intellectual analysis is inevitably fatal, is proof of the distance which he had been carried (by the rationalizing tendencies of the human mind) from the possibility of the tragic solution which he sought; and the confused, half-insane violence of his work will reveal, by the contrast which it affords with the serenity of the tragic writers whom he admired, how great was his failure.

Fundamentally this failure was, moreover, conditioned by exactly the same thing which has conditioned the failure of all modern attempts to achieve what he attempted — by the fact, that is to say, that tragedy must have a hero if it is not to be merely an accusation against, instead of a justification of, the world in which it occurs. Tragedy is, as Aristotle said, an imitation of noble actions, and Nietzsche, for all his enthusiasm for the Greek tragic writers, was palsied by the universally modern incapacity to conceive man as noble. Out of this dilemma, out of his need to find a hero who could give to life as he saw it the only possible justification, was born the idea of the Superman, but the Superman is, after all, only a hypothetical being, destined to become what man actually was in the eyes of the great tragic writers — a creature (as Hamlet said) "how infinite in capacities, in understanding how like a god." Thus Nietzsche lived half in the past through his literary enthusiasms and half in the future through his grandiose dreams, but for all his professed determination to justify existence he was no more able than the rest of us to find the present acceptable. Life, he said in effect, is not a Tragedy now but perhaps it will be when the Ape-man has been transformed into a hero (the *Übermensch*), and trying to find that sufficient, he went mad.

He failed, as all moderns must fail when they attempt, like him, to embrace the tragic spirit as a religious faith, because the resurgence of that faith is not an intellectual but a vital phenomenon, something not achieved by taking thought but born, on the contrary, out of an instinctive confidence in life which is nearer to the animal's unquestioning allegiance to the scheme of nature than it is to that critical intelligence characteristic of a fully developed humanism. And like other faiths it is not to be recaptured merely by reaching an intellectual conviction that it would be desirable to do so.

Modern psychology has discovered (or at least strongly emphasized) the fact that under certain conditions desire produces belief, and having discovered also that the more primitive a given mentality the more completely are its opinions determined by its wishes, modern psychology has concluded that the best mind is that which most resists the tendency to believe a thing simply because it would be pleasant or advantageous to do so. But justified as this conclusion may be from the intellectual point of view, it fails to take into account the fact that in a universe as badly adapted as this one to human as distinguished from animal needs this ability to will a belief may bestow an enormous vital advantage as it did, for instance, in the case at present under discussion where it made possible for Shakespeare the compensations of a tragic faith completely inaccessible to Nietzsche. Pure intelligence, incapable of being influenced by desire and therefore also incapable of choosing one opinion rather than another simply because

the one chosen is the more fruitful or beneficent, is doubtless a relatively perfect instrument for the pursuit of truth, but the question (likely, it would seem, to be answered in the negative) is simply whether or not the spirit of man can endure the literal and inhuman truth.

Certain ages and simple people have conceived of the action which passes upon the stage of the universe as of something in the nature of a Divine Comedy, as something, that is to say, which will reach its end with the words "and they lived happily ever after." Others, less naïve and therefore more aware of those maladjustments whose reality, at least so far as outward events are concerned, they could not escape, have imposed upon it another artistic form and called it a Divine Tragedy, accepting its catastrophe as we accept the catastrophe of an *Othello,* because of its grandeur. But a Tragedy, Divine or otherwise, must, it may again be repeated, have a hero, and from the universe as we see it both the Glory of God and the Glory of Man have departed. Our cosmos may be farcical or it may be pathetic but it has not the dignity of tragedy and we cannot accept it as such.

Yet our need for the consolations of tragedy has not passed with the passing of our ability to conceive it. Indeed, the dissonances which it was tragedy's function to resolve grow more insistent instead of diminishing. Our passions, our disappointments, and our sufferings remain important to us though important to nothing else and they thrust themselves upon us with an urgency which makes it impossible for us to dismiss them as the mere trivialities which, so our intellects tell us, they are. And yet, in the absence of tragic faith or the possibility of achieving it, we have no way in which we may succeed in giving them the dignity which would not only render them tolerable but transform them as they were transformed by the great ages into joys. The death of tragedy is, like the death of love, one of those emotional fatalities as the result of which the human as distinguished from the natural world grows more and more a desert.

Poetry, said Santayana in his famous phrase, is "religion which is no longer believed," but it depends, nevertheless, upon its power to revive in us a sort of temporary or provisional credence and the nearer it can come to producing an illusion of belief the greater is its power as poetry. Once the Tragic Spirit was a living faith and out of it tragedies were written. Today these great expressions of a great faith have declined, not merely into poetry, but into a kind of poetry whose premises are so far from any we can really accept that we can only partially and dimly grasp its meaning.

We read but we do not write tragedies. The tragic solution of the problem of existence, the reconciliation to life by means of the tragic spirit is, that is to say, now only a fiction surviving in art. When that art itself has become, as it probably will, completely meaningless, when we have ceased not only to write but to *read* tragic works, then it will be lost and in all real senses forgotten, since the devolution from Religion to Art to Document will be complete.

EUGENE O'NEILL

Eugene O'Neill was born in New York City in 1888, a son of the popular romantic actor James O'Neill. His early education was fragmentary, but he managed to get one year of college — Princeton. In 1909 he began a series of trips abroad in search of adventure; fell ill, tried office work again, and again set forth to see the world. There followed work on shipboard, in offices, periods without a job, brief spells of acting and managing with traveling theater companies, and finally a job as newspaper man in Connecticut. This was followed by ill-health, retirement to a sanitarium, and an effort at playwriting. In 1914–15 he studied under Professor Baker at Harvard, and in 1916 he first became connected with the Provincetown Players whose New York Theater gave him a chance to see his work competently acted on a stage. For the next few years he was closely associated with the Players, but in 1920 his *Beyond the Horizon* (first full-length play to receive regular Broadway production) achieved considerable popular success. From 1920 onward, O'Neill spent practically all his time writing, even during the twelve-year period (1934–46) when he would allow no new play of his to be produced. O'Neill's few published interviews yield very little of his ideas on dramatic technique, and the occasional brief pronouncements on his art are very little concerned with technical problems. His personal letters, on the other hand, few of which have been printed, abound in long and detailed discussions of esthetic

and practical matters. Excerpts from some letters may be consulted in Arthur Hobson Quinn's *A History of the American Drama From the Civil War to the Present Day* (1936); Isaac Goldberg's *The Theater of George Jean Nathan* (1926); several volumes of George Jean Nathan's collected writings; and Barrett H. Clark's *Eugene O'Neill, the Man and His Plays* (rev. ed., 1947). Among the short notes by O'Neill touching on drama or theater may be mentioned *Strindberg and Our Theater* (Provincetown Playbill, season 1923–24); a *Letter to the New York Times* (April 11, 1920); *Are the Actors to Blame?* (Provincetown Playbill, Season 1925–26); *Eugene O'Neill Writes About His Latest Play* [*The Great God Brown*] (New York *Evening Post*, Feb. 13, 1926); *O'Neill Talks About "Beyond the Horizon"* (New York *Evening Post*, Nov. 27, 1926); *O'Neill's Own Story of "Electra" in the Making* (New York *Herald Tribune*, Nov. 3, 1931). These statements and others by O'Neill are collected in *O'Neill and His Plays*, edited by Oscar Cargill, N. Bryllion Fagin, and William J. Fisher (1961).

The Iceman Cometh (1946), an exploration in detail of the need for illusion, was the last O'Neill play performed on Broadway in his lifetime. Illness compelled him to retire into seclusion, and he died in 1953. Several plays have been produced posthumously, including *Long Day's Journey into Night,* in which he returned to the style of his early realism; it is regarded by many as his best play.

(For a detailed list of O'Neill's plays and other publications, see *A Bibliography of the Works of Eugene O'Neill,* by Ralph Sanborn and Barrett H. Clark, 1931, and the bibliographical appendices included in the above-mentioned volume, *O'Neill and His Plays.*)

O'NEILL TALKS ABOUT HIS PLAYS [1]

(1924)

I am no longer interested in the one-act play. It is an unsatisfactory form—cannot go far enough. The one-act play, however, is a fine vehicle for something poetical, for something spiritual in feeling that cannot be carried through a long play. In the case of my cycle at the Provincetown Theatre the individual plays are complete in themselves, yet the identity of the crew goes through the series and welds the four one-acts into a long play. I do not claim any originality though for this idea, as Schnitzler has already done the same thing in *Anatol.* And doubtless others.

Many of the characters in my plays were suggested to me by people in real life, especially the sea characters. In special pleading I do not believe. Gorky's *A Night's Lodging,* the great proletarian revolutionary play, is really more wonderful propaganda for the submerged than any other play ever written, simply because it contains no propaganda, but simply shows humanity as it is—truth in terms of human life. As soon as an author slips propaganda into a play everyone feels it and the play becomes simply an argument.

The Hairy Ape was propaganda in the sense that it was a symbol of man, who has lost his old harmony with nature, the harmony which he used to have as an animal and has not yet acquired in a spiritual way. Thus, not being able to find it on earth nor in heaven, he's in the middle, trying to make peace, taking the "woist punches from bot' of 'em." This idea was expressed in Yank's speech. The public saw just the stoker, not the symbol, and the symbol makes the play either important or just another play. Yank can't go forward, and so he tries

to go back. This is what his shaking hands with the gorilla meant. But he can't go back to "belonging" either. The gorilla kills him. The subject here is the same ancient one that always was and always will be the one subject for drama, and that is man and his struggle with his own fate. The struggle used to be with the gods, but is now with himself, his own past, his attempt "to belong."

The most perfect plotless plays are those of Chekhov. But the newest thing now in playwriting is the opposite of the character play. It is the expressionistic play. For expressionism denies the value of characterization. As I understand it, expressionism tries to minimize everything on the stage that stands between the author and the audience. It strives to get the author talking directly to the audience. Their theory, as far as I can make it out, is that the character gets interested in the kind of man he is and what he does instead of the idea. But plenty of people will probably damn me for saying this, because everyone has a different idea of expressionism and mine is just what I have acquired through reading about it.

I personally do not believe that an idea can be readily put over to an audience except through characters. When it sees "A Man" and "A Woman"—just abstractions, it loses the human contact by which it identifies itself with the protagonist of the play. An example of this sort of expression is *Morn Till Midnight,* with character abstractions like "A Bank Clerk." This is the point at which I disagree with the theory. I do not believe that the character gets between the author's idea and the audience. The real contribution of the expressionist has been in the dynamic qualities of his plays. They express something in modern life better than did the old plays. I have something of this method in *The Hairy*

[1] From an interview in the New York *Herald Tribune,* November 16, 1924. Used by permission of the New York *Herald Tribune.* —Ed.

Ape. But the character Yank remains a man and everyone recognizes him as such.

I believe that *What Price Glory?* is one of the most significant events in the history of our theatre. It is a splendid thing that the first fine, true war play should come from the most reactionary country in the world. It is still more wonderful and encouraging to all who love the theatre that there should be such a great public for it, because even two years ago it would have been possible only at special matinees or for invited audiences.

I hardly ever go to the theatre, although I read all the plays I can get. I don't go to the theatre because I can always do a better production in my mind than the one on the stage. I have a better time and I am not bothered by the audience. No one sneezes during the scenes that interest me. Nor do I ever go to see one of my own plays—have seen only three of them since they started coming out. My real reason for this is that I was practically brought up in the theatre—in the wings—and I know all the technique of acting. I know everything that everyone is doing from the electrician to the stage hands. So I see the machinery going around all the time unless the play is wonderfully acted and produced. Then, too, in my own plays all the time I watch them I am acting all the parts and living them so intensely that by the time the performance is over I am exhausted—as if I had gone through a clothes wringer.

MEMORANDA ON MASKS [2]

(1932)

Not masks for all plays, naturally. Obviously not for plays conceived in purely realistic terms. But masks for certain types of plays, especially for the new modern play, as yet only dimly foreshadowed in a few groping specimens, but which must inevitably be written in the future. For I hold more and more surely to the conviction that the use of masks will be discovered eventually to be the freest solution of the modern dramatist's problem as to how—with the greatest possible dramatic clarity and economy of means—he can express those profound hidden conflicts of the mind which the probings of psychology continue to disclose to us. He must find some method to present this inner drama in his work, or confess himself incapable of portraying one of the most characteristic preoccupations and uniquely significant, spiritual impulses of his time. With his old—and more than a bit senile! —standby of realistic technique, he can do no more than, at best, obscurely hint at it through a realistically disguised surface symbolism, superficial and misleading. But that, while sufficiently beguiling to the sentimentally mystical, is hardly enough. A comprehensive expression is demanded here, a chance for eloquent presentation, a new form of drama projected from a fresh insight into the inner forces motivating the actions and reactions of men and women (a new and truer characterization, in other words), a drama of souls, and the adventures of "Free wills," with the masks that govern them and constitute their fates.

For what, at bottom, is the new psychological insight into human cause and effect but a study in masks, an exercise in unmasking? Whether we think the attempted unmasking has been successful, or has only created for itself new masks, is of no importance here. What is valid, what is unquestionable, is that this insight has uncovered the mask, has impressed the idea of mask as a symbol of inner reality upon all intelligent people of today; and I know they would welcome the use of masks in the theatre as a necessary, dramatically revealing new convention, and not regard them as any "stunty" resurrection of archaic props.

This was strikingly demonstrated for me in practical experience by *The Great God Brown*, which ran in New York for

2 From *The American Spectator,* November 1932. Used by permission of Mrs. Eugene O'Neill.—Ed.

eight months, nearly all of that time in Broadway theatres—a play in which the use of masks was an integral part of the theme. There was some misunderstanding, of course. But so is there always misunderstanding in the thing beyond what is contained in a human-interest newspaper story. In the main, however, *The Great God Brown* was accepted and appreciated by both critics and public— a fairly extensive public, as its run gives evidence.

I emphasize this play's success because the fact that a mask drama, the main values of which are psychological, mystical, and abstract, could be played in New York for eight months, has always seemed to me a more significant proof of the deeply responsive possibilities in our public than anything that has happened in our modern theatre before or since.

2. Looked at from even the most practical standpoint of the practicing playwright, the mask *is* dramatic in itself, *has always* been dramatic in itself, *is a* proven weapon of attack. At its best, it is more subtly, imaginatively, suggestively dramatic than any actor's face can ever be. Let anyone who doubts this study the Japanese Noh masks, or Chinese theatre masks, or African primitive masks—or right here in America the faces of the big marionettes Robert Edmond Jones made for the production of Stravinsky's *Oedipus*, or Benda's famous masks, or even photographs of them.

3. *Dogma for the new masked drama.* One's outer life passes in a solititude haunted by the masks of others; one's inner life passes in a solitude hounded by the masks of oneself.

4. With masked mob a new type of play may be written in which the Mob as King, Hero, Villain, or Fool will be the main character—The Great Democratic Play!

5. Why not give all future Classical revivals entirely in masks? *Hamlet,* for example. Masks would liberate this play from its present confining status as exclusively a "star vehicle." We would be able to see the great drama we are now only privileged to read, to identify ourselves with the figure of Hamlet as a symbolic projection of a fate that is in each of us, instead of merely watching a star giving us his version of a great acting role. We would even be able to hear the sublime poetry as the innate expression of the spirit of the drama itself, instead of listening to it as realistic recitation—or ranting—by familiar actors.

6. Consider Goethe's *Faust,* which, psychologically speaking, should be the closest to us of all the Classics. In producing this play, I would have Mephistopheles wearing the Mephisthophelean mask of the face of Faust. For is not the whole of Goethe's truth *for our time* just that Mephistopheles and Faust are one and the same—*are* Faust?

NEGLECTED POET [3]

It's not in me to pose much as a "misunderstood one," but it does seem discouragingly (that is, if one lacked a sense of ironic humor!) evident to me that most of my critics don't want to see what I'm trying to do or how I'm trying to do it, although I flatter myself that end and means are characteristic, individual and positive enough not to be mistaken for anyone's else, or for those of any "modern" or "pre-modern" school. To be called a "sordid realist" one day,

3 From a letter to Arthur Hobson Quinn, published in Quinn's *A History of the American Drama* (New York, 1945). Used by permission of Mrs. Eugene O'Neill.—Ed.

a "grim, pessimistic Naturalist" the next, a "lying Moral Romanticist" the next, etc. is quite perplexing—not to add the *Times* editorial that settled *Desire* once and for all by calling it a "Neo-Primitive," a Matisse of the drama, as it were! So I'm really longing to explain and try and convince some sympathetic ear that I've tried to make myself a melting pot for all these methods, seeing some virtues for my ends in each of them, and thereby, if there is enough real fire in me, boil down to my own technique. But where I feel myself most neglected is just where I set most store by myself— as a bit of a poet, who has labored with the spoken word to evolve original rhythms of beauty, where beauty apparently isn't—*Jones, Ape, God's Chillun, Desire,* etc.—and to see the transfiguring nobility of tragedy, in as near the Greek sense as one can grasp it, in seemingly the most ignoble, debased lives. And just here is where I am a most confirmed mystic, too, for I'm always, always trying to interpret Life in terms of lives, never just lives in terms of character. I'm always acutely conscious of the Force behind—Fate, God, our biological past creating our present, whatever one calls it—Mystery certainly—and of the one eternal tragedy of Man in his glorious, self-destructive struggle to make the Force express him instead of being, as an animal is, an infinitesimal incident in its expression. And my profound conviction is that this is the only subject worth writing about and that it is possible—or can be—to develop a tragic expression in terms of transfigured modern values and symbols in the theatre which may to some degree bring home to members of a modern audience their ennobling identity with the tragic figures on the stage. Of course, this is very much of a dream, but where the theatre is concerned, one must have a dream, and the Greek dream in tragedy is the noblest ever!

JOHN HOWARD LAWSON

John Howard Lawson was born in New York City in 1894. After his graduation from Williams College in 1914 he went into journalism and for three years was connected with Reuters' Press Cables, the New York office. From 1917 to 1919 he served with the Volunteer Ambulance Service, first with the French Army and later with the American Red Cross. In the summer of 1917 he served at the Front in France, and later in Italy. Since 1919 he has spent most of his time writing plays and motion pictures, in New York and on the West Coast. His first play, an experimental work, was *Roger Bloomer,* produced in New York in 1923. *Processional,* another experimental, and highly successful, play, was produced by the Theater Guild in 1925, and revived not long after. This was followed by *Nirvana* (1926), *Loudspeaker* (1927), and *The International* (1928), the two latter sponsored by The New Playwrights' Theater, an organization devoted to plays and productions of a generally novel or "Radical" nature. *Success Story* (1934) was a Group Theater offering. Three (commercially) unsuccessful plays followed: *Gentlewoman* (1934), *The Pure in Heart* (1934), and *Marching Song* (1937), the last-named a Theater Union production. *The Pure in Heart* and *Gentlewoman* were published in a volume called *With a Reckless Preface* (1934), a challenging attack on the drama reviewers. Lawson's *Theory and Technique of Playwriting* was published in 1936. He is author of several motion pictures, an active participant in the affairs of the Screen Writers' Guild and other organizations devoted to the interests of writers, and a contributing editor of New Masses. For several years he has been at work on an ambitious book that will treat of American social and economic history.

THE LAW OF CONFLICT [1]
[From *Theory and Technique of Playwriting*]
(1936)

Since the drama deals with social rela-

[1] Reprinted in full from *Theory and Technique of Playwriting* (1936), by permission of the author, and the publisher, G. P. Putnam's Sons. Copyright, 1936, by John Howard Lawson.

tionships, a dramatic conflict must be a *social* conflict. We can imagine a dramatic struggle between man and other men, or between man and his environment, including social forces or forces of nature. But it is difficult to imagine a play in which forces of nature are pitted against other forces of nature.

Dramatic conflict is also predicated on the exercise of conscious will. A conflict without conscious will is either wholly subjective or wholly objective; since such a conflict would not deal with the conduct of men in relation to other men or to their environment, it would not be a social conflict.

The following definition may serve as a basis for discussion. The essential character of drama is social conflict in which the conscious will is exerted: persons are pitted against other persons, or individuals against groups, or groups against other groups, or individuals or groups against social or natural forces.

The first impression of this definition is that it is still too broad to be of any practical value: a prize fight is a conflict between two persons which has dramatic qualities and a slight but appreciable social meaning. A world war is a conflict between groups and other groups, which has deep social implications.

Either a prize fight or a war might furnish the materials for a dramatic conflict. This is not merely a matter of compression and selection — although both compression and selection are obviously necessary. The dramatic element (which transforms a prize fight or a war from potential material of drama into the actual stuff of drama) seems to lie in the *way* in which the expectations and motives of the persons or groups are projected. This is not a matter solely of the use of the conscious will; it involves the *kind* and *degree* of conscious will exerted.

Brunetière tells us that the conscious will must be directed toward a specific goal: he compares Lesage's novel, *Gil Blas*, to the play, *The Marriage of Figaro*, which Beaumarchais made from the novel. "Gil Blas, like everybody else, wants to live, and if possible to live agreeably. That is not what we call having a will. But Figaro wants a certain definite thing, which is to prevent Count Almaviva from exercising on Susanne the seigneurial privilege. He finally succeeds — and I grant, since the statement has been made, that it is not exactly through the means which he had chosen, most of which turn against him; but nevertheless he has constantly willed what he willed. He had not ceased to devise means of attaining it, and when these means have failed, he has not ceased to invent new ones."

William Archer objects to Brunetière's theory on the ground that, "while it describes the matter of a good many dramas, it does not lay down any true differentia, any characteristic common to all true drama, and possessed by no other form of fiction." Archer's objections seem to be chiefly directed against the idea of *specific volition:* He mentions a number of plays in which he feels that there is no genuine conflict of will. He contends that *Oedipus* and *Ghosts* do not come within the limits of Brunetière's formula. He evidently means that the clash of wills between *persons* is not sufficiently defined in these dramas. He says: "No one can say that the balcony scene in *Romeo and Juliet* is undramatic, or the 'Galeoto fu il libro' scene in Mr. Stephen Phillips' *Paolo and Francesca;* yet the point of these scenes is not a clash, but an ecstatic concordance, of wills."

This confuses a conflict between persons with a conflict in which a conscious and definite aim has been set up in defiance of other persons or social forces. To be sure, the "clash of wills" in the balcony scene in *Romeo and Juliet* is not between the two persons on the stage. It would be absurd to suggest that the dramatist arbitrarily confine his art to the presentation of personal quarrels. Brunetière never maintains that any such direct opposition is required. On the contrary, he tells us that the theatre shows "the development of the human will, attacking the obstacles opposed to it by destiny, fortune, or circumstances." And again: "This is what may be called *will,* to set up a goal, and to direct everything toward it, to strive to bring everything into line with it." Can there be any doubt that Romeo and Juliet are setting up a goal and striving "to bring everything into line with it?" They know exactly what they want, and are conscious of the difficulties which they must meet. This is equally true of the tragic lovers in *Paolo and Francesca.*

Archer's use of *Oedipus* and *Ghosts* as examples is of considerable interest, because it shows the trend of his thought. He says that Oedipus " does not struggle at all. His struggles insofar as that word can be applied to his misguided efforts to escape from the toils of fate, are all things of the past; in the actual course of the tragedy he simply writhes under one revelation after another of bygone error and unwitting crime."

Archer's objection to the law of conflict goes far deeper than the question of *specific acts of volition:* although he disclaims any interest in the philosophic implications of the theory, his own point of view is essentially metaphysical; he accepts the idea of an absolute necessity which denies and paralyzes the will.

Archer neglects an important technical feature of *Oedipus* and *Ghosts.* Both plays employ the technique of beginning at a crisis. This necessarily means that a large part of the action is retrospective. But this does not mean that the action is passive, either in retrospect or in the crucial activity included in the play's structure. *Oedipus* is a series of conscious acts, directed toward sharply defined ends — the acts of men and women of strong will determined to prevent an impending danger. Their acts lead directly to a goal they are striving to avoid; one cannot assume that the exercise of the conscious will presupposes that the will accomplishes its aim. Indeed the intensity and meaning of the conflict lies in the disparity between the aim and the result, between the purpose and the achievement.

Oedipus is in no sense a passive victim. At the opening of the play he is aware of a problem, which he consciously strives to solve. This leads him to a violent conflict of will with Creon. Then Jocasta realizes the direction in which Oedipus' search is moving; she is faced with a terrible inner conflict; she tries to warn Oedipus, but he refuses to turn back from what he has *willed;* come what may, he must trace his own origin. When Oedipus faces the unbearable truth, he commits a conscious act: he blinds himself; and in the final scene with his two daughters, Antigone and Ismene, he is *still* facing the purport of the events which have crushed him; considering the future, the effect of his own acts upon his children, the measure of his own responsibility.

I have already stated that *Ghosts* is Ibsen's most vital study of personal and social responsibility. Mrs. Alving's life is a long, conscious fight to control her environment. Oswald does not accept his fate; he opposes it with all the force of his will. The end of the play shows Mrs. Alving faced with a terrible decision, a decision which strains her will to the breaking point — she must decide whether or not to kill her own son who has gone insane.

What would *Ghosts* be like if it were (as Archer maintains it to be) a play without a conscious struggle of wills? It is very difficult to conceive of the play in this way: the only events which would be partly unchanged would be Oswald's insanity and the burning of the orphanage. But there would be no action whatsoever leading to these situations. And even Oswald's cry, " give me the sun," would of necessity be omitted, since it expresses conscious will. Furthermore, if no exercise of conscious will were concerned, the orphanage would never have been built.

While denying that conflict is invariably present in drama, Archer does not agree with the Maeterlinckian theory which denies action and finds dramatic power in a man " submitting with bent head to the presence of his soul and his destiny." Archer is well aware that the theatre must deal with *situations* which affect the lives and emotions of human beings. Since he disapproves of the idea of a conflict of will, he suggests that the word, *crisis,* is more universally characteristic of dramatic representation. " The drama," he says, " may be called the art of crises, as fiction is the art of gradual developments." While this is not an inclusive definition, there can be no question that the idea of *crisis* adds something very pertinent to our conception of dramatic conflict. One can readily imagine a conflict which does not reach a crisis; in our daily lives we take continuous part in such conflicts. A struggle which fails to reach a crisis is undramatic. Nevertheless we cannot be satisfied with Archer's statement that " the essence of drama is crisis." An eartnquake is a crisis, but its dramatic significance lies in the reactions and acts of human beings. If *Ghosts* consisted only of Oswald's insanity and the burning of the orphanage it would include two crises, but no conscious will and no *preparation.* When human beings are involved in events which lead to a crisis, they do not stand idly by and watch the climax approach. Human beings seek to shape events for their own advantage, to extricate themselves from difficulties which are partially foreseen. The activity of the conscious will, seeking a way out, creates the very conditions which precipitate the crisis.

Henry Arthur Jones, in analyzing the points of view of Brunetière and Archer, tries to combine them by defining a play as "a succession of suspenses and crises, or as a succession of conflicts impending and conflicts raging, carried on in ascending and accelerated climaxes from the beginning to the end of a connected scheme."

This is a richly suggestive definition. But it is a definition of dramatic *construction* rather than of dramatic *principle.* It tells us a great deal about construction, particularly in the mention of "ascending and accelerated climaxes." But it does not mention the conscious will, and therefore throws very little light on the psychological factor which gives these climaxes their social and emotional significance. The meaning of the situations lies in the degree and kind of conscious will exerted, and in how it *works;* the crisis, the dramatic explosion, is created by *the gap between the aim and the result* — that is, by a shift of equilibrium between the force of will and the force of social necessity. A crisis is the point at which the balance of forces is so strained that something cracks, thus causing a realignment of forces, a new pattern of relationships.

The will which creates drama is directed toward a specific goal. But the goal which it selects must be sufficiently *realistic* to enable the will to have some effect on *reality.* We in the audience

must be able to understand the goal and the possibility of its fulfillment. The kind of will exerted must spring from a consciousness of reality which corresponds to our own. This is a variable factor, which can be accurately determined by an analysis of the social viewpoint of the audience.

But we are concerned not only with the *consciousness* of will, but with the *strength* of will. The exercise of will must be sufficiently vigorous to sustain and develop the conflict to a point of issue. A conflict which fails to reach a crisis is a conflict of weak wills. In Greek and Elizabethan tragedy, the point of maximum strain is generally reached in the death of the hero: he is crushed by the forces which oppose him, or he takes his own life in recognition of his defeat.

Brunetière concludes that strength of will is the only test of dramatic value: "One drama is superior to another drama according as the quantity of will exerted is greater or less, as the share of chance is less and that of necessity greater." One cannot accept this mechanical formulation. In the first place, there is no way to measure the quantity of will exerted. In the second place, the struggle is relative and not absolute. Necessity is simply the totality of the environment, and is, as we have observed, a variable quantity, depending on social concepts. This is a matter of quality as well as quantity. Our conception of the quality of the will and the quality of the forces to which it is opposed determines our acknowledgment of the depth and scope of the conflict. The highest dramatic art is not achieved by pitting the most gigantic will against the most absolute necessity. The agonized struggle of a weak will, seeking to adjust itself to an inhospitable environment, may contain elements of poignant drama.

But however weak the will may be, it must be *sufficiently strong* to sustain the conflict. Drama cannot deal with people whose wills are atrophied, who are unable to make decisions which have even temporary meaning, who adopt no conscious attitude toward events, who make no effort to control their environment. The precise degree of strength of will required is the strength needed to bring the action to an issue, to create a change of equilibrium between the individual and the environment.

The definition with which we begin this chapter may be re-examined and re-phrased as follows:

The essential character of drama is social conflict — persons against other persons, or individuals against groups, or groups against other groups, or individuals or groups against social or natural forces — in which the conscious will, exerted for the accomplishment of specific and understandable aims, is sufficiently strong to bring the conflict to a point of crisis.

MAXWELL ANDERSON

Maxwell Anderson was born in Atlantic, Pa., in 1888. His college education was received at the University of North Dakota, where he was graduated in 1911. He taught school for a short time in California, and then went into newspaper work. Coming East he contributed to the *New Republic,* and later held down jobs on the *Globe* and the *World* in New York. At about the same time, or perhaps a little earlier, he began writing verse. His first play, *White Desert,* was produced in New York in 1923, and failed. Then, in 1924, came *What Price Glory?,* a forthright and highly successful war play written in collaboration with Laurence Stallings. Two other plays were also written with the same collaborator, but neither was successful. Several plays followed during the next few years, *Saturday's Children* (1927); *Gods of the Lightning* (1928, written with Harold Hickerson); *Elizabeth the Queen* (1930); *Night Over Taos* (1932); and *Both Your Houses* (1933). The following years were equally productive, among the more distinguished titles being *Mary of Scotland* (1933); *Winterset* (1935); *High Tor* (1936); *Knickerbocker Holiday* (1938); *The Eve of St. Mark* (1942), *Joan of Lorraine* (1946); *Anne of the Thousand Days* (1948); and *Lost in the Stars* (1949).

During the early years of his career as playwright Anderson had almost nothing to say in public about the art and craft of his profession, believing that his plays should speak for themselves, but during the 1930's, in particular, he wrote a few prefaces to certain of his published plays, and two or three articles; also a few addresses, most of which are of particular interest as throwing light on the aims and ideals of the writer of tragedy. Some of these were collected in a slender volume under the title *The Essence of Tragedy and Other Footnotes and Papers,* and published in 1939. This volume includes *The Essence of Tragedy, Whatever Hope We Have, A Prelude to Poetry in the Theater, The Politics of Knickerbocker Holiday,* and *Yes, By the Eternal.* See also *The Theater as Religion,* an address originally entitled *By Way of Preface: The Theater as Religion,* delivered at Rutgers University, and later reprinted in the New York *Times; Cut is the Branch That Might Have Grown Full Straight* (an address delivered at the Theater Convention and published in the *Authors' League Bulletin,* 1937); and *How Storm Operation Grew* (*National Theatre Conference Bulletin,* Cleveland, 1944). Anderson's pronouncements on theatre and drama are clearly the outgrowth of his basic philosophy (foreshadowed in his volume of published verse, *You Who Have Dreams* 1925), and of his concern as craftsman and artist in shaping his plays for production in the contemporary theatre. A later collection of his essays on the theatre, *Off Broadway,* was published in 1947. Anderson died in 1959.

THE ESSENCE OF TRAGEDY [1]
[From *The Essence of Tragedy and Other Footnotes and Papers*]
(1938)

Anybody who dares to discuss the making of tragedy lays himself open to critical assault and general barrage, for the theorists have been hunting for the essence of tragedy since Aristotle without entire success. There is no doubt that playwrights have occasionally written tragedy successfully, from Aeschylus on, and there is no doubt that Aristotle came very close to a definition of what tragedy is in his famous passage on catharsis. But why the performance of a tragedy should have a cleansing effect on the audience, why an audience is willing to listen to tragedy, why tragedy has a place in the education of men, has never, to my knowledge, been convincingly stated. I must begin by saying that I have not solved the Sphinx's riddle which fifty generations of skillful brains have left in shadow. But I have one suggestion which I think might lead to a solution if it were put to laboratory tests by those who know something about philosophical analysis and dialectic.

There seems no way to get at this suggestion except through a reference to my own adventures in playwriting, so I ask your tolerance while I use myself as an instance. A man who has written successful plays is usually supposed to know something about the theory of playwriting, and perhaps he usually does. In my own case, however, I must confess that I came into the theatre unexpectedly, without preparation, and stayed in it because I had a certain amount of rather accidental success. It was not until after I had fumbled my way through a good many successes and an appalling number of failures that I began to doubt the sufficiency of dramatic instinct and to wonder whether or not there were general laws governing dramatic structure which so poor a head for theory as my own might

grasp and use. I had read the *Poetics* long before I tried playwriting, and I had looked doubtfully into a few well-known handbooks on dramatic structure, but the maxims and theories propounded always drifted by me in a luminous haze — brilliant, true, profound in context, yet quite without meaning for me when I considered the plan for a play or tried to clarify an emotion in dialogue. So far as I could make out every play was a new problem, and the old rules were inapplicable. There were so many rules, so many landmarks, so many pitfalls, so many essential reckonings, that it seemed impossible to find your way through the jungle except by plunging ahead, trusting to your sense of direction and keeping your wits about you as you went.

But as the seasons went by and my failures fell as regularly as the leaves in autumn I began to search again among the theorists of the past for a word of wisdom that might take some of the gamble out of playwriting. What I needed most of all, I felt, was a working definition of what a play is, or perhaps a formula which would include all the elements necessary to a play structure. A play is almost always, probably, an attempt to recapture a vision for the stage. But when you are working in the theatre it's most unsatisfactory to follow the gleam without a compass, quite risky to trust "the light that never was on sea or land" without making sure beforehand that you are not being led straight into a slough of despond. In other words you must make a choice among visions, and you must check your chosen vision carefully before assuming that it will make a play. But by what rules, what maps, what fields of reference can you check so intangible a substance as a revelation, a dream, an inspiration, or any similar nudge from the subconscious mind?

I shan't trouble you with the details of my search for a criterion, partly because I can't remember it in detail. But I reread Aristotle's *Poetics* in the light of some bitter experience, and one of his observations led me to a comparison of

1 Reprinted in full from *The Essence of Tragedy and Other Footnotes and Papers*, Washington, D. C., 1939, by permission of the author and the publisher. Copyright, 1939, by Maxwell Anderson. This paper was read at a session of the Modern Language Association in New York City in January 1938.

ancient and modern playwriting methods. In discussing construction he made a point of the recognition scene as essential to tragedy. The recognition scene, as Aristotle isolated it in the tragedies of the Greeks, was generally an artificial device, a central scene in which the leading character saw through a disguise, recognized as a friend or as an enemy, perhaps as a lover or a member of his own family, some person whose identity had been hidden. Iphigeneia, for example, acting as priestess in an alien country, receives a victim for sacrifice and then recognizes her own brother in this victim. There is an instant and profound emotional reaction, instantly her direction in the play is altered. But occasionally, in the greatest of the plays, the recognition turned on a situation far more convincing, though no less contrived. Oedipus, hunting savagely for the criminal who has brought the plague upon Thebes, discovers that he is himself that criminal — and since this is a discovery that affects not only the physical well-being and happiness of the hero, but the whole structure of his life, the effect on him and on the direction of the story is incalculably greater than could result from the more superficial revelation made to Iphigeneia.

Now scenes of exactly this sort are rare in the modern drama except in detective stories adapted for the stage. But when I probed a little more deeply into the memorable pieces of Shakespeare's theatre and our own I began to see that though modern recognition scenes are subtler and harder to find, they are none the less present in the plays we choose to remember. They seldom have to do with anything so naïve as disguise or the unveiling of a personal identity. But the element of discovery is just as important as ever. For the mainspring in the mechanism of a modern play is almost invariably a discovery by the hero of some element in his environment or in his own soul of which he has not been aware — or which he has not taken sufficiently into account. Moreover, nearly every teacher of playwriting has had some inkling of this, though it was not until after I had worked out my own theory that what they said on this point took on accurate meaning for me. I still think that the rule which I formulated for my own guidance is more concise than any other, and so I give it here: A play should lead up to and away from a central crisis, and this crisis should consist in a discovery by the leading character which has an indelible effect on his thought and emotion and completely alters his course of action. The leading character, let me say again, must make the discovery; it must affect him emotionally; and it must alter his direction in the play.

Try that formula on any play you think worthy of study, and you will find that, with few exceptions, it follows this pattern or some variation of this pattern. The turning point of *The Green Pastures*, for example, is the discovery of God, who is the leading character, that even he must learn and grow, that a God who is to endure must conform to the laws of change. The turning point of *Hamlet* is Hamlet's discovery, in the play-scene, that his uncle was unquestionably the murderer of his father. In *Abe Lincoln in Illinois* Lincoln's discovery is that he has been a coward, that he has stayed out of the fight for the Union because he was afraid. In each case, you will note, the discovery has a profound emotional effect on the hero, and gives an entirely new direction to his action in the play.

I'm not writing a disquisition on playwriting and wouldn't be competent to write one, but I do want to make a point of the superlative usefulness of this one touchstone for play-structure. When a man sets out to write a play his first problem is his subject and the possibilities of that subject as a story to be projected from the stage. His choice of subject matter is his personal problem, and one that takes its answer from his personal relation to his times. But if he wants to know a possible play subject when he finds it, if he wants to know how to mould the subject into play form after he has found it, I doubt that he'll ever discover another standard as satisfactory as the modern version of Aristotle which I have suggested. If the plot he has in mind does not contain a playable episode in which the hero or heroine makes an emotional discovery, a discovery that practically dictates the end of the story, then such an episode must be inserted — and if no place can be found for it the subject is almost certainly a poor one for the theatre. If this emotional discovery is contained in the story, but is not central, then it must be made central, and the whole action must revolve around it. In a three-act play it should fall near the end of the second act, though it may be delayed till the last; in a five-act play it will usually be found near the end of the third, though here also it can be delayed. Everything else in the play should be subordinated to this one episode — should lead up to or away from it.

Now this prime rule has a corollary which is just as important as the rule itself. The hero who is to make the central discovery in a play must not be a perfect man. He must have some variation of what Aristotle calls a tragic fault — and the reason he must have it is that when he makes his discovery he must change both in himself and in his action — and he must change for the better. The fault can be a very simple one — a mere unawareness, for example — but if he has no fault he cannot change for the better, but only for the worse, and for a reason which I shall discuss later, it is necessary that he must become more admirable, and not less so, at the end of the play. In other words, a hero must pass through an experience which opens his eyes to an error of his own. He must learn through suffering. In a tragedy he suffers death itself as a consequence of his fault or his attempt to correct it, but before he dies he has become a nobler person because of his recognition of his fault and the consequent alteration of his course of action. In a serious play which does not end in death he suffers a lesser punishment, but the pattern remains the same. In both forms he has a fault to begin with, he discovers that fault during the course of the action, and he does what he can to rectify it at the end. In *The Green Pastures* God's fault was that he believed himself perfect. He discovered that he was not perfect, and he resolved to change and grow. Hamlet's fault was that he could not make up his mind to act. He offers many excuses for his indecision until he discovers that there is no real reason for hesitation and that he has delayed out of cowardice. Lincoln, in *Abe Lincoln in Illinois,* has exactly the same difficulty. In the climactic scene it is revealed to him that he

had hesitated to take sides through fear of the consequences to himself, and he then chooses to go ahead without regard for what may be in store for him. From the point of view of the playwright, then, the essence of a tragedy, or even of a serious play, is the spiritual awakening, or regeneration, of his hero.

When a playwright attempts to reverse the formula, when his hero makes a discovery which has an evil effect, or one which the audience interprets as evil, on his character, the play is inevitably a failure on the stage. In *Troilus and Cressida* Troilus discovers that Cressida is a light woman. He draws from her defection the inference that all women are faithless — that faith in woman is the possession of fools. As a consequence he turns away from life and seeks death in a cause as empty as the love he has given up, the cause of the strumpet Helen. All the glory of Shakespeare's verse cannot rescue the play for an audience, and save in *Macbeth* Shakespeare nowhere wrote so richly, so wisely, or with such a flow of brilliant metaphor.

For the audience will always insist that the alteration in the hero be for the better — or for what it believes to be the better. As audiences change the standards of good and evil change, though slowly and unpredictably, and the meanings of plays change with the centuries. One thing only is certain: that an audience watching a play will go along with it only when the leading character responds in the end to what it considers a higher moral impulse than moved him at the beginning of the story, though the audience will of course define morality as it pleases and in the terms of its own day. It may be that there is no absolute up or down in this world, but the race believes that there is, and will not hear of any denial.

And now at last I come to the point toward which I've been struggling so laboriously. Why does the audience come to the theatre to look on while an imaginary hero is put to an imaginary trial and comes out of it with credit to the race and to himself? It was this question that prompted my essay, and unless I've been led astray by my own predilections there is a very possible answer in the rules for playwriting which I have just cited. The theatre originated in two complementary religious ceremonies, one celebrating the animal in man and one celebrating the god. Old Greek Comedy was dedicated to the spirits of lust and riot and earth, spirits which are certainly necessary to the health and continuance of the race. Greek tragedy was dedicated to man's aspiration, to his kinship with the gods, to his unending, blind attempt to lift himself above his lusts and his pure animalism into a world where there are other values than pleasure and survival. However unaware of it we may be, our theatre has followed the Greek patterns with no change in essence, from Aristophanes and Euripides to our own day. Our more ribald musical comedies are simply our approximation of the Bacchic rites of Old Comedy. In the rest of our theatre we sometimes follow Sophocles, whose tragedy is always an exaltation of the human spirit, sometimes Euripides, whose tragi-comedy follows the same pattern of an excellence achieved through suffering. The forms of both tragedy and comedy have changed a good deal in nonessentials, but in essentials — and especially in the core of meaning which they must have for audiences — they are in the main the same religious rites which grew up around the altars of Attica long ago.

It is for this reason that when you write for the theatre you must choose between your version of a phallic revel and your vision of what mankind may or should become. Your vision may be faulty, or shallow, or sentimental, but it must conform to some aspiration in the audience, or the audience will reject it. Old Comedy, the celebration of the animal in us, still has a place in our theatre, as it had in Athens, but here, as there, that part of the theatre which celebrated man's virtue and his regeneration in hours of crisis is accepted as having the more important function. Our comedy is largely the Greek New Comedy, which grew out of Euripides' tragi-comedy, and is separated from tragedy only in that it presents a happier scene and puts its protagonist through an ordeal which is less than lethal.

And since our plays, aside from those which are basically Old Comedy, are exaltations of the human spirit, since that is what an audience expects when it comes to the theatre, the playwright gradually discovers, as he puts plays before audiences, that he must follow the ancient Aristotelian rule: he must build his plot around a scene wherein his hero discovers some mortal frailty or stupidity in himself and faces life armed with a new wisdom. He must so arrange his story that it will prove to the audience that men pass through suffering purified, that, animal though we are, despicable though we are in many ways, there is in us all some divine, incalculable fire that urges us to be better than we are.

It could be argued that what the audience demands of a hero is only conformity to race morality, to the code which seems to the spectators most likely to make for race survival. In many cases, especially in comedy, and obviously in the comedy of Molière, this is true. But in the majority of ancient and modern plays it seems to me that what the audience wants to believe is that men have a desire to break the moulds of earth which encase them and claim a kinship with a higher morality than that which hems them in. The rebellion of Antigone, who breaks the laws of men through adherence to a higher law of affection, the rebellion of Prometheus, who breaks the law of the gods to bring fire to men, the rebellion of God in *The Green Pastures* against the rigid doctrine of the Old Testament, the rebellion of Tony in *They Knew What they Wanted* against the convention that called on him to repudiate his cuckold child, the rebellion of Liliom against the heavenly law which asked him to betray his own integrity and make a hypocrisy of his affection, even the repudiation of the old forms and the affirmation of new by the heroes of Ibsen and Shaw, these are all instances to me of the groping of men toward an excellence dimly apprehended, seldom possible of definition. They are evidence to me that the theatre at its best is a religious affirmation, an age-old rite restating and reassuring man's belief in his own destiny and his ultimate hope. The theatre is much older than the doctrine of evolution, but its one faith, asseverated again and again for every age and every year, is a faith in evolution, in the reaching and the climb of men toward distant goals, glimpsed but never seen, perhaps never achieved, or achieved only to be passed impatiently on the way to a more distant horizon.

JOHN GASSNER

John Gassner received all his formal education in New York City, where he was born in 1903. He received a Master's degree from Columbia University in 1925 and as recipient of a William Mitchell Fellowship in arts and letters did some work toward a Ph.D. degree. A student of Brander Matthews and George C. D. Odell, he specialized in creative and critical writing, and after leaving the University he did book reviewing and published occasional verse; was editorial adviser to various publishers, lectured at the Labor Temple School, and helped found *The Psychoanalytic Quarterly*. In 1928 he became an instructor at Hunter College, and in 1931 joined the Theater Guild, remaining as head of its Play Department until 1944, when he established a play department for Columbia Pictures Corporation. He has lectured and conducted classes at Bryn Mawr, Northwestern University, and the New School for Social Research; since 1956 he has been the Sterling Professor of Playwriting and Dramatic Literature at Yale. He has been a more or less regular contributor to various papers and magazines. He is author, editor or co-editor of a number of books on the theatre and drama and their related arts. Among them are *Best American Plays* series, 7 vols., covering the period 1916–63; *Masters of the Drama* (1940); *Producing the Play* (1941); *Our Heritage of World Literature* (1942); *The Theatre in Our Times* (1954); and *Theatre at the Crossroads* (1960). He has likewise adapted and dramatized a number of plays.

While Gassner's activities in the theater have brought him into constant touch with the practical economic problems which are a necessary part of it, he has at the same time familiarized himself with its historical, theoretical, and philosophic backgrounds.

Nearly all his critical and expository writings are concerned with the clarification of fundamental issues considered in the light of present-day attitudes.

CATHARSIS AND THE MODERN THEATER [1]
[From *One-Act Play Magazine and Theater Review*]
(1937–1946)

I

It is difficult to think of a more academic concept than that of catharsis. It is encrusted with antiquity and bears the rust of much speculation justly suspect to the practical worker. The concept is, nevertheless, one of those insights that philosophers sometimes achieve in spite

[1] The present text, condensed, revised and to a great extent rewritten by the author, appeared in its original form in the August, 1937, number of *One Act Play Magazine and Theater Review*. Printed here by permission of the author.

of themselves. Aristotle touched bottom when he declared the effect of tragedy to be purgation of the soul by pity and fear.

The Aristotelian formula, supremely empirical, has a dual importance: the spectator is given a definition of his experience, and the playwright is provided with a goal for which certain means are requisite, the goal set for him being no other than the effect he must achieve if he is to hold an audience with high and serious matter of a painful nature. Unfortunately, however, Aristotle's analysis was altogether too fragmentary, and his *Poetics* has come down to us as little more than a collection of notes. We do not even know precisely what catharsis meant for him and how he thought "pity and fear" produced the purgation.

The subject has exercised commentators since the Renaissance when they seized upon the short passage: "Tragedy through pity and fear effects a purgation of such emotions." Each age has added its own interpretation, naturally reflecting its own interests and its own kind of drama. According to the Sixteenth Century pundits, including the famous Castelvetro, tragedy hardened the spectator to suffering by subjecting him to pity- and fear-inducing scenes of misery and violence. Corneille, who gave much thought to his craft, held that tragedy forced the spectator to fear for himself when he observed a character's passions causing disaster, and that the resolve to rule one's own passions effected the purgation. Others, including John Milton, took the homeopathic view that pity and terror on the stage counteracted the disturbing elements of pity and terror in the spectator. For the liberals or humanitarians of the Enlightenment, including the author of *Nathan the Wise*, tragedy purified the observer by enabling him to exercise his sympathies. For Hegel tragedy reconciled conflicting views, thereby effecting catharsis. And so it went until Jacob Bernays, Wilhelm Stekel, and other psychologists arrived at the view that accords most easily with both the findings of psychopathology and common sense — namely, that catharsis is simply the expulsion of disturbing drives and conflicts.

Without adhering to any specific school of psychopathology, it is safe to say that if Aristotelian catharsis is a valid definition of tragic effect (and I believe it is), it means one thing above all: In the tragic experience we temporarily expel troublesome inner complications. We expel "pity" and "fear," to use Aristotle's terms, and the terms are broad enough to cover the most pathological or near-pathological elements — namely, anxieties, fears, morbid grief or self-pity, sadistic or masochistic desires, and the sense of guilt that these engender and are engendered by. In a successful tragedy we see these drives enacted on the stage directly or through their results by characters with whom we can identify ourselves. They are our proxies, so to speak.

We must observe, however, that the expulsion would certainly prove ephemeral and perhaps even incomplete or ineffective if the expelled matter were merely brought to the surface (to our "pre-conscious," if you will) instead of being fully recognized by our consciousness. Evoked "pity and fear" on the tragic stage may effect expulsion, but at least one other force is needed if real recognition is to be effectuated.

That something more is needed is evidenced by the whole history of the theater. The distinction between tragedy and melodrama is grounded in the opinion that excitement is not enough, that it does not produce the most satisfactory effects. Where the excitement emanates plausibly and serves an end beyond itself there is, we say, tragedy. Where the excitement exists solely for itself and is accomplished without the operation of reason or credibility we have melodrama. If purgation in tragedy were confined solely to the effects of pity and fear there could be little dramatic distinction between *Hamlet* and *The Bat*.

Has it not always been recognized that the superiority of the great tragedies, if we exclude purely stylistic differences, has resided in their powerful blending of passion with enlightenment? This is what we mean when we attribute their superiority to the significance of their content, the depth and scope of their conflict, or the relevance of their action to the major aspects and problems of humanity. In tragedy there is always a precipitate of final enlightenment — some inherent, cumulatively realized, understanding. We have seen an experience enacted on the stage, and have externalized its inner counterpart in ourselves by the process of vibrating to the acted passions; or possibly by some other means, since unconscious processes are open to infinite debate. Then, ensuring the externalization of the inner drives, we have given them form and meaning — that is, understood their causes and effects, which brings us to the furthest point from the unconscious, or from nebulous emotion, ever reached by the individual. Enlightenment is, therefore, the third component of the process of purgation.

It exists in perfect harmony with the components of "pity and fear," and it is even supported by them, just as enlightenment supports them. "Pity and fear," (using these terms to cover the emotional experience) are the *fixatives* of tragic enlightenment, for without their agency the meaning of a play would be superficial and fleeting; enlightenment unrooted in the emotions or unsupported and unevoked by them would be something imposed from without, unprecipitated from the struggle of the drama, and devoid of persuasive growth or cumulative effect. Moreover, pity and terror have mnemonic values which the drama cannot dispense with, because of its rapid course of action. Who would remember the significances of *Hamlet* without its anguish?

Finally, but keeping the above qualifications strictly in mind, we can maintain that enlightenment is not only the third element in catharsis, but the decisive one. The ultimate relief comes when the dramatist brings the tragic struggle to a state of rest. This cannot occur so long as we are left in a state of tension. No matter how well the action or the main character's destiny is resolved and concluded, the anarchic forces, "the pity and fear," evoked by the tragedy cannot establish a suitable inner equilibrium. Only enlightenment, a clear comprehension of what was involved in the struggle, an understanding of cause and effect, a judgment on what we have witnessed, and an induced state of mind that places it above the riot of passion — can effect this necessary equilibrium. And it is a necessary one if there is to be purgation, and if for the moment we are to be healed of the wounds self-inflicted in the unconscious, inflicted on us from without by external circumstance before they settle our inmost self, then inflicted once more by the tragic story enacted before our eyes on the stage. Only enlightenment can therefore round out the esthetic experience in tragedy, can actually ensure complete esthetic gratification. True tragic exaltation, which we require of a tragedy, also lies in this. For the exaltation comes only if we have prevailed over the anarchy of our inner life and the ever present and ever pressing life around us; and

how can we master this anarchy without understanding it, without putting order into this house of disorder?

Had Aristotle pursued his investigation of classic drama further, he would have surely arrived at this view himself. The author of the *Nichomachean Ethics* and the *Politics* could not have failed to discover the conclusive element of enlightenment in the purgation afforded by the tragedies of Æschylus, Sophocles, and Euripides. To adopt Nietzschean (*The Birth of Tragedy*) terminology, Greek tragedy imposed the Apollonian world of light and reason upon the dynamic Dionysian world of passion. The Apollonian element in the warp and woof of the plays, including the great choral passages, ordered and so mastered the Dionysiac excitement or disequilibrium. I believe the same thing can be demonstrated in Elizabethan tragedy, in the work of Corneille and Racine, and in modern tragedy.

To conclude this argument, I should, I suppose, try to disabuse anyone who would look askance at this insistence on enlightenment because it suggests a moral in the outmoded Victorian sense. The "moral" is imposed from without by a convention; that was the prime limitation of William Winter's criticism. Enlightenment is not actually imposed, but wells up from the stream of the play itself, from the enacted events, actions, and reactions. The moral, in other words, is a predigested judgment, whereas enlightenment is empirical. The moral is a summation or tag; enlightenment is a process. The moral of a play can be put into a sententious sentence. The element of enlightenment can also be summarized, but the summary is only a portion of the whole. It is a state of grace, so to speak, a civilized attitude achieved in the course of experiencing the play: an Apollonian attitude, Santayana's "life of reason," a clarity of mind and spirit, a resilience and cheerfulness even. The moral is a law. The enlightenment is a state of mind, and includes specific conclusions only as a necessary concomitant of every state of mind that is not vacuous. It is even a kind of poetry of the mind, no matter how earnest, somber or sultry.

II

Acceptance of the function of enlightenment in tragic catharsis is particularly essential if we are to cope with the modern drama, if we are to understand, write, and produce it. In the case of modern drama, many problems arise and many distinctions must be made. For instance, we must realize that many serious modern plays are not tragedies at all but a new form of tragi-comedy for which no term has yet been found. In this essay let us, however, continue to hew close to the matter of enlightenment.

The fact is that many who would grant my premise, out of conviction or from sheer exhaustion, will stickle at one other point as much as they would at the possibility that "enlightenment" is just an undercover term for a moral. They will insist on confining the matter of enlightenment to "universals" and proceed to flail post-Ibsen drama because it so often treats immediate issues and problems.

I have nothing against "universals," but it seems to me that the only universals these critics favor are *dead* ones; or let us say that, for reasons that could bear some scrutiny, they prefer them to be conveniently remote from contemporary social conflicts. Otherwise a universal is not universal for them. A fallacy, I believe, since how can something be universal if it no longer functions, what life is there in it if it lacks direct applicability to what pinches us, and what is left in it but a platitude that fobs us off with a cold compress while the diseased body teems with microbes.

A hard and fast distinction between the topical and the universal is impossible in practice. We live amid the immediacies of our time and place. Are these distinguishable, can these be separated from, fundamental realities and human drives? The immediate realities contain and project the universal ones. Even our most unvarnished economic and political struggles relate to the universals of anxiety, fear of deprivation, pain and extinction; they involve love and hate, loyalty and treason, selfishness and self-sacrifice, honor and dishonor, falsehood and truth, good and evil. And all this is also only another way of saying that anything we call universal is only a generalization of immediate and specific interests or concerns. If we could put ourselves in the place of an Athenian spectator at the first performance of *The Trojan Women*, the Oresteian trilogy, or any other tragedy that stirred that spectator either as an individual or as a member of a group, we would not speak so glibly of universals. It is safe to conjecture that everything we consider universal in these plays was once very immediate — socially, politically, psychologically.

No, the failure of any contemporary topical or even downright propaganda play as tragic art has other causes than the substitution of the "topical" for the "universal." These cannot be examined in this essay; they are many, and they also require particularization in individual cases. Still hewing to my theme, I should like to add only that perhaps the overall cause will be found in the social dramatist's and the propagandist's failure to achieve a catharsis. He fails chiefly because in striving so conscientiously for enlightenment, he so often substitutes statement for dramatic process and neglects to effectuate the "pity and fear" — that is, the tensions and emotional rapport or identification implicit in the Aristotelian terms. Although it is the combination of "pity," "fear," and "enlightenment" that produces tragic catharsis, his assault strategy makes the frontal attack with "enlightenment" but forgets about the flanks. The general assault fails, and the unsupported frontal attack soon crumbles, since there is no effective enlightenment when the play fails. There is even a school of social drama that in one way or other denies the value of catharsis. According to Berthold Brecht, the champion of the epic or "learning-play" (*Lehrstück*), sympathy and emotional identification (*Einfühlung*) represent enticements or evasions of social understanding and action. He objects to "all the illusion which whips up the spectator for two hours and leaves him exhausted and full of vague recollection and vaguer hope." Brecht's view is only a forthright version of an attitude that underlies much social drama which, regardless of its merits, must remain fundamentally untragic. Perhaps proponents of anti-emotional drama should go one step further and arraign tragedy itself as wrong for their purposes.[1]

[1] In fairness to Berthold Brecht it is worth noting that there are theatrical *non-tragic*

uses and effects in the "learning-play" and in such variants as the "living newspaper" (*Power, One-Third of a Nation.*) It is also open to question whether so potent a poet as Brecht does not go beyond the intent of a *Lehrstück,* in so far as his music and imagery exert a spell on the spectator. Brecht, the poet, is not always collaborating with Brecht the theoretician. J. G.

JOHN MASON BROWN

John Mason Brown was born in Louisville, Ky., in 1900. Graduated from Harvard in 1923, he began his very active career as dramatic critic, lecturer and instructor—after a short period of newspaper apprenticeship on the Louisville *Courier-Journal* in 1917 — when he became associate editor and dramatic critic of *Theatre Arts Monthly* in 1924, where he served until 1928. At various times he has conducted courses on drama at the University of Montana, Middlebury College, Harvard, Yale, The American Laboratory Theatre and elsewhere. From 1929 to 1941 he was dramatic critic for the New York *Evening Post,* and in 1941 and 1942 for the New York *World-Telegram;* after serving in the Navy, in

Europe, he became associate editor and dramatic critic of the *Saturday Review of Literature,* beginning late in December of 1944 and continuing until 1953. He is author and editor of several books, most of them concerned with the theatre or drama, among them *The American Theatre as Seen by Its Critics* (1934, with Montrose J. Moses); *The Modern Theatre in Revolt* (1929); *Upstage— The American Theatre in Performance* (1930); *Letters from Greenroom Ghosts* (1934); *The Art of Playgoing* (1936); *Two on an Aisle* (1938); *Broadway in Review* (1940); *Seeing Things* (1946); *Seeing More Things* (1948); *Still Seeing Things* (1950); and *Dramatis Personae* (1963).

THE TRAGIC BLUEPRINT[1]
[From *Broadway in Review*]
(1940)

In no way are the differences between what is patternless in our living and the pattern which the drama can superimpose upon life made clearer than in those differences which exist between death, as most of us are bound to face it, and death as it is encountered by the heroes and heroines of so-called high, or formal tragedy.

The finest statement of what is enduring in high tragedy's timeless blueprint is not to be found in the *Poetics* but in the Book of Job. Although Aristotle

[1] Reprinted in full from *Broadway in Review*, New York, 1940, by permission of the author, and the publisher, W. W. Norton & Company, Inc. Copyright, 1940, by W. W. Norton & Company, Inc.

was on the threshold of truth when he spoke of tragedy's being an imitation of an action, serious, complete, and of a certain magnitude, and insisted, however erroneously, upon its effecting through pity and fear the proper purgation of these emotions, the sage of Stagira halted at truth's portal as Eliphaz, the Temanite, did not when he was exhorting that prince of suffering known as Job.

"Man is born unto trouble," said the Temanite, "as the sparks fly upward. I would seek unto God, and unto God would I commit my cause: Which doeth great things and unsearchable; marvelous things without number. . . . Behold, happy *is* the man whom God correcteth: therefore despise not thou the chastening of the Almighty: For he maketh sore, and bindeth up: he woundeth, and his hands make whole."

In all tragedies concerned with the unsearchable, hence high because of the altitude of their search no less than because of the elevation of their agony, the sparks fly upward as men and women, born unto trouble, are made whole by their suffering. By these sparks, which are great words struck from the anvil of great sorrow, are we kept warm in the presence of the pain endured by those wounded men and women who are tragedy's favorite sons and daughters, and illumined in what would otherwise be the darkness of their dying.

That we are able to attend their deaths without tears; that the yield of their anguish is in us a pleasant ecstasy greater than is our sympathy with their distress; that we experience no desire to save them from their fates and would, indeed, feel cheated were they to be robbed of the self-realization which, on the brink of oblivion, is so often theirs — should warn us of how far the Stagirite was from truth when he spoke of tragedy as an imitation of life. One thing is certain. Regardless of the extent to which they may pretend to imitate life as their heroes and heroines are hastened to their deaths, high tragedies discard all pretense of such imitation when death, not life, becomes their high concern. If they extend life while dealing with the living, they transcend it when death is their subject. Then it is most markedly that their feigned reality, however slight, surrenders to the "beneficent illusion" and the arbitrary pattern is consolingly superimposed upon the patternless. The lies they tell at such supreme moments are among the most resplendent and sustaining truths they have to offer.

Whatever our deathbed fates may be, this much we know. Our dying will not be similar to the dying of the heroes and the heroines of high tragedy. When they die, these men and women are apt to be possessors of a talent for verbalization such as we can never aspire to even in our hardiest moments of health. By a convention, born of beauty and of our need, they are fated to leave this earth spiritually cross-ventilated. Furthermore, they die without benefit of hospitaliza-

tion. Always they go as victims of a design, with a toll to be paid either for a defect unmistakably established or a misdeed meriting punishment.

Our bodies, not our characters, are to blame if we have weak lungs or weak hearts. Thrombosis can switch off our consciousness at any moment without giving us time to light up spiritually or signifying divine disapproval. The arteries of saints no less than sinners can harden with old age. In everyday life longevity is the result neither of moral grandeur nor of Sunday-school applause. The good are asked to suffer with the bad, usually more often and to a greater extent. Cause and effect do not need to be on speaking terms to have any one of us snuffed out. Infantile paralysis is not an affliction which the innocent at five or eleven or at any age can be said to have earned. Death rides through life, not as a moral logician, inexorable in his demands, but as a hit-and-run driver. We who live in cities are aware that, while crossing the street — any street, at any hour, and even with the lights in our favor — to do the best good deed of which we are capable, we run the risk of being struck down by a truck, the driver of which will never have had anything against us except his truck at an unfortunate moment of impact. We say these haphazard misfortunes are beyond our understanding.

So they are, even as they are beyond the possibilities of high tragedy. Melodramas, when hard pushed, may enjoy dalliance with such disasters; never high tragedies. Although their concern is often the inexplicable, they take pains to state their gropings in understandable terms. They take few chances with chance. Where we, as actual men and women, may be confused by the injustice of our lot, the heroes and the heroines of high tragedy live lives and die deaths clearly motivated. They are not ruled by coincidence in our fashion. They are deliberate parts of a visible design, even when, in our manner, their search is to comprehend their place in a larger design, infinite as it is inscrutable.

For them the tree of life is always cut with a single purpose — to make a cross. If they shape their crosses for themselves, it is because they belong to a race apart, these men and women who, by their suffering, give high tragedy its grandeur. In spite of what the church basements may have told us, there would have been no such thing as high tragedy had the world been peopled exclusively by Boy Scouts and Girl Scouts. More often than not the record of high tragedy is the record of splendid sinners who, always *after* sinning — if to no other extent than shirking their manifest duties, or surrendering to their defects — redeem themselves spiritually just before the moment of their taking off. This is but a part of the pattern of high tragedy, and of its moral obligation, too.

We, in our living, are aware every time we pass a hospital, magnificent and indispensable as it may be, that we are in the presence of a brick-and-stone reminder of the frailties of the human body. The body, and all its sickroom failings, figures to a humiliating extent in our more leisurely deaths. In high tragedy what matters is always the flame and never the lamp; never the body and always the spirit.

This lifts high tragedy beyond tears even as it lifts it beyond pain. Run over the long list of the heroes and heroines of high tragedy and you will find that though these men and women have died from multifarious causes — have stabbed themselves or been stabbed, been poisoned, fallen like Romans on their swords, or died from snakebite, more classically known as aspbite — not one of them, at the moment of intense pain and imminent death, has ever surrendered to the mortal luxury of an "ouch." This is why even in an age of realism, no attempt wisely is ever made to deal realistically with their wounds. Their spirits spill the only blood that matters; and it is life-giving even when life is being taken.

Sinners or not, the heroes and heroines of high tragedy belong (as Edith Hamilton has pointed out) to the only genuine aristocracy known to this world — the aristocracy of truly passionate souls. In spite of economists or the most hopeful of Utopians, there is one respect in which men and women are doomed forever to be unequally endowed. This lies in their capacity to suffer. If this capacity is among the most ineradicable of mortal

inequalities, it is among the most notable gifts of high tragedy's heroes and heroines. Their genius is to suffer greatly, and in their sufferings to ring music from the very dissonances of life.

By convention they not only feel acutely and speak greatly for their authors and all the rest of us while speaking for themselves, but always have what we shall never have when our lungs are exhausted on hospital cots, and that is the last word. A poet's endowment enables them to sing their way into heaven. They trumpet themselves into paradise, releasing such verbal splendors that we forget their agonies and are sustained by the music with which they orchestrate death.

Pathos is everywhere one of the most common of emotional commodities. In no country is it held in higher esteem than here where we have Sealpack handkerchiefs to keep up with it and Hollywood to see to it that what might be our sympathetic dust bowls are in no danger of not being moist. Although it is as widespread as are the mishaps briefly reported in every daily newspaper, the pathetic is never the tragic. It is only the tragedy of the small-souled, the average, the commonplace. Its dividend is at the least sighs, at the most tears, and never ecstasy because it is no more than unhappy and can claim no fortune in misfortune.

The theatre knows a host of pathetic plays. It knows its tragedies, too — welcome enough, often dissolving, sometimes provocative, occasionally exquisite in their poignancy — which seek to deal with nothing more than the worries of men and women as they hurt, or are hurt by, one another or their neighbors. But high tragedies are more than earthbound. They are translunary as opposed to terrestrial, if for no other reason than that their heroes and heroines are bent upon facing imponderables. They extend their interest beyond their neighbors to the forces controlling their destinies. There are more things in the heaven and earth of these turbulent worldlings than are dreamt of in the philosophies of the tamer Horatios of this planet, however good or kind. If as characters these heroes and heroines take on spiritually the dimensions of their interests, their inter-

est is not unrequited. The gods, the stars,
and nature itself may direct their misad-
ventures, but they care for these people
as these people care for them.   Cries
Hecuba:

O thou who does uphold the world
Whose throne is high above the world
Thou, past our seeking to find, what art
*   thou?*
God, or Necessity of what must be,
Or reason of our reason,
Whate'er thou art, I pray to thee,
Seeing the silent road by which
All mortal things are led by thee to
*   justice.*[1]

And her cry, in one form or another,
addressed to Jove, to God, to Destiny, to
Heaven, to Dat Ole Davil Sea, Mother
Dynamo, or the godhead in one's self, is
apt, sooner or later, to be 'the cry of all
the men and women whose authors have
sought to follow the tragic blueprint.
Part of the greatness of these characters
is that with their eyes they at least dare
to look for the unseeable, and with their
ears they hear harmonies to which most
of us are deaf.
When they die, self-realized by their
suffering, they do not relinquish life but
are at last released from it. They fall as
mortals so complete that they have lost
both their desire and excuse for living.
Death for them is not a cessation of life.
It is a fulfillment of self. Their living
on, when the book is closed, would only
mean for them and us the letdown of a
sequel. Hence they and we can be happy
in their dying. Macbeth is the only one
of Shakespeare's major tragic characters
who dies unworthily, self-despising and
despised. The others feel to varying degrees, in language appropriate to their
natures, the exaltation of Mark Antony's:

*   I will be*
A bridegroom in my death, and run into't
As to a lover's bed.

Or they die as monarchs of their own
spirits in Cleopatra's fashion, when she
utters the superb speech beginning:

Give me my robe, put on my crown; I

[1] Edith Hamilton's translation.

have
Immortal longings in me. . . .
*   husband, I come.*
Now to that name my courage prove my
*   title!*
I am fire and air; my other elements
I give to baser life.

No wonder, in the presence of such a
spirit, one feels that Death himself has
struggled for its surrender. Or that
Charmian, when the asp has done its
tragic duty, can say as she surveys the
body of the dead queen:

*   So fare thee well,*
Now boast thee, death, in thy possession
*   lies*
A lass unparallel'd.

If those words form the finest caption
for the "beneficent illusion" of high tragedy known to our language, there are
plenty of others scarcely less noble or
sustaining. When Kent salutes the body
of the dead Lear with:

Vex not his ghost: O, let him pass! he
*   hates him much*
That would upon the rack of this tough
*   world*
Stretch him out longer

he is speaking one of these, and following
the pattern of death, made painless by its
verbal and spiritual splendors, in high
tragedy. Although many have tried and
only a handful have succeeded, all dramatists, before and after Shakespeare,
seeking to write high tragedy have
worked, however variously, from the
same blueprint. Recently, for example,
in *Murder in the Cathedral,* a play which
managed to become a play in spite of
T. S. Eliot, Mr. Eliot had his Thomas à
Becket sing, and sing beautifully, tragedy's timeless song. When his Becket
knew his murderers to be at the gates of
Canterbury, Mr. Eliot had him send away
his protecting priests with these magical
words:

I have had a tremor of bliss, a wink of
*   heaven, a whisper,*
And I would no longer be denied; all
*   things*
Proceed to a joyful consummation.

In our living we know only too well that, New Deal or no New Deal, few things ever proceed to a joyful consummation. The moral pleasure, and one of the aesthetic delights, of high tragedy is to persuade us that all things might so proceed, if only we were or could be better than our clay.

In the following pages three tragedies written according to the tragic pattern are discussed. Two of them are by William Shakespeare; one is by Maxwell Anderson. If *Romeo and Juliet*, however acted, is no more than a youthful groping after the tragic, *Hamlet* is of course one of the wonders of our literature. Hamlet may be an indecisive prince, but he is a great soul in distress. His interests are not limited to the court at Elsinore. Flights of angels sing him to his rest.

No contemporary understands the exaltation of the tragic pattern better than Maxwell Anderson. No one has written about it with more fervor or eloquence. Mr. Anderson is well aware that if we save our necks by losing our souls we might better be six feet under. As a dramatist whose understanding of the tragic is profound, however disappointing his tragedies may be, he knows the mere act of being alive does not mean any one of us is living. He is as conscious as we all are that the number of unburied living who clutter up the earth's surface is legion. He is no less aware that the spiritual and intellectual zombies to be met with daily are countless. As a dramatist, at least aiming at the tragic, he is not interested in these zombies except as they redeem themselves. As such a dramatist, he knows it is only by losing our necks that we can save our souls.

Mr. Anderson shows his wisdom in *Key Largo* by realizing that in high tragedy, or tragedy which aims at being high, the geographical whereabouts of God matters as little as does the name He may be given. In his prologue, the best part of an unsatisfactory play, Mr. Anderson has one of his young Americans, fighting at the front for Loyalist Spain, speak a speech in the best tragic manner. He is the young American who refuses to desert when Mr. Anderson's hero tries to persuade him to do so by telling him he and his comrades have been betrayed. What the young American says is:

I have to believe
there's something in the world that isn't
evil —
I have to believe there's something in the
world
that would rather die than accept injus-
tice — something
positive for good — that can't be killed —
or I'll die inside. And now that the sky's
found empty
a man has to be his own god for him-
self —
has to prove to himself that a man can die
for what he believes — if ever the time
comes to him
when he's asked to choose, and it just so
happens
it's up to me tonight.— And I stay here.
I don't say it's up to you — I couldn't
tell
about another man — or any of you —
but I know it's up to me.

When in the last act of *Key Largo* Mr. Anderson's hero is dying, after saving his soul by losing his neck in a silly gangster plot on the island off Florida which gives the play its title, Mr. Anderson once again follows the tragic pattern. "Is this dying?" his hero asks, when the gangster's bullet is in his stomach,

Then it's more enviable than the Ever-
glades,
to fight where you can win, in a narrow
room,
and to win, dying.

Mr. Anderson follows the same pattern again when, after his hero's death, the detective, playing a faint echo to Shakespeare's Kent, says:

You can't be sorry
for a man that planned it, and it all
worked out,
and he got what he wanted —

Much as one may regret that the fly of this emotion has not been embalmed in the amber of great language, one is also forced to realize that when Mr. Anderson follows the tragic pattern he is too well aware of its theory for his own creative good. He writes of ecstasy by rote rather than inspiration. And the pattern shrinks whenever it is memorized, not felt and rediscovered by the spiritual needs of each dramatist who feels the great need of employing it.

FRANCIS FERGUSSON

Born in 1904 in Albuquerque, New Mexico, Fergusson studied at Harvard and, as a Rhodes Scholar, at Oxford. He worked with the experimental American Laboratory Theatre in New York from 1926 to 1930. He has translated Sophocles' *Electra*, written drama criticism, and lectured at colleges and universities, including the New School for Social Research, Bennington College, Princeton University, and Rutgers University. He has published two books on the drama: *The Idea of a Theater* (1949), a study of ten great plays beginning with *Oedipus Rex;* and *The Human Image in Dramatic* *Literature*, a collection of essays (1957). In interpreting a play, his ultimate purpose is to discover its "action," that is, the intention or aim that governs the plot; usually, as Stanislavsky pointed out, the action can be briefly, if incompletely, stated in an infinitive—as, in *Oedipus Rex*, "to find the culprit in order to purify human life." Fergusson supports the theories of the British scholar Gilbert Murray (1866–1957), who found in Greek tragedy traces of their ritual origin. Fergusson's quest for ritual structure has not been confined to Greek drama.

OEDIPUS REX [1]

(1949)

The Cambridge School of Classical Anthropologists has shown in great detail that the form of Greek tragedy follows the form of a very ancient ritual, that of the *Enniautos-Daimon*, or seasonal god.[2] This was one of the most influential discoveries of the last few generations, and it gives us new insights into *Oedipus* which I think are not yet completely explored. The clue to Sophocles' dramatizing of the myth of Oedipus is to be found in this ancient ritual, which had a similar form and meaning—that is, it also moved in the "tragic rhythm."

Experts in classical anthropology, like experts in other fields, dispute innumerable questions of fact and of interpreta-

1 Extracts from Chapter I of *The Idea of a Theatre*, © 1949 by Princeton University Press. Used by permission of the publisher. —Ed.
2 See especially Jane Ellen Harrison's *Ancient Art and Ritual*, and her *Themis* which contains an "Excursus on the ritual forms preserved in Greek Tragedy" by Professor Gilbert Murray.

tion which the layman can only pass over in respectful silence. One of the thornier questions seems to be whether myth or ritual came first. Is the ancient ceremony merely an enactment of the Ur-Myth of the year-god—Attis, or Adonis, or Osiris, or the "Fisher-King"—in any case that Hero-King-Father-High-Priest who fights with his rival, is slain and dismembered, then rises anew with the spring season? Or did the innumerable myths of this kind arise to "explain" a ritual which was perhaps mimed or danced or sung to celebrate the annual change of season?

For the purpose of understanding the form and meaning of *Oedipus,* it is not necessary to worry about the answer to this question of historic fact. The figure of Oedipus himself fulfils all the requirements of the scapegoat, the dismembered king or god-figure. The situation in which Thebes is presented at the beginning of the play—in peril of its life; its crops, its herds, its women mysteriously infertile, signs of a mortal disease of the City, and the disfavor of the gods —is like the withering which winter brings, and calls, in the same way, for struggle, dismemberment, death, and renewal. And this tragic sequence is the substance of the play. It is enough to know that myth and ritual are close together in their genesis, two direct imitations of the perennial experience of the race.

But when one considers *Oedipus* as a ritual one understands it in ways which one cannot by thinking of it merely as a dramatization of a story, even that story. Harrison has shown that the Festival of Dionysos, based ultimately upon the yearly vegetation ceremonies, included *rites de passage,* like that celebrating the assumption of adulthood—celebrations of the mystery of individual growth and development. At the same time, it was a prayer for the welfare of the whole City; and this welfare was understood not only as material prosperity, but also as the natural order of the family, the ancestors, the present members, and the generations still to come, and, by the same token, obedience to the gods who were jealous, each in his own province, of this natural and divinely sanctioned order and proportion. . . .

I have indicated how Sophocles presents the life of the mythic Oedipus in the tragic rhythm, the mysterious quest of life. Oedipus is shown seeking his own true being; but at the same time and by the same token, the welfare of the City. When one considers the ritual form of the whole play, it becomes evident that it presents the tragic but perennial, even normal, quest of the whole City for its well-being. In this larger action, Oedipus is only the protagonist, the first and most important champion. This tragic quest is realized by all the characters in their various ways; but in the development of the action as a whole it is the chorus alone that plays a part as important as that of Oedipus; its counterpart, in fact. The chorus holds the balance between Oedipus and his antagonists, marks the progress of their struggles, and restates the main theme, and its new variation, after each dialogue or agon. The ancient ritual was probably performed by a chorus alone without individual developments and varia-

tions, and the chorus, in *Oedipus,* is still the element that throws most light on the ritual form of the play as a whole.

The chorus consists of twelve or fifteen "Elders of Thebes." This group is not intended to represent literally all of the citizens either of Thebes or of Athens. The play opens with a large delegation of Theban citizens before Oedipus' palace, and the chorus proper does not enter until after the prologue. Nor does the chorus speak directly for the Athenian audience; we are asked throughout to make-believe that the theatre is the agora at Thebes; and at the same time Sophocles' audience is witnessing a ritual. It would, I think, be more accurate to say that the chorus represents the point of view and the faith of Thebes as a whole, and, by analogy, of the Athenian audience. Their errand before Oedipus' palace is like that of Sophocles' audience in the theatre: they are watching a sacred combat, in the issue of which they have an all-important and official stake. Thus they represent the audience and the citizens in a particular way—not as a mob formed in response to some momentary feeling, but rather as an organ of a highly self-conscious community: something closer to the "conscience of the race" than to the overheated affectivity of a mob. . . .

If one thinks of the movement of the play, it appears that the tragic rhythm analyzes human action temporally into successive modes, as a crystal analyzes a white beam of light spatially into the colored bands of the spectrum. The chorus, always present, represents one of these modes, and at the recurrent moments when reasoned purpose is gone, it takes the stage with its faith-informed passion, moving through an ordered succession of modes of suffering, to a new perception of the immediate situation.

Oedipus Rex is a changing image of human life and action which could have been formed only in the mirror of the tragic theatre of the Festival of Dionysos. The perspectives of the myth, of the rituals, and of the traditional *hodos,* the way of life of the City—"habits of thought and feeling" which constitute the traditional wisdom of the race—were all required to make this play possible. That is why we have to try to regain these perspectives if we are to understand the written play which has come down to us: the analysis of the play leads to an analysis of the theatre in which it was formed.

But though the theatre was there, everyone could not use it to the full: Sophocles was required. This becomes clear if one considers the very different use which Euripides, Sophocles' contemporary, makes of the tragic theatre and its ritual forms.

Professor Gilbert Murray has explained in detail how the tragic form is derived from the ritual form; and he has demonstrated the ritual forms which are preserved in each of the extant Greek tragedies. In general, the ritual had its agon, or sacred combat, between the old King, or god or hero, and the new, corresponding to the agons in the tragedies, and the clear "purpose" moment of the tragic rhythm. It had its *Sparagmos*, in which the royal victim was literally or symbolically torn asunder, followed by the lamentation and/or rejoicing of the chorus: elements which correspond to the moments of "passion." The ritual had its messenger, its recognition scene, and its epiphany; various plot devices for representing the moment of "perception" which follows the "pathos." Professor Murray, in a word, studies the art or tragedy in the light of ritual forms, and thus, throws a really new light upon Aristotle's *Poetics*. The parts of the ritual would appear to correspond to parts of the plot, like recognitions and scenes of suffering, which Aristotle mentions, but, in the text which has come down to us, fails to expound completely. In this view, both the ritual and the more highly elaborated and individualized art of tragedy would be "imitating" action in the tragic rhythm; the parts of the ritual, and the parts of the plot, would both be devices for showing forth the three moments of this rhythm.

Professor Murray, however, does not make precisely these deductions. Unlike Aristotle, he takes the plays of Euripides, rather than Sophocles' *Oedipus,* as the patterns of the tragic form. That is because his attitude to the ritual forms is like Euripides' own: he responds to their purely theatrical effectiveness, but has no interest or belief in the prerational image of human nature and destiny which the ritual conveyed; which Sophocles felt as still alive and significant for

his generation, and presented once more in *Oedipus.* Professor Murray shows that Euripides restored the literal ritual much more accurately than Sophocles—his epiphanies, for example, are usually the bodily showing-forth of a very human god, who cynically expounds his cruel part in the proceedings; while the "epiphany" in *Oedipus,* the final tableau of the blind old man with his incestuous brood, merely conveys the moral truth which underlay the action, and implies the anagoge: human dependence upon a mysterious and divine order of nature. Perhaps these distinctions may be summarized as follows: Professor Murray is interested in the ritual forms in abstraction from all content; Sophocles saw also the spiritual content of the old forms: understood them at a level deeper than the literal, as imitations of an action still "true" to life in his sophisticated age. . . .

The general notion we used to compare the forms and spiritual content of tragedy and of ancient ritual was the "imitation of action." Ritual imitates action in one way, tragedy in another; and Sophocles' use of ritual forms indicates that he sensed the tragic rhythm common to both.

But the language, plot, characters of the play may also be understood in more detail and in relation to each other as imitations, in their various media, of the one action. I have already quoted Coleridge on the unity of action: "not properly a rule," he calls it, "but in itself the great end, not only of the drama, but of the epic, lyric, even to the candle-flame cone of an epigram—not only of poetry, but of poesy in general, as the proper generic term inclusive of all the fine arts, as its species." [3] Probably the influence of Coleridge partly accounts for the revival of this notion of action which underlies the recent studies of poetry which I have mentioned. Mr. Burke's [4] phrase, "language as symbolic action;" expresses the idea, and so does his dictum: "The poet spontaneously knows that 'beauty *is* as beauty *does*' (that the 'state' must be embodied in an 'actualization')." (*Four Tropes.*)

This idea of action, and of the play as the imitation of an action, is ultimately

[3] The essay on *Othello.*
[4] Kenneth Burke.—Ed.

derived fruɯ. the *Poetics*. . . . At this point I wish to show how the complex form of *Oedipus*—its plot, characters, and discourse—may be understood as the imitation of a certain action.

The action of the play is the quest for Laius' slayer. That is the over-all aim which informs it—"to find the culprit in order to purify human life," as it may be put. Sophocles must have seen this seeking action as the real life of the Oedipus myth, discerning it through the personages and events as one discerns "life in a plant through the green leaves." Moreover, he must have seen this particular action as a type, or crucial instance, of human life in general; and hence he was able to present it in the form of the ancient ritual which also presents and celebrates the perennial mystery of human life and action. Thus by "action" I do not mean the events of the story but the focus or aim of psychic life from which the events, in that situation, result.

If Sophocles was imitating action in this sense, one may schematically imagine his work of composition in three stages, three mimetic acts: 1. He makes the plot: i.e., arranges the events of the story in such a way as to reveal the seeking action from which they come. 2. He develops the characters of the story as individualized forms of "quest." 3. He expresses or realizes their actions by means of the words they utter in the various situations of the plot. This scheme, of course, has nothing to do with the temporal order which the poet may really have followed in elaborating his composition, nor to the order we follow in becoming acquainted with it; we start with the words, the "green leaves." The scheme refers to the "hierarchy of actualizations" which we may eventually learn to see in the completed work.

1. The first act of imitation consists in making the plot or arrangement of incidents. Aristotle says that the tragic poet is primarily a maker of plots, for the plot is the "soul of a tragedy," its formal cause. The arrangement which Sophocles made of the events of the story —starting near the end, and rehearsing the past in relation to what is happening now—already to some degree actualizes the tragic quest he wishes to show, even before we sense the characters as

individuals or hear them speak and sing. (The reader must be warned that this conception of the plot is rather unfamiliar to us. Usually we do not distinguish between the plot as the form of the play and the plot as producing a certain effect upon the audience—excitement, "interest," suspense, and the like. Aristotle also uses "plot" in this second sense. The mimicry of art has a further purpose, or final—as distinguished from its formal—cause, i.e., to reach the audience. Thinking of the Athenian theatre, he describes the plot as intended to show the "universal," or to rouse and purge the emotions of pity and terror. These two meanings of the word—the form of the action, and the device for reaching the audience. . . . At this point I am using the word *plot* in the first sense: as the form, the first actualization, of the tragic action.)

2. The characters, or agents, are the second actualization of the action. According to Aristotle, "the agents are imitated mainly with a view to the action"—i.e., the soul of the tragedy is there already in the order of events, the tragic rhythm of the life of Oedipus and Thebes; but this action may be more sharply realized and more elaborately shown forth by developing individual variations upon it. It was with this principle in mind that Ibsen wrote to his publisher, after two years' of work on *The Wild Duck,* that the play was nearly complete, and he could now proceed to "the more energetic individuation of the characters."

If one considers the Oedipus-Tiresias scene . . . , one can see how the characters serve to realize the action of the whole. They reveal, at any moment, a "spectrum of action" like that which the tragic rhythm spread before us in temporal succession, at the same time offering concrete instances of almost photographic sharpness. Thus Tiresias "suffers" in the darkness of his blindness while Oedipus pursues his reasoned "purpose"; and then Tiresias effectuates his "purpose" of serving his mantic vision of the truth, while Oedipus "suffers" a blinding passion of fear and anger. The agents also serve to move the action ahead, develop it in time, through their conflicts. The chorus meanwhile, in some respects between, in others deeper, than the antagonists, represents the interests of that resolution, that final chord of feeling, in which the end of the action, seen ironically and sympathetically as one, will be realized.

3. The third actualization is in the words of the play. The seeking action which is the substance of the play is imitated first in the plot, second in the characters, and third in the words, concepts, and forms of discourse wherein the characters "actualize" their psychic life in its shifting forms, in response to the everchanging situations of the play. If one thinks of plotting, characterization, and poetry as successive "acts of imitation" by the author, one may also say that they constitute, in the completed work, a hierarchy of forms; and that the words of the play are its "highest individuation." They are the "green leaves" which we actually perceive; the product and the sign of the one "life of the plant" which, by an imaginative effort, one may divine behind them all.

At this point one encounters again Mr. Burke's theory of "language as symbolic action," and the many contemporary studies of the arts of poetry which have been made from this point of view. It would be appropriate to offer a detailed study of Sophocles' language, using the modern tools of analysis, to substantiate my main point. But this would require the kind of knowledge of Greek which a Jebb spent his life to acquire; and I must be content to try to show, in very general terms, that the varied forms of the poetry of *Oedipus* can only be understood on a histrionic basis: i.e., as coming out of a direct sense of the tragic rhythm of *action*.

In the Oedipus-Tiresias scene, there is a "spectrum of the forms of discourse" corresponding to the "spectrum of action" which I have described. It extends from Oedipus' opening speech—a reasoned exposition not, of course, without feeling but based essentially upon clear ideas and a logical order—to the choral chant, based upon sensuous imagery and the "logic of feeling." Thus it employs, in the beginning, the principle of composition which Mr. Burke calls "syllogistic progression," and, at the other end of the spectrum, Mr. Burke's "progression by association and contrast." When the

Neoclassic and rationalistic critics of the seventeenth century read *Oedipus,* they saw only the order of reason; they did not know what to make of the chorus. Hence Racine's drama of "Action as Rational": a drama of static situations, of clear concepts and merely illustrative images. Nietzsche, on the other hand, saw only the passion of the chorus; for his insight was based on *Tristan,* which is composed essentially in sensuous images, and moves by association and contrast according to the logic of feeling: the drama which takes "action as passion." Neither point of view enables one to see how the scene, as a whole, hangs together.

If the speeches of the characters and the songs of the chorus are only the foliage of the plant, this is as much as to say that the life and meaning of the whole is never literally and completely present in any one formulation. It takes *all* of the elements—the shifting situation, the changing and developing characters, and their reasoned or lyric utterances, to indicate, in the round, the action Sophocles wishes to convey. Because this action takes the form of reason as well as passion, and of contemplation by way of symbols; because it is essentially moving (in the tragic rhythm); and because it is shared in different ways by all the characters, the play has neither literal unity nor the rational unity of the truly abstract idea, or "univocal concept." Its parts and its moments are one only "by analogy"; and just as the Saints warn us that we must believe in order to understand, so we must "make believe," by a sympathetic and imitative act of the histrionic sensibility, in order to get what Sophocles intended by his play.

It is the histrionic basis of Sophocles' art which makes it mysterious to us, with our demands for conceptual clarity, or for the luxury of yielding to a stream of feeling and subjective imagery. But it is this also which makes it so crucial an instance of the art of the theatre in its completeness, as though the author understood "song, spectacle, thought, and diction" in their primitive and subtle roots. And it is the histrionic basis of drama which "undercuts theology and science."

TENNESSEE WILLIAMS

The playwright was born Thomas Lanier Williams in Columbus, Mississippi, 1911; he first called himself Tennessee when he published a short story in 1939. In 1918, the family moved to St. Louis. Williams was educated at the University of Missouri, Washington University, and the State University of Iowa. He published stories and wrote plays, some of them produced in little theatres. By 1940, he was studying playwriting with John Gassner in New York. His *Battle of Angels* opened and closed in Boston in that year. His first Broadway success was *The Glass Menagerie* (1945), "a memory play." *A Streetcar Named Desire* (1947), concerning the collision between a possible nymphomaniac and her brutal brother-in-law, confirmed his promise. In later plays, he continued his employment of bold sexual patterns, symbolism, and Southern settings. In *Sweet Bird of Youth* (1959), some social criticism is apparent. Other plays include *Summer and Smoke* (1948), *The Rose Tattoo* (1951), *Camino Real* (1953), *Cat on a Hot Tin Roof* (1955), *Orpheus Descending* (1957, a revision of *Battle of Angels*), *Garden District* (1958, two one-act plays performed off Broadway), *Period of Adjustment* (1960, a comedy of married life), and *The Night of the Iguana* (1961). Most of Williams' longer plays have been filmed, and Williams is himself the author of the script for the film *Baby Doll,* based on two of his one-act plays. He has received two Pulitzer Prizes and three awards of the Drama Critics Circle. He is generally regarded as the leading American dramatist.

THE TIMELESS WORLD OF A PLAY [1]

(1951)

Carson McCullers concludes one of her lyric poems with the line: "Time, the endless idiot, runs screaming 'round the world." It is this continual rush of time, so violent that it appears to be screaming, that deprives our actual lives of so much dignity and meaning, and it is, perhaps more than anything else, the *arrest of time* which has taken place in a completed work of art that gives to certain plays their feeling of depth and significance. In the London notices of *Death of a Salesman* a certain notoriously skeptical critic made the remark that Willy Loman was the sort of man that almost any member of the audience had kicked out of an office had he applied for a job or detained one for conversation about his troubles. The remark itself possibly holds some truth. But the implication that Willy Loman is consequently a character with whom we have no reason to concern ourselves in drama,

1 The author's preface to *The Rose Tattoo.* © 1950, 1951 by Tennessee Williams. Used by permission of New Directions.—Ed.

reveals a strikingly false conception of what plays are. Contemplation is something that exists outside of time, and so is the tragic sense. Even in the actual world of commerce, there exists in some persons a sensibility to the unfortunate situations of others, a capacity for concern and compassion, surviving from a more tender period of life outside the present whirling wire-cage of business activity. Facing Willy Loman across an office desk, meeting his nervous glance and hearing his querulous voice, we would be very likely to glance at our wrist watch and our schedule of other appointments. We would not kick him out of the office, no, but we would certainly *ease* him out with more expedition than Willy had feebly hoped for. But suppose there had been no wrist watch or office clock and suppose there had *not* been the schedule of pressing appointments, and suppose that we were not actually facing Willy across a desk—and facing a person is *not* the best way to *see* him!—suppose, in other words, that the meeting with Willy Loman had somehow occurred in a world *outside* of time. Then I think we would receive him with concern and kindness and even with respect. If the world of a play did not offer us this occasion to view its characters under that special condition of a *world without time,* then, indeed, the characters and occurrences of drama would become equally pointless, equally trivial, as corresponding meetings and happenings in life.

The classic tragedies of Greece had tremendous nobility. The actors wore great masks, movements were formal, dance-like, and the speeches had an epic quality which doubtless were as removed from the normal conversation of their contemporary society as they seem today. Yet they did not seem false to the Greek audiences: the magnitude of the events and the passions aroused by them did not seem ridiculously out of proportion to common experience. And I wonder if this was not because the Greek audiences knew, instinctively or by training, that the created world of a play is removed from that element which makes people *little* and their emotions fairly inconsequential.

Great sculpture often follows the lines of the human body: yet the repose of great sculpture suddenly transmutes those human lines to something that has an absoluteness, a purity, a beauty, which would not be possible in a living mobile form.

A play may be violent, full of motion: yet it has that special kind of repose which allows contemplation and produces the climate in which tragic importance is a possible thing, provided that certain modern conditions are met.

In actual existence the moments of love are succeeded by the moments of satiety and sleep. The sincere remark is followed by a cynical distrust. Truth is fragmentary, at best: we love and betray each other not in quite the same breath but in two breaths that occur in fairly close sequence. But the fact that passion occurred in *passing,* that it then declined into a more familiar sense of indifference, should not be regarded as proof of its inconsequence. And this is the very truth that drama wishes to bring us . . .

Whether or not we admit it to ourselves, we are all haunted by a truly awful sense of impermanence. I have always had a particularly keen sense of this at New York cocktail parties, and perhaps that is why I drink the martinis almost as fast as I can snatch them from the tray. This sense is the febrile thing that hangs in the air. Horror of insincerity, of *not meaning,* overhangs these affairs like the cloud of cigarette smoke and the hectic chatter. This horror is the only thing, almost, that is left unsaid at such functions. All social functions involving a group of people not intimately known to each other are always under this shadow. They are almost always (in an unconscious way) like that last dinner of the condemned: where steak or turkey, whatever the doomed man wants, is served in his cell as a mockingly cruel reminder of what the great-big-little-transitory world had to offer.

In a play, time is arrested in the sense of being confined. By a sort of legerdemain, events are made to remain *events,* rather than being reduced so quickly to mere *occurrences.* The audience can sit back in a comforting dusk to watch a world which is flooded with light and in which emotion and action have a dimension and dignity that they would likewise have in real existence, if only the shattering intrusion of time could be locked out.

About their lives people ought to remember that when they are finished, everything in them will be contained in a marvelous state of repose which is the same as that which they unconsciously admired in drama. The rush is temporary. The great and only possible dignity of man lies in his power deliberately to choose certain moral values by which to live as steadfastly as if he, too, like a character in a play, were immured against the corrupting rush of time. Snatching the eternal out of the desperately fleeting is the great magic trick of human existence. As far as we know, as far as there exists any kind of empiric evidence, there is no way to beat the game of *being* against *non-being,* in which non-being is the predestined victor on realistic levels.

Yet plays in the tragic tradition offer us a view of certain moral values in violent juxtaposition. Because we do not participate, except as spectators, we can view them clearly, within the limits of our emotional equipment. These people on the stage do not return our looks. We do not have to answer their questions nor make any sign of being in company with them, nor do we have to compete with their virtues nor resist their offences. All at once, for this reason, we are able to *see* them! Our hearts are wrung by recognition and pity, so that the dusky shell of the auditorium where we are gathered anonymously together is flooded with an almost liquid warmth of unchecked human sympathies, relieved of self-consciousness, allowed to function ...

Men pity and love each other more deeply than they permit themselves to know. The moment after the phone has been hung up, the hand reaches for a scratch pad and scrawls a notation: "Funeral Tuesday at five, Church of the Holy Redeemer, don't forget flowers." And the same hand is only a little shakier than usual as it reaches, some minutes later, for a highball glass that will pour a stupefaction over the kindled nerves. Fear and evasion are the two little beasts that chase each other's tails in the revolving wire-cage of our nervous world. They distract us from feeling too much about things. Time rushes toward us with its hospital tray of infinitely varied narcotics, even while it is preparing us for its inevitably fatal operation ...

So successfully have we disguised from ourselves the intensity of our own feelings, the sensibility of our own hearts, that plays in the tragic tradition have begun to seem untrue. For a couple of hours we may surrender ourselves to a world of fiercely illuminated values in conflict, but when the stage is covered and the auditorium lighted, almost immediately there is a recoil of disbelief. "Well, well!" we say as we shuffle back up the aisle, while the play dwindles behind us with the sudden perspective of an early Chirico painting. By the time we have arrived at Sardi's, if not as soon as we pass beneath the marquee, we have convinced ourselves once more that life has as little resemblance to the curiously stirring and meaningful occurrences on the stage as a jingle has to an elegy of Rilke.

This modern condition of his theatre audience is something that an author must know in advance. The diminishing influence of life's destroyer, time, must be somehow worked into the context of his play. Perhaps it is a certain foolery, a certain distortion toward the grotesque, which will solve the problem for him. Perhaps it is only restraint, putting a mute on the strings that would like to break all bounds. But almost surely, unless he contrives in some way to relate the dimensions of his tragedy to the dimensions of a world in which time is *included*—he will be left among his magnificent debris on a dark stage, muttering to himself: "Those fools ..."

And if they could hear him above the clatter of tongues, glasses, chinaware and silver, they would give him this answer: "But you have shown us a world not ravaged by time. We admire your innocence. But we have seen our photographs, past and present. Yesterday evening we passed our first wife on the street. We smiled as we spoke but we didn't really see her! It's too bad, but we know what is true and not true, and at 3 A.M. your disgrace will be in print!"

NORTHROP FRYE

Northrop Frye, born in 1912, is professor of English at Victoria College, University of Toronto. His first book, *Fearful Symmetry: A Study of William Blake,* was followed by *Anatomy of Criticism* (1957), a full study of the nature, the subject matter, and the technique of literary criticism. Profoundly influenced by modern anthropology and by the Swiss psychologist Carl Jung, Frye conceives of criticism as a science comparable to anthropology and other social sciences. The critic's first function—or Fry's first function as a critic —is to analyze the archetype of a literary genre, that is, to find its basic quality and its category. The archetype is ultimately the product of what Jung would have called the collective unconscious of the human race; it is created over centuries of use and re-use, and it takes such forms as the association of comedy with courtship, conversion, and triumph over the father; of tragedy with sacrifice and the hero's fall; of romance with wish-fulfillment and the quest.

SPECIFIC FORMS OF DRAMA [1]

(1957)

. . . The division of dramas into tragedies and comedies . . . is a conception based entirely on verbal drama, and does not include or account for types of drama, such as the opera or masque, in which music and scenery have a more organic place. Yet verbal drama, whether tragic or comic, has clearly developed a long way from the primitive idea of drama, which is to present a powerful sensational focus for a community. The scriptural plays of the Middle Ages are primitive in this sense: they present to the audience a myth already familiar to and significant for that audience, and they are designed to remind the audience of their communal possession of this myth.

The scriptural play is a form of a spectacular dramatic genre which we may provisionally call a "myth-play." It is a somewhat negative and receptive form, and takes on the mood of the myth it represents. The crucifixion play in the Towneley cycle is tragic because the Crucifixion is; but it is not a tragedy in the sense that *Othello* is a tragedy. It does not, that is, make a tragic *point;* it simply presents the story because it is familiar and significant. It would be nonsense to apply such tragic conceptions as hybris to the figure of Christ in that play, and while pity and terror are raised, they remain attached to the subject, and there is no catharsis of them. The characteristic mood and resolution of the myth-play are pensive, and pensiveness, in this context, implies a continuing imaginative subjection to the story. The myth-play emphasizes dramatically the symbol of spiritual and corporeal communion. The scriptural plays themselves were associated with

1 Extracts from a section of the Fourth Essay, "Rhetorical Criticism: Theory of Genres," in *Anatomy of Criticism.* © 1957 by Princeton University Press. Used by permission of the publisher.—Ed.

the festival of Corpus Christi, and Calderon's religious plays are explicitly *autos sacramentales* or Eucharist plays. The appeal of the myth-play is a curious mixture of the popular and the esoteric; it is popular for its immediate audience, but those outside its circle have to make a conscious effort to appreciate it. In a controversial atmosphere it disappears, as it cannot deal with controversial issues unless it selects its audience. In view of the ambiguities attaching to the word myth, we shall speak of this genre as the *auto.*

When there is no clear-cut distinction between gods and heroes in a society's mythology, or between the ideals of the nobility and the priesthood, the *auto* may present a legend which is secular and sacred at once. An example is the No drama of Japan, which with its unification of chivalric and otherworldly symbols and its dreamy un-tragic, un-comic mood so strongly attracted Yeats. It is interesting to see how Yeats, both in his theory of the *anima mundi* and in his desire to get his play as physically close to the audience as possible, reverts to the archaic idea of corporeal communion. In Greek drama, too, there is no sharp boundary line between the divine and the heroic protagonist. But in Christian societies we can see glimpses of a secular *auto,* a romantic drama presenting the exploits of a hero, which is closely related to tragedy, the end of a hero's exploit being eventually his death, but which in itself is neither tragic nor comic, being primarily spectacular.

Tamburlaine is such a play: there the relation between the hero's hybris and his death is more casual than causal. This genre has had varying luck: more in Spain, for instance, than in France, where the establishing of tragedy was part of an intellectual revolution. The two attempts in France to move tragedy back towards heroic romance, *Le Cid* and

Hernani, each precipitated a big row. In Germany, on the other hand, it is clear that the actual genre of many plays by Goethe and Schiller is the heroic romance, however much affected they have been by the prestige of tragedy. In Wagner, who expands the heroic form all the way back to a sacramental drama of gods, the symbol of communion again occupies a conspicuous place, negatively in *Tristan,* positively in *Parsifal.* In proportion as it moves closer to tragedy and further from the sacred *auto,* drama tends to make less use of music. If we look at the earliest extant play of Aeschylus, *The Suppliants,* we can see that close behind it is a predominantly musical structure of which the modern counterpart would normally be the oratorio —it is perhaps possible to describe Wagner's operas as fermented oratorios.

In Renaissance England the audience was too bourgeois for a chivalric drama to get firmly established, and the Elizabethan secular *auto* eventually became the history-play. With the history-play we move from spectacle to a more purely verbal drama, and the symbols of communion become much attenuated, although they are still there. The central theme of Elizabethan history is the unifying of the nation and the binding of the audience into the myth as the inheritors of that unity, set over against the disasters of civil war and weak leadership. One may even recognize a secular Eucharist symbol in the red and white rose, just as one may recognize in the plays that end by pointing to Elizabeth, like Peele's *Arraignment of Paris,* a secular counterpart of a mystery play of the Virgin. But the emphasis and characteristic resolution of the history play are in terms of continuity and the closing up both of tragic catastrophe and (as in the case of Falstaff) of the comic festival. One may compare Shaw's "chronicle play" of *Saint Joan,* where the end of the play is a tragedy, followed by an epilogue in which the rejection of Joan is, like the rejection of Falstaff, historical, suggesting continuity rather than a rounded finish.

The history merges so gradually into tragedy that we often cannot be sure when communion has turned into catharsis. *Richard II* and *Richard III* are tragedies insofar as they resolve on those defeated kings; they are histories insofar as they resolve on Bolingbroke and Richmond, and the most one can say is that they lean toward history. *Hamlet* and *Macbeth* lean toward tragedy, but Fortinbras and Malcolm, the continuing characters, indicate the historical element in the tragic resolution. There seems to be a far less direct connection between history and comedy: the comic scenes in the histories are, so to speak, subversive. *Henry V* ends in triumph and marriage, but an action that kills Falstaff, hangs Bardolph and debases Pistol is not related to comedy in the way that *Richard II* is related to tragedy.

We are here concerned only with tragedy as a species of drama. Tragic drama derives from the *auto* its central heroic figure, but the association of heroism with downfall is due to the simultaneous presence of irony. The nearer the tragedy is to *auto,* the more closely associated the hero is with divinity; the nearer to irony, the more human the hero is, and the more the catastrophe appears to be a social rather than a cosmological event. Elizabethan tragedy shows a historical development from Marlowe, who presents his heroes more or less as demigods moving in a kind of social ether, to Webster, whose tragedies are almost clinical analyses of a sick society. Greek tragedy never broke completely from the *auto,* and so never developed a social form, though there are tendencies to it in Euripides. But whatever the proportions of heroism and irony, tragedy shows itself to be primarily a vision of the supremacy of the event or *mythos.* The response to tragedy is "this must be," or, perhaps more accurately, "this does happen": the event is primary, the explanation of it secondary and variable.

As tragedy moves over towards irony, the sense of inevitable event begins to fade out, and the sources of catastrophe come into view. In irony catastrophe is either arbitrary and meaningless, the impact of an unconscious (or, in the pathetic fallacy, malignant) world on conscious man, or the result of more or less definable social and psychological forces. Tragedy's "this must be" becomes irony's "this at least is," a concentration on foreground facts and a rejection of mythical superstructures. Thus the ironic drama is a vision of what in theology is called the fallen world, of simple humanity, man as natural man and in conflict with both human and non-human nature. In nineteenth-century drama the tragic vision is often identical with the ironic one, hence nineteenth-century tragedies tend to be either *Schicksal* dramas dealing with the arbitrary ironies of fate, or (clearly the more rewarding form) studies of the frustrating and smothering of human activity by the combined pressure of a reactionary society without and a disorganized soul within. Such irony is difficult to sustain in the theatre because it tends toward a stasis of action. In those parts of Chekhov, notably the last act of *The Three Sisters,* where the characters one by one withdraw from each other into their subjective prison-cells, we are coming about as close to pure irony as the stage can get. . . .

Ironic comedy presents us of course with "the way of the world," but as soon as we find sympathetic or even neutral characters in a comedy, we move into the more familiar comic area where we have a group of humors outwitted by the opposing group. Just as tragedy is a vision of the supremacy of *mythos* or thing done, and just as irony is a vision of *ethos,* or character individualized against environment, so comedy is a vision of *dianoia,* a significance which is ultimately social significance, the establishing of a desirable society. As an imitation of life, drama is, in terms of *mythos,* conflict; in terms of *ethos,* a representative image; in terms of *dianoia,* the final harmonic chord revealing the tonality under the narrative movement, it is community. The further comedy moves from irony, the more it becomes what we here call ideal comedy, the vision not of the way of the world, but of what you will, life as you like it. Shakespeare's main interest is in getting away from the son-father conflict of ironic comedy towards a vision of a serene community, a vision most prominent in *The Tempest.* Here the action is polarized around a younger and an older man working in harmony together, a lover and a benevolent teacher.

The next step brings us to the extreme limit of social comedy, the symposium, the structure of which is, as we should expect, clearest in Plato, whose Socrates is both teacher and lover, and whose vision moves toward an integration of society in a form like that of the symposium itself, the dialectic festivity which, as is explained in the opening of the *Laws,* is the controlling force that holds society together. It is easy to see that Plato's dialogue form is dramatic and has affinities with comedy and mime; and while there is much in Plato's thought that contradicts the spirit of comedy as we have outlined it, it is significant that he contradicts it directly, tries to kidnap it, so to speak. It seems almost a rule that the more he does this, the further he moves into pure exposition or dictatorial monologue and away from drama. The most dramatic of his dialogues, such as *Euthydemus,* are regularly the most indecisive in philosophical "position."

In our own day Bernard Shaw has tried hard to keep the symposium in the theatre. His early manifesto, *The Quintessence of Ibsenism,* states that a play should be an intelligent discussion of a serious problem, and in his preface to *Getting Married* he remarks approvingly on the fact that it observes the unities of time and place. For comedy of Shaw's type tends to a symposium form which occupies the same amount of time in its action that the audience consumes in watching it. However, Shaw discovered in practice that what emerges from the theatrical symposium is not a dialectic that compels to a course of action or thought, but one that emancipates from formulated principles of conduct. The shape of such a comedy is very clear in the bright little sketch *In Good King Charles's Golden Days,* where even the most highly developed human types, the saintly Fox and the philosophical Newton, are shown to be comic humors by the mere presence of other types of people. Yet the central symposium figure of the haranguing lover bulks formidably in *Man and Superman,* and even the renunciation of love for mathematics at the end of *Back to Methusaleh* is consistent with the symposium spirit. . . .

The further comedy moves from irony, and the more it rejoices in the free movement of its happy society, the more readily it takes to music and dancing. As music and scenery increase in importance, the ideal comedy crosses the boundary line of spectacular drama and becomes the masque. In Shakespeare's ideal comedies, especially *A Midsummer Night's Dream* and *The Tempest,* the close affinity with the masque is not hard to see. The masque—or at least the kind of masque that is nearest to comedy, and which we shall here call the ideal masque—is still in the area of *dianoia:* it is usually a compliment to the audience, or an important member of it, and leads up to an idealization of the society represented by that audience. Its plots and characters are fairly stock, as they exist only in relation to the significance of the occasion.

It thus differs from comedy in its more intimate attitude to the audience: there is more insistence on the connection between the audience and the community on the stage. The members of a masque are ordinarily disguised members of the audience, and there is a final gesture of surrender when the actors unmask and join the audience in a dance. The ideal masque is in fact a myth-play like the *auto,* to which it is related much as comedy is to tragedy. It is designed to emphasize, not the ideals to be achieved by discipline or faith, but ideals which are desired or considered to be already possessed. Its settings are seldom remote from magic and fairyland, from Arcadias and visions of earthly Paradise. It uses gods freely, like the *auto,* but possessively, and without imaginative subjection. In Western drama, from the Renaissance to the end of the eighteenth century, masque and ideal comedy make great use of Classical mythology, which the audience is not obliged to accept as "true."

The rather limited masque throws some light on the structure and characteristics of its two far more important and versatile neighbors. For the masque is flanked on one side by the musically organized drama which we call opera, and on the other by a scenically organized drama, which has now settled in the movie. Puppet-plays and the vast Chinese romances where, as in the movie, the audience enters and leaves unpredictably, are examples of pre-camera scenic masques. Both opera and movie are, like the masque, proverbial for lavish display, and part of the reason for it in the movie is that many movies are actually bourgeois myth-plays, as half a dozen critics suddenly and almost simultaneously discovered a few years ago. The predominance of the private life of the actor in the imaginations of many moviegoers may perhaps have some analogy with the consciously assumed disguise of the masque. . . .

For our next step we must return to the masque proper. The further comedy moves from irony, the less social power is allowed to the humors. In the masque, where the ideal society is still more in the ascendant, the humors become degraded into the uncouth figures of the Jonsonian antimasque, who are said to be descended from a dramatic form far older than the rest of the masque. Farce, being a non-mimetic form of comedy, has a natural place in the masque, though in the ideal masque its natural place is that of a rigorously controlled interlude. In *The Tempest,* a comedy so profound that it seems to draw the whole masque into itself, Stephano and Trinculo are comic humors and Caliban an antimasque figure, and the group shows the transition very clearly. The main theme of the masque involves gods, fairies, and personifications of virtues; the figures of the antimasque thus tend to become demonic, and dramatic characterization begins to split into an antithesis of virtue and vice, god and devil, fairy and monster. The tension between them partly accounts for the importance of the theme of magic in the masque. At the comic end this magic is held by the benevolent side, as in *The Tempest;* but as we move further away from comedy, the conflict becomes increasingly serious, and the antimasque figures less ridiculous and more sinister, possessed in their turn of powers of enchantment. This is the stage represented by *Comus,* which is very close to the open conflict of good and evil in the morality play. With the morality play we pass into another area of masque which we shall here call the archetypal masque, the prevailing form of most twentieth-century highbrow drama, at least in continental Europe, as well as of many experimental operas and unpopular movies.

The ideal masque tends to individualize its audience by pointing to the central member of it: even the movie audience, sitting in the dark in small units (usually of two), is a relatively individualized one. A growing sense of loneliness is noticeable as we move away from comedy. The archetypal masque, like all forms of spectacular drama, tends to detach its settings from time and space, but instead of the Arcadias of the ideal masque, we find ourselves frequently in a sinister limbo, like the threshold of death in *Everyman*, the sealed underworld crypts of Maeterlinck, or the nightmares of the future in expressionist plays. As we get nearer the rationale of the form, we see that the *auto* symbol of communion in one body is reappearing, but in a psychological and subjective form, and without gods. The action of the archetypal masque takes place in a world of human types, which at its most concentrated becomes the interior of the human mind. This is explicit even in the old moralities, like *Mankynd* and *The Castell of Perseverance*, and at least implicit in a good deal of Maeterlinck, Pirandello, Andreyev, and Strindberg.

Naturally, with such a setting, characterization has to break down into elements and fragments of personality. This is why I call the form the archetypal masque, the word archetype being in this context used in Jung's sense of an aspect of the personality capable of dramatic projection. Jung's persona and anima and counsellor and shadow throw a great deal of light on the characterization of modern allegorical, psychic, and expressionist dramas, with their circus barkers and wraith-like females and inscrutable sages and obsessed demons. The abstract entities of the morality play and the stock types of the commedia dell' arte (this latter representing one of the primitive roots of the genre) are similar constructions.

A sense of confusion and fear accompanies the sense of loneliness: Maeterlinck's early plays are almost dedicated to fear, and the constant undermining of the distinction between illusion and reality, as mental projections become physical bodies and vice versa, splits the action up into a kaleidoscopic chaos of reflecting mirrors. The mob scenes of German expressionist plays and the mechanical fantasies of the Capeks show the same disintegration at work in a social context. From the generic point of view, one of the most interesting archetypal plays is Andreyev's powerful *The Black Maskers,* in which its author saw reflected not only the destruction of an individual's *nobile castello,* which is its explicit theme, but the whole social collapse of modern Russia. This play distinguishes two groups of dissociative elements of personality, one group connected with self-accusation and the other with the death-wish, and it exhibits the human soul as a castle possessed by a legion of demons. It is evident that the further the archetypal masque gets from the ideal masque, the more clearly it reveals itself as the emancipated antimasque, a revel of satyrs who have got out of control. The progress of sophisticated drama appears to be towards an *anagnorisis* or recognition of the most primitive of all dramatic forms.

At the far end of the archetypal masque, where it joins the *auto,* we reach the point indicated by Nietzsche as the point of the birth of tragedy, where the revel of satyrs impinges on the appearance of a commanding god, and Dionysos is brought into line with Apollo. We may call this fourth cardinal point of drama the epiphany, the dramatic apocalypse or separation of the divine and the demonic, a point directly opposite the mime, which presents the simply human mixture. This point is the dramatic form of the point of epiphany, most familiar as the point at which the Book of Job, after describing a complete circuit from tragedy through symposium, finally ends. Here the two monsters behemoth and leviathan replace the more frequent demonic animals.

The Classical critics, from Aristotle to Horace, were puzzled to understand why a disorganized ribald farce like the satyr-play should be the source of tragedy, though they were clear that it was. In medieval drama, where the progression through sacred and heroic *auto* to tragedy is so much less foreshortened, the development is plainer. The most clearly epiphanic form of scriptural drama is the Harrowing of Hell play, which depicts the triumph of a divine redeemer over demonic resistance. The devils of that play are the Christian forms of figures very like the Greek satyrs, and dramatic groups generically very close to the satyrs are never far from any scriptural play that deals directly with Christ, whether tamed and awed as in the *Secunda Pastorum,* or triumphantly villainous, as in the crucifixion and Herod plays. And just as Greek tragedy retained and developed the satyr-play, so Elizabethan tragedy retains a satyric counterpoint in its clown scenes and the farcical underplots of *Faustus* and many later tragedies. The same element provides those superb episodes of the porter in *Macbeth,* the grave-diggers in *Hamlet,* and the serpent-bearer in *Antony and Cleopatra,* which so baffled Classically-minded critics who had forgotten about the satyr-play. Perhaps we could make more dramatic sense out of *Titus Andronicus* if we could see it as an unharrowed hell, a satyr-play of obscene and gibbering demons.

The two nodes of the scriptural play are Christmas and Easter: the latter presents the triumphant god, the former the quiet virgin mother who gathers to herself the processional masque of the kings and shepherds. This figure is at the opposite end of the masque from the watching queen or peeress of an ideal masque, with the virtuous but paralyzed Lady of *Comus* halfway between. A female figure symbolizing some kind of reconciling unity and order appears dimly at the end of the great panoramic masques of *Faust* and *Peer Gynt,* the "eternal feminine" of the former having some of its traditional links. Modern examples of the same epiphanic form range from Claudel's Annunciation play to Yeats's *Countess Cathleen,* where the heroine is really a female and Irish Jesus, sacrificing herself for her people and then cheating the devils by the purity of her nature, very much as in the pre-Anselm theory of the atonement. As Yeats remarks in a note, the story represents one of the supreme parables of the world.

ARTHUR MILLER

Miller, born in New York in 1915, attended the University of Michigan where he won several Avery Hopwood prizes in writing. He worked at odd jobs and for the WPA Federal Theatre. Gathering material for a war film, he incidentially provided himself with material for a book of journalism about America at war, *Situation Normal* (1944). He also wrote a novel about anti-Semitism, *Focus* (1945), and several short stories, one of which he eventually converted into the script of a film, *The Misfits* (1961). His first Broadway play, *The Man Who Had All the Luck* (1944), was a quick failure, but it was soon followed by the successful *All My Sons* (1947), about a manufacturer who supplies shoddy goods to the army during the war and encounters the just rage of his son. Departing from conventional realism, Miller employed a somewhat expressionistic method in his best-received play, *Death of a Salesman* (1949), in which a typical American salesman surveys his life and blindly refuses to see his errors. In *The Crucible* (1953), Miller used the Salem witch trials to make an indirect but emphatic comment upon McCarthyism in American life. Two one-act plays were performed in 1955, *A Memory of Two Mondays,* a casual presentation of workers in an automobile-parts warehouse, and *A View from the Bridge,* a longer work which aspired to tragedy with its pitiful account of a Brooklyn longshoreman. Although this last play invaded Tennessee Williams' area of peculiar sexual motivation—the longshoreman has unacknowledged incestuous feelings— Miller continues to be considered to be our leading social dramatist. The Lincoln Center Repertory Company produced his latest play, *After the Fall,* for its opening performance early in 1964.

TRAGEDY AND THE COMMON MAN [1]

(1949)

In this age few tragedies are written. It has often been held that the lack is due to a paucity of heroes among us, or else that modern man has had the blood drawn out of his organs of belief by the skepticism of science, and the heroic attack on life cannot feed on an attitude of reserve and circumspection. For one reason or another, we are often held to be below tragedy—or tragedy above us. The inevitable conclusion is, of course, that the tragic mode is archaic, fit only for the very highly placed, the kings or the kingly, and where this admission is not made in so many words it is most often implied.

I believe that the common man is as apt a subject for tragedy in its highest sense as kings were. On the face of it this ought to be obvious in the light of modern psychiatry, which bases its analysis upon classific formulations, such as the Oedipus and Orestes complexes, for instance, which were enacted by royal beings, but which apply to everyone in similar emotional situations.

More simply, when the question of tragedy in art is not at issue, we never hesitate to attribute to the well-placed and the exalted the very same mental processes as the lowly. And finally, if the exaltation of tragic action were truly a property of the high-bred character alone, it is inconceivable that the mass of mankind should cherish tragedy above all other forms, let alone be capable of understanding it.

As a general rule, to which there may be exceptions unknown to me, I think the tragic feeling is evoked in us when we are in the presence of a character who is ready to lay down his life, if need be, to secure one thing—his sense of personal dignity. From Orestes to Hamlet, Medea to Macbeth, the underlying struggle is that of the individual attempting to gain

1 This article appeared in *The New York Times,* February 27, 1949, following the opening of *Death of a Salesman.* © 1949 by the New York Times Company. Used by permission of *The New York Times* and Ashley-Steiner, Inc.—Ed.

his "rightful" position in his society.

Sometimes he is one who has been displaced from it, sometimes one who seeks to attain it for the first time, but the fateful wound from which the inevitable events spiral is the wound of indignity, and its dominant force is indignation. Tragedy, then, is the consequence of a man's total compulsion to evaluate himself justly.

In the sense of having been initiated by the hero himself, the tale always reveals what has been called his "tragic flaw," a failing that is not peculiar to grand or elevated characters. Nor is it necessarily a weakness. The flaw, or crack in the character, is really nothing—and need be nothing—but his inherent unwillingness to remain passive in the face of what he conceives to be a challenge to his dignity, his image of his rightful status. Only the passive, only those who accept their lot without active retaliation, are "flawless." Most of us are in that category.

But there are among us today, as there always have been, those who act against the scheme of things that degrades them, and in the process of action everything we have accepted out of fear or insensitivity or ignorance is shaken before us and examined, and from this total onslaught by an individual against the seemingly stable cosmos surrounding us —from this total examination of the "unchangeable" environment—comes the terror and the fear that is classically associated with tragedy.

More important, from this total questioning of what has been previously unquestioned, we learn. And such a process is not beyond the common man. In revolutions around the world, these past thirty years, he has demonstrated again and again this inner dynamic of all tragedy.

Insistence upon the rank of the tragic hero, or the so-called nobility of his character, is really but a clinging to the outward forms of tragedy. If rank or nobility of character was indispensable, then it would follow that the problems of those with rank were the particular problems of tragedy. But surely the right of one monarch to capture the domain from another no longer raises our passions, nor are our concepts of justice what they were to the mind of an Elizabethan king.

The quality in such plays that does shake us, however, derives from the underlying fear of being displaced, the disaster inherent in being torn away from our chosen image of what and who we are in this world. Among us today this fear is as strong, and perhaps stronger, than it ever was. In fact, it is the common man who knows this fear best.

Now, if it is true that tragedy is the consequence of a man's total compulsion to evaluate himself justly, his destruction in the attempt posits a wrong or an evil in his environment. And this is precisely the morality of tragedy and its lesson. The discovery of the moral law, which is what the enlightenment of tragedy consists of, is not the discovery of some abstract or metaphysical quantity.

The tragic right is a condition of life, a condition in which the human personality is able to flower and realize itself. The wrong is the condition which suppresses man, perverts the flowing out of his love and creative instinct. Tragedy enlightens—and it must, in that it points the heroic finger at the enemy of man's freedom. The thrust for freedom is the quality in tragedy which exalts. The revolutionary questioning of the stable environment is what terrifies. In no way is the common man debarred from such thoughts or such actions.

Seen in this light, our lack of tragedy may be partially accounted for by the turn which modern literature has taken toward the purely psychiatric view of life, or the purely sociological. If all our miseries, our indignities, are born and bred within our minds, then all action, let alone the heroic action, is obviously impossible.

And if society alone is responsible for the cramping of our lives, then the protagonist must needs be so pure and faultless as to force us to deny his validity as a character. From neither of these views can tragedy derive, simply because neither represents a balanced concept of life. Above all else, tragedy requires the finest appreciation by the writer of cause and effect.

No tragedy can therefore come about when its author fears to question absolutely everything, when he regards any institution, habit or custom as being either everlasting, immutable or inevitable. In the tragic view the need of man to wholly realize himself is the only fixed star, and whatever it is that hedges his nature and lowers it is ripe for attack and examination. Which is not to say that tragedy must preach revolution.

The Greeks could probe the very heavenly origin of their ways and return to confirm the rightness of laws. And Job could face God in anger, demanding his right, and end in submission. But for a moment everything is in suspension, nothing is accepted, and in this stretching and tearing apart of the cosmos, in the very action of so doing, the character gains "size," the tragic stature which is spuriously attached to the royal or the high born in our minds. The commonest of men may take on that stature to the extent of his willingness to throw all he has into the contest, the battle to secure his rightful place in his world.

There is a misconception of tragedy with which I have been struck in review after review, and in many conversations with writers and readers alike. It is the ideal that tragedy is of necessity allied to pessimism. Even the dictionary says nothing more about the word than that it means a story with a sad or unhappy ending. This impression is so firmly fixed that I almost hesitate to claim that in truth tragedy implies more optimism in its author than does comedy, and that its final result ought to be the reinforcement of the onlooker's brightest opinions of the human animal.

For, if it is true to say that in essence the tragic hero is intent upon claiming his whole due as a personality, and if this struggle must be total and without reservation, then it automatically demonstrates the indestructible will of man to achieve his humanity.

The possibility of victory must be there in tragedy. Where pathos rules, where pathos is finally derived, a character has fought a battle he could not possibly have won. The pathetic is achieved when the protagonist is, by virtue of his witlessness, his insensitivity, or the very air he gives off, incapable of grappling with a much superior force:

Pathos truly is the mode for the pessimist. But tragedy requires a nicer balance between what is possible and what is impossible. And it is curious, although edifying, that the plays we revere, century after century, are the tragedies. In them, and in them alone, lies the belief—optimistic, if you will—in the perfectibility of man.

It is time, I think, that we who are without kings, took up this bright thread of our history and followed it to the only place it can possibly lead in our time—the heart and spirit of the average man.

ERIC BENTLEY

Born in Bolton, England, in 1916, Bentley studied music and was later a student at Oxford, where he did some acting, including a performance in *Richard II*, directed by John Gielgud. He earned his doctorate in comparative literature at Yale; *A Century of Hero-Worship,* based on his dissertation, appeared in 1944. Subsequent books included *The Playwright as Thinker* (1946), *Bernard Shaw* (1947), *In Search of Theater* (1953), *The Dramatic Event* (1954), and *What is Theatre?* (1956). The last two volumes consist mainly of reviews contributed to the *New Republic* while Bentley was its drama critic. In addition, Bentley has translated plays by Brecht, Pirandello, and others and has edited many collections of plays.

He has taught principally at the University of Minnesota and at Columbia University, where he has been Brander Matthews Professor of Dramatic Literature since 1954. He has had considerable experience as a director, much of it in Europe—Dublin, Salzburg, Zurich, Padua, and Munich—and in Munich he assisted Brecht in a production of *Mother Courage.* In his drama criticism, he has championed writers new to the American theatre, like Brecht and Sartre, and he has restored shaky reputations, like those of Strindberg and Pirandello. His comic flair has been a useful tool of his drama criticism, helping him to expose pomposity and insincerity.

WHAT IS THEATRE? A POINT OF VIEW [1]

. . . Two mistakes are made. First, playwriting is regarded simply as a craft. Now, clearly, playwriting *is* a craft, just as fiction is a craft, *among other things.* It is another question whether it is advisable to isolate the craft from those other things, thus in effect replacing the playwright with the play-doctor, which is rather like replacing fathers and mothers with midwives. The notion has spread among writers, play-doctors, critics, producers, actors, public, that plays are "not written, but re-written"; that is, not written, but pieced together, not composed with one man's passion and intellect, but assembled by the ingenuity of all who stop by at the hotel bedroom, preferably during the rehearsal period. In this way, dramaturgy is demoted from the fine to the useful arts; and is unique among the latter by not really being useful.

The second mistake is to write with the audience consciously in mind, instead of in the faith that there *will* be an audience for good work. Obviously, when we say that a play is not a writer's exploration of reality but just a calculated arrangement of effects, there is no need to ask: effects upon whom? The *raison d'être* of these effects is to interest and please the audience. All writers, of course, *hope* to interest and please an audience; the exploratory writer decidedly hopes that his explorations will in-

1 Extracts from the title essay of *What Is Theatre?* © 1956 by Eric Bentley. Used by permission of Horizon Press, Inc.—Ed.

terest and please an audience. But for the non-exploratory writer, hope is not enough. He is not prepared to leave it, as it were, to chance. He puts his whole mind on audience, audience, audience—by God, he'll *make* them like it—and, perhaps, by foregoing his claim to be an artist, becomes a remarkable craftsman. An artist cannot give *all* his attention to the audience; he needs to keep so much of it for his characters, his story, his subject.[2]

... I have been maintaining that the "serious" modern playwright is, or should be, engaged, along with other modern writers, in the search for the human essence. If it is possible to state in a word what moral quality the artist engaged in this quest needs above all others, I should say that it is audacity. Conversely, artists who are not searching, not reaching out for anything, but working comfortably within their established resources, and who are completely lacking in daring, who never "cock a snoot," "take a crack" at anything, "stick their necks out"—for them should be reserved the harshest adjective in the critical vocabulary: innocuous. In life there are worse things than innocuousness—forms of rampant evil which render innocuousness praiseworthy by comparison. But the Devil doesn't write plays. And when Mussolini wrote them he didn't succeed in projecting anything of the force of his iniquity. Like many a better man, he only succeeded in writing innocuously. But that is the worst type of writing there is.

With the two conceptions of work—art and pastime, exploration and craft—go two conceptions of the worker. The master of pastime is the well-adjusted person, happily holding hands with the audience.[3] The artist, if not malad-

2 In his book *The Inmost Leaf*, Alfred Kazin speaks of "that morbid overconsciousness of the audience that afflicts even the most serious writers in this country." The problem is one, not for the theatre alone, but for our culture generally.

3 "The secret of your theatrical prosperity," Scribe was told in the speech that welcomed him into the Academy, "is to have happily seized upon the spirit of your century and to have made the kind of play which it takes to most readily and which most closely corresponds to its nature." Allowing for differences in vocabulary, isn't this what a Broadway critic would say when conferring an award on a Broadway playwright?

justed, and I believe he is not, is not well-adjusted either; perhaps we should follow Peter Viereck's suggestion and invent a third category, that of the *un*-adjusted man, the healthy rebel. At any rate, it has been known, at least since Plato, that the artist is a dangerous character, and consequently that art is a subversive activity. I am not speaking of the philosophy, much less of the politics, of artists. Artists are disturbing, unsettling people, not by what they preach but by what they are, conservatives like Dante and Shakespeare being far more disturbing and unsettling than our little revolutionaries. The greater the artist the greater the upset.

In the voice of every artist, however full-throated and mellow, there is an undertone of something very like insolence. The small boy who said to Mme. de Pompadour: *"Why* can't you kiss me? The queen kisses me,"* was not the devastating Voltaire but the "mild" Mozart. "To kindle art to the whitest heat, there must always be some fanaticism behind it": Bernard Shaw was inspired to write this by seeing, not Ibsen's *Ghosts,* but the music-hall sketches and cabaret songs of Yvette Guilbert. The famous Tramp of Charlie Chaplin was gentle, and beloved by all the world, yet when I heard a candid spectator say of Charlie: "I can't stand the man," I realized how many others would say the same if they rigorously examined their responses; because, for all the charm and the high spirits, Chaplin is an alarming artist. Again, I am not referring to politics (though doubtless Chaplin took up Stalinism because he *thought* it was radical; there, history's joke was on Charlie). About any film of his, however slight, there is an air of menace; whereas most other comedians, for all that they make a lot more noise, are quite harmless.

Henri de Montherlant devoted an essay to the analogy of playwriting and bullfighting; and I have heard Martha Graham compare the dancer to the matador, and that, not in point of similarity of movement, but similarity of psychology: the dancer will attain to that razor-edge keenness when each move, each fall, each leap has that degree of urgency, that heightened sense of hazard.

"Live dangerously!" The artist follows Nietzsche's recommendation. Ortega y Gasset says there is some vulgarity in it because life is of its nature dangerous. True; but, as the fact is ignored and implicitly denied by modern culture as such, Nietzsche was fully justified in shouting it from the housetops. Even now, though editorials can be uselessly shrill about hydrogen bombs, though facts like the murder of 6,000,000 Jews are common knowledge, that fundamental complacency of middle-class culture—the most imperturbable of all imperturbabilities—is still with us. The works of Nietzsche have not "dated." Nor has the artist's sense of danger: precisely from his "subversiveness" stems his utility to society.

And the theatre could make a special contribution. For though it has sometimes chosen to be the most unenterprising of the arts, the genius, and even the very technics, of the medium tend all the other way. Theatricality is, *by definition,* audacious. A comedian is, *by definition,* a zany. The impertinence, insolence, effrontery that I have speculatively attributed to the artist in general, none would deny to the clown in particular. But have we begun to draw the logical inferences? We have been told often enough of all the gradual, thorough, and fine-spun things that the novel can do and that the stage fails to do, but have we explored the possibilities of theatre in the opposite direction—the realm of the sudden, the astonishing, the extravagant? The theatre is the place for the anarchist to throw his bomb.

Or perhaps for anyone *but* the anarchist to throw his bomb. For while theatre is the art of explosions, the trick is to have them go off at the right time in the right spot. Audacity has no place in the arts until it is brought under iron control. The rhythm of theatre derives from an alternation of explosion and silence; more precisely, there is preparation, explosion, and subsiding. The man of the theatre must not merely bring explosives in his bag; he must know exactly how to prepare the explosions and how to handle their subsidence. For the interplay between audacity and control produces the supreme artistic effects; the work of the masters of dramatic literature abounds in examples. And stage directing calls for the same combination of powers, though usually, even from the

expert, we get either audacity without control, or control without audacity. The only man I know of who is endowed with both gifts to the greatest possible extent—and in both fields, playwriting and directing—is Bertolt Brecht. In that fact—and not in the theory and practice of propaganda—lies the secret of his unique importance in the theatre today.

But I am not coming forward with a messiah. No one man will provide the answer to our problem, and to part of it Brecht provides, in my opinion, the wrong answer. He is one of those writers who search less and less after what I have been calling the human essence, because they are more and more convinced that they have already found it. Even supposing that Brecht *has* found it, that fact would not augur well for him as an artist. The only artists today who remain artists after conversion to causes which claim a monopoly of the truth are those who are not wholly convinced. Graham Greene's work derives its vitality now from the fact that he is always fighting his own Catholicism. The minute he says to himself, "I am a Catholic writer," begins to ask the alleged truth of his beliefs to do duty for his personal grasp of truth, however tentative and unsure, he is through. I am not objecting here either to Communism or Catholicism but, rather, pointing out what kind of adherence to these causes, or any other that makes comparable claims for itself, is damaging to an artist. The audacity for which I have praised Brecht was not the product of such an adherence but, on the contrary, of that bourgeois freedom in which Brecht gradually came to disbelieve. As he was an artist by virtue of his subversive activities, and socially and overtly subversive activities at that, absolutely necessary to his art was a society which, first, he wished to subvert and which, second, would permit him to try and subvert it. Bourgeois capitalism met both conditions; Soviet communism neither. And so the *enfant terrible* of the Weimar Republic tried to convert himself into the yes-man of the Soviet bureaucracy and the DDR (Deutsche Demokratische Republik). Only in relation to the West could this political writer even try to remain audacious, and this is that easy audacity (common also among anti-communists) which is no audacity at all.[4] Meanwhile, those larger works which Brecht hopes will have some lasting value are most alive where some unresolved inner conflict forces its way in despite the author and the watching bureaucrats. Into both *Galileo* and *Mother Courage* have been smuggled elements which are as subversive to Communism as *The Threepenny Opera* is to capitalism. The Communist press has not been entirely happy about either play.

It is a mistake even to *hope* that an ideal will find its realization in a single man. It is a mistake to expect that the ideal situation will ever be realized at all. And it is above all a mistake to think that ages of great theatre come about through the critics' explaining how to write plays, or even how not to write them. The critic's influence is not directly on the creative act but on public opinion (the playwright being, however, a member of the public). What the critic influences is morale.

The theatre today is demoralized. It suffers from hysterical oscillation between cheap cynicism and idealistic euphoria. This could be because dramatic art nowadays attracts chiefly manic de-

4 My comments on Tennessee Williams and Arthur Miller in this book and *The Dramatic Event* are an attempt to describe the phenomenon of easy, or false, audacity in current American drama. This is not to deny that both these authors are capable of real audacity; their superiority to most of their colleagues derives to a large extent from their greater daring.

pressives, though to say so only provokes the query: how has this come to be so? Between flat despair and yeasty zeal, why is there nothing but a vacuum? The question puts the cart before the horse: it is precisely because of this vacuum, this void, this *néant,* that men can only admit defeat or simulate success, descend to cynicism or rise to feverish and showy enthusiasm. Which is to repeat that they are demoralized.

Now, if it isn't too late, what do we do about demoralization in any institution—the church, the army, the nation—but try to recall people to a sense of the past, the glorious origin of the institution, its great men, its highest moments? And this is what I have been doing in the course of this brief attempt to answer the question: What Is Theatre? (or rather, this lengthy attempt to ask that question). We of the theatre need the inspiration and the discipline of Shakespeare and Molière exactly as a musician needs the inspiration and discipline of Bach and Mozart. And we need a sense of where it all came from, this theatre of ours, and where it has been going, and where it seems to be going now. For the task that inexorably confronts us—the task of continuing—we need, also, to assign ourselves a master objective. I have been suggesting that it is to search for our lost humanity. And, as weapons in this quest, I have been commending two that have been there from the beginning without losing any of their efficacity with the passage of time—the audacity of Dionysos and the controlling hand of Apollo.

BIBLIOGRAPHY

NOTE FOR THE REVISED EDITION: Where the previous editor refers readers to George Saintsbury's *History of Criticism*, this reference should be supplemented with more modern works on the subject, including the following: William K. Wimsatt, Jr., and Cleanth Brooks, *Literary Criticism: A Short History* (New York, 1957); René Wellek, *A History of Modern Criticism, 1750–1950* (vols I and II: *The Later Eighteenth Century* and *The Romantic Age,* New Haven, 1955); Vernon Hall, Jr., *A Short History of Literary Criticism* (New York, 1963).

For bibliographical information on selections included in the text, see footnotes at the beginning of each passage.

GREECE

General works on Greek literature, criticism and critics:

W. Christ, *Geschichte der griechischen Literatur* (in Müller's *Handbuch der klassischen Altertumswissenschaft.* Bd. VII, München, 1890).

A. et M. Croiset, *Histoire de la Littérature grecque.* (Abridged ed., Paris, 1900. Translated as *An Abridged History of Greek Literature,* by George F. Heffelbower, (New York, 1904).

Emile Egger, *Essai sur l'histoire de la Critique chez les Grecs* (Paris, 3rd ed., 1887).

Edith Hamilton, *The Greek Way* (New York, 1930).

Werner Jaeger, *Paideia,* 3 vols. (New York, 1943–45).

Paul Masqueray, *Bibliographie pratique de la Litterature grecque, des origines à la fin de la période romaine* (Paris, 1914).

Gilbert Murray, *A History of Ancient Greek Literature* (New York, new ed., 1900).

General works on tragedy:

L. D. Barnett, *Greek Drama,* (London, 1900).

Lewis Campbell, *A Guide to Greek Tragedy, etc.* (London, 1891).

G. A. Grube, *The Drama of Euripides* (London, 1941).

A. E. Haigh, *The Attic Theater* (Oxford, 1898). *The Tragic Drama of the Greeks* (Oxford, 1896).

H. D. F. Kitto, *Greek Tragedy* (London, 1939, 1950).

——, *Form and Meaning in Drama* (London, 1956).

C.-A.-N. Maignien, *Du Théâtre tragique des Grecs, etc.* (Lyon, 1839).

R. G. Moulton, *The Ancient Classical Drama* (Oxford, 1898).

Gilbert Murray, *Euripides and His Age* (London, 1913, 1946).

——, *Aeschylus, the Creator of Tragedy* (Oxford, 1940).

Gilbert Norwood, *Greek Tragedy* (London, 1948).

Patin, *Etudes sur les tragiques grecs,* 4 vols. (Paris, 1841).

A. W. Pickard-Cambridge, *Dithyramb Tragedy and Comedy* (Oxford, 1927, 1962).

——, *The Theatre of Dionysus in Athens* (Oxford, 1946).

George Thomson, *Aeschylus and Athens* (London, 1941).

L. M. Watt, *Attic and Elizabethan Tragedy* (London, 1908).

H. Weil, *Etudes sur le drame antique* (Paris, 1897).

F. C. Welcker, *Die griechischen Tragödien,* 3 vols. (Bonn, 1839.)

Cedric H. Whitman, *Sophocles* (Cambridge, Mass., 1951).

General works on comedy:

Artaud, *Fragments pour servir à l'histoire de la comédie attique* (Paris, 1863).

William Wilson Baker, *De Comicis
græcis litterarum judicibus* (*Harvard
Studies in Class. Phil.*, vol. 15, pp. 121–
240. Cambridge, 1904).

Faustin Colin, *Clef de l'Histoire de la
Comédie grecque* (Paris, 1856).

F. M. Cornford, *The Origin of Attic
Comedy* (London, 1914).

Demetrius Detscheff, *De Tragœdiarum
Græcarum conformatione scœnica ac
dramatica* (Göttingen, 1904).

M.-G. Guizot, *Ménandre; étude historique
et littéraire sur la comédie et la société
grecque* (Paris, 1855).

José Hillebrand, *Esthetica Litteraria
Antiqua Classica*, etc. (Maguntiae,
1828).

Gilbert Norwood, *Greek Comedy* (New
York, 1931).

General works on criticism:

J. W. H. Atkins, *Literary Criticism in
Antiquity*, 2 vols. (Cambridge, Eng.,
1934).

C. S. Baldwin, *Ancient Rhetoric and Poetic* (New York, 1924).

Ernst Howald, *Die Anfänge der literarischen Kritik bei den Grieschen* (Kirch-
hain, 1910).

Abbé Jacquet, *Parallèle des tragiques
grecs et françois* (Lille et Lyon, 1760).

Ph. E. Legrand, *Pour l'Histoire de la
Comédie nouvelle* (*Rev. des Etudes
grecques*, vol. XV, Paris, 1902).

E. du Méril, *Histoire de la Comédie ancienne*, 2 vols. (Paris, 1864–69).

E. Müller, *Geschichte der Theorie der
Kunst bei den Alten*, 2 vols. (Breslau,
1834–37).

W. R. Roberts, *Greek Rhetoric and Literary Theory* (New York, 1928).

J.-J. Rousseau, *De l'Imitation théâtrale,
essai tiré des Dialogues de Platon*
(Amsterdam, 1764).

George Saintsbury, *A History of Criticism*, vol. 1 (2nd ed., New York, 1902).

A. Théry, *Histoire des opinions littéraires*
(2nd ed., Paris, 1849).

Ad. Trendelemburg, *Grammaticorum
Græcorum de arte tragica judiciorum
reliquiæ* (Bonn, 1867).

Leslie Morton Turner, *Du Conflit tragique chez les Grecs et dans Shakespeare* (Paris, 1913).

ARISTOTLE

Editions:

Among the many hundred editions of
Aristotle, it is necessary to mention only
a few. Practically all the emendations,
commentary, and theory of earlier editions are to be found in I. Bywater's
Aristotle on the Art of Poetry (text,
translation, and notes, Oxford, 1909), and
in S. H. Butcher's *Aristotle's Theory of
Poetry and Fine Art* (with text of the
Poetics, translation, bibliography, and
commentary, 4th edition, revised, London, 1911). Briefer editions — translation and notes only — are *Aristotle's
Treatise on Rhetoric and Poetic*, translated, with analysis and examination
questions, by Theodore Buckley (Bohn
ed., London, 1914); A. O. Prickard,
Aristotle on the Art of Poetry (London,
1891); and Lane Cooper, *Aristotle on the
Art of Poetry* (Boston, 1913, Ithaca,
1947). Also W. Hamilton Fyfe, *Aristotle's Art of Poetry* (Oxford, 1940), and
L. J. Potts, *Aristotle on the Art of Fiction* (Cambridge, Eng., 1953).

On Aristotle and his works:

Notes, etc. in above editions.

Charles Batteux, *Les Quatre Poétiques
d'Aristote, d'Horace, de Vida, de Despréaux, avec les traductions et des remarques* (Paris, 1771).

Ronald S. Crane, ed., *Critics and Criticism* (Chicago, 1952).

André Dacier, *La Poétique traduite en
François, avec des remarques critiques*
(Paris, 1692).

Gerald F. Else, *Aristotle's Poetics: The
Argument* (Cambridge, Mass., 1957).

Humphry House, *Aristotle's Poetics*
(London, 1956).

John Jones, *On Aristotle and Greek
Tragedy* (London, 1962).

F. L. Lucas, *Tragedy in Relation to Aristotle's Poetics* (London, 1927).

George Saintsbury, *A History of Criticism*, vol. 1 (New York, 1900).

Moise Schwab, *Bibliographie d'Aristote*
(Paris, 1896).

J. E. Spingarn, *A History of Literary
Criticism in the Renaissance* (2nd ed.,
New York, 1908).

ROME

References on Latin literature in general:

J. C. F. Baehr, *Geschichte der römischen Literatur*, 4 vols. (Karlsruhe, 2d ed., 1868-72).

G. Bernhardy, *Grundriss der römischen Literatur* (Braunschweig, 5th ed., 1872).

R. W. Browne, *A History of Roman Classical Literature* (London 1853).

M. S. Dimsdale, *A History of Latin Literature* (London & New York, 1915).

J. Wight Duff, *A Literary History of Rome* (New York, 1909).

Harold N. Fowler, *A History of Roman Literature* (New York, 1932).

E. Hübner, *Bibliographie der klassischen Altertumwissenschaft; Grundriss zu Vorlesungen über die Geschichte und Encyklopädie der klassischen Philologie* (Berlin, 2nd ed., 1889).

H. Joachim, *Geschichte der römischen Literatur* (Leipzig, 1896).

J. W. Mackail, *Latin Literature* (New York, 1895).

Henry Nettleship, *Lectures and Essays* (Oxford, 1885).

Henry Nettleship, *Lectures and Essays* (2d series, Oxford, 1895).

George Saintsbury, *A History of Criticism*, vol. 1, (New York, 1900).

J. E. Sandys, *A History of Classical Scholarship*, 3 vols. (Cambridge, 1903).

M. Schanz, *Geschichte der römischen Literature*, 3 parts (München, 1890-1901).

W. S. Teuffel, *Geschichte der römischen Literatur*, 3 parts (München, 1890- Eng. tr. from revised and enlarged ed. by L. Schwabe by G. C. W. Warr, 2 vols., London, 1891-92).

On Latin drama:

Gaston Boissier, *Le Poète Attius. Etude sur la Tragédie latine pendant la République* (Paris, 1857).

Philippe Fabia, *Les Théâtres de Rome au temps de Plaute et de Térence* (Rev. de Phil., XXI, Paris, 1897).

J. F. D'Alton, *Horace and His Age* (London, 1917. See especially chapter on literary criticism).

——, *Roman Literary Theory and Criticism* (New York, 1931).

G. Michaut, *Sur les Tréteaux latins* (Paris, 1912).

Grant Showerman, *Horace and His Influence* (Boston, 1922).

On Latin criticism:

W. R. Hardie, *Literary Criticism at Rome* (*In Lectures on Classical Subjects*, London, 1903).

HORACE

Editions:

Of the numerous Latin texts of Horace, that of Bentley is on the whole the best, though there are numerous others. This was reëdited by Zangemeister in 1869. Among modern commentaries are that of J. C. Orelli (4th ed. revised by O. Hirschfelder and J. Mewes, 1886-90), and of A. Kiessling (revised by R. Heinze, 1898-1908). The standard English commentary is the two-volume edition of E. C. Wickham (1874-96).

English translations abound. Among the early versions is *The Works of Horace*, translated by several hands [Dryden, Congreve, etc.] 2 vols., London, 1757-59. See also *The Works of Horace*, translated by C. Smart, revised by T. A. Buckley (late Bohn editions, n. d. ; *The Works of Horace*, translated by I. Lonsdale and S. Lee (London, 1873); and *A Poetical Translation of the Works of Horace*, by P. Francis, 2 vols. (ed. London, 1831).

On Horace and his works:

Gaston Boissier, *L'Art poétique d'Horace et la Tragédie romaine* (Rev., de Philol., Vol. XXII, Paris, 1898).

Albert S. Cook, *The Art of Poetry. The Poetical Treatises of Horace, Vida, and Boileau, with the Translations by Howes, Pitt, and Soame*, (with notes and intro., Boston, 1892).

George Converse Fiske, *Lucilius, The Ars Poetica of Horace, and Persius* (*Harvard Studies in Class. Philol.*, Vol. XXIV, Cambridge, 1913).

Paul Lejay, *La Date et le but de l'Art poétique d'Horce* (*Rev. de l'instruction pub. en Belgique*, vols. XLV and XLVI, Bruxelles, 1902-3).

H. H. Milman, *The Works of Horace, with English Notes critical and explanatory*, by C. Anthon. (New edition, with *Life of Horace*, by H. H. Milman, New York, 1875.)

Henry Nettleship, *Lectures and Essays* (Oxford, 1885).

E. Norden, *Die Komposition und Literaturgattung der horäzischen Epistola ad Pisones* (*Hermes*, vol. 40, Berlin, 1905).

Alois Patin, *Der Aufbau der Ars poetica*

des Horaz (*Studien zur Geschichte und Kultur des Altertums*, Bd. 4, Heft 1, Paderborn, 1910).

George Saintsbury, *A History of Criticism*, vol. 1 (New York, 1900).

Rev. W. Tuckwell, *Horace* (London, 1905).

Johann Vahlen, *Ueber Horatius' Brief an die Pisonen* (*Kön.-preuss. Akad. d. Wissensch. Sitzungsb.*, p. 589, Berlin, 1906).

THE MIDDLE AGES

General references on the literature of the Middle Ages:

J. W. H. Atkins, *English Literary Criticism: The Medieval Phase* (Cambridge, Eng., 1943).

C. S. Baldwin, *Medieval Rhetoric and Poetic* (New York, 1928).

Karl Borinski, *Die Antike in Poetik und Kunsttheorie. I. Mittelalter, Renaissance, Barock* (Leipzig, 1914).

Léon Clédat, *Le Théâtre au moyen-age* (Paris, 1897).

A. Ebert, *Allgemeine Geschichte der Literatur des Mittelalters im Abendlande*, 3 vols. (Leipzig, 1874–87).

Henry Hallam, *Introduction to the Literature of Europe, in the Fifteenth, Sixteenth, and Sevententh Centuries* (new ed., London, 1872).

A. H. L. Heeren, *Geschichte der klassischen Literatur im Mittelalter, 2* vols. (330–1400 A.D.) (Göttingen, 1822).

Amable Jourdain, *Recherches critiques sur l'age et l'origine des traductions latines d'Aristote, et sur les commentaires grecs ou arabes employés par les docteurs scolastiques* (2nd ed., Paris, 1843).

W. P. Ker, *The Dark Ages* (New York, 1904).

Max Manitius, *Geschichte der lateinischen Literatur des Mittelalters*. Teil I. (From Justinian to the middle of the 10th century.) (München, 1911.)

George Saintsbury, *A History of Criticism*, vol. I (New York, 1900).

J. E. Sandys, *A History of Classical Scholarship from the Sixth Century B.C. to the end of the Middle Ages* (Cambridge, 1903).

G. Gregory Smith, *The Transition Period* (New York, 1900).

F. J. Snell, *The Fourteenth Century* (New York, 1899).

J. E. Spingarn, *A History of Literary Criticism in the Renaissance* (2nd ed., New York, 1908). For additional matter, fuller bibl. and notes, see Fusco's translation, as *La Critica Letteraria nel Rinascimento*, with a preface by Croce (Bari, 1905).

DONATUS

Editions:

P. Wessner, *Aeli Donati quod tertur Comentum Terenti, 2* vols. (Leipzig, 1902–05).

Donati Fragmentum de Comœdia et Tragœdia (in Gronovius' *Thesaurus Graecarum Antiquitatum*), vol. VIII (Venetiis, 1735).[1]

The first printed edition of the Commentaries on Terence was published at Cologne, 1470–72, and was followed by three others in the same century.— Most of these contained the *De Comœdia et Tragœdia*.

On Donatus and his works:

Biographie universelle, vol. 11 (Paris, 1852).

Wilhelm Cloetta, *Beiträge zur Litteraturgeschichte des Mittelalters und der Renaissance* (Halle, 1890–92).

[1] Together with this fragment is another, entitled *Eranthii et Donati de Tragœdia et Comœdia.*— Ed.

Encyclopedia Britannica, 11th ed., vol. 8 (Cambridge, 1910).

H. T. Karsten, *De comm. Don. ad Terenti fabulas origine et compositione* (Leiden, 1907).

Gustave Lanson, *L'Idée de la tragédie avant Jodelle* (in *Revue d'histoire littéraire de la France,* Paris, 1904).

Nouvelle Biographie générale, vol. 14 (Paris, 1855).

G. Saintsbury, *A History of Criticism,* vol. 2 (New York, 1902).

J. E. Sandys, *A History of Classical Scholarship,* vol. I (Cambridge, 1903).

Ludwig Schopen, *De Terentio et Donato eius interprete* (Bonn, 1821).

J. E. Spingarn, *A History of Literary Criticism in the Renaissance* (New York, 1908).

Minton Warren, *On Five New Manuscripts of the Commentary of Donatus to Terence* (in *Harvard Studies in Classical Philology,* vol. XVII, Cambridge, U. S. A., 1906).

DANTE

Editions:

Among the standard texts of Dante containing the *Epistolæ* is *Tutte le opere di Dante Alighieri; nuovamente rivedute nel testo dal Dr. E. Moore,* etd., with dictionary, indexes, etc., by Paget Toynbee (3rd ed., Oxford, 1904), and Karl Witte's *Dantis Alighieri Epistolae quae extant, cum notis* (Patavii, 1827). Besides the translation here used, are: P. H. Wicksteed, *Translation of the Latin Works of Dante* (London, 1904), and Katharine Hilliard's translation of the *Convito* (London, 1889).

On Dante and his works:

Cesare Balbo, *Vita di Dante* (augmented ed., Firenze, 1853).

Charles Allen Dinsmore, *Aids to the Study of Dante* (Boston, 1903).

Étienne Gilson, *Dante the Philosopher* (London, 1948).

C. H. Grandgent, *Dante* (New York, 1916).

Vittorio Imbriani, *Studi Danteschi* (Firenze, 1891).

Edward Moore, *Studies in Dante,* 4 series (Oxford, 1896–1917).

George Saintsbury, *A History of Criticism,* vol. 1 (New York, 1902).

G. A. Scartazzini, *Enciclopedia Dantesca,* 2 vols. (Milano, 1905).

J. R. Smith, *The Earliest Lives of Dante* (New York, 1901).

F. J. Snell, *Handbook to the Works of Dante* (London, 1909).

Paget Toynbee, *Dante Alighieri, His Life and his Works* (4th ed., New York, 1910).

Paget Toynbee, *Dante Studies and Researches* (London, 1902).

Karl Witte, *Dante-Forschungen,* 1st and 2nd series (Halle, 1869, Heilbronn, 1876. Translated by C. Mabel Lawrence and Philip H. Wicksteed as *Essays on Dante,* Boston, 1898).

Special references on the *Epistle to Can Grande:*

C. H. Herford, *Dante's Theory of Poetry* (In *Quarterly Review,* v. 213, London, 1910).

C. S. Latham, *A Translation of Dante's Eleven Epistles* (Boston, 1892).

Francesco d'Ovidio, *L'Epistola a Cangrande* (In *Revista d'Italia,* anno 2, v. 3, Roma, 1899).

Francesco Torraca, *L'Epistola a Cangrande* (In *Revista d'Italia,* anno 2, pp. 601–636, Roma, 1899).

RENAISSANCE ITALY

References on Italian literature in general:

A. D'Ancona e O. Bacci, *Manuale della letteratura italiana,* 5 vols. (Torino, 1897–1900).

Robert F. Arnold, *Kultur der Renaissance* (Leipzig, 1905).

A. Bartoli, *Storia della letteratura italiana,* 7 vols. (Firenze, 1878–89).

V. Canello, *Storia della letteratura italiana nel secolo XVI* (Milano, 1880).

Francis Henry Cliffe, *A Manual of Italian Literature* (London, 1896).

W. Cloetta, *Beiträge zur Litteraturgeschichte des Mittelalters und der Renaissance,* 2 vols. (Halle, 1890–92).

B. Croce, *La Critica letteraria* (2nd ed., Roma, 1896).

——, *Estetica come scienza dell' espressione e linguistica generale* (2nd ed., Milano, 1904).

——, *La letteratura della Nuova Italia,* 6 vols. (Bari, 1921–40).

——, *Per la storia della critica e storiografia letteraria* (Napoli, 1903).

——, *Saggi sulla letteratura italiana del seicento* (Bari, 1910).

A. Ebert, *Allgemeine Geschichte der Literatur des Mittelalters im Abendland,* 3 vols. (Leipzig, 1874-87).

F. Flamini, *Studi di storia letteraria italiana e straniera* (Livorno, 1895)

Richard Garnett, *A History of ιtalιαn Literature* (New York, 1898).

A. Gaspary, *Geschichte der italienischen Literatur,* 2 vols. (Strassburg, 1885–88).

G. Koerting, *Geschichte der Literatur Italiens im Zeitalter der Renaissance* 3 vols. (Leipzig, 1878-84).

Kritischer Jahresbericht über die Fortschritte der Romanischen Philologie (München, Leipzig, Erlangen, etc., 1890 to date), is always useful.

G. Mazzoni, *Avviamento allo studio critico delle lettere italiane* (Firenze, 1907).

F. De Sanctis, *Storia della letteratura italiana,* 2 vols. (6th ed. Napoli, 1893).

J. A. Symonds, *Renaissance in Italy,* 7 vols. (New York, 1888).

G. Tiraboschi, *Storia della letteratura italiana,* 9 vols. (Firenze, 1805–1813).

J. H. Whitfield, *A Short History of Italian Literature* (London, 1950).

E. H. Wilkins, *A History of Italian Literature* (Cambridge, Mass., 1954).

Nicola Zingarelli, *Storia letteraria d'Italia* (Milano, 1903).

References on Italian drama:

A. d'Ancona, *Origini del teatro italiano,* 2 vols. (2nd ed., Torino, 1891).

G. Apollinaire, *Le Théâtre italien* (Paris, 1910)

E. Bertana, *La Tragedia* (In the *Storie dei generi letterati italiani,* Milano, 1906).

P. Bettoli, *Storia del teatro drammatico italiano dalla fine del secolo XV alla fine del secolo XIX* (Bergamo, 1901).

A. Biancale, *La Tragedia italiana del 500* (Roma, 1901).

Des Boulmiers, *Histoire anécdotique et raisonnée du théâtre italien,* etc., 7 vols. (Paris, 1769).

P. Emiliani-Giudici, *Storia del teatro in Italia* (Milano, 1860).

Marvin T. Herrick, *Italian Comedy in the Renaissance* (Urbana, 1960).

Joseph Spencer Kennard, *The Italian Theatre,* 2 vols. (New York, 1932).

J. L. Klein, *Geschichte des italienischen Dramas* (Leipzig, 1868).

E. Masi, *Studi sulla storia del teatro italiano* (Firenze, 1891).

F. Neri, *La tragedia italiana del cinquecento* (Roma, 1904).

D'Origny, *Annales du Théâtre italien depuis son origine jusqu'à nos jours,* 3 vols. (Paris, 1788).

F. et C. Parfaict, *Histoire de l'ancien théâtre italien,* etc. (Paris, 1767).

G. B. Pellizzaro, *La commedia del secolo XVI* (Vicenza, 1901).

L. Riccoboni, *Histoire du théâtre italien,* etc. (Paris, 1730).

——, *Dell' Arte Rappresentativa, Capitoli sei* (London, 1728).

Luigi Tonelli, *Il Teatro italiano* (Milano, 1924).

References on the literature of the Italian Renaissance, especially on dramatic criticism:

C. S. Baldwin, *Renaissance Literary Theory and Practice* (New York, 1939).

A. Benoist, *Les Théories dramatiques avant les Discours de Corneille* (In *Annales de la Faculté des Lettres de Bordeaux,* 1891).

K. Borinski, *Die Poetik der Renaissance, und die Anfänge der litterarischen Kritik in Deutschland* (Berlin, 1886).

——, *Die Antike in Poetik und Kunsttheorie. I, Mittelalter, Renaissance, Barock* (Leipzig, 1914).

H. Breitinger, *Les Unités d'Aristote avant le Cid de Corneille* (2nd ed., Genève, 1895).

L. Ceci, *Un' occhiata allo svolgimento storico della critica letteraria e politica del seicento* (Firenze, 1878).

R. J. Clements, *Picta Poesis: Literary*

and Humanistic Theory in Renaissance Emblem Books (Rome, 1960).

Dannheisser, *Zur Geschichte der Einheiten* (In *Zeitschrift für französische Sprache und Litteratur,* v. XIV (1892).

J. Ebner, *Beitrag zu einer Geschichte der dramatischen Einheiten in Italien* (Erlangen, 1898).

W. K. Ferguson, *The Renaissance in Historical Thought* (Boston, 1948).

F. Foffano, *Ricerche letterarie* (Livorno, 1897).

A. Graf, *Attraverso il Cinquecento* (Torino, 1888).

Vernon Hall, Jr., *Renaissance Literary Criticism: A Study of Its Social Content* (New York, 1945).

Baxter Hathaway, *The Age of Criticism: The Late Renaissance* (Ithaca, 1962).

M. T. Herrick, *The Fusion of Horatian and Aristotelian Literary Criticism* (Urbana, 1946).

——, *Comic Theory in the Sixteenth Century* (Urbana, 1960).

I. G. Isoia, *Critica del Rinascimento,* 2 vols. (Livorno, 1907).

T. Klette, *Beiträge zur Geschichte und Litteratur der italienischen Gelehrtenrenaissance,* 3 parts (Greifswald, 1888–90).

Alfredo Rolla, *Storia delle idee estitiche in Italia* (Torino, 1905).

George Saintsbury, *A History of Criticism,* vol. 2 (New York, 1902).

J. E. Sandys, *A History of Classical Scholarship,* vol. 2 (Cambridge, 1903).

J. E. Spingarn, *A History of Literary Criticism in the Renaissance* (2d ed., New York, 1908. Italian translation, *La Critica letteraria nel Rinascimento,* by Antonio Fusco, Bari, 1905, contains additional material and full bibliography).

Aug. Théry, *Histoire des opinions littéraires chez les anciens et chez les modernes,* 2 vols. (new ed., Paris, 1849).

K. Vossler, *Poetische Theorien in der italienischen Frührenaissance* (Berlin, 1900).

Bernard Weinberg, *A History of Literary Criticism in the Italian Renaissance* (Chicago, 1961).

Max J. Wolff, *Die Theorie der italienischen Tragödie im 16. Jahrhundert* (In *Archiv für der neueren Sprachen und Literaturen,* Bd. 128, n. serie, bd. 28, Braunschweig, 1912).

DANIELLO

Edition:

The only edition of Daniello's *Poetic* is that printed at Venice in 1536: *La Poetica di Bernardino Daniello Lucchese.*

On Daniello and his works:

Colle, *Storia scientifica-letteraria dello studio in Padua* (Padova, 1824–25).

George Saintsbury, *A History of Criticism,* vol. 2 (New York, 1902).

J. E. Spingarn, *A History of Literary Criticism in the Renaissance* (New York, 1908).

MINTURNO

Editions:

The *De Poeta Libri Sex* was published at Venice in 1559, the *Arte Poetica,* also at Venice, in 1563. Neither has been translated. In H. B. Charlton's *Castelvetro's Theory of Poetry* (Manchester, 1913), there are many quotations from both works.

On Minturno and his works:

Nouvelle Biographie générale, vol. 38 (Paris, 1861).

Nuova Enciclopedia italiano, vol. 14 (Torino, 1882).

H. Breitinger, *Les Unités d'Aristote avant le Cid de Corneille* (Genève, 1895).

Crescimbeni, *Istoria della vulgar poesia* Lib. II (Roma, 1698, and later).

René Rapin, *Avertissement* (In *Réflexions touchant la Poétique,* Paris, 1674. His critical *Works,* translated, appeared in London in 1706).

George Saintsbury, *A History of Criticism,* vol. 2 (New York, 1902).

J. E. Spingarn, *A History of Literary Criticism in the Renaissance* (2nd ed., New York, 1908).

Ughelli, *Italia Sacra,* vol. IX (ed. 1721)

SCALIGER

Editions:

The *Poetices Libri Septem* was first published at Lyons in 1561. Often reprinted during the sixteenth and seventeenth centuries. The only English translation is a slim volume of selections: *Select Translations from Scaliger's Poetics,* by F. M. Padelford (New York, 1905).

On Scaliger and his works:

Antoine Benoist, *Les Théories dramatiques avant les Discours de Corneille* (In *Annales des Facultés des lettres de Bordeaux,* 1892).
Victor Beranek, *Martin Optiz in seinem Verhältnis zu Scaliger und Ronsard* (Wien, 1883).
Jakob Bernays, *Zwei Abhandlungen über die aristotelische Theorie des Dramas* (Berlin, 1880).
Biographie universelle, vol. 38 (Paris, 1861).
Bourrousse de Laffore, *Etude sur Jules César de Lescale* (Agen, 1860).
H. Breitinger, *Les Unités d'Aristote avant le Cid de Corneille* (2nd ed., Genève, 1895).
Eduard Brinkschulte, *Julius Cæsar Scaligers kunsttheoretische Anschauungen* (Bonn, 1913).
Vernon Hall, Jr., *Life of Julius Caesar Scaliger, 1484–1580* (Philadelphia, 1950).
E. Lintilhac, *De J.-C. Scaligeri Poetica* (Paris, 1887).
Magen, *Documents sur Julius Cæsar Scaliger et sa famille* (Agen, 1873).
Charles Nisard, *Les Gladiateurs de la République des lettres au XVᵉ, XVIᵉ, et XVIIᵉ siècles,* 2 vols. (Paris, 1860).
George Saintsbury, *A History of Criticism,* vol. 2 (New York, 1902).
Joseph Justus Scaliger, *De Vetustate et splendore gentis Scaligeræ et Julii Cæseris Scaligeri* (Leyden, 1594).
Scaligeriana, 2 series (complete ed., Amsterdam, 1740).
J. E. Spingarn, *A History of Literary Criticism in the Renaissance* (New York, 1908).

CASTELVETRO

Editions:

The *Poetica d'Aristotele vulgarizzata e esposta* was first published at Vienna in 1570. But the second edition (Basle, 1576) contains important additions. The *Opera Varie Critiche,* with Muratori's Life of Castelvetro, appeared in Milan in 1727. The only English translation of the *Poetica* consists in the important passages, quoted in H. B. Charlton's *Castelvetro's Theory of Poetry* (Manchester, 1913).

On Castelvetro and his work:

Bayle, *Dictionary* (2nd ed., London, 1735).
A. Benoist, *Les Théories dramatiques avant les Discours de Corneille* (in *Annales de la Faculté des lettres de Bordeaux,* 1891).
H. Breitinger, *Les Unités d'Aristote avant le Cid de Corneille* (Genève, 1895).
A. Caro, *Apologia degli Academici di Bianchi di Roma contra M. Lodovico Castelvetro* (Parma, 1588).
Cavazzuti, *Lodovico Castelvetro* (Modena, 1903).
H. B. Charlton, *Castelvetro's Theory of Poetry* (Manchester Univ. Press, 1913).
A. Fusco, *La Poetica di Lodovico Castelvetro* (Napoli, 1904).
L. Muratori, *Vita dell' autore* (in the *Opere Varie Critiche,* Milano, 1727).
Nouvelle Biographie générale, vol. 9 (Paris, 1854).
A. Plonchar, *Della Vita e delle opere di L. Castelvetro* (Conegliano, 1878).
George Saintsbury, *A History of Criticism,* vol. 2 (New York, 1902).
J. E. Spingarn, *A History of Literary Criticism in the Renaissance* (2nd ed., New York, 1908).

RENAISSANCE FRANCE

General References on French literature:

L.-P. Betz, *La littérature comparée* (2nd ed., Strasbourg, 1904).
Geoffrey Brereton, *A Short History of French Literature* (London, 1954).
Ferdinand Brunetière, *Histoire de la littérature française classique,* 3 vols. (Paris, 1905–12).

——, *Manuel de l'histoire de la littérature française* (Paris, 1897).

J. Demogeot, *Histoire de la littérature française* (24th ed., Paris, 1892).

René Doumic, *Histoire de la littérature française* (Paris, 1900).

Edward Dowden, *A History of French Literature* (New York, 1897).

Emile Faguet, *Histoire de la littérature française*, 2 vols. (Paris, 1900).

Charles Gidel, *Histoire de la littérature française, depuis son origine jusqu'à la Renaissance,* (Paris, 1875).

——, *The same: . . . depuis la Renaissance jusqu'à la fin du XVII* siècle* (Paris, 1877).

F. Godefroy, *Histoire de la littérature française depuis le XVI* siècle jusqu'à nos jours,* 10 vols. (2nd ed., Paris, 1878–79).

P.-L. Jacob (ed.), *Bibliothèque dramatique de Monsieur de Soleinne* (catalog), 5 vols. (Paris, 1843–44).

René Jasinski, *Histoire de la littérature française,* 2 vols. (Paris, 1947).

H. P. Junker, *Grundriss der Geschichte der französischen Literatur,* (2nd ed., Münster, 1894).

Gustave Lanson, *Histoire de la littérature française* (12th ed., Paris, 1912).

——, *Manuel bibliographique de la littérature française moderne, 1500–1900,* 5 vols. (Paris, 1909–14).

[La Vallière] *Bibliothèque du Théâtre François,* 3 vols. (Dresde, 1768).

De Léris, *Dictionnaire portatif historique et littéraire des théâtres* (2nd ed., Paris, 1763).

Nicéron, *Mémoires pour servir à l'histoire des hommes illustres dans la république des lettres,* 43 vols. (Paris, 1729–45).

L. Petit de Julleville (editor), *Histoire de la langue et de la littérature française des origines à 1900,* 8 vols. (Paris, 1896–99).

C. H. Conrad Wright, *A History of French Literature* (Oxford, 1912).

General references on French drama:

Germain Bapst, *Essai sur l'histoire du théâtre* (Paris, 1893).

C. Barthélemy, *Histoire de la Comédie en France* (Paris, 1886).

J. Baudrais, *Essais historiques sur l'origine et les progrès de l'art dramatique*

en France 3 vols. (Paris, 1791).

Beauchamps, *Recherches sur les Théâtres de France* (Paris, 1735).

Ferdinand Brunetière, *Les Epoques du Théâtre français* (1636–1850). (Paris, 1892.)

——, *L'Evolution d'un genre: la Tragédie (In Etudes critiques sur l'histoire de la littérature française,* 7 ème série, Paris, 1905).

S. Chappuzeau, *Le Théâtre françois* (ed., Paris, 1876).

Gustave Cohen, *Le Théâtre en France au moyen age,* 2 vols. (Paris, 1947).

W. Creizenach, *Geschichte des neueren Dramas,* 3 vols. (Halle, 1893–1909).

Fontenelle, *Histoire du Théâtre françois* (In vol. III, *Œuvres,* Paris, 1790).

J.-L. Geoffroy, *Cours de littérature dramatique,* 6 vols. (Paris, 1819–20).

D. Germano, *Evolution historique du théâtre français* (Caltanissetta, 1902).

Frederick Hawkins, *Annals of the French Stage,* 2 vols. (London, 1884).

J. L. Klein, *Geschichte des Dramas,* 13 vols. (Leipzig, 1865–76).

Julien Le Rousseau, *Le Progrès de la littérature dramatique* (Paris, 1865).

Léon Levrault, *Drame et Tragédie* (Paris, n. d.).

——, *La Comédie* (Paris, n. d.).

Eugène Lintilhac, *Histoire générale du théâtre en France,* 5 vols. (Paris, 1904–11).

H.-J.-J. Lucas, *Histoire philosophique et littéraire du théâtre français depuis son origine jusqu'à nos jours,* 3 vols. (2nd ed., Bruxelles, 1862–63).

Karl Mantzius, *A History of Theatrical Art,* trans. by Louise von Cossel, 6 vols. (London, 1903–09).

Chevalier de Mouhy, *Abrégé de l'histoire du théâtre françois,* 3 vols. (Paris, 1780).

François et Claude Parfaict, *Histoire du Théâtre François depuis son origine jusqu'à présent* (Paris, 1754–55).

L. Petit de Julleville, *Le Théâtre en France* (7th ed., Paris, 1908).

A. Royer, *Histoire universelle du théâtre,* 6 vols. (Paris, 1869–70).

Paul de Saint-Victor, *Les Deux Masques,* 3 vols. (Paris, 1880–84).

References on early French literature and criticism:

Paul Albert, *La Littérature française des*

origines à la fin du XVI *siècle* (Paris, 1894).

Charles Arnaud, *Les Théories drama-tiques au XVII* *siècle. Etude sur la vie et les œuvres de l'Abbé d'Aubignac* (Paris, 1887).

A. Benoist, *Les Théories dramatiques avant les Discours de Corneille* (In *Annales de la Faculté des Lettres de Bordeaux,* 1891)

René Bray, *La Tragédie cornélienne de-vant la critique classique* (Paris, 1927).

H. Breitinger, *Les Unités d'Aristote avant le Cid de Corneille* (2nd ed., Genève, 1895).

Ferdinand Brunetière, *L'Evolution des genres dans l'histoire de la littérature. Introduction: L'Evolution de la crit-ique depuis la Renaissance jusqu'à nos jours* (6th ed., Paris, 1914).

Henri Carton, *Histoire de la critique littéraire en France* (Paris, 1886).

Emile Chasles, *La Comédie en France au XVI* *siècle* (Paris, 1862).

Philarète Chasles, *Etudes sur le seizième siècle en France* (Paris, 1848).

M.-A.-A. Chassang, *Des essais drama-tiques imités de l'antiquité au XIV* *et XV* *siècles* (Paris, 1852).

R. J. Clements, *Critical Theory and Practice of the Pléiade* (Cambridge, Mass., 1942).

E. Cougny, *Des Représentations drama-tiques et particulièrement de la comé-die politique dans les collèges au seiz-ième siècle* (Paris, 1868).

J. W Cunliffe, *Early French Tragedy in the Light of Recent Scholarship* (*Jour-nal of Comparative Literature,* I, 1903).

A. Darmsteter et A. Hatzfeld, *Le Seiz-ième siècle en France* (Paris, 1878).

Adolf Ebert, *Entwicklungsgeschichte der französische Tragödie, vornehmlich im XVI. Jahrhundert.* (Gotha, 1858).

Emile Egger, *L'Hellénisme en France,* 2 vols. (Paris, 1869).

Emile Faguet, *Le Seizième siècle* (Paris, 1893).

——, *La Tragédie française au XVI* *siècle* (2nd ed., Paris, 1912).

——, *Les Manifestes dramatiques avant Corneille* (In *Revue des cours et con-férences,* IX, No. 6, Paris, 1900).

Jules Guillemot, *L'Evolution de l'idée dramatique* etc. (Paris, 1910).

Jules Haraszti, *La Comédie française de la Renaissance et la scène* (In *Revue d'histoire littéraire de la France,* Paris, 1905).

Hecq et Paris, *La Poétique française au Moyen-âge et à la Renaissance* (Brux-elles, 1896).

Marcel Hervier, *Les Ecrivains français jugés par leurs contemporains. I. VI* *et XVII* *siècles* (Paris, 1911).

Edith Kern, *The Influence of Heinsius and Vossius upon French Dramatic Theory* (Baltimore, 1949).

H. C. Lancaster, *A Neglected Passage on the Three Unities of the French Classical Drama* (In *Modern Language Ass'n Publications,* vol. XXIII, Cam-bridge, Mass., 1908).

——, *The French Tragi-comedy: its Or-igin and Development from 1552 to 1628* (Baltimore, 1907).

E. Langlois, *De Artibus Rhetoricæ Rhythmicæ* (Paris, 1890).

Gustave Lanson, *Le Théâtre français au temps d'Alexandre Hardy* (In *Hom-mes et Livres,* Paris, 1895).

——, *Les Origines de la tragédie clas-sique en France* (In *Revue d'histoire littéraire de la France,* Paris, 1903).

——, *L'Idée de la tragédie avant Jodelle* (In *Revue d'histoire littéraire de la France,* Paris, 1904).

——, *La Substitution de la tragédie aux mystères et aux moralités* (*Revue d'histoire littéraire de la France,* Paris, 1903).

——, *La Tragédie en France avant Cor-neille* (In *Bulletin de l'Association des Elèves de Sèvres,* 1906).

Léon Levrault, *La Critique littéraire* (Paris, n. d.).

Eugène Lintilhac, *La Théorie du théâtre en France de Scaliger à Victor Hugo* (In *Nouvelle Revue,* N. S., IX, Paris, 1901).

J. Marsan, *La Pastorale dramatique en France à la fin du XVI* *siècle et au commencement du XVII* *siècle* (Paris, 1905).

Ernest Martineche, *La Comédie es-pagnole en France* (Paris, 1900).

Alfred Michiels, *Histoire des idées lit-téraires en France,* 2 vols. (Bruxelles, 3rd ed., 1848)

Heinrich Morf, *Geschichte der französi-schen Literatur im Zeitalter der Ren-aissance* (2nd ed., Strassburg, 1914).

W. F. Patterson, *Three Centuries of French Poetic Theory* (Ann Arbor, 1935).

Georges Péllissier, *Les Arts Poétiques antérieurs à Vauquelin* (In *L'Art Poétique de Vauquelin de la Fresnaye*, Paris, 1885).

B. Pifteau and J. Goujon, *Histoire du théâtre en France des origines au Cid (1398–1630)* (Paris, 1879).

E. J. B. Rathery, *Influence de l'Italie sur les lettres françaises depuis le XIII° siècle jusqu'au règne de Louis XIV* (Paris, 1853).

Eugène Rigal, *De Jodelle à Moliere* (Paris, 1911).

——, *Le Théâtre français avant la période classique* (Paris, 1901).

——, *Alexandre Hardy et le théâtre français à la fin du XVI° siècle et au commencement du XVII° siècle* (Paris, 1889).

A. Rosenbauer, *Die poetischen Theorien der Plejade nach Ronsard und Dubellay* (Erlangen, 1895).

Emile Roy, *Étude sur le Théâtre français du XIV° et XV° siècles* (Paris, 1901).

T. Rucktäschel, *Einige Arts poétiques aus der Zeit Ronsard's und Malherbe's* (Leipzig, 1889).

C.-A. Sainte-Beuve, *Tableau historique et critique de la Poésie française et du théâtre français au XVI° siècle* (Revised and augmented eds., Paris, 1842 and after).

George Saintsbury, *A History of Criticism*, vol. 2 (New York, 1902).

G. Gregory Smith, *The Transition Period* (New York, 1900).

J. E. Spingarn, *A History of Literary Criticism in the Renaissance* (2nd ed., New York, 1908).

Joseph Texte, *L'influence italienne dans la Renaissance française* (In *Etudes de littérature européene*, Paris, 1898).

Arthur Tilley, *From Montaigne to Molière* (London, 1908).

——, *The Literature of the French Renaissance*, 2 vols. (Cambridge, 1904).

Henri Tivier, *Histoire de la littérature dramatique en France depuis ses origines jusqu'au Cid* (Paris, 1873).

Pierre Toldo, *La Comédie française de la Renaissance* (In *Revue d'histoire littéraire de la France*, Paris, 1897–98–99, 1900).

P. Villey, *Les Sources d'idées au XVI°*

siècle. *Textes choisis et commentés* (Paris, 1912).

SEBILLET

Editions:

The *Art Poétique François pour l'instruction des jeunes studieus et encor peu avancez en la poésie françoise* was first published at Paris in 1548. It went through seven editions in a little over twenty-five years. It has been re-printed by the *Société des Textes français modernes*, and edited by Félix Gaiffe, Paris, 1910.

Among Sebillet's other works are political tracts, various translations (1581 and 1584), and a translation of Euripides *Iphigenia* (Paris, 1549).

On Sebillet and his work:

Biographie universelle, vol. 39.

Ferdinand Brunetière, *Histoire de la Littérature française classique*, vol. 1 (Paris, 1905).

Félix Gaiffe, Introduction to re-print of the *Art Poétique* (Paris, 1910).

Erich Lüken, *Du Bellay's Deffence et illustration de la largue françoyse in ihrem Verhältnis zu Sebillets Art Poétique* (Oldenburg, 1913).

Nouvelle Biographie générale, vol. 43 (Paris, 1867).

George Saintsbury, *A History of Criticism*, vol. 2 (New York, 1902).

J. E. Spingarn, *A History of Literary Criticism in the Renaissance* (2nd ed., New York, 1908).

TAILLE

On the drama:

Preface to *Les Corrivaux* (1562). *Art de la Tragédie*, in *Saül le furieux* (1572).

Editions:

With the exception of the very rare first edition of Taille's *Saül le furieux* (1572) which contains the *Art de la Tragédie*, there are only two editions, the reprint of the *Art* by itself in Hugo Schlensog's dissertation on the *Lucelles* of Louis le Jars and Jacques Duhamel (Freiburg i. Br., 1906), and the more recent edition *De l'Art de la tragédie,* edited by Fred West (Manchester, 1939). Taille's comedy *Les Corrivaux* (1562) with prefatory matter touching upon the drama, is reprinted in the *Œuvres* (see below). Taille's works, including two plays besides those already mentioned, but excluding *Saül* and the *Art de la Tragédie,* and with a *Notice* on the author, are reprinted: *Œuvres,* 4 vols., edited by René de Maulde (Paris, 1878).

On Taille and his works:

Prefaces to the editions cited.

G. Baguenault de Puchesse, *Jean et Jacques de la Taille* (In *Lectures et Mémoires de Sainte-Croix,* vol., VI, Orléans, 1889).
Biographie universelle, vol. 40 (Paris).
J. E. Spingarn, *A History of Literary Criticism in the Renaissance* (2nd ed., New York, 1908).
A. Werner, *Jean de la Taille und sein' Saül le furieux* (Leipzig, 1908).

SPAIN—THE GOLDEN AGE
TO THE PRESENT

General references on Spanish literature:

José Manuel Aicardo, *De literaturia contemporánea* (2d ed., Madrid, 1905).
P. A. Becker, *Geschichte der spanishen Literatur* (Strassburg, 1904).
Rudolf Beer, *Spanische Literaturgeschichte,* 2 vols. (Leipzig, 1903).
A. F. G. Bell, *Castilian Literature* (Oxford, 1938).
F. Bouterwek, *History of Spanish Literature* (Trans. by T. Ross, London, 1847).
Gerald Brenan, *The Literature of the Spanish People* (Cambridge, Eng., 1951).
Julio Cejador y Frauca, *Historia de la lengua y literatura castellana,* 5 vols. to date (Madrid, 1915-16).
H. B. Clarke, *Spanish Literature: an Elementary Handbook* (2nd ed., London, 1909).
James Fitzmaurice-Kelly, *Bibliographie de l'histoire de la littérature espagnole* (Paris, 1913).
——, *History of Spanish Literature* (London, 1898).
P. F. B. García, *La Literatura española en el siglo XIX* (Madrid, 1891).
William Hanssler, *A Handy Bibliographical Guide to the Study of the Spanish Language and Literature, etc.* (St. Louis, 1915)
Hispanic Society of America (pub.) *Bibliographie hispanique* (New York, annual nos. 1905 to date).

M. Menéndez y Pelayo, *Estudios de critica literaria,* 5 vols. (Madrid, 1893–1908).
Ernest Mérimée, *Précis d'histoire de la littérature espagnole* (Paris, 1908).
—— and S. Griswold Morley, *A History of Spanish Literature* (New York, 1930).
A. Morel-Fatio, *L'Espagne au XVIe et au XVIIe siècle* (Heilbronn, 1878).
——, *Etudes sur l'Espagne,* 2 vols. (2nd ed., Paris, 1895–1906).
Heinrich Morf, *Die romanishen Literaturen und Sprachen* (Berlin, 1909).
George Tyler Northrup, *An Introduction to Spanish Literature* (Chicago, 1925).
A. Puibusque, *Histoire comparée des littératures espagnole et française,* 2 vols. (Paris, 1843).
B. de los Rios de Lampérez, *Del siglo d'oro (Estudios literarios)* (Madrid, 1910).
Angel Salcedo y Ruiz, *La Literatura Española,* 3 vols. (2nd ed., Madrid, 1915–16).
J. C. L. S. de Sismondi, *De la Littérature du midi de l'Europe* (3rd ed., 4 vols., Paris, 1829. Translated as *Historical View of the Literature of the South of Europe,* 2 vols. Bohn ed., London, 1853).
Spanish Literature [a bibliography] (in *Pratt Institute Lectures,* nos. 30–31, Brooklyn, 1894–95).
Boris de Tannenberg, *L'Espagne littéraire, portraits d'hier et d'aujourd'-*

hui (Paris, 1903).

George Ticknor, *History of Spanish Literature*, 3 vols. (6th ed., Boston, 1888. Spanish translation, with additions and corrections, by Gayangos and Vedia, 4 vols., Madrid, 1851-56).

F. Wolf, *Studien zur Geschichte der spanischen und portugiesischen Nationalliteratur* (Berlin, 1859).

General references on Spanish drama:

The. G. Ahrens, *Zur Charakteristik des spanischen Dramas im Anfang des XVII. Jahrhunderts* (Halle, 1911).

A. Anaya, *An Essay on Spanish Literature . . . followed by a History of the Spanish Drama* (London, 1818).

C. A. de la Barrera y Leirado, *Catálogo bibliográfico del teatro antiguo Español desde sus orígenes hasta mediados del siglo XVIII* (Madrid, 1860).

A. J. Bastinos, *Arte dramático español contemporáneo* (Barcelona, 1914).

J.-J.-A. Bertrand, *L. Tieck et le théâtre espagnol* (Paris, 1914).

Jean-Paul Borel, *Théâtre de l'impossible* (Neuchâtel, 1963).

Manuel Bueno, *Teatro Españoi contemporáneo* (Madrid, 1909).

Manuel Cañete, *Teatro Español del siglo XVI* (Madrid, 1885).

Antonio Cánovas del Castillo, *El Teatro español* (Barcelona, 1906).

F. W. Chandler, *Aspects of Modern Drama* (New York, 1914).

John Chorley, *Notes on the National Drama in Spain* (*Fraser's Magazine*, London, July, 1859).

Barrett H. Clark, *The Continental Drama of Today* (2nd ed., New York, 1914).

——, *A Study of Modern Drama* (New York, rev. ed., 1928).

Cotarelo y Mori, *Bibliografía de las controversias sobre la Licitud del Teatro en España* (Madrid, 1904).

J. P. W. Crawford, *Spanish Drama Before Lope de Vega* (Philadelphia, 1922).

——, *The Spanish Pastoral Drama* (Philadelphia, 1915).

M. Damas-Hinard, *Discours sur l'histoire et l'esprit du théâtre espagnol* (Paris, 1847).

——, *Le Théâtre espagnol au siècle d'or* (Paris, 1853).

J. Ebner, *Zur Geschichte des klassischen Dramas in Spanien* (Passau, 1908).

Tomas de Erauso y Zavaleta, *Discurso Crítico sobre . . . las Comedias de España* (Madrid, 1750).

Juan Nicolás Böhl von Faber, *Teatro Español anterior á Lope de Vega* (Hamburgo, 1832).

M. A. Fée, *Etudes sur l'ancien théâtre espagnol* (Paris, 1873).

Alfred Gassier, *Le Théâtre espagnol* (Paris, 1898).

Franz Grillparzer, *Studien zum spanischen Theater* (in vol. 17, Cotta ed. *Grillparzers sämtliche Werke*).

David Hannay, *The Later Renaissance* (New York, 1898).

G. H. Lewes, *The Spanish Drama* (London, 1845).

H. Lucas, *Le Théâtre espagnol* (Paris, 1851).

Henry Lyonnet, *Le Théâtre en Espagne* (Paris, 1897).

Henri Mérimée, *L'Art dramatique à Valencia, depuis les origines jusqu' au commencement du XVIIe siècle* (Toulouse, 1913).

A. Morel-Fatio, *La Comedia espagnole du XVIIe siècle* (Paris, 1885).

——, *Les défenseurs de la Comedia* (in the *Bulletin hispanique Bordeaux*, 1902).

—— and L. Rouanet, *Le Théâtre espagnol* (Paris, 1900).

A. A. Parker, *The Allegorical Dramas of Calderón* (Oxford, 1943).

——, "The Approach to the Spanish Drama of the Golden Age," *Tulane Drama Review*, IV (1959), pp. 42-59.

C. Pérez Pastor, *Nuevos Datos acerca del Histrionismo español en los siglos XVI-XVII* (Madrid, 1901).

Casiano Pellicer, *Tratado historico sobre el Origen y progresos de la Comedia y del histrionismo en España* (Madrid, 1804).

H. A. Rennert, *The Spanish Stage in the Time of Lope de Vega* (New York, 1909).

José Francos Rodréguez, *El Teatro en España* (Madrid, 1908).

J. Sánchez Arjona, *Noticias referentes á los anales del teatro en Sevilla desde Lope de Rueda hasta fines del siglo XVII* (Sevilla, 1898).

A. F. von Schack, *Geschichte des drama-*

tischen Literatur und Kunst in Spanien, 2 vols. (Berlin, 1845–46).

——, Nachträge, etc. (Frankfurt a/M., 1854).

Adolf Schaeffer, Geschichte des spanischen Nationaldramas, 2 vols. (Leipzig, 1890).

A. Ludwig Stiefel, Spanisches Drama bis 1800 (in Kritischer Jahresbericht über die Fortschritte der romanischen Philologie, vol. 7, 1905).

L. Viardot, Etudes sur l'histoire des institutions de la littérature, du théâtre, et des beaux-arts en Espagne (Paris, 1835).

Louis de Viel-Castel, Essai sur le Théâtre espagnol, 2 vols. (Paris, 1882).

Bruce W. Wardropper, Introducción al teatro religioso del Siglo de Oro (Madrid, 1954).

José Yxart, El arte escénico en España (Madrid, 1894–96).

References on Spanish criticism:

H. Breitinger, Les Unités d'Aristote avant le Cid de Corneille (Genève, 1895).

H. J. Chaytor, Dramatic Theory in Spain (Cambridge, 1925).

F. Fernandez y Gonzalez, Historia de la Crítica literaria en España, etc. (Madrid, 1870).

Marcelino Menéndez y Pelayo, Historia de las Ideas estéticas en España, 9 vols. (2nd ed., Madrid, 1890, and following).

George Saintsbury, A History of Criticism, vol. 2 (New York, 1902).

J. E. Spingarn, A History of Literary Criticism in the Renaissance (2nd ed., New York, 1908).

CERVANTES

On the drama:

Don Quixote, part 1, chapter 48 (1605).
Viaje del Parnaso (1614).
Preface to Ocho comedias y ocho entremeses nuevos (1615).
[The play] El Rufián Dichoso (1615).

Editions:

The first part of Don Quixote was published at Madrid in 1605. There are innumerable editions, among the best of which is that in the Hartzenbusch edition of the Obras completas, 12 vols. (Madrid, 1863–64). The Complete Works have been published in English under the editorship of James Fitzmaurice-Kelly, 8 vols. (Glasgow, 1901–06). Among the editions of Don Quixote may be mentioned those of Clemencin, 6 vols. (Madrid, 1833–39), and Fitzmaurice-Kelley and Ormsby, 2 vols. (London, 1899–1900), though the best is Samuel Putnam's translation with notes, variant readings, etc., 2 vols. (New York, 1949). There are other English translations by Motteux, Shelton, Smollett, Ormsby, Walter Starkie, J. M. Cohen, and others. An English translation of the Interludes, by S. Griswold Morley (Princeton, 1948), contains notes and the Spanish text. There is a French translation of some of Cervantes' plays, together with the Preface referred to: Théâtre de Michel Cervantes, translated by Alphonse Royer (Paris, n.d.). The Viaje del Parnaso, with an interesting appendix, is translated by James Y. Gibson (London, 1883).

On Cervantes and his works:

A. F. G. Bell, Cervantes (Oklahoma City, 1947).

M. A. Buchanan, Cervantes as a Dramatist (in Modern Language Notes, vol. 33, 1908).

N. Díaz de Escovar, Apuntes escénicos cervantinos, etc. (Madrid, 1905).

Marcel Dieulafoy, Le Théâtre édifiant (Paris, 1907).

W. J. Entwistle, Cervantes (New York, 1940).

Martin Fernandez de Navarrete, Vida de Miguel de Cervantes Saavedra (Madrid, 1819).

James Fitzmaurice-Kelly, Miguel de Cervantes Saavedra, a Memoir (Oxford, 1913)

A. Flores and M. J. Benardete, eds., Cervantes Across the Centuries (New York, 1947).

S. Salas Garrido, Exposición de las ideas estéticas de Miguel de Cervantes Saavedra (Malaga, 1905).

R. L. Grismer, Cervantes: A Bibliography (New York, 1946).

Leopold Rius, Bibliografía crítica de las obras de Miguel de Cervantes Saavedra, 3 vols. (Madrid, 1895–1905).

R. Schevill, Cervantes (New York, 1919).

LOPE DE VEGA

On the drama:

Prefaces and dedications to the various *Comedias,* especially in *Partes* IX (1618), XIII (1620), XVII (1622), XIX (1627), and XXIII (1638). These are reprinted in *Obras* ed. by Menéndez y Pelayo for the Real Academia Española, 13 vols. (Madrid, 1890–1902). The *Arte nuevo de hacer comedias en este tiempo* originally appeared in the *Rimas* (Madrid, 1609). The *Rimas* are published in facsimile by the Hispanic Society of America (New York, 1903). The *Arte* by Morel-Fatio, with notes, in the *Bulletin hispanique* (Paris, Oct.–Dec., 1904). Also in H. J. Chaytor's *Dramatic Theory in Spain* (Cambridge, 1925). It is translated as *The New Art of Making Plays in This Age,* by William T. Brewster, with an introduction by Brander Matthews (Dramatic Museum of Columbia University, New York, 1914).

On Lope de Vega and his works:

Cayetano Alberto de la Barrera, *Nueva Biografía de Lope de Vega* (Madrid, 1890).

James Fitzmaurice-Kelly, *Lope de Vega and the Spanish Drama* (London, 1902).

Henry Richard, Lord Holland, *Some Account of the Lives and Writings of Lope Felix de Vega Carpio and Guillen de Castro* (London, 1817).

Camille Le Senne and Guillot de Saix, *Lope de Vega, L'Etoile de Séville. Etude et version française intégrale. Préface par Henry Roujon* (Paris, 1912).

Brander Matthews, *Introduction* to *The New Art of Writing Plays,* etc. (New York, 1914).

Pérez de Montalban, *Fama Póstuma* (Madrid, 1636).

——, *Para todos* (Madrid, 1632).

Alfred Morel-Fatio, *Les Origines de Lope de Vega* (In the *Bulletin hispanique,* VII, p. 38, Paris, 1905).

Cristóbal Pérez Pastor, *Datos desconocidos para la Vida de Lope de Vega* (In *Homenaje á Menéndez y Pelayo.* Madrid, 1900. New ed., in Tomillo's *Proceso de Lope de Vega,* etc., Madrid, 1901).

Camille Pitollet, *La Poétique de Lope* (In *Le Siècle, Paris,* Nov., 1905).

Hugo Albert Rennert, *The Life of Lope de Vega* (London, 1904).

——, *The Spanish Stage in the Time of Lope de Vega* (New York, 1909).

Rudolph Schevill, *The Dramatic Art of Lope de Vega* (Berkeley, Cal., 1918).

TIRSO DE MOLINA

On the drama:

Tirso's only remarks on dramatic theory are found in the *Cigarrales de Toledo* (1624).

Editions:

The various editions of the plays contain biographies, and in some cases extracts from the *Cigarrales de Toledo.* The passages on the drama are quoted fully in Menéndez y Peláyo's *Historia de las ideas estéticas en España* (2nd ed., Madrid 1890, ff.). Reprinted in H. J. Chaytor's *Dramatic Theory in Spain* (Cambridge, 1925). The plays are found in the *Comedias escogidas,* 2 vols. (Madrid, 1850), and in the *Comedias de Tirso de Molina,* 2 vols. (Madrid, 1906–07).

On Tirso de Molina and his works:

Artículos biográficos y críticos de varios autores acerca de . . . Tellez y sus obras (In the *Biblioteca de autores españoles,* vol. 5, pp. xi-xxxv, Madrid, 1850).

A. H. Bushee, *Three Centuries of Tirso de Molina* (Oxford, 1939).

I. L. McClelland, *Tirso de Molina: Studies in Dramatic Realism* (Liverpool, 1948).

M. Menéndez y Pelayo, *Estudios de crítica literaria,* 5 vols. (2nd series, Madrid, 1893–1908).

P. Muñoz Peña, *El teatro del Maestro Tirso de Molina* (Madrid, 1889).

B. de los Ríos de Lampérez, *Tirso de Molina* (Madrid, 1906).

LORCA

Editions:

The *Obras Completas* was published in Madrid in 1955. Translations of *Amor de don Perlimplín, La zapatera prod-igiosa, Doña Rosita la soltera,* and *Yerma* are included in *From Lorca's Theatre* (New York, 1941). *Blood Wedding, Yerma,* and *Bernarda Alba* are included in *Three Tragedies* (New York, 1947).

On Lorca and his works:

Arturo Barea, *Lorca: The Poet and His People* (New York, 1949).
Roy Campbell, *Lorca: An Appreciation of His Poetry* (New Haven, 1952).
Manuel Duran, ed., *Lorca* (Englewood Cliffs, 1962).
Edwin Honig, *Garcia Lorca* (Norfolk, Conn., 1944).
Robert Lima, *The Theatre of Garcia Lorca* (New York, 1963).

ELIZABETHAN ENGLAND

General references on English literature:

Albert C. Baugh, ed., *A Literary History of England* (New York, 1948).
Hardin Craig, ed., *A History of English Literature* (New York, 1950).
Stopford A. Brooke, *English Literature* (Ed., New York, 1907).
E. Engel, *A History of English Literature* (London, 1902).
Boris Ford, ed., *A Guide to English Literature,* 7 vols. (London, 1954–61).
Richard Garnett and Edmund Gosse, *English Literature,* 4 vols. (New York, 1908).
R. P. Halleck, *History of English Literature* (New York, 1900).
G. Körting, *Grundriss der Geschichte der englischen Literatur* (3rd ed., Münster, 1899).
Andrew Lang, *History of English Literature* (London, 1912).
Emile Legouis and Louis Cazamian, *A History of English Literature* (New York, rev., 1935).
C. S. Lewis, *English Literature in the Sixteenth Century* (Oxford, 1954). On non-dramatic literature.
M. L. Mézières, *Histoire critique de la littérature anglaise,* 3 vols. (Paris, 1834).
William Vaughn Moody and R. M. Lovett, *A History of English Literature* (New York, 1911).
Henry Morley, *English Writers,* 11 vols. (London, 1887–95).
Helen Morris, *Elizabethan Literature* (London, 1958).
W. R. Nicoll and T. Seccombe, *A History of English Literature,* 3 vols. (New York, 1907).
H. S. Pancoast, *An Introduction to Eng-lish Literature* (New York, 1894. See 3rd ed.).
John Peter, *Complaint and Satire in Early English Literature* (Oxford, 1956).
George Saintsbury, *A Short History of English Literature* (New York, 1898).
Leslie Stephen and Sidney Lee, *Dictionary of National Biography,* 66 vols. (London, 1885–1901).
A. W. Ward and A. R. Waller, editors, *The Cambridge History of English Literature,* 14 vols. (Cambridge and New York, 1907–17).

General references on English drama:

K. L. Bates and L. B. Godfrey, *English Drama, a Working Basis* (Wellesley, 1896).
David Erskine Baker, *Biographia Dramatica,* etc., 3 vols. (Continuation, London, 1811).
——, *The Companion to the Playhouse,* 2 vols. (London, 1764).
Benjamin Brawley, *A Short History of the English Drama* (New York, 1921)
E. K. Chambers, *The Mediæval Stage,* 2 vols. (Oxford, 1903).
L. N. Chase, *The English Heroic Play* (New York, 1903).
W. R. Chetwood, *The British Theatre* (Dublin, 1750).
W. Creizenach, *Geschichte des neueren Dramas* (Halle, 1893–1909; vol. iv translated by Cécile Hugon as *The English Drama in the Age of Shakespeare,* London, 1916).
Charles Dibdin, *A Complete History of the Stage,* 5 vols. (London, 1800).
John Doran, *Annals of the English Stage,* 2 vols. (London, 1864).

Alan S. Downer, *The British Drama* (New York, 1950).

John Downes, *Roscius Anglicanus, or a historical view of the Stage,* etc. (new ed., London, 1789).

S. A. Dunham, *Lives of British Dramatists,* 2 vols. (London, 1847).

Percy Fitzgerald, *New History of the English Stage* (London, 1882).

F. G. Fleay, *A Biographical Chronicle of the English Drama* (London, 1891).

John Genest, *Some Account of the English Stage,* 10 vols. (Bath, 1832).

Thomas Gilliland, *The Dramatic Mirror: containing the History of the Stage. from the earliest period to the present time,* etc., 2 vols. (London, 1808).

T. Hawkins, *The Origin of the English Drama,* 3 vols. (Oxford, 1773).

J. L. Klein, *Geschichte des Dramas,* vols. 12 and 13 (Leipzig, 1865–76).

G. Wilson Knight, *The Golden Labyrinth: A Study of British Drama* (London, 1962).

R. W. Lowe, *Bibliographical Account of English Theatrical Literature* (London, 1888).

Agnes M. Mackenzie, *The Playgoer's Handbook to the English Renaissance Drama* (London, n. d.).

E. Malone, *Historical Account of the Rise and Progress of the English Stage* (in 3rd vol., ed. of Shakespeare, London, 1821).

Jeanette Marks, *English Pastoral Drama* (London, 1908).

Watson Nicholson, *The Struggle for a Free Stage in London* (Boston, 1906).

Allardyce Nicoll, *British Drama* (London, 1925, 1932).

Moody E. Prior, *The Language of Tragedy* (New York, 1947).

A. S. Rappoport, *The English Drama* (London, n. d.).

A. W. Reed, *Early Tudor Drama* (London, 1926).

F. H. Ristine, *English Tragicomedy* (New York, 1910).

Felix E. Schelling, *The English Chronicle Play* (New York, 1902).

——, *English Drama* (New York, 1914).

R. F. Sharp, *A Short History of the English Stage* (London, 1909).

Donald Clive Stuart, *The Development of Dramatic Art* (New York, 1928).

A. H. Thorndike, *Tragedy* (Boston, 1908).

A. W. Ward, *History of English Dramatic Literature to the Death of Queen Anne,* 3 vols. (New York, 1899).

W. K. Wimsatt, Jr., ed., *English Stage Comedy* (New York, 1955).

Arnold Wynne, *The Growth of English Drama* (Oxford, 1914).

References on Elizabethan drama:

Peter Alexander, *Hamlet: Father and Son* (Oxford, 1955).

Howard Baker, *Induction to Tragedy* (Baton Rouge, 1939).

C. L. Barber, *Shakespeare's Festive Comedy* (Princeton, 1959).

S. L. Bethell, *Shakespeare and the Popular Dramatic Tradition* (London, 1944).

David M. Bevington, *From Mankind to Marlowe* (Cambridge, Mass., 1962).

Max Bluestone and Norman Rabkin, eds., *Shakespeare's Contemporaries* (New York, 1961).

F. S. Boas, *An Introduction to Stuart Drama* (Oxford, 1946).

——, *An Introduction to Tudor Drama* (Oxford, 1933).

——, ed., *Shakespeare and His Predecessors* (New York, 1904).

Fredson S. Bowers, *Elizabethan Revenge Tragedy* (Princeton, 1940).

M. C. Bradbrook, *The Growth and Structure of Elizabethan Comedy* (London, 1955).

——, *Themes and Conventions of Elizabethan Tragedy* (Cambridge, Eng., 1935).

John Russell Brown and Bernard Harris, eds., *Jacobean Theatre* (London, 1960).

O. J. Campbell, *Comicall Satyre and Shakespeare's Troilus and Cressida* (San Marino, 1938).

E. K. Chambers, *The Elizabethan Stage,* 4 vols. (New York, 1923).

Wolfgang Clemen, *English Tragedy before Shakespeare* (London, 1961).

J. P. Collier, ed., *The Alleyn Papers* (London, 1843).

——, *The History of English Dramatic Poetry to the Time of Shakespeare and Annals of the Stage to the Restoration,* 3 vols. (London, new ed., 1879).

W. J. Courthope, *History of English Poetry,* vols. I–III (London, 1895–1903).

J. W. Cunliffe, *The Influence of Italian on Early Elizabethan Drama* (in Mod-

ern Philology, 4, 1906).
——, The Influence of Seneca on Elizabethan Tragedy (London, 1893).
Madeleine Doran, Endeavors of Art (Madison, 1954).
N. Drake, Shakespeare and His Times (London, 1817).
L. Einstein, The Italian Renaissance in England (New York, 1902).
T. S. Eliot, Essays on Elizabethan Drama (New York, 1956).
Una Ellis-Fermor, The Jacobean Drama (London, 1936, 1947).
Harriet Ely Fansler, The Evolution of Technique in Elizabethan Tragedy (Chicago, 1914).
Willard Farnham, The Medieval Heritage of Elizabethan Tragedy (Berkeley, 1936).
F. G. Fleay, A Chronicle History of the London Stage (1559–1642) (London, 1890).
Henri Fluchère, Shakespeare (London, 1953).
F. Guizot, Shakespeare and His Times (trans., New York, 1855).
William Hazlitt, Lectures on the Dramatic Literature of the Age of Queen Elizabeth (London, 1821).
[W. C. Hazlitt. ed.] The English Drama and Stage Under the Tudor and Stuart Princes—1543-1664—Illustrated by a Series of Documents, Treatises, and Poems, etc. (London, 1869).
Marvin T. Herrick, Tragicomedy (Urbana, 1955).
J.-J. Jusserand, Le Théâtre en Angleterre jusqu' aux prédécesseurs immédiats de Shakespeare (2nd ed., Paris, 1881).
Ralph J. Kaufmann, ed., Elizabethan Drama: Modern Essays in Criticism (New York, 1961).
David Klein, The Elizabethan Dramatists as Critics (New York, 1963).
L. C. Knights, Drama and Society in the Age of Jonson (London, 1937).
Clifford Leech, Shakespeare's Tragedies (New York, 1950).
J. A. Lester, Connections Between the Drama of France and Great Britain, particularly in the Elizabethan Period (Cambridge. Mass., 1902).
A. Mézières, Prédécesseurs et contemporains de Shakespeare (Paris, 1881).
——, Contemporains et successeurs de Shakespeare (Paris, 1881).
Robert Ornstein, The Moral Vision of

Jacobean Tragedy (Madison, 1960).
T. M. Parrott and R. H. Ball, A Short View of Elizabethan Drama (New York, 1943).
E. C. Pettet, Shakespeare and the Romance Tradition (London, 1949).
Irving Ribner, The English History Play in the Age of Shakespeare (Princeton, 1957).
——, Jacobean Tragedy (London, 1962).
J. M. Robertson, Elizabethan Literature (New York, 1914).
A. P. Rossiter, English Drama from Early Times to the Elizabethans (London, 1950).
George Saintsbury, History of Elizabethan Literature (ed., London. 1906).
Felix E. Schelling, Elizabethan Drama, 2 vols. (Boston, 1908).
——, Elizabethan Playwrights (New York, 1925).
——, English Literature During the Lifetime of Shakespeare (New York, 1910).
M. A. Scott, The Elizabethan Drama, especially in its Relations to the Italians of the Renaissance (New Haven, 1894).
T. Seccombe and J. W. Allen, The Age of Shakespeare, 2 vols. (London, 1903).
A. C. Swinburne, The Age of Shakespeare (London, 1908).
J. A. Symonds, Shakespeare's Predecessors in the English Drama (London, 1881).
E. M. W. Tillyard, Shakespeare's History Plays (New York, 1946).
Eugene M. Waith, The Pattern of Tragicomedy in Beaumont and Fletcher (New Haven, 1952).
Barrett Wendell, The Temper of the Seventeenth Century in English Literature (New York, 1904).
E. P. Whipple, Literature of the Age of Elizabeth (Boston, 1869).

References on English criticism, Elizabethan in particular:

J. W. H. Atkins, English Literary Criticism: The Renascence (London, 1947, 1951).
L. S. Friedland, Dramatic Unities in England (in Journal of English and Germanic Philology, vol. 10, no. 1, 1911).
P. Hamelius, Die Kritik in der englischen Litteratur der 17. und 18. Jahrhunderts

(Leipzig, 1897).

David Klein, *Literary Criticism from the Elizabethan Dramatists* (New York, 1910).

C. W. Moulton, *The Library of Literary Criticism of English and American Authors*, 8 vols. (Buffalo, 1901–05).

George Saintsbury, *A History of English Criticism* (New York, 1911).

Felix E. Schelling, *Poetic and Verse Criticism of the Reign of Elizabeth* (Philadelphia, 1891).

G. Gregory Smith, *Elizabethan Critical Essays*, 2 vols. (Oxford, 1904).

J. E. Spingarn, *A History of Literary Criticism in the Renaissance* (2nd ed., New York, 1908).

H. S. Symmes, *Les Débuts de la critique dramatique en Angleterre jusqu' à la mort de Shakespeare* (Paris, 1903).

Laura J. Wylie, *Studies in the Evolution of English Criticism* (Boston, 1894).

SIDNEY

Editions:

Two editions appeared at London in 1595: *The Defence of Poesie*, and *An Apologie for Poetrie*. The latter is generally regarded as the better text of the two. It is re-printed in Arber's *English Reprints* and in the first volume of G. Gregory Smith's *Elizabethan Critical Essays*, 2 vols. (Oxford, 1904).

On Sidney and his works:

Prefaces to the Arber, Grosart, and Smith eds. of Sidney's works.

Fox Bourne, *Memoir of Sir Philip Sidney* (London, 1862).

E. J. M. Buxton, *Sir Philip Sidney and the English Renaissance* (London, 1954).

Collins, *Sidney Papers*, 2 vols. (London, 1745).

Fulke Greville, *Life of Sidney* (London, 1652).

Julius Lloyd, *Life of Sir Philip Sidney* (London, 1862).

Kenneth O. Myrick, *Sir Philip Sidney as a Literary Craftsman* (Cambridge, Mass., 1935).

M. Poirier, *Sir Philip Sidney* (Lille, 1948).

George Saintsbury, *A History of Criticism*, vol. 2 (New York, 1902).

J. E. Spingarn, *A History of Literary Criticism in the Renaissance* (2nd ed., New York, 1908).

J. A. Symonds, *Sir Philip Sidney* (*English Men of Letters Series*, late ed., London, 1906).

JONSON

On the drama:

Jonson's critical utterances are scattered through the prologues and in the dialogue of *Every Man in his Humour, Every Man Out of his Humour,* and *The Poetaster.*

The more important criticisms are:

To the Readers, in *Sejanus* (printed 1605).

To the Most Noble and Most Equal Sisters, the two Famous Universities, etc., in *Volpone, or the Fox* (printed 1607).

Prologue to *Epicœne* (printed 1609?).

Timber; or, Discoveries made upon Men and Matter (1641).

Ben Jonson's Conversations with William Drummond of Hawthornden (published London, 1842).

Editions:

The first and second folios of Jonson' works appeared respectively in 1616 and 1640. The first modern edition is that of Gifford, 9 vols., London, 1816. This is re-printed in 3 vols. (London, 1870). The most recent and certainly most completely annotated is *The Works of Ben Jonson,* edited by C. H. Herford and Percy and Evelyn Simpson, 11 vols. (Oxford, 1925–52). There are numerous other editions, among them a 2-volume selection of the plays (Mermaid Series, London and New York, 1893–94).

The *Discoveries* have been often re-printed: by Felix E. Schelling (Boston, 1892); by J. E. Spingarn, *Critical Essays of the Seventeenth Century,* vol. 1 (Oxford, 1908); Maurice Castelain (Paris, 1907); and H. Morley (London, 1892).

On Jonson and his works:

Prefatory material to editions cited.

P. Aronstein, *Ben Jonson's Theorie des*

Lustspiels (in *Anglia,* vol. 17, Halle, 1894).

Jonas A. Barish, ed., *Ben Jonson* (New York, 1963).

——, *Ben Jonson and the Language of Prose Comedy* (Cambridge, Mass., 1960).

Charles Read Baskervill, *English Elements in Jonson's Early Comedy* (Austin, 1911).

W. H. T. Baudissin, *Ben Jonson und seine Schule,* 2 vols. (Leipzig, 1836).

Helena Watts Baum, *The Satiric and the Didactic in Ben Jonson's Comedy* (Chapel Hill, 1947).

M. Castelain, *Ben Jonson, l'homme et l'œuvre* (Paris, 1907).

Esther Cloudman Dunn, *Ben Jonson's Art* (Northampton, Mass., 1925).

John J. Enck, *Jonson and the Comic Truth* (Madison, 1957).

H. Grossmann, *Ben Jonson als Kritiker* (Berlin, 1898).

C. H. Herford, *Ben Jonson* (in *Dictionary of National Biography,* vol. 30, London, 1892).

Edward B. Partridge, *The Broken Compass* (London, 1958).

H. Reinsch, *Jonson's Poetik und seine*

Beziehungen zu Horaz (Naumburg, 1898).

Alexander H. Sackton, *Rhetoric as a Dramatic Language in Ben Jonson* (New York, 1947).

Felix E. Schelling, *Jonson and the Classical School* (*Modern Language Association Publications,* Baltimore, 1898).

P. Simpson, " *Tanquam Explorator*": *Jonson's Method in the Discoveries* (*Modern Language Review,* vol. 2, 1907).

R. A. Small. *The Stage-quarrel Between Ben Jonson and the so-called Poetasters* (in *Forschungen zu englische Sprache und Literatur,* Breslau, 1899).

G. Gregory Smith, *Ben Jonson* (London, 1919).

J. E. Spingarn, *Sources of Jonson's* " *Discoveries* " (in *Modern Philology,* vol. 2, 1905).

A. C. Swinburne, *A Study of Ben Jonson* (London, 1889).

J. A. Symonds, *Ben Jonson* (London, 1886).

C. G. Thayer, *Ben Jonson* (Oklahoma City, 1963).

Freda L. Townsend, *Apologie for Bartholomew Fayre* (New York, 1947).

SEVENTEENTH-CENTURY
FRANCE

General references for seventeenth-century French literature.

A. Adam, *Histoire de la littérature française au XVIIe siècle,* 4 vols. (Paris, 1948–56).

Paul Albert, *La Littérature française au XVIIᵉ siècle* (Paris, 1895).

E. B. O. Borgerhoff, *The Freedom of French Classicism* (Princeton, 1950).

R. Bray, *Formation de la doctrine classique en France* (Lausanne, 1934).

Demogeot, *Tableau de la Littérature française au XVIIᵉ siècle avant Corneille et Descartes* (Paris, 1859).

A. Dupuy, *Histoire de la littérature française au XVIIᵉ siècle* (Paris, 1892).

Emile Faguet, *Le Dix-septième siècle* (Paris, 1890).

L.-H. Follioley, *Histoire de la littérature*

française au XVIIᵉ siècle, 3 vols. (Tours, 1885).

F. Guizot, *Corneille et son temps* (new ed., Paris, 1852. Translated as *Corneille and his Times,* New York, 1871).

Paul Lacroix, *XVIIᵉ Siècle: Lettres, Sciences, et arts* (Paris, 1882).

Georges Longhaye, *Histoire de la littérature française au XVIIᵉ siècle,* 5 parts (Paris, 1895–98).

F. Lotheissen, *Geschichte der französischen Literatur im 17. Jahrhundert,* 4 vols. (Wien, 1874–84).

W. G. Moore, *French Classical Literature* (Oxford, 1961).

D. Mornet, *Histoire de la littérature française classique, 1660–1700* (Paris, 1947).

Henri Peyre, *Le Classicisme français* (New York, 1942).

Voltaire, *Le Siècle de Louis XIV* (Paris, 1751).

On the drama of the seventeenth century:

G. Attinger, *L'Esprit de la commedia dell'arte dans le théâtre français* (Neuchâtel, 1950).
Jules Bonnassies, *Les Auteurs dramatiques. et la Comédie française à Paris aux XVIIe et XVIIIe siècles* (Paris, 1874).
F. Delavigne, *La Tragédie chrétienne au XVIIe siècle. Etudes littéraires* (Toulouse, 1847).
Eugène Despois, *Le Théâtre français sous Louis XIV* (Paris, 1874).
G. Fagniez, *L'Art dramatique et le goût public dans la première moitié du XVIIe siècle* (in the *Correspondant*, N. S., vol. 216, Paris, 1913).
Victor Fournel, *La Littérature indépendante et les écrivains oubliés au XVIIe siècle* (Paris, 1862).
Eleanor Jourdain, *An Introduction to the French Classical Drama* (Oxford, 1912).
H. C. Lancaster, *A History of French Dramatic Literature, 1610–1700,* 9 vols. (Baltimore, 1929–42).
Gustave Lanson, *Esquisse d'une histoire de la tragédie française* (Paris, 1927).
Jules Lemaître, *La Comedie après Molière et le Théâtre de Dancourt* (Paris, 1882).
Eugène Lintilhac, *La Comédie: XVIIe siècle* (Paris, 1908).
Pierre Mélèse, *Le Théâtre et le public à Paris sous Louis XIV, 1659–1715* (Paris, 1934).
Eugène Rigal, *Le Théâtre français avant la période classique* (Paris, 1901).
D. Roaten, *Structural Forms in the French Theater, 1500–1700* (Philadelphia, 1960).
Jacques Schérer, *La Dramaturge classique en France* (Paris, n.d.).
I. A. Schwartz, *The Commedia dell'arte and Its Influence on French Comedy in the Seventeenth Century* (New York, 1933).
Martin Turnell, *The Classical Moment* (London, 1947).

On French criticism in the seventeenth century:

Charles Arnaud, *Les Théories dramatiques au XVIIe siècle. Etude sur la vie et les œuvres de l'Abbé d'Aubignac* (Paris, 1888).
Auguste Bourgoin, *Les Maîtres de la critique au XVIIe siècle* (Paris, 1889).
F. Delfour, *Les Ennemis de Racine au XVIIe siècle* (Paris, 1859).
Charles Livet, *Précieux et ridicules* (2nd ed., Paris, 1870).
George Saintsbury, *A History of Criticism,* vol. 2 (New York, 1902).
Francisque Vial et Louis Denise, *Idées et doctrines du XVIIe siècle* (Paris, 1906).
M. Wilmotte, *La Critique littéraire au XVII siècle* (in *Etudes critiques sur la tradition littéraire en France,* Paris, 1909).

General references on the *Académie française:*

G. Boissier, *L'Académie française sous l'Ancien Régime* (Paris, 1909).
A. Fabre, *Chapelain et nos deux premières Académies* (Paris, 1890).
Charles Marty-Laveaux, *Les Régistres de l'Académie française,* 3 vols. (Paris, 1893).
Paul Mesnard, *Histoire de l'Académie française* (Paris, 1857).
Pellisson et d'Olivet, *Histoire de l'Académie françoise* (new ed., 2 vols., Paris, 1858).
L. Petit de Julleville, *Histoire de la langue et de la Littérature française,* vol. 4 (Paris, 1897).
C.-A. Sainte-Beuve, *L'Académie française* (in *Nouveaux Lundis,* vol. 12, Paris, 1863–70).
Leon Vincent, *The French Academy* (Boston, 1901).

OGIER

Editions:

The second edition of Schélandre's *Tyr et Sidon,* which contains Ogier's preface, was published at Paris in 1628. Its exact title is *Préface au Lecteur, par F.O.P.* [François Ogier, Parisien]. The *Préface* and play are re-printed in the eighth volume of Viollet-le-duc's *Ancien Théâtre françois* (Paris, 1856).

On Ogier and his work:

Aulard, article in *Bulletin de la Faculté des lettres de Poitiers* (Avril, 1883).

Bayle, *Dictionnaire* (English ed., London, 1735).

Nouvelle Biographie générale, vol. 38 (Paris, 1861).

George Saintsbury, *A History of Criticism,* vol. 2 (New York, 1902).

CHAPELAIN

On the drama:

The *Lettres* belong to two different periods, and are full of literary discussions, criticism, and ideas. The first group includes the correspondence with Balzac, and belongs to the years 1632-40. The second, written to many European scholars, including Gronovius, Huet, Heinsius, and Vossius, belong to the period 1659-73. The principal edition is the selection of *Lettres,* 2 vols. (edited by Ph. Tamizey de Larroque, Paris, 1880-83). Selections from the *Lettres* and miscellaneous material are found in Camusat's *Mélanges de Littérature, tirez des Lettres manuscrites de M. Chapelain* (Paris, 1726). The last section of this book, on the men of letters of the day, is re-printed in Collas' *Chapelain,* cited below.
A great many letters and other MSS. of Chapelain have never been printed. There are three of interest, however, re-printed in the appendix of Charles Arnaud's *Les Théories dramatiques au XVIIᵉ siècle* (Paris, 1887). The first of these, *Trois Dissertations inédites de Chapelain,* is a *Démonstration de la Règle des Vingt-quatre heures et Réfutation des Objections,* dated 1630; the second, a *Sommaire d'une Poétique dramatique;* and the third (undated, like the preceding) a *Variante du Sommaire précédent.* This last is translated in the present volume.

Editions:

Les Sentimens de l'Académie françoise sur la Tragi-comédie du Cid was first published in 1637, though the title-page bears the date of 1638. It was re-printed in 1678, probably in 1693, and in 1701; also in the Marty-Laveaux edition of *Les Œuvres de Pierre Cor-* *neille,* vol. 12 (Paris, 1862). in Gasté's *La Querelle du Cid* (Paris, 1898), in Georges Collas' *Jean Chapelain* (Paris, 1911), and in Colbert Searles' *Les Sentiments de L'Académie française sur la Tragi-comédie du Cid* (Univ. of Minnesota, Minneapolis, 1916). This edition contains in parallel columns Chapelain's original MS., the corrections, and the printed version.

On Chapelain and his works:

Introductions to the Thamizey de Larroque, Camusat, and Searles editions above cited.

Charles Arnaud, *Les Théories dramatiques au XVIIᵉ siècle. Étude sur la vie et les œuvres de l'Abbé d'Aubignac* (Paris, 1887).

Adrien Baillet, *Jugement des savants,* 8 vols. (Paris, 1722-30).

Biographie universelle, vol. 7 (Paris, 1844).

A. Bourgoin, *Les Maîtres de la critique au XVIIᵉ siècle* (Paris, 1889).

Pierre Brun, *Jean Chapelain* (in *Revue d'histoire littéraire de la France,* Paris, 1902).

Georges Collas, *Jean Chapelain* (Paris, 1911).

Abbé Fabre, *Les Ennemis de Chapelain* (Paris, 1888).

J.-E. Fidao-Justiniani, *L'Esprit classique et la Préciosité au XVIIᵉ siècle* (Paris, 1914).

Goujet, *Bibliothèque françoise,* 18 vols. (Paris, 1701-26. See vol. 17).

La Grande Encyclopédie, vol. 10 (Paris).

F. Guizot, *Corneille et son Temps,* translated as *Corneille and his Times,* New York. 1871 (chap. on *Chapelain*).

E. Hunger, *Der Cidstreit in chronologischen Ordnung* (Leipzig, 1891).

René Kerviter, *La Bretagne a l'Académie française au XVIIᵉ siècle* (Paris, 1879).

H. Moulin, *Chapelain, Huet, Menage* (Caën, 1882).

Alois Mühlan, *Jean Chapelain als litterarischer Kritiker* (Leipzig, 1884).

Nouvelle Biographie générale, vol. 9 (Paris, 1854).

Segrais, *Segraisiana,* 2 vols. (Paris, 1721; Amsterdam, 1723).

D'AUBIGNAC

On the drama:

D'Aubignac's dramatic writings are not confined to the *Pratique du théâtre*, though this is his most important contribution to the subject. He carried on a long and rather absurd discussion with Ménage on the .duration of the action in the *Heautontimorumenos* of Terence. The first published work of d'Aubignac on the subject was the *Discours sur la troisième comédie de Térence, intitulée: "Héautontimorumenos,"* published at Paris anonymously in 1640. The next was the *Térence justifié,* published in 1656. Both were re-printed under the title of *Térence justifié* in the Amsterdam 2-volume edition of the *Pratique,* in 1715. In 1663 came the *Deux Dissertations en forme de remarques sur deux tragédies de M. Corneille* (Paris, 1663), and, later in the same year, the *Troisième et Quatrième Dissertations* on further plays of Corneille. These are vitriolic attacks on Corneille. The *Dissertation sur la condamnation des Théâtres* was published in 1666. He is likewise the author of two plays, *Cyminde* (1642), and *Zénobie* (1647).

Editions:

La Pratique du théâtre was first published at Paris in 1657, and re-printed there in 1669. The same work, together with the *Discours* on Terence, and one of Ménage, was re-printed in 2 vols. (Amsterdam, 1715). It was translated, anonymously; as *The Whole Art of the Stage, now made English* (London, 1684). Several passages of the original French are quoted in Arnaud's life of d'Aubignac.

On the Abbé d'Aubignac and his works:

Charles Arnaud, *Les Théories dramatiques au XVIIᵉ siècle. Etude sur la vie et les œuvres de l'Abbé d'Aubignac* (Paris, 1887).
Adrien Baillet, *Jugement des savants* (new ed., Paris, 1722–30).
Saint-Marc Girardin, *J.-J. Rosseau* (in vol. 2, Paris, 1870).

Charles Livet, *Précieux et ridicules* (2nd ed., Paris, 1870).
George Saintsbury, *A History of Criticism,* vol. 2 (New York, 1902).

CORNEILLE

Of the various prefaces, notices, dedications, exclusive of the *Examens,* the following may be consulted on the subject of the drama:

Préface to *Clitandre* (1632).
Au Lecteur in *La Veuve* (1634).
A Monsieur XXX in *La Suivante* (1637).
A Monsieur P. T. N. G. in *Médée* (1635).
Mariana (*Avertissement*) in *Le Cid* (1648 ed.).
Epître in *Le Menteur* (1644).
Au Lecteur in *La Mort de Pompée* (1644).
Epître in *La Suite du Menteur* (1645).
Appian Alexandrin (*Avertissement*) in *Rodogune* (1647).
Au Lecteur in *Héraclius* (1647).
A Monsieur de Zuylichem in *Don Sanche d'Aragon* (1650).
Au Lecteur in *Nicomède* (1651).
Au Lecteur in *Œdipe* (1659).
Au Lecteur in *Sertorius* (1662).
Au Lecteur in *Sophonisbe* (1663).
Au Lecteur in *Othon* (1665).
Au Lecteur in *Agésilas* (1666).
Au Lecteur in *Attila* (1668).

Editions:

Corneille's earlier works were published separately and in small collections prior to 1660 (when the *Théâtre de Corneille* was published at Paris, in three volumes). Each of these contained one of the *Discours;* the *Examens* also appeared in this edition for the first time. Voltaire's edition, with his full commentaries, appeared at Geneva, as the *Théâtre de Pierre Corneille,* in 12 vols. The standard modern edition of the complete works (with biography, an album, notes, etc.) is in the *Grands Ecrivains* series: *Œuvres de P. Corneille,* edited by Ch. Marty-Laveaux, 12 vols. (Paris, 1862–68).
The edition of 1660 contains the three *Discours — De l'Utilité et des parties du poëme dramatique; De la Tragédie,*

et des moyens de la traiter selon le vraisemblable et le nécessaire; and *Des Trois Unités, d'Action, de Jour, et de Lieu.* Each is printed in a volume, prefatory to the plays. All the early plays are each accompanied with an *Examen;* the plays from *Sertorius* to *Suréna* are without them. Among the *Œuvres diverses* in the Marty-Laveaux edition are a few letters and verses touching upon the drama. The most interesting of these is the already cited *Lettre apologétique* to Scudéry; there is another, *To Zuylichem* (no. 14, dated 1650) that is also curious. The editions of 1644 (first part), 1648 (second part), and 1663, of Corneille's plays, each contains an *Au Lecteur.* The prefaces, etc., are almost invariably printed in any edition of Corneille, the *Discours* occasionally. Outside the Marty-Laveaux edition, they are to be found in the *Œuvres des deux Corneille* (Pierre and Thomas), in two volumes, edited by Charles Louandre (Paris, 1889), and in the Calmann-Lévy re-print.

On Corneille and his works:

See introductions to Voltaire, Louandre, and Marty-Laveaux eds. above referred to.
See references to the *Cid* Quarrel under *Chapelain.*

Charles Arnaud, *Les Théories dramatiques au XVIIe siècle. Etude sur la vie et les œuvres de l'Abbé d'Aubignac* (Paris, 1887).
J.-L. G. de Balzac, *Dissertations sur la gloire,* and *Sur le Romain* (in *Œuvres,* 2 vols., Paris, 1665).
J. Boehm, *Die dramatischen Theorien P. Corneille's* (Berlin, 1901).
F. Bouquet, *Points obscurs et nouveaux de la vie de Corneille* (Paris, 1888).
Robert Brasillach, *Corneille* (Paris, 1938).
Ferdinand Brunetière, *Corneille* (in *Etudes critiques sur l'histoire de la littérature française,* vol. 6, 3rd ed., Paris, 1911).
Emile Deschanel, *Le Romantisme des classiques Ière série, Corneille, Rotrou, Molière, les don Juan de toutes les littératures* (Paris, 1882).

Bernard Dort, *Corneille dramaturge* (Paris, 1957).
René Doumic, *Corneille* (in *Etudes sur la littérature française,* vol. 5, Paris, 1906).
Emile Faguet, *Propos de théâtre,* vols. 1 & 2 (Paris, 1903–08).
——, *En Lisant Corneille* (Paris, 1913).
——, *Drame ancien, drame moderne* (Paris, 1898).
——, *XVIIe Siècle* (Paris, 1890).
Fontenelle, *Vie de Corneille* (in *Œuvres,* vol. 3, 1790 ed.).
——, *Parallèle de Corneille et de Racine* (in *Œuvres,* vol. 3, 1790 ed.).
Prosser Hall Frye, *Corneille: the Neoclassic Tragedy and the Greek* (in *Literary Reviews and Criticisms,* New York, 1908).
Abbé Granet, *Recueils de dissertations sur plusieurs tragédies de Corneille et de Racine,* 2 vols. (Paris, 1740).
F. Guizot, *Corneille et son Temps* (2nd ed., Paris, 1852. Translated as *Corneille and his Times,* New York, 1871).
Guillaume Huszar, *Corneille et le théâtre espagnol* (Paris, 1903).
Dr. Kewitsch, *Sur les théories dramatiques de Corneille, d'après ses Discours et ses examens* (Paris, 1852).
Gustave Lanson, *Corneille* (4th ed., Paris, 1913).
——, *Sur les Discours de Corneille* (in the *Revue des Cours et Conférences,* Paris, 1900–01).
R. Le Brun, *Corneille devant trois siècles* (Paris, 1906).
Jules Lemaître, *Corneille et la Poétique d'Aristote* (Paris, 1888).
P. Le Verdier et Ed. Pelay, *Additions à la Bibliographie cornélienne* (Paris, 1908).
J.-A. Lisle, *Essai sur les théories dramatiques de Corneille d'après des discours et ses examens* (Paris, 1852).
G. May, *Tragédie cornélienne, tragédie racinienne* (Urbana, 1948).
Hippolyte Parigot, *Le Génie et le métier de Corneille* (in *Génie et métier,* Paris, 1894).
E. Picot, *Bibliographie cornélienne* (Paris, 1876).
Eugène Rambert, *Corneille, Racine, et Molière, deux cours sur la poésie dramatique française au XVIIe siècle* (Paris, 1862).
Saegert, *Essai sur les théories dra-*

matiques de Corneille, d'après ses discours et ses examens (Colberg, 1860).

C.-A. Sainte-Beuve, *Portraits littéraires,* vol. 1 (Paris, 1862).

——, *Nouveaux Lundis,* vol. 7 (Paris, 1863–70).

——, *Port-Royal* (3rd ed., 7 vols., 1869–71).

Francisque Sarcey, *Quarante ans de théâtre,* vol. 2 (Paris, 1900).

Jean Schlumberger, *Plaisir à Corneille* (Paris, 1936).

J. B. Segall, *Corneille and the Spanish Drama* (New York, 1902).

St. René Taillandier, *Corneille et ses contemporains* (Paris, 1864).

M. J. Taschereau, *Histoire de la vie et des ouvrages de P. Corneille* (Paris, 1855).

Henry M. Trollope, *Corneille and Racine* (Philadelphia, 1881).

Leon H. Vincent, *Corneille* (Boston, 1901).

P. J. Yarrow, *Corneille* (London, 1963).

MOLIÈRE

On the drama:

Préface to *Les Précieuses ridicules* (1660).

Avertissement to *Les Fâcheux* (1662).

Préface to *L'Ecole des femmes* (1663), *La Critique de l'Ecole des femmes* (1663).

L'Impromptu de Versailles (produced 1663, printed 1682).

Préface (1st ed., 1669) and *Placets au Roi* (2nd ed., 1669), in *Tartufe.*

Au Lecteur in *L'Amour médecin* (1676).

Editions:

The first complete edition of the works of Molière is *Les Œuvres de Monsieur de Molière,* 8 vols. (Paris, 1682). Among the numerous modern editions, see that edited by Despois and Mesnard in the *Grands Ecrivains* series: *Œuvres de Molière,* 13 vols. (Paris, 1873–1900). See also, Henri Van Laun's *The Dramatic Works of J. B. Poquelin Molière,* 6 vols. (Edinburgh, 1878), and Katharine Prescott Wormeley's translation of seventeen plays: *Molière,* 6 vols. (Boston, 1894).

On Molière and his works:

H. Ashton, *Molière* (London, 1930).

Jacques Audiberti, *Molière dramaturge* (Paris, 1954).

René Bray, *Molière, homme du théâtre* (Paris, 1954).

J.-F. Cailhava, *Etudes sur Molière, etc.* (Paris, 1802).

H. C. Chatfield-Taylor, *Molière, a Biography* (New York, 1906).

Jules Claretie, *Molière, sa vie et ses œuvres* (Paris, 1873).

Henri Davignon, *Molière et la vie* (Paris, 1904).

Emile Faguet, *En Lisant Molière* (Paris, 1914).

Ramon Fernandez, *Molière: The Man Seen Through the Plays* (New York, 1958).

Edouard Fournier, *Etudes sur la vie et les œuvres de Molière* (Paris, 1885).

J.-L. Le G. Grimarest, *La Vie de M. de Molière* (Paris, 1705).

J. D. Hubert, *Molière and the Comedy of Intellect* (Berkeley, 1962).

R. Jasinski, *Molière et le Misanthrope* (Paris, 1951).

Gustave Larroumet, *La Comédie de Molière* (Paris, 1886).

Jules Loiseleur, *Les Points obscurs dans la vie de Molière* (Paris, 1877).

A. P. Malassis, *Molière jugé pas ses contemporains* (Paris, 1877).

E. Martineche, *Molière et le Théâtre espagnol* (Paris, 1905).

Sir F. T. Marzials, *Molière* (London, 1906).

Brander Matthews, *Molière, his Life and his Works* (New York, 1910).

Paul Mesnard, *Notice biographique sur Molière* (in vol. X of the *Grands Ecricains* series, Paris, 1889).

Louis Moland, *Vie de J.-B. P. Molière* (Paris, 1892).

——, *Molière et la comédie italienne* (Paris, 2nd ed., 1867).

W. G. Moore, *Molière: A New Criticism* (Oxford, 1949).

Daniel Mornet, *Molière* (Paris, 1943).

John Palmer, *Molière, His Life and Works* (London, 1930).

Louis Riccoboni, *Observations sur la Comédie et sur le génie de Molière* (Paris, 1736).

C.-A. Sainte-Beuve, *Port-Royal,* 6 vols. (6th ed., Paris, 1901).

——, *Causeries du Lundi,* 13 vols. (Paris, 1851–57).

Alfred Simon, *Molière par lui-même* (Paris, 1960).

Eud. Soulié, *Recherches sur Molière et sur sa famille* (Paris, 1863).

Jules-Antoine Taschereau, *Histoire de la vie et des ouvrages de Molière* (Paris, 1825).

Henry M. Trollope, *The Life of Molière* (New York, 1905).

Charles Varlet de La Grange, *Régistre* (1658–1685).

Leon H. Vincent, *Molière* (Boston, 1902).

Special bibliographies and reprints of documents may be found in Lacroix's *Collection Molièresque* (Paris, 1867–75); Lacroix and Monval's *Nouvelle Collection Molièresque* (Paris, 1879–90); Monval's *Le Molièriste*, 10 vols. (Paris, 1879–89); Lacroix's *Bibliographie Molièresque* (Paris, 1875); Arthur Desfeuilles' *Notice bibliographique* in vol. 9 in the Mesnard-Despois *Molière;* the *Catalogue of the Molière Collection* in Harvard College Library; and the Bibliography in Chatfield-Taylor's *Molière.*

RACINE

On the drama:

Préface to *La Thébaïde* (1664).
Première Préface (1666), to *Alexandre le grand,* and *Seconde Préface* (1676).
Première Préface (1668) to *Andromaque; Seconde Préface* (1676).
Au Lecteur to *Les Plaideurs* (1669).
Première Préface (1670) to *Britannicus,* and *Seconde Préface* (1676).
Préface to *Bérenice* (1674).
Première Préface (1672) to *Bajazet; Seconde Préface* (1676).
Préface to *Mithridate* (1673).
Préface to *Iphigénie* (1675).
Préface to *Phèdre* (1677).
Préface to *Esther* (1689).
Préface to *Athalie* (1691).

The *Lettres* in volumes VI and VII of the Mesnard edition are interesting, but contain little on the drama. The *Fragments de la Poétique d'Aristote* are to be found in vol. V of the same edition.

Editions:

The standard edition of the complete works is the *Œuvres de J. Racine,* edited by Paul Mesnard, in the *Grands Ecrivains* series, 8 vols. (Paris, 1865–73).

On Racine and his works:

Roland Barthes, *Sur Racine* (Paris, 1963).

Charles Baudoin, *Jean Racine l'enfant du désert* (Paris, 1963).

Geoffrey Brereton, *Jean Racine* (London, 1951).

Ferdinand Brunetière, *Racine* (in *Etudes critiques sur l'histoire de la littérature française,* vol. 1, 7th ed., Paris, 1911).

A. F. B. Clark, *Jean Racine* (Cambridge, Mass., 1937).

F. Deltour, *Les Ennemis de Racine au XVIIᵉ siècle* (Paris, 1859).

E. Deschanel, *Le Romantisme des classiques. Racine* (Paris, 1883).

Emile Faguet, *Propos de théâtre,* vol. 1 (Paris, 1903).

Fontenelle, *Parallèle de Corneille et de Racine* (Paris, 1693).

Jean Giraudoux, *Racine* (Paris, 1950).

Lucien Goldmann, *Racine dramaturge* (Paris, 1956).

R. Jasinski, *Vers le vrai Racine* (Paris, 1958).

John C. Lapp, *Aspects of Racinian Tragedy* (Toronto, 1955).

Gustave Larroumet, *Racine* (4th ed., Paris, 1911).

Jules Lemaître, *Impressions de théâtre,* vols. 1, 2, and 4 (Paris, 1888–90).

——, *Jean Racine* (Paris, 1908).

Paul Mesnard, Introduction to *Grands Ecrivains* ed. of *Œuvres* (cited above. Also Bibliography in vol. 7).

P. Monceaux, *Racine* (Paris, 1892).

F. Mauriac, *La Vie de Racine* (Paris, 1928).

Daniel Mornet, *Jean Racine* (Paris, 1943).

Louis Racine, *Mémoires sur la vie de Jean Racine,* 2 vols. (Lausanne and Genève, 1747. Reprinted in vol. I of the Mesnard ed.).

P. Robert, *La Poétique de Racine* (Paris, 1890).

C.-A. Sainte-Beuve, *Portraits littéraires,* vol. I (Paris, 1830).

——, *Port-Royal,* vol. 6 (Paris, 1860).

——, *Nouveaux Lundis,* vols. 3 and 10 (Paris, 1862 ff).

Francisque Sarcey, *Quarante Ans de théâtre*, vol. *2* (Paris, 1900).

P. Stapfer, *Racine et Victor Hugo* (Paris, 1887).

Stendhal, *Racine et Shakespeare* (Paris, 1823).

H. Taine, *Nouveaux essais de critique et d'histoire* (Paris, 1865).

Thierry-Maulnier, *Racine* (Paris, 1935).

Eugène Vinaver, *Racine and Poetic Tragedy* (Manchester, 1955).

BOILEAU

On the drama:

The *Art poétique* (1674), is practically Boileau's only drama criticism, though he incidentally touches upon the subject in a few of his *Epîtres* and *Satires*.

Editions:

The *Art poétique* first appeared in the *Œuvres diverses* in 1674. Of the " original " editions the best are in the *Œuvres* published in 1674, 1694, 1701, and 1713. Among the annotated *Œuvres,* see the 4-volume ed. by Berriat Saint-Prix, 1830; the 4-volume Gidel ed., 1873, and the Pauly 2-volume ed., 1891. The best ed. of the *Art poétique* is in the single volume, with notes and introduction by Brunetière (7th ed., Paris, 1911). The *Works of Monsieur Boileau* were translated " by several hands " and with a Life by Des Maizéaux in 2 vols., London, 1712. *The Art of Poetry* was translated by Sir William Soames, " revised by Dryden," London, 1683. This is reprinted in Albert S. Cook's *The Art of Poetry,* together with the similar treatises of Horace and Vida, Boston, 1892.

On Boileau and his work:

D'Alembert, *Eloge de Despréaux* (Paris, 1779).

Bolœana (Paris, 1713).

A. Bourgoin, *Les Maîtres de la critique au XVIIᵉ siècle* (Paris, 1889).

Ferdinand Brunetière, Article on *Boileau* in *La Grande Encyclopédie,* vol. 7 (Paris).

——, Introduction to *L'Art Poétique* (7th ed., Paris, 1911).

——, *L'Esthétique de Boileau* (in *Etudes critiques sur l'histoire de la littérature française,* vol. 6, Paris, 3rd ed., 1911).

A. F. B. Clark, *Boileau and the French Classical Critics in England (1660–1830)* (Paris, 1935).

Charles Dejob, *Lessing et Boileau* (in the *Revue des Cours et Conférences,* Paris, 1897).

P. Desmaizéaux, *La Vie de Monsieur Boileau-Despréaux* (Paris, 1712).

Marie Philip Haley, *Racine and the Art poétique of Boileau* (Baltimore, 1938).

D. Nisard, *Examen des Poétiques d'Aristote, d'Horace, et de Boileau* (St. Cloud, 1845).

C.-A. Sainte-Beuve, *Port-Royal,* vol. 6 (latest ed., Paris, 1901).

——, *Portraits littéraires,* vol. 1 (Paris, 1862).

——, *Causeries du Lundi,* vol. 6 (Paris, 1851–62).

George Saintsbury, *A History of Criticism,* vol. *2* (New York, 1902).

SAINT-EVREMOND

On the drama:

Dissertation sur la tragédie de Racine intitulée: Alexandre le Grand (1666).

Résponse de M. de Saint-Evremond à M. de Corneille (1668).

De la Tragédie ancienne et moderne (1672).

Sur les Caractères des tragédies (1672).

A un auteur qui me demandait mon sentiment d'une pièce où l'héroïne ne faisait que se lamenter (1672).

Sur les tragédies (1677).

Sur nos comédies, excepté celles de Molière, où l'on trouve le vrai esprit de la comédie, et sur la comédie espagnole (1677).

De la comédie italienne (1677).

De la comédie anglaise (1677).

Sur les opéras (1677).

Défense de quelques pièces de théâtre de M. Corneille (1677).[1]

(All the above are in the English translation cited.)

Editions:

With the exception of the works already

[1] The dates in each case refer to writing All these essays were first published in 1705.— Ed.

mentioned, very little of Saint-Evremond was published during his lifetime. The first authorized edition, which is not, however, complete, was the *Œuvres meslées*, 3 vols., London, 1705. This was followed by the 7-vol. ed. of 1708, the Amsterdam ed. in 1727, and Paris ed. in 1740. Among the modern editions, see the *Œuvres mêlées*, edited in 3 vols. by Giraud (Paris, 1865), and Ch. Gidel's single-volume ed. of the *Œuvres choisis* (Garnier, Paris, after 1866). The *Œuvres* were translated as *The Works of Monsieur de St. Evremond*, 3 vols. (London, 1714. This contains a *Life* by P. Des Maizéeaux).

On Saint-Evremond and his works:

Introductions to the various editions cited.

A. Bourgoin, *Les Maîtres de la critique au XVIIe siècle* (Paris, 1889).

W. Melville Daniels, *Saint-Evremond en Angleterre* (Versailles, 1907).

Gilbert et Gidel, *Eloges de Saint-Evremond* (Paris, 1866).

La Grande Encyclopédie, vol. 29 (Paris).

G. Merlet, *Saint-Evremond* (Paris, 1869).

F. Pastrello, *Etude sur Saint-Evremond et son influence* (Trieste, 1875).

C.-A. Sainte-Beuve, *Causeries du Lundi*, vol. 4 (Paris, 1857-62).

George Saintsbury, *A History of Criticism*, vol. 2 (New York, 1902).

RESTORATION AND EIGHTEENTH-CENTURY ENGLAND

General references Restoration and eighteenth-century literature:

A. Beljame, *Le Public et les hommes de lettres en Angleterre au dix-huitième siècle* (2nd ed., Paris, 1897).

John Dennis, *The Age of Pope* (London, 1899).

R. Garnett, *The Age of Dryden* (London, 1903).

Edmund Gosse, *A History of Eighteenth Century Literature* (London, 1889).

——, *Seventeenth Century Studies* (London, 1883).

Alan D. McKillop, *English Literature from Dryden to Burns* (New York, 1958).

T. S. Perry, *English Literature of the Eighteenth Century* (New York, 1883).

George Saintsbury, *The Peace of the Augustans* (London, 1916).

Leslie Stephen, *English Literature and Society in the Eighteenth Century* (London, ed., 1910).

——, *History of English Thought in the Eighteenth Century*, 2 vols. (ed. New York, 1877).

John Harold Wilson, *The Court Wits of the Restoration* (Princeton, 1948).

General references on the drama:

F. W. Bateson, *English Comic Drama 1700-1750* (Oxford, 1929).

Ernest Bernbaum, *The Drama of Sensibility (1696-1780)* (Boston, 1915).

Thomas Betterton (?), *The History of the English Stage, from the Restoration to the Present Time*, etc. (London, 1741).

F. S. Boas, *An Introduction to Eighteenth-Century Drama* (Oxford, 1953).

Theophilus Cibber, *Dissertations on the Theatres*, etc. (London, 1756).

William Cooke, *Memoirs of Charles Macklin . . . forming an History of the Stage during almost the whole of the last century* (2nd ed., London, 1806).

Bonamy Dobrée, *Restoration Comedy* (Oxford, 1924).

——, *Restoration Tragedy* (Oxford, 1929).

Downs, John, *Roscius Anglicanus, or, An Historical Review of the Stage . . . from 1660 to 1706* (London, 1708. "With additions," by Davies, 1789).

Malcolm Elwin, *The Playgoer's Handbook to Restoration Drama* (London, 1928).

Percy Fitzgerald, *A New History of the English Stage, from the Restoration to the Liberty of the Theatres*, etc. (London, 1882).

T. H. Fujimura, *The Restoration Comedy of Wit* (Princeton, 1952).

A.-A. de Grisy, *Histoire de la comédia anglaise au dix-septième siècle* (Paris, 1878).

W. Harvey-Jellie, *Les Sources du théâtre anglais à l'époque de la Restauration* (Paris, 1906).

Norman N. Holland, *The First Modern Comedies* (Cambridge, Mass., 1959).

L. C. Knights, "Restoration Comedy: The Reality and the Myth," in *Explorations* (New York, 1947).

Joseph Wood Krutch, *Comedy and Conscience After the Restoration* (New York, 1924).

John Loftis, *Comedy and Society from Congreve to Fielding* (Stanford, 1959).

Kathleen M. Lynch, *The Social Mode of Restoration Comedy* (New York, 1926).

D. H. Miles, *The Influence of Molière on Restoration Comedy* (New York, 1910).

J. Fitzgerald Molloy, *Famous Plays, with a Discourse by way of Prologue on the Playhouses of the Restoration* (London, 1886).

G. H. Nettleton, *English Drama of the Restoration and Eighteenth Century* (New York, 1914).

Allardyce Nicoll, *A History of Restoration Drama* (Cambridge, 1923).

——, *A History of Early Eighteenth Century Drama* (Cambridge, 1925).

——, *A History of Late Eighteenth Century Drama* (Cambridge, 1927).

John Palmer, *The Comedy of Manners* (New York, 1913).

——, *Comedy* (New York, n. d.).

H. T. E Perry, *The Comic Spirit in Restoration Drama* (New Haven, 1925)

Arthur Sherbo, *English Sentimental Drama* (East Lansing, Mich., 1957).

J. H. Smith, *The Gay Couple in Restoration Comedy* (Cambridge, Mass., 1948).

Alwin Thaler, *Shakspere to Sheridan*, (Cambridge, Mass., 1922).

E. N. S. Thompson, *The Controversy Between the Puritans and the Stage* (New Haven, 1903).

Dale Underwood, *Etherege and the Seventeenth-Century Comedy of Manners* (New Haven, 1957).

O. Waterhouse, *The Development of English Sentimental Comedy in the 18th Century* (in *Anglia*, vol. 30, Halle, 1907).

Ernest B. Watson, *Sheridan to Robertson* (Cambridge, Mass., 1926).

Special works on criticism:

H. H. Adams and Baxter Hathaway, eds., *Dramatic Essays of the Neoclassic Age* (New York, 1950).

A. Beljame, *Le Public et les hommes de lettres en Angleterre au dix-huitième siècle* (2nd ed., Paris, 1897).

Clarence C. Green, *The Neo-Classic Theory of Tragedy in England during the Eighteenth Century* (Cambridge, Mass., 1934).

P. Hamelius, *Die Kritik in der englischen Literatur der 17. und 18. Jahrhunderts* (Leipzig, 1897).

George Saintsbury, *A History of Criticism*, vol. 2 (New York, 1902).

——, *A History of English Criticism* (New York, 1911).

For collections of contemporary essays, see J. E. Spingarn, *Critical Essays of the Seventeenth Century*, 3 vols. (Oxford, 1908–09); W. H. Durham, *Critical Essays of the Eighteenth Century* (New Haven, 1915); R. M. Alden, *Readings in English Prose of the Eighteenth Century* (Boston, 1911).

DRYDEN

On the drama:

Epistle Dedicatory, in *The Rival Ladies* (1664).

An Essay of Dramatick Poesie, with its *Epistle Dedicatory* (1668).

A Defence of an Essay of Dramatique Poesie (1668).

Dedication to *The Indian Emperor* (1667).

Preface to *Secret Love, or, The Maiden Queen* (1668).

Preface to *The Wild Gallant* (1669).

Preface to *The Tempest* (1670).

Preface to *Tyrannick Love* (1670).

Preface to *The Mock Astrologer* (1671).

Of Heroick Plays, in *The Conquest of Granada* (1672).

Epilogue, and *Defence of the Epilogue* to the second part of *The Conquest of Granada* (1672).

Epistle Dedicatory in *Marriage a-la-Mode* (1673).

Epistle Dedicatory in *The Assignation* (1673).

Preface to *The State of Innocence* (1675).

Dedication to *Aurengzebe* (1676).
Preface to *All for Love* (1678).
Dedication of *Limberham* (1678).
Preface to *Œdipus* (1679).
Preface to *Troilus and Cressida* (1679).
Dedication of *The Spanish Fryar* (1681).
The Vindication of the Duke de Guise (1683).
Preface to *Albion and Albanius* (1685).
Preface to *Don Sebastian* (1690).
Dedication of *Amphitryon* (1690).
Preface to *Cleomenes* (1692).
A Discourse on the Origin and Progress of Satire (preface to Dryden's and others' translation of *Juvenal,* 1693).
Dedication of *Third Part of Poetical Miscellanies* (1693).
Dedication of *Love Triumphant* (1694).
A Parallel of Poetry and Painting (in Dryden's translation of Du Fresnoy's *De Arte Graphica,* 1695).
Preface to Dryden's son's *The Husband his own Cuckold* (1696).
A Discourse on Epick Poetry (preface to Dryden's translation of the *Æneid,* 1697).

Editions:

The Comedies, Tragedies and Operas written by John Dryden, Esq., were published in 2 vols. (London, 1701). Congreve edited the *Dramatick Works* in 6 vols. (London, 1717). The first collected edition of the *Works* was edited by Sir Walter Scott, 18 vols. (1808). This edition, revised and corrected by George Saintsbury (18 vols., Edinburgh, 1882–93) is the standard. Edmund Malone edited the prose works as *Critical and Miscellaneous Prose Works,* 4 vols. (London, 1800). The important essays are edited as *Essays of John Dryden,* by W. P. Ker, 2 vols. (Oxford, 1900). *The Best Plays of John Dryden,* 2 vols., edited by Saintsbury (New York, n.d.) contain numerous essays. *Dramatic Essays of John Dryden,* edited by W. H. Hudson, are published in *Everyman's Library* (New York, n.d.). There are annotated editions of the *Essays of Dramatick Poesie* by T. Arnold (Oxford, 1903), and Von Schunck (New York, 1899). *Essays on the Drama,* edited by W. Strunk (1908). *Essays,* edited by W. P. Ker, 2 vols. (Oxford, 1926).

The *Letters* may be consulted for biographical data. One (No. IX, Malone ed.) refers to Rymer and his ideas. The *Heads of an Answer to Rymer* (1711); and the *Preface to Notes and Observations on the Empress of Morocco* (1674, attributed to Dryden), may be consulted, as well as the *Notes and Observations,* etc., 2nd edition, by Settle (1687).

On Dryden and his works:

Prefaces to works cited.

A. Beljame, *Le Public et les hommes de lettres en Angleterre, 1660–1744* (2nd ed., Paris, 1897).
F. Bobertag, *Dryden's Theorie des Dramas* (in *Englische Studien,* vol. 4, Heilbronn, 1881).
William E. Bohn, *The Development of John Dryden's Criticism* (in *Modern Language Association Publications,* vol. 22, Cambridge, U. S. A., 1907).
L. I. Bredvold, *The Intellectual Milieu of John Dryden* (Ann Arbor, 1934).
G. S. Collins, *Dryden's Dramatic Theory and Praxis* (Leipzig, 1892).
J. Churton Collins, *Essays and Studies* (London, 1895).
W. J. Courthope, *History of English Poetry,* vols. 3 and 4 (London, 1903).
N. Delius, *Dryden und Shakespeare* (Berlin, 1869).
P. H. Frye, *Dryden and the Critical Canons of the Eighteenth Century* (in *Literary Reviews and Criticisms,* New York, 1908).
R. Garnett, *The Age of Dryden* (London, 1895).
P. Hamelius, *Die Kritik in der englischer Litteratur der 17. und 18. Jahrhunderts* (Leipzig, 1897).
F. L. Huntley, *On Dryden's "Essay of Dramatic Poesy"* (Ann Arbor, 1951).
Samuel Johnson, *John Dryden* (in *Lives of the Most Eminent English Poets* (ed., London, 1871).
James Russell Lowell, *Among My Books* (Boston, 1870).
T. B. Macaulay, *Dryden* (in *Critical and Miscellaneous Essays,* in *Complete Works,* London, 1879).
F. Ohlsen, *Dryden as a Dramatist and Critic* (Altona, 1883).
George Saintsbury, *John Dryden* (in

English Men of Letters series, London, 1881).

Margaret Sherwood, *Dryden's Dramatic Theory and Practice* (New Haven, 1898).

D. Nicol Smith, *John Dryden* (Cambridge, Eng., 1950).

F. Weselmann, *Dryden als Kritiker* (Göttingen, 1893).

MILTON

On the drama:

Of that sort of Dramatic Poem which is call'd Tragedy (1671).

Editions:

The Works of John Milton, etc., 8 vols., ed. by I. Mitford (London, 1851). See See aso *The Poetical Works of John Milton,* edited by John Masson (Globe ed., London, 1877 ff). For special editions of *Samson Agonistes,* see those edited by J. C. Collins (Oxford, 1883), and by A. W. Verity (Cambridge, 1892). The Preface alone is re-printed in the second volume of J. E. Spingarn's *Critical Essays of the Seventeenth Century* (Oxford, 1908).

On Milton and his works:

Matthew Arnold, *Essays in Criticism,* 2nd series (London, 1888).

——, *Mixed Essays* (London, 1879).

S. A. Brooke, *Milton* (London, 1879).

I. Bywater, *Milton and the Aristotelian Definition of Tragedy* (In *Jour. of Phil.,* xxvii, p. 267, 1900).

R. Garnett, *Life of John Milton* (London, 1890).

Ida Langdon, *Milton's Theory of Poetry and Fine Art* (New Haven, 1924).

D. Masson, *The Life of John Milton,* 6 vols. (Cambridge, 1859–80. Index vol., 1894).

W. R. Parker, *Milton's Debt to Greek Tragedy in Samson Agonistes* (Baltimore, 1937).

W. A. Raleigh, *Milton* (London, 1890).

A. Schmidt, *Miltons dramatische Dichtungen* (Königsberg, 1864).

W. P. Trent, *John Milton* (New York, 1899).

RYMER

On the drama:

The Preface of the Translator, in Rapin's *Reflexions on Aristotle's Treatise of Poesie* (1674).

The Tragedies of the Last Age Consider'd and Examin'd by the Practice of the Ancients and by the Common Sense of All Ages (1678).

A Short View of Tragedy, Its Original Excellency and Corruption, With Some Reflections on Shakespear and Other Practitioners for the Stage (1693).

Editions:

The *Preface* to Rapin, and excerpts from *The Tragedies of the Last Age* and *A Short View* are reprinted in the second volume of Spingarn's *Critical Essays of the Seventeenth Century* (Oxford, 1908), and in Rymer's *Critical Works,* edited by Curt Zimansky (New Haven, 1956).

On Rymer and his works:

Encyclopedia Britannica, vol. 23 (11th ed., Cambridge, 1910).

A. Hofherr, *Thomas Rymer's dramatische Kritik* (Heidelberg, 1908).

Samuel Johnson, *Dryden* (in *Lives of the Poets;* ed., Oxford, 1908).

George Saintsbury, *A History of Criticism,* vol. 2 (New York, 1902)

Introduction to the first volume of Spingarn's *Critical Essays of the Seventeenth Century* (Oxford, 1908).

Sir T. N. Talfourd, *Critical and Miscellaneous Writings,* 3rd American ed., Boston, 1854).

CONGREVE

On the drama:

Epistles Dedicatory to *The Double-Dealer* (1694).

Concerning Humour in Comedy (in *Letters upon Several Occasions,* etc., 1696).

Dedication to *The Mourning Bride* (1697).

Amendments upon Mr. Collier's False and Imperfect Citations, etc. (1698).

Dedication to *The Way of the World* (1700).

Editions:

The first edition of Congreve's collected *Works* appeared in 3 vols. (London, 1710). The dramatic works have been often reprinted: *The Dramatic Works of Wycherley, Congreve, Vanbrugh and Farquhar,* by Leigh Hunt (London, 1849); *The Comedies of William Congreve,* edited by W. G. S. Street, 2 vols. (London, 1895); *The Best Plays of William Congreve,* edited by A. C. Ewald (*Mermaid* ed., New York, 1903). A number of Congreve's letters are found in Monck Berkeley's *Literary Relics. Concerning Humour in Comedy* is reprinted by J. E. Spingarn in vol. 3, of *Critical Essays of the Seventeenth Century* (Oxford, 1909). More recent editions are the *Complete Works,* edited by Montague Summers, 4 vols. (1923); the *Works,* edited by F. W. Bateson (1930); and the *Comedies,* edited by Bonamy Dobree (Oxford, 1925).

On Congreve and his works:

Prefaces to editions cited.

C. F. Armstrong, *William Congreve* (in *From Shakespeare to Shaw,* London, 1913).
A. Bennewitz, *Congreve und Molière* (Leipzig, 1890).
Edmund Gosse, *Life of William Congreve* (London, new ed., 1924).
William Hazlitt, *Lectures on the English Comic Writers,* etc. (London, 1818. Reprint in *Everyman's Library,* New York, n.d.).
John C. Hodges, *Congreve the Man* (New York, 1944).
Samuel Johnson, *Congreve* (in *Lives of the Poets,* eds. cited).
Charles Lamb, *The Artificial Comedy of the Last Century* (in *Essays of Elia,* E. V. Lucas ed. of the *Works,* London, 1907).
T. B. Macaulay, *Leigh Hunt* (in *Critical and Miscellaneous Essays,* ed. Montague, London, 1903).
George Meredith, *An Essay on Comedy* (London, 1897).
D. Schmid, *Congreve, sein Leben und seine Lustspiele* (Wien, 1897).

Leslie Stephen, *William Congreve* (in *Dictionary of National Biography,* vol. 12, London, 1887).
A. C. Swinburne, *Miscellanies* (London, 1886).
D. Crane Taylor, *William Congreve* (Oxford, 1931).
W. M. Thackeray, *The English Humourists of the Eighteenth Century,* etc. (London, 1853. Reprinted in *Everyman's Library,* New York, n.d.; also *Biographical* ed., vol. 7, London, 1897).
Charles Wilson, *Memoirs of the Life, Writings and Amours of W. Congreve, Esq.,* etc. (London, 1730).

FARQUHAR

On the drama:

Preface: To the Reader, in *The Constant Couple* (1700).
Prologue to *Sir Harry Wildair* (1701).
A Discourse Upon Comedy in Reference to the English Stage (1702).
Preface to *The Inconstant* (1703).
Preface to *The Twin-Rivals* (1705).
To All Friends round the Wrekin, in *The Recruiting Officer* (1706).

Editions:

The first collected edition of the plays is *The Comedies of Mr. George Farquhar,* published at London in 1709. The *Discourse* appeared in the *Works,* in 1714. It was first published in 1702, in the volume entitled *Love and Business.* The *Letters* are published in most of the editions after 1728, together with biographical notices. The *Discourse* is reprinted in *A Discourse upon Comedy, The Recruiting Officer, and The Beaux Stratagem,* by Louis A. Strauss (Boston, 1914), and by W. H. Durham, in *Critical Essays of the Eighteenth Century* (New Haven, 1915). The *Dramatic Works,* edited by A. C. Ewald in 2 vols., are reprinted (London, 1892), and *Four Plays,* edited by William Archer, *Mermaid Series* (New York, 1905); also in Leigh Hunt's *Dramatic Works of Wycherley, Congreve, Vanbrugh, and Farquhar* (London, 1849 ff.). His *Complete Works* were edited by C. A. Stonehill, 2 vols. (London, 1930).

On Farquhar and his works:

Prefatory matter to editions cited.

Willard Connely, *Young George Farquhar* (London, 1949).
Heinrich Döring, *George Farquhar* (in *Encyclopädie der Wissenschaften und Kunste,* Leipzig, 1818).
Edmund Gosse, *Gossip in a Library* (London, 1891).
Otto Hallbauer, *Life and Works of George Farquhar* (Holzminden, 1880).
J. G. Robertson, *Lessing and Farquhar* (In *Modern Language Review,* vol. 2, 1907).
Christian Heinrich Schmid, *George Farquhar* (in *Englisches Theater,* erster theil, Introduction, Leipzig, 1772).
David Schmid, *George Farquhar; sein Leben, und seine Original-Dramen* (Wien, 1904).
Leslie Stephen, *George Farquhar* (in *Dictionary of National Biography,* vol. 18, London, 1889).

ADDISON

On the drama:

The Spectator, nos. 39, 40, 41, 42, 44, 45, 58, 59, 60, 61, 62, 63, 258, 290, 296, 419, and 446 (1711-12).

Editions:

The best modern edition of the complete works, is Hurd's *The Works of Joseph Addison,* 6 vols. (Bohn ed., London, 1854–56)). A convenient edition of *The Spectator* is the reprint of the first edition, in Everyman's Library, 4 vols. (London and New York, 1906). See Thomas Arnold's *Selections from Addison's papers contributed to the Spectator* (Oxford, 1866 ff.).

On Addison and his works:

Lucy Aikin, *The Life of Joseph Addison,* 2 vols. (London, 1843).
W. J. Courthope, *Addison* (London, 1884).
Thomas Tickell, *Life of Joseph Addison* (*Preface* to 1st ed. of Addison's *Works,* London, 1721).

JOHNSON

On the drama:

Lives of the Poets (especially *Rowe, Congreve, Dryden, Otway, Addison,* and *Gay*); in *The Rambler* (especially Nos. 125, 139, and 156); the *Preface to Shakespeare* (1765).

Editions:

The first collected edition — *The Works of Samuel Johnson,* edited by Arthur Murphy, in 12 vols.,— appeared in London in 1792. The Oxford Edition of the *Works* (11 vols., Oxford, 1825) is a standard. A good modern edition is *The Works of Samuel Johnson,* 16 vols. (Troy, N. Y., 1903). Special editions of the *Lives of the Poets* are edited by Mrs. Alex. Napier, 3 vols. (London, 1890), and by Arthur Waugh, 6 vols. (London, 1896). See also Matthew Arnold's *Six Chief "Lives of the Poets,"* with a preface (London, 1878). The *Letters of Samuel Johnson,* collected and edited by G. Birkbeck Hill, 2 vols. (Oxford, 1892), and *Johnsonian Miscellanies,* arranged and edited by the same, 2 vols. (Oxford, 1892-97); together with *The Essays of Samuel Johnson,* edited by Stuart J. Reid (London, 1888), should be consulted. Also Raleigh's *Johnson on Shakespeare* (London, 1908). See also *Samuel Johnson on Shakespeare,* edited by W. K. Wimsatt, Jr. (New York, 1960), and *The Critical Opinions of Samuel Johnson,* edited by J. E. Brown, 2 vols. (Princeton, 1936).

On Johnson and his works:

See prefatory matter to editions cited above.

W. J. Bate, *The Achievement of Samuel Johnson* (New York, 1955).
James Boswell, *Life of Samuel Johnson,* 2 vols. (London, 1791). Standard edition by G. Birkbeck Hill, 6 vols., Oxford, 1887).
W. P. Courtney, *A Bibliography of Samuel Johnson* (Oxford, 1905).
John Dennis, *Dr. Johnson* (London, 1905).
Lieut.-Col. F. Grant, *Samuel Johnson* (London, 1887).
Jean Hagstrum, *Samuel Johnson's Literary Criticism* (Minneapolis, 1952).
Sir John Hawkins, *Life of Samuel Johnson* (London, 1787).
G. Birkbeck Hill, *Johnson; his Friends*

and Critics (London, 1878).

Joseph Wood Krutch, *Samuel Johnson* (New York, 1944).

T. B. Macaulay, *Samuel Johnson* (in *Works*, London, 1879).

George Saintsbury, *A History of Criticism*, vol. 2 (New York, 1902).

Thomas Seccombe, *The Age of Johnson* (London, 1900).

Leslie Stephen, *Samuel Johnson* (London, 1878).

GOLDSMITH

On the drama:

An Enquiry into the Present State of Polite Learning in Europe (London, 1759). (The *Citizen of the World* and *The Bee* may also be consulted for occasional references to the drama.)

Preface to *The Good-natur'd Man* (1768).

An Essay on the Theatre; or, a Comparison Between Laughing and Sentimental Comedy (1772).

Editions:

The first general edition of Goldsmith is the *Miscellaneous Works* (London, 1775). The best modern edition is the *Works*, edited by J. W. M. Gibbs, 5 vols. (London, 1884–86). A good annotated edition of the plays, with a bibliography and reprint of the *Essay on the Theatre*, is *The Good-natur'd Man* and *She Stoops to Conquer*, with

an introduction by Austin Dobson (Boston, 1911).

On Goldsmith and his works:

William Black, *Goldsmith* (London, 1878).

Austin Dobson, *Life of Oliver Goldsmith* (revised ed., New York, 1899).

John Forster, *The Life and Adventures of Oliver Goldsmith*, 2 vols. (2nd ed. London, 1854).

Washington Irving, *The Life of Oliver Goldsmith*, 2 vols. (New York, 1844 ff.).

A. Norman Jeffares, *Oliver Goldsmith* (London, 1959).

F. F. Moore, *The Life of Oliver Goldsmith* (latest ed., New York. 1911).

Sir James Prior, *The Life of Oliver Goldsmith*, 2 vols. (London, 1837).

W. M. Thackeray, *The English Humourists of the Eighteenth Century* (modern reprint in Everyman's Library, n.d.)

Ralph M. Wardle, *Oliver Goldsmith* (Lawrence, Kan., 1957).

HUME

On Hume and his works:

E. C. Mossner, *The Forgotten Hume* (New York, 1943).

N. K. Smith, *The Philosophy of David Hume* (London, 1941).

ITALY—SEVENTEENTH
CENTURY TO THE PRESENT

General references on Italian literature from the Renaissance to the present day:

A. d'Ancona e O. Bacci, *Manuale della letteratura italiana*, 6 vols. (Firenze, 1904–08).

L. Collison-Morley, *Modern Italian Literature* (Boston, 1912).

Tullio Concari, *Il Settecento* (in series *Storia letteraria*, etc., Milano, 1898–1900).

L. Etienne, *Histoire de la littérature italienne* (Paris, 1884).

Richard Garnett, *A History of Italian Literature* (New York, 1909).

H. Hauvette, *La Littérature italienne* (Paris, 1906).

M. Landau, *Geschichte der italienischen Literatur im 18. Jahrhundert* (Berlin, 1899

Vernon Lee, *Studies of the Eighteenth Century in Italy* (2nd ed., Chicago, 1908).

G. Mazzoni, *L'Ottocento* (in series, *Storia letteraria*, etc., Milano, 1898–1913).

M. Mignon, *Etudes de littérature italienne* (Paris, 1912).

Sergio Pacifici, *A Guide to Contemporary Italian Literature* (New York, 1962).

V. Rossi, *Storia aella letteratura italiana per uso dei licei*, 3 vols. (Milano, 1907).

Amédée Roux, *Histoire de la littérature contemporaine en Italie*, etc. (1859–74) (Paris, 1896).

References on Italian drama from the Renaissance to the present day:

Silvio d'Amico, *Il teatro italiano* (Trier, 1933).

Anonymous, *An Essay upon the Present State of the Theatre in France, England, and Italy* (London, 1760).

P. F. Biancolelli, *Nouveau Théâtre italien* (Anvers, 1713).

Charles Burney, *Memoirs of the Life and Writings of the Abate Metastasio,* etc., 3 vols. (London, 1796).

Eugenio Camerini, *I Precursori del Goldoni* (Milano, 1872).

H. C. Chatfield-Taylor, *Goldoni, a Biography* (New York, 1913).

Nicola Chiaramonte, *La situazione drammatica* (Milan, 1960).

Barrett H. Clark, *A Study of the Modern Drama* (2nd ed., New York, 1928)

G. Costetti, *Il Teatro italiano nel 1800* (Rocca di S. Cassiano, 1901).

Nathan Haskell Dole, *A Teacher of Dante,* etc. (New York, 1908).

Jean Dornis, *Le Théâtre italien contemporain* (Paris, 1898).

Carlo Goldoni, *Mémoires* (Paris, 1787. Reprinted with preface and notes by Guido Mazzoni in two volumes as *Memorie di Carlo Goldoni,* Firenze, 1907. Translated by John Black as *Memoirs of Carlo Goldoni, 2* vols., London, 1814. Abridged ed., edited by W. D. Howells, Boston, 1877).

——, *Lettere* (Modern edition, Bologna, 1907).

Carlo Gozzi, *Memorie inutili,* etc., 3 vols. (Venezia, 1797. Translated, with an introduction, by J. A. Symonds, as *Memoirs of Carlo Gozzi, 2* vols., London, 1890. The Symonds translation reissued, edited, revised, and abridged by Philip Horne, with an introduction

by Harold Acton, as *Useless Memoirs of Carlo Gozzi,* London, 1962).

Giuseppe Guerzoni, *Il Teatro italiano nel secolo XVIII* (Milano, 1876).

A. Lalia-Paternostro, *Studi drammatici* (Napoli, 1903).

E. M. Leopardi, *Il Melodramma del Metastasio e la sua fortuna nel secolo XVIII* (Napoli, 1909).

Cesare Levi, *Letteratura drammatica* (Milano, 1900).

Henry Lyonnet, *Le Théâtre en Italie* (Paris, 1900).

——, *Pulcinella et Cie* (Paris, 1901).

Lander MacClintock, *The Age of Pirandello* (Bloomington, 1950).

Giovanni Battista Magrini, *I Tempi, la Vita e gli Scritti di Carlo Gozzi* (Benevento, 1883).

O. Marchini-Capasso, *Goldoni e la Commedia dell' Arte* (Napoli, 1912).

F. Martini, *Al teatro* (Firenze, 1908).

E. Masi, *Studi sulla Storia del teatro italiano* (Firenze, 1891).

Addison McLeod, *Plays and Players of Modern Italy* (London, 1912).

Philippe Monnier, *Venise au XVIIIᵉ siècle* (Lausanne, 1907. Translated anonymously, Boston, 1910).

Charles Rabany, *Carlo Goldoni. Le Théâtre et la vie en Italie au XVIIIᵉ siècle* (Paris, 1896).

L. Riccoboni, *Histoire du Théâtre italien* (Paris, 1731).

G. G. de Rossi, *Del Moderno teatro italiano* (Bassano, 1794).

G. M. Scalinger, *Teatro sociologico* (Napoli, 1902).

Michele Scherillo, *La Commodia dell' Arte in Italia* (Torino, 1880).

Winifred Smith, *The Commedia dell' Arte* (New York, 1912).

L. Stoppate, *La Commedia popolare in Italia* (Padova, 1887).

Adriano Tilgher, *Studi sul teatro contemporaneo* (Rome, 1928).

J. C. Walker, *Historical and Critical Essay on the Revival of the Drama in Italy* (Edinburgh, 1805).

——, *Historical Memoir on Italian Tragedy,* etc. (London, 1799).

Gaetano Zocchi, *Il Teatro italiano a' tempi nostri* (Prato, 1885).

References on Italian dramatic criticism and theory from the Renaissance to the present day:

P. Ferrieri, *Francesco de Sanctis e la critica letteraria* (Milano, 1888).

A. Galletti, *Le Teorie drammatiche e la tragedia in Italia nel secolo XVIII* (Cremona, 1901).

Lander MacClintock, *The Contemporary Drama of Italy* (Boston, 1920).

L. Morandi, *Antologia della nostra critica letteraria moderna* (4th ed., Città di Castello, 1889).

George Saintsbury, *A History of Criticism,* vols. 2 and 3 (New York, 1902–04).

G. Trezza, *La critica moderna* (2nd ed., Bologna, 1880).

GOLDONI

On the drama:

Outside the many prefaces to the various editions, Goldoni's principal writings on the drama are in the *Teatro Comico* (1751) and the *Mémoires* (1787).

Editions:

The early editions are not complete, and there is considerable confusion in collating them. The *Pasquali* edition, in 17 vols. (Venice, 1761, and following), authorized by Goldoni, is the best of the early editions. The Tasso edition, 45 vols. (Venice, 1823–27), is a good modern edition, while the *Opere complete,* published by the Municipality of Venice in 20 vols. (1907–17) is now considered the definitive edition. The *Mémoires de M. Goldoni pour servir à l'histoire de sa vie et à celle de son théâtre,* were published in three vols., Paris, 1787. The best modern edition is the reprint, *Memorie di Carlo Goldoni,* with preface and notes by Guido Mazzoni, in 2 vols. (Firenze, 1907). These are translated as *Memoirs of Goldoni,* translated by John Black, 2 vols. (London, 1814. Reprinted in *A Collection of the Most Instructive and Amusing Lives ever Published,* vol. 23, London, 1828). An abridgement, with an essay by W. D. Howells, was published at Boston in 1877. H. C. Chatfield-Taylor's biography (see below) contains translated extracts from the plays, prefaces, and *Memoirs.*

On Goldoni and his works:

Prefaces to various editions of the works.

Alfonso Aloi, *Il Goldoni e la Commedia dell' Arte* (Catania, 1883).

V. de Amicis, *La Commedia popolare latina e la commedia dell' arte* (Napoli, 1882).

G. Bertoni, *Carlo Goldoni e il teatro francese del suo tempo* (Modena, 1907).

Carlo Borghi, *Memorie sulla Vita di Carlo Goldoni* (Modena, 1859).

Virgilio Brocchi, *Carlo Goldoni a Venezia nel secolo XVIII* (Bologna, 1907).

Giulio Caprin, *Carlo Goldoni, la sua vita, le sue opere* (Milano, 1907).

Luigi Carrer, *Saggi su la vita e le opere di Carlo Goldoni,* 3 vols. (Venezia, 1824).

H. C. Chatfield-Taylor, *Goldoni, a Biography* (New York, 1913).

Edward Copping, *Alfieri and Goldoni* (London, 1857).

A. Cuman, *La Riforma del Teatro comico italiano e Carlo Goldoni* (in *Ateneo veneto,* vols. 22 & 23, Venezia, 1899–1900).

Giovanni Gherardini, *Vita di Carlo Goldoni* (Milano, 1821).

Angelo de Gubernatis, *Carlo Goldoni* (Firenze, 1911).

J. S. Kennard, *Goldoni and the Venice of his Time* (New York, 1920).

Vernon Lee, *Studies of the Eighteenth Century in Italy* (2nd ed., Chicago, 1906).

E. Von Lohner, *Carlo Goldoni e le sue Memorie* (in *Archivio veneto,* vols. 23 & 24, Venezia, 1882).

Olga Marchini-Capasso, *Goldoni e la commedia dell' arte* (Bergamo, 1907).

Ferdinando Meneghezzi, *Della Vita e delle opere di Carlo Goldoni* (Milano, 1827).

P. G. Molmenti, *Carlo Goldoni* (2nd ed., Venezia, 1880).

Giuseppe Ortolani, *Della Vita e dell' arte di Carlo Goldoni* (Venezia, 1907).

E. Pasqualini, *Carlo Goldoni* (Assisi, 1909).

P. Petrocchi, *Carlo Goldoni e la commedia* (Milano, 1893).

Charles Rabany, *Carlo Goldoni* (Paris, 1896).

Michele Scherillo, *La Commedia dell' arte in Italia* (Torino, 1884).

Winifred Smith, *The Commedia dell' Arte* (New York, 1912).

Marietta Tovini, *Studio su Carlo Goldoni* (Firenze, 1900).

GOZZI

Editions:

The *Memorie inutili della vita di Carlo Gozzi scritte da lui medesimo e pubblicate por umiltà* was first published in 3 vols. (Venice, 1797–98). It was translated by John Addington Symonds as *Memoirs of Carlo Gozzi*, 2 vols. (London, 1890); this translation has been revised and abridged by Philip Horne and reissued as *Useless Memoirs of Carlo Gozzi* (London, 1962).

On Gozzi and his works:

Giovanni Battista Magrini, *I Tempi, la Vita e gli Scritti di Carlo Gozzi* (Benevento, 1883).

PIRANDELLO

On Pirandello and his works:

Luigi Baccolo, *Luigi Pirandello* (Milan, 1949).

Thomas Bishop, *Pirandello and the French Theatre* (New York, 1960).

Massimo Bontempelli, *Pirandello, Leopardi, D'Annunzio* (Verona, 1939).

Umberto Cantoro, *Luigi Pirandello e il problema della personalità* (Bologna, 1954).

J. Chaix-Ruy, *Luigi Pirandello* (Paris, 1957).

Edoardo Crema, *Il dramma della creazione in Pirandello* (Siena, 1953).

Guy Dumur, *Pirandello dramaturge* (Paris, 1955).

Arminio Janner, *Luigi Pirandello* (Florence, 1948).

Manlio Lo Vecchio Musti, *Bibliografia di Pirandello*, 2 vols. (Milan, 1937–40).

——, *L'opera di Luigi Pirandello* (Turin, 1939).

Federico Vittori Nardelli, *L'uomo segreto* (Milan, 1944).

J.-Th. Paolantonacci, *Le Théâtre de Luigi Pirandello* (Paris, n.d.).

Antonio di Pietro, *Pirandello* (Milan, 1951).

Walter Starkie, *Luigi Pirandello* (New York, 1937).

Domenico Vittorini, *The Drama of Luigi Pirandello* (Philadelphia, 1935; New York, 1957).

GERMANY—
THE BEGINNINGS TO LESSING

General references on German literature:

K. Breul, *Handy Bibliographical Guide to the German Language and Literature* (London, 1895).

Kuno Francke, *History of German Literature as Determined by Social Forces* (New York, 1911).

G. G. Gervinus, *Geschichte der poetischen Nationalliteratur der Deutschen* (New ed. by K. Bartsch, 5 vols., Leipzig, 1871–74).

K. Goedeke, *Grundriss zur Geschichte der deutschen Dichtung*, 4 vols. (Dresden, 1859–81).

Jahresberichte für neuere deutsche Literaturgeschichte, 14 vols. (Berlin, 1892 ff).

K. A. Koberstein, *Grundriss zur Geschichte der deutschen Nationalliteratur* (New ed. by K. Bartsch, 5 vols., Leipzig, 1872–74).

J. G. Robinson, *A History of German Literature* (New York, 1902).

Ernst Rose, *A History of German Literature* (New York, 1960).

W. Scherer, *Geschichte der deutschen Literatur* (latest ed., Berlin, 1905).

Calvin Thomas, *A History of German Literature* (New York, 1908).

A. F. C. Vilmar, *Geschichte der deutschen Nationalliteratur* (ed. by A. Stern, 1906).

W. Wackernagel, *Geschichte der deutschen Literatur* (new ed. and continuation by E. Martin, 2 vols., Basel, 1879, 1885–94).

General references on German drama:

R. F. Arnold et al., *Das deutsche Drama* (Munich, 1925).
Carl Heine, *Das Theater in Deutschland* (1891).
Otto Mann, *Geschichte des deutschen Dramas* (Stuttgart, 1960).
Roeert E. Prutz, *Vorlesungen über die Geschichte des deutschen Theaters* (Leipzig, 1847).
R. Prölss, *Katechismus der Dramaturgie* (2nd ed., Leipzig, 1890).
——, *Geschichte der neueren Dramas*, 3 vols. (Leipzig, 1880–83).
Carl Weitbrecht, *Das deutsche Drama* (Berlin, 1900).
Benno von Wiese, ed., *Das deutsche Drama*, 2 vols. (Dusseldorf, 1960).
——, *Die deutsche Tragödie von Lessing bis Hebbel* (Hamburg, 1958).

References on early German drama and German criticism:

B. Aiken-Sneath, *Comedy in Germany in the First Half of the Eighteenth Century* (Oxford, 1936).
Richard Beckherrn, *M. Opitz, P. Ronsard und D. Heinsius* (Königsberg, 1888).
G. Belouin, *De Gottsched à Lessing* (Paris, 1909).
J. Bintz, *Der Einfluss der Ars Poetica des Horaz auf die deutsche Literatur des xviii. Jahrhundert* (Hamburg, 1892).
Karl Borinski, *Die Poetik der Renaissance und die Anfänge der literarischen Kritik in Deutschland* (Berlin, 1886).
Friedrich Braitmaier, *Geschichte der poetischen Theorie und Kritik von den Diskursen der Maler bis auf Lessing* (Frauenfeld, 1889).
J. C. Brandes, *Meine Lebengeschichte* (Munich, 1923).
F. Brüggemann, *Gottscheds Lebens- und Kunstreform* (Leipzig, 1935).
Ida Bruhning, *Le Théátre en Allemagne* (Paris, 1887).
Johann Cruger, *J. C. Gottsched und die Schweizer* (Berlin, 1884).
Danzel, *Gottsched und seine Zeit* (Leipzig, 1848).
Hugo Dinger, *Dramaturgie als Wissenschaft*, 2 vols. (Leipzig, 1904–05).

A. Eloesser, *Das bürgerliche Drama* (Berlin, 1898).
W. Flemming, *Barockdrama*, 6 vols. (Leipzig, 1930–33).
C. M. Gayley and F. N. Scott, *An Introduction to the Methods and Materials of Literary Criticism* (Boston, 1899).
J. C. Gottsched, *Gesammelte Schriften*, 4 vols. (Berlin, 1902–12).
E. Grucker, *Histoire des Doctrines littéraires et esthétiques en Allemagne* (Paris, 1883).
Karl Holl, *Zur Geschichte der Lustspieltheorie* (Berlin, 1911).
Max Koch, *Gottsched und die Reform der deutschen Literatur im 18. Jahrhundert* (Hamburg, 1887).
T. S. Perry, *From Opitz to Lessing* (Boston, 1885).
Max Poensgen, *Geschichte der Theorie der Tragödie von Gottsched bis Lessing* (Leipzig, 1899).
E. Reichel, *Gottsched*, 2 vols. (Berlin, 1908, 1912).
George Saintsbury, *A History of Criticism*, vol. 2 (New York, 1902).
Walter Schinz, *Le Problème de la tragédie en Allemagne* (Paris, 1903).
A. W. Schlegel, *Vorlesungen über dramatische Kunst und Literatur* (Berlin, 1809–11). Translated by J. Black, as *Lectures on Dramatic Art and Literature;* Bohn ed., London, 1914).
Wilhelm von Scholz, *Deutsche Dramaturgie*, 3 vols. (München, 1912–14).
Madame de Staël, *De l'Allemagne* (1810).
G. Waniek, *Gottsched und die deutsche Literatur seiner Zeit* (Leipzig, 1897).
R. Weitbrecht, *Blätter fur literarische Unterhaltung* (1891–11: 625, *Kritiker und Dichter*).
O. Wichmann, *L'Art poétique de Boileau dans celui de Gottsched* (Berlin, 1879).

LESSING

On the drama:

Beiträge zur Historie und Aufnahme des Theaters (1750).
Theatralische Bibliothek (1754–58).
Vorrede zu Thomsons Trauerspielen (1756).
Vorrede des Uebersetzers in *Das Theater des Herrn Diderot* (1760).
Briefe, die neueste Litteratur betreffend

(1759, 1760).
Hamburgische Dramaturgie (1769).
Leben des Sophokles (1760–90).
Dramaturgische Entwürfe und Fragmente (posthumous).
Kollektaneen zur Litteratur (vol. 20, *Cotta* ed. also contain casual references to the drama).
The *Briefe*, likewise. See also especially *Lessings Briefwechsel mit Mendelssohn und Nicolai über das Trauerspiel* (in *Philosophische Bib.*, vol. 2, Leipzig, 1910).

Editions:

G. E. Lessings Schriften, 6 vols. (Berlin, 1753–55), and *G E. Lessings sämmtliche Schriften*, 30 vols. (1771–94) were the only collected editions appearing during the author's life-time. Among the modern editions are the Lachmann-Muncker 15 vols. ed. (1900), and the Boxburger and Blumner eds., 14 vols. (1883–90). A convenient and accessible edition is the *Cotta* edition, under the supervision of Hugo Göring, 20 vols. (Stuttgart and Berlin, n. d.). A more recent edition is the *Werke*, J. Petersen and W. von Olshausen, eds. (1925–35). There are numerous editions of the *Hamburgische Dramaturgie:* the first edition appeared in Hamburg, 2 vols. (1769). See in abovementioned collected works.

On Lessing and his works:

Hermann Baumgart, *Aristoteles, Lessing, und Goethe. Ueber das ethische und das aesthetische Princip der Tragödie* (Leipzig, 1877).
Emil Brenning, *Lessing als Dramatiker und Lessings Nathan der Weise* (Bremen, 1878).
Wilhelm Cosack, *Materialen zu G. E. Lessings Hamburgischer Dramaturgie, etc.* (Paderborn, 1876).
T. W. Danzel, *Gotthold Ephraim Lessing, sein Leben und seine Werke,* 2 vols. (2nd ed., Berlin, 1880–81).
W. Dilthey, *Das Erlebnis und die Dichtung* (Leipzig & Berlin, 1906).
Heinrich Düntzer, *Lessings Leben* (Leipzig, 1882).
L. Eckart, *Lessing und das erst deutsche Nationaltheater in Hamburg* (Hamburg, 1864).
H. B. Garland, *Lessing: The Founder of Modern German Literature* (London, 1962).
Emil Gotschlich, *Lessings aristotelische Studien und der Einfluss derselben auf seine Werke* (Berlin, 1876).
J. Kont, *Lessing et la définition de la tragédie par Aristote* (in *Rev. des Etudes grecques*, p. 387, Paris, 1893).
C. G. Lessing, *G. E. Lessings Leben, etc.,* 3 parts (Berlin, 1793).
Otto Mann, *Lessing* (Hamburg, 1949).
J. G. Robertson, *Lessing's Dramatic Theory* (Cambridge, Eng., 1939).
T. W. Rolleston, *Lessing* (London, n. d.).
Erich Schmidt, *Lessing. Geschichte seines Lebens und seiner Schriften* (Berlin, 1884).
Eugen Sierke, *G. E. Lessing als angehender Dramatiker,* etc. (Königsberg, 1869).
James Sime, *Lessing,* 2 vols. (London, 1877).
Adolph Stahr, *G. E. Lessing, sein Leben und seine Werke,* 2 parts (Berlin, 1859).
(Translation of the above: *The Life and Works of G. E. Lessing,* translated by E. P. Evans, 2 vols., Boston, 1866.)
Benno von Wiese, *Lessing* (Leipzig, 1931).

EIGHTEENTH-CENTURY FRANCE

General references on eighteenth century French literature:

Paul Albert, *La Littérature française au dix-huitième siècle* (10th ed., Paris, 1908).
Adrien Baillet, *Jugemens des savans sur les principaux ouvrages des auteurs,* 8 vols. (Augmented ed., Paris, 1722–30).
De Baranti, *Tableau de la littérature française au XVIII*e *siècle* (5th ed., Paris, 1809).
E. Bersot, *Etudes sur le XVIII*e *siècle* 2 vols. (Paris, 1855).

Ferdinand Brunetière, *Etudes sur le XVIII⁰ siècle* (Paris, 1911).

E. Caro, *La Fin du XVIII⁰ siècle,* 2 vols. (Paris, 1880).

Emile Faguet, *Dix-huitième siècle* (37th ed., Paris, n. d.).

Paul Hazard, *European Thought in the Eighteenth Century* (New York, 1954).

D. Mornet, *Le Romantisme au 18e siècle* (Paris, 1912).

A. F. Villemain, *Tableau de la littérature française au XVIII⁰ siècle,* 2 vols. (New ed., Paris, 1891).

Vinet, *Histoire de la littérature française au dix-huitième siècle,* 2 vols. (Paris, 1853).

Special references on eighteenth century French drama:

Victor du Bled, *La Comédie de société au XVIII⁰ siècle* (Paris, 1893).

C. Desprez de Boissy, *Lettres sur les spectacles avec une histoire des ouvrages pour et contre les Théâtres* (Paris, 1774).

G. Desnoiresterres, *La Comédie satirique au XVIII⁰ siècle* (Paris, 1885).

Emile Faguet, *Rousseau contre Molière* (Paris, 1912).

Léon Fontaine, *Le Théâtre et la philosophie au XVIII⁰ siècle* (Paris, 1878).

Frederick Hawkins, *The French Stage in the Eighteenth Century,* 2 vols. (London, 1888).

Theodore Hook, *The French Stage and the French People,* 2 vols. (London, 1841).

G. Huszar, *L'Influence de l'Espagne sur le théâtre français des XVIII⁰ et XIX⁰ siècles* (Paris, 1912).

Gustave Lanson, *La Comédie au XVIII⁰ siècle* (In *Hommes et livres,* Paris, 1895).

C. Lenient, *La Comédie en France au XVIII⁰ siècle,* 2 vols. (Paris, 1888).

Romain Rolland, *Le Théâtre du Peuple* (Paris, new ed., 1913. Translated by Barrett H. Clark, as *The People's Theater,* New York, 1918).

On the drama:

M. M. D. C. [de Chaussiron], *Réflexions sur le Comique-larmoyant* (Paris, 1749).

Eloesser, *Das bürgerliche Drama, seine Geschichte im XVIII. und XIX. Jahrhundert* (Berlin, 1898).

F. Gaiffe, *Le Drame en France au XVIII⁰ siècle* (Paris, 1910).

La Harpe, *Lycée ou Cours de Littérature ancienne et moderne,* 19 vols. (see vols. 11, 12, and 13. Paris, An VII and following).

Gustave Lanson, *Nivelle de la Chaussée et la Comédie larmoyante* (2nd ed., Paris, 1903).

Alexis Pitou, *Les Origines du mélodrame à la fin du XVIII⁰ siècle* (in *Rev. d'Hist. lit. de la France,* v. 18, Paris, 1911).

E. Rigal, *Le Romantisme au théâtre avant les Romantiques* (in *Rev. d'Hist. lit. de la France,* Paris, 1915).

Jean-Jacques Rousseau, *Politics and the Arts* (Glencoe, 1960).

A. W. Schlegel, *Lectures on Dramatic Art and Literature* (Trans. by John Black, 2nd ed., Bohn Lib., London, 1914).

Je la Viéville, *Lettre à M. de Milcent, jeune littérateur, sur les Drames bourgeois ou larmoyans* (Amsterdam, 1775)

Wetz, *Die Anfänge der ernsten bürgerlichen Dichtung der achzehnten Jahrhundert* (Strassburg, 1885).

References on criticism, especially dramatic:

René Doumic, *Etudes sur la littérature française,* 5ème série (Paris, 1906).

Emile Faguet, *Propos de théâtre,* 2ème série (Paris, 1905).

Eleanor F. Jourdain, *Dramatic Theory and Practice in France, 1690-1808* (London, 1921).

Daniel Mornet, *La Question des règles au XVIII⁰ siècle* (in *Rev. d'Hist. lit. de la France,* Paris, 1914).

Amilda A. Pons, *Jean-Jacques Rousseau et le théâtre* (Genève, 1909).

H. Rigault, *Histoire de la querelle des Anciens et des Modernes* (Paris, 1859).

J. Rocafort, *Les Questions de littérature dramatique dans l'Encyclopédie* (Paris, 1890)

George Saintsbury, *A History of Criticism,* vols. 2 and 3 (New York, 1902–04).

Joseph Texte, *L'Italie et la critique française au XVIII⁰ siècle* (in *Rev. des cours et conférences,* Paris, 16 Jan., 1896).

Francisque Vial et Louis Denise, *Idées et doctrines du XVIII⁰ siècle* (Paris, n.d.).

VOLTAIRE

On the drama:

Lettres écrites en 1719, qui contiennent la critique de l'Œdipe de Sophocle, de celui de Corneille, et de celui de l'auteur [7 letters]; the *Préface* to the ed. [a reply to La Motte]. Also a *Lettre au Père Porée, Jésuite.* All in *Œdipe* (1730).
Préface, in *La Mort de César* (1736
Discours sur la tragédie, in *Brutus* (1731).
Discours prononcé avant la représentation d'Eriphyle, in *Eryphile* (1732).
Epître dédicatoire à M. Falkener, Marchand anglais, in *Zaïre* (1733).
A M. le Chevalier Falkener, etc., in *Zaïre* (ed. 1736).
Préface, in *La Mort de César* (1736 ed.).
Epitre à Madame la marquise du Chastelet, in *Alzire* (1736), and *Discours préliminaire* to the same.
Préface to *L'Enfant prodigue* (1738).
A Mademoiselle Clairon, in *Zulime* (1761).
Avis de l'éditeur [by Voltaire], in *Le Fanatisme, ou Mahomet le prophète* (1743).
A M. le Marquis Scipion Maffei, and *Réponse à M. de la Lindelle,* in *Mérope* (1744).
Dissertation sur la tragédie ancienne et moderne, etc., in *Sémiramis* (1748).
Prologue to *L'Echange* (1747).
Préface to *Nanine* (1749).
Epitre to the Duchesse du Maine, in *Oreste* (1750).
Préface to *Rome sauvée* (1752).
A Monseigneur le Maréschal duc de Richelieu, in *L'Orphelin de la Chine* (1755).
Préface to *Socrate* (1759).
Epître dédicatoire . . . à M. le Comte de Lauragnais, in *L'Ecossaise* (1760). Also *Préface.*
A Madame la Marquise de Pompadour, in *Tancrède* (1760).
Avertissement du traducteur, in the *Jules César de Shakespeare* (1735); also *Observations sur le Jules César de Shakespeare.*
Préface de l'éditeur [Voltaire], in *Le Triumvirat* (1767).
Préfaces to *Les Scythes* (1767 and 1768).
Notes in *Olympie* (1764).
Discours historique et critique, in *Les Guèbres* (1769).
A Monsieur le duc de la Vallière, in *Sophonisbe* (1770).
Fragment d'une lettre, in *Les Pélopides* (1772).
Epître dédicatoire and *Notes,* in *Les Lois de Minos* (1773).
Epître dédicatoire à M. d'Alembert, in *Don Pèdre;* also *Discours historique et critique sur la tragédie de Don Pèdre* (1774).
Lettre à l'Académie française, in *Irène* (1778).

In the miscellaneous writings of Voltaire will be found numerous references to the drama. The most important are in the following:

Siècle de Louis XIV (1751).
Lettres philosophiques sur les anglais (1734).
Dictionnaire philosophique (esp. articles: *Aristote, Art dramatique, Art poétique, Critique.* 1764).
Commentaires sur Corneille (1764. Reprinted separately, Paris, 1886).
Les Anciens et les modernes, ou la Toilette de Madame de Pompadour (1765).
Vie de Molière (1739).
Eloge de M. de Crébillon (1762).

Editions:

The first of the collected editions of Voltaire with any pretense to completeness is the so-called *Kehl* edition, edited by Beaumarchais, Condorcet, and Decroix, in 70 vols. (Paris, 1784–90). The *Beuchot* edition, also in 70 vols., was published at Paris, 1828 and following. The *Siècle* edition, edited by E. de La Bedollière and Georges Avenel, in 8 vols., was published at Paris, 1867–70. The Charles Lahure edition, in 35 vols., was published at Paris in 1859. Probably the best edition is that published by Garnier, edited by Moland, 50 vols., Paris, 1877–83. This was followed by the *Table générale et analytique,* by Charles Pierrot, 2 vols. (Paris, 1885). Since the appearance of this edition, a number of volumes of unpublished correspondence and other matter have made their appearance, the most interesting of which are the *Lettres inédites à Louis Racine,* edited by Tamizey de

584

Larroque (Paris, 1893).

The *Lettres*, of which there are at least 10,000, contain numerous references to drama. (Among these, see: *Au Marquis Capacelli*, Dec. 4, 1758; *A d'Argental*, June 18, 1759; *A Mlle. Clairon*, Oct. 16, 1760; *A Le Kain*, Dec. 16, 1760; and *A. H. Walpole*, July 15, 1768.) Most of the above have been translated, in various collected and separate editions. See especially the latest collected editions of the works. Among contemporary translations, the volume *Critical Essays on Dramatic Poetry by Monsieur de Voltaire* (London, 1761) will be found to include many of the important dramatic theories of the author. *The Dramatic Works of M. de Voltaire*, translated by Hugh Downman (1781), contain a number of *Prefaces*. Among modern translations, vol. 19 of the *Works of Voltaire* (New York, 1901) contains half a dozen prefaces to plays.

The *Life of Molière* is translated by Barrett H. Clark (in *Great Short Biographies of the World*, New York, 1928).

On Voltaire and his works:

Richard Aldington, *Voltaire* (London, 1925).
G. Bengesco, *Voltaire: bibliographie de ses œuvres*, 4 vols. (Paris, 1882–90).
B. Bonieux, *Critique des tragédies de Corneille et de Racine par Voltaire* (Clermont-Ferrand, 1866).
Henry N. Brailsford, *Voltaire* (London, 1935).
Ferdinand Brunetière, *Voltaire* (in *Etudes critiques sur l'histoire de la littérature française*, I, 7th ed., Paris, 1911).
——, *Voltaire et Rousseau* (in same, III, Paris, 1887).
——, *Voltaire* (in same, IV, Paris, 1891).
——, *Voltaire* (in *Etudes sur le XVIIIe siècle*, Paris, 1911).
E. Champion, *Voltaire. Etudes critiques.* (Paris, 1892).
M. Clément, *De la Tragédie, pour servir de suite aux lettres à Voltaire*, 2 vols. (Amsterdam, 1784).
Comte Alexandre Collini, *Mon séjour auprès de Voltaire* (Paris, 1807).
Marquis de Condorcet, *Vie de Voltaire* (mod. ed., Paris, 1895.—*The Life of Voltaire*, translated from the French, 2 vols., London, 1790).

L. Crouslé, *La Vie et les œuvres de Voltaire*, 2 vols. (Paris, 1899).
Emile Deschanel, *Le Romantisme des classiques: Le Théâtre de Voltaire* (Paris, 1888).
Francis Espinasse, *Life of Voltaire* (London, 1892).
Emile Faguet, *Voltaire* (in *Collection des classiques populaires*. Paris, 1895).
——, *XVIIIe siècle* (37th ed., Paris, n.d.).
E. B. Hamley, *Voltaire* (Edinburgh, 1877).
Eloi Johanneau, *Rhétorique et Poétique de Voltaire* (Paris, 1828).
H. Jürging, *Voltaires dramatische Theorie* (Münster, 1885).
Lacombe, *Poétique de M. de Voltaire, ou Observations recueillies de ses ouvrages*, etc., 2 vols. (Paris et Genève, 1776).
Gustave Lanson, *Voltaire* (Paris, 1906).
Oliver H. G. Leigh, *Voltaire: Index to his Works* (in vol. 22, *Works of Voltaire*, New York, 1901).
H.-G.-M. Lion, *Les Tragédies et les théories dramatiques de Voltaire* (Paris, 1895).
Lonchamp et Wagnière, *Mémoires sur Voltaire et ses ouvrages* (Paris, 1825).
Thomas R. Lounsbury, *Shakespeare and Voltaire* (New York, 1902).
Robert Lowenstein, *Voltaire as an Historian of the Seventeenth Century French Drama* (Baltimore, 1935).
G. Maugras, *Voltaire et Jean-Jacques Rousseau* (Paris, 1886).
John Morley, *Voltaire* (London, 1878).
Raymond Naves, *Voltaire* (Paris, 1942).
Charles Nisard, *Les Ennemis de Voltaire* (Paris, 1833).
Jean-Jacques Olivier, *Voltaire et les comédiens interprètes de son théâtre*, etc. (Paris, 1900).
James Parton, *Life of Voltaire*, 2 vols. (Boston, 1881).
René Pomeau, *Voltaire par lui-même* (Paris, 1955).
Georges Renard, *Vie de Voltaire* (Paris, 1883).
T. W. Russell, *Voltaire, Dryden, and Heroic Tragedy* (New York, 1946).
C.-A. Sainte-Beuve, *Causeries du Lundi*, 2, 7, 13, 15 (Paris, 1857–62).
K. Schirmacher, *Voltaire, eine Biographie* (Leipzig, 1898).
A. Schmitz, *Le Commentaire de Voltaire sur Corneille* (Erfurt, 1876).
S. G. Tallentyre, *The Life of Voltaire*

(New York, n.d.).
——, *Voltaire in His Letters* (New York, 1919).
Norman L. Torrey, *The Spirit of Voltaire* (New York, 1938).

DIDEROT

On the drama:

Notice préliminaire and *Entretiens (Dorval et moi)* in *Le Fils naturel* (1757).
Epître dédicatoire and *De la Poésie dramatique*, in *Le Père de famille* (1758).
Lettre de Madame Riccoboni . . . à Monsieur Diderot (1758); *Réponse à la lettre de Mme. Riccoboni* (1758). (In vol. 7, Assézat ed.)
Réflexions sur Terence (1762).
Observations sur Garrick (1770).
Miscellanéa dramatiques (under this title were published 21 essays, letters, prefaces, and fragments, some of them never before printed. See vol. 8, Assézat ed.).
Lettres (vols. 18, 19, 20, Assézat ed. Also the *Correspondance littéraire*, of Grimm, Diderot, etc., 16 vols., Paris, 1877–82).
For incidental references on the drama, see *Les Bijoux indiscrets*, chaps. 37 and 38 (1748); *Paradoxe sur le comédien* (first published in 1830); see special *édition critique* of Ernest Dupuy, Paris, 1902. Translated as *The Paradox of Acting*, by W. H. Pollock (London, 1883).

Editions:

The early editions — 15 vols., 1798, and 21 vols., 1821–22 — are far from complete. The most recent and most nearly complete edition is that under the direction of J. Assézat, as the *Œuvres complètes de Diderot*, 20 vols., Paris, 1875–77. This was followed by the *Correspondance littéraire* of Grimm, Diderot, Raynal, Meister, etc., 16 vols., Paris, 1877–82.

On Diderot and his works:

A. Bailly, *Vie de Diderot* (Paris, 1932).
J. Barbey d'Aurevilly, *Goethe et Diderot* (Paris, 1882).
E. Bersot, *Diderot* (Paris, 1851).
J. Block, *Beiträge zu einer Würdigung*

Diderot's als Dramatiker (Königsberg, 1888).
Ferdinand Brunetière, *Diderot* (in *Etudes critiques sur l'histoire de la littérature française*, 2^{cme} série, Paris, 1882).
A. Collignon, *Diderot, sa vie et ses œuvres* (Paris, 1875).
C. Y. Cousin d'Avallon, *Diderotiana* (Paris, 1810–11).
Lester G. Crocker, *The Embattled Philosopher* (East Lansing, 1954).
René Doumic, *Diderot* (in *Etudes sur la littérature française*, vol. 1, Paris, 1896).
——, *Diderot* (In same, vol. 5, Paris, 1906).
Havelock Ellis, *The New Spirit* (London, 1891).
Emile Faguet, *Diderot* (in *XVIIIe siècle*, Paris, 1911).
——, *Propos de théâtre*, 2eme série (Paris, 1905).
Otis Fellows and Gita May, *Diderot Studies III* (Geneva, 1961).
Otis Fellows and Norman Torrey, *Diderot Studies I & II* (Syracuse, 1949, 1953).
Alice Green Fredman, *Diderot and Sterne* (New York, 1950).
La Grande Encyclopédie, vol. 14 (Paris).
J. J. C. L. [Leids], *Principaux écrits relatifs à la personné et aux œuvres au temps et à l'influence de Diderot, compilation critique et chronologique* (Amsterdam and Paris, 1887).
J. Robert Loy, *Diderot's Determined Fatalist* (New York, 1950).
John Morley, *Diderot and the Encyclopedists*, 2 vols. (New ed., New York, 1905).
Joseph Reinach, *Diderot* (Paris, 1894).
Rosenkranz, *Diderot's Leben und Werke*, 2 vols. (Leipzig, 1866).
C.-A. Sainte-Beuve, *Causeries du Lundi*, vol. 3 (Paris, 1857–62).
——, *Nouveaux Lundis*, vol. 9 (Paris, 1863–70).
——, *Portraits littéraires*, vol. I (Paris, 1862).
——, *Premiers Lundis*, vol. 1 (Paris, 1874).
Edmond Scherer, *Diderot* (Paris, 1880).
A. Séché et J. Bertaut, *Diderot* (Paris, n. d.).
Mme. de Vandeul, *Mémoires pour servir à l'histoire de la vie et des ouvrages*

de Diderot (re-printed with other early notices in vol. 1, Assézat ed.).

Arthur M. Wilson, *Diderot: The Testing Years, 1713–1759* (New York, 1957).

BEAUMARCHAIS

On the drama:

Essai sur le genre dramatique sérieux, in *Eugénie,* and separately (1767).

Lettre modérée sur la chûte et la critique du Barbier de Séville, in *Le Barbie· de Séville* (1775).

Préface, in *La Folle Journée ou le Mariage de Figaro* (Paris, 1784).

Un Mot sur la Mère coupable, in *L'Autre Tartuffe ou la Mère coupable* (1797).

The *Mémoires* (originally published in parts, 1773–74) are reprinted with a notice by Sainte-Beuve (Paris, n.d.). They may be consulted for biographical data. The *Lettres,* printed in modern editions, contain occasional references to drama, while the *Compte rendu de l'affaire des auteurs dramatiques et des comédiens français,* etc., and *Rapport fait aux auteurs dramatiques,* etc., are interesting documents on the quarrel over authors' rights.

Editions:

The first edition of the *Œuvres complètes* was edited by Gudin de La Brenellerie, 7 vols. (Paris, 1809). The best modern complete editions are *Théâtre complet de Beaumarchais,* edited by G. d'Heylli and F. de Marescot, 4 vols. (Paris, 1869–71), and *Œuvres complètes de Beaumarchais,* edited by Edouard Fournier (Paris, 1867). Among the more recent editions is the *Théâtre illustré,* with notes and introduction by M. Roustan, 2 vols. (Paris, n.d.). This edition contains all the prefaces, and extracts from the plays.

On Beaumarchais and his works:

See prefaces to various editions cited:

Auguste Bailly, *Beaumarchais* (Paris, 1945).

Anton Bettelheim, *Beaumarchais* (2nd ed., München, 1911).

Paul Bonnefon, *Beaumarchais* (Paris, 1887).

Gudin de la Brenellerie, *Histoire de Beaumarchais* (Paris, 1888).

Maurice Chevrier, *Discours sur Beaumarchais* (Paris, 1887).

Henri Cordier, *Bibliographie des œuvres de Beaumarchais* (Paris, 1883).

Cousin d'Avallon, *Vie privée, politique et littéraire de Beaumarchais* (Paris, 1802).

Cynthia Cox, *The Real Figaro* (New York, 1963).

René Dalsemé, *Beaumarchais* (New York, 1929).

La Grande Encyclopédie, vol. 5 (Paris, 1888).

Evelyn B. Hall, *The Friends of Voltaire* (New York, 1907).

André Hallays, *Beaumarchais* (Paris, 1897).

Elizabeth Kite, *Beaumarchais and the War of American Independence* (Boston, 1918).

Louis Latzarus, *Beaumarchais* (Paris, 1930).

M. de Lescure, *Eloge de Beaumarchais* (Paris, 1886).

Eugène Lintilhac, *Beaumarchais et ses œuvres* (Paris, 1887).

Louis de Loménie, *Beaumarchais et son temps,* 2 vols. (4th ed., Paris, 1880). Translated by H. S. Edwards, as *Beaumarchais and his Times,* 4 vols. (London, 1856).

J. B. Ratermanis and W. R. Irwin, *The Comic Style of Beaumarchais* (Seattle, 1961).

John Rivers, *Figaro: the Life of Beaumarchais* (New York, n.d.).

C.-A. Sainte-Beuve, *Causeries du Lundi* vol. 6 (Paris, 1857–62).

Jacques Schérer, *La Dramaturgie de Beaumarchais* (Paris, 1954).

GERMANY— ROMANTIC PERIOD TO THE PRESENT

General references on modern German literature:

Adolf Bartels, *Die neuere Literatur* (vol.

2 of the *Geschichte der deutschen Literatur,* 5th and 6th ed., Leipzig, 1909).

Félix Bertaux, *Panorama of German Literature from 1871 to 1931* (New York,

1935).

Alfred Biese, *Deutsche Literaturge-schichte,* vol. 3 (Leipzig, 1910).

Jethro Bithell, *Modern German Litera-ture, 1880–1950* (London, 1959).

H. H. Boyesen, *Essays on German Lit-erature* (New York, 1892).

G. Brandes, *The Main Currents of Nine-teenth Century Literature,* 5 vols. (New York, 1906).

E. M. Butler, *The Tyranny of Greece over Germany* (Cambridge, Eng., 1935).

Kasimir Edschmid, *Über Expressionis-mus in der Literatur* (Berlin, 1919).

Arthur Eloesser, *Modern German Litera-ture* (New York, 1933).

R. von Gottschall, *Die deutsche National-literatur des 19. Jahrhunderts,* 4 vols. (5th ed.; Breslau, 1881).

Michael Hamburger, *Reason and En-ergy: Studies in German Literature* (New York, 1957).

Erich Heller, *The Disinherited Mind* (Cambridge, Eng., 1952).

J. Hillebrand, *Die deutsche National-literatur im 18. und 19. Jahrhundert,* 3 vols. (3rd ed., Gotha, 1875).

M. Koch, *Nationalität und Nationallit-eratur* (Berlin, 1891).

A. Köster, *Die deutsche Literatur der Aufklärungzeit* (Heidelberg, 1925).

Friedrich Kummer, *Deutsche Literatur des 19. Jahrhunderts* (Dresden, 1909).

Victor Lange, *Modern German Litera-ture, 1870–1940* (New York, 1945).

G. R. Mason, *From Gottsched to Hebbel* (London, 1961).

Richard M. Meyer, *Die deutsche Litera-tur des 19. Jahrhunderts* (Berlin, 1906).

Richard Samuel and R. Hinton Thomas, *Expressionism in German Life, Litera-ture and the Theatre* (Cambridge, Eng., 1934).

Walter H. Sokel, *The Writer in Ex-tremis: Expressionism in Twentieth-Century German Literature* (Stanford, 1959).

Adolf Stern, *Die deutsch Nationallitera-tur von Tode Goethes bis zur Gegen-wart* (Marburg, 1886).

——, *Geschichte der neueren Literatur* (Leipzig, 1882–85).

Karl Storck, *Deutsche Literaturge-schichte* (6th and 7th ed., Stuttgart, 1913).

Georg Witkowski, *Die Entwicklung der deutschen Literatur seit 1830* (Leipzig, 1912).

Eugen Wolff, *Geschichte der deutschen Literatur in der Gegenwart* (Leipzig, 1896).

General references on German drama since Lessing:

Robert F. Arnold, *Das moderne Drama* (Strassburg, 1912).

——, *Bibliographie der deutschen Büh-nen seit 1830* (Strassburg, 1909).

Julius Bab, *Die Chronik des deutschen Dramas,* 5 vols. (Berlin, 1922–26).

——, *Kritik der Bühne* (Berlin, 1908).

——, *Neue Wege zum Drama* (Berlin, 1911).

——, *Das Theater der Gegenwart* (Leip-zig, 1928).

——, *Uber den Tag hinaus* (Heidelberg, 1960).

——, *Wege zum Drama* (Berlin, 1906).

——, *Der Wille zum Drama* (Berlin, 1919).

Hermann Bahr, *Dialog vom Tragischen* (Berlin, 1904).

——, *Premieren* (München, 1902).

——, *Studien zur Kritik der Moderne* (Frankfurt, 1894).

——, *Die Ueberwindung des Naturalis-mus* (Dresden, 1891).

——, *Wiener Theater (1892–98)* (Ber-lin, 1899).

——, *Zur Kritik der Moderne* (Zurich, 1889).

Louis Benoist-Hanappier, *Le Drame nat-uraliste en Allemagne* (Paris, 1905).

A. von Berger, *Dramaturgische Vor-träge* (Wien, 1890–91).

A. Berger, *Meine Hamburgische Drama-turgie* (Wien, 1910).

Otto Brahm, *Kritische Schriften über Drama und Theater* (Berlin, 1913).

W. H. Bruford, *Theatre, Drama and Au-dience in Goethe's Germany* (London, 1950).

Heinrich Bulthaupt, *Dramaturgie des Schauspiels,* 4 vols. (12th ed., Olden-burg, 1908).

Max Bürger, *Dramaturgisches* (Leip-zig, 1910).

Barrett H. Clark, *A Study of the Mod-ern Drama* (2nd ed., New York, 1928).

Bernhard Diebold, *Anarchie im Drama* (Frankfurt, 1921).

Arthur Eloesser, *Das bürgerliche Drama. Seine Geschichte im 18. und 19. Jahr-*

hundert (Berlin, 1898).

Karl Frenzel, *Berliner Dramaturgie,* 2 vols. (Erfurt, 1877).

Gustav Freytag, *Aufsätze zur Geschichte, Literatur, und Kunst* (Leipzig, 1888).

——, *Die Technik des Dramas* (Leipzig, 1863). In English: *The Technique of the Drama,* Elias J. MacEwan, tr. (Chicago, 1895 ff.).

S. Friedmann, *Das deutsche Drama des neunzehnten Jahrhunderts. Neuere und neuste Zeit* (11th ed., Berlin, 1904).

H. F. Garten, *Modern German Drama* (London, 1959).

Rudolf von Gottschall, *Zur Kritik des modernen Literatur* (12th ed., Berlin, 1900).

A. von Hanstein, *Das jüngste Deutschland* (Leipzig, 1905).

Otto Heller, *Studies in Modern German Literature* (Boston, 1905).

Arno Holz, *Die Kunst, ihr Wesen und ihre Gesetze* (Berlin, 1891).

——, *Neue Folge* (Berlin, 1893).

Herbert Jhering, *Von Reinhardt bis Brecht,* 3 vols. (Berlin, 1961).

Rudolf Kayser, *Das junge deutsche Drama* (Berlin, 1924).

Alfred Kerr, *Das neue Drama* (Berlin, 1909).

——, *Die Welt im Drama* (Cologne, 1954).

Marianne Kesting, *Das epische Theater* (Stuttgart, 1959).

Eugen Killian, *Aus der Praxis der moderne Dramaturgie* (München, 1914).

——, *Dramaturgische Blätter (Erste Reihe)* (München, 1905).

Wilhelm Kosch, *Das deutsche Theater und Drama im 19. Jahrhundert* (Leipzig, 1913).

Ludwig Lewisohn, *The Modern Drama* (New York, 1915).

——, *The Spirit of Modern German Literature* (New York, 1917).

Berthold Litzmann, *Das deutsche Drama in den literarischen Bewegungen der Gegenwart* (4th ed., Hamburg, 1897).

Walther Lohmeyer, *Die Dramaturgie der Massen* (Berlin, 1913).

Max Martersteig, *Das deutsche Theater im 19. Jahrhundert* (Leipzig, 1904).

Siegfried Melchinger, *Dramaturgie des Sturms und Drangs* (Gotha, 1929).

——, *Theater der Gegenwart* (Frankfurt, 1956).

Robert Petsch, *Deutsche Dramaturgie von Lessing bis Hebbel* (Berlin, 1912).

Erwin Piscator, *Das politische Theater* (Berlin, 1929). In French: *Le Théâtre politique* (Paris, 1962).

Percival Pollard, *Masks and Minstrels of New Germany* (Boston, 1911).

Robert Prölss, *Geschichte des neueren Dramas,* 3 vols. (Leipzig, 1880–83).

Paul Reiff, *Views of Tragedy Among the Early German Romanticists* (in *Modern Language Notes,* 1904).

Robert Ress, *Arno Holz und seine künstlerische und weltkulturelle Bedeutung* (Dresden, 1913).

Jürgen Rühle, *Das gefesselte Theater* (Cologne, 1957).

Paul Schlenther, *Gerhart Hauptmann, Leben und Werke* (new ed., Berlin, 1912).

Friedrich Spielhagen, *Neue Beiträge zur Theorie und Technik der Epik und Dramatik* (Leipzig, 1898).

Edgar Steiger, *Das Werden des neueren Dramas,* 2 vols. (Berlin, 1903).

Clara Stockmeyer, *Soziale Probleme in Drama des Sturmes und Dranges* (Frankfurt, 1922).

Alfred Stoeckius, *Naturalism in the Recent German Drama with special reference to Gerhart Hauptmann* (New York, 1903).

Hermann Sudermann, *Verrohung in der Theater Kritik* (Stuttgart, 1902).

Bertha E. Trebein, *Theodor Fontane as a Critic of the Drama* [bibliographies] (New York, 1916).

Frank Wedekind, *Schauspielkunst* (München, 1910).

Ernst von Wildenbruch, *Das deutsche Drama* (Leipzig, 1906).

Georg Witkowski, *Das deutsche Drama des neunzehnten Jahrhunderts in seiner Entwicklung dargestellt* (2nd ed., Leipzig, 1906. Translated by L. E. Horning as *The German Drama of the Nineteenth Century,* New York, 1909).

Klaus Ziegler, *Das deutsche Drama der Neuzeit* (Berlin, 1954).

SCHILLER

On the drama:

Vorrede to *Die Räuber* (1781).
Ueber das gegenwärtige deutsche Theater (1782).
Die Schaubühne als eine moralische Anstalt betrachtet (1784).
Vorrede to *Die Verschwörung des Fiesco*

zu Genova (1787).
Briefe über Don Carlos (1788).
Ueber Egmont, Trauerspiel von Goethe (1788).
Ueber den Grund des Vergnügens an tragischen Gegenstänаder (1792).
Ueber die tragische Kunst (1792).
(The *Kleinere Schriften* contain a few minor reviews of plays. See, among these: *Erste Vorrede der "Räuber"; Vorrede zur zweiten Auflage der "Räuber"; Ueber die "Räuber"; Anhang über die Vorstellung der "Räuber";* and *Ankündigung der Rheinischen Thalia.*)
Editions:

The first so-called complete edition of Schiller was the Körner edition, 12 volumes published by Cotta (Stuttgart, 1812–15). This was supplemented by additional material in Hoffmeister's *Supplemente zu Schillers Werken* (1840–41). Goedeke's edition of the *Sämtliche Schriften,* 15 volumes, appeared at Stuttgart between 1868 and 1876. Among the best modern editions are those under the supervision of Boxberger and Birlingen, in 12 voumes (Stuttgart, 1882–91), and L. Bellermann, in 14 volumes (Leipzig, 1895 and following). Critical editions include that from the house of Cotta, in 16 volumes (Stuttgart, completed in 1894), and the *Sämtliche Werke* edited by Otto Guntter and George Witkowski, 20 volumes (Leipzig, 1909–11). The letters are found in Jonas' edition of Schiller's *Briefe,* 7 volumes (Stuttgart, 1892 ff.).
Schiller's Works, translated by several hands, are published in 7 vols., in the Bohn edition. The sixth volume contains the more important essays on the drama: *Essays, Æsthetical and Philosophical.* The *Correspondence Between Schiller and Goethe* is in 2 vols. (same ed.).
There is another edition of the *Complete Works,* edited by Hempel, 2 vols. (Philadelphia, 1879). Also *Schiller's Works,* translated by R. D. Boylan and Joseph Mellish, edited by N. H. Dole (Boston, 1902).

On Schiller and his works:

For bibliography, see Goedeke's *Grundriss zur Geschichte der deutschen Dichtung,* 2te Aufl. (Dresden, 1893),

and Nevinson's *Life* (see below).
The first biography was Körner's in his edition (1812–15).

Victor Basch, *La Poétique de Schiller* (Paris, 2nd ed., 1911).
K. Berger, *Die Entwicklung von Schillers Æsthetik* (Weimar, 1894).
F. A. Blanchet, *Du Théâtre de Schiller* (Strassburg, 1855).
Wilhelm Bolze, *Schillers philosophische Begründung der Æsthetik der Tragödie* (Leipzig, 1913).
H. H. Boyesen, *Goethe and Schiller* (New York, 1882).
Reinhard Buchwald, *Schiller* (Leipzig, 1937).
Thomas Carlyle, *Life of Friedrich Schiller* (London, 1825).
Herbart Cysarz, *Schiller* (Halle, 1934).
Wilhelm Dilthey, *Schiller* (Göttingen, 1957).
H. B. Garland, *Schiller* (London, 1949).
Melitta Gerhard, *Schiller* (Bern, 1950).
Karl Hoffmeister, *Schillers Leben* (in the 1838–42 ed. of the Works.)
W. G. Howard, *Schiller and Hebbel* (in *Mod. Lang. Ass'n Pubs.,* v. 22, Cambridge, Mass., 1907).
F. W. Kaufman, *Schiller, Poet of Philosophical Idealism* (Oberlin, 1942).
William F. Mainland, *Schiller and the Changing Past* (London, 1957).
Thomas Mann, "On Schiller," in *Last Essays* (New York, 1959).
Kurt May, *Friedrich Schiller, Idee und Wirklichkeit im Drama* (Göttingen, 1948).
Heinrich Meng, *Schillers Abhandlung über naive und sentimentalische Dichtung* (Frauenfeld, 1936).
F.-J.-G. Montargis, *L'Esthétique de Schiller* (Paris, 1890).
Henry W. Nevinson, *Life of Friedrich Schiller* (London, 1889).
Hermann Oertel, *Schillers Theorie der Tragödie* (Dresden, 1934).
J. Peterson, *Schiller und die Bühne* (Berlin, 1904).
Otto Pietsch, *Schiller als Kritiker* (Konigsberg, 1898).
J. G. Robertson, *Schiller after a Century* (Edinburgh, 1905).
E. L. Stahl, *Schiller's Drama: Theory and Practice* (Oxford, 1954).
Calvin Thomas, *The Life and Works of Friedrich Schiller* (New York, 1901).
Benno von Wiese, *Die Dramen Schillers*

(Leipzig, 1938).
——, *Schiller* (Leipzig, 1955).
William Witte, *Schiller* (Oxford, 1949).

GOETHE

On the drama:

The many editions, including certain articles under different titles, make it next to impossible to put the dramatic writings in chronological order. The following references are to the Weimar editions (Weimar, 143 vols., 1887–1920) unless otherwise indicated. The more important articles are specifically mentioned.

Tag- und Jahres-Hefte als Ergänzung meiner sonstigen Bekentnisse, von 1749 bis 1806, and the same from 1807 to 1822. Also *Biographische Einzelheiten* (especially *Zum Jahre 1815 — Theater*). In vols. 35 and 36 (1892–93.)

Zum Shakespeares Tag; Recensionen in die Frankfürter gelehrten Anzeigen (1772); *Auf Goethes Brieftasche — Mercier — Wagner, Neuer Versuch uber die Schauspielkunst.* In vol. 37 (1896).

Theater und Schauspielkunst (20 articles and fragments); and *Literatur (Beiträge zur Jenaischen Allgemeinen Literaturzeitung und Alteres* 1787–1807). 29 articles, many on the drama, vol. 40 (1901).

Literatur. (Beiträge zum Morgenblatt für gebildete Stände, 1807–16.) 3 articles on drama. *Ueber Kunst und Alterthum. Mittheilungen im ersten bis dritten Bande.* 1816–22. 6 articles on drama. Continuation of same in second vol., 1823–32. About 20 articles on the drama. Vol. 41, first and second parts (1902–03).

Ankündigungen. Geleitworte, 1813–30. (Contains the *Theilname Goethes an Manzoni.*) In first part, vol. 42 (1904).

Literatur. Aus dem Nachlass. (Contains *Das Wesen der antiken Trcyödie*, 1827); and *Maximen und Reflexionen über Literatur und Ethik, aus Kunst und Alterthum.* In vol. 42, second part (1907).

The Weimar Edition also includes 63 volumes of the *Briefe und Tagebücher*, in which are numerous references to the drama.

Aus meinem Leben, Dichtung und Wahrheit, part I (Thubingen, 1811); other parts up to 1833.

[Johann P. Eckermann], *Gespräche mit Goethe in den letzten Jahren seines Lebens, 1823–1832*, 2 vols. (with the supplementary volume containing Soret's notes, Leipzig, 1836–48).

Wilhelm Meisters theatralische Sendung (1st published Stuttgart, 1911).

Wilhelm Meisters Lehrjahre, 4 vols. (Berlin, 1795–96).

Wilhelm Meisters Wanderjahre, part I (Stuttgart, 1821). The novel as a whole was eventually published in 3 vols. in the 1830 ed. of the *Werke*.

Editions:

In order to facilitate reference, the miscellaneous criticisms referred to in the Weimar Edition — not including *Kunst und Alterthum* — are to be found in the easily accessible, though not entirely trustworthy *Cotta* Edition of the *Sämtliche Werke*, in 36 vols., Stuttgart, n.d. These are found in vols. 4, 14, 26, 27, 28, and 36. See also the Hempel Edition, and the *Jubiläums-Ausgabe* (Stuttgart, 1905). Not all the criticisms have been translated into English. The *Maxims of Goethe*, however, contain a number of the more important short maxims and fragments. This is published under the title *Criticisms, Reflections, and Maxims of Goethe*, translated by W. B. Rönnfeldt (London, n.d.). The *Dichtung und Wahrheit* is translated by John Oxenford as *The Autobiography of Goethe*, 2 vols. (Bohn ed., London, revised ed., 1897). The second vol. of this ed. contains a translation of the *Tag- und Jahres-Hefte*, by Charles Nisbet, as *Annals or Day and Year Papers.* Eckermann's *Gespräche* are translated by John Oxenford as *Conversations of Goethe with Eckermann and Soret.* Eckermann himself added a third vol. in 1848 with the Soret conversations (revised Bohn ed., London, 1913). *Wilhelm Meisters Lehrjahre* and *Wilhelm Meisters Wanderjahre* are translated by Thomas Carlyle as *Wilhelm Meister's Apprenticeship and Travels* (Edinburgh, 1824ff). See especially Gräf's *Goethe über seine Dichtungen*, 9 vols. (1901–

14). Max Morris's *Der junge Goethe,* 6 vols. (1909–12), contains much matter not in any other editions. See also Goethe's *Literary Essays,* edited by Joel E. Spingarn (New York, 1921).

On Goethe and his works:

Dichtung und Wahrheit, and Eckermann, *Gespräche* (see above). For bibliography, see Goedeke's well-known *Grundriss.* For general biography and bibliography, see the *Goethe-Jahrbuch* (Frankfurt, 1880–1913), and the *Schriften der Goethe-Gesellschaft,* 28 vols. (Weimar, 1885–1913).

Jeanne Ancelet-Hustache, *Goethe* (New York, 1960).
Bertram Barnes, *Goethe's Knowledge of French Literature* (Oxford, 1937).
J. Barbey d'Aurevilly, *Goethe et Diderot* (Paris, 1880).
Arnold Bergstraesser, ed., *Goethe and the Modern Age* (Chicago, 1950).
A. Bielschowsky, *Goethe; sein Leben und seine Werke,* 2 vols. (München, 1896–1904. Translated by W. A. Cooper as *The Life of Goethe,* 3 vols., New York, 1905–08).
Wilhelm Bode, *Goethes Aesthetik* (Berlin, 1901).
Ewald A. Boucke, *Goethes Weltanschauung auf historischer Grundlage* (Stuttgart, 1907).
James Boyd, *Goethe's Knowledge of English Literature* (Oxford, 1932).
H. H. Boyesen, *Goethe and Schiller* (New York, 1879).
Georg Brandes, *Goethe* (New York, 1924).
Thomas Carlyle, *Essays on Goethe* [reprints] (New York, 1881).
Jean-Marie Carré, *Goethe* (New York, 1929).
Ernst Cassirer, *Goethe und die geschichtliche Welt* (Berlin, 1932).
Benedetto Croce, *Goethe* (London, 1923).
Heinrich Düntzer, *Goethes Leben* (Leipzig, 1880. Translated as *Life of Goethe,* by Thomas W. Lyster, popular ed., London, 1908).
E. Engel, *Goethe. Der Mann und das Werk* (Berlin, 1910).
Barker Fairley, *Goethe as Revealed in His Poetry* (London, 1932).
——, *A Study of Goethe* (Oxford, 1947).
Henry Hatfield, *Goethe* (Norfolk, Conn.,

1963).
K. Heinemann, *Goethe,* 2 vols. (Leipzig, 1895).
G. H. Lewes, *The Life and Works of Goethe,* 2 vols. (London, 1855. 3rd ed., revised, 2 vols., Leipzig, 1882. Cheap reprint in Everyman's Library).
Ludwig Lewisohn, ed., *Goethe, the Story of a Man,* 2 vols. (New York, 1949).
Michael Lex, *Die Idee im Drama bei Goethe, Schiller, Grillparzer, Kleist* (München, 1904).
Hippolyte Loiseau, *Goethe et la France* (Paris, 1930).
Emil Ludwig, *Goethe,* trans. by Ethel C. Mayne (New York, 1928).
Georg Lukács, *Goethe und seine Zeit* (Bonn, 1947). In French: *Goethe et son époque* (Paris, 1949).
Thomas Mann, *Freud, Goethe, Wagner* (New York, 1937).
R. M. Meyer, *Goethe,* 2 vols. (3rd ed., Berlin, 1905).
Jean Paris, *Johann Wolfgang Goethe dramaturge* (Paris, 1956).
Ronald Peacock, *Goethe's Major Plays* (New York, 1959).
Walther Rehm, *Griechentum und Goethezeit* (Bern, 3rd ed., 1952).
J. G. Robertson, *The Life and Works of Goethe 1749–1832* (London, 1932).
William Rose, ed., *Essays on Goethe* (London, 1949).
F. W. Rudloff, *Shakespeare. Schiller, and Goethe Relatively Considered* (Brighton, 1848).
George Santayana, *Three Philosophical Poets* (Cambridge, Mass., 1910).
George Simmel, *Goethe* (Berlin, 1913).
Otto Stelzer, *Goethe und die bildende Kunst* (Braunschweig, 1949).
Fritz Strich, *Goethe and World Literature* (London, 1949).
Calvin Thomas, *Goethe* (New York, 1917).
P. E. Titsworth, *The Attitude of Goethe and his School Toward French Classical Drama* (in *Jour. of Eng. and Germanic Phil.,* Oct., 1912).
Valerius Tornius, *Goethe als Dramaturg* (Leipzig, 1909).
Humphry Trevelyan, *Goethe and the Greeks* (Cambridge, Eng., 1942).
H. Viehoff, *Goethe's Leben,* 4 vols. (2nd ed., Stuttgart, 1854).
Karl Vietor, *Goethe the Poet* (Cambridge, Mass., 1949).

——, *Goethe the Thinker* (Cambridge, Mass., 1950).

Ferdinand Weinhandl, *Die Metaphysik Goethes* (Berlin, 1932).

E. M. Wilkinson and L. A. Willoughby, *Goethe, Poet and Thinker* (London, 1962)

G. Witkowsky, *Goethe* (Leipzig, 1899).

SCHLEGEL

On the drama:

Schlegel's chief contributions to dramatic theory are for the most part confined to the *Vorlesungen,* although the *Characteristiken und Kritiken* and *Kritische Scriften* include references to the subject.

Editions:

The works of Schlegel were collected by E. Böcking, who edited them as *Sämtliche Werke,* 12 vols. (1846–47). The works in French were edited, by the same, as the *Œuvres écrites en français,* 3 vols. (Leipzig, 1847). The *Vorlesungen über dramatische Kunst und Literatur* are translated as *Lectures on Dramatic Art and Literature,* by John Black (2nd ed., revised by Rev. A. J. W. Morrison, Bohn Lib. ed., London, 1914).

On Schlegel and his works:

M. Bernays, *Zur Entstehungsgeschichte des Schlegelschen Shakespeare* (Leipzig, 1872).

Bernard von Brentano, *August Wilhelm Schlegel* (Stuttgart, 1949).

August Emmersleben, *Die Antike in der romantischen Theorie: Die Gebrüder Schlegel und die Antike* (Berlin, 1937).

R. Genée, *Schlegel und Shakespeare* (Leipzig, 1905).

Anna Augusta Helmholtz, *The Indebtedness of Samuel Taylor Coleridge to August Wilhelm Schlegel* (Madison, 1907).

Josef Körner, *Die Botschaft der deutschen Romantik an Europa* (Augsburg, 1929).

——, *Romantiker und Klassiker* (Berlin, 1924).

Jean de Pange, *Schlegel et Madame de Staël* (Paris, 1938).

Wilhelm Schwartz, *A. W. Schegels Verhaltnis zur spanischen und portugiesischen Literatur* (Halle, 1913).

Hans Zehnder, *Die Anfänge von August W. Schlegels kritischer Tätigkeit* (Mulhouse, 1930).

WAGNER

On the drama:

In practically all Wagner's theoretical writings, in his letters, his autobiography, and criticisms, there are references to the drama. The most important of these are:

Das Kunstwerk der Zukunft (1849).
Oper und Drama (1851).
Eine Mittheilung an meine Freunde (1851).
Zur Widmung der zweiten Auflage von "Oper und Drama" (1868).
Ueber die Bestimmung der Oper (1871).
Ueber die Anwendung der Musik auf das Drama (1879). (These appeared as articles, letters, etc., at different times between 1835 and 1883.)

All the above are translated by William Ashton Ellis in *Richard Wagner's Prose Works,* 8 vols. (London, 1892 ff).

Selections from a number of the more characteristic writings are translated by Edward L. Burlingame in *Art Life and Theories of Richard Wagner* (New York, 1875). *The Purpose of the Opera* in this volume is a translation of *Die Bestimmung der Oper.*

Editions:

The complete works are *Gesammelte Schriften und Dichtungen von Richard Wagner,* 10 vols. (Leipzig, 1871–83). These are translated (the plays and poems omitted) as *Richard Wagner's Prose Works,* by William Ashton Ellis, 8 vols. (London, 1892–99).

On Wagner and his works:

Jacques Barzun, *Darwin, Marx, Wagner* (New York, 1941).

Paul Bekker, *Richard Wagner: His Life and Work* (New York, 1931).

Eric Bentley, *A Century of Hero-Worship* (Philadelphia, 1944).

H. S. Chamberlain, *Richard Wagner* (München, 1896. Translated as the same by G. Ainslie Hight, London, 1900).
——, *The Wagnerian Drama* (New York, 1915).
A. E. F. Dickinson, *The Musical Design of the Ring* (Oxford, 1926).
Edwin Evans, *An Introduction to the Study of Wagner's Prose Works* (London, 1913).
C. F. Glasenapp, *Das Leben Richard Wagners*, 6 vols. (3rd ed., Leipzig, 1894–1911).
E. H. Krehbiel, *Studies in the Wagnerian Drama* (New York, 1898).
Ernest Newman, *A Study of Wagner* (New York, 1899).
——, *Wagner as Man and Artist* (London, 1914).
——, *The Wagner Operas* (New York, 1949).
George Bernard Shaw, *The Perfect Wagnerite* (London, 1898).
Jack M. Stein, *Richard Wagner and the Synthesis of the Arts* (Detroit, 1960).
Richard Wagner, *Mein Leben, 2* vols. (München, 1911).
Oscar Walzel, *Richard Wagner in seiner Zeit und nach seiner Zeit* (Munich, 1913).

NIETZSCHE

Editions:

The collected works were edited by Gast and Horneffer, 20 vols. (Leipzig, 2nd ed., 1910–26). The authorized English translation was done by Oscar Levy, 18 vols. (Edinburgh & London, 1909–13).

On Nietzsche and his works:

Charles Andler, *Nietzsche, sa vie et sa pensée*, 6 vols. (Paris, 1920–31).
Eric Bentley, *A Century of Hero-Worship* (Philadelphia, 1944).
Georg Brandes, *Friedrich Nietzsche* (London, 1914).
Crane Brinton, *Nietzsche* (Cambridge, Mass., 1941).
F. Copleston, *Friedrich Nietzsche, Philosopher of Culture* (London, 1942).
Benno Filser, *Die Aesthetik Nietzsches in der Geburt der Tragödie* (Passau, n.d.).

E. Förster-Nietzsche, *The Life of Nietzsche*, 2 vols. (New York, 1912).
——, ed., *The Nietzsche-Wagner Correspondence* (New York, 1921).
Erich Heller, *The Disinherited Mind* (London, 1954).
Karl Jaspers, *Nietzsche* (Berlin, 1936).
Walter Kaufmann, *Nietzsche, Philosopher, Psychologist, Antichrist* (Princeton, 1950).
A. H. J. Knight, *Aspects of the Life and Work of Nietzsche* (Cambridge, Eng., 1933).
G. Wilson Knight, *Christ and Nietzsche* (London, 1948).
Janko Lavrin, *Nietzsche, An Approach* (London, 1949).
F. A. Lea, *The Tragic Philosopher: A Study of Friedrich Nietzsche* (New York, 1957).
Anthony Ludovici, *Nietzsche and Art* (Boston, 1912).
Thomas Mann, *Last Essays* (New York, 1959).
George A. Morgan, Jr., *What Nietzsche Means* (Cambridge, Mass., 1941).
Leo Shestov, *Tolstoi and Nietzsche* (London, 1923).
W. D. Williams, *Nietzsche and the French* (Oxford, 1952).

FREUD

Works reflecting Freud's views on art include the following in English translations:
Character and Culture (New York, 1963).
Delusion and Dream (New York, 1917; Boston, 1956).
The Interpretation of Dreams (London, 1932).
Leonardo da Vinci (New York, 1910).
On Creativity and the Unconscious (New York, 1958).
Wit and Its Relation to the Unconscious (London, 1922).

Editions:
The Standard Edition of Freud's Complete Psychological Works in 24 vols., newly translated under the general editorship of James Strachey, began publication in London, 1953.

On Freud, his works, and his approach to art:

A. A. Brill, *Freud's Contribution to Psychiatry* (New York, 1944).
L. B. Fraiberg, *Psychoanalysis and American Literary Criticism* (Detroit, 1960).
Erich Fromm, *The Forgotten Language: An Introduction to the Understanding of Dreams, Fairy Tales and Myths* (New York, 1951).
Ernest Jones, *Hamlet and Oedipus* (New York, 1949).
——, *The Life and Work of Sigmund Freud,* 3 vols. (New York, 1953–57).
Herbert Marcuse, *Eros and Civilization* (Boston, 1955).
William Phillips, ed., *Art and Psychoanalysis* (New York, 1957).
Otto Rank, *Art and the Artist* (New York, 1932).
——, *The Myth of the Birth of the Hero* (New York, 1914).
Philip Rieff, *Freud: The Mind of the Moralist* (New York, 1959).
Wayne Shumaker, *Literature and the Irrational* (Englewood Cliffs, 1960).

BRECHT

Editions:

.The following have been published so far: *Versuche,* 15 vols. (Berlin, 1930–32, 1949–57). *Stücke,* 12 vols. (Berlin, 1953—). *Theaterarbeit: 6 Aufführungen des Berliner Ensembles* (Dresden, 1952). *Schriften zum Theater* (Berlin, 1957). The most comprehensive collections of his plays in English are in *Plays,* 2 vols. (London, 1960, 1962), and *Seven Plays,* edited by Eric Bentley (New York, 1961). A few of his writings on the theatre have appeared in English in various periodicals and anthologies. See the issue of the *Tulane Drama Review* devoted to Brecht (Autumn, 1961).

On Brecht and his works:

Eric Bentley, *The Playwright as Thinker* (New York, 1946). (See also Bentley's other books.)
Peter Demetz, ed., *Brecht* (Englewood Cliffs, 1962).
Jacques Desuche, *Bertolt Brecht* (Paris, 1963).
Bernard Dort, *Lecture de Brecht* (Paris, 1960).
Martin Esslin, *Brecht* (New York, 1960).
Ronald Gray, *Bertolt Brecht* (Edinburgh, 1961).
Reinhold Grimm, *Bertolt Brecht* (Stuttgart, 1961).
——, *Bertolt Brecht: Die Struktur seines Werkes* (Nuremberg, 1959).
Werner Hecht, *Brechts Weg sum epischen Theater* (Berlin, 1962).
Walter Hink, *Die Dramaturgie des späten Brecht* (Göttingen, 1959).
Volker Klotz, *Bertolt Brecht: Versuch über das Werk* (Darmstadt, 1957).
Hans Mayer, *Bertolt Brecht und die Tradition* (Pfullingen, 1961).
Siegfried Melchinger et al., *Das ärgernis Brecht* (Basel, 1961).
Ernst Schumacher, *Die dramatischen Versuche Bertolt Brechts 1918–1933* (Berlin, 1955).
Geneviève Serreau, *Bertolt Brecht dramaturge* (Paris, 1954).
Sinn und Form (Berlin, 1949, 1957: special issues of Brecht).
Walter Weideli, *The Art of Bertolt Brecht* (New York, 1963).
John Willett, *The Theatre of Bertolt Brecht* (London, 1959).

DUERRENMATT

Editions:

The Visit has been published in the English adaptation by Maurice Valency (New York, 1958), and in the translation by Patrick Bowles (New York, 1962). *The Physicists* has been translated by James Kirkup (New York, 1964). None of the other plays have yet appeared in translation, though several novels have.

On Duerrenmatt and his works:

Hans Banziger, *Frisch und Dürrenmatt* (Bern, 1960).
Elizabeth Brock-Sulzer, *Dürrenmatt* (Zurich, 1960).

SCANDINAVIA

General works on Scandinavian literature:

Harald Beyer, *A History of Norwegian Literature* (New York, 1956).
Frederika Blankner, ed., *The History of the Scandinavian Literatures* (New York, 1938).
Illit Gr⌀ndahl and Ola Raknes, *Chapters in Norwegian Literature* (London, 1923).
Alrik Gustafson, *A History of Swedish Literature* (Minneapolis, 1961).
Theodore Jorgenson, *History of Norwegian Literature* (New York, 1933).
P. Mitchell, *A History of Danish Literature* (New York, 1958).
H. G. Topsöe-Jensen, *Scandinavian Literature from Brandes to Our Day* (New York, 1939).

IBSEN

Editions:

The collected works were translated by William Archer et al., 10 vols. (London, 1906–12).
Muriel C. Bradbrook, *Ibsen the Norwegian* (London, 1946).
Georg Brandes, *Henrik Ibsen, Bjørnstjerne Bjørnson* (London, 1899).
Brian W. Downs, *Ibsen: The Intellectual Background* (Cambridge, Eng., 1946).
——, *A Study of Six Plays by Ibsen* (Cambridge, Eng., 1960).
Angel Flores, ed., *Ibsen: A Marxist Analysis* (New York, 1937).
Edmund Gosse, *Ibsen* (London, 1907).
Henrik Jaeger, *Henrik Ibsen* (London, 1890).
G. Wilson Knight, *Henrik Ibsen* (New York, 1962).
Halvdan Koht, *The Life of Ibsen*, 2 vols. (New York, 1931).
F. L. Lucas, *Ibsen and Strindberg* (London, 1962).

James W. McFarlane, *Ibsen and the Temper of Norwegian Literature* (London, 1960).
John Northam, *Ibsen's Dramatic Method* (London, 1953).
George Bernard Shaw, *The Quintessence of Ibsenism* (London, 1891).

P. F. D. Tennant, *Ibsen's Dramatic Technique* (Cambridge, Eng., 1948).
Hermann J. Weigand, *The Modern Ibsen* (New York, 1925).
Adolph E. Zucker, *Ibsen, the Master Builder* (London, 1929).

STRINDBERG

Editions:

The standard edition is the *Samlade Skrifter,* edited by J. Landquist, 55 vols. (Stockholm, 1912–21).

On Strindberg and his works:

Arthur Adamov, *Strindberg dramaturge* (Paris, 1955).
Joan Bulman, *Strindberg and Shakespeare* (London, 1933).
G. A. Campbell, *Strindberg* (New York, 1933).
Carl E. W. L. Dahlström, *Strindberg's Dramatic Expressionism* (Ann Arbor, 1930).
Walter Johnson, *Strindberg and the Historical Drama* (Seattle, 1963).
F. L. Lucas, *Ibsen and Strindberg* (London, 1962).
B. G. Madsen, *Strindberg's Naturalistic Theatre* (Seattle, 1962).
Brita M. E. Mortensen and Brian W. Downs, *Strindberg: An Introduction to His Life and Works* (Cambridge, Eng., 1949).
Elizabeth Sprigge, *The Strange Life of August Strindberg* (New York, 1949).

RUSSIA

General works on Russian literature:

Vera Alexandrovna, *A History of Soviet Literature 1917–1962* (New York, 1963).
Vissarion Belinsky, Nicolay Chernyshevsky, and Nicolay Dobrolyubov, *Selected Criticism* (New York, 1962).

Jospeh Freeman, J. Kunitz, and L. Lozo-
wick, *Voices of October: Art and
Literature in Soviet Literature* (New
York, 1930).

Richard Hare, *Russian Literature from
Pushkin to the Present Day* (London.
1947).

D. S. Mirsky, *A History of Russian Literature*, ed. by Francis J. Whitfield
(New York, 1949).

·Helen Muchnic, *From Gorky to Paster
nak* (New York, 1961).

——, *An Introduction to Russian Literature* (New York, 1947).

George Reavey, *Soviet Literature To-
Day* (London, 1946).

E. J. Simmons, *An Outline of Modern
Russian Literature (1880–1940)* (Ithaca, 1943).

Marc Slonim, *The Epic of Russian Literature: From Its Origins through Tolstoy* (New York, 1950).

——, *Modern Russian Literature: From
Chekhov to the Present* (New York,
1953).

Ivar Spector, *The Golden Age of Russian Literature* (Caldwell, Ida., 1943).

Gleb Struve, *25 Years of Soviet Russian Literature (1918–1943)* (London,
1944).

Leon Trotsky, *Literature and Revolution* (New York, 1925).

References on the drama:

Alexander Bakshy, *The Path of the Modern Russian Stage* (Boston, 1918).

Faubion Bowers, *Broadway, U.S.S.R.*
(New York, 1959).

Ben W. Brown, *Theatre at the Left*
(Providence, 1938).

Huntly Carter, *The New Spirit in the
Russian Theatre, 1917–1928* (London,
1929).

H. W. L. Dana, *Drama in Wartime Russia* (New York, 1943).

——, *Handbook on Soviet Drama* (New
York, 1938).

René Fülöp-Miller and Joseph Gregor,
The Russian Theatre (Philadelphia,
1930).

Nikolai A. Gorchakov, *The Theatre in
Soviet Russia* (New York, 1957).

Norris Houghton, *Moscow Rehearsals*
(New York, 1936).

——, *Return Engagement* (New York,
1962).

Joseph MacLeod, *Actors Cross the Volga*

(London, 1946).

——, *The New Soviet Theatre* (London,
1943).

P. A. Markov, *The Soviet Theatre* (London, 1934).

Vsevolod Meyerhold, *Le Théâtre thé-
âtral* (Paris, 1963).

Vladimir Nemirovich-Danchenko, *My
Life in the Russian Theatre* (London,
1937).

Oliver M. Sayler, *Inside the Moscow Art
Theatre* (New York, 1925).

——, *The Russian Theatre* (New York,
1920, 1922, 1923).

Marc Slonim, *Russian Theatre: From
the Empire to the Soviets* (New York,
1961).

André Van Gyseghem, *Theatre in Soviet
Russia* (London, 1943).

Leo Wiener, *The Contemporary Drama
of Russia* (Boston, 1924).

Peter Yershov, *Comedy in the Soviet
Theater* (New York, 1956).

CHEKHOV

On Chekhov and his works:

W. H. Bruford, *Chekhov* (London,
1957).

——, *Chekhov and His Russia* (London,
1947).

William Gerhardi, *Anton Chekhov* (New
York, 1923).

Ronald Hingley, *Chekhov* (London,
1950).

S. S. Koteliansky, ed., *Anton Chekhov:
Literary and Theatrical Reminiscences*
(London, 1927).

—— and P. Tomlinson, *Life and Letters
of Anton Chekhov* (New York, 1925).

David Magarshack, *Chekhov: A Life*
(New York, 1953).

——, *Chekhov the Dramatist* (London,
1952).

Ernest Simmons, *Chekhov: A Biography*
(Boston, 1962).

Vladimir Yermilov, *A. P. Chekhov* (Moscow, n.d.).

STANISLAVSKY

On the drama:

An Actor Prepares (New York, 1948).
Building a Character (New York, 1949).

Creating a Role (New York, 1961).
My Life in Art (Boston, 1924).
The Seagull Produced by Stanislavsky (New York, 1952).
Stanislavsky on the Art of the Stage (London, 1950).
Stanislavsky Produces Othello (London, 1948).
Stanislavski's Legacy (New York, 1958).

On Stanislavsky:

Nikolai M. Gorchakov, *Stanislavsky Directs* (New York, 1954).
Robert Lewis, *Method—Or Madness?* (New York, 1958).
David Magarshack, *Stanislavsky* (London, 1953).

Charles Marowitz, *The Method as Means* (London, 1961).

PLEKHANOV

On the drama:

Art and Society (New York, 1936).
"Ibsen, Petty Bourgeois Revolutionist" in *Ibsen: A Marxist Analysis,* ed. by Angel Flores (New York, 1937).

On Plekhanov:

S. H. Baron, *Plekhanov* (Stanford, 1963).

FRANCE—NINETEENTH AND TWENTIETH CENTURIES

General references on nineteenth- and twentieth-century French literature:

Anna Balakian, *Literary Origins of Surrealism* (New York, 1947).
A. Bailly, *L'Époque contemporaine* (Paris, 1956).
——, *L'Époque 1900* (Paris, 1951).
P. de Boisdeffre, *Métamorphose de la littérature,* 2 vols. (Paris, 1950–51).
J.-P. Charpentier, *La Littérature française au XIXe siècle* (Paris, 1875).
H. Clouard, *Histoire de la littérature française du symbolisme à nos jours, 1885 à 1940* (Paris, 1940).
Emile Faguet, *Le Dix-neuvième siècle* (Paris, 1887).
Wallace Fowlie, *Age of Surrealism* (Denver, 1950).
——, *A Guide to Contemporary French Literature* (New York, 1957).
Marcel Girardi, *Guide illustré de la littérature française moderne, 1918–1949* (Paris, 1949, 1954).
C. Le Goffic, *La Littérature française au XIXe siècle* (Paris, 1910).
R. Lalou, *Histoire de la littérature française contemporaine,* 2 vols. (Paris, 1941).
Georges Lemaître, *From Cubism to Surrealism in French Literature* (Cambridge, Mass., 1941).
G. Pellissier, *Le Mouvement littéraire au XIXe siècle* (5th ed., Paris, 1898).

——, *Etudes de Littérature contemporaine,* 2 series (Paris, 1901).
Marcel Raymond, *From Baudelaire to Surrealism* (New York, 1949).
Roger Shattuck, *The Banquet Years* (New York, 1958).
M. Souriau, *Histoire du romantisme en France,* 3 vols. (Paris, 1927–28).
F. Strowski, *Histoire de la littérature française au XIXe siècle* (Paris, 1912).
A. Thibaudet, *Histoire de la littérature française de 1789 à nos jours* (Paris, 1936).
Hugo P. Thième, *Guide bibliographique de la Littérature française de 1800 à 1906* (Paris, 1907).
Edmund Wilson, *Axel's Castle* (New York, 1931).

References on nineteenth- and twentieth-century French drama:

André Antoine, *Mes Souvenirs sur le Théâtre Libre* (Paris, 1921).
N. C. Arvin, *Eugène Scribe and the French Theatre 1815–1860* (Cambridge, Mass., 1924).
J. Barbey D'Aurevilly, *Le Théâtre contemporan,* 3 vols. (Paris, 1887–92).
Jean-Louis Barrault, *Reflections on the Theatre* (London, 1951).
——, *The Theatre of Jean-Louis Barrault* (New York, 1961).
Henri-Martin Barzun, *L'Ere du drame*

(Paris, 1912).

Henry Bataille, *Ecrits sur le théâtre* (Paris, 1917).

Marc Beigbeder, *Le Théâtre en France depuis la liberation* (Paris, 1959).

A. Benoist, *Essais de critique dramatique* (Paris, 1898).

——, *Le Théâtre d'aujourd'hui*, 2 vols. (Paris, 1911).

Léon Blum, *Au Théâtre*, 4 vols. (Paris, 1906ff).

Robert Brasillach, *Animateurs de théâtre* (Paris, 1936, 1954).

Adolphe Brisson, *Le Théâtre* (Paris, annually from 1907 to date).

Pierre Brisson, *Au Hasard des soirées* (Paris, 1935).

——, *Propos de théâtre* (Paris, 1957).

——, *Le Théâtre des années folles* (Geneva, 1943).

Ferdinand Brunetière, *Essais sur la littérature contemporaine* (Paris, 1892).

Alfred Capus, *Le Théâtre* (Paris, n.d.).

——, *Notre époque et le théâtre* (Paris, 1906).

Frank W. Chandler, *The Contemporary Drama of France* (Boston, 1920).

Joseph Chiari, *The Contemporary French Theatre: The Flight from Naturalism* (Lodon, 1958).

Barrett H. Clark, *Four Plays of the Free Theater*. Preface by Brieux (Cincinnati, 1915).

——, *Contemporary French Dramatists* (2nd ed., Cincinnati, 1916).

——, *The Continental Drama of Today* (2nd ed., New York, 1914).

——, *A Study of the Modern Drama* (2nd ed., New York, 1928).

Jacques Copeau, *Critiques d'un autre temps* (Paris, 1923).

——, *Souvenirs du Vieux-Colombier* (Paris, 1931).

A. Delaforest, *Théâtre moderne. Cours de littérature dramatique*, 2 vols. (Paris, 1836).

M. Descotes, *Le Drame romantique et ses grands créateurs* (Paris, 1955).

F. W. M. Draper, *The Rise and Fall of the French Romantic Drama* (New York, n.d.).

Alexandre Dumas, *Mes Mémoires* (Paris, 1852–54).

——, *Souvenirs dramatiques* (Paris, 1868).

D. O. Evans, *Le Théâtre pendant le période romantiaue* (Paris, 1925).

Emile Faguet, *Notes sur le théâtre contemporain,* 7 vols. (Paris, 1889–95).

——, *Propos de théâtre*, 5 vols. (Paris, 1903–10).

——, *Drame ancien, Drame moderne* (Paris, 1898).

Augustin Filon, *De Dumas à Rostand* (Paris, 1898. Translated as *Modern French Drama* by Janet E. Hogarth, London, 1898).

C. Formentin, *Essais sur les origines du drame moderne en France* (Aix, 1879).

Wallace Fowlie, *Dionysus in France: A Guide to Contemporary French Theatre* (New York, 1960).

R. Gallet, *L'Art nouveau au Théâtre libre* (Paris, 1890).

Jean-Jacques Gautier, *Deux Fauteuils d'orchestre* (Paris, 1962).

——, *Paris-sur-Scène* (Paris, 1951).

Théophile Gautier, *Histoire de l'art dramatique en France depuis 25 ans,* 6 vols. (Paris, 1858–59).

——, *Souvenirs de théâtre, d'art et de critique* (Paris, 1883).

Henri Gouhier, *L'Essence du théâtre* (Paris, 1943).

——, *L'Œuvre théâtrale* (Paris, 1958).

——, *Le Théâtre et l'existence* (Paris, 1952).

C. M. Des Granges, *La Comédie et les mœurs sous la Restauration et la monarchie de juillet* (Paris, 1904).

——, *Geoffroy et la critique dramatique sous le Consulat et l'Empire* (1800–1814) (Paris, 1897).

David 1. Grossvogel, *The Self-Conscious Stage in Modern French Drama* (New York, 1958). Reprinted, 1961, as *20th Century French Drama.*

——, *Four Playwrights and a Postscript* (Ithaca, 1962).

J. Guex, *Le Théâtre et la société française de 1815 à 1848* (Vévey, 1900).

Jacques Guicharnaud (with June Beckelman), *Modern French Theatre from Giraudoux to Beckett* (New Haven, 1961).

Harold Hobson, *The French Theatre of Today* (London, 1953).

Jules Janin, *Histoire de l'art dramatique,* 6 vols. (Paris, 1853–58).

Gertrude R. Jasper, *Adventure in the Theatre: Lugné-Poë and the Théâtre de l'Œuvre to 1899* (New Brunswick, 1947).

Louis Jouvet, *Témoignages sur le théâtre* (Paris, 1952).

Jean Jullien, *Le Théâtre vivant*, 2 vols. (Paris, 1892–96).

Armand Kahn, *Le Théâtre social en France* (Paris, 1907).

Robert Kemp, *La Vie du théâtre* (Paris, 1956).

René Lalou, *Le Théâtre en France depuis 1900* (Paris, 1958).

Gustave Larroumet, *Etudes de critique dramatique*, 2 vols. (Paris, 1892).

——, *Nouvelles études d'histoire et de critique dramatique* (Paris, 1899).

A. Le Breton, *Le Théâtre romantique* (Paris, 1922).

Jules Lemaître, *Impressions de théâtre*, 10 vols. (Paris, 1888–98).

——, *Theatrical Impressions* (London, 1924).

——, *Théories et impressions* (Paris, 1903).

Charles Lenient, *La Comédie en France au XIXe siècle*, 2 vols. (Paris, 1898).

Eugène Lintilhac, *La Comédie: De la Révolution au Second Empire* (Paris, 1909).

——, *Conférences dramatiques* (Paris, 1898).

Gabriel Marcel, *L'Heure théâtrale* (Paris, 1960).

Brander Matthews, *French Dramatists of the Nineteenth Century* (4th ed., New York, 1905).

Charles Maurice, *Histoire anécdotique du théâtre*, etc., 2 vols. (Paris, 1856).

E. Mazères, *Comédies et souvenirs* (Paris, 1855).

Catulle Mendes, *L'Art au théâtre*, 3 vols. (Paris, 1896–98).

E. Montégut, *Dramaturges et romanciers* (Paris, 1890).

Édouard Noël et Edmond Stoullig, *Les Annales du théâtre et de la musique* (Paris, annual volumes since 1875).

H. Parigot, *Le Théâtre d'hier* (Paris, 1893).

Leonard Cabell Pronko, *Avant-Garde: The Experimental Theater in France* (Berkeley, 1962).

Oreste F. Pucciani, ed., *The French Theater since 1930* (Boston, 1954).

Romain Rolland, *Le Théâtre du peuple* (Paris, 1903. Translated by Barrett H. Clark, as *The People's Theater*, New York, 1918).

E. de Saint-Auban, *L'Idée sociale au théâtre* (Paris, 1901).

Paul de Saint-Victor, *Les Deux masques*, 3 vols. (Paris, 1867).

——, *Le Théâtre contemporain* (Paris, 1889).

Francisque Sarcey, *Quarante ans de théâtre*, 8 vols. (Paris, 1900–02).

A. Séché and Jules Bertaut, *L'Evolution du théâtre contemporain* (Paris, 1908).

Edmond Sée, *Petits dialogues sur le théâtre et l'art dramatique* (Paris, 1913).

Pierre Henri Simon, *Théâtre-Destin* (Paris, 1959).

H. A. Smith, *Main Currents of Modern French Drama* (New York, 1925).

A. Soubies, *Le Théâtre en France de 1871 à 1892* (Paris, 1893).

A. Thalasso, *Le Théâtre libre* (Paris, 1909).

Pierre-Aimé Touchard, *Dionysos, apologie pour le théâtre* (Paris, 1949).

François Veuillot, *Les Prédicateurs de la scène* (Paris, 1904).

Jean Vilar, *De la tradition théâtrale* (Paris, 1955).

S. M. Waxman, *Antoine and the Théâtre Libre* (Cambridge, Mass., 1926).

J.-J. Weiss, *Le Théâtre et les mœurs* (Paris, 1889).

——, *Trois années de théâtre (1883–85)*, 4 vols. (Paris, 1892–96).

Emile Zola, *Le Naturalisme au théâtre* (Paris, 1881).

——, *Nos Auteurs dramatiques* (Paris, 1881).

References on criticism:

Irving Babbitt, *Masters of Modern French Criticism* (Boston, 1912).

Alexandre Belis, *La Critique française à la fin du XIXe siècle* (Paris, 1926).

Maurice Eloy, *Critiques d'aujourd'hui* (Paris, 1889).

A. Michiels, *Histoire des idées littéraires en France au dix-neuvième siècle, et de leurs origines dans les siècles antérieurs* (4th ed., Paris, 1863).

Georges Renard, *Les Princes de la jeune critique* (Paris, 1890).

Ernest Tissot, *Les Evolutions de la critique française* (Paris, 1890).

STENDHAL

Editions:

The most recent edition of his collected works is the Divan edition, 79 vols. (Paris, 1926–37). *Racine and Shake-*

speare, with a foreword by André Maurois (New York, 1962), was translated by Guy Daniels.

On Stendhal and his works:

Paul Arbelet, *La Jeunesse de Stendhal* (Paris, 1919).

Léon Blum, *Stendhal et le Beylisme* (Paris, 1930).

Victor Brombert, ed., *Stendhal* (Englewood Cliffs, 1962).

Jean Dutourd, *The Man of Sensibility* (New York, 1961).

Harry Levin, *Toward Stendhal* (Murray, Utah, 1945).

Vittorio del Litto, *La Vie intellectuelle de Stendhal* (Paris, 1959).

Henri Martineau, *Le Cœur de Stendhal,* 2 vols. (Paris, 1952, 1953).

Jean Prévost, *La Création chez Stendhal* (Paris, 1951).

HUGO

On the drama:

Preface to *Cromwell* (originally published in the separate volume of the play, Paris, 1827).
Preface to *Hernani* (1830).
Preface to *Marion de Lorme* (1831).
Preface to *Le Roi s'amuse* (1832).
Preface to *Lucrèce Borgia* (1833).
Preface to *Marie Tudor* (1833).
Preface to *Angelo* (1835).
Preface to *La Esmeralda* (1836).
Preface to *Ruy Blas* (1838).
Preface to *Les Burgraves* (1843).
William Shakespeare (Paris, 1864).

Editions:

The definitive edition of the complete works — exclusive of the posthumous pieces — is the *Œuvres complètes,* 46 vols. (Paris, 1880–85). The *Théâtre,* in 4 vols. (Paris, 1867), contains all the prefaces, and all but the latest plays. *William Shakespeare* was published in Paris in 1864. The plays are translated by various hands, in the *Dramatic Works* of Hugo, 3 vols. (latest ed., Boston, 1909). This edition contains all the prefaces. *William Shakespeare* is translated by Melville B. Anderson (Chicago, 1887). Maurice Souriau edits a critical edition of the *Préface*

de Cromwell (Paris, 1897). There is another edition, by J. R. Ettinger, Jr.: *Préface de Cromwell and Hernani* (Chicago, 1900), and one by E. Wahl (Oxford, 1909).

On Hugo and his works:

A. Acerra, *Influenza di A. Manzoni sopra V. Hugo nelle dottrine drammatiche* (Napoli, 1907).

Alfred Asseline, *Victor Hugo intime* (Paris, 1885).

Alfred Barbou, *Victor Hugo et son temps* (Paris, 1881. Translated as *Victor Hugo and his Time,* by Ellen E. Frewer, New York, 1882).

J.-B. Barrère, *La Fantaisie de Victor Hugo* (Paris, 1949).

——, *Hugo, l'homme et l'œuvre* (Paris, 1952).

P. Berret, *Victor Hugo* (Paris, 1927).

Eugene Blanchet, *Victor Hugo et la renaissance théâtrale au XIXe siècle* (Meaux, 1879).

James Cappon, *Victor Hugo; a Memoir and a Study* (Edinburgh, 1885).

J. Ch. Dabas, *A Propos de Shakespeare ou le nouveau livre de Victor Hugo* (Bordeaux, 1864).

J. Gaudon, *Hugo dramaturge* (Paris, 1955).

Théophile Gautier, *Histoire du Romantisme* (Paris, 1874).

P. et V. Glachant, *Essai critique sur le théâtre de Victor Hugo,* 2 vols. (Paris, 1902–03).

E. M. Grant, *The Career of Victor Hugo* (Cambridge, Mass., 1945).

F. Gregh, *L'Œuvre de Victor Hugo* (Paris, 1933).

Henri Guillemin, *Victor Hugo par lui-même* (Paris, 1951).

Matthew Josephson, *Victor Hugo* (New York, 1942).

Albert Le Roy, *L'Aube du théâtre romantique* (Paris, 1904).

G. Lote, *En Préface à Hernani, cent ans après* (Paris, 1930).

Jules Marsan, *Le Théâtre historique et le Romantisme* (1818–1829) (in *Rev. d'Hist. lit. de la France,* Paris, 1910).

W. Martin, *Victor Hugos dramatische Technik* (in the *Zeitschrift für französische Sprache,* etc., 1904–05).

Frank T. Marzials, *Life of Victor Hugo* (London, 1888).

Brander Matthews, *French Dramatists of the Nineteenth Century* (4th ed., New York, 1905).

André Maurois, *Olympio, the Life of Victor Hugo* (New York, 1956).

Emile Montégut, *Mélanges critiques* (Paris, 1888).

Pierre Nebout, *Le Drame romantique* (Paris, 1895).

——, *Victor Hugo* (in *Hommes et idées du XIXe siècle*, Paris, 1903).

W. D. Pendell, *Victor Hugo's Acted Dramas and the Contemporary Press* (Baltimore, 1957).

Charles Renouvier, *Victor Hugo le philosophe* (Paris, 1900).

——, *Victor Hugo le poète* (Paris, 1893).

Charles-Albert Rossé, *Les Théories littéraires de Victor Hugo* (Délémont, 1903).

P. Souchon, *Auteur de Ruy Blas* (Paris, 1939).

M. Souriau, *La Préface de Cromwell* (n.d.).

M.-A. Souriau, *De la Convention dans la tragédie et dans le drame romantique* (Paris, 1885).

Paul Stapfer, *Racine et Victor Hugo* (Paris, 1887).

Algernon Charles Swinburne, *A Study of Victor Hugo* (London, 1886).

John Hayward Thomas, *L'Angleterre dans l'œuvre de Victor Hugo* (Paris, 1933).

DUMAS FILS

On the drama:

Au Lecteur, in vol. 1 of the *Théâtre complet* (Paris, 1868).

A Propos de la Dame aux camélias (1867).

Prefatory note to *Diane de Lys* (1868).

A Henri Lavoix, prefatory note to *Le Bijou de la Reine* (1868).

Avant-Propos to *Le Demi-Monde* (1868).

A Charles Marchal, preface to *La Question d'argent* (1868).

Préface to *Le Fils naturel* (1868).

Préface to *Un Père prodigue* (1868).

Préface to *l'Ami des femmes* (1869).

Préface to *Les Idées de Madame Aubray* (1870).

Préface to *Une Visite de noces* (1871).

Au Public, preface to *La Princesse Georges* (1877).

A M. Cuvillier-Fleury, preface to *La Femme de Claude* (1873).

Préface to *Monsieur Alphonse* (1873).

Préface to *L'Etrangère* (1879).

Notes de la Princesse de Bagdad (1892).

Notes sur Denise (1892).

Notes sur Francillon (1892).

Préface to *Le Théâtre des autres*, vol. 1 (1894).

Préface to *Un Mariage dans un chapeau* (1894).

Préface to *Le Supplice d'une femme* (1894).

Préface to *Héloïse Paranquet* (1894).

Préface to vol. 2 of the *Théâtre des autres* (1895).

The *Edition des Comédiens* of the *Théâtre complet*, 7 vols. (Paris, 1895), contains new prefaces and notes which have since been collected into a single volume (*Notes*), and included in the regular edition of the *Théâtre complet* as vol. 8 (n.d.).

Miscellaneous essays, many of them on the drama, are collected in the *Entr'actes*, 3 vols. (Paris, 1877–79), and the single volume of *Nouveaux Entr' actes* (Paris, 1890).

Dumas fils wrote prefaces to some forty books, a complete list of which is found in Carlos M. Noël's *Les Idées sociales dans le théâtre de A. Dumas fils* (Paris, 1912).

Editions:

The Calmann-Lévy edition of the *Théâtre complet*, in 8 vols. (Paris, 1895), is the authoritative edition for plays and prefaces. The same publishers also issue the *Entr' actes* in 3, and the *Nouveaux Entr' actes* in 1 vol. (see latest editions). The only preface that has appeared in English is that to *Un Père prodigue*, translated by Barrett H. Clark, as *The Technic of Playwriting* (in *The Drama*, Chicago, Feb., 1917).

On Dumas fils and his works:

Antoine Benoist, *Essais de critique dramatique* (Paris, 1898).

Paul Bourget, *Nouveaux essais de psychologie contemporaine* (Paris, 1885).

René Doumic, *Portraits d'écrivains* (Paris, 1892).

——, *De Scribe à Ibsen* (Paris, 1896).

Augustin Filon, *De Dumas à Rostand* (Paris, 1898).

Anatole France, *M. Alexandre Dumas moraliste* (in *La Vie littéraire*, I, Paris, 1888. Translated by A. W. Evans as *On Life and Letters*, First Series, London and New York, 1911).

Théophile Gautier, *Portraits contemporains et questions actuelles* (Paris, 1873).

Léopold Lacour, *Trois Théâtres* (Paris, 1880).

H. de Lapommeraye, *Histoire du début d'A. Dumas fils au théâtre* (Paris, 1873).

Jules Lemaître, *Impressions de théâtre*, V and VI (Paris, 1892).

Brander Matthews, *French Dramatists of the Nineteenth Century* (4th ed., New York, 1905).

Carlos M. Noël, *Les Idées sociales dans le théâtre de A. Dumas fils* (Paris, 1912).

Hippolyte Parigot, *Le Théâtre d'hier* (Paris, 1893).

Paul de Saint-Victor, *Théâtre contemporain* (Paris, 1889).

H. Stanley Schwarz, *Alexandre Dumas, fils, Dramatist* (New York, 1927).

Frank A. Taylor, *The Theatre of Alexandre Dumas Fils* (Oxford, 1937).

Emile Zola, *Nos Auteurs dramatiques* (Paris, 1881).

ZOLA

On the drama:

Préface to the *Théâtre* (Paris, 1878).
Préface to *Thérèse Raquin* (1873).
Préface to *Les Héritiers Rabourdin* (1874).
Préface to *Le Bouton de rose* (1874).
Le Naturalisme au théâtre (Paris, 1881).
Nos Auteurs dramatiques (Paris, 1881).

Editions:

The *Théâtre*, in a single volume, and the collected essays, *Nos Auteurs dramatiques* and *Le Naturalisme au Théâtre*, have been frequently reprinted. The dates of original appearance are indicated above.

On Zola and his works:

G. Bornhack, *Zola als Dramatiker* (in *Zeitschrift für französische Sprache und Literatur*, vol. II, 1889).

F. L. Doucet, *L'Esthétique de Zola et son application à la critique* (The Hague, 1923).

Emile Faguet, *Zola* (Paris, 1903).

F. W. Hemmings, *Emile Zola* (Oxford, 1953).

Abel Hermant, *Essais de critique* (Paris, 1913).

Matthew Josephson, *Zola and His Time* (New York, 1928).

Jules Lemaître, *Impressions de théâtre*, vol. 7 (6th ed., Paris, 1901).

P. Martino, *Le Naturalisme français* (Paris, 1923).

Brander Matthews, *French Dramatists of the Nineteenth Century* (4th ed., New York, 1905)

Georges Pellissier, *Emile Zola* (in *Nouveaux Essais de littérature contemporaire*, Paris, 1895).

F. Sarcey, *Quarante ans de théâtre*, vol. 7 (Paris, 1902).

Angus Wilson, *Emile Zola* (London, 1952).

BRUNETIÈRE

On the drama:

Dernières recherches sur la vie de Molière (1877).
Voltaire (1878).
Les Ennemis de Racine au XVII⁰ siècle (1879).
La Comédie de Marivaux (1881).
Le Théâtre de la Révolution (1881).
La Tragédie de Racine (1884).
Marivaux (1884).
Trois Moliéristes (1885).
A propos du Théâtre chinois (1886).
Le Théâtre de Voltaire (1886).
Sur Victor Hugo (1886).
Voltaire (1886).
L'Esthétique de Boileau (1889).
Le Naturalisme au théâtre (1889).
Alexandre Hardy (1890).
La Philosophie de Molière (1890).
La Réforme du théâtre (1890).
Octave Feuillet (1890).
Voltaire (1890).
L'Evolution des genres dans l'histoire de la littérature, tome 1. Introduction. Evolution de la critique depuis la

Renaissance jusqu'à nos jours (1890).
Pierre Corneille (1891).
Victor Hugo après 1830 (1891).
Les Epoques du Théâtre français (1892).
La Loi du théâtre (1894).
La Doctrine évolutive et l'histoire de la littérature (1898).
L'Evolution d'un genre: la Tragédie (1901).

Mélodrame ou tragédie? (1904).
Les Epoques de la Comédie de Molière (1906).

The first fourteen essays in the above list are reprinted in the *Etudes critiques sur l'histoire de la littérature française*, 8 vols. (Paris, 1880 ff.); *Les Epoques du Théâtre français* was published in Paris in 1892; *L'Evolution des genres*, etc., of which only one volume appeared, Paris, 1890; *La Loi du théâtre* as a preface to Noël and Stoullig's *Les Annales du théâtre et de la musique*, 1894; *Le Naturalisme au théâtre* and *La Réforme du théâtre* in *Essais sur la littérature contemporaine*, 1892; *Mélodrame ou tragédie?*, in *Variétés littéraires*, 1904; *Voltaire* in the posthumous *Etudes sur le XVIIIe siècle*, 1911; *Victor Hugo après 1830* and *Octave Feuillet* in *Nouveaux essais sur la littérature contemporaine*, 1895; the last five in volumes 2 and 3 of *Histoire et littérature*, 3 vols., 1898. Occasional references to the drama are also found in Brunetière's *Manuel de l'histoire de la littérature française* (1898), *Histoire de la littérature française classique*, 3 vols. (1903 and ff.), *Victor Hugo*, 2 vols. (1902), and his various prefaces to *Boileau Déspreaux* (1889) *Pierre Corneille: Chefs-d'œuvre* (1894), etc. *La Loi du théâtre* is translated as *The Law of the Drama*, by Philip M. Hayden, with an introduction by Henry Arthur Jones (Dramatic Museum of Columbia University, New York, 1914). *Brunetière's Essays in French Literature* (a selection) is translated by D. N. Smith (New York, 1898); and the *Manuel* as *Manual of French Literature*, translated by R. D. Derechef (New York, 1898).

On Brunetière and his works:

William Archer, *Playwriting* (Boston, 1912).
Irving Babbitt, *The Masters of Modern French Criticism* (Boston, 1912).

Victor Basch, *Les Idées de M. Brunetière* (in *La Grande revue*, Paris, 1899).
L.-J. Bondy, *Le Classicisme de Ferdinand Brunetière* (Baltimore, 1930).
Barrett H. Clark, *The Continental Drama of To-day* (2nd ed., New York, 1914).
——, *The British and American Drama of To-day* (New York, 1914).
Ernst Robert Curtius, *Ferdinand Brunetière: Beitrag zur Geschichte des französischen Kritik* (Strassburg, 1914).
René Doumic, *Ferdinand Brunetière* (in *Ecrivains d'aujourd'hui*, Paris, 1894)
Victor Giraud, *Ferdinand Brunetière* (in the *Revue des deux mondes*, Paris, 1908).
Clayton Hamilton, *The Theory of the Theatre* (New York, 1910).
——, *Studies in Stagecraft* (New York, 1914).
——, *Problems of the Playwright* (New York, 1917).
Elton Hocking, *Ferdinand Brunetière: The Evolution of a Critic* (Madison, 1936).
Henry Arthur Jones, *Introduction* to the translation of *The Law of the Drama* (see above).
Brander Matthews, *The Development of the Drama* (New York, 1903).
——, *A Study of the Drama* (Boston, 1910).
Jacques Nonteuil, *Ferdinand Brunetière* (Paris, 1933).
L. R. Richard, *F. Brunetière* (Paris, 1905).
Melchior de Vogüe, *Ferdinand Brunetière* (in the *Revue des deux mondes*, Paris, 1907).

BERGSON

On Bergson and his work:

A. O. Lovejoy, *Bergson and Romantic Evolutionism* (Berkeley, 1914).
Louise Mathewson, *Bergson's Theory of the Comic in the Light of English Comedy* (Lincoln, 1920).
A. Szathmary, *The Aesthetic Theory of Bergson* (Cambridge, Mass., 1937).

MAETERLINCK

On the drama:

Letter inserted in the program of Van
Lerberghe's *Les Flaireurs* (1892).
Article on Ibsen (1894).
Menus Propos. Le Théâtre (1890).
Préface to Alfred Sutro's *The Cave of
Illusion* (1900).
Preface to Maeterlinck's *Théâtre* (I)
(1901).
Le Tragique quotidien (1896).
L'Etoile (1896).
Le Réveil de l'âme (1896).
Préface to *The Plays of Maurice Mae-
terlinck,* 2nd series (1896).
La Sagesse et la destinée (1898).
Le Drame moderne (1904).
A Propos du " Roi Lear" (1907).
Preface to Maeterlinck's translation of
Macbeth (1910).

Editions:

The volumes of collected essays in which
the above are included are: *Le
Trésor des humbles* (Paris, 1896); *La
Sagesse et la destinée* (Paris, 1898);
Le Temple enseveli (Paris, 1902); *Le
double Jardin* (Paris, 1904); and *L'In-
telligence des fleurs* (Paris, 1907).
These are translated as *The Treasure
of the Humble* (by Alfred Sutro, New
York, 1897); *Wisdom and Destiny* (by
Alfred Sutro, New York, 1898); *The
Buried Temple* (New York, 1902);
The Double Garden (by A. T. de Mattos, New York, 1904); and *The Measure of the Hours* (by A. T. de Mattos,
New York, 1907). The *Letter* from
the program of *Les Flaireurs* is quoted
at length in Remy de Gourmont's *La
Belgique littéraire* (Paris, 1915). Sections from the article on Ibsen are
quoted in Moses' *Maurice Maeterlinck,
a Study* (New York, 1911). The article *Menus Propos,* etc., is quoted in
the same volume. *The Cave of Illusion*
appeared in London, 1900. The *Théâtre,* vol. I, was published at Brussels,
1901. *Le Tragique quotidien, L'Etoile,*
and *Le Réveil de l'ame* are in *Le
Trésor des humbles* (Paris, 1896).
The *Préface* to the Plays—in French
—is included in the English translation of *Pelléas et Mélisande* (New
York, 1896). *La Sagesse et la des-*

tinée was published at Paris in 1898.
Le Drame moderne originally appeared in *Le double Jardin* (Paris,
1904). *A Propos du " Roi Lear"* appeared in *L'Intelligence des fleurs*
(Paris, 1907). Maeterlinck's *Préface*
to his translation of *Macbeth* is affixed to the edition of that play (Paris,
1910).

On Maeterlinck and his works:

Ad. van Bever, *Maurice Maeterlinck*
(Paris, 1904).
Jethro Bithell, *Life and Writings of
Maurice Maeterlinck* (London, 1913).
Barrett H. Clark, *The Continental Drama
of To-day* (New York, 2nd ed., 1915).
——, *A Study of the Modern Drama*
(2nd ed., New York, 1928).
Macdonald Clark, *Maurice Maeterlinck,
Poet and Philosopher* (New York,
1916).
May Daniels, *The French Drama of the
Unspoken* (Edinburgh, 1953).
M. Esch, *L'Œuvre de Maurice Maeter-
linck* (Paris, 1912).
W. D. Halls, *Maurice Maeterlinck* (Ox-
ford, 1960).
Gerard Harry, *Maurice Maeterlinck*
(Bruxelles, 1909).
Archibald Henderson, *Interpreters of
Life and the Modern Spirit* (New
York, 1905).
James Huneker, *Iconoclasts* (New York,
1905).
Georges Leneveu, *Ibsen et Maeterlinck*
(Paris, 1902).
Montrose J. Moses, *Maurice Maeterlinck,
a Study* (New York, 1911).
Johannes Schlaf, *Maurice Maeterlinck*
(Berlin, 1906).
S. C. de Soissons, *Maeterlinck as a Re-
former of the Drama* (in *Contem-
porary Review,* vol. 86, London, 1904).
Arthur Symons, *Plays, Acting, and
Music* (New York, 1909).
Una Taylor, *Maurice Maeterlinck, a
Critical Study* (New York, 1915).
Edward Thomas, *Maurice Maeterlinck*
(New York, 1911).

ARTAUD

On the drama:

Œuvres complètes, Vol. I (Paris, 1956)

Le Théâtre et son double (Paris, 1938). Translated as *The Theater and Its Double* (New York, 1958).
Lettres à Jean-Louis Barrault (Paris, 1952).

On Artaud:

Special issues of *Cahiers Renaud-Barrault* (May, 1958) and *La Tour du Feu* (December, 1959).

SARTRE

On Sartre and his work:

R. M. Albérès, *Jean-Paul Sartre* (Paris, 1953).

Maurice Cranston, *Jean-Paul Sartre* (Edinburgh, 1962).

Edith Kern, ed., *Sartre* (Englewood Cliffs, 1962).
Iris Murdoch, *Sartre* (New Haven, 1953).
Philip Thody, *Jean-Paul Sartre* (London, 1960).

IONESCO

On Ionesco and his work:

Richard Coe, *Ionesco* (Edinburgh, 1961).
Martin Esslin, *The Theatre of the Absurd* (Garden City, 1961).

BRITAIN—NINETEENTH
AND TWENTIETH CENTURIES

General references on nineteenth- and twentieth-century British literature:

Douglas Bush, *Mythology and the Romantic Tradition in English Poetry* (Cambridge, Mass., 1937).
G. K. Chesterton, *The Victorian Age in Literature* (New York, 1913).
A. S. Collins, *English Literature of the Twentieth Century* (London, 1951, 1960).
Bonamy Dobree, ed., *From Anne to Victoria* (London, 1937).
G. S. Fraser, *The Modern Writer and His World* (London, 1953).
Granville Hicks, *Figures of Transition* (New York, 1939).
J. Isaacs, *An Assessment of Twentieth Century Literature* (London, 1951).
Ian Jack, *English Literature 1815–1832* (New York, 1963).
Holbrook Jackson, *The Eighteen Nineties* (New York, 1913).
J. M. Kennedy, *English Literature, 1880–1913* (London, 1913).
L. Magnus, *English Literature in the Nineteenth Century* (New York, 1909).
W. L. Renwick, *English Literature 1789–1815* (New York, 1963).
George Saintsbury, *A History of Nineteenth Century Literature* (New York, 1904).

William York Tindall, *Forces in Modern British Literature 1885–1946* (New York, 1947).
Basil Willey, *More Nineteenth Century Studies* (London, 1956),
——, *Nineteenth Century Studies* (London, 1949).

General references on nineteenth- and twentieth-century British drama:

James Agate, *An Anthology* (London, 1961).
——, *The Contemporary Theatre, 1923–26*, 4 vols. (London, 1924–27).
——, ed., *The English Dramatic Critics* (New York, n.d.).
——, *A Short View of the English Stage* (London, 1926).
William Archer, *About the Theatre* (London, 1886).
——, *English Dramatists of Today* (London, 1882).
——, *The Old Drama and the New* (London, 1923).
——, *Playmaking* (Boston, 1912).
——, *Study and Stage* (London, 1899).
——, *The Theatrical World*, 5 vols. (London, 1894–98).
H. B. Baker, *The London Stage, 1576–1903* (London, 1904).

Max Beerbohm, *Around Theatres* (London, 1953).

Mario Borsa, *The English Stage of Today* (London, 1908).

Arthur Bouchier, *Some Reflections on the Drama—and Shakespeare* (Oxford, 1911).

Maurice Bourgeois, *Synge and the Irish Theatre* (London, 1913).

G. Boyle, *English and American Poets and Dramatists of the Victorian Age* (Frankfurt, 1886).

Ivor Brown, *Masques and Phases* (London, 1926).

——, *Parties of the Play* (London, 1928).

John Russell Brown and Russell Harris, eds., *Contemporary Theatre* (London, 1962).

Gilbert Cannan, *The Dramatic Sense* (in *English Review*, v. 5, London, 1910).

Huntley Carter, *The New Spirit in Drama and Art* (London, 1912).

F. W. Chandler, *Aspects of Modern Drama* (New York, 1914).

Barrett H. Clark, *The British and American Drama of Today* (New York, 1915).

——, *A Study of the Modern Drama* (new ed., New York, 1928).

J. Coleman, *Players and Playwrights I Have Known* (London, 1888).

Dutton Cook, *The Book of the Play* (London, 1876).

——, *Nights at the Play* (London, 1883).

——, *On the Stage* (London, 1883).

J. W. Cunliffe, *Modern English Playwrights* (New York, 1927).

A. Darbyshire, *Art of the Victorian Stage* (Manchester, 1907).

Thomas H. Dickinson, *The Contemporary Drama of England* (Boston, 1917).

M. Willson Disher, *Blood and Thunder* (London, 1949).

——, *Melodrama: Plots that Thrilled* (London, 1954).

Denis Donoghue, *The Third Voice: Modern British and American Verse Drama* (Princeton, 1959).

Ashley Dukes, *Drama* (New York, 1926).

——, *Modern Dramatists* (London, 1911).

——, *The World to Play With* (New York, 1928).

——, *The Youngest Drama* (Chicago, 1924).

Una Ellis-Fermor, *The Irish Dramatic Movement* (London, 1939; revised, 1954).

Augustin Filon, *The English Stage* (London, 1897).

E. Fitzball, *Thirty-five Years of a Dramatic Author's Life* (London, 1858).

W. L. George, *Dramatic Actualities* (London, 1914).

Lady Gregory, *Our Irish Theatre* (New York, 1913).

J. T. Grein, *Dramatic Criticism* (London, 1899).

——, *Dramatic Criticism* (London, 1901).

——, *Dramatic Criticism* (London, 1904).

——, *The New World of the Theatre* (London, 1924).

——, *Premières of the Year* (London, 1900).

——, *The Theater and the World* (London, 1921).

William Hazlitt, *A View of the English Stage* (reprint London, 1906).

R. H. Hirne, *The New Spirit of the Age* (London, 1845).

Harold Hobson, *Verdict at Midnight* (London, 1952).

P. P. Howe, *Dramatic Portraits* (London, 1913).

Leigh Hunt, *Dramatic Essays of Leigh Hunt,* edited by William Archer and R. W. Lowe (London, 1894).

H. B. Irving, *Occasional Papers, Dramatic and Historical* (Boston, 1907).

Henry Arthur Jones, *The Foundations of a National Drama* (New York, 1913).

——, *The Renascence of the English Drama* (New York, 1895).

Laurence Kitchin, *Mid-Century Drama* (London, 1960).

Peter Kavanagh, *The Abbey Theatre* (New York, 1950).

Ludwig Lewisohn, *The Modern Drama* (New York, 1915).

Desmond MacCarthy, *Theatre* (London, 1955).

W. C. Macready, *Diary and Reminiscences* (London, 1875–76).

A. E. Malone, *The Irish Drama* (London, 1929).

C. E. Montague, *Dramatic Values* (London, 1911).

George Moore, *Hail and Farewell,* 3 vols. (New York, 1911–13).

Henry Morley, *The Journal of a London Playgoer* (London, 1866).

Mowbray Morris, *Essays in Theatrical Criticism* (London, 1882).

Sean O'Casey, *The Green Crow* (New York, 1956).

John Palmer, *The Future of the Theatre* (London, 1913).

Ronald Peacock, *The Poet in the Theatre* (New York, 1946, 1960).

J. R. Planché, *Recollections and Reflections*. 2 vols. (London, 1872).

"Q," *Dramatists of the Present Day* (London, 1871).

Ernest Reynolds, *Modern English Drama* (London, 1949).

Lennox Robinson, *Ireland's Abbey Theatre* (London, 1951).

——, ed., *The Irish Theatre* (London, 1939).

G. Rowell, *The Victorian Theatre* (London, 1956).

Newell W. Sawyer, *The Comedy of Manners from Sheridan to Maugham* (Philadelphia, 1931).

Clement Scott, *The Drama of Yesterday and To-day*, 2 vols. (London, 1899).

Bernard Shaw, *Dramatic Opinions and Essays*, 2 vols. (New York, 1906).

——, *Our Theatres in the Nineties*, 3 vols. (London, 1932).

——, *Shaw on Theatre* (New York, 1958).

Alan Simpson, *Beckett and Behan and a Theatre in Dublin* (London, 1962).

E. F. S[pence], *Our Stage and its Critics* (London, 1910).

E. L. Stahl, *Das englische Theater im 19. Jahrhundert* (Leipzig, 1914).

Graham Sutton, *Some Contemporary Dramatists* (New York, 1926).

John Russell Taylor, *Anger and After: A Guide to the New British Drama* (London, 1962).

Winton Tolles, *Tom Taylor and the Victorian Drama* (New York, 1940).

J. C. Trewin, *Dramatists of Today* (London, 1954).

Kenneth Tynan, *Curtains* (New York, 1961).

——, *He That Plays the King* (London, 1950).

A. B. Walkley, *Drama and Life* (London, 1908).

——, *Playhouse Impressions* (London, 1892).

Cornelius Weygandt, *Irish Plays and Playwrights* (Boston, 1913).

Glynne Wickham, *Drama in a World of Science* (London, 1962).

Raymond Williams, *Drama from Ibsen to Eliot* (New York, 1953).

T. C. Worsley, *The Fugitive Art* (London, 1952).

COLERIDGE

On the drama:

The *Literary Remains,* 4 vols. (London, 1836–39) contain most of Coleridge's *Lectures* on Shakespeare, the Greek dramatists, and the English poets. However, most of his other critical volumes may be consulted for miscellaneous remarks on the drama, especially *Biographia Literaria* (1817), *Table-Talk* (1835), *Anima Poetæ* (1895), *Biographia Epistolaris* (1911), and *Letters, 1785–1834, 2* vols. (1895).

Editions:

The *Works* are printed in the Bohn edition (see recent reprint). Convenient editions of the *Lectures* are in Everyman's Library (n.d.). See also J. W. Mackail's *Coleridge's Literary Criticism* (Oxford, 1908); *Shakespearean Criticism,* ed. T. M. Raysor, 2 vols. (London, 1930); *Miscellaneous Criticism,* ed. T. M. Raysor (London, 1936).

On Coleridge and his works:

Thomas Allsop, *Letters, Conversations, and Recollections of Samuel Taylor Coleridge* (London, 1836. Later ed., London, 1864).

Hall Caine, *Samuel Taylor Coleridge* (London, 1887).

James Dykes Campbell, *Samuel Taylor Coleridge* (London, 1894).

Joseph Cottle, *Early Recollections, chiefly relating to the late Samuel Taylor Coleridge, during his long residence in Bristol, 2* vols. (London, 1837. Later edition in new form, as *Reminiscences of Samuel Taylor Coleridge and Robert Southey,* London, 1847).

R. H. Fogle, *The Idea of Coleridge's Criticism* (Berkeley, 1962).

Richard Garnett, *Coleridge* (London, 1904).

James Gillman, *The Life of Samuel Tay-*

lor *Coleridge,* only 1 vol. published (London, 1838).

John Louis Haney, *A Bibliography of Samuel Taylor Coleridge* (Philadelphia 1903).

Gordon McKenzie, *Organic Unity in Coleridge* (Berkeley, 1939).

J. H. Muirhead, *Coleridge as Philosopher* (London, 1930).

William Francis Prideaux, *The Bibliography of Coleridge* (London, 1900).

Herbert Read, *Coleridge as Critic* (London, 1949).

I. A. Richards, *Coleridge on Imagination* (London, 1934).

Henry D. Traill, *Coleridge* (in *English Men of Letters,* London, 1884).

Basil Willey, *Coleridge on Imagination and Fancy* (Oxford, 1946).

LAMB

On the drama:

Notes in the *Specimens of English Dramatic Poets who lived about the Time of Shakespeare* (1808).

On the Tragedies of Shakespeare (1811). *On the Artificial Comedy of the Last Century* (1823).

John Kemble and Godwin's Tragedy of " Antonio " (1822).

Of the numerous other essays more or less on the drama, but chiefly dealing with acting, the most interesting are: *On the Custom of Hissing at the Theatres* (1811), *Biographical Memoir of Mr. Liston* (1825), *The Religion of Actors* (1826), *On a Passage in " The Tempest"* (1823), *The Death of Munden* (1832), *My First Play* (1823), *On Some of the Old Actors* (1823), *On the Acting of Munden* (1823), *Stage Illusion* (1833), *To the Shade of Elliston* (1833), *Ellistoniana* (1833), *Barbara S——* (1833), and the five "criticisms" included in *Eliana.* For numerous occasional remarks on the drama see the *Letters* (Ainger ed., 1904).

Editions:

Lamb's Works and Correspondence, edited by Alfred Ainger, 12 vols. (London, 1883–88). See also *The Works of Charles Lamb,* edited by W. Macdon-

ald, 12 vols. (London, 1903–04), and by E. V. Lucas, 7 vols. (London, 1903–04).

On the Artificial Comedy of the Last Century (to which *John Kemble and Godwin's Tragedy of " Antonio "* was originally affixed), is in the *Essays of Elia* (1823); also, *My First Play, On Some of the Old Actors,* and *On the Acting of Munden.* The *Last Essays of Elia* (1833) include *Stage Illusion, To the Shade of Elliston, Ellistoniana,* and *Barbara S——.* The remaining essays are found in the *Works* (see above), while in his *Dramatic Essays of Charles Lamb* (New York, 1891), Brander Matthews has included all the essays on the drama. Percy Fitzgerald's *The Art of the Stage as Set Out in Lamb's Dramatic Essays* (London, 1885) contains practically the same material. The *Eliana,* with the five criticisms, was first collected by J. E. Babson (Boston, 1865). The plays and selected essays on the drama are edited by Rudolf Dircks in the *Plays and Dramatic Essays by Charles Lamb* (London, n. d.). There are innumerable re-prints of the *Elia* essays; a convenient edition is that in Everyman's Library, with an introduction by Augustine Birrell (New York, 1906). The *Letters* are published as *Letters of Charles Lamb,* edited by Alfred Ainger, 2 vols. (new ed., London, 1904). There is also a two-volume edition of these in Everyman's Library. See also *Lamb's Criticism,* ed. E. M. W. Tillyard (Cambridge, Eng., 1923), and *The Works of Charles and Mary Lamb,* ed. Thomas Hutchinson, 2 vols. (Oxford, 1924).

On Lamb and his works:

Alfred Ainger, *Charles Lamb* (in *English Men of Letters* series. Revised ed., London, 1888).

Edmund C. Blunden, *Charles Lamb and His Contemporaries* (Cambridge, Eng., 1933).

Barry Cornwall, *Charles Lamb: a Memoir* (London, 1866).

Bertram Dobbell, *Sidelights on Charles Lamb* (London, 1903).

Percy Fitzgerald, *Lamb, his Friends, Haunts, Books* (London, 1866).

W. C. Hazlitt, *The Lambs: New Particu-*

lars (London, 1897).

W. C. Hazlitt, editor, *Lamb and Hazlitt: Further Letters and Records, Hitherto Unpublished* (London, 1900).

Walter Jerrold, *Charles Lamb* (London, 1905).

E. V. Lucas, *Life of Charles Lamb*, 2 vols. (London, 1905).

T. B. Macaulay, *Leigh Hunt* (London, 1841. Reprinted in Critical and Historical Essays; many eds.).

B. E. Martin, *In the Footprints of Lamb* (London, 1891).

F. W. Roe, *Charles Lamb and Shakespeare* (Madison, 1916).

HAZLITT

On the drama:

On Modern Comedy (1815).
Schlegel on the Drama (1816).
A View of the English Stage (1818).
On Wit and Humour (1819).
On the Comic Writers of the Last Century (1819).
On Dramatic Poetry (1820).
Lectures on the Dramatic Literature of the Reign of Queen Elizabeth (1820).

The above are the chief single articles and works concerned with the drama. The following works, however, should be consulted for occasional essays and remarks: *The Characters of Shakespear's Plays* (1817), *The Round Table* (1817), *Lectures on the English Comic Writers* (1819), *Lectures on the English Poets* (1818–19), *Table Talk* (1821–22), *The Spirit of the Age* (1825), *The Plain Speaker* (1826), and *Notes of a Journey Through France and Italy* (1826).

Editions:

The standard edition of the complete writings (with the exception of the life of Bonaparte, is *The Collected Works of William Hazlitt*, edited by Waller and Glover, 12 vols. (London, 1902–04). The last 3 volumes contain some new material, and include a number of articles hitherto found only in miscellaneous editions. The second edition (London, 1854) of the *View of the English Stage*, includes *On Modern Comedy*, *On Dramatic Poetry*, and *Explanations*, etc. *Schlegel on the Drama* is in vol. 10 of the *Collected Works*. *On Wit and Humour*, and *On the Comic Writers of the Last Century* are in *Lectures on the English Comic Writers*. Convenient modern reprints are in Everyman's Library: *The Characters of Shakespeare's Plays* (1906); *Lectures on the English Comic Writers, and Miscellaneous Essays* (1910); *Lectures on The English Poets, and The Spirit of the Age* (1910); and *Table Talk, or Original Essays* (1908). Most of the works are in the 7-volume Bohn Library edition (London and New York, various dates).

Previous editions have been superseded by the *Complete Works,* edited by P. P. Howe, 21 vols. (London, 1930–34).

On Hazlitt and his works:

Herschel Baker, *William Hazlitt* (Cambridge, Mass., 1962).

Augustine Birrell, *Res Judicatæ* (New York, 1903).

Jules Douady, *Liste chronologique des œuvres de William Hazlitt* (Paris, 1906).

——, *Vie de William Hazlitt, l'essayiste* (Paris, 1906).

W. C. Hazlitt, *Lamb and Hazlitt. Further Letters and Records Hitherto Unpublished* (New York, 1899).

——, *Memoirs of William Hazlitt*, 2 vols. (London, 1867).

P. P. Howe, *Life of William Hazlitt* (London, 3rd ed., 1928).

Alexander Ireland, *List of the Writings of William Hazlitt and Leigh Hunt,* etc. (London, 1868).

C. M. Maclean, *Born under Saturn* (London, 1943).

Elisabeth Schneider, *The Aesthetics of William Hazlitt* (Philadelphia, 1933).

MEREDITH

On Meredith and his works:

J. W. Beach, *The Comic Spirit of George Meredith* (New York, 1911).

G. T. Milnes, *George Meredith and the Comic Spirit* (London, 1925).

Lionel Stevenson, *The Ordeal of George Meredith* (New York, 1953).

G. M. Trevelyan, *The Poetry and Philosophy of George Meredith* (London, 1906).

W. F. Wright, *Art and Substance in George Meredith* (Lincoln, 1953).

SHAW

On the drama:

Since there are a great many articles contributed to newspapers and magazines which have never been collected, it is impossible to mention every one. The following are, however, the most important. It has not been thought necessary to indicate each separate preface to separate volume and play. Practically every play (and every volume) contains a preface more or less concerned with the drama.

The Quintessence of Ibsenism (1891).

Preface and *Appendices* to the Independent Theater Edition of *Widowers' Houses* (1893).

A Dramatic Realist to his Critics (1894).

Preface to *Archer's Theatrical World of 1894* (1895).

The Problem Play (1895).

The Perfect Wagnerite (1901).

The Author's Apology (1902).

Ibsen (1906).

Letter from Mr. G. Bernard Shaw in *Tolstoy on Shakespeare* (1906).

Dramatic Opinions and Essays, 2 vols. (New York, 1907).

The Sanity of Art (1908).

Statement of the Evidence in Chief of George Bernard Shaw before the Joint Committee on Stage Plays (Censorship and Theatre Licensing) (1909).

The New Drama (1911).

Preface to *Three Plays by Brieux* (New York, 1911).

Letter on The Principles that Govern the Dramatist in his Selection of Themes and Methods of Treatment (1912).

The Art and Craft of Playwriting (1914).

Sixteen Self-Sketches (1949).

For letters and reports of conversations, see Archibald Henderson's biographies of Shaw (cited below) and the following volumes of correspondence:

Ellen Terry and Bernard Shaw: A Correspondence (New York, 1931).

Bernard Shaw and Mrs. Patrick Campbell: Their Correspondence (New York, 1952).

Advice to a Young Critic and Other Letters (New York, 1955).

Bernard Shaw's Letters to Granville Barker (New York, 1956).

See also Shaw's collected music criticism.

Editions:

Shaw's collected works, including all the plays with their prefaces, are published by Constable in London, and Dodd, Mead in New York. The Independent Theatre Edition of *Widowers' Houses* appeared in London, 1893. Archer's *Theatrical World of 1894* was published in London (1895). The *Dramatic Opinions and Essays* are a selection of the best criticisms contributed to the *Saturday Review*. They are edited with an introduction by James Huneker, 2 vols. (New York, 1907), and published complete in 3 vols. as *Our Theatres in the Nineties* (London, 1932). *A Dramatic Realist to His Critics* and *The Problem Play* are included in *Shaw on Theatre,* ed. by E. J. West (New York, 1958). *The Author's Apology from "Mrs. Warren's Profession"* is printed separately, with an introduction by John Corbin (New York, 1905). The article on *Ibsen* appeared in the *Clarion*, London, June 1, 1906. *Tolstoy on Shakespeare* was printed in New York, 1906. *The New Drama, Letter on the Principles*, etc., appeared respectively in the London *Times,* Nov. 10, 1911, and the New York *Times,* June 2, 1912. *The Quintessence of Ibsenism* originally appeared in New York in 1891, but a new edition, "Now completed to the Death of Ibsen," was issued (New York) in 1913. It is included with *The Perfect Wagerite* and *The Sanity of Art* in *Major Critical Essays* (London, 1931). *The Art and Craft of Playwriting* was first printed as a reported lecture in the Oxford (England) *Chronicle* (March 6, 1914). The *Preface* to the *Plays by Brieux* is published in that volume (New York, 1911). *The Sanity of Art* originally appeared in separate form in London (1908). *The Perfect Wagnerite* appeared in New York

(1901). Shaw's remarks on the Censorship problem are included in full in his Preface to *The Shewing-Up of Blanco Posnet* (1909). A number of previously uncollected articles are included in *Shaw on Theatre* (see above) and *Shaw on Shakespeare,* ed. by Edwin Wilson (New York, 1961). Shaw's music criticism for the *Star* and the *World* is published in *London Music in 1888–89* (London, 1937), and *Music in London: 1890–94,* 3 vols. (London, 1931); *Shaw on Music* (New York, 1955), ed. by Eric Bentley, contains some essays from other sources.

On Shaw and his works:

William Archer, *The Theatrical World,* 5 vols. (London, 1894–98).
Julius Bab, *Bernard Shaw* (Berlin, 1910).
Eric Bentley, *Bernard Shaw* (Norfolk, Conn., 1947; New York, rev. ed., 1957).
Richard Burton, *Bernard Shaw, the Man and the Mask* (New York, 1916).
Charles Cestre, *Bernard Shaw et son œuvre* (Paris, 1912).
G. K. Chesterton, *George Bernard Shaw* (New York, 1909).
J. S. Collis, *Shaw* (New York, 1925).
St. John Ervine, *Bernard Shaw* (New York, 1956).
Augustin Hamon, *Le Molière du XX⁶ siècle: Bernard Shaw* (Paris, 1913. Translated by Eden and Cedar Paul as *The Twentieth Century Molière: Bernard Shaw,* New York, 1916).
Archibald Henderson, *Bernard Shaw: Playboy and Prophet* (New York, 1932).
——, *George Bernard Shaw: His Life and Works* (Cincinnati, 1911).
——, *George Bernard Shaw: Man of the Century* (New York, 1956).
——, *Table-Talk of G. B. S.* (New York, 1925).
P. P. Howe, *Bernard Shaw* (New York, 1915).
William Irvine, *The Universe of G. B. S.* (New York, 1949).
Holbrook Jackson, *Bernard Shaw* (London, 1907).
C. E. M. Joad, *Shaw* (London, 1949).
Louis Kronenberger, ed., *Shaw: A Critical Survey* (Cleveland, 1953).
Desmond MacCarthy, *Shaw* (London, 1951).

Joseph McCabe, *George Bernard Shaw* (New York, 1914).
Martin Meisel, *Shaw and the Nineteenth-Century Theater* (Princeton, 1963).
H. L. Mencken, *George Bernard Shaw, His Plays* (Boston, 1905).
Arthur H. Nethercot, *Men and Supermen* (Cambridge, Mass., 1954).
Richard M. Ohmann, *Shaw: The Style and the Man* (Middletown, 1962).
John Palmer, *George Bernard Shaw, Harlequin or Patriot?* (New York, 1915).
Hesketh Pearson, *G. B. S.: A Full Length Portrait* (New York, 1942).
——, *G. B. S.: A Postscript* (New York, 1950).
C. B. Purdom, *A Guide to the Plays of Bernard Shaw* (New York, 1963).
R. F. Rattray, *Bernard Shaw: A Chronicle* (New York, 1951).
Edward Shanks, *Bernard Shaw* (London, 1924).
Alick West, *A Good Man Fallen Among Fabians* (London, 1950).
Homer Woodbridge, *G. B. Shaw: Creative Artist* (Carbondale, 1963).

ARCHER

On the drama:

English Dramatists of Today (1882).
About the Theatre (1886).
The Theatrical World, 1894–98, 5 vols. (1894–98).
Study and Stage (1899).
Playmaking (1912).
The Old Drama and the New (Boston, 1923).

In the introductions and prefaces to the *Collected Works of Henrik Ibsen* (translated by Archer, his brother, and others, 10 vols., London and New York, 1906–08), Archer has supplied much material on the drama. His editions of *The Dramatic Essays* of Leigh Hunt, Hazlitt, John Forster, and G. H. Lewes (London, 1894–96) may likewise be consulted. Further prefatory matter is in the English translation of Mantzius' *History of Theatrical Art,* vol. 1 (London, 1903), the Mermaid edition of George Farquhar (London, 1906), and to W. S. Gilbert's *A Stage Play* (New York, 1916). Archer's biographies and other books contain references and occasionally separate essays on dramatists: *Henry Irving, Actor and Manager* (1883), *Life of Macready* (1890), *Masks or Faces?* (1888), *Real Conversations* (1907), (and, together with Granville-Barker) *Schemes and Estimates for a National Theatre* (1907).

On Archer and his works:

Mario Borsa, *The English Stage of To-day* (New York, 1908).
Clayton Hamilton, *Problems of the Playwright* (New York, 1917).
——, *Studies in Stagecraft* (New York, 1914).
Brander Matthews, *A critic of the Acted Drama: William Archer* (in *The Historical Novel*, New York, 1901).
Bernard Shaw, *Foreword to Three Plays by William Archer* (London, 1927).

YEATS

On the drama:

Yeats's writings on the drama may be found in various collections of his essays, particularly the following volumes:

Plays and Controversies (New York, 1924).
Autobiographies (New York, 1953).
Essays and Introductions (New York, 1961).
Explorations (London, 1962).

Studies of Yeats and his works:

Richard Ellmann, *The Identity of Yeats* (New York, 1954).
——, *Yeats, the Man and the Masks* (New York, 1949).
James Hall and Martin Steinmann, eds., *The Permanence of Yeats* (New York, 1950).
T. R. Henn, *The Lonely Tower* (London, 1950).
A. Norman Jeffares, *Yeats, Man and Poet* (New Haven, 1949).
George Brandon Saul, *Prolegomena to the Study of Yeats's Plays* (Philadelphia, 1958).
Peter Ure, *Yeats the Playwright* (London, 1963).
Helen Hennessy Vendler, *Yeats's Vision and the Later Plays* (Cambridge,

Mass., 1953).
F. A. C. Wilson, *W. B. Yeats and Tradition* (New York, 1958).
——, *Yeats's Iconography* (London, 1960).

SYNGE

Editions:

The Complete Works of John M. Synge was first issued in 1910, and later published in a Modern Library edition (New York, 1935). *The Complete Plays* are published separately (New York, 1960).

On Synge and his works:

David H. Greene and Edward M. Stephens, *J. M. Synge 1871–1909* (New York, 1959).
Alan Price, *Synge and Anglo-Irish Drama* (London, 1961).
W. B. Yeats, *John Millington Synge and the Ireland of His Time* (London, 1911).

O'CASEY

On the drama:

The Green Crow (New York, 1956).
See also his autobiography in 6 vols., beginning with *I Knock at the Door* (1939), and concluding with *Sunset and Evening Star* (1954).

On O'Casey and his works:

Robert Hogan, *The Experiments of Sean O'Casey* (New York, 1960).
David Krause, *Sean O'Casey: The Man and His Work* (London, 1960).

ELIOT

On the drama:

The Use of Poetry and the Use of Criticism (Cambridge, Mass., 1933).
Selected Essays (New York, 1950).
Essays on Elizabethan Drama (New York, 1956).
On Poetry and Poets (New York, 1957).

On Eliot and his works:
Helen Gardner, *The Art of T. S. Eliot*

(London, 1949).
D. S. Jones, *The Plays of T. S. Eliot* (London, 1960).
Hugh Kenner, ed., *T. S. Eliot* (Englewood Cliffs, 1962).
F. O. Matthiessen, *The Achievement of T. S. Eliot* (New York, 3rd ed., 1958).
D. E. S. Maxwell, *The Poetry of T. S.*

Eliot (London, 1952).
Carol H. Smith, *T. S. Eliot's Dramatic Theory and Practice* (Princeton, 1963).
Grover Smith, Jr., *T. S. Eliot's Poetry and Plays* (Chicago, 1956).
Leonard Unger, ed., *T. S. Eliot: A Selected Critique* (New York, 1948).

NORTH AMERICA

For a bibliography of American drama criticism, see the Preface to that section of the text. See also bibliographical information included in the introductions to individual authors, as well as the following:

BAKER

Wisner Payne Kinne, *George Pierce Baker and the American Theatre* (Cambridge, Mass., 1954).

NATHAN

On the drama:

The Theatre Book of the Year, 1942–43 (New York, 1943). This series continues through 1950–51.
The Theatre in the Fifties (New York, 1953).

On Nathan and his work:

Constance Frick, *The Dramatic Criticism of George Jean Nathan* (Ithaca, 1943).

O'NEILL

On O'Neill and his works:

Edwin Engel, *The Haunted Heroes of Eugene O'Neill* (Cambridge, Mass., 1953).
Doris Falk, *Eugene O'Neill and the Tragic Vision* (New Brunswick, 1958).
John Gassner, *Eugene O'Neill* (Minneapolis, 1960).
Arthur and Barbara Gelb, *O'Neill* (New York, 1962).
Clifford Leech, *Eugene O'Neill* (Edinburgh, 1963).

Richard Dana Skinner, *Eugene O'Neill: A Poet's Quest* (New York, 1935).
Sophus Keith Winther, *Eugene O'Neill* (New York, 1934; rev. ed., 1961).

ANDERSON

On Anderson and his works:

Mabel Driscoll Bailey, *Maxwell Anderson: The Playwright as Prophet* (New York, 1957).

WILLIAMS

On Williams and his work:

Signi Falk, *Tennessee Williams* (New York, 1961).
John D. Hurrell, ed., *Two Modern American Tragedies: Reviews and Criticism of "Death of a Salesman" and "A Streetcar Named Desire"* (New York, 1961).
Benjamin Nelson, *Tennessee Williams: His Life and Work* (London, 1961).
Nancy M. Tischler, *Tennessee Williams: Rebellious Puritan* (New York, 1961).

MILLER

On Miller and his work:

John D. Hurrell, ed., *Two Modern American Tragedies: Reviews and Criticism of "Death of a Salesman" and "A Streetcar Named Desire"* (New York, 1961).
Dennis Welland, *Arthur Miller* (Edinburgh, 1961).